Financial Aid
for Native Americans
2017-2019

Gail Ann Schlachter
R. David Weber

A Listing of Scholarships, Fellowships, Grants, Awards, and
Other Sources of Free Money Available Primarily or
Exclusively to Native Americans Plus a Set of Six Indexes
(Program Title, Sponsoring Organization, Residency,
Tenability, Subject, and Deadline Date)

AdmitHub
Boston, Massachusetts

AdmitHub
Harvard Innovation Launch Lab
114 Western Ave.
Boston, MA 02134
      (617) 575-9369
      E-mail: rsp@admithub.com
Visit our web site: www.admithub.com

Manufactured in the United States of America

Contents

Foreword

About Dr. Gail Schlachter and Reference Service Press

Dr. Gail Ann Schlachter (1943-2015), original founder of Reference Service Press, was working as a librarian in the mid-1970s when she recognized that women applying for college faced significant obstacles finding information about financial aid resources designed to help them. This challenge inspired her to publish her ground-breaking book, Directory of Financial Aids for Women, in 1977. The book's success prompted additional financial aid directories for other underserved communities, including the present volume for Native Americans.

By 1985, the business had become so successful that she left her job as a publishing company executive to run her company, Reference Service Press, full-time. Over the years, the company's offerings expanded to over two dozen financial aid titles covering many different types of students—law students, business students, students studying abroad, and many more. The company's success was driven by its database of tens of thousands of financial aid programs, laboriously hand-built over the decades and kept current to exacting specifications. In 1995, Reference Service Press once again broke new ground by launching one of the first-ever searchable electronic databases of financial aid resources (initially through America Online). For more background about the founding and success of Reference Service Press, see Katina Strauch's 1997 "Against the Grain" interview with Dr. Schlachter, available at http://docs.lib.purdue.edu/cgi/viewcontent.cgi?article=2216&context=atg.

Dr. Schlachter was also a major figure in the library community for nearly five decades. She served: as reference book review editor for RQ (now Reference and User Services Quarterly) for 10 years; as president of the American Library Association's Reference and User Services Association; as editor of the Reference and User Services Association Quarterly; seven terms on the American Library Association's governing council; and as a member of the association's Executive Board at the time of her death. She was posthumously inducted into the California Library Association Hall of Fame. The University of Wisconsin School of Library and Information Studies named Dr. Schlachter an "Alumna of the Year," and she was recognized with both the Isadore Gilbert Mudge Citation and the Louis Shores/Oryx Press Award.

Dr. Schlachter will be remembered for how her financial aid directories helped thousands of students achieve their educational and professional dreams. She also will be remembered for her countless contributions to the library profession. And, as an American Library Association Executive Board resolution from June 2015 says, she will be remembered, "most importantly, for her mentorship, friendship, and infectious smile." Yet, despite her impressive lifetime of professional accomplishments, Dr. Schlachter always was most proud of her family, including her husband Stuart Hauser, her daughter Dr. Sandy Hirsh (and Jay Hirsh) and son Eric Goldman (and Lisa Goldman), and her grandchildren Hayley, Leah, Jacob, and Dina.

Introduction

WHY THIS DIRECTORY IS NEEDED

Despite our country's ongoing economic problems and increased college costs, the financial aid picture for minorities has never looked brighter. Currently, billions of dollars are set aside each year specifically for Native Americans, African Americans, Asian Americans, and Hispanic Americans. This funding is open to minorities at any level (high school through postdoctoral and professional) for a variety of activities, including study, research, travel, training, career development, and creative projects.

While numerous print or online listings have been prepared to identify and describe general financial aid opportunities (those open to all segments of society), those resources have never covered more than a small portion of the programs designed primarily or exclusively for minorities. As a result, many advisors, librarians, scholars, researchers, and students often have been unaware of the extensive funding available to Native Americans and other minorities. But, with the ongoing publication of *Financial Aid for Native Americans,* that has all changed. Here, in just one place, Native American students, professionals, and postdoctorates now have current and detailed information about the special resources set aside specifically for them.

Financial Aid for Native Americans is prepared biennially as part of Reference Service Press' four-volume *Minority Funding Set* (the other volumes in the set cover funding for Asian Americans, African Americans, and Hispanic Americans). Each of the volumes in this set is sold separately, or the complete set can be purchased at a discounted price.

No other source, in print or online, offers the extensive coverage provided by these titles. That's why the Grantsmanship Center labeled the set "a must for every organization serving minorities," *Reference Sources for Small and Medium-Sized Libraries* called the titles "the absolute best guides for finding funding," and *Reference Books Bulletin* selected each of the volumes in the *Minority Funding Set* as their "Editor's Choice." *Financial Aid for Native Americans,* itself, has also received rave reviews. According to *Choice,* "This is a unique and valuable resource" which is "highly recommended." *Reference Books Bulletin* calls it a "landmark resource" and *EMIE Bulletin* concluded that the directory is "definitely designed to ease what can be a very stressful process." Perhaps *American Reference Books Annual* sums up best the critical reaction to *Financial Aid for Native Americans:* "extraordinarily useful...absolutely essential."

WHAT'S UPDATED?

The preparation of each new edition of *Financial Aid for Native Americans* involves extensive updating and revision. To make sure that the information included here is both reliable and current, the editors at Reference Service Press 1) reviewed and updated all relevant programs covered in the previous edition of the directory, 2) collected information on all programs open to Native Americans that were added to Reference Service Press' funding database since the last edition of the directory, and then 3) searched extensively for new program leads in a variety of sources, including printed directories, news reports, journals, newsletters, house organs, annual reports, and sites on the Internet. We only include program descriptions that are written directly from information supplied by the sponsoring organization in print or online (no information is ever taken from secondary sources). When that information could not be found, we sent up to four data collection letters (followed by up to three telephone or email inquiries, if necessary) to those sponsors. Despite our best efforts, however, some sponsoring organizations still failed to respond and, as a result, their programs are not included in this edition of the directory.

7

The 2017-2019 edition of *Financial Aid for Native Americans* completely revises and updates the previous (eighth) edition. Programs that have ceased operations have been dropped from the listing. Similarly, programs that have broadened their scope and no longer focus on Native Americans have also been removed from the listing. Profiles of continuing programs have been rewritten to reflect current requirements; nearly 75 percent of the continuing programs reported substantive changes in their locations, requirements (particularly application deadline), benefits, or eligibility requirements since the 2014-2016 edition. In addition, hundreds of new entries have been added to the program section of the directory. The resulting listing describes the 1,360 biggest and best sources of free money available to Native Americans, including scholarships, fellowships, grants, awards, and other funding opportunities.

WHAT MAKES THIS DIRECTORY UNIQUE?

The 2017-2019 edition of *Financial Aid for Native Americans* will help American Indians, Native Alaskans (including Eskimos and Aleuts), and Native Hawaiians tap into the billions of dollars available to them, as minorities, for study, research, creative activities, past accomplishments, future projects, professional development, work experience, and many other activities. The listings cover every major subject area, are sponsored by more than 900 different private and public agencies and organizations, and are open to Native Americans at any level, from college-bound high school students through professionals and postdoctorates.

Not only does *Financial Aid for Native Americans* provide the most comprehensive coverage of available funding (1,360 entries), but it also displays the most informative program descriptions (on the average, more than twice the detail found in any other listing). In addition to this extensive and focused coverage, *Financial Aid for Native Americans* also offers several other unique features. First of all, hundreds of funding opportunities listed here have never been covered in any other source. So, even if you have checked elsewhere, you will want to look at *Financial Aid for Native Americans* for additional leads. And, here's another plus: all of the funding programs in this edition of the directory offer "free" money; not one of the programs will ever require you to pay anything back (provided, of course, that you meet the program requirements).

Further, unlike other funding directories, which generally follow a straight alphabetical arrangement, *Financial Aid for Native Americans* groups entries by intended recipients (undergraduates, graduate students, or professionals/postdoctorates), to make it easy for you to search for appropriate programs. This same convenience is offered in the indexes, where program title, sponsoring organization, geographic, subject, and deadline date entries are each subdivided by recipient group.

Finally, we have tried to anticipate all the ways you might wish to search for funding. The volume is organized so you can identify programs not only by intended recipient, but also by subject focus, sponsoring organization, program title, residency requirements, where the money can be spent, and even deadline date. Plus, we've included all the information you'll need to decide if a program is right for you: purpose, eligibility requirements, financial data, duration, special features, limitations, number awarded, and application date. You even get fax numbers, toll-free numbers, e-mail addresses, and web sites (when available), along with complete contact information.

WHAT'S EXCLUDED?

While this book is intended to be the most comprehensive source of information on funding available to Native Americans, there are some programs we've specifically excluded from the directory:

- *Programs that do not accept applications from U.S. citizens or residents.* If a program is open only to foreign nationals or excludes Americans from applying, it is not covered.

- *Programs that are open equally to all segments of the population.* Only funding opportunities set aside primarily or exclusively for American Indians, Native Alaskans, and/or Native Hawaiians are included here.

- *Money for study or research outside the United States.*   Since there are comprehensive and up-to-date directories that describe the available funding for study, research, or other activities abroad (see the list of Reference Service Press publications opposite this directory's title page), only programs that fund activities in the United States are covered here.

- *Very restrictive programs.*   In general, programs are excluded if they are open only to a limited geographic area (such as single Alaska Native villages; only scholarships offered by the 13 regional Native Corporations are available for Alaska Natives) or offer limited financial support (less than $1,000). Note, however, that the vast majority of programs included here go way beyond that, paying up to full tuition or stipends that exceed $25,000 a year!

- *Programs administered by individual academic institutions solely for their own students.*   The directory identifies "portable" programs—ones that can be used at any number of schools. Financial aid administered by individual schools specifically for their own students is not covered. Write directly to the schools you are considering to get information on their offerings.

- *Money that must be repaid.*   Only "free money" is identified here. If a program requires repayment or charges interest, it's not listed. Now you can find out about billions of dollars in aid and know (if you meet the program requirements) that not one dollar of that will ever need to be repaid.

HOW THE DIRECTORY IS ORGANIZED

Financial Aid for Native Americans is divided into two sections: 1) a detailed list of funding opportunities open to Native Americans and 2) a set of six indexes to help you pinpoint appropriate funding programs.

Financial Aid Programs Open to Native Americans.   The first section of the directory describes 1,360 sources of free money available to American Indians, Native Alaskans, and/or Native Hawaiians. The focus is on financial aid aimed at American citizens or residents to support study, research, or other activities in the United States. The programs listed here are sponsored by more than 900 different government agencies, professional organizations, corporations, sororities and fraternities, foundations, religious groups, educational associations, and military/veterans organizations. All areas of the sciences, social sciences, and humanities are covered.

To help you focus your search, the entries in this section are grouped into the following three chapters:

- **Undergraduates:**   Included here are nearly 700 scholarships, grants, awards, and other sources of free money that support undergraduate study, training, research, or creative activities. These programs are open to high school seniors, high school graduates, currently-enrolled college students, and students returning to college after an absence. Money is available to support these students in any type of public or private postsecondary institution, ranging from technical schools and community colleges to major universities in the United States.

- **Graduate Students:**   Described here are 573 fellowships, grants, awards, and other sources of free money that support post-baccalaureate study, training, research, and creative activities. These programs are open to students applying to, currently enrolled in, or returning to a master's, doctoral, professional, or specialist program in public or private graduate schools in the United States.

- **Professionals/Postdoctorates:**   Included here are nearly 100 funding programs for U.S. citizens or residents who 1) are in professional positions (e.g., artists, writers), whether or not they have an advanced degree; 2) are master's or professional degree recipients; 3) have earned a doctoral degree or its equivalent (e.g., Ph.D., Ed.D., M.D.); or 4) have recognized stature as established scientists, scholars, academicians, or researchers.

Within each of these three chapters, entries appear alphabetically by program title. Since some of the programs supply assistance to more than one specific group, those are listed in all relevant chapters. For example, the A.T. Anderson Memorial Scholarship Program supports students working on either an undergraduate or graduate degree, so the program is described in both the Undergraduates *and* Graduate Students chapters.

Each program entry has been designed to give you a concise profile that, as the sample on page 7 illustrates, includes information (when available) on organization address and telephone numbers (including toll-free and fax numbers), e-mail addresses and web site, purpose, eligibility, money awarded, duration, special features, limitations, number of awards, and application deadline.

The information reported for each of the programs in this section was gathered from research conducted through the middle of 2017. While the listing is intended to cover as comprehensively as possible the biggest and best sources of free money available to Native Americans, some sponsoring organizations did not post information online or respond to our research inquiries and, consequently, are not included in this edition of the directory.

Indexes.　To help you find the aid you need, we have constructed six indexes; these will let you access the listings by program title, sponsoring organization, residency, tenability, subject focus, and deadline date. These indexes use a word-by-word alphabetical arrangement. Note: numbers in the index refer to entry numbers, not to page numbers in the book.

Program Title Index.　If you know the name of a particular funding program and want to find out where it is covered in the directory, use the Program Title Index. To assist you in your search, every program is listed by all its known names, former names, and abbreviations. Since one program can be included in more than one place (e.g., a program providing assistance to both undergraduate and graduate students is described in both the first and second chapter), each entry number in the index has been coded to indicate the intended recipient group ("U" = Undergraduates; "G" = Graduate Students; "P" = Professionals/Postdoctorates). By using this coding system, you can avoid duplicate entries and turn directly to the programs that match your eligibility characteristics.

Sponsoring Organization Index.　This index makes it easy to identify agencies that offer funding primarily or exclusively to Native Americans. More than 900 organizations are indexed here. As in the Program Title Index, we've used a code to help you determine which organizations sponsor programs that match your educational level.

Residency Index.　Some programs listed in this book are restricted to Native Americans in a particular state or region. Others are open to Native Americans wherever they live. This index helps you identify programs available only to residents in your area as well as programs that have no residency requirements. Further, to assist you in your search, we've also indicated the recipient level for the funding offered to residents in each of the areas listed in the index.

Tenability Index.　This index identifies the geographic locations where the funding described in *Financial Aid for Native Americans* may be used. Index entries (city, county, state, region) are arranged alphabetically (word by word) and subdivided by recipient group. Use this index when you are looking for money to support your activities in a particular geographic area.

Subject Index.　This index allows you to identify the subject focus of each of the financial aid opportunities described in *Financial Aid for Native Americans*. More than 250 different subject terms are listed. Extensive "see" and "see also" references, as well as recipient group subdivisions, will help you locate appropriate funding opportunities.

Calendar Index.　Since most financial aid programs have specific deadline dates, some may have closed by the time you begin to look for funding. You can use the Calendar Index to determine which programs are still open. This index is arranged by recipient group (Undergraduates, Graduate Students, and Professionals/Postdoctorates) and subdivided by month during which the deadline falls. Filing dates can and quite often do vary from year to year; consequently, this index should be used only as a guide for deadlines beyond 2016.

HOW TO USE THE DIRECTORY

Here are some tips to help you get the most out the funding opportunities listed in *Financial Aid for Native Americans.*

To Locate Funding by Recipient Group. To bring together programs with a similar educational focus, this directory is divided into three chapters: Undergraduates, Graduate Students, and Professionals/Postdoctorates. If you want to get an overall picture of the sources of free money available to Native Americans in any of these categories, turn to the appropriate chapter and then review the entries there. Since each of these chapters functions as a self-contained entity, you can browse through any of them without having to first consulting an index.

To Find Information on a Particular Financial Aid Program. If you know the name of a particular financial aid program, and the group eligible for that award, then go directly to the appropriate chapter in the directory (e.g., Undergraduates, Graduate Students), where you will find the program profiles arranged alphabetically by title. To save time, though, you should always check the Program Title Index first if you know the name of a specific award but are not sure in which chapter it has been listed. Plus, since we index each program by all its known names and abbreviations, you'll also be able to track down a program there when you only know the popular rather than official name.

To Locate Programs Sponsored by a Particular Organization. The Sponsoring Organization Index makes it easy to identify agencies that provide financial assistance to Native Americans or to identify specific financial aid programs offered by a particular organization. Each entry number in the index is coded to identify recipient group (Undergraduates, Graduate Students, Professionals/Postdoctorates), so that you can easily target appropriate entries.

To Browse Quickly Through the Listings. Look at the listings in the chapter that relates to you (Undergraduates, Graduate Students, or Professionals/Postdoctorates) and read the "Summary" paragraph in each entry. In seconds, you'll know if this is an opportunity that you might want to pursue. If it is, be sure to read the rest of the information in the entry, to make sure you meet all of the program requirements before writing or going online for an application form. Please save your time and energy. Don't apply if you don't qualify!

To Locate Funding Available to Native Americans from or Tenable in a Particular City, County, or State. The Residency Index identifies financial aid programs open to Native Americans in a specific state, region, etc. The Tenability Index shows where the money can be spent. In both indexes, "see" and "see also" references are used liberally, and index entries for a particular geographic area are subdivided by recipient group (Undergraduates, Graduate Students, and Professionals/Postdoctorates) to help you identify the funding that's right for you. When using these indexes, always check the listings under the term "United States," since the programs indexed there have no geographic restrictions and can be used in any area.

To Locate Financial Aid Programs Open to Native Americans in a Particular Subject Area. Turn to the Subject Index first if you are interested in identifying funding programs for Native Americans that are focused on a particular subject area (more than 250 different subject fields are listed there). To make your search easier, the intended recipient groups (Undergraduates, Graduate Students, Professionals/Postdoctorates) are clearly labeled in each of the subject listings. Extensive cross-references are also provided. Since a large number of programs are not restricted by subject, be sure to check the references listed under the "General programs" heading in the index, in addition to the specific terms that directly relate to your interest areas. The listings under "General programs" can be used to fund activities in any subject area (although the programs may be restricted in other ways).

To Locate Financial Aid Programs for Native Americans by Deadline Date. If you are working with specific time constraints and want to weed out the financial aid programs whose filing dates you won't be able to meet, turn first to the Calendar Index and check the program references listed under the appropriate recipient group and month. Note: not all sponsoring organizations supplied deadline information; those programs are listed under the "Deadline not specified" entries in the index. To identify every relevant financial aid program, regardless of filing date, go the appropriate chapter and read through all the entries there that match your educational level.

To Locate Financial Aid Programs Open to All Segments of the Population. Only programs available to Native Americans are listed in this publication. However, there are thousands of other programs that are open equally to all segments of the population. To identify these programs, talk to your local librarian, check with your financial aid office on campus, look at the list of RSP print resources on the page opposite the title page in this directory, or see if your library subscribes to Reference Service Press' interactive online funding database *RSP FundingFinder.* For more information on that award-winning resource, go online to: www.rspfunding.com/esubscriptions.html.

PLANS TO UPDATE THE DIRECTORY

This volume, covering 2017-2019, is the ninth edition of *Financial Aid for Native Americans.* The next biennial edition will cover the years 2019-2021 and will be issued by the beginning of 2019.

ACKNOWLEDGEMENTS

A debt of gratitude is owed all the organizations that contributed information to the 2017-2019 edition of *Financial Aid for Native Americans.* Their generous cooperation has helped to make this publication a current and comprehensive survey of awards.

SAMPLE ENTRY

(1) **[240]**

(2) **Ford Motor Company Tribal College Scholarship**

(3) American Indian College Fund
Attn: Scholarship Department
8333 Greenwood Boulevard
Denver, CO 80221
(303) 426-8900
(800) 776-FUND   Fax: (303) 426-1200
E-mail: scholarships@collegefund.org
Web: www.collegefund.org/content/full_circle_scholarships_listings

(4) **Summary**   To provide financial assistance to Native Americans who are interested in attending a Tribal College or University (TCU) and majoring in specified fields.

(5) **Eligibility**   This program is open to American Indians or Alaska Natives who are enrolled or planning to enroll full time at an eligible TCU; first preference is given to students at TCUs in Michigan. Applicants must have a GPA of 3.0 or higher and be able to demonstrate exceptional academic achievement or financial need. They must have declared a major in mathematics, science, engineering, business, teacher training, or environmental science. Applications are available only online and include required essays on specified topics. U.S. citizenship is required.

(6) **Financial data**   The stipend is $3,000.

(7) **Duration**   1 year.

(8) **Additional information**   This program is funded by the Ford Motor Company in partnership with the American Indian College Fund.

(9) **Number awarded**   1 or more each year.

(10) **Deadline**   May of each year.

DEFINITION

(1) **Entry number:**   The consecutive number that is given to each entry and used to identify the entry in the index.

(2) **Program title:**   Title of scholarship, fellowship, grant, award, or other source of free money described in the directory.

(3) **Sponsoring organization:**   Name, address, and telephone number, toll-free number, fax number, e-mail address, and/or web site (when information was available) for organization sponsoring the program.

(4) **Summary:**   Identifies the major program requirements; read the rest of the entry for additional detail.

(5) **Eligibility:**   Qualifications required of applicants, plus information on application procedure and selection process.

(6) **Financial data:**   Financial details of the program, including fixed sum, average amount, or range of funds offered, expenses for which funds may and may not be applied, and cash-related benefits supplied (e.g., room and board).

(7) **Duration:**   Period for which support is provided; renewal prospects.

(8) **Additional information:**   Any unusual (generally nonmonetary) benefits, features, restrictions, or limitations associated with the program.

(9) **Number awarded:**   Total number of recipients each year or other specified period.

(10) **Deadline:**   The month by which applications must be submitted.

ABOUT THE AUTHORS

Dr. Gail Ann Schlachter (1943-2015) worked for more than three decades as a library manager, a library educator, and an administrator of library-related publishing companies. Among the reference books to her credit are the biennially-issued *Directory of Financial Aids for Women* and two award-winning bibliographic guides: *Minorities and Women: A Guide to Reference Literature in the Social Sciences* (which was chosen as an "outstanding reference book of the year" by *Choice)* and *Reference Sources in Library and Information Services* (which won the first Knowledge Industry Publications "Award for Library Literature"). She was the reference book review editor for *RQ* (now *Reference and User Services Quarterly)* for 10 years, was a past president of the American Library Association's Reference and User Services Association, was the editor-in-chief of the *Reference and User Services Association Quarterly,* and was serving her sixth term on the American Library Association's governing council at the time of her death. In recognition of her outstanding contributions to reference service, Dr. Schlachter was named the University of Wisconsin School of Library and Information Studies "Alumna of the Year" and was awarded both the Isadore Gilbert Mudge Citation and the Louis Shores/Oryx Press Award.

Dr. R. David Weber taught history and economics at Los Angeles Harbor College (in Wilmington, California) for many years and continues to teach history as an emeritus professor. During his years of full-time teaching there, and at East Los Angeles College, he directed the Honors Program and was frequently chosen the "Teacher of the Year." He has written a number of critically-acclaimed reference works, including *Dissertations in Urban History* and the three-volume *Energy Information Guide.* With Gail Schlachter, he is the author of Reference Service Press' *Financial Aid for Persons with Disabilities and Their Families,* which was selected by *Library Journal* as one of the "best reference books of the year," and a number of other award-winning financial aid titles, including the *College Student's Guide to Merit and Other No-Need Funding,* which was chosen as one of the "outstanding reference books of the year" by *Choice.*

Financial Aid Programs
Open to Native Americans

Undergraduates ●

Graduate Students ●

Professionals/Postdoctorates ●

Undergraduates

Listed alphabetically by program title and described in detail here are 693 scholarships, grants, awards, and other sources of "free money" set aside for college-bound high school seniors and continuing or returning undergraduate students of American Indian, Native Alaskan (including Eskimos and Aleuts), and Native Hawaiian descent. This funding is available to support study, training, research, and/or creative activities in the United States.

[1]
AAAE FOUNDATION SCHOLARSHIPS FOR NATIVE AMERICANS

American Association of Airport Executives Foundation
Attn: AAAE Foundation Scholarship Program
601 Madison Street, Suite 400
Alexandria, VA 22314
(703) 824-0500, ext. 148   Fax: (703) 820-1395
E-mail: cindy.gunderson@aaae.org
Web: www.aaae.org

Summary To provide financial assistance to Native American upper-division college students who are majoring in aviation.

Eligibility This program is open to full-time Native American college juniors or seniors who are enrolled in an aviation program and have a GPA of 3.0 or higher. Each college or university may nominate only 1 student for this scholarship. Selection is based on academic record, financial need, participation in school and community activities, work experience, and a personal statement.

Financial data The stipend is $1,000.

Duration 1 year.

Number awarded 1 or more each year.

Deadline March of each year.

[2]
ACCENTURE AMERICAN INDIAN SCHOLARSHIPS

American Indian Graduate Center
Attn: Executive Director
3701 San Mateo Boulevard, N.E., Suite 200
Albuquerque, NM 87110-1249
(505) 881-4584   Toll Free: (800) 628-1920
Fax: (505) 884-0427   E-mail: fellowships@aigc.com
Web: www.aigcs.org

Summary To provide financial assistance for college to Native American high school seniors interested in majoring in fields of business and technology.

Eligibility This program is open to enrolled members of federally-recognized American Indian tribes and Alaska Native groups who can provide a Certificate of Degree of Indian Blood (CDIB). Applicants must be entering freshmen at an accredited U.S. college or university, planning to work full time on a bachelor's degree in engineering, computer science, operations management, finance, marketing, management, or other business-oriented fields. They must have a GPA of 3.25 or higher. Along with their application, they must submit an essay describing their character, personal merit, and commitment to community and American Indian or Alaska Native heritage. Selection is based on academic excellence, demonstrated leadership, and commitment to preserving American Indian culture and communities.

Financial data The stipend is $5,000 per year.

Duration 4 years.

Additional information This program, established in 2005, is supported by Accenture.

Number awarded 3 each year.

Deadline January of each year.

[3]
ACCESS PATH TO PSYCHOLOGY AND LAW EXPERIENCE (APPLE) PROGRAM

American Psychological Association
Attn: Division 41 (American Psychology-Law Society)
c/o Jennifer Hunt, Minority Affairs Committee Chair
Buffalo State University of New York, Psychology
  Department
Classroom Building C308
1300 Elmwood Avenue
Buffalo, NY 14222
(716) 878-3421   E-mail: huntjs@buffalostate.edu
Web: www.apadivisions.org

Summary To provide an opportunity for Native American and other undergraduate students from underrepresented groups to gain research and other experience to prepare them for graduate work in psychology and law.

Eligibility This program is open to undergraduate students who are members of underrepresented groups, including, but are not limited to, racial and ethnic minorities; first-generation college students; lesbian, gay, bisexual, and transgender students; and physically disabled students. Applicants must be interested in participating in a program in which they work on research for approximately 10 hours per week; participate in GRE classes and/or other development opportunities; attend a conference of the American Psychology-Law Society (AP-LS); submit a proposal to present their research at an AP-LS conference or in the Division 41 program of an American Psychological Association (APA) conference; submit a summary of their research experience to the AP-LS Minority Affairs Committee chair within 1 month of its completion; and correspond with a secondary mentor from the Minority Affairs Committee to participate in the ongoing assessment of this program. Selection is based on the quality of the proposed research and mentoring experience and the potential for the student to become a successful graduate student.

Financial data Grants range up to $3,000, including a stipend of $1,200 per semester or $800 per quarter or summer, $100 for research expenses, and up to $500 to attend the AP-LS conference.

Duration Up to 1 year.

Number awarded 6 each year.

Deadline November of each year.

[4]
ACCOUNTANCY BOARD OF OHIO EDUCATION ASSISTANCE PROGRAM

Accountancy Board of Ohio
Attn: Executive Director
77 South High Street, Suite 1802
Columbus, OH 43215-6128
(614) 466-4135   Fax: (614) 466-2628
E-mail: john.e.patterson@acc.ohio.gov
Web: www.acc.ohio.gov

Summary To provide financial assistance to Native American and other minority or financially disadvantaged students enrolled in an accounting education program at Ohio academic institutions approved by the Accountancy Board of Ohio.

Eligibility This program is open to minority and financially disadvantaged Ohio residents who apply as full-time juniors or seniors in an accounting program at an accredited college or university in the state. Students who remain in good standing at their institutions and who enter a qualified fifth-year program are then eligible to receive these funds. Minority is defined as Blacks, Native Americans, Hispanics, and Asian. Financial disadvantage is defined according to information provided on the Free Application for Federal Student Aid (FAFSA). U.S. citizenship or permanent resident status is required.

Financial data The amount of the stipend is determined annually but does not exceed the in-state tuition at Ohio public universities (currently, $13,067).

Duration 1 year (the fifth year of an accounting program). Funds committed to students who apply as juniors must be used within 4 years and funds committed to students who apply as seniors must be used within 3 years. The award is nonrenewable and may only be used when the student enrolls in the fifth year of a program.

Number awarded Several each year.

Deadline Applications may be submitted at any time.

[5]
ACT SIX SCHOLARSHIPS

Act Six
c/o Degrees of Change
1109 A Street, Suite 101
P.O. Box 1573
Tacoma, WA 98401
(253) 642-6712   E-mail: tim.herron@actsix.org
Web: www.actsix.org

Summary To provide financial assistance to Native American and other residents of Washington and Oregon who come from diverse backgrounds and are interested in attending designated private faith-based universities in those states.

Eligibility This program is open to high school seniors or recent graduates and planning to enter college as freshmen who come from diverse, multicultural backgrounds. Applicants must be residents of the following regions and interested in attending designated colleges for that region: Portland: George Fox University or Warner Pacific College; Spokane: Gonzaga University or Whitworth University; Tacoma-Seattle: Gonzaga University, Northwest University, Pacific Lutheran University, or Whitworth University; or Yakima Valley: Heritage University. Students are not required to make a faith commitment, but they must be willing to explore Christian spirituality as it relates to service and leadership. Ethnicity and family income are considered as factors in selecting an intentionally diverse group of scholars, but there are no income restrictions and students from all ethnic backgrounds are encouraged to apply.

Financial data The program makes up the difference between any other assistance the student receives and full tuition. For recipients who demonstrate financial need in excess of tuition, awards cover some or all of the cost of room and board, books, travel, and personal expenses.

Duration 1 year; may be renewed.

Number awarded Varies each year; recently, 56 were awarded.

Deadline November of each year.

[6]
ACTUARIAL DIVERSITY SCHOLARSHIPS

Actuarial Foundation
Attn: Actuarial Education and Research Fund Committee
475 North Martingale Road, Suite 600
Schaumburg, IL 60173-2226
(847) 706-3535   Fax: (847) 706-3599
E-mail: scholarships@actfnd.org
Web: www.actuarialfoundation.org

Summary To provide financial assistance to Native American and other minority undergraduate students who are preparing for a career in actuarial science.

Eligibility This program is open to members of minority groups, defined as having at least 1 birth parent who is Black/African American, Hispanic, Native North American, or Pacific Islander. Applicants must be graduating high school seniors or current full-time undergraduate students working on or planning to work on a degree at an accredited 2- or 4-year college or university that may lead to a career in the actuarial profession. They must have a GPA of 3.0 or higher; high school seniors must also have a minimum score of 28 on the ACT mathematics examination or 600 on the SAT mathematics examination. Along with their application, they must submit a 1- or 2-page personal statement that covers why they are interested in becoming an actuary, the steps they are taking to enter the actuarial profession, participation in actuarial internships, and participation in extracurricular activities. Financial need is not considered in the selection process.

Financial data Annual stipends are $1,000 for high school seniors applying for freshman year, $2,000 for college freshmen applying for sophomore year, $3,000 for college sophomores applying for junior year, or $4,000 for college juniors applying for senior year.

Duration 1 year; may be renewed, provided the recipient remains enrolled full time, in good academic standing, in a course of study that may lead to a career in the actuarial profession, and (for college juniors and higher) passes actuarial examinations.

Additional information This program began in 1977 by the Casualty Actuarial Society and the Society of Actuaries. In 2008, it was transferred to the Actuarial Foundation.

Number awarded Varies each year; recently, 40 were awarded.

Deadline April of each year.

[7]
ACXIOM DIVERSITY SCHOLARSHIP PROGRAM

Acxiom Corporation
601 East Third Street
P.O. Box 8190
Little Rock, AR 72203-8190
(501) 342-1000   Toll Free: (877) 314-2049
E-mail: Candice.Davis@acxiom.com
Web: www.acxiom.com/about-acxiom/careers

Summary To provide financial assistance and possible work experience to Native American and other upper-division and graduate students who are members of a diverse population that historically has been underrepresented in the information technology work force.

Eligibility This program is open to juniors, seniors, and graduate students who are working full time on a degree in a field of information technology, including computer science, computer information systems, management information systems, information quality, information systems, engineering, mathematics, statistics, or related areas of study. Women, veterans, minorities, and individuals with disabilities are encouraged to apply. Applicants must have a GPA of 3.0 or higher. Along with their application, they must submit a 500-word essay describing how the scholarship will help them achieve their academic, professional, and personal goals. Selection is based on academic achievement, relationship of field of study to information technology, and relationship of areas of professional interest to the sponsor's business needs.

Financial data The stipend is $5,000 per year.

Duration 1 year; may be renewed 1 additional year, provided the recipient remains enrolled full time, maintains a GPA of 3.0 or higher, and (if offered an internship) continues to meet internship expectations.

Additional information Recipients may be offered an internship (fall, spring, summer, year-round) at 1 of the sponsor's offices in Austin (Texas), Conway (Arkansas), Downers Grove (Illinois), Little Rock (Arkansas), Nashville (Tennessee), New York (New York), or Redwood City (California).

Number awarded Up to 5 each year.

Deadline December of each year.

[8]
A.D. OSHERMAN SCHOLARSHIP FUND

Greater Houston Community Foundation
Attn: Scholarships Assistant
5120 Woodway Drive, Suite 6000
Houston, TX 77056
(713) 333-2236   Fax: (713) 333-2220
E-mail: jlauver@ghcf.org
Web: www.ghcfscholar.org

Summary To provide financial assistance to residents of Texas who are Native Americans or members of other designated groups and are interested in attending college in any state.

Eligibility This program is open to Texas residents who are graduating high school seniors or full-time freshmen, sophomores, or juniors at an accredited public 2- or 4-year college or university in any state. Applicants must qualify as a member of a recognized minority group, the first in their family to attend college, or a veteran with active service, particularly service in Iraq or Afghanistan. They must have a GPA of 2.75 or higher and a history of community service. Financial need is considered in the selection process.

Financial data The stipend is $2,500 per year for students at 4-year universities or $1,500 per year for students at 2-year colleges.

Duration 1 year; recipients may reapply.

Number awarded 2 each year.

Deadline March of each year.

[9]
ADDIE B. MORRIS SCHOLARSHIP

American Association of Railroad Superintendents
P.O. Box 200
La Fox, IL 60147
(331) 643-3369   E-mail: aars@supt.org
Web: www.railroadsuperintendents.org/Scholarships

Summary To provide financial assistance to undergraduate and graduate students, especially Native Americans and other minorities working on a degree in transportation.

Eligibility This program is open to full-time undergraduate and graduate students enrolled at accredited colleges and universities in Canada or the United States. Applicants must have completed enough credits to have standing as a sophomore and must have a GPA of 2.75 or higher. Preference is given to minority students enrolled in the transportation field who can demonstrate financial need.

Financial data The stipend is $1,000. Funds are sent directly to the recipient's institution.

Duration 1 year.

Number awarded 1 or more each year.

Deadline June of each year.

[10]
ADOLPH VAN PELT SCHOLARSHIPS

Association on American Indian Affairs, Inc.
Attn: Director of Scholarship Programs
966 Hungerford Drive, Suite 12-B
Rockville, MD 20850
(240) 314-7155   Fax: (240) 314-7159
E-mail: general.aaia@indian-affairs.org
Web: www.indian-affairs.org

Summary To provide financial assistance to Native American undergraduate students.

Eligibility This program is open to Native American students interested in working on an undergraduate degree on a full-time basis. Applicants must submit proof of tribal enrollment and an essay of 2 to 3 pages on 1 of the following topics: 1) why the sponsor's International Repatriation Project is important and how they would inform others about it; 2) the Annie E. Casey Foundation's Juvenile Detention Alternatives Initiative and tribal and community-based alternatives to detention for juveniles; or 3) how tribal leaders can promote higher education in their family and community. They must have a GPA of 2.5 or higher. Selection is based on merit and need.

Financial data The stipend is $1,500.

Duration 1 year; recipients may reapply.

Number awarded Varies each year; recently, 8 were awarded.

Deadline May of each year.

[11]
ADULT VOCATIONAL TRAINING SERVICES OF THE CHEYENNE RIVER SIOUX TRIBE

Cheyenne River Sioux Tribe
Attn: Education Services Office
2001 Main Street
P.O. Box 590
Eagle Butte, SD 57625
(605) 964-8311   E-mail: dal7882@lakotanetwork.com
Web: www.sioux.org/educational-services-department.html

Summary To provide financial assistance for vocational training in any state to members of the Cheyenne River Sioux Tribe and other tribal members who reside on the Cheyenne River Reservation.

Eligibility This program is open to enrolled Cheyenne River Sioux tribal members and other eligible Indian tribal members who reside on the Cheyenne River Reservation. Applicants must be a high school graduate or GED recipient interested in a program of vocational training in any state. They must be able to demonstrate financial need.

Financial data A stipend is awarded (amount not specified).

Duration 1 year; may be renewed.

Additional information Funding for this program is provided by the U.S. Bureau of Indian Affairs (BIA).

Number awarded Varies each year.

Deadline Applications may be submitted at any time; awards are granted on a first-come, first-served basis.

[12]
AFSCME UNION SCHOLARSHIPS OF THE THURGOOD MARSHALL COLLEGE FUND

Thurgood Marshall College Fund
Attn: Senior Manager of Scholarship Programs
901 F Street, N.W., Suite 300
Washington, DC 20004
(202) 507-4851   Fax: (202) 652-2934
E-mail: deshuandra.walker@tmcfund.org
Web: www.tmcf.org

Summary To provide financial assistance and work experience with the American Federation of State, County and Municipal Employees (AFSCME) to Native Americans and other students of color interested in preparing for a career in the labor union movement.

Eligibility This program is open to students of color (African American, American Indian/Alaskan Native, Asian Pacific Islander American, Latino American) who are currently enrolled as sophomores or juniors at a college or university in any state. Applicants must be interested in participating in a summer field placement in a union organizing campaign at 1 of several locations across the country followed by a year of academic study at their college or university. They must have a current GPA of 2.5 or higher and a demonstrated interest in working through the union labor movement. Along with their application, they must submit a personal statement on an assigned topic, a letter of recommendation, and their current academic transcript.

Financial data The program provides 1) a stipend of up to $4,000 (provided by AFSCME) and on-site housing for the summer field placement; and 2) an academic scholarship of up to $6,300 for the school year, based on successful completion of the summer program and financial need.

Duration 10 weeks for the summer field placement; students who enter the program as sophomores are eligible for a second placement at AFSCME headquarters in Washington, D.C.; 1 year for the academic scholarship.

Additional information This program is sponsored by AFSCME.

Number awarded Varies each year.

Deadline February of each year.

[13]
AGA INVESTING IN THE FUTURE STUDENT RESEARCH FELLOWSHIPS

American Gastroenterological Association
Attn: AGA Research Foundation
Research Awards Manager
4930 Del Ray Avenue
Bethesda, MD 20814-2512
(301) 222-4012   Fax: (301) 654-5920
E-mail: awards@gastro.org
Web: www.gastro.org

Summary To provide funding for research on digestive diseases or nutrition to Native American and other undergraduate and medical students from underrepresented minority groups.

Eligibility This program is open to undergraduate and medical students at accredited U.S. institutions who are African Americans, Hispanic/Latino Americans, Alaska Natives, American Indians, or Natives of the U.S. Pacific Islands. Applicants must be interested in conducting research on digestive diseases or nutrition. They may not hold similar salary support awards from other agencies (e.g., American Liver Foundation, Crohn's and Colitis Foundation). Research must be conducted under the supervision of a preceptor who is a full-time faculty member at an institution in a state other than the student's, directing a research project in a gastroenterology-related area, and a member of the American Gastroenterological Association (AGA).

Financial data Fellowships provide payment of housing, travel, and a stipend of $5,000.

Duration 8 to 10 weeks. The work may take place at any time during the year.

Additional information This program is supported by the National Institute of Diabetes and Digestive and Kidney Diseases (NIDDKD) of the U.S. National Institutes of Health (NIH).

Number awarded 12 each year.

Deadline February of each year.

[14]
AHTNA HERITAGE FOUNDATION COMPETITIVE SCHOLARSHIP

Ahtna, Incorporated
Attn: Ahtna Heritage Foundation
P.O. Box 213
Glennallen, AK 99588
(907) 822-5778   Fax: (907) 822-5338
E-mail: ahtnaheritage@yahoo.com
Web: www.ahtnaheritagefoundation.com/scholarships.html

Summary To provide financial assistance to shareholders of Ahtna, Incorporated in Alaska and their descendants who plan to work on an undergraduate degree at a school in any state.

Eligibility This program is open to Ahtna shareholders (original or Class L) who are high school graduates or GED recipients. Applicants must be enrolled or planning to enroll full or part time at a college, university, or vocational school in any state as an undergraduate or graduate student. They must have a GPA of 3.0 or higher and be able to demonstrate financial need. Along with their application, they must submit 1) a 1- to 2-page personal biography that includes information about their family, community, business and other interests, and future and educational goals; 2) letters of recommendation; and 3) a 2-page essay on how their education will impact the Ahtna people.

Financial data The stipend is $5,000 per year.

Duration 1 year; may be renewed, provided the recipient maintains a GPA of 3.0 or higher.

Additional information Ahtna, Incorporated is 1 of 13 regional corporations established according to the terms of the Alaska Native Claims Settlement Act (ANCSA) of 1971.

Number awarded 1 each year.

Deadline July of each year.

[15]
AHTNA HERITAGE FOUNDATION HIGH SCHOOL DUAL CREDIT SCHOLARSHIP PROGRAM

Ahtna, Incorporated
Attn: Ahtna Heritage Foundation
P.O. Box 213
Glennallen, AK 99588
(907) 822-5778   Fax: (907) 822-5338
E-mail: ahtnaheritage@yahoo.com
Web: www.ahtnaheritagefoundation.com/scholarships.html

Summary To provide financial assistance to shareholders of Ahtna, Incorporated in Alaska and their descendants who are interested in taking college classes while still enrolled in high school.

Eligibility This program is open to Ahtna shareholders (original or Class L) who are taking college courses while enrolled full time in high school. Applicants must have a GPA of 3.0 or higher in high school and in any college classes already completed. Along with their application, they must submit a 1-page essay describing their future and educational goals.

Financial data The stipend is $500 per semester.

Duration 1 semester; may be renewed, provided the recipient maintains a GPA of 3.0 or higher.

Additional information Ahtna, Incorporated is 1 of 13 regional corporations established according to the terms of the Alaska Native Claims Settlement Act (ANCSA) of 1971.

Number awarded 20 each semester.

Deadline Applications may be submitted at any time; awards are granted on a first-come, first-served basis.

[16]
AHTNA HERITAGE FOUNDATION SUMMER SCHOLARSHIPS

Ahtna, Incorporated
Attn: Ahtna Heritage Foundation
P.O. Box 213
Glennallen, AK 99588
(907) 822-5778   Fax: (907) 822-5338
E-mail: ahtnaheritage@yahoo.com
Web: www.ahtnaheritagefoundation.com/scholarships.html

Summary To provide financial assistance to shareholders of Ahtna, Incorporated in Alaska and their descendants who plan to attend summer school in any state.

Eligibility This program is open to Ahtna shareholders (original or Class L) who are high school graduates or GED recipients. Applicants must be enrolled or planning to enroll in summer school at a college, university, or vocational school in any state as an undergraduate or graduate student. They must have a GPA of 2.0 or higher and be able to demonstrate financial need.

Financial data The stipend is $2,000 for full-time students or $1,000 for part-time students.

Duration 1 year; may be renewed for up to 5 summers as an undergraduate and 5 summers as a graduate student, provided the recipient maintains a GPA of 2.0 or higher.

Additional information Ahtna, Incorporated is 1 of 13 regional corporations established according to the terms of the Alaska Native Claims Settlement Act (ANCSA) of 1971.

Number awarded Varies each year.

Deadline May of each year.

[17]
AIA/F DIVERSITY ADVANCEMENT SCHOLARSHIP

American Institute of Architects
Attn: AIA Foundation
1799 New York Avenue, N.W.
Washington, DC 20006-5292
(202) 626-7511   Fax: (202) 626-7420
E-mail: divscholarship@aia.org
Web: www.aia.org/about/initiatives/AIAB101856

Summary To provide financial assistance to Native American and other high school and college students from diverse backgrounds who are interested in studying architecture in college.

Eligibility This program is open to students from minority and/or financially disadvantaged backgrounds who are high school seniors, students in a community college or technical school transferring to an accredited architectural program, or college freshmen entering a professional degree program at an accredited program of architecture. Students who have completed 1 or more years of a 4-year college curriculum are not eligible. Applicants must submit 2 or 3 drawings, including 1 freehand sketch of any real life object (e.g., buildings, people, objects, self-portrait) and 1 or 2 additional images of drawings or drafted floor plans or drawings using computer-aided design (CAD). Selection is based on those drawings and financial need.

Financial data Stipends range from $3,000 to $4,000 per year, depending upon individual need. Students must apply for supplementary funds from other sources.

Duration 1 year; may be renewed for up to 4 additional years or until completion of a degree.

Additional information This program was established in 1970 as the AIA/AAF Minority Disadvantaged Scholarship Program.

Number awarded 2 each year.

Deadline April of each year.

[18]
AIET MINORITIES AND WOMEN EDUCATIONAL SCHOLARSHIP PROGRAM

Appraisal Institute
Attn: Appraisal Institute Education Trust
200 West Madison Street, Suite 1500
Chicago, IL 60606
(312) 335-4133   Fax: (312) 335-4134
E-mail: educationtrust@appraisalinstitute.org
Web: www.appraisalinstitute.org

Summary To provide financial assistance to Native American and other underrepresented undergraduate students majoring in real estate or allied fields.

Eligibility This program is open to members of groups underrepresented in the real estate appraisal profession. Those groups include women, American Indians, Alaska Natives, Asians and Pacific Islanders, Blacks or African Americans, and Hispanics. Applicants must be full- or part-time students enrolled in real estate courses within a degree-granting college, university, or junior college. They must have a GPA of 2.5 or higher and be able to demonstrate financial need. U.S. citizenship is required.

Financial data The stipend is $1,000. Funds are paid directly to the recipient's institution to be used for tuition and fees.

Duration 1 year.

Number awarded At least 1 each year.

Deadline April of each year.

[19]
AINAHAU O KALEPONI HAWAIIAN CIVIC CLUB ACADEMIC, VOCATIONAL, AND TRADE SCHOLARSHIP

Ainahau o Kaleponi Hawaiian Civic Club
Attn: Scholarship Committee
12534 Valley View Street, Number 343
Garden Grove, CA 92845
E-mail: edyehill@yahoo.com
Web: www.aokhcc.org

Summary To provide financial assistance for undergraduate, graduate, or vocational study to residents of any state who have ties to the Native Hawaiian community.

Eligibility This program is open to students enrolled or entering an academic, vocational, trade, or graduate school in any state. Applicants must submit a 300-word essay that includes a short biography, what they have accomplished this past year, extracurricular activities or work experience in the past year, community service or volunteer work in the past year, participation in Hawaiian organization in the past year, and possible future contributions to Hawaiian community culture. Special consideration is given to members of the Ainahau o Kaleponi Hawaiian Civic Club (AOKHCC) and to appli-

cants whose family has been actively involved in AOKHCC. Financial need is not considered in the selection process.

Financial data A stipend is awarded (amount not specified).

Duration 1 year.

Number awarded 1 or more each year.

Deadline April of each year.

[20]
AINTA SCHOLARSHIPS

American Indian Alaska Native Tourism Association
Attn: Scholarship Program
2401 12th Street N.W.
Albuquerque, NM 87104
(505) 724-3592   Fax: (505) 212-7023
E-mail: sbowman@aianta.org
Web: www.aianta.org/Education_and_Training.aspx

Summary To provide financial assistance to Native American students preparing for a career in the tourism industry.

Eligibility This program is open to students of American Indian, Native Hawaiian, or Alaska Native heritage who can document their ancestry. Applicants must be enrolled or planning to full or part time at a 2- or 4-year college, university, or vocational/technical school with a concentration in hospitality, tourism, recreation, or culinary arts. They may be working on a certificate, associate, bachelor's, or master's degree and have a GPA of 2.5 or higher. Along with their application, they must submit a 500-word essay about themselves, including information on any special circumstances or obstacles they have had to overcome to attend college, why they have selected the hospitality/tourism field, their ultimate career goal, their service to their tribal community, any leadership or community service, and their financial need.

Financial data The stipend is $1,000 per year.

Duration 1 year; may be renewed, provided the recipient provides 12 volunteer hours to a tribe, national park, or public land institution.

Number awarded 3 each year.

Deadline July of each year for fall semester; December of each year for spring semester.

[21]
AISES INTEL SCHOLARSHIPS

American Indian Science and Engineering Society
Attn: Director of Membership and Communications
2305 Renard Place, S.E., Suite 200
Albuquerque, NM 87106
(505) 765-1052, ext. 110   Fax: (505) 765-5608
E-mail: lpaz@aises.org
Web: www.aises.org/scholoarships/intel-scholarship

Summary To provide financial assistance to members of the American Indian Science and Engineering Society (AISES) who are working on an undergraduate or graduate degree in a field of computer science or engineering.

Eligibility This program is open to AISES members who are full-time undergraduate or graduate students at an accredited 4-year college or university. Applicants must be American Indian tribal members, Alaskan Natives, or Native Hawaiians and have a Certificate of Degree of Indian or Alaska Native Blood (CDIB) showing at least 25% Native blood. They must have a GPA of 3.0 or higher and be working on a degree in computer science, computer engineering, electrical engineering, chemical engineering, or material science. Selection is based on academic performance, a personal statement, letters of recommendation, and activities (e.g., jobs, volunteer efforts, internships, extracurricular involvement, hobbies).

Financial data The stipend is $5,000 for undergraduates or $10,000 for graduate students.

Duration 1 year; nonrenewable.

Additional information This program is funded by Intel.

Number awarded Up to 5 each year.

Deadline April of each year.

[22]
ALABAMA INDIAN AFFAIRS COMMISSION SCHOLARSHIP

Alabama Indian Affairs Commission
771 South Lawrence Street, Suite 106
Montgomery, AL 36104-5005
(334) 240-0998   Toll Free: (800) 436-8261
Fax: (334) 240-3408   E-mail: aiac@att.net
Web: www.aiac.state.al.us/Prog_Scholarships.aspx

Summary To provide financial assistance to American Indians residing in Alabama and attending college in the state.

Eligibility This program is open to residents of Alabama who have been enrolled in a state- or federally-recognized Indian tribe for at least 3 years. Applicants must be attending or planning to attend an academic institution in the state. Special consideration is given to nursing, medical, veterinary, and pharmacy students, who may attend school in other states because of the limited availability of spaces in Alabama schools. Financial need is not considered in the selection process.

Financial data A stipend is awarded (amount not specified).

Duration 1 year; recipients may reapply.

Number awarded 1 or more each year.

Deadline April of each year.

[23]
ALEUT FOUNDATION PART-TIME SCHOLARSHIPS

The Aleut Corporation
Attn: Aleut Foundation
703 West Tudor Road, Suite 102
Anchorage, AK 99503-6650
(907) 646-1929   Toll Free: (800) 232-4882
Fax: (907) 646-1949   E-mail: taf@thealeutfoundation.org
Web: www.thealeutfoundation.org

Summary To provide financial assistance for college or graduate school to Native Alaskans who are shareholders of The Aleut Corporation or their descendants and are enrolled part time.

Eligibility This program is open to Native Alaskans who are original enrollees or descendants of original enrollees of The Aleut Corporation (TAC). Applicants must be enrolled in an associate, bachelor's, or higher degree program as a part-time student (at least 3 credit hours). They must have a GPA of 2.0 or higher. Along with their application, they must include a letter of intent, up to 500 words in length, that

describes their educational goals and objectives and their expected graduation date.

Financial data The stipend depends on the number of credit hours in the undergraduate or graduate program, to a maximum of $1,200 per year.

Duration 1 year.

Additional information The Aleut Corporation is 1 of 13 Alaska Native Regional Corporations created under the Alaska Native Claims Settlement Act of 1971. The foundation began awarding scholarships in 1987.

Number awarded Varies each year; recently, 2 were awarded.

Deadline June of each year for annual scholarships; November of each year for spring scholarships; April of each year for summer school.

[24]
ALEUT FOUNDATION SCHOLARSHIP PROGRAM

The Aleut Corporation
Attn: Aleut Foundation
703 West Tudor Road, Suite 102
Anchorage, AK 99503-6650
(907) 646-1929   Toll Free: (800) 232-4882
Fax: (907) 646-1949   E-mail: taf@thealeutfoundation.org
Web: www.thealeutfoundation.org

Summary To provide financial assistance to Native Alaskans who are shareholders of The Aleut Corporation or their descendants and plan to attend college in any state.

Eligibility This program is open to Native Alaskans who are original enrollees or descendants of original enrollees of The Aleut Corporation (TAC). Applicants must be enrolled or planning to enroll full time at a college or university in any state to work on an undergraduate degree. They must have earned a GPA of 3.5 or higher for the Honors Scholarship, 3.0 or higher for the Exceptional Scholarship, 2.5 or higher for the Achievement Scholarship, or 2.0 or higher for the Merit Scholarship. Along with their application, they must include a letter of intent, up to 500 words in length, that describes their educational goals and objectives and their expected graduation date.

Financial data Annual stipends are $3,000 for Honors Scholarships, $2,500 for Exceptional Scholarships, $2,000 for Achievement Scholarships, or $1,500 for Merit Scholarships.

Duration 1 year; may be renewed.

Additional information The Aleut Corporation is 1 of 13 Alaska Native Regional Corporations created under the Alaska Native Claims Settlement Act of 1971. The foundation began awarding scholarships in 1987.

Number awarded Varies each year.

Deadline June of each year for annual scholarships; November of each year for spring scholarships; April of each year for summer school.

[25]
ALEUT FOUNDATION VOCATIONAL-TECHNICAL SCHOLARSHIPS

The Aleut Corporation
Attn: Aleut Foundation
703 West Tudor Road, Suite 102
Anchorage, AK 99503-6650
(907) 646-1929   Toll Free: (800) 232-4882
Fax: (907) 646-1949   E-mail: taf@thealeutfoundation.org
Web: www.thealeutfoundation.org

Summary To provide financial assistance for vocational school in any state to Native Alaskans who are shareholders of The Aleut Corporation or their descendants.

Eligibility This program is open to Native Alaskans who are original enrollees or descendants of original enrollees of The Aleut Corporation (TAC). Applicants must be enrolled in or accepted to a vocational program in any state on a full-time basis. Along with their application, they must include a letter of intent, up to 500 words in length, that describes their educational goals and objectives and their expected graduation date.

Financial data The stipend is $1,700 per year.

Duration 1 semester (at least 6 weeks); may be renewed.

Additional information The Aleut Corporation is 1 of 13 Alaska Native Regional Corporations created under the Alaska Native Claims Settlement Act of 1971. The foundation began awarding scholarships in 1987.

Number awarded Varies each year; recently, 4 were awarded.

Deadline June of each year for annual scholarships; November of each year for spring scholarships; April of each year for summer school.

[26]
ALLOGAN SLAGLE MEMORIAL SCHOLARSHIP

Association on American Indian Affairs, Inc.
Attn: Director of Scholarship Programs
966 Hungerford Drive, Suite 12-B
Rockville, MD 20850
(240) 314-7155   Fax: (240) 314-7159
E-mail: general.aaia@indian-affairs.org
Web: www.indian-affairs.org

Summary To provide financial assistance for college or graduate school to Native American students whose tribe is not federally recognized.

Eligibility This program is open to American Indian and Native Alaskan full-time undergraduate and graduate students. Applicants must be members of tribes that are either state-recognized or that are not federally-recognized but are seeking federal recognition. Along with their application, they must submit proof of tribal enrollment and an essay of 2 to 3 pages on 1 of the following topics: 1) why the sponsor's International Repatriation Project is important and how they would inform others about it; 2) the Annie E. Casey Foundation's Juvenile Detention Alternatives Initiative and tribal and community-based alternatives to detention for juveniles; or 3) how tribal leaders can promote higher education in their family and community. They must have a GPA of 2.5 or higher. Selection is based on merit and need.

Financial data The stipend is $1,500.

Duration 1 year; recipients may reapply.

Number awarded Varies each year; recently, 7 were awarded.

Deadline May of each year.

[27]
ALMA EXLEY SCHOLARSHIP

Community Foundation of Greater New Britain
Attn: Scholarship Manager
74A Vine Street
New Britain, CT 06052-1431
(860) 229-6018, ext. 305   Fax: (860) 225-2666
E-mail: cfarmer@cfgnb.org
Web: www.cfgnb.org

Summary To provide financial assistance to Native American and other minority college students in Connecticut who are interested in preparing for a teaching career.

Eligibility This program is open to students of color (African Americans, Asian Americans, Hispanic Americans, and Native Americans) enrolled in a teacher preparation program in Connecticut. Applicant must 1) have been admitted to a traditional teacher preparation program at an accredited 4-year college or university in the state; or 2) be participating in the Alternate Route to Certification (ARC) program sponsored by the Connecticut Department of Higher Education.

Financial data The stipend is $1,500 per year for students at a 4-year college or university or $500 for a student in the ARC program.

Duration 2 years for students at 4-year colleges or universities; 1 year for students in the ARC program.

Number awarded 2 each year: 1 to a 4-year student and 1 to an ARC student.

Deadline October of each year.

[28]
ALYESKA MATCH SCHOLARSHIPS

Cook Inlet Tribal Council, Inc.
c/o The CIRI Foundation
3600 San Jeronimo Drive, Suite 256
Anchorage, AK 99508-2870
(907) 793-3575   Toll Free: (800) 764-3382
Fax: (907) 793-3585   E-mail: tcf@thecirifoundation.org
Web: www.thecirifoundation.org/citc-scholarship

Summary To provide financial assistance to Alaska Natives who are working on an undergraduate degree or certificate at a school in any state in fields that will prepare them for employment on the Trans-Alaska Pipeline System (TAPS).

Eligibility This program is open to Alaska Natives who are enrolled full time in college or a vocational training program in any state. Applicants must be studying a field specified by Alyeska Pipeline Service Company that relates to future employment on the TAPS. Recently, those were limited to engineering (chemical/process, civil, electrical, mechanical); business (management information systems, technology, engineering management, environmental quality engineering science, project management, construction management, project controls); environmental (biology, chemistry); planner scheduler (accounting, finance, economics, mathematics, statistics, engineering); quality assurance (engineering, safety, business); technical (process technology, supervisory control and data acquisition (SCADA), instrument, welding). Applicants must have a GPA of 2.5 or higher and be able to demonstrate unmet financial need even though they are receiving other funding. Awards are granted on a first-come, first-served basis.

Financial data Stipends range up to $7,500 per year.

Duration 1 year; may be renewed up to 4 additional years, provided the recipient maintains a GPA of 2.0 or higher.

Additional information Funding for this program is provided by Alyeska Pipeline Service Company as part of its commitment under Section 29 of the Right of Way Agreement to provide scholarships to Alaska Natives.

Number awarded Varies each year.

Deadline May of each year for fall; November of each year for spring.

[29]
ALYESKA PIPELINE PIPELINE SERVICE COMPANY ALASKA NATIVE PROGRAM

Bristol Bay Native Corporation
Attn: BBNC Education Foundation
111 West 16th Avenue, Suite 400
Anchorage, AK 99501-6299
(907) 278-3602   Toll Free: (800) 426-3602
Fax: (907) 265-7886   E-mail: bbncef@bbnc.net
Web: www.bbnc.net

Summary To provide financial assistance for college in any state to shareholders of Bristol Bay Native Corporation (BBNC) who are studying specified fields to prepare for employment with the Alyeska Pipeline Service Company (APSC) or in the oilfields.

Eligibility This program is open to BBNC shareholders who are enrolled full time as an upper-division student at a college or university in any state and working on a degree in accounting, business administration, computer science, construction and project management, economics, engineering, environment, finance, health and safety, information technology, instrumentation, management information systems, process technology, or project controls. Applicants must be interested in preparing for employment with APSC or in the oilfields. They have a GPA of 2.5 or higher and be able to demonstrate financial need. Along with their application, they must submit an essay on how they became interested in their proposed field of study, any special circumstances they want to be considered, and their desire to work in the region or for a BBNC subsidiary company. Selection is based on the essay (30%), cumulative GPA (40%), financial need (20%), a resume (5%), and letters of recommendation (5%).

Financial data Stipend amounts vary.

Duration 1 year.

Additional information The BBNC is 1 of 13 Alaska Native Regional Corporations created under the Alaska Native Claims Settlement Act of 1971. This program, sponsored by APSC, began in 2015.

Number awarded 1 or more each year.

Deadline April of each year.

[30]
ALYESKA PIPELINE SERVICE COMPANY SCHOLARSHIP OF KONIAG INCORPORATED

Koniag Incorporated
Attn: Koniag Education Foundation
4241 B Street, Suite 303B
Anchorage, AK 99503
(907) 562-9093   Toll Free: (888) 562-9093
Fax: (907) 562-9023   E-mail: kef@koniageducation.org
Web: www.koniageducation.org/scholarships/alyeska

Summary To provide financial assistance to Alaska Natives who are Koniag Incorporated shareholders or descendants and enrolled in undergraduate or graduate study in a field of interest to the Alyeska Pipeline Service Company.

Eligibility This program is open to undergraduates who are Alaska Native shareholders of Koniag Incorporated or descendants of those original enrollees. Applicants must be preparing for a career with Alyeska and on the Trans Alaska Pipeline System (TAPS) or other oil industry-related jobs. They may be majoring in business planning and related fields (accounting, economics, finance), engineering (chemical, civil, electrical, mechanical), environment, health, information technology, inspection, quality, project and construction management, safety, security, or technical fields (e.g., instrument, SCADA, process technology, communications) Along with their application, they must submit a 300-word essay about their personal and family history, community involvement, volunteer activities, and educational and life goals. Financial need is not considered in the selection process.

Financial data The maximum stipend is $7,500 per year. Funds are sent directly to the recipient's school and may be used for tuition, books, supplies, room, board, and transportation.

Duration 1 year; may be renewed.

Additional information Koniag Incorporated is 1 of 13 Alaska Native Regional Corporations created under the Alaska Native Claims Settlement Act of 1971. It manages this program with support from the Alyeska Pipeline Service Company as part of its commitment under Section 29 of the Right of Way Agreement to provide scholarships to Alaska Natives.

Number awarded 1 each year.

Deadline May of each year.

[31]
AMAC MEMBER AWARD

Airport Minority Advisory Council
Attn: AMAC Foundation
2001 Jefferson Davis Highway, Suite 500
Arlington, VA 22202
(703) 414-2622   Fax: (703) 414-2686
E-mail: terrifrierson@palladiumholdingsco.com
Web: amac-org.com/amac-foundation/scholarships

Summary To provide financial assistance to Native American and other underrepresented high school seniors and undergraduates who are preparing for a career in the aviation industry and are connected to Airport Minority Advisory Council (AMAC).

Eligibility This program is open to minority and female high school seniors and current undergraduates who have a

GPA of 2.5 or higher and a record of involvement in community and extracurricular activities. Applicants must be interested in working on a bachelor's degree in accounting, architecture, aviation, business administration, engineering, or finance as preparation for a career in the aviation or airport industry. They must be AMAC members, family of members, or mentees of member. Along with their application, they must submit a 750-word essay on how they have overcome barriers in life to achieve their academic and/or career goals; their dedication to succeed in the aviation industry and how AMAC can help them achieve their goal; and the most important issues that the aviation industry is facing today and how they see themselves changing those. Financial need is not considered in the selection process. U.S. citizenship is required.

Financial data   The stipend is $2,000 per year.

Duration   1 year; recipients may reapply.

Number awarded   4 each year.

Deadline   May of each year.

[32]
AMELIA KEMP MEMORIAL SCHOLARSHIP

Women of the Evangelical Lutheran Church in America
Attn: Scholarships
8765 West Higgins Road
Chicago, IL 60631-4101
(773) 380-2741   Toll Free: (800) 638-3522, ext. 2741
Fax: (773) 380-2419   E-mail: valora.starr@elca.org
Web: www.womenoftheelca.org

Summary   To provide financial assistance to Native American and other lay women of color who are members of Evangelical Lutheran Church of America (ELCA) congregations and who wish to study on the undergraduate, graduate, professional, or vocational school level.

Eligibility   This program is open to ELCA lay women of color who are at least 21 years of age and have experienced an interruption of at least 2 years in their education since high school. Applicants must have been admitted to an educational institution to prepare for a career in other than ordained ministry. U.S. citizenship is required.

Financial data   The maximum stipend is $1,000 per year.

Duration   1 year; recipients may reapply for 1 additional year.

Number awarded   1 or more each year.

Deadline   February of each year.

[33]
AMERICAN ASSOCIATION OF PHYSICISTS IN MEDICINE DIVERSITY RECRUITMENT THROUGH EDUCATION AND MENTORING (DREAM) PROGRAM

American Association of Physicists in Medicine
Attn: AAPM Education and Research Fund
One Physics Ellipse
College Park, MD 20740
(301) 209-3350   Fax: (301) 209-0862
E-mail: jackie@aapm.org
Web: www.aapm.org/education/GrantsFellowships.asp

Summary   To provide an opportunity for Native American and other minority upper-division students to gain summer work experience performing research in a medical physics laboratory or assisting with clinical service at a clinical facility.

Eligibility   This program is open to minority undergraduates who are entering their junior or senior year at an Historically Black College or University (HBCU), Minority Serving Institution (MSI), or non-Minority Serving Institution. Applicants must be interested in gaining experience in medical physics by performing research in a laboratory or assisting with clinical service at a clinical facility. Preference is given to those who have declared a major in physics, engineering, or other science that requires mathematics at least through differential equations and junior-level courses in modern physics or quantum mechanics and electricity and magnetism or equivalent courses in engineering sciences. They must be U.S. citizens, U.S. permanent residents, or Canadian citizens. Work must be conducted under the supervision of a mentor who is a member of the American Association of Physicists in Medicine (AAPM) employed by a university, hospital, clinical facility, or radiological industry within the United States.

Financial data   The stipend is $5,000.

Duration   10 weeks during the summer.

Additional information   This program was formerly known as the American Association of Physicists in Medicine Minority Undergraduate Experience Program.

Number awarded   Varies each year; recently, 9 were awarded.

Deadline   February of each year.

[34]
AMERICAN BUS ASSOCIATION DIVERSITY SCHOLARSHIPS

American Bus Association
Attn: ABA Foundation
111 K Street, N.E., Ninth Floor
Washington, DC 20002
(202) 842-1645   Toll Free: (800) 283-2877
Fax: (202) 842-0850   E-mail: abainfo@buses.org
Web: www.buses.org/aba-foundation/scholarships/diversity

Summary   To provide financial assistance for college to Native American and members of other traditionally underrepresented groups who are preparing for a career in the transportation, travel, hospitality, and tourism industry.

Eligibility   This program is open to members of traditionally underrepresented groups who have completed at least 1 year of study at a 2- or 4-year college or university. Applicants must be working on a degree in a course of study related to the transportation, travel, hospitality, and tourism industry. They must have a GPA of 3.0 or higher. Along with their application, they must submit a 500-word essay on the role they hope to play in advancing the future of the transportation, travel, hospitality, and tourism industry. Selection is based on academic achievement, character, leadership, financial need, and commitment to advancing the transportation, travel, hospitality, and tourism industry. Additional consideration is given to applicants who are affiliated with a company that is a member of the American Bus Association (ABA).

Financial data   The stipend is $2,500.

Duration   1 or more each year.

Deadline   April of each year.

[35]
AMERICAN CHEMICAL SOCIETY SCHOLARS PROGRAM

American Chemical Society
Attn: Scholars Program
1155 16th Street, N.W.
Washington, DC 20036
(202) 872-6250   Toll Free: (800) 227-5558, ext. 6250
Fax: (202) 872-4361   E-mail: scholars@acs.org
Web: www.acs.org

Summary To provide financial assistance to Native American and other underrepresented minority students who have a strong interest in chemistry and a desire to prepare for a career in a chemically-related science.

Eligibility This program is open to 1) college-bound high school seniors; 2) freshmen, sophomores, and juniors enrolled full time at an accredited college or university; 3) community college students planning to transfer to a 4-year school; and 4) community college students working on a 2-year degree. Applicants must be African American, Hispanic/Latino, or Native American. They must be majoring or planning to major in chemistry, biochemistry, chemical engineering, or other chemically-related fields, such as environmental science, materials science, or toxicology, in preparation for a career in the chemical sciences or chemical technology. Students planning careers in medicine or pharmacy are not eligible. U.S. citizenship or permanent resident status is required. Selection is based on academic record (GPA of 3.0 or higher), career objective, leadership ability, participation in school activities, community service, and financial need.

Financial data Stipends range up to $5,000 per year, depending on the availability of funding, the number of scholarships awarded, and the need of the recipient. Funds are sent directly to the recipient's college or university.

Duration 1 year; may be renewed.

Additional information This program began in 1994.

Number awarded Varies each year; recently, 309 students received these awards.

Deadline February of each year.

[36]
AMERICAN INDIAN CHAMBER OF COMMERCE OF CALIFORNIA SCHOLARSHIP

American Indian Chamber of Commerce of California
Attn: AICC Scholarship
555 West Fifth Street, 31st Floor
Los Angeles, CA 90013
(213) 440-3232   E-mail: stateadmin@aicccal.org
Web: www.aicccal.org/scholar_forms/default.html

Summary To provide financial assistance for college or graduate school to American Indians who live or attend school in California.

Eligibility This program is open to American Indians who 1) are on a federal- or state-recognized tribal roll and identified by a tribal enrollment card; or 2) have an official letter from a federal- or state-recognized tribe or agency verifying tribal membership or Indian blood. Applicants must be full-time degree candidates at an accredited institution of higher learning (junior college, trade/vocational school, 4-year university, graduate school) in California or residents of California attending an institution of higher learning elsewhere in the

United States. Along with their application, they must submit an educational commitment essay describing their chosen field of study, educational goals, career goals, involvement in the Indian community, and how this scholarship will help in furthering their education. Selection is based on transcripts (30 points), a letter of recommendation (20 points), the educational commitment essay (50 points), and major chosen (bonus 10 points if majoring in business).

Financial data Stipends are $2,500 or $1,500.

Duration 1 year.

Additional information This program began in 1999.

Number awarded 6 each year: 1 at $2,500 and up to 5 at $1,500.

Deadline November of each year.

[37]
AMERICAN INDIAN CHAMBER OF COMMERCE OF WISCONSIN SCHOLARSHIPS

American Indian Chamber of Commerce of Wisconsin, Inc.
Attn: Scholarship Program
10809 West Lincoln Avenue, Suite 102
West Allis, WI 53227
(414) 604-2044   Toll Free: (877) 603-2044
Fax: (414) 604-2070   E-mail: beverly@aiccw.org
Web: www.aiccw.org/welcome/scholarship-program

Summary To provide financial assistance to American Indian students from Wisconsin who are interested in attending college or graduate school in any state.

Eligibility This program is open to residents of Wisconsin who can provide proof of enrollment in an American Indian tribe by at least 1 parent. Applicants must be enrolled full time at a 4-year college or university or graduate school in any state and have a GPA of 3.0 or higher. Along with their application, they must submit a 1-page statement on their personal background, their academic background, their educational and career goals, any hardships or obstacles they have overcome, and how this scholarship will help them to achieve their goals. Selection is based on academic achievement and financial need.

Financial data The stipend ranges from $1,000 to $2,500.

Duration 1 year.

Additional information This program began in 2005.

Number awarded 1 or more each year; since the program began, it has awarded more than $300,000 to 154 students.

Deadline June of each year.

[38]
AMERICAN INDIAN COMMUNITY COLLEGE SCHOLARSHIP

Scholarship Administrative Services, Inc.
Attn: MEFUSA Program
13730 Loumont Street
Whittier, CA 90601

Summary To provide financial assistance to American Indian high school seniors who are interested in attending a community college.

Eligibility This program is open to American Indian seniors graduating from high schools anywhere in the United States. Applicants must be enrolled members of a federally-recognized tribal organization and planning to attend a community college on a full-time basis. Along with their application, they must submit a 1,000-word essay on their educational and career goals, how a community college education will help them to achieve those goals, and how they plan to serve the American Indian community after completing their education. Selection is based on the essay, high school GPA (2.5 or higher), SAT or ACT scores, involvement in the American Indian community, and financial need.

Financial data   The stipend is $5,000 per year.

Duration   1 year; may be renewed 1 additional year if the recipient maintains full-time enrollment and a GPA of 2.5 or higher.

Additional information   This program is sponsored by the Minority Educational Foundation of the United States of America (MEFUSA) and administered by Scholarship Administrative Services, Inc. MEFUSA was established in 2001 to meet the needs of minority students who "show a determination to get a college degree," but who, for financial or other personal reasons, are not able to attend a 4-year college or university. Requests for applications should be accompanied by a self-addressed stamped envelope, the student's e-mail address, and the name of the source where they found the scholarship information.

Number awarded   Up to 100 each year.

Deadline   April of each year.

[39]
AMERICAN INDIAN EDUCATION FUND SCHOLARSHIP PROGRAM

American Indian Education Fund
2401 Eglin Street
Rapid City, SD 57703
Toll Free: (866) 866-8642
E-mail: rschad@nativepartnership.org
Web: www.nrcprograms.org

Summary   To provide financial assistance for college to American Indian and Alaskan Native students.

Eligibility   This program is open to full-time students of Native American or Alaskan Native descent who are currently attending or planning to attend a 2-year college, a 4-year college or university, or a vocational/technical school. Applicants may be either graduating high school seniors or undergraduates who are entering, continuing, or returning to school. Along with their application, they must submit a 4-page essay in which they describe themselves as a student, their ultimate career goals, their plans for working in or with the Indian community, and their participation in leadership and/or community service activities. A GPA between 2.0 to 3.4 is desirable, but all current or future undergraduate students are encouraged to apply. An ACT score of 14 or higher is desirable. Financial need is considered in the selection process.

Financial data   The stipend is $2,000 per year. Funds are paid directly to the recipient's college or university.

Duration   1 year; may be renewed, provided the recipient maintains a GPA of 2.0 or higher.

Additional information   The American Indian Education Fund, formerly the American Indian Education Foundation, is a component of Partnership with Native Americans, formerly National Relief Charities.

Number awarded   Approximately 225 each year.

Deadline   April of each year.

[40]
AMERICAN INDIAN FELLOWSHIP IN BUSINESS SCHOLARSHIP

National Center for American Indian Enterprise
  Development
Attn: Scholarship Committee
953 East Juanita Avenue
Mesa, AZ 85204
Toll Free: (800) 462-2433, ext. 250   Fax: (480) 545-4208
E-mail: scholarships@ncaied.org
Web: www.ncaied.org/programs/scholarships

Summary   To provide financial assistance to American Indians and Alaska Natives working on a bachelor's or master's degree in business.

Eligibility   This program is open to enrolled members of American Indian tribes and Alaska Native villages. Applicants must be enrolled full time as a junior, senior, or master's degree student in business at a college or university in the United States. Along with their application, they must submit 3 essays of 150 to 250 words each on their community involvement, personal challenges, or business experience (paid or volunteer). Selection is based on the quality of those essays (5%), grades (30%), community involvement (30%), personal challenges (25%), and business experience (10%).

Financial data   A stipend is awarded (amount not specified).

Duration   1 year.

Additional information   Recipients must attend the sponsor's annual conference, named Reservation Economic Summit (RES Oklahoma), in association with the Indian Progress in Business (INPRO) Event in Tulsa in November. The sponsor will pay all expenses of attending, including lodging, ground transportation, and airfare. Students who are unable to attend must forfeit their scholarship.

Number awarded   Varies each year; recently, 10 were awarded.

Deadline   September of each year.

[41]
AMERICAN INDIAN MUSEUM FELLOWSHIP

Minnesota Historical Society
Attn: Education Outreach
345 Kellogg Boulevard West
St. Paul, MN 55102
(651) 259-3440   Fax: (651) 259-3434
E-mail: coral.moore@mnhs.org
Web: www.mnhs.org/internships/fellows/americanindian

Summary   To provide an opportunity for American Indian students from any state to learn about tribal historic preservation and museum studies during a summer program at sites in Minnesota.

Eligibility   This program is open to American Indian undergraduates who are 1) residents of Minnesota; 2) residents of other states attending a higher education institution in Minnesota; and 3) members of Dakota, Lakota, and Nakota communities outside of Minnesota attending college in any state. Applicants are not required to be tribally enrolled, but they must be interested in a summer training program in tribal historic preservation and museum studies. Along with their application, they must submit brief descriptions of 1) why they are interested in this program; 2) any relevant course work completed and/or involvement with museum work or tribal historic preservation; 3) how they believe their participation might benefit their community; and 4) how their academic and personal experiences will contribute to seminar discussions related to tribal historic preservation and the representation of American Indian communities in historical organizations.

Financial data The program provides payment of all travel expenses, housing, meals, and a $1,000 stipend upon completion.

Duration 2 and a half weeks during the summer.

Additional information This program operates as a partnership between the Minnesota Indian Affairs Council and the Minnesota Historical Society. Funding is provided by the Arts and Cultural Heritage Fund of the state of Minnesota and the David and Rosemary Good Family Foundation.

Number awarded 15 each year.

Deadline March of each year.

[42]
AMERICAN INDIAN NURSE SCHOLARSHIP PROGRAM

National Society of the Colonial Dames of America
c/o Dumbarton House
2715 Q Street, N.W.
Washington, DC 20007-3071
(202) 337-2288   Fax: (202) 337-0348
Web: www.nscda.org

Summary To provide financial assistance to American Indians interested in preparing for a career in nursing.

Eligibility This program is open to American Indians who are high school graduates (or the equivalent) and enrolled full time in a nursing program at an accredited school. Applicants must have maintained the scholastic average required by their school, be recommended by their counselor or school officer, not be receiving an Indian Health Service Scholarship, have a career goal directly related to the needs of the Indian people, and be in financial need. They must expect to graduate within 2 years if in an associate degree program or within 4 years if in a bachelor's degree program; graduate students are also eligible.

Financial data The stipend is $1,500 per semester ($3,000 per year). Funds are to be used for tuition or fees. The money is sent directly to the recipient's school.

Duration 1 semester; those students who continue to meet the eligibility requirements and have been recommended for continuation are given priority consideration for additional periods of support.

Additional information This program began in 1928.

Number awarded 10 to 15 each year.

Deadline May of each year for fall; November of each year for spring.

[43]
AMERICAN INDIAN SCHOLARSHIPS

Daughters of the American Revolution-National Society
Attn: Committee Services Office, Scholarships
1776 D Street, N.W.
Washington, DC 20006-5303
(202) 628-1776
Web: www.dar.org

Summary To provide supplementary financial assistance to Native American students who are interested in working on an undergraduate or graduate degree.

Eligibility This program is open to Native Americans of any age, any tribe, in any state who are enrolled or planning to enroll in a college, university, or vocational school. Applicants must have a GPA of 3.25 or higher. Graduate students are eligible, but undergraduate students receive preference. Selection is based on academic achievement and financial need.

Financial data The stipend is $4,000. The funds are paid directly to the recipient's college.

Duration 1 year; nonrenewable.

Number awarded 1 each year.

Deadline February of each year.

[44]
AMERICAN INDIAN SCHOLARSHIPS OF SOUTHERN CALIFORNIA

American Indian Scholarship Fund of Southern California
23705 Vanowen Street
PMB 154
West Hills, CA 91307
Web: www.aisfsc.org/scholarship-application

Summary To provide financial assistance to American Indians attending college in southern California.

Eligibility This program is open to American Indians currently enrolled at a college, university, or community college in southern California. Applicants must submit 3 letters of recommendation, transcripts, proof of tribal membership or enrollment, and a 1-page essay discussing their adversities, accomplishments, and ambitions for the future. They must be able to demonstrate financial need.

Financial data A stipend is awarded (amount not specified).

Duration 1 year; recipients may reapply.

Additional information This program began in 1975 but became inactive in 1992. It was revived in 2002.

Number awarded Varies each year; recently, 2 were awarded.

Deadline Deadline not specified.

[45]
AMERICAN INDIAN SCIENCE AND ENGINEERING SOCIETY INTERNSHIP PROGRAM

American Indian Science and Engineering Society
Attn: Director of Membership and Communications
2305 Renard Place, S.E., Suite 200
Albuquerque, NM 87106
(505) 765-1052, ext. 110   Fax: (505) 765-5608
E-mail: lpaz@aises.org
Web: www.aises.org/scholarships/internships

Summary To provide summer work experience with federal agencies or other partner organizations to American Indian and Alaska Native college students who are members of the American Indian Science and Engineering Society (AISES).

Eligibility This program is open to AISES members who are full-time college or university sophomores, juniors, seniors, or graduate students with a GPA of 3.0 or higher. Applicants must be American Indians or Alaska Natives interested in working at selected sites with a partner organization. They must submit an application that includes an essay on their reasons for participating in the program, how it relates to their academic and career goals, what makes them a strong candidate for the program, what they hope to learn and gain as a result, and their leadership skills and experience. U.S. citizenship is required for most positions, although permanent residents may be eligible at some agencies.

Financial data   Interns receive a weekly stipend of $550, dormitory lodging, round-trip airfare or mileage to the internship site, and a weekly allowance of $70 for local transportation.

Duration   10 weeks during the summer.

Additional information   Recently, internships were available at the Bonneville Power Administration (in Vancouver and Cle Elum, Washington), the U.S. Bureau of Land Management (in Arizona), the U.S. Department of Veterans Affairs (in Washington, D.C.), and the U.S. Department of Agriculture Food Safety and Inspection Services (in Washington, D.C.).

Number awarded   Varies each year.

Deadline   February of each year.

[46]
AMERICAN INDIAN SERVICES SCHOLARSHIP PROGRAM

American Indian Services
1902 North Canyon Road, Suite 100
Provo, UT 84604
(801) 375-1777   Toll Free: (888) 227-4120
Fax: (801) 375-1643
E-mail: scholarship@americanindianservices.org
Web: www.americanindianservices.org/students.html

Summary   To provide financial assistance for college to Native Americans who demonstrate financial need.

Eligibility   This program is open to undergraduate students who have completed no more than 150 semester credits at a university, college, junior college, or technical school with a GPA of 2.25 or higher. Applicants must be able to document their Indian heritage with a Certificate of Degree of Indian Blood (CDIB), another official document, or an official document for their parent or grandparent. They must have at least one-quarter North American Native Indian blood. Along with their application, they must submit a 1-page letter about themselves, including their tribe, where they are from, the school they are attending, their area of study, their educational goals and future plans, and why they feel they need this scholarship. Selection is based on financial need, academic status, and availability of funds.

Financial data   Students are expected to arrange for payment of half their tuition. This program pays the other half, from $500 to $1,500.

Duration   1 semester; may be renewed if the recipient maintains a GPA of 2.25 or higher.

Number awarded   Recently, more than 1,500 were awarded.

Deadline   February of each year for classes starting in April or May; May of each year for classes starting in June; August of each year for classes starting in August or September; November of each year for classes starting in January.

[47]
AMERICAN SEAFOODS BBNC SCHOLARSHIP

Bristol Bay Native Corporation
Attn: BBNC Education Foundation
111 West 16th Avenue, Suite 400
Anchorage, AK 99501-6299
(907) 278-3602   Toll Free: (800) 426-3602
Fax: (907) 265-7886   E-mail: bbncef@bbnc.net
Web: www.bbnc.net

Summary   To provide financial assistance to shareholders of Bristol Bay Native Corporation (BBNC) who are currently working on an undergraduate degree in fisheries, biology, or science at a college in any state.

Eligibility   This program is open to BBNC shareholders who are enrolled full time as an upper-division student at a college or university in any state and working on a degree in fisheries, biology, or science. Applicants must have a GPA of 2.5 or higher and be able to demonstrate financial need. Along with their application, they must submit an essay on how they became interested in their proposed field of study, any special circumstances they want to be considered, and their desire to work in the region or for a BBNC subsidiary company. Selection is based on the essay (30%), cumulative GPA (40%), financial need (20%), a resume (5%), and letters of recommendation (5%).

Financial data   Stipend amounts vary.

Duration   1 year.

Additional information   The BBNC is 1 of 13 Alaska Native Regional Corporations created under the Alaska Native Claims Settlement Act of 1971. This program, sponsored by American Seafoods, began in 2011.

Number awarded   1 or more each year.

Deadline   April of each year.

[48]
AMS MINORITY SCHOLARSHIPS

American Meteorological Society
Attn: Development and Student Program Manager
45 Beacon Street
Boston, MA 02108-3693
(617) 227-2426, ext. 3907   Fax: (617) 742-8718
E-mail: dFernandez@ametsoc.org
Web: www2.ametsoc.org

Summary   To provide financial assistance to Native American and other underrepresented minority students entering college and planning to major in meteorology or an aspect of atmospheric sciences.

Eligibility   This program is open to members of minority groups traditionally underrepresented in the sciences (especially Hispanics, Native Americans, and Blacks/African Americans) who are entering their freshman year at a college or university and planning to work on a degree in the atmospheric or related oceanic and hydrologic sciences. Applicants must submit an official high school transcript showing grades from the past 3 years, a letter of recommendation from a high school teacher or guidance counselor, a copy of scores from an SAT or similar national entrance exam, and a 500-word essay on a topic that changes annually; recently, applicants were invited to write on global change and how they would use their college education in atmospheric science (or a closely-related field) to make their community a better place in which to live. Selection is based on the essay and academic performance in high school.

Financial data The stipend is $3,000 per year.

Duration 1 year; may be renewed for the second year of college study.

Additional information This program is funded by grants from industry and by donations to the American Meteorological Society (AMS) 21st Century Campaign. Requests for an application must be accompanied by a self-addressed stamped envelope.

Number awarded Varies each year; recently, 3 were awarded.

Deadline February of each year.

[49]
AMY HUNTER-WILSON, M.D. MEMORIAL SCHOLARSHIP

Wisconsin Medical Society
Attn: Wisconsin Medical Society Foundation
330 East Lakeside Street
Madison, WI 53715
(608) 442-3789   Toll Free: (866) 442-3800, ext. 3789
Fax: (608) 442-3802 E-mail: elizabeth.ringle@wismed.org
Web: www.wisconsinmedicalsociety.org

Summary To provide financial assistance to American Indians interested in working on a degree in medicine, nursing, or allied health care.

Eligibility This program is open to members of federally-recognized American Indian tribes who are 1) full-time students enrolled in a health career program at an accredited institution; 2) adults returning to school in an allied health field; and 3) adults working in a non-professional health-related field returning for a professional license or degree. Applicants must be working on a degree or advanced training as a doctor of medicine, nurse, physician assistant, technician, or other health-related professional. Along with their application, they must submit a personal statement of 1 to 2 pages on their family background, achievements, current higher educational status, career goals, and financial need. Preference is given to residents of Wisconsin who are students at educational institutions in the state. U.S. citizenship is required. Selection is based on financial need, academic achievement, personal qualities and strengths, and letters of recommendation.

Financial data Stipends range from $2,000 to $4,000.

Duration 1 year.

Number awarded Varies each year; recently, 1 at $4,000, 1 at $2,500, and 2 at $2,000 each were awarded.

Deadline January of each year.

[50]
ANA MULTICULTURAL EXCELLENCE SCHOLARSHIP

American Association of Advertising Agencies
Attn: AAAA Foundation
1065 Avenue of the Americas, 16th Floor
New York, NY 10018
(212) 262-2500   E-mail: ameadows@aaaa.org
Web: www.aaaa.org

Summary To provide financial assistance to Native American and other multicultural students who are working on an undergraduate degree in advertising.

Eligibility This program is open to undergraduate students who are U.S. citizens of proven multicultural heritage and have at least 1 grandparent of multicultural heritage. Applicants must be participating in the Multicultural Advertising Intern Program (MAIP). They must be entering their senior year at an accredited college or university in the United States and have a GPA of 3.0 or higher. Selection is based on academic ability.

Financial data The stipend is $2,500.

Duration 1 year.

Additional information This program was established by the Association of National Advertisers (ANA) in 2001. The American Association of Advertising Agencies (AAAA) assumed administration in 2003.

Number awarded 2 each year.

Deadline Deadline not specified.

[51]
ANAC STUDENT DIVERSITY MENTORSHIP SCHOLARSHIP

Association of Nurses in AIDS Care
Attn: Awards Committee
3538 Ridgewood Road
Akron, OH 44333-3122
(330) 670-0101   Toll Free: (800) 260-6780
Fax: (330) 670-0109   E-mail: anac@anacnet.org
Web: www.nursesinaidscare.org

Summary To provide financial assistance to student nurses from Native American and other minority groups who are interested in HIV/AIDS nursing and in attending the national conference of the Association of Nurses in AIDS Care (ANAC).

Eligibility This program is open to student nurses from a diverse racial or ethnic background, defined to include African Americans, Hispanics/Latinos, Asians/Pacific Islanders, and American Indians/Alaskan Natives. Candidates must have a genuine interest in HIV/AIDS nursing, be interested in attending the ANAC national conference, and desire to develop a mentorship relationship with a member of the ANAC Diversity Specialty Committee. They may be 1) pre-licensure students enrolled in an initial R.N. or L.P.N./L.V.N. program (i.e. L.P.N./L.V.N., A.D.N., diploma, B.S./B.S.N.); or 2) current licensed R.N. students with an associate or diploma degree who are enrolled in a bachelor's degree program. Nominees may be recommended by themselves, nursing faculty members, or ANAC members, but their nomination must be supported by an ANAC member. Along with their nomination form, they must submit a 2,000-character essay describing their interest or experience in HIV/AIDS care and why they want to attend the ANAC conference.

Financial data Recipients are awarded a $1,000 scholarship (paid directly to the school), up to $599 in reimbursement of travel expenses to attend the ANAC annual conference, free conference registration, an award plaque, a free ticket to the awards ceremony at the conference, and a 2-year ANAC membership.

Duration 1 year.

Additional information The mentor will be assigned at the conference and will maintain contact during the period of study.

Number awarded 1 each year.

Deadline August of each year.

[52]
ANAGI LEADERSHIP AWARD

Arctic Slope Regional Corporation
Attn: Arctic Education Foundation
P.O. Box 129
Barrow, AK 99723
(907) 852-8633   Toll Free: (800) 770-2772
Fax: (907) 852-2774   E-mail: arcticed@asrc.com
Web: www.arcticed.com

Summary To provide financial assistance to shareholders or descendants of shareholders of the Arctic Slope Regional Corporation (ASRC) who have demonstrated leadership and are interested in attending college in any state.

Eligibility This program is open to original shareholders of the ASRC and direct lineal descendants of original ASRC shareholders. Applicants must be attending or planning to attend a college, university, or vocational/technical school in any state. They must have maintained a GPA of 2.0 or higher throughout high school and during college or training (if applicable), have been involved in school and community extracurricular activities, and have demonstrated leadership qualities. Along with their application, they must an essay describing their leadership experience, their goals in attending college or training, and their plans after completion of college or training. Selection is based on academic performance, demonstrated leadership ability, and community service achievements.

Financial data The award provides for payment of tuition, fees, books, room, and board, to a maximum of $20,000 per year.

Duration Up to 4 years.

Additional information The Arctic Slope Regional Corporation is 1 of 13 Alaska Native Regional Corporations created under the Alaska Native Claims Settlement Act of 1971.

Number awarded 1 each year.

Deadline April of each year.

[53]
ANDREW GRONHOLDT SCHOLARSHIP AWARD

The Aleut Corporation
Attn: Aleut Foundation
703 West Tudor Road, Suite 102
Anchorage, AK 99503-6650
(907) 646-1929   Toll Free: (800) 232-4882
Fax: (907) 646-1949   E-mail: taf@thealeutfoundation.org
Web: www.thealeutfoundation.org

Summary To provide financial assistance to Native Alaskans who are shareholders of The Aleut Corporation or their descendants and working on a degree in the arts at a school in any state.

Eligibility This program is open to Native Alaskans who are original enrollees or descendants of original enrollees of The Aleut Corporation (TAC). Applicants must have completed at least 1 year of a bachelor's, 2- or 4-year vocational, or master's degree in the arts at a school in any state. They

must be enrolled full time and have a GPA of 3.0 or higher. Along with their application, they must include a letter of intent, up to 500 words in length, that describes their educational goals and objectives and their expected graduation date.

Financial data A stipend is awarded (amount not specified).

Duration 1 year.

Additional information The Aleut Corporation is 1 of 13 Alaska Native Regional Corporations created under the Alaska Native Claims Settlement Act of 1971.

Number awarded 1 each year.

Deadline June of each year.

[54]
ANN EUBANK HEALTH SCHOLARSHIP

Chickasaw Foundation
2020 Arlington, Suite 4
P.O. Box 1726
Ada, OK 74821-1726
(580) 421-9030   Fax: (580) 421-9031
E-mail: ChickasawFoundation@chickasaw.net
Web: www.chickasawfoundation.org/Scholarships.aspx

Summary To provide financial assistance to members of the Chickasaw Nation who are working or an undergraduate or graduate degree in a health care field.

Eligibility This program is open to Chickasaw students who are currently working full time on an undergraduate or graduate degree in a health care-related field. Applicants must have a GPA of 3.0 or higher. They must submit 2 letters of recommendation; a copy of their Chickasaw Nation citizenship card; official high school or college transcripts; ACT or SAT scores; a 2-page list of honors, achievements, awards, club memberships, societies, and civic involvement; and a 1-page essay on their long-term goals and plans for achieving those. Financial need is not considered in the selection process.

Financial data A stipend is awarded (amount not specified).

Duration 1 year.

Number awarded 1 each year.

Deadline June of each year.

[55]
ANNA BELLE MITCHELL MEMORIAL SCHOLARSHIP

Cherokee Nation Foundation
800 South Muskogee
Tahlequah, OK 74464
(918) 207-0950   Fax: (918) 207-0951
E-mail: contact@cherokeenationfoundation.org
Web: www.cherokeenationfoundation.org/scholarships

Summary To provide financial assistance to citizens of the Cherokee Nation who are interested in attending a university in any state and majoring in art, especially pottery.

Eligibility This program is open to citizens of the Cherokee Nation who are high school seniors or students currently enrolled full time at a 4-year college or university in any state. Applicants must have a GPA of 3.0 or higher and be majoring in art, especially pottery. They are not required to reside in the Cherokee Nation area. Along with their application, they must submit 3 samples of their work and an 800-word essay on their desire to pursue higher education, their chosen field of study, how they plan to serve the Cherokee people after they complete their higher education, and whether or not they speak the Cherokee language. Selection is based on the clarity and presentation of the essay; academic information (including transcripts and ACT scores); school, cultural and community activities; future plans to serve Cherokee people; and financial need.

Financial data A stipend is awarded (amount not specified).

Duration 1 year; may be renewed up to 4 additional years, provided the recipient maintains a GPA of 3.0 or higher.

Number awarded 1 or more each year.

Deadline January of each year.

[56]
ANNA K. GOWER AND ANNABELLE K. GOWER SCHOLARSHIP FUND

Hawai'i Community Foundation
Attn: Scholarship Department
827 Fort Street Mall
Honolulu, HI 96813
(808) 566-5570   Toll Free: (888) 731-3863
Fax: (808) 521-6286
E-mail: scholarships@hcf-hawaii.org
Web: hcf.scholarships.ngwebsolutions.com

Summary To provide financial assistance to residents of Hawaii of native ancestry who are interested in working on an undergraduate degree at a school in any state.

Eligibility This program is open to residents of Hawaii who are of Native Hawaiian ancestry and enrolled full time at a 2- or 4-year college or university in any state. Applicants must be able to demonstrate academic achievement (GPA of 2.7 or higher), good moral character, and financial need. Along with their application, they must submit a short statement indicating their reasons for attending college, their planned course of study, their career goals, what community service means to them, and how they plan to use their knowledge to serve the needs of the Native Hawaiian community.

Financial data The amounts of the awards depend on the availability of funds and the need of the recipient. Recently, the average value of the scholarships awarded by the foundation was $2,800.

Duration 1 year.

Number awarded 1 or more each year.

Deadline February of each year.

[57]
ANNE SHEN SMITH ENDOWED SCHOLARSHIP

Society of Women Engineers
Attn: Scholarship Selection Committee
203 North LaSalle Street, Suite 1675
Chicago, IL 60601-1269
(312) 596-5223   Toll Free: (877) SWE-INFO
Fax: (312) 644-8557   E-mail: scholarships@swe.org
Web: societyofwomenengineers.swe.org

Summary To provide financial assistance to women, especially those from Native American or other underrepresented groups, working on an undergraduate degree in engineering at colleges in California.

Eligibility This program is open to women who are entering their sophomore, junior, or senior year at a 4-year ABET-accredited college or university in California. Applicants must be working full time on a degree in computer science or any field of engineering. Preference is given to members of groups underrepresented in engineering. U.S. citizenship is required. Selection is based on merit.

Financial data The stipend is $1,000.

Duration 1 year.

Additional information This program began in 2015.

Number awarded 1 each year.

Deadline February of each year.

[58]
ANONYMOUS FOUNDATION SCHOLARSHIP FOR NON-TRIBAL COLLEGE STUDENTS

American Indian College Fund
Attn: Scholarship Department
8333 Greenwood Boulevard
Denver, CO 80221
(303) 426-8900   Toll Free: (800) 776-FUND
Fax: (303) 426-1200
E-mail: scholarships@collegefund.org
Web: www.collegefund.org

Summary To provide financial assistance to Native American college students from California who are interested in attending mainstream colleges and universities in any state.

Eligibility This program is open to American Indians and Alaska Natives who have proof of enrollment or descendancy and are residents of California or members or descendants of a California-based tribe. Applicants must be enrolled or planning to enroll full time at a mainstream college or university in any state. They must have a GPA of 2.0 or higher and be able to demonstrate exceptional academic achievement or financial need. Applications are available only online and include required essays on specified topics. U.S. citizenship is required.

Financial data The stipend is $5,500.

Duration 1 year.

Number awarded 1 or more each year.

Deadline May of each year.

[59]
ANONYMOUS FOUNDATION SCHOLARSHIP FOR TRIBAL COLLEGE STUDENTS

American Indian College Fund
Attn: Scholarship Department
8333 Greenwood Boulevard
Denver, CO 80221
(303) 426-8900   Toll Free: (800) 776-FUND
Fax: (303) 426-1200
E-mail: scholarships@collegefund.org
Web: www.collegefund.org

Summary To provide financial assistance to Native American college students from California who are interested in attending Tribal Colleges and Universities (TCUs) in any state.

Eligibility This program is open to American Indians and Alaska Natives who have proof of enrollment or descendancy and are residents of California or members or descendants of a California-based tribe. Applicants must be enrolled or planning to enroll full time at an eligible TCU in any state. They must have a GPA of 2.0 or higher and be able to demonstrate exceptional academic achievement or financial need. Applications are available only online and include required essays on specified topics. U.S. citizenship is required.

Financial data The stipend is $4,600.

Duration 1 year.

Number awarded 1 or more each year.

Deadline May of each year.

[60]
ANTHC SCHOLARSHIPS

Alaska Native Tribal Health Consortium
Attn: Education, Development and Training Department
3900 Ambassador Drive, Suite 101
Anchorage, AK 99508
(907) 729-1301   Toll Free: (800) 684-8361
Fax: (907) 729-3638   E-mail: learning@anthc.org
Web: www.anthc.org/scholarship-opportunities

Summary To provide financial assistance for college or graduate school to Natives and American Indians who are residents of Alaska and interested in a career in health care.

Eligibility This program is open to Alaska Natives and American Indians who are undergraduate or graduate students interested in preparing for a career in the field of health care. Applicants must be residents of Alaska working full time on an associate, bachelor's, master's, or Ph.D. degree. Along with their application, they must submit a personal statement answering several questions on their interest in Alaska Native health care. Selection is based on the statement, letters of recommendation, presentation of the application, and involvement in the Native community.

Financial data The stipend is $5,000 per year.

Duration 1 year; may be renewed if recipients maintain a GPA of 2.5 or higher and complete at least 6 credits each term.

Number awarded 10 each year.

Deadline June of each year.

[61]
ANTHONY A. WELMAS SCHOLARSHIP

American Indian College Fund
Attn: Scholarship Department
8333 Greenwood Boulevard
Denver, CO 80221
(303) 426-8900   Toll Free: (800) 776-FUND
Fax: (303) 426-1200
E-mail: scholarships@collegefund.org
Web: www.collegefund.org

Summary To provide financial assistance to Native American college students who are interested in attending Tribal Colleges and Universities (TCUs) or other colleges or universities in any state.

Eligibility This program is open to American Indians and Alaska Natives who have proof of enrollment or descendancy in a federally-recognized tribe. Applicants must be working on or planning to work on an associate or bachelor's degree at an eligible TCU or other college or university in any state. They must have a GPA of 3.0 or higher. Applications are available only online and include required essays on specified topics. U.S. citizenship is required.

Financial data The stipend is $1,000.

Duration 1 year.

Number awarded 1 or more each year.

Deadline May of each year.

[62]
APS/FOUR CORNERS POWER PLANT NAVAJO SCHOLARSHIPS

Pinnacle West Capital Corporation
Attn: Four Corners Power Plant Program
Scholarship Committee
P.O. Box 355
MS 4918
Fruitland, NM 87416
(505) 598-8213   E-mail: Corrine.Yazzie@aps.com
Web: s.com

Summary To provide financial assistance to members of the Navajo Nation who live near the Four Corners and are interested in attending college in any state to prepare for a career in the electric utility industry.

Eligibility This program is open to members of the Navajo Nation who live near the Four Corners and are attending or planning to attend a college or university in any state as a full-time student. Applicants must intend to major in a field that will prepare them for a career in the electric utility industry, including accounting, business administration, chemistry, computer science, engineering, human resources, nursing, occupational safety, or vocational programs (e.g., automotive, electrical, instrumentation, machinist, water treatment, welding). They must have a cumulative GPA of 2.5 or higher. Along with their application, they must submit 3 essays of 300 words each on 1) their career plans, why they have chosen that field, and what they have done to demonstrate their interest in that field; 2) their ability to deal with others effectively; and 3) how society will benefit from their education.

Financial data The stipend ranges from $1,000 to $1,500 per year.

Duration 1 year; may be renewed, provided the recipient continues to meet eligibility requirements.

Additional information This program began in 1995.

Number awarded Varies each year.

Deadline June of each year.

[63]
APS/IBM RESEARCH INTERNSHIP FOR UNDERREPRESENTED MINORITY STUDENTS

American Physical Society
Attn: Committee on Minorities
One Physics Ellipse
College Park, MD 20740-3844
(301) 209-3232   Fax: (301) 209-0865
E-mail: apsibmin@us.ibm.com
Web: www.aps.org

Summary To provide an opportunity for Native American and other underrepresented minority students to participate in a summer research internship in science or engineering at facilities of IBM.

Eligibility This program is open to members of underrepresented minority groups currently enrolled as sophomores or juniors and majoring in biology, chemistry, chemical engineering, computer science or engineering, electrical engineering, materials science or engineering, mechanical engineering, or physics. Applicants are not required to be U.S. citizens, but they must be enrolled at a college or university in the United States. They must be interested in working as a research intern at a participating IBM laboratory. A GPA of at least 3.0 is required. Selection is based on commitment to and interest in their major field of study.

Financial data Interns receive a competitive salary of approximately $8,000 for the summer.

Duration 10 weeks during the summer.

Additional information Participating IBM laboratories are the Almaden Research Center in San Jose, California, the Watson Research Center in Yorktown Heights, New York, or the Austin Research Laboratory in Austin, Texas.

Number awarded 1 each year.

Deadline February of each year.

[64]
AQQALUK TRUST SCHOLARSHIPS

Robert Aqqaluk Newlin, Sr. Memorial Trust
Attn: Education Coordinator
P.O. Box 509
Kotzebue, AK 99752
(907) 442-8143   Toll Free: (866) 442-1607
Fax: (907) 442-2289
E-mail: aqqaluk.trust@aqqaluktrust.com
Web: www.aqqaluktrust.com/education

Summary To provide financial assistance to Alaska Natives who are associated with the Northwest Alaska Native Association (NANA) Regional Corporation and interested in attending college in any state.

Eligibility This program is open to NANA shareholders, descendants of NANA shareholders, and dependents of NANA shareholders and their descendants. Applicants must have a GED or high school diploma with a cumulative GPA of 2.0 or higher and be enrolled or accepted for enrollment at an accredited or authorized college, university, or vocational technical skills program in any state. Along with their application, they must submit a statement that explains how they intend to use their education to enhance Inupiaq values and culture, summarizes their accomplishments, and describes their educational and career goals.

Financial data Stipends are $2,000 per semester for full-time students or $1,000 per semester for part-time students. Funds must be used for tuition, fees, books, course-related supplies, room, board, and similar expenses.

Duration 1 semester; recipients may reapply by providing a letter updating their educational and career goals, explaining how they are moving toward their goals, and reporting how the previous funds were spend.

Additional information The NANA Regional Corporation is 1 of 13 regional corporations established according to the terms of the Alaska Native Claims Settlement Act (ANCSA) of 1971. It originally administered its scholarship program, but later transferred its education department to the Robert Aqqaluk Newlin, Sr. Memorial Trust. Sponsors of the program include the NANA Regional Corporation, Teck Alaska Inc., and Qivliq, LLC.

Number awarded Varies each year, depending upon the availability of funds and qualified applicants.

Deadline College and university students must apply by July of each year for fall semester or quarter, October of each year for winter quarter, January of each year for spring semester, February of each year for spring quarter, or May of each year for summer school. Vocational/technical students must apply before the start of training.

[65]
ARCTIC EDUCATION FOUNDATION SCHOLARSHIPS

Arctic Slope Regional Corporation
Attn: Arctic Education Foundation
P.O. Box 129
Barrow, AK 99723
(907) 852-8633   Toll Free: (800) 770-2772
Fax: (907) 852-2774   E-mail: arcticed@asrc.com
Web: www.arcticed.com

Summary To provide financial assistance to Inupiat Natives who are shareholders or descendants of shareholders of the Arctic Slope Regional Corporation (ASRC) and interested in attending college or graduate school in any state.

Eligibility This program is open to U.S. citizens who are 1) a northern Alaskan Inupiat Native currently residing in the Arctic Slope region of Alaska; 2) an original shareholder of the ASRC; or 3) a direct lineal descendant of an original ASRC shareholder. Applicants must be attending or planning to attend a college, university, or vocational/technical school in any state as a full- or part-time undergraduate or graduate student. Along with their application, they must submit documentation of financial need and a short paragraph on their personal plans upon completion of study.

Financial data For students in vocational training programs, the maximum stipend is $2,875 per semester ($5,750 per year). For full-time undergraduate students at 4-year colleges and universities, the maximum stipend is $6,750 per year. For graduate students, the maximum stipend is $10,750 per year.

Duration 1 year; may be renewed.

Additional information The Arctic Slope Regional Corporation is 1 of 13 Alaska Native Regional Corporations created under the Alaska Native Claims Settlement Act of 1971.

Number awarded Varies each year.

Deadline February of each year for spring quarter; April of each year for summer school; July of each year for fall semester or quarter; or November of each year for spring semester or winter quarter.

[66]
ARIZONA PUBLIC SERVICE HOPI SCHOLARS PROGRAM

Hopi Tribe
Attn: Grants and Scholarships Program
P.O. Box 123
Kykotsmovi, AZ 86039
(928) 734-3542   Toll Free: (800) 762-9630
Fax: (928) 734-9575   E-mail: JTorivio@hopi.nsn.us
Web: www.hopi-nsn.gov

Summary   To provide financial assistance to Hopi students who are working on an undergraduate degree in an area of science, technology, engineering, or mathematics (STEM), education, or nursing.

Eligibility   This program is open to enrolled members of the Hopi Tribe who are full-time college sophomores, juniors, or seniors working on an associate or bachelor's degree. First priority is given to students majoring in a field of STEM; other priorities include education and nursing. Applicants must have a GPA of 2.5 or higher and have applied for all federal, state, and institutional aid. They must be willing to perform 40 hours of community service that will benefit the Hopi community. Along with their application, they must submit a 1-page essay on their commitment to giving back to the Hopi community.

Financial data   The stipend is $4,000.

Duration   1 year.

Additional information   This program began in 2010 with support from Arizona Public Service.

Number awarded   8 each year: 2 sophomores, 3 juniors, and 3 seniors.

Deadline   January of each year.

[67]
ARIZONA PUBLIC SERVICE NAVAJO SCHOLARS PROGRAM FOR NON-TRIBAL COLLEGE STUDENTS

American Indian College Fund
Attn: Scholarship Department
8333 Greenwood Boulevard
Denver, CO 80221
(303) 426-8900   Toll Free: (800) 776-FUND
Fax: (303) 426-1200
E-mail: scholarships@collegefund.org
Web: www.collegefund.org

Summary   To provide financial assistance to members of the Navajo Nation who are interested in majoring in fields of science, technology, engineering, or mathematics (STEM) at a college in Arizona or New Mexico.

Eligibility   This program is open to enrolled members of the Navajo Nation at any Shiprock Agency Chapter who are enrolled or planning to enroll at a college or university in Arizona or New Mexico. Applicants must have a GPA of 2.8 or higher and be majoring in a field or subfield of STEM. They must be interested in interning or working for Arizona Public Service. Applications are available only online and include required essays on specified topics. U.S. citizenship is required.

Financial data   The stipend is $6,000.

Duration   1 year.

Additional information   This program is sponsored by Arizona Public Service in partnership with the American Indian College Fund. Recipients must participate in the American Indian Higher Education Consortium (AIHEC) summer leadership conference; all expenses are paid.

Number awarded   1 or more each year.

Deadline   May of each year.

[68]
ARIZONA PUBLIC SERVICE NAVAJO SCHOLARS PROGRAM FOR TRIBAL COLLEGE STUDENTS

American Indian College Fund
Attn: Scholarship Department
8333 Greenwood Boulevard
Denver, CO 80221
(303) 426-8900   Toll Free: (800) 776-FUND
Fax: (303) 426-1200
E-mail: scholarships@collegefund.org
Web: www.collegefund.org

Summary   To provide financial assistance to members of the Navajo Nation who are interested in majoring in fields of science, technology, engineering, or mathematics (STEM) at designated Tribal Colleges and Universities (TCUs) in Arizona or New Mexico.

Eligibility   This program is open to enrolled members of the Navajo Nation at any Shiprock Agency Chapter who are enrolled or planning to enroll at Diné College (Tsaile, Arizona), Navajo Technical College (Chinle Arizona, Crownpoint, New Mexico, or Teec Nos Pos, Arizona), or Southwest Indian Polytechnic Institute (Albuquerque, New Mexico). Applicants must have a GPA of 2.8 or higher and be majoring in a field or subfield of STEM. They must be interested in interning or working for Arizona Public Service. Applications are available only online and include required essays on specified topics. U.S. citizenship is required.

Financial data   The stipend is $6,000.

Duration   1 year.

Additional information   This program is sponsored by Arizona Public Service in partnership with the American Indian College Fund. Recipients must participate in the American Indian Higher Education Consortium (AIHEC) summer leadership conference; all expenses are paid.

Number awarded   1 or more each year.

Deadline   May of each year.

[69]
ARKANSAS CONFERENCE ETHNIC AND LANGUAGE CONCERNS COMMITTEE SCHOLARSHIPS

United Methodist Church-Arkansas Conference
Attn: Committee on Ethnic and Language Concerns
800 Daisy Bates Drive
Little Rock, AR 72202
(501) 324-8045   Toll Free: (877) 646-1816
Fax: (501) 324-8018   E-mail: mallen@arumc.org
Web: www.arumc.org/docs-and-forms

Summary   To provide financial assistance to Native American and other ethnic minority Methodist students from Arkansas who are interested in attending college or graduate school in any state.

Eligibility   This program is open to ethnic minority undergraduate and graduate students who are active members of local congregations affiliated with the Arkansas Conference of the United Methodist Church (UMC). Applicants must be currently enrolled in an accredited institution of higher education in any state. Along with their application, they must submit an essay explaining how this scholarship will make them a leader in the UMC. Preference is given to students attending a UMC-affiliated college or university.

Financial data The stipend is $500 per semester ($1,000 per year) for undergraduates or $1,000 per semester ($2,000 per year) for graduate students.

Duration 1 year; may be renewed.

Number awarded 5 each year: 1 in each UMC Arkansas district.

Deadline February or September of each year.

[70]
ARTHUR C. PARKER SCHOLARSHIPS

Society for American Archaeology
Attn: Native American Scholarship Fund
1111 14th Street, N.W., Suite 800
Washington, DC 20005-5622
(202) 789-8200   Fax: (202) 789-0284
E-mail: nasf@saa.org
Web: ecommerce.saa.org

Summary To provide financial assistance to Native American students and professionals interested in additional training in archaeological methods.

Eligibility This program is open to high school seniors, college undergraduates, graduate students, and personnel of tribal or other Native cultural preservation programs. Applicants must be Native Americans or Pacific Islanders from the United States, including U.S. Trust Territories, or indigenous people from Canada. They must be interested in attending a training program in archaeological methods offered by an accredited college or university, including field work, analytical techniques, and curation. Individuals may apply themselves, or they may be nominated by a high school teacher, current professor, or cultural preservation program supervisor. Along with the application, they must submit a 2-page personal statement describing why they are interested in their proposed program and in archaeology, and the contributions they hope to make to the future of archaeology.

Financial data The stipend is $4,000.

Duration 1 year.

Additional information Partial support of this program is provided by the National Science Foundation (NSF).

Number awarded 4 each year: 1 funded by the Society for American Archaeology and 3 by the NSF.

Deadline December of each year.

[71]
ARTHUR H. GOODMAN MEMORIAL SCHOLARSHIP

San Diego Foundation
Attn: Community Scholarships
2508 Historic Decatur Road, Suite 200
San Diego, CA 92106
(619) 814-1343   Fax: (619) 239-1710
E-mail: scholarships@sdfoundation.org
Web: www.sdfoundation.org

Summary To provide financial assistance to Native American and other underrepresented community college students in California or Arizona planning to transfer to a 4-year school in any state to prepare for a career in economic development.

Eligibility This program is open to women and minorities currently enrolled at a community college in California or Arizona and planning to transfer as a full- or part-time student at a 4-year school in any state. Applicants must submit informa-

tion on their long-term career goal, a list of volunteer and extracurricular activities, documentation of financial need, and a 3-page personal statement on their commitment to community involvement and desire to prepare for a career in the field of economic development.

Financial data Stipends range from $1,500 to $3,000.

Duration 1 year.

Additional information This program was established in 1998 by the CDC Small Business Finance Corporation.

Number awarded Varies each year; recently, 5 were awarded.

Deadline April of each year.

[72]
ASCPA EDUCATIONAL FOUNDATION DIVERSITY SCHOLARSHIPS

Alabama Society of Certified Public Accountants
Attn: ASCPA Educational Foundation
1041 Longfield Court
P.O. Box 242987
Montgomery, AL 36124-2987
(334) 834-7650   Toll Free: (800) 227-1711 (within AL)
Fax: (334) 834-7603
Web: www.ascpa.org

Summary To provide financial assistance to Native American and other minority accounting students at colleges and universities in Alabama.

Eligibility This program is open to minority (Black or African American, Hispanic or Latino, Native American, or Asian) residents of any state enrolled at least half time at colleges and universities in Alabama with at least 1 full year of school remaining. Applicants must have declared a major in accounting and have completed intermediate accounting courses. They must have a GPA of 3.0 or higher overall and in all accounting classes. Along with their application, they must submit a 25-word essay on why the scholarship is important to them. Financial need is not considered in the selection process. Preference is given to students who have a strong interest in a career as a C.P.A. in Alabama. U.S. citizenship or permanent resident status is required.

Financial data The stipend is $2,500.

Duration 1 year.

Additional information This program began in 2012.

Number awarded 5 each year.

Deadline March of each year.

[73]
ASLA COUNCIL OF FELLOWS SCHOLARSHIPS

Landscape Architecture Foundation
Attn: Leadership in Landscape Scholarship Program
1129 20th Street, N.W., Suite 202
Washington, DC 20036
(202) 331-7070   Fax: (202) 331-7079
E-mail: scholarships@lafoundation.org
Web: www.lafoundation.org

Summary To provide financial assistance to upper-division students, especially those from Native American and other disadvantaged and underrepresented groups, working on a degree in landscape architecture.

Eligibility This program is open to landscape architecture students in the third, fourth, or fifth year of undergraduate work. Preference is given to, and 1 scholarship is reserved for, members of underrepresented ethnic or cultural groups. Applicants must submit a 500-word essay on how they envision themselves contributing to the profession of landscape architecture, 2 letters of recommendation, documentation of financial need, and (for students applying for the scholarship reserved for underrepresented groups) a statement identifying their association with a specific ethnic or cultural group. U.S. citizenship or permanent resident status is required.

Financial data The stipend is $4,000. Students also receive a 1-year membership in the American Society of Landscape Architects (ASLA), general registration fees for the ASLA annual meeting, and a travel stipend to attend the meeting.

Duration 1 year.

Additional information This program is sponsored by ASLA and administered by the Landscape Architecture Foundation.

Number awarded 3 each year, of which 1 is reserved for a member of an underrepresented group.

Deadline February of each year.

[74]
ASSE DIVERSITY COMMITTEE UNDERGRADUATE SCHOLARSHIP

American Society of Safety Engineers
Attn: ASSE Foundation
Scholarship Award Program
520 North Northwest Highway
Park Ridge, IL 60068-2538
(847) 699-2929   Fax: (847) 296-3769
E-mail: assefoundation@asse.org
Web: foundation.asse.org/scholarships-and-grants

Summary To provide financial assistance to upper-division students who are Native Americans or members of other diverse groups and are working on a degree related to occupational safety.

Eligibility This program is open to students who are working on an undergraduate degree in occupational safety, health, environment, industrial hygiene, occupational health nursing, or a closely-related field (e.g., industrial or environmental engineering). Applicants must be full-time students who have completed at least 60 semester hours and have a GPA of 3.0 or higher. A goal of this program is to support individuals regardless of race, ethnicity, gender, religion, personal beliefs, age, sexual orientation, physical challenges, geographic location, university, or specific area of study. U.S. citizenship is not required. Membership in the American Society of Safety Engineers (ASSE) is not required, but preference is given to members.

Financial data The stipend is $1,000 per year.

Duration 1 year; recipients may reapply.

Number awarded 1 each year.

Deadline November of each year.

[75]
ASSOCIATED FOOD AND PETROLEUM DEALERS MINORITY SCHOLARSHIPS

Associated Food and Petroleum Dealers
Attn: AFPD Foundation
5779 West Maple Road
West Bloomfield, MI 48322
(248) 671-9600   Toll Free: (800) 666-6233
Fax: (866) 601-9610   E-mail: info@afpdonline.org
Web: www.afpdonline.org/michigan-scholarship.php

Summary To provide financial assistance to Native American and othr minority high school seniors and current college students from Michigan who are enrolled or planning to enroll at a college in any state.

Eligibility This program is open to Michigan residents who are high school seniors or college freshmen, sophomores, or juniors. Applicants must be members of 1 of the following minority groups: African American, Hispanic, Asian, Native American, or Arab/Chaldean. They must be enrolled or planning to enroll full time at a college or university in any state. Preferential consideration is given to applicants with a membership affiliation in the Associated Food and Petroleum Dealers (AFPD), although membership is not required. Selection is based on academic performance, leadership, and participation in school and community activities; college grades are considered if the applicant is already enrolled in college.

Financial data The stipend is $1,500 per year.

Duration 1 year; may be renewed 1 additional year.

Additional information This program is administered by International Scholarship and Tuition Services, Inc. The AFPD was formed in 2006 by a merger of the Associated Food Dealers of Michigan and the Great Lakes Petroleum Retailers and Allied Trades Association.

Number awarded At least 10 each year, of which at least 3 must be awarded to member customers.

Deadline March of each year.

[76]
ASSOCIATION FOR WOMEN GEOSCIENTISTS MINORITY SCHOLARSHIP

Association for Women Geoscientists
Attn: AWG Foundation
12000 North Washington Street, Suite 285
Thornton, CO 80241
(303) 412-6219   Fax: (303) 253-9220
E-mail: office@awg.org
Web: www.awg.org/eas/minority.htm

Summary To provide financial assistance to Native American and other underrepresented minority women who are interested in working on an undergraduate degree in the geosciences.

Eligibility This program is open to women who are African American, Hispanic, or Native American (including Eskimo, Hawaiian, Samoan, or American Indian). Applicants must be full-time students working on, or planning to work on, an undergraduate degree in the geosciences (including geology, geophysics, geochemistry, hydrology, meteorology, physical oceanography, planetary geology, or earth science education). They must submit a 500-word essay on their academic and career goals, 2 letters of recommendation, high school and/or college transcripts, and SAT or ACT scores. Financial need is not considered in the selection process. U.S. citizenship is required.

Financial data A total of $6,000 is available for this program each year.

Duration 1 year; may be renewed.

Additional information This program, first offered in 2004, is supported by ExxonMobil Foundation.

Number awarded 1 or more each year.

Deadline June of each year.

[77]
ASSOCIATION ON AMERICAN INDIAN AFFAIRS DISPLACED HOMEMAKER SCHOLARSHIPS

Association on American Indian Affairs, Inc.
Attn: Director of Scholarship Programs
966 Hungerford Drive, Suite 12-B
Rockville, MD 20850
(240) 314-7155   Fax: (240) 314-7159
E-mail: general.aaia@indian-affairs.org
Web: www.indian-affairs.org

Summary To provide financial assistance to Native American displaced homemakers who are trying to complete their college education.

Eligibility This program is open to full-time college students who are Native Americans and have special needs because of family responsibilities. Examples of displaced homemakers include students who are attending college for the first time, usually 35 years of age or older, because they have put off higher education to raise their children, students who are entering or returning to college after their children enter elementary school, and men or women who have been divorced and had to leave college to care for children and are now returning. Applicants must submit proof of tribal enrollment and an essay of 2 to 3 pages on 1 of the following topics: 1) why the sponsor's International Repatriation Project is important and how they would inform others about it; 2) the Annie E. Casey Foundation's Juvenile Detention Alternatives Initiative and tribal and community-based alternatives to detention for juveniles; or 3) how tribal leaders can promote higher education in their family and community. They must have a GPA of 2.5 or higher. Selection is based on merit and need.

Financial data The stipend is $1,500. Awards are intended to assist recipients with child care, transportation, and some basic living expenses as well as educational costs.

Duration 1 year; recipients may reapply.

Number awarded Varies each year; recently, 2 were awarded.

Deadline May of each year.

[78]
A.T. ANDERSON MEMORIAL SCHOLARSHIP

American Indian Science and Engineering Society
Attn: Director of Membership and Communications
2305 Renard Place, S.E., Suite 200
Albuquerque, NM 87106
(505) 765-1052, ext. 110   Fax: (505) 765-5608
E-mail: lpaz@aises.org
Web: www.aises.org/scholarships/at-anderson

Summary To provide financial assistance to members of the American Indian Science and Engineering Society (AISES) who are majoring in designated fields as undergraduate or graduate students.

Eligibility This program is open to AISES members who are full-time undergraduate or graduate students at an accredited 4-year college or university. Applicants must be American Indian tribal members, Alaskan Natives, or Native Hawaiians and have a Certificate of Degree of Indian or Alaska Native Blood (CDIB) showing at least 25% Native blood. They must have a GPA of 3.0 or higher and be working on a degree in engineering, mathematics, medical sciences, natural resources, physical science, technology, or the sciences. Selection is based on academic performance, a personal statement, letters of recommendation, and activities (e.g., jobs, volunteer efforts, internships, extracurricular involvement, hobbies).

Financial data The annual stipend is $1,000 for undergraduates or $2,000 for graduate students.

Duration 1 year; nonrenewable.

Additional information This program began in 1983. Current sponsors include the AMB Foundation, Bayer, Boeing, Chrysler, Helen Roberti Foundation, Lockheed Martin, Northrup Grumman, Oracle, and the San Manuel Band of Mission Indians.

Number awarded Varies each year; recently, 80 were awarded.

Deadline April of each year.

[79]
ATALOA MEMORIAL SCHOLARSHIP

Chickasaw Foundation
2020 Arlington, Suite 4
P.O. Box 1726
Ada, OK 74821-1726
(580) 421-9030   Fax: (580) 421-9031
E-mail: ChickasawFoundation@chickasaw.net
Web: www.chickasawfoundation.org/Scholarships.aspx

Summary To provide financial assistance to members of the Chickasaw Nation who are working on an undergraduate degree in music or a related field.

Eligibility This program is open to Chickasaw students who are currently enrolled full time at a college or university and working on an undergraduate degree in music, including vocal, Native American, composition, music education, or a related field. Applicants must submit high school or college transcripts; 2 letters of recommendation; a copy of their Chickasaw Nation citizenship card; a 2-page list of honors, achievements, awards, club memberships, societies, and civic involvement; and a 1-page essay on their long-term goals and plans for achieving those. Financial need is not considered in the selection process.

Financial data A stipend is awarded (amount not specified).

Duration 1 year.

Number awarded 1 each year.

Deadline June of each year.

[80]
ATKINS NORTH AMERICA ACHIEVEMENT COLLEGE SCHOLARSHIP

Conference of Minority Transportation Officials
Attn: National Scholarship Program
100 M Street, S.E., Suite 917
Washington, DC 20003
(202) 506-2917   E-mail: info@comto.org
Web: www.comto.org/page/scholarships

Summary To provide financial assistance to Native American and other minority undergraduates interested in working on a degree in transportation or a related field.

Eligibility This program is open to minority students who have completed at least 12 semester hours as full-time undergraduates. Applicants must be studying transportation, engineering, planning, or a related discipline. Along with their application they must submit a cover letter on their transportation-related career goals and life aspirations. Financial need is not considered in the selection process.

Financial data The stipend is $2,000. Funds are paid directly to the recipient's college or university.

Duration 1 year.

Additional information This program is sponsored by Atkins North America.

Number awarded 1 each year.

Deadline April of each year.

[81]
ATKINS NORTH AMERICA ACHIEVEMENT HIGH SCHOOL SCHOLARSHIP

Conference of Minority Transportation Officials
Attn: National Scholarship Program
100 M Street, S.E., Suite 917
Washington, DC 20003
(202) 506-2917   E-mail: info@comto.org
Web: www.comto.org/page/scholarships

Summary To provide financial assistance to Native American and other minority high school seniors interested in working on a degree in transportation or a related field.

Eligibility This program is open to minority seniors graduating from high school with a GPA of 3.0 or higher. Applicants must be planning to study aspects of transportation, including technology, engineering, planning, or management. Along with their application they must submit a cover letter on their transportation-related career goals and life aspirations. Financial need is not considered in the selection process.

Financial data The stipend is $2,000. Funds are paid directly to the recipient's college or university.

Duration 1 year.

Additional information This program is sponsored by Atkins North America.

Number awarded 1 each year.

Deadline April of each year.

[82]
ATKINS NORTH AMERICA LEADERSHIP SCHOLARSHIP

Conference of Minority Transportation Officials
Attn: National Scholarship Program
100 M Street, S.E., Suite 917
Washington, DC 20003
(202) 506-2917   E-mail: info@comto.org
Web: www.comto.org/page/scholarships

Summary To provide financial assistance to Native American and other minority undergraduate and graduate students interested in working on a degree in transportation or a related field.

Eligibility This program is open to minority 1) undergraduates who have completed at least 12 semester hours of study; and 2) graduate students. Applicants must be studying transportation, engineering, planning, or a related discipline. Along with their application they must submit a cover letter on their transportation-related career goals and life aspirations. Financial need is not considered in the selection process.

Financial data The stipend is $3,000. Funds are paid directly to the recipient's college or university.

Duration 1 year.

Additional information This program is sponsored by Atkins North America.

Number awarded 1 each year.

Deadline April of each year.

[83]
AT-LARGE TRIBAL COUNCIL AWARD

Cherokee Nation Foundation
800 South Muskogee
Tahlequah, OK 74464
(918) 207-0950   Fax: (918) 207-0951
E-mail: contact@cherokeenationfoundation.org
Web: cherokeenation.academicworks.com

Summary To provide financial assistance to high school senior citizens of the Cherokee Nation who are planning to attend college in any state and who reside outside the tribal jurisdictional boundaries.

Eligibility This program is open to citizens of the Cherokee Nation who are graduating from high schools outside the jurisdictional area of the tribe. Applicants must be planning to enroll at a college, university, or vocational/technical school in any state. Along with their application, they must submit an 800-word essay on their desire to pursue higher education, their chosen field of study, how they plan to serve the Cherokee people after they complete their higher education, and whether or not they speak the Cherokee language. Selection is based on the clarity and presentation of the essay; academic information (including transcripts and ACT scores); school, cultural and community activities; future plans to serve Cherokee people; and financial need.

Financial data The stipend is $1,500 per semester ($3,000 per year).

Duration 1 year. Renewal for the second semester requires the recipient to earn a GPA of 3.0 or higher in the first semester.

Additional information These scholarships were first awarded in 2008.

Number awarded Varies each year; recently, 3 were awarded.

Deadline January of each year.

[84]
AUSTIN FAMILY SCHOLARSHIP ENDOWMENT FOR TRIBAL COLLEGE STUDENTS

American Indian College Fund
Attn: Scholarship Department
8333 Greenwood Boulevard
Denver, CO 80221
(303) 426-8900   Toll Free: (800) 776-FUND
Fax: (303) 426-1200
E-mail: scholarships@collegefund.org
Web: www.collegefund.org

Summary To provide financial assistance to members of American Indian tribes in Oklahoma who are interested in attending Tribal Colleges and Universities (TCUs) in any state.

Eligibility This program is open to residents of Oklahoma who are members or descendants of an American Indian tribe in the state. Applicants must be enrolled or planning to enroll full time at an eligible TCU in any state and have a GPA of 2.0 or higher. Applications are available only online and include required essays on specified topics. U.S. citizenship is required.

Financial data The stipend is $1,085.

Duration 1 year.

Number awarded 1 or more each year.

Deadline May of each year.

[85]
AVIATION AND PROFESSIONAL DEVELOPMENT SCHOLARSHIP

Airport Minority Advisory Council
Attn: AMAC Foundation
2001 Jefferson Davis Highway, Suite 500
Arlington, VA 22202
(703) 414-2622   Fax: (703) 414-2686
E-mail: terrifrierson@palladiumholdingsco.com
Web: amac-org.com/amac-foundation/scholarships

Summary To provide financial assistance to Native American and other minority high school seniors and undergraduates who are preparing for a career in the aviation industry and interested in participating in activities of the Airport Minority Advisory Council (AMAC).

Eligibility This program is open to minority and female high school seniors and current undergraduates who have a GPA of 2.5 or higher and a record of involvement in community and extracurricular activities. Applicants must be interested in working on a bachelor's degree in accounting, architecture, aviation, business administration, engineering, or finance as preparation for a career in the aviation or airport industry. They must be interested in participating in the AMAC program, including becoming a member if they are awarded a scholarship, and communicating with AMAC once each semester during the term of the scholarship. Along with their application, they must submit a 750-word essay on how they have overcome barriers in life to achieve their academic and/or career goals; their dedication to succeed in the aviation industry and how AMAC can help them achieve their goal;

and the most important issues that the aviation industry is facing today and how they see themselves changing those. Financial need is not considered in the selection process. U.S. citizenship is required.

Financial data The stipend is $2,000 per year.

Duration 1 year; recipients may reapply.

Number awarded 4 each year.

Deadline May of each year.

[86]
BANK2 BANKING SCHOLARSHIP

Chickasaw Foundation
2020 Arlington, Suite 4
P.O. Box 1726
Ada, OK 74821-1726
(580) 421-9030   Fax: (580) 421-9031
E-mail: ChickasawFoundation@chickasaw.net
Web: www.chickasawfoundation.org/Scholarships.aspx

Summary To provide financial assistance to members of the Chickasaw Nation who are preparing for a career in banking.

Eligibility This program is open to Chickasaw students who are currently enrolled at a 4-year college or university as a full-time undergraduate student. Applicants must be majoring in finance, business, or accounting and preparing for a career in banking. Along with their application, they must submit high school or college transcripts; 2 letters of recommendation; a copy of their Chickasaw Nation citizenship card; a 2-page list of honors, achievements, awards, club memberships, societies, and civic involvement; and a 1-page essay on their long-term goals and plans for achieving those. Financial need is not considered in the selection process.

Financial data A stipend is awarded (amount not specified).

Duration 1 year.

Additional information This program is supported by Bank2, headquartered in Oklahoma City and owned by the Chickasaw Nation.

Number awarded 1 each year.

Deadline June of each year.

[87]
BANK2 TA-OSSAA-ASHA' SCHOLARSHIPS

Chickasaw Foundation
2020 Arlington, Suite 4
P.O. Box 1726
Ada, OK 74821-1726
(580) 421-9030   Fax: (580) 421-9031
E-mail: ChickasawFoundation@chickasaw.net
Web: www.chickasawfoundation.org/Scholarships.aspx

Summary To provide financial assistance to members of the Chickasaw Nation who are preparing for a career in banking.

Eligibility This program is open to Chickasaw students who are currently enrolled at an accredited institution of higher education as a full-time undergraduate student. Applicants must be majoring in finance, business, or accounting and preparing for a career in banking. Along with their application, they must submit high school or college transcripts; 2 letters of recommendation; a copy of their Chickasaw Nation citizenship card; a 2-page list of honors, achievements, awards, club memberships, societies, and civic involvement; and a 1-page essay on their long-term goals and plans for achieving those. Financial need is not considered in the selection process.

Financial data A stipend is awarded (amount not specified).

Duration 1 year.

Additional information This program is supported by Bank2, headquartered in Oklahoma City and owned by the Chickasaw Nation.

Number awarded 4 each year.

Deadline June of each year.

[88]
BARNEY UHART MEMORIAL SCHOLARSHIP PROGRAM

Chugach Alaska Corporation
Attn: Chugach Heritage Foundation
3800 Centerpoint Drive, Suite 1200
Anchorage, AK 99503
(907) 261-0400   Toll Free: (800) 858-2768
Fax: (907) 261-8896 E-mail: scholarships@chugach.com
Web: www.chugachheritagefoundation.org

Summary To provide financial assistance to college seniors and graduate students who are original shareholders of the Chugach Alaska Corporation or their descendants and interested in an internship with the Corporation or a subsidiary.

Eligibility This program is open to original shareholders and the descendants of original enrollees of the Chugach Alaska Corporation who are willing to relocate temporarily to intern with a Corporation subsidiary or at corporate headquarters. Applicants must be enrolled or planning to enroll full time at an accredited college or university in any state as a senior or graduate student and have a GPA of 3.0 or higher. They must be working on a degree in specified fields; recently, those were accounting, business, communications, education, engineering, finance, or information technology. Selection is based on academic excellence, community involvement, leadership qualities, and management interest.

Financial data The stipend is $5,000; the internship is a paid position.

Duration 1 year.

Additional information The Chugach Alaska Corporation is 1 of 13 Alaska Native Regional Corporations created under the Alaska Native Claims Settlement Act of 1971.

Number awarded 2 each year.

Deadline January of each year.

[89]
BARRY AND DEANNA SNYDER, SR. CHAIRMAN'S SCHOLARSHIP

Seneca Diabetes Foundation
Attn: Secretary/Treasurer
P.O. Box 309
Irving, NY 14081
(716) 532-4900   E-mail: white@sni.org
Web: www.senecadiabetesfoundation.org/scholarships

Summary To provide financial assistance to members of the Seneca Nation who are interested in attending college to prepare for a career in the health or human services professions and have experience in a leadership position.

Eligibility This program is open to members of the Seneca Nation who are interested in attending college to assist the Seneca people, especially in regard to the fight against diabetes, by working on a degree in health or human services. Applicants must be able to demonstrate experience in a leadership position. Along with their application, they must submit brief statements on 1) the professional, community, or cultural services and activities in which they have participated; 2) how this scholarship would help further their education; 3) their goals or plan for using their education and training to benefit the Seneca Nation and its people; and 4) an example of a time when they served in a leadership position, the successes and challenges that they faced, the lessons they learned, and how they can apply those lessons to other life experiences. In the selection process, primary consideration is given to financial need, but involvement in community and cultural activities, personal assets, and desire to improve the quality of life for the Seneca people are also considered.

Financial data The stipend is $5,000 per year.

Duration 2 years.

Number awarded Varies each year; recently, 3 were awarded.

Deadline August of each year.

[90]
BBNC EDUCATION FOUNDATION SHORT-TERM VOCATIONAL/TECHNICAL EDUCATION SCHOLARSHIPS

Bristol Bay Native Corporation
Attn: BBNC Education Foundation
111 West 16th Avenue, Suite 400
Anchorage, AK 99501-6299
(907) 278-3602   Toll Free: (800) 426-3602
Fax: (907) 265-7886   E-mail: bbncef@bbnc.net
Web: www.bbnc.net

Summary To provide financial assistance to Alaska Natives who are shareholders of Bristol Bay Native Corporation (BBNC) and interested in taking short-term educational training at a school in any state.

Eligibility This program is open to BBNC shareholders and lineal descendants of shareholders. Applicants must be enrolled or planning to enroll at a vocational school in any state for short-term training to enhance their work or career opportunities. Along with their application, they must submit a letter of request that includes their employment goals, how their training will relate to their employment goals, and employment opportunities after completion of their training.

Financial data The stipend ranges up to $1,000.

Duration 1 year.

Additional information The BBNC is 1 of 13 Alaska Native Regional Corporations created under the Alaska Native Claims Settlement Act of 1971.

Number awarded Varies each year.

Deadline Applications may be submitted at any time. Awards are granted on a first-come, first-served basis.

[91]
BEAUTIFUL MINDS SCHOLARSHIP

RentDeals.com
Attn: Scholarships
14173 Northwest Freeway, Suite 190
Houston, TX 77040
Toll Free: (800) 644-5012
Web: www.rentdeals.com/scholarship.php

Summary To provide financial assistance to Native American and other minority high school seniors who submit outstanding essays on finding their purpose and plan to attend college.

Eligibility This program is open to graduating high school seniors who are members of minority groups and have a GPA of 3.0 or higher. Applicants must be planning to enroll at an accredited postsecondary institution and major in any field. Selection is based primarily on an essay on the topic, "Finding My Purpose."

Financial data The stipend is $1,000.

Duration 1 year.

Number awarded 1 each year.

Deadline March of each year.

[92]
BECHTEL UNDERGRADUATE FELLOWSHIP AWARD

National Action Council for Minorities in Engineering
Attn: Director, Scholarships and University Relations
440 Hamilton Avenue, Suite 302
White Plains, NY 10601-1813
(914) 539-4316   Fax: (914) 539-4032
E-mail: scholars@nacme.org
Web: www.nacme.org/scholarships

Summary To provide financial assistance to American Indian and other underrepresented minority college juniors majoring in construction engineering.

Eligibility This program is open to African American, Latino, and American Indian college juniors who have a GPA of 3.0 or higher and have demonstrated academic excellence, leadership skills, and a commitment to science and engineering as a career. Applicants must be enrolled full time at an ABET-accredited engineering program and preparing for a career in a construction-related engineering discipline.

Financial data The stipend is $2,500 per year. Funds are sent directly to the recipient's university.

Duration Up to 2 years.

Additional information This program was established by the Bechtel Group Foundation.

Number awarded 2 each year.

Deadline April of each year.

[93]
BERING STRAITS FOUNDATION HIGHER EDUCATION SCHOLARSHIPS

Bering Straits Native Corporation
Attn: Bering Straits Foundation
110 Front Street, Suite 300
P.O. Box 1008
Nome, AK 99762-1008
(907) 443-4305   Toll Free: (800) 478-5079 (within AK)
Fax: (907) 443-8129
E-mail: foundation@beringstraits.com
Web: www.beringstraits.com/foundation/scholarships

Summary To provide financial assistance to Alaska Natives who are shareholders or descendants of shareholders of the Bering Straits Native Corporation and entering or enrolled in an undergraduate or graduate program in any state.

Eligibility This program is open to Native Alaskans who are shareholders or lineal descendants of shareholders of the Bering Straits Native Corporation. Applicants must be graduating or have graduated from high school with a GPA of 3.0 or higher (or have earned a GED). They must be accepted or currently enrolled (as an undergraduate or graduate student) at an accredited college or university in any state as a full-time student and be able to demonstrate financial need. Along with their application, they must submit a personal statement on their educational goals and objectives, their community and school activities, and honors and awards they have received.

Financial data The stipend is $1,000 per semester for students who maintain a GPA of 3.0 or higher or $400 per semester for students whose GPA is from 2.5 to 2.99. Funds are paid directly to the recipient's school.

Duration 1 semester; may be renewed if the recipient maintains a GPA of 2.5 or higher.

Additional information The Bering Straits Native Corporation is 1 of 13 Alaska Native Regional Corporations created under the Alaska Native Claims Settlement Act of 1971.

Number awarded Varies each year.

Deadline April of each year for high school seniors; June of each year for the fall semester for continuing undergraduates; December of each year for the spring semester.

[94]
BERING STRAITS FOUNDATION VOCATIONAL TRAINING SCHOLARSHIPS

Bering Straits Native Corporation
Attn: Bering Straits Foundation
110 Front Street, Suite 300
P.O. Box 1008
Nome, AK 99762-1008
(907) 443-4305   Toll Free: (800) 478-5079 (within AK)
Fax: (907) 443-2985
E-mail: foundation@beringstraits.com
Web: www.beringstraits.com/foundation/scholarships

Summary To provide financial assistance to Alaska Natives who are shareholders or descendants of shareholders of the Bering Straits Native Corporation and entering or enrolled in a vocational training program in any state.

Eligibility This program is open to Native Alaskans who are shareholders or lineal descendants of shareholders of the

Bering Straits Native Corporation. Applicants must be high school graduates with a GPA of 2.5 or higher. They must be accepted or currently enrolled at an accredited vocational school in any state as a full-time student and be able to demonstrate financial need. Along with their application, they must submit a personal statement on their educational goals and objectives, their community and school activities, their hobbies and interests, and honors and awards they have received.

Financial data   The stipend is $500 per semester. Funds are paid directly to the recipient's school.

Duration   1 semester; may be renewed if the recipient maintains a GPA of 2.0 or higher during the first semester and 2.5 or higher in succeeding semesters.

Additional information   The Bering Straits Native Corporation is 1 of 13 Alaska Native Regional Corporations created under the Alaska Native Claims Settlement Act of 1971.

Number awarded   Varies each year.

Deadline   Applications may be submitted at any time, but they must be received at least 2 weeks prior to the start of class.

[95]
BIA HIGHER EDUCATION GRANTS FOR HOPI TRIBAL MEMBERS

Hopi Tribe
Attn: Grants and Scholarships Program
P.O. Box 123
Kykotsmovi, AZ 86039
(928) 734-3542   Toll Free: (800) 762-9630
Fax: (928) 734-9575   E-mail: JTorivio@hopi.nsn.us
Web: www.hopi-nsn.gov

Summary   To provide financial assistance to students of Hopi ancestry who are working on an undergraduate, graduate, or postgraduate degree.

Eligibility   This program is open to students who are working or planning to work full time on an associate, baccalaureate, graduate, or postgraduate degree. Applicants must be enrolled members of the Hopi Tribe and able to demonstrate financial need. They must have a GPA of 2.0 or higher as an incoming freshman, 2.25 or higher as an entering sophomore, 2.5 as an entering junior or senior, or 3.0 as a graduate or professional student.

Financial data   The maximum grant is $2,500 per semester ($5,000 per year).

Duration   1 semester; may be renewed for up to 10 terms of undergraduate study or up to 5 terms of graduate study, provided the recipient remains enrolled full time and meets the required GPA for their academic level.

Additional information   This program is funded by the Bureau of Indian Affairs (BIA).

Number awarded   Varies each year.

Deadline   June of each year for fall; October of each year for winter; November of each year for spring.

[96]
BILL BERNBACH DIVERSITY SCHOLARSHIPS

American Association of Advertising Agencies
Attn: AAAA Foundation
1065 Avenue of the Americas, 16th Floor
New York, NY 10018
(212) 262-2500   E-mail: bbscholarship@ddb.com
Web: www.aaaa.org

Summary   To provide financial assistance to Native American and other multicultural students interested in working on an undergraduate or graduate degree in advertising at designated schools.

Eligibility   This program is open to African Americans, Asian Americans, Hispanic Americans, and Native Americans (including American Indians, Alaska Natives, Native Hawaiians, and other Pacific Islanders) who are interested in studying the advertising creative arts at designated institutions as a full-time student. Applicants must be working on or have already received an undergraduate degree and be able to demonstrate creative talent and promise. They must be U.S. citizens, nationals, or permanent residents. Along with their application, they must submit 10 samples of creative work in their respective field of expertise.

Financial data   The stipend is $5,000.

Duration   1 year.

Additional information   This program, which began in 1998, is currently sponsored by DDB Worldwide. The participating schools are the Art Center College of Design (Pasadena, California), Creative Circus (Atlanta, Georgia), Miami Ad School (Miami Beach, Florida), University of Oklahoma (Norman, Oklahoma), University of Texas at Austin, VCU Brandcenter (Richmond, Virginia), Savannah College of Art and Design (Savannah, Georgia), University of Oregon (Eugene), City College of New York, School of Visual Arts (New York, New York), Fashion Institute of Technology (New York, New York), and Howard University (Washington, D.C.).

Number awarded   3 each year.

Deadline   May of each year.

[97]
BILL DICKEY GOLF SCHOLARSHIPS

Bill Dickey Scholarship Association
Attn: Scholarship Committee
1241 East Washington Street, Suite 101
Phoenix, AZ 85034
(602) 258-7851   Fax: (602) 258-3412
E-mail: andrea@bdscholar.org
Web: www.nmjgsa.org/scholarships.php

Summary   To provide financial assistance to Native American and other minority high school seniors and undergraduate students who excel at golf.

Eligibility   This program is open to graduating high school seniors and current undergraduate students who are members of minority groups (African American, Asian/Pacific Islander, Hispanic, or American Indian/Alaskan Native). Applicants must submit a 500-word essay on a topic that changes annually but relates to minorities and golf. Selection is based on academic achievement, leadership, evidence of community service, golfing ability, and financial need.

Financial data Stipends range from 1-time awards of $1,000 to 4-year awards of $3,500 per year. Funds are paid directly to the recipient's college.

Duration 1 year or longer.

Additional information This sponsor was established in 1984 as the National Minority Junior Golf Association and given its current name in 2006. Support is provided by the Jackie Robinson Foundation, PGA of America, Anheuser-Busch, the Tiger Woods Foundation, and other cooperating organizations.

Number awarded Varies; generally 80 or more each year.

Deadline May of each year.

[98]
BILL FRYREAR MEMORIAL SCHOLARSHIPS

Chickasaw Foundation
2020 Arlington, Suite 4
P.O. Box 1726
Ada, OK 74821-1726
(580) 421-9030   Fax: (580) 421-9031
E-mail: ChickasawFoundation@chickasaw.net
Web: www.chickasawfoundation.org/Scholarships.aspx

Summary To provide financial assistance to members of the Chickasaw Nation who are working on an undergraduate degree in art or history.

Eligibility This program is open to Chickasaw students who are currently enrolled at an accredited institution of higher education as a full-time undergraduate student. Applicants must be majoring in art or history. Along with their application, they must submit high school or college transcripts; 2 letters of recommendation; a copy of their Chickasaw Nation citizenship card; a 2-page list of honors, achievements, awards, club memberships, societies, and civic involvement; and a 1-page essay on their long-term goals and plans for achieving those. Financial need is not considered in the selection process.

Financial data A stipend is awarded (amount not specified).

Duration 1 year.

Number awarded 1 each year.

Deadline June of each year.

[99]
BILL RABBIT LEGACY ART SCHOLARSHIP

Cherokee Nation Foundation
800 South Muskogee
Tahlequah, OK 74464
(918) 207-0950   Fax: (918) 207-0951
E-mail: contact@cherokeenationfoundation.org
Web: cherokeenation.academicworks.com

Summary To provide financial assistance to citizens of the Cherokee Nation who are interested in attending a university in any state and majoring in specified fields of art.

Eligibility This program is open to citizens of the Cherokee Nation who are high school seniors or students currently enrolled as full-time undergraduate or graduate students at a 4-year college or university in any state. Applicants must have a GPA of 3.0 or higher and be studying drawing, painting, sculpture, pottery, traditional beadwork, or textiles. They are not required to reside in the Cherokee Nation area. Along with their application, they must submit 3 samples of their work, a 650-word essay on the world they come from and how it has shaped their dreams and aspiration, and a 500-word essay on their desire to pursue higher education, their chosen field of study, how they plan to serve the Cherokee people after they complete their higher education, and whether or not they speak the Cherokee language. Selection is based on the clarity and presentation of the essay; academic information (including transcripts and ACT scores); school, cultural and community activities; future plans to serve Cherokee people; and financial need.

Financial data A stipend is awarded (amount not specified).

Duration 1 year; may be renewed up to 3 additional years, provided the recipient maintains a GPA of 3.0 or higher.

Number awarded 1 or more each year.

Deadline January of each year.

[100]
BLACKFEET ADULT VOCATIONAL TRAINING GRANTS

Blackfeet Nation
Attn: Higher Education Program
1 Agency Square
P.O. Box 850
Browning, MT 59417
(406) 338-7539   Fax: (406) 338-7529
E-mail: bhep@3rivers.net
Web: www.blackfeetnation.com

Summary To provide financial assistance for vocational training to members of the Blackfeet and other tribes.

Eligibility This program is open to enrolled members of a federally-recognized tribe between 18 and 35 years of age in need of training to obtain reasonable and satisfactory employment. Applicants must be willing to accept full-time employment as soon as possible after completion of training. Along with their application they must submit high school or GED transcripts, college transcripts (if they have ever attended college), a copy of the admission letter from the school they plan to attend, a financial needs analysis, a Certificate of Degree of Indian Blood (CDIB), a copy of their marriage license (if a spouse is claimed as financially dependent), a copy of birth certificates for any family members claimed as financially dependent, and military discharge papers (if applicable). Grants are awarded according to the following priorities: 1) Blackfeet tribal members residing on or near the Blackfeet Reservation; 2) Blackfeet tribal members residing off the Blackfeet Reservation; 3) members of other federally-recognized tribes (as funding permits); and 4) second training grant applicants (as funding permits).

Financial data The amount awarded varies, depending upon the recipient's educational requirements and financial needs. The maximum for an unmarried student with no dependents is $3,200 per year; for a student with 3 or more dependents; the maximum stipend is $3,800 per year. Funds are sent to the school's financial aid officer.

Duration Up to 24 months (36 months for registered nursing students) of full-time training.

Number awarded Varies each year.

Deadline February of each year.

[101]
BLACKFEET HIGHER EDUCATION GRANTS

Blackfeet Nation
Attn: Higher Education Program
1 Agency Square
P.O. Box 850
Browning, MT 59417
(406) 338-7539   Fax: (406) 338-7529
E-mail: bhep@3rivers.net
Web: www.blackfeetnation.com

Summary To provide financial assistance to members of the Blackfeet Tribe who are interested in working on an undergraduate degree at a college or university in any state.

Eligibility Applicants must be enrolled members of the Blackfeet Tribe and be enrolled or accepted for enrollment as an undergraduate at an academically recognized college or university in any state. They must submit a 1-page letter describing their career goals and academic plans, high school or GED transcripts, college transcripts (if they have previously attended college), a copy of the admission letter from the college or university they plan to attend, a financial needs analysis, and a Certificate of Degree of Indian Blood (CDIB). Scholarships are awarded according to the following priorities: 1) renewal of grants to students currently funded who are in good academic and financial aid standing and submit the application packet on time; 2) college seniors not currently funded who can graduate within the current academic year; 3) 2-year degree graduates who apply within 1 year of earning their associate degree; 4) high school seniors who apply within 1 year of earning their high school diploma; 5) applicants previously funded who are in good academic and financial aid standing and submit the application packet in a timely manner; and 6) candidates who submit late applications (supported only if funding permits).

Financial data The amount awarded varies, depending upon the recipient's educational requirements and financial needs. The maximum for an unmarried student with no dependents is $3,200 per year; for a student with 3 or more dependents; the maximum stipend is $3,800 per year. Funds are sent to the school's financial aid officer.

Duration 1 year; may be renewed up to a total of 10 semesters or 15 quarters.

Additional information Recipients must enroll as full-time students and earn no less than 12 credit hours per term with a GPA of 2.0 or higher as freshmen, 13 credits and 2.2 as sophomores, 14 credits and 2.4 as juniors, and 15 credits and 2.6 as seniors. Students who attend private schools or institutions outside of Montana must pay the difference in tuition, unless no comparable program exists at Montana public institutions.

Number awarded Varies each year.

Deadline February of each year; March of each year for summer term.

[102]
BLOSSOM KALAMA EVANS MEMORIAL SCHOLARSHIPS

Hawai'i Community Foundation
Attn: Scholarship Department
827 Fort Street Mall
Honolulu, HI 96813
(808) 566-5570   Toll Free: (888) 731-3863
Fax: (808) 521-6286
E-mail: scholarships@hcf-hawaii.org
Web: hcf.scholarships.ngwebsolutions.com

Summary To provide financial assistance to residents of Hawaii of native ancestry who are interested in working on an undergraduate or graduate degree at a school in the state.

Eligibility This program is open to residents of Hawaii who are of Native Hawaiian ancestry and enrolled as full-time juniors, seniors, or graduate students at a 4-year college or university in the state. Applicants must be able to demonstrate academic achievement (GPA of 2.7 or higher), good moral character, and financial need. Along with their application, they must submit a short statement indicating their reasons for attending college, their planned course of study, their career goals, what community service means to them, and how they plan to use their knowledge to serve the needs of the Native Hawaiian community. Preference is given to applicants interested in studying Hawaiian language or Hawaiian studies.

Financial data The amounts of the awards depend on the availability of funds and the need of the recipient. Recently, the average value of the scholarships awarded by the foundation was $2,800.

Duration 1 year.

Number awarded Varies each year; recently, 9 were awarded.

Deadline February of each year.

[103]
BLUECROSS BLUESHIELD OF TENNESSEE COMMUNITY TRUST DIVERSITY SCHOLARSHIP

National Association of Health Services Executives-
   Memphis Chapter
Attn: Selection Committee
P.O. Box 40051
Memphis, TN 38174-0051
E-mail: nahsememphis@gmail.com
Web: www.bcbst.com

Summary This program is open to Native American and other minority students who are residents of Tennessee working on an undergraduate degree in a field of health care at a college in the state.

Eligibility This program is open to minority residents of Tennessee who are currently enrolled as full-time sophomores or juniors at an accredited college or university in the state. Applicants must be working on a degree in a field of health care and have a GPA of 2.5 or higher. They must be U.S. citizens between 18 and 23 years of age. Along with their application, they must submit a 500-word essay on their particular field of study, why they chose to prepare for a career in health care, and how they plan to use their skills or knowledge to help raise awareness of health issues in their community.

Financial data The stipend is $10,000. Funds are paid directly to the recipient's university.

Duration 1 year.

Additional information This program is sponsored by BlueCross BlueShield of Tennessee in collaboration with the Memphis Chapter of the National Association of Health Services Executives (NAHSE).

Number awarded 3 each year: 1 each for the west, middle, and east region of Tennessee.

Deadline March of each year.

[104]
BOIS FORTE HIGHER EDUCATION PROGRAM

Bois Forte Band of Chippewa
Attn: Department of Education and Training
5344 Lakeshore Drive
P.O. Box 16
Nett Lake, MN 55772
(218) 757-3124   Toll Free: (800) 221-8129
Fax: (218) 757-3126 E-mail: bmason@boisforte-NSN.gov
Web: www.boisforte.com/divisions/education.htm

Summary To provide financial assistance for undergraduate or graduate study to enrolled members of the Bois Forte Band of Chippewa Indians.

Eligibility Eligible to apply for this assistance are enrolled members of the Bois Forte Band of Chippewa Indians. Applicants must have been accepted at an institution of higher education and had their financial need determined by that institution based on the Free Application for Federal Student Aid (FAFSA). Minnesota residents must apply to the Indian Scholarship Assistance Program of the Minnesota Indian Scholarship Program. Applicants wishing to attend school outside of Minnesota must complete an out-of-state application form. Applicants must also apply for financial assistance from all other available sources, including but not limited to public and private grants and scholarships. They must not be in default of any tribal, federal, or state student education loan or in non-compliance with child support payments. Applicants are interviewed. Financial assistance is awarded on a first-come, first-served basis.

Financial data The maximum amount awarded is $5,000 per year for undergraduates or $6,250 per year for graduate students.

Duration 1 year; may be renewed for a total of 10 semesters of full-time enrollment or part-time equivalent provided recipients maintain a GPA of 2.0 or higher.

Additional information Students may receive financial assistance for summer school.

Number awarded Varies each year.

Deadline Applications may be submitted any time after January 1 but should be received no later than 8 weeks prior to the first day of school.

[105]
BOX ENGINEERING DIVERSITY SCHOLARSHIP

Box, Inc.
Attn: Scholarship
4440 El Camino Real
Los Altos, CA 94022
Toll Free: (877) 729-4269   E-mail: scholarship@box.com
Web: www.boxdiversityscholarship.com

Summary To provide financial assistance to college students majoring in designated fields of technology who are Native Americans or members of other groups underrepresented in those fields.

Eligibility This program is open to U.S. citizens currently enrolled as sophomores or juniors at a 4-year college or university who are majoring in science, engineering, information technology, mathematics, or a related field. Applicants must identify with an underrepresented minority (e.g., female, LGBT, Hispanic, African American, or Native American). Finalists are invited to the sponsor's headquarters in Los Altos, California.

Financial data Stipends are $20,000 or $4,000.

Duration 1 year.

Number awarded 1 at $20,000 and 4 at $4,000 each year.

Deadline October of each year.

[106]
BREAKTHROUGH TO NURSING SCHOLARSHIPS

National Student Nurses' Association
Attn: Foundation
45 Main Street, Suite 606
Brooklyn, NY 11201
(718) 210-0705   Fax: (718) 210-0710
E-mail: nsna@nsna.org
Web: www.nsna.org

Summary To provide financial assistance to Native American and other minority undergraduate and graduate students who wish to prepare for careers in nursing.

Eligibility This program is open to students currently enrolled in state-approved schools of nursing or pre-nursing associate degree, baccalaureate, diploma, generic master's, generic doctoral, R.N. to B.S.N., R.N. to M.S.N., or L.P.N./ L.V.N. to R.N. programs. Graduating high school seniors are not eligible. Support for graduate education is provided only for a first degree in nursing. Applicants must be members of a racial or ethnic minority underrepresented among registered nurses (American Indian or Alaska Native, Hispanic or Latino, Native Hawaiian or other Pacific Islander, Black or African American, or Asian). They must be committed to providing quality health care services to underserved populations. Along with their application, they must submit a 200-word description of their professional and educational goals and how this scholarship will help them achieve those goals. Selection is based on academic achievement, financial need, and involvement in student nursing organizations and community health activities. U.S. citizenship or permanent resident status is required.

Financial data Stipends range from $1,000 to $2,000.

Duration 1 year.

Additional information Applications must be accompanied by a $10 processing fee.

Number awarded Varies each year; recently, 13 were awarded: 10 sponsored by the American Association of Critical-Care Nurses and 3 sponsored by the Mayo Clinic.

Deadline January of each year.

[107]
BRISTOL BAY NATIVE CORPORATION EDUCATION FOUNDATION HIGHER EDUCATION SCHOLARSHIPS

Bristol Bay Native Corporation
Attn: BBNC Education Foundation
111 West 16th Avenue, Suite 400
Anchorage, AK 99501-6299
(907) 278-3602   Toll Free: (800) 426-3602
Fax: (907) 265-7886   E-mail: bbncef@bbnc.net
Web: www.bbnc.net

Summary To provide financial assistance to shareholders of Bristol Bay Native Corporation (BBNC) who are interested in attending college in any state.

Eligibility This program is open to BBNC shareholders who have a high school diploma or equivalent and are enrolled or planning to enroll in an accredited college or university. Applicants must have a GPA of 2.0 or higher and be able to demonstrate financial need. They must enroll either full time or part time with at least 6 credit hours. Along with their application, they must submit an essay on how they became interested in their proposed field of study, any special circumstances they want to be considered, and their desire to work in the region or for a BBNC subsidiary company. Selection is based on the essay (30%), cumulative GPA (40%), financial need (20%), a resume (5%), and letters of recommendation (5%).

Financial data Stipends recently ranged from $1,000 to $5,000 per year.

Duration 1 year.

Additional information The BBNC is 1 of 13 Alaska Native Regional Corporations created under the Alaska Native Claims Settlement Act of 1971.

Number awarded Approximately 100 each year.

Deadline April of each year.

[108]
BRISTOL BAY NATIVE CORPORATION EDUCATION FOUNDATION VOCATIONAL EDUCATION SCHOLARSHIPS

Bristol Bay Native Corporation
Attn: BBNC Education Foundation
111 West 16th Avenue, Suite 400
Anchorage, AK 99501-6299
(907) 278-3602   Toll Free: (800) 426-3602
Fax: (907) 265-7886   E-mail: bbncef@bbnc.net
Web: www.bbnc.net

Summary To provide financial assistance for vocational education in any state to shareholders of Bristol Bay Native Corporation (BBNC).

Eligibility This program is open to BBNC shareholders who have a high school diploma or equivalent (GED). Applicants must be enrolled or planning to enroll in an accredited vocational institution in any state as a part- or full-time student. They must have a GPA of 2.0 or higher and be able to demonstrate financial need. Along with their application, they must submit an essay on how they became interested in their proposed field of study, any special circumstances they want to be considered, and their desire to work in the region or for a BBNC subsidiary company. Selection is based on the essay

(30%), cumulative GPA (40%), financial need (20%), a resume (5%), and letters of recommendation (5%).

Financial data The stipend ranges from $1,000 to $2,000.

Duration 1 year.

Additional information The BBNC is 1 of 13 Alaska Native Regional Corporations created under the Alaska Native Claims Settlement Act of 1971.

Number awarded Varies each year; recently, 20 were awarded.

Deadline April of each year.

[109]
BROWN AND CALDWELL MINORITY SCHOLARSHIP

Brown and Caldwell
Attn: HR/Scholarship Program
1527 Cole Boulevard, Suite 300
Lakewood, CO 80401
(303) 239-5400   Fax: (303) 239-5454
E-mail: scholarships@brwncald.com
Web: www.brownandcaldwell.com/Scholarships.asp?id=1

Summary To provide financial assistance to Native American and other minority students working on an undergraduate or graduate degree in an environmental or engineering field.

Eligibility This program is open to members of minority groups (African Americans, Hispanics, Asians, Pacific Islanders, Native Americans, or Alaska Natives) who are full-time juniors, seniors, or graduate students at an accredited 4-year college or university. Applicants must have a GPA of 3.0 or higher and a declared major in civil, chemical, or environmental engineering or an environmental science (e.g., biology, ecology, geology, hydrogeology). They must be U.S. citizens or permanent residents. Along with their application, they must submit an essay (up to 250 words) on a topic that changes annually but relates to their personal development. Financial need is not considered in the selection process.

Financial data The stipend is $5,000.

Duration 1 year.

Number awarded 1 each year.

Deadline May of each year.

[110]
BROWN AND CALDWELL NAVAJO NATION SCHOLARSHIP

Brown and Caldwell
Attn: Jay Yazzie
6955 Union Park Center, Suite 270
Midvale, UT 84047-4135
(801) 316-9810   Fax: (801) 565-7330
E-mail: jyazzie@brwncald.com
Web: www.brownandcaldwell.com/Scholarships.asp?id=6

Summary To provide financial assistance to members of the Navajo Nation who are interested in working on an undergraduate degree in an environmental or engineering field.

Eligibility This program is open to members of the Navajo Nation who are high school seniors or full-time students at an accredited 2- or 4-year college or university. Applicants must have a GPA of 3.0 or higher and an interest in majoring in civil, chemical, or environmental engineering or an environmental science (e.g., biology, ecology, geology, hydrogeology). They must be U.S. citizens or permanent residents.

Along with their application, they must submit an essay (up to 500 words) on a topic that changes annually but relates to environmental science. Financial need is not considered in the selection process.

Financial data The stipend is $1,000 per year.

Duration 1 year; may be renewed up to 3 additional years.

Number awarded 1 each year.

Deadline May of each year.

[111]
BURLINGTON NORTHERN SANTA FE FOUNDATION SCHOLARSHIPS

American Indian Science and Engineering Society
Attn: Director of Membership and Communications
2305 Renard Place, S.E., Suite 200
Albuquerque, NM 87106
(505) 765-1052, ext. 110   Fax: (505) 765-5608
E-mail: lpaz@aises.org
Web: www.aises.org/scholarships

Summary To provide financial assistance for college to outstanding American Indian and Alaskan Native high school seniors from designated states who are members of American Indian Science and Engineering Society (AISES).

Eligibility This program is open to AISES members who are seniors graduating from high schools in the service area of the BNSF Railway and its affiliated companies: (Arizona, California, Colorado, Kansas, Minnesota, Montana, New Mexico, North Dakota, Oklahoma, Oregon, South Dakota, Texas, and Washington). Applicants must be planning to attend an accredited 4-year college or university in any state and major in business, education, engineering, mathematics, medicine or health administration, natural or physical sciences, or technology. They must have a GPA of 2.0 or higher and be able to document ancestry as an American Indian, Alaskan Native, or Native Hawaiian. Selection is based on academic performance, a personal statement, letters of recommendation, and activities (e.g., jobs, volunteer efforts, internships, extracurricular involvement, hobbies).

Financial data The stipend is $2,500 per year.

Duration 4 years or until completion of a baccalaureate degree, whichever occurs first. Renewal requires that they maintain a GPA of 2.0 or higher for their freshman and sophomore years and 3.0 or higher for their junior and senior years.

Additional information This program is funded by the BNSF Railway Foundation and administered by AISES.

Number awarded 5 new awards are made each year.

Deadline April of each year.

[112]
CADDO NATION HIGHER EDUCATION GRANT PROGRAM

Caddo Nation
Attn: Education Coordinator
P.O. Box 487
Binger, OK 73009
(405) 656-2344   Fax: (405) 656-2964
E-mail: cbotone@caddonation.org
Web: www.caddonaton-nsn.gov/higher-education

Summary To provide financial assistance to members of the Caddo Nation interested in attending college.

Eligibility This program is open to enrolled members of the Caddo Nation who are attending or planning to attend a college or university in any state as a full or part time student. Applicants must have a GPA of 2.0 or higher. Applicants must submit brief statements on why they chose to continue their education, why they chose the college they are planning to attend, who influenced them to go to college or continue their education, if they are a first generation college student in their family, their anticipated graduation date, their degree program and field of study, the educational goals they have set for themselves, their intent after they have reached those goals, and if they plan to return to the Caddo Nation to bring their knowledge and expertise.

Financial data Stipends range from $500 to $1,800 per term, provided the recipient maintains a GPA of 2.0 or higher.

Duration 1 term; may be renewed up to 9 additional terms.

Number awarded Varies each year.

Deadline July of each year for fall term; November of each year for spring term.

[113]
CALIFORNIA PLANNING FOUNDATION DIVERSITY IN PLANNING SCHOLARSHIP

American Planning Association-California Chapter
Attn: California Planning Foundation
c/o Kelly Main
California Polytechnic State University at San Luis Obispo
City and Regional Planning Department
Office 21-116B
San Luis Obispo, CA 93407-0283
(805) 756-2285   Fax: (805) 756-1340
E-mail: cpfapplications@gmail.com
Web: www.californiaplanningfoundation.org

Summary To provide financial assistance to Native Americans and other undergraduate and graduate students in accredited planning programs at California universities who will increase diversity in the profession.

Eligibility This program is open to students entering their final year for an undergraduate or master's degree in an accredited planning program at a university in California. Applicants must be students who will increase diversity in the planning profession. Along with their application, they must submit 1) a 500-word personal statement explaining why planning is important to them, their potential contribution to the profession of planning in California, and how this scholarship would help them to complete their degree; 2) a 500-word description of their experience in planning (e.g., internships, volunteer experiences, employment); and 3) a 500-word essay on what they consider to be 1 of the greatest planning challenges in California today. Selection is based on academic performance, increasing diversity in the planning profession, commitment to serve the planning profession in California, and financial need.

Financial data The stipend is $3,000. The award includes a 1-year student membership in the American Planning Association (APA) and payment of registration for the APA California Conference.

Duration 1 year.

Additional information The accredited planning programs are at 3 campuses of the California State University system (California State Polytechnic University at Pomona, California Polytechnic State University at San Luis Obispo, and San Jose State University), 3 campuses of the University of California (Berkeley, Irvine, and Los Angeles), and the University of Southern California.

Number awarded 1 each year.

Deadline March of each year.

[114]
CALISTA EDUCATION AND CULTURE SCHOLARSHIP PROGRAM

Calista Corporation
Attn: Calista Education and Culture, Inc.
5015 Business Park Boulevard, Suite 3000
Anchorage, AK 99503
(907) 275-2800　　　　Toll Free: (800) 277-5516
Fax: (907) 275-2936
E-mail: scholarships@calistacorp.com
Web: www.calistaeducation.org/scholarships.html

Summary To provide financial assistance to Alaska Natives who are shareholders or descendants of shareholders of the Calista Corporation and interested in working on an undergraduate or graduate degree at a school in any state.

Eligibility This program is open to Alaska Natives who are shareholders or lineal descendants of shareholders of the Calista Corporation. Applicants must be at least a high school graduate or have earned a GED and be in good academic standing with a GPA of 2.0 or higher. They must be working on an undergraduate or graduate degree at a college or university in any state. Along with their application, they must submit a 1-page essay on their educational and career goals. Financial need is considered in the selection process.

Financial data The amount awarded for undergraduates depends upon the recipient's GPA: awards for full-time students are $500 per semester for a GPA of 2.0 to 2.49, $750 per semester for a GPA of 2.5 to 2.99, and $1,000 per semester a GPA of 3.0 or higher. Awards for part-time students are half those amounts. Stipends are $750 per semester for full-time trade school students or $375 per semester for part-time trade school student. For graduate students, the stipend is $1,500 per semester for full-time students or $750 for part-time students. The funds are paid in 2 equal installments; the second semester check is not issued until grades from the previous semester's work are received.

Duration 1 year; recipients may reapply.

Additional information The Calista Corporation is 1 of 13 Alaska Native Regional Corporations created under the Alaska Native Claims Settlement Act of 1971. This program was established in 1994.

Number awarded Varies each year; recently, scholarships worth $309,125 were awarded.

Deadline June of each year for fall term; November of each year for spring trm.

[115]
CALTECH AMGEN SCHOLARS PROGRAM

California Institute of Technology
Attn: Student-Faculty Programs
1200 East California Boulevard
MailCode 330-87
Pasadena, CA 91125
(626) 395-2885　　　　Fax: (626) 389-5467
E-mail: sfp@clatech.edu
Web: sfp.caltech.edu/programs/amgen_scholars

Summary To provide an opportunity for undergraduate students, especially Native Americans and those from other diverse populations, to participate in biological and chemical summer research at the California Institute of Technology (Caltech).

Eligibility This program is open to sophomores, juniors, and non-graduating seniors at 4-year colleges and universities in the United States, Puerto Rico, and other U.S. territories. Applicants must be U.S. citizens or permanent residents who have a cumulative GPA of 3.2 or higher and an interest in preparing for a Ph.D. or M.D./Ph.D. They must be interested in working on a summer research project at Caltech in biology, chemistry, or biotechnical-related fields. Applications are encouraged from, but not limited to, underrepresented minorities, women, first-generation college students, geographically underrepresented students, educationally and financially disadvantaged students, and students with disabilities.

Financial data Scholars receive a stipend of $6,000, campus housing, a modest board allowance, and travel to and from Pasadena.

Duration 10 weeks during the summer.

Additional information This program serves as the Cal Tech component of the Amgen Scholars Program, which operates at 8 other U.S. universities (and the National Institutes of Health) and is funded by the Amgen Foundation.

Number awarded Varies each year.

Deadline February of each year.

[116]
CAND FOUNDATION AMERICAN INDIAN/ ALASKA NATIVE SCHOLARSHIP

California Academy of Nutrition and Dietetics
Attn: CAND Foundation
7740 Manchester Avenue, Suite 102
Playa del Rey, CA 90293-8499
(310) 822-0177　　　　Fax: (310) 823-0264
E-mail: scholarships@dietitian.org
Web: www.dietitian.org/d_cdaf/cdaf_outreach.html

Summary To provide financial assistance to Native Americans from California who are members of the Academy of Nutrition and Dietetics (AND) and interested in working on an undergraduate degree at a school in any state.

Eligibility This program is open to enrolled members of federally-recognized Indian tribes and Native Alaskan villages who currently reside in California (although they may attend school in any state). Applicants must be juniors or seniors accepted into a Registered Dietetic Technician (DTR) program, a Didactic Program in Dietetics (DPD), a Coordinated Program (CP) in dietetics, or a Supervised Practice Program. They must have at least a "B" average in high school, a 2.75 or higher overall college GPA (for DTR students), or a GPA of 2.75 or higher in didactic courses for the DPD, CP, or Supervised Practice Program. AND membership is required. Along with their application, they must submit a letter of application that includes a discussion of their career goals. Selection is based on that letter (15%), academic ability (25%), work or volunteer experience (15%), letters of recommendation (15%), extracurricular activities (5%), and financial need (25%).

Financial data   The stipend is $2,000.

Duration   1 year.

Additional information   The California Academy of Nutrition and Dietetics is the California affiliate of the AND.

Number awarded   1 each year.

Deadline   April of each year.

[117]
CANFIT PROGRAM CULINARY ARTS SCHOLARSHIPS

Communities-Adolescents-Nutrition-Fitness
Attn: Scholarship Program
P.O. Box 3989
Berkeley, CA 94703
(510) 644-1533, ext. 112   Toll Free: (800) 200-3131
Fax: (510) 843-9705   E-mail: info@canfit.org
Web: www.canfit.org/scholarships

Summary   To provide financial assistance to Native American and other minority culinary arts students in California.

Eligibility   This program is open to American Indians, Alaska Natives, African Americans, Asian Americans, Pacific Islanders, and Latinos/Hispanics from California who are enrolled at a culinary arts college in the state. Applicants are not required to have completed any college units. Along with their application, they must submit 1) documentation of financial need; 2) letters of recommendation from 2 individuals; 3) a 1-to 2-page letter describing their academic goals and involvement in community nutrition and/or physical education activities; and 4) an essay of 500 to 1,000 words on a topic related to healthy foods for youth from low-income communities of color.

Financial data   A stipend is awarded (amount not specified).

Number awarded   1 or more each year.

Deadline   March of each year.

[118]
CANFIT PROGRAM UNDERGRADUATE SCHOLARSHIPS

Communities-Adolescents-Nutrition-Fitness
Attn: Scholarship Program
P.O. Box 3989
Berkeley, CA 94703
(510) 644-1533, ext. 112   Toll Free: (800) 200-3131
Fax: (510) 843-9705   E-mail: info@canfit.org
Web: www.canfit.org/scholarships

Summary   To provide financial assistance to Native American and other minority undergraduate students who are working on a degree in nutrition, culinary arts, or physical education in California.

Eligibility   This program is open to American Indians, Alaska Natives, African Americans, Asian Americans, Pacific Islanders, and Latinos/Hispanics from California who are

enrolled in an approved bachelor's degree program in nutrition, culinary arts, or physical education in the state. Applicants must have completed at least 50 semester units and have a GPA of 2.5 or higher. Along with their application, they must submit 1) documentation of financial need; 2) letters of recommendation from 2 individuals; 3) a 1-to 2-page letter describing their academic goals and involvement in community nutrition and/or physical education activities; and 4) an essay of 500 to 1,000 words on a topic related to healthy foods for youth from low-income communities of color.

Financial data   A stipend is awarded (amount not specified).

Number awarded   1 or more each year.

Deadline   March of each year.

[119]
CAP LATHROP BROADCAST AND TELECOMMUNICATIONS SCHOLARSHIP

Cook Inlet Region, Inc.
Attn: The CIRI Foundation
3600 San Jeronimo Drive, Suite 256
Anchorage, AK 99508-2870
(907) 793-3575   Toll Free: (800) 764-3382
Fax: (907) 793-3585   E-mail: tcf@thecirifoundation.org
Web: www.thecirifoundation.org/scholarships

Summary   To provide financial assistance for undergraduate or graduate studies in media-related fields to Alaska Natives and their lineal descendants.

Eligibility   This program is open to Alaska Native enrollees under the Alaska Native Claims Settlement Act (ANCSA) of 1971 and their lineal descendants. Applicants may be enrollees of any of the 13 ANCSA regional corporations, but preference is given to original enrollees/descendants of Cook Inlet Region, Inc. (CIRI) who have a GPA of 2.5 or higher. There are no Alaska residency requirements or age limitations. Applicants must be accepted or enrolled full time in a 2-year undergraduate, 4-year undergraduate, or graduate degree program. They must be majoring in a media-related field (e.g., telecommunications, broadcast, business, engineering, journalism) and planning to work in the telecommunications or broadcast industry in Alaska after graduation. Along with their application, they must submit a 500-word statement on their educational and career goals and how they are contributing, or planning to contribute, to a positive Alaska Native community. Selection is based on that statement, academic achievement, rigor of course work or degree program, student financial contribution, financial need, grade level, previous work performance, community service, and relationship of degree program to career goals.

Financial data   The stipend is $4,000 per year. Funds must be used for tuition, university fees, books, required class supplies, and campus housing and meal plans for students who must live away from their permanent home to attend college. Checks are sent directly to the recipient's school.

Duration   1 year (2 semesters).

Additional information   CIRI is 1 of 13 regional corporations established according to the terms of the Alaska Native Claims Settlement Act (ANCSA) of 1971. This program began in 1997. Recipients must plan to work in the broadcast or telecommunications industry in Alaska upon completion of their academic degree.

Number awarded   1 each year.

Deadline   May of each year.

[120]
CARL H. MARRS SCHOLARSHIP FUND

Cook Inlet Region, Inc.
Attn: The CIRI Foundation
3600 San Jeronimo Drive, Suite 256
Anchorage, AK 99508-2870
(907) 793-3575   Toll Free: (800) 764-3382
Fax: (907) 793-3585   E-mail: tcf@thecirifoundation.org
Web: www.thecirifoundation.org/about/donors

Summary   To provide financial assistance for undergraduate or graduate studies in business-related fields to Alaska Natives who are original enrollees to Cook Inlet Region, Inc. (CIRI) and their lineal descendants.

Eligibility   This program is open to Alaska Native enrollees to CIRI under the Alaska Native Claims Settlement Act (ANCSA) of 1971 and their lineal descendants. There are no Alaska residency requirements or age limitations. Applicants must be accepted or enrolled full time in a 4-year undergraduate or a graduate degree program in business administration, economics, finance, organizational management, accounting, or a similar field. They must have a GPA of 3.7 or higher. Along with their application, they must submit a 500-word statement on their educational and career goals and how they are contributing, or planning to contribute, to a positive Alaska Native community. Selection is based on that statement, academic achievement, rigor of course work or degree program, student financial contribution, financial need, grade level, previous work performance, community service, and relationship of degree program to career goals.

Financial data   The stipend is $20,000 per year.

Duration   1 year; may be renewed.

Additional information   CIRI is 1 of 13 regional corporations established according to the terms of the Alaska Native Claims Settlement Act (ANCSA) of 1971. This program began in 2001.

Number awarded   Varies each year; recently, 2 were awarded.

Deadline   May of each year.

[121]
CARMEN E. TURNER SCHOLARSHIPS

Conference of Minority Transportation Officials
Attn: National Scholarship Program
100 M Street, S.E., Suite 917
Washington, DC 20003
(202) 506-2917   E-mail: info@comto.org
Web: www.comto.org/page/scholarships

Summary   To provide financial assistance for college or graduate school to members of the Conference of Minority Transportation Officials (COMTO) and their families.

Eligibility   This program is open to undergraduate and graduate students who have been members or whose parents, guardians, or grandparents have been members of COMTO for at least 1 year. Applicants must be working on a degree in a field related to transportation and have a GPA of 2.5 or higher. Along with their application they must submit a cover letter on their transportation-related career goals and

life aspirations. Financial need is not considered in the selection process.

Financial data   The stipend is $3,500. Funds are paid directly to the recipient's college or university.

Duration   1 year.

Number awarded   1 each year.

Deadline   April of each year.

[122]
CAROL JORGENSEN SCHOLARSHIP FOR ENVIRONMENTAL STEWARDSHIP

Society of American Indian Government Employees
c/o Luke Jones
U.S. Environmental Protection Agency
American Indian Environmental Office (2690-M)
1200 Pennsylvania Avenue, N.W.
Washington, DC 20460
(202) 564-0303   Fax: (202) 564-0298
E-mail: jones.luke@epa.gov
Web: www.saige.org/scholar/cjscholarship.html

Summary   To provide financial assistance to Native Americans working on an undergraduate degree in a field related to environmental stewardship.

Eligibility   This program is open to full-time undergraduate students who are affiliated with a federally-recognized tribe of Native Americans. Tribal enrollment is not required, but tribal affiliation must be verified by a letter of support from a current or former tribal government official or respected member of the tribal community. Applicants must be working on a degree in an environmental stewardship discipline (e.g., environmental studies, natural resource management, the natural sciences, public policy or administration with an environmental focus). Along with their application, they must submit a 2-page personal statement that describes how their undergraduate studies support their commitment to environmental stewardship.

Financial data   The stipend is $1,000.

Duration   1 year.

Additional information   This program began in 2010.

Number awarded   1 each year.

Deadline   June of each year.

[123]
CAROLE SIMPSON RTDNF SCHOLARSHIP

Radio Television Digital News Foundation
Attn: Membership and Programs Manager
529 14th Street, N.W., Suite 1240
Washington, DC 20045
(202) 536-8356   Fax: (202) 223-4007
E-mail: karenh@rtdna.org
Web: www.rtdna.org/content/carole_simpson_scholarship

Summary   To provide financial assistance to Native American and other minority undergraduate students who are interested in preparing for a career in electronic journalism.

Eligibility   This program is open to sophomore or more advanced minority undergraduate students enrolled in an electronic journalism sequence at an accredited or nationally-recognized college or university. Applicants must submit a cover letter that discusses their current and past journalism experience, describes how they would use the funds if they were to receive the scholarship, discusses their reasons for preparing for a career in electronic journalism, and includes 3 to 5 links to their best and most relevant work samples.

Financial data The stipend is $2,000, paid in semiannual installments of $1,000 each.

Duration 1 year.

Additional information The Radio Television Digital News Foundation (RTDNF) also provides an all-expense paid trip to the Excellence in Journalism conference held that year. The RTDNF was formerly the Radio and Television News Directors Foundation (RTNDF).

Number awarded 1 each year.

Deadline April of each year.

[124]
CATCHING THE DREAM SCHOLARSHIPS

Catching the Dream
Attn: Scholarship Affairs Office
8200 Mountain Road, N.E., Suite 203
Albuquerque, NM 87110-7835
(505) 262-2351   Fax: (505) 262-0534
E-mail: NScholarsh@aol.com
Web: www.catchingthedream.org

Summary To provide financial assistance for college to American Indian undergraduate and graduate students interested in studying a field related to economic development for tribes.

Eligibility This program is open to American Indians who can provide proof that they are at least one-quarter Indian blood and a member of a U.S. tribe that is federally-recognized, state-recognized, or terminated. Applicants must be enrolled or planning to enroll full time at an accredited U.S. college or university as entering freshmen, undergraduate students, graduate students, or Ph.D. candidates. Along with their application, they must submit 1) documentation that they have read the sponsor's web site on "How to Find and Win Scholarships" and have applied for at least 50 other scholarships or financial aid programs; 2) official transcripts including standardized test scores (ACT, SAT, GRE, MCAT, LSAT, etc.); and 3) an essay of 3 to 5 pages explaining their career plans (especially how those plans include working with and benefiting Indians), what their Indian heritage means to them, and their leadership experience. Selection is based on merit and potential for improving the lives of Indian people.

Financial data Stipends range from $500 to $5,000 per year.

Duration 1 year.

Additional information The sponsor formerly offered 3 separate programs: the MESBEC (Mathematics, Engineering, Science, Business, Education, Computers) Program; the Native American Leadership in Education (NALE) Program; and the Tribal Business Management (TBM) Program.

Number awarded Varies; generally, 30 to 35 each year.

Deadline April of each year for fall semester or quarter; September of each year for spring semester or winter quarter; March of each year for summer school.

[125]
CERT COLLEGE SCHOLARSHIPS

Council of Energy Resource Tribes
Attn: Program Assistant
3545 South Tamarac Drive, Suite 320
Denver, CO 80237
(303) 282-7576, ext. 12   Fax: (303) 282-7584
E-mail: clebeau@certredearth.com
Web: 74.63.154.129/tribaladvance-education-college.html

Summary To provide financial assistance to American Indians who are interested in studying fields related to mathematics, business, science, engineering, or other technical fields on the undergraduate or graduate school level.

Eligibility This program is open to Indian high school seniors, college students, and graduate students who have participated in a qualifying program conducted by the Council of Energy Resource Tribes (CERT). Applicants must be enrolled or planning to enroll full time at an accredited 2- or 4-year tribal, public, or private college or university and major in business, engineering, science, mathematics, computer technology, or a related field. Along with their application, they must submit official tribal affiliation documents, university or college enrollment verification, and their most recent academic transcripts. Financial need is not considered in the selection process.

Financial data The stipend is $1,000 per year.

Duration 1 year; may be renewed up to 4 additional years, provided the recipient maintains a GPA of 2.5 or higher.

Number awarded Varies each year.

Deadline September of each year for fall semester; February of each year for spring semester.

[126]
CESDA DIVERSITY SCHOLARSHIPS

Colorado Educational Services and Development
   Association
P.O. Box 40214
Denver, CO 80204
(303) 492-2178   E-mail: Maria.Barajas@colorado.edu
Web: www.cesda.org/#!scholarships/crq5

Summary To provide financial assistance to high school seniors in Colorado who are planning to attend college in the state and are first-generation college students, Native American, or members of other underrepresented ethnic or racial minorities.

Eligibility This program is open to seniors graduating from high schools in Colorado who are 1) the first member of their family to attend college; 2) a member of an underrepresented ethnic or racial minority (African American, Asian/Pacific Islander, American Indian, Hispanic/Chicano/Latino); and/or 3) able to demonstrate financial need. Applicants must have a GPA of 2.8 or higher and be planning to enroll at a 2- or 4-year college or university in Colorado. U.S. citizenship or permanent resident status is required. Selection is based on leadership and community service (particularly within minority communities), past academic performance, personal and professional accomplishments, personal attributes, special abilities, academic goals, and financial need.

Financial data The stipend is $1,000.

Duration 1 year; nonrenewable.

Number awarded Varies each year.

Deadline March of each year.

[127]
CH2M HILL INDUSTRY PARTNER SCHOLARSHIP

Conference of Minority Transportation Officials
Attn: National Scholarship Program
100 M Street, S.E., Suite 917
Washington, DC 20003
(202) 506-2917   E-mail: info@comto.org
Web: www.comto.org/page/scholarships

Summary To provide financial assistance to Native American and other minority high school and college students interested in working on a degree in a field related to transportation.

Eligibility This program is open to minority high school seniors and current undergraduates who have a GPA of 3.0 or higher. Applicants must be working on or planning to work on a degree in engineering with a focus on the field of transportation. Along with their application they must submit a cover letter on their transportation-related career goals and life aspirations. Financial need is not considered in the selection process.

Financial data The stipend is $3,000. Funds are paid directly to the recipient's college or university.

Duration 1 year.

Additional information This program is sponsored by CH2M Hill.

Number awarded 1 each year.

Deadline April of each year.

[128]
CHAHTA FOUNDATION INCOMING FRESHMAN SCHOLARSHIP

Chahta Foundation
Attn: Scholarship Specialist
P.O. Box 1849
Durant, OK 74702
(580) 924-8280, ext. 2546
Toll Free: (800) 522-6170, ext. 2546
Fax: (580) 745-9023
E-mail: scholarship@chahtafoundation.com
Web: www.chahtafoundation.com

Summary To provide financial assistance to Choctaw tribal members who are high school seniors and interested in attending college in any state.

Eligibility This program is open to members of the Choctaw nation who are graduating from high schools in any state. Applicants must be planning to enroll at a college, university, or vocational/technical institution. They must have a GPA of 2.5 or higher. Along with their application, they must submit a list of honors, extracurricular activities, community volunteer services, and any recent work history. Financial need is not considered in the selection process.

Financial data The stipend is $2,000.

Duration 1 year; nonrenewable.

Number awarded 1 each year.

Deadline March of each year.

[129]
CHAHTA FOUNDATION UNDERGRADUATE SCHOLARSHIPS

Chahta Foundation
Attn: Scholarship Specialist
P.O. Box 1849
Durant, OK 74702
(580) 924-8280, ext. 2546
Toll Free: (800) 522-6170, ext. 2546
Fax: (580) 745-9023
E-mail: scholarship@chahtafoundation.com
Web: www.chahtafoundation.com

Summary To provide financial assistance to Choctaw tribal members who are working on a bachelor's degree in any field at a college in any state.

Eligibility This program is open to members of the Choctaw nation who have completed at least 1 year toward a bachelor's degree in any field. Applicants must be enrolled full time at a college or university in any state. They must have a GPA of 3.0 or higher and be able to demonstrate financial need. Along with their application, they must submit a 500-word essay on why being Choctaw is important to them.

Financial data The stipend is $3,000.

Duration 1 year; nonrenewable.

Number awarded 1 or more each year.

Deadline March of each year.

[130]
CHEROKEE NATION BUSINESSES SCHOLARSHIP

Cherokee Nation Foundation
800 South Muskogee
Tahlequah, OK 74464
(918) 207-0950   Fax: (918) 207-0951
E-mail: contact@cherokeenationfoundation.org
Web: www.cherokeenationfoundation.org/scholarships

Summary To provide scholarship/loans and work experience to citizens of the Cherokee Nation who are interested in completing a bachelor's or master's degree in a business-related field at a university in any state and working for Cherokee Nation Businesses.

Eligibility This program is open to citizens of the Cherokee Nation who are currently enrolled full time at a college or university in any state and working on an upper level bachelor's, professional, or master's degree. Their field of study must be accounting, corporate law, finance, engineering (biomedical, chemical, electrical, or mechanical), marketing, or mass communications. Applicants must be willing to 1) complete a paid summer internship for Cherokee Nation Businesses; and 2) sign a contract to work for Cherokee Nation Businesses for 2 years after graduation. They are not required to reside in the Cherokee Nation area. Along with their application, they must submit an 800-word essay on their desire to pursue higher education, their chosen field of study, how they plan to serve the Cherokee people after they complete their higher education, and whether or not they speak the Cherokee language. Financial need is considered in the selection process.

Financial data A stipend is awarded (amount not specified).

Duration 1 year; may be renewed up to 3 additional years, provided the recipient maintains a GPA that is in good standing at their school, performs the required internship, and completes a course in Cherokee Nation history.

Number awarded 1 or more each year.

Deadline January of each year.

[131]
CHEROKEE NATION UNDERGRADUATE SCHOLARSHIP PROGRAM

Cherokee Nation
Attn: College Resource Center
22361 Bald Hill Road
P.O. Box 948
Tahlequah, OK 74465
(918) 453-5465
Toll Free: (800) 256-0671, ext. 5465 (within OK)
Fax: (918) 458-6195 E-mail: scholarships@cherokee.org
Web: www.cherokee.org

Summary To provide financial assistance for undergraduate study in any state to citizens of the Cherokee Nation.

Eligibility This program is open to citizens of the Cherokee Nation who are attending or planning to attend a college or university in any state. Applicants must have a GPA of 2.0 or higher. There are no residency requirements, but applicants who live outside the Cherokee nation area, defined as those counties within and contiguous to the Cherokee Nation boundaries, must qualify for the federal Pell Grant through their FAFSA.

Financial data The stipend is $2,000 per semester for full-time study or $1,000 per semester for part-time study.

Duration Up to 8 semesters.

Additional information The Cherokee Nation area covers all or part of the following Oklahoma counties: Adair, Cherokee, Craig, Delaware, Mayes, McIntosh, Muskogee, Nowata, Ottawa, Rogers, Sequoyah, Tulsa, Wagoner, and Washington. Contiguous counties include Haskell, Le Flore, Osage, and Pittsburg counties in Oklahoma; Benton, Crawford, and Washington counties in Arkansas; Cherokee, Labette, and Montgomery counties in Kansas; and McDonald County in Missouri. Recipients must agree to perform 1 hour of community service to the Cherokee Nation for every $100 awarded.

Number awarded Varies each year; nearly 1,600 students receive support annually.

Deadline August of each year for fall semester; January of each year for spring semester.

[132]
CHEVRON CORPORATION SCHOLARSHIPS OF THE AMERICAN INDIAN SCIENCE AND ENGINEERING SOCIETY

American Indian Science and Engineering Society
Attn: Director of Membership and Communications
2305 Renard Place, S.E., Suite 200
Albuquerque, NM 87106
(505) 765-1052, ext. 110   Fax: (505) 765-5608
E-mail: lpaz@aises.org
Web: www.aises.org

Summary To provide financial assistance to members of the American Indian Science and Engineering Society (AISES) who are working on an undergraduate or graduate degree in a field of interest to Chevron Corporation.

Eligibility This program is open to AISES members who are full-time undergraduate or graduate students at an accredited 4-year college or university. Applicants must be American Indian tribal members, Alaskan Natives, Native Hawaiians, First Nations members, or other indigenous peoples of North America and have a Certificate of Degree of Indian or Alaska Native Blood (CDIB) showing at least 25% Native blood. They must have a GPA of 3.3 or higher and be working on a degree in business or a field of science, technology, engineering, or mathematics (STEM) that is beneficial to Chevron. In the selection process, priority is given to 1) freshmen and sophomores who have a related internship or non-technical work experience; 2) juniors who have at least 1 leadership role in AISES and at least 1 technical internship related to their field of study; 3) seniors who have least 1 leadership role in AISES, at least 1 technical internship related to their field of study, and have not committed to an offer of employment with a company other than Chevron; and graduate students who have a least 1 technical internship related to their field of study and a master's thesis or doctoral dissertation on a topic that is related to the energy industry. All applicants must be able to demonstrate knowledge and interest in Chevron and the energy industry and have at least 1 noteworthy achievement or recognition.

Financial data The stipend is $5,000.

Duration 1 year; nonrenewable.

Additional information This program is funded by Chevron Corporation.

Number awarded 1 or more each year.

Deadline April of each year.

[133]
CHEYENNE AND ARAPAHO HIGHER EDUCATION GRANTS

Cheyenne and Arapaho Tribes of Oklahoma
Attn: Higher Education Program
100 Red Moon Circle
P.O. Box 167
Concho, OK 73022
(405) 422-7653   Toll Free: (800) 247-4612
Fax: (405) 422-8211   E-mail: heducation@c-a-tribes.org
Web: www.c-a-tribes.org/higher-education

Summary To provide financial assistance to enrolled Cheyenne-Arapaho tribal members who are interested in working on an undergraduate or graduate degree at a college in any state.

Eligibility This program is open to Cheyenne-Arapaho Indians who reside in any state and are at least a high school graduate (or the equivalent), approved for admission by a college or university, and in financial need. Applicants may be enrolled or planning to enroll at a 2- or 4-year college or university (not a vocational or technical school) in any state. The vast majority of students assisted under this program are at the undergraduate level, although graduate and/or married students are eligible for consideration and assistance. Summer and part-time students may apply as well, as long as application is made well in advance of enrollment and is accompanied by an official need evaluation.

Financial data The stipend is $2,000 per year.

Duration 1 year; renewable.

Number awarded 40 to 80 each year.

Deadline May of each year for fall semester; October for spring semester; or March for summer session.

[134]
CHEYENNE RIVER SIOUX TRIBE SCHOLARSHIP

Cheyenne River Sioux Tribe
Attn: Education Services Office
2001 Main Street
P.O. Box 590
Eagle Butte, SD 57625
(605) 964-8311   E-mail: dal7882@lakotanetwork.com
Web: www.sioux.org/educational-services-department.html

Summary To provide financial assistance to members of the Cheyenne River Sioux Tribe who are interested in attending college in any state but are not eligible for funding through other tribal programs.

Eligibility This program is open to enrolled Cheyenne River Sioux tribal members who are attending or planning to attend a college, university, or vocational/technical school in any state. Applicants must be high school graduates or GED recipients and planning to enroll full time. They must be eligible for the tribe's Higher Education Program, but they must have been denied funding because of 1) lack of funds available through that program; 2) inability to meet the financial need requirement of that program; or 3) exhaustion of the number of semesters allowed by that program.

Financial data A stipend is awarded (amount not specified).

Duration 1 year; may be renewed, provided the recipient remains enrolled full time and maintains a GPA of 2.0 or higher.

Number awarded Varies each year.

Deadline July of each year for the academic year; December of each year for spring semester only.

[135]
CHF/ALYESKA MATCH SCHOLARSHIPS

Chugach Alaska Corporation
Attn: Chugach Heritage Foundation
3800 Centerpoint Drive, Suite 1200
Anchorage, AK 99503
(907) 261-0400   Toll Free: (800) 858-2768
Fax: (907) 261-8896 E-mail: scholarships@chugach.com
Web: www.chugachheritagefoundation.org

Summary To provide financial assistance to undergraduate and graduate students who are original shareholders of the Chugach Alaska Corporation or their descendants and attending college in any state to prepare for a career in the oil industry.

Eligibility This program is open to original shareholders and the descendants of original enrollees of the Chugach Alaska Corporation. Applicants must be enrolled or planning to enroll at an accredited college or university in any state as an undergraduate or graduate student to work on a degree in engineering (chemical, civil, electrical, mechanical; environmental health and safety; construction and project management; computer science, information technology, management information systems; instrumentation, process technology, supervisory control and data acquisition (SCADA); accounting, business administration, economics, of finance; or applied technology and industry trades such as welding,

diesel and heavy equipment, electrician, maritime, culinary. They must have a GPA of 2.5 or higher and an interest in working within the Trans-Alaska Pipeline Services (TAPS) and the oil industry. Along with their application, a personal statement of career goals.

Financial data The stipend is $7,500 per academic year.

Duration 1 year; may be renewed.

Additional information The Chugach Alaska Corporation is 1 of 13 Alaska Native Regional Corporations created under the Alaska Native Claims Settlement Act of 1971. This program is sponsored by the Alyeska Pipeline Service Company.

Number awarded Varies each year.

Deadline Students must submit applications within 4 weeks after the start of the term. Awards are presented on a first-come, first-served basis.

[136]
CHICKASAW FOUNDATION CAREER TECHNOLOGY SCHOLARSHIP

Chickasaw Foundation
2020 Arlington, Suite 4
P.O. Box 1726
Ada, OK 74821-1726
(580) 421-9030   Fax: (580) 421-9031
E-mail: ChickasawFoundation@chickasaw.net
Web: www.chickasawfoundation.org/Scholarships.aspx

Summary To provide financial assistance for vocational school to employees of the Chickasaw Nation.

Eligibility This program is open to employees of the Chickasaw Nation who are currently enrolled at a career technology, vocational/technical, or trade school. Applicants must be at least 18 years of age and have a GPA of 2.0 or higher. Along with their application, they must submit high school or college transcripts; 2 letters of recommendation; a copy of their Chickasaw Nation citizenship card; a copy of their Chickasaw Nation employee identification badge; a 2-page list of honors, achievements, awards, club memberships, societies, and civic involvement; and a 1-page essay on their long-term goals and plans for achieving those. Financial need is not considered in the selection process.

Financial data A stipend is awarded (amount not specified).

Duration 1 year.

Number awarded 1 each year.

Deadline June or February of each year.

[137]
CHICKASAW FOUNDATION FINE ARTS SCHOLARSHIP

Chickasaw Foundation
2020 Arlington, Suite 4
P.O. Box 1726
Ada, OK 74821-1726
(580) 421-9030   Fax: (580) 421-9031
E-mail: ChickasawFoundation@chickasaw.net
Web: www.chickasawfoundation.org/Scholarships.aspx

Summary To provide financial assistance to Native Americans interested in studying fine arts in college.

Eligibility This program is open to Native American students who are currently enrolled full time as a junior or senior at an accredited 4-year college. Applicants must be majoring in fine arts (dance, dramatics, art, music) and have a GPA of 3.0 or higher. Along with their application, they must submit high school or college transcripts; 2 letters of recommendation; a copy of their Chickasaw Nation citizenship card; a copy of their Certificate of Degree of Indian Blood (CDIB); a 2-page list of honors, achievements, awards, club memberships, societies, and civic involvement; and a 1-page essay on their long-term goals and plans for achieving those. Financial need is not considered in the selection process.

Financial data A stipend is awarded (amount not specified).

Duration 1 year.

Number awarded 2 each year.

Deadline June of each year.

[138]
CHICKASAW FOUNDATION GENERAL PURPOSE EDUCATION SCHOLARSHIPS

Chickasaw Foundation
2020 Arlington, Suite 4
P.O. Box 1726
Ada, OK 74821-1726
(580) 421-9030   Fax: (580) 421-9031
E-mail: ChickasawFoundation@chickasaw.net
Web: www.chickasawfoundation.org/Scholarships.aspx

Summary To provide financial assistance to members of the Chickasaw Nation who are interested in working on an undergraduate or graduate degree.

Eligibility This program is open to Chickasaw students who are currently enrolled at an accredited institution of higher education as a full-time undergraduate or graduate student. Applicants may be majoring in any field, but they must have a GPA of 2.0 or higher. Along with their application, they must submit high school or college transcripts; 2 letters of recommendation; a copy of their Chickasaw Nation citizenship card; a 2-page list of honors, achievements, awards, club memberships, societies, and civic involvement; and a 1-page essay on their long-term goals and plans for achieving those. Financial need is not considered in the selection process.

Financial data A stipend is awarded (amount not specified).

Duration 1 year.

Number awarded Varies each year; recently, 5 were awarded.

Deadline June of each year.

[139]
CHICKASAW FOUNDATION HEALTH PROFESSIONS SCHOLARSHIP

Chickasaw Foundation
2020 Arlington, Suite 4
P.O. Box 1726
Ada, OK 74821-1726
(580) 421-9030   Fax: (580) 421-9031
E-mail: ChickasawFoundation@chickasaw.net
Web: www.chickasawfoundation.org/Scholarships.aspx

Summary To provide financial assistance to members of the Chickasaw Nation who are interested in working on an undergraduate, graduate, or vocational/technical degree in a health-related field.

Eligibility This program is open to undergraduate, graduate, and vocational/technical students who are members of the Chickasaw Nation. Academic students must be preparing for a career as a dentist, dental hygienist, nurse, physician assistant, nurse practitioner, medical doctor, laboratory technologist, pharmacist, imaging technologist, behavioral health counselor, or biomedical engineer. Vocational students must be engaged in training as an emergency medical technician, licensed practical nurse, or electrician or plumber for the health arena. Applicants must have a GPA of 3.0 or higher. Along with their application, they must submit high school or college transcripts; 2 letters of recommendation; a copy of their Certificate of Degree of Indian Blood (CDIB) if relevant; a copy of their Chickasaw Nation citizenship card; a 2-page list of honors, achievements, awards, club memberships, societies, and civic involvement; and a 1-page essay on their long-term goals and plans for achieving those. Financial need is not considered in the selection process.

Financial data A stipend is awarded (amount not specified).

Duration 1 year.

Number awarded 1 each year.

Deadline June of each year.

[140]
CHICKASAW FOUNDATION JUDICIAL SCHOLARSHIP

Chickasaw Foundation
2020 Arlington, Suite 4
P.O. Box 1726
Ada, OK 74821-1726
(580) 421-9030   Fax: (580) 421-9031
E-mail: ChickasawFoundation@chickasaw.net
Web: www.chickasawfoundation.org/Scholarships.aspx

Summary To provide financial assistance to members of the Chickasaw Nation who are interested in working on an undergraduate or graduate degree in a field related to law.

Eligibility This program is open to Chickasaw students who are currently enrolled at an accredited 4-year college or university as a full-time undergraduate or law student. Applicants must be working on a degree in law, pre-law, legal studies, paralegal, or any major associated with law or a bachelor's degree obtained with the intention of pursuing a law degree. They must have a GPA of 3.2 or higher. Along with their application, they must submit high school, college, and/or law school transcripts; 2 letters of recommendation; a copy of their Chickasaw Nation citizenship card; a 2-page list of honors, achievements, awards, club memberships, societies, and civic involvement; and a 1-page essay on their long-term goals and plans for achieving those. Financial need is not considered in the selection process.

Financial data A stipend is awarded (amount not specified).

Duration 1 year.

Number awarded 1 each year.

Deadline June of each year.

[141]
CHICKASAW FOUNDATION NONPROFIT MANAGEMENT SCHOLARSHIP

Chickasaw Foundation
2020 Arlington, Suite 4
P.O. Box 1726
Ada, OK 74821-1726
(580) 421-9030   Fax: (580) 421-9031
E-mail: ChickasawFoundation@chickasaw.net
Web: www.chickasawfoundation.org/Scholarships.aspx

Summary To provide financial assistance to members of the Chickasaw Nation working on an undergraduate or graduate degree in a field related to nonprofit management.

Eligibility This program is open to members of the Chickasaw Nation who are currently enrolled as full-time graduate students or undergraduates at a 4-year college or university. Applicants must be working on nonprofit management certification or another field of study related to the nonprofit sector. They must have a GPA of 3.0 or higher. Along with their application, they must submit high school or college transcripts; 2 letters of recommendation; a copy of their Chickasaw Nation citizenship card; a 2-page list of honors, achievements, awards, club memberships, societies, and civic involvement; and a 1-page essay on their long-term goals and plans for achieving those. Financial need is not considered in the selection process.

Financial data A stipend is awarded (amount not specified).

Duration 1 year.

Number awarded 1 each year.

Deadline June of each year.

[142]
CHICKASAW NATION ADA WELLNESS PROGRAM SCHOLARSHIP

Chickasaw Foundation
2020 Arlington, Suite 4
P.O. Box 1726
Ada, OK 74821-1726
(580) 421-9030   Fax: (580) 421-9031
E-mail: ChickasawFoundation@chickasaw.net
Web: www.chickasawfoundation.org/Scholarships.aspx

Summary To provide financial assistance to members of the Chickasaw Nation who are working on an undergraduate degree in kinesiology or recreation.

Eligibility This program is open to members of the Chickasaw Nation who are currently enrolled as undergraduates at a college or university. Applicants must be working on a degree in kinesiology or recreation and have a GPA of 2.0 or higher. Along with their application, they must submit high school or college transcripts; 2 letters of recommendation; a copy of their Chickasaw Nation citizenship card; a 2-page list of honors, achievements, awards, club memberships, societies, and civic involvement; and a 1-page essay on their long-term goals and plans for achieving those. Financial need is not considered in the selection process.

Financial data A stipend is awarded (amount not specified).

Duration 1 year.

Number awarded 1 each year.

Deadline June of each year.

[143]
CHICKASAW NATION DIVISION OF SOCIAL SERVICES GENERAL EDUCATIONAL SCHOLARSHIP

Chickasaw Foundation
2020 Arlington, Suite 4
P.O. Box 1726
Ada, OK 74821-1726
(580) 421-9030   Fax: (580) 421-9031
E-mail: ChickasawFoundation@chickasaw.net
Web: www.chickasawfoundation.org/Scholarships.aspx

Summary To provide financial assistance for college to members of the Chickasaw Nation.

Eligibility This program is open to Chickasaw students who are currently enrolled as a full-time undergraduate student. Applicants may be majoring in any field, but they must have a GPA of 2.5 or higher. Along with their application, they must submit high school or college transcripts; 2 letters of recommendation; a copy of their Chickasaw Nation citizenship card; a 2-page list of honors, achievements, awards, club memberships, societies, and civic involvement; and a 1-page essay on their long-term goals and plans for achieving those. Financial need is not considered in the selection process.

Financial data A stipend is awarded (amount not specified).

Duration 1 year.

Number awarded 1 each year.

Deadline June of each year.

[144]
CHICKASAW NATION DIVISION ON AGING SCHOLARSHIP

Chickasaw Foundation
2020 Arlington, Suite 4
P.O. Box 1726
Ada, OK 74821-1726
(580) 421-9030   Fax: (580) 421-9031
E-mail: ChickasawFoundation@chickasaw.net
Web: www.chickasawfoundation.org/Scholarships.aspx

Summary To provide financial assistance to members of the Chickasaw Nation who are upper-division students in geriatrics.

Eligibility This program is open to Chickasaw students who are currently enrolled full time at an accredited institution of higher education. Applicants must be classified as juniors or seniors at a 4-year college and have a GPA of 3.0 or higher. They must be majoring in a field related to geriatrics, including nursing, social work, physical therapy, or psychiatry. Along with their application, they must submit high school or college transcripts; 2 letters of recommendation; a copy of their Chickasaw Nation citizenship card; a 2-page list of honors, achievements, awards, club memberships, societies, and civic involvement; and a 1-page essay on their long-term goals and plans for achieving those. Financial need is not considered in the selection process.

Financial data A stipend is awarded (amount not specified).

Duration 1 year.

Number awarded 1 each year.

Deadline June of each year.

[145] CHICKASAW NATION LIGHTHORSE SCHOLARSHIP

Chickasaw Foundation
2020 Arlington, Suite 4
P.O. Box 1726
Ada, OK 74821-1726
(580) 421-9030   Fax: (580) 421-9031
E-mail: ChickasawFoundation@chickasaw.net
Web: www.chickasawfoundation.org/Scholarships.aspx

Summary To provide financial assistance to members of the Chickasaw Nation who are working on an undergraduate degree in a field related to law enforcement.

Eligibility This program is open to Chickasaw students who are currently enrolled full time at a 2- or 4-year college or university and working on an undergraduate degree in criminal justice, police science, or another field related to law enforcement. Applicants must have a GPA of 3.0 or higher. Along with their application, they must submit high school or college transcripts; 2 letters of recommendation; a copy of their Chickasaw Nation citizenship card; a 2-page list of honors, achievements, awards, club memberships, societies, and civic involvement; and a 1-page essay on their long-term goals and plans for achieving those. Financial need is not considered in the selection process.

Financial data A stipend is awarded (amount not specified).

Duration 1 year.

Number awarded 1 each year.

Deadline June of each year.

[146] CHICKASAW NATION OF OKLAHOMA SCHOLARSHIPS

Oklahoma Youth Expo
Attn: Scholarship Program
500 N.W. 30th Street
Oklahoma City, OK 73118
(405) 235-0404   Fax: (405) 235-1727
Web: www.okyouthexpo.com

Summary To provide financial assistance to members of the Chickasaw Nation who are high school seniors, exhibit at the Oklahoma Youth Expo (OYE), and plan to attend college in Oklahoma to major in any subject.

Eligibility This program is open to members of the Chickasaw Nation who are high school seniors and exhibit at the OYE (membership in an Oklahoma 4-H Club or Oklahoma FFA chapter is required to exhibit). Applicants must be planning to enroll full time at an institution of higher education in Oklahoma where they may major in any subject field. They must have a Chickasaw Nation CDIB card and a Chickasaw Nation Membership Card. Along with their application, they must submit 500-word essays on 1) how the junior livestock program has contributed to their higher educational and career pursuits; and 2) their 10-year goals in life and how those pursuits will help make Oklahoma a better place. Selection is based on academics, community involvement, and junior agriculture program participation.

Financial data The stipend is $2,500.

Duration 1 year; nonrenewable.

Additional information This program is sponsored by the Chickasaw Nation.

Number awarded 3 each year.

Deadline November of each year.

[147] CHIEF MANUELITO SCHOLARSHIP PROGRAM

Navajo Nation
Attn: Office of Navajo Nation Scholarship and Financial Assistance
P.O. Box 1870
Window Rock, AZ 86515-1870
(928) 871-7444   Toll Free: (800) 243-2956
Fax: (928) 871-7410
E-mail: rosegraham@navajo-nsn.gov
Web: www.onnsfa.org/FundingTypes/ChiefManuelito.aspx

Summary To provide financial assistance to academically superior members of the Navajo Nation who are interested in working on an undergraduate degree.

Eligibility This program is open to enrolled members of the Navajo Nation who are attending or planning to enroll as full-time students at an accredited 4-year college or university. Applicants who are graduating high school seniors must have the following minimum combinations of ACT score and GPA: 21 and 3.8, 22 and 3.7, 23 and 3.6, 24 and 3.5, 25 and 3.4, 26 and 3.3, 27 and 3.2, 28 and 3.1, or 29 and 3.0. They must have completed in high school at least 1 unit of Navajo language and at least half a unit of Navajo government. Applicants who are current undergraduate students must have completed at least 24 semester credit hours with an overall GPA of 3.0 or higher.

Financial data The stipend is $7,000 per year.

Duration 1 year; may be renewed if the recipient maintains full-time status and a GPA of 3.0 or higher.

Additional information This program began in 1980.

Number awarded Varies each year; recently, 79 were awarded.

Deadline June of each year for fall and academic year applicants; November of each year for winter and spring term.

[148] CHIEF TONY TANNER SCHOLARSHIP

Coquille Indian Tribe
Attn: Department of Culture, Education and Library Services
495 Miluk Drive
Coos Bay, OR 97420
(541) 756-0904   Toll Free: (800) 622-5869
Fax: (541) 888-2418
E-mail: bridgettwheeler@coquilletribe.org
Web: www.coquilletribe.org/higheredprograms.htm

Summary To provide financial assistance to members of the Coquille Indian Tribe who are attending college in any state.

Eligibility This program is open to enrolled members of the Coquille Indian Tribe who are entering their sophomore, junior, or senior year at an accredited college or university in any state. Along with their application, they must submit a personal essay on their career goals, why they chose their educational field, and if they plan to use their education to benefit the Coquille Indian Tribe. Selection is based on academic achievement, community and/or cultural involvement, and leadership.

Financial data　The stipend is $5,000.

Duration　1 year; nonrenewable.

Number awarded　Varies each year; recently, 4 were awarded.

Deadline　June of each year.

[149]
CHIPS QUINN SCHOLARS PROGRAM

Newseum Institute
Attn: Chips Quinn Scholars Program
555 Pennsylvania Avenue, N.W.
Washington, DC 20001
(202) 292-6271　　　　　　Fax: (202) 292-6275
E-mail: kcatone@freedomforum.org
Web: www.newseuminstitute.org

Summary　To provide work experience to Native American and other minority college students and recent graduates who are majoring in journalism.

Eligibility　This program is open to students of color who are college juniors, seniors, graduate students, or recent graduates with journalism majors or career goals in newspapers. Candidates must be nominated or endorsed by journalism faculty, campus media advisers, editors of newspapers, or leaders of minority journalism associations. Along with their application, they must submit a resume, transcripts, 2 letters of recommendation, and an essay of 200 to 400 words on why they want to be a Chips Quinn Scholar. Reporters and copy editors must also submit 6 samples of published articles they have written; photographers must submit 15 to 25 photographs on a DVD; multimedia journalists and graphic designers should submit 6 to 10 samples of their work on a DVD. Applicants must have a car and be available to work as a full-time intern during the spring or summer. U.S. citizenship or permanent resident status is required. Campus newspaper experience is strongly encouraged.

Financial data　Students chosen for this program receive a travel stipend to attend a Multimedia training program in Nashville, Tennessee prior to reporting for their internship, a $500 housing allowance from the Freedom Forum, and a competitive salary during their internship.

Duration　Internships are for 10 to 12 weeks, in spring or summer.

Additional information　This program began in 1991 in memory of the late John D. Quinn Jr., managing editor of the *Poughkeepsie Journal*. Funding is provided by the Freedom Forum, formerly the Gannett Foundation. After graduating from college and obtaining employment with a newspaper, alumni of this program are eligible to apply for fellowship support to attend professional journalism development activities.

Number awarded　Approximately 70 each year. Since the program began, more than 1,300 scholars have been selected.

Deadline　September of each year.

[150]
CHOCTAW NATION HIGHER EDUCATION GRANTS

Choctaw Nation
Attn: Higher Education Department
16th and Locust
P.O. Box 1210
Durant, OK 74702-1210
(580) 924-8280
Toll Free: (800) 522-6170, ext. 2547 (within OK)
Fax: (580) 924-1267
E-mail: hepapplication@choctawnation.com
Web: www.choctawnation.com

Summary　To provide financial assistance to Choctaw Indians who are interested in working on an undergraduate degree and can demonstrate financial need.

Eligibility　This program is open to students who are attending or planning to attend an accredited college or university and have a Certificate of Degree of Indian Blood (CDIB) and tribal membership card showing Choctaw descent. Students in vocational and technical schools or correspondence courses are not eligible. Applicants must be able to demonstrate financial need.

Financial data　The stipend depends on the need, class level, and enrollment status of the recipient; maximum awards are $400 per semester for part-time students, $500 per semester for full-time freshmen, $600 per semester for full-time sophomores, $700 per semester for full-time juniors, or $800 per semester for full-time seniors.

Duration　1 year; may be renewed for up to 4 additional years as long as the recipient enrolls in at least 12 hours per semester (or at least 6 hours for part-time students) with a GPA of 2.0 or higher.

Additional information　This program began in 1984 with funding from the Bureau of Indian Affairs.

Number awarded　Varies each year.

Deadline　September of each year for fall semester; February of each year for spring semester.

[151]
CHOCTAW NATION HIGHER EDUCATION SCHOLARSHIPS

Choctaw Nation
Attn: Higher Education Department
16th and Locust
P.O. Box 1210
Durant, OK 74702-1210
(580) 924-8280
Toll Free: (800) 522-6170, ext. 2547 (within OK)
Fax: (580) 924-1267
E-mail: hepapplication@choctawnation.com
Web: www.choctawnation.com

Summary　To provide financial assistance to Choctaw Indians who are interested in working on an undergraduate degree.

Eligibility　This program is open to students who are attending or planning to attend an accredited college or university and have a Certificate of Degree of Indian Blood (CDIB) and tribal membership card showing Choctaw descent. Students in vocational and technical schools or correspondence courses are not eligible. Applicants must have a

GPA of 2.5 or higher. Financial need is not considered in the selection process.

Financial data The stipend depends on GPA: $500 per semester for full-time students with a GPA less than 2.50; $600 per semester for full-time students with a GPA of 2.50 to 2.99, $800 per semester for full-time students with a GPA of 3.00 to 3.49, or $1,000 per semester for full-time students with a GPA of 3.50 to 4.00. Part-time students receive $500 per semester regardless of GPA.

Duration 1 year; may be renewed for up to 4 additional years as long as the recipient enrolls in at least 12 hours per semester (or at least 6 hours for part-time students) with a GPA of 2.5 or higher.

Additional information The Choctaw Nation established this program in 1998.

Number awarded Varies each year.

Deadline September of each year for fall semester; February of each year for spring semester.

[152]
CHOCTAW NATION OF OKLAHOMA SCHOLARSHIPS

Oklahoma Youth Expo
Attn: Scholarship Program
500 N.W. 30th Street
Oklahoma City, OK 73118
(405) 235-0404   Fax: (405) 235-1727
Web: www.okyouthexpo.com

Summary To provide financial assistance to members of the Choctaw Nation who are high school seniors, exhibit at the Oklahoma Youth Expo (OYE), and plan to attend college in Oklahoma to major in any subject.

Eligibility This program is open to members of the Choctaw Nation who are high school seniors and exhibit at the OYE (membership in an Oklahoma 4-H Club or Oklahoma FFA chapter is required to exhibit). Applicants must be planning to enroll full time at an institution of higher education in Oklahoma where they may major in any subject field. They must have a Choctaw Nation CDIB card and a Choctaw Nation Membership Card. Along with their application, they must submit 500-word essays on 1) how the junior livestock program has contributed to their higher educational and career pursuits; and 2) their 10-year goals in life and how those pursuits will help make Oklahoma a better place. Selection is based on academics, community involvement, and junior agriculture program participation.

Financial data The stipend is $2,500.

Duration 1 year; nonrenewable.

Additional information This program is sponsored by the Choctaw Nation.

Number awarded 2 each year.

Deadline November of each year.

[153]
CHUGACH HERITAGE FOUNDATION UNDERGRADUATE SCHOLARSHIPS

Chugach Alaska Corporation
Attn: Chugach Heritage Foundation
3800 Centerpoint Drive, Suite 1200
Anchorage, AK 99503
(907) 261-0400   Toll Free: (800) 858-2768
Fax: (907) 261-8896 E-mail: scholarships@chugach.com
Web: www.chugachheritagefoundation.org

Summary To provide financial assistance to undergraduate students who are original shareholders of the Chugach Alaska Corporation or their descendants and attending college in any state.

Eligibility This program is open to original shareholders and the descendants of original enrollees of the Chugach Alaska Corporation. Applicants must be enrolled or planning to enroll at an accredited college or university in any state as an undergraduate student. They must have a GPA of 2.0 or higher.

Financial data For full-time students, stipends are $5,000 per year for freshmen and sophomores or associate degree students or $6,300 per year for juniors and seniors in bachelor's degree programs. Stipends for part-time students are prorated appropriately.

Duration 1 year; may be renewed if the recipient maintains a GPA of 2.0 or higher.

Additional information The Chugach Alaska Corporation is 1 of 13 Alaska Native Regional Corporations created under the Alaska Native Claims Settlement Act of 1971.

Number awarded Varies each year.

Deadline Students must submit applications within 4 weeks after the start of the term.

[154]
CHUGACH HERITAGE FOUNDATION VOCATIONAL TRAINING FUNDING

Chugach Alaska Corporation
Attn: Chugach Heritage Foundation
3800 Centerpoint Drive, Suite 1200
Anchorage, AK 99503
(907) 261-0400   Toll Free: (800) 858-2768
Fax: (907) 261-8896 E-mail: scholarships@chugach.com
Web: www.chugachheritagefoundation.org

Summary To provide financial assistance to students who are original enrollees of the Chugach Alaska Corporation or their descendants and enrolled in a vocational training program in any state.

Eligibility This program is open to original enrollees and the descendants of original enrollees of the Chugach Alaska Corporation. Applicants must be registered for training that will broaden their employment opportunities or maintain their skill level at a school in any state. They must have a GPA of 2.0 or higher.

Financial data The stipend is $4,200 per calendar year.

Duration 1 year; may be renewed if the recipient maintains a GPA of 2.0 or higher.

Additional information The Chugach Alaska Corporation is 1 of 13 Alaska Native Regional Corporations created under the Alaska Native Claims Settlement Act of 1971.

Number awarded Varies each year.

Deadline Applications may be submitted at any time, but they must be received at least 30 days prior to the first day of class.

[155]
CIGNA FOUNDATION SCHOLARS HEALTHCARE SCHOLARSHIP

American Indian College Fund
Attn: Scholarship Department
8333 Greenwood Boulevard
Denver, CO 80221
(303) 426-8900   Toll Free: (800) 776-FUND
Fax: (303) 426-1200
E-mail: scholarships@collegefund.org
Web: www.collegefund.org

Summary To provide financial assistance to Native American college students who are interested in studying designated health-related fields at mainstream colleges and universities in Arizona, California, Colorado, or Washington.

Eligibility This program is open to American Indians and Alaska Natives from any state who have proof of enrollment or descendancy. Applicants must be entering their junior or senior year at a college or university in Arizona, California, Colorado, or Washington. They must have a GPA of 3.0 or higher and be studying pre-medicine, pharmacy, dentistry, health technologies, or nursing. Applications are available only online and include required essays on specified topics. U.S. citizenship is required.

Financial data The stipend is $2,666.

Duration 1 year.

Additional information This program is sponsored by the CIGNA Foundation.

Number awarded 1 or more each year.

Deadline May of each year.

[156]
CIGNA FOUNDATION TRIBAL SCHOLARS HEALTHCARE SCHOLARSHIP

American Indian College Fund
Attn: Scholarship Department
8333 Greenwood Boulevard
Denver, CO 80221
(303) 426-8900   Toll Free: (800) 776-FUND
Fax: (303) 426-1200
E-mail: scholarships@collegefund.org
Web: www.collegefund.org

Summary To provide financial assistance to Native American college students who are interested in studying designated health-related fields at Tribal Colleges and Universities (TCUs) in Arizona, Washington, or Wisconsin.

Eligibility This program is open to American Indians and Alaska Natives from any state who have proof of enrollment or descendancy. Applicants must be enrolled or planning to enroll as freshmen, sophomores, juniors, or seniors at an eligible TCU in Arizona, Washington, or Wisconsin. They must have a GPA of 3.0 or higher and be working on a degree in social and behavioral science, public health, chemical dependency studies, medical office mid-management, medical assistant, pre-health information management, pre-nursing, medical transcriptionist, or nursing. Applications are available only online and include required essays on specified topics. In the selection process, consideration is given to leadership qualities and involvement in the Native community. U.S. citizenship is required.

Financial data The stipend is $2,000.

Duration 1 year.

Additional information This program is sponsored by the CIGNA Foundation.

Number awarded 1 or more each year.

Deadline May of each year.

[157]
CIRI FOUNDATION ACHIEVEMENT SCHOLARSHIPS

Cook Inlet Region, Inc.
Attn: The CIRI Foundation
3600 San Jeronimo Drive, Suite 256
Anchorage, AK 99508-2870
(907) 793-3575   Toll Free: (800) 764-3382
Fax: (907) 793-3585   E-mail: tcf@thecirifoundation.org
Web: www.thecirifoundation.org/scholarships

Summary To provide financial assistance for undergraduate or graduate studies to Alaska Natives who are original enrollees to Cook Inlet Region, Inc. (CIRI) and their lineal descendants.

Eligibility This program is open to Alaska Native enrollees to CIRI under the Alaska Native Claims Settlement Act (ANCSA) of 1971 and their lineal descendants. There are no Alaska residency requirements or age limitations. Applicants must be accepted or enrolled full time in a 4-year or graduate degree program. They must have a GPA of 3.0 or higher. Along with their application, they must submit a 500-word statement on their educational and career goals and how they are contributing, or planning to contribute, to a positive Alaska Native community. Selection is based on that statement, academic achievement, rigor of course work or degree program, student financial contribution, financial need, grade level, previous work performance, community service, and relationship of degree program to career goals.

Financial data The stipend is $8,000 per year.

Duration 1 year (2 semesters).

Additional information CIRI is 1 of 13 regional corporations established according to the terms of the Alaska Native Claims Settlement Act (ANCSA) of 1971.

Number awarded Varies each year.

Deadline May of each year.

[158]
CIRI FOUNDATION EXCELLENCE SCHOLARSHIPS

Cook Inlet Region, Inc.
Attn: The CIRI Foundation
3600 San Jeronimo Drive, Suite 256
Anchorage, AK 99508-2870
(907) 793-3575   Toll Free: (800) 764-3382
Fax: (907) 793-3585   E-mail: tcf@thecirifoundation.org
Web: www.thecirifoundation.org/scholarships

Summary To provide financial assistance for undergraduate or graduate studies to Alaska Natives who are original enrollees to Cook Inlet Region, Inc. (CIRI) and their lineal descendants.

Eligibility This program is open to Alaska Native enrollees to CIRI under the Alaska Native Claims Settlement Act (ANCSA) of 1971 and their lineal descendants. There are no Alaska residency requirements or age limitations. Applicants must be accepted or enrolled full time in a 4-year undergraduate or a graduate degree program. They must have a GPA of 3.5 or higher. Along with their application, they must submit a 500-word statement on their educational and career goals and how they are contributing, or planning to contribute, to a positive Alaska Native community. Selection is based on that statement, academic achievement, rigor of course work or degree program, student financial contribution, financial need, grade level, previous work performance, community service, and relationship of degree program to career goals.

Financial data The stipend is $10,000 per year.

Duration 1 year (2 semesters).

Additional information CIRI is 1 of 13 regional corporations established according to the terms of the Alaska Native Claims Settlement Act (ANCSA) of 1971.

Number awarded Varies each year; recently, 7 were awarded.

Deadline May of each year.

[159]
CIRI FOUNDATION GENERAL SEMESTER SCHOLARSHIPS

Cook Inlet Region, Inc.
Attn: The CIRI Foundation
3600 San Jeronimo Drive, Suite 256
Anchorage, AK 99508-2870
(907) 793-3575   Toll Free: (800) 764-3382
Fax: (907) 793-3585   E-mail: tcf@thecirifoundation.org
Web: www.thecirifoundation.org/scholarships

Summary To provide financial assistance for undergraduate or graduate studies to Alaska Natives who are original enrollees to Cook Inlet Region, Inc. (CIRI) and their lineal descendants.

Eligibility This program is open to Alaska Native enrollees to CIRI under the Alaska Native Claims Settlement Act (ANCSA) of 1971 and their lineal descendants. There are no Alaska residency requirements or age limitations. Applicants must be accepted or enrolled full or part time in a 2-year, 4-year, or graduate degree program. They must have a GPA of 2.5 or higher. Along with their application, they must submit a 500-word statement on their educational and career goals and how they are contributing, or planning to contribute, to a positive Alaska Native community. Selection is based on that statement, academic achievement, rigor of course work or degree program, student financial contribution, financial need, grade level, previous work performance, community service, and relationship of degree program to career goals.

Financial data The stipend is $2,500 per semester for full-time students or $2,250 per semester for part-time students.

Duration 1 semester; recipients may reapply.

Additional information CIRI is 1 of 13 regional corporations established according to the terms of the Alaska Native Claims Settlement Act (ANCSA) of 1971.

Number awarded Varies each year; recently, 213 were awarded.

Deadline May or November of each year.

[160]
CIRI FOUNDATION INTERNSHIP PROGRAM

Cook Inlet Region, Inc.
Attn: The CIRI Foundation
3600 San Jeronimo Drive, Suite 256
Anchorage, AK 99508-2870
(907) 793-3575   Toll Free: (800) 764-3382
Fax: (907) 793-3585   E-mail: tcf@thecirifoundation.org
Web: www.thecirifoundation.org/internships

Summary To provide on-the-job training to Alaska Natives who are original enrollees to the Cook Inlet Region, Inc. (CIRI) and their lineal descendants.

Eligibility This program is open to Alaska Native enrollees to CIRI under the Alaska Native Claims Settlement Act (ANCSA) of 1971 and their lineal descendants. Applicants must 1) be enrolled in a 2- or 4-year academic or graduate degree program with a GPA of 2.5 or higher; 2) have recently completed an undergraduate or graduate degree program; or 3) be enrolled or have recently completed a technical skills training program at an accredited or otherwise approved postsecondary institution. Along with their application, they must submit a 500-word statement on their areas of interest, their educational and career goals, how their career goals relate to their educational goals, and the type of work experience they would like to gain as it relates to their career and educational goals.

Financial data The intern's wage is based on a trainee position and is determined by the employer of the intern with the approval of the foundation (which pays one half of the intern's wages).

Duration Internships are approved on a quarterly basis for 480 hours of part-time or full-time employment. Interns may reapply on a quarter-by-quarter basis, not to exceed 12 consecutive months.

Additional information The foundation and the intern applicant work together to identify an appropriate placement experience. The employer hires the intern. Placement may be with Cook Inlet Region, Inc. (CIRI), a firm related to the foundation, or a business or service organization located anywhere in the United States. The intern may be placed with more than 1 company during the internship period. Interns may receive academic credit. CIRI is 1 of 13 regional corporations established according to the terms of the Alaska Native Claims Settlement Act (ANCSA) of 1971.

Number awarded Varies each year.

Deadline March, June, September, or November of each year.

[161]
CIRI FOUNDATION SPECIAL EXCELLENCE SCHOLARSHIPS

Cook Inlet Region, Inc.
Attn: The CIRI Foundation
3600 San Jeronimo Drive, Suite 256
Anchorage, AK 99508-2870
(907) 793-3575   Toll Free: (800) 764-3382
Fax: (907) 793-3585   E-mail: tcf@thecirifoundation.org
Web: www.thecirifoundation.org/scholarships

Summary To provide financial assistance for undergraduate or graduate studies in selected fields to Alaska Natives who are original enrollees to Cook Inlet Region, Inc. (CIRI) and their lineal descendants.

Eligibility This program is open to Alaska Native enrollees to CIRI under the Alaska Native Claims Settlement Act (ANCSA) of 1971 and their lineal descendants. There are no Alaska residency requirements or age limitations. Applicants must be accepted or enrolled full time in a 4-year undergraduate or a graduate degree program. They must have a GPA of 3.7 or higher. Preference is given to students working on a degree in business, education, mathematics, sciences, health services, or engineering. Along with their application, they must submit a 500-word statement on their educational and career goals and how they are contributing, or planning to contribute, to a positive Alaska Native community. Selection is based on that statement, academic achievement, rigor of course work or degree program, student financial contribution, financial need, grade level, previous work performance, community service, and relationship of degree program to career goals.

Financial data The stipend is $20,000 per year.

Duration 1 year; may be renewed.

Additional information CIRI is 1 of 13 regional corporations established according to the terms of the Alaska Native Claims Settlement Act (ANCSA) of 1971. This program began in 1997.

Number awarded 1 or more each year.

Deadline May of each year.

[162]
CIRI FOUNDATION VOCATIONAL TRAINING GRANTS

Cook Inlet Region, Inc.
Attn: The CIRI Foundation
3600 San Jeronimo Drive, Suite 256
Anchorage, AK 99508-2870
(907) 793-3575   Toll Free: (800) 764-3382
Fax: (907) 793-3585   E-mail: tcf@thecirifoundation.org
Web: www.thecirifoundation.org/vocational-training

Summary To provide financial assistance for professional preparation after high school to Alaska Natives who are original enrollees to the Cook Inlet Region, Inc. (CIRI) and their lineal descendants.

Eligibility This program is open to Alaska Native enrollees to CIRI under the Alaska Native Claims Settlement Act (ANCSA) of 1971 and their lineal descendants. Applicants should have a high school diploma or GED, have a GPA of 2.5 or higher, and be able to document the availability of employment upon completion of the training. They must be accepted or enrolled part or full time in a technical skills certificate or degree program, such as (but not limited to) craft/trade, automotive technology, office occupations, and computer technology. Alaska residency is not required. Along with their application, they must submit a 500-word statement on their educational and career goals and how they are contributing, or planning to contribute, to a positive Alaska Native community. Selection is based on that statement, academic achievement, rigor of course work or degree program, student financial contribution, financial need, grade level, previous work performance, community service, and relationship of degree program to career goals.

Financial data The maximum stipend is $4,500 per calendar year.

Duration 1 quarter; recipients may reapply.

Additional information CIRI is 1 of 13 regional corporations established according to the terms of the Alaska Native Claims Settlement Act (ANCSA) of 1971.

Number awarded Varies each year; recently, 42 were awarded.

Deadline March, June, September, or November of each year.

[163]
CITIZEN POTAWATOMI NATION TRIBAL ROLLS SCHOLARSHIPS

Citizen Potawatomi Nation
Attn: Office of Tribal Rolls
1601 South Gordon Cooper Drive
Shawnee, OK 74801-9002
(405) 878-5779   Toll Free: (800) 880-9880
Fax: (405) 878-4653
Web: www.potawatomi.org/services/education

Summary To provide financial assistance for college or graduate school to members of the Citizen Potawatomi Nation.

Eligibility This program is open to enrolled members of the Citizen Potawatomi Nation who are attending or planning to attend an undergraduate or graduate degree program, vocational technical career courses, or other accredited educational program in any state. Applicants must have a GPA of 2.0 or higher and be able to demonstrate financial need.

Financial data Stipends are $1,500 per semester for full-time students or $750 per semester for part-time students.

Duration 1 semester; may be renewed, provided the recipient maintains a GPA of 2.0 or higher.

Number awarded Varies each year; recently, 125 were awarded, including 94 to undergraduates, 10 to vocational/technical students, and 21 to graduate students.

Deadline July of each year for fall session, November of each year for spring or winter session, or May for summer session.

[164]
CLAY FORD MINORITY SCHOLARSHIPS

Florida Board of Accountancy
Florida Department of Business and Professional Regulation
Attn: Division of Certified Public Accounting
240 N.W. 76th Drive, Suite A
Gainesville, FL 32607-6656
(352) 333-2505   Fax: (352) 333-2508
E-mail: CPA.Applications@dbpr.state.fl.us
Web: www.myfloridalicense.com

Summary To provide financial assistance to Native American and other minority residents of Florida who are entering the fifth year of an accounting program.

Eligibility This program is open to Florida residents who have completed at least 120 credit hours at a college or university in the state and have a GPA of 2.5 or higher. Applicants must be planning to remain in school as a full-time student for the fifth year required to sit for the C.P.A. examination. They must be members of a minority group, defined to include African Americans, Hispanic Americans, Asian Americans, Native Americans, or women. Selection is based on scholastic ability and performance and financial need.

Financial data Stipends range from $3,000 to $6,000 per semester.

Duration 1 semester; may be renewed 1 additional semester.

Number awarded Varies each year; a total of $200,000 is available for this program annually.

Deadline May of each year.

[165]
CLEM JUDD, JR. MEMORIAL SCHOLARSHIP

Hawai'i Lodging & Tourism Association
Attn: Hawaii Hotel Industry Foundation
2270 Kalakaua Avenue, Suite 1702
Honolulu, HI 96815-2519
(808) 923-0407   Fax: (808) 924-3843
E-mail: info@hawaiilodging.org
Web: www.hawaiilodging.org/scholarship-opportunities.html

Summary To provide financial assistance to Native Hawaiians who are upper-division students working on a degree in hotel management at a school in any state.

Eligibility This program is open to Hawaii residents who can provide proof of their Native Hawaiian ancestry through birth certificates of their parents or grandparents. Applicants must be a junior or senior at an accredited college or university (in any state) and majoring in hotel management. They must have a GPA of 3.0 or higher. Financial need is not considered in the selection process.

Financial data The stipend ranges from $1,000 to $2,500.

Duration 1 year.

Additional information This program began in 1996.

Number awarded Up to 2 each year.

Deadline June of each year.

[166]
COBELL SCHOLARSHIPS

Indigenous Education, Inc.
6501 Americas Parkway, N.E., Suite 825
P.O. Box 26837
Albuquerque, NM 87125
(505) 313-0032   Toll Free: (844) 551-0650
Web: www.cobellscholar.org

Summary To provide financial assistance to Native Americans interested in attending college.

Eligibility This program is open to American Indians and Alaska Natives who submit a tribal enrollment form. Applicants must be enrolled or planning to enroll in a vocational diploma, associate, bachelor's, master's, doctoral, or professional degree or certificate. They must be able to demonstrate financial need.

Financial data Recently, stipends averaged more than $5,000.

Duration 1 year; nonrenewable.

Additional information This program was established in 2009 with $3.4 billion as settlement of a lawsuit filed by Elouise Cobell against the federal government for misuse of Indian Trust funds.

Number awarded Varies each year; recently, 368 students received more than $1,900,000 in scholarships (more than $1,500,000 for undergraduates and nearly $400,000 for graduate students.

Deadline May of each year.

[167]
COCA-COLA FIRST GENERATION SCHOLARSHIP

American Indian College Fund
Attn: Scholarship Department
8333 Greenwood Boulevard
Denver, CO 80221
(303) 426-8900   Toll Free: (800) 776-FUND
Fax: (303) 426-1200
E-mail: scholarships@collegefund.org
Web: www.collegefund.org

Summary To provide financial assistance to Native Americans who are interested in attending a Tribal College or University (TCU) and are the first in their family to attend college.

Eligibility This program is open to American Indians or Alaska Natives who are planning to enroll full time in their freshman year at an eligible TCU. Applicants must have a GPA of 3.0 or higher and be able to demonstrate financial need. They must be the first in their immediate family to attend college. Applications are available only online and include required essays on specified topics. U.S. citizenship is required.

Financial data The stipend is $5,000 per year.

Duration 1 year; may be renewed, provided the recipient maintains a GPA of 3.0 or higher and participates actively in campus and community life.

Additional information This program is sponsored by the Coca-Cola Company in partnership with the American Indian College Fund. Recipients must participate in the American Indian Higher Education Consortium (AIHEC) summer leadership conference; all expenses are paid.

Number awarded 1 or more each year.

Deadline May of each year.

[168]
COLBERT "BUD" BAKER SCHOLARSHIP

Chickasaw Foundation
2020 Arlington, Suite 4
P.O. Box 1726
Ada, OK 74821-1726
(580) 421-9030   Fax: (580) 421-9031
E-mail: ChickasawFoundation@chickasaw.net
Web: www.chickasawfoundation.org/Scholarships.aspx

Summary To provide financial assistance to members of the Chickasaw Nation who are majoring or minoring in American history, education, or pre-law.

Eligibility This program is open to Chickasaw students who are currently enrolled full time at an accredited institution of higher education. Applicants must be classified as juniors or seniors at a 4-year college. They must be 1) majoring in history; or 2) majoring in education or pre-law with a minor in history. The history emphasis must be on Chickasaw tribal history or Native American studies. Along with their application, they must submit high school or college transcripts; 2 letters of recommendation; a copy of their Chickasaw Nation citizenship card; a 2-page list of honors, achievements, awards, club memberships, societies, and civic involvement; and a 1-

page essay on their long-term goals and plans for achieving those. Financial need is not considered in the selection process.

Financial data A stipend is awarded (amount not specified).

Duration 1 year.

Number awarded 1 or more each year.

Deadline June of each year.

[169]
COLGATE "BRIGHT SMILES, BRIGHT FUTURES" MINORITY SCHOLARSHIPS

American Dental Hygienists' Association
Attn: Institute for Oral Health
444 North Michigan Avenue, Suite 3400
Chicago, IL 60611-3980
(312) 440-8900, ext. 244   Fax: (312) 440-6726
E-mail: institute@adha.net
Web: www.adha.org/ioh-associate-certificate-scholarships

Summary To provide financial assistance to Native American and other minority students who are members of the American Dental Hygienists' Association (ADHA) and enrolled in certificate programs in dental hygiene.

Eligibility This program is open to members of groups currently underrepresented in the dental hygiene profession (Native Americans, African Americans, Hispanics, Asians, and males) who are student or active members of the ADHA. Applicants must have a GPA of 3.5 or higher and have completed at least 1 year of full-time enrollment in an accredited dental hygiene certificate or associate degree program in the United States.

Financial data The stipend is $1,250.

Duration 1 year; nonrenewable.

Additional information These scholarships are sponsored by the Colgate-Palmolive Company.

Number awarded 2 each year.

Deadline January of each year.

[170]
COLLEGE STUDENT PRE-COMMISSIONING INITIATIVE

U.S. Coast Guard
Attn: Recruiting Command
2300 Wilson Boulevard, Suite 500
Arlington, VA 22201
(703) 235-1775   Toll Free: (877) NOW-USCG, ext. 205
Fax: (703) 235-1881
E-mail: Margaret.A.Jackson@uscg.mil
Web: www.gocoastguard.com

Summary To provide financial assistance to college students at Native American or other designated minority institutions who are willing to serve in the Coast Guard following graduation.

Eligibility This program is open to students entering their junior or senior year at a college or university designated as an Historically Black College or University (HBCU), Hispanic Serving Institution (HSI), Tribal College or University (TCU), or the University of Guam, the University of Hawaii (at Manoa, Hilo, or West Oahu), Argosy University (Hawaii), or the Institute of American Indian and Alaska Native Culture (Santa Fe, New Mexico). Applicants must be U.S. citizens; have a GPA

of 2.5 or higher; have scores of 1100 or higher on the critical reading and mathematics SAT, 23 or higher on the ACT, 4AQR/4PFAR on the ASTB, or 109 or higher on the SVAB GT; be between 19 and 27 years of age; and meet all physical requirements for a Coast Guard commission. They must agree to attend the Coast Guard Officer Candidate School following graduation and serve on active duty as an officer for at least 3 years.

Financial data Those selected to participate receive full payment of tuition, books, and fees; monthly housing and food allowances; medical and life insurance; special training in leadership, management, law enforcement, navigation, and marine science; 30 days of paid vacation per year; and a Coast Guard monthly salary of up to $2,200.

Duration Up to 2 years.

Number awarded Varies each year.

Deadline January of each year.

[171]
COLORADO EDUCATION ASSOCIATION MINORITY STUDENT SCHOLARSHIPS

Colorado Education Association
Attn: Ethnic Minority Advisory Council
1500 Grant Street
Denver, CO 80203
(303) 837-1500   Toll Free: (800) 332-5939
Web: www.coloradoea.org

Summary To provide financial assistance to Native American and other minority high school seniors in Colorado who are children of members of the Colorado Education Association (CEA) and planning to attend college in any state.

Eligibility This program is open to seniors graduating from high schools in Colorado who are members of a minority ethnic group, defined to include American Indians/Alaska Natives, Asians, Blacks, Hispanics, Native Hawaiians/Pacific Islanders, and multi-ethnic. Applicants must be the dependent child of an active, retired, or deceased CEA member. They must be planning to attend an accredited institution of higher education in any state. Along with their application, they must submit brief statements on 1) their need for this scholarship; and 2) why they plan to pursue a college education.

Financial data The stipend is $1,000.

Duration 1 year; nonrenewable.

Number awarded 4 each year.

Deadline April of each year.

[172]
COLORADO INDIAN EDUCATION FOUNDATION SCHOLARS PROGRAM

Colorado Indian Education Foundation
P.O. Box 40325
Denver, CO 80204
(303) 875-4631   E-mail: info@coief.org
Web: www.coief.org/scholars-applications

Summary To provide financial assistance to American Indians from Colorado who are interested in attending college in the state.

Eligibility This program is open to American Indian residents of Colorado who can verify that they 1) are on a federal or state-recognized tribal roll and are identified by a tribal enrollment card; 2) have an official letter from a federal or state recognized tribe or agency stating tribal membership or Indian blood; 3) have a family tree and officially sealed birth certificates establishing that at least 1 parent is Indian; or 4) are an enrolled official member of a terminated tribe. Applicants must be enrolled or planning to enroll full time at an accredited college, university, or vocational/trade school in Colorado. They must have a GPA of 2.5 or higher. Along with their application, they must submit a 2-page essay describing their chosen field of study, educational goals, career goals, involvement in the Indian community, and how this scholarship will help them in furthering their education. Financial need is not considered in the selection process.

Financial data The stipend ranges from $1,000 to $2,000.

Duration 1 year.

Number awarded Varies each year; recently, 21 were awarded.

Deadline October of each year.

[173]
COMMISSION ON DIETETIC REGISTRATION DIVERSITY SCHOLARSHIPS

Academy of Nutrition and Dietetics
Attn: Foundation
120 South Riverside Plaza, Suite 2000
Chicago, IL 60606-6995
(312) 899-4821   Toll Free: (800) 877-1600, ext. 4821
Fax: (312) 899-4796   E-mail: blabrador@eatright.org
Web: www.eatrightfoundation.org/foundation/scholarships

Summary To provide financial assistance to Native Americans and members of other underrepresented minority groups who are enrolled in an undergraduate or graduate program in dietetics.

Eligibility This program is open to students enrolled at a CADE-accredited/approved college or university in the undergraduate coordinated dietetics program, the undergraduate didactic program in dietetics, a dietetic internship program, a dietetic technician program, or a dietetic graduate program. Applicants must be members of underrepresented minority groups (African American, Hispanic, Native American). They must be U.S. citizens or permanent residents and show promise of being a valuable, contributing member of the profession. Membership in the Academy of Nutrition and Dietetics is encouraged but not required.

Financial data The stipend is $5,000.

Duration 1 year.

Number awarded 20 each year.

Deadline March of each year.

[174]
COMMUNICATIONS INTERNSHIP AWARD FOR STUDENTS OF COLOR

College and University Public Relations and Allied
  Professionals
237 South Fraser Street
P.O. Box 10034
State College, PA 16805-0034
Fax: (814) 863-3428   E-mail: ehanson@cuprap.org
Web: www.cuprap.org/awards/communications-internships

Summary To provide an opportunity for Native Americans and other students of color at institutions that are members of the College and University Public Relations and Allied Professionals (CUPRAP) to complete an internship in communications.

Eligibility This program is open to students of color (i.e., African Americans, Asian/Pacific Islanders, Hispanics/Latinos, and Native Americans) who have completed the first year of college and are enrolled as a degree candidate in the second year or higher. Applicants must obtain and complete a verifiable internship of at least 150 hours in a communications-related field (e.g., print media, radio, television, public relations, advertising, graphic/web design). They must be enrolled full time at an accredited 2- or 4-year college or university that is a member of CUPRAP. Selection is based on financial need, academic ability, communication skills, and creativity as demonstrated through work samples.

Financial data The stipend is $2,000, paid upon confirmation of employment in an internship position.

Duration The internship award is presented annually; recipients may reapply.

Additional information This internship award was first presented in 1983.

Number awarded 1 each year.

Deadline January of each year.

[175]
COMPUTERCRAFT CORPORATION SCHOLARSHIP

Chickasaw Foundation
2020 Arlington, Suite 4
P.O. Box 1726
Ada, OK 74821-1726
(580) 421-9030   Fax: (580) 421-9031
E-mail: ChickasawFoundation@chickasaw.net
Web: www.chickasawfoundation.org/Scholarships.aspx

Summary To provide financial assistance to members of the Chickasaw Nation who are majoring in fields of interest to ComputerCraft Corporation.

Eligibility This program is open to Chickasaw students who are currently enrolled full time as an undergraduate student. The sponsor recruits computer engineers, graphic designers, biologists, conference managers, and international trade specialists. Preference may be given to those majors, but all fields of study are eligible. Applicants must have a GPA of 2.5 or higher. Along with their application, they must submit high school or college transcripts; 2 letters of recommendation; a copy of their Chickasaw Nation citizenship card; a 2-page list of honors, achievements, awards, club memberships, societies, and civic involvement; and a 1-page essay on their long-term goals and plans for achieving those. Financial need is not considered in the selection process.

Financial data A stipend is awarded (amount not specified).

Duration 1 year.

Number awarded 1 each year.

Deadline June of each year.

[176]
COMTO COLORADO SCHOLARSHIPS

Conference of Minority Transportation Officials-Colorado
  Chapter
Attn: Scholarship Committee
1114 West Seventh Avenue
P.O. Box 13582
Denver, CO 80201
E-mail: DrMaryDavis@aol.com
Web: www.comtocolorado.org/scholarship-program

Summary   To provide financial assistance to Native American and other minority high school seniors in Colorado who are interested in studying a transportation-related field at a college or university in any state.

Eligibility   This program is open to minority seniors graduating from high schools in Colorado with a GPA of 2.5 or higher. Applicants must be planning to attend an accredited college, university, or trade school in any state. They must be planning to major in archaeology and/or cultural resources, architecture, aviation, engineering (chemical, civil, electrical, mechanical, or structural), computer aided design, computer science, construction engineering technology, construction and/or construction management, diesel mechanics, electrical, electronics, environmental science and related fields, geology and/or geotechnical engineering, heating and air conditioning, hydraulic and/or elevator mechanics, public information and outreach programs, security systems, urban planning, or vehicle design and maintenance. Along with their application, they must submit an essay of 500 to 700 words on why they chose their planned field of study, how they think their course work and life experiences have helped them prepare for their college studies and the future, and why they are an excellent candidate for this scholarship. Selection is based on that essay (20%), GPA (15%), participation in career-related activities (10%), letters of recommendation (15%), high school citizenship (15%), and an interview (25%).

Financial data   A stipend is awarded (amount not specified). Funds may be used for tuition, books, and/or room and board expenses.

Duration   1 year.

Number awarded   Up to 10 each year.

Deadline   March of each year.

[177]
CONNECTICUT EDUCATION FOUNDATION SCHOLARSHIPS FOR MINORITY HIGH SCHOOL STUDENTS

Connecticut Education Association
Attn: Connecticut Education Foundation, Inc.
21 Oak Street, Suite 500
Hartford, CT 06106-8001
(860) 525-5641   Toll Free: (800) 842-4316
Fax: (860) 725-6323   E-mail: jeffl@cea.org
Web: www.cea.org/cef/ethnic-minority-scholarship-fund

Summary   To provide financial assistance to Native American and other minority high school seniors in Connecticut who are interested in attending college in the state to prepare for a teaching career.

Eligibility   This program is open to minority seniors (Blacks, Native Americans or Alaskan Natives, Asian or Pacific Islanders, and Hispanics or Latinos) graduating from high schools in Connecticut. Applicants have been accepted at an accredited 2- or 4-year college or university in the state and be planning to enter the teaching profession. They must have a GPA of 2.75 or higher. Finalists may be interviewed. Financial need is considered in the selection process.

Financial data   The stipend is $2,000 per year.

Duration   1 year; may be renewed.

Number awarded   At least 1 each year.

Deadline   April of each year.

[178]
CONNECTICUT MINORITY TEACHER INCENTIVE GRANTS

Connecticut Office of Higher Education
Attn: Minority Teacher Incentive Grant Program
61 Woodland Street
Hartford, CT 06105-2326
(860) 947-1855   Toll Free: (800) 842-0229 (within CT)
Fax: (860) 947-1313   E-mail: mtip@ctohe.org
Web: www.ctohe.org/sfa/sfa.shtml

Summary   To provide financial assistance and loan repayment to Native American and other minority upper-division college students in Connecticut who are interested in teaching at public schools in the state.

Eligibility   This program is open to juniors and seniors enrolled full time in Connecticut college and university teacher preparation programs. Applicants must be members of a minority group, defined as African American, Hispanic/Latino, Asian American, or Native American. They must be nominated by the education dean at their institution.

Financial data   The maximum stipend is $5,000 per year. In addition, if recipients complete a credential and begin teaching at a public school in Connecticut within 16 months of graduation, they may receive up to $2,500 per year, for up to 4 years, to help pay off college loans.

Duration   Up to 2 years.

Number awarded   Varies each year.

Deadline   October of each year.

[179]
CONNECTICUT NATIVE AMERICAN INTERTRIBAL URBAN COUNCIL SCHOLARSHIP

Connecticut Native American Intertribal Urban Council
Attn: Scholarship Committee
545 Whalley Avenue
New Haven, CT 06511
(203) 215-1521
Web: www.cnaituc.org/

Summary   To provide financial assistance to Native American residents of Connecticut, Massachusetts, and Rhode Island who wish to study nursing or pharmacy at a school in their state.

Eligibility   This program is open to Native American students who reside and attend school in Connecticut, Massachusetts, or Rhode Island. Applicants must be enrolled in or accepted to a school of pharmacy or nursing. They must have a GPA of 2.0 or higher. Along with their application, they must submit a multimedia project or essay on a topic of their choice. Selection is based on that project/essay, academic record, community service, and work experience.

Financial data A stipend is awarded (amount not specified).

Duration 1 year.

Additional information Funding for this program is provided by CVS Pharmacy.

Number awarded Varies each year.

Deadline April of each year.

[180]
CONNECTICUT SOCIETY OF CERTIFIED PUBLIC ACCOUNTANTS DIVERSITY SCHOLARSHIPS

Connecticut Society of Certified Public Accountants
Attn: CTCPA Educational Trust Fund
716 Brook Street, Suite 100
Rocky Hill, CT 06067-3433
(860) 258-0239   Toll Free: (800) 232-2232 (within CT)
Fax: (860) 258-4859   E-mail: jillb@ctcpas.org
Web: www.ctcpas.org/Content/ETF/Apply.aspx

Summary To provide financial assistance to Native Americans and members of other traditionally underrepresented groups who are upper-division students from Connecticut and majoring in accounting.

Eligibility This program is open to members of groups traditionally underrepresented in accounting. Applicants must be juniors or seniors who are residents of Connecticut and/or currently attending a college or university in that state that is recognized by the Connecticut State Board of Accountancy. They must have a GPA of 3.0 or higher and a major in accounting.

Financial data The stipend is $1,000.

Duration 1 year.

Number awarded 1 each year.

Deadline September of each year.

[181]
CONTINENTAL SOCIETY DAUGHTERS OF INDIAN WARS SCHOLARSHIP

Continental Society Daughters of Indian Wars
c/o Nona Thompson Quinn, Scholarship Chair
224 S.W. Landmark Circle
Geronimo, OK 73545-5142
(580) 353-2888   E-mail: nptquinn@aol.com
Web: www.csdiw.org/scholarships.html

Summary To provide financial assistance to Native American college students who are interested in preparing for a career in education or social service.

Eligibility This program is open to enrolled tribal members of a federally-recognized tribe who are accepted at or already attending an accredited college or university. Applicants must be planning to work with a tribe or nation in the field of education or social service. They must have a GPA of 3.0 or higher and be carrying at least 10 quarter hours or 8 semester hours. Preference is given to students entering their junior year. Financial need is considered in the selection process.

Financial data The stipend is $5,000 per year.

Duration 1 year; may be renewed.

Number awarded 1 each year.

Deadline June of each year.

[182]
COOK INLET TRIBAL COUNCIL TRIBAL HIGHER EDUCATION PROGRAM

Cook Inlet Tribal Council, Inc.
c/o The CIRI Foundation
3600 San Jeronimo Drive, Suite 256
Anchorage, AK 99508-2870
(907) 793-3575   Toll Free: (800) 764-3382
Fax: (907) 793-3585   E-mail: tcf@thecirifoundation.org
Web: www.thecirifoundation.org/citc-scholarship

Summary To provide financial assistance to Alaska Native shareholders of the Cook Inlet Region, Inc. (CIRI) and their descendants who are working on an undergraduate or graduate degree.

Eligibility This program is open to Alaska Native shareholders of CIRI and their descendants, regardless of residence, who are enrolled or planning to enroll full time at an accredited college, university, training institution, or vocational/technical school. Applicants must be working on a certificate, associate, bachelor's, master's, or doctoral degree. Along with their application they must submit a letter of reference, a 200-word statement of purpose, their Certificate of Degree of Alaska Native Blood (CDIB), a letter of acceptance from the school, transcripts, their Student Aid Report, a budget forecast, and (for males) documentation of Selective Service registration. Awards are presented on a first-come, first-served basis as long as funds are available.

Financial data This program provides supplementary matching financial aid. Awards are intended to be applied to tuition, fees, course-required books and supplies, and on-campus housing and meal plans only. Total funding over a lifetime educational career is limited to $30,000 for undergraduate degrees and certificates, $20,000 for a master's degree, or $20,000 for a doctoral degree.

Duration 1 year; may be renewed up to 4 additional years if the recipient maintains a GPA of 2.0 or higher.

Additional information Students whose CDIB gives their village as Tyonek, Kenai, Ninilchik, Knik, or Salamatof must apply directly to their village organization.

Number awarded Varies each year, depending on the availability of funds.

Deadline May of each year for fall; November of each year for spring.

[183]
COQUILLE INDIAN TRIBE ADULT VOCATIONAL TRAINING GRANTS

Coquille Indian Tribe
Attn: Department of Culture, Education and Library
  Services
495 Miluk Drive
Coos Bay, OR 97420
(541) 756-0904   Toll Free: (800) 622-5869
Fax: (541) 888-2418
E-mail: bridgettwheeler@coquilletribe.org
Web: www.coquilletribe.org/higheredprograms.htm

Summary To provide financial assistance to members of the Coquille Indian Tribe who are attending or planning to attend vocational school in any state.

Eligibility This program is open to enrolled members of the Coquille Indian Tribe who are entering or continuing at a vocational/technical school in any state. Along with their application, they must submit a personal essay on their vocational goals and how the tribe will benefit by sending them to this training institute.

Financial data The program provides payment of tuition, supplies, licensing or certification fees, and a stipend of $500 per month to help cover expenses for travel, lodging, or other costs related to being able to attend the course.

Duration 1 year; may be renewed, provided the recipient maintains a GPA of 2.0 or higher.

Number awarded Varies each year.

Deadline Deadline not specified.

[184]
COQUILLE INDIAN TRIBE COMPUTER EQUIPMENT PROGRAM

Coquille Indian Tribe
Attn: Department of Culture, Education and Library
  Services
495 Miluk Drive
Coos Bay, OR 97420
(541) 756-0904   Toll Free: (800) 622-5869
Fax: (541) 888-2418
E-mail: rhondaferguson@coquilletribe.org
Web: www.coquilletribe.org/higheredprograms.htm

Summary To provide funding for the purchase of computer equipment to members of the Coquille Indian Tribe who are working full time on an undergraduate or graduate degree.

Eligibility This program is open to enrolled members of the Coquille Indian Tribe who have been enrolled for at least 2 semesters as a full- or part-time undergraduate or graduate student at an accredited college, university, or community college in any state. Applicants must be seeking funding for the purchase of computer equipment.

Financial data The grant is $1,200; funds must be used for purchase of computer equipment or programming, and not for training, shipping, and/or maintenance of equipment.

Duration This is a 1-time grant.

Number awarded Varies each year.

Deadline Deadline not specified.

[185]
COQUILLE INDIAN TRIBE HIGHER EDUCATION GRANTS

Coquille Indian Tribe
Attn: Department of Culture, Education and Library
  Services
495 Miluk Drive
Coos Bay, OR 97420
(541) 756-0904   Toll Free: (800) 622-5869
Fax: (541) 888-2418
E-mail: bridgettwheeler@coquilletribe.org
Web: www.coquilletribe.org/higheredprograms.htm

Summary To provide financial assistance to members of the Coquille Indian Tribe who are attending or planning to attend college or graduate school in any state.

Eligibility This program is open to enrolled members of the Coquille Indian Tribe who are entering or continuing undergraduate or graduate students at an accredited college, university, or community college in any state. Along with their application, they must submit a personal statement on their

short- and long-term career goals and if they plan to work for the tribe after graduation. Financial need is also considered in the selection process.

Financial data Maximum stipends are $12,000 per year for graduate students, $9,000 per year for full-time undergraduates at 4-year colleges and universities or $7,500 per year for students at 2-year community colleges. Part-time students are eligible to receive funding for tuition and books only.

Duration 1 year; may be renewed up to 4 additional years.

Number awarded Varies each year.

Deadline June of each year for fall semester or quarter, October of each year for spring semester or winter quarter; January of each year for spring quarter; March of each year for summer term.

[186]
CREEK NATION OF OKLAHOMA SCHOLARSHIP GRANTS

Muscogee (Creek) Nation of Oklahoma
Attn: Higher Education Program
P.O. Box 580
Okmulgee, OK 74447
(918) 732-7661   Toll Free: (800) 482-1979, ext. 7661
Fax: (918) 732-7694   E-mail: highered@mcn-nsn.gov
Web: www.muscogeenation-nsn.gov

Summary To provide financial assistance to needy Creek undergraduate students who plan to attend college in any state.

Eligibility This program is open to Creek students of any degree of Indian blood who are attending or planning to attend an accredited institution of higher learning in any state. Applicants must be eligible to receive Pell Grants. They must submit copies of their Certificate of Degree of Indian Blood (CDIB) and tribal citizenship card.

Financial data Maximum stipends are $1,000 per semester for single students, $1,500 per semester for independent students, or $2,000 per semester for married or head of household students.

Duration 1 year; may be renewed for a maximum of 10 semesters of funding as long as the recipient enrolls in at least 15 hours per term and maintains a GPA of 2.0 or higher.

Additional information The Muscogee (Creek) Nation of Oklahoma administers the Higher Education Program with funding provided by the Bureau of Indian Affairs (BIA).

Number awarded Varies each year.

Deadline May of each year for fall semester; December of each year for spring semester.

[187]
CREEK NATION TRIBAL FUNDS GRANT PROGRAM

Muscogee (Creek) Nation of Oklahoma
Attn: Higher Education Program
P.O. Box 580
Okmulgee, OK 74447
(918) 732-7661   Toll Free: (800) 482-1979, ext. 7661
Fax: (918) 732-7694   E-mail: highered@mcn-nsn.gov
Web: www.muscogeenation-nsn.gov

Summary To provide financial assistance to enrolled citizens of the Muscogee (Creek) Nation attending an accredited college or university in any state.

Eligibility This program is open to enrolled citizens of the Muscogee (Creek) Nation (with no minimum blood quantum required) who are enrolled or planning to enroll in an accredited college or university in any state. Applicants must submit copies of their tribal citizenship card and a 250-word essay on their educational goals. Financial need is not required.

Financial data The stipend is $125 per credit hour per semester, to a maximum of $4,500 per year for full-time students or $2,750 per year for part-time students. The award may be used to supplement other financial aid sources.

Duration 1 semester; may be renewed up to 9 additional semesters, provided the recipient maintains at least a 2.5 GPA.

Number awarded Varies each year.

Deadline May of each year for fall semester; December of each year for spring semester.

[188]
CREEK NATION TRIBAL INCENTIVE GRANT PROGRAM

Muscogee (Creek) Nation of Oklahoma
Attn: Higher Education Program
P.O. Box 580
Okmulgee, OK 74447
(918) 732-7661   Toll Free: (800) 482-1979, ext. 7661
Fax: (918) 732-7694   E-mail: highered@mcn-nsn.gov
Web: www.muscogeenation-nsn.gov

Summary To provide financial assistance to enrolled citizens of the Muscogee (Creek) Nation who have an excellent academic record and are attending an accredited college or university in any state.

Eligibility This program is open to enrolled citizens of the Muscogee (Creek) Nation (with no minimum blood quantum required) who are enrolled or planning to enroll in an accredited college or university in any state. Applicants must have a GPA of 3.0 or higher. They must submit copies of their Certificate of Degree of Indian Blood (CDIB) and tribal enrollment card.

Financial data The maximum stipend is $700 per semester for full-time students (12 credit hours or more per semester) or $350 per semester for part-time students (less than 12 hours). Support may not exceed $1,400 per year. The award may be used to supplement other financial aid sources.

Duration 1 semester; may be renewed for up to 9 additional semesters.

Number awarded Varies each year.

Deadline Fall transcripts must be submitted by January of each year; spring transcripts are due by June of each year.

[189]
CRST EDUCATION HARDSHIP GRANT

Cheyenne River Sioux Tribe
Attn: Education Services Office
2001 Main Street
P.O. Box 590
Eagle Butte, SD 57625
(605) 964-8311   E-mail: dal7882@lakotanetwork.com
Web: www.sioux.org/educational-services-department.html

Summary To provide financial assistance to members of the Cheyenne River Sioux Tribe who are attending college or graduate school in any state but are not eligible for funding through other tribal programs.

Eligibility This program is open to enrolled Cheyenne River Sioux tribal members who are attending a college, university, or vocational/technical school in any state. Applicants must be ineligible for other tribal education programs because they 1) are graduate students (master's degree only); 2) have been suspended from the tribe's higher education or adult vocational training programs; or 3) have exceeded the number of semesters allowed by the higher education program. Funding is awarded in the following priority order: undergraduate students attending college off-reservation, moving expenses for students attending college off-reservation, undergraduate students at Oglala Lakota College, graduate students attending college off-reservation, and graduate students enrolled in online distance learning programs.

Financial data A stipend is awarded (amount not specified).

Duration 1 year; may be renewed.

Number awarded Varies each year.

Deadline September of each year for fall semester; February of each year for spring semester.

[190]
CUBA WADLINGTON, JR. AND MICHAEL P. JOHNSON SCHOLARSHIP

Tulsa Community Foundation
Attn: Scholarships
7030 South Yale Avenue, Suite 600
Tulsa, OK 74136
(918) 494-8823   Fax: (918) 494-9826
E-mail: scholarships@tulsacf.org
Web: www.tulsacf.org/whatwedo/education/scholarships

Summary To provide financial assistance to upper-division students at colleges in any state who are Native Americans or members of other underrepresented groups in the energy industry.

Eligibility This program is open to students entering their junior or senior year at a college or university in any state and preparing for a career in the energy industry with a major in accounting, engineering, finance, or technology. Applicants must be members of a group underrepresented in the energy industry (women and ethnic minorities). They must have a GPA of 3.0 or higher. Along with their application, they must submit a 2-page personal essay that includes their future or academic career goals, any adversity or challenge they have overcome or anticipate in pursuit of their educational goals, and the importance of diversity in the workplace and how dealing with diversity in their own life has shaped them. Financial need is not considered in the selection process.

Financial data The stipend is $2,000. Funds are paid directly to the university.

Duration 1 year; nonrenewable.

Additional information This program is supported by the Williams Companies of Tulsa, Oklahoma.

Number awarded Varies each year.

Deadline June of each year.

[191]
CYPRUS TOHONO CORPORATION FOUR YEAR SCHOLARSHIP

Phoenix Indian Center, Inc.
4520 North Central Avenue, Suite 250
Phoenix, AZ 85012
(602) 264-6768   Fax: (602) 274-7486
E-mail: fmscholarshp@phxindcenter.org
Web: www.phxindcenter.org

Summary To provide financial assistance to members of Indian tribes in Arizona who are interested in attending college in the state to major in designated fields.

Eligibility This program is open to enrolled members of Native American tribes in Arizona; preference is given to members of the Tohono O'odham Nation. They must be enrolled or planning to enroll full time as incoming freshmen, sophomores, or juniors at a community college or 4-year public university in Arizona. In the selection process, first preference is given to students whose major is a field of engineering related to minerals (e.g., chemical, environmental, geological, metallurgical, or mining); second preference is given to students with majors in business or business-related fields (e.g., accounting, economics, finance, mathematics), teaching of STEM-related fields, occupational safety, environmental sustainability, or natural sciences (e.g., chemistry, physics). Applicants must have a GPA of 2.5 or higher. Along with their application, they must submit an essay of 300 to 500 words on 1) their motivations for attending college; 2) some of their personal, educational, and professional goals; and 3) some successes, accomplishments, obstacles, or challenges they have overcome in life.

Financial data The scholarship covers tuition, fees, books, and room and board at the rate paid by Arizona residents.

Duration 1 year; may be renewed 3 additional years; provided the recipient maintains a cumulative GPA of 2.0 during freshman year and 3.0 for subsequent years. Students at community colleges must transfer to an accredited 4-year university to continue to receive the scholarship.

Additional information This program is funded by the Freeport-McMoran Foundation and administered by the Phoenix Indian Center. .

Number awarded 1 each year.

Deadline June of each year.

[192]
DAKOTA INDIAN FOUNDATION SCHOLARSHIP

Dakota Indian Foundation
209 North Main Street
P.O. Box 340
Chamberlain, SD 57325-0340
(605) 234-5472   Fax: (605) 234-5858
Web: www.dakotaindianfoundation.org

Summary To provide financial assistance to American Indians (especially those of Sioux heritage) who are currently enrolled in college.

Eligibility This program is open to American Indians (priority given to those of Lakota, Dakota, or Nakota heritage) who are currently enrolled full time at a college or university in any state as a sophomore, junior, or senior. A copy of tribal registration must be provided. Applicants may be studying in any field. Along with their application, they must submit a personal statement that includes their qualifications for a scholarship, educational interest, career plans, extracurricular activities, and need for financial assistance.

Financial data The stipend is $1,000 per semester ($2,000 per year).

Duration 1 semester; may be renewed, provided the recipient remains enrolled full time and maintains a GPA of 2.5 or higher.

Number awarded Varies each year; recently, 122 students were receiving support from this foundation.

Deadline July of each year for the fall semester; January of each year for the spring semester.

[193]
DAMON P. MOORE SCHOLARSHIP

Indiana State Teachers Association
Attn: Scholarships
150 West Market Street, Suite 900
Indianapolis, IN 46204-2875
(317) 263-3400   Toll Free: (800) 382-4037
Fax: (800) 777-6128   E-mail: mshoup@ista-in.org
Web: www.ista-in.org/damon-p-moore-scholarship

Summary To provide financial assistance to Native American and other ethnic minority high school seniors in Indiana who are interested in studying education at a college in any state.

Eligibility This program is open to ethnic minority public high school seniors in Indiana who are interested in studying education in college. Selection is based on academic achievement, leadership ability as expressed through co-curricular activities and community involvement, recommendations, and a 300-word essay on their educational goals and how they plan to use this scholarship.

Financial data The stipend is $1,000.

Duration 1 year; may be renewed for 3 additional years if the recipient maintains at least a "C+" average and continues to pursue a teaching credential.

Additional information This program began in 1987.

Number awarded 1 each year.

Deadline February of each year.

[194]
DAVID SANKEY MINORITY SCHOLARSHIP IN METEOROLOGY

National Weather Association
Attn: Executive Director
3100 Monitor Avenue, Suite 123
Norman, OK 73072
(405) 701-5167   Fax: (405) 701-5227
E-mail: exdir@nwas.org
Web: www.nwas.org

Summary To provide financial assistance to Native Americans and members of other underrepresented groups working on an undergraduate or graduate degree in meteorology.

Eligibility This program is open to members of underrepresented ethnic groups who are either entering their sophomore or higher year of undergraduate study or enrolled as graduate students. Applicants must be working on a degree in meteorology. Along with their application, they must submit a 1-page statement explaining why they are applying for this scholarship. Selection is based on that statement, academic achievement, and 2 letters of recommendation.

Financial data The stipend is $1,000.

Duration 1 year.

Additional information This program began in 2002.

Number awarded 1 each year.

Deadline April of each year.

[195]
DELAWARE ATHLETIC TRAINERS' ASSOCIATION ETHNIC DIVERSITY ADVISORY COMMITTEE SCHOLARSHIP

Delaware Athletic Trainers' Association
c/o Education Committee Chair
University of Delaware
159 Fred Rust Ice Arena
Newark, DE 19716
(302) 831-6402   E-mail: kaminski@udel.edu
Web: www.delata.org/scholarship-applications.html

Summary To provide financial assistance to Native Americans and other ethnic minority members of the National Athletic Trainers' Association (NATA) from Delaware who are working on an undergraduate or graduate degree in the field.

Eligibility This program is open to NATA members who are members of ethnic diversity groups and residents of Delaware or attending college in that state. Applicants must be enrolled full time in an undergraduate athletic training education program or a graduate athletic training program and have a GPA of 2.5 or higher. They must intend to prepare for the profession of athletic training. Along with their application, they must submit an 800-word statement on their athletic training background, experience, philosophy, and goals. Selection is based equally on academic performance and athletic training clinical achievement.

Financial data A stipend is awarded (amount not specified).

Duration 1 year.

Number awarded 1 or more each year.

Deadline February of each year.

[196]
DIGITASLBI MULTICULTURAL SCHOLARSHIP

American Association of Advertising Agencies
Attn: AAAA Foundation
1065 Avenue of the Americas, 16th Floor
New York, NY 10018
(212) 262-2500   E-mail: ameadows@aaaa.org
Web: www.aaaa.org

Summary To provide financial assistance to Native American and other multicultural students who are working on an undergraduate degree in advertising.

Eligibility This program is open to undergraduate students of proven multicultural heritage. Applicants must be participating in the Multicultural Advertising Intern Program (MAIP). They must be enrolled at an accredited college or university in the United States and be able to demonstrate financial need.

Financial data The stipend is $5,000.

Duration 1 year.

Additional information This program is funded by DigitasLBi.

Number awarded 1 each year.

Deadline July of each year.

[197]
DISTRIBUTED RESEARCH EXPERIENCES FOR UNDERGRADUATES

Computing Research Association
1828 L Street, N.W., Suite 800
Washington, DC 20036-4632
(202) 234-2111   Fax: (202) 667-1066
E-mail: dreu@cra.org
Web: www.cra.org/cra-w/dreu

Summary To provide an opportunity for Native American and other underrepresented undergraduate students to work on a summer research project in computer science or engineering.

Eligibility This program is open to members of underrepresented groups (women, Hispanics, African Americans, American Indians, students with disabilities) who are entering their junior or senior year of college. Applicants must be interested in conducting a summer research project directly related to computer science or computer engineering under the mentorship of a faculty member at the mentor's home university. They must be U.S. citizens or permanent residents. Selection is based on the student's potential for success in graduate school, the extent of the student's experience and skills, the student's potential gain from the experience, and the potential that the student's participation will advance the goals of the program.

Financial data Students receive a stipend of $7,000 plus relocation travel assistance up to $500 if appropriate.

Duration 10 weeks during the summer.

Additional information This program began in 1994 as the Distributed Mentor Project (DMP) by the Computing Research Association's Committee on the Status of Women in Computing Research (CRA-W). In 2007, the Coalition to Diversify Computing (CDC) became a cosponsor of the program and in 2009 it was given its current name. From the beginning, funding has been provided by the National Science Foundation.

Number awarded Varies each year; recently, 46 students were selected to participate in this program.

Deadline February of each year.

[198]
DIVERSITY IN PSYCHOLOGY AND LAW RESEARCH AWARD

American Psychological Association
Attn: Division 41 (American Psychology-Law Society)
c/o Kathy Gaskey, Administrative Officer
P.O. Box 11488
Southport, NC 28461-3936
(910) 933-4018   Fax: (910) 933-4018
E-mail: apls@ec.rr.com
Web: www.apadivisions.org

Summary To provide funding to Native American and other student members of the American Psychology-Law Society (AP-LS) who are interested in conducting a research project related to diversity.

Eligibility This program is open to undergraduate and graduate student members of AP-LS who are interested in conducting research on issues related to psychology, law, multiculturalism, and/or diversity (e.g., research pertaining to psycholegal issues on race, gender, culture, sexual orientation). Students from underrepresented groups are strongly encouraged to apply; underrepresented groups include, but are not limited to: racial and ethnic minorities; first-generation college students; lesbian, gay, bisexual, and transgender students; and students with physical disabilities. Applicants must submit a project description that includes a statement of the research problem, the project's likely impact on the field of psychology and law broadly, methodology, budget, and an overview of relevant literature. Selection is based on the impact of the project on diversity and multiculturalism and the expected completion within the allocated time.

Financial data　The grant is $1,000.

Duration　The project must be completed within 1 year.

Number awarded　Up to 5 each year.

Deadline　November of each year.

[199]
DIVERSITY SUMMER HEALTH-RELATED RESEARCH EDUCATION PROGRAM

Medical College of Wisconsin
Attn: Office of Student Diversity Affairs
8701 Watertown Plank Road
Milwaukee, WI 53226
(414) 955-8735　　　　　　　　Fax: (414) 955-0129
E-mail: studentdiversity@mcw.edu
Web: www.mcw.edu/Diversity-Programs.htm

Summary　To provide an opportunity for Native American and other undergraduate residents of any state who come from diverse backgrounds to participate in a summer research training experience at the Medical College of Wisconsin.

Eligibility　This program is open to U.S. citizens and permanent residents who come from an ethnically, economically, and/or educationally disadvantaged backgrounds. The program targets African Americans, Mexican-Americans, Native Americans (American Indians, Alaska Natives, and Native Hawaiians), Pacific Islanders, Hmong, mainland Puerto Ricans, and individuals with disabilities. Applicants must be interested in participating in a summer research training program at the Medical College of Wisconsin. They must have completed at least 1 year of undergraduate study at an accredited college or university (or be a community college student enrolled in at least 3 courses per academic term) and have a GPA of 3.4 or higher.

Financial data　The stipend is $10 per hour for a 40-hour week. Housing is provided for students who live outside Milwaukee County and travel expenses are paid for those who live outside Wisconsin.

Duration　10 weeks during the summer.

Additional information　Students are "matched" with a full-time faculty investigator to participate in a research project addressing the causes, prevention, and treatment of cardiovascular, pulmonary, or hematological diseases. This program is funded by the National Heart, Lung, and Blood Institute (NHLBI) of the National Institutes of Health (NIH). Participants are required to prepare an abstract of their research and make a brief oral presentation of their project at the conclusion of the summer.

Number awarded　Approximately 12 each year.

Deadline　January of each year.

[200]
DOC AND BARBARA CARTWRIGHT ENDOWED SCHOLARSHIP

American Indian College Fund
Attn: Scholarship Department
8333 Greenwood Boulevard
Denver, CO 80221
(303) 426-8900　　　　　　　　Toll Free: (800) 776-FUND
Fax: (303) 426-1200
E-mail: scholarships@collegefund.org
Web: www.collegefund.org

Summary　To provide financial assistance to American Indian men interested in attending tribal colleges and universities.

Eligibility　This program is open to male American Indians registered as a member of a tribe or a descendant of at least 1 grandparent or parent who is an enrolled tribal member. Applicants must be enrolled or planning to enroll at a tribal college or university in any state and have a GPA of 3.0 or higher. They must serve as mentors and role models to encourage other American Indian men to pursue higher education and actively recruit other American Indian men to attend college. Applications are available only online and include required essays on specified topics. U.S. citizenship is required.

Financial data　The stipend is $3,000.

Duration　1 year.

Number awarded　1 or more each year.

Deadline　May of each year.

[201]
DOMINION DIVERSITY SCHOLARSHIP PROGRAM

Dominion Resources Inc.
Attn: Diversity Team
701 East Cary Street, 13th Floor
Richmond, VA 23219
(804) 819-2000　　　　　　　　E-mail: diversity@dom.com
Web: www.dom.com

Summary　To provide financial assistance and work experience to Native American and other high school seniors and college students who will contribute to the diversity of the sponsor.

Eligibility　This program is open to high school seniors and current college students who will not graduate for at least 2 years. Community college students must be enrolled in a program that will prepare them to transfer to a 4-year institution. Applicants must commit to a paid intern work session during the summer following their first year of scholarship support. Along with their application, they must submit an essay of 1,000 to 1,250 words that 1) describes the experiences or ideas they would bring to the diversity of the sponsor; 2) includes the new perspectives or new talents they will contribute to the sponsor; and 3) describes how this diversity scholarship program will help them achieve their career goals. The sponsor defines diversity to include minorities, women, protected veterans, and individuals with disabilities.

Financial data The scholarship stipend is $5,000. A competitive salary is paid for the internship.

Duration 1 year for the scholarship; 10 to 12 weeks during the summer for the internship.

Additional information The sponsor operates electric distribution and transmission companies in North Carolina and Virginia and natural gas distribution companies in Ohio and West Virginia.

Number awarded 30 each year.

Deadline May of each year.

[202]
DON CORP SCHOLARSHIP

Sault Tribe of Chippewa Indians
Attn: Higher Education Department
523 Ashmun Street
Sault Ste. Marie, MI 49783
(906) 635-6050, ext. 26312   Toll Free: (800) 793-0660
Fax: (906) 635-7785   E-mail: BMacArthur@saulttribe.net
Web: www.saulttribe.com

Summary To provide financial assistance to members of the Sault Tribe of Chippewa Indians who are interested in working on an undergraduate degree in a field related to history.

Eligibility This program is open to members of the Sault Tribe who are enrolled or planning to enroll full time at a 2- or 4-year college or university in any state. Applicants must be interested in working on an undergraduate degree in history, museum studies, historical preservation, or other history-related field. Along with their application, they must submit an essay of 1,000 to 2,000 words on a topic that changes annually but relates to their Indian heritage.

Financial data The stipend is $1,000.

Duration 1 year.

Number awarded 1 each year.

Deadline May of each year.

[203]
DON SAHLI–KATHY WOODALL MINORITY STUDENT SCHOLARSHIP

Tennessee Education Association
Attn: Sahli-Woodall Scholarship Fund
801 Second Avenue North
Nashville, TN 37201-1099
(615) 242-8392   Toll Free: (800) 342-8367
Fax: (615) 259-4581   E-mail: jdemain@tea.nea.org
Web: www.teateachers.org

Summary To provide financial assistance to Native American and other minority high school seniors in Tennessee who are interested in majoring in education at a college or university in the state.

Eligibility This program is open to minority high school seniors in Tennessee who are planning to attend a college or university in the state and major in education. Application must be made either by a Future Teachers of America chapter affiliated with the Tennessee Education Association (TEA) or by the student with the recommendation of an active TEA member. Selection is based on academic record, leadership ability, financial need, and demonstrated interest in becoming a teacher.

Financial data The stipend is $1,000.

Duration 1 year.

Number awarded 1 each year.

Deadline February of each year.

[204]
DONALD AND ITASKER THORNTON MEMORIAL SCHOLARSHIP

Thornton Sisters Foundation
P.O. Box 21
Atlantic Highlands, NJ 07716-0021
(732) 872-1353   E-mail: tsfoundation2001@yahoo.com
Web: www.thornton-sisters.com/ttsf.htm

Summary To provide financial assistance for college to Native American and other women of color in New Jersey.

Eligibility This program is open to women of color (defined as African Americans, Latino Americans, Caribbean Americans, and Native Americans) who are graduating from high schools in New Jersey. Applicants must have a grade average of "C+" or higher and be able to document financial need. They must be planning to attend an accredited 4-year college or university. Along with their application, they must submit a 500-word essay describing their family background, personal and financial hardships, honors or academic distinctions, and community involvement and activities.

Financial data A stipend is awarded (amount not specified). Funds are to be used for tuition and/or books.

Duration 1 year; nonrenewable.

Number awarded 1 or more each year.

Deadline May of each year.

[205]
DONALD D. AND J. WENONAH GUNNING MEMORIAL SCHOLARSHIP

Chickasaw Foundation
2020 Arlington, Suite 4
P.O. Box 1726
Ada, OK 74821-1726
(580) 421-9030   Fax: (580) 421-9031
E-mail: ChickasawFoundation@chickasaw.net
Web: www.chickasawfoundation.org/Scholarships.aspx

Summary To provide financial assistance to members of the Chickasaw Nation who are beginning undergraduate study.

Eligibility This program is open to Chickasaw students who are entering their freshman year at a 2- or 4-year college. All academic majors are eligible. Along with their application, they must submit high school or college transcripts; 2 letters of recommendation; a copy of their Chickasaw Nation citizenship card; documentation of financial need; a 2-page list of honors, achievements, awards, club memberships, societies, and civic involvement; and a 1-page essay on their long-term goals and plans for achieving those.

Financial data A stipend is awarded (amount not specified).

Duration 1 year.

Number awarded 1 each year.

Deadline June of each year.

[206]
DOYON FOUNDATION BASIC SCHOLARSHIPS

Doyon, Limited
Attn: Doyon Foundation
615 Bidwell Avenue, Suite 101
Fairbanks, AK 99701
(907) 459-2048   Toll Free: (888) 478-4755, ext. 2048
Fax: (907) 459-2065   E-mail: foundation@doyon.com
Web: www.doyonfoundation.com/static/facts.aspx

Summary To provide financial assistance to undergraduate and graduate students at schools in any state who are shareholders or descendants of shareholders of Doyon, Limited.

Eligibility This program is open to undergraduate or graduate students who are shareholders or the descendants of shareholders of Doyon, Limited. Applicants must be accepted or enrolled at an accredited college, university, technical institute, or vocational school. Both part-time and full-time students are eligible, but full-time students must be accepted into a degree program.

Financial data Stipends are $1,200 per semester for full-time students or $800 per semester for part-time students.

Duration 1 year. Undergraduate students may reapply if they maintain a GPA of 2.0 or higher; graduate or master's degree students may reapply if they maintain a GPA of 3.0 or higher; and specialist or doctoral students may reapply if they maintain a GPA of 3.25 or higher.

Additional information Doyon, Limited is 1 of 13 Alaska Native Regional Corporations created under the Alaska Native Claims Settlement Act of 1971.

Number awarded Varies each year; recently, scholarships were awarded to 175 full-time students and 57 part-time students.

Deadline March of each year for summer school, May of each year for fall semester, November of each year for spring semester.

[207]
DOYON FOUNDATION COMPETITIVE SCHOLARSHIPS

Doyon, Limited
Attn: Doyon Foundation
615 Bidwell Avenue, Suite 101
Fairbanks, AK 99701
(907) 459-2048   Toll Free: (888) 478-4755, ext. 2048
Fax: (907) 459-2065   E-mail: foundation@doyon.com
Web: www.doyonfoundation.com/static/facts.aspx

Summary To provide financial assistance to undergraduate and graduate students at schools in any state who are shareholders or descendants of shareholders of Doyon, Limited.

Eligibility This program is open to undergraduate or graduate students who are shareholders or the descendants of shareholders of Doyon, Limited. Applicants must be accepted or enrolled full or part time at an accredited college, university, or vocational/technical school in any state. Undergraduates must be enrolled in a 4-year bachelor's degree program; graduate students must be enrolled in any post-baccalaureate program; vocational/technical students must be enrolled in a 1- to 3-year certificate or associate degree program. Along with their application, they must submit a personal essay on their educational goals, professional goals, extra-curricular and community service activities or volunteerism, and cultural awareness and contributions to a healthy Native community. Selection is based on the essay (40 points), GPA (40 points), letters of recommendation (30 points), and personal impression (10 points).

Financial data Stipends are $5,000 per year for undergraduates, $7,000 per year for master's students, and $9,000 per year for doctoral students.

Duration 1 year. Undergraduate students may reapply if they maintain a GPA of 2.0 or higher; graduate or master's degree students may reapply if they maintain a GPA of 3.0 or higher; and specialist or doctoral students may reapply if they maintain a GPA of 3.25 or higher.

Additional information Doyon, Limited is 1 of 13 Alaska Native Regional Corporations created under the Alaska Native Claims Settlement Act of 1971. This program includes the Morris Thompson Scholarship Fund and the Rosemarie Maher Memorial Fund. Recipients must attend school on a full-time basis. Scholarship recipients of $5,000 or more are encouraged to complete at least 1 summer internship during their 4 years of study. Scholarship recipients of less than $5,000 are encouraged to do 1 of the following: serve on a local or regional board or commission, volunteer at least 20 hours, or give presentations on their field of study. A written report detailing the internship or service and lessons learned is required upon completion of the internship.

Number awarded Varies each year; recently, 26 were awarded.

Deadline May of each year for academic year scholarships; November of each year for spring semester.

[208]
DOYON FOUNDATION SHORT-TERM VOCATIONAL PROGRAM

Doyon, Limited
Attn: Doyon Foundation
615 Bidwell Avenue, Suite 101
Fairbanks, AK 99701
(907) 459-2048   Toll Free: (888) 478-4755, ext. 2048
Fax: (907) 459-2065   E-mail: foundation@doyon.com
Web: www.doyonfoundation.com/static/facts.aspx

Summary To provide financial assistance for vocational training in any state to shareholders or descendants of shareholders of Doyon, Limited.

Eligibility This program is open to shareholders or the descendants of shareholders of Doyon, Limited. Applicants must be accepted or enrolled at an accredited college, university, or vocational/technical school in any state in a program that lasts less than 6 weeks or 120 hours.

Financial data The program pays the actual cost of the course or program, to a maximum of $1,000.

Duration Funding is provided for a single short-term course or program. Students may apply for only 1 such award per year.

Additional information Doyon, Limited is 1 of 13 Alaska Native Regional Corporations created under the Alaska Native Claims Settlement Act of 1971.

Number awarded Varies each year.

Deadline Applications may be submitted at any time.

[209]
DR. JO ANN OTA FUJIOKA SCHOLARSHIP

Phi Delta Kappa International
Attn: PDK Educational Foundation
320 West Eighth Street, Suite 216
P.O. Box 7888
Bloomington, IN 47407-7888
(812) 339-1156   Toll Free: (800) 766-1156
Fax: (812) 339-0018   E-mail: scholarships@pdkintl.org
Web: www.pdkintl.org

Summary To provide financial assistance to Native American and other high school seniors and undergraduates of color who plan to study education at a college in any state and have a connection to Phi Delta Kappa (PDK).

Eligibility This program is open to high school seniors and undergraduates of color who are majoring or planning to major in education and can meet 1 of the following criteria: 1) is a member of Educators Rising (formerly the Future Educators Association); 2) is the child or grandchild of a PDK member; or 3) has a reference letter written by a PDK member. Also eligible are undergraduate members of PDK or Educators Rising who are enrolled in a college education program. Applicants must submit a 500-word essay on a topic related to education that changes annually. Selection is based on the essay, academic standing, letters of recommendation, service activities, educational activities, and leadership activities; financial need is not considered.

Financial data The stipend is $2,000.

Duration 1 year.

Additional information This program began in 2006.

Number awarded 1 each year.

Deadline March of each year.

[210]
DR. ROE B. LEWIS MEMORIAL SCHOLARSHIPS

Southwest Indian Agricultural Association
1664 East Florence boulevard
Casa Grande, AZ 85122-4779
(520) 562-6722   Fax: (520) 562-2840
E-mail: swiaa@g.com
Web: www.swindianag.com/construction.html

Summary To provide financial assistance to American Indians working on an undergraduate or graduate degree in a field related to agriculture or natural resources.

Eligibility This program is open to American Indians enrolled in a federally-recognized band, nation, or tribe. Applicants must be working on an undergraduate or graduate degree in agriculture or natural resources at an accredited college, university, or vocational/technical school. Along with their application, they must submit an essay explaining how they plan to use their education to promote, educate, and/or improve agriculture on southwest reservations. First-year undergraduates must have a GPA of 2.5 or higher; all other students must have a GPA of 3.0 or higher. Financial need is not considered in the selection process.

Financial data The stipend is $1,000.

Duration 1 year.

Number awarded 3 each year: 2 to undergraduates and 1 to a graduate student.

Deadline November of each year.

[211]
DWIGHT MOSLEY SCHOLARSHIPS

United States Tennis Association
Attn: USTA Foundation
70 West Red Oak Lane
White Plains, NY 10604
(914) 696-7223   Fax: (914) 697-2307
E-mail: foundation@usta.com
Web: www.ustafoundation.com

Summary To provide financial assistance to Native American and other high school seniors who are from diverse ethnic backgrounds, have participated in an organized community tennis program, and plan to attend college in any state.

Eligibility This program is open to high school seniors from diverse ethnic backgrounds who have excelled academically, demonstrated achievements in leadership, and participated extensively in an organized community tennis program. Applicants must be planning to enroll as a full-time undergraduate student at a 4-year college or university. They must have a GPA of 3.0 or higher and be able to demonstrate financial need and sportsmanship. Along with their application, they must submit an essay of 1 to 2 pages about how their participation in a tennis and education program has influenced their life, including examples of special mentors, volunteer service, and future goals. Females and males are considered separately.

Financial data The stipend is $2,500 per year. Funds are paid directly to the recipient's college or university.

Duration 4 years.

Number awarded 2 each year: 1 female and 1 male.

Deadline February of each year.

[212]
ECOTRUST NATIVE AMERICAN SCHOLARSHIP

American Indian College Fund
Attn: Scholarship Department
8333 Greenwood Boulevard
Denver, CO 80221
(303) 426-8900   Toll Free: (800) 776-FUND
Fax: (303) 426-1200
E-mail: scholarships@collegefund.org
Web: www.collegefund.org

Summary To provide financial assistance to Native American college students from any state who are interested in studying fields related to environmentalism at mainstream colleges and universities in California or Oregon.

Eligibility This program is open to American Indians and Alaska Natives from any state who have proof of enrollment or descendancy. Applicants must be enrolled or planning to enroll as freshmen, sophomores, juniors, or seniors at a college or university in California or Oregon. They must have a GPA of 2.5 or higher and be working on a degree in economic development, environmental studies, natural resource management, public health, or social sciences. Financial need and demonstrated leadership are considered in the selection process. Applications are available only online and include required essays on specified topics. U.S. citizenship is required.

Financial data The stipend is $3,000.

Duration 1 year.

Number awarded 1 or more each year.

Deadline May of each year.

[213]
ED BRADLEY SCHOLARSHIP

Radio Television Digital News Foundation
Attn: Membership and Programs Manager
529 14th Street, N.W., Suite 1240
Washington, DC 20045
(202) 536-8356   Fax: (202) 223-4007
E-mail: karenh@rtdna.org
Web: www.rtdna.org/content/ed_bradley_scholarship

Summary To provide financial assistance to Native American and other minority undergraduate students who are preparing for a career in electronic journalism.

Eligibility This program is open to sophomore or more advanced minority undergraduate students enrolled in an electronic journalism sequence at an accredited or nationally-recognized college or university. Applicants must submit a cover letter that discusses their current and past journalism experience, describes how they would use the funds if they were to receive the scholarship, discusses their reasons for preparing for a career in electronic journalism, and includes 3 to 5 links to their best and most relevant work samples.

Financial data The stipend is $10,000, paid in semiannual installments of $5,000 each.

Duration 1 year.

Additional information The Radio Television Digital News Foundation (RTDNF) was formerly the Radio and Television News Directors Foundation (RTNDF).

Number awarded 1 each year.

Deadline April of each year.

[214]
EDITH KANAKA'OLE FOUNDATION HIGHER EDUCATION SCHOLARSHIP

Edith Kanaka'ole Foundation
Attn: Higher Education Scholarship
1500 Kalaniana'ole Avenue
Hilo, HI 96720-4914
(808) 961-5242   Fax: (808) 961-4789
Web: www.edithkanakaolefoundation.org/scholarships

Summary To provide financial assistance to Native Hawaiians who are attending or planning to attend a college or university on the island of Hawai'i.

Eligibility This program is open to students who are of Native Hawaiian ancestry in whole or in part. Applicants must be enrolled or planning to enroll full time at a college or university on Hawai'i island. They must have a GPA of 2.5 or higher and agree to complete a "give back" program. Financial need is considered in the selection process.

Financial data A stipend is awarded (amount not specified); funds are not intended to be the recipient's primary source of higher education funding.

Duration 1 year; may be renewed if the recipient maintains a GPA of 3.0 or higher.

Number awarded 1 or more each year.

Deadline Deadline not specified.

[215]
EDSA MINORITY SCHOLARSHIP

Landscape Architecture Foundation
Attn: Leadership in Landscape Scholarship Program
1129 20th Street, N.W., Suite 202
Washington, DC 20036
(202) 331-7070   Fax: (202) 331-7079
E-mail: scholarships@lafoundation.org
Web: www.lafoundation.org

Summary To provide financial assistance to Native American and other minority college students who are interested in studying landscape architecture.

Eligibility This program is open to African American, Hispanic, Native American, and minority college students of other cultural and ethnic backgrounds. Applicants must be entering their final 2 years of undergraduate study in landscape architecture or working on a graduate degree in that field. Along with their application, they must submit a 500-word essay on a design or research effort they plan to pursue (explaining how it will contribute to the advancement of the profession and to their ethnic heritage), 3 work samples, and 2 letters of recommendation. Selection is based on professional experience, community involvement, extracurricular activities, and financial need.

Financial data The stipend is $5,000.

Additional information This scholarship was formerly designated the Edward D. Stone, Jr. and Associates Minority Scholarship.

Number awarded 1 each year.

Deadline February of each year.

[216]
EDUCATIONAL FOUNDATION OF THE COLORADO SOCIETY OF CERTIFIED PUBLIC ACCOUNTANTS MINORITY SCHOLARSHIPS

Colorado Society of Certified Public Accountants
Attn: Educational Foundation
7887 East Belleview Avenue, Suite 200
Englewood, CO 80111
(303) 773-2877   Toll Free: (800) 523-9082 (within CO)
Fax: (303) 773-6344
Web: www.cocpa.org

Summary To provide financial assistance to Native American and other minority upper-division and graduate students in Colorado who are majoring in accounting.

Eligibility This program is open to Colorado minority residents (Black or African American, Hispanic or Latino, Native American, Asian American) who are upper-division or graduate students at colleges and universities in the state and have completed at least 6 semester hours of accounting courses. Applicants must have a GPA of at least 3.0 overall and 3.25 in accounting classes. They must be U.S. citizens or noncitizens legally living and studying in Colorado with a valid visa that enables them to become employed. Financial need is not considered in the selection process.

Financial data The stipend is $2,500. Funds are paid directly to the recipient's school to be used for books, C.P.A. review materials, tuition, fees, and dormitory room and board.

Duration 1 year; recipients may reapply.

Number awarded 1 or more each year.

Deadline May of each year for fall semester or quarter; November of each year for winter quarter or spring semester.

[217]
EIGHT NORTHERN INDIAN PUEBLOS COUNCIL ADULT VOCATIONAL TRAINING PROGRAM

Eight Northern Indian Pueblos Council, Inc.
Attn: Adult Vocational Training Program
327 Eagle Drive
P.O. 969
Ohkay Owingeh, NM 87566
(505) 747-1593, ext. 115   Fax: (505) 747-1599
E-mail: jnelson@enipc.org
Web: www.enipc.org

Summary To provide financial assistance to members of designated Pueblos in New Mexico who are interested in a program of adult vocational training.

Eligibility This program is open to enrolled members of the following Pueblos: Nambe, Picuris, Pojoaque, San Ildefonso, and Tesuque. Applicants must be interested in working full time for a GED, associate degree, or certificate program. They must be in need of training in order to obtain reasonable and satisfactory employment and be currently unemployed or underemployed. Students working on a bachelor's degree are not eligible.

Financial data For students in a semester program, the stipend is $800 for the fall semester, $800 for the spring semester, and $400 for summer school. For students in a quarter or certificate program, the stipend is $500 per quarter.

Duration Participants are eligible for 24 months of full-time training (36 months for nursing students).

Number awarded Varies each year.

Deadline Deadline not specified.

[218]
EIGHT NORTHERN INDIAN PUEBLOS COUNCIL HIGHER EDUCATION GRANT PROGRAM

Eight Northern Indian Pueblos Council, Inc.
Attn: Higher Education Scholarship
327 Eagle Drive
P.O. Box 969
Ohkay Owingeh, NM 87566
(505) 747-1593   Fax: (505) 747-1599
E-mail: jnelson@enipc.org
Web: www.enipc.org

Summary To provide financial assistance for college to members of designated Pueblos in New Mexico.

Eligibility This program is open to enrolled members of the following Pueblos: Tesuque, Pojoaque, and Picuris. Applicants must be enrolled or planning to enroll full time in an associate or baccalaureate degree program and have a GPA of 2.0 or higher. They may major in any subject area. Financial need is considered in determining the amount of the award.

Financial data The amount awarded varies, depending upon the recipient's financial need, up to $5,000 per year. Generally, however, scholarships range between $1,000 and $1,800 per year.

Duration 1 year; may be renewed for up to 4 additional years.

Number awarded Approximately 50 each year.

Deadline July of each year.

[219]
ELIZABETH AND SHERMAN ASCHE MEMORIAL SCHOLARSHIP

Association on American Indian Affairs, Inc.
Attn: Director of Scholarship Programs
966 Hungerford Drive, Suite 12-B
Rockville, MD 20850
(240) 314-7155   Fax: (240) 314-7159
E-mail: general.aaia@indian-affairs.org
Web: www.indian-affairs.org

Summary To provide financial assistance to Native Americans interested in working on an undergraduate or graduate degree in health or science.

Eligibility This program is open to American Indian and Alaskan Native full-time undergraduate and graduate students working on a degree in health or science. Applicants must submit proof of tribal enrollment and an essay of 2 to 3 pages on 1 of the following topics: 1) why the sponsor's International Repatriation Project is important and how they would inform others about it; 2) the Annie E. Casey Foundation's Juvenile Detention Alternatives Initiative and tribal and community-based alternatives to detention for juveniles; or 3) how tribal leaders can promote higher education in their family and community. They must have a GPA of 2.5 or higher. Selection is based on merit and need.

Financial data The stipend is $1,500.

Duration 1 year. Recipients may reapply.

Number awarded Varies each year; recently, 6 were awarded.

Deadline May of each year.

[220]
ELLIS INJURY LAW DIVERSITY SCHOLARSHIPS

Ellis Law Corporation
Attn: Scholarship
883 North Douglas Street
El Segundo, CA 90245
Toll Free: (888) 559-7672
E-mail: scholarships@alelaw.com
Web: www.ellisinjurylaw.com/scholarships

Summary To provide financial assistance to pre-law and law students who either are members of an ethnic minority group or have been involved in diversity issues.

Eligibility This program is open to students accepted or enrolled at 1) a 4-year college or university with the intention of working on a law degree; and 2) an ABA-accredited law school. Applicants must be either members of an ethnic/racial minority or individuals who have made a demonstrative commitment to diversity within their school and/or community. They must have a GPA of 3.0 or higher. Along with their application, they must submit an essay of 1,500 to 2,000 words answering 3 questions about recent Supreme Court decisions regarding affirmative action. Selection is based on that essay and transcripts.

Financial data The stipend is $1,000.

Duration 1 year.

Additional information   This program began in 2014.

Number awarded   3 each year.

Deadline   December of each year.

[221]
EMERGING ARCHIVAL SCHOLARS PROGRAM

Archival Education and Research Institute
Center for Information as Evidence
c/o UCLA Graduate School of Education and Information
  Studies
Office of External Relations
2043 Moore Hall
Los Angeles, CA 90095-1521
(310) 206-0375   Fax: (310) 794-5324
Web: aeri.gseis.ucla.edu/fellowships.htm

Summary   To provide an opportunity for Native American and other minority undergraduate and graduate students to learn more about the field of archival studies and to be exposed to research in the field.

Eligibility   This program is open to undergraduates who have completed their junior year and to students who have completed the first year of a master's degree program. Applicants must be African American, Hispanic/Latino, Asian/Pacific Islander, Native American, Puerto Rican, or any other person who will add diversity to the field of archival studies. They must have a GPA of 3.0 or higher, but they may be working on a degree in any field and are not required to have prior knowledge of or experience in archival studies. U.S. citizenship or permanent resident status is required. Applicants must be interested in attending the week-long Archival Education and Research Institute (AERI), held at a different university each summer, where they are assigned both a faculty research mentor and a Ph.D. student mentor who introduce them to doctoral research and careers in archival studies.

Financial data   Grants provide payment of round-trip travel, accommodation, and most meals.

Duration   These grants are offered annually.

Additional information   This program, first offered in 2009, is supported by the Institute of Museum and Library Services. Scholars who indicate an interest in continuing on to a doctoral program in archival studies after completing the AERI may be invited to participate in a supervised research project that will last up to 1 year and to present results of their research in a poster session at the AERI of the following year.

Number awarded   Up to 7 each year.

Deadline   April of each year.

[222]
EMMA L. BOWEN FOUNDATION INTERNSHIPS

Emma L. Bowen Foundation
Attn: Senior Vice President, Eastern Region and National
  Recruitment
30 Rockefeller Plaza
(Campus 1221 Avenue of the Americas #28A41)
New York, NY 10112
(212) 975-2545   E-mail: sdrice@cbs.com
Web: www.emmabowenfoundation.com

Summary   To provide financial assistance and work experience to Native American and other minority students interested in preparing for a career in the media industry.

Eligibility   This program is open to minority students who are rising high school seniors, graduating high school seniors, or college freshmen. Applicants must be interested in working at a media company during the summer and school breaks until they graduate from college. They must have a GPA of 3.0 or higher, plans to attend an accredited 4-year college or university, and an interest in the media industry as a career. Along with their application, they must submit an essay of 500 to 1,000 words on how the media industry helps to create the images that influence our decisions and perceptions on a daily basis. U.S. citizenship or permanent resident status is required.

Financial data   Interns receive a stipend of $2,500 to $3,000 and matching compensation of $2,500 to $3,000 to help pay for college tuition and other expenses.

Duration   1 summer for the internship; 1 academic year for the educational support; may be renewed until the intern graduates from college if he or she maintains a GPA of 3.0 or higher.

Additional information   This program began in 1989. The sponsoring companies have included Broadcast Music Inc., CBS Incorporated, Charter Communications, Comcast NBC Universal, C-SPAN, Cox Communications, Fox Television Stations, Inc., Gannett Television, National Association of Broadcasters Educational Foundation, Turner Entertainment Networks.

Number awarded   Approximately 60 to 70 new interns are selected each year.

Deadline   Applications may be submitted at any time.

[223]
EMPIRE STATE DIVERSITY HONORS SCHOLARSHIP PROGRAM

State University of New York
Attn: Office of Diversity, Equity and Inclusion
State University Plaza, T1000A
353 Broadway
Albany, NY 12246
(518) 320-1189   E-mail: carlos.medina@suny.edu
Web: system.suny.edu/odei/diversity-programs

Summary   To provide financial assistance to residents of New York who are attending campuses of the State University of New York (SUNY) and contribute to the diversity of the student body.

Eligibility   This program is open to U.S. citizens and permanent residents who are New York residents and enrolled as undergraduate students at any of the participating SUNY colleges. Applicants must be able to demonstrate 1) how they will contribute to the diversity of the student body, primarily by having overcome a disadvantage or other impediment to success in higher education; and 2) high academic achievement. Economic disadvantage, although not a requirement, may be the basis for eligibility. Membership in a racial or ethnic group that is underrepresented at the applicant's school or program may serve as a plus factor in making awards, but may not form the sole basis of selection.

Financial data   The maximum stipend provided by the SUNY system is half the student's cost of attendance or $3,000, whichever is less. The individual campus must match the SUNY award in an equal amount.

Duration   1 year; renewable.

Number awarded Varies each year; recently, 929 students at 41 SUNY institutions received support from this program.

Deadline Deadline not specified.

[224]
ENCOURAGE MINORITY PARTICIPATION IN OCCUPATIONS WITH EMPHASIS ON REHABILITATION

Allina Health System
Courage Kenny Rehabilitation Institute-Volunteer Services
Attn: EMPOWER Scholarship Committee
3915 Golden Valley Road
Minneapolis, MN 55422
(612) 775-2728   E-mail: ckriempower@allina.com
Web: www.allinahealth.org

Summary To provide financial assistance to Native American and other students of color from Minnesota and western Wisconsin interested in attending college in any state to prepare for a career in the medical rehabilitation field.

Eligibility This program is open to ethnically diverse students accepted at or enrolled in an institution of higher learning in any state. Applicants must be residents of Minnesota or western Wisconsin (Burnett, Pierce, Polk, and St. Croix counties). They must be able to demonstrate a career interest in the medical rehabilitation field by a record of volunteer involvement related to health care and must have a GPA of 2.0 or higher. Along with their application, they must submit a 1-page essay that covers their medical/rehabilitation career-related volunteer service, including detailed information about patients or clients with whom they worked, what they did, what they think they accomplished and gained from their experience and how it will assist them in your future endeavors. Financial need is considered in the selection process.

Financial data The stipend is $1,500.

Duration 1 year.

Additional information This program, established in 1995 by the Courage Center, is also identified by its acronym as the EMPOWER Scholarship Award. The Courage Kenny Rehabilitation Institute was established in 2013 when Courage Center merged with the Sister Kenny Rehabilitation Institute and became part of Allina Health.

Number awarded 2 each year.

Deadline May of each year.

[225]
EO NA PUNAWAI SCHOLARSHIP FUND

Hawai'i Community Foundation
Attn: Scholarship Department
827 Fort Street Mall
Honolulu, HI 96813
(808) 566-5570   Toll Free: (888) 731-3863
Fax: (808) 521-6286
E-mail: scholarships@hcf-hawaii.org
Web: hcf.scholarships.ngwebsolutions.com

Summary To provide financial assistance to residents of Hawaii, especially those of Native Hawaiian ancestry, who are studying a field of science, technology, engineering, or mathematics (STEM) at a college in any state.

Eligibility This program is open to residents of Hawaii who are attending a 4-year accredited college or university in any state as a full-time undergraduate student. Preference is given to students of Native Hawaiian ancestry. Applicants must be majoring in a field of STEM. They must be able to demonstrate academic achievement (GPA of 3.0 or higher), good moral character, leadership in community service, and financial need. Along with their application, they must submit a short statement indicating their reasons for attending college, their planned course of study, their career goals, and what community service means to them.

Financial data The amounts of the awards depend on the availability of funds and the need of the recipient. Recently, the average value of the scholarships awarded by the foundation was $2,800.

Duration 1 year.

Additional information This program began in 2015.

Number awarded Varies each year.

Deadline February of each year.

[226]
ESA FOUNDATION SCHOLARSHIP PROGRAM

Entertainment Software Association
Attn: ESA Foundation
317 Madison Avenue, 22nd Floor
New York, NY 10017
(917) 522-3250
Web: www.esafoundation.org/scholarship.asp

Summary To provide financial assistance to Native American and members of other minority groups who are interested in attending college to prepare for a career in computer and video game arts.

Eligibility This program is open to women and members of minority groups who are high school seniors or undergraduates currently enrolled full time at an accredited 4-year college or university. Applicants must be interested in working on a degree leading to a career in computer and video game arts. They must be U.S. citizens and have a GPA of 2.75 or higher.

Financial data The stipend is $3,000.

Duration 1 year; nonrenewable.

Additional information This program began in 2007.

Number awarded Up to 30 each year: 15 to graduating high school seniors and 15 to current undergraduates.

Deadline March of each year.

[227]
ESTEE LAUDER TRIBAL SCHOLARSHIP

American Indian College Fund
Attn: Scholarship Department
8333 Greenwood Boulevard
Denver, CO 80221
(303) 426-8900   Toll Free: (800) 776-FUND
Fax: (303) 426-1200
E-mail: scholarships@collegefund.org
Web: www.collegefund.org

Summary To provide financial assistance to Native American college students who are interested in studying business or environmental fields at Tribal Colleges and Universities (TCUs) in Minnesota.

Eligibility This program is open to American Indians and Alaska Natives from any state who have proof of enrollment or descendancy. Applicants must be enrolled or planning to enroll as freshmen, sophomores, juniors, or seniors at an eligible TCU in Minnesota. They must have a GPA of 3.0 or higher and be working on a degree in business, marketing, environmental science, or a related field. Applications are available only online and include required essays on specified topics. U.S. citizenship is required.

Financial data The stipend is $1,000.

Duration 1 year.

Additional information This program is sponsored by Estée Lauder.

Number awarded 1 or more each year.

Deadline May of each year.

[228]
ETHEL AND EMERY FAST SCHOLARSHIP

Ethel and Emery Fast Scholarship Foundation, Inc.
12620 Rolling Road
Potomac, MD 20854
(301) 762-1102   Fax: (301) 279-0201
E-mail: qccarol@erols.com

Summary To provide financial assistance to qualified Native Americans enrolled as undergraduates or graduate students.

Eligibility Applicants must 1) be Native Americans enrolled in a federally-recognized tribe; 2) have successfully completed 1 year of their undergraduate or graduate school program; 3) be enrolled in school full time; and 4) be able to demonstrate financial need. Along with their application, they must submit documentation of Native American eligibility, an original transcript, a letter confirming enrollment, a federal income tax return, a statement of financial need, and a personal statement (up to 2 pages) describing their current situation, their future aspirations in terms of their academic pursuits, and how this scholarship will assist them in attaining their goals.

Financial data A stipend is awarded (amount not specified). Funds are paid directly to the recipient's college or university and can only be used to pay for tuition, room, board, and fees.

Duration 1 year.

Number awarded Varies each year.

Deadline August of each year for the fall semester; January of each year for the spring semester.

[229]
ETHEL CURRY SCHOLARSHIPS

Minnesota Department of Education
Attn: Manager, Minnesota Indian Education
1500 Highway 36 West
Roseville, MN 55113-4266
(651) 582-8832   Toll Free: (800) 657-3927
E-mail: ladonna.mustin@state.mn.us
Web: www.education.state.mn.us

Summary To provide financial assistance to Native Americans in Minnesota who are interested in working on an undergraduate or graduate degree.

Eligibility This program is open to Indians who are enrolled in a Minnesota-based tribe or community. Applicants must be attending or planning to attend an accredited post-secondary institution in Minnesota as an undergraduate or graduate student. Undergraduates must have a GPA of 2.0 or higher; graduate students must have a GPA of 3.0 or higher. Along with their application, they must submit a 400-word essay on why they should be awarded this scholarship. Selection is based on merit.

Financial data A stipend is awarded (amount not specified).

Duration Up to 4 years.

Number awarded Varies each year; recently, 9 were awarded.

Deadline May of each year.

[230]
EUGENE DANIEL SCHOLARSHIPS

Osage Nation Education Department
Attn: Career Training and Scholarship
105 Buffalo Avenue
Hominy, OK 74035
(918) 287-5301   Fax: (918) 885-2136
E-mail: scholarship@osagenation-nsn.gov
Web: www.osagenation-nsn.gov

Summary To provide financial assistance to members of the Osage Nation who are interested in working on an undergraduate or graduate degree in a medical-related field.

Eligibility This program is open to Osage tribal students who are enrolled full time in a certification, associate, baccalaureate, master's, or doctoral program at an accredited college or technical school. Applicants must be working on a degree in a medical-related field and have a GPA of 3.0 or higher. They must be able to demonstrate financial need.

Financial data The stipend is $500 per semester. Funds are paid directly to the student's school to be applied toward tuition, fees, and books.

Duration 2 semesters.

Number awarded 4 each year.

Deadline June of each year.

[231]
EXXONMOBIL GEOSCIENCES SCHOLARSHIP PROGRAM

American Indian Science and Engineering Society
Attn: Director of Membership and Communications
2305 Renard Place, S.E., Suite 200
Albuquerque, NM 87106
(505) 765-1052, ext. 110   Fax: (505) 765-5608
E-mail: lpaz@aises.org
Web: www.aises.org/scholoarships/aises-exxonmobil

Summary To provide funding to members of the American Indian Science and Engineering Society (AISES) who are interested in conducting field work or research related to geosciences.

Eligibility This program is open to AISES members who are full-time undergraduate or graduate students at an accredited 4-year college or university. Applicants must be American Indian tribal members, Alaskan Natives, or Native Hawaiians and have a Certificate of Degree of Indian or Alaska Native Blood (CDIB) showing at least 25% Native blood. They must be seeking funding for geosciences field camps (normally undergraduates) or field-based research (typically master's or doctoral students). Along with their application, they must submit documentation of acceptance into a geoscience field camp or an approved plan for field-based research. A GPA of at least 3.0 is required.

Financial data The stipend is $3,000.

Duration 1 year; nonrenewable.

Additional information This program is funded by Exxon-Mobil.

Number awarded Up to 7 each year.

Deadline April of each year.

[232]
EXXONMOBIL SCHOLARSHIP OF KONIAG INCORPORATED

Koniag Incorporated
Attn: Koniag Education Foundation
4241 B Street, Suite 303B
Anchorage, AK 99503
(907) 562-9093   Toll Free: (888) 562-9093
Fax: (907) 562-9023
E-mail: scholarships@koniageducation.org
Web: www.koniageducation.org

Summary To provide financial assistance to Alaska Natives who are Koniag Incorporated shareholders or descendants and working on an undergraduate or graduate degree in science or mathematics related to the oil and gas industry.

Eligibility This program is open to undergraduate and graduate students who are Alaska Native shareholders of Koniag Incorporated or descendants of those original enrollees. Applicants must have a GPA of 3.0 or higher and be working full time on a degree in a field of science or mathematics related to the oil and gas industry. Along with their application, they must submit a 300-word essay about their personal and family history, community involvement, volunteer activities, and educational and life goals. Financial need is not considered in the selection process.

Financial data The stipend is $5,000 per year. Funds are sent directly to the recipient's school and may be used for tuition, books, supplies, room, board, and transportation.

Duration 1 year; may be renewed.

Additional information Koniag Incorporated is 1 of 13 Alaska Native Regional Corporations created under the Alaska Native Claims Settlement Act of 1971. This program is supported by ExxonMobil.

Number awarded 1 to 3 each year.

Deadline May of each year.

[233]
FIRST GENERATION INDIAN DESCENT TUITION ASSISTANCE PROGRAM

Poarch Band of Creek Indians
Attn: Tuition Program Coordinator
5811 Jack Springs Road
Atmore, AL 36502
(251) 368-9136, ext. 2535   Fax: (251) 368-4502
E-mail: mjohnson@pci-nsn.gov
Web: www.poarchcreekindians.org

Summary To provide financial assistance to undergraduate and graduate students who are first-generation descendants of members of the Poarch Band of Creek Indians.

Eligibility This program is open to first-generation descendants of enrolled tribal members of the Poarch Band of Creek Indians. Applicants must be attending or planning to attend an approved postsecondary institution as an undergraduate or graduate student. They must have a GPA of 2.0 or higher and be able to document financial need.

Financial data Total maximum awards are $5,000 for students participating in a certificate program not culminating in a degree and not part of the federal student aid program, $10,000 for students participating in a certificate program not culminating in a degree but part of the federal student aid program, $20,000 for an associate degree program, or $50,000 for a bachelor's, master's, or graduate degree program.

Duration 1 year; may be renewed until the recipient reaches a lifetime benefit cap of $50,000.

Additional information This program began in 2006 and was named the Fred L. McGhee First Generation Indian Descent Scholarship Program. The current name was adopted in 2013.

Number awarded Varies each year.

Deadline Applications may be submitted at any time.

[234]
FIRST TRANSIT SCHOLARSHIP

Conference of Minority Transportation Officials
Attn: National Scholarship Program
100 M Street, S.E., Suite 917
Washington, DC 20003
(202) 506-2917   E-mail: info@comto.org
Web: www.comto.org/page/scholarships

Summary To provide financial assistance to Native American and other minority upper-division and graduate students in engineering or other field related to transportation.

Eligibility This program is open to minority juniors, seniors, and graduate students in transporation, planning, engineering or other technical transportation-related disciplines. Applicants must submit a cover letter on their transportation-related career goals and life aspirations. Financial need is not considered in the selection process.

Financial data The stipend is $6,000. Funds are paid directly to the recipient's college or university.

Duration 1 year.

Additional information This program is sponsored by First Transit Inc.

Number awarded 1 each year.

Deadline April of each year.

[235]
FLANDREAU SANTEE SIOUX ADULT VOCATIONAL TRAINING GRANTS

Flandreau Santee Sioux Tribe
Attn: Education Coordinator
P.O. Box 283
Flandreau, SD 57028
(605) 997-2859   Fax: (605) 573-0310
E-mail: kellyn.james@fsst.org
Web: www.santeesioux.com/Agnesrossedu_main.html

Summary To provide financial assistance to members of the Flandreau Santee Sioux Tribe and other Indians who live near the reservation and are interested in attending vocational school.

Eligibility This program is open to enrolled members of the Flandreau Santee Sioux Tribe and members of other federally-recognized tribes who live within 50 miles of Tribal Headquarters. Applicants must be between 18 and 35 years of age and in need of training at a vocational/technical institute to obtain reasonable and satisfactory employment. They must apply for all available federal funding, using the Free Application for Student Aid (FAFSA). Awards are granted on a first-come, first-served basis.

Financial data The stipend is $500 per semester. Funds are for tuition and fees and are paid directly to the institution.

Duration Up to 24 months of full-time training or equivalent in part-time training is provided.

Additional information Funding for this program is provided by the U.S. Bureau of Indian Affairs (BIA).

Number awarded Varies each year.

Deadline July of each year for fall semester or quarter; December of each year for spring semester or winter quarter; January of each year for spring quarter; May of each year for summer session.

[236]
FLANDREAU SANTEE SIOUX BIA HIGHER EDUCATION GRANTS

Flandreau Santee Sioux Tribe
Attn: Education Coordinator
P.O. Box 283
Flandreau, SD 57028
(605) 997-2859   Fax: (605) 573-0310
E-mail: kellyn.james@fsst.org
Web: www.santeesioux.com/Agnesrossedu_main.html

Summary To provide financial assistance to members of the Flandreau Santee Sioux Tribe who are interested in attending college in any state.

Eligibility This program is open to enrolled members of the tribe who are attending or planning to attend a college or university in any state. Applicants must intend to complete a baccalaureate degree or an associate degree that leads to a baccalaureate degree. They must apply for all available federal funding, using the Free Application for Student Aid (FAFSA). In the selection process, first priority is given to continuing students, second to new students, and third to returning students. Within those categories, additional consideration is given to class rank (upperclassmen are funded before lowerclassmen), financial need (students with unmet financial need are funded before students with no financial need), and residency (students who are on reservation are funded before students who are off reservation).

Financial data For the first semester of each year, full-time students receive $1,000 as freshmen, $1,100 as sophomores, $1,200 as juniors, or $1,300 as seniors. For the second semester of each year, full-time students who have a GPA of 2.0 to 3.0 during the first semester receive the same amounts; those who have less than 2.0 receive $800 as freshmen, $880 as sophomores, $960 as juniors, or $1,040 as seniors; those who have more than 3.0 receive $1,100 as freshmen, $1,200 as sophomores, $1,300 as juniors, or $1,400 as seniors. Part-time students receive stipends equal to half the amount of full-time students in the same category. Funds are for tuition and fees and are paid directly to the institution.

Duration 1 semester; may be renewed for a total of 89 semester credits for an associate degree or a total of 154 semester credits for a bachelor's degree (including funded associate degree credits). Renewal requires that recipients maintain a GPA of 2.0 or higher.

Additional information Funding for this program is provided by the U.S. Bureau of Indian Affairs (BIA).

Number awarded Varies each year.

Deadline July of each year for fall semester or quarter; December of each year for spring semester or winter quarter; January of each year for spring quarter; May of each year for summer session.

[237]
FLORIDA JOB TRAINING AND EDUCATION PROGRAM

Florida Governor's Council on Indian Affairs
Attn: Workforce Development Services
625 North Adams Street
Tallahassee, FL 32301
(850) 488-0730   Toll Free: (800) 322-9186
Fax: (850) 488-5875   E-mail: info@fgcia.com
Web: www.fgcia.org/training

Summary To provide financial assistance to needy Native Americans in Florida or Georgia who are interested in obtaining additional education or training.

Eligibility This program is open to Native Americans (Native Hawaiians, Alaskan Natives, American Indians) who are residents of Florida or Georgia. Applicants must be unemployed, underemployed, or economically disadvantaged. They must be interested in enrolling full or part time at a GED training site, vocational or technical school, or community college. Along with their application, they must submit a brief statement describing their educational and career goals.

Financial data Tuition and other services are offered to recipients.

Duration Up to 1 year.

Number awarded Varies each year.

Deadline Deadline not specified.

[238]
FOOL SOLDIER SCHOLARSHIP

Sioux Falls Area Community Foundation
Attn: Scholarship Coordinator
200 North Cherapa Place
Sioux Falls, SD 57103-2205
(605) 336-7055, ext. 20   Fax: (605) 336-0038
E-mail: pgale@sfacf.org
Web: www.sfacf.org/statewide-students-college-bound

Summary To provide financial assistance to descendants of specified Indians in South Dakota who are interested in attending college in any state.

Eligibility This program is open to enrolled members of South Dakota Indian tribes who are graduating from high school. Applicants must have a GPA of 2.0 or higher and be able to demonstrate financial need. They must be planning to attend an accredited college, university, or technical school in any state. Along with their application, they must document descendancy from 1 or more of the Fool Soldiers, a group of Teton Lakota men who ransomed the freedom of 2 white women and 6 children held captive by a band of Dakota Indians in 1862.

Financial data The stipend is $1,250. Funds are paid in 2 equal installments and are to be used for tuition, fees, and/or books.

Duration 1 year.

Additional information This program began in 1997.

Number awarded 1 or more each year.

Deadline March of each year.

[239]
FORD MOTOR COMPANY SCHOLARSHIPS

American Indian College Fund
Attn: Scholarship Department
8333 Greenwood Boulevard
Denver, CO 80221
(303) 426-8900   Toll Free: (800) 776-FUND
Fax: (303) 426-1200
E-mail: scholarships@collegefund.org
Web: www.collegefund.org

Summary To provide financial assistance to Native American college students who are interested in majoring in designated fields at mainstream colleges and universities, especially those in Michigan.

Eligibility This program is open to American Indians and Alaska Natives who have proof of enrollment or descendancy and are enrolled or planning to enroll full time in a bachelor's degree program at a mainstream institution; first preference is given to students at colleges and universities in Michigan. Applicants must have a GPA of 3.0 or higher and be able to demonstrate exceptional academic achievement or financial need. They must have declared a major in accounting, computer science, engineering, finance, marketing, or operations management. Applications are available only online and include required essays on specified topics. U.S. citizenship is required.

Financial data The stipend is $3,000 per year.

Duration 1 year; may be renewed.

Additional information This program is funded by the Ford Motor Company in partnership with the American Indian College Fund.

Number awarded Varies each year.

Deadline May of each year.

[240]
FORD MOTOR COMPANY TRIBAL COLLEGE SCHOLARSHIP

American Indian College Fund
Attn: Scholarship Department
8333 Greenwood Boulevard
Denver, CO 80221
(303) 426-8900   Toll Free: (800) 776-FUND
Fax: (303) 426-1200
E-mail: scholarships@collegefund.org
Web: www.collegefund.org

Summary To provide financial assistance to Native Americans who are interested in attending a Tribal College or University (TCU) and majoring in specified fields.

Eligibility This program is open to American Indians or Alaska Natives who are enrolled or planning to enroll full time at an eligible TCU; first preference is given to students at

TCUs in Michigan. Applicants must have a GPA of 3.0 or higher and be able to demonstrate exceptional academic achievement or financial need. They must have declared a major in mathematics, science, engineering, business, teacher training, or environmental science. Applications are available only online and include required essays on specified topics. U.S. citizenship is required.

Financial data The stipend is $3,000.

Duration 1 year.

Additional information This program is funded by the Ford Motor Company in partnership with the American Indian College Fund.

Number awarded 1 or more each year.

Deadline May of each year.

[241]
FORT PECK TRIBES ADULT VOCATIONAL TRAINING PROGRAM

Fort Peck Assiniboine and Sioux Tribes
Attn: Education Department
501 Medicine Bear Road
P.O. Box 1027
Poplar, MT 59255-1027
(406) 768-5136   Toll Free: (800) 799-2926
Fax: (406) 768-3556
Web: www.fortpecktribes.org/education.html

Summary To provide financial assistance for vocational training to Assiniboine and Sioux members of the Fort Peck Tribes in Montana.

Eligibility This program is open to enrolled members of the Fort Peck Assiniboine and Sioux Tribes between 17 and 35 years of age. Applicants must have a high school diploma or GED, be actively pursuing a certificate of completion in an adult vocational training program, and be able to demonstrate expectation of employment. Along with their application, they must submit a copy of their high school diploma or GED, a Certificate of Degree of Indian Blood (CDIB), evidence of financial need, and, if relevant, a marriage license, birth certificates for all family members claimed as financial dependents, and military discharge papers. First priority is given to enrolled tribal members living on or near the Fort Peck Reservation and second to enrolled tribal members living off the reservation. Members of other tribes are eligible if funding permits.

Financial data Stipends depend on the need of the recipient.

Duration Up to 24 months (or 36 months for nursing students).

Number awarded Varies each year.

Deadline July of each year for fall; December of each year for spring.

[242]
FORT PECK TRIBES HIGHER EDUCATION SCHOLARSHIPS

Fort Peck Assiniboine and Sioux Tribes
Attn: Education Department
501 Medicine Bear Road
P.O. Box 1027
Poplar, MT 59255-1027
(406) 768-5136   Toll Free: (800) 799-2926
Fax: (406) 768-3556
Web: www.fortpecktribes.org/education.html

Summary To provide financial assistance to members of the Fort Peck Assiniboine and Sioux Tribes who are interested in attending college in any state.

Eligibility This program is open to enrolled members of the Fort Peck Assiniboine and Sioux Tribes who have or will have a high school diploma or GED certificate. Applicants must be enrolled or planning to enroll at an institution of higher education in any state. They must be able to document financial need. Priority in funding is given to college seniors, juniors, sophomores, and freshmen, in that order.

Financial data The maximum stipend recently was $3,600 per year for students who live off the reservation or $1,800 per year for students who live on the reservation. Funding is the same, regardless of whether the student attends school in Montana or another state.

Duration 1 year; may be renewed up to 4 additional years, provided the recipient maintains a GPA of 2.0 or higher.

Number awarded Varies each year.

Deadline July of each year.

[243]
FORUM FOR CONCERNS OF MINORITIES SCHOLARSHIPS

American Society for Clinical Laboratory Science
Attn: Forum for Concerns of Minorities
1861 International Drive, Suite 200
McLean, VA 22102
(571) 748-3770   E-mail: ascls@ascls.org
Web: www.ascls.org/forum-for-concerns-of-minorities

Summary To provide financial assistance to Native American and other minority students in clinical laboratory scientist and clinical laboratory technician programs.

Eligibility This program is open to minority students who are enrolled in a program in clinical laboratory science, including clinical laboratory science/medical technology (CLS/MT) and clinical laboratory technician/medical laboratory technician (CLT/MLT). Applicants must be able to demonstrate financial need. Membership in the American Society for Clinical Laboratory Science is encouraged but not required.

Financial data Stipends depend on the need of the recipients and the availability of funds.

Duration 1 year.

Number awarded 2 each year: 1 to a CLS/MT student and 1 to a CLT/MLT student.

Deadline March of each year.

[244]
FOUR DIRECTIONS SUMMER RESEARCH PROGRAM

Brigham and Women's Hospital
Attn: Center for Faculty Development and Diversity
Office for Multicultural Faculty Careers
1620 Tremont Street 3-014
Boston, MA 02120
(617) 525-8356   Fax: (617) 264-5110
E-mail: FourDirections@partners.org
Web: fdsrp.partners.org/program_overview

Summary To provide an opportunity undergraduate students with a commitment to the Native American community to participate in a summer research project at Harvard Medical School.

Eligibility This program is open to U.S. citizens and permanent residents who are interested in preparing for a career in medicine, public health, or biomedical research and have a demonstrated interest and commitment to Native American communities. Applicants must have completed at least 1 year of undergraduate study at a 4-year institution and have taken at least 1 introductory science course (may include biology or chemistry). They must be interested in working on a summer research project at Harvard Medical School under the supervision of a scientist engaged in medical, public health, or biomedical research. Along with their application, they must submit 250-word essays on 1) their involvement in the Native American Community, including any hobbies, cultural activities or volunteer work that may demonstrate their contribution to the lives of Native People; and 2) their interest in medicine or biomedical research, including their goals and how they hope to benefit themselves and their people by participating in this program.

Financial data The program provides a stipend (amount not specified), transportation, and lodging expenses.

Duration 8 weeks during the summer.

Additional information This program, which began in 1994, is administered jointly by Harvard Medical School and Brigham and Women's Hospital. Participants may not take the summer MCAT, as the time constraints of this program do not allow time to study for that examination.

Number awarded 6 each year.

Deadline February of each year.

[245]
FRANCES CRAWFORD MARVIN AMERICAN INDIAN SCHOLARSHIP

Daughters of the American Revolution-National Society
Attn: Committee Services Office, Scholarships
1776 D Street, N.W.
Washington, DC 20006-5303
(202) 628-1776
Web: www.dar.org

Summary To provide financial assistance to Native American students who are working on an undergraduate degree.

Eligibility This program is open to Native Americans enrolled full time at a 2- or 4-year college or university. Applicants must have a GPA of 3.25 or higher. Selection is based on academic achievement and financial need.

Financial data The stipend depends on the availability of funds.

Duration 1 year; recipients may reapply.

Number awarded 1 each year.

Deadline February of each year.

[246]
FRANCIS M. KEVILLE MEMORIAL SCHOLARSHIP

Construction Management Association of America
Attn: CMAA Foundation
7926 Jones Branch Drive, Suite 800
McLean, VA 22101-3303
(703) 677-3361   E-mail: foundation@cmaanet.org
Web: www.cmaafoundation.org

Summary To provide financial assistance to Native American and other minority undergraduate and graduate students working on a degree in construction management.

Eligibility This program is open to women and members of minority groups who are enrolled as full-time undergraduate or graduate students. Applicants must have completed at least 1 year of study and have at least 1 full year remaining for a bachelor's or master's degree in construction management or a related field. Along with their application, they must submit essays on why they are interested in a career in construction management and why they should be awarded this scholarship. Selection is based on that essay (20%), academic performance (40%), recommendation of the faculty adviser (15%), and extracurricular activities (25%); a bonus of 5% is given to student members of the Construction Management Association of America (CMAA).

Financial data The stipend is $5,000. Funds are disbursed directly to the student's university.

Duration 1 year.

Number awarded 1 each year.

Deadline April of each year.

[247]
FRANK GILBERT MEMORIAL SCHOLARSHIP

South Carolina Professional Association for Access and Equity
Attn: Financial Secretary
P.O. Box 71297
North Charleston, SC 29415
(843) 670-4890   E-mail: anderson4569@bellsouth.net
Web: www.scpaae.org/#!scholarships/c11tv

Summary To provide financial assistance to Native American and other undergraduate students at colleges and universities in South Carolina who are recognized as underrepresented minorities on their campus and have been involved in public service.

Eligibility This program is open to residents of any state who have completed at least 12 semester hours at a college or university in South Carolina. Applicants must be recognized as an underrepresented ethnic minority on their campus. They must have a GPA of 3.5 or higher. Along with their application, they must submit 1) a personal letter on their public service, academic and career goals, honors and awards, leadership skills and organization participation, community service, and a statement of why they would like to receive this scholarship; and 2) a paragraph defining access and equity and describing how they can assist in achieving access and

equity within South Carolina. Financial need is not considered in the selection process.

Financial data The stipend is $1,500.

Duration 1 year.

Number awarded 1 or more each year.

Deadline February of each year.

[248]
FRANK J. CAVERLY SCHOLARSHIP

Inter Tribal Council of Arizona, Inc.
Attn: Kathy Davis
2214 North Central Avenue, Suite 100
Phoenix, AZ 85004
(602) 258-4822   Fax: (602) 258-4825
E-mail: info@itcaonline.com
Web: www.itcaonline.com/?page_id=168

Summary To provide financial assistance for college to American Indians.

Eligibility This program is open to American Indians who are members of a federally- or state-recognized tribe and high school graduates or equivalent. Applicants must be enrolled or planning to enroll at a college, university, junior college, or recognized vocational/technical school. They must have a GPA of 3.0 or higher and an educational objective that will benefit tribal communities, directly or indirectly. Along with their application, they must submit a 2-page essay that includes their achievements, activities, educational goals, and career goals for service to the Indian community.

Financial data Awards depend on need and are intended to provide partial payment of costs of tuition, books, and fees; room and board may also be considered in some cases.

Duration 1 academic term; may be renewed 1 additional term, provided the recipient remains in good academic standing.

Number awarded Varies each year.

Deadline Applications are reviewed on a quarterly basis.

[249]
FRANK W. HILL MEMORIAL SCHOLARSHIP

Bristol Bay Native Corporation
Attn: BBNC Education Foundation
111 West 16th Avenue, Suite 400
Anchorage, AK 99501-6299
(907) 278-3602   Toll Free: (800) 426-3602
Fax: (907) 265-7886   E-mail: bbncef@bbnc.net
Web: www.bbnc.net

Summary To provide financial assistance to shareholders of Bristol Bay Native Corporation (BBNC) who are currently working on an undergraduate or graduate degree in education at a college in any state.

Eligibility This program is open to BBNC shareholders who are enrolled full time as a junior, senior, or graduate student at a college or university in any state and working on a degree in education. Applicants must have a GPA of 2.5 or higher and be able to demonstrate financial need. Along with their application, they must submit an essay on how they became interested in their proposed field of study, any special circumstances they want to be considered, and their desire to work in the region or for a BBNC subsidiary company. Selection is based on the essay (30%), cumulative GPA (40%), financial need (20%), a resume (5%), and letters of recommendation (5%).

Financial data The stipend is $1,000.

Duration 1 year.

Additional information The BBNC is 1 of 13 Alaska Native Regional Corporations created under the Alaska Native Claims Settlement Act of 1971. This program began in 2012.

Number awarded 1 or more each year.

Deadline April of each year.

[250]
FRED L. HATCH MEMORIAL TEACHER EDUCATION SCHOLARSHIP

Sault Tribe of Chippewa Indians
Attn: Higher Education Department
523 Ashmun Street
Sault Ste. Marie, MI 49783
(906) 635-6050, ext. 26312   Toll Free: (800) 793-0660
Fax: (906) 635-7785   E-mail: BMacArthur@saulttribe.net
Web: www.saulttribe.com

Summary To provide financial assistance to members of the Sault Tribe who are enrolled in a teacher education program at a college in Michigan.

Eligibility This program is open to members of the Sault Tribe who are college juniors or higher and are one-quarter Indian blood quantum or more. Applicants must be enrolled full time in a teacher education program at an accredited Michigan 4-year public college or university. They must have a cumulative GPA of 3.0 or higher. Along with their application, they must submit an essay of 1,000 to 2,000 words on a topic that changes annually but relates to their Indian heritage.

Financial data The stipend is $1,000 per year.

Duration 1 year; may be renewed.

Number awarded 1 each year.

Deadline May of each year.

[251]
FREEPORT-MCMORAN SCHOLARSHIP PROGRAM

Phoenix Indian Center, Inc.
4520 North Central Avenue, Suite 250
Phoenix, AZ 85012
(602) 264-6768   Fax: (602) 274-7486
E-mail: fmscholarshp@phxindcenter.org
Web: www.phxindcenter.org

Summary To provide financial assistance to members of designated Indian tribes in Arizona who are interested in attending college in the state to major in designated fields.

Eligibility This program is open to enrolled members of the following tribes: Hualapai, San Carlos Apache, Tohono O'odham, or White Mountain Apache. They must be enrolled or planning to enroll full time as incoming freshmen, sophomores, or juniors at a community college or 4-year public university in Arizona. In the selection process, first preference is given to students whose major is a field of engineering related to minerals (e.g., chemical, environmental, geological, metallurgical, or mining); second preference is given to students with majors in business or business-related fields (e.g., accounting, economics, finance, mathematics), occupational

safety, environmental sustainability, or natural sciences (e.g., chemistry, physics). Applicants must have a GPA of 2.5 or higher. Along with their application, they must submit an essay of 300 to 500 words on 1) their motivations for attending college; 2) some of their personal, educational, and professional goals; and 3) some successes, accomplishments, obstacles, or challenges they have overcome in life.

Financial data The stipend is $2,500 per semester at 4-year universities or $1,250 per semester at community colleges.

Duration 1 semester; may be renewed, provided the recipient maintains good academic standing and a GPA of 2.5 or higher.

Additional information This program is funded by the Freeport-McMoran Foundation and administered by the Phoenix Indian Center. .

Number awarded 25 to 40 each year.

Deadline May of each year.

[252]
FRIENDS OF HUBBELL SCHOLARSHIPS

Friends of Hubbell Trading Post National Historic Site, Inc.
Attn: Scholarship Committee
4111 South La Corta Drive
Tempe, AZ 85282
E-mail: chairman@friendsofhubbell.org
Web: www.friendsofhubbell.org/Scholarships.htm

Summary To provide financial assistance to members of the Hopi and Navajo Nations who are attending college in the Four Corners Region.

Eligibility This program is open to enrolled members of the Hopi and Navajo Nations who are attending a 4-year college or university in the Four Corners Region of Arizona, New Mexico, Colorado, and Utah. Applicants must have a GPA of 3.0 or higher and be entering their junior or senior year of college. They must have a declared major or be in a special degree program. Along with their application, they must submit information on their financial status and an essay on their educational goals, career plans, and how those relate to the Navajo or Hopi Nation.

Financial data Recently, stipends were $2,500.

Duration 1 year.

Number awarded Varies each year; recently, 10 were awarded.

Deadline June of each year.

[253]
GABE STEPETIN SCHOLARSHIP AWARD

The Aleut Corporation
Attn: Aleut Foundation
703 West Tudor Road, Suite 102
Anchorage, AK 99503-6650
(907) 646-1929   Toll Free: (800) 232-4882
Fax: (907) 646-1949   E-mail: taf@thealeutfoundation.org
Web: www.thealeutfoundation.org

Summary To provide financial assistance to Native Alaskans who are shareholders of The Aleut Corporation or their descendants and working on a degree in business at a school in any state.

Eligibility This program is open to Native Alaskans who are original enrollees or descendants of original enrollees of

The Aleut Corporation (TAC). Applicants must have completed at least 1 year of a bachelor's, 2- or 4-year vocational, or master's degree in business at a school in any state. They must be enrolled full time and have a GPA of 3.0 or higher. Along with their application, they must include a letter of intent, up to 500 words in length, that describes their educational goals and objectives and their expected graduation date.

Financial data A stipend is awarded (amount not specified).

Duration 1 year.

Additional information The Aleut Corporation is 1 of 13 Alaska Native Regional Corporations created under the Alaska Native Claims Settlement Act of 1971.

Number awarded 1 each year.

Deadline June of each year.

[254]
GARRETT A. MORGAN TRANSPORTATION ACHIEVEMENT SCHOLARSHIP

Conference of Minority Transportation Officials-Michigan
  Chapter
Attn: President
P.O. Box 32439
Detroit, MI 48232
(269) 491-7279   E-mail: averyk@michigan.gov
Web: www.comtomichigan.org/scholarships.html

Summary To provide financial assistance to Native American and other minority high school seniors in Michigan who plan to attend college in any state to major in a transportation-related field.

Eligibility This program is open to seniors graduating from high schools in Michigan who are members of minority groups. Applicants must be planning to attend an accredited college, university, or vocational/technical institute and major in the field of transportation or a transportation-related discipline. They must have a GPA of 2.5 or higher. U.S. citizenship or legal resident status is required.

Financial data The stipend ranges from $500 to $3,000. Funds are paid directly to the student.

Duration 1 year.

Number awarded 1 or more each year.

Deadline April of each year.

[255]
GATES MILLENNIUM SCHOLARS PROGRAM

Bill and Melinda Gates Foundation
P.O. Box 10500
Fairfax, VA 22031-8044
Toll Free: (877) 690-GMSP   Fax: (703) 205-2079
Web: www.gmsp.org

Summary To provide financial assistance to outstanding low-income minority students, particularly those interested in majoring in specific fields in college.

Eligibility This program is open to African Americans, Alaska Natives, American Indians, Hispanic Americans, and Asian Pacific Islander Americans who are graduating high school seniors with a GPA of 3.3 or higher. Principals, teachers, guidance counselors, tribal higher education representatives, and other professional educators are invited to nominate students with outstanding academic qualifications, par-

ticularly those likely to succeed in the fields of computer science, education, engineering, library science, mathematics, public health, or science. Nominees should have significant financial need and have demonstrated leadership abilities through participation in community service, extracurricular, or other activities. U.S. citizenship, nationality, or permanent resident status is required. Nominees must be planning to enter an accredited college or university as a full-time, degree-seeking freshman in the following fall.

Financial data The program covers the cost of tuition, fees, books, and living expenses not paid for by grants and scholarships already committed as part of the recipient's financial aid package.

Duration 4 years or the completion of the undergraduate degree, if the recipient maintains at least a 3.0 GPA.

Additional information This program, established in 1999, is funded by the Bill and Melinda Gates Foundation and administered by the United Negro College Fund with support from the American Indian Graduate Center, the Hispanic Scholarship Fund, and the Asian & Pacific Islander American Scholarship Fund.

Number awarded 1,000 new scholarships are awarded each year.

Deadline January of each year.

[256]
GATEWAYS TO THE LABORATORY PROGRAM

Cornell University
Attn: Weill Cornell/Rockefeller/Sloan-Kettering Tri-
  Institutional MD-PhD Program
Gateways to the Laboratory Program
1300 York Avenue, Room C-103
New York, NY 10065-4805
(212) 746-6023   Fax: (212) 746-8678
E-mail: mdphd@med.cornell.edu
Web: weill.cornell.edu/mdphd/summerprogram

Summary To provide Native American and other underrepresented minority and disadvantaged college freshmen and sophomores with an opportunity to participate in a summer research internship in New York City through the Tri-Institutional MD-PhD Program of Weill Cornell Medical College, Rockefeller University, and Sloan-Kettering Institute.

Eligibility This program is open to college freshmen and sophomores who are defined by the National Institutes of Health (NIH) as in need of special recruitment and retention, i.e., members of racial and ethnic groups underrepresented in health-related sciences (American Indians or Alaska Natives, Blacks or African Americans, Hispanics or Latinos, and Native Hawaiians or Other Pacific Islanders), persons with disabilities, and individuals from disadvantaged backgrounds (low-income or from a rural or inner-city environment). Applicants must be interested in continuing on to a combined M.D./Ph.D. program following completion of their undergraduate degree. They should have a GPA of 3.0 or higher and have completed a college level calculus class. Along with their application, they must submit an essay summarizing their laboratory experience, research interests, and goals. U.S. citizenship or permanent resident status is required.

Financial data Students receive a stipend of $4,300 and reimbursement of travel expenses. At the end of the summer, 1 family member receives airfare and hotel accommodations to come to New York for the final presentations.

Duration 10 weeks, during the summer.

Additional information Interns work independently on a research project at Weill Cornell Medical College, Rockefeller University, or Memorial Sloan-Kettering Cancer Center, all located across the street from each other on the Upper East Side of New York City.

Number awarded 15 each year.

Deadline January of each year.

[257]
GCI/UUI SCHOLARSHIPS

United Utilities, Inc.
Attn: Scholarship Committee
5450 A Street
Anchorage, AK 99518
(907) 273-5214   Toll Free: (800) 478-2020, ext. 5214
Fax: (907) 273-5325   E-mail: tamp@uui-alaska.com
Web: www.uui-alaska.com

Summary To provide financial assistance to residents of selected Native communities in Alaska who are interested in attending college in any state.

Eligibility This program is open to high school seniors and graduates who live in a Native Alaska community where United Utilities, Inc. or an affiliate (United-KUC or Yukon Telephone) provide communications services. Applicants must be enrolled or planning to enroll full or part time at a college, university, or vocational/trade school in any state. They must have a GPA of 2.0 or higher. Along with their application, they must submit a current transcript with GPA, the name of the college they plan to attend, estimated cost of education for 1 year, and a 350-word essay describing their educational and career goals, their plans upon graduation, why they are interested in this scholarship program, and their intended field of study.

Financial data The stipend is $2,000.

Duration 1 year.

Additional information United Utilities, Inc. is currently owned by GCI. Among the communities it serves are Lower Kuskokwim School District, Lower Yukon School District, Bering Straits School District, Kashunamiut School, and St. Mary's School District.

Number awarded Approximately 150 each year.

Deadline April of each year.

[258]
GENERATION GOOGLE SCHOLARSHIPS FOR CURRENT UNIVERSITY STUDENTS

Google Inc.
Attn: Scholarships
1600 Amphitheatre Parkway
Mountain View, CA 94043-8303
(650) 253-0000   Fax: (650) 253-0001
E-mail: generationgoogle@google.com
Web: www.google.com

Summary To provide financial assistance to Native Americans and members of other underrepresented groups enrolled as undergraduate or graduate students in a computer-related field.

Eligibility This program is open to students enrolled as full-time undergraduate or graduate students at a college or university in the United States or Canada. Applicants must be members of a group underrepresented in computer science: African Americans, Hispanics, American Indians, or Filipinos/Native Hawaiians/Pacific Islanders. They must be working on a degree in computer science, computer engineering, or a closely-related field. Selection is based on academic achievement, leadership, and passion for computer science and technology.

Financial data The stipend is $10,000 per year for U.S. students or $C5,000 for Canadian students.

Duration 1 year; may be renewed.

Additional information Recipients are also invited to attend Google's Computer Science Summer Institute at Mountain View, California, Seattle, Washington, or Cambridge, Massachusetts in the summer.

Number awarded Varies each year.

Deadline February of each year.

[259]
GENERATION GOOGLE SCHOLARSHIPS FOR HIGH SCHOOL SENIORS

Google Inc.
Attn: Scholarships
1600 Amphitheatre Parkway
Mountain View, CA 94043-8303
(650) 253-0000   Fax: (650) 253-0001
E-mail: generationgoogle@google.com
Web: www.google.com

Summary To provide financial assistance to Native Americans and members of other underrepresented groups planning to work on a bachelor's degree in a computer-related field.

Eligibility This program is open to high school seniors planning to enroll full time at a college or university in the United States or Canada. Applicants must be members of a group underrepresented in computer science: African Americans, Hispanics, American Indians, Filipinos/Native Hawaiians/Pacific Islanders, women, or people with a disability. They must be interested in working on a bachelor's degree in computer science, computer engineering, or a closely-related field. Selection is based on academic achievement, leadership, and passion for computer science and technology.

Financial data The stipend is $10,000 per year for U.S. students or $C5,000 for Canadian students.

Duration 1 year; may be renewed for up to 3 additional years or until graduation, whichever comes first.

Additional information Recipients are required to attend Google's Computer Science Summer Institute at Mountain View, California, Seattle, Washington, or Cambridge, Massachusetts in the summer.

Number awarded Varies each year.

Deadline February of each year.

[260]
GEOCORPS AMERICA DIVERSITY INTERNSHIPS

Geological Society of America
Attn: Program Officer, GeoCorps America
3300 Penrose Place
P.O. Box 9140
Boulder, CO 80301-9140
(303) 357-1025   Toll Free: (800) 472-1988, ext. 1025
Fax: (303) 357-1070   E-mail: mdawson@geosociety.org
Web: rock.geosociety.org

Summary   To provide work experience at national parks to student members of the Geological Society of America (GSA) who are Native Americans or members of other underrepresented groups.

Eligibility   This program is open to all GSA members, but applications are especially encouraged from groups historically underrepresented in the sciences (African Americans, American Indians, Alaska Natives, Hispanics, Native Hawaiians, other Pacific Islanders, and persons with disabilities). Applicants must be interested in a short-term work experience in facilities of the U.S. government. Geoscience knowledge and skills are a significant requirement for most positions, but students from diverse disciplines (e.g., chemistry, physics, engineering, mathematics, computer science, ecology, hydrology, meteorology, the social sciences, and the humanities) are also invited to apply. Activities involve research; interpretation and education; inventory and monitoring; or mapping, surveying, and GIS. Prior interns are not eligible. U.S. citizenship or possession of a proper visa is required.

Financial data   Each internship provides a $2,750 stipend. Also provided are free housing or a housing allowance of $1,500 to $2,000.

Duration   3 months during the spring, summer, fall, or winter.

Additional information   This program is offered by the GSA in partnership with the National Park Service, the U.S. Forest Service, and the Bureau of Land Management.

Number awarded   Varies each year.

Deadline   March of each year for spring or summer positions; June of each year for fall or winter positions.

[261]
GEOCORPS AMERICAN INDIAN INTERNSHIPS

Geological Society of America
Attn: Program Officer, GeoCorps America
3300 Penrose Place
P.O. Box 9140
Boulder, CO 80301-9140
(303) 357-1025   Toll Free: (800) 472-1988, ext. 1025
Fax: (303) 357-1070   E-mail: mdawson@geosociety.org
Web: rock.geosociety.org

Summary   To provide work experience in national parks to American Indians and Native Alaskans who are student members of the Geological Society of America (GSA).

Eligibility   This program is open to all GSA members, but applications are especially encouraged from American Indians, Alaska Natives, and persons with a strong connection to an American Indian tribe or community. Applicants must be interested in a short-term work experience in facilities of the U.S. government. Geoscience knowledge and skills are a significant requirement for most positions, but students from

diverse disciplines (e.g., chemistry, physics, engineering, mathematics, computer science, ecology, hydrology, meteorology, the social sciences, and the humanities) are also invited to apply. Activities involve research; interpretation and education; inventory and monitoring; or mapping, surveying, and GIS. Prior interns are not eligible. U.S. citizenship or permanent resident status is required.

Financial data   Each internship provides a $2,750 stipend. A travel allowance of $500 (or $1,000 for positions in Alaska) and free housing or a housing allowance of $1,500 to $2,000 are also provided.

Duration   3 months during the spring, summer, fall, or winter.

Additional information   This program is offered by the GSA in partnership with the National Park Service.

Number awarded   1 or more each year.

Deadline   March of each year for spring or summer positions; June of each year for fall or winter positions.

[262]
GEOLOGICAL SOCIETY OF AMERICA MINORITY STUDENT SCHOLARSHIP PROGRAM

Geological Society of America
Attn: Program Officer-Grants, Awards and Recognition
3300 Penrose Place
P.O. Box 9140
Boulder, CO 80301-9140
(303) 357-1060   Toll Free: (888) 443-4472, ext. 1060
Fax: (303) 357-1070   E-mail: awards@geosociety.org
Web: www.geosociety.org

Summary   To provide financial assistance to Native American and other minority undergraduate student members of the Geological Society of America (GSA) working on a degree in geoscience.

Eligibility   This program is open to GSA members who are U.S. citizens and members of a minority group working on an undergraduate degree. Applicants must have taken at least 2 introductory geoscience courses and be enrolled in additional geoscience courses for the upcoming academic year. Selection is based on the scientific merits of the proposal, the capability of the investigator, and the reasonableness of the budget.

Financial data   The stipend is $1,500. Funds may be used to pay college fees, purchase text books, or attend GSA field courses or conferences. Winners also receive meeting registration for the GSA annual meeting where the awards are presented and a complimentary GSA membership for the following year.

Duration   1 year.

Additional information   This program is sponsored by ExxonMobil.

Number awarded   6 each year: 1 in each GSA geographic section.

Deadline   January of each year.

[263]
GEORGE CAMPBELL, JR. FELLOWSHIP IN ENGINEERING

National Action Council for Minorities in Engineering
Attn: Director, Scholarships and University Relations
440 Hamilton Avenue, Suite 302
White Plains, NY 10601-1813
(914) 539-4316   Fax: (914) 539-4032
E-mail: scholars@nacme.org
Web: www.nacme.org/scholarships

Summary   To provide financial assistance to Native American and other underrepresented minority college sophomores majoring in engineering or related fields.

Eligibility   This program is open to African American, Latino, and American Indian college sophomores who have a GPA of 3.0 or higher and have demonstrated academic excellence, leadership skills, and a commitment to science and engineering as a career. Applicants must be enrolled full time at an ABET-accredited engineering program. Fields of study include all areas of engineering as well as computer science, materials science, mathematics, operations research, or physics.

Financial data   The stipend is $5,000 per year. Funds are sent directly to the recipient's university.

Duration   Up to 3 years.

Number awarded   1 each year.

Deadline   April of each year.

[264]
GEORGE K. NOLAN TRIBAL JUDICIAL SCHOLARSHIP

Sault Tribe of Chippewa Indians
Attn: Higher Education Department
523 Ashmun Street
Sault Ste. Marie, MI 49783
(906) 635-6050, ext. 26312   Toll Free: (800) 793-0660
Fax: (906) 635-7785   E-mail: BMacArthur@saulttribe.net
Web: www.saulttribe.com

Summary   To provide financial assistance to members of the Sault Tribe of Chippewa Indians who are working on an undergraduate or graduate degree in a field related to law.

Eligibility   This program is open to members of the Sault Tribe who are attending a 2- or 4-year college or university as a full-time sophomore or higher. Applicants must be working on an undergraduate or graduate degree in law enforcement, legal studies, political science, public administration, or tribal law. Along with their application, they must submit an essay of 1,000 to 2,000 words on a topic that changes annually but relates to their Indian heritage.

Financial data   The stipend is $1,000.

Duration   1 year.

Number awarded   1 each year.

Deadline   May of each year.

[265]
GERALDINE MEMMO SCHOLARSHIP

Seneca Diabetes Foundation
Attn: Secretary/Treasurer
P.O. Box 309
Irving, NY 14081
(716) 532-4900   E-mail: white@sni.org
Web: www.senecadiabetesfoundation.org/scholarships

Summary   To provide financial assistance to members of the Seneca Nation who are interested in attending college to prepare for a career in the health or human services professions and have also demonstrated an interest in Seneca and Native American history.

Eligibility   This program is open to members of the Seneca Nation who are interested in attending college to assist the Seneca people, especially in regard to the fight against diabetes, by working on a degree in health or social services. Applicants must be able to demonstrate an interest in Seneca and Native American history. Along with their application, they must submit brief statements on 1) the professional, community, or cultural services and activities in which they have participated; 2) how this scholarship would help further their education; 3) their goals or plan for using their experience to benefit the Seneca Nation and its people; and 4) how their interest in Seneca and Native American history came about, how they research the subject, how they have applied their knowledge, and the most interesting aspect to them of Seneca and Native American heritage. In the selection process, primary consideration is given to financial need, but involvement in community and cultural activities, interest in research on Seneca and Native American history and heritage, and desire to improve the quality of life for the Seneca people are also considered.

Financial data   The stipend is $5,000.

Duration   1 year.

Number awarded   1 each year.

Deadline   August of each year.

[266]
GILA RIVER INDIAN COMMUNITY HIGHER EDUCATION PROGRAM

Gila River Indian Community
Attn: Student Services Department
555 B Street
P.O. Box 97
Sacaton, AZ 85147
(520) 562-3316   Fax: (520) 562-2924
E-mail: Jennifer.Hinton@gric.nsn.us
Web: www.mygilariver.com/gricted/studentservices.html

Summary   To provide financial assistance for college to members of the Gila River Indian Community.

Eligibility   This program is open to enrolled members of the Gila River Indian Community who have a high school diploma or GED. Applicants must be attending or planning to attend an accredited college or university in any state to earn a degree, diploma, or certificate in any field. Along with their application, they must submit transcripts, their Certificate of Indian Blood (CIB), documentation of financial need, and a 200-word essay on their educational goals and future plans.

Financial data   A stipend is awarded (amount not specified).

Duration 1 year; may be renewed.

Number awarded Varies each year.

Deadline June of each year for fall semester; November of each year for spring semester; April of each year for summer semester.

[267]
GLENN GODFREY MEMORIAL SCHOLARSHIP

Koniag Incorporated
Attn: Koniag Education Foundation
4241 B Street, Suite 303B
Anchorage, AK 99503
(907) 562-9093   Toll Free: (888) 562-9093
Fax: (907) 562-9023
E-mail: scholarships@koniageducation.org
Web: www.koniageducation.org/scholarships/glenn-godfrey

Summary To provide financial assistance to Alaska Natives who are Koniag Incorporated shareholders or descendants and have demonstrated leadership and plans to attend college in any state.

Eligibility This program is open to college sophomores, juniors, and seniors who are Alaska Native shareholders of Koniag Incorporated or descendants of those original enrollees. Applicants must be enrolled or planning to enroll full time at an accredited college, university, or vocational school in any state. They must have a GPA of 2.5 or higher and be able to demonstrate leadership in school, community, athletics, church, or Native culture activities. Along with their application, they must submit a 300-word essay about their personal and family history, community involvement, volunteer activities, and educational and life goals. Financial need is not considered in the selection process.

Financial data The stipend is $5,000. Funds are sent directly to the recipient's school and may be used for tuition, fees, books, and on-campus room and meals.

Duration 1 year; may be renewed up to 2 additional years, provided the recipient maintains a GPA of 2.5 or higher and participates in school, community, or church activities.

Additional information Koniag Incorporated is 1 of 13 Alaska Native Regional Corporations created under the Alaska Native Claims Settlement Act of 1971.

Number awarded 1 each year.

Deadline May of each year.

[268]
GO RED MULTICULTURAL SCHOLARSHIP FUND

American Heart Association
Attn: Go Red for Women
7272 Greenville Avenue
Dallas, TX 75231-4596
Toll Free: (800) AHA-USA1
E-mail: GoRedScholarship@heart.org
Web: www.goredforwomen.org

Summary To provide financial assistance to Native American women and others from from multicultural backgrounds who are preparing for a career in a field of health care.

Eligibility This program is open to women who are currently enrolled at an accredited college, university, health care institution, or program and have a GPA of 3.0 or higher. Applicants must be U.S. citizens or permanent residents of Hispanic, African American, Asian/Pacific Islander, Native American, or other minority origin. They must be working on an undergraduate or graduate degree as preparation for a career as a nurse, physician, or allied health care worker. Selection is based on community involvement, a personal essay, transcripts, and 2 letters of recommendation.

Financial data The stipend is $2,500.

Duration 1 year.

Additional information This program, which began in 2012, is supported by Macy's.

Number awarded 16 each year.

Deadline December of each year.

[269]
GOLDMAN SACHS SCHOLARSHIP FOR EXCELLENCE

Goldman Sachs
Attn: Human Capital Management
200 West Street, 25th Floor
New York, NY 10282
E-mail: Iris.Birungi@gs.com
Web: www.goldmansachs.com

Summary To provide financial assistance and work experience to Native American and other underrepresented minority students preparing for a career in the financial services industry.

Eligibility This program is open to undergraduate students of Black, Latino, or Native American heritage. Applicants must be entering their sophomore or junior year and have a GPA of 3.4 or higher. Students with all majors and disciplines are encouraged to apply, but they must be able to demonstrate an interest in the financial services industry. Along with their application, they must submit 2 essays on the following topics: 1) the business principle of the sponsoring firm that resonates most with them personally, professionally or academically, and how they have exemplified this principle through their experiences; and 2) how they will embody the business principle they selected throughout their summer internship and as a campus ambassador of the firm. Selection is based on academic achievement, interest in the financial services industry, community involvement, and demonstrated leadership and teamwork capabilities.

Financial data Sophomores receive a stipend of $10,000, a summer internship at Goldman Sachs, an opportunity to receive a second award upon successful completion of the internship, and an offer to return for a second summer internship. Juniors receive a stipend of $15,000 and a summer internship at Goldman Sachs.

Duration Up to 2 years.

Additional information This program was initiated in 1994 when it served only students at 4 designated Historically Black Colleges and Universities: Florida A&M University, Howard University, Morehouse College, and Spelman College. It has since been expanded to serve underrepresented minority students in all states.

Number awarded 1 or more each year.

Deadline December of each year.

[270]
GORDON STAFFORD SCHOLARSHIP IN ARCHITECTURE

Stafford King Wiese Architects
Attn: Scholarship Selection Committee
622 20th Street
Sacramento, CA 95811
(916) 930-5900   Fax: (916) 290-0100
E-mail: info@skwaia.com
Web: www.skwarchitects.com/about/scholarship

Summary   To provide financial assistance to Native Americans and members of other minority groups from California interested in studying architecture at a college in any state.

Eligibility   This program is open to California residents currently enrolled at accredited schools of architecture in any state as first-year new or first-year transfer students and working on a bachelor's or 5-year master's degree. Applicants must be able to demonstrate minority status (defined as Black, Hispanic, Native American, Pacific Asian, or Asian Indian). They must submit a 500-word statement expressing their desire to prepare for a career in architecture. Finalists are interviewed and must travel to Sacramento, California at their own expense for the interview.

Financial data   The stipend is $3,000 per year. That includes $1,500 deposited in the recipient's school account and $1,500 paid to the recipient directly.

Duration   1 year; may be renewed up to 4 additional years.

Additional information   This program began in 1995.

Number awarded   Up to 5 each year.

Deadline   June of each year.

[271]
GRAND PORTAGE TRIBAL SCHOLARSHIP PROGRAM

Grand Portage Reservation Tribal Council
Attn: Education Director
P.O. Box 428
Grand Portage, MN 55605
(218) 475-2812   Fax: (218) 475-2284

Summary   To provide financial assistance for undergraduate or graduate study to Grand Portage Reservation Chippewa Tribe members in Minnesota.

Eligibility   This program is open to enrolled members of the Grand Portage Reservation of Chippewa who are residents of Minnesota. Applicants must be enrolled or planning to enroll at an accredited college, university, or vocational school in Minnesota at least three-quarter time as an undergraduate or half time as a graduate student They must be able to demonstrate financial need.

Financial data   The amount of the award is based on the need of the recipient.

Duration   1 year; may be renewed for a total of 10 semesters or 15 quarters to complete a 4-year degree program if recipients maintain full-time enrollment and a GPA of 2.0 or higher. Adjustments are considered for part-time and/or graduate study.

Number awarded   Varies each year.

Deadline   At least 2 weeks before school starts.

[272]
GRAND TRAVERSE BAND ADULT VOCATIONAL TRAINING GRANTS

Grand Traverse Band of Ottawa and Chippewa Indians
Attn: Higher Education Specialist
845 Business Park Drive
Traverse City, MI 49686
(231) 534-7760   Toll Free: (866) 534-7760
Fax: (231) 534-7773
E-mail: melissa.alberts@gtbindians.com
Web: www.gtbindians.org/higher_education.asp

Summary   To provide financial assistance to members of the Grand Traverse Band (GTB) of Ottawa and Chippewa Indians who are interested in attending a vocational/technical institute in Michigan.

Eligibility   This program is open to enrolled GTB members who are working on or planning to work on licensing or certification in a vocational field. Applicants must be able to document financial need. They must be interested in attending an accredited training facility in Michigan. Along with their application, they must submit a personal statement on how they plan to serve their Indian community after they have successfully completed their course of study.

Financial data   Stipends are $5 per clock hour, to a maximum of $7,200 per year. Recipients are also entitled to a grant of up to $500 per year for licensing fees, certifications, and state board fees.

Duration   Students must be able to complete their programs within 3 years.

Number awarded   Varies each year.

Deadline   Deadline not specified.

[273]
GRAND TRAVERSE BAND HIGHER EDUCATION GRANTS

Grand Traverse Band of Ottawa and Chippewa Indians
Attn: Higher Education Specialist
845 Business Park Drive
Traverse City, MI 49686
(231) 534-7760   Toll Free: (866) 534-7760
Fax: (231) 534-7773
E-mail: melissa.alberts@gtbindians.com
Web: www.gtbindians.org/higher_education.asp

Summary   To provide financial assistance to members of the Grand Traverse Band (GTB) of Ottawa and Chippewa Indians who are interested in attending college or graduate school in any state.

Eligibility   This program is open to enrolled GTB members who are working on or planning to work on an associate, bachelor's, master's, or doctoral degree at a public college or university in Michigan. Applicants must be able to document financial need. Along with their application, they must submit a personal statement on how they plan to serve their Indian community after they have successfully completed their course of study.

Financial data   Stipends for associate degree students are $200 per credit hour, to a maximum of $7,200 per year; stipends for bachelor's degree students are $250 per credit hour, to a maximum of $9,000 per year; stipends for graduate students are $600 per credit hour, to a maximum of $10,800 per year.

Duration 1 semester; may be renewed as long as the recipient maintains a GPA of 2.0 or higher. Support is provided for up to 12 credits above the number required for an undergraduate degree or up to 6 credits above the number required for a graduate degree.

Number awarded Varies each year.

Deadline Deadline not specified.

[274]
GREAT LAKES SECTION IFT DIVERSITY SCHOLARSHIP

Institute of Food Technologists-Great Lakes Section
c/o Andrea Kirk, Scholarship Chair
Post Foods, LLC
275 Cliff Street
Battle Creek, MI 49014
E-mail: greatlakesift@gmail.com
Web: www.greatlakesift.org/student-scholarships

Summary To provide financial assistance to Native American and other minority members of the Great Lakes Section of the Institute of Food Technologists (IFT) from any state who are working on an undergraduate or graduate degree related to food technology at a college in Michigan.

Eligibility This program is open to minority residents of any state who are members of the IFT Great Lakes Section (GLS) and working full time on an undergraduate or graduate degree in food science, nutrition, food engineering, food packaging, or related fields at a college or university in Michigan. Applicants must have a GPA of 3.0 or higher and plans for a career in the food industry. Along with their application, they must submit a 1-page personal statement that covers their academic program, future plans and career goals, extracurricular activities (including involvement in community, university, GLS, or national IFT activities), and work experience. Financial need is not considered in the selection process.

Financial data The stipend is $1,000.

Duration 1 year; nonrenewable.

Number awarded 1 each year.

Deadline February of each year.

[275]
H. NOBLE DICK SCHOLARSHIP

Bristol Bay Native Corporation
Attn: BBNC Education Foundation
111 West 16th Avenue, Suite 400
Anchorage, AK 99501-6299
(907) 278-3602   Toll Free: (800) 426-3602
Fax: (907) 265-7886   E-mail: bbncef@bbnc.net
Web: www.bbnc.net

Summary To provide financial assistance to shareholders of Bristol Bay Native Corporation (BBNC) who are currently majoring in business or accounting at a college in any state.

Eligibility This program is open to BBNC shareholders who are enrolled full time as a junior or senior at a college or university in any state and majoring in accounting or business management. Applicants must have a GPA of 2.5 or higher and be able to demonstrate financial need. Along with their application, they must submit an essay on how they became interested in their proposed field of study, any special circumstances they want to be considered, and their desire to work in the region or for a BBNC subsidiary company. Selection is

based on the essay (30%), cumulative GPA (40%), financial need (20%), a resume (5%), and letters of recommendation (5%).

Financial data The stipend is $1,000.

Duration 1 year.

Additional information The BBNC is 1 of 13 Alaska Native Regional Corporations created under the Alaska Native Claims Settlement Act of 1971.

Number awarded 1 or more each year.

Deadline April of each year.

[276]
HANA SCHOLARSHIPS

United Methodist Church
Attn: General Board of Higher Education and Ministry
Office of Loans and Scholarships
1001 19th Avenue South
P.O. Box 340007
Nashville, TN 37203-0007
(615) 340-7342   Fax: (615) 340-7367
E-mail: umscholar@gbhem.org
Web: www.gbhem.org

Summary To provide financial assistance to upper-division and graduate Methodist students who are of Hispanic, Asian, Native American, or Pacific Islander ancestry.

Eligibility This program is open to full-time juniors, seniors, and graduate students at accredited colleges and universities in the United States who have been active, full members of a United Methodist Church (UMC) for at least 3 years prior to applying. Applicants must have at least 1 parent who is Hispanic, Asian, or Native American. They must be able to demonstrate involvement in their Hispanic, Asian, or Native American (HANA) community in the UMC. Selection is based on that involvement, academic ability (GPA of at least 2.85), and financial need. U.S. citizenship or permanent resident status is required.

Financial data Stipends range from $1,000 to $3,000.

Duration 1 year; recipients may reapply.

Number awarded 50 each year.

Deadline February of each year.

[277]
HARVARD SCHOOL OF PUBLIC HEALTH SUMMER INTERNSHIPS IN BIOLOGICAL SCIENCES IN PUBLIC HEALTH

Harvard T.H. Chan School of Public Health
Attn: Summer Program Coordinator
677 Huntington Avenue, SPH2-119
Boston, MA 02115
(617) 432-4397   Fax: (617) 432-0433
E-mail: BPH@hsph.harvard.edu
Web: www.hsph.harvard.edu

Summary To enable Native American and other disadvantaged minority college science students to participate in a summer research internship in biological sciences at Harvard School of Public Health.

Eligibility This program is open to U.S. citizens, nationals, and permanent residents who are 1) members of ethnic groups underrepresented in graduate education (African Americans, Hispanics/Latinos, American Indians, Alaskan Natives, Pacific Islanders, and Native Hawaiians); 2) first-generation college students; and 3) students from an economically disadvantaged background. Applicants must be entering their junior or senior year with a GPA of 3.0 or higher and be interested in preparing for a research career in the biological sciences. They must be interested in participating in a summer research project related to biological science questions that are important to the prevention of disease, especially such public health questions as cancer, infections (malaria, tuberculosis, parasites), lung diseases, common diseases of aging, diabetes, and obesity.

Financial data The program provides a stipend of at least $3,600, a travel allowance of up to $500, and free dormitory housing.

Duration 8 weeks, beginning in mid-June.

Additional information Interns conduct research under the mentorship of Harvard faculty members who are specialists in cancer cell biology, immunology and infectious diseases, molecular and cellular toxicology, environmental health sciences, nutrition, and cardiovascular research. Funding for this program is provided by the National Institutes of Health.

Number awarded Up to 10 each year.

Deadline January of each year.

[278]
HATTIE J. HILLIARD SCHOLARSHIP

Wisconsin Women of Color Network, Inc.
c/o P.E. Kiram
756 North 35th Street, Suite 101
Milwaukee, WI 53208
(414) 899-2329   E-mail: pekiram64@gmail.com

Summary To provide financial assistance to Native American and other women of color from Wisconsin who are interested in studying art at a school in any state.

Eligibility This program is open to residents of Wisconsin who are women of color enrolled or planning to enroll at a college, university, or vocational/technical school in any state. Applicants must be a member of 1 of the following groups: African American, Asian, American Indian, or Hispanic. Their field of study must be art, graphic art, commercial art, or a related area. They must be able to demonstrate financial need. Along with their application, they must submit a 1-page essay on how this scholarship will help them accomplish their educational goal. U.S. citizenship is required.

Financial data A stipend is awarded (amount not specified).

Duration 1 year.

Additional information This program began in 1995.

Number awarded 1 each year.

Deadline May of each year.

[279]
HAWAIIAN CIVIC CLUB OF HONOLULU SCHOLARSHIP

Hawaiian Civic Club of Honolulu
Attn: Scholarship Committee
P.O. Box 1513
Honolulu, HI 96806
E-mail: hcchmotherclub@gmail.com
Web: www.hcchonolulu.org/scholarship-program

Summary To provide financial assistance for undergraduate studies in any state to residents of Hawaii, especially those of Native Hawaiian descent.

Eligibility This program is open to residents of Hawaii who are enrolled or planning to enroll full time at an accredited 2- or 4-year college, university, or vocational school in any state. Applicants must have a GPA of 2.5 or higher. Priority is given to members of the Hawaiian Civic Club of Honolulu and their families; membership in the club is limited to persons of Native Hawaiian descent (descendants of the aboriginal inhabitants of the Hawaiian Islands prior to 1778). The club's founding objectives are to elevate the social status of Hawaiians, elevate the intellectual status of Hawaiians, and increase pride in race heritage and Hawaiian identify. Along with their application, they must submit 750-word essays on 2 of the following topics: 1) an experience in their family or community that impacted at least 1 of the club's funding objectives; 2) the actions in their life that sustain their well-being as a kanaka maoli; or 3) the familial or community influences that will promote self-determination in their life and why. Selection is based on the quality of the essays, academic standing, financial need, and the completeness of the application package.

Financial data The amount of the stipend varies; recently, awards averaged approximately $1,440.

Duration 1 year.

Number awarded Varies each year; recently, 50 of these scholarships, worth $72,000, were awarded.

Deadline April of each year.

[280]
HAWAI'I'S DAUGHTERS GUILD OF CALIFORNIA SCHOLARSHIPS

Hawai'i's Daughters Guild of California
P.O. Box 3305
Gardena, CA 90247
E-mail: HDG.Scholarship@gmail.com
Web: www.hawaiidaughtersguild.webs.com

Summary To provide financial assistance for college or graduate school to women of Polynesian ancestry from California.

Eligibility This program is open to California residents who are women of Polynesian ancestry and graduating high school seniors, full-time undergraduates, or full-time graduate students. Applicants must have a GPA of 3.0 or higher and be able to demonstrate financial need. Along with their application, they must submit transcripts, 3 letters of recommendation, an autobiographical essay, and proof of ancestry. Selection is based on goals as described in the autobiographical essay, academic achievement, extracurricular activities, community service, and financial need.

Financial data A stipend is awarded (amount not specified).

Duration 1 year.

Number awarded Varies each year.

Deadline March of each year.

[281]
HAYNES/HETTING AWARD

Philanthrofund Foundation
Attn: Scholarship Committee
1409 Willow Street, Suite 109
Minneapolis, MN 55403-2241
(612) 870-1806   Toll Free: (800) 435-1402
Fax: (612) 871-6587   E-mail: info@PfundOnline.org
Web: www.pfundonline.org/scholarships.html

Summary To provide funds to African American and Native American Minnesota students who have supported gay, lesbian, bisexual, and transgender (GLBT) activities.

Eligibility This program is open to residents of Minnesota and students attending a Minnesota educational institution who are African American or Native American. Applicants must be self-identified as GLBT or from a GLBT family. They may be attending or planning to attend a trade school, technical college, college, or university (as an undergraduate or graduate student). Selection is based on the applicant's 1) affirmation of GLBT or allied identity; 2) evidence of experience and skills in service and leadership; and 3) evidence of service, leading, and working for change in GLBT communities, including serving as a role model, mentor, and/or adviser.

Financial data The stipend is $5,000. Funds must be used for tuition, books, fees, or dissertation expenses.

Duration 1 year.

Number awarded 1 each year.

Deadline January of each year.

[282]
HEALTH PROFESSIONS PRE-GRADUATE SCHOLARSHIP PROGRAM

Indian Health Service
Attn: Scholarship Program
5600 Fishers Lane
Mail Stop OHR (11E53A)
Rockville, MD 20857
(301) 443-6197   Fax: (301) 443-6048
Web: www.ihs.gov/scholarship/scholarships

Summary To provide financial support to American Indian and Alaska Native students interested in majoring in pre-medicine, pre-podiatry, pre-optometry, or pre-dentistry in college.

Eligibility This program is open to American Indians and Alaska Natives who are members or descendants of members of state- or federally-recognized tribes. Applicants must be high school graduates or the equivalent; have the capacity to complete a health professions course of study; and be enrolled or accepted for enrollment in a baccalaureate degree program to prepare for entry into a school of medicine, podiatry, optometry, or dentistry. They must intend to serve Indian people upon completion of their professional health care education. Priority is given to students entering their junior or senior year; support is provided to freshmen and sophomores only if remaining funds are available. Along with their application, they must submit a brief narrative that includes why they are requesting the scholarship, their career goals, and how those goals will help to meet the health needs of American Indian and Alaska Native people. Selection is based on that narrative (30 points); academic performance (40 points); and faculty, employer, and tribal recommendations (30 points).

Financial data Awards provide a living stipend of at least $1,500 per month for 10 months; a payment directly to the school for tuition and required fees; a lump sum to cover the costs of books, laboratory expenses, and other necessary educational expenses; a payment of $300 for travel expenses; and up to $400 for approved tutorial costs.

Duration Up to 4 years of full-time study or up to 8 years of part-time study.

Number awarded Varies each year.

Deadline February of each year for continuing students; March of each year for new applicants.

[283]
HEALTH PROFESSIONS PREPARATORY SCHOLARSHIP PROGRAM

Indian Health Service
Attn: Scholarship Program
5600 Fishers Lane
Mail Stop OHR (11E53A)
Rockville, MD 20857
(301) 443-6197   Fax: (301) 443-6048
Web: www.ihs.gov/scholarship/scholarships

Summary To provide financial assistance to Native American students who need compensatory or pre-professional education to qualify for enrollment in a health professions school.

Eligibility This program is open to American Indians and Alaska Natives who are members or descendants of members of state- or federally-recognized tribes. Applicants must be high school graduates or the equivalent; have the capacity to complete a health professions course of study; and be enrolled or accepted for enrollment in a compensatory or pre-professional general education course or curriculum. The qualifying fields of study may vary annually, but recently they included pre-nursing (for courses leading to a B.S. degree in nursing), pre-pharmacy (for courses leading to a Pharm.D. degree), pre-social work (for juniors and seniors preparing for an M.S. degree in social work), and pre-clinical psychology (for juniors and seniors). They must intend to serve Indian people upon completion of their professional health care education as a health care provider in the discipline for which they are enrolled at the pregraduate level. Along with their application, they must submit a brief narrative that includes why they are requesting the scholarship, their career goals, and how those goals will help to meet the health needs of American Indian and Alaska Native people. Selection is based on that narrative (30 points); academic performance (40 points); and faculty, employer, and tribal recommendations (30 points).

Financial data Awards provide a living stipend of at least $1,500 per month for 10 months; a payment directly to the school for tuition and required fees; a lump sum to cover the costs of books, laboratory expenses, and other necessary educational expenses; a payment of $300 for travel expenses; and up to $400 for approved tutorial costs.

Duration Up to 2 years of full-time study or up to 4 years of part-time study.

Number awarded Varies each year.

Deadline February of each year for continuing students; March of each year for new applicants.

[284]
HEALTH PROFESSIONS SCHOLARSHIP PROGRAM

Indian Health Service
Attn: Scholarship Program
5600 Fishers Lane
Mail Stop OHR (11E53A)
Rockville, MD 20857
(301) 443-6197   Fax: (301) 443-6048
Web: www.ihs.gov/scholarship/scholarships

Summary To provide loans-for-service to American Indian and Alaska Native students enrolled in health professions and allied health professions programs.

Eligibility This program is open to American Indians and Alaska Natives who are members of federally-recognized tribes. Applicants must be at least high school graduates and enrolled in a full-time study program leading to a degree in a health-related professions school within the United States. Priority is given to upper-division and graduate students. Qualifying fields of study recently included chemical dependency counseling (master's degree), clinical psychology (Ph.D. or Psy.D.), coding specialist (A.A.S.), counseling psychology (Ph.D.), dentistry (D.D.S. or D.M.D.), diagnostic radiology technology (associate or B.S.), environmental engineering (B.S., junior or senior), environmental health/sanitarian (B.S., junior or senior), health records administration (R.H.I.T. or R.H.I.A.), medical technology (B.S., junior or senior), allopathic and osteopathic medicine (M.D. or D.O.), nursing (A.D.N., B.S.N., C.R.N.A., N.P., certified nurse midwife, certified registered nurse anesthetist, geriatric nursing, pediatric nursing, psychiatric and mental health nursing, women's health nursing), optometry (O.D.), pharmacy (Pharm.D.), physician assistant (P.A.C.), physical therapy (M.S. or D.P.T.), podiatry (D.P.M.), public health nutritionist (M.S.), respiratory therapy (B.S.), social work (master's degree with concentration in direct or clinical practice), or ultrasonography (B.S. or certificate). Along with their application, they must submit a brief narrative that includes why they are requesting the scholarship, their career goals, and how those goals will help to meet the health needs of American Indian and Alaska Native people. Selection is based on that narrative (30 points); academic performance (40 points); and faculty, employer, and tribal recommendations (30 points).

Financial data Awards provide a payment directly to the school for tuition and required fees; a stipend for living expenses of at least $1,500 per month for 12 months; a lump sum to cover the costs of books, laboratory expenses, and other necessary educational expenses; a payment of $300 for travel expenses; and up to $400 for approved tutorial costs. Upon completion of their program of study, recipients are required to provide payback service of 1 year for each year of scholarship support at the Indian Health Service, at a tribal health program, at an urban Indian health program, or in private practice in a designated health professional shortage area serving a substantial number of Indians. Recipients who fail to complete their service obligation must repay all funds received (although no interest is charged).

Duration 1 year; may be renewed for up to 3 additional years.

Number awarded Varies each year.

Deadline February of each year for continuing students; March of each year for new applicants.

[285]
HEART OF THE WARRIOR SCHOLARSHIP

Chahta Foundation
Attn: Scholarship Specialist
P.O. Box 1849
Durant, OK 74702
(580) 924-8280, ext. 2546
Toll Free: (800) 522-6170, ext. 2546
Fax: (580) 745-9023
E-mail: scholarship@chahtafoundation.com
Web: www.chahtafoundation.com

Summary To provide financial assistance to Choctaw Indian students who are attending a university in any state and who submit an outstanding essay on the impact of the wars in Iraq and Afghanistan on their lives.

Eligibility This program is open to Choctaw students who are currently enrolled at an accredited college or university in any state. Applicants must submit a 500-word essay on 1) an individual, event, or story from the Iraq or Afghanistan wars that has impacted their life); and 2) how the individual, event, or story may or may not have impacted their decisions on their educational and/or future goals. Selection is based on the essay's content (40%), originality (20%), structure and writing (20%), and grammar and spelling (20%).

Financial data The stipend is $2,000.

Duration 1 year; nonrenewable.

Number awarded 1 each year.

Deadline March of each year.

[286]
HELEN K. AND ARTHUR E. JOHNSON FOUNDATION SCHOLARSHIP

American Indian College Fund
Attn: Scholarship Department
8333 Greenwood Boulevard
Denver, CO 80221
(303) 426-8900   Toll Free: (800) 776-FUND
Fax: (303) 426-1200
E-mail: scholarships@collegefund.org
Web: www.collegefund.org

Summary To provide financial assistance to Native American college students from Colorado who are interested in attending Tribal Colleges and Universities (TCUs) or other colleges or universities in any state.

Eligibility This program is open to American Indians and Alaska Natives who have proof of enrollment or descendancy and are residents of Colorado or members or descendants of the Southern Ute or Ute Mountain tribe. Applicants must be enrolled or planning to enroll full time at an eligible TCU or other college or university in any state. They must have a GPA of 2.0 or higher. Applications are available only online and include required essays on specified topics. U.S. citizenship is required.

Financial data The stipend is $2,600 for students at TCUs or $2,400 for students at other colleges and universities.

Duration 1 year.
Number awarded 1 or more each year.
Deadline May of each year.

[287]
HELEN TRUEHEART COX ART SCHOLARSHIP FOR A NATIVE AMERICAN WOMAN

National League of American Pen Women
1300 17th Street, N.W.
Washington, DC 20036-1973
(202) 785-1997   Fax: (202) 452-8868
E-mail: contact@nlapw.org
Web: www.nlapw.org/grants-and-scholarships

Summary To provide financial assistance to Native American women interested in studying art in college.

Eligibility This program is open to women between 18 and 25 years of age who are members of a Native American tribe. Applicants must be interested in attending a college, university, or trade school in any state and majoring in art. They must submit 3 prints (4 by 6 inches) in any media (e.g., oil, water color, original works on paper, sculpture, acrylic) or 3 prints (8 by 10 inches) of photographic works. Financial need is considered in the selection process.

Financial data The stipend is $1,000.

Duration 1 year.

Additional information A fee of $20 must accompany each application.

Number awarded 1 each even-numbered year.

Deadline October of odd-numbered years.

[288]
HERSHEY COMPANY COLLEGE SCHOLARSHIP

American Indian College Fund
Attn: Scholarship Department
8333 Greenwood Boulevard
Denver, CO 80221
(303) 426-8900   Toll Free: (800) 776-FUND
Fax: (303) 426-1200
E-mail: scholarships@collegefund.org
Web: www.collegefund.org

Summary To provide financial assistance to Native American college students from designated states who are interested in studying business or fields of science, technology, engineering, or mathematics (STEM) at mainstream colleges and universities.

Eligibility This program is open to American Indians and Alaska Natives who have proof of enrollment or descendancy. Applicants must be enrolled or planning to enroll as freshmen, sophomores, juniors, or seniors at a college or university. They must have a GPA of 3.0 or higher and be working on a degree in business or a field of STEM. Priority is given to students who attend college or reside in Illinois, Pennsylvania, Tennessee, or Virginia. Applications are available only online and include required essays on specified topics. U.S. citizenship is required.

Financial data The stipend is $2,500.

Duration 1 year.

Additional information This program is sponsored by the Hershey Company. Recipients are strongly encouraged to apply to that company's internship program.

Number awarded 1 or more each year.
Deadline May of each year.

[289]
HERSHEY COMPANY TRIBAL SCHOLARSHIP

American Indian College Fund
Attn: Scholarship Department
8333 Greenwood Boulevard
Denver, CO 80221
(303) 426-8900   Toll Free: (800) 776-FUND
Fax: (303) 426-1200
E-mail: scholarships@collegefund.org
Web: www.collegefund.org

Summary To provide financial assistance to Native American college students who are interested in studying business or fields of science, technology, engineering, or mathematics (STEM) at Tribal Colleges and Universities (TCUs).

Eligibility This program is open to American Indians and Alaska Natives from any state who have proof of enrollment or descendancy. Applicants must be enrolled or planning to enroll as freshmen, sophomores, juniors, or seniors at an eligible TCU. They must have a GPA of 3.0 or higher and be working on a degree in business or a field of STEM. Applications are available only online and include required essays on specified topics. U.S. citizenship is required.

Financial data The stipend is $1,250.

Duration 1 year.

Additional information This program is sponsored by the Hershey Company. Recipients are strongly encouraged to apply to that company's internship program.

Number awarded 1 or more each year.
Deadline May of each year.

[290]
HIGHER EDUCATION PROGRAM OF THE CHEYENNE RIVER SIOUX TRIBE

Cheyenne River Sioux Tribe
Attn: Education Services Office
2001 Main Street
P.O. Box 590
Eagle Butte, SD 57625
(605) 964-8311   E-mail: dal7882@lakotanetwork.com
Web: www.sioux.org/educational-services-department.html

Summary To provide financial assistance to members of the Cheyenne River Sioux Tribe who are interested in attending college in any state.

Eligibility This program is open to enrolled Cheyenne River Sioux tribal members and other eligible Indian tribal members who reside on the Cheyenne River Reservation. Applicants must be high school graduates or GED recipients and enrolled or planning to enroll full time at a college, university, or vocational/technical school in any state. They must be able to demonstrate financial need. First priority is given to college seniors, then juniors, then sophomores, and then freshmen.

Financial data A stipend is awarded (amount not specified).

Duration 1 year; may be renewed, provided the recipient remains enrolled full time and maintains a GPA of 2.0 or higher.

Additional information Funding for this program is provided by the U.S. Bureau of Indian Affairs (BIA).

Number awarded Varies each year.

Deadline June of each year for the academic year; November of each year for spring semester only; April of each year for summer session.

[291]
HILTON WORLDWIDE TRIBAL COLLEGE HOSPITALITY SCHOLARSHIP

American Indian College Fund
Attn: Scholarship Department
8333 Greenwood Boulevard
Denver, CO 80221
(303) 426-8900   Toll Free: (800) 776-FUND
Fax: (303) 426-1200
E-mail: scholarships@collegefund.org
Web: www.collegefund.org

Summary To provide financial assistance to Native American college students who are interested in studying business or hospitality at designated Tribal Colleges and Universities (TCUs).

Eligibility This program is open to American Indians and Alaska Natives from any state who have proof of enrollment or descendancy. Applicants must be enrolled or planning to enroll as freshmen, sophomores, juniors, or seniors at Blackfeet Community College, Lac Courte Oreilles Ojibwa Community College, or Southwestern Indian Polytechnic Institute. They must have a GPA of 3.0 or higher and be working on a degree in business or hospitality. Applications are available only online and include required essays on specified topics. U.S. citizenship is required.

Financial data The stipend is $1,000.

Duration 1 year.

Additional information This program is sponsored by Hilton Worldwide. Recipients are strongly encouraged to apply for internship openings with that company.

Number awarded 1 or more each year.

Deadline May of each year.

[292]
HNTB SCHOLARSHIP

Conference of Minority Transportation Officials
Attn: National Scholarship Program
100 M Street, S.E., Suite 917
Washington, DC 20003
(202) 506-2917   E-mail: info@comto.org
Web: www.comto.org/page/scholarships

Summary To provide financial assistance to Native American and other minority high school seniors interested in working on a degree in transportation or a related field.

Eligibility This program is open to minority seniors graduating from high school with a GPA of 3.0 or higher. Applicants must have been accepted at an accredited university or technical college with the intent to study transportation or a transportation-related discipline. They must be able to demonstrate leadership skills and activities. Along with their application they must submit a cover letter on their transportation-related career goals and life aspirations. Financial need is not considered in the selection process.

Financial data The stipend is $5,000. Funds are paid directly to the recipient's college or university.

Duration 1 year.

Additional information This program is sponsored by HNTB Corporation.

Number awarded 1 each year.

Deadline April of each year.

[293]
HO-CHUNK NATION HIGHER EDUCATION SCHOLARSHIPS

Ho-Chunk Nation
Attn: Higher Education Division
P.O. Box 667
Black River Falls, WI 54615
(715) 284-4915   Toll Free: (800) 362-4476
Fax: (715) 284-1760
E-mail: higher.education@ho-chunk.com
Web: www.ho-chunknation.com/highered/scholarships.aspx

Summary To provide financial assistance to undergraduate students who are enrolled members of the Ho-Chunk Nation.

Eligibility Applicants must be enrolled members of the Ho-Chunk Nation who have been accepted at an accredited college, university, or vocational college in the United States as an undergraduate student. Applicants must plan to attend a nonprofit institution that is accredited by a regional agency and by the U.S. Department of Education as eligible to receive student financial aid funds. If they are determined by their school's financial aid office to have no financial need, they are eligible to receive no-need grants. If their school determines that they have financial need, they are eligible for need-based grants. Along with their application, they must submit an essay about their educational and career goals and information on financial need.

Financial data No-need grants cover direct costs of tuition, required fees, and books, up to the maximum award of $9,000 per academic year for full-time students or $7,000 per year for part-time students. Need-based grants provide full payment of allowable education-related expenses. Funds are paid directly to the recipient's school.

Duration 1 year; may be renewed for a total of 6 semesters for a technical diploma or 2-year degree or 10 semesters for a bachelor's degree.

Number awarded Varies each year.

Deadline The absolute deadline for applications is the first day of classes.

[294]
HO-CHUNK NATION SUMMER PROGRAM AWARDS

Ho-Chunk Nation
Attn: Higher Education Division
P.O. Box 667
Black River Falls, WI 54615
(715) 284-4915   Toll Free: (800) 362-4476
Fax: (715) 284-1760
E-mail: higher.education@ho-chunk.com
Web: www.ho-chunknation.com/highered/scholarships.aspx

Summary To provide financial assistance to Ho-Chunk undergraduate or graduate students who wish to continue their postsecondary studies during the summer.
Eligibility Applicants must be enrolled members of the Ho-Chunk Nation; have been accepted at an accredited public vocational or technical school, college, or university in the United States in an undergraduate or graduate program; and be interested in attending summer school on a full-time basis.
Financial data This program pays up to $3,500 to undergraduate recipients and up to $9,000 to graduate school recipients. Funds must be used for tuition, fees, or books. Funds are paid directly to the recipient's school.
Duration 1 term for a 1-year degree or certificate, 3 terms for an associate degree, 6 terms for a bachelor's degree, 8 terms for a master's degree, or 10 terms for a doctoral or professional degree.
Additional information Undergraduate recipients must earn a GPA of 2.0 or higher in the summer classes; graduate school recipients must earn 3.0 or higher.
Number awarded Varies each year.
Deadline February of each year.

[295]
HOMER "DEE" WELLS MEMORIAL SCHOLARSHIP

Chickasaw Foundation
2020 Arlington, Suite 4
P.O. Box 1726
Ada, OK 74821-1726
(580) 421-9030 Fax: (580) 421-9031
E-mail: ChickasawFoundation@chickasaw.net
Web: www.chickasawfoundation.org/Scholarships.aspx

Summary To provide financial assistance to members of the Chickasaw Nation who are working on an undergraduate or graduate degree in construction management or engineering.
Eligibility This program is open to members of the Chickasaw Nation who are currently enrolled full time in the second year of an associate degree program, as a junior or senior in an undergraduate program, or as a graduate student. Applicants must be working on a degree in construction management or engineering. They must have a GPA of 3.0 or higher. Along with their application, they must submit high school or college transcripts; 2 letters of recommendation; a copy of their Chickasaw Nation citizenship card; a 2-page list of honors, achievements, awards, club memberships, societies, and civic involvement; and a 1-page essay on their long-term goals and plans for achieving those. Financial need is not considered in the selection process.
Financial data A stipend is awarded (amount not specified).
Duration 1 year.
Number awarded 1 or more each year.
Deadline June of each year.

[296]
HONDA SWE SCHOLARSHIPS

Society of Women Engineers
Attn: Scholarship Selection Committee
203 North LaSalle Street, Suite 1675
Chicago, IL 60601-1269
(312) 596-5223 Toll Free: (877) SWE-INFO
Fax: (312) 644-8557 E-mail: scholarships@swe.org
Web: societyofwomenengineers.swe.org

Summary To provide financial assistance to undergraduate women from designated states, especially Native Americans and members of other underrepresented groups, who are majoring in designated engineering specialties.
Eligibility This program is open to SWE members who are entering their junior or senior year at a 4-year ABET-accredited college or university. Preference is given to members of underrepresented ethnic or racial groups, candidates with disabilities, and veterans. Applicants must be U.S. citizens working full time on a degree in automotive engineering, chemical engineering, computer science, electrical engineering, engineering technology, manufacturing engineering, materials science and engineering, or mechanical engineering. They must be residents of or attending college in Illinois, Indiana, Michigan, Ohio, Pennsylvania, or Wisconsin. Financial need is considered in the selection process.
Financial data The stipend is $1,000.
Duration 1 year.
Additional information This program is sponsored by American Honda Motor Company.
Number awarded 5 each year.
Deadline February of each year.

[297]
HONEYWELL SCHOLARSHIPS

Society of Women Engineers
Attn: Scholarship Selection Committee
203 North LaSalle Street, Suite 1675
Chicago, IL 60601-1269
(312) 596-5223 Toll Free: (877) SWE-INFO
Fax: (312) 644-8557 E-mail: scholarships@swe.org
Web: societyofwomenengineers.swe.org

Summary To provide financial assistance to members of the Society of Women Engineers (SWE) from designated states, especially Native Americans members of other underrepresented groups, interested in studying specified fields of engineering in college.
Eligibility This program is open to SWE members who are rising college sophomores, juniors, or seniors and have a GPA of 3.5 or higher. Applicants must be enrolled full time at an ABET-accredited 4-year college or university and major in computer science or aerospace, automotive, chemical, computer, electrical, industrial, manufacturing, materials, mechanical, or petroleum engineering. They must reside or attend college in Arizona, California, Florida, Indiana, Kansas, Minnesota, New Mexico, Puerto Rico, Texas, or Washington. Preference is given to members of groups underrepresented in computer science and engineering who can demonstrate financial need. U.S. citizenship is required.
Financial data The stipend is $5,000.
Duration 1 year.

Additional information This program is sponsored by Honeywell International Inc.

Number awarded 3 each year.

Deadline February of each year for current college students; May of each year for high school seniors.

[298]
HOPI ADULT VOCATIONAL TRAINING PROGRAM

Hopi Tribe
Attn: Adult Vocational Training Program
P.O. Box 123
Kykotsmovi, AZ 86039
(928) 734-3542   Toll Free: (800) 762-9630
Fax: (928) 734-9575   E-mail: JTorivio@hopi.nsn.us
Web: www.hopi-nsn.gov

Summary To provide financial assistance to members of the Hopi Tribe who are interested in vocational training.

Eligibility This program is open to enrolled members of the Hopi Tribe who are unskilled, unemployed, or underemployed. Applicants must be between 17 and 35 years of age and residing on or near the Hopi Reservation. They must be interested in full-time vocational training at an accredited private or public institution approved by the Hopi Tribe Adult Vocational Training Program to acquire marketable vocational skills.

Financial data A stipend is awarded (amount not specified).

Duration Support is provided until completion of the program.

Number awarded Varies each year.

Deadline Deadline not specified.

[299]
HOPI EDUCATION AWARDS PROGRAM

Hopi Tribe
Attn: Grants and Scholarships Program
P.O. Box 123
Kykotsmovi, AZ 86039
(928) 734-3542   Toll Free: (800) 762-9630
Fax: (928) 734-9575   E-mail: JTorivio@hopi.nsn.us
Web: www.hopi-nsn.gov

Summary To provide financial assistance to needy students of Hopi ancestry who are working on an undergraduate, graduate, or postgraduate degree.

Eligibility This program is open to students who are working full time on an associate, baccalaureate, graduate, or postgraduate degree. Applicants must be enrolled members of the Hopi Tribe and able to demonstrate financial need. Undergraduates must have a GPA of 2.5 or higher and graduate students must have a GPA of 3.0 or higher.

Financial data The maximum grant is $2,500 per semester ($5,000 per year).

Duration 1 semester; may be renewed for up to 10 terms of undergraduate study or up to 5 terms of graduate study, provided the recipient maintains full-time enrollment and a GPA of 2.5 or higher as an undergraduate or 3.0 or higher as a graduate student.

Additional information This grant is awarded as a secondary source of financial aid to eligible students who are also receiving aid from the Bureau of Indian Affairs (BIA) Higher Education program.

Number awarded Varies each year.

Deadline June of each year for fall; October of each year for winter; November of each year for spring.

[300]
HOPI TRIBAL PRIORITY AWARDS

Hopi Tribe
Attn: Grants and Scholarships Program
P.O. Box 123
Kykotsmovi, AZ 86039
(928) 734-3542   Toll Free: (800) 762-9630
Fax: (928) 734-9575   E-mail: JTorivio@hopi.nsn.us
Web: www.hopi-nsn.gov

Summary To provide scholarship/loans to Hopi students who are interested in working on a graduate degree in an area of interest to the Hopi Tribe.

Eligibility This program is open to enrolled members of the Hopi Tribe who are full-time graduate students working on a degree in a subject area that is of priority interest to the Hopi Tribe. Recently, those areas were law, economic development, business/finance, environmental/natural resources, education, or social sciences. Applicants must have a GPA of 3.5 or higher. Along with their application, they must submit personal statements on their reasons for applying for this scholarship, their career goals as related to the Hopi Tribe priorities, and how they intend to apply directly their educational goals to meet the needs of the Hopi People.

Financial data This program provides payment of all tuition and fees, books and supplies, transportation, room and board, and a stipend of $1,500 per month. Recipients must agree to provide 1 year of professional services to the Hopi Tribe or other service agencies that serve the Hopi People for each year funding is awarded.

Duration 1 year; may be renewed, provided the recipient maintains a GPA of 3.5 or higher.

Number awarded Up to 5 each year.

Deadline June of each year.

[301]
HOPI TUITION AND BOOK AWARD

Hopi Tribe
Attn: Grants and Scholarships Program
P.O. Box 123
Kykotsmovi, AZ 86039
(928) 734-3542   Toll Free: (800) 762-9630
Fax: (928) 734-9575   E-mail: JTorivio@hopi.nsn.us
Web: www.hopi-nsn.gov

Summary To provide financial assistance to students of Hopi ancestry who are interested in working on an undergraduate or graduate degree at a college in any state but cannot demonstrate financial need.

Eligibility This program is open to students who are interested in working full or part time on an associate, baccalaureate, graduate, or postgraduate degree. Applicants must be enrolled members of the Hopi Tribe who have no unmet financial need. Undergraduates must have a GPA of 2.5 or higher and graduate students must have a GPA of 3.0 or higher.

Financial data The maximum grant is $2,500 per semester ($5,000 per year).

Duration 1 semester; may be renewed for up to 10 terms of undergraduate study or up to 5 terms of graduate study, provided the recipient maintains full-time enrollment and a GPA of 2.5 or higher as an undergraduate or 3.0 or higher as a graduate student.

Number awarded Varies each year.

Deadline June of each year for fall; October of each year for winter; November of each year for spring.

[302]
HORACE AND SUSIE REVELS CAYTON SCHOLARSHIP

Public Relations Society of America-Puget Sound
  Chapter
Attn: Diane Bevins
1006 Industry Drive
P.O. Box 58530
Seattle, WA 98138-1530
(206) 623-8632   Fax: (206) 575-9255
E-mail: prsascholarship@asi-seattle.net
Web: www.prsapugetsound.org/Page.aspx?nid=73

Summary To provide financial assistance to Native American and other minority upperclassmen from Washington who are interested in preparing for a career in public relations.

Eligibility This program is open to U.S. citizens who are members of minority groups, defined as African Americans, Asian Americans, Hispanic/Latino Americans, Native Americans, and Pacific Islanders. Applicants must be full-time juniors or seniors attending a college in Washington or Washington students (who graduated from a Washington high school or whose parents live in the state year-round) attending college elsewhere. They must have overcome barriers in pursuit of personal or academic goals. Selection is based on academic achievement, financial need, and demonstrated aptitude in public relations and related courses, activities, and/or internships.

Financial data The stipend is $3,500.

Duration 1 year.

Additional information This program began in 1992.

Number awarded 1 each year.

Deadline May of each year.

[303]
HOWARD KECK/WESTMIN ENDOWMENT SCHOLARSHIP FUND

Cook Inlet Region, Inc.
Attn: The CIRI Foundation
3600 San Jeronimo Drive, Suite 256
Anchorage, AK 99508-2870
(907) 793-3575   Toll Free: (800) 764-3382
Fax: (907) 793-3585   E-mail: tcf@thecirifoundation.org
Web: www.thecirifoundation.org/about/donors

Summary To provide financial assistance for undergraduate or graduate studies in any field to Alaska Natives who are original enrollees to Cook Inlet Region, Inc. (CIRI) and their lineal descendants.

Eligibility This program is open to Alaska Native enrollees to CIRI under the Alaska Native Claims Settlement Act (ANCSA) of 1971 and their lineal descendants. There are no Alaska residency requirements or age limitations. Applicants must be accepted or enrolled full time in a 2-year undergraduate, 4-year undergraduate, or graduate degree program. They may be studying in any field but must have a GPA of 2.5

or higher. Along with their application, they must submit a 500-word statement on their educational and career goals and how they are contributing, or planning to contribute, to a positive Alaska Native community. Selection is based on that statement, academic achievement, rigor of course work or degree program, student financial contribution, financial need, grade level, previous work performance, community service, and relationship of degree program to career goals.

Financial data The stipend is $20,000 per year, $10,000 per year, $8,000 per year, or $2,500 per semester, depending on GPA.

Duration 1 semester or 1 year.

Additional information CIRI is 1 of 13 regional corporations established according to the terms of the Alaska Native Claims Settlement Act (ANCSA) of 1971. This fund was established in 1986 by Howard Keck/Westmin Ltd.

Number awarded Varies each year; recently, 5 were awarded.

Deadline May of each year for annual scholarships; May or November of each year for semester scholarships.

[304]
HP ENGINEERING INC SCHOLARSHIP

Cherokee Nation Foundation
800 South Muskogee
Tahlequah, OK 74464
(918) 207-0950   Fax: (918) 207-0951
E-mail: contact@cherokeenationfoundation.org
Web: cherokeenation.academicworks.com

Summary To provide financial assistance to citizens of several Cherokee nations who are enrolled at a college or university in any state and working on an undergraduate or graduate degree in electrical or mechanical engineering.

Eligibility This program is open to citizens of the Cherokee Nation, the United Keetoowah Band, or the Eastern Band of Cherokee Indians. Applicants must be juniors, seniors, or graduate students in an ABET-accredited undergraduate or graduate program in electrical or mechanical engineering. They must agree to spend a 2-day job shadow experience at HP Engineering offices in Tulsa, Oklahoma and Rogers, Arkansas. Along with their application, they must submit a description of their most meaningful achievements and how those relate to their field of study and their future goals. Selection is based on the clarity and presentation of the essay; academic information (including transcripts and ACT scores); school, cultural and community activities; future plans to serve Cherokee people; and financial need.

Financial data The stipend is $1,000.

Duration 1 year.

Additional information This program is sponsored by HP Engineering Inc.

Number awarded 1 or more each year.

Deadline February of each year.

[305]
HYATT HOTELS FUND FOR MINORITY LODGING MANAGEMENT STUDENTS

American Hotel & Lodging Educational Foundation
Attn: Manager of Foundation Programs
1250 I Street, N.W., Suite 1100
Washington, DC 20005-5904
(202) 289-3180   Fax: (202) 289-3199
E-mail: foundation@ahlef.org
Web: www.ahlef.org

Summary   To provide financial assistance to Native American and other minority college students working on a degree in hotel management.

Eligibility   This program is open to students majoring in hospitality management at a 4-year college or university as at least a junior. Applicants must be members of a minority group (African American, Hispanic, American Indian, Alaskan Native, Asian, or Pacific Islander). They must be enrolled full time. Along with their application, they must submit a 500-word essay on their personal background, including when they became interested in the hospitality field, the traits they possess or will need to succeed in the industry, and their plans as related to their educational and career objectives and future goals. Selection is based on industry-related work experience; financial need; academic record and educational qualifications; professional, community, and extracurricular activities; personal attributes, including career goals; the essay; and neatness and completeness of the application. U.S. citizenship or permanent resident status is required.

Financial data   The stipend is $2,000.

Duration   1 year.

Additional information   Funding for this program, established in 1988, is provided by Hyatt Hotels & Resorts.

Number awarded   Varies each year; recently, 18 were awarded. Since this program was established, it has awarded scholarships worth $702,000 to 351 minority students.

Deadline   April of each year.

[306]
IBM TRIBAL COLLEGE SCHOLARSHIP

American Indian College Fund
Attn: Scholarship Department
8333 Greenwood Boulevard
Denver, CO 80221
(303) 426-8900   Toll Free: (800) 776-FUND
Fax: (303) 426-1200
E-mail: scholarships@collegefund.org
Web: www.collegefund.org

Summary   To provide financial assistance to Native American college students who are interested in studying business or fields of science, technology, engineering, or mathematics (STEM) at Tribal Colleges and Universities (TCUs) and are interested in an internship with IBM.

Eligibility   This program is open to American Indians and Alaska Natives from any state who have proof of enrollment or descendancy. Applicants must be enrolled or planning to enroll as freshmen, sophomores, juniors, or seniors at an eligible TCU. They must have a GPA of 3.0 or higher, be working on a degree in business or a field of STEM, have an interest in interning for IBM, and be able to demonstrate leadership and commitment to the American Indian community. Applica-

tions are available only online and include required essays on specified topics. U.S. citizenship is required.

Financial data   The stipend is $2,000.

Duration   1 year.

Additional information   This program is sponsored by IBM.

Number awarded   1 or more each year.

Deadline   May of each year.

[307]
IDA M. POPE MEMORIAL SCHOLARSHIPS

Hawai'i Community Foundation
Attn: Scholarship Department
827 Fort Street Mall
Honolulu, HI 96813
(808) 566-5570   Toll Free: (888) 731-3863
Fax: (808) 521-6286
E-mail: scholarships@hcf-hawaii.org
Web: hcf.scholarships.ngwebsolutions.com

Summary   To provide financial assistance to Native Hawaiian women who are interested in working on an undergraduate or graduate degree in designated fields at a school in any state.

Eligibility   This program is open to female residents of Hawaii who are Native Hawaiian, defined as a descendant of the aboriginal inhabitants of the Hawaiian islands prior to 1778. Applicants must be enrolled full time at a 2- or 4-year college or university in any state and working on an undergraduate or graduate degree in health, science, mathematics, or education (including counseling and social work). They must be able to demonstrate academic achievement (GPA of 3.5 or higher), good moral character, and financial need. Along with their application, they must submit a short statement indicating their reasons for attending college, their planned course of study, their career goals, and what community service means to them.

Financial data   The amounts of the awards depend on the availability of funds and the need of the recipient. Recently, the average value of the scholarships awarded by the foundation was $2,800.

Duration   1 year; may be renewed.

Number awarded   Varies each year; recently, 61 were awarded.

Deadline   February of each year.

[308]
ILLINOIS BROADCASTERS ASSOCIATION MULTICULTURAL INTERNSHIPS

Illinois Broadcasters Association
Attn: MIP Coordinator
200 Missouri Avenue
Carterville, IL 62918
(618) 985-5555   Fax: (618) 985-6070
E-mail: iba@ilba.org
Web: www.ilba.org/careers/internship-program

Summary   To provide funding to Native American and other minority college students in Illinois who are majoring in broadcasting and interested in interning at a radio or television station in the state.

Eligibility   This program is open to currently-enrolled minority students majoring in broadcasting at a college or university in Illinois. Applicants must be interested in a fall, spring, or summer internship at a radio or television station that is a member of the Illinois Broadcasters Association. Along with their application, they must submit 1) a 250-word essay on how they expect to benefit from a grant through this program; and 2) at least 2 letters of recommendation from a broadcasting faculty member or professional familiar with their career potential and 1 other letter. The internship coordinator of the sponsoring organization selects those students nominated by their schools who have the best opportunity to make it in the world of broadcasting and matches them with internship opportunities that would otherwise be unpaid.

Financial data This program provides a grant to pay the living expenses for the interns in the Illinois communities where they are assigned. The amount of the grant depends on the length of the internship.

Duration 16 weeks in the fall and spring terms or 12 weeks in the summer.

Number awarded 12 each year: 4 in each of the 3 terms.

Deadline Deadline not specified.

[309]
ILLINOIS NURSES FOUNDATION CENTENNIAL SCHOLARSHIP

Illinois Nurses Association
Attn: Illinois Nurses Foundation
P.O. Box 636
Manteno, IL 60950
(815) 468-8804   Fax: (773) 304-1419
E-mail: info@ana-illinois.org
Web: www.ana-illinois.org

Summary To provide financial assistance to nursing undergraduate and graduate students who are American Indians or members of other underrepresented groups.

Eligibility This program is open to students working on an associate, bachelor's, or master's degree at an accredited NLNAC or CCNE school of nursing. Applicants must be members of a group underrepresented in nursing (African Americans, Hispanics, American Indians, Asians, and males). Undergraduates must have earned a passing grade in all nursing courses taken to date and have a GPA of 2.85 or higher. Graduate students must have completed at least 12 semester hours of graduate work and have a GPA of 3.0 or higher. All applicants must be willing to 1) act as a spokesperson to other student groups on the value of the scholarship to continuing their nursing education; and 2) be profiled in any media or marketing materials developed by the Illinois Nurses Foundation. Along with their application, they must submit a narrative of 250 to 500 words on how they, as nurses, plan to affect policy at either the state or national level that impacts on nursing or health care generally, or how they believe they will impact the nursing profession in general.

Financial data A stipend is awarded (amount not specified).

Duration 1 year.

Number awarded 1 or more each year.

Deadline March of each year.

[310]
INDIANA INDUSTRY LIAISON GROUP SCHOLARSHIP

Indiana Industry Liaison Group
c/o Candee Chambers, Vice Chair
DirectEmployers Association
9002 North Purdue Road, Suite 100
Indianapolis, IN 46268
(317) 874-9000   Toll Free: (866) 268-6202
E-mail: vchair@indianailg.org
Web: www.indianailg.org

Summary To provide financial assistance to Native American and other students from any state enrolled at colleges and universities in Indiana who have been involved in activities to promote diversity.

Eligibility This program is open to residents of any state currently enrolled at an accredited college or university in Indiana. Applicants must either 1) be enrolled in programs or classes related to diversity/Affirmative Action (AA)/Equal Employment Opportunity (EEO); or 2) have work or volunteer experience with diversity/AA/EEO organizations. Along with their application, they must submit an essay of 400 to 500 words on 1 of the following topics: 1) their personal commitment to diversity/AA/EEO within their community or business; 2) a time or situation in which they were able to establish and/or sustain a commitment to diversity; 3) a time when they have taken a position in favor of affirmative action and/or diversity; or 4) activities in which they have participated within their community that demonstrate their personal commitment to moving the community's diversity agenda forward. Financial need is not considered in the selection process.

Financial data The stipend is $1,000.

Duration 1 year.

Number awarded 1 each year.

Deadline January of each year.

[311]
INFRASTRUCTURE ENGINEERING SCHOLARSHIP

Conference of Minority Transportation Officials
Attn: National Scholarship Program
100 M Street, S.E., Suite 917
Washington, DC 20003
(202) 506-2917   E-mail: info@comto.org
Web: www.comto.org/page/scholarships

Summary To provide financial assistance to Native American and other minority upper-division and graduate students interested in working on a degree in transportation or a related field.

Eligibility This program is open to minority juniors, seniors, and graduate student at an accredited college, university, or vocational/technical school. Applicants must be studying transportation, engineering, planning, or a related discipline. They must have a GPA of 2.5 or higher. Along with their application they must submit a cover letter on their transportation-related career goals and life aspirations. Financial need is not considered in the selection process. Membership in the Conference of Minority Transportation Officials is considered a plus but is not required.

Financial data The stipend is $2,500. Funds are paid directly to the recipient's college or university.

Duration 1 year.

Additional information This program is sponsored by Infrastructure Engineering Inc.

Number awarded 1 each year.

Deadline April of each year.

[312]
INROADS NATIONAL COLLEGE INTERNSHIPS

INROADS, Inc.
10 South Broadway, Suite 300
St. Louis, MO 63102
(314) 241-7488   Fax: (314) 241-9325
E-mail: info@inroads.org
Web: www.inroads.org

Summary To provide an opportunity for Native American and other young people of color to gain work experience in business or industry.

Eligibility This program is open to African Americans, Hispanics, and Native Americans who reside in the areas served by INROADS. Applicants must be interested in preparing for a career in accounting, business, computer sciences, economics. engineering, finance, health care, management information systems, retail store management, or supply chain management. They must be high school seniors or freshmen or sophomores in 4-year colleges and universities and have a GPA of 3.0 or higher. International students may apply if they have appropriate visas.

Financial data Salaries vary, depending upon the specific internship assigned; recently, the range was from $170 to $750 per week.

Duration Up to 4 years.

Additional information INROADS places interns in Fortune 1000 companies, where training focuses on preparing them for corporate and community leadership. The INROADS organization offers internship opportunities through 35 local affiliates in 26 states, Canada, and Mexico.

Number awarded Approximately 2,000 high school and college students are currently working for more than 200 corporate sponsors nationwide.

Deadline March of each year.

[313]
INTERMOUNTAIN SECTION AWWA DIVERSITY SCHOLARSHIP

American Water Works Association-Intermountain
  Section
Attn: Member Services Coordinator
3430 East Danish Road
Sandy, UT 84093
(801) 712-1619, ext. 2   Fax: (801) 487-6699
E-mail: nicoleb@ims-awwa.org
Web: ims-awwa.site-ym.com/group/StudentPO

Summary To provide financial assistance to Native American and other minority undergraduate and graduate students working on a degree in the field of water quality, supply, and treatment at a university in the Intermountain West.

Eligibility This program is open to 1) women; and 2) students who identify as Hispanic or Latino, Black or African American, Native Hawaiian or other Pacific Islander, Asian, or American Indian or Alaska Native. Applicants must be entering or enrolled in an undergraduate or graduate program at a college or university in the Intermountain West (defined to include all or portions of Arizona, Colorado, Idaho, Montana, Nevada, New Mexico, Utah, or Wyoming) that relates to water quality, supply, or treatment. Along with their application, they must submit a 2-page essay on their academic interests and career goals and how those relate to water quality, supply, or treatment. Selection is based on that essay, letters of recommendation, and potential to contribute to the field of water quality, supply, and treatment in the Intermountain West.

Financial data The stipend is $1,000. The winner also receives a 1-year student membership in the Intermountain Section of the American Water Works Association (AWWA).

Duration 1 year; nonrenewable.

Number awarded 1 each year.

Deadline November of each year.

[314]
INTERPUBLIC GROUP SCHOLARSHIP AND INTERNSHIP

New York Women in Communications, Inc.
Attn: NYWICI Foundation
355 Lexington Avenue, 15th Floor
New York, NY 10017-6603
(212) 297-2133   Fax: (212) 370-9047
E-mail: nywicipr@nywici.org
Web: www.nywici.org/foundation/scholarships

Summary To provide financial assistance and work experience to Native American women and those from other ethnically diverse groups who are residents of designated eastern states and enrolled as juniors at a college in any state to prepare for a career in advertising or public relations.

Eligibility This program is open to female residents of New York, New Jersey, Connecticut, or Pennsylvania who are from ethnically diverse groups and currently enrolled as juniors at a college or university in any state. Also eligible are women who reside outside the 4 states but are currently enrolled at a college or university within 1 of the 5 boroughs of New York City. Applicants must be preparing for a career in advertising or public relations and have a GPA of 3.2 or higher. They must be available for a summer internship with Interpublic Group (IPG) in New York City. Along with their application, they must submit a 2-page resume; a personal essay of 300 words on an assigned topic that changes annually; 2 letters of recommendation; and an official transcript. Selection is based on academic record, need, demonstrated leadership, participation in school and community activities, honors and other awards or recognition, work experience, goals and aspirations, and unusual personal and/or family circumstances. U.S. citizenship or permanent status is required.

Financial data The scholarship stipend ranges up to $10,000; the internship is salaried (amount not specified).

Duration 1 year.

Additional information This program is sponsored by IPG, a holding company for a large number of firms in the advertising industry.

Number awarded 2 each year.

Deadline January of each year.

[315]
INTERTRIBAL AGRICULTURE COUNCIL SCHOLARSHIPS

Intertribal Agriculture Council
100 North 27th Street, Suite 500
Billings, MT 59101-2054
(406) 259-3525   Fax: (406) 256-9980
Web: www.indianaglink.com/youth

Summary To provide financial assistance to Native Americans interested in working on a bachelor's degree in fields related to agriculture.

Eligibility This program is open to enrolled members of federally-recognized tribes or Alaska Native corporations. Applicants must be attending or accepted for attendance as a full-time student at an accredited college or university in any state. They must be working on a bachelor's degree in agriculture, agribusiness, agricultural education, agricultural engineering, animal science, environmental management, horticulture, natural resource management, range management, soil science, veterinary medicine, or a related field. Along with their application, they must submit an essay of 500 to 1,000 words on how the use of this scholarship will enhance future management of tribal natural resources.

Financial data The stipend is $1,000 per semester ($2,000 per year).

Duration 1 year; may be renewed until completion of a bachelor's degree, provided the recipient remains enrolled full time and maintains a GPA of 2.0 or higher.

Additional information Awards are presented in each of the following areas represented by an IAC board member: Alaska; Northwest (Idaho, Oregon, Washington); Pacific (California, Nevada); Rocky Mountain (Montana, Wyoming); Navajo (southeastern Utah, northeastern Arizona, southwestern Colorado); Southwest (Colorado, New Mexico, except the Navajo Nation); Western (Arizona, Utah, except the Navajo Nation); Great Plains (Nebraska, North Dakota, South Dakota); eastern Oklahoma; Southern Plains (Kansas, western Oklahoma, Texas); Midwest (Illinois, Iowa, Michigan, Minnesota, Wisconsin); East (all other states).

Number awarded 12 each year: 1 from each of the areas.

Deadline Deadline not specified.

[316]
INTER-TRIBAL COUNCIL OF AT&T EMPLOYEES SCHOLARSHIP PROGRAM

Inter-Tribal Council of AT&T Employees
c/o Margo Bernath
1 AT&T Way, Room 2B207A
Bedminster, NJ 07921
E-mail: membership@icae4nativeamericans.org
Web: www.icae4nativeamericans.org/links.htm

Summary To provide financial assistance for college to Native American students.

Eligibility This program is open to Native Americans who are graduating high school seniors or undergraduates already enrolled full time at an accredited college or university. Applicants must submit a 1,000-word essay on a topic that changes annually but relates to issues of concern to Native Americans; recently, students were invited to write on how they, as a Native American, would use the current technologies to improve the quality of life within their tribal community. Selection is based on scholastic discipline, personal achievement, and community involvement. U.S. citizenship or permanent resident status is required.

Financial data Stipends are $2,000, $1,000, or $500.

Duration 1 year; recipients may reapply.

Number awarded Varies each year; recently, 27 were awarded: 1 at $2,000, 18 at $1,000 and 8 at $500.

Deadline October of each year.

[317]
IOLA M. HENHAWK NURSING SCHOLARSHIP

Seneca Nation of Indians
Attn: Allegany Education Department
P.O. Box 231
Salamanca, NY 14779
(716) 945-1790, ext. 3103   Fax: (716) 945-7170
E-mail: AllganyHEP@sni.org

Summary To provide financial assistance to members of the Seneca Nation of Indians who are interested in studying nursing in college.

Eligibility This program is open to enrolled Seneca Indians interested in preparing for a career in nursing. Both high school seniors and students already enrolled in college are eligible. Applicants must submit a certificate of tribal affiliation, letter of acceptance from the college, transcript, and personal letter describing their need and the proposed use of the funds.

Financial data The stipend is $1,000 per year. Funds are paid directly to the college financial aid office to be used for tuition or such course-related expenses as laboratory fees or books.

Duration 1 year.

Additional information This program began in 1993.

Number awarded 1 or more each year.

Deadline June of each year.

[318]
IRA L. AND MARY L. HARRISON MEMORIAL SCHOLARSHIP

Baptist Convention of New Mexico
Attn: Missions Mobilization Team
5325 Wyoming Boulevard, N.E.
P.O. Box 94485
Albuquerque, NM 87199-4485
(505) 924-2315   Toll Free: (800) 898-8544
Fax: (505) 924-2320   E-mail: cpairett@bcnm.com
Web: www.bcnm.com/scholarships

Summary To provide financial assistance to Native American Southern Baptist students from New Mexico who are attending designated colleges or Baptist seminaries.

Eligibility This program is open to undergraduate and seminary students who are Native American members of churches affiliated with the Baptist Convention of New Mexico. Applicants must have a GPA of 2.0 or higher and be able to demonstrate financial need. Undergraduates must be attending Wayland Baptist University at its main campus in Plainview, Texas or at its New Mexico external campuses in Clovis or Albuquerque. Graduate students must be attending 1 of the 6 Southern Baptist seminaries: Southeastern Baptist Theological Seminary (Wake Forest, North Carolina); Southern Baptist Theological Seminary (Louisville, Kentucky);

Southwestern Baptist Theological Seminary (Fort Worth, Texas); New Orleans Baptist Theological Seminary (New Orleans, Louisiana); Midwestern Baptist Theological Seminary (Kansas City, Missouri); or Golden Gate Baptist Theological Seminary (Mill Valley, California).

Financial data A stipend is awarded (amount not specified).

Duration 1 year; may be renewed.

Number awarded 1 or more each year.

Deadline March, June, August, or December of each year.

[319]
IRENE C. HOWARD MEMORIAL SCHOLARSHIPS

Chickasaw Foundation
2020 Arlington, Suite 4
P.O. Box 1726
Ada, OK 74821-1726
(580) 421-9030   Fax: (580) 421-9031
E-mail: ChickasawFoundation@chickasaw.net
Web: www.chickasawfoundation.org/Scholarships.aspx

Summary To provide financial assistance to members of the Chickasaw Nation who are working on a college degree in specified fields.

Eligibility This program is open to Chickasaw students who are currently enrolled at an accredited institution of higher education as a full-time undergraduate student. Applicants must be majoring in science, liberal arts, or nutrition science. They must have a GPA of 3.5 or higher. Along with their application, they must submit high school or college transcripts; 2 letters of recommendation; a copy of their Chickasaw Nation citizenship card; a 2-page list of honors, achievements, awards, club memberships, societies, and civic involvement; and a 1-page essay on their long-term goals and plans for achieving those. Financial need is not considered in the selection process.

Financial data The stipend recently was $8,000.

Duration 1 year.

Number awarded 1 each year.

Deadline June of each year.

[320]
ITHANA (EDUCATION) SCHOLARSHIP

Chickasaw Foundation
2020 Arlington, Suite 4
P.O. Box 1726
Ada, OK 74821-1726
(580) 421-9030   Fax: (580) 421-9031
E-mail: ChickasawFoundation@chickasaw.net
Web: www.chickasawfoundation.org/Scholarships.aspx

Summary To provide financial assistance to members of the Chickasaw Nation who can demonstrate financial need and are working on an undergraduate or graduate degree in any field.

Eligibility This program is open to members of the Chickasaw Nation who are currently working full-time on an undergraduate or graduate degree in any field. Applicants must be able to demonstrate that they are a leader or contributor to society with a strong Christian character. They must have a GPA of 2.5 or higher. Along with their application, they must submit high school or college transcripts; 2 letters of recommendation; a copy of their Chickasaw Nation citizenship card;

documentation of financial need; a 2-page list of honors, achievements, awards, club memberships, societies, and civic involvement; and a 1-page essay on their long-term goals and plans for achieving those.

Financial data A stipend is awarded (amount not specified).

Duration 1 year.

Number awarded Varies each year; recently, 3 were awarded.

Deadline June of each year.

[321]
IVALU SCHOLARSHIP

Arctic Slope Regional Corporation
Attn: Arctic Education Foundation
P.O. Box 129
Barrow, AK 99723
(907) 852-8633   Toll Free: (800) 770-2772
Fax: (907) 852-2774   E-mail: arcticed@asrc.com
Web: www.arcticed.com

Summary To provide financial assistance to shareholders or descendants of shareholders of the Arctic Slope Regional Corporation (ASRC) who have demonstrated commitment to Inupiaq value and are interested in attending college in any state.

Eligibility This program is open to original shareholders of the ASRC and direct lineal descendants of original ASRC shareholders. Applicants must be attending or planning to attend a college, university, or vocational/technical school in any state. They must have maintained a GPA of 2.0 or higher throughout high school and during college or training (if applicable), and have demonstrated cultural community service commitment through activities, abilities, and efforts that involve the Inupiaq core values (respect for our elders and each other, family and kinship, humility, humor, compassion, knowledge of language, sharing, cooperation, avoidance of conflict, spirituality, hunting traditions, and respect for nature). Along with their application, they must an essay describing their cultural community service commitments and how those have utilized Inupiaq values, their goals in attending college or training, and their plans after completion of college or training. Selection is based on academic performance, demonstrated leadership ability, and community service achievements.

Financial data The award provides for payment of tuition, fees, books, room, and board, to a maximum of $15,000 per year.

Duration Up to 4 years.

Additional information The Arctic Slope Regional Corporation is 1 of 13 Alaska Native Regional Corporations created under the Alaska Native Claims Settlement Act of 1971.

Number awarded 1 each year.

Deadline April of each year.

[322]
J. MICHAEL PRINCE UNDERGRADUATE SCHOLARSHIP

Chahta Foundation
Attn: Scholarship Specialist
P.O. Box 1849
Durant, OK 74702
(580) 924-8280, ext. 2546
Toll Free: (800) 522-6170, ext. 2546
Fax: (580) 745-9023
E-mail: scholarship@chahtafoundation.com
Web: www.chahtafoundation.com

Summary To provide financial assistance to Choctaw tribal members who are working on an undergraduate degree in business or fashion at a school in any state.

Eligibility This program is open to members of the Choctaw nation who are entering their junior year at a college or university in any state. Applicants must be majoring in business or fashion. They must have a GPA of 3.0 or higher. Along with their application, they must submit a resume, transcript, a financial need analysis, and a letter of recommendation.

Financial data The stipend is $1,000.

Duration 1 year.

Additional information This program began in 2014.

Number awarded A selected number are awarded each year.

Deadline March of each year.

[323]
JACOBS ENGINEERING SCHOLARSHIP

Conference of Minority Transportation Officials
Attn: National Scholarship Program
100 M Street, S.E., Suite 917
Washington, DC 20003
(202) 506-2917   E-mail: info@comto.org
Web: www.comto.org/page/scholarships

Summary To provide financial assistance to Native American and other minority upper-division and graduate student members of the Conference of Minority Transportation Officials (COMTO) working on a degree in transportation or a related field.

Eligibility This program is open to minority juniors, seniors, and graduate student who are COMTO members. Applicants must be studying transportation, engineering (civil, construction, or environmental), safety, urban planning, or a related discipline. They must have a GPA of 3.0 or higher. Along with their application they must submit a cover letter on their transportation-related career goals and life aspirations. Financial need is not considered in the selection process. Membership in the Conference of Minority Transportation Officials is considered a plus but is not required.

Financial data The stipend is $2,500. Funds are paid directly to the recipient's college or university.

Duration 1 year.

Additional information This program is sponsored by Jacobs Engineering Group.

Number awarded 1 or more each year.

Deadline April of each year.

[324]
JACOBS ENGINEERING TRANSPORTATION SCHOLARSHIP

Conference of Minority Transportation Officials
Attn: National Scholarship Program
100 M Street, S.E., Suite 917
Washington, DC 20003
(202) 506-2917   E-mail: info@comto.org
Web: www.comto.org/page/scholarships

Summary To provide financial assistance to Native American and other minority upper-division and graduate student members of the Conference of Minority Transportation Officials (COMTO) and family of members working on a degree in transportation or a related field.

Eligibility This program is open to minority juniors, seniors, and graduate student who are COMTO members or whose parents, guardians, or grandparents are members. Applicants must be studying transportation, engineering (civil, construction, or environmental), safety, urban planning, or a related discipline. They must have a GPA of 3.0 or higher. Along with their application they must submit a cover letter on their transportation-related career goals and life aspirations. Financial need is not considered in the selection process.

Financial data The stipend is $2,500. Funds are paid directly to the recipient's college or university.

Duration 1 year.

Additional information This program is sponsored by Jacobs Engineering Group.

Number awarded 1 or more each year.

Deadline April of each year.

[325]
JAMES AND CAROLEE CUNDIFF GRANTS

Chickasaw Foundation
2020 Arlington, Suite 4
P.O. Box 1726
Ada, OK 74821-1726
(580) 421-9030   Fax: (580) 421-9031
E-mail: ChickasawFoundation@chickasaw.net
Web: www.chickasawfoundation.org/Scholarships.aspx

Summary To provide financial assistance to members of the Chickasaw Nation who can demonstrate financial need and are working on an undergraduate or graduate degree in any field.

Eligibility This program is open to members of the Chickasaw Nation who are currently enrolled as full-time undergraduate or graduate students at a 2- or 4-year college or university in any state. Applicants must be able to demonstrate that they are a leader or contributor to society with a strong Christian character. Along with their application, they must submit high school or college transcripts; 2 letters of recommendation; a copy of their Chickasaw Nation citizenship card; documentation of financial need; a 2-page list of honors, achievements, awards, club memberships, societies, and civic involvement; and a 1-page essay on their long-term goals and plans for achieving those.

Financial data A stipend is awarded (amount not specified).

Duration 1 year.

Number awarded 10 each year.

Deadline June of each year.

[326]
JAMES B. MORRIS SCHOLARSHIPS

James B. Morris Scholarship Fund
Attn: Scholarship Selection Committee
P.O. Box 12145
Des Moines, IA 50312
(515) 864-0922
Web: www.morrisscholarship.org

Summary   To provide financial assistance to Native American and other minority undergraduate, graduate, and law students from Iowa.

Eligibility   This program is open to minority students (African Americans, Asian/Pacific Islanders, Hispanics, or Native Americans) who are interested in working on an undergraduate or graduate degree. Applicants must be either Iowa residents attending a college or university anywhere in the United States or non-Iowa residents who are attending a college or university in Iowa. Along with their application, they must submit an essay of 250 to 500 words on why they are applying for this scholarship, activities or organizations in which they are involved, and their future plans. Selection is based on the essay, academic achievement (GPA of 2.5 or higher), community service, and financial need. U.S. citizenship is required.

Financial data   The stipend ranges from $1,000 to $2,500 per year.

Duration   1 year; may be renewed.

Additional information   This fund was established in 1978 in honor of the J.B. Morris family, who founded the Iowa branch of the National Association for the Advancement of Colored People and published the *Iowa Bystander* newspaper. The program includes the Ann Chapman Scholarships, the Vincent Chapman, Sr. Scholarships, the Catherine Williams Scholarships, and the Brittany Hall Memorial Scholarships. Support for additional scholarships is provided by EMC Insurance Group and Wells Fargo Bank.

Number awarded   Varies each year; recently, 22 were awarded.

Deadline   February of each year.

[327]
JAMES ECHOLS SCHOLARSHIP

California Association for Health, Physical Education, Recreation and Dance
Attn: Chair, Scholarship Committee
1501 El Camino Avenue, Suite 3
Sacramento, CA 95815-2748
(916) 922-3596   Toll Free: (800) 499-3596 (within CA)
Fax: (916) 922-0133   E-mail: reception@cahperd.org
Web: www.cahperd.org

Summary   To provide financial assistance to Native American and other minority student members of the California Association for Health, Physical Education, Recreation and Dance.

Eligibility   This program is open to California residents who have been members of the association for at least 60 days and are attending a 2- or 4-year college or university in the state. Applicants must be undergraduate or graduate students working on a degree in health education, physical education, recreation, or dance and have completed at least 60 semester hours of college work. Selection is based on scholastic proficiency (a GPA of 3.0 or higher); leadership ability in school, community, and professional activities; and personal qualities of enthusiasm, cooperativeness, responsibility, initiative, and ability to work with others. This scholarship is awarded to the highest-ranked minority (Asian, African American, Latino, or Native American) applicant.

Financial data   The stipend is $1,000.

Duration   1 year.

Number awarded   1 each year.

Deadline   November of each year.

[328]
JAMES MICHAEL "MIKE" DUNN MEMORIAL SCHOLARSHIP

Chickasaw Foundation
2020 Arlington, Suite 4
P.O. Box 1726
Ada, OK 74821-1726
(580) 421-9030   Fax: (580) 421-9031
E-mail: ChickasawFoundation@chickasaw.net
Web: www.chickasawfoundation.org/Scholarships.aspx

Summary   To provide financial assistance for college or vocational school to members of the Chickasaw Nation.

Eligibility   This program is open to Chickasaw students who are currently enrolled as a full-time undergraduate or vocational/technical student. Applicants may be majoring in any field, but they must have a GPA of 2.5 or higher. Along with their application, they must submit high school or college transcripts; 2 letters of recommendation; a copy of their Chickasaw Nation citizenship card; a 2-page list of honors, achievements, awards, club memberships, societies, and civic involvement; and a 1-page essay on their long-term goals and plans for achieving those. Financial need is not considered in the selection process.

Financial data   A stipend is awarded (amount not specified).

Duration   1 year.

Number awarded   1 each year.

Deadline   June of each year.

[329]
JANET SHALEY JAMES MEMORIAL SCHOLARSHIP

Chickasaw Foundation
2020 Arlington, Suite 4
P.O. Box 1726
Ada, OK 74821-1726
(580) 421-9030   Fax: (580) 421-9031
E-mail: ChickasawFoundation@chickasaw.net
Web: www.chickasawfoundation.org/Scholarships.aspx

Summary   To provide financial assistance for college to members of the Chickasaw Nation.

Eligibility   This program is open to Chickasaw students who are currently enrolled as a full-time undergraduate student. Applicants may be majoring in any field, but they must have a GPA of 3.0 or higher. Along with their application, they must submit high school or college transcripts; 2 letters of recommendation; a copy of their Chickasaw Nation citizenship card; a 2-page list of honors, achievements, awards, club memberships, societies, and civic involvement; and a 1-page essay on their long-term goals and plans for achieving those. Financial need is not considered in the selection process.

Financial data A stipend is awarded (amount not specified).

Duration 1 year.

Number awarded 1 each year.

Deadline June of each year.

[330]
JANIE HARDWICK BENSON MEMORIAL SCHOLARSHIP

Chickasaw Foundation
2020 Arlington, Suite 4
P.O. Box 1726
Ada, OK 74821-1726
(580) 421-9030   Fax: (580) 421-9031
E-mail: ChickasawFoundation@chickasaw.net
Web: www.chickasawfoundation.org/Scholarships.aspx

Summary To provide financial assistance to members of the Chickasaw Nation who are working or an undergraduate or graduate degree in nursing.

Eligibility This program is open to Chickasaw students who are currently working full time on an undergraduate or graduate degree in nursing (A.D.N., B.S.N., or M.S.N.). Applicants must have a GPA of 2.75 or higher. Along with their application, they must submit high school or college transcripts; 2 letters of recommendation; a copy of their Chickasaw Nation citizenship card; a 2-page list of honors, achievements, awards, club memberships, societies, and civic involvement; and a 1-page essay on their long-term goals and plans for achieving those. Financial need is not considered in the selection process.

Financial data A stipend is awarded (amount not specified).

Duration 1 year.

Number awarded 1 each year.

Deadline June of each year.

[331]
JEAN CHARLEY-CALL NURSING SCHOLARSHIPS

Hopi Tribe
Attn: Grants and Scholarships Program
P.O. Box 123
Kykotsmovi, AZ 86039
(928) 734-3542   Toll Free: (800) 762-9630
Fax: (928) 734-9575   E-mail: JTorivio@hopi.nsn.us
Web: www.hopi-nsn.gov

Summary To provide financial assistance to Hopi students who are interested in working on a degree in nursing.

Eligibility This program is open to enrolled members of the Hopi Tribe who are high school graduates or GED recipients and enrolled or planning to enroll full time in a nursing program at an accredited college or university in any state. Applicants must have a GPA of 2.5 or higher and have applied for all federal, state, and institutional aid. Along with their application, they must submit a 1-page essay on their inspiration for choosing the nursing field and their plans upon completion of their program.

Financial data The stipend is $1,000.

Duration 1 year.

Number awarded 2 each year.

Deadline August of each year.

[332]
JESS GREEN MEMORIAL LAW SCHOLARSHIP

Chickasaw Foundation
2020 Arlington, Suite 4
P.O. Box 1726
Ada, OK 74821-1726
(580) 421-9030   Fax: (580) 421-9031
E-mail: ChickasawFoundation@chickasaw.net
Web: www.chickasawfoundation.org/Scholarships.aspx

Summary To provide financial assistance to members of the Chickasaw Nation who are interested in working on an undergraduate degree in a field related to law.

Eligibility This program is open to Chickasaw students who are currently enrolled as juniors or seniors at an accredited 4-year college or university as a full-time pre-law student. Applicants must be working on a degree in law, pre-law, legal studies, paralegal, or any major associated with law or a bachelor's degree obtained with the intention of pursuing a law degree. They must have a GPA of 3.0 or higher. Along with their application, they must submit high school or college transcripts; 2 letters of recommendation; a copy of their Chickasaw Nation citizenship card; a 2-page list of honors, achievements, awards, club memberships, societies, and civic involvement; and a 1-page essay on their long-term goals and plans for achieving those. Financial need is not considered in the selection process.

Financial data A stipend is awarded (amount not specified).

Duration 1 year.

Number awarded 1 each year.

Deadline June of each year.

[333]
JEWELL HILTON BONNER SCHOLARSHIP

Navy League of the United States
Attn: Scholarships
2300 Wilson Boulevard, Suite 200
Arlington, VA 22201-5424
(703) 528-1775   Toll Free: (800) 356-5760
Fax: (703) 528-2333
E-mail: scholarships@navyleague.org
Web: navyleaguefoundation.awardspring.com

Summary To provide financial assistance for college to dependent children of sea service personnel, especially Native Americans.

Eligibility This program is open to U.S. citizens who are 1) dependents or direct descendants of an active, Reserve, retired, or honorably discharged member of the U.S. sea service (including the Navy, Marine Corps, Coast Guard, or Merchant Marines); or 2) current active members of the Naval Sea Cadet Corps. Applicants must be entering their freshman year at an accredited college or university. They must have a GPA of 3.0 or higher. Along with their application, they must submit transcripts, 2 letters of recommendation, SAT/ACT scores, documentation of financial need, proof of qualifying sea service duty, and a 1-page personal statement on why they should be considered for this scholarship. Preference is given to applicants of Native American heritage.

Financial data The stipend is $2,500 per year.

Duration 4 years, provided the recipient maintains a GPA of 3.0 or higher.

Number awarded 1 each year.

Deadline February of each year.

[334]
JIMMY A. YOUNG MEMORIAL EDUCATION RECOGNITION AWARD

American Association for Respiratory Care
Attn: American Respiratory Care Foundation
9425 North MacArthur Boulevard, Suite 100
Irving, TX 75063-4706
(972) 243-2272   Fax: (972) 484-2720
E-mail: info@arcfoundation.org
Web: www.arcfoundation.org

Summary To provide financial assistance to college students, especially Native Americans and other minorities, interested in becoming respiratory therapists.

Eligibility Candidates must be enrolled in an accredited respiratory therapy program, have completed at least 1 semester/quarter of the program, and have a GPA of 3.0 or higher. Preference is given to nominees of minority origin. Applications must include 6 copies of an original referenced paper on some aspect of respiratory care and letters of recommendation. The foundation prefers that the candidates be nominated by a school or program, but any student may initiate a request for sponsorship by a school (in order that a deserving candidate is not denied the opportunity to compete simply because the school does not initiate the application).

Financial data The stipend is $1,000. The award also provides airfare, 1 night's lodging, and registration for the association's international congress.

Duration 1 year.

Number awarded 1 each year.

Deadline June of each year.

[335]
JOAN HAMILTON MEMORIAL SCHOLARSHIP

American Civil Liberties Union of Alaska
1057 West Fireweed Lane, Suite 207
Anchorage, AK 99503
(907) 258-0044   Fax: (907) 258-0288
E-mail: scholarship@acluak.org
Web: www.acluak.org/pages/joan-hamilton-scholarship.html

Summary To provide financial assistance to Alaska residents who are interested in attending college or law school in any state to prepare for a career serving Alaska Natives and/or residents of rural Alaska.

Eligibility This program is open to residents of Alaska who are enrolled in a postsecondary educational or vocational program in any state. Applicants must be preparing for a career related to the law (e.g., lawyer, VSO, *guardian ad litem,* paralegal) in order to become advocates of Alaska Native rights and "defend the constitutional rights and civil liberties of the peoples of rural Alaska." Along with their application, they must submit an essay of 2 to 4 pages that includes what they consider important challenges facing Alaska Native communities and/or residents of rural Alaska, the actions they have taken and plan to take to support Native Alaska communities and/or residents of rural Alaska, how a law-

related career would enable them to address the challenges facing Alaska Native communities and/or residents of rural Alaska, and how they envision their education to allow them to further the work of this program's sponsor and namesake.

Financial data The stipend is $2,500 per year.

Duration 1 year; may be renewed.

Number awarded 1 each year.

Deadline March of each year.

[336]
JOHANNA DREW CLUNEY FUND

Hawai'i Community Foundation
Attn: Scholarship Department
827 Fort Street Mall
Honolulu, HI 96813
(808) 566-5570   Toll Free: (888) 731-3863
Fax: (808) 521-6286
E-mail: scholarships@hcf-hawaii.org
Web: hcf.scholarships.ngwebsolutions.com

Summary To provide financial assistance to residents of Hawaii, especially those of Native ancestry, who are interested in enrolling in a vocational training program in the state.

Eligibility This program is open to residents of Hawaii who are enrolled or planning to enroll full time at a vocational college or institution that is part of the University of Hawaii community college system. Applicants must be able to demonstrate academic achievement (GPA of 2.0 or higher), good moral character, and financial need. Along with their application, they must submit a short statement indicating their reasons for attending college, their planned course of study, their career goals, and what community service means to them. Preference is given to students of Hawaiian ancestry.

Financial data The amounts of the awards depend on the availability of funds and the need of the recipient. Recently, the average value of the scholarships awarded by the foundation was $2,800.

Duration 1 year.

Additional information This program began in 2006.

Number awarded Varies each year; recently, 35 were awarded.

Deadline February of each year.

[337]
JOHN BENNETT HERRINGTON SCHOLARSHIP

Chickasaw Foundation
2020 Arlington, Suite 4
P.O. Box 1726
Ada, OK 74821-1726
(580) 421-9030   Fax: (580) 421-9031
E-mail: ChickasawFoundation@chickasaw.net
Web: www.chickasawfoundation.org/Scholarships.aspx

Summary To provide financial assistance to members of the Chickasaw Nation who are preparing for a career in space aeronautics.

Eligibility This program is open to Chickasaw students who are currently enrolled full time at an accredited institution of higher education. Applicants must be classified as juniors or seniors at a 4-year college and have a GPA of 2.5 or higher. They must be majoring in chemistry, engineering, geophysics, mathematics, natural science, physics, or a related field. Their career interest must relate to space aeronautics. Along with their application, they must submit high school or college transcripts; 2 letters of recommendation; a copy of their Chickasaw Nation citizenship card; a 2-page list of honors, achievements, awards, club memberships, societies, and civic involvement; and a 1-page essay on their long-term goals and plans for achieving those. Financial need is not considered in the selection process.

Financial data The stipend recently was $10,000 per year.

Duration Up to 2 years.

Number awarded 1 each year.

Deadline June or February of each year.

[338]
JOHN DEERE SCHOLARSHIP FOR FEMALE AND MINORITY STUDENTS

American Welding Society
Attn: AWS Foundation, Inc.
8669 N.W. 36th Street, Suite 130
Doral, FL 33166-6672
(305) 443-9353   Toll Free: (800) 443-9353, ext. 250
Fax: (305) 443-7559   E-mail: nprado-pulido@aws.org
Web: www.aws.org/foundation/page/john-deere-scholarship

Summary To provide financial assistance to Native American and other minority undergraduate students, especially those from designated states, who are working on a degree in welding engineering or welding engineering technology at a university in any state.

Eligibility This award is available to U.S. citizens who are women or members of minority groups. Preference is given to residents of Illinois, Iowa, Kansas Minnesota, Missouri, Nebraska, North Dakota, South Dakota, or Wisconsin. Applicants must have completed at least 1 semester of full-time study in a 4-year undergraduate program of welding engineering, welding engineering technology, or mechanical or manufacturing engineering with a welding emphasis. They must have a GPA of 3.0 or higher. Along with their application, they must submit a statement of unmet financial need (although financial need is not required to apply), transcripts, 2 letters of recommendation, and a personal statement that provides their personal objectives and values, their career objectives with a statement of why they want to prepare for a career in welding, participation and leadership in campus and outside organizations, participation in American Welding Society (AWS) student and section activities, and general background information.

Financial data The stipend is $2,500.

Duration 1 year; nonrenewable.

Additional information This program is sponsored by John Deere.

Number awarded 1 each year.

Deadline February of each year.

[339]
JOHN N. COLBERG SCHOLARSHIP FUND

Cook Inlet Region, Inc.
Attn: The CIRI Foundation
3600 San Jeronimo Drive, Suite 256
Anchorage, AK 99508-2870
(907) 793-3575   Toll Free: (800) 764-3382
Fax: (907) 793-3585   E-mail: tcf@thecirifoundation.org
Web: www.thecirifoundation.org/about/donors

Summary To provide financial assistance for undergraduate or graduate studies leading to a career in the law to Alaska Natives who are original enrollees to Cook Inlet Region, Inc. (CIRI) and their lineal descendants.

Eligibility This program is open to Alaska Native enrollees to CIRI under the Alaska Native Claims Settlement Act (ANCSA) of 1971 and their lineal descendants. There are no Alaska residency requirements or age limitations. Applicants must be accepted or enrolled full time in a 4-year undergraduate or a graduate degree program. Preference is given to students who are working on a degree leading to the study of law and have a GPA of 2.5 or higher. Along with their application, they must submit a 500-word statement on their educational and career goals and how they are contributing, or planning to contribute, to a positive Alaska Native community. Selection is based on that statement, academic achievement, rigor of course work or degree program, student financial contribution, financial need, grade level, previous work performance, community service, and relationship of degree program to career goals.

Financial data The stipend is $2,500 per semester.

Duration 1 semester or 1 year.

Additional information CIRI is 1 of 13 regional corporations established according to the terms of the Alaska Native Claims Settlement Act (ANCSA) of 1971. This program began in 2003.

Number awarded 1 or more each year.

Deadline May of each year.

[340]
JOHN SHURR JOURNALISM AWARD

Cherokee Nation Foundation
800 South Muskogee
Tahlequah, OK 74464
(918) 207-0950   Fax: (918) 207-0951
E-mail: contact@cherokeenationfoundation.org
Web: cherokeenation.academicworks.com

Summary To provide financial assistance to citizens of the Cherokee Nation who are enrolled at a college or university in any state and working on an undergraduate or graduate degree in journalism.

Eligibility This program is open to citizens of the Cherokee Nation who are currently enrolled in an undergraduate or graduate program in journalism or mass communications at a college or university in any state. Applicants must have a GPA of 3.0 or higher. They are not required to reside in the Cherokee Nation area. Along with their application, they must submit writing samples and an essay describing their journalism career goals. Selection is based on the clarity and presentation of the essay; academic information (including transcripts and ACT scores); school, cultural and community activities; future plans to serve Cherokee people; and financial need.

Financial data The stipend is $1,000 per semester ($2,000 per year).

Duration 1 year. Renewal for the second semester requires the recipient to earn a GPA of 3.0 or higher in the first semester.

Additional information Recipients are expected to apply for an 8-week paid internship with *The Cherokee Phoenix* newspaper in Tahlequah, Oklahoma during the summer following their scholarship year.

Number awarded 1 each year.
Deadline January of each year.

[341]
JOHN SWAGERTY II AWARD FOR AGRICULTURE STUDENTS

Pueblo of Jemez
Attn: Education Services Center
5117 Highway 4
P.O. Box 100
Jemez Pueblo, NM 87024
(575) 834-9102   Toll Free: (888) 834-3936
Fax: (575) 834-7900
E-mail: higher_ed@jemezpueblo.org
Web: www.jemezpueblo.org

Summary To provide financial assistance to Jemez Pueblo students who are interested in studying an agriculture-related field at a school in any state.

Eligibility This program is open to Jemez Pueblo students working on or planning to work on a degree at an accredited institution of higher education in any state as a full-time student. Applicants must have a GPA of 2.0 or higher and be majoring in agricultural economics, agricultural engineering, agricultural mechanization, agronomy and crop science, animal sciences, fishing and fisheries sciences and management, greenhouse operations and management, natural resources, plant physiology, plant sciences, rural sociology, or soil sciences. They must be at least one quarter Jemez and recognized by the Jemez Pueblo census office (a Certificate of Indian Blood must be provided). Along with their application, they must submit 2 letters of recommendation, a copy of their letter of acceptance from the institution they are attending or planning to attend, a personal statement on why they chose their specific agricultural program and what they will do with the degree or certificate they receive, and an official transcript from the high school or college they last attended.

Financial data The stipend depends on the need of the recipient.

Duration 1 semester; may be renewed if the recipient remains enrolled full time with a GPA of 2.5 or higher.

Number awarded Varies each year.

Deadline January of each year.

[342]
JONES-BOWMAN LEADERSHIP AWARD

Cherokee Preservation Foundation
71 John Crowe Hill Road
P.O. Box 504
Cherokee, NC 28719
(828) 497-5550   Toll Free: (888) 886-8524
Fax: (828) 497-8929   E-mail: info@cpfdn.org
Web: www.cherokeepreservation.org

Summary To provide financial assistance to members of the Eastern Band of Cherokee Indians who are interested in working on an undergraduate degree in order to enhance their leadership skills.

Eligibility This program is open to enrolled members of the Eastern Band of Cherokee Indians who are enrolled or planning to enroll in formal undergraduate study. Applicants must be interested in working on a 2- or 4-year degree while they also develop an individually designed plan of leadership learning, Cherokee culture, and community service. The plan should be developed in coordination with an assigned mentor and may include attendance at national or international conferences or training workshops, summer community service or experiential learning activities, domestic or foreign travel, academic enrichment and tutoring programs, or leadership development training. Selection is based primarily on leadership potential; financial need is not considered.

Financial data The stipend is approximately $4,000 per year.

Duration 1 year; may be renewed up to 3 additional years, provided the recipient maintains a GPA of 2.5 or higher for the first year and 3.0 or higher for subsequent years.

Additional information This program began in 2007. Fellows are expected to contribute at least 40 hours of unpaid community service each year. For the first 2 years, that service should be performed in the Cherokee Preservation Foundation's 7-county service area.

Number awarded Varies each year; recently, 6 were awarded.

Deadline May of each year.

[343]
JOSEPH K. LUMSDEN MEMORIAL SCHOLARSHIP

Sault Tribe of Chippewa Indians
Attn: Higher Education Department
523 Ashmun Street
Sault Ste. Marie, MI 49783
(906) 635-6050, ext. 26312   Toll Free: (800) 793-0660
Fax: (906) 635-7785   E-mail: BMacArthur@saulttribe.net
Web: www.saulttribe.com

Summary To provide financial assistance to members of the Sault Tribe of Chippewa Indians who are upper-division or graduate students at a university in any state.

Eligibility This program is open to members of the Sault Tribe who are college juniors or higher and are one-quarter Indian blood quantum or more. Applicants must be enrolled full time at a 4-year college or university in any state and have a cumulative GPA of 3.0 or higher. Along with their application, they must submit an essay of 1,000 to 2,000 words on a topic that changes annually but relates to their Indian heritage.

Financial data The stipend is $1,000 per year.

Duration 1 year; may be renewed.

Number awarded 1 each year.

Deadline May of each year.

[344]
JUDITH MCMANUS PRICE SCHOLARSHIPS

American Planning Association
Attn: Leadership Affairs Associate
205 North Michigan Avenue, Suite 1200
Chicago, IL 60601
(312) 431-9100   Fax: (312) 786-6700
E-mail: mgroh@planning.org
Web: www.planning.org/scholarships/apa

Summary To provide financial assistance to Native American and other underrepresented students enrolled in undergraduate or graduate degree programs at recognized planning schools.

Eligibility This program is open to undergraduate and graduate students in urban and regional planning who are women or members of the following minority groups: African American, Hispanic American, or Native American. Applicants must be citizens of the United States and able to document financial need. They must intend to work as practicing planners in the public sector. Along with their application, they must submit a 2-page personal and background statement describing how their education will be applied to career goals and why they chose planning as a career path. Selection is based (in order of importance), on: 1) commitment to planning as reflected in their personal statement and on their resume; 2) academic achievement and/or improvement during the past 2 years; 3) letters of recommendation; 4) financial need; and 5) professional presentation.

Financial data Stipends range from $2,000 to $4,000 per year. The money may be applied to tuition and living expenses only. Payment is made to the recipient's university and divided by terms in the school year.

Duration 1 year; recipients may reapply.

Additional information This program began in 2002.

Number awarded Varies each year; recently, 3 were awarded.

Deadline April of each year.

[345]
JUDITH TEMPEST LAWALL AWARD FOR FUTURE HEALTH CARE CAREERS

Pueblo of Jemez
Attn: Education Services Center
5117 Highway 4
P.O. Box 100
Jemez Pueblo, NM 87024
(575) 834-9102   Toll Free: (888) 834-3936
Fax: (575) 834-7900
E-mail: higher_ed@jemezpueblo.org
Web: www.jemezpueblo.org

Summary To provide financial assistance to Jemez Pueblo students who demonstrate academic merit and are interested in earning a college degree at a school in any state.

Eligibility This program is open to Jemez Pueblo students working on or planning to work on an associate or bachelor's degree at an accredited institution of higher education in any state as a full-time student. Applicants must have a GPA of 2.5 or higher and be majoring in a health-related field. They must be at least one quarter Jemez and recognized by the Jemez Pueblo census office (a Certificate of Indian Blood must be provided). Along with their application, they must submit 2 letters of recommendation, a copy of their letter of acceptance from the institution they are attending or planning to attend, a personal statement on why they chose their specific health care program and what they will do with the degree or certificate they receive, and an official transcript from the high school or college they last attended.

Financial data The stipend depends on the need of the recipient.

Duration 1 semester; may be renewed if the recipient remains enrolled full time with a GPA of 2.5 or higher.

Number awarded Varies each year.

Deadline June of each year.

[346]
JUDSON L. BROWN ENDOWMENT FUND SCHOLARSHIP

Sealaska Corporation
Attn: Sealaska Heritage Institute
105 South Seward Street, Suite 201
Juneau, AK 99801
(907) 463-4844   E-mail: scholarships@sealaska.com
Web: www.sealaska.com

Summary To provide financial assistance to Native Alaskan undergraduate and graduate students who have a connection to the Sealaska Corporation.

Eligibility This program is open to 1) Alaska Natives who are shareholders of Sealaska Corporation; and 2) Native lineal descendants of Alaska Natives enrolled to Sealaska Corporation, whether or not they own Sealaska Corporation stock. Applicants must be entering their junior or senior year at a college or university in any state. They must be able to provide documentation of the involvement in tribal governments and Alaska Native organizations or programs that promote advancement of cultural, social, and economic development for Native Peoples. Along with their application, they must submit an essay on how they have been involved in Native activities and how they plan to use their education to promote the cultural, social, and economic well-being of the Native Peoples and communities. Financial need is also considered in the selection process.

Financial data The stipend is $5,000.

Duration 1 year.

Additional information Sealaska Corporation is 1 of 13 Alaska Native Regional Corporations created under the Alaska Native Claims Settlement Act of 1971.

Number awarded 1 each year.

Deadline February of each year.

[347]
JUNE CURRAN PORCARO SCHOLARSHIP

Sault Tribe of Chippewa Indians
Attn: Higher Education Department
523 Ashmun Street
Sault Ste. Marie, MI 49783
(906) 635-6050, ext. 26312   Toll Free: (800) 793-0660
Fax: (906) 635-7785   E-mail: BMacArthur@saulttribe.net
Web: www.saulttribe.com

Summary To provide financial assistance to members of the Sault Tribe of Chippewa Indians who have been homeless, displaced, or in the foster care system and are interested in attending college or graduate school in any state to work on a degree in human services.

Eligibility This program is open to members of the Sault Tribe who have been homeless, displaced, or in the foster care system. Applicants must be working on an undergraduate or graduate degree in human services at a college or university in any state to prepare for a career of helping people who are homeless, displaced, or involved in the foster care system. They must be able to demonstrate financial need. Along with their application, they must submit an essay of 1,000 to 2,000 words on a topic that changes annually but relates to their Indian heritage.

Financial data The stipend is $1,000.

Duration 1 year.

Additional information   Recipients must agree to provide at least 40 hours of volunteer service at an accredited homeless shelter during the school year for which they receive the award.

Number awarded   1 each year.

Deadline   May of each year.

[348]
JUSTINE E. GRANNER MEMORIAL SCHOLARSHIP

Iowa United Methodist Foundation
2301 Rittenhouse Street
Des Moines, IA 50321
(515) 974-8927
Web: www.iumf.org/scholarships/general

Summary   To provide financial assistance to members of United Methodist churches in Iowa who are Native Americans or other ethnic minorities interested in majoring in a health-related field.

Eligibility   This program is open to ethnic minority students who are members of United Methodist churches and preparing for a career in nursing, public health, or a related field at a college or school of nursing in Iowa. Preference is given to graduates of Iowa high schools. Applicants must have a GPA of 3.0 or higher. They must submit transcripts, 3 letters of recommendation, ACT and/or SAT scores, and documentation of financial need.

Financial data   The stipend is $1,000.

Duration   1 year.

Number awarded   1 each year.

Deadline   February of each year.

[349]
KAISER PERMANENTE COLORADO DIVERSITY SCHOLARSHIP PROGRAM

Kaiser Permanente
Attn: Diversity Development Department
10065 East Harvard Avenue, Suite 400
Denver, CO 80231
Toll Free: (877) 457-4772
E-mail: co-diversitydevelopment@kp.org

Summary   To provide financial assistance to Colorado residents who are Native Americans of members of other underrepresented groups and interested in working on an undergraduate or graduate degree in a health care field at a public college in the state.

Eligibility   This program is open to all residents of Colorado, including those who identify as 1 or more of the following: African American, Asian Pacific, Latino, lesbian, gay, bisexual, transgender, intersex, Native American, U.S. veteran, and/or a person with a disability. Applicants must be enrolled or planning to enroll full time at a publicly-funded college, university, or technical school in Colorado as 1) a graduating high school senior with a GPA of 2.7 or higher; 2) a GED recipient with a GED score of 520 or higher; 3) an undergraduate student; or 4) a graduate or doctoral student. They must be preparing for a career in health care (e.g., athletic training, audiology, cardiovascular perfusion technology, clinical medical assisting, cytotechnology, dental assisting, dental hygiene, diagnostic medicine, dietetics, emergency medical technology, medicine, nursing, occupational therapy, pharmacy, phlebotomy, physical therapy, physician assistant, radiology, respiratory therapy, social work, sports medicine, surgical technology). Selection is based on academic achievement, character qualities, community outreach and volunteering, and financial need.

Financial data   Stipends range from $1,400 to $2,600 per year.

Duration   1 year; may be renewed.

Number awarded   Varies each year; recently, 17 were awarded.

Deadline   March of each year.

[350]
KA'IULANI HOME FOR GIRLS TRUST SCHOLARSHIP

Hawai'i Community Foundation
Attn: Scholarship Department
827 Fort Street Mall
Honolulu, HI 96813
(808) 566-5570   Toll Free: (888) 731-3863
Fax: (808) 521-6286
E-mail: scholarships@hcf-hawaii.org
Web: hcf.scholarships.ngwebsolutions.com

Summary   To provide financial assistance to women of Native Hawaiian ancestry who are attending college in any state.

Eligibility   This program is open to women of Native Hawaiian ancestry who are full-time freshmen or sophomores at an accredited 2- or 4-year college or university in any state. Applicants must demonstrate academic achievement (GPA of 3.3 or higher), good moral character, and financial need. Along with their application, they must submit a short statement indicating their reasons for attending college, their planned course of study, their career goals, and what community service means to them.

Financial data   The amounts of the awards depend on the availability of funds and the need of the recipient. Recently, the average value of the scholarships awarded by the foundation was $2,800.

Duration   1 year; may be renewed.

Additional information   This fund was established in 1963 when the Ka'iulani Home for Girls, formerly used to provide boarding home facilities for young women of Native Hawaiian ancestry, was demolished and the property sold.

Number awarded   Varies each year.

Deadline   February of each year.

[351]
KANSAS ETHNIC MINORITY SCHOLARSHIP PROGRAM

Kansas Board of Regents
Attn: Student Financial Assistance
1000 S.W. Jackson Street, Suite 520
Topeka, KS 66612-1368
(785) 296-3518   Fax: (785) 296-0983
E-mail: loldhamburns@ksbor.org
Web: www.kansasregents.org/scholarships_and_grants

Summary   To provide financial assistance to Native Americans and other minority students in Kansas who are interested in attending college in the state.

Eligibility Eligible to apply are Kansas residents who fall into 1 of these minority groups: American Indian, Alaskan Native, African American, Asian, Pacific Islander, or Hispanic. Applicants may be current college students (enrolled in community colleges, colleges, or universities in Kansas), but high school seniors graduating in the current year receive priority consideration. Minimum academic requirements include 1 of the following: 1) ACT score of 21 or higher or combined mathematics and critical reading SAT score of 990 or higher; 2) cumulative GPA of 3.0 or higher; 3) high school rank in upper 33%; 4) completion of the Kansas Scholars Curriculum (4 years of English, 4 years of mathematics, 3 years of science, 3 years of social studies, and 2 years of foreign language); 5) selection by the National Merit Corporation in any category; or 6) selection by the College Board as a Hispanic Scholar. Selection is based primarily on financial need.

Financial data A stipend of up to $1,850 is provided, depending on financial need and availability of state funds.

Duration 1 year; may be renewed for up to 3 additional years (4 additional years for designated 5-year programs), provided the recipient maintains a 2.0 cumulative GPA and has financial need.

Number awarded Approximately 200 each year.

Deadline April of each year.

[352]
KANSAS SPJ MINORITY STUDENT SCHOLARSHIP

Society of Professional Journalists-Kansas Professional Chapter
c/o Denise Neil, Scholarship Committee
Wichita Eagle
825 East Douglas Avenue
P.O. Box 820
Wichita, KS 67201-0820
(316) 268-6327   E-mail: dneil@wichitaeagle.com

Summary To provide financial assistance to residents of any state enrolled at colleges and universities in Kansas who are Native Americans or members of other racial or ethnic minority groups and interested in a career in journalism.

Eligibility This program is open to residents of any state who are members of a racial or ethnic minority group and entering their junior or senior year at colleges and universities in Kansas. Applicants must be seriously considering a career in journalism. They must be enrolled at least half time and have a GPA of 2.5 or higher. Along with their application, they must submit a professional resume, 4 to 6 examples of their best work (clips or stories, copies of photographs, tapes or transcripts of broadcasts, printouts of web pages) and a 1-page cover letter about themselves, how they came to be interested in journalism, their professional goals, and (if appropriate) their financial need for this scholarship.

Financial data The stipend is $1,000.

Duration 1 year.

Number awarded 1 each year.

Deadline March of each year.

[353]
KATHY MANN MEMORIAL SCHOLARSHIP

Wisconsin Education Association Council
Attn: Scholarship Committee
33 Nob Hill Drive
P.O. Box 8003
Madison, WI 53708-8003
(608) 276-7711   Toll Free: (800) 362-8034, ext. 278
Fax: (608) 276-8203   E-mail: BrisackM@weac.org
Web: www.weac.org

Summary To provide financial assistance to Native American and other minority high school seniors whose parent is a member of the Wisconsin Education Association Council (WEAC) and who plan to study education at a college in any state.

Eligibility This program is open to high school seniors whose parent is an active WEAC member, an active retired member, or a person who died while holding a WEAC membership. Applicants must be members of a minority group (American Indian, Eskimo or Aleut, Hispanic, Asian or Pacific Islander, or Black). They must rank in the top 25% of their graduating class or have a GPA of 3.0 or higher, plan to major or minor in education at a college in any state, and intend to teach in Wisconsin. Selection is based on an essay on why they want to enter the education profession and what they hope to accomplish, GPA, letters of recommendation, school and community activities, and financial need.

Financial data The stipend is $1,450 per year.

Duration 4 years, provided the recipient maintains a GPA of 3.0 or higher.

Number awarded 1 each year.

Deadline February of each year.

[354]
KAY LONGCOPE SCHOLARSHIP AWARD

National Lesbian & Gay Journalists Association
2120 L Street, N.W., Suite 850
Washington, DC 20037
(202) 588-9888   Fax: (202) 588-1818
E-mail: info@nlgfa.org
Web: www.nlgja.org/resources/longcope

Summary To provide financial assistance to lesbian, gay, bisexual, and transgender (LGBT) undergraduate and graduate students of color who are interested in preparing for a career in journalism.

Eligibility This program is open to LGBT students of color who are current or incoming undergraduate or graduate students at a college, university, or community college. Applicants must be planning a career in journalism and be committed to furthering the sponsoring organization's mission of fair and accurate coverage of the LGBT community. They must demonstrate an awareness of the issues facing the LGBT community and the importance of fair and accurate news coverage. For undergraduates, a declared major in journalism and/or communications is desirable but not required; non-journalism majors may demonstrate their commitment to a journalism career through work samples, internships, and work on a school news publication, online news service, or broadcast affiliate. Graduate students must be enrolled in a journalism program. Along with their application, they must submit a 1-page resume, 5 work samples, official transcripts, 3 letters of recommendation, and a 750-word news story on a designated subject involving the LGBT community. U.S. citizenship or permanent resident status is required. Selection is based on journalistic and scholastic ability.

Financial data The stipend is $3,000.

Duration 1 year.

Additional information This program began in 2008.

Number awarded 1 each year.

Deadline May of each year.

[355]
KEN MCCOY G.E.D. COLLEGE SCHOLARSHIP

Sault Tribe of Chippewa Indians
Attn: Higher Education Department
523 Ashmun Street
Sault Ste. Marie, MI 49783
(906) 635-6050, ext. 26312   Toll Free: (800) 793-0660
Fax: (906) 635-7785   E-mail: BMacArthur@saulttribe.net
Web: www.saulttribe.com

Summary To provide financial assistance to members of the Sault Tribe of Chippewa Indians who completed a GED certificate and are interested in attending college in any state to work on an undergraduate degree in any field.

Eligibility This program is open to members of the Sault Tribe who are enrolled or planning to enroll full time at a 2- or 4-year college or university in any state. Applicants must have previously completed a GED certificate. They must be working on or planning to work on an undergraduate degree in any field. Along with their application, they must submit an essay of 1,000 to 2,000 words on a topic that changes annually but relates to their Indian heritage.

Financial data The stipend is $1,000.

Duration 1 year.

Number awarded 1 each year.

Deadline May of each year.

[356]
KENTUCKY LIBRARY ASSOCIATION SCHOLARSHIP FOR MINORITY STUDENTS

Kentucky Library Association
c/o Executive Director
5932 Timber Ridge Drive, Suite 101
Prospect, KY 40059
(502) 223-5322   Fax: (502) 223-4937
E-mail: info@kylibasn.org
Web: www.klaonline.org/scholarships965.cfm

Summary To provide financial assistance to Native Americans and members of other minority groups who are residents of Kentucky or attending school there and are working on an undergraduate or graduate degree in library science.

Eligibility This program is open to members of minority groups (defined as American Indian, Alaskan Native, Black, Hispanic, Pacific Islander, or other ethnic group) who are entering or continuing at a graduate library school accredited by the American Library Association (ALA) or an undergraduate library program accredited by the National Council for Teacher Education (NCATE). Applicants must be residents of Kentucky or a student in a library program in the state. Along with their application, they must submit a statement of their career objectives, why they have chosen librarianship as a career, and their reasons for applying for this scholarship. Selection is based on that statement, cumulative undergrad-

uate and graduate GPA (if applicable), academic merit and potential, and letters of recommendation. U.S. citizenship or permanent resident status is required.

Financial data The stipend is $1,000.

Duration 1 year; nonrenewable.

Number awarded 1 or more each year.

Deadline June of each year.

[357]
KENTUCKY MINORITY EDUCATOR RECRUITMENT AND RETENTION SCHOLARSHIPS

Kentucky Department of Education
Attn: Office of Next-Generation Learners
500 Mero Street, 19th Floor
Frankfort, KY 40601
(502) 564-1479   Fax: (502) 564-4007
TDD: (502) 564-4970
E-mail: jennifer.baker@education.ky.gov
Web: www.education.ky.gov

Summary To provide forgivable loans to Native Americans and other minority undergraduate and graduate students enrolled in Kentucky public institutions who want to become teachers.

Eligibility This program is open to residents of Kentucky who are undergraduate or graduate students pursuing initial teacher certification at a public university or community college in the state. Applicants must have a GPA of 2.75 or higher and either maintain full-time enrollment or be a part-time student within 18 semester hours of receiving a teacher education degree. They must be U.S. citizens and meet the Kentucky definition of a minority student.

Financial data Stipends are $5,000 per year at the 8 state universities in Kentucky or $2,000 per year at community and technical colleges. This is a scholarship/loan program. Recipients are required to teach 1 semester in Kentucky for each semester or summer term the scholarship is received. If they fail to fulfill that requirement, the scholarship converts to a loan payable at 6% annually.

Duration 1 year; may be renewed up to 3 additional years.

Additional information The Kentucky General Assembly established this program in 1992.

Number awarded Varies each year.

Deadline Each state college of teacher education sets its own deadline.

[358]
KIRBY MCDONALD EDUCATION ENDOWMENT FUND

Cook Inlet Region, Inc.
Attn: The CIRI Foundation
3600 San Jeronimo Drive, Suite 256
Anchorage, AK 99508-2870
(907) 793-3575   Toll Free: (800) 764-3382
Fax: (907) 793-3585   E-mail: tcf@thecirifoundation.org
Web: www.thecirifoundation.org/about/donors

Summary To provide financial assistance for undergraduate or graduate studies in designated fields to Alaska Natives who are original enrollees to Cook Inlet Region, Inc. (CIRI) and their lineal descendants.

Eligibility This program is open to Alaska Native enrollees to CIRI under the Alaska Native Claims Settlement Act (ANCSA) of 1971 and their lineal descendants. There are no Alaska residency requirements or age limitations. Applicants must be accepted or enrolled full time in a 4-year undergraduate or a graduate degree program. Preference is given to students in the culinary arts, business administration, or engineering. They must have a GPA of 2.5 or higher. Along with their application, they must submit a 500-word statement on their educational and career goals and how they are contributing, or planning to contribute, to a positive Alaska Native community. Selection is based on that statement, academic achievement, rigor of course work or degree program, student financial contribution, financial need, grade level, previous work performance, community service, and relationship of degree program to career goals.

Financial data The stipend is $10,000 per year, $8,000 per year, or $2,500 per semester, depending on GPA.

Duration 1 semester or 1 year.

Additional information CIRI is 1 of 13 regional corporations established according to the terms of the Alaska Native Claims Settlement Act (ANCSA) of 1971. This program began in 1991.

Number awarded 1 or more each year.

Deadline May of each year for annual scholarships; May or November of each year for semester scholarships.

[359]
KONIAG ANGAYUK SCHOLARSHIP AND INTERNSHIP

Koniag Incorporated
Attn: Koniag Education Foundation
4241 B Street, Suite 303B
Anchorage, AK 99503
(907) 562-9093   Toll Free: (888) 562-9093
Fax: (907) 562-9023
E-mail: scholarships@koniageducation.org
Web: www.koniageducation.org

Summary To provide financial assistance and work experience to Alaska Natives who are Koniag Incorporated shareholders or descendants and interested in attending college in any state.

Eligibility This program is open to undergraduate students who are Alaska Native shareholders of Koniag Incorporated or descendants of those original enrollees. Applicants must have a GPA of 3.0 or higher and be working full time on a degree in any field. They must be interested in interning during the summer at a subsidiary of Koniag Development Corporation. Along with their application, they must submit a 300-word essay about their personal and family history, community involvement, volunteer activities, and educational and life goals. Financial need is not considered in the selection process.

Financial data The scholarship stipend is $10,000 per year. The internships provide a competitive salary and reimbursement of travel and lodging costs.

Duration The scholarship is for 1 academic year and may be renewed, provided the recipient maintains a GPA of 3.0 or higher and full-time status. The internship is for 6 to 10 weeks during the summer.

Additional information Koniag Incorporated is 1 of 13 Alaska Native Regional Corporations created under the Alaska Native Claims Settlement Act of 1971.

Number awarded 1 each year.

Deadline January of each year.

[360]
KONIAG EDUCATION FOUNDATION CAREER DEVELOPMENT GRANTS

Koniag Incorporated
Attn: Koniag Education Foundation
4241 B Street, Suite 303B
Anchorage, AK 99503
(907) 562-9093   Toll Free: (888) 562-9093
Fax: (907) 562-9023
E-mail: scholarships@koniageducation.org
Web: www.koniageducation.org

Summary To provide financial assistance to Alaska Natives who are Koniag Incorporated shareholders or descendants and interested in attending a short-term career development course.

Eligibility This program is open to high school seniors, high school graduates, and currently-enrolled vocational school students who are Alaska Native shareholders of Koniag Incorporated or descendants of those original enrollees. Applicants must be interested in attending an accredited career development activity, including non-degree, part-time, short-term courses of study that will increase their opportunities for employment or job advancement. Along with their application, they must submit a letter providing information about their personal history (including their involvement in the Alaska Native community and how their education would contribute to that community) and the educational plans. Financial need is not considered in the selection process.

Financial data Stipends range up to $1,000.

Duration Up to 6 weeks. Students may obtain only 2 of these grants each year.

Additional information Koniag Incorporated is 1 of 13 Alaska Native Regional Corporations created under the Alaska Native Claims Settlement Act of 1971.

Number awarded Varies each year.

Deadline Applications may be submitted at any time.

[361]
KONIAG EDUCATION FOUNDATION GENERAL SCHOLARSHIPS

Koniag Incorporated
Attn: Koniag Education Foundation
4241 B Street, Suite 303B
Anchorage, AK 99503
(907) 562-9093   Toll Free: (888) 562-9093
Fax: (907) 562-9023
E-mail: scholarships@koniageducation.org
Web: www.koniageducation.org/scholarships/general

Summary To provide financial assistance to Alaska Natives who are Koniag Incorporated shareholders or descendants and plan to attend college or graduate school in any state.

Eligibility This program is open to high school seniors, high school and GED graduates, college students, and graduate students who are Alaska Native shareholders of Koniag

Incorporated or descendants of those original enrollees. Applicants must have a GPA of 2.5 or higher and be enrolled or planning to enroll full or part time at a college or university in any state. Along with their application, they must submit a 300-word essay about their personal and family history, community involvement, volunteer activities, and educational and life goals. Financial need is not considered in the selection process.

Financial data   Stipends range up to $2,500 per year. Funds are sent directly to the recipient's school and may be used for tuition, books, supplies, room, board, and transportation.

Duration   1 year; may be renewed, provided recipients maintain a GPA of 2.0 or higher.

Additional information   Koniag Incorporated is 1 of 13 Alaska Native Regional Corporations created under the Alaska Native Claims Settlement Act of 1971.

Number awarded   Varies each year.

Deadline   March of each year.

[362]
LAC DU FLAMBEAU UNDERGRADUATE ASSISTANCE PROGRAM

Lac du Flambeau Band of Lake Superior Chippewa
  Indians
Attn: Gikendaasowin (Education) Center
562 Peace Pipe Road
P.O. Box 67
Lac du Flambeau, WI 54538
(715) 588-7925   Fax: (715) 588-9063
E-mail: ldfedu@ldftribe.com
Web: www.ldftribe.com

Summary   To provide financial assistance to tribal members of the Lac du Flambeau Band of Lake Superior Chippewa Indians who are interested in working on an undergraduate degree.

Eligibility   This program is open to enrolled Lac du Flambeau members who are working on or planning to work full or part time on an undergraduate degree. Applicants must be able to demonstrate financial need.

Financial data   The maximum stipend is $1,750 per semester for full-time students, $1,313 per semester for part-time students enrolled in 9 to 11 credits, or $875 per semester for part-time students enrolled in 6 to 8 credits.

Duration   1 semester; may be renewed up to 9 additional semesters, provided the recipient maintains a GPA of 2.0 or higher.

Number awarded   Varies each year.

Deadline   The priority deadline is June of each year for fall semester, November of each year for spring semester, or March of each year for summer session.

[363]
LAGRANT FOUNDATION UNDERGRADUATE SCHOLARSHIPS

Lagrant Foundation
Attn: Senior Talent Acquisition and Fundraising Manager
633 West Fifth Street, 48th Floor
Los Angeles, CA 90071
(323) 469-8680, ext. 223   Fax: (323) 469-8683
E-mail: erickainiguez@lagrant.com
Web: www.lagrantfoundation.org/Scholarship%20Program

Summary   To provide financial assistance to Native American and other minority college students who are interested in majoring in advertising, public relations, or marketing.

Eligibility   This program is open to African Americans, Asian Americans/Pacific Islanders, Hispanics/Latinos, and Native Americans/American Indians who are full-time students at a 4-year accredited institution. Applicants must have a GPA of 2.75 or higher and be either majoring in advertising, marketing, or public relations or minoring in communications with plans to prepare for a career in advertising, marketing, or public relations. Along with their application, they must submit 1) a 1- to 2-page essay outlining their career goals; what steps they will take to increase ethnic representation in the fields of advertising, marketing, and public relations; and the role of an advertising, marketing, or public relations practitioner; 2) a paragraph describing the college and/or community activities in which they are involved; 3) a brief paragraph describing any honors and awards they have received; 4) a letter of reference; 5) a resume; and 6) an official transcript. U.S. citizenship or permanent resident status is required.

Financial data   The stipend is $2,500.

Duration   1 year.

Number awarded   Varies each year; recently, 22 were awarded.

Deadline   February of each year.

[364]
LAGUNA ACOMA CONNECTIONS PROGRAM

Pueblo of Laguna
Attn: Partners for Success
11 Rodeo Drive, Building A
P.O. Box 207
Laguna, NM 87026
(505) 552-9322   Fax: (505) 552-0623
E-mail: p.solimon@lagunaed.net
Web: partnersforsuccess.us/pfs—apply.html

Summary   To provide vocational rehabilitation to American Indian adults with disabilities who reside on the Laguna and Acoma reservations in New Mexico.

Eligibility   This program is open to residents of the Laguna and Acoma reservations who either apply directly or are referred by an agency, family member, or community member. Applicants must have a physical or mental impairment that is a barrier to employment and require services in order to prepare for, enter, or obtain employment. Along with their applicatiopn, they must submit a 3-paragraph statement that covers 1) the type of degree or certificate they plan to earn; 2) the type of work they will seek upon completion; 3) their personal commitment or desire to complete a program; 4) any personal achievements; and 5) previous education.

Financial data This program provides services based on individual need and interest, availability of jobs, and selection of career goals.

Duration Services are provided until the participant obtains employment.

Number awarded Varies each year; recently, this program served 57 Indians with disabilities.

Deadline Applications may be submitted at any time.

[365]
LANNAN SCHOLARSHIP

American Indian College Fund
Attn: Scholarship Department
8333 Greenwood Boulevard
Denver, CO 80221
(303) 426-8900   Toll Free: (800) 776-FUND
Fax: (303) 426-1200
E-mail: scholarships@collegefund.org
Web: www.collegefund.org

Summary To provide financial assistance to Native American students enrolling in a bachelor's degree program at a Tribal College or University (TCU).

Eligibility This program is open to American Indians and Alaska Natives who can document proof of enrollment or descendancy. Applicants must be enrolled or planning to enroll full time in a bachelor's degree program at an approved TCU. They must have a GPA of 3.0 or higher and be able to demonstrate leadership and commitment to an American Indian community. Applications are available only online and include required essays on specified topics. U.S. citizenship is required.

Financial data The stipend is $3,000 per year.

Duration 1 year; may be renewed.

Number awarded 1 or more each year.

Deadline May of each year.

[366]
LARRY MATFAY SCHOLARSHIP

Koniag Incorporated
Attn: Koniag Education Foundation
4241 B Street, Suite 303B
Anchorage, AK 99503
(907) 562-9093   Toll Free: (888) 562-9093
Fax: (907) 562-9023
E-mail: scholarships@koniageducation.org
Web: www.koniageducation.org/scholarships/larry-matfay

Summary To provide financial assistance to Alaska Natives who are Koniag Incorporated shareholders or descendants and enrolled in undergraduate or graduate study in a field related to Alutiiq culture.

Eligibility This program is open to college juniors, seniors, and graduate students who are Alaska Native shareholders of Koniag Incorporated or descendants of those original enrollees. Applicants must have a GPA of 2.5 or higher and be working full time on a degree in Alaska Native or American Indian studies, anthropology, health care, history, linguistics, rural development, or another discipline that involves research and learning about Alutiiq culture. Along with their application, they must submit a 300-word essay about their personal and family history, community involvement, volun-

teer activities, and educational and life goals. Financial need is not considered in the selection process.

Financial data The stipend is $1,000 per year. Funds are sent directly to the recipient's school and may be used for tuition, books, supplies, room, board, and transportation.

Duration 1 year; may be renewed.

Additional information Koniag Incorporated is 1 of 13 Alaska Native Regional Corporations created under the Alaska Native Claims Settlement Act of 1971.

Number awarded 1 each year.

Deadline May of each year.

[367]
LAUNCHING LEADERS UNDERGRADUATE SCHOLARSHIP

JPMorgan Chase
Campus Recruiting
Attn: Launching Leaders
277 Park Avenue, Second Floor
New York, NY 10172
(212) 270-6000
E-mail: bronwen.x.baumgardner@jpmorgan.com
Web: careers.jpmorgan.com

Summary To provide financial assistance and work experience to Native American and other underrepresented minority undergraduate students interested in a career in financial services.

Eligibility This program is open to Black, Hispanic, and Native American students enrolled as sophomores or juniors and interested in financial services. Applicants must have a GPA of 3.5 or higher. Along with their application, they must submit 500-word essays on 1) why they should be considered potential candidates for CEO of the sponsoring bank in 2020; and 2) the special background and attributes they would contribute to the sponsor's diversity agenda. They must be interested in a summer associate position in the sponsor's investment banking, sales and trading, or research divisions.

Financial data The stipend is $5,000 for recipients accepted as sophomores or $10,000 for recipients accepted as juniors. For students accepted as sophomores and whose scholarship is renewed for a second year, the stipend is $15,000. The summer internship is a paid position.

Duration 1 year; may be renewed 1 additional year if the recipient successfully completes the 10-week summer intern program and maintains a GPA of 3.5 or higher.

Number awarded Approximately 12 each year.

Deadline October of each year.

[368]
LAWRENCE MATSON MEMORIAL ENDOWMENT FUND SCHOLARSHIPS

Cook Inlet Region, Inc.
Attn: The CIRI Foundation
3600 San Jeronimo Drive, Suite 256
Anchorage, AK 99508-2870
(907) 793-3575   Toll Free: (800) 764-3382
Fax: (907) 793-3585   E-mail: tcf@thecirifoundation.org
Web: www.thecirifoundation.org/about/donors

Summary To provide financial assistance for undergraduate or graduate studies in selected liberal arts to Alaska

Natives who are original enrollees to Cook Inlet Region, Inc. (CIRI) and their lineal descendants.

Eligibility This program is open to Alaska Native enrollees to CIRI under the Alaska Native Claims Settlement Act (ANCSA) of 1971 and their lineal descendants. There are no Alaska residency requirements or age limitations. Applicants must be accepted or enrolled full time in a 4-year undergraduate or a graduate degree program in the following liberal arts fields: language, education, social sciences, arts, communications, or law. They must have a GPA of 2.5 or higher. Along with their application, they must submit a 500-word statement on their educational and career goals and how they are contributing, or planning to contribute, to a positive Alaska Native community. Selection is based on that statement, academic achievement, rigor of course work or degree program, student financial contribution, financial need, grade level, previous work performance, community service, and relationship of degree program to career goals.

Financial data The stipend is $10,000 per year, $8,000 per year, or $2,500 per semester, depending on GPA.

Duration 1 semester or 1 year.

Additional information CIRI is 1 of 13 regional corporations established according to the terms of the Alaska Native Claims Settlement Act (ANCSA) of 1971. This fund was established in 1989.

Number awarded Varies each year; recently, 3 were awarded: 1 at $10,000 per year, 1 at $8,000 per year, and 1 at $2,500 per semester.

Deadline May of each year for annual scholarships; May or November of each year for semester scholarships.

[369]
LCDR JANET COCHRAN AND CDR CONNIE GREENE SCHOLARSHIP

National Naval Officers Association-Washington, D.C.
 Chapter
c/o LCDR Stephen Williams
P.O. Box 30784
Alexandria, VA 22310
(703) 566-3840 Fax: (703) 566-3813
E-mail: Stephen.Williams@Navy.mil
Web: dcnnoa.memberlodge.com/page-309002

Summary To provide financial assistance to female Native American and other minority high school seniors from the Washington, D.C. area who are interested in attending college in any state.

Eligibility This program is open to female minority seniors graduating from high schools in the Washington, D.C. metropolitan area who plan to enroll full time at an accredited 2- or 4-year college or university in any state. Applicants must have a GPA of 2.5 or higher and be U.S. citizens or permanent residents. Selection is based on academic achievement, community involvement, and financial need.

Financial data The stipend is $1,500.

Duration 1 year; nonrenewable.

Additional information Recipients are not required to join or affiliate with the military in any way.

Number awarded 1 each year.

Deadline March of each year.

[370]
LEADERSHIP FOR DIVERSITY SCHOLARSHIP

California School Library Association
Attn: CSL Foundation
6444 East Spring Street, Number 237
Long Beach, CA 90815-1553
Toll Free: (888) 655-8480 Fax: (888) 655-8480
E-mail: info@csla.net
Web: www.csla.net/awards-2/scholarships

Summary To provide financial assistance to Native American and other students who reflect the diversity of California's population and are interested in earning a credential as a library media teacher in the state.

Eligibility This program is open to students who are members of a traditionally underrepresented group enrolled in a college or university library media teacher credential program in California. Applicants must intend to work as a library media teacher in a California school library media center for a minimum of 3 years. Along with their application, they must submit a 250-word statement on what they can contribute to the profession, their commitment to serving the needs of multicultural and multilingual students, and their financial need.

Financial data The stipend is $1,500.

Duration 1 year.

Number awarded 1 each year.

Deadline September of each year.

[371]
LEDGENT DIVERSITY UNDERGRADUATE SCHOLARSHIPS

Accounting and Financial Women's Alliance
Attn: Educational Foundation
2365 Harrodsburg Road, A325
Lexington, KY 40504
(859) 219-3532 Toll Free: (800) 326-2163
Fax: (859) 219-3577 E-mail: foundation@afwa.org
Web: www.afwa.org/foundation/scholarships

Summary To provide financial assistance to Native American and other minority undergraduates interested in preparing for a career in accounting or finance.

Eligibility This program is open to members of minority groups (African Americans, Hispanic Americans, Native Americans, or Asian Americans) who are entering their third, fourth, or fifth year of undergraduate study at a college, university, or professional school of accounting. Applicants must have completed at least 60 semester hours with a declared major in accounting or finance and a GPA of 3.0 or higher. Along with their application, they must submit an essay of 150 to 250 words on their career goals and objectives, the impact they want to have on the accounting world, community involvement, and leadership examples. Selection is based on leadership, character, communication skills, scholastic average, and financial need. Membership in the Accounting and Financial Women's Alliance (AFWA) is not required. Applications must be submitted to a local ASWA chapter.

Financial data A stipend is awarded (amount not specified).

Duration 1 year; recipients may reapply.

Additional information This program is sponsored by Ledgent.

Number awarded 1 each year.

Deadline Local chapters must submit their candidates to the national office by September of each year.

[372]
LEECH LAKE POSTSECONDARY GRANT PROGRAM

Leech Lake Band of Ojibwe
Attn: Education Division
190 Sailstar Drive, N.W.
Cass Lake, MN 56633
(218) 335-8253   Toll Free: (866) 638-7738
Fax: (218) 335-8339
Web: www.llojibwe.com

Summary To provide financial assistance to Minnesota Chippewa Tribe members who are interested in postsecondary education at a school in any state.

Eligibility This program is open to enrolled members of the Leech Lake Band of Ojibwe who have been residents of Minnesota for at least 1 year. Applicants may be high school seniors or graduates, current undergraduates, short-term training students, or full- or part-time graduate students. They must be interested in attending a postsecondary institution in any state. Financial need is considered in the selection process.

Financial data Stipends range up to $3,000 per year, depending on need.

Duration 1 year; may be renewed.

Additional information Applicants for this program must also apply for the Minnesota Indian Scholarship Program, financial aid administered by their institution, and any other aid for which they may be eligible (e.g., work-study, Social Security, veteran's benefits).

Number awarded Varies each year.

Deadline For vocational school students, at least 8 weeks before school starts; for college or university students, June of each year.

[373]
LEON BRADLEY SCHOLARSHIPS

American Association of School Personnel Administrators
Attn: Scholarship Program
11863 West 112th Street, Suite 100
Overland Park, KS 66210
(913) 327-1222   Fax: (913) 327-1223
E-mail: aaspa@aaspa.org
Web: www.aaspa.org/leon-bradley-scholarship

Summary To provide financial assistance to Native American and other minority undergraduates, paraprofessionals, and graduate students preparing for a career in teaching and school leadership at colleges in designated southeastern states.

Eligibility This program is open to members of minority groups (American Indian, Alaskan Native, Asian, Pacific Islander, Black, Hispanic, Middle Easterner) currently enrolled full time at a college or university in Alabama, Florida, Georgia, Kentucky, North Carolina, South Carolina, Tennessee, or Virginia. Applicants must be 1) undergraduates in their final year (including student teaching) of an initial teaching certification program; 2) paraprofessional career-changers in their final year (including student teaching) of an initial teaching certification program; or 3) graduate students who have served as a licensed teacher and are working on a school administrator credential. They must have an overall GPA of 3.0 or higher. Priority is given to applicants who 1) can demonstrate work experience that has been applied to college expenses; 2) have received other scholarship or financial aid support; or 3) are seeking initial certification and/or endorsement in a state-identified critical area.

Financial data Stipends are $2,500 for undergraduates in their final year, $1,500 for paraprofessionals in their final year, and $1,500 for graduate students.

Duration 1 year.

Number awarded 4 each year: 1 undergraduate, 1 paraprofessional, and 2 graduate students.

Deadline May of each year.

[374]
LEONARD M. PERRYMAN COMMUNICATIONS SCHOLARSHIP FOR ETHNIC MINORITY STUDENTS

United Methodist Communications
Attn: Communications Ministry Team
810 12th Avenue South
P.O. Box 320
Nashville, TN 37202-0320
(615) 742-5481   Toll Free: (888) CRT-4UMC
Fax: (615) 742-5485   E-mail: scholarships@umcom.org
Web: www.umcom.org

Summary To provide financial assistance to Native American and other minority United Methodist college students who are interested in careers in religious communications.

Eligibility This program is open to United Methodist ethnic minority students enrolled in accredited institutions of higher education as juniors or seniors. Applicants must be interested in preparing for a career in religious communications. For the purposes of this program, "communications" is meant to cover audiovisual, electronic, and print journalism. Selection is based on Christian commitment and involvement in the life of the United Methodist church, academic achievement, journalistic experience, clarity of purpose, and professional potential as a religion communicator.

Financial data The stipend is $2,500 per year.

Duration 1 year.

Additional information The scholarship may be used at any accredited institution of higher education.

Number awarded 1 each year.

Deadline March of each year.

[375]
LEROY C. SCHMIDT, CPA MINORITY 150-HOUR ACCOUNTING SCHOLARSHIPS

Wisconsin Institute of Certified Public Accountants
Attn: WICPA Educational Foundation
W233N2080 Ridgeview Parkway, Suite 201
Waukesha, WI 53188
(262) 785-0445, ext. 3025
Toll Free: (800) 772-6939 (within WI)
Fax: (262) 785-0838   E-mail: jessica@wicpa.org
Web: www.wicpa.org

Summary To provide financial assistance to Native American and other underrepresented minority residents of Wisconsin enrolled at a college or university in the state and working to meet the requirements to sit for the Certified Public Accountant (C.P.A.) examination.

Eligibility This program is open to minority residents of Wisconsin (African American, Native American/Alaska Native, Pacific Islander, or Hispanic) who have completed 120 credit hours at a college or university in the state in a degree program that qualifies them to sit for the Uniform C.P.A. Examination. Applicants must be entering their fifth-year requirement and eligible to receive a master's degree in business, a double major/minor, or additional courses for credit to satisfy the 150-hour requirement. They must be enrolled full time, have a GPA of 3.0 or higher, and be U.S. citizens.

Financial data The stipend is $5,000 or $2,500.

Duration 1 year.

Number awarded Varies each year; recently, 2 were awarded: 1 at $5,000 and 1 at $2,500.

Deadline February of each year.

[376]
LILLE HOPE MCGARVEY SCHOLARSHIP AWARD

The Aleut Corporation
Attn: Aleut Foundation
703 West Tudor Road, Suite 102
Anchorage, AK 99503-6650
(907) 646-1929   Toll Free: (800) 232-4882
Fax: (907) 646-1949   E-mail: taf@thealeutfoundation.org
Web: www.thealeutfoundation.org

Summary To provide financial assistance to Native Alaskans who are shareholders of The Aleut Corporation or their descendants and working on a degree in the medical field at a school in any state.

Eligibility This program is open to Native Alaskans who are original enrollees or descendants of original enrollees of The Aleut Corporation (TAC). Applicants must have completed at least 1 year of a bachelor's, 2- or 4-year vocational, or master's degree in a medical field at a school in any state. They must be enrolled full time and have a GPA of 3.0 or higher. Along with their application, they must include a letter of intent, up to 500 words in length, that describes their educational goals and objectives and their expected graduation date.

Financial data A stipend is awarded (amount not specified).

Duration 1 year.

Additional information The Aleut Corporation is 1 of 13 Alaska Native Regional Corporations created under the Alaska Native Claims Settlement Act of 1971.

Number awarded 1 each year.

Deadline June of each year.

[377]
LILLIAN FOWLER MEMORIAL SCHOLARSHIP

Chickasaw Foundation
2020 Arlington, Suite 4
P.O. Box 1726
Ada, OK 74821-1726
(580) 421-9030   Fax: (580) 421-9031
E-mail: ChickasawFoundation@chickasaw.net
Web: www.chickasawfoundation.org/Scholarships.aspx

Summary To provide financial assistance to members of the Chickasaw Nation who are working or an undergraduate or graduate degree in health care or social work.

Eligibility This program is open to Chickasaw students who are currently working full time on an undergraduate or graduate degree in social work or a health Applicants must have a GPA of 3.0 or higher. Along with their application, they must submit high school or college transcripts; 2 letters of recommendation; a copy of their Chickasaw Nation citizenship card; a 2-page list of honors, achievements, awards, club memberships, societies, and civic involvement; and a 1-page essay on their long-term goals and plans for achieving those. Financial need is not considered in the selection process.

Financial data A stipend is awarded (amount not specified).

Duration 1 year.

Number awarded 1 each year.

Deadline June of each year.

[378]
LITTLE EAGLE FREE SCHOLARSHIPS

Little Eagle Free, Inc.
P.O. Box 10102
Fullerton, CA 92838
E-mail: littleeaglefreeinc@gmail.com
Web: www.littleeaglefree.org

Summary To provide financial assistance to American Indians attending college in California.

Eligibility This program is open to American Indians who can identify their ancestry or affiliation. Applicants must be working on an associate or bachelor's degree at a college or university in California. As part of their application, they must provide information on their extracurricular activities, financial situation, and how they plan to give back to the Indian community following graduation. They must also submit a 2-page essay about themselves; their goals, hopes, and expectations; and how education will influence their future.

Financial data A stipend is awarded (amount not specified).

Duration 1 year.

Number awarded 1 or more each year.

Deadline July of each year.

[379]
LITTLE RIVER BAND OF OTTAWA INDIANS HIGHER EDUCATION SCHOLARSHIP

Little River Band of Ottawa Indians
Attn: Education Department
2608 Government Center Drive
Manistee, MI 49660
(231) 398-6735   Toll Free: (888) 723-8288
Fax: (231) 398-6655   E-mail: yparsons@lrboi-nsn.gov
Web: www.lrboi-nsn.gov/membership-services/education

Summary To provide financial assistance to members of the Little River Band of Ottawa Indians who are interested in attending college or graduate school.

Eligibility This program is open to tribal citizens of the Little River Band of Ottawa Indians who are attending or planning to attend an accredited college or university. Applicants must be interested in working on an associate, bachelor's, master's, or Ph.D. degree. They must have applied for all other available financial aid and still show unmet need. In the selection process, priority is given first to residents of Michigan, second to students attending schools in Michigan, and third to students attending schools in other states.

Financial data The stipend is $3,500 per semester ($7,000 per year). Recipients are also eligible to apply for book stipends of $200 to $500 (depending on the number of credits in which they are enrolled). Funds are paid to the recipient's institution.

Duration 1 year; may be renewed, provided the recipient maintains a GPA of 2.0 or higher.

Number awarded Varies each year.

Deadline Deadline not specified.

[380]
LITTLE RIVER BAND OF OTTAWA INDIANS VOCATIONAL EDUCATION ASSISTANCE PROGRAM

Little River Band of Ottawa Indians
Attn: Education Department
2608 Government Center Drive
Manistee, MI 49660
(231) 398-6735   Toll Free: (888) 723-8288
Fax: (231) 398-6655   E-mail: yparsons@lrboi-nsn.gov
Web: www.lrboi-nsn.gov/membership-services/education

Summary To provide financial assistance to members of the Little River Band of Ottawa Indians who are interested in attending vocational school.

Eligibility This program is open to tribal citizens of the Little River Band of Ottawa Indians who are at least 18 years of age. Applicants must be interested in attending an accredited vocational/technical program for training to obtain reasonable and satisfactory employment. They must have applied for all other available financial aid and still show unmet need. In the selection process, priority is given first to residents of Michigan, second to students attending schools in Michigan, and third to students attending schools in other states.

Financial data The stipend is $4,000 per term. Funds are paid to the recipient's institution.

Duration Recipients are entitled to a maximum of 24 months of support (or 36 months for nursing programs).

Number awarded Varies each year.

Deadline Deadline not specified.

[381]
LORI JUMP SURVIVOR HONORARY SCHOLARSHIP

Sault Tribe of Chippewa Indians
Attn: Higher Education Department
523 Ashmun Street
Sault Ste. Marie, MI 49783
(906) 635-6050, ext. 26312   Toll Free: (800) 793-0660
Fax: (906) 635-7785   E-mail: BMacArthur@saulttribe.net
Web: www.saulttribe.com

Summary To provide financial assistance to members of the Sault Tribe of Chippewa Indians who are attending college in any state and working on an undergraduate degree in social services or social work.

Eligibility This program is open to members of the Sault Tribe who are enrolled full time at a 2- or 4-year college or university in any state. Applicants must be working on an under-

graduate degree in social work or social services. Along with their application, they must submit an essay of 1,000 to 2,000 words on a topic that changes annually but relates to their Indian heritage.

Financial data The stipend is $1,000.

Duration 1 year.

Number awarded 1 each year.

Deadline May of each year.

[382]
LOUIS B. RUSSELL, JR. MEMORIAL SCHOLARSHIP

Indiana State Teachers Association
Attn: Scholarships
150 West Market Street, Suite 900
Indianapolis, IN 46204-2875
(317) 263-3369   Toll Free: (800) 382-4037
Fax: (800) 777-6128   E-mail: mshoup@ista-in.org
Web: www.ista-in.org/louis-b-russell-scholarship

Summary To provide financial assistance to Native American and other ethnic minority high school seniors in Indiana who are interested in attending vocational school in any state.

Eligibility This program is open to ethnic minority high school seniors in Indiana who are interested in continuing their education in the area of industrial arts, vocational education, or technical preparation at an accredited postsecondary institution in any state. Selection is based on academic achievement, leadership ability as expressed through co-curricular activities and community involvement, recommendations, and a 300-word essay on their educational goals and how they plan to achieve those goals.

Financial data The stipend is $1,000.

Duration 1 year; may be renewed for 1 additional year, provided the recipient maintains a GPA of "C+" or higher.

Number awarded 1 each year.

Deadline February of each year.

[383]
LOVE SCHOLARSHIP FOR DIVERSITY

International Council of Shopping Centers
Attn: ICSC Foundation
1221 Avenue of the Americas, 41st Floor
New York, NY 10020-1099
(646) 728-3628   Fax: (732) 694-1690
E-mail: foundation@icsc.org
Web: www.icsc.org

Summary To provide financial assistance to Native American and other minority undergraduate students who are preparing for a career as a retail real estate professional.

Eligibility This program is open to U.S. citizens who are full-time juniors or seniors working on a degree related to the retail real estate profession. Applicants must be a member of an underrepresented ethnic minority group (American Indian or Alaskan Native, Asian or Pacific Islander, African American, Hispanic, Caribbean). They must have a GPA of 3.0 or higher.

Financial data The stipend is $1,000.

Duration 1 year.

Number awarded 1 or more each year.

Deadline January of each year.

[384]
LSAMP UNDERGRADUATE SUMMER RESEARCH PROGRAM

Cornell University
College of Engineering
Attn: Diversity Programs in Engineering
146 Olin Hall
Ithaca, NY 14853-5201
(607) 255-6403   Fax: (607) 255-2834
E-mail: dpeng@cornell.edu
Web: www.engineering.cornell.edu

Summary To provide an opportunity for Native American and other traditionally underrepresented minority groups in the sciences and engineering to participate in a summer research program in a field of science, technology, engineering, or mathematics (STEM) at Cornell University.

Eligibility This program is open to members of minority groups traditionally underrepresented in the sciences and engineering who are entering their sophomore, junior, or senior year at a college or university anywhere in the country. Applicants must be interested in working on a research project in a field of STEM under the guidance of a faculty or research mentor at Cornell University. They must have a GPA of 3.0 or higher and be U.S. citizens or permanent residents.

Financial data Participating students receive a stipend of $4,000, a round-trip travel stipend of up to $300, a double room in a campus residential hall, and access to laboratories, libraries, computer facilities, and study lounges.

Duration 10 weeks during the summer.

Additional information This program is part of the Louis Stokes Alliance for Minority Participation (LSAMP), supported by the National Science Foundation as part of its Research Experiences for Undergraduates (REU) program. Students are encouraged to enter and present their research at their affiliated National Society of Black Engineers (NSBE), Society of Hispanic Professional Engineers (SHPE), or American Indian Science and Engineering Society (AISES) or professional conference.

Number awarded Varies each year; recently, 9 were accepted.

Deadline February of each year.

[385]
LTK ENGINEERING SCHOLARSHIP

Conference of Minority Transportation Officials
Attn: National Scholarship Program
100 M Street, S.E., Suite 917
Washington, DC 20003
(202) 506-2917   E-mail: info@comto.org
Web: www.comto.org/page/scholarships

Summary To provide financial assistance to Native American and other minority upper-division and graduate students in engineering or other field related to transportation.

Eligibility This program is open to full-time minority juniors, seniors, and graduate students in engineering or other technical transportation-related disciplines. Applicants must have a GPA of 3.0 or higher. Along with their application they must submit a cover letter on their transportation-related career goals and life aspirations. Financial need is not considered in the selection process.

Financial data The stipend is $6,000. Funds are paid directly to the recipient's college or university.

Duration 1 year.

Additional information This program is sponsored by LTK Engineering Services.

Number awarded 1 each year.

Deadline April of each year.

[386]
LTK ENGINEERING TRANSPORTATION PLANNING SCHOLARSHIP

Conference of Minority Transportation Officials
Attn: National Scholarship Program
100 M Street, S.E., Suite 917
Washington, DC 20003
(202) 506-2917   E-mail: info@comto.org
Web: www.comto.org/page/scholarships

Summary To provide financial assistance to Native American and other minority upper-division and graduate students in planning or other field related to transportation.

Eligibility This program is open to full-time minority juniors, seniors, and graduate students in planning of other technical transportation-related disciplines. Applicants must have a GPA of 3.0 or higher. Along with their application they must submit a cover letter on their transportation-related career goals and life aspirations. Financial need is not considered in the selection process.

Financial data The stipend is $5,000. Funds are paid directly to the recipient's college or university.

Duration 1 year.

Additional information This program is sponsored by LTK Engineering Services.

Number awarded 1 each year.

Deadline April of each year.

[387]
LULA BYNUM BOURLAND MEMORIAL SCHOLARSHIP

Chickasaw Foundation
2020 Arlington, Suite 4
P.O. Box 1726
Ada, OK 74821-1726
(580) 421-9030   Fax: (580) 421-9031
E-mail: ChickasawFoundation@chickasaw.net
Web: www.chickasawfoundation.org/Scholarships.aspx

Summary To provide financial assistance to members of the Chickasaw Nation who are working on an undergraduate or graduate degree in Native American studies, peace education studies, or alternatives to growth.

Eligibility This program is open to members of the Chickasaw Nation who are currently enrolled as full-time juniors, seniors, or graduate students at a 4-year college or university. Applicants must be working on a degree in Native American studies, peace education studies, sustainable resource studies, or a related field of alternatives to perpetual growth as an economic model. Along with their application, they must submit high school or college transcripts; 2 letters of recommendation; a copy of their Chickasaw Nation citizenship card; a 2-page list of honors, achievements, awards, club memberships, societies, and civic involvement; and a 1-page essay on their long-term goals and plans for achieving those. Financial need is not considered in the selection process.

Financial data A stipend is awarded (amount not specified).

Duration 1 year.

Number awarded 1 or more each year.

Deadline June of each year.

[388]
LYNN C. GIBSON MEMORIAL SCHOLARSHIP

Chickasaw Foundation
2020 Arlington, Suite 4
P.O. Box 1726
Ada, OK 74821-1726
(580) 421-9030   Fax: (580) 421-9031
E-mail: ChickasawFoundation@chickasaw.net
Web: www.chickasawfoundation.org/Scholarships.aspx

Summary To provide financial assistance for vocational study of secretarial science to members of the Chickasaw Nation.

Eligibility This program is open to members of the Chickasaw Nation who are currently enrolled in a career technology program that leads to certification as a secretarial or administrative assistant. Applicants must have a grade average of "B" or higher. Along with their application, they must submit high school or college transcripts; 2 letters of recommendation; a copy of their Chickasaw Nation citizenship card; a 2-page list of honors, achievements, awards, club memberships, societies, and civic involvement; and a 1-page essay on their long-term goals and plans for achieving those. Financial need is not considered in the selection process.

Financial data A stipend is awarded (amount not specified).

Duration 1 year.

Number awarded 1 each year.

Deadline June or February of each year.

[389]
MABEL SMITH MEMORIAL SCHOLARSHIP

Wisconsin Women of Color Network, Inc.
c/o P.E. Kiram
756 North 35th Street, Suite 101
Milwaukee, WI 53208
(414) 899-2329   E-mail: pekiram64@gmail.com

Summary To provide financial assistance for vocation/technical school or community college to Native American and other minority residents of Wisconsin.

Eligibility This program is open to residents of Wisconsin who are high school or GED-equivalent graduating seniors planning to continue their education at a vocational/technical school or community college in any state. Applicants must be a member of 1 of the following groups: African American, Asian, American Indian, Latina, or biracial. They must have a GPA of 2.0 or higher and be able to demonstrate financial need. Along with their application, they must submit a 1-page essay on how this scholarship will help them accomplish their educational goal. U.S. citizenship is required.

Financial data A stipend is awarded (amount not specified).

Duration 1 year.

Additional information This program began in 1990.

Number awarded 1 each year.

Deadline May of each year.

[390]
MAE LASSLEY/OSAGE SCHOLARSHIPS

Osage Scholarship Fund
c/o Roman Catholic Diocese of Tulsa
P.O. Box 690240
Tulsa, OK 74169-0240
(918) 294-1904   Fax: (918) 294-0920
E-mail: sarah.jameson@dioceseoftulsa.org
Web: www.osagenation-nsn.gov

Summary To provide financial assistance to Osage Indians who are Roman Catholics attending college or graduate school.

Eligibility This program is open to Roman Catholics who are attending or planning to attend a college or university as a full-time undergraduate or graduate student. Applicants must be Osage Indians on the rolls in Pawhuska, Oklahoma and have a copy of their Certificate of Degree of Indian Blood (CDIB) or Osage tribal membership card. Undergraduates must have a GPA of 2.5 or higher; graduate students must have a GPA of 3.0 or higher. Selection is based on academic ability and financial need.

Financial data The stipend is $1,000 per year.

Duration 1 year; may be renewed if the recipient maintains full-time enrollment and a GPA of 2.5 or higher as an undergraduate or 3.0 or higher as a graduate student.

Number awarded Normally, 10 each year: 2 for students attending St. Gregory's University in Shawnee, Oklahoma as freshmen and 8 for any college or university.

Deadline April of each year.

[391]
MAGNEL LARSEN DRABEK SCHOLARSHIP

Koniag Incorporated
Attn: Koniag Education Foundation
4241 B Street, Suite 303B
Anchorage, AK 99503
(907) 562-9093   Toll Free: (888) 562-9093
Fax: (907) 562-9023
E-mail: scholarships@koniageducation.org
Web: www.koniageducation.org

Summary To provide financial assistance to Alaska Natives who are Koniag Incorporated shareholders or descendants and working on an undergraduate or graduate degree in education, arts, or cultural studies.

Eligibility This program is open to undergraduate and graduate students who are Alaska Native shareholders of Koniag Incorporated or descendants of those original enrollees. Applicants must have a GPA of 2.5 or higher and be working full time on a degree in education, arts, or cultural studies. Along with their application, they must submit a 300-word essay about their personal and family history, community involvement, volunteer activities, and educational and life goals. Financial need is not considered in the selection process.

Financial data The stipend is $2,000 per year. Funds are sent directly to the recipient's school and may be used for tuition, books, supplies, room, board, and transportation.

Duration 1 year; may be renewed.

Additional information Koniag Incorporated is 1 of 13 Alaska Native Regional Corporations created under the Alaska Native Claims Settlement Act of 1971.

Number awarded 1 each year.

Deadline May of each year.

[392]
MARCIA SILVERMAN MINORITY STUDENT AWARD

Public Relations Student Society of America
Attn: Vice President of Member Services
33 Maiden Lane, 11th Floor
New York, NY 10038-5150
(212) 460-1474   Fax: (212) 995-0757
E-mail: prssa@prsa.org
Web: www.prssa.prsa.org

Summary To provide financial assistance to Native American and other minority college seniors who are interested in preparing for a career in public relations.

Eligibility This program is open to minority (African American/Black, Hispanic/Latino, Asian, Native American, Alaskan Native, or Pacific Islander) students who are entering their senior year at an accredited 4-year college or university. Applicants must have a GPA of 3.0 or higher and be working on a degree in public relations, journalism, or other field to prepare for a career in public relations. Along with their application, they must submit an essay on their view of the public relations profession and their public relations career goals. Selection is based on academic achievement, demonstrated leadership, practical experience, commitment to public relations, writing skills, and letters of recommendation.

Financial data The stipend is $5,000.

Duration 1 year.

Additional information This program began in 2010.

Number awarded 1 each year.

Deadline June of each year.

[393]
MARGARET L. BROWN SCHOLARSHIP FUND

Cook Inlet Region, Inc.
Attn: The CIRI Foundation
3600 San Jeronimo Drive, Suite 256
Anchorage, AK 99508-2870
(907) 793-3575   Toll Free: (800) 764-3382
Fax: (907) 793-3585   E-mail: tcf@thecirifoundation.org
Web: www.thecirifoundation.org/about/donors

Summary To provide financial assistance for undergraduate or graduate studies in designated fields to Alaska Natives who are original enrollees to Cook Inlet Region, Inc. (CIRI) and their lineal descendants.

Eligibility This program is open to Alaska Native enrollees to CIRI under the Alaska Native Claims Settlement Act (ANCSA) of 1971 and their lineal descendants. There are no Alaska residency requirements or age limitations. Applicants must be accepted or enrolled full time in a 4-year undergraduate or a graduate degree program in land use policy and planning, conversation economics, environmental science, education policy, or related fields. They must have a GPA of 3.7 or higher. Along with their application, they must submit a 500-word statement on their educational and career goals

and how they are contributing, or planning to contribute, to a positive Alaska Native community. Selection is based on that statement, academic achievement, rigor of course work or degree program, student financial contribution, financial need, grade level, previous work performance, community service, and relationship of degree program to career goals.

Financial data The stipend is $20,000 per year.

Duration 1 year; may be renewed.

Additional information CIRI is 1 of 13 regional corporations established according to the terms of the Alaska Native Claims Settlement Act (ANCSA) of 1971. This program began in 2013.

Number awarded 1 or more each year.

Deadline May of each year.

[394]
MARJORIE BOWENS-WHEATLEY SCHOLARSHIPS

Unitarian Universalist Association
Attn: UU Women's Federation
258 Harvard Street
Brookline, MA 02446
(617) 838-6989   E-mail: uuwf@uua.org
Web: www.uuwf.org

Summary To provide financial assistance to Native American and other women of color who are working on an undergraduate or graduate degree to prepare for Unitarian Universalist ministry or service.

Eligibility This program is open to women of color who are either 1) aspirants or candidates for the Unitarian Universalist ministry; or 2) candidates in the Unitarian Universalist Association's professional religious education or music leadership credentialing programs. Applicants must submit a 1- to 2-page narrative that covers their call to UU ministry, religious education, or music leadership; their passions; how their racial/ethnic/cultural background influences their goals for their calling; and how the work of the program's namesake relates to their dreams and plans for their UU service.

Financial data The stipend is $1,500.

Duration 1 year.

Additional information This program began in 2009.

Number awarded Varies each year; recently, 2 were awarded.

Deadline March of each year.

[395]
MARTHA J. (MARTI) ALESHIRE FARRINGTON SCHOLARSHIP

Cherokee Nation Foundation
800 South Muskogee
Tahlequah, OK 74464
(918) 207-0950   Fax: (918) 207-0951
E-mail: contact@cherokeenationfoundation.org
Web: cherokeenation.academicworks.com

Summary To provide financial assistance to citizens of the Cherokee Nation who are interested in attending a 4-year university in any state and majoring in any field.

Eligibility This program is open to citizens of the Cherokee Nation who are enrolled or planning to enroll at a 4-year college or university in any state. Applicants must have a GPA of 3.0 or higher. They are not required to reside in the Cherokee

Nation area. Along with their application, they must submit an 800-word essay on their desire to pursue higher education, their chosen field of study, how they plan to serve the Cherokee people after they complete their higher education, and whether or not they speak the Cherokee language. Selection is based on the clarity and presentation of the essay; academic information (including transcripts and ACT scores); school, cultural and community activities; future plans to serve Cherokee people; and financial need.

Financial data The stipend is $1,000 per year.

Duration 1 year; may be renewed up to 4 additional years, provided the recipient maintains a GPA of 3.0 or higher.

Number awarded 1 or more each year.

Deadline January of each year.

[396]
MARTHA MILLER TRIBUTARY SCHOLARSHIP

Sault Tribe of Chippewa Indians
Attn: Higher Education Department
523 Ashmun Street
Sault Ste. Marie, MI 49783
(906) 635-6050, ext. 26312   Toll Free: (800) 793-0660
Fax: (906) 635-7785   E-mail: BMacArthur@saulttribe.net
Web: www.saulttribe.com

Summary To provide financial assistance to members of the Sault Tribe of Chippewa Indians who are attending college in any state and working on an undergraduate or graduate degree in human services or social work.

Eligibility This program is open to members of the Sault Tribe who are enrolled full time at a 2- or 4-year college or university in any state. Applicants must be working on an undergraduate or graduate degree in social work, social services, or other field of study related to human services. Along with their application, they must submit an essay of 1,000 to 2,000 words on a topic that changes annually but relates to their Indian heritage.

Financial data The stipend is $1,000.

Duration 1 year.

Number awarded 1 each year.

Deadline May of each year.

[397]
MARTIN LUTHER KING, JR. MEMORIAL SCHOLARSHIP FUND

California Teachers Association
Attn: CTA Foundation for Teaching and Learning
1705 Murchison Drive
P.O. Box 921
Burlingame, CA 94011-0921
(650) 697-1400   E-mail: scholarships@cta.org
Web: www.cta.org

Summary To provide financial assistance for college or graduate school to Native Americans and other racial and ethnic minorities who are members of the California Teachers Association (CTA), children of members, or members of the Student CTA.

Eligibility This program is open to members of racial or ethnic minority groups (African Americans, American Indians/ Alaska Natives, Asians/Pacific Islanders, and Hispanics) who are 1) active CTA members; 2) dependent children of active, retired, or deceased CTA members; or 3) members of Student CTA. Applicants must be interested in preparing for a teaching career in public education or already engaged in such a career.

Financial data Stipends vary each year; recently, they ranged up to $6,000.

Duration 1 year.

Number awarded Varies each year; recently, 24 were awarded: 1 to a CTA member, 10 to children of CTA members, and 13 to Student CTA members.

Deadline February of each year.

[398]
MARTIN LUTHER KING JR. SCHOLARSHIP AWARDS

American Correctional Association
Attn: Scholarship Award Committee
206 North Washington Street, Suite 200
Alexandria, VA 22314
(703) 224-0000   Toll Free: (800) ACA-JOIN
Fax: (703) 224-0179   E-mail: execoffice@aca.org
Web: www.aca.org

Summary To provide financial assistance for undergraduate or graduate study to Native American and other minorities interested in a career in the criminal justice field.

Eligibility Members of the American Correctional Association (ACA) may nominate a minority person for these awards. Nominees do not need to be ACA members, but they must have been accepted to or be enrolled in an undergraduate or graduate program in criminal justice at a 4-year college or university. Along with the nomination package, they must submit a 250-word essay describing their reflections on the ideals and philosophies of Dr. Martin Luther King and how they have attempted to emulate those qualities in their lives. They must provide documentation of financial need, academic achievement, and commitment to the principles of Dr. King.

Financial data A stipend is awarded (amount not specified). Funds are paid directly to the recipient's college or university.

Duration 1 year.

Number awarded 1 each year.

Deadline May of each year.

[399]
MARY AND HAROLD "CUB" MCKERCHIE TRIBUTARY SCHOLARSHIP

Sault Tribe of Chippewa Indians
Attn: Higher Education Department
523 Ashmun Street
Sault Ste. Marie, MI 49783
(906) 635-6050, ext. 26312   Toll Free: (800) 793-0660
Fax: (906) 635-7785   E-mail: BMacArthur@saulttribe.net
Web: www.saulttribe.com

Summary To provide financial assistance to members of the Sault Tribe of Chippewa Indians who are nontraditional students and interested in attending college in any state to work on an undergraduate degree in any field.

Eligibility This program is open to members of the Sault Tribe who are nontraditional students enrolled or planning to enroll full time at a 2- or 4-year college or university in any state. Applicants must be working on or planning to work on an undergraduate degree in any field. Along with their application, they must submit an essay of 1,000 to 2,000 words on a topic that changes annually but relates to their Indian heritage.

Financial data The stipend is $1,000.

Duration 1 year.

Number awarded 1 each year.

Deadline May of each year.

[400]
MARY E. BORDER SCHOLARSHIP

Kansas 4-H
c/o K-State Research and Extension
201 Umberger Hall
Manhattan, KS 66506-3404
(785) 532-5800   Fax: (785) 532-5981
Web: www.kansas4-h.org/p.aspx?tabid=479

Summary To provide financial assistance to members of Kansas 4-H who are Native Americans or other economically-disadvantaged minority high school seniors or returning adults planning to enroll at a college in any state and major in any field.

Eligibility This program is open to residents of Kansas who have completed at least 1 year of 4-H work and are planning to enrolled at a college in any state and major in any field. Applicants may be 1) economically-disadvantaged high school seniors; 2) high school seniors who are members of minority groups (African American, Asian/Pacific Islander, American Indian/Alaska Native, Hispanic/Latino); or 3) adults returning to college. Along with their application, they must submit a 1-page summary of 4-H leadership, community service, participation, and recognition; a 1-page essay on how 4-H has impacted them; and a 1-page summary of non-4-H leadership, community service, participation, and recognition in school and community. Selection is based on 4-H leadership (40%), 4-H citizenship and community service (30%), 4-H participation and recognition (20%), and non-4-H leadership, citizenship, and recognition (10%).

Financial data The stipend is $1,500.

Duration 1 year.

Number awarded 1 each year.

Deadline January of each year.

[401]
MARY HILL DAVIS ETHNIC/MINORITY SCHOLARSHIP PROGRAM

Baptist General Convention of Texas
Attn: Theological Education
7557 Rambler Road, Suite 1200
Dallas, TX 75231-2388
(214) 828-5252   Toll Free: (888) 244-9400
Fax: (214) 828-5261   E-mail: institutions@bgct.org
Web: www.texasbaptists.org

Summary To provide financial assistance for college to Native American and other ethnic minority residents of Texas who are members of Texas Baptist congregations.

Eligibility This program is open to members of Texas Baptist congregations who are of African American, Hispanic, Native American, or other intercultural heritage. Applicants must be attending or planning to attend a university affiliated with the Baptist General Convention of Texas to work on a bachelor's degree as preparation for service as a future lay or vocational ministry leader in a Texas Baptist ethnic/minority church. They must have been active in their respective ethnic/minority community. Along with their application, they must submit a letter of recommendation from their pastor and transcripts. Students still in high school must have a GPA of at least 3.0; students previously enrolled in a college must have at least a 2.0 GPA. U.S. citizenship or permanent resident status is required.

Financial data Stipends are $800 per semester ($1,600 per year) for full-time students or $400 per semester ($800 per year) for part-time students.

Duration 1 semester; may be renewed up to 7 additional semesters.

Additional information The scholarships are funded through the Week of Prayer and the Mary Hill Davis Offering for state missions sponsored annually by Women's Missionary Union of Texas. The eligible institutions are Baptist University of The Americas, Baylor University, Dallas Baptist University, East Texas Baptist University, Hardin Simmons University, Houston Baptist University, Howard Payne University, University of Mary Hardin Baylor, and Wayland Baptist University.

Number awarded Varies each year.

Deadline April of each year.

[402]
MARY K. MORELAND AND DANIEL T. JENKS SCHOLARSHIP

Chickasaw Foundation
2020 Arlington, Suite 4
P.O. Box 1726
Ada, OK 74821-1726
(580) 421-9030   Fax: (580) 421-9031
E-mail: ChickasawFoundation@chickasaw.net
Web: www.chickasawfoundation.org/Scholarships.aspx

Summary To provide financial assistance to members of the Chickasaw Nation interested in studying education in college.

Eligibility This program is open to Chickasaw students who are currently enrolled full time as an undergraduate at an accredited 4-year college or university. Applicants must be majoring in education and have a GPA of 3.0 or higher. Along with their application, they must submit high school or college transcripts; 2 letters of recommendation; a copy of their Chickasaw Nation citizenship card; a 2-page list of honors, achievements, awards, club memberships, societies, and civic involvement; and a 1-page essay on their long-term goals and plans for achieving those. Financial need is not considered in the selection process.

Financial data A stipend is awarded (amount not specified).

Duration 1 year.

Number awarded 1 each year.

Deadline June of each year.

[403]
MASSACHUSETTS NATIVE AMERICAN TUITION WAIVER PROGRAM

Massachusetts Office of Student Financial Assistance
454 Broadway, Suite 200
Revere, MA 02151
(617) 391-6070   Fax: (617) 727-0667
E-mail: osfa@osfa.mass.edu
Web: www.mass.edu/osfa/programs/categorical.asp

Summary To provide financial assistance for college to Massachusetts residents who are Native Americans.

Eligibility Applicants for this assistance must have been permanent legal residents of Massachusetts for at least 1 year and certified by the Bureau of Indian Affairs as Native Americans. They may not be in default on any federal student loan. U.S. citizenship or permanent resident status is required.

Financial data Eligible students are exempt from any tuition payments for an undergraduate degree or certificate program at public colleges or universities in Massachusetts.

Duration Up to 4 academic years, for a total of 130 semester hours.

Additional information Recipients may enroll either part or full time in a Massachusetts publicly-supported institution.

Number awarded Varies each year.

Deadline April of each year.

[404]
MASSASOIT (SUPREME SACHEM) WAMPANOAG SCHOLARSHIP

Society of Mayflower Descendants in Pennsylvania
c/o Billie J. Gailey
3661 Perrysville Avenue
Pittsburgh, PA 15214
Web: www.sail1620.org/Society-News/scholarships

Summary To provide financial assistance to high school seniors and current undergraduates who are affiliated with the Wampanoag Tribe and interested in attending college in any state.

Eligibility This program is open to high school seniors and continuing students at colleges in any state who are members of the Wampanoag tribe. Applicants must submit a 500-word essay on the topic, "Identify the positive and negative influences of the Plimoth Colonists on the Wampanoag Nation and describe the effects over time." Selection is based on the essay's adherence to topic, organization, historical accuracy, reasoning, appropriate word choice, and correct grammar, spelling, and punctuation.

Financial data The stipend is $1,000. Funds are paid directly to the student.

Duration 1 year.

Number awarded 1 each year.

Deadline April of each year.

[405]
MAUREEN L. AND HOWARD N. BLITMAN, P.E. SCHOLARSHIP TO PROMOTE DIVERSITY IN ENGINEERING

National Society of Professional Engineers
Attn: NSPE Educational Foundation
1420 King Street
Alexandria, VA 22314-2794
(703) 684-2833   Toll Free: (888) 285-NSPE
Fax: (703) 684-2821   E-mail: education@nspe.org
Web: www.nspe.org

Summary To provide financial assistance for college to Native Americans and members of other underrepresented ethnic minority groups interested in preparing for a career in engineering.

Eligibility This program is open to members of underrepresented ethnic minorities (African Americans, Hispanics, or Native Americans) who are high school seniors accepted into an ABET-accredited engineering program at a 4-year college or university. Applicants must have a GPA of 3.5 or higher, verbal SAT score of 600 or higher, and math SAT score of 700 or higher (or English ACT score of 29 or higher and math ACT score of 29 or higher). They must submit brief essays on 4 assigned topics. Selection is based on those essays, GPA, internship/co-op experience and community involvement, 2 faculty recommendations, and honors/scholarships/awards. U.S. citizenship is required.

Financial data The stipend is $5,000 per year; funds are paid directly to the recipient's institution.

Duration 1 year; nonrenewable.

Number awarded 1 each year.

Deadline February of each year.

[406]
MCGHEE-TULLIS TUITION ASSISTANCE PROGRAM

Poarch Band of Creek Indians
Attn: Tuition Program Coordinator
5811 Jack Springs Road
Atmore, AL 36502
(251) 368-9136, ext. 2535   Fax: (251) 368-4502
E-mail: mjohnson@pci-nsn.gov
Web: www.poarchcreekindians.org

Summary To provide funding to members of the Poarch Band of Creek Indians for payment of tuition or repayment of educational loans.

Eligibility This program is open to enrolled members of the Poarch Band of Creek Indians who are enrolled or planning to enroll in 1) a certificate program leading to an increased chance of employment and/or increase in salary; 2) a vocational/technical school; or 3) a college or university program leading to an undergraduate, graduate, or professional degree. Applicants must be seeking funding 1) to pay the cost of tuition, books, and mandatory fees; or 2) to repay their educational loans incurred prior to their current enrollment.

Financial data Total maximum awards are $10,000 for students participating in a certificate program not culminating in a degree and not part of the federal student aid program, $20,000 for students participating in a certificate program not culminating in a degree but part of the federal student aid program, $30,000 for an associate degree program, $50,000 for a bachelor's degree, $75,000 for a master's degree, or $100,000 for a doctoral degree; those limits are cumulative. Tribal members may also apply for a supplemental grant for purchase of specialized tools required for their program and a 1-time grant of $1,000 for the purchase of a laptop or desktop computer.

Duration Available funds are disbursed as requested, until exhaustion of the lifetime allotment.

Number awarded Varies each year.

Deadline Applications may be submitted at any time.

[407]
MCKINNEY FAMILY FUND SCHOLARSHIP

Cleveland Foundation
Attn: Scholarship Processing
1422 Euclid Avenue, Suite 1300
Cleveland, OH 44115-2001
(216) 861-3810　　　　　　　　Fax: (216) 861-1729
E-mail: mbaker@clevefdn.org
Web: www.clevelandfoundation.org

Summary To provide financial assistance to residents of Ohio, especially Native Americans and members of other minority groups, who are interested in attending college or graduate school in any state.

Eligibility This program is open to U.S. citizens who have been residents of Ohio for at least 2 years. Applicants must be high school seniors or graduate students and interested in working full or part time on an associate, bachelor's, master's, or doctoral degree at an accredited college or university in any state. They must have a GPA of 2.5 or higher. Preference is given to applicants of minority descent. Selection is based on evidence of sincerity toward obtaining an academic credential. Financial need may be used as a tiebreaker.

Financial data The stipend is $2,000 per year. Funds are paid directly to the school and must be applied to tuition, fees, books, supplies, and equipment required for course work.

Duration 1 year; may be renewed up to 3 additional.

Number awarded 1 or more each year.

Deadline March of each year.

[408]
MEDIA GENERAL MINORITY SCHOLARSHIP AND TRAINING PROGRAM

Media General
Attn: Angie Cartwright, Human Resources
9101 Burnet Road
Austin, TX 78758
(512) 380-4400
Web: www.mediageneral.com/careers/scholarship.html

Summary To provide scholarship/loans to Native American and other minority undergraduates interested in earning a degree in a field related to broadcast journalism and working at a station owned by LIN Television Corporation.

Eligibility This program is open to U.S. citizens and permanent residents of non-white origin who are enrolled as a sophomore or junior at a college or university. Applicants must have a declared major in broadcast journalism, digital multimedia, mass/speech/digital communication, television production, or marketing and a GPA of 3.0 or higher. Along with their application, they must submit a list of organizations and activities in which they have held leadership positions, 3

references, a 50-word description of their career goals, a list of personal achievements and honors, and a 500-word essay about themselves. Financial need is not considered in the selection process.

Financial data The program pays for tuition and fees, books, and room and board, to a maximum of $10,000 per year. Recipients must sign an employment agreement that guarantees them part-time employment as an intern during school and a 2-year regular position at a television station owned by Media General following graduation. If they fail to honor the employment agreement, they must repay all scholarship funds received.

Duration 2 years.

Additional information This program began in 1998 under LIN Television Corporation, which was acquired by Media General in 2014. Media General owns 71 television stations in 48 media markets in the United States. Recipients of these scholarships must work at a station selected by Media General management.

Number awarded 2 each year: 1 for a student in broadcast television and 1 for a student in digital media.

Deadline January of each year.

[409]
MELLON UNDERGRADUATE CURATORIAL FELLOWSHIP PROGRAM

Art Institute of Chicago
Attn: Coordinator, Andrew W. Mellon Academic Programs
111 South Michigan Avenue
Chicago, IL 60603
(312) 443-3581　　　　　　　　E-mail: fmings@artic.edu
Web: www.artic.edu/mellon

Summary To provide an opportunity for Native American and other undergraduates from groups historically underrepresented in the curatorial field to gain academic training and work experience to prepare for a career as an art curator.

Eligibility This program is open to undergraduates (typically freshmen or sophomores) who can commit 2 years to a program of preparation for a career as an art curator. Applicants must be studying art history, art, or the museum field at a college or university in the vicinity of 5 designated art museums. They must be members of groups historically underrepresented in the curatorial field and interested in continuing on to graduate school for advanced study in a relevant academic discipline. They must also be available to work with a mentor at the museum during the academic year to gain experience with curators and staff on exhibitions, collections, and programs and to participate in a summer internship. Interested students first apply to participate in a Summer Academy at the museum in their area. Selection for the Academy is based on academic record, extracurricular activities, background or other experiences, and expected contribution to the program. Based on performance during the Academy and personal interviews, Curatorial Fellows are selected at each of the 5 museums.

Financial data Students selected for the Summer Academies receive a per diem allowance. Students selected as fellows receive an academic stipend of $4,000 per year and a grant of $6,000 for the summer internship.

Duration The Summer Academy lasts 1 week. The fellowship is 2 years, including 10-week summer internships.

Additional information The Andrew W. Mellon Foundation established this program in 2013. In addition to the Art Institute of Chicago, it also operates at the High Museum of Art in Atlanta, the Los Angeles County Museum of Art, the Museum of Fine Arts, Houston, and the Nelson-Atkins Museum of Art in Kansas City. Students who attend college in the vicinity of those museums should contact them about this program.

Number awarded 15 students at each of the 5 museums are selected each year to participate in the Summer Academy. Of those, 2 are selected at each museum to receive the Curatorial Fellowship.

Deadline February of each year.

[410]
MESCALERO APACHE TRIBAL SCHOLARSHIP

Mescalero Apache Tribe
Attn: Tribal Education Department
148 Cottonwood Drive
P.O. Box 227
Mescalero, NM 88340
(575) 464-9243   Fax: (575) 464-4506
E-mail: mescaleroed@matisp.net
Web: mescaleroapachetribe.com/tribaledu

Summary To provide financial assistance for undergraduate or graduate education to members of the Mescalero Apache Tribe.

Eligibility This program is open to enrolled members of the Mescalero Apache Tribe who are high school seniors, high school graduates, or currently-enrolled undergraduate or graduate students. Applicants must have a GPA of 2.0 or higher and be able to demonstrate financial need. They must enroll full or part time at an accredited college, university, or community college in any state.

Financial data The amount awarded varies, up to $10,000 per year.

Duration 1 year; may be renewed for up to 3 additional years, provided the recipient maintains a GPA of 2.0 or higher as an undergraduate or 3.0 or higher as a graduate student.

Number awarded Varies each year.

Deadline May of each year for the academic year and fall term; October of each year for the spring term; March of each year for the summer session.

[411]
MICHAEL BAKER SCHOLARSHIP FOR DIVERSITY IN ENGINEERING

Association of Independent Colleges and Universities of Pennsylvania
101 North Front Street
Harrisburg, PA 17101-1404
(717) 232-8649   Fax: (717) 233-8574
E-mail: info@aicup.org
Web: www.aicup.org/Foundation-Scholarships

Summary To provide financial assistance to Native American and other minority students from any state enrolled at member institutions of the Association of Independent Colleges and Universities of Pennsylvania (AICUP) who are majoring in designated fields of engineering.

Eligibility This program is open to full-time undergraduate students from any state enrolled at designated AICUP col-

leges and universities who are women and/or members of the following minority groups: American Indians, Alaska Natives, Asians, Blacks/African Americans, Hispanics/Latinos, Native Hawaiians, or Pacific Islanders. Applicants must be juniors majoring in architectural, civil, or environmental engineering with a GPA of 3.0 or higher. Along with their application, they must submit a 2-page essay on what they believe will be the greatest challenge facing the engineering profession over the next decade, and why.

Financial data The stipend is $2,500 per year.

Duration 1 year; may be renewed 1 additional year if the recipient maintains appropriate academic standards.

Additional information This program, sponsored by the Michael Baker Corporation, is available at the 88 private colleges and universities in Pennsylvania that comprise the AICUP.

Number awarded 1 each year.

Deadline April of each year.

[412]
MICHIGAN CHAPTER COMTO SCHOLARSHIPS

Conference of Minority Transportation Officials-Michigan Chapter
Attn: President
P.O. Box 32439
Detroit, MI 48232
(269) 491-7279   E-mail: averyk@michigan.gov
Web: www.comtomichigan.org/scholarships.html

Summary To provide financial assistance to Native American and other minority undergraduate and graduate students in Michigan who are working on a degree in a transportation-related field.

Eligibility This program is open to members of minority groups enrolled full time as sophomores, juniors, seniors, or graduate students at colleges or universities in Michigan. Applicants must be working on a degree in engineering, planning, or other transportation-related discipline. Graduate students must be members of the Conference of Minority Transportation Officials (COMTO); if undergraduates are not already members, they must become a member within 30 days of the scholarship award. U.S. citizenship or legal resident status is required.

Financial data The stipend ranges from $500 to $3,000. Funds are paid directly to the student.

Duration 1 year.

Number awarded Varies each year; recently, 7 were awarded: 1 at $3,000, 1 at $2,000, 2 at $1,000, and 3 at $500.

Deadline April of each year.

[413]
MICHIGAN INDIAN ELDERS ASSOCIATION SCHOLARSHIP

Michigan Indian Elders Association
c/o Mike Duschene, Scholarship Committee Coordinator
P.O. Box 624
Baraga, MI 49908
(231) 348-3918   E-mail: mduschene@charter.net
Web: michiganindianelders.org/students.php

Summary To provide financial assistance to members of constituent tribes and bands of the Michigan Indian Elders

Association (MIEA) who are interested in attending college in any state.

Eligibility This program is open to enrolled members of the 11 MIEA constituent tribes and bands and their direct descendants. Applicants must be 1) graduating high school seniors who have a GPA of 3.0 or higher; 2) students currently enrolled in college, university, or trade school who have a GPA of 3.0 or higher; or 3) holders of a GED certificate who passed all 5 GED equivalency tests with a minimum score of at least 40 and an average score of at least 45. They must be attending or planning to enroll full time at a college, university, or trade school in any state. Financial need is not considered in the selection process.

Financial data Stipends are $1,000 or $500.

Duration 1 year.

Additional information The constituent tribes and bands are the Grand Traverse Band of Ottawa and Chippewa Indians, Hannahville Band of Potawatomi Indians, Keweenaw Bay Indian Community, Lac Vieux Desert Band of Lake Superior Chippewa Indians, Little River Band of Ottawa Indians, Little Traverse Bay Band of Odawa Indians, Match-E-Be-Nash-She-Wish Band of Potawatomi Indians (Gun Lake Tribe), Nottawaseppi Huron Band of the Potawatomi, Pokagon Band of Potawatomi Indians, Saginaw Chippewa Indian Tribe, and Sault Ste. Marie Tribe of Chippewa Indians.

Number awarded At least 10 each year, including 4 at $1,000 and at least 6 at $500.

Deadline June of each year.

[414]
MICHIGAN INDIAN TUITION WAIVER PROGRAM

Michigan Department of Civil Rights
Attn: Michigan Indian Tuition Waiver
110 West Michigan Avenue, Suite 800
Lansing, MI 48933
(517) 335-3165　　　　　　　　Fax: (517) 241-0546
TDD: (517) 241-1965
E-mail: MDCR-INFO@michigan.gov
Web: www.michigan.gov

Summary To exempt members of Indian tribes from tuition at Michigan postsecondary institutions.

Eligibility This program is open to Michigan residents who have lived in the state for at least 12 months and can certify at least one-quarter North American Indian blood from a federally-recognized tribe. Applicants must be attending a public college, university, or community college in Michigan. The program includes full- and part-time study, academic-year and summer school, and undergraduate and graduate work.

Financial data All qualified applicants are entitled to waiver of tuition at Michigan public institutions.

Duration Indian students are entitled to the waiver as long as they attend college in Michigan.

Additional information This program began in 1976 as the result of an agreement between the state of Michigan and the federal government under which the state agreed to provide free tuition to North American Indians in exchange for the Mt. Pleasant Indian School, which the state acquired as a training facility for the developmentally disabled.

Number awarded Varies each year.

Deadline Deadline not specified.

[415]
MICKEY LELAND ENERGY FELLOWSHIPS

Oak Ridge Institute for Science and Education
Attn: MLEF Fellowship Program
1299 Bethel Valley Road, Building SC-200
P.O. Box 117, MS 36
Oak Ridge, TN 37831-0117
(865) 574-6440　　　　　　　　Fax: (865) 576-0734
E-mail: barbara.dunkin@orau.org
Web: orise.orau.gov/mlef/index.html

Summary To provide summer work experience at fossil energy sites of the Department of Energy (DOE) to Native American, other underrepresented minority, and female students or postdoctorates.

Eligibility This program is open to U.S. citizens currently enrolled full time at an accredited college or university. Applicants must be undergraduate, graduate, or postdoctoral students in fields of science, technology (IT), engineering, or mathematics (STEM) and have a GPA of 3.0 or higher. They must be interested in a summer work experience at a DOE fossil energy research facility. Along with their application, they must submit a 100-word statement on why they want to participate in this program. A goal of the program is to recruit women and underrepresented minorities into careers related to fossil energy, although all qualified students are encouraged to apply.

Financial data Weekly stipends are $600 for undergraduates, $750 for master's degree students, or $850 for doctoral and postdoctoral students. Travel costs for a round trip to and from the site and for a trip to a designated place for technical presentations are also paid.

Duration 10 weeks during the summer.

Additional information This program began as 3 separate activities: the Historically Black Colleges and Universities Internship Program established in 1995, the Hispanic Internship Program established in 1998, and the Tribal Colleges and Universities Internship Program, established in 2000. Those 3 programs were merged into the Fossil Energy Minority Education Initiative, renamed the Mickey Leland Energy Fellowship Program in 2000. Sites to which interns may be assigned include the National Energy Technology Laboratory (Morgantown, West Virginia, Albany, Oregon and Pittsburgh, Pennsylvania), Pacific Northwest National Laboratory (Richland, Washington), Sandia National Laboratory (Livermore, California), Lawrence Berkeley National Laboratory (Berkeley, California), Los Alamos National Laboratory (Los Alamos, New Mexico), Strategic Petroleum Reserve Project Management Office (New Orleans, Louisiana), or U.S. Department of Energy Headquarters (Washington, D.C.).

Number awarded Varies each year; recently, 30 students participated in this program.

Deadline December of each year.

[416]
MIDWIVES OF COLOR-WATSON MIDWIFERY STUDENT SCHOLARSHIP

American College of Nurse-Midwives
Attn: ACNM Foundation, Inc.
8403 Colesville Road, Suite 1550
Silver Spring, MD 20910-6374
(240) 485-1850   Fax: (240) 485-1818
E-mail: foundation@acnmf.org
Web: www.midwife.org

Summary To provide financial assistance for midwifery education to Native American and other students of color who belong to the American College of Nurse-Midwives (ACNM).

Eligibility This program is open to ACNM members of color who are currently enrolled in an accredited basic midwife education program and have successfully completed 1 academic or clinical semester/quarter or clinical module. Applicants must submit they must submit a 150-word essay on their 5-year midwifery career plans; a 150-word essay on their intended future participation in the local, regional, and/or national activities of the ACNM; a 150-word essay on their need for financial assistance; and a 100-word statement on how they would use the funds if they receive the scholarship. Selection is based on academic excellence, leadership potential, and financial need.

Financial data The stipend is $3,000.

Duration 1 year.

Number awarded Varies each year; recently, 3 were awarded.

Deadline February of each year.

[417]
MINNESOTA INDIAN SCHOLARSHIP PROGRAM

Minnesota Office of Higher Education
Attn: Minnesota Indian Scholarship Program
1450 Energy Park Drive, Suite 350
St. Paul, MN 55108-5227
(651) 642-0567   Toll Free: (800) 657-3866
Fax: (651) 642-0675   TDD: (800) 627-3529
E-mail: info.ohe@state.mn.us
Web: www.ohe.state.mn.us/mPg.cfm?pageID=149

Summary To provide financial assistance to Native Americans in Minnesota who are interested in working on an undergraduate or graduate degree in any field.

Eligibility Applicants must be at least one-fourth degree Indian ancestry; members of a recognized Indian tribe; at least high school graduates (or approved equivalent); accepted by an accredited college, university, or vocational school in Minnesota; and residents of Minnesota for at least 1 year. Undergraduates must be attending college at least three-fourths time; graduate students must be enrolled at least half time.

Financial data The stipend depends on need, to a maximum of $4,000 per year for undergraduates or $6,000 per year for graduate students. Awards are paid directly to the student's school or college.

Duration 1 year; may be renewed up to 4 additional years plus an additional 5 years of graduate study.

Number awarded Approximately 700 each year.

Deadline June of each year.

[418]
MINNESOTA SOCIAL SERVICE ASSOCIATION DIVERSITY SCHOLARSHIP

Minnesota Social Service Association
Attn: Membership and Diversity Committee
125 Charles Avenue
St. Paul, MN 55103
(651) 644-0556   Fax: (651) 224-6540
E-mail: ajorgensen@mnssa.org
Web: www.mnssa.org

Summary To provide financial assistance to Native Americans and other students from a diverse background who are enrolled in an undergraduate program in the health and human services field at a college in the upper Midwest.

Eligibility This program is open to residents of any state entering their junior or senior year at a college or university in Iowa, Minnesota, North Dakota, South Dakota, or Wisconsin. Applicants must be working full time on a degree in the health and human services field and have a GPA of 3.0 or higher. They must be from a diverse background, which may be along the dimensions of race, ethnicity, gender, sexual orientation, socioeconomic status, age, physical ability, religion, or other ideology. Financial need is considered in the selection process.

Financial data The stipend is $1,000.

Duration 1 year.

Number awarded 1 each year.

Deadline May of each year.

[419]
MINORITIES IN GOVERNMENT FINANCE SCHOLARSHIP

Government Finance Officers Association
Attn: Scholarship Committee
203 North LaSalle Street, Suite 2700
Chicago, IL 60601-1210
(312) 977-9700   Fax: (312) 977-4806
Web: www.gfoa.org

Summary To provide financial assistance to Native American and other minority upper-division and graduate students who are preparing for a career in state and local government finance.

Eligibility This program is open to upper-division and graduate students who are preparing for a career in public finance by working on a degree in public administration, accounting, finance, political science, economics, or business administration (with a specific focus on government or nonprofit management). Applicants must be members of a minority group, citizens or permanent residents of the United States or Canada, and able to provide a letter of recommendation from a representative of their school. Selection is based on career plans, academic record, plan of study, letters of recommendation, and GPA. Financial need is not considered.

Financial data The stipend is $6,000.

Duration 1 year.

Additional information This program defines minorities as Blacks or African Americans, American Indians or Alaskan Natives, Hispanics or Latinos, Native Hawaiians or other Pacific Islanders, or Asians.

Number awarded 1 each year.

Deadline February of each year.

[420]
MINORITY AFFAIRS COMMITTEE'S AWARD FOR OUTSTANDING SCHOLASTIC ACHIEVEMENT

American Institute of Chemical Engineers
Attn: Minority Affairs Committee
120 Wall Street, FL 23
New York, NY 10005-4020
Toll Free: (800) 242-4363   Fax: (203) 775-5177
E-mail: awards@aiche.org
Web: www.aiche.org

Summary To recognize and reward Native American and other underrepresented minority students majoring in chemical engineering who serve as role models for other minority students.

Eligibility Members of the American Institute of Chemical Engineers (AIChE) may nominate any chemical engineering student who serves as a role model for minority students in that field. Nominees must be members of a minority group that is underrepresented in chemical engineering (i.e., African American, Hispanic, Native American, Alaskan Native). They must have a GPA of 3.0 or higher. Along with their application, they must submit a 300-word essay on their immediate plans after graduation, areas of chemical engineering of most interest, and long-range career plans. Selection is based on that essay, academic record, participation in AIChE student chapter and professional or civic activities, and financial need.

Financial data The award consists of a plaque and a $1,500 honorarium.

Duration The award is presented annually.

Additional information This award was first presented in 1996.

Number awarded 1 each year.

Deadline Nominations must be submitted by May of each year.

[421]
MINORITY AND UNDERREPRESENTED ENVIRONMENTAL LITERACY PROGRAM

Missouri Department of Higher Education
Attn: Student Financial Assistance
205 Jefferson Street
P.O. Box 1469
Jefferson City, MO 65102-1469
(573) 751-2361   Toll Free: (800) 473-6757
Fax: (573) 751-6635   E-mail: info@dhe.mo.gov
Web: www.dhe.mo.gov/ppc/grants/muelp_0310_final.php

Summary To provide financial assistance to Native American and other underrepresented students from Missouri who are or will be working on a bachelor's or master's degree in an environmental field.

Eligibility This program is open to residents of Missouri who are high school seniors or current undergraduate or graduate students enrolled or planning to enroll full time at a college or university in the state. Priority is given to members of the following underrepresented minority ethnic groups: African Americans, Hispanic or Latino Americans, Native Americans and Alaska Natives, and Native Hawaiians and Pacific Islanders. Applicants must be working on or planning to work on a bachelor's or master's degree in 1) engineering (civil, chemical, environmental, mechanical, or agricultural);

2) environmental studies (geology, biology, wildlife management, natural resource planning, natural resources, or a closely-related course of study); 3) environmental chemistry; or 4) environmental law enforcement. They must be U.S. citizens or permanent residents or otherwise lawfully present in the United States. Graduating high school seniors must have a GPA of 3.0 or higher; students currently enrolled in college or graduate school must have a GPA of 2.5 or higher. Along with their application, they must submit a 1-page essay on why they are applying for this scholarship, 3 letters of recommendation, a resume of school and community activities, and transcripts that include SAT or ACT scores. Financial need is not considered in the selection process.

Financial data Stipends vary each year; recently, they averaged approximately $3,045 per year.

Duration 1 year; may be renewed if the recipient maintains a GPA of 2.5 or higher and full-time enrollment.

Additional information This program was established by the Missouri Department of Natural Resources but transferred to the Department of Higher Education in 2009.

Number awarded Varies each year.

Deadline May of each year.

[422]
MINORITY SCHOLARSHIP AWARD FOR ACADEMIC EXCELLENCE IN PHYSICAL THERAPY

American Physical Therapy Association
Attn: Honors and Awards Program
1111 North Fairfax Street
Alexandria, VA 22314-1488
(703) 684-APTA   Toll Free: (800) 999-APTA, ext. 8082
Fax: (703) 684-7343   TDD: (703) 683-6748
E-mail: honorsandawards@apta.org
Web: www.apta.org

Summary To provide financial assistance to Native American and other minority students who are interested in becoming a physical therapist or physical therapy assistant.

Eligibility This program is open to U.S. citizens and permanent residents who are members of the following minority groups: African American or Black, Asian, Native Hawaiian or other Pacific Islander, American Indian or Alaska Native, or Hispanic/Latino. Applicants must be in the final year of a professional physical therapy or physical therapy assistant education program. They must submit a personal essay outlining their professional goals and minority service. U.S. citizenship or permanent resident status is required. Selection is based on 1) demonstrated evidence of contributions in the area of minority affairs and services with an emphasis on contributions made while enrolled in a physical therapy program; 2) potential to contribute to the profession of physical therapy; and 3) scholastic achievement. Preference is given to members of the American Physical Therapy Association (APTA).

Financial data The stipend varies; recently, stipends were $5,000 for physical therapy professional education students or $2,000 for physical therapy assistant students.

Duration 1 year.

Number awarded Varies each year; recently, 7 professional education students and 1 physical therapy assistant student received awards.

Deadline November of each year.

[423]
MINORITY SCHOLARSHIP AWARDS FOR COLLEGE STUDENTS IN CHEMICAL ENGINEERING

American Institute of Chemical Engineers
Attn: Minority Affairs Committee
120 Wall Street, FL 23
New York, NY 10005-4020
Toll Free: (800) 242-4363   Fax: (203) 775-5177
E-mail: awards@aiche.org
Web: www.aiche.org

Summary To provide financial assistance for the undergraduate study of chemical engineering to Native American and other underrepresented minority college student members of the American Institute of Chemical Engineers (AIChE).

Eligibility This program is open to undergraduate student AIChE members who are also members of a minority group that is underrepresented in chemical engineering (African Americans, Hispanics, Native Americans, Alaskan Natives, and Pacific Islanders). They must have a GPA of 3.0 or higher. Along with their application, they must submit a 300-word essay on their immediate plans after graduation, areas of chemical engineering of most interest, and long-range career plans. Selection is based on that essay, academic record, participation in AIChE student chapter and professional or civic activities, and financial need.

Financial data The stipend is $1,000.

Duration 1 year; nonrenewable.

Number awarded Varies each year; recently, 16 were awarded.

Deadline June of each year.

[424]
MINORITY SCHOLARSHIP AWARDS FOR INCOMING COLLEGE FRESHMEN IN CHEMICAL ENGINEERING

American Institute of Chemical Engineers
Attn: Minority Affairs Committee
120 Wall Street, FL 23
New York, NY 10005-4020
Toll Free: (800) 242-4363   Fax: (203) 775-5177
E-mail: awards@aiche.org
Web: www.aiche.org

Summary To provide financial assistance to incoming Native American and other minority freshmen interested in studying science or engineering in college.

Eligibility Eligible are members of a minority group that is underrepresented in chemical engineering (African Americans, Hispanics, Native Americans, Alaskan Natives, and Pacific Islanders). Applicants must be graduating high school seniors planning to enroll at a 4-year university with a major in science or engineering. They must be nominated by an American Institute of Chemical Engineers (AIChE) local section. Selection is based on academic record (including a GPA of 3.0 or higher), participation in school and work activities, a 300-word letter outlining the reasons for choosing science or engineering, and financial need.

Financial data The stipend is $1,000.

Duration 1 year; nonrenewable.

Number awarded Approximately 10 each year.

Deadline Nominations must be submitted by June of each year.

[425]
MINORITY SCHOLARSHIP IN CLASSICS AND CLASSICAL ARCHAEOLOGY

Society for Classical Studies
Attn: Executive Director
New York University
20 Cooper Square
New York, NY 10003
(212) 992-7828   Fax: (212) 995-3531
E-mail: xd@classicalstudies.org
Web: www.classicalstudies.org

Summary To provide Native American and other minority undergraduates with summer training as preparation for advanced work in the classics or classical archaeology.

Eligibility Eligible to apply are minority (African American, Hispanic American, Asian American, and Native American) undergraduate students who wish to engage in summer study as preparation for graduate work in the classics or classical archaeology. Applicants may propose participation in summer programs in Italy, Greece, Egypt, or other classical centers; language training at institutions in the United States, Canada, or Europe; or other relevant courses of study. Selection is based on academic qualifications, especially in classics; demonstrated ability in at least 1 classical language; quality of the proposal for study with respect to preparation for a career in classics; and financial need.

Financial data The maximum award is $4,500.

Duration 1 summer.

Additional information This program includes 1 scholarship supported by the Gladys Krieble Delmas Foundation.

Number awarded 2 each year.

Deadline December of each year.

[426]
MINORITY TEACHER EDUCATION SCHOLARSHIPS

Florida Fund for Minority Teachers, Inc.
Attn: Executive Director
G415 Norman Hall
618 S.W. 12th Street
P.O. Box 117045
Gainesville, FL 32611-7045
(352) 392-9196   Fax: (352) 846-3011
E-mail: info@ffmt.org
Web: www.ffmt.org/mtes-application-active

Summary To provide scholarship/loans to Florida residents who are Native Americans or members of other minority groups preparing for a career as a teacher.

Eligibility This program is open to Florida residents who are African American/Black, Hispanic/Latino, Asian American/Pacific Islander, or American Indian/Alaskan Native. Applicants must be entering their junior year in a teacher education program at a participating college or university in Florida. Along with their application, they must submit an essay of 100 to 300 words on how their life experiences have impacted them to go into the field of education. Special consideration is given to community college graduates. Selection is based on writing ability, communication skills, overall academic performance, and evidence of commitment to the youth of America (preferably demonstrated through volunteer activities).

Financial data The stipend is $4,000 per year. Recipients are required to teach 1 year in a Florida public school for each year they receive the scholarship. If they fail to teach in a public school, they are required to repay the total amount of support received at an annual interest rate of 8%.

Duration Up to 2 consecutive years, provided the recipient remains enrolled full time with a GPA of 2.5 or higher.

Additional information For a list of the 22 participating public institutions and the 16 participating private institutions, contact the Florida Fund for Minority Teachers (FFMT). Recipients are also required to attend the annual (FFMT) recruitment and retention conference.

Number awarded Varies each year.

Deadline June of each year for fall semester; October of each year for spring semester.

[427]
MINORITY TEACHERS OF ILLINOIS SCHOLARSHIP PROGRAM

Illinois Student Assistance Commission
Attn: Scholarship and Grant Services
1755 Lake Cook Road
Deerfield, IL 60015-5209
(847) 948-8550   Toll Free: (800) 899-ISAC
Fax: (847) 831-8549   TDD: (800) 526-0844
E-mail: isac.studentservices@isac.illinois.gov
Web: www.isac.org

Summary To provide scholarship/loans to Native Americans and other minority students in Illinois who plan to become teachers at the preschool, elementary, or secondary level.

Eligibility Applicants must be Illinois residents, U.S. citizens or eligible noncitizens, members of a minority group (African American/Black, Hispanic American, Asian American, or Native American), and high school graduates or holders of a General Educational Development (GED) certificate. They must be enrolled at least half time as an undergraduate or graduate student, have a GPA of 2.5 or higher, not be in default on any student loan, and be enrolled or accepted for enrollment in a teacher education program.

Financial data Grants up to $5,000 per year are awarded. This is a scholarship/loan program. Recipients must agree to teach full time 1 year for each year of support received. The teaching agreement may be fulfilled at a public, private, or parochial preschool, elementary school, or secondary school in Illinois; at least 30% of the student body at those schools must be minority. It must be fulfilled within the 5-year period following the completion of the undergraduate program for which the scholarship was awarded. The time period may be extended if the recipient serves in the U.S. armed forces, enrolls full time in a graduate program related to teaching, becomes temporarily disabled, is unable to find employment as a teacher at a qualifying school, or takes additional courses on at least a half-time basis to obtain certification as a teacher in Illinois. Recipients who fail to honor this work obligation must repay the award with 5% interest.

Duration 1 year; may be renewed for a total of 8 semesters or 12 quarters.

Number awarded Varies each year.

Deadline Priority consideration is given to applications received by February of each year.

[428]
MISS CHEROKEE SCHOLARSHIPS

Cherokee Nation
Attn: Miss Cherokee Committee
P.O. Box 948
Tahlequah, OK 74465
(918) 207-3577   Fax: (918) 458-5580
E-mail: cultural@cherokee.org
Web: www.cherokee.org

Summary To recognize and reward, with college scholarships, women selected in the Miss Cherokee competition.

Eligibility This competition is open to women who are Cherokee Nation tribal citizens, reside within the 14-county tribal jurisdiction, are between 17 and 22 years of age, have graduated from high school or received a GED certificate, have never been married or cohabited, and have no children. Applicants must submit information on Cherokee cultural activities in which they participate, their community service, and their leadership skills.

Financial data The winner receives a $3,000 scholarship, first runner-up a $2,000 scholarship, and second runner-up a $1,000 scholarship. Funds are paid directly to the institution of higher education that the recipient is attending.

Duration The competition is held annually.

Number awarded 3 scholarships are awarded each year.

Deadline July of each year.

[429]
MISSOURI MINORITY TEACHING SCHOLARSHIP PROGRAM

Missouri Department of Higher Education
Attn: Student Financial Assistance
205 Jefferson Street
P.O. Box 1469
Jefferson City, MO 65102-1469
(573) 751-2361   Toll Free: (800) 473-6757
Fax: (573) 751-6635   E-mail: info@dhe.mo.gov
Web: www.dhe.mo.gov/ppc/grants/minorityteaching.php

Summary To provide scholarships and forgivable loans to Native American and other minority high school seniors, high school graduates, and college students in Missouri who are interested in preparing for a teaching career in mathematics or science.

Eligibility This program is open to Missouri residents who are African American, Asian American, Hispanic American, or Native American. Applicants must be 1) high school seniors, college students, or returning adults (without a degree) who rank in the top 25% of their high school class and have scores in the top 25% of the ACT or SAT examination (recently, that meant a composite score of 24 or higher on the ACT or 1360 or higher on the composite critical reading and mathematics SAT); or 2) baccalaureate degree-holders who are returning to an approved mathematics or science teacher education program. They must be a U.S. citizen or permanent resident or otherwise lawfully present in the United States. All applicants must be enrolled full time in an approved teacher education program at a community college,

4-year college, or university in Missouri. Selection is based on high school class rank, ACT or SAT scores, school and community activities, career interest in teaching, leadership skills, employment experience, and recommendations.

Financial data The stipend is $3,000 per year, of which $2,000 is provided by the state as a forgivable loan and $1,000 is provided by the school as a scholarship. Recipients must commit to teaching in a Missouri public elementary or secondary school for 5 years following graduation. If they fail to fulfill that obligation, they must repay the state portion of the scholarship with interest at 9.5%.

Duration Up to 4 years.

Number awarded Up to 100 each year.

Deadline May of each year.

[430]
MITCH MUSGROVE MEMORIAL SCHOLARSHIP

Chickasaw Foundation
2020 Arlington, Suite 4
P.O. Box 1726
Ada, OK 74821-1726
(580) 421-9030   Fax: (580) 421-9031
E-mail: ChickasawFoundation@chickasaw.net
Web: www.chickasawfoundation.org/Scholarships.aspx

Summary To provide financial assistance to members of the Chickasaw Nation who are working on a degree in finance or accounting.

Eligibility This program is open to Chickasaw students who are currently enrolled part or full time at an accredited 2- or 4-year college or university. Applicants must be majoring in finance or accounting and have a GPA of 2.0 or higher. Along with their application, they must submit high school or college transcripts; 2 letters of recommendation; a copy of their Chickasaw Nation citizenship card; a 2-page list of honors, achievements, awards, club memberships, societies, and civic involvement; and a 1-page essay on their long-term goals and plans for achieving those. Financial need is not considered in the selection process.

Financial data A stipend is awarded (amount not specified).

Duration 1 year.

Number awarded 1 each year.

Deadline June of each year.

[431]
MITCH SPERRY MEMORIAL LAW SCHOLARSHIP

Chickasaw Foundation
2020 Arlington, Suite 4
P.O. Box 1726
Ada, OK 74821-1726
(580) 421-9030   Fax: (580) 421-9031
E-mail: ChickasawFoundation@chickasaw.net
Web: www.chickasawfoundation.org/Scholarships.aspx

Summary To provide financial assistance to members of the Chickasaw Nation who are interested in working on an undergraduate or graduate degree in a field related to law.

Eligibility This program is open to Chickasaw students who are currently enrolled at an accredited 4-year college or university as a full-time undergraduate or law student. Applicants must be working on a degree in law, pre-law, legal studies, paralegal, or any major associated with law or a bache-

lor's degree obtained with the intention of pursuing a law degree. They must have a GPA of 3.0 or higher. Along with their application, they must submit high school, college, and/or law school transcripts; 2 letters of recommendation; a copy of their Chickasaw Nation citizenship card; a 2-page list of honors, achievements, awards, club memberships, societies, and civic involvement; and a 1-page essay on their long-term goals and plans for achieving those. Financial need is not considered in the selection process.

Financial data A stipend is awarded (amount not specified).

Duration 1 year.

Number awarded 1 each year.

Deadline June of each year.

[432]
MNACC STUDENT OF COLOR SCHOLARSHIP

Minnesota Association of Counselors of Color
c/o Cristina Montañez, Scholarship Committee
University of Minnesota at Morris
600 East Fourth Street
Morris, MN 56267
E-mail: scholarships@mnacc.org
Web: www.mnacc.org

Summary To provide financial assistance to Native American and other high school seniors of color in Minnesota who plan to attend college in the area.

Eligibility This program is open to seniors graduating from public and private high schools in Minnesota who are students of color. Applicants must be planning to enroll full time at a 4-year college or university, a 2-year college, or a trade or technical college that is a member of the Minnesota Association of Counselors of Color (MnACC). Along with their application, they must submit an essay, up to 500 words in length, on their choice of assigned topics.

Financial data Stipends are $1,000 or $500.

Duration 1 year; nonrenewable.

Additional information These scholarships may be used at approximately 67 MnACC member institutions, including colleges, universities, and technical schools in Minnesota as well as selected schools in Iowa, Michigan, North Dakota, South Dakota, and Wisconsin.

Number awarded Varies each year; recently, 26 were awarded.

Deadline March of each year.

[433]
MOHAWK HIGHER EDUCATION PROGRAM

St. Regis Mohawk Tribe
Attn: Higher Education
Community Building
412 State Route 37
Akwesasne, NY 13655-3109
(518) 358-2272, ext. 247   Toll Free: (800) 800-8679
Fax: (518) 358-3203   E-mail: rcook@srmt-nsn.gov
Web: www.srmt-nsn.gov

Summary To provide financial assistance to members of the St. Regis Mohawk Tribe who are interested in attending college in any state.

Eligibility This program is open to members of the St. Regis Mohawk Tribe who are enrolled full time at an accredited 2- or 4-year college or university in any state. Applicants must be able to demonstrate unmet financial need after receipt of all other financial aid (e.g., federal Pell Grants, New York TAP Awards). First priority is given to enrolled members who live on the reservation, second to enrolled members who live near the reservation, and third to one-quarter degree descendants of enrolled members who live in any state. Awards are presented on a first-come, first-served basis.

Financial data The stipend depends on the need of the recipient.

Duration 1 year; may be renewed, provided the recipient maintains a GPA of 2.0 or higher as a freshman or 2.5 or higher afterwards.

Additional information This program began in 1986.

Number awarded Varies each year.

Deadline July of each year for fall; December of each year for spring.

[434]
MONTANA AMERICAN INDIAN STUDENT WAIVER

Office of the Commissioner of Higher Education
Attn: Montana University System
State Scholarship Coordinator
2500 Broadway
P.O. Box 203201
Helena, MT 59620-3201
(406) 444-6570   Toll Free: (800) 537-7508
Fax: (406) 444-1469   E-mail: snewlun@montana.edu
Web: www.mus.edu

Summary To provide financial assistance to Montana Indians interested in attending college or graduate school in the state.

Eligibility Eligible to apply are Native American students (one-quarter Indian blood or more) who have been residents of Montana for at least 1 year prior to application, have graduated from an accredited high school or federal Indian school, and can demonstrate financial need.

Financial data Students eligible for this benefit are entitled to attend any unit of the Montana University System without payment of undergraduate or graduate registration or incidental fees.

Duration Students are eligible for continued fee waiver as long as they maintain reasonable academic progress and full-time status (12 or more credits for undergraduates, 9 or more credits for graduate students).

Number awarded Varies; more than $1 million in waivers are approved each year.

Deadline Deadline not specified.

[435]
MONTGOMERY SUMMER RESEARCH DIVERSITY FELLOWSHIPS

American Bar Foundation
Attn: Summer Research Diversity Fellowship
750 North Lake Shore Drive
Chicago, IL 60611-4403
(312) 988-6515   Fax: (312) 988-6579
E-mail: fellowships@abfn.org
Web: www.americanbarfoundation.org

Summary To provide an opportunity for Native American and other undergraduate students from diverse backgrounds to work on a summer research project in the field of law and social science.

Eligibility This program is open to U.S. citizens and permanent residents who are African Americans, Hispanic/Latinos, Asians, Puerto Ricans, Native Americans, or other individuals who will add diversity to the field of law and social science such as persons with disabilities and LGBTQ individuals. Applicants must be sophomores or juniors in college, have a GPA of 3.0 or higher, be majoring in the social sciences or humanities, and be willing to consider an academic or research career. Along with their application, they must submit a 200-word essay on their future plans and why this fellowship would contribute to them, another essay on an assigned topic, official transcripts, and a letter of recommendation from a faculty member familiar with their work.

Financial data Participants receive a stipend of $3,600.

Duration 35 hours per week for 8 weeks during the summer.

Additional information Students are assigned to an American Bar Foundation Research Professor who involves the student in the design and conduct of the professor's research project and who acts as mentor during the student's tenure.

Number awarded 4 each year.

Deadline February of each year.

[436]
MOONIENE OGEE MEMORIAL SCHOLARSHIP

Chickasaw Foundation
2020 Arlington, Suite 4
P.O. Box 1726
Ada, OK 74821-1726
(580) 421-9030   Fax: (580) 421-9031
E-mail: ChickasawFoundation@chickasaw.net
Web: www.chickasawfoundation.org/Scholarships.aspx

Summary To provide financial assistance to members of the Chickasaw Nation who are working on an undergraduate or graduate degree in education.

Eligibility This program is open to Chickasaw students who are currently working full time on an undergraduate, graduate, or doctoral degree in education. Applicants must have a GPA of 2.5 or higher. Along with their application, they must submit high school or college transcripts; 2 letters of recommendation; a copy of their Chickasaw Nation citizenship card; a 2-page list of honors, achievements, awards, club memberships, societies, and civic involvement; and a 1-page essay on their long-term goals and plans for achieving those. Financial need is not considered in the selection process.

Financial data A stipend is awarded (amount not specified).

Duration 1 year.

Number awarded 1 each year.

Deadline June of each year.

[437]
MORGAN STANLEY TRIBAL SCHOLARS PROGRAM

American Indian College Fund
Attn: Scholarship Department
8333 Greenwood Boulevard
Denver, CO 80221
(303) 426-8900   Toll Free: (800) 776-FUND
Fax: (303) 426-1200
E-mail: scholarships@collegefund.org
Web: www.collegefund.org

Summary To provide financial assistance to Native American students interested in attending a Tribal College or University (TCU) or mainstream university to prepare for a career in business and the financial services industry.

Eligibility This program is open to American Indians and Alaska Natives who are enrolled or planning to enroll full time at an eligible TCU or mainstream university. Applicants must have declared a major in business or a related field and have a GPA of 3.0 or higher. They must be able to demonstrate an interest in the financial services industry and a commitment to the American Indian community. Applications are available only online and include required essays on specified topics. Selection is based on exceptional academic achievement. U.S. citizenship is required.

Financial data The stipend is $5,000 at mainstream universities or $2,500 at TCUs.

Duration 1 year.

Additional information This scholarship is sponsored by Morgan Stanley, in partnership with the American Indian College Fund.

Number awarded 15 each year: 10 at TCUs and 5 at mainstream universities.

Deadline May of each year.

[438]
MORRIS K. UDALL SCHOLARSHIPS

Morris K. Udall and Stewart L. Udall Foundation
Attn: Program Manager, Scholarship Program
130 South Scott Avenue
Tucson, AZ 85701-1922
(520) 901-8564   Fax: (520) 670-5530
E-mail: info@udall.gov
Web: www.udall.gov

Summary To provide financial assistance to 1) college sophomores and juniors who intend to prepare for a career in environmental public policy; and 2) Native American and Alaska Native students who intend to prepare for a career in health care or tribal public policy.

Eligibility Each 2- and 4-year college and university in the United States and its possessions may nominate up to 6 sophomores or juniors for either or both categories of this program: 1) students who intend to prepare for a career in environmental public policy; and 2) Native American and Alaska Native students who intend to prepare for a career in health care or tribal public policy. For the first category, the program seeks future leaders across a wide spectrum of environmental fields, such as policy, engineering, science, education, urban planning and renewal, business, health, justice, or economics. For the second category, the program seeks future Native American and Alaska Native leaders in either 1) health care, including counseling, dentistry, health care administration, medicine, social work, and research into health conditions affecting Native American communities; or 2) tribal public policy, including tribal sovereignty, tribal law, Native American justice, cultural preservation and revitalization, natural resource management, Native American economic development, or Native American education. Nominees must be U.S. citizens, nationals, or permanent residents with a GPA of 3.0 or higher. Along with their application, they must submit an 800-word essay on a speech, legislative act, book, or public policy statement by either Morris K. Udall or Stewart L. Udall and its impact on their interests and goals. Selection is based on academic achievement; demonstrated commitment to their field; leadership, public service, consensus building, and integrity; and understanding of the Udall legacy as demonstrated by the essay.

Financial data The maximum stipend is $7,000 per year. Funds are to be used for tuition, fees, books, room, and board.

Duration 1 year; recipients nominated as sophomores may be renominated in their junior year.

Number awarded Approximately 60 each year, including at least 20 reserved for students in tribal public policy and native health care.

Deadline Faculty representatives must submit their nominations by early March of each year.

[439]
MOSS ADAMS DIVERSITY SCHOLARSHIPS

Moss Adams LLP
Attn: Moss Adams Foundation
999 Third Avenue, Suite 3300
Seattle, WA 98104
(206) 302-6800   Toll Free: (800) 243-4936
Fax: (206) 652-2098   E-mail: careers@mossadams.com
Web: www.mossadams.com/about/careers/home

Summary To provide financial assistance to Native American and other students who will promote diversity in the accounting profession.

Eligibility This program is open to sophomores working on a bachelor's degree in accounting. Applicants should be able to promote diversity, defined to include students from diverse racial and ethnic backgrounds, women, LGBT individuals, military veterans, and people with disabilities. They must have a GPA of 3.0 or higher. Selection is based on academic achievement, demonstrated leadership skills, extracurricular activities (particularly those in leadership roles in diversity organizations), and communication skills.

Financial data The stipend is $2,500.

Duration 1 year.

Number awarded Up to 12 each year.

Deadline March of each year.

[440]
MOSS ADAMS FOUNDATION DIVERSITY SCHOLARSHIPS

Moss Adams LLP
Attn: Moss Adams Foundation
999 Third Avenue, Suite 3300
Seattle, WA 98104
(206) 302-6800   Toll Free: (800) 243-4936
Fax: (206) 652-2098   E-mail: careers@mossadams.com
Web: www.mossadams.com/about/careers/home

Summary   To provide financial assistance to Native American and other students who are working on a bachelor's degree in accounting and who will promote diversity in the profession.

Eligibility   This program is open to students entering their junior year of a bachelor's degree program in accounting who have a GPA of 3.0 or higher. Applicants must be members of diverse racial and ethnic backgrounds, women, LGBT individuals, military veterans, or people with disabilities. Selection is based on academic achievement, demonstrated leadership skills, extracurricular activities (particularly those in leadership roles in diversity organizations, and effective communication skills.

Financial data   The stipend is $2,500.

Duration   1 year.

Number awarded   Approximately 7 each year.

Deadline   March of each year.

[441]
MOSS ADAMS FOUNDATION SCHOLARSHIP

Educational Foundation for Women in Accounting
Attn: Foundation Administrator
136 South Keowee Street
Dayton, OH 45402
(937) 424-3391   Fax: (937) 222-5749
E-mail: info@efwa.org
Web: www.efwa.org/scholarships_graduate.php

Summary   To provide financial support to women, including minority women, who are working on an accounting degree.

Eligibility   This program is open to women who are enrolled in an accounting degree program at an accredited college or university. Applicants must meet 1 of the following criteria: 1) women pursuing a fifth-year requirement either through general studies or within a graduate program; 2) women returning to school as current or reentry juniors or seniors; or 3) minority women. Selection is based on aptitude for accounting and business, commitment to the goal of working on a degree in accounting (including evidence of continued commitment after receiving this award), clear evidence that the candidate has established goals and a plan for achieving those goals (both personal and professional), financial need, and a demonstration of how the scholarship will impact her life. U.S. citizenship is required.

Financial data   The stipend is $1,000.

Duration   1 year.

Additional information   This program was established by Rowling, Dold & Associates LLP, a woman-owned C.P.A. firm based in San Diego. It was renamed when that firm merged with Moss Adams LLP.

Number awarded   2 each year: 1 to an undergraduate and 1 to a graduate student.

Deadline   April of each year.

[442]
MSCPA MINORITY SCHOLARSHIPS

Missouri Society of Certified Public Accountants
Attn: MSCPA Educational Foundation
540 Maryville Centre Drive, Suite 200
P.O. Box 958868
St. Louis, MO 63195-8868
(314) 997-7966   Toll Free: (800) 264-7966 (within MO)
Fax: (314) 997-2592   E-mail: dhull@mocpa.org
Web: www.mocpa.org/students/scholarships

Summary   To provide financial assistance to Native American and other minority residents of Missouri who are working on an undergraduate or graduate degree in accounting at a university in the state.

Eligibility   This program is open to members of minority groups underrepresented in the accounting profession (Black/African American, Hispanic/Latino, Native American, Asian American) who are currently working full time on an undergraduate or graduate degree in accounting at a college or university in Missouri. Applicants must either be residents of Missouri or the children of members of the Missouri Society of Certified Public Accountants (MSCPA). They must be U.S. citizens, have completed at least 30 semester hours of college work, have a GPA of 3.3 or higher, and be student members of the MSCPA. Selection is based on the GPA, involvement in MSCPA, educator recommendations, and leadership potential. Financial need is not considered.

Financial data   The stipend is $1,250 per year.

Duration   1 year; may be renewed.

Number awarded   Varies each year; recently, 3 were awarded.

Deadline   February of each year.

[443]
MSIPP INTERNSHIPS

Department of Energy
Office of Environmental Management
Savannah River National Laboratory
Attn: MSIPP Program Manager
Building 773-41A, 232
Aiken, SC 29808
(803) 725-9032   E-mail: connie.yung@srnl.doe.gov
Web: srnl.doe.gov/msipp/internships.htm

Summary   To provide an opportunity for undergraduate and graduate students at Minority Serving Institutions (MSIs) to work on a summer research project at designated National Laboratories of the U.S. Department of Energy (DOE).

Eligibility   This program is open to full-time undergraduate and graduate students enrolled at an accredited MSI. Applicants must be interested in working during the summer on a research project at a participating DOE National Laboratory. They must be working on a degree in a field of science, technology, engineering, or mathematics (STEM); the specific field depends on the particular project on which they wish to work. Their GPA must be 3.0 or higher. U.S. citizenship is required.

Financial data The stipend depends on the cost of living at the location of the host laboratory.

Duration 10 weeks during the summer.

Additional information This program is administered at the Savannah River National Laboratory (SRNL) in Aiken, South Carolina, which serves as the National Laboratory for the DOE Office of Environmental Management. The other participating National Laboratories are Argonne National Laboratory (ANL) in Argonne, Illinois, Idaho National Laboratory (INL) in Idaho Falls, Idaho, Los Alamos National Laboratory (LANL) in Los Alamos, New Mexico, Oak Ridge National Laboratory (ORNL) in Oak Ridge, Tennessee, and Pacific Northwest National Laboratory (PNNL) in Richland, Washington. The program began in 2016.

Number awarded Varies each year. Recently, the program offered 11 research projects at SRNL, 12 at ANL, 1 at INL, 7 at LANL, 4 at ORNL, and 7 at PNNL.

Deadline March of each year.

[444]
MULTICULTURAL AUDIENCE DEVELOPMENT INITIATIVE INTERNSHIPS

Metropolitan Museum of Art
Attn: Internship Programs
1000 Fifth Avenue
New York, NY 10028-0198
(212) 570-3710   Fax: (212) 570-3782
E-mail: mmainterns@metmuseum.org
Web: www.metmuseum.org

Summary To provide summer work experience at the Metropolitan Museum of Art to Native American and other college undergraduates, graduate students, and recent graduates from diverse backgrounds.

Eligibility This program is open to members of diverse groups who are undergraduate juniors and seniors, students currently working on a master's degree, or individuals who completed a bachelor's or master's degree within the past year. Ph.D. students may be eligible to apply during the first 12 months of their program, provided they have not yet achieved candidacy. Students from various academic backgrounds are encouraged to apply, but they must be interested in preparing for a career in the arts and museum fields. Freshmen and sophomores are not eligible.

Financial data The stipend is $3,750.

Duration 10 weeks, beginning in June.

Additional information Interns are assigned to departmental projects (curatorial, administration, or education) at the Metropolitan Museum of Art; other assignments may include giving gallery talks and working at the Visitor Information Center. The assignment is for 35 hours a week. The internships are funded by the Multicultural Audience Initiative at the museum.

Number awarded 1 or more each year.

Deadline January of each year.

[445]
MULTICULTURAL UNDERGRADUATE INTERNSHIPS AT THE GETTY CENTER

Getty Foundation
Attn: Multicultural Undergraduate Internships
1200 Getty Center Drive, Suite 800
Los Angeles, CA 90049-1685
(310) 440-7320   Fax: (310) 440-7703
E-mail: summerinterns@getty.edu
Web: www.getty.edu

Summary To provide summer work experience at facilities of the Getty Center to Native American and other minority undergraduates with ties to Los Angeles County, California.

Eligibility This program is open to currently-enrolled undergraduates who either reside or attend college in Los Angeles County, California. Applicants must be members of groups currently underrepresented in museum professions and fields related to the visual arts and humanities: individuals of African American, Asian, Latino/Hispanic, Native American, or Pacific Islander descent. They may be majoring in any field, including the sciences and technology, and are not required to have demonstrated a previous commitment to the visual arts. Along with their application, they must submit a personal statement of up to 500 words on why they are interested in this internship, including what they hope to gain from the program, their interest or involvement in issues of multiculturalism, aspects of their past experience that they feel are most relevant to the application, and any specific career or educational avenues they are interested in exploring. U.S. citizenship or permanent resident status is required.

Financial data The stipend is $5,000.

Duration 10 weeks during the summer.

Additional information Internships are available at the Getty Center in Los Angeles, the Getty Villa in Malibu, and approximately 65 arts and museum organizations in Los Angeles County.

Number awarded 15 to 20 each year.

Deadline January of each year.

[446]
MUTUAL OF OMAHA ACTUARIAL SCHOLARSHIP FOR MINORITY STUDENTS

Mutual of Omaha
Attn: Strategic Staffing-Actuarial Recruitment
3300 Mutual of Omaha Plaza
Omaha, NE 68175
Toll Free: (800) 365-1405
E-mail: diversity@mutualofomaha.com
Web: www.mutualofomaha.com

Summary To provide financial assistance and work experience to Native American and other minority undergraduate students who are preparing for an actuarial career.

Eligibility This program is open to members of minority groups (African American, Hispanic, Native American, Asian or Pacific Islander, or Alaskan Eskimo) who have completed at least 24 semester hours of full-time study. Applicants must be working on an actuarial or mathematics-related degree with the goal of preparing for an actuarial career. They must have a GPA of 3.4 or higher and have passed at least 1 actuarial examination. Prior to accepting the award, they must be available to complete a summer internship at the sponsor's home office in Omaha, Nebraska. Along with their application, they must submit a 1-page personal statement on why they are interested in becoming an actuary and how they are preparing themselves for an actuarial career. Status as a U.S. citizen, permanent resident, asylee, or refugee must be established.

Financial data   The scholarship stipend is $5,000 per year. Funds are paid directly to the student. For the internship, students receive an hourly rate of pay, subsidized housing, and financial incentives for successful examination results received during the internship period.

Duration   1 year. Recipients may reapply if they maintain a cumulative GPA of 3.4 or higher.

Number awarded   Varies each year.

Deadline   October of each year.

[447]
MV TRANSIT COLLEGE SCHOLARSHIP

Conference of Minority Transportation Officials
Attn: National Scholarship Program
100 M Street, S.E., Suite 917
Washington, DC 20003
(202) 506-2917   E-mail: info@comto.org
Web: www.comto.org/page/scholarships

Summary   To provide financial assistance to Native American and other minority college student members of the Conference of Minority Transportation Officials (COMTO) and family of members working on a degree in transportation or a related field.

Eligibility   This program is open to minority undergraduate students who have been COMTO members or whose parents, guardians, or grandparents have been members for at least 1 year. Applicants must be majoring in transportation, engineering, planning, or a related discipline. They must have a GPA of 2.0 or higher. Along with their application they must submit a cover letter on their transportation-related career goals and life aspirations. Financial need is not considered in the selection process.

Financial data   The stipend is $4,000. Funds are paid directly to the recipient's college or university.

Duration   1 year.

Additional information   This program is sponsored by MV Transportation, Inc.

Number awarded   1 or more each year.

Deadline   April of each year.

[448]
MV TRANSIT HIGH SCHOOL SENIOR SCHOLARSHIP

Conference of Minority Transportation Officials
Attn: National Scholarship Program
100 M Street, S.E., Suite 917
Washington, DC 20003
(202) 506-2917   E-mail: info@comto.org
Web: www.comto.org/page/scholarships

Summary   To provide financial assistance to Native American and other minority high school seniors who are members of the Conference of Minority Transportation Officials (COMTO) or family of members and interested in working on a degree in transportation or a related field.

Eligibility   This program is open to minority high school seniors who have been COMTO members or whose parents, guardians, or grandparents have been members for at least 1 year. Applicants must be planning to enroll at an accredited college, university, or vocational/technical institute and major in a transportation-related field. They must have a GPA of 2.0 or higher. Along with their application they must submit a cover letter on their transportation-related career goals and life aspirations. Financial need is not considered in the selection process.

Financial data   The stipend is $3,500. Funds are paid directly to the recipient's college or university.

Duration   1 year.

Additional information   This program is sponsored by MV Transportation, Inc.

Number awarded   1 or more each year.

Deadline   April of each year.

[449]
NASA SCHOLARSHIP AND RESEARCH OPPORTUNITIES (SRO) MINORITY UNIVERSITY RESEARCH AND EDUCATION PROJECT (MUREP) SCHOLARSHIPS

National Aeronautics and Space Administration
Attn: National Scholarship Deputy Program Manager
Office of Education and Public Outreach
Ames Research Center
Moffett Field, CA 94035
(650) 604-6958   E-mail: elizabeth.a.cartier@nasa.gov
Web: intern.nasa.gov

Summary   To provide financial assistance and summer research experience at National Aeronautics and Space Administration (NASA) facilities to Native American and other undergraduate students majoring in designated fields of science, technology, engineering, or mathematics (STEM) at a Minority Serving Institution (MSI).

Eligibility   This program is open to U.S. citizens and nationals who are working on an undergraduate degree at an MSI and have a GPA of 3.0 or higher with at least 2 years of full-time study remaining. Applicants must be majoring in chemistry, computer and information science and engineering, engineering (aeronautical and aerospace, biomedical, chemical, civil, computer, electrical and electronic, environmental, industrial and operations research, materials, mechanical, nuclear, ocean, optical, polymer, or systems) geosciences (including geophysics, hydrology, physical and dynamic meteorology, physical oceanography, planetary science), life sciences (including biochemistry, cell biology, developmental biology, evolutionary biology, genetics, physiology), materials research, mathematical sciences, or physics and astronomy. They must be available for an internship at a NASA center performing aeronautical research during the summer between their junior and senior years. Along with their application, they must submit a 1,000-word essay on 1) their professional goals and what attracted them to their intended STEM field of study; 2) the events and individuals that have been critical in influencing their academic and career decisions; and 3) how receiving the MUREP scholarship would help them accomplish their professional goals. Financial need is not considered in the selection process.

Financial data Students receive 75% of their tuition and education-related costs, up to $9,000 per academic year. The stipend for the summer internship is $6,000.

Duration 2 years.

Number awarded Up to 20 each year.

Deadline March of each year.

[450]
NATIONAL INDIAN GAMING ASSOCIATION TRIBAL COLLEGE SCHOLARSHIPS

American Indian College Fund
Attn: Scholarship Department
8333 Greenwood Boulevard
Denver, CO 80221
(303) 426-8900   Toll Free: (800) 776-FUND
Fax: (303) 426-1200
E-mail: scholarships@collegefund.org
Web: www.collegefund.org

Summary To provide financial assistance to Native American students interested in attending a Tribal College or University (TCU), especially those majoring in designated fields.

Eligibility This program is open to American Indians and Alaska Natives who are enrolled or planning to enroll full time at an eligible TCU. Applicants may be studying any field, but preference is given to business, hospitality, information technology, or marketing majors. They must have a GPA of 3.0 or higher. Applications are available only online and include required essays on specified topics. U.S. citizenship is required.

Financial data The stipend is $2,000.

Duration 1 year.

Additional information This scholarship is sponsored by the National Indian Gaming Association, in partnership with the American Indian College Fund.

Number awarded 1 or more each year.

Deadline May of each year.

[451]
NATIONAL INSTITUTES OF HEALTH UNDERGRADUATE SCHOLARSHIP PROGRAM

National Institutes of Health
Attn: Office of Intramural Training and Education
2 Center Drive
Building 2, Room 2E24
Bethesda, MD 20892-0230
(301) 594-2222   Fax: (301) 594-9606
TDD: (888) 352-3001   E-mail: ugsp@nih.gov
Web: www.training.nih.gov/programs/ugsp

Summary To provide loans-for-service for undergraduate education in the life sciences to Native Americans and other students from disadvantaged backgrounds.

Eligibility This program is open to U.S. citizens, nationals, and permanent residents who are enrolled or accepted for enrollment as full-time students at accredited 4-year institutions of higher education and committed to careers in biomedical, behavioral, and social science health-related research. Applicants must come from a family that meets federal standards of low income, currently defined as a family with an annual income below $23,540 for a 1-person family, ranging to below $81,780 for families of 8 or more. They must have a GPA of 3.3 or higher or be in the top 5% of their class.

Selection is based on commitment to a career in biomedical, behavioral, or social science health-related research as an employee of the National Institutes of Health (NIH); academic achievements; recommendations and evaluations of skills, abilities, and goals; and relevant extracurricular activities. Applicants are ranked according to the following priorities: first, juniors and seniors who have completed 2 years of undergraduate course work including 4 core science courses in biology, chemistry, physics, and calculus; second, other undergraduates who have completed those 4 core science courses; third, freshmen and sophomores at accredited undergraduate institutions; and fourth, high school seniors who have been accepted for enrollment as full-time students at accredited undergraduate institutions. The sponsor especially encourages applications from underrepresented minorities, women, and individuals with disabilities.

Financial data Stipends are available up to $20,000 per year, to be used for tuition, educational expenses (such as books and lab fees), and qualified living expenses while attending a college or university. Recipients incur a service obligation to work as an employee of the NIH in Bethesda, Maryland for 10 consecutive weeks (during the summer) during the sponsored year and, upon graduation, for 52 weeks for each academic year of scholarship support. The NIH 52-week employment obligation may be deferred if the recipient goes to graduate or medical school.

Duration 1 year; may be renewed for up to 3 additional years.

Number awarded 15 each year.

Deadline March of each year.

[452]
NATIONAL MUSEUM OF THE AMERICAN INDIAN 10-WEEK INTERNSHIPS IN CONSERVATION

National Museum of the American Indian
Attn: Conservation Office
Cultural Resources Center
4220 Silver Hill Road, MRC 538
Suitland, MD 20746-2863
(301) 238-1424   Fax: (301) 238-3201
E-mail: NMAIcrcconserv@si.edu
Web: www.nmai.si.edu

Summary To provide undergraduate and graduate students with an opportunity to learn more about conservation during an internship at the Smithsonian Institution's National Museum of the American Indian (NMAI).

Eligibility This program is open to undergraduate and graduate students with a background in studio art, anthropology, art history, museum studies, chemistry, or biology. Native American students interested in conservation and museum care practices are especially welcome. Applicants must be interested in participating in a program at the NMAI Cultural Resources Center in Suitland, Maryland that involves collaboration with Native people in developing appropriate methods of handling, preserving, and interpreting cultural materials.

Financial data Interns receive a stipend (amount not specified).

Duration 10 weeks, in summer or winter.

Number awarded Varies each year.

Deadline February of each year for summer; September of each year for winter.

[453]
NATIONAL OCEANIC AND ATMOSPHERIC ADMINISTRATION EDUCATIONAL PARTNERSHIP PROGRAM WITH MINORITY SERVING INSTITUTIONS UNDERGRADUATE SCHOLARSHIPS

National Oceanic and Atmospheric Administration
Attn: Office of Education
1315 East-West Highway
SSMC3, Room 10600
Silver Spring, MD 20910-6233
(301) 628-2900   E-mail: EPP.USP@noaa.gov
Web: www.noaa.gov

Summary To provide financial assistance and research experience to undergraduate students at Tribal Colleges and Universities and other Minority Serving Institutions who are majoring in scientific fields of interest to the National Oceanic and Atmospheric Administration (NOAA).

Eligibility This program is open to full-time juniors at Minority Serving Institutions, including Hispanic Serving Institutions (HSIs), Historically Black Colleges and Universities (HBCUs), Tribal Colleges and Universities (TCUs), Alaskan Native Serving Institutions, and Native Hawaiian Serving Institutions. Applicants must have a GPA of 3.2 or higher and a major in atmospheric science, biology, computer science, engineering, environmental science, geography, hydrology, mathematics, oceanography, physical science, physics, remote sensing, social science, or other field that supports NOAA's programs and mission. They must also be interested in participating in a research internship at an NOAA site. Selection is based on relevant course work (30%), education plan and statement of career interest (40%), recommendations (20%), and additional experience related to diversity of education, extracurricular activities, honors and awards, non-academic and volunteer work, and communication skills (10%). U.S. citizenship is required.

Financial data Total support for 2 academic years and 2 summer internships is $45,000.

Duration 2 academic years and 2 summer internships.

Number awarded Up to 15 each year.

Deadline February of each year.

[454]
NATIONAL PRESS CLUB SCHOLARSHIP FOR JOURNALISM DIVERSITY

National Press Club
Attn: Executive Director's Office
529 14th Street, N.W., 13th Floor
Washington, DC 20045
(202) 662-7599
Web: www.press.org/about/scholarships/diversity

Summary To provide funding to Native American and other high school seniors who are planning to major in journalism in college and who will bring diversity to the field.

Eligibility This program is open to high school seniors who have been accepted to college and plan to prepare for a career in journalism. Applicants must submit 1) a 500-word essay explaining how they would add diversity to U.S. journalism; 2) up to 5 work samples demonstrating an ongoing interest in journalism through work on a high school newspaper or other media; 3) letters of recommendation from 3 people; 4) a copy of their high school transcript; 5) documentation of financial need; 6) a letter of acceptance from the college or university of their choice; and 7) a brief description of how they have pursued journalism in high school.

Financial data The stipend is $2,000 for the first year and $2,500 for each subsequent year. The program also provides an additional $500 book stipend, designated the Ellen Masin Persina Scholarship, for the first year.

Duration 4 years.

Additional information The program began in 1990.

Number awarded 1 each year.

Deadline February of each year.

[455]
NATIONAL SPACE GRANT COLLEGE AND FELLOWSHIP PROGRAM

National Aeronautics and Space Administration
Attn: Office of Education
300 E Street, S.W.
Mail Suite 6M35
Washington, DC 20546-0001
(202) 358-1069   Fax: (202) 358-7097
E-mail: aleksandra.korobov@nasa.gov
Web: www.nasa.gov

Summary To provide financial assistance to Native American and other undergraduate and graduate students interested in preparing for a career in a space-related field.

Eligibility This program is open to undergraduate and graduate students at colleges and universities that participate in the National Space Grant program of the U.S. National Aeronautics and Space Administration (NASA) through their state consortium. Applicants must be interested in a program of study and/or research in a field of science, technology, engineering, or mathematics (STEM) related to space. A specific goal of the program is to recruit and train U.S. citizens, especially underrepresented minorities, women, and persons with disabilities, for careers in aerospace science and technology. Financial need is not considered in the selection process.

Financial data Each consortium establishes the terms of the fellowship program in its state.

Additional information NASA established the Space Grant program in 1989. It operates through 52 consortia in each state, the District of Columbia, and Puerto Rico. Each consortium includes selected colleges and universities in that state as well as other affiliates from industry, museums, science centers, and state and local agencies.

Number awarded Varies each year.

Deadline Each consortium sets its own deadlines.

[456]
NATIONAL TRIBAL GAMING COMMISSIONS/ REGULATORS SCHOLARSHIPS

National Tribal Gaming Commissions/Regulators
Attn: Scholarship Committee
P.O. Box 454
Oneida, WI 54155
E-mail: dawnr@thehillgroup.org
Web: www.ntgcr.com/scholarships

Summary To provide financial assistance to Native Americans interested in working on an undergraduate or graduate degree in a field related to the gaming industry.

Eligibility This program is open to enrolled members of federally-recognized American Indian tribes and Alaska Native groups. Applicants must be high school seniors, rising undergraduates, or potential graduate students enrolled or planning to enroll full time at an accredited college or university in the United States and have a GPA of 2.5 or higher. They must be preparing for a career in the gaming, business, financial, or hospitality industries. Along with their application, they must submit a 4-page essay on their personal background (including whether or not they speak their tribal language or are learning their tribal language and other cultural skills), their degree plan for higher education, why they have chosen that field of study, how they plan to serve their tribal people when they complete their higher education, and why they should be selected for this scholarship. Selection is based on the essay, academic ability (judged on GPA, class rank, SAT and/or ACT scores, and curriculum rigor), leadership, honors and awards received, community involvement, 3 letters of recommendation, intellectual skills beyond the classroom, accomplishments, professional development, and financial need.

Financial data The stipend is $2,500.

Duration 1 year.

Number awarded 2 each year.

Deadline June of each year for fall semester; December of each year for spring semester.

[457]
NATIVE AGRICULTURE AND FOOD SYSTEMS COLLEGE SCHOLARSHIP PROGRAM

First Nations Development Institute
Attn: Senior Program Officer
2432 Main Street
Longmont, CO 80501
(303) 774-7836, ext. 208   Fax: (303) 774-7841
E-mail: mwhiting@firstnations.org
Web: www.firstnations.org/grantmaking/scholarship

Summary To provide financial assistance to Native Americans who are working on an undergraduate or graduate degree in an agriculture-related field.

Eligibility This program is open to enrolled members of a current or terminated federal or state tribe who are enrolled as full-time undergraduate or graduate students and can demonstrate a commitment to helping their Native community reclaim local food-system control. Applicants must be working on a degree in agriculture or a related field, including (but not limited to) agribusiness management, agriscience technologies, agronomy, animal husbandry, aquaponics, fisheries and wildlife, food production and safety, food-related policy and legislation, horticulture, irrigation science, plant-based nutrition, and sustainable agriculture or food systems. They must have a GPA of 3.0 or higher. Along with their application, they must submit an essay of 250 to 500 words on how they have been involved in their tribal community and how they will use their degree to help their tribe reclaim control of their traditional or local food system.

Financial data The stipend is $1,000.

Duration 1 year.

Additional information This program began in 2014.

Number awarded 6 each year.

Deadline November of each year.

[458]
NATIVE AMERICAN EDUCATION GRANTS

Presbyterian Church (USA)
Attn: Office of Financial Aid for Service
100 Witherspoon Street
Louisville, KY 40202-1396
(502) 569-5224   Toll Free: (888) 728-7228, ext. 5224
Fax: (502) 569-8766   TDD: (800) 833-5955
E-mail: finaid@pcusa.org
Web: www.presbyterianmission.org

Summary To provide financial assistance to Native American students interested in continuing their college education.

Eligibility This program is open to Alaska Native and Native American students who are enrolled or planning to enroll full time at an accredited institution in the United States. Applicants must be able to provide documentation of membership in a Native American or Alaska Native tribe. They must have a GPA of 2.5 or higher and be able to demonstrate financial need. Along with their application, they must submit a 500-word essay on what they plan to study and their plans for their education or career after college. Students from all faith traditions are encouraged to apply, but preference is given to members of the PCUSA.

Financial data Stipends range up to $3,000 per year, depending upon the recipient's financial need.

Duration 1 year; may be renewed up to 3 additional years.

Number awarded Up to 30 each year.

Deadline May of each year.

[459]
NATIVE AMERICAN HEALTH EDUCATION FUND SCHOLARSHIP

Triangle Community Foundation
Attn: Scholarships and Donor Services Officer
P.O. Box 12729
Durham, NC 27701
(919) 474-8370, ext. 4015   Fax: (919) 941-9208
E-mail: sarah@trianglecf.org
Web: www.trianglecf.org

Summary To provide financial assistance to Native Americans who are attending college or graduate school to prepare for a career in a health-related field.

Eligibility This program is open to Native American students currently enrolled at a college or graduate school. Applicants must be preparing for a career in medicine, nursing, dietetics and nutrition, medical technology, physical therapy, pharmacy, social work, medical research (biochemistry), or other health-related fields. They must be able to demonstrate a desire to return to their community or Reservation to improve health care.

Financial data The stipend ranges up to $1,000.

Duration 1 year.

Additional information This program, sponsored by the Native American Health Education Fund, awarded its first scholarship in 1990.

Number awarded Varies each year. Since the program began, it has awarded 106 scholarships.

Deadline June of each year.

[460]
NATIVE AMERICAN JOURNALISTS ASSOCIATION SCHOLARSHIPS

Native American Journalists Association
c/o University of Oklahoma
Gaylord College
395 West Lindsey Street
Norman, OK 73019-4201
(405) 325-1649   Fax: (405) 325-6945
E-mail: info@naja.com
Web: www.naja.com/students/naja-scholarships

Summary To provide financial assistance to student members of the Native American Journalists Association (NAJA) who are interested in a career in journalism or journalism education.

Eligibility This program is open to NAJA members who are high school seniors, undergraduates, or graduate students working on or planning to work on a degree in journalism. Applicants must include proof of enrollment in a federal- or state-recognized tribe; work samples; transcripts; a cover letter on their financial need, area of interest (print, broadcast, photojournalism, new media, journalism education), and reasons for preparing for a career in journalism; and 2 letters of recommendation.

Financial data The stipend is $1,000.

Duration 1 year.

Additional information Support for this program is provided by the Joseph Grimm Foundation, the Haskell Indian Nations University, and CNN.

Number awarded Varies each year; recently, 3 were awarded.

Deadline March of each year.

[461]
NATIVE AMERICAN NATURAL RESOURCE RESEARCH SCHOLARSHIP

Intertribal Timber Council
Attn: Education Committee
1112 N.E. 21st Avenue, Suite 4
Portland, OR 97232-2114
(503) 282-4296   Fax: (503) 282-1274
E-mail: itc1@teleport.com
Web: www.itcnet.org/about_us/scholarships.html

Summary Io provide funding to Native American undergraduate or graduate students interested in conducting tribally-relevant research on a natural resource issue.

Eligibility This program is open to undergraduate or graduate students who are enrolled members of a federally-recognized Indian tribe or Alaska Native Corporation. Applicants must be planning to conduct natural resource research that is tribally-relevant. They must submit a 4-page research proposal that includes 1) an abstract that explains the merit of the research and how it is relevant to tribal natural resource interests; 2) a timeline and methodology; 3) a dissemination plan, including a tribal component; and 4) budget and budget justification.

Financial data The grant ranges up to $4,000.

Duration 1 year.

Additional information This program is offered in partnership with the U.S. Forest Service.

Number awarded 1 each year.

Deadline January of each year.

[462]
NATIVE AMERICAN SCIENCE SCHOLARSHIPS

Denver Museum of Nature & Science
Attn: Department of Anthropology
Native American Science Initiative
2001 Colorado Boulevard
Denver, CO 80205
(303) 370-6367   E-mail: nascience@dmns.org
Web: www.dmns.org

Summary To provide financial assistance to Native Americans from Colorado who are interested in preparing for a science career.

Eligibility This program is open to students who have demonstrated leadership, academic achievement, and an interest in a science career. Preference is given to Native Americans who are either 1) seniors graduating from a high school in Colorado and planning to major in science at a college or university in any state; or 2) undergraduates from any state currently majoring in science at a college or university in Colorado. Applicants must submit 150-word essays on 1) their academic achievements; 2) their educational and career goals; and 3) why they should be selected for the program.

Financial data A stipend is awarded (amount not specified).

Duration 1 year.

Number awarded 1 or more each year.

Deadline September of each year.

[463]
NATIVE HAWAIIAN HEALTH SCHOLARSHIP PROGRAM

Papa Ola Lokahi, Inc.
Attn: Native Hawaiian Health Scholarship Program
894 Queen Street
Honolulu, HI 96813
(808) 597-6550   Fax: (808) 597-6552
E-mail: adminassist@nhhsp.org
Web: www.papaolalokahi.org

Summary To provide scholarship/loans to Native Hawaiians for training in the health professions in exchange for service, after graduation, in a federally-designated health professional shortage area (HPSA) or other facility for Native Hawaiians.

Eligibility Applicants must be Native Hawaiians training in allopathic or osteopathic medicine (M.D. or D.O.); dentistry (D.D.S. or D.M.D.); clinical psychology (Ph.D. or Psy.D.); nursing (A.D.N., B.S.N. or M.S.N.); nurse midwifery (M.S.N.); primary care nurse practitioner, including adult/geriatrics, community/public health, family health, pediatrics, and women's health (M.S.N.); social work, (M.S.W.); dental hygiene (D.H.); primary care physician assistant (master's level); optometry (O.D.): pharmacy (Pharm.D.); public health (M.P.H.); dietitian or nutritionist (master's level); or marriage and family therapy (M.F.T.). They may be studying in any state. Recipients must agree to serve in a designated health care facility in Hawaii upon completion of training. First priority is given to former scholars who have completed their previous service obligation and are seeking another year of support. Second priority is given to applicants who appear to have characteristics that increase the probability they will continue to serve underserved Native Hawaiians after the completion of their service obligations.

Financial data Full coverage of tuition and fees is paid directly to the health professional school. A stipend, recently set at $1,330 per month, is paid directly to the scholar. This is a scholarship/loan program. Participants are obligated to provide full-time clinical primary health care services to populations in 1) a Native Hawaiian Health Care System; or 2) an HPSA in Hawaii, medically underserved area (MUA), or another area or facility in Hawaii designated by the U.S. Department of Health and Human Services. Participants owe 1 year of service in the National Health Service Corps for each full or partial year of support received under this program. The minimum service obligation is 2 years.

Duration 1 year; may be renewed for up to 3 additional years.

Additional information This program, which began in 1991, is administered by the U.S. Health Resources and Services Administration, Bureau of Health Professions, through a contract with Papa Ola Lokahi, Inc.

Number awarded Normally, 10 each year.

Deadline February of each year.

[464]
NATIVE VISION SCHOLARSHIPS

Native Vision
c/o Johns Hopkins University
Center for American Indian Health
415 North Washington Street, Fourth Floor
Baltimore, MD 21231
(410) 955-6931　　　　　　　Fax: (410) 955-2010
E-mail: mhammen@jhsph.edu
Web: www.nativevision.org

Summary To provide financial assistance for college to American Indian high school seniors who participate in a sports camp.

Eligibility This program is open to graduating high school seniors who are enrolled members of a federally-recognized tribe. Applicants must have been admitted to an accredited community college or 4-year undergraduate program. They must be able to demonstrate a sustained involvement in the community, an applied interest in American Indian issues and initiatives, a GPA of 3.0 or higher, and involvement in extracurricular and/or athletic activities. Along with their application, they must submit a high school transcript, 2 letters of recommendation, and a 200-word essay on their goals for the future and how this scholarship will help them achieve their dreams; their essay should emphasize how their goals relate to their continued involvement in American Indian communities. The program is intended for students who also participate in the sponsor's summer Sports and Life Skills camp.

Financial data The stipend is $5,000.

Duration 1 year.

Additional information Native Vision was established in 2001 by the Center for American Indian Health at the Johns Hopkins Bloomberg School of Public Health and the National Football League Players Association. Each year, it sponsors a Sports and Life Skills camp, hosted by a tribal organization, for approximately 800 Native American students. In addition to training clinics in baseball, football, basketball, soccer, volleyball, and track, it conducts workshops on such topics as financial aid for college, leadership, crafts, and drunk driving prevention.

Number awarded 2 each year.

Deadline May of each year.

[465]
NAVAJO ENGINEERING AND CONSTRUCTION AUTHORITY SCHOLARSHIP PROGRAM

Navajo Engineering and Construction Authority
1 Uranium Boulevard
Shiprock, NM 87420
(505) 368-5151　　　　　　　Fax: (505) 368-3050
Web: www.navajo.net/scholarships

Summary To provide financial assistance to members of the Navajo Nation who are working on an undergraduate degree in specified fields at designated colleges.

Eligibility This program is open to enrolled members of the Navajo Nation who have a high school or college GPA of 2.7 or higher. Applicants must be enrolled at 1 of 8 designated colleges or universities and working on a degree in engineering, construction management/technology, finance, business management, accounting, pre-medicine, nursing, or teaching. They must be able to demonstrate financial need.

Financial data The stipend is $1,500 per semester ($3,000 per year). Funds are paid directly to the recipient's institution.

Duration 1 semester; may be renewed until graduation.

Additional information The eligible institutions are University of New Mexico, New Mexico State University, San Juan College, University of Arizona, Northern Arizona University, Diné College, Brigham Young University, and Fort Lewis College.

Number awarded 1 or more each year.

Deadline Deadline not specified.

[466]
NAVAJO GENERATING STATION NAVAJO SCHOLARSHIP

Salt River Project
Navajo Generating Station
Attn: Scholarship Committee
P.O. Box 850
Page, AZ 86040
(928) 645-6277　　　　E-mail: Rachelle.Lane@srpnet.com
Web: www.srpnet.com/education/grants/navajo.aspx

Summary To provide financial assistance to members of the Navajo Nation who have completed at least 2 years of college, particularly those who are majoring in selected sciences.

Eligibility This program is open to enrolled members of the Navajo Nation who are full-time students at an accredited college or university. Applicants must be entering their junior year of college and have a GPA of 3.0 or higher. Preference is given to students majoring in business or fields of science, technology, engineering, and mathematics (STEM). Along with their application, they must submit a 1-page letter explaining their career goals, reasons for selecting that field of study, and why they believe the sponsor should provide funds; a current resume; official transcripts; 2 letters of recommendation; documentation of financial need; and a Certificate of Indian Blood (CIB). Selection is based on field of study, academic excellence, and achievement.

Financial data The stipend depends on the need of the recipient.

Duration 1 year; may be renewed until completion of a bachelor's degree.

Additional information This program began in 1976.

Number awarded Varies each year; recently, 7 were awarded.

Deadline May of each year.

[467]
NAVAJO NATION COLLEGE DEVELOPMENTAL STUDIES PROGRAM

Navajo Nation
Attn: Office of Navajo Nation Scholarship and Financial Assistance
P.O. Box 1870
Window Rock, AZ 86515-1870
(928) 871-7444   Toll Free: (800) 243-2956
Fax: (928) 871-7410
E-mail: rosegraham@navajo-nsn.gov
Web: www.onnsfa.org/Documents/DocumentList.aspx

Summary To provide financial assistance to members of the Navajo Nation who require remedial education at the college level.

Eligibility This program is open to enrolled members of the Navajo Nation who are taking developmental studies courses to improve deficiencies in math, reading, or writing skills. Preference is given to students at Diné College. Selection is based on financial need.

Financial data The amount of the award depends on the need of the recipient.

Duration Recipients may enroll in up to 12 semester credit hours of college development courses during their first year in college.

Number awarded Varies each year.

Deadline June of each year for fall term; November of each year for winter or spring terms; April of each year for summer session.

[468]
NAVAJO NATION FINANCIAL NEED-BASED ASSISTANCE PROGRAM

Navajo Nation
Attn: Office of Navajo Nation Scholarship and Financial Assistance
P.O. Box 1870
Window Rock, AZ 86515-1870
(928) 871-7444   Toll Free: (800) 243-2956
Fax: (928) 871-7410
E-mail: rosegraham@navajo-nsn.gov
Web: www.onnsfa.org/Documents/DocumentList.aspx

Summary To provide financial assistance for college to members of the Navajo Nation.

Eligibility This program is open to enrolled members of the Navajo Nation who have proof of one-quarter or more Navajo Indian blood quantum on their Certificate of Degree of Indian Blood (CDIB). Applicants must be attending or planning to attend an accredited institution of higher education to work on an associate or baccalaureate degree. Financial need must be demonstrated.

Financial data The stipend is $1,500 per year.

Duration 1 year; may be renewed (if the recipient maintains at least a 2.0 GPA) for up to a total of 10 semesters of full-time undergraduate study, 5 academic terms or 64 semester credit hours at 2-year institutions, or 50 semester credit hours of part-time undergraduate study.

Number awarded Varies each year; recently, 3,714 were awarded.

Deadline June of each year for fall term; November of each year for winter or spring terms; April of each year for summer session.

[469]
NAVAJO NATION OIL AND GAS COMPANY SCHOLARSHIPS

Navajo Nation Oil and Gas Company
Attn: Scholarship Department
P.O. Box 4439
Window Rock, AZ 86515
(928) 871-4880   Toll Free: (888) 871-4880
Fax: (928) 871-4882   E-mail: scholarship@nnogc.com
Web: www.nnogc.com/scholarship.html

Summary To provide financial assistance to members of the Navajo Nation interested in attending college to prepare for a career in the petroleum industry.

Eligibility This program is open to high school seniors and undergraduates who are enrolled members of the Navajo Nation. Applicants must be enrolled or planning to enroll full time at a college or university and work on a bachelor's degree in accounting, business administration, engineering (civil, electrical, environmental, mechanical, mining, or petroleum), geology, human resource management, marketing, or natural resource management. They must be able to demonstrate financial need.

Financial data Scholarships provide full payment of tuition, room and board on campus, and books.

Duration 4 years, provided the recipient remains enrolled full time and maintains a GPA of 3.0 or higher.

Number awarded Up to 2 each year.

Deadline June of each year.

[470]
NAVAJO NATION TEACHER EDUCATION PROGRAM

Navajo Nation
Navajo Nation Scholarship and Financial Assistance
Attn: Navajo Nation Teacher Education Program
P.O. Box 1870
Window Rock, AZ 86515-1870
(928) 871-7453   Toll Free: (800) 243-2956
Fax: (928) 871-7410
E-mail: rosegraham@navajo-nsn.gov
Web: www.onnsfa.org/Documents/DocumentList.aspx

Summary To provide financial assistance to members of the Navajo Nation who wish to prepare for a career as a bilingual or bicultural teacher.

Eligibility This program is open to enrolled members of the Navajo Nation who are enrolled in or planning to enroll full or part time in an undergraduate degree program at a school on or near the Navajo Nation. Applicants must complete an emphasis in either Navajo Language or Navajo Culture, taken concurrently each semester with teacher education courses. They may be specializing in elementary education, early childhood education, bilingual multicultural education, special education, educational leadership, school counseling, curriculum and instruction, library science, or science and mathematics secondary education. Priority is given to 1) applicants fluent in the Navajo language and wishing to teach on the Navajo Nation; and 2) applicants who are paraprofessionals and/or Head Start staff currently teaching on the Navajo Nation or that serve a majority of Navajo students. Graduate students are not eligible. Financial need is not considered in the selection process.

Financial data A stipend is awarded (amount not specified).

Duration 1 semester; may be renewed for up to 5 additional semesters of full-time study or 11 additional semesters or part-time study.

Additional information Eligible institutions include Arizona State University, Diné College, San Juan College, Fort Lewis College, Northern Arizona University, Western New Mexico University, University of New Mexico at Gallup, University of Northern Colorado, or Prescott College.

Number awarded Varies each year; recently, 250 students were participating in the program.

Deadline Each eligible university or college sets its own deadline.

[471]
NAVAJO NATION VOCATIONAL EDUCATION PROGRAM

Navajo Nation
Attn: Office of Navajo Nation Scholarship and Financial Assistance
P.O. Box 1870
Window Rock, AZ 86515-1870
(928) 871-7444   Toll Free: (800) 243-2956
Fax: (928) 871-7410
E-mail: rosegraham@navajo-nsn.gov
Web: www.onnsfa.org/Documents/DocumentList.aspx

Summary To provide financial assistance for vocational education to members of the Navajo Nation.

Eligibility This program is open to enrolled members of the Navajo Nation who are enrolled or planning to enroll full time at a regionally-accredited vocational institution. Applicants must be interested in working on an associate of applied science degree or a vocational certificate. Selection is based on financial need.

Financial data The amount of the award depends on the need of the recipient.

Duration 1 year; may be renewed.

Number awarded Varies each year.

Deadline June of each year for fall term; November of each year for winter or spring terms; April of each year for summer session.

[472]
NAVAL RESEARCH LABORATORY SUMMER RESEARCH PROGRAM FOR HBCU/MI UNDERGRADUATES AND GRADUATES

Naval Research Laboratory
Attn: Personnel Operations Branch
4555 Overlook Avenue, S.W.
Washington, DC 20375-5320
(202) 767-8313
Web: www.nrl.navy.mil/hbcu/description

Summary To provide research experience at the Naval Research Laboratory (NRL) to undergraduate and graduate students in fields of science, technology, engineering, and mathematics (STEM) at Tribal Colleges and Universities and other minority institutions.

Eligibility This program is open to undergraduate and graduate students who have completed at least 1 year of study at an Historically Black College or University (HBCU), Minority Institution (MI), or Tribal College or University (TCU). Applicants must be working on a degree in a field of STEM and have a cumulative GPA of 3.0 or higher. They must be interested in participating in a research program at NRL under the mentorship of a senior staff scientist. U.S. citizenship or permanent resident status is required.

Financial data The stipend is $810 per week for undergraduates or $1,050 per week for graduate students. Subsidized housing is provided at a motel in the area.

Duration 10 weeks during the summer.

Additional information This program is conducted in accordance with a planned schedule and a working agreement between NRL, the educational institution, and the student.

Number awarded Varies each year.

Deadline February of each year.

[473]
NAVAL SEA SYSTEMS COMMAND (NAVSEA) AND STRATEGIC SYSTEMS PROGRAMS SCHOLARSHIP

American Indian Science and Engineering Society
Attn: Director of Membership and Communications
2305 Renard Place, S.E., Suite 200
Albuquerque, NM 87106
(505) 765-1052, ext. 110   Fax: (505) 765-5608
E-mail: lpaz@aises.org
Web: www.aises.org/scholarships/NAVSEA

Summary To provide financial assistance to high school senior members of the American Indian Science and Engineering Society (AISES) who are interested in studying Navy-related fields of science, technology, engineering, and mathematics (STEM) in college.

Eligibility This program is open to AISES members who are high school seniors planning to enroll full time at an ABET-accredited minority-serving 4-year college or university and major in a STEM field of relevant to the U.S. Navy. Applicants must be American Indian tribal members, Alaskan Natives, or Native Hawaiians and have a Certificate of Degree of Indian or Alaska Native Blood (CDIB) showing at least 25% Native blood. They must have a GPA of 3.0 or higher and be able to demonstrate financial need. U.S. citizenship is required.

Financial data The stipend is $10,000. Recipients are also eligible to apply for summer employment that provides up to $15,000 per year in continuing tuition assistance.

Duration 1 year; may be continued.

Additional information This program is sponsored by the Naval Sea Systems Command (NAVSEA) and the Strategic Systems Programs (SSP) of the U.S. Navy.

Number awarded 1 or more each year.

Deadline August of each year.

[474]
NAVY/MARINE CORPS JROTC SCHOLARSHIP

National Naval Officers Association-Washington, D.C.
  Chapter
c/o LCDR Stephen Williams
P.O. Box 30784
Alexandria, VA 22310
(703) 566-3840   Fax: (703) 566-3813
E-mail: Stephen.Williams@navy.mil
Web: dcnnoa.memberlodge.com/page-309002

Summary To provide financial assistance to Native American and other minority high school seniors from the Washington, D.C. area who have participated in Navy or Marine Corps Junior Reserve Officers Training Corps (JROTC) and are planning to attend college in any state.

Eligibility This program is open to minority seniors graduating from high schools in the Washington, D.C. metropolitan area who have participated in Navy or Marine Corps JROTC. Applicants must be planning to enroll full time at an accredited 2- or 4-year college or university in any state. They must have a GPA of 2.5 or higher. Selection is based on academic achievement, community involvement, and financial need. U.S. citizenship or permanent resident status is required.

Financial data The stipend is $1,000.

Duration 1 year; nonrenewable.

Additional information Recipients are not required to join or affiliate with the military in any way after college.

Number awarded 1 each year.

Deadline March of each year.

[475]
NBC UNIVERSAL SCHOLARSHIP

American Indian College Fund
Attn: Scholarship Department
8333 Greenwood Boulevard
Denver, CO 80221
(303) 426-8900   Toll Free: (800) 776-FUND
Fax: (303) 426-1200
E-mail: scholarships@collegefund.org
Web: www.collegefund.org

Summary To provide financial assistance to Native American students interested in attending a Tribal College or University (TCU) or mainstream university to prepare for a career in media.

Eligibility This program is open to American Indians and Alaska Natives who are planning to enroll as an undergraduate or graduate student at an eligible TCU or mainstream university. Applicants must have declared a major in broadcasting, entertainment, film, journalism, media, or telecommunications and have a GPA of 3.0 or higher. They must be able to demonstrate an interest in a career in media (either in front of

or behind the camera) and an internship in the Los Angeles or New York offices of NBC Universal. Applications are available only online and include required essays on specified topics. U.S. citizenship is required.

Financial data The stipend is $5,000 at mainstream universities or $5,250 at TCUs.

Duration 1 year.

Additional information This scholarship is sponsored by NBCUniversal, in partnership with the American Indian College Fund.

Number awarded 1 or more each year.

Deadline May of each year.

[476]
NELLIE STONE JOHNSON SCHOLARSHIP

Nellie Stone Johnson Scholarship Program
P.O. Box 40309
St. Paul, MN 55104
(651) 738-1404   Toll Free: (866) 738-5238
E-mail: info@nelliestone.org
Web: www.nelliestone.org/scholarship-program

Summary To provide financial assistance to Native American and other racial minority union members and their families who are interested in working on an undergraduate or graduate degree in any field at a Minnesota state college or university.

Eligibility This program is open to students in undergraduate and graduate programs at a 2- or 4-year institution that is a component of Minnesota State Colleges and Universities (MnSCU). Applicants must be a minority (Asian, American Indian, Alaska Native, Black/African American, Chicano(a) or Latino(a), Native Hawaiian, or Pacific Islander) and a union member or the child, grandchild, or spouse of a minority union member. They must submit a 2-page essay about their background, educational goals, career goals, and commitment to the causes of human or civil rights. Undergraduates must have a GPA of 2.0 or higher; graduate students must have a GPA of 3.0 or higher. Preference is given to Minnesota residents. Selection is based on the essay, commitment to human or civil rights, extracurricular activities, volunteer activities, community involvement, academic standing, and union verification.

Financial data Stipends are $1,200 per year for full-time students or $500 per year for part-time students.

Duration 1 year; may be renewed up to 3 additional years for students working on a bachelor's degree, 1 additional year for students working on a master's degree, or 1 additional year for students in a community or technical college program.

Number awarded Varies each year; recently, 18 were awarded.

Deadline May of each year.

[477]
NEW YORK EXCEPTIONAL UNDERGRADUATE/ GRADUATE STUDENT SCHOLARSHIP

Conference of Minority Transportation Officials
Attn: National Scholarship Program
100 M Street, S.E., Suite 917
Washington, DC 20003
(202) 506-2917   E-mail: info@comto.org
Web: www.comto.org/page/scholarships

Summary To provide financial assistance to Native American or other minority students who are members or relatives of members of the Conference of Minority Transportation Officials (COMTO) in New York and working on an undergraduate or graduate degree in transportation.

Eligibility This program is open to minorities who have been members or relatives of members of COMTO in New York for at least 1 year. Applicants must be enrolled full time at an accredited college, university, or vocational/technical institute and working on an undergraduate or graduate degree in a transportation-related discipline. They must have a GPA of 3.5 or higher. Along with their application they must submit a cover letter on their transportation-related career goals and life aspirations. Financial need is not considered in the selection process.

Financial data The stipend is $5,000. Funds are paid directly to the recipient's college or university.

Duration 1 year.

Number awarded 1 each year.

Deadline April of each year.

[478]
NEXTERA ENERGY-FORD DRY LAKE SCHOLARSHIP PROGRAM

American Indian Science and Engineering Society
Attn: Director of Membership and Communications
2305 Renard Place, S.E., Suite 200
Albuquerque, NM 87106
(505) 765-1052, ext. 110   Fax: (505) 765-5608
E-mail: lpaz@aises.org
Web: www.aises.org/scholoarships/nextera-energy

Summary To provide financial assistance to citizens of designated Native American nations in Arizona and California who are members of American Indian Science and Engineering Society (AISES) and working on an undergraduate or graduate degree in designated science and engineering fields.

Eligibility This program is open to AISES members in Arizona and California who are enrolled citizens of the following particpating tribal communities: Agua Caliente Band of Cahuilla Indians, Chemehueva Indian Tribe, Cahuilla Indian Tribe, Cocopah Indian Tribe, Colorado Indian River Tribes (Mohave, Chemehuevi, Hopi, Navajo), Fort Mohave Indian Tribe, Morongo Band of Mission Indians, Quechan Indian Tribe, Soboba Band of Luiseno Indians, Torres Martinez Desert Cahuilla Indians, or Twenty-Nine Palms Band of Mission Indians. Applicants must be enrolled full time at an accredited 2- or 4-year college, university, or vocational school in any state and working on an undergraduate or graduate degree in chemical engineering, computer engineering, computer science, electrical engineering, or material science. Along with their application, they must submit a 1,500-word personal statement on their educational and career goals, letters of recommendation, transcripts, and Certificate of Indian Blood (CIB) or proof of tribal enrollment. Selection is based on academic performance, the personal statement, letters of recommendation, and activities (e.g., jobs, volunteer efforts, internships, extracurricular involvement, hobbies).

Financial data The stipend is $5,000 per semester.

Duration 1 semester; may be renewed up to 5 additional semesters or until completion of a degree, whichever occurs first. Renewal requires that they maintain a GPA of 2.0 or higher.

Additional information This program is funded by the NextEra Energy Foundation and administered by AISES.

Number awarded 1 or more each year.

Deadline April of each year.

[479]
NIDDK DIVERSITY SUMMER RESEARCH TRAINING PROGRAM (DSRTP) FOR UNDERGRADUATE STUDENTS

National Institute of Diabetes and Digestive and Kidney Diseases
Attn: Office of Minority Health Research Coordination
6707 Democracy Boulevard, Room 906A
Bethesda, MD 20892-5454
(301) 435-2988   Fax: (301) 594-9358
E-mail: MartinezW@mail.nih.gov
Web: www.niddk.nih.gov

Summary To provide Native American and other underrepresented minority undergraduate students with an opportunity to conduct research in the laboratory of a National Institute of Diabetes and Digestive and Kidney Diseases (NIDDK) intramural scientist during the summer.

Eligibility This program is open to undergraduate students who come from backgrounds underrepresented in biomedical research, including individuals from disadvantaged backgrounds and those from of underrepresented racial and ethnic groups. Applicants must be interested in participating in a research project conducted at an intramural research laboratory of NIDDK in Bethesda, Maryland or Phoenix, Arizona. They must have completed at least 1 year at an accredited institution and have a GPA of 3.0 or higher. Along with their application, they must submit a 2-page personal statement of their research interest, career goals, and reasons for applying for training at NIDDK. U.S. citizenship or permanent resident status is required.

Financial data Students receive a stipend of $2,600, housing, and (for those who live outside the Washington metropolitan area or the state of Arizona) a travel allowance of $700.

Duration 10 weeks during the summer.

Number awarded Varies each year.

Deadline February of each year.

[480]
NIHEWAN SCHOLARSHIPS

Nihewan Foundation for Native American Education
9595 Wilshire Boulevard, Suite 1020
Beverly Hills, CA 90212
(808) 822-3111　　　　　Fax: (310) 278-0238
E-mail: info@nihewan.org
Web: www.nihewan.org/programs.html

Summary To provide financial assistance to Native Americans interested in studying about their culture in college.

Eligibility This program is open to enrolled members of a Native American tribe or Canadian First nation. Applicants must be interested in working on a college degree in Native American/indigenous studies. Along with their application, they must include 3 essays: 1) their goals with regard to Native American/indigenous studies; 2) other foundations that are helping finance their studies (must have applied to at least 2 other foundations and still have unmet need); and 3) their current school expenses.

Financial data A stipend is awarded (amount not specified).

Duration 1 year.

Additional information The Nihewan Foundation was established by singer-songwriter Buffy Sainte-Marie in 1969.

Number awarded 1 or more each year.

Deadline Deadline not specified.

[481]
NINILCHIK NATIVE ASSOCIATION SCHOLARSHIP AND VOCATIONAL GRANT

Cook Inlet Region, Inc.
Attn: The CIRI Foundation
3600 San Jeronimo Drive, Suite 256
Anchorage, AK 99508-2870
(907) 793-3575　　　　　Toll Free: (800) 764-3382
Fax: (907) 793-3585　　　E-mail: tcf@thecirifoundation.org
Web: www.thecirifoundation.org

Summary To provide financial assistance for professional preparation after high school to Alaska Natives who are original enrollees or descendants of the Ninilchik Native Association.

Eligibility This program is open to 1) Alaska Native enrollees of the Ninilchik Native Association under the Alaska Native Claims Settlement Act (ANCSA) of 1971; and 2) their lineal descendants. Proof of eligibility must be submitted. There is no residency requirement. Applicants for the scholarships must be accepted or enrolled full time in an accredited or otherwise approved postsecondary college or university; applicants for the grants may be enrolled either part or full time in a technical skills certificate or degree program. All applicants should have a GPA of 2.5 or higher. Along with their application, they must submit a 500-word statement on their educational and career goals and how they are contributing, or planning to contribute, to a positive Alaska Native community. Selection is based on that statement, academic achievement, rigor of course work or degree program, student financial contribution, financial need, grade level, previous work performance, community service, and relationship of degree program to career goals.

Financial data The stipend is $1,500.

Duration 1 semester for the general scholarship and 1 calendar year for the vocational technical grant; recipients may reapply.

Additional information This program began in 1992 and is currently administered by the The CIRI Foundation on behalf of the Ninilchik Native Association, Inc.

Number awarded Varies each year.

Deadline May or November of each year for academic scholarships; June of each year for vocational grants.

[482]
NISSAN NORTH AMERICA SCHOLARSHIP

American Indian College Fund
Attn: Scholarship Department
8333 Greenwood Boulevard
Denver, CO 80221
(303) 426-8900　　　　　Toll Free: (800) 776-FUND
Fax: (303) 426-1200
E-mail: scholarships@collegefund.org
Web: www.collegefund.org

Summary To provide financial assistance to Native American students enrolling in a bachelor's degree program at a Tribal College or University (TCU) or other institution.

Eligibility This program is open to American Indians and Alaska Natives who can document proof of enrollment or descendancy. Applicants must be enrolled or planning to enroll full time in a bachelor's degree program at a TCU or other institution. They must have a GPA of 2.5 or higher and be able to demonstrate leadership and commitment to an American Indian community. Applications are available only online and include required essays on specified topics. Selection is based on exceptional academic achievement. U.S. citizenship is required.

Financial data The stipend is $3,000 per year.

Duration 1 year; may be renewed.

Additional information This scholarship is sponsored by Nissan North America, Inc., in partnership with the American Indian College Fund.

Number awarded 20 each year.

Deadline May of each year.

[483]
NJUA EXCELLENCE IN DIVERSITY SCHOLARSHIP

New Jersey Utilities Association
50 West State Street, Suite 1117
Trenton, NJ 08608
(609) 392-1000　　　　　Fax: (609) 396-4231
E-mail: info@njua.com
Web: www.njua.com/excellence_in_diversity_scholarship

Summary To provide financial assistance to minority, female, and disabled high school seniors in New Jersey interested in attending college in any state.

Eligibility This program is open to seniors graduating from high schools in New Jersey who are women, minorities (Black or African American, Hispanic or Latino, American Indian or Alaska Native, Asian, Native Hawaiian or Pacific Islander, or 2 or more races), and persons with disabilities. Applicants must be planning to work on a bachelor's degree at a college or university in any state. Along with their application, they must submit a 500-word essay explaining their career ambition and why they have chosen that career. Children of employees of any New Jersey Utilities Association-member company are ineligible. Selection is based on overall academic excellence and demonstrated financial need. U.S. citizenship or permanent resident status is required.

Financial data The stipend is $1,500 per year. Funds are paid to the recipient's college or university.

Duration 4 years.

Number awarded 1 each year.

Deadline April of each year.

[484]
NMAI INTERNSHIP PROGRAM

National Museum of the American Indian
Attn: Internship Program
Fourth Street and Independence Avenue, S.W.
MRC 590
P.O. Box 37012
Washington, DC 20013
(202) 633-6645   Fax: (202) 633-6899
E-mail: NMAIinterns@si.edu
Web: www.nmai.si.edu/connect/internships/

Summary To provide work and/or research opportunities for Native American students in the area of museum practice and related programming at the Smithsonian Institution's National Museum of the American Indian (NMAI).

Eligibility These internships are intended primarily for American Indian, Native Hawaiian, and Alaska Native students currently enrolled in undergraduate or graduate academic programs with a cumulative GPA of 3.0 or higher. Applicants must be interested in guided work/research experiences using the resources of the NMAI or other Smithsonian Institution facilities. Along with their application, they must submit a personal statement on their interest in the museum field, what they hope to accomplish through an internship, how it would relate to their academic and professional development, and what in particular about the NMAI interests them and leads them to apply for an internship.

Financial data Stipends range from $100 to $400 per week.

Duration 3 sessions of 10 weeks each are held annually.

Additional information Intern projects vary by department. Most projects provide the intern with museum practice and program development experience. Some projects may be more research oriented. Interns who receive a stipend must work 40 hours per week. Positions are available at the Cultural Resources Center in Suitland, Maryland, the George Gustav Heye Center in New York, or the administrative offices in Washington, D.C.

Number awarded Varies each year. More than 100 students have participated in the program since it began in 1994.

Deadline February of each year for summer; July of each year for fall; November of each year for spring.

[485]
NOAH THOMAS LEASK FAMILY SCHOLARSHIPS

Sault Tribe of Chippewa Indians
Attn: Higher Education Department
523 Ashmun Street
Sault Ste. Marie, MI 49783
(906) 635-6050, ext. 26312   Toll Free: (800) 793-0660
Fax: (906) 635-7785   E-mail: BMacArthur@saulttribe.net
Web: www.saulttribe.com

Summary To provide financial assistance to members of the Sault Tribe of Chippewa Indians interested in attending college in any state to work on an undergraduate or graduate degree in any field.

Eligibility This program is open to members of the Sault Tribe who are enrolled full time at a 2- or 4-year college or university in any state. Applicants must be working on an undergraduate or graduate degree in any field. Along with their application, they must submit an essay of 1,000 to 2,000 words on a topic that changes annually but relates to their Indian heritage.

Financial data The stipend is $1,000.

Duration 1 year.

Number awarded 35 each year.

Deadline May of each year.

[486]
NOKIA BELL LABORATORIES INTERN PROGRAM

Nokia Bell Laboratories
Attn: Special Programs Manager
600-700 Mountain Avenue
Murray Hill, NJ 07974
(908) 582-3000   E-mail: info@bell-labs.com
Web: www.bell-labs.com/connect/internships

Summary To provide technical work experience at facilities of Nokia Bell Laboratories during the summer to Native Americans and other underrepresented undergraduate students.

Eligibility This program is open to women and members of minority groups (African Americans, Hispanics, and Native American Indians) who are underrepresented in the sciences. Applicants must be interested in pursuing technical employment experience in research and development facilities of Nokia Bell Laboratories. The program is primarily directed at undergraduate students who have completed their second or third year of college. Emphasis is placed on the following disciplines: business modeling, chemical engineering, chemistry, computer science and engineering, economics, electrical engineering, engineering mechanics, industrial engineering, manufacturing engineering, mathematics, mechanical engineering, operations research, physics, statistics, systems engineering, and telecommunications. U.S. citizenship or permanent resident status is required. Selection is based on academic achievement, personal motivation, and compatibility of student interests with current Nokia Bell Laboratories activities.

Financial data Salaries are commensurate with those of regular Nokia Bell Laboratories employees with comparable education. Interns are reimbursed for travel expenses up to the cost of round-trip economy-class airfare.

Duration 10 weeks during the summer.

Additional information Nokia Bell Laboratories facilities are located in central and northern New Jersey and in Naperville, Illinois.

Number awarded Varies each year.

Deadline November of each year.

[487]
NORMA T. MCGUIRE NATIVE AMERICAN SCHOLARSHIP

Florida Society Colonial Dames XVII Century
c/o Betty Jane Stewart
3155 Highland Grove Drive
Orange Park, FL 32065-6856

Summary To provide financial assistance to Native American high school seniors in Florida who plan to attend college in the state.

Eligibility This program is open to high school seniors in Florida who can provide proof of Native American descent from a U.S. tribe. Applicants must be planning to enroll full-time at a 2- or 4-year college or university in Florida. They must have a GPA of 3.5 or higher and be able to demonstrate financial need. Along with their application, they must submit a 1-page summary of their aims, ambitions, and why they need financial aid.

Financial data The stipend is $1,000.

Duration 1 year; nonrenewable.

Number awarded 1 each year.

Deadline April of each year.

[488]
NORTH CAROLINA AMERICAN INDIAN FUND SCHOLARSHIPS

Triangle Community Foundation
Attn: Scholarships and Donor Services Officer
P.O. Box 12729
Durham, NC 27701
(919) 474-8370, ext. 4015   Fax: (919) 941-9208
E-mail: sarah@trianglecf.org
Web: www.trianglecf.org

Summary To provide financial assistance to American Indian high school seniors from North Carolina who plan to attend college in the state.

Eligibility This program is open to residents of North Carolina who are enrolled members of a state or federally-recognized tribe. Applicants must be enrolled or planning to enroll full time at an accredited public or private college, university, community college, or trade school in North Carolina. They must have a GPA of 2.0 or higher. Along with their application, they must submit an essay on their past involvement in American Indian communities and their plans to address American Indian concerns and initiatives. Selection is based on academic merit and performance; commitment to and plan to give back to the American Indian community in the future; involvement in extracurricular, volunteer, and community activities; and demonstrated financial need.

Financial data The stipend is $1,000 per year; funds must be used for tuition, required fees, and textbooks.

Duration 1 year; recipients may reapply.

Additional information This program began in 2001.

Number awarded 1 or more each year.

Deadline April of each year.

[489]
NORTH CAROLINA CPA FOUNDATION OUTSTANDING MINORITY ACCOUNTING STUDENT SCHOLARSHIPS

North Carolina Association of Certified Public Accountants
Attn: North Carolina CPA Foundation, Inc.
P.O. Box 80188
Raleigh, NC 27623-0188
(919) 469-1040, ext. 130   Toll Free: (800) 722-2836
Fax: (919) 378-2000   E-mail: nccpafound@ncacpa.org
Web: www.ncacpa.org/scholarship-recipients

Summary To provide financial assistance to Native American and other minority undergraduate students working on a degree in accounting at colleges and universities in North Carolina.

Eligibility This program is open to North Carolina residents who are members of a minority group, defined as Black, Native American/Alaskan Native, Middle-Eastern, Asian or Pacific Islander, or Hispanic, and enrolled full time in an accounting program at a college or university in the state. Applicants must have completed at least 36 semester hours, including at least 1 college or university-level accounting course, and have a GPA of 3.0 or higher. They must be sponsored by an accounting faculty member. Selection is based on the content of an essay on a topic related to the public accounting profession (35%), essay grammar (35%), and extracurricular activities (30%).

Financial data Stipends are $2,000 or $1,000.

Duration 1 year; may be renewed up to 2 additional years.

Number awarded 2 each year: 1 at $2,000 and 1 at $1,000.

Deadline February of each year.

[490]
NORTH DAKOTA INDIAN SCHOLARSHIP PROGRAM

North Dakota University System
Attn: Financial Aid Office
State Capitol, Judicial Wing, Room 103
600 East Boulevard Avenue, Department 21
Bismarck, ND 58505-0602
(701) 328-2906   Fax: (701) 328-2979
E-mail: ndfinaid@ndus.edu
Web: www.ndus.nodak.edu

Summary To provide financial assistance to Native American students in North Dakota colleges and universities.

Eligibility Applicants must have at least one-quarter degree Indian blood, be residents of North Dakota or enrolled members of a tribe resident in North Dakota, and be accepted as full-time undergraduate students by an institution of higher learning or vocational education in North Dakota. Students with a GPA of 2.0 to 3.499 must be able to demonstrate financial need; those with a GPA of 3.5 or higher can qualify on the basis of merit.

Financial data The stipend ranges up to $2,000 depending on scholastic ability, funds available, total number of applicants, and financial need. The award is divided into semester or quarter payments. The money is to be used to pay registration, health fees, board, room, books, and other necessary items handled by the institution. Any remaining balance may be used to cover the student's personal expenses.

Duration 1 academic year; renewable up to 3 additional years, if the recipient maintains a 2.0 GPA and continues to be in financial need.

Number awarded Varies; approximately 150 to 175 each year.

Deadline July of each year.

[491]
NORTH TEXAS EXCEPTIONAL HIGH SCHOOL STUDENT SCHOLARSHIP

Conference of Minority Transportation Officials
Attn: National Scholarship Program
100 M Street, S.E., Suite 917
Washington, DC 20003
(202) 506-2917   E-mail: info@comto.org
Web: www.comto.org/page/scholarships

Summary To provide financial assistance to Native American and other minority high school seniors who are members or family of members of the Conference of Minority Transportation Officials (COMTO) in New York and planning to work on a degree in transportation.

Eligibility This program is open to minority residents of Texas who have been members or whose parents, guardians, or grandparents have been members of COMTO for at least 1 year. Applicants must be high school seniors who have been accepted at an accredited college, university, or vocational/technical institute and planning to work on a degree in a transportation-related discipline. They must have a GPA of 2.0 or higher. Along with their application they must submit a cover letter on their transportation-related career goals and life aspirations. Financial need is not considered in the selection process.

Financial data The stipend is $3,000. Funds are paid directly to the recipient's college or university.

Duration 1 year.

Number awarded 1 each year.

Deadline April of each year.

[492]
NORTH TEXAS EXCEPTIONAL UNDERGRADUATE/GRADUATE STUDENT SCHOLARSHIP

Conference of Minority Transportation Officials
Attn: National Scholarship Program
100 M Street, S.E., Suite 917
Washington, DC 20003
(202) 506-2917   E-mail: info@comto.org
Web: www.comto.org/page/scholarships

Summary To provide financial assistance to Native American and other minority residents of Texas who are working on an undergraduate or graduate degree in transportation.

Eligibility This program is open to minorities who are residents of Texas enrolled at an accredited college, university, or vocational/technical institute and working on an undergraduate or graduate degree in a transportation-related discipline. Applicants must have a GPA of 2.5 or higher. Along with their application they must submit a cover letter on their transpor-

tation-related career goals and life aspirations. Financial need is not considered in the selection process. Membership in the Conference of Minority Transportation Officials (COMTO) is considered a plus but is not required.

Financial data The stipend is $4,500. Funds are paid directly to the recipient's college or university.

Duration 1 year.

Number awarded 1 each year.

Deadline April of each year.

[493]
NORTHERN ARAPAHO TRIBAL SCHOLARSHIPS

Northern Arapaho Tribe
Attn: Sky People Higher Education
533 Ethete Road
P.O. Box 920
Fort Washakie WY 82514
(307) 332-5286   Toll Free: (800) 815-6795
Fax: (307) 332-9104 E-mail: assistant@skypeopleed.org
Web: www.skypeopleed.org/?page_id=117

Summary To provide financial assistance for college or graduate school to members of the Northern Arapaho Tribe.

Eligibility This program is open to anyone who can certify at least one-fourth degree Northern Arapaho Indian Blood, but preference is given to enrolled members of the Northern Arapaho tribe. Applicants must be enrolled or planning to enroll full time at an accredited college, university, or graduate school in any state. Funding priorities are 1) high school seniors ready to graduate; 2) continuing students with a GPA of 2.25 or higher; 3) high school or GED graduates; and 4) late applicants.

Financial data The amount of the awards depends on the financial need of the recipients.

Duration 1 year; may be renewed for a total of 5 academic years, provided the recipient remains enrolled full time and maintains a GPA of 2.25 or higher.

Additional information This program is supported by Northern Arapaho tribal funds.

Number awarded Varies each year.

Deadline June of each year for the academic year; November of each year for the spring semester; April of each year for summer school.

[494]
NORTHWEST FARM CREDIT SERVICES MINORITY SCHOLARSHIPS

Northwest Farm Credit Services
Attn: Public Relations and Events Manager
P.O. Box 2515
Spokane, WA 99220-2515
(509) 340-5467   Toll Free: (800) 743-2125
Fax: (800) 255-1789
E-mail: heidi.whitman@northwestfcs.com
Web: www.northwestfcs.com

Summary To provide financial assistance to Native American and other minority students who are majoring in a field related to agricultural business at universities in designated northwestern states.

Eligibility This program is open to members of minority ethnic groups (African American or Black, American Indian or Alaska Native, Asian, Latino/Hispanic, or Pacific Islander) currently enrolled as full-time sophomores or higher at 4-year universities in Alaska, Idaho, Montana, Oregon, Utah, or Washington. Applicants must be studying accounting, business, finance, agricultural business, or economics. They must have a GPA of 3.0 or higher and be U.S. citizens or legal residents. Along with their application, they must submit a 1-page essay on how they will use their education and degree to make a positive impact. Selection is based on that essay (20%), academic achievement (20%), leadership (25%), participation in extracurricular activities (25%), and letters of recommendation (10%).

Financial data   The stipend is $2,000.

Duration   1 year; nonrenewable.

Number awarded   4 each year.

Deadline   February of each year.

[495]
NORTHWEST INDIAN HOUSING ASSOCIATION YOUTH SCHOLARSHIP PROGRAM

Northwest Indian Housing Association
c/o Laurie Ann Cloud, Educational Scholarship
  Committee
Nez Perce Tribal Housing Authority
P.O. Bo 188
Lapwai, ID 83540
(208) 843-2229   E-mail: lauriec@nezperce.org
Web: www.nwiha.org/youth-scholarship-program

Summary   To provide financial assistance to members of Indian tribes affiliated with the Northwest Indian Housing Association (NWIHA) who are interested in attending college in any state.

Eligibility   This program is open to individuals younger than 24 years of age who are enrolled in Indian tribes that are NWIHA voting members. Applicants must be attending or planning to attend a 2- or 4-year college or university in any state. They must be sponsored by an NWIHA member organization, including a tribal department, an Indian housing authority, or a Tribally Designated Housing Entity (TDHE). Along with their application, they must submit an essay on their need for funds, how the funds will be used, and how the educational activity or training will improve their life.

Financial data   A stipend is awarded (amount not specified).

Duration   1 year.

Number awarded   1 or more each year.

Deadline   March of each year.

[496]
NORTHWEST JOURNALISTS OF COLOR SCHOLARSHIP AWARDS

Northwest Journalists of Color
c/o Anika Anand
The Evergrey
P.O. Box 30854
Seattle, WA 98113
E-mail: anikaanand00@gmail.com
Web: www.aajaseattle.org/scholarships

Summary   To provide financial assistance to students from Washington state who demonstrate a commitment to the importance of diverse cultural backgrounds and are interested in careers in journalism.

Eligibility   This program is open to students who are 1) current high school juniors or seniors in Washington; 2) residents of any state attending a 2- or 4-year college, university, or vocational school in Washington; or 3) seniors graduating from Washington high schools and planning to attend a 2- or 4-year college, university, or vocational school in any state. Applicants must be preparing for a career in broadcast, photo, or print journalism. They do not need to identify as a student of color, but strong preference is given to applicants who demonstrate an understanding of and commitment to the importance of diverse cultural backgrounds and experiences in newsrooms. Along with their application, they must submit 1) a 500-word essay about their interest in a career as a journalist; 2) link to a resume; 3) up to 3 work samples; and 4) a 250-word statement of financial need.

Financial data   Stipends range up to $2,500 per year.

Duration   1 year; may be renewed.

Additional information   This program, established in 1986, is sponsored by local chapters of the Asian American Journalists Association, the Native American Journalists Association, the Black Journalists Association of Seattle, and the National Association of Hispanic Journalists.

Number awarded   Varies each year.

Deadline   April of each year.

[497]
NOTAY BEGAY III SCHOLARSHIP PROGRAM

Albuquerque Community Foundation
Attn: Scholarship Program
624 Tijeras Avenue, N.W.
P.O. Box 25266
Albuquerque, NM 87125-5266
(505) 883-6240   Fax: (505) 883-3629
E-mail: foundation@albuquerquefoundation.org
Web: www.albuquerquefoundation.org

Summary   To provide financial assistance to Native American high school seniors in New Mexico who have participated in athletics and plan to attend college in any state.

Eligibility   This program is open to seniors graduating from high schools in New Mexico who are Native Americans. Applicants must be scholar-athletes with a varsity-level sports background and a GPA of 3.0 or higher. They must be planning to attend a college or university in any state as a full-time student. Along with their application, they must submit 1) a personal statement describing why they are going to college, what they plan to study, their career goals, any unusual challenges they face in continuing their education, and how they plan to give back to their community after college; 2) transcripts; 3) a reference from a current academic teacher or counselor; 4) a reference from an athletic coach; and 5) proof of tribal enrollment or Certificate of Degree of Indian Blood (at least 25%).

Financial data   The stipend is $1,400.

Duration   1 year; nonrenewable.

Additional information   This program began in 1999.

Number awarded   1 or 2 each year.

Deadline   March of each year.

[498]
NOVA CORPORATION SCHOLARSHIP

NOVA Corporation
1445 Sheffler Drive
Chambersburg, PA 17201
(717) 262-9750   Fax: (717) 262-9730
Web: www.nova-dine.com/scholarships-education

Summary To provide financial assistance to members of the Navajo Nation interested in working on a degree related to information technology.

Eligibility This program is open to members of the Navajo Nation who are enrolled as sophomores or higher at a college or university. Applicants must be majoring in a field related to information technology (e.g., management information systems, computer information systems, computer engineering) or that is crucial to its business functions (e.g., accounting, business management, communication, finance, marketing). They must have a GPA of 2.0 or higher. Along with their application, they must submit an essay of 500 to 800 words on why they should be considered for this scholarship. Special consideration is given to students from low-income families who have been unsuccessful in obtaining financial assistance through the normal FAFSA sources.

Financial data The stipend is $500 per semester ($1,000 per year).

Duration 1 year.

Additional information NOVA Corporation is an information technology firm owned by the Navajo Nation.

Number awarded 1 or more each year.

Deadline August of each year.

[499]
NSCA MINORITY SCHOLARSHIPS

National Strength and Conditioning Association
Attn: NSCA Foundation
1885 Bob Johnson Drive
Colorado Springs, CO 80906-4000
(719) 632-6722, ext. 152   Toll Free: (800) 815-6826
Fax: (719) 632-6367   E-mail: foundation@nsca.org
Web: www.nsca.com/foundation/nsca-scholarships

Summary To provide financial assistance to Native Americans and other minorities who are interested in working on an undergraduate or graduate degree in strength training and conditioning.

Eligibility This program is open to Blacks, Hispanics, Asian Americans, and Native Americans who are 17 years of age and older. Applicants must have been accepted into an accredited postsecondary institution to work on an undergraduate or graduate degree in the strength and conditioning field. Along with their application, they must submit a 500-word essay on their personal and professional goals and how receiving this scholarship will assist them in achieving those goals. Selection is based on that essay, academic achievement, strength and conditioning experience, honors and awards, community involvement, letters of recommendation, and involvement in the National Strength and Conditioning Association (NSCA).

Financial data The stipend is $1,500.

Duration 1 year.

Additional information The NSCA is a nonprofit organization of strength and conditioning professionals, including coaches, athletic trainers, physical therapists, educators, researchers, and physicians. This program was first offered in 2003.

Number awarded Varies each year; recently, 5 were awarded.

Deadline March of each year.

[500]
NSHSS NATIVE AMERICAN SCHOLAR AWARDS

National Society of High School Scholars Foundation
Attn: Scholarships
1936 North Druid Hills Road
Atlanta, GA 30319
(404) 235-5500   Toll Free: (866) 343-1800
Fax: (404) 235-5510
E-mail: scholarships@nshssfoundation.org
Web: www.nhss.org/member-benefits/scholarships

Summary To provide financial assistance to Native American high school juniors and seniors who are affiliated with the National Society of High School Scholars (NSHSS) and planning to attend college in any state.

Eligibility This program is open to high school juniors and seniors who are affiliated with the NSHSS and can document their Native American heritage. Applicants must be planning to major in any field at a college in any state. Along with their application, they must submit a resume, transcript, recommendation, photograph, personal statement, and name and e-mail address of their high school principal and counselor.

Financial data The stipend is $1,000.

Duration 1 year.

Number awarded 3 each year.

Deadline March of each year.

[501]
NTUA ENHANCED SCHOLARSHIP WITH INTERNSHIP

Navajo Tribal Utility Authority
Attn: HR Division/Training Department
P.O. Box 170
Fort Defiance, AZ 86504
(928) 729-5721, ext. 2152
Web: www.ntua.com/ntuascholarship.html

Summary To provide financial assistance and work experience to members of the Navajo Nation who are interested in working on an undergraduate or master's degree as preparation for a career in the utility industry.

Eligibility This program is open to enrolled members of the Navajo Nation who are enrolled to planning to enroll as full-time undergraduate or graduate students. Applicants must be preparing for a career in the multi-service utility industry by working on a degree in business, management, administration, accounting, engineering (civil, electrical, or environmental), information technology, or environment. They must also be interested in an internship with the Navajo Tribal Utility Authority (NTUA). Undergraduates must have a GPA of 2.0 or higher and graduate students must have at least a 3.0 GPA. Along with their application, they must submit a business letter describing their interest in the scholarship and describing how their degree aligns with the multi-service utility industry.

Financial data The stipend is $2,500 per year. The internship is paid.

Duration 1 year; may be renewed, provided undergraduates maintain a GPA of 2.0 or higher and graduate students maintain a GPA of 3.0 or higher.

Number awarded 1 or more each year.

Deadline April of each year.

[502]
NTUA SCHOLARSHIP

Navajo Tribal Utility Authority
Attn: HR Division/Training Department
P.O. Box 170
Fort Defiance, AZ 86504
(928) 729-5721, ext. 2152
Web: www.ntua.com/ntuascholarship.html

Summary To provide financial assistance to members of the Navajo Nation who are interested in working on an undergraduate or master's degree as preparation for a career in the utility industry.

Eligibility This program is open to enrolled members of the Navajo Nation who are enrolled to planning to enroll as full-time undergraduate or graduate students. Applicants must be preparing for a career in the multi-service utility industry by working on a degree in business, management, administration, accounting, engineering (civil, electrical, or environmental), information technology, or environment. Undergraduates must have a GPA of 2.0 or higher and graduate students must have at least a 3.0 GPA. Along with their application, they must submit a business letter describing their interest in the scholarship and describing how their degree aligns with the multi-service utility industry.

Financial data The stipend is $2,000 per year.

Duration 1 year; may be renewed, provided undergraduates maintain a GPA of 2.0 or higher and graduate students maintain a GPA of 3.0 or higher.

Number awarded 1 or more each year.

Deadline April of each year.

[503]
NYAL BRINGS UNDERGRADUATE SCHOLARSHIP

Dakota Indian Foundation
209 North Main Street
P.O. Box 340
Chamberlain, SD 57325-0340
(605) 234-5472   Fax: (605) 234-5858
Web: www.dakotaindianfoundation.org

Summary To provide financial assistance to American Indians (especially those of Sioux heritage) who have participated in college track and are majoring or minoring in Native American studies.

Eligibility This program is open to American Indians (priority given to those of Lakota, Dakota, or Nakota heritage) who are currently enrolled full time at a college or university in any state as a sophomore, junior, or senior. Applicants must be a college level athlete in track; other sports may be considered. They must major or minor in Native American studies, Lakota in particular. Along with their application, they must submit a personal statement that includes their qualifications for a scholarship, educational interest, career plans, extracurricular activities, and need for financial assistance.

Financial data The stipend is $1,000 per semester ($2,000 per year).

Duration 1 semester; recipients may reapply, provided they maintain a GPA of 2.0 or higher and demonstrate academic potential.

Number awarded Varies each year.

Deadline July of each year for the fall semester; January of each year for the spring semester.

[504]
NYS AID TO NATIVE AMERICANS

New York State Education Department
Attn: Native American Education Unit
Education Building Annex, Room 475
89 Washington Avenue
Albany, NY 12234
(518) 474-0537   Fax: (518) 474-3666
E-mail: emscosigen@mail.nysed.gov
Web: www.hesc.ny.gov

Summary To provide financial assistance to Native Americans in New York who are interested in attending college in the state.

Eligibility This program is open to Native Americans who meet these qualifications: are on official tribal rolls of a New York tribe or are the child of an enrolled member; are residents of New York; and are or will be graduates of an accredited high school or have a New York State General Equivalency Diploma or are enrolled in college credit programs working for the State High School Equivalency Diploma. Recipients must be accepted by an approved accredited postsecondary institution within New York.

Financial data The stipend is $2,000 per year for full-time study (at least 12 credit hours per semester or 24 credit hours per year); students registering for less than full-time study are funded on a prorated basis. Funding is available for summer course work on a special needs basis. Funds spent for summer school are deducted from the recipient's maximum entitlement.

Duration 1 year; renewable for up to 3 additional years (4 additional years for specific programs requiring 5 years to complete degree requirements).

Additional information The New York tribes include members of the Iroquoian tribes (St. Regis Mohawk, Oneida, Onondaga, Cayuga, Seneca Nation, Tonawanda Band of Seneca, and Tuscarora), the Shinnecock tribe, and the Poospatuck tribe. Remedial, non-credit, and college preparation courses are not funded.

Number awarded Varies; approximately 500 each year.

Deadline July of each year for fall semester; December of each year for spring semester; May of each year for summer session.

[505]
OFFICE OF HAWAIIAN AFFAIRS HIGHER EDUCATION SCHOLARSHIP PROGRAM

Hawai'i Community Foundation
Attn: Scholarship Department
827 Fort Street Mall
Honolulu, HI 96813
(808) 566-5570   Toll Free: (888) 731-3863
Fax: (808) 521-6286
E-mail: scholarships@hcf-hawaii.org
Web: hcf.scholarships.ngwebsolutions.com

Summary To provide financial assistance for college or graduate school to Native Hawaiian residents of any state.

Eligibility This program is open to residents of any state who can document Native Hawaiian ancestry through the Office of Hawaiian Affairs Hawaiian Registry Program. Applicants must be enrolled full or part time at an accredited 2- or 4-year college or university as an undergraduate or graduate student. They must be able to demonstrate academic achievement (GPA of 2.0 or higher for undergraduates or 3.0 or higher for graduate students), good moral character, and financial need. Along with their application, they must submit a short statement indicating their reasons for attending college, their planned course of study, their career goals, and what community service means to them.

Financial data The amounts of the awards depend on the availability of funds and the need of the recipient. Recently, the average value of the scholarships awarded by the foundation was $2,800.

Duration 1 year; may be renewed.

Number awarded Varies each year.

Deadline February of each year.

[506]
OGLALA SIOUX TRIBE HIGHER EDUCATION GRANT PROGRAM

Oglala Sioux Tribe
Attn: Higher Education
P.O. Box 562
Pine Ridge, SD 57770-0562
(605) 867-5338   Toll Free: (800) 832-3651
Fax: (605) 867-1390   E-mail: highered@gwtc.net

Summary To provide financial assistance to members of the Oglala Sioux Tribe who are interested in working on a baccalaureate degree at a college in any state.

Eligibility This program is open to members of the Oglala Sioux Tribe who are enrolled or planning to enroll at a 4-year college or university in any state. Applicants must be interested in working on a baccalaureate degree in any field; certificate and diploma programs do not qualify. Along with their application, they must submit their Certificate of Indian Blood (CIB), a letter of acceptance from the college they will attend, college transcripts of an official grade report, and a financial needs analysis form. Awards are granted on a first-come, first-served basis, contingent upon academic progress, financial need, and availability of funds.

Financial data A stipend is awarded (amount not specified).

Duration 1 year; may be renewed up to 4 additional years.

Number awarded Varies each year.

Deadline June of each year for academic year and fall semester or quarter; November of each year for spring term; March of each year for summer sessions.

[507]
OHIO HIGH SCHOOL ATHLETIC ASSOCIATION MINORITY SCHOLAR ATHLETE SCHOLARSHIPS

Ohio High School Athletic Association
Attn: Foundation
4080 Roselea Place
Columbus, OH 43214
(614) 267-2502   Fax: (614) 267-1677
Web: www.ohsaa.org/School-Resources

Summary To provide financial assistance to Native American and other minority high school seniors in Ohio who have participated in athletics and plan to attend college in any state.

Eligibility This program is open to minority seniors graduating from high schools in Ohio that are members of the Ohio High School Athletic Association (OHSAA). Applicants must have received at least 3 varsity letters in 1 sport or 4 letters in 2 sports and have a GPA of 3.25 or higher. They must be planning to attend a college or university in any state. Along with their application, they must submit a 1-page essay on the role that interscholastic athletics has played in their life and how such participation will benefit them in the future. Selection is based on that essay, GPA, ACT and SAT scores, varsity letters earned, and athletic honors.

Financial data The stipend is $1,000.

Duration 1 year.

Number awarded 6 each year: 1 in each OHSSA District.

Deadline April of each year.

[508]
OHIO NEWSPAPERS FOUNDATION MINORITY SCHOLARSHIPS

Ohio Newspaper Association
Attn: Foundation
1335 Dublin Road, Suite 216-B
Columbus, OH 43215-7038
(614) 486-6677, ext. 1010   Fax: (614) 486-6373
E-mail: ariggs@ohionews.org
Web: www.ohionews.org/aws/ONA/pt/sp/scholarships

Summary To provide financial assistance to American Indian and other minority high school seniors in Ohio planning to attend college in any state to prepare for a career in the newspaper industry.

Eligibility This program is open to high school seniors in Ohio who are members of minority groups (African American, Hispanic, Asian American, or American Indian) and planning to prepare for a career in the newspaper industry, especially advertising, communications, journalism, or marketing. Applicants must have a high school GPA of 2.5 or higher and demonstrate writing ability in an autobiography of 750 to 1,000 words that describes their academic and career interests, awards, extracurricular activities, and journalism-related activities. They must be planning to attend a college or university in Ohio.

Financial data The stipend is $1,500.

Duration 1 year; nonrenewable.

Additional information   This program began in 1990.
Number awarded   1 each year.
Deadline   March of each year.

[509]
OHIO NURSES FOUNDATION MINORITY STUDENT SCHOLARSHIP

Ohio Nurses Association
Attn: Ohio Nurses Foundation
4000 East Main Street
Columbus, OH 43213-2983
(614) 237-5414   Fax: (614) 237-6081
E-mail: info@ohionursesfoundation.org
Web: www.ohionursesfoundation.org

Summary   To provide financial assistance to Native American and other minority residents of Ohio who are interested in working on a degree in nursing at a school in any state.

Eligibility   This program is open to residents of Ohio who are members of a minority group and interested in attending college in any state to prepare for a career as a nurse. Applicants must be attending or have attended a high school in the state. If still in high school, they must have a cumulative GPA of 3.5 or higher at the end of their junior year. If out of high school, they may not have had a break of more than 2 years between high school and enrollment in a nursing program. Selection is based on a personal statement, high school or college academic records, school activities, and community services.

Financial data   The stipend is $1,000.

Duration   1 year; recipients may reapply for 1 additional year if they remain enrolled full time and maintain a cumulative GPA of 2.5 or higher.

Number awarded   1 or more each year.

Deadline   January of each year.

[510]
OKLAHOMA CAREERTECH FOUNDATION TEACHER RECRUITMENT/RETENTION SCHOLARSHIP FOR STUDENTS

Oklahoma CareerTech Foundation
Attn: Administrator
1500 West Seventh Avenue
Stillwater, OK 74074-4364
(405) 743-5453   Fax: (405) 743-5541
E-mail: leden@careertech.ok.gov
Web: www.okcareertech.org

Summary   To provide financial assistance to Native American and other residents of Oklahoma who reflect the diversity of the state and are attending a college or university in the state to prepare for a career in the Oklahoma CareerTech system.

Eligibility   This program is open to residents of Oklahoma who are juniors or seniors at an institution of higher education in the state. Applicants must be working on a bachelor's degree and teacher certification in Oklahoma's CareerTech system. They must reflect the ethnic diversity of the state. Along with their application, they must submit brief statements on their interest and commitment to the CareerTech teaching profession and their financial need.

Financial data   The stipend ranges from $500 per semester to $1,500 per year.

Duration   1 semester; may be renewed, provided the recipient maintains a GPA of 2.5 or higher.
Number awarded   1 or more each year.
Deadline   May of each year.

[511]
OLFIELD DUKES MULTICULTURAL STUDENT AWARD

Public Relations Student Society of America
Attn: Vice President of Member Services
33 Maiden Lane, 11th Floor
New York, NY 10038-5150
(212) 460-1474   Fax: (212) 995-0757
E-mail: DukesScholarship@prsa.org
Web: www.prssa.prsa.org

Summary   To provide financial assistance to Native American and other multicultural college seniors who are interested in preparing for a career in public relations.

Eligibility   This program is open to multicultural (African American/Black, Hispanic/Latino, Asian, Native American, Alaskan Native, or Pacific Islander) students who are entering their junior year at an accredited 4-year college or university. Applicants must have a GPA of 3.0 or higher and be working on a degree in public relations, journalism, or other field to prepare for a career in public relations. Selection is based on academic achievement, specific examples of commitment to service and social responsibility, awards and honors received for academic or extracurricular achievements, writing skills, and letters of recommendation.

Financial data   The stipend is $1,000.

Duration   1 year.

Additional information   This program began in 2013 with support from Prudential Financial and Weber Shandwick.

Number awarded   1 each year.

Deadline   June of each year.

[512]
OLIVE WHITMAN MEMORIAL SCHOLARSHIP

Daughters of the American Revolution-New York State Organization
c/o Nancy Goodnough
59 Susquehanna Avenue
Coopertown, NY 13326
(607) 547-8794   E-mail: ngoodnaugh@gmail.com
Web: www.nydar.org

Summary   To provide financial assistance for college or graduate school to Native American women in New York.

Eligibility   This program is open to women who are at least 50% Native American and residents of New York. Applicants must be graduating or have graduated from a high school in the state with a "B+" average. They must be attending or planning to attend an accredited college, university, or graduate school in the state.

Financial data   The stipend is $1,000.

Duration   1 year.

Number awarded   1 each year.

Deadline   April of each year.

[513]
OPERATION JUMP START III SCHOLARSHIPS

American Association of Advertising Agencies
Attn: AAAA Foundation
1065 Avenue of the Americas, 16th Floor
New York, NY 10018
(212) 262-2500   E-mail: ameadows@aaaa.org
Web: www.aaaa.org

Summary To provide financial assistance to Native American and other multicultural art directors and copywriters interested in working on an undergraduate or graduate degree in advertising.

Eligibility This program is open to African Americans, Asian Americans, Hispanic Americans, and Native Americans who are U.S. citizens or permanent residents. Applicants must be incoming graduate students at 1 of 6 designated portfolio schools or full-time juniors at 1 of 2 designated colleges. They must be able to demonstrate extreme financial need, creative talent, and promise. Along with their application, they must submit 10 samples of creative work in their respective field of expertise.

Financial data The stipend is $5,000 per year.

Duration Most awards are for 2 years.

Additional information Operation Jump Start began in 1997 and was followed by Operation Jump Start II in 2002. The current program began in 2006. The 6 designated portfolio schools are the AdCenter at Virginia Commonwealth University, the Creative Circus in Atlanta, the Portfolio Center in Atlanta, the Miami Ad School, the University of Texas at Austin, and Pratt Institute. The 2 designated colleges are the Minneapolis College of Art and Design and the Art Center College of Design at Pasadena, California.

Number awarded 20 each year.

Deadline Deadline not specified.

[514]
OREGON ALLIANCE OF INDEPENDENT COLLEGES AND UNIVERSITIES NAMED SCHOLARSHIP FOR UNDERREPRESENTED POPULATIONS

Oregon Alliance of Independent Colleges and Universities
Attn: Vice President
16101 S.W. 72nd Avenue, Suite 100
Portland, OR 97224
(503) 639-4541   Fax: (503) 639-4851
E-mail: brent@oaicu.org
Web: www.oaicu.org

Summary To provide financial assistance to Native Americans and members of other underrepresented populations who are residents of Oregon and interested in studying at an independent college in the state.

Eligibility This program is open to Oregon residents who are members of underrepresented populations and are enrolled or planning to enroll full time at a college or university that is a member of the Oregon Alliance of Independent Colleges and Universities (OAICU). Applicants must be planning to major in a field related to the business focus of designated sponsors. Selection is based on academic record in high school, achievements in school or community activities, financial need, and a written statement, up to 500 words, on the meaning of good citizenship and how the fulfillment of their personal goals will help applicants live up to that definition.

Financial data Stipends awarded by OAICU normally average approximately $2,500.

Duration 1 year.

Additional information The OAICU member institutions are Concordia University, Corban University, George Fox University, Lewis and Clark College, Linfield College, Marylhurst University, Northwest Christian University, Pacific University, Reed College, University of Portland, Warner Pacific College, and Willamette University. Recent sponsors included the BNSF Railway Foundation, Costco Wholesale, KeyBank, NW Natural, UPS Foundation, and Wells Fargo Bank.

Number awarded Varies each year.

Deadline March of each year.

[515]
OREGON NATIVE AMERICAN CHAMBER OF COMMERCE SCHOLARSHIPS

Oregon Native American Chamber of Commerce
Attn: Scholarship Committee Chair
P.O. Box 69593
Portland, OR 97239
(503) 894-4525   E-mail: ep.sherman@onacc.org
Web: www.onacc.org/si.html

Summary To provide financial assistance to Native American students from Oregon and southwestern Washington who are attending college in any state.

Eligibility This program is open to Native American residents of Oregon and southwestern Washington who are currently enrolled at an accredited community college or 4-year college or university in any state. Applicants must submit 300-word statements on how receiving this scholarship would benefit them and their educational needs, how they are involved in their Native American community on or off campus, what they plan to do with their education to help "give back" to Native Americans after graduation, and how they view their Native American heritage and its importance to them. Financial need is not considered in the selection process.

Financial data The stipend is $1,000.

Duration 1 year.

Additional information This program began in 2000. Recipients must attend the sponsor's annual gathering to receive their awards.

Number awarded Varies each year; recently, 10 were awarded.

Deadline July of each year.

[516]
OSAGE NATION CAREER TRAINING SCHOLARSHIPS

Osage Nation Education Department
Attn: Career Training and Scholarship
105 Buffalo Avenue
Hominy, OK 74035
(918) 287-5301   Fax: (918) 885-2136
E-mail: scholarship@osagenation-nsn.gov
Web: www.osagenation-nsn.gov

Summary To provide financial assistance for career training to members of the Osage Nation.

Eligibility This program is open to Osage tribal students who are enrolled or planning to enroll in community education (defined as continued education) or an accredited training institution that offers licensure or certification. Applicants are eligible for funding through 1 or more of the following types of aid: tuition and fees, books, and school supplies. They must be able to demonstrate financial need.

Financial data Grants provide payment of tuition for community education, to a maximum of $500 per course. For students at career institutions, the stipend is $180 per credit hour, or a maximum of $2,700 per semester for up to 15 credit hours, $1,620 per quarter for up to 9 credit hours, or $1,080 per semester of summer study for up to 6 credit hours.

Duration Students may receive support for up to 3 courses of community education per year or up to 15 credit hours per semester or 9 credit hours per quarter plus 6 credit hours for summer school at a career institution. Support is provided until completion of licensure or certification, provided the student maintains a GPA of 2.0 or higher.

Number awarded Varies each year.

Deadline June of each year for all semesters or quarters.

[517]
OSAGE NATION HIGHER EDUCATION SCHOLARSHIPS

Osage Nation Education Department
Attn: Career Training and Scholarship
105 Buffalo Avenue
Hominy, OK 74035
(918) 287-5301   Fax: (918) 885-2136
E-mail: scholarship@osagenation-nsn.gov
Web: www.osagenation-nsn.gov

Summary To provide financial assistance for college or graduate school to members of the Osage Nation.

Eligibility This program is open to Osage tribal students who are enrolled or planning to enroll at a 2- or 4-year college or university. Applicants are eligible for funding through 1 or more of the following types of aid: tuition and fees, books, room and board, and supplies and equipment. They must be able to demonstrate financial need.

Financial data Stipends are $150 per credit hour for students at associate degree colleges, $290 per credit hour for students at baccalaureate colleges, $330 per credit hour at research universities, or $360 per credit hour for students enrolled in professional or graduate programs.

Duration Students may receive support for up to 36 credit hours per academic year plus 12 credit hours for summer school.

Number awarded Varies each year.

Deadline June of each year for all semesters.

[518]
OSMANN FAMILY NATIVE AMERICAN SCHOLARSHIP

Sioux Falls Area Community Foundation
Attn: Scholarship Coordinator
200 North Cherapa Place
Sioux Falls, SD 57103-2205
(605) 336-7055, ext. 20   Fax: (605) 336-0038
E-mail: pgale@sfacf.org
Web: www.sfacf.org/statewide-students-college-bound

Summary To provide financial assistance to members of Indian tribes in South Dakota who are interested in attending college in the state.

Eligibility This program is open to enrolled members of South Dakota Indian tribes who are graduating from high school. Applicants must have a GPA of 2.5 or higher and a record of participation in school or community activities. They must be planning to attend an institution that is a member of the South Dakota university system or a vocational/technical school in Sioux Falls, Watertown, Mitchell, or Rapid City. Along with their application, they must submit a 250-word essay describing their educational goals.

Financial data The stipend is $1,000. Funds are paid in 2 equal installments and are to be used for tuition, fees, and/or books.

Duration 1 year.

Additional information This program began in 1998.

Number awarded 1 or more each year.

Deadline March of each year.

[519]
OWANAH ANDERSON SCHOLARSHIPS

Association on American Indian Affairs, Inc.
Attn: Director of Scholarship Programs
966 Hungerford Drive, Suite 12-B
Rockville, MD 20850
(240) 314-7155   Fax: (240) 314-7159
E-mail: general.aaia@indian-affairs.org
Web: www.indian-affairs.org

Summary To provide financial assistance to female Native American upper-division students.

Eligibility This program is open to female Native American students enrolled as full-time juniors and majoring in any field. Applicants must submit proof of tribal enrollment and an essay of 2 to 3 pages on 1 of the following topics: 1) why the sponsor's International Repatriation Project is important and how they would inform others about it; 2) the Annie E. Casey Foundation's Juvenile Detention Alternatives Initiative and tribal and community-based alternatives to detention for juveniles; or 3) how tribal leaders can promote higher education in their family and community. They must have a GPA of 2.5 or higher. Selection is based on merit and need.

Financial data The stipend is $1,500 per year.

Duration 2 years.

Number awarded Varies each year; recently, 3 were awarded.

Deadline May of each year.

[520]
PA STUDENT SCHOLARSHIPS

American Academy of Physician Assistants
Attn: Physician Assistant Foundation
2318 Mill Road, Suite 1300
Alexandria, VA 22314-6868
(703) 836-2272   Fax: (703) 684-1924
E-mail: pafoundation@aapa.org
Web: www.pa-foundation.org

Summary To provide financial assistance to student members of the American Academy of Physician Assistants (AAPA) who are Native American or other underrepresented minorities or disadvantaged students.

Eligibility This program is open to AAPA student members attending a physician assistant program accredited by the Commission on Accreditation of Allied Health Education Programs. Applicants must qualify as 1) an underrepresented minority (American Indian, Alaska Native, Black or African American, Hispanic or Latino, Native Hawaiian or other Pacific Islander, or Asian other than Chinese, Filipino, Japanese, Korean, Asian Indian, or Thai); 2) economically disadvantaged (with income below a specified level); or 3) educationally disadvantaged (from a high school with low SAT scores, from a school district in which less than half of graduates go on to college, has a diagnosed physical or mental impairment, English is not their primary language, the first member of their family to attend college). They must have completed at least 1 semester of PA studies.

Financial data Stipends are $2,500, $2,000, or $1,000.

Duration 1 year; nonrenewable.

Additional information This program includes the AAPA Past Presidents Scholarship, the Bristol-Myers Squibb Endowed Scholarship, the National Commission on Certification of Physician Assistants Endowed Scholarships, the Procter & Gamble Endowed Scholarship, and the PA Foundation Scholarships.

Number awarded Varies each year; recently, 32 were awarded: 3 at $2,500, 27 at $2,000, and 2 at $1,000.

Deadline January of each year.

[521]
PACIFIC ISLANDER HEALTH PARTNERSHIP SCHOLARSHIPS

Pacific Islander Health Partnership
c/o Toaono Vaifale
1505 East 17th Street, Number 117
Santa Ana, CA 92705-8520
(714) 625-6880
E-mail: tvaifale@pacifichealthpartners.org
Web: www.pacifichealthpartners.org/scholarships.html

Summary To provide financial assistance to Native Hawaiians and Pacific Islanders who are interested in studying a field of science, technology, engineering, or mathematics (STEM).

Eligibility This program is open to students who self-identify as Native Hawaiian or Pacific Island and desire to advocate in the Pacific Islander communities. Applicants must be enrolled or planning to enroll at a 2- or 4-year college, university, or vocational school in any state. They must be majoring in a field of STEM and have a GPA of 3.0 or higher.

Financial data Stipends range from $250 to $1,000.

Duration 1 year.

Number awarded Varies each year; recently, 11 were awarded.

Deadline April of each year.

[522]
PAGE EDUCATION FOUNDATION GRANTS

Page Education Foundation
901 North Third Street, Suite 355
P.O. Box 581254
Minneapolis, MN 55458-1254
(612) 332-0406   Fax: (612) 332-0403
E-mail: info@page-ed.org
Web: www.page-ed.org

Summary To provide funding to Native American and other high school seniors of color in Minnesota who plan to attend college in the state.

Eligibility This program is open to students of color who are graduating from high schools in Minnesota and planning to enroll full time at a postsecondary school in the state. Applicants must submit a 500-word essay that deals with why they believe education is important, their plans for the future, and the service-to-children project they would like to complete in the coming school year. Selection is based on the essay, 3 letters of recommendation, and financial need.

Financial data Stipends range from $1,000 to $2,500 per year.

Duration 1 year; may be renewed up to 3 additional years.

Additional information This program was founded in 1988 by Alan Page, a former football player for the Minnesota Vikings. While attending college, the Page Scholars fulfill a 50-hour service-to-children contract that brings them into contact with K-8 students of color.

Number awarded Varies each year; recently, 503 Page Scholars (210 new recipients and 293 renewals) were enrolled, of whom 260 were African American, 141 Asian American, 70 Chicano/Latino, 13 American Indian, and 19 biracial or multiracial.

Deadline April of each year.

[523]
PAUAHI FOUNDATION SCHOLARSHIP PROGRAM

Pauahi Foundation
Attn: Scholarships
567 South King Street, Suite 160
Honolulu, HI 96813-3036
(808) 534-3966   Fax: (808) 534-3890
E-mail: scholarships@pauahi.org
Web: www.pauahi.org/scholarships

Summary To provide financial assistance to college and graduate students, especially Native Hawaiians, who are working on a degree in various fields.

Eligibility This program includes many scholarships with different specifications, but all of them give preference to Native Hawaiians (descendants of the aboriginal inhabitants of the Hawaiian Islands prior to 1778). Most are for both undergraduate and graduate students, although some specify 1 or the other. Most are based on merit only, but some include or require financial need. Eligible fields of study cover a wide range of topics, and many are open to all fields. Most require full-time study, but some also allow half-time enrollment. Most are for residents and students in any state, but some require residence and/or study in Hawaii. Many, but not all, specify a minimum GPA. For a list of all the scholarships with their individual requirements, contact the foundation.

Financial data Stipends range from $500 to $5,000 per year.

Duration Most scholarships are for 1 year; some are renewable.

Number awarded Varies each year; the program includes 100 distinct scholarships, most of which provide only 1 award although some offer as many as 6.

Deadline February of each year.

[524]
PCMA EDUCATION FOUNDATION DIVERSITY SCHOLARSHIP

Professional Convention Management Association
Attn: PCMA Education Foundation
35 East Wacker Drive, Suite 500
Chicago, IL 60601
(312) 423-7262   Toll Free: (877) 827-7262
Fax: (312) 423-7222   E-mail: foundation@pcma.org
Web: www.pcma.org

Summary To provide financial assistance to student members of the Professional Convention Management Association (PCMA) who are Native Americans or members of other underrepresented groups and majoring in a field related to the meetings or hospitality industry.

Eligibility This program is open to PCMA members who are currently enrolled in at least 6 credit hours with a major directly related to the meetings or hospitality industry. Applicants must be students traditionally underrepresented in the industry, including (but not limited to) those identifying by a certain race, sex, color, religion, creed, sexual orientation, gender identity or expression, or disability, as well as those with a history of overcoming adversity. They must have a GPA of 2.75 or higher. Along with their application, they must submit a 750-word essay that details how they became interested in the meetings and events industry and a short paragraph describing the potential impact receiving this scholarship would have for them. Selection is based on that essay, academic record, meetings industry experience, and a letter of recommendation.

Financial data The stipend is $2,500.

Duration 1 year.

Number awarded 1 each year.

Deadline March of each year.

[525]
PDEF MICKEY WILLIAMS MINORITY SCHOLARSHIPS

Society of Nuclear Medicine and Molecular Imaging
Attn: Grants and Awards
1850 Samuel Morse Drive
Reston, VA 20190-5316
(703) 708-9000, ext. 1255   Fax: (703) 708-9015
E-mail: grantinfo@snm.org
Web: www.snmmi.org

Summary To provide financial support to Native American and other minority students working on an associate or bachelor's degree in nuclear medicine technology.

Eligibility This program is open to members of the Technologist Section of the Society of Nuclear Medicine and Molecular Imaging (SNMMI-TS) who are accepted or enrolled in a baccalaureate or associate degree program in nuclear medicine technology. Applicants must be members of a minority group: African American, Native American (including American Indian, Eskimo, Hawaiian, and Samoan), Hispanic American, Asian American, or Pacific Islander. They must have a cumulative GPA of 2.5 or higher and be able to demonstrate financial need. Along with their application, they must submit an essay on their reasons for entering the nuclear medicine technology field, their career goals, and their financial need. U.S. citizenship or permanent resident status is required.

Financial data The stipend is $2,500.

Duration 1 year; may be renewed for 1 additional year.

Additional information This program is supported by corporate sponsors of the Professional Development and Education Fund (PDEF) of the SNMMI-TS.

Number awarded Varies each year; recently, 2 were awarded.

Deadline December of each year.

[526]
PEGGY PETERMAN SCHOLARSHIP

Tampa Bay Times
Attn: Director of Corporate Giving
490 First Avenue South
St. Petersburg, FL 33701
(727) 893-8780   Toll Free: (800) 333-7505, ext. 8780
Fax: (727) 892-2257   E-mail: waclawek@tampabay.com
Web: www.tampabay.com

Summary To provide financial assistance to Native American and other minority undergraduate and graduate students who are interested in preparing for a career in the newspaper industry and who accept an internship at the *Tampa Bay Times*.

Eligibility This program is open to minority college sophomores, juniors, seniors, and graduate students from any state who are interested in preparing for a career in the newspaper industry. Applicants must be interested in an internship at the *Tampa Bay Times* and must apply for that at the same time as they apply for this scholarship. They should have experience working on a college publication and at least 1 professional internship.

Financial data The stipend is $5,000.

Duration Internships are for 12 weeks during the summer. Scholarships are for 1 year.

Number awarded 1 each year.

Deadline October of each year.

[527]
PENNSYLVANIA ACADEMY OF NUTRITION AND DIETETICS FOUNDATION DIVERSITY SCHOLARSHIP

Pennsylvania Academy of Nutrition and Dietetics
Attn: Foundation
96 Northwoods Boulevard, Suite B2
Columbus, OH 43235
(614) 436-6136   Fax: (614) 436-6181
E-mail: padafoundation@eatrightpa.org
Web: www.eatrightpa.org/scholarshipapp.cfm

Summary To provide financial assistance to members of the Pennsylvania Academy of Nutrition and Dietetics who are

Native Americans or members of other minority groups and working on an associate or bachelor's degree in dietetics.

Eligibility This program is open to academy members who are Black, Hispanic, Asian or Pacific Islander, or Native American (Alaskan Native, American Indian, or Hawaiian Native). Applicants must be 1) enrolled in the first year of study in an accredited dietetic technology program; or 2) enrolled in the third year of study in an accredited undergraduate or coordinated program in dietetics. They must have a GPA of 2.5 or higher. Along with their application, they must submit a letter indicating their intent and the reason they are applying for the scholarship, including a description of their personal financial situation. Selection is based on academic achievement (20%), commitment to the dietetic profession (30%), leadership ability (30%), and financial need (20%).

Financial data The stipend is $1,000.

Duration 1 year.

Additional information The Pennsylvania Academy of Nutrition and Dietetics is the Pennsylvania affiliate of the Academy of Nutrition and Dietetics.

Number awarded 1 or more each year.

Deadline April of each year.

[528]
PETER DOCTOR MEMORIAL INDIAN INCENTIVE GRANTS

Peter Doctor Memorial Indian Scholarship Foundation, Inc.
c/o Clara Hill, Treasurer
P.O. Box 431
Basom, NY 14013
(716) 542-2025   E-mail: ceh3936@hughes.net

Summary To provide financial assistance to New York Iroquois Indians who are graduating high school seniors and planning to attend college in any state.

Eligibility This program is open to enrolled New York Iroquois Indians who are graduating from high school and have been accepted at an accredited college or university in any state. Interviews may be required. Applicants must have tribal certification. Selection is based on need.

Financial data Stipends range from $700 to $1,500.

Duration 1 year.

Number awarded 1 from each tribe.

Deadline May of each year.

[529]
PETER DOCTOR MEMORIAL INDIAN SCHOLARSHIP GRANTS

Peter Doctor Memorial Indian Scholarship Foundation, Inc.
c/o Clara Hill, Treasurer
P.O. Box 731
Basom, NY 14013
(716) 542-2025   E-mail: ceh3936@hughes.net

Summary To provide financial assistance to New York Iroquois Indians currently enrolled at a college in any state on the undergraduate or graduate school level.

Eligibility This program is open to enrolled New York Iroquois Indian students who have completed at least 1 year at a technical school, college, or university in any state. Both undergraduate and graduate students are eligible. There are

no age limits or GPA requirements. Interviews may be required. Applicants must have tribal certification. Selection is based on need.

Financial data Stipends range up to $1,500.

Duration 2 years for medical students; 1 year for all other recipients.

Number awarded Varies each year.

Deadline May of each year.

[530]
PETER KALIFORNSKY MEMORIAL ENDOWMENT SCHOLARSHIP FUND

Cook Inlet Region, Inc.
Attn: The CIRI Foundation
3600 San Jeronimo Drive, Suite 256
Anchorage, AK 99508-2870
(907) 793-3575   Toll Free: (800) 764-3382
Fax: (907) 793-3585   E-mail: tcf@thecirifoundation.org
Web: www.thecirifoundation.org/about/donors

Summary To provide financial assistance for undergraduate or graduate studies, especially in Alaska Native studies, to Alaska Natives who are original enrollees to Cook Inlet Region, Inc. (CIRI) and their lineal descendants.

Eligibility This program is open to Alaska Native enrollees to CIRI under the Alaska Native Claims Settlement Act (ANCSA) of 1971 and their lineal descendants. There are no Alaska residency requirements or age limitations. Applicants must be accepted or enrolled full time in a 4-year undergraduate or a graduate degree program. Preference is given to students in Alaska Native studies. They must have a GPA of 2.5 or higher. Along with their application, they must submit a 500-word statement on their educational and career goals and how they are contributing, or planning to contribute, to a positive Alaska Native community. Selection is based on that statement, academic achievement, rigor of course work or degree program, student financial contribution, financial need, grade level, previous work performance, community service, and relationship of degree program to career goals.

Financial data The stipend is $10,000 per year, $8,000 per year, or $2,500 per semester, depending on GPA.

Duration 1 semester or 1 year.

Additional information CIRI is 1 of 13 regional corporations established according to the terms of the Alaska Native Claims Settlement Act (ANCSA) of 1971. This program began in 1993.

Number awarded 1 or more each year.

Deadline May of each year for annual scholarships; May or November of each year for semester scholarships.

[531]
PFATS-NFL CHARITIES MINORITY SCHOLARSHIPS

Professional Football Athletic Trainers Society
c/o Britt Brown, ATC, Associate Athletic Trainer
Dallas Cowboys
One Cowboys Parkway
Irving, TX 75063
(972) 497-4992   E-mail: bbrown@dallascowboys.net
Web: www.pfats.com/about/scholarships

Summary To provide financial assistance to Native American and other ethnic minority undergraduate and graduate students working on a degree in athletic training.

Eligibility This program is open to ethnic minority students who are working on an undergraduate or graduate degree in athletic training. Applicants must have a GPA of 2.5 or higher. Along with their application, they must submit a cover letter, a curriculum vitae, and a letter of recommendation from their supervising athletic trainer. Female athletic training students are encouraged to apply.

Financial data A stipend is awarded (amount not specified).

Duration 1 year.

Additional information Recipients also have an opportunity to work at summer training camp of a National Football League (NFL) team. Support for this program, which began in 1993, is provided by NFL Charities.

Number awarded 1 or more each year.

Deadline March of each year.

[532]
PGA OF AMERICA DIVERSITY SCHOLARSHIP PROGRAM

Professional Golfers' Association of America
Attn: PGA Foundation
100 Avenue of the Champions
Palm Beach Gardens, FL 33418
Toll Free: (888) 532-6662 E-mail: sjubb@pgahq.com
Web: www.pgafoundation.com

Summary To provide financial assistance to Native American and other minorities interested in attending a designated college or university to prepare for a career as a golf professional.

Eligibility This program is open to women and minorities interested in becoming a licensed PGA Professional. Applicants must be interested in attending 1 of 20 colleges and universities that offer the Professional Golf Management (PGM) curriculum sanctioned by the PGA.

Financial data The stipend is $3,000 per year.

Duration 1 year; may be renewed.

Additional information This program began in 1993. Programs are offered at the following universities: Arizona State University (Tempe), Campbell University (Buies Creek, North Carolina), Clemson University (Clemson, South Carolina), Coastal Carolina University (Conway, South Carolina), Eastern Kentucky University (Richmond), Ferris State University (Big Rapids, Michigan), Florida State University (Tallahassee), Florida Gulf Coast University (Fort Myers), Methodist University (Fayetteville, North Carolina), Mississippi State University (Mississippi State), New Mexico State University (Las Cruces), North Carolina State University (Raleigh), Pennsylvania State University (University Park), Sam Houston State University (Huntsville), University of Central Oklahoma (Edmond), University of Colorado at Colorado Springs, University of Idaho (Moscow), University of Maryland Eastern Shore (Princess Anne), University of Nebraska at Lincoln, and University of Nevada at Las Vegas.

Number awarded Varies each year; recently, 20 were awarded.

Deadline Deadline not specified.

[533]
PHILADELPHIA CHAPTER AABE SCHOLARSHIPS

American Association of Blacks in Energy-Philadelphia Chapter
Attn: Scholarship Committee
P.O. Box 34282
Philadelphia, PA 19104
(267) 882-7385 E-mail: Sherri.Pennington@pgworks.com
Web: www.aabe.org/index.php?component=pages&id=706

Summary To provide financial assistance to Native Americans and members of other underrepresented minority groups who are high school seniors in Delaware and Pennsylvania and planning to major in an energy-related field at a college in any state.

Eligibility This program is open to seniors graduating from high schools in Delaware or Pennsylvania and planning to work on a bachelor's degree at a college or university in any state. Applicants must be African Americans, Hispanics, or Native Americans who have a GPA of 3.0 or higher and have taken the ACT and/or SAT test. Their intended major must be a field of business, engineering, physical sciences, mathematics, or technology related to energy. Along with their application, they must submit a 350-word essay that includes 1) when they discovered their interest in the field of energy and what sparked their interest; and 2) either what excites them about the field of energy or how they expect their education to prepare them for the field of energy. Financial need is not considered in the selection process.

Financial data The stipend is $2,000.

Duration 1 year; nonrenewable.

Additional information Winners are eligible to compete for regional and national scholarships.

Number awarded 6 each year.

Deadline March of each year.

[534]
PHILLIP D. REED UNDERGRADUATE ENDOWMENT FELLOWSHIP

National Action Council for Minorities in Engineering
Attn: Director, Scholarships and University Relations
440 Hamilton Avenue, Suite 302
White Plains, NY 10601-1813
(914) 539-4316 Fax: (914) 539-4032
E-mail: scholars@nacme.org
Web: www.nacme.org/scholarships

Summary To provide financial assistance to Amrican Indian and other underrepresented minority college sophomores majoring in engineering or related fields.

Eligibility This program is open to African American, Latino, and American Indian college sophomores who have a GPA of 3.0 or higher and have demonstrated academic excellence, leadership skills, and a commitment to science and engineering as a career. Applicants must be enrolled full time at an ABET-accredited engineering program. Fields of study include all areas of engineering as well as computer science, materials science, mathematics, operations research, or physics.

Financial data The stipend is $5,000 per year. Funds are sent directly to the recipient's university.

Duration Up to 3 years.

Number awarded 1 each year.

Deadline April of each year.

[535]
PHOENIX AISES SCHOLARSHIP

American Indian Science and Engineering Society-
Phoenix Professional Chapter
Attn: Scholarships
P.O. Box 16483
Phoenix, AZ 85011
E-mail: phxaises1@gmail.com
Web: www.phxaises.com/scholarship

Summary To provide financial assistance to Native Americans who attend school in Arizona and are members of the American Indian Science and Engineering Society (AISES).

Eligibility This program is open to AISES members who are also members of American Indian tribes, members of Native Alaskan communities, or Native Hawaiians. Applicants must be high school seniors planning to enroll full time at an accredited 2- or 4-year college or university in Arizona or students currently enrolled at such an institution. They must have a GPA of 3.0 or higher and be majoring in a field of science, technology, engineering, or mathematics (STEM). Along with their application, they must submit a 500-word essay including reasons why they chose their field of study, their career aspirations, obstacles they have faced as a student, and their involvement and commitment to tribal community life.

Financial data The stipend is $500 for high school seniors entering college or $1,000 for students already enrolled.

Duration 1 year.

Number awarded Varies each year.

Deadline August of each year.

[536]
PHOENIX BENNER NATIVE & FIRST NATIONS SCHOLARSHIP

Pride Foundation
Attn: Educational Programs Director
2014 East Madison Street, Suite 300
Seattle, WA 98122
(206) 323-3318   Toll Free: (800) 735-7287
Fax: (206) 323-1017
E-mail: scholarships@pridefoundation.org
Web: www.pridefoundation.org

Summary To provide financial assistance to Native and First Nations lesbian, gay, bisexual, transgender, or queer (LGBTQ) residents of the Northwest who are interested in attending college in any state.

Eligibility This program is open to LGBTQ residents of Alaska, Idaho, Montana, Oregon, or Washington who are Native or First Nations students and attending or planning to attend a college, university, or vocational school in any state. Applicants must be able to demonstrate a current or future activism and/or leadership in the Native community. Selection is based on demonstrated commitment to social justice and LGBTQ concerns, leadership in their communities, the ability to be academically and personally successful, and (to some extent) financial need.

Financial data Recently, the average stipend for all scholarships awarded by the foundation was approximately $3,400. Funds are paid directly to the recipient's school.

Duration 1 year; recipients may reapply.

Number awarded 1 each year. Since it began offering scholarships in 1993, the foundation has awarded a total of more than $3.5 million to nearly 1,400 recipients.

Deadline January of each year.

[537]
PHYLLIS G. MEEKINS SCHOLARSHIP

Ladies Professional Golf Association
Attn: LPGA Foundation
100 International Golf Drive
Daytona Beach, FL 32124-1082
(386) 274-6200   Fax: (386) 274-1099
E-mail: foundation.scholarships@lpga.com
Web: www.lpga.com

Summary To provide financial assistance to Native American and other minority female graduating high school seniors who played golf in high school and plan to continue to play in college.

Eligibility This program is open to female high school seniors who are members of a recognized minority group. Applicants must have a GPA of 3.0 or higher and a background in golf. They must be planning to enroll full time at a college or university in the United States and play competitive golf. Along with their application, they must submit a letter that describes how golf has been an integral part of their lives and includes their personal, academic, and professional goals; their chosen discipline of study; and how this scholarship will be of assistance. Financial need is considered in the selection process. U.S. citizenship or legal resident status is required.

Financial data The stipend is $1,250.

Duration 1 year.

Additional information This program began in 2006.

Number awarded 1 each year.

Deadline May of each year.

[538]
PI STATE NATIVE AMERICAN GRANTS-IN-AID

Delta Kappa Gamma Society International-Pi State
Organization
c/o Arlene Ida, Native American Committee Chair
3 Sherwood Park Drive
Burnt Hills, NY 12027
E-mail: aiddski@nucap.rr.com
Web: www.deltakappagamma.org/NY

Summary To provide funding to Native American women from New York who plan to work in education or another service field.

Eligibility This program is open to Native American women from New York who are attending a 2- or 4-year college in the state. Applicants must be planning to work in education or another service field, but preference is given to those majoring in education. Both undergraduate and graduate students are eligible.

Financial data The grant is $500 per semester ($1,000 per year). Funds may be used for any career-related purpose, including purchase of textbooks.

Duration 1 semester; may be renewed for a total of 5 years and a total of $5,000 over a recipient's lifetime.

Number awarded Up to 5 each year.

Deadline May of each year for fall; January of each year for winter or spring.

[539]
PLAINS ANTHROPOLOGICAL SOCIETY NATIVE AMERICAN STUDENT AWARDS

Plains Anthropological Society
c/o Mark Muñiz
St. Cloud State University
262 Stewart Hall
720 Fourth Avenue South
St. Cloud, MN 56301-4498
(320) 308-4162   E-mail: mpmuniz@stcloudstate.edu
Web: www.plainsanthropologicalsociety.org/scholarship

Summary To provide financial assistance to Native Americans working on an undergraduate or graduate degree in anthropology or archaeology at a college in the Great Plains area of the United States or Canada.

Eligibility This program is open to Native American students currently enrolled full time at a 4-year college or university and working on an undergraduate or graduate degree in anthropology or archaeology. Undergraduates may be attending a college or university in the United States or Canada that provides course work or research covering the Great Plains area of the United States (all or part of the states of Colorado, Kansas, Montana, Nebraska, New Mexico, North Dakota, Oklahoma, South Dakota, Texas, or Wyoming) or Canada (all or part of the provinces of Alberta, Manitoba, or Saskatchewan). Graduate students must be conducting research that relates to an aspect of the Great Plains, but they do not need to be attending a university located in that region. All applicants must submit documentation of tribal enrollment, a letter of recommendation from a faculty member focusing on their accomplishments or potential in the field of anthropology, and a letter of interest outlining their prior experience and future goals in studying anthropology.

Financial data The stipend is $1,000.

Duration 1 year.

Number awarded 1 or more each year.

Deadline September of each year.

[540]
P.O. PISTILLI SCHOLARSHIPS

Design Automation Conference
c/o Andrew B. Kahng, Scholarship Director
University of California at San Diego-Jacobs School of
  Engineering
Jacobs Hall, EBU3B, Rpp, 2134
9500 Gilman Drive
La Jolla, CA 92093-0404
(858) 822-4884   Fax: (858) 534-7029
E-mail: abk@cs.ucsd.edu
Web: www.dac.com

Summary To provide financial assistance to female, minority, or disabled high school seniors who are interested in preparing for a career in computer science or electrical engineering.

Eligibility This program is open to graduating high school seniors who are members of underrepresented groups: women, African Americans, Hispanics, Native Americans, and students with disabilities. Applicants must be interested in preparing for a career in electrical engineering, computer engineering, or computer science. They must have at least a 3.0 GPA, have demonstrated high achievements in math and science courses, have demonstrated involvement in activities associated with the underrepresented group they represent, and be able to demonstrate significant financial need. U.S. citizenship is not required, but applicants must be U.S. residents when they apply and must plan to attend an accredited U.S. college or university. Along with their application, they must submit 3 letters of recommendation, official transcripts, ACT/SAT and/or PSAT scores, a personal statement outlining future goals and why they think they should receive this scholarship, and documentation of financial need.

Financial data Stipends are $4,000 per year. Awards are paid each year in 2 equal installments.

Duration 1 year; may be renewed up to 4 additional years.

Additional information This program is funded by the Design Automation Conference of the Association for Computing Machinery's Special Interest Group on Design Automation.

Number awarded 2 to 7 each year.

Deadline January of each year.

[541]
POARCH BAND OF CREEK INDIANS ACADEMIC ACHIEVEMENT BONUS

Poarch Band of Creek Indians
Attn: Tuition Program Coordinator
5811 Jack Springs Road
Atmore, AL 36502
(251) 368-9136, ext. 2535   Fax: (251) 368-4502
E-mail: mjohnson@pci-nsn.gov
Web: www.poarchcreekindians.org

Summary To recognize and reward members of the Poarch Band of Creek Indians who achieve academic excellence while working on an undergraduate or graduate degree.

Eligibility These awards are presented to enrolled members of the Poarch Band of Creek Indians who are completing an associate, bachelor's, or master's degree program at a college or university in any state and have been enrolled in the tribe's tuition assistance program. To qualify, they must maintain a GPA of 3.5 or higher upon graduation.

Financial data The award is $2,000 for associate degree students, $4,000 for bachelor's degree students, or $2,000 for master's degree students. Other professional degree students are evaluated on a case-by-case basis.

Duration Each student is eligible to receive 1 of these awards.

Number awarded Varies each year.

Deadline Deadline not specified.

[542]
PRINCE KUHI'O HAWAIIAN CIVIC CLUB SCHOLARSHIP

Prince Kuhi'o Hawaiian Civic Club
Attn: Scholarship Chair
P.O. Box 4728
Honolulu, HI 96812
(808) 678-0231   E-mail: pkhcc64@gmail.com
Web: www.pkhcc.com/scholarship.html

Summary To provide financial assistance for undergraduate or graduate studies to persons of Native Hawaiian descent.

Eligibility This program is open to high school seniors and full-time undergraduate or graduate students who are of Native Hawaiian descent (descendants of the aboriginal inhabitants of the Hawaiian Islands prior to 1778). Graduating high school seniors and current undergraduate students must have a GPA of 2.5 or higher; graduate students must have at least a 3.3 GPA. Along with their application, they must submit an essay on a topic that changes annually; recently, students were asked to write on the Hawaiian issue that influenced their decision to pursue their course of study at a college or university. Priority is given to members of the Prince Kuhi'o Hawaiian Civic Club in good standing, including directly-related family members. Special consideration is given to applicants majoring in Hawaiian studies and culture, Hawaiian language, education, or journalism. Selection is based on academic achievement and leadership potential.

Financial data Stipends range from $500 to $1,000 per year.

Duration 1 year; may be renewed.

Number awarded Varies each year.

Deadline March of each year.

[543]
PRINCETON SUMMER UNDERGRADUATE RESEARCH EXPERIENCE

Princeton University
Attn: Graduate School
Office of Academic Affairs and Diversity
Clio Hall
Princeton, NJ 08544-0255
(609) 258-2066   E-mail: diverse@princeton.edu
Web: gradschool.princeton.edu

Summary To provide an opportunity for Native American and other minority or disadvantaged students to assist Princeton faculty in any area during the summer.

Eligibility This program is open to full-time sophomores and juniors at all colleges and universities in the United States who are majoring in any academic discipline and have a GPA of 3.5 or higher in their major. Current college freshmen and graduating seniors are not eligible. Applicants must be interested in working during the summer with a Princeton faculty member. They should have a goal of continuing on for a Ph.D. and preparing for a career in college or university teaching and research. Students in the sciences and engineering normally work in a laboratory group on an aspect of the faculty member's current research. Students in the humanities and social sciences might assist a faculty member engaged in a particular research, editing, bibliographical, or course-preparation project; alternatively, they may work on a research paper under faculty supervision. Members of racial and ethnic minority groups underrepresented in doctoral research programs, students from socioeconomically disadvantaged backgrounds, and students at small liberal arts colleges are especially encouraged to apply.

Financial data Participants receive a stipend of $3,750, housing in a campus dormitory, a $150 meal card, and up to $500 in reimbursement of travel costs.

Duration 8 weeks during the summer.

Number awarded Up to 20 each year.

Deadline January of each year.

[544]
PRSA DIVERSITY MULTICULTURAL SCHOLARSHIPS

Public Relations Student Society of America
Attn: Vice President of Member Services
33 Maiden Lane, 11th Floor
New York, NY 10038-5150
(212) 460-1474   Fax: (212) 995-0757
E-mail: prssa@prsa.org
Web: www.prssa.prsa.org

Summary To provide financial assistance to Native American and other minority college students who are interested in preparing for a career in public relations.

Eligibility This program is open to minority (African American/Black, Hispanic/Latino, Asian, Native American, Alaskan Native, or Pacific Islander) students who are at least juniors at an accredited 4-year college or university. Applicants must be enrolled full time, be able to demonstrate financial need, and have a GPA of 3.0 or higher. Membership in the Public Relations Student Society of America is preferred but not required. A major or minor in public relations is preferred; students who attend a school that does not offer a public relations degree or program must be enrolled in a communications degree program (e.g., journalism, mass communications).

Financial data The stipend is $1,500.

Duration 1 year.

Additional information This program began in 1989.

Number awarded 2 each year.

Deadline May of each year.

[545]
PUEBLO OF ACOMA HIGHER EDUCATION PROGRAM

Pueblo of Acoma
Attn: Higher Education Coordinator
P.O. Box 307
Acoma, NM 87034
(505) 552-5135   Fax: (505) 552-6812
E-mail: highered@puebloofacoma.org
Web: www.puebloofacoma.org

Summary To provide financial assistance to of Acoma enrolled members who are interested in attending college in any state.

Eligibility This program is open to members of the Pueblo of Acoma who are enrolled or planning to enroll full or part time at an accredited college or university in any state to work on an associate or bachelor's degree. Applicants must submit their Certificate of Degree of Indian Blood (CDIB) and tribal enrollment, 2 letters of recommendation, high school or college transcripts, ACT or SAT scores, a copy of their class schedule, and documentation of financial need.

Financial data The amount awarded varies, depending upon the recipient's financial need. Generally, scholarships are considered supplemental funds.

Duration 1 year; may be renewed, provided the recipient maintains a GPA of 2.0 or higher.

Additional information Funding for this program is provided by the U.S. Bureau of Indian Affairs.

Number awarded Varies each year.

Deadline April of each year for the fall term; September of each year for the spring term.

[546]
PUEBLO OF ISLETA HIGHER EDUCATION PROGRAM

Pueblo of Isleta
Attn: Scholarship Coordinator
P.O. Box 1270
Isleta, NM 87022
(505) 869-9790, ext. 9794   Fax: (505) 869-7573
E-mail: poi08001@isletapueblo.com
Web: www.isletapueblo.com/isleta-higher-education.html

Summary To provide financial assistance to members of the Pueblo of Isleta who are interested in attending college or graduate school in any state.

Eligibility This program is open to undergraduate and graduate students who are tribally enrolled members of the Pueblo of Isleta and can document at least one-half Isleta blood. Applicants must have applied for federal aid by submitting a Free Application for Federal Student Aid (FAFSA).

Financial data For full-time students who can demonstrate financial need, the maximum stipend for a 4-year undergraduate degree or graduate degree is $3,000 per academic term. For part-time students who can demonstrate financial need, the maximum stipend is $1,000 per academic term. For students enrolled in a course of study that normally does not lead to a 4-year degree, the maximum stipend is $1,000 per academic term. For students who are designated as "no-need" by their institution and are ineligible to receive other assistance, the maximum stipend is $5,000 per academic term. Students enrolled in special legal summer programs in preparation for entrance to an accredited institution for the following semester can receive up to a maximum award of $2,500.

Duration 1 year; students may receive support for an undergraduate degree for up to 5 years, for a master's degree for 2 years beyond the bachelor's degree, or for a doctoral degree for 3 years beyond the master's degree.

Number awarded Varies each year.

Deadline June of each year for the full academic year or fall semester; October of each year for the spring semester or winter quarter; March of each year for summer term.

[547]
PUEBLO OF JEMEZ FINANCIAL NEED SCHOLARSHIP PROGRAM

Pueblo of Jemez
Attn: Education Services Center
5117 Highway 4
P.O. Box 100
Jemez Pueblo, NM 87024
(575) 834-9102   Toll Free: (888) 834-3936
Fax: (575) 834-7900
E-mail: higher_ed@jemezpueblo.org
Web: www.jemezpueblo.org

Summary To provide financial assistance to Jemez Pueblo students who demonstrate financial need and are interested in earning a college degree at a school in any state.

Eligibility This program is open to Jemez Pueblo students working on or planning to work on an associate or bachelor's degree at an accredited institution of higher education in any state as a full-time student. Applicants must have a GPA of 2.0 or higher and be able to demonstrate financial need. They must be at least one quarter Jemez and recognized by the Jemez Pueblo census office (a Certificate of Indian Blood must be provided). Along with their application, they must submit 2 letters of recommendation, a copy of their letter of acceptance from the institution they are attending or planning to attend, and an official transcript from the high school or college they last attended.

Financial data The stipend depends on the need of the recipient.

Duration 1 semester; may be renewed if the recipient remains enrolled full time with a GPA of 2.5 or higher.

Number awarded Varies each year.

Deadline June of each year for fall; January of each year for spring.

[548]
PUEBLO OF JEMEZ MERIT SCHOLARSHIP PROGRAM

Pueblo of Jemez
Attn: Education Services Center
5117 Highway 4
P.O. Box 100
Jemez Pueblo, NM 87024
(575) 834-9102   Toll Free: (888) 834-3936
Fax: (575) 834-7900
E-mail: higher_ed@jemezpueblo.org
Web: www.jemezpueblo.org

Summary To provide financial assistance to Jemez Pueblo students who demonstrate academic merit and are interested in earning a college degree at a school in any state.

Eligibility This program is open to Jemez Pueblo students working on or planning to work on an associate or bachelor's degree at an accredited institution of higher education in any state as a full-time student. Applicants must have a GPA of 3.0 or higher and be able to demonstrate academic merit. They must be at least one quarter Jemez and recognized by the Jemez Pueblo census office (a Certificate of Indian Blood must be provided). Along with their application, they must submit 2 letters of recommendation, a copy of their letter of acceptance from the institution they are attending or planning to attend, and an official transcript from the high school or college they last attended.

Financial data The stipend depends on the need of the recipient.

Duration 1 semester; may be renewed if the recipient remains enrolled full time with a GPA of 3.5 or higher.

Number awarded Varies each year.

Deadline June of each year for fall; January of each year for spring.

[549]
PUEBLO OF LAGUNA GOVERNOR'S SCHOLARSHIP PROGRAM

Pueblo of Laguna
Attn: Partners for Success
11 Rodeo Drive, Building A
P.O. Box 207
Laguna, NM 87026
(505) 552-9322   Fax: (505) 552-0623
E-mail: p.solimon@lagunaed.net
Web: partnersforsuccess.us/pfs—direct-education.html

Summary To provide financial assistance to members of the Pueblo of Laguna who demonstrate awareness of Pueblo issues and are interested in attending college in any state.

Eligibility This program is open to graduating high school seniors who are regular enrolled members of the Pueblo of Laguna. Applicants must be planning to work on a bachelor's degree at an accredited college or university in the United States. Along with their application, they must submit an essay, from 1 to 3 pages in length, on 1 or more of the following priority areas the Pueblo is highly committed to improving: education, health care, financial stability, housing, and/or work force excellence. They must also submit transcripts with GPA of 3.0 or higher and ACT/SAT scores and be available for an interview.

Financial data The stipend is $1,000 per year.

Duration Up to 4 years.

Additional information The winner of the Governor's Scholarship is offered an opportunity to speak to Tribal leadership and share ideas and recommendations.

Number awarded 1 each year.

Deadline July of each year.

[550]
PUEBLO OF LAGUNA HIGHER EDUCATION UNDERGRADUATE PROGRAM

Pueblo of Laguna
Attn: Partners for Success
11 Rodeo Drive, Building A
P.O. Box 207
Laguna, NM 87026
(505) 552-9322   Fax: (505) 552-0623
E-mail: p.solimon@lagunaed.net
Web: partnersforsuccess.us/pfs—direct-education.html

Summary To provide financial assistance to members of the Pueblo of Laguna who are interested in attending college in any state.

Eligibility This program is open to regular enrolled members of the Pueblo of Laguna. Applicants must have a high school diploma or GED certificate and be working on a bachelor's or transferable associate degree. They must have been accepted by an accredited college or university in the United States as a full-time student. Along with their application, they

must submit documentation of financial need, a 1-page personal statement on their purpose in working on a degree in their chosen field of study and their career or professional goals, high school and/or college transcripts, ACT scores, and verification of tribal membership or Indian blood. Vocational students, part-time students, and "naturalized" Laguna tribal members are not eligible.

Financial data The stipend is $4,000 for the first year, $5,000 for the second year, $6,000 for the third year, and $8,000 for the fourth year.

Duration 1 year; may be renewed for up to 3 additional years (students may submit an appeal for a fifth year of study), provided the recipient maintains a GPA of 2.0 or higher and full-time enrollment.

Number awarded Varies each year; recently, 120 new and renewal scholarships were awarded.

Deadline July of each year.

[551]
PUEBLO OF POJOAQUE HIGHER EDUCATION SCHOLARSHIP PROGRAM

Pueblo of Pojoaque
Attn: Higher Education
101 C Lightning Loop
Santa Fe, NM 87506
(505) 455-3369   Fax: (505) 455-3360
E-mail: pueblooofpojoaque@gmail.com
Web: www.pueblooofpojoaque.blogspot.com

Summary To provide financial assistance to Pueblo of Pojoaque tribal members interested in working on an undergraduate or graduate degree at a school in any state.

Eligibility This program is open to Pueblo of Pojoaque tribal members who can provide a certificate of tribal verification. Applicants must be working on or planning to work on a certificate, associate, bachelor's, master's, or doctoral degree at a school of higher education in any state. They must be able to verify that they have applied for all other available financial aid and that they still have financial need. Both full- and part-time undergraduate students are eligible, but graduate students must be enrolled full time.

Financial data Both full- and part-time students receive a grant to cover tuition, fees, and books, to a maximum of $2,000 per year. In addition, full-time students receive a monthly stipend (amount not specified).

Duration Support to full-time students is available for 1 year for certificate programs, 3 years for associate degrees, 5 years for bachelor's degrees, or 4 years for graduate degrees. Support to part-time students is available for 2 years for certificate programs, 4 years for associate degrees, or 7 years for bachelor's degrees. Renewal for full-time students requires that they complete at least 20 hours of nonprofit community service per semester. Renewal for all students requires that they maintain a GPA of 2.0 or higher.

Number awarded Varies each year.

Deadline April of each year.

[552]
PWC TRIBAL COLLEGE ACCOUNTING SCHOLARSHIP

American Indian College Fund
Attn: Scholarship Department
8333 Greenwood Boulevard
Denver, CO 80221
(303) 426-8900   Toll Free: (800) 776-FUND
Fax: (303) 426-1200
E-mail: scholarships@collegefund.org
Web: www.collegefund.org

Summary To provide financial assistance to Native American students working on an accounting degree at a Tribal College or University (TCU).

Eligibility This program is open to American Indians and Alaska Natives who can document proof of enrollment or descendancy. Applicants must be enrolled as sophomores or juniors majoring in accounting at an approved TCU. They must have a GPA of 2.8 or higher and be able to demonstrate an interest in internship opportunities. Applications are available only online and include required essays on specified topics. U.S. citizenship is required.

Financial data The stipend is $9,000.

Duration 1 year.

Additional information This scholarship is sponsored by PricewaterhouseCoopers (PwC) in partnership with the American Indian College Fund.

Number awarded 1 or more each year.

Deadline May of each year.

[553]
RACE RELATIONS MULTIRACIAL STUDENT SCHOLARSHIP

Christian Reformed Church
Attn: Office of Race Relations
1700 28th Street, S.E.
Grand Rapids, MI 49508
(616) 224-5883   Toll Free: (877) 864-3977
Fax: (616) 224-0834   E-mail: elugo@crcna.org
Web: www.crcna.org/race/scholarships

Summary To provide financial assistance to Native American and other undergraduate and graduate minority students interested in attending colleges related to the Christian Reformed Church in North America (CRCNA).

Eligibility This program is open to students of color in the United States and Canada. Normally, applicants are expected to be members of CRCNA congregations who plan to pursue their educational goals at Calvin Theological Seminary or any of the colleges affiliated with the CRCNA. They must be interested in training for the ministry of racial reconciliation in church and/or in society. Along with their application, they must submit paragraphs about their personal history and family, Christian faith, and Christian leadership goals. Students who have no prior history with the CRCNA must attend a CRCNA-related college or seminary for a full academic year before they are eligible to apply for this program. Students entering their sophomore year must have earned a GPA of 2.0 or higher as freshmen; students entering their junior year must have earned a GPA of 2.3 or higher as sophomores; students entering their senior year must have earned a GPA of 2.6 or higher as juniors.

Financial data First-year students receive $500 per semester. Other levels of students may receive up to $2,000 per academic year.

Duration 1 year.

Additional information This program was first established in 1971 and revised in 1991. Recipients are expected to train to engage actively in the ministry of racial reconciliation in church and in society. They must be able to work in the United States or Canada upon graduating and must consider working for 1 of the agencies of the CRCNA.

Number awarded Varies each year; recently, 31 students received a total of $21,000 in support.

Deadline March of each year.

[554]
RALPH BUNCHE SUMMER INSTITUTE

American Political Science Association
Attn: Diversity and Inclusion Programs
1527 New Hampshire Avenue, N.W.
Washington, DC 20036-1206
(202) 349-9362   Fax: (202) 483-2657
E-mail: kmealy@apsanet.org
Web: www.apsanet.org/rbsi

Summary To introduce Native American and other underrepresented minority undergraduate students to the world of graduate study and to encourage their eventual application to a Ph.D. program in political science.

Eligibility This program is open to African American, Latino(a), Native American, and Pacific Islander college students completing their junior year. Applicants must be interested in attending graduate school and working on a degree in a field related to political science. Along with their application, they must submit a 2-page personal statement on their reasons for wanting to participate in this program and their future academic and professional plans. U.S. citizenship is required.

Financial data Participants receive a stipend of $200 per week plus full support of tuition, transportation, room, board, books, and instructional materials.

Duration 5 weeks during the summer.

Additional information The institute includes 2 transferable credit courses (1 in quantitative analysis and the other on race and American politics). In addition, guest lecturers and recruiters from Ph.D. programs visit the students. Classes are held on the campus of Duke University. Most students who attend the institute excel in their senior year and go on to graduate school, many with full graduate fellowships and teaching assistantships. This program is funded by the National Science Foundation.

Number awarded 20 each year.

Deadline January of each year.

[555]
RDW GROUP, INC. MINORITY SCHOLARSHIP FOR COMMUNICATIONS

Rhode Island Foundation
Attn: Donor Services Administrator
One Union Station
Providence, RI 02903
(401) 427-4011　　　　　　　Fax: (401) 331-8085
E-mail: rbogert@rifoundation.org
Web: www.rifoundation.org

Summary　To provide financial assistance to Native American and other undergraduate and graduate students of color in Rhode Island who are interested in preparing for a career in communications at a school in any state.

Eligibility　This program is open to undergraduate and graduate students at colleges and universities in any state who are Rhode Island residents of color. Applicants must intend to work on a degree in communications (including computer graphics, art, cinematography, or other fields that would prepare them for a career in advertising). They must be able to demonstrate financial need and a commitment to a career in communications. Along with their application, they must submit an essay (up to 300 words) on the impact they would like to have on the communications field.

Financial data　The stipend is approximately $2,000 per year.

Duration　1 year; recipients may reapply.

Additional information　This program is sponsored by the RDW Group, Inc.

Number awarded　1 each year.

Deadline　April of each year.

[556]
RED CLIFF BAND HIGHER EDUCATION GRANTS PROGRAM

Red Cliff Band of Lake Superior Chippewa
Attn: Education Department
88385 Pike Road, Highway 13
Bayfield, WI 54814
(715) 779-3706, ext. 229　　　　Fax: (715) 779-3704
E-mail: Dee.Gokee@redcliff-nsn.gov
Web: www.redcliff-nsn.gov

Summary　To provide financial assistance for college or graduate school to members of the Red Cliff Band of Lake Superior Chippewa.

Eligibility　This program is open to enrolled tribal members of the Red Cliff Band who are working on or planning to work on an undergraduate or graduate degree. Applicants must be able to demonstrate financial need. In the selection process, first priority is given to enrolled members of the tribe who reside within the reservation, including the communities of Bayfield and LaPointe; second to enrolled members who reside in the neighboring communities of Cornucopia, Washburn, or Ashland; third to enrolled members of the tribe who reside in the state of Wisconsin and are attending school full time or, only if funding allows, part time; and fourth to enrolled members of the tribe who live in other states and are attending school full time or, only if funding allows, part time.

Financial data　The maximum stipend for undergraduate students is $3,000 per academic year for full-time students or $1,500 per academic year for part-time students. The maxi-

mum stipend for graduate students is $2,500 per academic year.

Duration　1 year; may be renewed for a total of 10 semesters for undergraduates or 4 semesters for graduate students, provided the recipient maintains a GPA of 2.0 or higher as an undergraduate or 3.0 or higher as a graduate student.

Number awarded　Varies each year.

Deadline　June of each year.

[557]
RED CLIFF BAND JOB TRAINING PROGRAM

Red Cliff Band of Lake Superior Chippewa
Attn: Education Department
88385 Pike Road, Highway 13
Bayfield, WI 54814
(715) 779-3706, ext. 229　　　　Fax: (715) 779-3704
E-mail: Dee.Gokee@redcliff-nsn.gov
Web: www.redcliff-nsn.gov

Summary　To provide financial assistance for technical or vocational training to adult members of the Red Cliff Band of Lake Superior Chippewa.

Eligibility　This program is open to enrolled tribal members of the Red Cliff Band who are working on or planning to work on a diploma, certificate, or associate degree. Applicants must be able to demonstrate financial need.

Financial data　The maximum stipend is $1,800 per academic year for full-time students or $900 per academic year for part-time students.

Duration　Up to 24 months at a vocational technical training institution or 36 months at a school of nursing, provided the recipient maintains a GPA of 2.0 or higher.

Number awarded　Varies each year.

Deadline　June of each year.

[558]
RENAE WASHINGTON-LORINE DUBOSE MEMORIAL SCHOLARSHIPS

Oklahoma CareerTech Foundation
Attn: Oklahoma Association of Minorities in Career and
　Technology Education
c/o Patti Pouncil, Scholarship Committee Chair
3 CT Circle
Drumright, OK 74030
918) 352-2551, ext. 285
Web: www.okcareertech.org

Summary　To provide financial assistance to Native American and other minority students enrolled at Oklahoma Career and Technology Education (CTE) centers.

Eligibility　This program is open to residents of Oklahoma who are members of an ethnic minority group (American Indian/Alaskan, Asian, African American, Hispanic, Native Hawaiian/Pacific Islander). Applicants must be enrolled full time at a CTE center in the state. Along with their application, they must submit a 100-word essay on why they have applied for this scholarship. Financial need is considered in the selection process.

Financial data　The stipend is $1,000.

Duration　1 year.

Number awarded　2 each year.

Deadline　May of each year.

[559]
RESEARCH AND ENGINEERING APPRENTICESHIP PROGRAM

Academy of Applied Science
Attn: REAP
24 Warren Street
Concord, NH 03301
(603) 228-4530   Fax: (603) 228-4730
E-mail: phampton@aas-world.org
Web: www.usaeop.com/programs/apprenticeships/reap

Summary To provide an opportunity for high school students who are Native Americans or members of other groups historically underrepresented in science, technology, engineering, or mathematics (STEM) to engage in a summer research apprenticeship.

Eligibility This program is open to high school students who meet at least 2 of the following requirements: 1) qualifies for free or reduced lunch; 2) is a member of a group historically underrepresented in STEM, including Blacks/African Americans, Hispanics, Native Americans, Alaskan Natives, Native Hawaiians, or other Pacific Islanders; 3) is a woman in physical science, computer science, mathematics, or engineering; 4) receives special education services; 5) has a disability; 6) speaks English as a second language; or 7) has parents who did not attend college. Applicants must be interested in working as an apprentice on a research project in the laboratory of a mentor scientist at a college or university near their home. Selection is based on demonstrated interests in STEM research and demonstrated potential for a successful career in STEM. They must be at least 16 years of age.

Financial data The stipend is $1,300.

Duration 5 to 8 weeks during the summer.

Additional information The program provides intensive summer training for high school students in the laboratories of scientists. The program, established in 1980, is funded by a grant from the U.S. Army Educational Outreach Program. Students must live at home while they participate in the program and must live in the area of an approved college or university. The program does not exist in every state.

Number awarded Varies; recently, approximately 120 students were funded at more than 50 universities nationwide.

Deadline February of each year.

[560]
RICHARD B. FISHER SCHOLARSHIP

Morgan Stanley
Attn: Diversity Recruiting
1585 Broadway
New York, NY 10036
(212) 762-0211   Toll Free: (888) 454-3965
Fax: (212) 507-4972
E-mail: richardbfisherprogram@morganstanley.com
Web: www.morganstanley.com

Summary To provide financial assistance and work experience to Native Americans and members of other underrepresented groups who are preparing for a career in technology within the financial services industry.

Eligibility This program is open to African American, Hispanic, Native American and lesbian/gay/bisexual/transgender students who are enrolled in their sophomore or junior year of college (or the third or fourth year of a 5-year program). Applicants must be enrolled full time and have a GPA of 3.4 or higher. They must be willing to commit to a paid summer internship in the Morgan Stanley Information Technology Division. All majors and disciplines are eligible, but preference is given to students preparing for a career in technology within the financial services industry. Along with their application, they must submit 1-page essays on 1) why they are applying for this scholarship and why they should be selected as a recipient; 2) a technical project on which they worked, either through a university course or previous work experience, their role in the project, and how they contributed to the end result; and 3) a software, hardware, or new innovative application of existing technology that they would create if they could and the impact it would have. Financial need is not considered in the selection process.

Financial data The stipend is $7,500 per year.

Duration 1 year (the junior year); may be renewed for the senior year.

Additional information The program, established in 1993, includes a paid summer internship in the Morgan Stanley Information Technology Division in the summer following the time of application.

Number awarded 1 or more each year.

Deadline December of each year.

[561]
RICHARD L. HOLMES COMMUNITY SERVICE AWARD

American Association of Blacks in Energy-Atlanta
  Chapter
Attn: Scholarship Committee
P.O. Box 55216
Atlanta, GA 30308-5216
(404) 506-6756
E-mail: G2AABEATCHAP@southernco.com
Web: www.aabe.org/atlanta

Summary To provide financial assistance to high school seniors who are Native Americans or members of other underrepresented minority groups in Georgia and have demonstrated outstanding community service and are planning to major in an energy-related field at a college in any state.

Eligibility This program is open to seniors graduating from high schools in Georgia and planning to attend a college or university in any state. Applicants must be African Americans, Hispanics, or Native Americans who have a GPA of 3.0 or higher and who have taken the ACT and/or SAT test. They must be able to demonstrate exceptional responsibility to give back to their community and/or to help others. Their intended major must be business, engineering, technology, mathematics, the physical sciences, or other energy-related field. Along with their application, they must submit a 350-word essay that includes 1) when they discovered their interest in the field of energy and what sparked their interest; and 2) either what excites them about the field of energy or how they expect their education to prepare them for the field of energy. Financial need is not considered in the selection process.

Financial data A stipend is awarded; amount not specified.

Duration 1 year.

Number awarded 1 each year.

Deadline March of each year.

[562]
RICHARD S. SMITH SCHOLARSHIP

United Methodist Church
Attn: General Board of Discipleship
Young People's Ministries
P.O. Box 340003
Nashville, TN 37203-0003
(615) 340-7184   Toll Free: (877) 899-2780, ext. 7184
Fax: (615) 340-7063
E-mail: youngpeople@umcdiscipleship.org
Web: www.umcyoungpeople.org/grants-scholarships

Summary To provide financial assistance to Native American and other minority high school seniors who wish to prepare for a Methodist church-related career.

Eligibility This program is open to graduating high school seniors who are members of racial/ethnic minority groups and have been active members of a United Methodist Church for at least 1 year. Applicants must have been admitted to an accredited college or university to prepare for a church-related career. They must have maintained at least a "C" average throughout high school and be able to demonstrate financial need. Along with their application, they must submit brief essays on their participation in church projects and activities, a leadership experience, the role their faith plays in their life, the church-related vocation to which God is calling them, and their extracurricular interests and activities. U.S. citizenship or permanent resident status is required.

Financial data The stipend is $1,000.

Duration 1 year; nonrenewable.

Additional information This program began in 1997. Recipients must enroll full time in their first year of undergraduate study.

Number awarded 2 each year.

Deadline May of each year.

[563]
ROBERT J. AND EVELYN CONLEY CREATIVE WRITING AWARD

Cherokee Nation Foundation
800 South Muskogee
Tahlequah, OK 74464
(918) 207-0950   Fax: (918) 207-0951
E-mail: contact@cherokeenationfoundation.org
Web: cherokeenation.academicworks.com

Summary To provide financial assistance to citizens of several Cherokee nations who are enrolled at a college or university in any state and working on an undergraduate or graduate degree in English or creative writing.

Eligibility This program is open to citizens of the Cherokee Nation, the United Keetoowah Band, or the Eastern Band of Cherokee Indians. Applicants must be currently enrolled in an undergraduate or graduate program in English or creative writing at a college or university in any state. They are not required to reside in the Cherokee Nation area. Along with their application, they must submit writing samples and an 800-word essay on their desire to pursue higher education, their chosen field of study, how they plan to serve the Cherokee people after they complete their higher education, and whether or not they speak the Cherokee language. Selection is based on the clarity and presentation of the essay; academic information (including transcripts and ACT scores);

school, cultural and community activities; future plans to serve Cherokee people; and financial need.

Financial data The stipend is $1,000 per semester ($2,000 per year).

Duration 1 year. Renewal for the second semester requires the recipient to earn a GPA of 3.0 or higher in the first semester.

Number awarded 1 each year.

Deadline January of each year.

[564]
RODNEY T. MATHEWS, JR. MEMORIAL SCHOLARSHIP FOR CALIFORNIA INDIANS

Morongo Band of Mission Indians
Attn: Scholarship Coordinator
12700 Pumarra Road
Banning, CA 92220
(951) 572-6185   E-mail: trisha.smith@morongo.org
Web: www.morongonation.org/content/education-services

Summary To provide financial assistance for college or graduate school in any state to California Indians.

Eligibility This program is open to enrolled members of federally-recognized California Indian tribes who have been actively involved in the Native American community. Applicants must submit documentation of financial need, an academic letter of recommendation, and a letter of recommendation from the American Indian community. They must be enrolled full time at an accredited college or university in any state. Undergraduates must have a GPA of 2.75 or higher; graduate students must have a GPA of 3.5 or higher. Along with their application, they must submit 1) a 2-page personal statement on their academic, career, and personal goals; any extenuating circumstances they wish to have considered; how they view their Native American heritage and its importance to them; how they plan to "give back" to Native Americans after graduation; and their on-going active involvement in the Native American community both on and off campus; and 2) a 2-page essay, either on what they feel are the most critical issues facing tribal communities today and how they see themselves working in relationship to those issues, or on where they see Native people in the 21st century in terms of survival, governance, and cultural preservation, and what role they see themselves playing in that future.

Financial data The maximum stipend is $10,000 per year. Funds are paid directly to the recipient's school for tuition, housing, textbooks, and required fees.

Duration 1 year; may be renewed 1 additional year.

Additional information Recipients are required to complete 60 hours of service with a designated California Indian community agency: California Indian Museum and Cultural Center, Indian Health Care Services, National Indian Justice Center, California Indian Legal Services, California Indian Professor Association, California Indian Culture and Awareness Conference, or California Democratic Party Native American Caucus.

Number awarded 4 each year.

Deadline March of each year.

[565]
ROSA L. PARKS COLLEGE SCHOLARSHIP

Conference of Minority Transportation Officials
Attn: National Scholarship Program
100 M Street, S.E., Suite 917
Washington, DC 20003
(202) 506-2917   E-mail: info@comto.org
Web: www.comto.org/page/scholarships

Summary To provide financial assistance to Native American and other students who have a tie to the Conference of Minority Transportation Officials (COMTO) and are interested in working on an undergraduate or master's degree in transportation.

Eligibility This program is open to 1) undergraduates who have completed at least 60 semester credit hours in a transportation discipline; and 2) students working on a master's degree in transportation who have completed at least 15 credits. Applicants must be or have a parent, guardian, or grandparent who has been a COMTO member for at least 1 year. They must have a GPA of 3.0 or higher. Along with their application they must submit a cover letter on their transportation-related career goals and life aspirations. Financial need is not considered in the selection process.

Financial data The stipend is $4,500. Funds are paid directly to the recipient's college or university.

Duration 1 year.

Number awarded 1 each year.

Deadline April of each year.

[566]
ROSA L. PARKS HIGH SCHOOL SCHOLARSHIP

Conference of Minority Transportation Officials
Attn: National Scholarship Program
100 M Street, S.E., Suite 917
Washington, DC 20003
(202) 506-2917   E-mail: info@comto.org
Web: www.comto.org/page/scholarships

Summary To provide financial assistance for college to children and grandchildren of members of the Conference of Minority Transportation Officials (COMTO) who are interested in studying any field.

Eligibility This program is open to high school seniors who are members or whose parent, guardian, or grandparent has been a COMTO member for at least 1 year and who have been accepted at an accredited college, university, or vocational/technical institution. Applicants must have a GPA of 3.0 or higher. Along with their application they must submit a cover letter on their transportation-related career goals and life aspirations. Financial need is not considered in the selection process.

Financial data The stipend is $4,500. Funds are paid directly to the recipient's college or university.

Duration 1 year.

Number awarded 1 each year.

Deadline April of each year.

[567]
ROSEBUD SIOUX TRIBE HIGHER EDUCATION SCHOLARSHIPS

Rosebud Sioux Tribe
Attn: Higher Education Services
P.O. Box 40
Rosebud, SD 57570-0130
(605) 747-2375   Toll Free: (877) 691-8183
Fax: (605) 747-5479   E-mail: rsthighered@gwtc.net
Web: www.rst-education-department.com

Summary To provide financial assistance for college to members of the Rosebud Sioux Tribe.

Eligibility This program is open to members of the Rosebud Sioux Tribe who are enrolled or planning to enroll full time at a college or university in any state. Licensure and diploma programs do not qualify. Applicants must have applied for a Pell Grant and be eligible for federal financial aid. In the selection process, first priority is given to continuing students who currently are receiving this assistance; second to students who received their high school diploma or GED certification from within the boundaries of the Rosebud Reservation in south central South Dakota; third to students from South Dakota but outside the reservation; and fourth to out-of-state students.

Financial data A stipend is awarded (amount not specified).

Duration 1 year; may be renewed, provided the recipient maintains minimum GPAs of 1.5 as a freshman, 2.0 as a sophomore, or 2.5 as a junior or senior.

Additional information This program is funded by the U.S. Bureau of Indian Affairs (BIA).

Number awarded Varies each year.

Deadline June of each year for academic year; November of each year for spring term only.

[568]
ROSEMARY GASKIN SCHOLARSHIP

Chippewa County Community Foundation
511 Ashmum Street, Suite 200
P.O. Box 1979
Sault Ste. Marie, MI 49783
(906) 635-1046   Fax: (775) 417-7368
E-mail: cccf@lighthouse.net
Web: www.cccf4good4ever.org/Scholarships.aspx

Summary To provide financial assistance to members of the Sault Ste. Marie Tribe of Chippewa Indians who are interested in attending a public college in any state.

Eligibility This program is open to enrolled members of the Sault Ste. Marie Tribe of Chippewa Indians who have been accepted for enrollment at a public institution of higher education in any state. Applicants are not required to demonstrate financial need, to enroll full time, or to have a minimum blood quantum level. Along with their application, they must submit a 500-word essay on their choice of the following topics: equality, American Indian rights, education, or reviving Indian culture and traditional beliefs.

Financial data The stipend is $1,000.

Duration 1 year.

Number awarded Varies each year; recently, 3 were awarded.

Deadline March of each year.

[569]
ROY M. HUHNDORF SCHOLARSHIP ENDOWMENT

Cook Inlet Region, Inc.
Attn: The CIRI Foundation
3600 San Jeronimo Drive, Suite 256
Anchorage, AK 99508-2870
(907) 793-3575   Toll Free: (800) 764-3382
Fax: (907) 793-3585   E-mail: tcf@thecirifoundation.org
Web: www.thecirifoundation.org/about/donors

Summary To provide financial assistance for undergraduate or graduate studies in health science to Alaska Natives who are original enrollees to Cook Inlet Region, Inc. (CIRI) and their lineal descendants.

Eligibility This program is open to Alaska Native enrollees to CIRI under the Alaska Native Claims Settlement Act (ANCSA) of 1971 and their lineal descendants. There are no Alaska residency requirements or age limitations. Applicants must be accepted or enrolled full time in a 4-year undergraduate or a graduate degree program. They must be working on a degree in health science and have a GPA of 2.5 or higher. Along with their application, they must submit a 500-word statement on their educational and career goals and how they are contributing, or planning to contribute, to a positive Alaska Native community. Selection is based on that statement, academic achievement, rigor of course work or degree program, student financial contribution, financial need, grade level, previous work performance, community service, and relationship of degree program to career goals.

Financial data The stipend is $10,000 per year, $8,000 per year, or $2,500 per semester, depending on GPA.

Duration 1 semester or 1 year.

Additional information CIRI is 1 of 13 regional corporations established according to the terms of the Alaska Native Claims Settlement Act (ANCSA) of 1971. This program began in 1995.

Number awarded 1 or more each year.

Deadline May of each year for annual scholarships; May or November of each year for semester scholarships.

[570]
ROYCE OSBORN MINORITY STUDENT SCHOLARSHIPS

American Society of Radiologic Technologists
Attn: ASRT Foundation
15000 Central Avenue, S.E.
Albuquerque, NM 87123-3909
(505) 298-4500, ext. 1392
Toll Free: (800) 444-2778, ext. 1392
Fax: (505) 298-5063   E-mail: foundation@asrt.org
Web: foundation.asrt.org/what-we-do/scholarships

Summary To provide financial assistance to Native American and other minority students enrolled in entry-level radiologic sciences programs.

Eligibility This program is open to Blacks or African Americans, American Indians or Alaska Natives, Hispanics or Latinos, Asians, and Native Hawaiians or other Pacific Islanders who are enrolled in an accredited entry-level program in radiography, sonography, magnetic resonance, or nuclear medicine. Applicants must be able to finish their degree or certificate in the year for which they are applying. They must be

U.S. citizens, nationals, or permanent residents have a GPA of 3.0 or higher. Along with their application, they must submit 9 essays of 200 words each on assigned topics related to their personal situation and interest in a career in radiologic science. Selection is based on those essays, academic and professional achievements, recommendations, and financial need.

Financial data The stipend is $4,000. Funds are paid directly to the recipient's institution.

Duration 1 year.

Number awarded 5 each year.

Deadline January of each year.

[571]
RUTH GOODE NURSING SCHOLARSHIP

Seneca Diabetes Foundation
Attn: Secretary/Treasurer
P.O. Box 309
Irving, NY 14081
(716) 532-4900   E-mail: white@sni.org
Web: www.senecadiabetesfoundation.org/scholarships

Summary To provide financial assistance to members of the Seneca Nation who are interested in attending college to work on a degree in nursing.

Eligibility This program is open to members of the Seneca Nation who are interested in attending college to work on a degree in nursing. Applicants must submit brief statements on 1) the professional, community, or cultural services and activities in which they have participated; 2) how this scholarship would help further their education; 3) their goals or plan for using their nursing experience to benefit the Seneca Nation and its people; and 4) the qualities about Ruth Goode's life, both personal and professional, they identify with the most. In the selection process, primary consideration is given to financial need, but involvement in community and cultural activities, personal assets, and desire to improve the quality of life for the Seneca people are also considered.

Financial data The stipend is $5,000.

Duration 1 year.

Number awarded 1 each year.

Deadline August of each year.

[572]
RUTH WEBB MINORITY SCHOLARSHIP

California Academy of Physician Assistants
2318 South Fairview Street
Santa Ana, CA 92704-4938
(714) 427-0321   Fax: (714) 427-0324
E-mail: capa@capanet.org
Web: www.capanet.org

Summary To provide financial assistance to Native American and other minority student members of the California Academy of Physician Assistants (CAPA) enrolled in physician assistant programs in California.

Eligibility This program is open to student members of CAPA enrolled in primary care physician assistant programs in California. Applicants must be members of a minority group (African American, Hispanic, Asian/Pacific Islander, or Native American/Alaskan Native). They must have maintained good academic standing and conducted activities to promote the physician assistant profession. Along with their application, they must submit an essay describing the activities they have performed to promote the physician assistant profession, the importance of representing minorities in their community, and why they should be awarded this scholarship. Financial need is considered in the selection process.

Financial data The stipend is $2,000.

Duration 1 year.

Number awarded 1 each year.

Deadline December of each year.

[573]
SAGINAW CHIPPEWA INDIAN TRIBAL SCHOLARSHIP PROGRAM

Saginaw Chippewa Indian Tribe of Michigan
Attn: Higher Education Coordinator
7070 East Broadway Road
Mt. Pleasant, MI 48858
(989) 775-4505   Fax: (989) 775-4529
E-mail: skutt@sagchip.org
Web: www.sagchipschool.net/higher-ed/Scholarships

Summary To provide financial assistance for college, graduate school, or vocational training to members of the Saginaw Chippewa Indian Tribe of Michigan.

Eligibility This program is open to enrolled members of the Saginaw Chippewa Indian Tribe of Michigan who are attending or planning to attend an accredited 2- or 4-year college, university, or vocational/trade institution in any state. Applicants must be interested in working on an undergraduate or graduate degree or vocational certificate as a full- or part-time student. They must apply for all available financial aid using the FAFSA standard form; residents of Michigan who plan to attend college in that state must also apply for the Michigan Indian Tuition Waiver. U.S. citizenship is required.

Financial data The stipend for vocational training is $125 per week, to a maximum of $2,000. The stipend for undergraduate and graduate study is $1,000 per semester ($2,000 per year) for part-time students enrolled in 6 to 8 undergraduate credit hours or 3 to 5 graduate credit hours, $1,500 per semester ($3,000 per year) for part-time students enrolled in 9 to 11 undergraduate credit hours or 6 to 8 graduate credit hours, or $2,000 per semester ($4,000 per year) for full-time students.

Duration 1 year; may be renewed, provided the recipient maintains a GPA of 2.0 or higher. Students are limited to receiving 1 each of vocational certificates, associate degree, bachelor's degree, master's degree, or doctoral degree.

Number awarded Varies each year.

Deadline October of each year for fall semester or quarter; February of each year for winter quarter or spring quarter or semester; or June of each year for summer term.

[574]
SALAMATOF NATIVE ASSOCIATION, INC. SCHOLARSHIP AND GRANT PROGRAM

Cook Inlet Region, Inc.
Attn: The CIRI Foundation
3600 San Jeronimo Drive, Suite 256
Anchorage, AK 99508-2870
(907) 793-3575   Toll Free: (800) 764-3382
Fax: (907) 793-3585   E-mail: tcf@thecirifoundation.org
Web: www.thecirifoundation.org

Summary To provide financial assistance for undergraduate or graduate studies to Alaska Natives who are original enrollees of the Salamatof Native Association, Inc. (SNAI) and their spouses and lineal descendants.

Eligibility This program is open to Alaska Native enrollees to SNAI under the Alaska Native Claims Settlement Act (ANCSA) of 1971 and their spouses and lineal descendants. There are no Alaska residency requirements or age limitations. Applicants must be accepted or enrolled full or part time in a 2-year, 4-year undergraduate, technical skills training, or graduate degree program. They must have a GPA of 2.5 or higher. Along with their application, they must submit a 500-word statement on their educational and career goals and how they are contributing, or planning to contribute, to a positive Alaska Native community. Selection is based on that statement, academic achievement, rigor of course work or degree program, student financial contribution, financial need, grade level, previous work performance, community service, and relationship of degree program to career goals.

Financial data Stipends range from $2,250 to $2,500 per term.

Duration 1 year; recipients must reapply each year.

Additional information Cook Inlet Region, Inc. (CIRI) is 1 of 13 regional corporations established according to the terms of the Alaska Native Claims Settlement Act (ANCSA) of 1971. This program began in 1992 by the Salamatof Native Association, Inc. which provides funds matched by the CIRI Foundation.

Number awarded Varies each year; recently, 3 were awarded.

Deadline May or December of each year for academic programs; June of each year for vocational programs.

[575]
SAN CARLOS APACHE TRIBE HIGHER EDUCATION GRANTS

San Carlos Apache Tribe
Attn: Department of Education
1 San Carlos Avenue
San Carlos, AZ 85550
(928) 475-2336   Fax: (928) 475-2507
Web: www.scateducationdepartment.com

Summary To provide financial assistance for college or graduate school in any state to members of the San Carlos Apache Tribe.

Eligibility This program is open to members of the San Carlos Apache Tribe who are attending or planning to attend an accredited 2- or 4-year college or university in any state. Applicants must be interested in working on an associate, baccalaureate, or graduate degree as a full- or part-time student. They must be able to demonstrate financial need and have 1) a GPA of 2.0 or higher or a GED score of 45 or higher; and 2) an ACT score of 22 or higher or an SAT combined critical reading and mathematics score of 930 or higher. In the selection process, awards are presented in the following priority order: first, full-time undergraduate students who reside on the San Carlos Reservation in southeastern Arizona; second, graduate students who reside on the reservation; third, part-time students who reside on the reservation; fourth, students who reside off the reservation; and fifth, students who do not demonstrate financial need (assisted only if funds are available).

Financial data The stipend depends on the financial need of the recipient, to a maximum of $4,000 per semester at a 2-year college or $5,000 per semester at a 4-year college or university.

Duration 1 year; may be renewed up to a total of 64 credit hours at a 2-year college, up to 125 credit hours at a 4-year college or university. Renewal requires the recipient to maintain a GPA of 2.0 or higher as an undergraduate or 3.0 or higher as a graduate student.

Number awarded Varies each year.

Deadline June of each year for fall semester; November of each year for spring semester.

[576]
SANTA FE NATURAL TOBACCO COMPANY FOUNDATION ACHIEVING THE DREAM SCHOLARSHIP

American Indian College Fund
Attn: Scholarship Department
8333 Greenwood Boulevard
Denver, CO 80221
(303) 426-8900   Toll Free: (800) 776-FUND
Fax: (303) 426-1200
E-mail: scholarships@collegefund.org
Web: www.collegefund.org

Summary To provide financial assistance to Native American college students who are single parents or first-year associate degree students and interested in studying any field at designated Tribal Colleges and Universities (TCUs).

Eligibility This program is open to American Indians and Alaska Natives from any state who have proof of enrollment or descendancy. Applicants must be entering their freshman or sophomore year at Diné College, Navajo Technical College, Sisseton Wahpeton College, Sinte Gleska University, or Oglala Lakota College and studying any field. They must have a GPA of 2.0 or higher and be single parents or first-year associate degree students. Applications are available only online and include required essays on specified topics. U.S. citizenship is required.

Financial data The stipend is $4,000.

Duration 1 year.

Additional information This program is sponsored by the Santa Fe Natural Tobacco Company Foundation.

Number awarded 15 each year.

Deadline May of each year.

[577]
SAULT TRIBE SPECIAL NEEDS SCHOLARSHIPS

Sault Tribe of Chippewa Indians
Attn: Higher Education Department
523 Ashmun Street
Sault Ste. Marie, MI 49783
(906) 635-6050, ext. 26312   Toll Free: (800) 793-0660
Fax: (906) 635-7785   E-mail: BMacArthur@saulttribe.net
Web: www.saulttribe.com

Summary To provide financial assistance for education at any level to members of the Sault Tribe of Chippewa Indians who have a disability.

Eligibility This program is open to members of the Sault Tribe who have a documented physical or emotional disability. Applicants must be enrolled in an educational program at any level. Along with their application, they must submit a letter from themselves or a parent describing the proposed use of the funds and an itemized list of the expected costs.

Financial data The stipend is $1,000.

Duration 1 year.

Number awarded 4 each year: 2 for students under 18 years of age and 2 for students 18 years of age or older.

Deadline May of each year.

[578]
SAULT TRIBE UNDERGRADUATE SCHOLARSHIPS

Sault Tribe of Chippewa Indians
Attn: Higher Education Department
523 Ashmun Street
Sault Ste. Marie, MI 49783
(906) 635-6050, ext. 26312   Toll Free: (800) 793-0660
Fax: (906) 635-7785   E-mail: BMacArthur@saulttribe.net
Web: www.saulttribe.com

Summary To provide financial assistance to members of the Sault Tribe of Chippewa Indians who are interested in attending college in any state.

Eligibility This program is open to members of the Sault Tribe who are enrolled or planning to enroll full time to work on an undergraduate degree in any field at a 2- or 4-year college or university in any state. Applicants must submit an essay of 1,000 to 2,000 words on a topic that changes annually but relates to their Indian heritage.

Financial data The stipend is $1,000.

Duration 1 year.

Additional information This program includes the following named scholarships: the Barb and Ed "Pie" Pine Tributary Scholarship, the Bernard Bouschor Honorary Scholarship, the Donald "Duck" Andress Honoree Tributary Scholarship, the Joe Gray Honoree Tributary Scholarship, the Lorrie Brackenbury Honoree Tributary Scholarship, and The Nokimos Scholarship: Mary Sabina Osagwin and Christine Muscoe Anderson.

Number awarded 6 named scholarships are awarded each year.

Deadline May of each year.

[579]
SCHOLARSHIPS FOR MINORITY ACCOUNTING STUDENTS

American Institute of Certified Public Accountants
Attn: Academic and Career Development Division
220 Leigh Farm Road
Durham, NC 27707-8110
(919) 402-4931   Fax: (919) 419-4705
E-mail: scholarships@aicpa.org
Web: www.aicpa.org

Summary To provide financial assistance to Native Americans and other minorities interested in studying accounting at the undergraduate or graduate school level.

Eligibility This program is open to minority undergraduate and graduate students, enrolled full time, who have a GPA of 3.3 or higher (both cumulatively and in their major) and intend to pursue a C.P.A. credential. The program defines minority students as those whose heritage is Black or African American, Hispanic or Latino, Native American, or Asian American.

Undergraduates must have completed at least 30 semester hours, including at least 6 semester hours of a major in accounting. Graduate students must be working on a master's degree in accounting, finance, taxation, or a related program. Applicants must be U.S. citizens or permanent residents and student affiliate members of the American Institute of Certified Public Accountants (AICPA). Along with their application, they must submit 500-word essays on 1) why they want to become a C.P.A. and how attaining that licensure will contribute to their goals; and 2) how they would spread the message about accounting and the C.P.A. profession in their community and school. In the selection process, some consideration is given to financial need.

Financial data Stipends range up to $5,000 per year. Funds are disbursed directly to the recipient's school.

Duration 1 year; may be renewed up to 3 additional years or until completion of a bachelor's or master's degree, whichever is earlier.

Additional information This program began in 1969. Additional support is provided by the Accounting Education Foundation of the Texas Society of Certified Public Accountants, the New Jersey Society of Certified Public Accountants, Robert Half International, and the Virgin Islands Society of Certified Public Accountants.

Number awarded Varies each year; recently, 97 students received funding through this program.

Deadline March of each year.

[580]
SCHOLARSHIPS FOR RACIAL JUSTICE

Higher Education Consortium for Urban Affairs
Attn: Student Services
2233 University Avenue West, Suite 210
St. Paul, MN 55114-1698
(651) 287-3300   Toll Free: (800) 554-1089
Fax: (651) 659-9421   E-mail: hecua@hecua.org
Web: www.hecua.org

Summary To provide financial assistance to Native American and other students of color who are enrolled in programs of the Higher Education Consortium for Urban Affairs (HECUA) at participating colleges and universities and are committed to undoing institutionalized racism.

Eligibility This program is open to students at member colleges and universities who are participating in HECUA programs. Applicants must be a student of color who can demonstrate a commitment to undoing institutionalized racism. Along with their application, they must submit a reflective essay of 550 to 1,700 words on the personal, social, or political influences in their lifetime that have motivated them to work on racial justice issues.

Financial data The stipend is $4,000.

Duration 1 semester.

Additional information This program began in 2012. Consortium members include Augsburg College (Minneapolis, Minnesota), Augustana College (Sioux Falls, South Dakota), Carleton College (Northfield, Minnesota), College of Saint Scholastica (Duluth, Minnesota), Colorado College (Colorado Springs, Colorado), Denison University (Granville, Ohio), Gustavus Adolphus College (St. Peter, Minnesota), Hamline University (St. Paul, Minnesota), Macalester College (St. Paul, Minnesota), Northland College (Ashland, Wisconsin), Saint Mary's University (Winona, Minnesota), Saint

Catherine University (St. Paul, Minnesota), Saint Olaf College (Northfield, Minnesota), Swarthmore College (Swarthmore, Pennsylvania), University of Minnesota (Twin Cities, Duluth, Morris, Crookston, Rochester), and University of Saint Thomas (St. Paul, Minnesota).

Number awarded Several each year.

Deadline April of each year for summer and fall programs; November of each year for January and spring programs.

[581]
SCIENCE AND ENGINEERING PROGRAMS FOR WOMEN AND MINORITIES AT BROOKHAVEN NATIONAL LABORATORY

Brookhaven National Laboratory
Attn: Diversity Office, Human Resources Division
Building 400B
P.O. Box 5000
Upton, New York 11973-5000
(631) 344-2703   Fax: (631) 344-5305
E-mail: palmore@bnl.gov
Web: www.bnl.gov/diversity/programs.asp

Summary To provide on-the-job training in scientific areas at Brookhaven National Laboratory (BNL) during the summer to Native Americans and other underrepresented minority students.

Eligibility This program at BNL is open to women and underrepresented minority (African American/Black, Hispanic, Native American, or Pacific Islander) students who have completed their freshman, sophomore, or junior year of college. Applicants must be U.S. citizens or permanent residents, at least 18 years of age, and majoring in applied mathematics, biology, chemistry, computer science, engineering, high and low energy particle accelerators, nuclear medicine, physics, or scientific writing. Since no transportation or housing allowance is provided, preference is given to students who reside in the BNL area.

Financial data Participants receive a competitive stipend.

Duration 10 to 12 weeks during the summer.

Additional information Students work with members of the scientific, technical, and professional staff of BNL in an educational training program developed to give research experience.

Number awarded Varies each year.

Deadline April of each year.

[582]
SC-PAAE SCHOLARSHIPS

South Carolina Professional Association for Access and Equity
Attn: Financial Secretary
P.O. Box 71297
North Charleston, SC 29415
(843) 670-4890   E-mail: anderson4569@bellsouth.net
Web: www.scpaae.org/#!scholarships/c11tv

Summary To provide financial assistance to undergraduate students at colleges and universities in South Carolina who are recognized as underrepresented minorities on their campus.

Eligibility This program is open to residents of any state who have completed at least 12 semester hours at a college or university in South Carolina. Applicants must be recognized as an underrepresented ethnic minority on their campus. They must have a GPA of 2.75 or higher. Along with their application, they must submit 1) a personal letter on their academic and career goals, honors and awards, leadership skills and organization participation, community service, and a statement of why they would like to receive this scholarship; and 2) a paragraph defining access and equity and describing how they can assist in achieving access and equity within South Carolina. Financial need is not considered in the selection process.

Financial data Stipends are $750 for students at 2-year institutions or $1,000 for students at 4-year institutions.

Duration 1 year.

Number awarded Varies each year.

Deadline February of each year.

[583]
SEALASKA CORPORATION INTERNSHIPS

Sealaska Corporation
Attn: Intern Program Coordinator
One Sealaska Plaza, Suite 400
Juneau, AK 99801-1276
(907) 586-1512   Toll Free: (800) 848-5921
Fax: (907) 586-2304   E-mail: interns@sealaska.com
Web: www.sealaska.com

Summary To provide work experience during the summer to Native Alaskan college students affiliated with Sealaska Corporation.

Eligibility This program is open to Sealaska Corporation shareholders, direct descendants of originally-enrolled shareholders, and spouses of shareholders and descendants. Applicants must have completed at least 2 years of college, have a GPA of 2.5 or higher, and be attending college in the following fall. They must be interested in working with Sealaska Corporation or its subsidiaries in the Pacific Northwest, Alaska, or Colorado. Relevant fields of study include accounting, administration, Alaska Native cultural and educational studies, communications, construction management and planning, economic development, environmental studies, finance, information technology, legal studies, marketing, natural resources, or nonprofit activities.

Financial data A competitive salary is paid, along with a housing stipend, transportation, and tuition for summer credit for the internship.

Duration Summer months.

Additional information Sealaska Corporation is 1 of 13 Alaska Native Regional Corporations created under the Alaska Native Claims Settlement Act of 1971.

Number awarded Varies each year; recently, 13 students received these internships.

Deadline March of each year.

[584]
SEALASKA HERITAGE INSTITUTE 7(I) SCHOLARSHIPS

Sealaska Corporation
Attn: Sealaska Heritage Institute
105 South Seward Street, Suite 201
Juneau, AK 99801
(907) 463-4844   E-mail: scholarships@sealaska.com
Web: scholarship.sealaskaheritage.org/Account/LogOn

Summary To provide financial assistance for undergraduate or graduate study in any state to Native Alaskans who have a connection to Sealaska Corporation and are majoring in designated fields.

Eligibility This program is open to 1) Alaska Natives who are shareholders of Sealaska Corporation; and 2) Native lineal descendants of Alaska Natives enrolled to Sealaska Corporation, whether or not the applicant owns Sealaska Corporation stock. Applicants must be enrolled or accepted for enrollment as full-time undergraduate or graduate students at a college or university in any state. Along with their application, they must submit 2 essays: 1) their personal history and educational goals; and 2) their expected contributions to the Alaska Native or Native American community. Financial need is also considered in the selection process. The following areas of study qualify for these awards: natural resources (environmental sciences, engineering, conservation biology, environmental law, fisheries, forestry, geology, marine science/biology, mining technology, wildlife management); business administration (accounting, computer information systems, economics, finance, human resources management, industrial management, information systems management, international business, international commerce and trade, and marketing); and other special fields (cadastral surveys, chemistry, equipment/machinery operators, industrial safety specialists, health specialists, plastics engineers, trade specialists, physics, mathematics, and marine trades and occupations).

Financial data The amount of the award depends on the availability of funds, the number of qualified applicants, class standing, and cumulative GPA.

Duration 1 year; may be renewed up to 6 years for a bachelor's degree, up to 3 years for a master's degree, up to 2 years for a doctorate, or up to 3 years for vocational study. The maximum total support is limited to 9 years. Renewal depends on recipients' maintaining full-time enrollment and a GPA of 2.0 or higher.

Additional information Funding for this program is provided from Alaska Native Claims Settlement Act (ANSCA) Section 7(i) revenue sharing provisions. Sealaska Corporation is 1 of 13 Alaska Native Regional Corporations created under the Alaska Native Claims Settlement Act of 1971.

Number awarded Varies each year.

Deadline February of each year.

[585]
SEALASKA HERITAGE SCHOLARSHIPS

Sealaska Corporation
Attn: Sealaska Heritage Institute
105 South Seward Street, Suite 201
Juneau, AK 99801
(907) 463-4844   E-mail: scholarships@sealaska.com
Web: scholarship.sealaskaheritage.org/Account/LogOn

Summary To provide financial assistance for undergraduate or graduate study in any state to Native Alaskans who have a connection to Sealaska Corporation.

Eligibility This program is open to 1) Alaska Natives who are shareholders of Sealaska Corporation; and 2) Native lineal descendants of Alaska Natives enrolled to Sealaska Corporation, whether or not they own Sealaska Corporation stock. Applicants must be enrolled or accepted for enrollment as full-time undergraduate or graduate students at a college or university in any state. Undergraduates must have a GPA of 2.0 or higher; graduate students must have a GPA of 3.0 or higher. Along with their application, they must submit 2 essays: 1) their personal history and educational goals; and 2) their expected contributions to the Alaska Native or Native American community. Financial need is also considered in the selection process.

Financial data The amount of the award depends on the availability of funds, the number of qualified applicants, class standing, and cumulative GPA.

Duration 1 year; may be renewed up to 6 years for a bachelor's degree, up to 3 years for a master's degree, up to 2 years for a doctorate, or up to 3 years for vocational study. The maximum total support is limited to 9 years. Renewal depends on recipients' maintaining full-time enrollment and a GPA of 2.0 or higher as an undergraduate or 3.0 or higher as a graduate student.

Additional information Sealaska Corporation is 1 of 13 Alaska Native Regional Corporations created under the Alaska Native Claims Settlement Act of 1971.

Number awarded Varies each year.

Deadline February of each year.

[586]
SENECA GAMING CORPORATION SCHOLARSHIP

Seneca Diabetes Foundation
Attn: Secretary/Treasurer
P.O. Box 309
Irving, NY 14081
(716) 532-4900   E-mail: white@sni.org
Web: www.senecadiabetesfoundation.org/scholarships

Summary To provide financial assistance to members of the Seneca Nation who are interested in attending college to prepare for a career in health care business and administration.

Eligibility This program is open to members of the Seneca Nation who are interested in attending college to assist the Seneca people, especially in regard to the fight against diabetes, by working on a degree in health care business and administration. Applicants must be able to demonstrate experience in a leadership position. Along with their application, they must submit brief statements on 1) the professional, community, or cultural services and activities in which they have participated; 2) how this scholarship would help further their education; 3) their goals or plan for using their education and training to benefit the Seneca Nation and its people; and 4) an example of a time when they served in a leadership position, the successes and challenges that they faced, the lessons they learned, and how they can apply those lessons to other life experiences. In the selection process, primary consideration is given to financial need, but involvement in community and cultural activities, personal assets, and desire to improve the quality of life for the Seneca people are also considered.

Financial data A stipend is awarded (amount not specified).

Duration 1 year.

Number awarded 1 each year.

Deadline August of each year.

[587]
SENECA NATION HIGHER EDUCATION PROGRAM

Seneca Nation of Indians
Attn: Higher Education Department, Cattaraugus Territory
12861 Route 438
Irving, NY 14081
(716) 532-3341   Fax: (716) 532-3269
E-mail: snihighered@sni.org
Web: sni.org

Summary To provide financial assistance for college or graduate school to members of the Seneca Nation of Indians in New York.

Eligibility This program is open to members of the Seneca Nation of Indians who are enrolled or planning to enroll in an associate, bachelor's, master's, or doctoral program. They must have applied for all other forms of financial aid for which they qualify, e.g., full-time undergraduates who are New York residents must apply for New York State Indian Aid (NYSIA) and the New York State Tuition Assistance Program (TAP); part-time undergraduates who are New York residents must apply for Aid for Part-Time Study (APTS); non-residents of New York must apply for funding from their state of residence; graduate students must apply for an American Indian Graduate Center (AIGC) fellowship. Applicants with permanent residence on the reservation qualify for level 1 awards; those with permanent residence within New York qualify for level 2 awards; those with permanent residence outside New York qualify for level 3 awards. Financial need is considered in the selection process.

Financial data Maximum awards per academic year for tuition and fees are $15,000 for level 1 students, $12,000 for level 2 students, or $10,000 for level 3 students. Other benefits for all recipients include $1,400 per year for books and supplies for full-time students or $140 per 3-credit hours for part-time students; payment of room and board in dormitories or college-approved housing for full-time students; a transportation allowance for commuters of $1,000 per year for full-time students or $100 per 3-credit hours for part-time students; a supplies allowance of $600 per year for full-time students or $60 per 3-credit hours for part-time students; a computer allowance of $1,200; a required equipment/tools allowance of $1,200; and a child care expense allowance of $750 per semester for full-time students or $375 per semester for part-time students.

Duration 1 year; may be renewed.

Number awarded Varies each year.

Deadline July of each year for fall semester or quarter; October of each year for winter quarter; December of each year for spring semester or quarter; May of each year for summer semester or quarter.

[588]
SEO UNDERGRADUATE CAREER PROGRAM

Sponsors for Educational Opportunity
Attn: Career Program
55 Exchange Place
New York, NY 10005
(212) 979-2040   Toll Free: (800) 462-2332
Fax: (646) 706-7113
E-mail: careerprogram@seo-usa.org
Web: www.seocareer.org

Summary To provide Native American and other undergraduate students of color with an opportunity to gain summer work experience in selected fields.

Eligibility This program is open to students of color at colleges and universities in the United States. Applicants must be interested in a summer internship in 1 of the following fields: asset management, consulting, engineering, finance and accounting, human resources, investment banking, investment research, marketing and sales, nonprofit sector, private equity, sales and trading, technology with banks, technology with global companies, or transaction services. Freshmen are not eligible. Sophomores are eligible for asset management, finance and accounting, investment banking, sales and trading, technology with banks, and transaction services. Juniors are eligible for all fields. Seniors and current graduate students are not eligible. All applicants must have a cumulative GPA of 3.0 or higher. Personal interviews are required.

Financial data Interns receive a competitive stipend of up to $1,300 per week.

Duration 10 weeks during the summer.

Additional information This program began in 1980. Corporate leadership internships are in the New York metro area, New Jersey, Connecticut, Iowa, Massachusetts, North Carolina, Ohio, California, and other areas; banking and private equity internships are in New York City with limited opportunities in New Jersey, Connecticut and possibly Miami or Houston; nonprofit internships are in New York City.

Number awarded Approximately 300 to 400 each year.

Deadline December of each year for sales and trading; January of each year for asset management, consulting, investment banking, investment research, nonprofit sector, private equity, and transaction services; February of each year for engineering, finance and accounting, human resources, marketing and sales, and technology.

[589]
SHELL INCENTIVE FUND SCHOLARSHIPS FOR HIGH SCHOOL SENIORS

Shell Oil Company
Attn: Scholarship Administrator
910 Louisiana, Suite 4476C
Houston, TX 77002
(713) 718-6379
E-mail: SI-Shell-US-Recruitment-Scholarships@shell.
   com
Web: www.shell.us

Summary To provide financial assistance to Native American and other minority high school seniors planning to major in specified engineering and geosciences fields in college.

Eligibility This program is open to graduating high school seniors who are members of underrepresented minority groups (Blacks, Hispanic/Latino, American Indian, Alaskan Native) and planning to enroll full time at 22 participating universities. Applicants must be planning to major in engineering (chemical, civil, electrical, geological, geophysical, mechanical, or petroleum) or geosciences (geology, geophysics, or physics). They must be U.S. citizens or authorized to work in the United States. Along with their application, they must submit a 100-word essay on the kind of work they plan to be doing in 10 years, both in their career and in their community; they should comment specifically on how they could potentially contribute to the petrochemical industry. Financial need is not considered in the selection process.

Financial data The stipend is $2,500.

Duration 1 year; nonrenewable, although recipients may apply for a Shell Incentive Fund Scholarship for Undergraduate Students to cover the remaining years of their undergraduate program.

Additional information This program is managed by International Scholarship and Tuition Services, Inc. The participating institutions are Colorado School of Mines, Cornell University, Florida A&M University, Georgia Institute of Technology, Louisiana State University, Massachusetts Institute of Technology, Michigan State University, North Carolina A&T State University, Ohio State University, Pennsylvania State University, Prairie View A&M University, Purdue University, Rice University, Stanford University, Texas A&M University, University of Colorado at Boulder, University of Houston, University of Illinois at Urbana-Champaign, University of Michigan, University of Oklahoma, University of Texas at Austin, and University of Texas at El Paso.

Number awarded Up to 20 each year.

Deadline February of each year.

[590]
SHELL INCENTIVE FUND SCHOLARSHIPS FOR UNDERGRADUATE STUDENTS

Shell Oil Company
Attn: Scholarship Administrator
910 Louisiana, Suite 4476C
Houston, TX 77002
(713) 718-6379
E-mail: SI-Shell-US-Recruitment-Scholarships@shell.
   com
Web: www.shell.us

Summary To provide financial assistance to Native American and other underrepresented minority students majoring in specified engineering and geosciences fields at designated universities.

Eligibility This program is open to students enrolled full time as sophomores, juniors, or seniors at 22 participating universities. Applicants must be U.S. citizens or authorized to work in the United States and members of a race or ethnicity underrepresented in the technical and scientific academic areas (Black, Hispanic/Latino, American Indian, or Alaskan Native). They must have a GPA of 3.2 or higher with a major in engineering (chemical, civil, electrical, geological, geophysical, mechanical, or petroleum) or geosciences (geology, geophysics, or physics). Along with their application, they must submit a 100-word essay on the kind of work they plan to be doing in 10 years, both in their career and in their community. Financial need is not considered in the selection process.

Financial data The stipend is $5,000 per year.

Duration 1 year; may be renewed up to 3 additional years, provided the recipient remains qualified and accepts a Shell Oil Company internship (if offered).

Additional information This program is managed by International Scholarship and Tuition Services Inc. The participating institutions are Colorado School of Mines, Cornell University, Florida A&M University, Georgia Institute of Technology, Louisiana State University, Massachusetts Institute of Technology, Michigan State University, North Carolina A&T

State University, Ohio State University, Pennsylvania State University, Prairie View A&M University, Purdue University, Rice University, Stanford University, Texas A&M University, University of Colorado at Boulder, University of Houston, University of Illinois at Urbana-Champaign, University of Michigan, University of Oklahoma, University of Texas at Austin, and University of Texas at El Paso.

Number awarded   Up to 20 each year.

Deadline   January of each year.

[591]
SIGNIFICANT OPPORTUNITIES IN ATMOSPHERIC RESEARCH AND SCIENCE (SOARS) PROGRAM

University Corporation for Atmospheric Research
Attn: SOARS Program Manager
3090 Center Green Drive
P.O. Box 3000
Boulder, CO 80307-3000
(303) 497-8622   Fax: (303) 497-8629
E-mail: soars@ucar.edu
Web: www.soars.ucar.edu

Summary   To provide summer work experience to undergraduate or graduate students, especially Native Americans and members of other underrepresented groups, who are interested in preparing for a career in atmospheric or a related science.

Eligibility   This program is open to U.S. citizens or permanent residents who have completed their sophomore year of college and are majoring in atmospheric science or a related field (e.g., biology, chemistry, computer science, earth science, engineering, environmental science, the geosciences, mathematics, meteorology, oceanography, physics, or social science). Applicants must have a GPA of 3.0 or higher and be planning to prepare for a career in the field of atmospheric or a related science. The program especially encourages applications from members of groups that are historically underrepresented in the atmospheric and related sciences, including Blacks/African Americans, Hispanics/Latinos, American Indians/Alaskan Natives, women, first-generation college students, and students with disabilities. It also welcomes applications from students who are gay, lesbian, bisexual, or transgender; have experienced, and worked to overcome, educational or economic disadvantage; or have personal or family circumstances that may complicate their continued progress in research careers.

Financial data   Participants receive a competitive stipend and a housing allowance. Round-trip travel between Boulder and any 1 location within the continental United States is also provided. Students who are accepted into a graduate program receive full scholarships (with SOARS and the participating universities each sharing the costs).

Duration   10 weeks during the summer. Students are encouraged to continue for 4 subsequent summers.

Additional information   This program began in 1996. Students are assigned positions with a research project. They are exposed to the research facilities at the National Center for Atmospheric Research (NCAR), including computers, libraries, laboratories, and aircraft. NCAR is operated by the University Corporation for Atmospheric Research (a consortium of more than 100 North American universities) with primary support from the National Science Foundation (NSF);

other sponsors include the Department of Energy, the Department of Defense, the National Aeronautics and Space Administration (NASA), the Environmental Protection Agency (EPA), the Federal Aviation Administration (FAA), and the National Oceanic and Atmospheric Administration (NOAA). Before completing their senior years, students are encouraged to apply to a master's or doctoral degree program at 1 of the participating universities.

Number awarded   Varies each year; recently, 17 were awarded.

Deadline   January of each year.

[592]
SMA NATIVE AMERICAN STEM SCHOLARSHIP

Souder, Miller & Associates
Attn: Scholarships
3451 Candelaria Road N.E., Suite D
Albuquerque, NM 87107
(505) 299-0942   Toll Free: (877) 299-0942
E-mail: nativeamerican.scholarship@soudermiller.com
Web: www.soudermiller.com/company/tss

Summary   To provide financial assistance to Native Americans who are interested in working on a bachelor's degree in a field of science, technology, engineering, or mathematics (STEM).

Eligibility   This program is open to enrolled members of federally-recognized pueblos, nations, or tribes who are graduating high school seniors or students currently enrolled in an accredited college or university. Preference is given to students who reside within the tribal lands. Applicants must be interested in working full time on a bachelor's degree in a field of STEM. They must have a GPA of 3.0 or higher. Along with their application, they must submit their Certificate of Indian Blood (CIB) and a 1-page letter on their future goals and how an education in STEM will benefit their community. Financial need is not considered in the selection process.

Financial data   The stipend is $1,500 per year; funds are paid directly to the recipient's college or university.

Duration   1 year; may be renewed up to 3 additional years, provided the recipient remains enrolled full time and maintains a GPA of 3.0 or higher.

Number awarded   Varies each year.

Deadline   June of each year.

[593]
SMITHSONIAN MINORITY AWARDS PROGRAM

Smithsonian Institution
Attn: Office of Fellowships and Internships
470 L'Enfant Plaza, Suite 7102
P.O. Box 37012, MRC 902
Washington, DC 20013-7012
(202) 633-7070   Fax: (202) 633-7069
E-mail: siofi@si.edu
Web: www.smithsonianofi.com

Summary   To provide funding to Native American and other minority undergraduate and graduate students interested in conducting research at the Smithsonian Institution.

Eligibility   This program is open to members of U.S. minority groups underrepresented in the Smithsonian's scholarly programs. Applicants must be undergraduates or beginning graduate students interested in conducting research in the

Institution's disciplines and in the museum field. They must be U.S. citizens or permanent residents and have a GPA of 3.0 or higher.

Financial data Students receive a grant of $600 per week.

Duration Up to 10 weeks.

Additional information Recipients must carry out independent research projects in association with the Smithsonian's research staff. Eligible fields of study currently include animal behavior, ecology, and environmental science (including an emphasis on the tropics); anthropology (including archaeology); astrophysics and astronomy; earth sciences and paleobiology; evolutionary and systematic biology; history of science and technology; history of art (especially American, contemporary, African, Asian, and 20th-century art); American crafts and decorative arts; social and cultural history of the United States; and folklife. Students are required to be in residence at the Smithsonian for the duration of the fellowship.

Number awarded Varies each year; recently, 25 were granted: 2 for fall, 19 for summer, and 4 for spring.

Deadline January of each year for summer and fall residency; September of each year for spring residency.

[594]
SMITHSONIAN MINORITY STUDENT INTERNSHIP

Smithsonian Institution
Attn: Office of Fellowships and Internships
470 L'Enfant, Suite 7102
P.O. Box 37012, MRC 902
Washington, DC 20013-7012
(202) 633-7070　　　　　　　Fax: (202) 633-7069
E-mail: siofi@si.edu
Web: www.smithsonianofi.com/minority-internship-program

Summary To provide Native American and other minority undergraduate or graduate students with the opportunity to work on research or museum procedure projects in specific areas of history, art, or science at the Smithsonian Institution.

Eligibility Internships are offered to minority students who are actively engaged in undergraduate or graduate study or have graduated within the past 4 months. Applicants must be U.S. citizens or permanent residents who have an overall GPA of 3.0 or higher. Applicants must be interested in conducting research in any of the following fields of interest to the Smithsonian: animal behavior, ecology, and environmental science (including an emphasis on the tropics); anthropology (including archaeology); astrophysics and astronomy; earth sciences and paleobiology; evolutionary and systematic biology; history of science and technology; history of art (especially American, contemporary, African, Asian, and 20th-century art); American crafts and decorative arts; social and cultural history of the United States; and folklife.

Financial data The program provides a stipend of $600 per week; travel allowances may also be offered.

Duration 10 weeks during the summer or academic year.

Number awarded Varies each year.

Deadline January of each year for summer or fall; September of each year for spring.

[595]
SMITHSONIAN NATIVE AMERICAN INTERNSHIPS

Smithsonian Institution
Attn: Office of Fellowships and Internships
Minority Awards Program
470 L'Enfant Plaza, Suite 7102
P.O. Box 37012, MRC 902
Washington, DC 20013-7012
(202) 633-7070　　　　　　　Fax: (202) 633-7069
E-mail: siofi@si.edu
Web: www.smithsonianofi.com

Summary To support Native American students interested in conducting projects related to Native American topics that require the use of Native American resources at the Smithsonian Institution.

Eligibility Applicants must be Native American students who are actively engaged in graduate or undergraduate study and are interested in working with Native American resources at the Smithsonian Institution. Along with their application, they must submit a 2- to 4-page essay in which they describe their past and present academic history and other experiences which they feel have prepared them for an internship, what they hope to accomplish through an internship and how it would relate to their academic and career goals, and what about the Smithsonian in particular interests them and leads them to apply for the internship.

Financial data Interns receive a stipend of $600 per week, a travel allowance, and a small research allowance.

Duration Up to 10 weeks.

Additional information Interns pursue directed research projects supervised by Smithsonian staff members. Recipients must be in residence at the Smithsonian Institution for the duration of the program.

Number awarded Varies each year.

Deadline January of each year for summer residency or fall residency; September of each year for spring residency.

[596]
SOCIETY FOR AMERICAN ARCHAEOLOGY NATIVE AMERICAN UNDERGRADUATE ARCHAEOLOGY SCHOLARSHIP

Society for American Archaeology
Attn: Native American Scholarship Fund
1111 14th Street, N.W., Suite 800
Washington, DC 20005-5622
(202) 789-8200　　　　　　　Fax: (202) 789-0284
E-mail: nasf@saa.org
Web: ecommerce.saa.org

Summary To provide financial assistance to Native Americans interested in working on an undergraduate degree in archaeology.

Eligibility This program is open to Native Americans who are enrolled or planning to enroll at an accredited college or university in an undergraduate program in archaeology. Applicants must submit a 2-page personal statement describing why they are interested in their proposed program and in archaeology, and the contributions they hope to make to the future of archaeology.

Financial data The stipend is $5,000.

Duration 1 year.

Additional information This program began in 2009.

Number awarded 1 each year.

Deadline December of each year.

[597]
SOCIETY OF AMERICAN INDIAN GOVERNMENT EMPLOYEES ACADEMIC SCHOLARSHIPS

Society of American Indian Government Employees
c/o Southern California Scholarship Committee
1340 South Ventura Road
Oxnard, CA 93033
E-mail: Vvmed4d@yahoo.com
Web: www.saige.org/scholar/acscholarship.html

Summary To provide financial assistance to members of the Society of American Indian Government Employees (SAIGE) who are interested in working on an undergraduate or graduate degree.

Eligibility This program is open to American Indians and Alaska Natives who have term, seasonal, career conditional, or career appointments as federal employees. Applicants must be interested in working on a bachelor's, master's, or Ph.D. degree at an accredited postsecondary school. They must have a GPA of 2.5 or higher and be members of SAIGE. Along with their application, they must submit a 1-page essay describing their educational and workforce advancement goals and how this scholarship will help them achieve their goals, a letter of recommendation, and a narrative of extracurricular and community service activities.

Financial data Stipends range from $300 to $500 per semester, or $500 to $1,000 per academic year. Funding is provided as reimbursement for tuition costs upon receipt of a passing grade.

Duration 1 semester; may be renewed upon reapplication.

Additional information This program began in 2005.

Number awarded 1 or more each semester.

Deadline May of each year for fall semester; October of each year for spring semester.

[598]
SOVEREIGN NATIONS SCHOLARSHIP FUND FOR NON-TRIBAL COLLEGE STUDENTS

American Indian College Fund
Attn: Scholarship Department
8333 Greenwood Boulevard
Denver, CO 80221
(303) 426-8900   Toll Free: (800) 776-FUND
Fax: (303) 426-1200
E-mail: scholarships@collegefund.org
Web: www.collegefund.org

Summary To provide financial assistance to Native American students who are interested in attending a mainstream university.

Eligibility This program is open to American Indians and Alaska Natives who can document proof of enrollment or descendancy. Applicants must be enrolled or planning to enroll full time in a bachelor's degree program at a mainstream institution. They must have a GPA of 2.0 or higher and be able to demonstrate exceptional academic achievement. Applications are available only online and include required essays on specified topics. U.S. citizenship is required.

Financial data The stipend is $2,000 per year.

Duration 1 year; may be renewed.

Number awarded Varies each year.

Deadline May of each year.

[599]
SOVEREIGN NATIONS SCHOLARSHIP FUND FOR TRIBAL COLLEGE STUDENTS

American Indian College Fund
Attn: Scholarship Department
8333 Greenwood Boulevard
Denver, CO 80221
(303) 426-8900   Toll Free: (800) 776-FUND
Fax: (303) 426-1200
E-mail: scholarships@collegefund.org
Web: www.collegefund.org

Summary To provide financial assistance for college to Native American students who are interested in attending a Tribal College or University (TCU) and working for a tribe or Indian organization after graduation.

Eligibility This program is open to American Indians and Alaska Natives who can document proof of enrollment or descendancy. Applicants must be planning to 1) enroll full time at a TCU; and 2) work for their tribe or an Indian organization after graduation. They must have a GPA of 3.0 or higher and be able to demonstrate exceptional academic achievement. Applications are available only online and include required essays on specified topics. U.S. citizenship is required.

Financial data The stipend is $2,000 per year.

Duration 1 year; may be renewed.

Number awarded Varies each year.

Deadline May of each year.

[600]
SSRP-AMGEN SCHOLARS PROGRAM

Stanford University
School of Medicine
Attn: Office of Graduate Education
MSOB X1C20
1265 Welch Road
Stanford, CA 94305-5421
(650) 725-8791   Fax: (650) 725-3867
E-mail: ssrpmail@stanford.edu
Web: biosciences.stanford.edu/prospective/diversity/ssrp

Summary To provide Native Americans and other underrepresented minority undergraduate students with a summer research experience at Stanford University in biological and biomedical sciences.

Eligibility This program is open to sophomores, juniors, and non-graduating seniors at 4-year colleges and universities in the United States, Puerto Rico, and U.S. territories. Students from all ethnic backgrounds are eligible, but the program especially encourages applications from African Americans, Latino/Hispanic Americans, Native Americans, Pacific Islanders, and other undergraduates who, by reason of their culture, class, race, ethnicity, background, work and life experiences, skills, and interests would bring diversity to graduate study in the biological and biomedical sciences (biochemistry, bioengineering, biology, biomedical informatics, biophysics, cancer biology, chemical and systems biology, developmental biology, genetics, immunology, microbiology, molecular and cellular physiology, neurosciences, stem cell and regenerative medicine, and structural biology). Applicants must have at least 1 year of undergraduate education remaining before graduation and should be planning to prepare for and enter a Ph.D. program in the biological or biomedical sciences. They must have a GPA of 3.2 or higher. U.S. citizenship or permanent resident status is required.

Financial data The program provides a stipend of $3,500, housing, meals, and transportation to and from the San Francisco Bay area.

Duration 9 weeks during the summer.

Additional information This program encompasses 1) the Stanford component of the Amgen Scholars Program, which operates at 8 other U.S. universities (and the National Institutes of Health) and is funded by the Amgen Foundation; 2) Genetics Department Funding; and 3) Stanford Medicine Dean's Funding.

Number awarded 30 to 35 each year.

Deadline January of each year.

[601]
ST. CROIX CHIPPEWA INDIANS HIGHER EDUCATION GRANTS PROGRAM

St. Croix Chippewa Indians of Wisconsin
Attn: Education Coordinator
24663 Angeline Avenue
Webster, WI 54893
(715) 349-2195, ext. 5300   Toll Free: (800) 236-2195
Fax: (715) 349-7905
Web: www.stcciw.com

Summary To provide financial assistance for college or graduate school to tribal members of the St. Croix Chippewa Indians of Wisconsin.

Eligibility This program is open to enrolled tribal members of the St. Croix Chippewa Indians who are working on or planning to work on an undergraduate or graduate degree at a 4-year college or university. Applicants must be able to demonstrate financial need. Along with their application, they must submit a 350-word personal essay that includes their strengths and weaknesses, how they feel their life experiences have prepared them for their life goals, and who has inspired them in their life.

Financial data Full-time (12 credits or more) undergraduates may receive up to $3,000 per semester, half-time (6 to 11 credits) up to $1,500 per semester, and part-time (less than 6 credits) up to $750 per semester. Funds may be used for tuition, fees, books, and room in a dormitory. Full-time (6 credits or more) graduate students may receive up to $2,500 for tuition and up to $500 for books per semester) and half-time (3 to 5 credits) up to $1,250 for tuition and $500 for books per semester. Summer students (6 credits or more) may receive up to $1,500 for tuition, fees, books, and room in a dormitory.

Duration 1 year; may be renewed for a total of 10 semesters, provided the recipient maintains a GPA of 2.0 or higher as an undergraduate or 3.0 or higher as a graduate student.

Number awarded Varies each year.

Deadline June of each year for fall term; October of each year for winter or spring term; March of each year for summer term.

[602]
ST. CROIX CHIPPEWA INDIANS JOB PLACEMENT AND TRAINING PROGRAM

St. Croix Chippewa Indians of Wisconsin
Attn: Education Coordinator
24663 Angeline Avenue
Webster, WI 54893
(715) 349-2195, ext. 5300   Toll Free: (800) 236-2195
Fax: (715) 349-7905
Web: www.stcciw.com

Summary To provide financial assistance for technical or vocational training to tribal members of the St. Croix Chippewa Indians of Wisconsin.

Eligibility This program is open to enrolled tribal members of the St. Croix Chippewa Indians who are working on or planning to work on a vocational degree at a 2-year college or vocational school. Applicants must be able to demonstrate financial need.

Financial data Stipends range up to $1,500 per semester for full-time (12 credits or more) students, $750 per semester for half-time (6 to 11 credits), $375 per semester for part-time (less than 6 credits), or $750 for summer (6 credits or more) students.

Duration Up to 24 months at a vocational technical training institution or 36 months at a school of nursing, provided the recipient maintains a GPA of 2.0 or higher.

Number awarded Varies each year.

Deadline June of each year for fall term; October of each year for winter or spring term; March of each year for summer term.

[603]
STANDING ROCK SIOUX TRIBE HIGHER EDUCATION SCHOLARSHIPS

Standing Rock Sioux Tribe
Standing Rock Administrative Service Center
Attn: Tribal Department of Education
P.O. Box D
Fort Yates, ND 58538
(701) 854-8545   Fax: (701) 854-2175
E-mail: cironeyes@standingrock.org
Web: www.standingrock.org

Summary To provide financial assistance for college to members of the Standing Rock Sioux Tribe.

Eligibility This program is open to enrolled members of the Standing Rock Sioux Tribe in North Dakota and South Dakota. Applicants must be attending or planning to attend an accredited college or university. They must be able to demonstrate financial need. Undergraduates must have a cumulative GPA of 2.0 or higher; graduate students must have a GPA of 2.5 or higher for the most recent college education. Undergraduates must submit a personal essay that covers their academic background, employment and non-academic experiences, significant accomplishments, and how they degree they are seeking will contribute to their career and long-term goals. Graduate student essays must explain how their degree will contribute to the advancement of the Standing Rock Sioux Tribe.

Financial data For undergraduates, the stipend depends on need, ranging up to $3,500 per semester. Graduate students receive up to $500 per semester credit hour and book reimbursement up to $500 per semester.

Duration   1 semester; may be renewed until completion of an undergraduate or graduate degree.

Number awarded   Varies each year.

Deadline   June of each year for fall semester; November of each year for spring semester; April of each year for summer school.

[604]
STATE COUNCIL ON ADAPTED PHYSICAL EDUCATION CULTURAL DIVERSITY STUDENT SCHOLARSHIP

California Association for Health, Physical Education, Recreation and Dance
Attn: State Council on Adapted Physical Education
1501 El Camino Avenue, Suite 3
Sacramento, CA 95815-2748
(916) 922-3596   Toll Free: (800) 499-3596 (within CA)
Fax: (916) 922-0133
E-mail: califstatecouncilape@gmail.com
Web: www.califstatecouncilape.org

Summary   To provide financial assistance to Native American and other culturally diverse members of the California Association for Health, Physical Education, Recreation and Dance (CAHPERD) who are preparing to become a student teacher in the field of adapted physical education.

Eligibility   This program is open to CAHPERD members who are attending a California college or university and specializing in the field of adapted physical education. Applicants must be members of an ethnic or cultural minority group (e.g., African American, American Indian/Native American, Asian American, Filipino, Mexican American, other Latino, Pacific Islander). They must be planning to become a student teacher during the following academic year. Along with their application, they must submit a 300-word statement of their professional goals and philosophy of physical education for individuals with disabilities. Selection is based on academic proficiency; leadership ability; personal qualities; school, community, and professional activities; and experience and interest in working with individuals with disabilities.

Financial data   The stipend is $1,000.

Duration   1 year.

Number awarded   1 each year.

Deadline   January of each year.

[605]
STEPHEN WASHBURN SCHOLARSHIP

Seneca Diabetes Foundation
Attn: Secretary/Treasurer
P.O. Box 309
Irving, NY 14081
(716) 532-4900   E-mail: white@sni.org
Web: www.senecadiabetesfoundation.org/scholarships

Summary   To provide financial assistance to members of the Seneca Nation, especially veterans, who are interested in attending college or graduate school to prepare for a career in a health-related field.

Eligibility   This program is open to members of the Seneca Nation who are interested in attending college or graduate school to assist the Seneca people, especially in regard to

the fight against diabetes, by working on a degree in a health-related field, including clinical studies or health administration. Service veterans receive preferential consideration. Along with their application, they must submit brief statements on 1) the professional, community, or cultural services and activities in which they have participated; 2) how this scholarship would help further their education; 3) their goals or plan for using their education and training to benefit the Seneca Nation and its people; and 4) an example of a time when they served in a leadership position, the successes and challenges that they faced, the lessons they learned, and how they can apply those lessons to other life experiences. In the selection process, primary consideration is given to financial need, but involvement in community and cultural activities, personal assets, and desire to improve the quality of life for the Seneca people are also considered.

Financial data   The stipend is $5,000.

Duration   1 year.

Number awarded   1 each year.

Deadline   August of each year.

[606]
STEPS TO SUCCESS-THE DOUG PAUL SCHOLARSHIP PROGRAM

Credit Suisse
Attn: Diversity and Inclusion Programs
Eleven Madison Avenue
New York, NY 10010-3629
(212) 325-2000   Fax: (212) 325-6665
E-mail: campus.diversity@credit-suisse.com
Web: www.credit-suisse.com

Summary   To provide financial assistance and work experience at Credit Suisse in New York to Native American and other underrepresented minority undergraduate students interested in a career in financial services.

Eligibility   This program is open to college students entering their junior year who are Black/African American, Hispanic/Latino, or Native American. Applicants must be preparing for a career in financial services by studying such fields as asset management, equity research, finance, investment banking, information technology, operations, and sales and trading. They must be interested in an internship in New York with Credit Suisse. Selection is based on academic excellence, leadership ability, and interest in the financial services industry.

Financial data   Students who complete the summer internship receive a stipend of $5,000 for the following year of academic study.

Duration   The internship is 10 weeks during the summer, followed by a year of academic study (the junior year) and a possible renewal of the internship the following summer.

Number awarded   1 or more each year.

Deadline   June of each year.

[607]
STEVEN THAYER HOPI SCHOLARSHIP

Arizona Community Foundation
Attn: Director of Scholarships
2201 East Camelback Road, Suite 405B
Phoenix, AZ 85016
(602) 381-1400   Toll Free: (800) 222-8221
Fax: (602) 381-1575
E-mail: scholarship@azfoundation.org
Web: azfoundation.academicworks.com/opportunities/2479

Summary To provide financial assistance to members of the Hopi Nation in Arizona who are interested in studying art at an institution of higher education in any state.

Eligibility This program is open to members of the Hopi Nation in Arizona who are majoring, or planning to major, in art at a recognized college, university, community college, or art institute in any state. Applicants must have a GPA of 3.0 or higher in high school and in any college studies. Along with their application, they must submit a portfolio with up to 10 images that demonstrate their skill as a Hopi artist and a 500-word essay about their goals and aspirations as a Hopi artist.

Financial data The stipend is approximately $3,600 per year.

Duration 1 year; recipients may reapply.

Number awarded Varies each year.

Deadline April of each year.

[608]
STUDENT OPPORTUNITY SCHOLARSHIPS OF THE PRESBYTERIAN CHURCH (USA)

Presbyterian Church (USA)
Attn: Office of Financial Aid for Service
100 Witherspoon Street
Louisville, KY 40202-1396
(502) 569-5224   Toll Free: (888) 728-7228, ext. 5224
Fax: (502) 569-8766   TDD: (800) 833-5955
E-mail: finaid@pcusa.org
Web: www.presbyterianmission.org

Summary To provide financial assistance to Presbyterian college students, especially Native Americans and others of racial/ethnic minority heritage.

Eligibility This program is open to active members of the Presbyterian Church (USA) who are entering their sophomore, junior, or senior year of college as full-time students in a bachelor's degree program. Preference is given to applicants who are members of racial/ethnic minority groups (Asian American, African American, Hispanic American, Native American, Alaska Native). Applicants must have a GPA of 2.5 or higher and be able to demonstrate financial need.

Financial data Stipends range up to $2,000 per year, depending upon the financial need of the recipient.

Duration 1 year; may be renewed if the recipient continues to need financial assistance and demonstrates satisfactory academic progress.

Number awarded Approximately 80 each year.

Deadline May of each year.

[609]
SUMMER CLINICAL AND TRANSLATIONAL RESEARCH PROGRAM

Harvard Medical School
Office for Diversity Inclusion and Community Partnership
Attn: Program for Faculty Development and Diversity Inclusion
164 Longwood Avenue, Second Floor
Boston, MA 02115-5810
(617) 432-1892   Fax: (617) 432-3834
E-mail: pfdd_dcp@hms.harvard.edu
Web: mfdp.med.harvard.edu

Summary To provide an opportunity for undergraduate students, especially Native Americans and other underrepresented minorities, to engage in research at Harvard Medical School during the summer.

Eligibility This program is open to undergraduate sophomores, juniors, and seniors who are preparing for a career in medical research. Priority is given to students at schools that receive funding from the Minority Biomedical Research Support (MBRS) or Minority Access to Research Careers (MARC) programs of the National Institute of Health (NIH), Historically Black Colleges and Universities (HBCUs), Hispanic Serving Institutions (HSIs), or Tribal Colleges and Universities (TCUs). Applicants must be interested in working on a summer research program at Harvard Medical School under the mentorship of a faculty advisor. They must be interested in a research and health-related career, especially in clinical or translational research or research that transforms scientific discoveries arising from laboratory, clinical, or population studies into clinical or population-based applications to improve health. U.S. citizenship, nationality, or permanent resident status is required.

Financial data Participants receive a stipend (amount not specified), housing, and reimbursement of transportation costs to Boston up to $400.

Duration 10 weeks during the summer.

Additional information This program, established in 2008, is funded by the National Center for Research Resources of the NIH. It is a joint enterprise of Harvard University, its 10 schools, its 17 Academic Healthcare Centers, Boston College School of Nursing, MIT, the Cambridge Health Alliance, and other community partners. Interns attend weekly seminars with Harvard faculty focusing on such topics as research methodology, health disparities, ethics, and career paths. They also have the opportunity to participate in offerings of other Harvard Medical School programs, such a career development seminars and networking dinners.

Number awarded Varies each year; recently, 10 college students were admitted to this program.

Deadline December of each year.

[610]
SUMMER HONORS UNDERGRADUATE RESEARCH PROGRAM

Harvard Medical School
Attn: Division of Medical Sciences
Diversity Programs Office
260 Longwood Avenue, T-MEC 335
Boston, MA 02115-5720
(617) 432-4980   Toll Free: (800) 367-9019
Fax: (617) 432-2644   E-mail: shurp@hms.harvard.edu
Web: www.hms.harvard.edu/dms/diversity/shurp

Summary To provide an opportunity for Native American and other underrepresented minority students to engage in research at Harvard Medical School during the summer.

Eligibility This program at Harvard Medical School is open to undergraduate students belonging to minority groups that are underrepresented in the sciences. Applicants must have had at least 1 summer (or equivalent) of experience in a research laboratory and have taken at least 1 upper-level biology course that includes molecular biology. They should be considering a career in biological or biomedical research. U.S. citizenship or permanent resident status is required.

Financial data The program provides a stipend of $450 per week, dormitory housing, travel costs, a meal card, and health insurance if it is needed.

Duration 10 weeks during the summer.

Number awarded Varies each year.

Deadline January of each year.

[611]
SUMMER PROGRAM IN BIOSTATISTICS AND COMPUTATIONAL BIOLOGY

Harvard T.H. Chan School of Public Health
Department of Biostatistics
Attn: Diversity Coordinator
677 Huntington Avenue, SPH2, Fourth Floor
Boston, MA 02115
(617) 432-3175   Fax: (617) 432-5619
E-mail: biostat_diversity@hsph.harvard.edu
Web: www.hsph.harvard.edu

Summary To enable Native Americans and other underrepresented minority or disadvantaged science undergraduates to participate in a summer research internship at Harvard T.H. Chan School of Public Health that focuses on biostatistics, epidemiology, and public health.

Eligibility This program is open to 1) members of ethnic groups underrepresented in graduate education (African Americans, Hispanic/Latinos, Native Americans, Pacific Islanders, biracial/multiracial); 2) first-generation college students; 3) low-income students; or 4) individuals with a disability. Applicants must be current undergraduates interested in participating in a summer program on the use of quantitative methods for biological, environmental, and medical research as preparation for graduate studies in biostatistics or computational biology. They must have a strong GPA, including course work in calculus, and a strong interest in mathematics, statistics, computer science, and other quantitative subjects. U.S. citizenship or permanent resident status is required.

Financial data Funding covers travel, housing, course materials, and a stipend to cover meals and incidentals.

Duration 6 weeks, starting in June.

Additional information Interns take non-credit classes in biostatistics and epidemiology, participate in a collaborative research project, and travel to local laboratories and research centers to observe public health research in action.

Number awarded Normally 12 each year.

Deadline January of each year.

[612]
SUMMER PROGRAM IN EPIDEMIOLOGY

Harvard T.H. Chan School of Public Health
Department of Epidemiology
655 Huntington Avenue
Boston, MA 02115
(617) 432-1050   Fax: (617) 566-7805
E-mail: edigiova@hsph.harvard.edu
Web: www.hsph.harvard.edu

Summary To enable Native American and other underrepresented minority or disadvantaged undergraduates to participate in a summer research program in epidemiology at Harvard T.H. Chan School of Public Health.

Eligibility This program is open to undergraduate students who 1) are U.S. citizens, nationals, or permanent residents; 2) have a GPA of 3.0 or higher; 3) have a quantitative science background or have taken several quantitative classes beyond introductory level courses; 4) can demonstrate an interest in public health; and 5) are from at least 1 underrepresented group in biomedical research, including people with disabilities, members of minority racial and ethnic groups (African Americans, Hispanic/Latinos, Native Americans, Pacific Islanders), people of disadvantaged and low socioeconomic status, members of families with annual income below established thresholds, and people from a rural, inner-city, or other environment that has inhibited them from getting the knowledge, skills, and abilities needed for a research career. They must be planning to apply to a graduate program to work on a master's or doctoral degree in epidemiology; students planning to apply to medical school and students already accepted to graduate school are not eligible.

Financial data Interns receive a salary (amount not specified) and support for travel.

Duration 5 weeks, during the summer.

Additional information The program includes introductory course work in epidemiology and biostatistics, formal lectures by faculty at the Harvard T.H. Chan School of Public Health, a group research project, and a Kaplan GRE course.

Number awarded Varies each year; recently, 8 were awarded.

Deadline February of each year.

[613]
SUMMER RESEARCH OPPORTUNITIES PROGRAM (SROP)

Committee on Institutional Cooperation
Attn: Academic and International Programs
1819 South Neil Street, Suite D
Champaign, IL 61820-7271
(217) 333-8475   Fax: (217) 244-7127
E-mail: cic@staff.cic.net
Web: www.cic.net/students/srop/introduction

Summary To provide an opportunity for Native Americans and other undergraduates from diverse backgrounds to gain research experience at member institutions of the Committee on Institutional Cooperation (CIC) during the summer.

Eligibility This program is open to students currently enrolled in a degree-granting program at a college or university who have a GPA of 3.0 or higher and an interest in continuing on to graduate school. Applicants must be interested in conducting a summer research project under the supervision of a faculty mentor at a CIC member institution. The program is designed to increase educational access for students from diverse backgrounds; members of racial and ethnic minority groups and low-income first-generation students are especially encouraged to apply. U.S. citizenship or permanent resident status is required.

Financial data Participants are paid a stipend that depends on the participating CIC member institution, but ranges from $3,000 to $6,000. Faculty mentors receive a $500 research allowance for the cost of materials.

Duration 8 to 10 weeks during the summer.

Additional information Participants work directly with faculty mentors at the institution of their choice and engage in other enrichment activities, such as workshops and social gatherings. In July, all participants come together at 1 of the CIC campuses for the annual SROP conference. The participating CIC member institutions are University of Illinois at Urbana-Champaign, University of Iowa, University of Michigan, University of Minnesota, University of Nebraska at Lincoln, University of Wisconsin at Madison, Michigan State University, Northwestern University, Ohio State University, Pennsylvania State University, Purdue University, and Rutgers University. Students are required to write a paper and an abstract describing their projects and to present the results of their work at a campus symposium.

Number awarded Varies each year.

Deadline February of each year.

[614]
SUMMER TRANSPORTATION INTERNSHIP PROGRAM FOR DIVERSE GROUPS

Department of Transportation
Attn: Summer Transportation Internship Program for Diverse Groups
Eighth Floor E81-105
1200 New Jersey Avenue, S.E.
Washington, DC 20590
(202) 366-2907   E-mail: Crystal.Taylor@dot.gov
Web: www.fhwa.dot.gov/education/stipdg.cfm

Summary To enable Native Americans and undergraduate, graduate, and law students from other diverse groups to gain work experience during the summer at facilities of the U.S. Department of Transportation (DOT).

Eligibility This program is open to all qualified applicants, but it is designed to provide women, persons with disabilities, and members of diverse social and ethnic groups with summer opportunities in transportation. Applicants must be U.S. citizens currently enrolled in a degree-granting program of study at an accredited institution of higher learning at the undergraduate (community or junior college, university, college, or Tribal College or University) or graduate level. Undergraduates must be entering their junior or senior year; students attending a Tribal or community college must have completed their first year of school; law students must be entering their second or third year of school. Students who

will graduate during the spring or summer are not eligible unless they have been accepted for enrollment in graduate school. The program accepts applications from students in all majors who are interested in working on transportation-related topics and issues. Preference is given to students with a GPA of 3.0 or higher. Undergraduates must submit a 1-page essay on their transportation interests and how participation in this program will enhance their educational and career plans and goals. Graduate students must submit a writing sample representing their educational and career plans and goals. Law students must submit a legal writing sample.

Financial data The stipend is $4,000 for undergraduates or $5,000 for graduate and law students. The program also provides housing and reimbursement of travel expenses from interns' homes to their assignment location.

Duration 10 weeks during the summer.

Additional information Assignments are at the DOT headquarters in Washington, D.C., a selected modal administration, or selected field offices around the country.

Number awarded 80 to 100 each year.

Deadline January of each year.

[615]
SURETY AND FIDELITY INDUSTRY SCHOLARSHIP PROGRAM

The Surety Foundation
Attn: Scholarship Program for Minority Students
1101 Connecticut Avenue, N.W., Suite 800
Washington, DC 20036
(202) 463-0600, ext. 638   Fax: (202) 463-0606
E-mail: scarradine@surety.org
Web: www.thesuretyfoundation.org

Summary To provide financial assistance to Native American and other minority undergraduates working on a degree in a field related to insurance.

Eligibility This program is open to full-time undergraduates who are U.S. citizens and members of a minority group (Black, Native American/Alaskan Native, Asian/Pacific Islander, Hispanic). Applicants must have completed at least 30 semester hours of study at an accredited 4-year college or university and have a declared major in insurance/risk management, accounting, business, or finance. They must have a GPA of 3.0 or higher and be able to demonstrate financial need.

Financial data The stipend is $5,000 per year.

Duration 1 year; recipients may reapply.

Additional information This program, established in 2003 by The Surety & Fidelity Association of America, includes the Adrienne Alexander Scholarship and the George W. McClellan Scholarship.

Number awarded Varies each year; recently, 3 were awarded.

Deadline January of each year.

[616]
SUSIE QIMMIQSAK BEVINS ENDOWMENT SCHOLARSHIP FUND

Cook Inlet Region, Inc.
Attn: The CIRI Foundation
3600 San Jeronimo Drive, Suite 256
Anchorage, AK 99508-2870
(907) 793-3575   Toll Free: (800) 764-3382
Fax: (907) 793-3585   E-mail: tcf@thecirifoundation.org
Web: www.thecirifoundation.org/about/donors

Summary To provide financial assistance for undergraduate or graduate studies in the literary, performing, and visual arts to Alaska Natives who are original enrollees to Cook Inlet Region, Inc. (CIRI) and their lineal descendants.

Eligibility This program is open to Alaska Native enrollees to CIRI under the Alaska Native Claims Settlement Act (ANCSA) of 1971 and their lineal descendants. There are no Alaska residency requirements or age limitations. Applicants must be accepted or enrolled full time in a 2-year, 4-year, or graduate degree program in the literary, visual, or performing arts. They should have a GPA of 2.5 or higher. Along with their application, they must submit a 500-word statement on their educational and career goals and how they are contributing, or planning to contribute, to a positive Alaska Native community. Selection is based on that statement, academic achievement, rigor of course work or degree program, student financial contribution, financial need, grade level, previous work performance, community service, and relationship of degree program to career goals.

Financial data The stipend is $2,000 per semester.

Duration 1 semester; recipients may reapply.

Additional information CIRI is 1 of 13 regional corporations established according to the terms of the Alaska Native Claims Settlement Act (ANCSA) of 1971. This program began in 1990.

Number awarded 1 or more each year.

Deadline May or November of each year.

[617]
SYNOD OF LAKES AND PRAIRIES RACIAL ETHNIC SCHOLARSHIPS

Synod of Lakes and Prairies
Attn: Committee on Racial Ethnic Ministry
2115 Cliff Drive
Eagen, MN 55122-3327
(651) 357-1140   Toll Free: (800) 328-1880, ext. 202
Fax: (651) 357-1141   E-mail: mkes@lakesandprairies.org
Web: www.lakesandprairies.org

Summary To provide financial assistance to Native American and other minority residents of the Presbyterian Church (USA) Synod of Lakes and Prairies who are working on an undergraduate or graduate degree at a college or seminary in any state as preparation for service to the church.

Eligibility This program is open to members of Presbyterian churches who reside within the Synod of Lakes and Prairies (Iowa, Minnesota, Nebraska, North Dakota, South Dakota, and Wisconsin). Applicants must be members of ethnic minority groups studying at least half time for service in the Presbyterian Church (USA) as a teaching elder, ordained minister, commissioned ruling elder, lay professional, or volunteer. They must be in good academic standing, making

progress toward an undergraduate or graduate degree, and able to demonstrate financial need. Along with their application, they must submit essays of 200 to 500 words on 1) what the church needs to do to be faithful to its mission in the world today; and 2) the people, practices, or events that influence their commitment to Christ in ways that renew their fair and strengthen their service.

Financial data Stipends range from $850 to $3,500.

Duration 1 year.

Number awarded Varies each year; recently, 9 were awarded.

Deadline September of each year.

[618]
TENNESSEE MINORITY TEACHING FELLOWS PROGRAM

Tennessee Student Assistance Corporation
Parkway Towers
404 James Robertson Parkway, Suite 1510
Nashville, TN 37243-0820
(615) 741-1346   Toll Free: (800) 342-1663
Fax: (615) 741-6101   E-mail: TSAC.Aidinfo@tn.gov
Web: www.tn.gov

Summary To provide scholarship/loans to Native American and other minority residents of Tennessee who wish to attend college in the state to prepare for a career in the teaching field.

Eligibility This program is open to minority residents of Tennessee who are either high school seniors planning to enroll full time at a college or university in the state or continuing college students at a Tennessee college or university. High school seniors must have a GPA of 2.75 or higher and an ACT score of at least 18 or a combined mathematics and critical reading SAT score of at least 860. Continuing college students must have a college GPA of 2.5 or higher. All applicants must agree to teach at the K-12 level in a Tennessee public school following graduation from college. Along with their application, they must submit a 250-word essay on why they chose teaching as a profession. U.S. citizenship is required.

Financial data The scholarship/loan is $5,000 per year. Recipients incur an obligation to teach at the preK-12 level in a Tennessee public school 1 year for each year the award is received.

Duration 1 year; may be renewed for up to 3 additional years, provided the recipient maintains full-time enrollment and a cumulative GPA of 2.5 or higher.

Additional information This program began in 1989.

Number awarded 20 new awards are granted each year.

Deadline April of each year.

[619]
TEWAARATON OUTSTANDING NATIVE AMERICAN SCHOLARSHIP

Tewaaraton Foundation
c/o The University Club
1135 16th Street, N.W.
Washington, DC 20036
(202) 255-1485   E-mail: sarah@tewaaraton.com
Web: www.tewaaraton.com/native-american-scholarships

Summary To provide financial assistance for college to male and female members of the Iroquois community, considered separately, who have played lacrosse in high school.

Eligibility This program is open to high school seniors who are members of the Iroquois community and planning to attend college. Applicants must have played lacrosse. They must submit an essay of 3 to 5 pages on what lacrosse means to them as an Iroquois student-athlete. Males and females are considered separately. Selection is based on academic achievement, athletic performance, and ambition.

Financial data The stipend is $5,000 per year. Funds are paid directly to the student's college or university.

Duration 2 years.

Additional information This program is supported by USA Lacrosse.

Number awarded 2 each year: 1 female and 1 male.

Deadline April of each year.

[620]
THANKSGIVING DAY AWARD

Massachusetts Society of Mayflower Descendants
175 Derby Street, Suite 13
Hingham, MA 02034-4036
(781) 875-3194   E-mail: info@massmayflower.org
Web: www.massmayflower.org

Summary To provide financial assistance to members of the Wampanoag Nation who are interested in attending college in any state.

Eligibility This program is open to Wampanoag Nation members who are enrolled or planning to enroll at a college or university in any state. Along with their application, they must submit a 500-word essay on their Native American heritage, transcripts that include SAT scores, and information on financial need.

Financial data The stipend is $1,500.

Duration 1 year; recipients may reapply.

Additional information Funding for this program is provided by the Massachusetts Society of Mayflower Descendants in recognition of the Wampanoag Nation's assistance to its Pilgrim ancestors.

Number awarded 2 each year.

Deadline April of each year.

[621]
THERESA A. MIKE SCHOLARSHIP

Theresa A. Mike Foundation
Attn: Scholarship Committee
46-200 Harrison Place
Coachella, CA 92236
(760) 863-5108
Web: www.theresamike.org/index-3.html

Summary To provide financial assistance to American Indians from any state and residents of the Coachella Valley of California who are interested in attending college or graduate school in any state.

Eligibility This program is open to 1) employees and dependents of employees of any entity of the Twenty-Nine Palms Band of Mission Indians; 2) enrolled members of a federally-recognized Native American Indian Tribe; or 3) current residents or graduates of high schools in the Coachella Valley or Morongo Basin of California. Applicants must be enrolled

or planning to enroll full time at a college or graduate school in any state. They must have a GPA of 3.0 or higher. Along with their application, they must submit an essay of at least 1,000 words that covers their career goals and how they became interested in their chosen career, why education is important to them, and how other aspects of their life relate to their educational and career goals. Financial need may also be considered in the selection process.

Financial data A stipend is awarded (amount not specified).

Duration 1 year.

Additional information This program began in 1997.

Number awarded Varies each year.

Deadline June of each year.

[622]
THOMAS DARGAN MINORITY SCHOLARSHIP

KATU-TV
Attn: Human Resources
2153 N.E. Sandy Boulevard
P.O. Box 2
Portland, OR 97207-0002
(503) 231-4222
Web: www.katu.com

Summary To provide financial assistance to Native American and other minority students from Oregon and Washington who are studying broadcasting or communications in college.

Eligibility This program is open to minority (Asian, Black/African American, Hispanic or Latino, Native Hawaiian or Pacific Islander, American Indian or Alaska Native) U.S. citizens, currently enrolled as a sophomore or higher at a 4-year college or university or an accredited community college in Oregon or Washington. Residents of Oregon or Washington enrolled at a school in any state are also eligible. Applicants must be majoring in broadcasting or communications and have a GPA of 3.0 or higher. Community college students must be enrolled in a broadcast curriculum that is transferable to a 4-year accredited university. Finalists are interviewed. Selection is based on financial need, academic achievement, and an essay on personal and professional goals.

Financial data The stipend is $6,000. Funds are sent directly to the recipient's school.

Duration 1 year; recipients may reapply if they have maintained a GPA of 3.0 or higher.

Additional information Winners are also eligible for a paid internship in selected departments at Fisher Broadcasting/KATU in Portland, Oregon.

Number awarded 1 each year.

Deadline April of each year.

[623]
THOMAS G. NEUSOM SCHOLARSHIPS

Conference of Minority Transportation Officials
Attn: National Scholarship Program
100 M Street, S.E., Suite 917
Washington, DC 20003
(202) 506-2917   E-mail: info@comto.org
Web: www.comto.org/page/scholarships

Summary To provide financial assistance for college or graduate school to Native American and other minority members of the Conference of Minority Transportation Officials (COMTO) and their families.

Eligibility This program is open to undergraduate and graduate students who have been members of COMTO or whose parents, guardians, or grandparents have been members for at least 1 year. Applicants must be working (either full or part time) on a degree in a field related to transportation and have a GPA of 2.5 or higher. Along with their application they must submit a cover letter on their transportation-related career goals and life aspirations. Financial need is not considered in the selection process.

Financial data The stipend is $5,500. Funds are paid directly to the recipient's college or university.

Duration 1 year.

Number awarded 1 each year.

Deadline April of each year.

[624]
THOMAS R. PICKERING FOREIGN AFFAIRS FELLOWSHIPS

The Washington Center for Internships
Attn: Foreign Affairs Fellowship Program
1333 16th Street, N.W.
Washington, DC 20036-2205
(202) 238-7900   Fax: (202) 238-7700
E-mail: info@twc.org
Web: www.twc.edu

Summary To provide forgivable loans to undergraduate and graduate students, especially Native Americans and members of other underrepresented groups, interested in preparing for a career with the Department of State's Foreign Service.

Eligibility This program is open to U.S. citizens who are entering their senior year of undergraduate study or their first year of graduate study. Applicants must be planning to work on a 2-year full-time master's degree program relevant to the work of the U.S. Foreign Service, including public policy, international affairs, public administration, business, economics, political science, sociology, or foreign languages. They must be preparing for a career in the Foreign Service. Applications are especially encouraged from women, members of minority groups historically underrepresented in the Foreign Service, and students with financial need.

Financial data The program pays for tuition, room, board, books, mandatory fees, and 1 round-trip ticket from the fellow's residence to academic institution, to a maximum of $37,500 per academic year.

Duration 2 years: the senior year of undergraduate study and the first year of graduate study for college seniors; the first 2 years of graduate school for entering graduate students.

Additional information This program is funded by the State Department and administered by The Washington Center for Internships. Fellows must commit to a minimum of 5 years of service in an appointment as a Foreign Service Officer following graduation and successful completion of the Foreign Service examination. If they fail to fulfill that commitment, they must refund all money received.

Number awarded Approximately 40 each year: 20 college seniors and 20 entering graduate students.

Deadline January of each year.

[625]
TOMIAR RUDY ORTEGA, SR. SCHOLARSHIP

Pukúu, Cultural Community Services
1019 Second Street, Suite 2
San Fernando, CA 91340
(818) 336-6105   Fax: (818) 837-0796
Web: www.pukuu.org/services/scholarship

Summary To provide financial assistance to Native Americans who live in California and are attending college or graduate school in any state.

Eligibility This program is open to American Indians and Alaskan Natives who live in California and can document tribal or village enrollment or descendancy. Applicants must be enrolled at an accredited college or university in any state. They must be able to document completion of community service within the previous 12 months. Undergraduates must have a GPA of 2.75 or higher and graduate students must have a GPA of 3.5 or higher. Along with their application, they must submit a 2-page essay on their academic, career, and personal goals, including how they view their Native American heritage and its importance to them, how they plan to "give back" to Native Americans after graduation, and their on-going active involvement in the Native American community both on and off campus.

Financial data The stipend is $1,000.

Duration 1 year.

Number awarded 2 each year.

Deadline August of each year.

[626]
TRAILBLAZER SCHOLARSHIP

Conference of Minority Transportation Officials
Attn: National Scholarship Program
100 M Street, S.E., Suite 917
Washington, DC 20003
(202) 506-2917   E-mail: info@comto.org
Web: www.comto.org/page/scholarships

Summary To provide financial assistance for college or graduate school to Native American and other minority members of the Conference of Minority Transportation Officials (COMTO) and their families.

Eligibility This program is open to undergraduate and graduate students who have been members of COMTO or whose parents, guardians, or grandparents have been members for at least 1 year. Applicants must be working (either full or part time) on a degree in a field related to transportation and have a GPA of 2.5 or higher. Along with their application they must submit a cover letter on their transportation-related career goals and life aspirations. Financial need is not considered in the selection process.

Financial data The stipend is $2,500. Funds are paid directly to the recipient's college or university.

Duration 1 year.

Number awarded 1 each year.

Deadline April of each year.

[627]
TRANS-PAC ALASKA SCHOLARSHIP

Koniag Incorporated
Attn: Koniag Education Foundation
4241 B Street, Suite 303B
Anchorage, AK 99503
(907) 562-9093   Toll Free: (888) 562-9093
Fax: (907) 562-9023
E-mail: scholarships@koniageducation.org
Web: www.koniageducation.org/scholarships

Summary To provide financial assistance to Alaska Natives who are Koniag Incorporated shareholders or descendants and enrolled in undergraduate or graduate study in a field related to natural resources.

Eligibility This program is open to college juniors, seniors, and graduate students who are Alaska Native shareholders of Koniag Incorporated or descendants of those original enrollees. Applicants must have a GPA of 3.0 or higher and be working full time on a degree related to natural resources (e.g., forestry). Along with their application, they must submit a 300-word essay about their personal and family history, community involvement, volunteer activities, and educational and life goals. Financial need is not considered in the selection process.

Financial data The stipend is $5,000 per year. Funds are sent directly to the recipient's school and may be used for tuition, books, supplies, room, board, and transportation.

Duration 1 year; may be renewed.

Additional information Koniag Incorporated is 1 of 13 Alaska Native Regional Corporations created under the Alaska Native Claims Settlement Act of 1971. This program is supported by Transpac Group, a log and lumber export company.

Number awarded 2 each year.

Deadline May of each year.

[628]
TRANSPORTATION INDUSTRY COLLEGE SCHOLARSHIP

Conference of Minority Transportation Officials-Fort
  Lauderdale Chapter
Attn: Scholarship Committee
Victor Garcia, South Florida Regional Transportation
  Authority
801 N.W. 33rd Street
Pompano Beach, FL 33064
(954) 788-7925   Toll Free: (800) GO-SFRTA
Fax: (854) 788-7961   TDD: (800) 273-7545
E-mail: victorgarcia@comtoftlauderdale.org
Web: www.comtoftlauderdale.org/scholarship-program

Summary To provide financial assistance to Native American and other minority students working on a transportation-related undergraduate degree at a college in Florida.

Eligibility This program is open to minority students currently enrolled at accredited colleges and universities in Florida. Applicants must be majoring in a transportation-related field and have a GPA of 2.5 or higher. They must be U.S. citizens or permanent residents. Along with their application, they must submit an essay of 500 to 750 words on their transportation-related career goals and life aspirations. Financial need is not considered in the selection process.

Financial data The stipend is $1,500.

Duration 1 year; nonrenewable.

Additional information This program began in 2015.

Number awarded 1 each year.

Deadline April of each year.

[629]
TRAVELER'S FOUNDATION SCHOLARSHIPS FOR NON-TRIBAL COLLEGE STUDENTS

American Indian College Fund
Attn: Scholarship Department
8333 Greenwood Boulevard
Denver, CO 80221
(303) 426-8900   Toll Free: (800) 776-FUND
Fax: (303) 426-1200
E-mail: scholarships@collegefund.org
Web: www.collegefund.org

Summary To provide financial assistance to Native American college students from designated states who are majoring in business-related fields at colleges and universities in their state.

Eligibility This program is open to American Indians and Alaska Natives who have proof of enrollment or descendancy and are currently enrolled full time at a public or private college or university. Preference is given to juniors and seniors. Applicants must be residents of or attending college in California, Colorado, Connecticut, Florida, Illinois, Minnesota, or Texas. They must have a GPA of 3.0 or higher and be able to demonstrate financial need and a commitment to community and leadership development. Their major must be accounting, business, computer science, computer technology, engineering, mathematics, or a related field. Applications are available only online and include required essays on specified topics. U.S. citizenship is required.

Financial data The stipend is $4,000.

Duration 1 year.

Additional information This program is funded by the Traveler's Foundation in partnership with the American Indian College Fund.

Number awarded 1 or more each year.

Deadline May of each year.

[630]
TRAVELER'S FOUNDATION TRIBAL COLLEGE SCHOLARSHIPS

American Indian College Fund
Attn: Scholarship Department
8333 Greenwood Boulevard
Denver, CO 80221
(303) 426-8900   Toll Free: (800) 776-FUND
Fax: (303) 426-1200
E-mail: scholarships@collegefund.org
Web: www.collegefund.org

Summary To provide financial assistance to Native American college students from designated states who are majoring in business-related fields at specified Tribal Colleges and Universities (TCUs).

Eligibility This program is open to American Indians and Alaska Natives who have proof of enrollment or descendancy and are enrolled full time at Fond du Lac Tribal and Community College, Haskell Indian Nations University, Leech Lake

Tribal College, Northwest Indian College, or White Earth Tribal and Community College. Preference is given to juniors and seniors. Applicants must be residents of California, Colorado, Connecticut, Florida, Illinois, Minnesota, or Texas. They must have a GPA of 3.0 or higher and be able to demonstrate financial need and a commitment to community and leadership development. Their major must be accounting, business, computer science, computer technology, engineering, mathematics, or a related field. Applications are available only online and include required essays on specified topics. U.S. citizenship is required.

Financial data The stipend is $4,000.

Duration 1 year.

Additional information This program is funded by the Traveler's Foundation in partnership with the American Indian College Fund.

Number awarded 1 or more each year.

Deadline May of each year.

[631]
TRIANGLE NATIVE AMERICAN SOCIETY SCHOLARSHIPS

Triangle Native American Society
P.O. Box 26841
Raleigh, NC 27611-6841
(919) 553-7449 E-mail: tnasscholarship@tnasweb.org
Web: www.tnasweb.org/tnasfinancialaidhome.htm

Summary To provide financial assistance to Native Americans in North Carolina who are enrolled at a public university in the state.

Eligibility This program is open to American Indians who have been North Carolina residents for at least 1 year and are entering their sophomore, junior, or senior year at a school in the University of North Carolina system. Applicants must be enrolled full time and have a GPA of 2.5 or higher. They must be able to demonstrate financial need, leadership abilities, and community involvement.

Financial data Stipends range from $500 to $1,000.

Duration 1 year; recipients may reapply.

Additional information This program was formerly known as the Mark Ulmer Native American Scholarship.

Number awarded Varies each year; recently, 3 of these scholarships were awarded.

Deadline June of each year.

[632]
TRUMAN D. PICARD SCHOLARSHIP PROGRAM

Intertribal Timber Council
Attn: Education Committee
1112 N.E. 21st Avenue, Suite 4
Portland, OR 97232-2114
(503) 282-4296 Fax: (503) 282-1274
E-mail: itc1@teleport.com
Web: www.itcnet.org/about_us/scholarships.html

Summary To provide financial assistance to American Indians or Alaskan Natives who are interested in studying natural resources in college.

Eligibility This program is open to 1) graduating high school seniors; and 2) currently-enrolled college students. Applicants must be enrolled in a federally-recognized tribe or Native Alaska corporation. They must be majoring or plan-

ning to major in natural resources. Selection is based on interest in natural resources; commitment to education, community, and culture; academic merit; and financial need.

Financial data The stipend is $2,000 for high school seniors entering college or $2,500 for students already enrolled in college.

Duration 1 year.

Additional information Recipients who attend the University of Washington (Seattle), Oregon State University, Northern Arizona University, Yale University, or Salish Kootenai College (Pablo, Montana) are also eligible for additional scholarships and tuition waivers.

Number awarded Varies each year; recently, 28 were awarded.

Deadline January of each year.

[633]
TURTLE MOUNTAIN BAND OF CHIPPEWA INDIANS SCHOLARSHIP PROGRAM

Turtle Mountain Band of Chippewa Indians
Attn: Tribal Scholarship Office
P.O. Box 900
Belcourt, ND 58316
(701) 477-8102 Fax: (701) 477-8053
Web: www.tmbci.org/programs/?program_id=35

Summary To provide financial assistance for full-time undergraduate or graduate study in any state to enrolled members of the Turtle Mountain Band of Chippewa.

Eligibility Applicants must be enrolled members of the Turtle Mountain Band of Chippewa, be full-time students enrolled in an academic program at an accredited postsecondary institution in any state on either the undergraduate or graduate school level, and have a GPA of 2.0 or higher. Undergraduate applicants must be enrolled for at least 12 quarter or 12 semester credit hours (or 6 semester/quarter hours for a summer session); graduate school applicants must be enrolled for at least 1 course. Along with their application, they must submit a Certificate of Degree of Indian Blood (CDIB), a letter of acceptance/admission from their college, the award notice sent by the college's financial aid office, a high school transcript or GED certificate, and any college transcripts. Priority is given to applicants in the following order: seniors who need to attend summer school in order to graduate, juniors who need summer school in order to become seniors, students who need summer school to acquire their 2-year degree, sophomores, freshmen, and graduate students.

Financial data A stipend is awarded (amount not specified).

Duration The maximum number of terms the scholarship program will fund a student for an undergraduate degree is 10 semesters or 15 quarters; the maximum number of terms for a student at a 2-year college is 3 years, 6 semesters, or 9 quarters.

Additional information Once recipients earn 65 or more credit hours at a 2-year college, they must transfer to a 4-year institution.

Number awarded Varies each year.

Deadline August of each year.

[634]
TUSCARORA NATION SCHOLARSHIP PROGRAM

Tuscarora Indian School
c/o Jamie Gilbert
Niagara Wheatfield School District
Tuscarora Elementary School
2015 Mount Hope Road
Lewiston, NY 14092
(716) 215-3652   E-mail: jgilbert@nwcsd.org
Web: www.nwcsd.k12.ny.us/Page/4416

Summary To provide financial assistance to members of the Tuscarora Nation who are interested in attending college in the State University of New York (SUNY) system.

Eligibility This program is open to enrolled members of the Tuscarora Nation who are attending or planning to attend a community college or university in the SUNY system. Applicants must submit an essay of 200 to 300 words on their educational and future goals. They must also submit a description of a community involvement project for the Tuscarora Nation that they propose to conduct over the course of 4 years if they are selected to receive a scholarship; the project may be in the area of environment, education, health and well-being, culture, administration, recreation, or history and the arts.

Financial data The program provides recipients with full payment of tuition at any SUNY college or university.

Duration 4 years.

Additional information This program began in 2007 as part of the relicensing agreement between the Power Authority of the State of New York and the Tuscarora Nation. Funding is provided by the Power Authority, but the Tuscarora Nation has sole responsibility for selecting the recipients.

Number awarded 2 each year.

Deadline April of each year.

[635]
UCSD MSTP SUMMER UNDERGRADUATE RESEARCH FELLOWSHIP PROGRAM

University of California at San Diego
Attn: School of Medicine
Medical Scientist Training Program
9500 Gilman Drive, MC 0661
La Jolla, CA 92093-0661
(858) 822-5631   Toll Free: (800) 925-8704
Fax: (858) 822-3067   E-mail: mstp@ucsd.edu
Web: mstp.ucsd.edu/surf/Pages/default.aspx

Summary To provide an opportunity for Native American and other undergraduate students from underrepresented groups to work during the summer on a research project in the biomedical sciences at the University of California at San Diego (UCSD).

Eligibility This program is open to undergraduate students at colleges in any state who are members of an underrepresented group (racial and ethnic groups that have been shown to be underrepresented in health-related sciences, individuals with disabilities, or individuals from a disadvantaged background). Applicants must be interested in working on a research project in the laboratory of a UCSD faculty member in the biomedical sciences. They must be U.S. citizens, permanent residents, or nationals. Along with their application, they must submit brief essays on 1) why they consider themselves an individual from a disadvantaged ethnicity or background or are underrepresented in the biomedical sciences; 2) their past research experiences; 3) the areas of research they wish to pursue in the program; 4) their educational and career plans and how this program will advance them towards their goals; and 5) anything else that might help to evaluate their application.

Financial data The program provides a stipend of $1,600 per month, room (but not board), and a $500 travel allowance.

Duration 8 weeks during the summer.

Additional information This program is sponsored by the National Heart, Lung, and Blood Institute (NHLBI) of the National Institutes of Health (NIH).

Number awarded Varies each year; recently, 11 students participated in this program.

Deadline February of each year.

[636]
UDALL FOUNDATION NATIVE AMERICAN CONGRESSIONAL INTERNSHIPS

Morris K. Udall and Stewart L. Udall Foundation
Attn: Program Manager, Internship Program
130 South Scott Avenue
Tucson, AZ 85701-1922
(520) 901-8561   Fax: (520) 670-5530
E-mail: info@udall.gov
Web: www.udall.gov

Summary To provide an opportunity for Native American upper-division and graduate students to work in a Congressional office during the summer.

Eligibility This program is open to American Indians and Alaska Natives who are enrolled members of recognized tribes and have an interest in tribal government and policy. Applicants must have a GPA of 3.0 or higher as a junior, senior, graduate student, law student, or recent graduate of a tribal or 4-year college. They must be able to participate in an internship in Washington, D.C., where they will gain practical experience in the legislative process, Congressional matters, and governmental proceedings that specifically relate to Native American issues. Fields of study of previous interns have included American Indian studies, political science, law and pre-law, psychology, social work, history, business and public administration, anthropology, community and urban planning, architecture, communications, health sciences, public health, biology, engineering, sociology, environmental studies and natural resources, economics, and justice studies. Applicants must demonstrate strong research and writing skills; organizational abilities and time management skills; maturity, responsibility, and flexibility; interest in learning how the federal government "really works;" commitment to their tribal community; knowledge of Congressman Morris K. Udall's legacy with regard to Native Americans; and awareness of issues and challenges currently facing Indian Country.

Financial data Interns receive round-trip airfare to Washington, D.C.; dormitory lodging at a local university; a $42 daily allowance sufficient for meals, transportation, and incidentals; and an educational stipend of $1,200 to be paid at the conclusion of the internship.

Duration 10 weeks during the summer.

Additional information These internships were first offered in 1996.

Number awarded 12 each year.

Deadline January of each year.

[637]
UNDERGRADUATE STUDENT RESEARCH EXPERIENCES AT FDA

National Science Foundation
Directorate for Engineering
Attn: Division of Chemical, Bioengineering,
  Environmental, and Transport Systems
4201 Wilson Boulevard, Room 565S
Arlington, VA 22230
(703) 292-7942   Fax: (703) 292-9098
TDD: (800) 281-8749   E-mail: lesterow@nsf.gov
Web: www.nsf.gov

Summary To provide an opportunity for Native American and other undergraduate students to work at an intramural research laboratory of the U.S. Food and Drug Administration (FDA).

Eligibility This program is open to undergraduate students in science, engineering, and mathematics fields of interest to the National Science Foundation (NSF). Applicants must be U.S. citizens, nationals, or permanent residents. They must be proposing a program of full- or part-time work at an FDA laboratory in an area related to their academic program under the guidance of an academic adviser and an FDA mentor. The program encourages applications from all citizens, including women and men, underrepresented minorities, and persons with disabilities.

Financial data Undergraduate students may receive stipends up to $450 per week; they may also receive some assistance with housing or travel expenses, or both. No indirect costs are allowed. The total award may be up to $8,000 for a fellowship for a single student. FDA provides office space, research facilities, research costs in the form of expendable and minor equipment purchases in the host laboratory, and the time of its research staff.

Duration Support may be provided for a summer project, or for 1 or 2 semesters of part- or full-time work.

Additional information This program is also offered by the NSF Directorate for Computer and Information Science and Engineering.

Number awarded A total of 3 to 10 grants for all FDA programs is awarded each year; total funding is approximately $500,000.

Deadline March of each year.

[638]
UNITED HEALTH FOUNDATION SCHOLARSHIP FOR NON-TRIBAL COLLEGE STUDENTS

American Indian College Fund
Attn: Scholarship Department
8333 Greenwood Boulevard
Denver, CO 80221
(303) 426-8900   Toll Free: (800) 776-FUND
Fax: (303) 426-1200
E-mail: scholarships@collegefund.org
Web: www.collegefund.org

Summary To provide financial assistance to Native American college students who are interested in majoring in health-related fields at designated mainstream colleges and universities in Arizona and New Mexico.

Eligibility This program is open to American Indians and Alaska Natives from any state who have proof of enrollment or descendancy and are enrolled or planning to enroll full time at Arizona State University, Northern Arizona University, University of Arizona, San Juan College (Farmington, New Mexico), University of New Mexico, or Western New Mexico University. Applicants must have a GPA of 3.0 or higher and be able to demonstrate exceptional academic achievement or financial need. They must have declared a major in health or a related program and have a demonstrated interest in serving communities in need. Applications are available only online and include required essays on specified topics. U.S. citizenship is required.

Financial data The stipend is $5,000.

Duration 1 year.

Additional information This program is funded by the United Health Foundation in partnership with the American Indian College Fund.

Number awarded 1 or more each year.

Deadline May of each year.

[639]
UNITED HEALTH FOUNDATION SCHOLARSHIP FOR TRIBAL COLLEGE STUDENTS

American Indian College Fund
Attn: Scholarship Department
8333 Greenwood Boulevard
Denver, CO 80221
(303) 426-8900   Toll Free: (800) 776-FUND
Fax: (303) 426-1200
E-mail: scholarships@collegefund.org
Web: www.collegefund.org

Summary To provide financial assistance to Native American college students who are interested in majoring in health-related fields at designated tribal colleges and universities in Arizona and New Mexico.

Eligibility This program is open to American Indians and Alaska Natives from any state who have proof of enrollment or descendancy and are entering their freshman or sophomore year at Diné College (Tsaile, Arizona), Tohono O'odham Community College (Sells, Arizona), or Navajo Technical College (Chinle, Arizona, Crownpoint, New Mexico, or Teec Nos Pos, Arizona). Applicants must have a GPA of 3.0 or higher and be able to demonstrate exceptional academic achievement or financial need. They must have declared a major in health or a related program and have a demonstrated interest in serving communities in need. Applications are available only online and include required essays on specified topics. U.S. citizenship is required.

Financial data The stipend is $5,000.

Duration 1 year.

Additional information This program is funded by the United Health Foundation in partnership with the American Indian College Fund.

Number awarded 1 or more each year.

Deadline May of each year.

[640]
UNITED PARCEL SERVICE SCHOLARSHIP FOR MINORITY STUDENTS

Institute of Industrial and Systems Engineers
Attn: Scholarship Coordinator
3577 Parkway Lane, Suite 200
Norcross, GA 30092
(770) 449-0461, ext. 105   Toll Free: (800) 494-0460
Fax: (770) 441-3295   E-mail: bcameron@iisenet.org
Web: www.iienet2.org/Details.aspx?id=857

Summary To provide financial assistance to Native American and other minority undergraduates who are studying industrial engineering at a school in the United States, Canada, or Mexico.

Eligibility Eligible to be nominated are minority undergraduate students enrolled at any school in the United States or its territories, Canada, or Mexico, provided the school's engineering program is accredited by an agency recognized by the Institute of Industrial and Systems Engineers (IISE) and the student is pursuing a full-time course of study in industrial engineering with a GPA of at least 3.4. Nominees must have at least 5 full quarters or 3 full semesters remaining until graduation. Students may not apply directly for these awards; they must be nominated by the head of their industrial engineering department. Nominees must be IISE members. Selection is based on scholastic ability, character, leadership, and potential service to the industrial engineering profession.

Financial data The stipend is $4,000.

Duration 1 year.

Additional information Funding for this program is provided by the UPS Foundation.

Number awarded 1 each year.

Deadline Schools must submit nominations by November of each year.

[641]
UNITED SOUTH AND EASTERN TRIBES SCHOLARSHIP FUND

United South and Eastern Tribes, Inc.
Attn: Scholarship Fund
711 Stewarts Ferry Pike, Suite 100
Nashville, TN 37214
(615) 467-1542   Fax: (615) 872-7417
E-mail: mstephens@usetinc.org
Web: www.usetinc.org/resources/scholarships

Summary To provide supplemental financial assistance for college to Native Americans who are in the United South and Eastern Tribes (USET) service area.

Eligibility This program is open to Indian students who live in the service area of the USET, which covers portions of the following states: Alabama, Connecticut, Florida, Louisiana, Maine, Massachusetts, Mississippi, New York, North Carolina, Rhode Island, South Carolina, and Texas. Special consideration is given to applicants who are enrolled members of 1 of the following 26 federally-recognized United South and Eastern Tribes: Alabama Coushatta Tribe of Texas; Aroostook Band of Micmac Indians (Maine); Catawba Indian Nation (South Carolina); Cayuga Nation (New York); Chitimacha Tribe of Louisiana; Coushatta Tribe of Louisiana; Eastern Band of Cherokee Indians (North Carolina); Houlton Band of Maliseet Indians (Maine); Jena Band of Choctaw Indians (Louisiana); Mashantucket Pequot Tribe (Connecticut); Mashpee Wampanoag Tribe (Massachusetts); Miccosukee Tribe of Florida; Mississippi Band of Choctaw Indians; Mohegan Tribe of Connecticut; Narragansett Tribe (Rhode Island); Oneida Nation (New York); Passamaquoddy Tribe Indian Township (Maine); Passamaquoddy Pleasant Point (Maine); Penobscot Nation (Maine); Poarch Band of Creek Indians (Alabama); Seminole Tribe of Florida; Seneca Nation (New York); Shinnecock Indian Nation (New York); St. Regis Band of Mohawk Indians (New York); Tunica Biloxi Tribe of Louisiana; Wampanoag Tribe of Gay Head (Massachusetts);. Applicants must be currently enrolled or accepted at a postsecondary educational institution, have satisfactory scholastic standing, and be able to demonstrate need for financial assistance. Undergraduates must submit a 250-word essay on their future goals, obstacles overcome, and challenges; graduate students must submit a 500-word essay on their future goals, reasons for attending graduate school, obstacles overcome, and challenges.

Financial data The stipend for undergraduates is at least $750 and for graduate students at least $1,000.

Duration 1 year.

Number awarded Varies each year.

Deadline April of each year.

[642]
UNTO THESE HILLS EDUCATIONAL FUND SCHOLARSHIP

Unto These Hills Educational Fund, Inc.
Attn: Secretary
P.O. Box 2453
Cherokee, NC 28719
(828) 497-5539   Fax: (828) 497-5554
E-mail: trista@cbcprinting.com

Summary To provide financial assistance to eastern Cherokee Indians who are interested in working on an undergraduate degree.

Eligibility This program is open to students who are enrolled members of the Eastern Band of Cherokee Indians, Cherokee, North Carolina or to students whose parents are enrolled members of the Eastern Band of Cherokee. Applicants must provide documentation of undergraduate enrollment and tribal membership. Selection is based on scholastic aptitude (a least a 2.0 GPA), achievement, career ambitions, and the relative financial need of the student. First priority is given to students at 4-year universities; second priority is given to community college students.

Financial data A stipend is awarded (amount not specified).

Duration 1 year; may be renewed.

Additional information This fund was established in the memory of the late Suzanne M. Davis, who was the costume designer for "Unto These Hills." The organization was originally chartered as the Suzanne M. Davis Educational Fund, Inc., but in 1979 the name of the organization was changed to Unto These Hills Educational Fund, Inc.

Number awarded Varies each year; recently, 13 were awarded.

Deadline March of each year.

[643]
UPS/CIC FOUNDATION SCHOLARSHIPS

Wisconsin Association of Independent Colleges and
  Universities
Attn: Senior Vice President for Educational Services
122 West Washington Avenue, Suite 700
Madison, WI 53703-2723
(608) 256-7761, ext. 223   Fax: (608) 256-7065
E-mail: carole.trone@waicu.org
Web: www.waicu.org

Summary   To provide financial assistance to students at
member institution of the Wisconsin Association of Independent Colleges and Universities (WAICU) who are Native
Americans or members of other designated target populations.

Eligibility   This program is open to students enrolled full
time at WAICU member colleges or universities. The background of applicants must reflect 1 or more of the components of the target population for the UPS Foundation and the
First Opportunity Program of the Council of Independent Colleges (CIC): first generation, low-income, minority, or new
American students.

Financial data   The stipend is $2,600.

Duration   1 year.

Additional information   The WAICU member schools are
Alverno College, Bellin College, Beloit College, Cardinal
Stritch University, Carroll College, Carthage College, Colum-
bia College of Nursing, Concordia University of Wisconsin,
Edgewood College, Lakeland College, Lawrence University,
Marian College, Marquette University, Medical College of
Wisconsin, Milwaukee Institute of Art & Design, Milwaukee
School of Engineering, Mount Mary College, Nashotah
House Theological Seminary, Northland College, Ripon Col-
lege, St. Norbert College, Silver Lake College of the Holy
Family, Viterbo University, and Wisconsin Lutheran College.
This program is supported by the UPS Foundation and
administered nationally through CIC.

Number awarded   Up to 24 each year: 1 at each of the
member schools.

Deadline   Each participating college sets its own deadline.

[644]
UPS DIVERSITY SCHOLARSHIPS OF THE
AMERICAN SOCIETY OF SAFETY ENGINEERS

American Society of Safety Engineers
Attn: ASSE Foundation
Scholarship Award Program
520 North Northwest Highway
Park Ridge, IL 60068-2538
(847) 699-2929   Fax: (847) 296-3769
E-mail: assefoundation@asse.org
Web: foundation.asse.org/scholarships-and-grants

Summary   To provide financial assistance to Native American and other minority upper-division students working on a
degree related to occupational safety.

Eligibility   This program is open to students who are U.S.
citizens and members of minority ethnic or racial groups.
Applicants must be majoring in occupational safety, health,
environment, industrial hygiene, occupational health nursing,
or a closely-related field (e.g., industrial or environmental
engineering). They must be full-time students who have com-

pleted at least 60 semester hours and have a GPA of 3.0 or
higher. Membership in the American Society of Safety Engineers (ASSE) is not required, but preference is given to members.

Financial data   The stipend is $5,250 per year.

Duration   1 year; recipients may reapply.

Additional information   Funding for this program is provided by the UPS Foundation. Recipients may also be provided with the opportunity to attend a professional development conference related to safety.

Number awarded   3 each year.

Deadline   November of each year.

[645]
USDA 1994 TRIBAL SCHOLARS PROGRAM

Department of Agriculture
Attn: Office of Advocacy and Outreach
USDA 1994 Tribal Scholarship Program
1400 Independence Avenue, S.W.
Washington, DC 20250-0603
(202) 720-7265
Web: www.outreach.usda.gov/education/1994tlgcu

Summary   To provide financial assistance to students
entering or enrolled at a 1994 Land-Grant Tribal College or
University who are interested in majoring in an agriculture-
related field.

Eligibility   This program is open to U.S. citizens who are
high school seniors or rising college sophomores or juniors at
a 1994 Land-Grant Tribal College or University. Applicants
must be interested in working on a bachelor's degree in agriculture or a related field (e.g., agricultural business and management, agricultural economics, agricultural engineering
and mechanics, agricultural production and technology,
agronomy or crop science, animal sciences, botany, computer science, environmental science, farm and range management, food sciences and technology, forestry and related
sciences, home economics and nutrition, horticulture, natural
resources management, soil conservation and science).
They must have a GPA of 2.75 or higher. Along with their
application, they must submit an essay of 50o to 800 word on
what motivates them to consider a career in public service
working for the U.S. Department of Agriculture (USDA); how
they became interested in studying food, agriculture, and natural resource sciences; and how USDA will benefit if they are
selected for this program.

Financial data   The program provides full payment of
tuition, a paid internship, employee benefits, fees, books, and
room and board.

Duration   1 year; may be renewed up to 3 additional years,
provided the recipient maintains a GPA of 3.0 or higher.

Additional information   For a list of the 35 participating
1994 Land-Grant Tribal Colleges and Universities, contact the
sponsor.

Number awarded   1 or more each year.

Deadline   February of each year.

[646]
VALLIERE/GIROUX SCHOLARSHIP FOR SINGLE WORKING MOMS

Wisconsin Indian Education Association
Attn: Scholarship Coordinator
P.O. Box 910
Keshena, WI 54135
(715) 799-5110   Fax: (715) 799-5102
E-mail: vnuske@mitw.org
Web: www.wiea.org/index.php/About/Scholarships

Summary To provide financial assistance to members of Wisconsin Indian tribes who are single mothers and interested in attending college in any state.

Eligibility This program is open to residents of Wisconsin who can provide proof of tribal enrollment. Applicants must be single mothers with children whom they are supporting financially. Applicants must have been accepted at a 4-year college or university in any state for enrollment in at least 6 credits per semester. They must have a GPA of 2.5 or higher. Along with their application, they must submit a 1-page personal essay on how they will apply their education and their educational goals. Selection is based on that essay (20 points), letters of recommendation (15 points), and GPA (15 points if 3.5 or higher, 10 points if 3.00 to 3.49, 5 points if 2.50 to 2.99). Financial need is not considered.

Financial data The stipend is $1,000.

Duration 1 year; nonrenewable.

Additional information Eligible tribes include Menominee, Oneida, Stockbridge-Munsee, Forest County Potowatomi, Ho-Chunk, Bad River Chippewa, Lac Courte Oreilles Ojibwe, St. Croix Chippewa, Red Cliff Chippewa, Sakoagon (Mole Lake) Chippewa, Brotherton, and Lac du Flambeau Chippewa.

Number awarded 1 each year.

Deadline March of each year.

[647]
VERA CLAUSSEN MEMORIAL "WANAPUM TRIBE" SCHOLARSHIP

Columbia Basin Foundation
234 First Avenue N.W., Suite B
Ephrata, WA 98823
(509) 754-4596
E-mail: info@columbiabasinfoundation.org
Web: www.columbiabasinfoundation.org

Summary To provide financial assistance for college to Wanapum Indians and their descendants.

Eligibility This program is open to Wanapum Indians as recognized by the Wanapum Tribal Council and descendants of Wanapums. Applicants may be of any age as long as they have graduated from high school or have earned a GED certificate and are enrolled or planning to enroll full time at an accredited college, university, or vocational school. They must have a GPA of 2.0 or higher from the high school at which they graduated or the last college they attended or are attending. Along with their application, they must submit 1) a list of programs or events specific to the Wanapum tribe in which they have participated; 2) a list of school or community activities in which they have participated; 3) a 300-word essay on their goals as those relate to their education, career,

and future plans; 4) a 200-word essay about themselves; and 5) information about their financial situation.

Financial data The stipend is $2,000.

Duration 1 year.

Number awarded 4 each year.

Deadline February of each year.

[648]
VERL AND DOROTHY MILLER NATIVE AMERICAN VOCATIONAL SCHOLARSHIP

Oregon Community Foundation
Attn: Scholarship Department
1221 S.W. Yamhill Street, Suite 100
Portland, OR 97205-2108
(503) 227-6846   Fax: (503) 274-7771
E-mail: mchee@oregoncf.org
Web: www.oregoncf.org/grants-scholarships/scholarships

Summary To provide financial assistance to American Indians from Oregon who are interested in studying at a trade or vocational school in the state.

Eligibility This program is open to American Indian residents of Oregon who can document tribal enrollment and/or blood quantum. Applicants must be attending or planning to attend a trade or vocational school in the state either full or part time. Selection is based on academic promise, participation in school or community activities, personal qualities (e.g., work ethic, dependability, stability, moral character, responsibility), aptitude for a particular trade or vocation, and financial need.

Financial data A stipend is awarded (amount not specified).

Duration 1 year; may be renewed up to 3 additional years.

Additional information This program began in 2002.

Number awarded 1 or more each year.

Deadline February of each year.

[649]
VICTOR MATSON, SR. TRIBUTARY SCHOLARSHIP

Sault Tribe of Chippewa Indians
Attn: Higher Education Department
523 Ashmun Street
Sault Ste. Marie, MI 49783
(906) 635-6050, ext. 26312   Toll Free: (800) 793-0660
Fax: (906) 635-7785   E-mail: BMacArthur@saulttribe.net
Web: www.saulttribe.com

Summary To provide financial assistance to members of the Sault Tribe of Chippewa Indians interested in attending college in any state to work on an undergraduate or graduate degree in a field related to fisheries or natural resources.

Eligibility This program is open to members of the Sault Tribe who are enrolled full time at a 2- or 4-year college or university in any state. Applicants must be working on an undergraduate or graduate degree in the field of fisheries or natural resources management or a related area. Along with their application, they must submit an essay of 1,000 to 2,000 words on a topic that changes annually but relates to their Indian heritage.

Financial data The stipend is $1,000.

Duration 1 year.

Number awarded 1 each year.

Deadline May of each year.

[650]
VSCPA MINORITY ACCOUNTING SCHOLARSHIPS

Virginia Society of Certified Public Accountants
Attn: Educational Foundation
4309 Cox Road
Glen Allen, VA 23060
(804) 612-9427   Toll Free: (800) 733-8272
Fax: (804) 273-1741   E-mail: foundation@vscpa.com
Web: www.vscpa.com

Summary To provide financial assistance to Native American and other minority students enrolled in an undergraduate accounting program in Virginia.

Eligibility Applicants must be minority students (African American or Black, Hispanic or Latino, American Indian or Native Alaskan, Asian, Native Hawaiian or other Pacific Islander) currently enrolled in a Virginia college or university undergraduate accounting program. They must be U.S. citizens, be majoring in accounting, have completed at least 3 hours of accounting, be currently registered for 3 more credit hours of accounting, and have a GPA of 3.0 or higher. Selection is based on an essay, transcripts, a current resume, a faculty letter of recommendation, and financial need.

Financial data The stipend is $1,000.

Duration 1 year.

Number awarded Approximately 3 each year.

Deadline March of each year.

[651]
WAH-TIAH-KAH SCHOLARSHIP

Osage Minerals Council
813 Grandview
P.O. Box 779
Pawhuska, OK 74056
(918) 287-5346
Web: www.osagenation-nsn.gov

Summary To provide financial assistance to Osage students who are interested in attending college or graduate school to prepare for a career in the petroleum industry.

Eligibility This program is open to full-time undergraduate and graduate students who can prove Osage Indian blood in any degree. Applicants must be working on or planning to work on a degree in a field related to petroleum. Along with their application, they must submit a copy of their Osage Certificate of Degree of Indian Blood (CDIB), transcripts, 2 letters of recommendation, ACT or SAT scores, and a personal statement of their educational and career goals.

Financial data A stipend is awarded (amount not specified).

Duration 1 semester; may be renewed for up to 7 additional semesters, provided the recipient reapplies each semester and maintains a GPA of 2.0 or higher.

Number awarded Varies each year.

Deadline June of each year for fall term; December of each year for spring term.

[652]
WAK-WEI SCHOLARSHIPS

Yakama Nation
Department of Human Services
Attn: Higher Education Program
107 Teo Road
P.O. Box 151
Toppenish, WA 98948
(509) 865-5121, ext. 4542   Toll Free: (800) 543-2802
Fax: (509) 865-6994   E-mail: murry@yakama.com
Web: www.yakama.us/programs.php

Summary To provide financial assistance to Yakama tribal members interested in working on an undergraduate or graduate degree at a school in any state.

Eligibility This program is open to enrolled members of the Yakama nation who are enrolled or planning to enroll full time at a 2- or 4-year college or university in any state. High school seniors must have a GPA of 3.0 or higher; students returning to college after an absence must have a GPA of 2.0 or higher. Financial need is the major factor in the selection process.

Financial data The stipend is $500 per year for freshmen and sophomores or $1,000 per year for juniors, seniors, and graduate students.

Duration 1 year; recipients may reapply.

Number awarded 7 each year: 4 for freshmen and sophomores and 3 for juniors and seniors.

Deadline June of each year.

[653]
WALMART STORES TRIBAL COLLEGE SCHOLARSHIP

American Indian College Fund
Attn: Scholarship Department
8333 Greenwood Boulevard
Denver, CO 80221
(303) 426-8900   Toll Free: (800) 776-FUND
Fax: (303) 426-1200
E-mail: scholarships@collegefund.org
Web: www.collegefund.org

Summary To provide financial assistance to Native Americans who are interested in attending a Tribal College or University (TCU) and are the first in their family to attend college.

Eligibility This program is open to American Indians or Alaska Natives who are planning to enroll full time in their freshman year at an eligible TCU. Applicants must have a GPA of 2.0 or higher. They must be the first in their immediate family to attend college. Applications are available only online and include required essays on specified topics. U.S. citizenship is required.

Financial data The stipend is $2,750.

Duration 1 year.

Additional information This program is sponsored by Walmart in partnership with the American Indian College Fund.

Number awarded 1 or more each year.

Deadline May of each year.

[654]
WALTER CHARLEY MEMORIAL SCHOLARSHIPS

Ahtna, Incorporated
Attn: Ahtna Heritage Foundation
P.O. Box 213
Glennallen, AK 99588
(907) 822-5778   Fax: (907) 822-5338
E-mail: ahtnaheritage@yahoo.com
Web: www.ahtnaheritagefoundation.com/scholarships.html

Summary To provide financial assistance to shareholders of Ahtna, Incorporated in Alaska and their descendants who plan to attend college or graduate school in any state.

Eligibility This program is open to Ahtna shareholders (original, gifted, inherited, or Class L) who are high school graduates or GED recipients. Applicants must be 1) attending or planning to attend a college, university, or vocational school in any state as an undergraduate or graduate student; or 2) accepted in a program specializing in a recognized area or field of study. They must have a GPA of 2.0 or higher and be able to demonstrate financial need.

Financial data For undergraduates, the stipend is $2,000 per semester ($4,000 per year) for full-time students or $1,000 per semester ($2,000 per year) for part-time students. For graduate students, the stipend is $3,000 per semester ($6,000 per year) for full-time students or $1,500 per semester ($3,000 per year) for part-time students.

Duration 1 year; may be renewed, provided the recipient maintains a GPA of 2.0 or higher.

Additional information Ahtna, Incorporated is 1 of 13 regional corporations established according to the terms of the Alaska Native Claims Settlement Act (ANCSA) of 1971.

Number awarded Varies each year.

Deadline July of each year for fall semester; December of each year for spring semester.

[655]
WARNER NORCROSS & JUDD PARALEGAL AND LEGAL SECRETARIAL SCHOLARSHIP

Grand Rapids Community Foundation
Attn: Education Program Officer
185 Oakes Street S.W.
Grand Rapids, MI 49503-4008
(616) 454-1751, ext. 103   Fax: (616) 454-6455
E-mail: rbishop@grfoundation.org
Web: www.grfoundation.org/scholarshipslist

Summary To provide financial assistance to Native American and other minority residents of Michigan who are interested in working on a paralegal or legal secretarial studies degree at an institution in the state.

Eligibility This program is open to residents of Michigan who are students of color attending or planning to attend an accredited public or private 2- or 4-year college or university in the state. Applicants must have a declared major in paralegal or legal secretarial studies. They must be U.S. citizens or permanent residents and have a GPA of 2.5 or higher. Financial need is considered in the selection process.

Financial data The stipend is $2,000. Funds are paid directly to the recipient's institution.

Duration 1 year.

Additional information Funding for this program is provided by the law firm Warner Norcross & Judd LLP.

Number awarded 1 each year.

Deadline March of each year.

[656]
WASHINGTON ADMIRAL'S FUND SCHOLARSHIP

National Naval Officers Association-Washington, D.C.
   Chapter
c/o LCDR Stephen Williams
P.O. Box 30784
Alexandria, VA 22310
(703) 566-3840   Fax: (703) 566-3813
E-mail: Stephen.Williams@navy.mil
Web: dcnnoa.memberlodge.com/page-309002

Summary To provide financial assistance to Native American and other minority high school seniors from the Washington, D.C. area who are interested in attending a college or university in any state and enrolling in the Navy Reserve Officers Training Corps (NROTC) program.

Eligibility This program is open to minority seniors graduating from high schools in the Washington, D.C. metropolitan area who plan to enroll full time at an accredited 2- or 4-year college or university in any state. Applicants must be planning to enroll in the NROTC program. They must have a GPA of 2.5 or higher and be U.S. citizens or permanent residents. Selection is based on academic achievement, community involvement, and financial need.

Financial data The stipend is $1,000.

Duration 1 year; nonrenewable.

Additional information If the recipient fails to enroll in the NROTC unit, all scholarship funds must be returned.

Number awarded 1 each year.

Deadline March of each year.

[657]
WASHINGTON AMERICAN INDIAN ENDOWED SCHOLARSHIP PROGRAM

Washington Student Achievement Council
Attn: American Indian Endowed Scholarship Program
917 Lakeridge Way
P.O. Box 43430
Olympia, WA 98504-3430
(360) 753-7843   Toll Free: (888) 535-0747
Fax: (360) 753-7808   TDD: (360) 753-7809
E-mail: aies@wsac.wa.gov
Web: www.wsac.wa.gov

Summary To provide financial assistance to American Indian undergraduate and graduate students in Washington.

Eligibility This program is open to Washington residents who have close social and cultural ties to an American Indian tribe and/or community in the state. Applicants must demonstrate financial need and be enrolled, or planning to enroll, as a full-time undergraduate or graduate student at a Washington state public or independent college, university, or career school. Along with their application, they must submit essays on 1) their close social and cultural ties to an American Indian community in Washington; and 2) how they plan to serve a Washington American Indian community upon completing their education and how their contribution is intended to affect the community. Selection is based on academic merit, financial need, and commitment to serve the American Indian community in Washington.

Financial data Stipends range from about $500 to $2,000 per year.

Duration 1 year, may be renewed up to 4 additional years.

Additional information This program was created by the Washington legislature in 1990 with a state appropriation to an endowment fund and matching contributions from tribes, individuals, and organizations.

Number awarded Varies each year; recently, 16 students received $17,300 in support from this program.

Deadline January of each year.

[658]
WASHINGTON DC AREA SUPPLY OFFICERS SCHOLARSHIP

National Naval Officers Association-Washington, D.C.
Chapter
c/o LCDR Stephen Williams
P.O. Box 30784
Alexandria, VA 22310
(703) 566-3840 Fax: (703) 566-3813
E-mail: Stephen.Williams@navy.mil
Web: dcnnoa.memberlodge.com/page-309002

Summary To provide financial assistance to Native American and other minority high school seniors from the Washington, D.C. area who are interested in attending college in any state.

Eligibility This program is open to minority seniors graduating from high schools in the Washington, D.C. metropolitan area who plan to enroll full time at an accredited 2- or 4-year college or university in any state. Applicants must have a GPA of 3.0 or higher and be U.S. citizens or permanent residents. Selection is based on academic achievement, community involvement, and financial need.

Financial data The stipend is $3,000.

Duration 1 year; nonrenewable.

Number awarded 1 each year.

Deadline March of each year.

[659]
WASHINGTON, D.C. CHAPTER NNOA SCHOLARSHIPS FOR MINORITY STUDENTS

National Naval Officers Association-Washington, D.C.
Chapter
c/o LCDR Stephen Williams
P.O. Box 30784
Alexandria, VA 22310
(703) 566-3840 Fax: (703) 566-3813
E-mail: Stephen.Williams@navy.mil
Web: dcnnoa.memberlodge.com/page-309002

Summary To provide financial assistance to Native American and other minority high school seniors from the Washington, D.C. area who are interested in attending college in any state.

Eligibility This program is open to minority seniors graduating from high schools in the Washington, D.C. metropolitan area who plan to enroll full time at an accredited 2- or 4-year college or university in any state. Applicants must have a GPA of 2.5 or higher and be U.S. citizens or permanent residents. Selection is based on academic achievement, community involvement, and financial need.

Financial data The stipend is $2,000 or $1,000.

Duration 1 year; nonrenewable.

Additional information Recipients are not required to join or affiliate with the military in any way. In addition to a number of scholarships with additional requirements, this program includes the following named general scholarships: the Ester Boone Memorial Scholarships, the Mr. Charlie Tompkins Scholarship, and the Navy Federal Credit Union Scholarship.

Number awarded Varies each year; recently, 3 were awarded: 1 at $2,000 and 2 at $1,000.

Deadline March of each year.

[660]
WASHOE TRIBE ADULT VOCATIONAL SCHOLARSHIPS

Washoe Tribe
Attn: Education Department
1246 Waterloo Lane
Gardnerville, NV 89410
(775) 782-6320, ext. 2808 Toll Free: (800) 76-WASHOE
Fax: (775) 782-6790 E-mail: education@washoetribe.us
Web: www.washoetribe.us

Summary To provide financial assistance to members of the Washoe Tribe who are interested in obtaining a diploma or certificate at a vocational or technical junior college.

Eligibility Eligible to apply for these scholarships are adult members of the Washoe Tribe in Nevada and California who are pursuing (or planning to pursue) vocational education. Applicants are required to seek all other sources of funding, in addition to applying for this program. They must submit brief essays on their educational and career goals, how the training will help them meet their educational goals, the license or certificate they will receive upon completion of their training program, their educational goals after completing their training program, and what they can contribute to their training finances.

Financial data A stipend is awarded (amount not specified).

Duration The maximum training period is generally 24 months.

Number awarded Varies each year; recently, 11 were awarded.

Deadline Applications may be submitted at any time.

[661]
WASHOE TRIBE HIGHER EDUCATION SCHOLARSHIP PROGRAM

Washoe Tribe
Attn: Education Department
1246 Waterloo Lane
Gardnerville, NV 89410
(775) 782-6320, ext. 2808 Toll Free: (800) 76-WASHOE
Fax: (775) 782-6790 E-mail: education@washoetribe.us
Web: www.washoetribe.us

Summary To provide financial assistance for college to members of the Washoe Tribe in Nevada and California.

Eligibility This program is open to members of the Washoe Tribe who are enrolled or planning to enroll full time in an associate or bachelor's degree program at a college or university in any state. Applicants are required to seek all other sources of funding, in addition to applying for this program. They must submit brief statements on their educational and career goals, their planned major or minor, their plans after completing their higher education, what they can contribute toward their college expenses, and other scholarships for which they have applied.

Financial data Recently, stipends were $1,005.

Duration 1 year; may be renewed if the recipient remains enrolled full time with a GPA of 2.0 or higher.

Number awarded Varies each year; recently, 10 were awarded.

Deadline July or December of each year.

[662]
WASHOE TRIBE INCENTIVE SCHOLARSHIPS

Washoe Tribe
Attn: Education Department
1246 Waterloo Lane
Gardnerville, NV 89410
(775) 782-6320, ext. 2808   Toll Free: (800) 76-WASHOE
Fax: (775) 782-6790   E-mail: education@washoetribe.us
Web: www.washoetribe.us

Summary To provide financial assistance to members of the Washoe Tribe working on an undergraduate or graduate degree at a school in any state.

Eligibility This program is open to members of the Washoe Tribe who are currently working full time on an associate, baccalaureate, graduate, or postgraduate degree at a school in any state. Applicants must have a GPA of 3.0 or higher. Along with their application they must submit proof of Washoe enrollment, a copy of their college grade report, and a copy of their current class schedule. Selection is based on a first-come, first-served basis; financial need is not considered.

Financial data The stipend varies each year; recently, stipends were $2,000 per semester.

Duration 1 year; recipients may reapply.

Number awarded 20 each year.

Deadline January or June of each year.

[663]
WAVE FELLOWS PROGRAM

California Institute of Technology
Student-Faculty Programs
1200 East California Boulevard
Mail Code 33-087
Pasadena, CA 91125
(626) 395-2885   Fax: (626) 389-5467
E-mail: sfp@caltech.edu
Web: sfp.caltech.edu/programs/wavefellows

Summary To provide an opportunity for Native American and other underrepresented college students to work in a research laboratory at California Institute of Technology (Caltech) during the summer.

Eligibility This program is open to underrepresented minorities, women, first-generation college students, geographically underrepresented students, educationally and financially disadvantaged students, and students with disabilities. Applicants must be interested in working during the summer in a modern academic research laboratory at Caltech under the guidance of experienced scientists and engineers. They must be undergraduate sophomores, juniors, or non-graduating seniors who have a GPA of 3.2 or higher and a major in a field of science, technology, engineer-

ing, or mathematics (STEM). U.S. citizenship or permanent resident status is required.

Financial data The stipend is $600 per week. A $500 housing allowance is also provided.

Duration 8 to 10 weeks during the summer, beginning in June.

Additional information Support for this program is provided by Edison International and the Genentech Foundation.

Number awarded Varies each year.

Deadline January of each year.

[664]
WELLS FARGO AMERICAN INDIAN SCHOLARSHIP

American Indian Graduate Center
Attn: Executive Director
3701 San Mateo Boulevard, N.E., Suite 200
Albuquerque, NM 87110-1249
(505) 881-4584   Toll Free: (800) 628-1920
Fax: (505) 884-0427   E-mail: fellowships@aigc.com
Web: www.aigcs.org

Summary To provide financial assistance to Native American upper-division students working on a business-related degree.

Eligibility This program is open to enrolled members of federally-recognized American Indian tribes and Alaska Native groups who can provide a Certificate of Degree of Indian Blood (CDIB). Applicants must be entering their junior or senior year as a full-time student and working on a degree to prepare for a career in banking, resort management, gaming operations, or management and administration, including accounting, finance, human resources, and information systems. They must have a GPA of 3.0 or higher and be able to demonstrate financial need. Along with their application, they must submit an essay on their personal, educational, and professional goals.

Financial data A stipend is awarded (amount not specified).

Duration 1 year.

Additional information This program is supported by Wells Fargo Bank.

Number awarded 1 or more each year.

Deadline May of each year.

[665]
WELLS FARGO-BBNC SCHOLARSHIP FUND

Bristol Bay Native Corporation
Attn: BBNC Education Foundation
111 West 16th Avenue, Suite 400
Anchorage, AK 99501-6299
(907) 278-3602   Toll Free: (800) 426-3602
Fax: (907) 265-7886   E-mail: bbncef@bbnc.net
Web: www.bbnc.net

Summary To provide financial assistance to shareholders of Bristol Bay Native Corporation (BBNC) who are majoring in banking at a college in any state.

Eligibility This program is open to BBNC shareholders who are enrolled full time as a junior or senior at a college or university in any state to prepare for a career in banking. Applicants must have a GPA of 2.0 or higher and be able to demonstrate financial need. Along with their application, they must submit an essay on how they became interested in their proposed field of study, any special circumstances they want to be considered, and their desire to work in the region or for a BBNC subsidiary company. Selection is based on the essay (30%), cumulative GPA (40%), financial need (20%), a resume (5%), and letters of recommendation (5%).

Financial data   The stipend is $5,000.

Duration   1 year.

Additional information   The BBNC is 1 of 13 Alaska Native Regional Corporations created under the Alaska Native Claims Settlement Act of 1971. The funding for this program is provided equally by Wells Fargo Bank and the BBNC Education Foundation.

Number awarded   1 or more each year.

Deadline   April of each year.

[666]
WHITE EARTH SCHOLARSHIP PROGRAM

White Earth Indian Reservation Tribal Council
Attn: Scholarship Program
P.O. Box 418
White Earth, MN 56591
(218) 983-3285, ext. 5304   Toll Free: (800) 950-3248
Fax: (218) 983-3705
E-mail: leslie.nessman@whiteearth-nsn.gov
Web: www.whiteearth.com

Summary   To provide financial assistance to Minnesota Chippewa Tribe members who are interested in attending college, vocational school, or graduate school in specified fields.

Eligibility   This program is open to enrolled members of the White Earth Band of the Minnesota Chippewa Tribe who can demonstrate financial need. Applicants must be attending or planning to attend a college, university, or vocational school in any state. Graduate students must be working on a degree in business, education, human services, law, or medicine.

Financial data   A stipend is awarded (amount not specified).

Duration   1 year; may be renewed, provided undergraduates maintain a GPA of 2.0 or higher and graduate students maintain a GPA of 3.0 or higher.

Additional information   Applicants for this program must also apply for financial aid administered by their institution and any other aid for which they may be eligible (e.g., work-study, Social Security, veteran's benefits).

Number awarded   Varies each year.

Deadline   May of each year.

[667]
WHITE MOUNTAIN APACHE TRIBAL SCHOLARSHIPS

White Mountain Apache Tribe
Attn: Office of Higher Education
205 West Fatco Road
P.O. Box 250
Whiteriver, AZ 85941
(928) 338-5800   Toll Free: (877) 7-APACHE
Fax: (928) 338-1869   E-mail: lgoklish@wmat.us
Web: www.wmat.nsn.us/high_ed.html

Summary   To provide financial assistance to members of the White Mountain Apache Tribe who are interested in attending college or graduate school in any state.

Eligibility   This program is open to members of the White Mountain Apache Tribe who are enrolled or planning to enroll full time at a college, university, or vocational/technical school in any state. Applicants must be interested in working on an undergraduate or graduate degree in any field. Along with their application, they must submit a 150-word essay on their educational goals and plans for utilizing their scholarship.

Financial data   A stipend is awarded (amount not specified).

Duration   1 year; may be renewed, provided the recipient remains enrolled full time and maintains a GPA of 1.7 or higher as a freshman, 2.0 as a sophomore through senior, or 3.0 as a graduate student.

Additional information   This program is funded by the U.S. Bureau of Indian Affairs (BIA).

Number awarded   Varies each year.

Deadline   March of each year for fall; September of each year for spring.

[668]
WICHITA HIGHER EDUCATION PROGRAM

Wichita and Affiliated Tribes
Attn: Higher Education
P.O. Box 729
Anadarko, OK 73005
(405) 247-8612   Fax: (405) 247-5687
E-mail: yolanda.walker@wichitatribe.com
Web: www.wichitatribe.com/programs/education.aspx

Summary   To provide financial assistance to Wichita tribal members who are interested in attending college in any state.

Eligibility   This program is open to Wichita tribal members who have been accepted to a college or university in any state as a full- or part-time student. Applicants must submit high school and/or college transcripts, tribal identification, and a letter of intent. Preference is given to students who are eligible for federal Pell grants.

Financial data   Stipends depend on the need of the recipient.

Duration   1 year; may be renewed as long as the recipient maintains a GPA of 2.0 or higher.

Number awarded   Varies each year.

Deadline   June of each year for the academic year; October of each year for spring semester only; March of each year for summer semester.

[669]
WIEA SCHOLARSHIPS

Wisconsin Indian Education Association
Attn: Scholarship Coordinator
P.O. Box 910
Keshena, WI 54135
(715) 799-5110   Fax: (715) 799-5102
E-mail: vnuske@mitw.org
Web: www.wiea.org/index.php/About/Scholarships

Summary   To provide financial assistance for undergraduate or graduate study to members of Wisconsin Indian tribes.

Eligibility   This program is open to residents of Wisconsin who can provide proof of tribal enrollment. Applicants must fall into 1 of the following categories: 1) entering freshman at a 4-year college or university; 2) new or continuing student at a tribal college or vocational/technical school; 3) undergraduate student at a 4-year college or university; or 4) graduate or Ph.D. student. All applicants must be full-time students. Along with their application, they must submit a 1-page personal essay on how they will apply their education. Selection is based on that essay (25 points), letters of recommendation (10 points), and GPA (15 points if 3.5 or higher, 10 points if 3.00 to 3.49, 5 points if 2.50 to 2.99). Financial need is not considered.

Financial data The stipend is $1,000.

Duration 1 year; nonrenewable.

Additional information This program began in 1997. Eligible tribes include Menominee, Oneida, Stockbridge-Munsee, Forest County Potowatomi, Ho-Chunk, Bad River Chippewa, Lac Courte Oreilles Ojibwe, St. Croix Chippewa, Red Cliff Chippewa, Sakoagon (Mole Lake) Chippewa, Brotherton, and Lac du Flambeau Chippewa.

Number awarded 4 each year: 1 in each of the 4 categories.

Deadline April of each year.

[670]
WIGA COLLEGE SCHOLARSHIPS

Washington Indian Gaming Association
1110 Capitol Way South, Suite 404
Olympia, WA 98501-2251
(360) 352-3248　　　　　　　Fax: (360) 352-4819
E-mail: abriel@reachone.com
Web: www.washingtonindiangaming.org

Summary To provide financial assistance to members of Indian tribes in Washington who are interested in attending college or graduate school in any state.

Eligibility This program is open to Washington residents who are enrolled members of tribes affiliated with the Washington Indian Gaming Association (WIGA) and to urban Indian students in the state. Applicants must be attending or accepted at a community college, undergraduate institution, or graduate school in any state. Native American students from outside Washington who attend college in the state are also eligible. Along with their application, they must submit a 250-word personal essay on why they are considering their intended major, how it will help them reach future career objectives, and how their education will benefit their home community (whether urban or rural). Financial need is also considered in the selection process.

Financial data Stipends are $2,200 per year for graduate or professional students, $2,000 per year for undergraduates at 4-year institutions, or $1,000 per year for students at community colleges or technical schools.

Duration 1 year; may be renewed, provided the recipient maintains a GPA of 2.5 or higher.

Number awarded Varies each year; recently, 41 were awarded: 7 to students at community colleges and technical schools, 25 to undergraduates at 4-year institutions, and 9 to graduate students.

Deadline March of each year.

[671]
WILLIAM D. PHILLIPS SCHOLARSHIP FUND

Cook Inlet Region, Inc.
Attn: The CIRI Foundation
3600 San Jeronimo Drive, Suite 256
Anchorage, AK 99508-2870
(907) 793-3575　　　　　　　Toll Free: (800) 764-3382
Fax: (907) 793-3585　　　E-mail: tcf@thecirifoundation.org
Web: www.thecirifoundation.org/about/donors

Summary To provide financial assistance for undergraduate or graduate studies in public policy fields to Alaska Natives who are original enrollees to Cook Inlet Region, Inc. (CIRI) and their lineal descendants.

Eligibility This program is open to Alaska Native enrollees to CIRI under the Alaska Native Claims Settlement Act (ANCSA) of 1971 and their lineal descendants. There are no Alaska residency requirements or age limitations. Applicants must be accepted or enrolled full time in a 4-year undergraduate or a graduate degree program in government, public policy, public administration, budget and public finance, social policy, education policy, or related fields. They must have a GPA of 3.7 or higher. Along with their application, they must submit a 500-word statement on their educational and career goals and how they are contributing, or planning to contribute, to a positive Alaska Native community. Selection is based on that statement, academic achievement, rigor of course work or degree program, student financial contribution, financial need, grade level, previous work performance, community service, and relationship of degree program to career goals.

Financial data The stipend is $20,000 per year.

Duration 1 year; may be renewed.

Additional information CIRI is 1 of 13 regional corporations established according to the terms of the Alaska Native Claims Settlement Act (ANCSA) of 1971.

Number awarded 1 or more each year.

Deadline May of each year.

[672]
WILLIAM K. SCHUBERT M.D. MINORITY NURSING SCHOLARSHIP

Cincinnati Children's Hospital Medical Center
Attn: Office of Diversity and Inclusion, MLC 9008
3333 Burnet Avenue
Cincinnati, OH 45229-3026
(513) 803-6416　　　　　　　Toll Free: (800) 344-2462
Fax: (513) 636-5643　　　　　　　TDD: (513) 636-4900
E-mail: diversity@cchmc.org
Web: www.cincinnatichildrens.org

Summary To provide financial assistance to Native Americans and members of other underrepresented groups interested in working on a bachelor's or master's degree in nursing to prepare for licensure in Ohio.

Eligibility This program is open to members of groups underrepresented in the nursing profession (males, American Indians or Alaska Natives, Blacks or African Americans, Hawaiian Natives or other Pacific Islanders, Hispanics or Latinos, or Asians). Applicants must be enrolled or accepted in a professional bachelor's or master's registered nurse program at an accredited school of nursing to prepare for initial licensure in Ohio. They must have a GPA of 2.75 or higher. Along with their application, they must submit a 750-word essay that covers 1) their long-range personal, educational, and professional goals; 2) why they chose nursing as a profession; 3) how their experience as a member of an underrepresented group has influenced a major professional and/or personal decision in their life; 4) any unique qualifications, experiences, or special talents that demonstrate their creativity; and 5) how their work experience has contributed to their personal development.

Financial data The stipend is $2,750 per year.

Duration 1 year. May be renewed up to 3 additional years for students working on a bachelor's degree or 1 additional year for students working on a master's degree; renewal requires that students maintain a GPA of 2.75 or higher.

Number awarded 1 or more each year.

Deadline April of each year.

[673]
WILLIAM RANDOLPH HEARST ENDOWMENT SCHOLARSHIPS

National Action Council for Minorities in Engineering
Attn: Director, Scholarships and University Relations
440 Hamilton Avenue, Suite 302
White Plains, NY 10601-1813
(914) 539-4316   Fax: (914) 539-4032
E-mail: scholars@nacme.org
Web: www.nacme.org/scholarships

Summary To provide financial assistance to Native American and other underrepresented minority college freshmen or sophomores majoring in engineering or related fields.

Eligibility This program is open to African American, Latino, and American Indian college freshmen and sophomores who have a GPA of 2.8 or higher and have demonstrated academic excellence, leadership skills, and a commitment to science and engineering as a career. Applicants must be enrolled full time at an ABET-accredited engineering program. Fields of study include all areas of engineering as well as computer science, materials science, mathematics, operations research, or physics.

Financial data The stipend is $2,500 per year. Funds are sent directly to the recipient's university.

Duration Up to 4 years.

Additional information This program was established by the William Randolph Hearst Foundation.

Number awarded 2 each year.

Deadline April of each year.

[674]
WILLIAM RUCKER GREENWOOD SCHOLARSHIP

Association for Women Geoscientists-Potomac Chapter
Attn: Scholarships
P.O. Box 6644
Arlington, VA 22206-0644
E-mail: awgpotomacschol@hotmail.com
Web: www.awg.org/members/po_scholarships.htm

Summary To provide financial assistance to Native American and other minority women from any state working on an undergraduate or graduate degree in the geosciences at a college in the Potomac Bay region.

Eligibility This program is open to minority women who are residents of any state and currently enrolled as full-time undergraduate or graduate geoscience majors at an accred-

ited, degree-granting college or university in Delaware, the District of Columbia, Maryland, Virginia, or West Virginia. Selection is based on the applicant's 1) participation in geoscience or earth science educational activities; and 2) potential for leadership as a future geoscience professional.

Financial data The stipend is $1,000. The recipient also is granted a 1-year membership in the Association for Women Geoscientists (AWG).

Duration 1 year.

Number awarded 1 each year.

Deadline April of each year.

[675]
WILLIE BRADSHAW MEMORIAL ENDOWED SCHOLARSHIPS

North Carolina High School Athletic Association
Attn: Director of Grants and Fundraising
222 Finley Golf Course Road
P.O. Box 3216
Chapel Hill, NC 27515-3216
(919) 240-7371   Fax: (919) 240-7399
E-mail: mary@nchsaa.org
Web: www.nchsaa.org

Summary To provide financial assistance to Native American and other minority seniors (males and females considered separately) at high schools in North Carolina who have participated in lacrosse and plan to attend college in any state.

Eligibility This program is open to American Indian/Alaska Native, African American, Hispanic American, and Asian Pacific Islander American seniors graduating from high schools that are members of the North Carolina High School Athletic Association (NCHSAA). Applicants must be U.S. citizens, nationals, or permanent residents planning to attend college in any state. They must have participated in a sanctioned varsity sport, demonstrate leadership abilities through participation in community service and extracurricular or other activities, have clean school and athletic disciplinary records, and have adjusted gross family income between $30,000 and $75,000 per year. Males and females are considered separately.

Financial data The stipend is $750 for regional winners; state winners receive an additional $1,000.

Duration 1 year; nonrenewable.

Number awarded 16 regional winners (1 male and 1 female in each of 8 regions) are selected each year; from those winners, 1 male and 1 female are selected as state winners.

Deadline February of each year.

[676]
WILSON-HOOPER SCHOLARSHIP

Chahta Foundation
Attn: Scholarship Specialist
P.O. Box 1849
Durant, OK 74702
(580) 924-8280, ext. 2546
Toll Free: (800) 522-6170, ext. 2546
Fax: (580) 745-9023
E-mail: scholarship@chahtafoundation.com
Web: www.chahtafoundation.com

Summary To provide financial assistance to members of the Choctaw Nation who are preparing for a career in veterinary technology or veterinary medicine.
Eligibility This program is open to Choctaw students who are attending an institution of higher education and working on an association degree in veterinary technology or a doctoral degree in veterinary medicine. They must have a GPA of 3.0 or higher. Along with their application, they must submit essays on 1) why they want to become a veterinarian; and 2) their preference in working with small animals, large animals, or exotics. In the selection process, emphasis is placed on desire and ability rather than financial need.
Financial data The stipend ranges from $500 to $4,000 per year.
Duration 1 year; recipients may reapply.
Additional information This program began in 2014.
Number awarded 1 or more each year.
Deadline May of each year.

[677]
WINNEBAGO TRIBE HIGHER EDUCATION ASSISTANCE

Winnebago Tribe of Nebraska
Attn: Higher Education Director
100 Bluff Street
P.O. Box 687
Winnebago, NE 68071
(402) 878-2631   Fax: (402) 878-2637
E-mail: patrice.bass@winnebagotribe.com
Web: www.winnebagotribe.com

Summary To provide financial assistance to members of the Winnebago Tribe of Nebraska who are interested in attending vocational school, college, or graduate school in any state.
Eligibility This program is open to enrolled members of the Winnebago Tribe of Nebraska who are attending or planning to attend an institution of higher education in any state. Applicants must be working full or part time on a vocational certificate or an associate, bachelor's, master's, or doctoral degree and have a GPA of 2.5 or higher. They must submit a copy of their Certificate of Degree of Indian Blood (CDIB), transcripts, and documentation of financial need. In the selection process, first priority is given to students who live on the reservation, second to students who live off the reservation, third to students who live in Nebraska, and fourth to students who live in other states.
Financial data For undergraduates, funding is intended only to supplement other assistance available to the student. For full-time graduate students, the stipend is $15,000 per year. For part-time graduate students, the stipend depends on the need of the recipient.
Duration 1 semester; may be renewed, provided the recipient maintains a GPA of 2.5 or higher as an undergraduate or 3.0 or higher as a graduate student.
Number awarded Varies each year.
Deadline April of each year for fall, academic year, or summer school; October of each year for spring or winter.

[678]
WINNERS FOR LIFE FOUNDATION SCHOLARSHIP

American Indian College Fund
Attn: Scholarship Department
8333 Greenwood Boulevard
Denver, CO 80221
(303) 426-8900   Toll Free: (800) 776-FUND
Fax: (303) 426-1200
E-mail: scholarships@collegefund.org
Web: www.collegefund.org

Summary To provide financial assistance to Native American college students who are interested in studying any field at Tribal Colleges and Universities (TCUs).
Eligibility This program is open to American Indians and Alaska Natives from any state who have proof of enrollment or descendancy. Applicants must be enrolled or planning to enroll as freshmen, sophomores, juniors, or seniors at an eligible TCU. They must have a GPA of 2.0 or higher and be working on a degree in any field. Applications are available only online and include required essays on specified topics. U.S. citizenship is required.
Financial data The stipend is $2,000.
Duration 1 year.
Additional information This program is sponsored by the Winners for Life Foundation.
Number awarded 1 or more each year.
Deadline May of each year.

[679]
WISCONSIN INDIAN STUDENT ASSISTANCE GRANTS

Wisconsin Higher Educational Aids Board
131 West Wilson Street, Suite 902
P.O. Box 7885
Madison, WI 53707-7885
(608) 266-0888   Fax: (608) 267-2808
E-mail: cindy.cooley@wi.gov
Web: www.heab.state.wi.us/programs.html

Summary To provide financial assistance to Native Americans in Wisconsin who are interested in attending college or graduate school in the state.
Eligibility Wisconsin residents who have at least 25% Native American blood (of a certified tribe or band) are eligible to apply if they are able to demonstrate financial need and are interested in attending college on the undergraduate or graduate school level. Applicants must attend a Wisconsin institution (public, independent, or proprietary). They may be enrolled either full or part time.
Financial data The stipend ranges from $250 to $1,100 per year. Additional funds are available on a matching basis from the U.S. Bureau of Indian Affairs.
Duration Up to 5 years.
Number awarded Varies each year.
Deadline Generally, applications can be submitted at any time.

[680]
WISCONSIN MINORITY UNDERGRADUATE RETENTION GRANTS

Wisconsin Higher Educational Aids Board
131 West Wilson Street, Suite 902
P.O. Box 7885
Madison, WI 53707-7885
(608) 267-2212   Fax: (608) 267-2808
E-mail: deanna.schulz@wi.gov
Web: www.heab.state.wi.us/programs.html

Summary To provide financial assistance to Native Americans and other minorities in Wisconsin who are currently enrolled at a college in the state.

Eligibility This program is open to residents of Wisconsin who are African Americans, Hispanic Americans, American Indians, or southeast Asians (students who were admitted to the United States after December 31, 1975 and who are a former citizen of Laos, Vietnam, or Cambodia or whose ancestor was a citizen of 1 of those countries). Applicants must be enrolled at least half time as sophomores, juniors, seniors, or fifth-year undergraduates at a Wisconsin technical college, tribal college, or independent college or university in the state. They must be nominated by their institution and be able to demonstrate financial need.

Financial data Stipends range from $250 to $2,500 per year, depending on the need of the recipient.

Duration Up to 4 years.

Additional information The Wisconsin Higher Educational Aids Board administers this program for students at private nonprofit institutions, technical colleges, and tribal colleges. The University of Wisconsin has a similar program for students attending any of the branches of that system. Eligible students should apply through their school's financial aid office.

Number awarded Varies each year.

Deadline Deadline dates vary by institution; check with your school's financial aid office.

[681]
WOKSAPE OYATE: "WISDOM OF THE PEOPLE" DISTINGUISHED SCHOLAR AWARD

American Indian College Fund
Attn: Scholarship Department
8333 Greenwood Boulevard
Denver, CO 80221
(303) 426-8900   Toll Free: (800) 776-FUND
Fax: (303) 426-1200
E-mail: scholarships@collegefund.org
Web: www.collegefund.org

Summary To provide financial assistance to Native American high school seniors who are the valedictorian or salutatorian of their class and planning to attend a Tribal College or University (TCU).

Eligibility This program is open to American Indians or Alaska Natives who are graduating from high school as the valedictorian or salutatorian of their class. Applicants must be planning to enroll full time at an eligible TCU. Applications are available only online and include required essays on specified topics. Selection is based on exceptional academic achievement. U.S. citizenship is required.

Financial data The stipend is $8,000. Funding is available only if the recipient maintains a GPA of 3.5 or higher.

Duration 1 year.

Additional information This program began in 2006 with an endowment grant from the Lilly Endowment.

Number awarded 1 each year.

Deadline May of each year.

[682]
WOKSAPE OYATE: "WISDOM OF THE PEOPLE" KEEPERS OF THE NEXT GENERATION AWARD

American Indian College Fund
Attn: Scholarship Department
8333 Greenwood Boulevard
Denver, CO 80221
(303) 426-8900   Toll Free: (800) 776-FUND
Fax: (303) 426-1200
E-mail: scholarships@collegefund.org
Web: www.collegefund.org

Summary To provide financial assistance to Native Americans who are single parents and attending or planning to attend a Tribal College or University (TCU).

Eligibility This program is open to American Indians or Alaska Natives who are single parents and enrolled or planning to enroll full time at an eligible TCU. Applicants must have a GPA of 2.0 or higher. Applications are available only online and include required essays on specified topics. Selection is based on exceptional academic achievement. U.S. citizenship is required.

Financial data The stipend is $8,000.

Duration 1 year.

Additional information This program began in 2006 with an endowment grant from the Lilly Endowment.

Number awarded 1 each year.

Deadline May of each year.

[683]
WOMAN WHO MOVES THE NATION SCHOLARSHIP

Conference of Minority Transportation Officials
Attn: National Scholarship Program
100 M Street, S.E., Suite 917
Washington, DC 20003
(202) 506-2917   E-mail: info@comto.org
Web: www.comto.org/page/scholarships

Summary To provide financial assistance to Native American and other minority women who are working on an undergraduate or graduate degree in specified fields to prepare for a management career in a transportation-related organization.

Eligibility This program is open to minority women who are working on an undergraduate or graduate degree with intent to lead in some capacity as a supervisor, manager, director, or other position in transit or a transportation-related organization. Applicants may be studying business, entrepreneurship, political science, or other specialized area. They must have a GPA of 3.0 or higher. Along with their application they must submit a cover letter on their transportation-related career goals and life aspirations. Financial need is not considered in the selection process.

Financial data The stipend is $5,000. Funds are paid directly to the recipient's college or university.

Duration 1 year.

Number awarded 1 each year.

Deadline April of each year.

[684]
WOODS HOLE OCEANOGRAPHIC INSTITUTION MINORITY FELLOWSHIPS

Woods Hole Oceanographic Institution
Attn: Academic Programs Office
Clark Laboratory 223, MS 31
360 Woods Hole Road
Woods Hole, MA 02543-1541
(508) 289-2219   Fax: (508) 457-2188
E-mail: education@whoi.edu
Web: www.whoi.edu/page.do?pid=9377

Summary To provide work experience to Native Americans and members of other minority groups who are interested in preparing for careers in the marine sciences, oceanographic engineering, or marine policy.

Eligibility This program is open to ethnic minority undergraduates enrolled in U.S. colleges or universities who have completed at least 1 year of study and who are interested in the physical or natural sciences, mathematics, engineering, or marine policy. Applicants must be U.S. citizens or permanent residents and African American or Black; Asian American; Chicano, Mexican American, Puerto Rican or other Hispanic; or Native American, Alaska Native, or Native Hawaiian. They must be interested in participating in a program of study and research at Woods Hole Oceanographic Institution. Selection is based on previous academic and scientific achievements and promise as future ocean scientists or ocean engineers.

Financial data The stipend is $500 per week; trainees also receive free housing and additional support for travel to Woods Hole.

Duration 10 to 12 weeks during the summer or 1 semester during the academic year; renewable.

Additional information Trainees are assigned advisers who supervise their research programs and supplementary study activities. Some traineeships involve field work or research cruises. This program is conducted as part of the Research Experiences for Undergraduates (REU) Program of the National Science Foundation.

Number awarded 4 to 5 each year.

Deadline February of each year.

[685]
WRIGHT-HATCH JOURNALISM SCHOLARSHIP

Sault Tribe of Chippewa Indians
Attn: Higher Education Department
523 Ashmun Street
Sault Ste. Marie, MI 49783
(906) 635-6050, ext. 26312   Toll Free: (800) 793-0660
Fax: (906) 635-7785   E-mail: BMacArthur@saulttribe.net
Web: www.saulttribe.com

Summary To provide financial assistance to members of the Sault Tribe of Chippewa Indians interested in attending college in any state to work on an undergraduate degree in journalism.

Eligibility This program is open to members of the Sault Tribe who are enrolled full time at a 2- or 4-year college or university in any state. Applicants must be working on an undergraduate degree in journalism. Along with their application, they must submit an essay of 1,000 to 2,000 words on a topic that changes annually but relates to their Indian heritage.

Financial data The stipend is $1,000.

Duration 1 year.

Number awarded 1 each year.

Deadline May of each year.

[686]
WSP/PARSONS BRINCKERHOFF ENGINEERING SCHOLARSHIP

Conference of Minority Transportation Officials
Attn: National Scholarship Program
100 M Street, S.E., Suite 917
Washington, DC 20003
(202) 506-2917   E-mail: info@comto.org
Web: www.comto.org/page/scholarships

Summary To provide financial assistance to Native American and other members of the Conference of Minority Transportation Officials (COMTO) and their families who are working on an undergraduate degree in engineering.

Eligibility This program is open to undergraduate students who are members and their parents, guardians, or grandparents who have been members of COMTO for at least 1 year. Applicants must be working on a degree in engineering and have a GPA of 3.0 or higher. Along with their application they must submit a cover letter on their transportation-related career goals and life aspirations. Financial need is not considered in the selection process.

Financial data The stipend is $2,500. Funds are paid directly to the recipient's college or university.

Duration 1 year.

Additional information This program is sponsored by WSP USA, formerly Parsons Brinckerhoff, Inc.

Number awarded 2 each year.

Deadline April of each year.

[687]
WSP/PARSONS BRINCKERHOFF GOLDEN APPLE SCHOLARSHIP

Conference of Minority Transportation Officials
Attn: National Scholarship Program
100 M Street, S.E., Suite 917
Washington, DC 20003
(202) 506-2917   E-mail: info@comto.org
Web: www.comto.org/page/scholarships

Summary To provide financial assistance to Native American and other members of the Conference of Minority Transportation Officials (COMTO) and their children who are high school seniors planning to attend college to prepare for a career in transportation.

Eligibility This program is open to graduating high school seniors who are members of COMTO or whose parents are members. Applicants must be planning to attend an accredited college, university, or vocational/technical institution to prepare for a career in transportation. They must have a GPA of 2.0 or higher. Along with their application they must submit a cover letter on their transportation-related career goals and life aspirations. Financial need is not considered in the selection process.

Financial data The stipend is $2,500. Funds are paid directly to the recipient's college or university.

Duration 1 year.

Additional information This program is sponsored by WSP USA, formerly Parsons Brinckerhoff, Inc.

Number awarded 2 each year.

Deadline April of each year.

[688]
XEROX TECHNICAL MINORITY SCHOLARSHIP PROGRAM

Xerox Corporation
Attn: Technical Minority Scholarship Program
150 State Street, Fourth Floor
Rochester, NY 14614
Toll Free: (877) 747-3625 E-mail: xtmsp@rballiance.com
Web: www.xerox.com/jobs/minority-scholarships/enus.html

Summary To provide financial assistance to Native Americans and other minorities interested in undergraduate or graduate education in the sciences and/or engineering.

Eligibility This program is open to minorities (people of African American, Asian, Pacific Islander, Native American, Native Alaskan, or Hispanic descent) working full time on a bachelor's, master's, or doctoral degree in chemistry, computing and software systems, engineering (chemical, computer, electrical, imaging, manufacturing, mechanical, optical, or software), information management, laser optics, materials science, physics, or printing management science. Applicants must be U.S. citizens or permanent residents with a GPA of 3.0 or higher and attending a 4-year college or university.

Financial data Stipends range from $1,000 to $10,000.

Duration 1 year.

Number awarded Varies each year, recently, 128 were awarded.

Deadline September of each year.

[689]
YAKAMA NATION CREDIT ENTERPRISE SCHOLARSHIP

Yakama Nation
Department of Human Services
Attn: Higher Education Program
107 Teo Road
P.O. Box 151
Toppenish, WA 98948
(509) 865-5121, ext. 4540   Toll Free: (800) 543-2802
Fax: (509) 865-6994   E-mail: murry@yakama.com
Web: www.yakama.us/programs.php

Summary To provide financial assistance to undergraduate and graduate students who are Yakama tribal members majoring in a business-related field at a school in any state.

Eligibility This program is open to enrolled members of the Yakama nation who are enrolled or planning to enroll full time at a college or university in any state. Applicants must be working on an undergraduate or graduate degree in accounting, banking, business, real estate, or a closely-related field.

Financial data A stipend is awarded (amount not specified).

Duration 1 year.

Number awarded 1 or more each year.

Deadline June of each year.

[690]
YAKAMA NATION HIGHER EDUCATION SCHOLARSHIP

Yakama Nation
Department of Human Services
Attn: Higher Education Program
107 Teo Road
P.O. Box 151
Toppenish, WA 98948
(509) 865-5121, ext. 4540   Toll Free: (800) 543-2802
Fax: (509) 865-6994   E-mail: murry@yakama.com
Web: www.yakama.us/programs.php

Summary To provide financial assistance to Yakama tribal members interested in working on an undergraduate or graduate degree at a school in any state.

Eligibility This program is open to enrolled members of the Yakama nation who are enrolled or planning to enroll at a postsecondary institution in any state. Applicants must be interested in working on an undergraduate or graduate degree on a part-time or full-time basis. Along with their application, they must submit a personal letter describing their educational and employment goals. Financial need is considered in the selection process.

Financial data The stipend is $1,500 per year for full-time undergraduates or $3,000 per year for full-time graduate students. Part-time students are eligible for funding for tuition and books only.

Duration 1 year; may be renewed.

Number awarded Varies each year.

Deadline June of each year for fall semester or quarter or for academic year; October of each year for spring semester or winter quarter; January of each year for spring quarter; April of each year for high school seniors and summer school.

[691]
YAVAPAI-APACHE NATION HIGHER EDUCATION GRANTS

Yavapai-Apache Nation
Attn: Higher Education Department
2400 West Datsi Street
Camp Verde, AZ 86322
(928) 649-7111   Fax: (928) 567-6485
Web: www.yavapai-apache.org/administration

Summary To provide financial assistance to members of the Yavapai-Apache Nation who are interested in attending college or graduate school in any state.

Eligibility This program is open to members of the Yavapai-Apache Nation who are enrolled or planning to enroll at an accredited institution of higher education in any state. Applicants must be interested in working full or part time on a vocational certificate or an associate, bachelor's, master's, or doctoral degree. Along with their application, they must submit 1) a brief essay on their educational goals and how they will utilize their education; and 2) documentation of financial need.

Financial data The stipend is $20,000 per year for under-graduate and vocational students or $30,000 per year for graduate students.

Duration 1 semester; may be renewed up to 5 additional full-time semesters for students working on an associate degree, 9 additional full-time semesters for students working on a bachelor's degree, 9 additional full-time semesters for students working on a graduate degree, or until completion of a program for vocational students. Renewal requires the recipient to maintain a GPA of 2.0 or higher.

Number awarded Varies each year.

Deadline June of each year for fall and academic year; September of each year for spring only; March of each year for summer; August of each year for vocational/technical school.

[692]
YOUNG NATIVE WRITERS ESSAY CONTEST

Holland & Knight Charitable Foundation, Inc.
201 North Franklin Street, 11th Floor
P.O. Box 2877
Tampa, FL 33601-2877
(813) 227-8500   Toll Free: (866) HK-CARES
E-mail: nativewriters@hklaw.com
Web: www.nativewriters.hklaw.com/index.asp

Summary To recognize and reward, with college scholar-ships, Native American high school students who submit out-standing essays on issues impacting their tribal communities.

Eligibility This competition is open to Native American high school students in grades 9-12 who have a significant and current relationship with a tribal community. Applicants must submit a 1,200-word essay on an assigned topic that changes every year but relates to Native American issues. Selection is based on 1) evidence of relevant reading and thoughtful use of resource materials; 2) treatment of the assigned theme; 3) clear and effective language, mechanics, and grammar; and 4) a coherent plan of organization.

Financial data First-place winners receive an all-expense paid trip to Washington, D.C. to visit the National Museum of the American Indian and other prominent sites. They also receive scholarships of $2,500 that are paid to their colleges or universities after they graduate from high school and upon receipt of proof of registration.

Duration The competition is held annually.

Additional information This program, which began in 2006, is sponsored by the National Museum of the American Indian and the National Indian Education Association.

Number awarded 4 each year.

Deadline April of each year.

[693]
ZUNI HIGHER EDUCATION SCHOLARSHIPS

Pueblo of Zuni
Attn: Education and Career Development Center
01 Twin Buttes Drive
P.O. Box 339
Zuni, NM 87327
(505) 782-5998   Fax: (505) 782-6080
E-mail: zecdc@ashiwi.org
Web: www.ashiwi.org/zecdc/Tribal.Scholarship.html

Summary To provide financial assistance for college or graduate school in any state to members of the Pueblo of Zuni.

Eligibility This program is open to enrolled members of the Pueblo of Zuni who are high school seniors or graduates. Applicants must have earned a GPA of 2.0 or higher and be interested in working on an associate, bachelor's, or graduate degree as a full-time student at a college or university in any state. They must have also applied for a federal Pell Grant. Along with their application, they must submit a personal statement on why they are seeking this scholarship.

Financial data The amount awarded depends on the need of the recipient, up to $5,000 per year.

Duration 1 year; may be renewed if the recipient maintains a GPA of 2.0 or higher.

Number awarded Varies each year.

Deadline June of each year for the fall semester; October of each year for the spring semester; April of each year for the summer session.

Graduate Students

Listed alphabetically by program title and described in detail here are 573 fellowships, grants, awards, and other sources of "free money" set aside for incoming, continuing, or returning graduate students of American Indian, Native Alaskan (including Eskimos and Aleuts), and Native Hawaiian descent who are working on a master's, doctoral, or professional degree. This funding is available to support study, training, research, and/or creative activities in the United States.

[694]
ACADEMIC LIBRARY ASSOCIATION OF OHIO DIVERSITY SCHOLARSHIP

Academic Library Association of Ohio
c/o Eileen Theodore-Shusta, Diversity Committee Chair
Ohio University
Library Administrative Services
422 Alden
30 Park Place
Athens, OH 45701
(740) 593-2989   E-mail: theodore@ohio.edu
Web: www.alaoweb.org/procmanual/policies.html#diversity

Summary To provide financial assistance to Native American and other residents of Ohio who are working on a master's degree in library science at a school in any state and will contribute to diversity in the profession.

Eligibility This program is open to residents of Ohio who are enrolled or entering an ALA-accredited program for a master's degree in library science, either on campus or via distance education. Applicants must be able to demonstrate how they will contribute to diversity in the profession, including (but not limited to) race or ethnicity, sexual orientation, life experience, physical ability, and a sense of commitment to those and other diversity issues. Along with their application, they must submit 1) a list of participation in honor societies or professional organizations, awards, scholarships, prizes, honors, or class offices; 2) a list of their community, civic, organizational, or volunteer experiences; and 3) an essay on their understanding of and commitment to diversity in libraries, including how they, as library school students and future professionals, might address the issue.

Financial data The stipend is $1,500.

Duration 1 year.

Number awarded 2 each year.

Deadline March of each year.

[695]
ACC GREATER PHILADELPHIA DIVERSITY CORPORATE SUMMER INTERNSHIP

Association of Corporate Counsel-Greater Philadelphia Chapter
c/o Anne Bancroft, Diversity Committee Co-Chair
Exelon Business Services Company
2301 Market Street, Suite 23
Philadelphia, PA 19103
Toll Free: (800) 494-4000
E-mail: anne.bancroft@exeloncorp.com
Web: www.acc.com

Summary To provide an opportunity for Native American and other law students from diverse backgrounds to gain summer work experience in corporate law at firms in the Philadelphia area.

Eligibility This program is open to students who are members of minority groups traditionally underrepresented in the legal profession (Asian/Pacific Islander, African American, Hispanic, American Indian/Alaska Native). Applications are solicited from law schools in the Philadelphia area, but students at all other law schools may be eligible if they are interested in a summer internship in corporate law at a firm in that area. Interested students must submit information about their financial status, a list of extracurricular activities, any relevant legal experience, a legal writing sample, and an essay of 250 to 500 words explaining why they qualify for this internship and what they hope to gain from the experience.

Financial data The stipend is $7,500.

Duration Summer months.

Number awarded Approximately 15 each year.

Deadline January of each year.

[696]
ACC NATIONAL CAPITAL REGION CORPORATE SCHOLARS PROGRAM

Association of Corporate Counsel-National Capital Region
Attn: Executive Director
P.O. Box 2147
Rockville, MD 20847-2147
(301) 881-3018   E-mail: Ilene.Reid-NCR@accglobal.com
Web: m.acc.com/chapters/ncr/scholars.cfm

Summary To provide an opportunity for summer work experience in the metropolitan Washington, D.C. area to Native American and other students at law schools in the area who will contribute to the diversity of the profession.

Eligibility This program is open to students entering their second or third year of part- or full-time study at law schools in the Washington, D.C. metropolitan area (including suburban Maryland and all of Virginia). Applicants must be able to demonstrate how they contribute to diversity in the legal profession, based not only on ideas about gender, race, and ethnicity, but also concepts of socioeconomic background and their individual educational and career path. They must be interested in working during the summer at a sponsoring private corporation and nonprofit organizations in the Washington, D.C. area. Along with their application, they must submit a personal statement of 250 to 500 words explaining why they qualify for this program, a writing sample, their law school transcript, and a resume.

Financial data The stipend is at least $9,000.

Duration 10 weeks during the summer.

Additional information The sponsor is the local chapter of the Association of Corporate Counsel (ACC). It established this program in 2004 with support from the Minority Corporate Counsel Association (MCCA).

Number awarded Varies each year; recently, 13 of these internships were awarded.

Deadline January of each year.

[697]
ACM/IEEE-CS GEORGE MICHAEL MEMORIAL HPC FELLOWSHIPS

Association for Computing Machinery
Attn: Awards Committee Liaison
2 Penn Plaza, Suite 701
New York, NY 10121-0701
(212) 626-0561   Toll Free: (800) 342-6626
Fax: (212) 944-1318   E-mail: acm-awards@acm.org
Web: awards.acm.org/hpcfell/nominations.cfm

Summary To provide financial assistance to Native American and other doctoral students from any country who are working on a degree in high performance computing (HPC) and will contribute to diversity in the field.

Eligibility This program is open to students from any country who have completed at least 1 year full-time study in a

Ph.D. program in HPC and have at least 1 year remaining before graduating. Applications from women, minorities, international students, and all who contribute to diversity are especially encouraged. Selection is based on overall potential for research excellence, degree to which technical interests align with those of the HPC community, demonstration of current and planned future use of HPC resources, evidence of a plan of student to enhance HPC-related skills, evidence of academic progress to date (including presentations and publications), and recommendation by faculty adviser.

Financial data The stipend is $5,000. Fellows also receive reimbursement of travel expenses to attend the conference of the Association for Computing Machinery (ACM).

Duration 1 year.

Additional information This program, which began in 2007, is sponsored by the IEEE Computer Society.

Number awarded Up to 6 each year.

Deadline April of each year.

[698]
ACM SIGHPC/INTEL COMPUTATIONAL AND DATA SCIENCE FELLOWSHIPS

Association for Computing Machinery
Attn: Special Interest Group on High Performance
  Computing (SIGHPC)
Office of SIG Services
2 Penn Plaza, Suite 701
New York, NY 10121-0701
(212) 626-0606   Toll Free: (800) 342-6626
Fax: (212) 944-1318   E-mail: cappo@hq.acm.org
Web: www.sighpc.org/fellowships

Summary To provide financial assistance to Native American and other underrepresented graduate students in any country who are working on a degree in computational or data science.

Eligibility This program is open to women and members of racial or ethnic backgrounds that have not traditionally participated in the computing field. Applicants must be enrolled as graduate students at a college or university in any country and working on a graduate degree in computational or data science. They must have completed less than half of their planning program of study; preference is given to students who are still early in their studies. Selection is based on overall potential for excellence in data science and/or computational science, likelihood of successfully completing a graduate degree, and extent to which applicants will increase diversity in the workplace.

Financial data The stipend is $15,000.

Duration 1 year.

Additional information This program was established in 2016 by Intel Corporation.

Number awarded Varies each year; recently, 14 were presented.

Deadline April of each year.

[699]
ACOUSTICAL SOCIETY OF AMERICA MINORITY FELLOWSHIP

Acoustical Society of America
Attn: Office Manager
1305 Walt Whitman Road, Suite 300
Melville, NY 11747-4300
(516) 576-2360   Fax: (631) 923-2875
E-mail: asa@acousticalsociety.org
Web: www.acousticalsociety.org

Summary To provide financial assistance to Native Americans and other underrepresented minorities who are working on a graduate degree involving acoustics.

Eligibility This program is open to U.S. and Canadian citizens and permanent residents who are members of a minority group that is underrepresented in the sciences (Hispanic, African American, or Native American). Applicants must be enrolled in or accepted to a graduate degree program as a full-time student. Their program of study may be in any field of pure or applied science and engineering directly related to acoustics, including acoustical oceanography, architectural acoustics, animal bioacoustics, biomedical ultrasound, bioresponse to vibration, engineering acoustics, musical acoustics, noise, physical acoustics, psychological acoustics, physiological acoustics, signal processing in acoustics, speech communication, structural acoustics and vibration, and underwater acoustics. Along with their application, student must submit a statement on why they are enrolled in their present academic program, including how they intend to use their graduate education to develop a career and how the study of acoustics is relevant to their career objectives.

Financial data The stipend is $20,000 per year. The sponsor strongly encourages the host educational institution to waive all tuition costs and assessed fees. Fellows also receive $1,000 for travel to attend a national meeting of the sponsor.

Duration 1 year; may be renewed for 1 additional year if the recipient is making normal progress toward a degree and is enrolled full time.

Additional information This program began in 1992.

Number awarded 1 each year.

Deadline March of each year.

[700]
ACXIOM DIVERSITY SCHOLARSHIP PROGRAM

Acxiom Corporation
601 East Third Street
P.O. Box 8190
Little Rock, AR 72203-8190
(501) 342-1000   Toll Free: (877) 314-2049
E-mail: Candice.Davis@acxiom.com
Web: www.acxiom.com/about-acxiom/careers

Summary To provide financial assistance and possible work experience to Native American and other upper-division and graduate students who are members of a diverse population that historically has been underrepresented in the information technology work force.

Eligibility This program is open to juniors, seniors, and graduate students who are working full time on a degree in a field of information technology, including computer science, computer information systems, management information systems, information quality, information systems, engineering, mathematics, statistics, or related areas of study. Women, veterans, minorities, and individuals with disabilities are encouraged to apply. Applicants must have a GPA of 3.0 or higher. Along with their application, they must submit a 500-word essay describing how the scholarship will help them achieve their academic, professional, and personal goals. Selection is based on academic achievement, relationship of field of study to information technology, and relationship of areas of professional interest to the sponsor's business needs.

Financial data The stipend is $5,000 per year.

Duration 1 year; may be renewed 1 additional year, provided the recipient remains enrolled full time, maintains a GPA of 3.0 or higher, and (if offered an internship) continues to meet internship expectations.

Additional information Recipients may be offered an internship (fall, spring, summer, year-round) at 1 of the sponsor's offices in Austin (Texas), Conway (Arkansas), Downers Grove (Illinois), Little Rock (Arkansas), Nashville (Tennessee), New York (New York), or Redwood City (California).

Number awarded Up to 5 each year.

Deadline December of each year.

[701]
ADDIE B. MORRIS SCHOLARSHIP

American Association of Railroad Superintendents
P.O. Box 200
La Fox, IL 60147
(331) 643-3369   E-mail: aars@supt.org
Web: www.railroadsuperintendents.org/Scholarships

Summary To provide financial assistance to undergraduate and graduate students, especially Native Americans and other minorities working on a degree in transportation.

Eligibility This program is open to full-time undergraduate and graduate students enrolled at accredited colleges and universities in Canada or the United States. Applicants must have completed enough credits to have standing as a sophomore and must have a GPA of 2.75 or higher. Preference is given to minority students enrolled in the transportation field who can demonstrate financial need.

Financial data The stipend is $1,000. Funds are sent directly to the recipient's institution.

Duration 1 year.

Number awarded 1 or more each year.

Deadline June of each year.

[702]
ADLER POLLOCK & SHEEHAN DIVERSITY SCHOLARSHIP

Adler Pollock & Sheehan P.C.
Attn: Marketing Manager
One Citizens Plaza, Eighth Floor
Providence, RI 02903
(401) 274-7200   Fax: (401) 751-0604
E-mail: Diversitycomm@apslaw.com
Web: www.apslaw.com/our-firm/diversity-commitment

Summary To provide financial assistance to residents of Massachusetts and Rhode Island who are Native Americans or members of other diverse groups and plan to attend law school in any state.

Eligibility This program is open to residents of Massachusetts and Rhode Island who are members of a diverse group, including African American, American Indian, Hispanic, Asian/Pacific Islander, gay/lesbian, or other minority group. Applicants must be entering their first year at an ABA-accredited law school in the United States. They must be able to demonstrate academic achievement, a desire to work and reside in Massachusetts or Rhode Island after graduation, a demonstrated commitment to the community, a vision of contributions to the profession and community after graduation, and financial need.

Financial data The stipend is $10,000.

Duration 1 year.

Number awarded 1 each year.

Deadline May of each year.

[703]
ADRIENNE M. AND CHARLES SHELBY ROOKS FELLOWSHIP FOR RACIAL AND ETHNIC THEOLOGICAL STUDENTS

United Church of Christ
Attn: Associate Director, Grant and Scholarship
  Administration
700 Prospect Avenue East
Cleveland, OH 44115-1100
(216) 736-2166   Toll Free: (866) 822-8224, ext. 2166
Fax: (216) 736-3783   E-mail: scholarships@ucc.org
Web: www.ucc.org/ministry_education_scholarships

Summary To provide financial assistance to Native Americans and other minority students who are either enrolled at an accredited seminary preparing for a career of service in the United Church of Christ (UCC) or working on a doctoral degree in the field of religion.

Eligibility This program is open to members of underrepresented ethnic groups (African American, Hispanic American, Asian American, Native American Indian, or Pacific Islander) who have been a member of a UCC congregation for at least 1 year. Applicants must be either 1) enrolled in an accredited school of theology in the United States or Canada and working on an M.Div. degree with the intent of becoming a pastor or teacher within the UCC; or 2) doctoral (Ph.D., Th.D., or Ed.D.) students preparing for a scholarly teaching vocation in the field of religion. Seminary students must have a GPA in all postsecondary work of 3.0 or higher and must have begun the in-care process; preference is given to students who have demonstrated leadership (through a history of service to the church) and scholarship (through exceptional academic performance). For doctoral students, preference is given to applicants who have demonstrated academic excellence, teaching effectiveness, and commitment to the UCC and who intend to become professors in colleges, seminaries, or graduate schools.

Financial data Grants range from $500 to $5,000 per year.

Duration 1 year; may be renewed.

Number awarded Varies each year; recently, 12 of these scholarships, including 8 for M.Div. students and 4 for doctoral students, were awarded.

Deadline February of each year.

[704]
AFPE UNDERREPRESENTED MINORITY PRE-DOCTORAL FELLOWSHIP

American Foundation for Pharmaceutical Education
Attn: Grants Manager
6076 Franconia Road, Suite C
Alexandria, VA 22310-1758
(703) 875-3095   Toll Free: (855) 624-9526
Fax: (703) 875-3098   E-mail: info@afpenet.org
Web: www.afpenet.org

Summary To provide funding for dissertation research to Native American and other underrepresented minority graduate students working on a Ph.D. in pharmaceutical science.

Eligibility This program is open to African American/Black, Hispanic/Latino, and Native American students who have completed at least 3 semesters of full-time graduate study and have no more than 3 and a half years remaining to complete a Ph.D. in pharmaceutical science at a U.S. school or college of pharmacy. Students enrolled in joint Pharm.D./Ph.D. programs are eligible if they have completed 3 full semesters of graduate credit toward the Ph.D. and if the Ph.D. degree will be awarded within 3 additional years. Applicants must be U.S. citizens or permanent residents. Selection is based on research plan and experience (50%), academic performance (35%), and leadership and character (15%).

Financial data The grant is $10,000 per year. Funds must be used to enable the students to make progress on their Ph.D. (e.g., student stipend, laboratory supplies, books, materials, travel) but not for indirect costs for the institution.

Duration 1 year; may be renewed 1 additional year.

Number awarded Up to 5 each year.

Deadline December of each year.

[705]
AGA INVESTING IN THE FUTURE STUDENT RESEARCH FELLOWSHIPS

American Gastroenterological Association
Attn: AGA Research Foundation
Research Awards Manager
4930 Del Ray Avenue
Bethesda, MD 20814-2512
(301) 222-4012   Fax: (301) 654-5920
E-mail: awards@gastro.org
Web: www.gastro.org

Summary To provide funding for research on digestive diseases or nutrition to Native American and other undergraduate and medical students from underrepresented minority groups.

Eligibility This program is open to undergraduate and medical students at accredited U.S. institutions who are African Americans, Hispanic/Latino Americans, Alaska Natives, American Indians, or Natives of the U.S. Pacific Islands. Applicants must be interested in conducting research on digestive diseases or nutrition. They may not hold similar salary support awards from other agencies (e.g., American Liver Foundation, Crohn's and Colitis Foundation). Research must be conducted under the supervision of a preceptor who is a full-time faculty member at an institution in a state other than the student's, directing a research project in a gastroenterology-related area, and a member of the American Gastroenterological Association (AGA).

Financial data Fellowships provide payment of housing, travel, and a stipend of $5,000.

Duration 8 to 10 weeks. The work may take place at any time during the year.

Additional information This program is supported by the National Institute of Diabetes and Digestive and Kidney Diseases (NIDDKD) of the U.S. National Institutes of Health (NIH).

Number awarded 12 each year.

Deadline February of each year.

[706]
AGING RESEARCH DISSERTATION AWARDS TO INCREASE DIVERSITY

National Institute on Aging
Attn: Office of Extramural Affairs
7201 Wisconsin Avenue, Suite 2C-218
Bethesda, MD 20814
(301) 402-4158   Fax: (301) 402-2945
TDD: (301) 451-0088   E-mail: hunterc@nia.nih.gov
Web: www.grants.nih.gov

Summary To provide financial assistance to Native American and other doctoral candidates from underrepresented groups who wish to conduct research on aging.

Eligibility This program is open to doctoral candidates conducting research on a dissertation with an aging-related focus, including the basic biology of aging; chronic, disabling, and degenerative diseases of aging, with a particular focus on Alzheimer's Disease; multiple morbidities; individual behavioral and social changes with aging; caregiving; longevity; and the consequences for society of an aging population. Applicants must be 1) members of an ethnic or racial group underrepresented in biomedical or behavioral research (Blacks or African Americans, Hispanics or Latinos, American Indians, Alaska Natives, Native Hawaiians, and other Pacific Islanders); 2) individuals with disabilities; or 3) individuals from socially, culturally, economically, or educationally disadvantaged backgrounds that have inhibited their ability to prepare for a career in health-related research. They must be U.S. citizens, nationals, or permanent residents.

Financial data Grants provide $23,376 per year for stipend and up to $20,000 for additional expenses. No funds may be used to pay for tuition or fees associated with completion of doctoral studies. The institution may receive up to 8% of direct costs as facilities and administrative costs per year.

Duration Up to 2 years.

Number awarded Up to 5 each year.

Deadline Applications must be submitted by February, June, or October of each year.

[707]
AHRQ GRANTS FOR HEALTH SERVICES RESEARCH DISSERTATIONS

Agency for Healthcare Research and Quality
Attn: Office of Extramural Research, Education and
  Priority Populations
540 Gaither Road
Rockville, MD 20850
(301) 427-1391   Fax: (301) 427-1561
TDD: (301) 451-0088
E-mail: Gregory.Stuppard@ahrq.hhs.gov
Web: www.grants.nih.gov

Summary To provide funding to Native American and other doctoral candidates engaged in research for a dissertation that examines an aspect of the health care system.

Eligibility This program is open to citizens, nationals, and permanent residents who are enrolled full time in an accredited research doctoral degree program at an institution in the United States. Applicants must have completed all requirements for the doctoral degree except for the dissertation in such fields as the social or behavioral sciences, mathematics, engineering, health services, nursing, epidemiology, biostatistics, health policy, or health informatics. Their proposed dissertation topic must relate to the strategic goals of the Agency for Healthcare Research and Quality (AHRQ): 1) reducing the risk of harm from health care services by promoting the delivery of appropriate care that achieves the best quality outcomes; 2) achieving wider access to effective health care services and reducing health care costs; and 3) assuring that providers and consumers/patients use beneficial and timely health care information to make informed decisions. Priority is given to proposals that address health services research issues critical to such priority population as individuals living in inner city and rural (including frontier) areas; low-income and minority groups; women, children, and the elderly; and individuals with special health care needs, including those with disabilities and those who need chronic or end-of-life health care. Members of underrepresented racial and ethnic groups, individuals from disadvantaged backgrounds, and individuals with disabilities are especially encouraged to apply.

Financial data This program provides up to $40,000 in direct costs, including $23,376 for the investigator's salary, direct project expenses (travel, data purchasing, data processing, and supplies), and matriculation fees. The institution will receive facilities and administrative costs of 8% of total allowable direct costs, exclusive of tuition and related fees, health insurance, and expenditures for equipment.

Duration 9 to 17 months.

Number awarded Up to 30 each year.

Deadline January, April, July, or October of each year.

[708]
AHTNA HERITAGE FOUNDATION SUMMER SCHOLARSHIPS

Ahtna, Incorporated
Attn: Ahtna Heritage Foundation
P.O. Box 213
Glennallen, AK 99588
(907) 822-5778   Fax: (907) 822-5338
E-mail: ahtnaheritage@yahoo.com
Web: www.ahtnaheritagefoundation.com/scholarships.html

Summary To provide financial assistance to shareholders of Ahtna, Incorporated in Alaska and their descendants who plan to attend summer school in any state.

Eligibility This program is open to Ahtna shareholders (original or Class L) who are high school graduates or GED recipients. Applicants must be enrolled or planning to enroll in summer school at a college, university, or vocational school in any state as an undergraduate or graduate student. They must have a GPA of 2.0 or higher and be able to demonstrate financial need.

Financial data The stipend is $2,000 for full-time students or $1,000 for part-time students.

Duration 1 year; may be renewed for up to 5 summers as an undergraduate and 5 summers as a graduate student, provided the recipient maintains a GPA of 2.0 or higher.

Additional information Ahtna, Incorporated is 1 of 13 regional corporations established according to the terms of the Alaska Native Claims Settlement Act (ANCSA) of 1971.

Number awarded Varies each year.

Deadline May of each year.

[709]
AICPA FELLOWSHIPS FOR MINORITY DOCTORAL STUDENTS

American Institute of Certified Public Accountants
Attn: Academic and Career Development Division
220 Leigh Farm Road
Durham, NC 27707-8110
(919) 402-4931   Fax: (919) 419-4705
E-mail: scholarships@aicpa.org
Web: www.aicpa.org

Summary To provide financial assistance to Native American and other underrepresented minority doctoral students who wish to prepare for a career teaching accounting at the college level.

Eligibility This program is open to underrepresented minority students who have applied to and/or been accepted into a doctoral program with a concentration in accounting. Applicants must have earned a master's degree or completed a minimum of 3 years of full-time work in accounting. They must be attending or planning to attend school full time and agree not to work full time in a paid position, teach more than 1 course as a teaching assistant, or work more than 25% as a research assistant. U.S. citizenship or permanent resident status is required. Preference is given to applicants who have attained a C.P.A. designation and/or are members of the American Institute of Certified Public Accountants (AICPA) and those who perform AICPA committee service. For purposes of this program, the AICPA defines minority students as those whose heritage is Black or African American, Hispanic or Latino, or Native American. Selection is based on academic and professional achievement, commitment to earning an accounting doctoral degree, and financial need.

Financial data The stipend is $12,000 per year.

Duration 1 year; may be renewed up to 4 additional years.

Number awarded Varies each year; recently, 22 were awarded.

Deadline March of each year.

[710]
AIGC BIE STEM LOAN FOR SERVICE

American Indian Graduate Center
Attn: Executive Director
3701 San Mateo Boulevard, N.E., Suite 200
Albuquerque, NM 87110-1249
(505) 881-4584   Toll Free: (800) 628-1920
Fax: (505) 884-0427   E-mail: fellowships@aigc.com
Web: www.aigcs.org/scholarships/graduate-fellowships

Summary To provide loans-for-service to Native American students interested in completing a graduate degree in a field of science, technology, engineering, or mathematics (STEM) and working for organizations affiliated with the Bureau of Indian Affairs (BIA) or tribal governments.

Eligibility This program is open to enrolled members of federally-recognized American Indian tribes and Alaska Native groups and other students who can document one-fourth degree federally-recognized Indian blood. Applicants must be enrolled as full-time students in a graduate or professional school in the United States working on a master's, doctoral, or professional degree in a field of STEM. They must have a GPA of 3.0 or higher. Along with their application, they must submit a 500-word statement on how their selected major will apply to the intent of this program as it applies to their personal commitment to serve the American Indian and Alaska Native community. Selection is based on that statement, academic achievement, and financial need.

Financial data Loans are based on each applicant's unmet financial need. No interest is charged. Loan repayment may be canceled at the rate of 1 year of loan payment for 1 year of employment with the BIA, the Bureau of Indian Education, a BIA-funded organization (on or off a reservation), or a tribal government.

Duration 1 year; may be renewed up to 1 additional year for master's degree students; up to 2 additional years for M.F.A. students; up to 3 additional years for doctoral degree students; up to 3 additional years for medicine, osteopathic medicine, dentistry, chiropractic, or veterinary degree students; or up to 2 additional years for law degree students.

Additional information This program is funded by the Bureau of Indian Education (BIE) of the BIA.

Number awarded Varies each year.

Deadline May of each year.

[711]
AIGC FELLOWSHIPS

American Indian Graduate Center
Attn: Executive Director
3701 San Mateo Boulevard, N.E., Suite 200
Albuquerque, NM 87110-1249
(505) 881-4584   Toll Free: (800) 628-1920
Fax: (505) 884-0427   E-mail: fellowships@aigc.com
Web: www.aigcs.org/scholarships/graduate-fellowships

Summary To provide financial assistance to Native American students interested in attending graduate school.

Eligibility This program is open to enrolled members of federally-recognized American Indian tribes and Alaska Native groups and other students who can document one-fourth degree federally-recognized Indian blood. Applicants must be enrolled as full-time students in a graduate or professional school in the United States working on a master's, doc-toral, or professional degree in any field. Along with their application, they must submit a 500-word essay on their extracurricular activities as they relate to American Indian programs at their institution, volunteer and community work as related to American Indian communities, tribal and community involvement, and plans to make positive changes in the American Indian community with their college education. Financial need is also considered in the selection process.

Financial data Stipends range from $1,000 to $5,000 per academic year, depending on the availability of funds and the recipient's unmet financial need.

Duration 1 year; may be renewed up to 1 additional year for master's degree students; up to 2 additional years for M.F.A. students; up to 3 additional years for doctoral degree students; up to 3 additional years for medicine, osteopathic medicine, dentistry, chiropractic, or veterinary degree students; or up to 2 additional years for law degree students.

Additional information This program is funded by the U.S. Bureau of Indian Affairs.

Number awarded More than 400 each year; a total of $1.2 million is available for this program annually.

Deadline May of each year.

[712]
AIGC LOAN FOR SERVICE

American Indian Graduate Center
Attn: Executive Director
3701 San Mateo Boulevard, N.E., Suite 200
Albuquerque, NM 87110-1249
(505) 881-4584   Toll Free: (800) 628-1920
Fax: (505) 884-0427   E-mail: fellowships@aigc.com
Web: www.aigcs.org/scholarships/graduate-fellowships

Summary To provide loans-for-service to Native American students interested in completing a graduate degree in any field and working for organizations affiliated with the Bureau of Indian Affairs (BIA) or tribal governments.

Eligibility This program is open to enrolled members of federally-recognized American Indian tribes and Alaska Native groups and other students who can document one-fourth degree federally-recognized Indian blood. Applicants must be enrolled as full-time students in a graduate or professional school in the United States working on a master's, doctoral, or professional degree in any field. They must have a GPA of 3.0 or higher. Along with their application, they must submit a 500-word statement on how their selected major will apply to the intent of this program as it applies to their personal commitment to serve the American Indian and Alaska Native community. Selection is based on that statement, academic achievement, and financial need.

Financial data Loans are based on each applicant's unmet financial need. No interest is charged. Loan repayment may be canceled at the rate of 1 year of loan payment for 1 year of employment with the BIA, the Bureau of Indian Education, a BIA-funded organization (on or off a reservation), or a tribal government.

Duration 1 year; may be renewed up to 1 additional year for master's degree students; up to 2 additional years for M.F.A. students; up to 3 additional years for doctoral degree students; up to 3 additional years for medicine, osteopathic medicine, dentistry, chiropractic, or veterinary degree students; or up to 2 additional years for law degree students.

Number awarded Varies each year.

Deadline May of each year.

[713]
AINTA SCHOLARSHIPS

American Indian Alaska Native Tourism Association
Attn: Scholarship Program
2401 12th Street N.W.
Albuquerque, NM 87104
(505) 724-3592   Fax: (505) 212-7023
E-mail: sbowman@aianta.org
Web: www.aianta.org/Education_and_Training.aspx

Summary To provide financial assistance to Native American students preparing for a career in the tourism industry.

Eligibility This program is open to students of American Indian, Native Hawaiian, or Alaska Native heritage who can document their ancestry. Applicants must be enrolled or planning to full or part time at a 2- or 4-year college, university, or vocational/technical school with a concentration in hospitality, tourism, recreation, or culinary arts. They may be working on a certificate, associate, bachelor's, or master's degree and have a GPA of 2.5 or higher. Along with their application, they must submit a 500-word essay about themselves, including information on any special circumstances or obstacles they have had to overcome to attend college, why they have selected the hospitality/tourism field, their ultimate career goal, their service to their tribal community, any leadership or community service, and their financial need.

Financial data The stipend is $1,000 per year.

Duration 1 year; may be renewed, provided the recipient provides 12 volunteer hours to a tribe, national park, or public land institution.

Number awarded 3 each year.

Deadline July of each year for fall semester; December of each year for spring semester.

[714]
AISES INTEL SCHOLARSHIPS

American Indian Science and Engineering Society
Attn: Director of Membership and Communications
2305 Renard Place, S.E., Suite 200
Albuquerque, NM 87106
(505) 765-1052, ext. 110   Fax: (505) 765-5608
E-mail: lpaz@aises.org
Web: www.aises.org/scholoarships/intel-scholarship

Summary To provide financial assistance to members of the American Indian Science and Engineering Society (AISES) who are working on an undergraduate or graduate degree in a field of computer science or engineering.

Eligibility This program is open to AISES members who are full-time undergraduate or graduate students at an accredited 4-year college or university. Applicants must be American Indian tribal members, Alaskan Natives, or Native Hawaiians and have a Certificate of Degree of Indian or Alaska Native Blood (CDIB) showing at least 25% Native blood. They must have a GPA of 3.0 or higher and be working on a degree in computer science, computer engineering, electrical engineering, chemical engineering, or material science. Selection is based on academic performance, a personal statement, letters of recommendation, and activities (e.g., jobs, volunteer efforts, internships, extracurricular involvement, hobbies).

Financial data The stipend is $5,000 for undergraduates or $10,000 for graduate students.

Duration 1 year; nonrenewable.

Additional information This program is funded by Intel.

Number awarded Up to 5 each year.

Deadline April of each year.

[715]
ALABAMA INDIAN AFFAIRS COMMISSION SCHOLARSHIP

Alabama Indian Affairs Commission
771 South Lawrence Street, Suite 106
Montgomery, AL 36104-5005
(334) 240-0998   Toll Free: (800) 436-8261
Fax: (334) 240-3408   E-mail: aiac@att.net
Web: www.aiac.state.al.us/Prog_Scholarships.aspx

Summary To provide financial assistance to American Indians residing in Alabama and attending college in the state.

Eligibility This program is open to residents of Alabama who have been enrolled in a state- or federally-recognized Indian tribe for at least 3 years. Applicants must be attending or planning to attend an academic institution in the state. Special consideration is given to nursing, medical, veterinary, and pharmacy students, who may attend school in other states because of the limited availability of spaces in Alabama schools. Financial need is not considered in the selection process.

Financial data A stipend is awarded (amount not specified).

Duration 1 year; recipients may reapply.

Number awarded 1 or more each year.

Deadline April of each year.

[716]
ALASKA LIBRARY ASSOCIATION GENERAL GRADUATE LIBRARY STUDIES SCHOLARSHIP

Alaska Library Association
Attn: Scholarship Committee
c/o Alaska State Library
395 Whittier Street
Juneau, AK 99801
(907) 465-2916   Toll Free: (888) 820-4525
Fax: (907) 465-2151
E-mail: julie.neiderhauser@alaska.gov
Web: www.akla.org/scholarships

Summary To provide financial assistance to Alaskan Natives and other residents of Alaska who are interested in working on a graduate library degree at a school in any state and, upon graduation, working in a library in Alaska.

Eligibility This program is open to Alaska residents who have earned a bachelor's degree or higher from an accredited college or university. Applicants must be eligible for acceptance or currently enrolled in an accredited graduate degree program in any state in library and information science; on-site or distance education students during the academic year, semester, or quarter for which the scholarship is awarded; and willing to make a commitment to work in an Alaska library for at least 1 year after graduation as a paid employee or volunteer. Preference is given to applicants meeting the federal definition of Alaska Native ethnicity. Selection is based on financial need, demonstrated scholastic ability and writing skills, an essay on professional goals and objectives, and 3 letters of recommendation (at least 1 of which must be from a librarian).

Financial data   The stipend is $4,000.

Duration   1 year.

Number awarded   1 each year.

Deadline   January of each year.

[717]
ALBERT W. DENT STUDENT SCHOLARSHIP

American College of Healthcare Executives
Attn: Scholarship Committee
One North Franklin Street, Suite 1700
Chicago, IL 60606-3529
(312) 424-2800   Fax: (312) 424-0023
E-mail: contact@ache.org
Web: www.ache.org

Summary   To provide financial assistance to Native American and other minority graduate student members of the American College of Healthcare Executives (ACHE).

Eligibility   This program is open to ACHE student associates entering their final year of classroom work in a health care management master's degree program. Applicants must be minority students, enrolled full time, able to demonstrate financial need, and U.S. or Canadian citizens. Along with their application, they must submit an 1- to 2-page essay describing their leadership abilities and experiences, their community and volunteer involvement, their goals as a health care executive, and how this scholarship can help them achieve their career goals.

Financial data   The stipend is $5,000.

Duration   1 year.

Additional information   The program was established and named in honor of Dr. Albert W. Dent, the foundation's first African American fellow and president emeritus of Dillard University.

Number awarded   Varies each year; the sponsor awards up to 20 scholarships through this and its other scholarship program.

Deadline   March of each year.

[718]
ALEUT FOUNDATION GRADUATE SCHOLARSHIPS

The Aleut Corporation
Attn: Aleut Foundation
703 West Tudor Road, Suite 102
Anchorage, AK 99503-6650
(907) 646-1929   Toll Free: (800) 232-4882
Fax: (907) 646-1949   E-mail: taf@thealeutfoundation.org
Web: www.thealeutfoundation.org

Summary   To provide financial assistance to Native Alaskans who are shareholders of The Aleut Corporation or their descendants and plan to attend graduate school in any state.

Eligibility   This program is open to Native Alaskans who are original enrollees or descendants of original enrollees of The Aleut Corporation (TAC). Applicants must be enrolled for at least 6 credit hours in a graduate degree program. They must have a GPA of 3.0 or higher. Along with their application,

they must include a letter of intent, up to 500 words in length, that describes their educational goals and objectives and their expected graduation date.

Financial data   The stipend is $3,000 per year.

Duration   1 year; may be renewed.

Additional information   The Aleut Corporation is 1 of 13 Alaska Native Regional Corporations created under the Alaska Native Claims Settlement Act of 1971. The foundation established this program in 2008.

Number awarded   Varies each year.

Deadline   June of each year for annual scholarships; November of each year for spring scholarships; April of each year for summer school.

[719]
ALEUT FOUNDATION PART-TIME SCHOLARSHIPS

The Aleut Corporation
Attn: Aleut Foundation
703 West Tudor Road, Suite 102
Anchorage, AK 99503-6650
(907) 646-1929   Toll Free: (800) 232-4882
Fax: (907) 646-1949   E-mail: taf@thealeutfoundation.org
Web: www.thealeutfoundation.org

Summary   To provide financial assistance for college or graduate school to Native Alaskans who are shareholders of The Aleut Corporation or their descendants and are enrolled part time.

Eligibility   This program is open to Native Alaskans who are original enrollees or descendants of original enrollees of The Aleut Corporation (TAC). Applicants must be enrolled in an associate, bachelor's, or higher degree program as a part-time student (at least 3 credit hours). They must have a GPA of 2.0 or higher. Along with their application, they must include a letter of intent, up to 500 words in length, that describes their educational goals and objectives and their expected graduation date.

Financial data   The stipend depends on the number of credit hours in the undergraduate or graduate program, to a maximum of $1,200 per year.

Duration   1 year.

Additional information   The Aleut Corporation is 1 of 13 Alaska Native Regional Corporations created under the Alaska Native Claims Settlement Act of 1971. The foundation began awarding scholarships in 1987.

Number awarded   Varies each year; recently, 2 were awarded.

Deadline   June of each year for annual scholarships; November of each year for spring scholarships; April of each year for summer school.

[720]
ALLAN R. BLOOMFIELD DIVERSITY SCHOLARSHIP

Allan R. Bloomfield
118-21 Queens Boulevard, Suite 617
Forest Hills, NY 11375
(718) 544-0500
Web: www.bankruptcyqueens.com/scholarship

Summary To provide financial assistance to Native Americans and members of other ethnic and racial minority groups who are attending law school.
Eligibility This program is open to ethnic and racial minorities who are currently enrolled full time in the first or second year of law school and contributing to the diversity of their student body. Applicants must be U.S. citizens or permanent residents and have a GPA of 3.0 or higher. Along with their application, they must submit a 1-page essay describing how they plan to utilize their law degree.
Financial data The stipend is $1,000.
Duration 1 year.
Number awarded 1 or more each year.
Deadline May of each year.

[721]
ALLOGAN SLAGLE MEMORIAL SCHOLARSHIP

Association on American Indian Affairs, Inc.
Attn: Director of Scholarship Programs
966 Hungerford Drive, Suite 12-B
Rockville, MD 20850
(240) 314-7155   Fax: (240) 314-7159
E-mail: general.aaia@indian-affairs.org
Web: www.indian-affairs.org

Summary To provide financial assistance for college or graduate school to Native American students whose tribe is not federally recognized.
Eligibility This program is open to American Indian and Native Alaskan full-time undergraduate and graduate students. Applicants must be members of tribes that are either state-recognized or that are not federally-recognized but are seeking federal recognition. Along with their application, they must submit proof of tribal enrollment and an essay of 2 to 3 pages on 1 of the following topics: 1) why the sponsor's International Repatriation Project is important and how they would inform others about it; 2) the Annie E. Casey Foundation's Juvenile Detention Alternatives Initiative and tribal and community-based alternatives to detention for juveniles; or 3) how tribal leaders can promote higher education in their family and community. They must have a GPA of 2.5 or higher. Selection is based on merit and need.
Financial data The stipend is $1,500.
Duration 1 year; recipients may reapply.
Number awarded Varies each year; recently, 7 were awarded.
Deadline May of each year.

[722]
AMA FOUNDATION MINORITY SCHOLARS AWARDS

American Medical Association
Attn: AMA Foundation
330 North Wabash Avenue, Suite 39300
Chicago, IL 60611-5885
(312) 464-5019   Fax: (312) 464-4142
E-mail: amafoundation@ama-assn.org
Web: www.ama-assn.org

Summary To provide financial assistance to medical school students who are Native Americans or members of other underrepresented minority groups.
Eligibility This program is open to first- and second-year medical students who are members of the following traditionally underrepresented groups in the medical profession: African American, American Indian, Native Hawaiian, Alaska Native, or Hispanic. Only nominations are accepted. Each medical school is invited to submit 2 nominees. U.S. citizenship or permanent resident status is required.
Financial data The stipend is $10,000.
Duration 1 year.
Additional information This program is offered by the AMA Foundation of the American Medical Association in collaboration with the Minority Affairs Consortium (MAC) and with support from the Pfizer Medical Humanities Initiative.
Number awarded Varies each year; recently, 20 were awarded.
Deadline March of each year.

[723]
AMAF VALUING DIVERSITY PH.D. SCHOLARSHIPS

American Marketing Association Foundation
Attn: Foundation Manager
311 South Wacker Drive, Suite 5800
Chicago, IL 60606
(312) 542-9015   Fax: (312) 542-9001
E-mail: jschnidman@ama.org
Web: www.themarketingfoundation.org

Summary To provide financial assistance to Native Americans and members of other underrepresented minority groups working on a doctoral degree in advertising or marketing.
Eligibility This program is open to African Americans, Hispanics, and Native Americans who have completed at least 1 year of a full-time Ph.D. program in advertising or marketing. Applicants must submit an essay that explains how receiving this scholarship will help them further their research efforts, including information on 1 of the following: 1) how their dissertation research incorporates conceptual, design, or methods issues related to diversity; 2) how their dissertation research contributes to advancing the field of marketing; or 3) how their dissertation research incorporates any innovative theories or advanced, cutting-edge designs, methods, or approaches. They must be U.S. citizens or permanent residents.
Financial data The stipend is $1,000.
Duration 1 year; recipients may reapply.
Additional information This program began in 2003.
Number awarded Varies each year; recently, 5 were awarded.
Deadline April of each year.

[724]
AMELIA KEMP MEMORIAL SCHOLARSHIP

Women of the Evangelical Lutheran Church in America
Attn: Scholarships
8765 West Higgins Road
Chicago, IL 60631-4101
(773) 380-2741   Toll Free: (800) 638-3522, ext. 2741
Fax: (773) 380-2419   E-mail: valora.starr@elca.org
Web: www.womenoftheelca.org

Summary To provide financial assistance to Native American and other lay women of color who are members of Evangelical Lutheran Church of America (ELCA) congregations and who wish to study on the undergraduate, graduate, professional, or vocational school level.

Eligibility This program is open to ELCA lay women of color who are at least 21 years of age and have experienced an interruption of at least 2 years in their education since high school. Applicants must have been admitted to an educational institution to prepare for a career in other than ordained ministry. U.S. citizenship is required.

Financial data The maximum stipend is $1,000 per year.

Duration 1 year; recipients may reapply for 1 additional year.

Number awarded 1 or more each year.

Deadline February of each year.

[725]
AMERICAN ANTHROPOLOGICAL ASSOCIATION MINORITY DISSERTATION FELLOWSHIP PROGRAM

American Anthropological Association
Attn: Committee on Minority Issues in Anthropology
2300 Clarendon Boulevard, Suite 1301
Arlington, VA 22201
(703) 528-1902   Fax: (703) 528-3546
E-mail: arussell@aaanet.org
Web: www.aaanet.org/cmtes/minority/Minfellow.cfm

Summary To provide funding to Native Americans and other minorities who are working on a Ph.D. dissertation in anthropology.

Eligibility This program is open to Native American, African American, Latino(a), Pacific Islander, and Asian American doctoral students who have been admitted to degree candidacy in anthropology. Applicants must be U.S. citizens, enrolled in a full-time academic program leading to a doctoral degree in anthropology, and members of the American Anthropological Association. They must have a record of outstanding academic success, have had their dissertation proposal approved by their dissertation committee prior to application, be writing a dissertation in an area of anthropological research, and need funding to complete the dissertation. Along with their application, they must submit a cover letter, a research plan summary, a curriculum vitae, a statement regarding employment, a disclosure statement providing information about other sources of available and pending financial support, 3 letters of recommendation, and an official transcript from their doctoral program. Selection is based on the quality of the submitted information and the judged likelihood that the applicant will have a good chance of completing the dissertation.

Financial data The grant is $10,000. Funds are sent in 2 installments (in September and in January) directly to the recipient.

Duration 1 year; nonrenewable.

Number awarded 1 each year.

Deadline February of each year.

[726]
AMERICAN BAR ASSOCIATION LEGAL OPPORTUNITY SCHOLARSHIP

American Bar Association
Attn: Fund for Justice and Education
321 North Clark Street, 21st Floor
Chicago, IL 60654-7598
(312) 988-5927   Fax: (312) 988-6392
E-mail: legalosf@staff.abanet.org
Web: www.americanbar.org

Summary To provide financial assistance to Native American and other racial and ethnic minority students who are interested in attending law school.

Eligibility This program is open to racial and ethnic minority college graduates who are interested in attending an ABA-accredited law school. Only students beginning law school may apply; students who have completed 1 or more semesters of law school are not eligible. Applicants must have a cumulative GPA of 2.5 or higher and be citizens or permanent residents of the United States. Along with their application, they must submit a 1,000-word statement describing their personal and family background, community service activities, and other connections to their racial and ethnic minority community. Financial need is also considered in the selection process.

Financial data The stipend is $5,000 per year.

Duration 1 year; may be renewed for 2 additional years if satisfactory performance in law school has been achieved.

Additional information This program began in the 2000-01 academic year.

Number awarded Approximately 20 each year.

Deadline February of each year.

[727]
AMERICAN EDUCATIONAL RESEARCH ASSOCIATION DISSERTATION GRANTS PROGRAM

American Educational Research Association
Attn: Grants Program
1430 K Street, N.W., Suite 1200
Washington, DC 20005
(202) 238-3200   Fax: (202) 238-3250
E-mail: grantsprogram@aera.net
Web: www.aera.net

Summary To provide funding to Native American and other underrepresented doctoral students writing their dissertation on educational policy.

Eligibility This program is open to advanced graduate students who are writing their dissertations in such disciplines as (but not limited to) education, sociology, economics, psychology, demography, statistics, or psychometrics. Applicants may be U.S. citizens, U.S. permanent residents, or non-U.S. citizens working at a U.S. institution. Underrepresented ethnic and racial minority researchers are strongly encouraged to apply. Dissertation topics may cover a wide range of policy-related issues, but priority is given to proposals that 1) develop or benefit from new quantitative measures or methodological approaches for addressing education issues; 2) incorporate subject matter expertise, especially when studying science, technology, engineering, or mathematics (STEM) learning; 3) analyze TIMSS, PISA, or other international data resources; or 4) include the integration and analysis of more than 1 data set. The research project must include the analysis of data from at least 1 of the large-scale nationally or internationally representative data sets, such as those of the National Science Foundation (NSF), National Center for Education Statistics (NCES), Department of Labor, Census Bureau, or National Institutes of Health (NIH). Selection is based on the importance of the proposed policy issue, strength of the methodological model and proposed statistical analysis of the study, and relevant experience or research record of the applicant.

Financial data The maximum grant is $20,000 per year. No support is provided for indirect costs to institutions. Funding is linked to approval of the recipient's progress report and final report. Grantees receive one-third of the total award at the beginning of the grant period, one-third upon acceptance of the progress report, and one-third upon acceptance of the final report. Funds can be sent either to the recipients or to their institutions.

Duration 1 year; nonrenewable.

Additional information Funding for this program is provided by the NSF. Grantees must submit a brief (3 to 6 pages) progress report midway through the grant period. A final report must be submitted at the end of the grant period. The final report may be either an article suitable for publication in a scholarly journal or a copy of the dissertation.

Number awarded Approximately 15 each year.

Deadline March or September of each year.

[728]
AMERICAN EDUCATIONAL RESEARCH ASSOCIATION MINORITY FELLOWSHIPS IN EDUCATION RESEARCH

American Educational Research Association
Attn: Fellowships Program
1430 K Street, N.W., Suite 1200
Washington, DC 20005
(202) 238-3200   Fax: (202) 238-3250
E-mail: fellowships@aera.net
Web: www.aera.net

Summary To provide funding to Native American and other minority doctoral students writing their dissertation on educational research.

Eligibility This program is open to U.S. citizens and permanent residents who have advanced to candidacy and successfully defended their Ph.D./Ed.D. dissertation research proposal. Applicants must plan to work full time on their dissertation in educational research, the humanities, or social or behavioral science disciplinary or interdisciplinary fields, such as economics, political science, psychology, or sociology. This program is targeted for members of groups historically underrepresented in higher education (African Americans, American Indians, Alaskan Natives, Asian Americans, Native Hawaiian or Pacific Islanders, and Hispanics or Latinos). Selection is based on scholarly achievements and publications, letters of recommendation, quality and significance of the proposed research, and commitment of the applicant's faculty mentor to the goals of the program.

Financial data The grant is $20,000, including up to $1,000 for travel to the sponsor's annual conference.

Duration 1 year; nonrenewable.

Additional information This program began in 1991.

Number awarded Up to 3 each year.

Deadline October of each year.

[729]
AMERICAN EPILEPSY SOCIETY PREDOCTORAL RESEARCH FELLOWSHIPS

American Epilepsy Society
135 South LaSalle Street, Suite 2850
Chicago, IL 60603
(312) 883-3800   Fax: (312) 896-5784
E-mail: info@aesnet.org
Web: www.aesnet.org

Summary To provide funding to Native American and other underrepresented doctoral candidates who are interested in conducting dissertation research related to epilepsy.

Eligibility This program is open full-time doctoral students conducting dissertation research with an epilepsy-related theme under the guidance of a mentor with expertise in epilepsy research. Applicants must have a defined research plan and access to institutional resources to conduct the proposed project. Selection is based on the applicant's potential and commitment to develop as an independent and productive epilepsy researcher, academic record, and research experience; the mentor's research qualifications; the research training plan; and the quality of the research facilities, resources, and training opportunities. Applications are especially encouraged from women, members of minority groups, and people with disabilities. U.S. citizenship is not required, but all research must be conducted in the United States.

Financial data Grants range up $30,000, including $29,000 as stipend and $1,000 for travel support and complimentary registration to attend the sponsor's annual meeting.

Duration 1 year; nonrenewable.

Additional information In addition to the funding provided by the American Epilepsy Society, support is available from the TESS Research Foundation for applications focused on epilepsy due to SLC13A5 mutations; the LGS Foundation for applications focused on Lennox-Gastaut-Syndrome; the PCDH19 Alliance for applications focused on epilepsy due to PCDH19 mutations; the Dravet Syndrome Foundation for applications focused on Dravet Syndrome; Wishes for Elliott for applications focused on epilepsy due to SCN8A mutations; and the TS Alliance for applications focused on epilepsy associated with tuberous sclerosis complex (TSC).

Number awarded Varies each year.

Deadline Letters of intent must be submitted by October of each year; final proposals are due in January.

[730]
AMERICAN INDIAN CHAMBER OF COMMERCE OF CALIFORNIA SCHOLARSHIP

American Indian Chamber of Commerce of California
Attn: AICC Scholarship
555 West Fifth Street, 31st Floor
Los Angeles, CA 90013
(213) 440-3232   E-mail: stateadmin@aicccal.org
Web: www.aicccal.org/scholar_forms/default.html

Summary To provide financial assistance for college or graduate school to American Indians who live or attend school in California.

Eligibility This program is open to American Indians who 1) are on a federal- or state-recognized tribal roll and identified by a tribal enrollment card; or 2) have an official letter from a federal- or state-recognized tribe or agency verifying tribal membership or Indian blood. Applicants must be full-time degree candidates at an accredited institution of higher learning (junior college, trade/vocational school, 4-year university, graduate school) in California or residents of California attending an institution of higher learning elsewhere in the United States. Along with their application, they must submit an educational commitment essay describing their chosen field of study, educational goals, career goals, involvement in the Indian community, and how this scholarship will help in furthering their education. Selection is based on transcripts (30 points), a letter of recommendation (20 points), the educational commitment essay (50 points), and major chosen (bonus 10 points if majoring in business).

Financial data Stipends are $2,500 or $1,500.

Duration 1 year.

Additional information This program began in 1999.

Number awarded 6 each year: 1 at $2,500 and up to 5 at $1,500.

Deadline November of each year.

[731]
AMERICAN INDIAN CHAMBER OF COMMERCE OF WISCONSIN SCHOLARSHIPS

American Indian Chamber of Commerce of Wisconsin, Inc.
Attn: Scholarship Program
10809 West Lincoln Avenue, Suite 102
West Allis, WI 53227
(414) 604-2044   Toll Free: (877) 603-2044
Fax: (414) 604-2070   E-mail: beverly@aiccw.org
Web: www.aiccw.org/welcome/scholarship-program

Summary To provide financial assistance to American Indian students from Wisconsin who are interested in attending college or graduate school in any state.

Eligibility This program is open to residents of Wisconsin who can provide proof of enrollment in an American Indian tribe by at least 1 parent. Applicants must be enrolled full time at a 4-year college or university or graduate school in any state and have a GPA of 3.0 or higher. Along with their application, they must submit a 1-page statement on their personal background, their academic background, their educational and career goals, any hardships or obstacles they have overcome, and how this scholarship will help them to achieve their goals. Selection is based on academic achievement and financial need.

Financial data The stipend ranges from $1,000 to $2,500.

Duration 1 year.

Additional information This program began in 2005.

Number awarded 1 or more each year; since the program began, it has awarded more than $300,000 to 154 students.

Deadline June of each year.

[732]
AMERICAN INDIAN EDUCATION FUND GRADUATE SCHOLARSHIPS

American Indian Education Fund
2401 Eglin Street
Rapid City, SD 57703
Toll Free: (866) 866-8642
E-mail: rschad@nativepartnership.org
Web: www.nrcprograms.org

Summary To provide financial assistance for graduate school to American Indian, Alaskan Native, and Native Hawaiian students.

Eligibility This program is open to students of Native American, Alaskan Native, or Native Hawaiian descent who are currently enrolled in between 6 and 18 credits in a master's or doctoral degree program. Students enrolled in online courses or at the ABD (all but dissertation) level are not eligible. Applicants should have a GPA between 2.5 and 3.5. Along with their application, they must submit a 500-word statement that includes why they should receive this scholarship, their most significant accomplishments and contributions, the impact of their selected studies or research, their financial need, and their tribal affiliation.

Financial data The stipend ranges from $1,000 to $2,000 per year. Funds are paid directly to the recipient's institution.

Duration 1 year; may be renewed.

Additional information The American Indian Education Fund, formerly the American Indian Education Foundation, is a component of Partnership with Native Americans, formerly National Relief Charities.

Number awarded Varies each year.

Deadline April of each year.

[733]
AMERICAN INDIAN FELLOWSHIP IN BUSINESS SCHOLARSHIP

National Center for American Indian Enterprise Development
Attn: Scholarship Committee
953 East Juanita Avenue
Mesa, AZ 85204
Toll Free: (800) 462-2433, ext. 250   Fax: (480) 545-4208
E-mail: scholarships@ncaied.org
Web: www.ncaied.org/programs/scholarships

Summary To provide financial assistance to American Indians and Alaska Natives working on a bachelor's or master's degree in business.

Eligibility This program is open to enrolled members of American Indian tribes and Alaska Native villages. Applicants must be enrolled full time as a junior, senior, or master's degree student in business at a college or university in the United States. Along with their application, they must submit 3 essays of 150 to 250 words each on their community involvement, personal challenges, or business experience (paid or volunteer). Selection is based on the quality of those essays (5%), grades (30%), community involvement (30%), personal challenges (25%), and business experience (10%).

Financial data A stipend is awarded (amount not specified).

Duration 1 year.

Additional information Recipients must attend the sponsor's annual conference, named Reservation Economic Summit (RES Oklahoma), in association with the Indian Progress in Business (INPRO) Event in Tulsa in November. The sponsor will pay all expenses of attending, including lodging, ground transportation, and airfare. Students who are unable to attend must forfeit their scholarship.

Number awarded Varies each year; recently, 10 were awarded.

Deadline September of each year.

[734]
AMERICAN INDIAN LAW REVIEW WRITING COMPETITION

American Indian Law Review
Attn: Editorial Advisor
University of Oklahoma Law Center
Andrew M. Coats Hall
300 Timberdell Road
Norman, OK 73019-0701
(405) 325-5191   Fax: (405) 325-6282
E-mail: mwaters@ou.edu
Web: www.law.ou.edu/content/writing-competition-1

Summary To recognize and reward outstanding unpublished papers written by law students on American Indian law.

Eligibility This competition is open to students at accredited law schools in the United States or Canada. They may submit an unpublished paper (from 20 to 50 pages in length) on any issue concerning American Indian law (although topics recently published in the *American Indian Law Review* are not encouraged). Selection is based on originality and timeliness of topic, knowledge and use of applicable legal principles, proper and articulate analysis of the issues, use of authorities, extent of research, logic and reasoning in analysis, ingenuity and ability to argue by analogy, clarity and organization, correctness of format and citations, grammar and writing style, and strength and logic of conclusions.

Financial data First prize is $1,000 and publication of the paper in the *American Indian Law Review*. Second prize is $500. Third prize is $250.

Duration The competition is held annually.

Number awarded 3 each year.

Deadline January of each year.

[735]
AMERICAN INDIAN NURSE SCHOLARSHIP PROGRAM

National Society of the Colonial Dames of America
c/o Dumbarton House
2715 Q Street, N.W.
Washington, DC 20007-3071
(202) 337-2288   Fax: (202) 337-0348
Web: www.nscda.org

Summary To provide financial assistance to American Indians interested in preparing for a career in nursing.

Eligibility This program is open to American Indians who are high school graduates (or the equivalent) and enrolled full time in a nursing program at an accredited school. Applicants must have maintained the scholastic average required by their school, be recommended by their counselor or school officer, not be receiving an Indian Health Service Scholarship,

have a career goal directly related to the needs of the Indian people, and be in financial need. They must expect to graduate within 2 years if in an associate degree program or within 4 years if in a bachelor's degree program; graduate students are also eligible.

Financial data The stipend is $1,500 per semester ($3,000 per year). Funds are to be used for tuition or fees. The money is sent directly to the recipient's school.

Duration 1 semester; those students who continue to meet the eligibility requirements and have been recommended for continuation are given priority consideration for additional periods of support.

Additional information This program began in 1928.

Number awarded 10 to 15 each year.

Deadline May of each year for fall; November of each year for spring.

[736]
AMERICAN INDIAN SCHOLARSHIPS

Daughters of the American Revolution-National Society
Attn: Committee Services Office, Scholarships
1776 D Street, N.W.
Washington, DC 20006-5303
(202) 628-1776
Web: www.dar.org

Summary To provide supplementary financial assistance to Native American students who are interested in working on an undergraduate or graduate degree.

Eligibility This program is open to Native Americans of any age, any tribe, in any state who are enrolled or planning to enroll in a college, university, or vocational school. Applicants must have a GPA of 3.25 or higher. Graduate students are eligible, but undergraduate students receive preference. Selection is based on academic achievement and financial need.

Financial data The stipend is $4,000. The funds are paid directly to the recipient's college.

Duration 1 year; nonrenewable.

Number awarded 1 each year.

Deadline February of each year.

[737]
AMERICAN INDIAN SCIENCE AND ENGINEERING SOCIETY INTERNSHIP PROGRAM

American Indian Science and Engineering Society
Attn: Director of Membership and Communications
2305 Renard Place, S.E., Suite 200
Albuquerque, NM 87106
(505) 765-1052, ext. 110   Fax: (505) 765-5608
E-mail: lpaz@aises.org
Web: www.aises.org/scholarships/internships

Summary To provide summer work experience with federal agencies or other partner organizations to American Indian and Alaska Native college students who are members of the American Indian Science and Engineering Society (AISES).

Eligibility This program is open to AISES members who are full-time college or university sophomores, juniors, seniors, or graduate students with a GPA of 3.0 or higher. Applicants must be American Indians or Alaska Natives interested in working at selected sites with a partner organization. They must submit an application that includes an essay on their reasons for participating in the program, how it relates to their academic and career goals, what makes them a strong candidate for the program, what they hope to learn and gain as a result, and their leadership skills and experience. U.S. citizenship is required for most positions, although permanent residents may be eligible at some agencies.

Financial data Interns receive a weekly stipend of $550, dormitory lodging, round-trip airfare or mileage to the internship site, and a weekly allowance of $70 for local transportation.

Duration 10 weeks during the summer.

Additional information Recently, internships were available at the Bonneville Power Administration (in Vancouver and Cle Elum, Washington), the U.S. Bureau of Land Management (in Arizona), the U.S. Department of Veterans Affairs (in Washington, D.C.), and the U.S. Department of Agriculture Food Safety and Inspection Services (in Washington, D.C.).

Number awarded Varies each year.

Deadline February of each year.

[738]
AMERICAN NURSES ASSOCIATION MINORITY FELLOWSHIP PROGRAM

American Nurses Association
Attn: SAMHSA Minority Fellowship Programs
8515 Georgia Avenue, Suite 400
Silver Spring, MD 20910-3492
(301) 628-5247   Toll Free: (800) 274-4ANA
Fax: (301) 628-5339 E-mail: janet.jackson@ana.org
Web: www.emfp.org

Summary To provide financial assistance to Native American and other minority nurses who are doctoral candidates interested in psychiatric, mental health, and substance abuse issues that impact the lives of ethnic minority people.

Eligibility This program is open to nurses who have a master's degree and are members of an ethnic or racial minority group, including but not limited to Blacks or African Americans, Hispanics or Latinos, American Indians and Alaska Natives, Asians and Asian Americans, and Native Hawaiians and other Pacific Islanders. Applicants must be enrolled full time in an accredited doctoral nursing program. They must be certified as a Mental Health Nurse Practitioner, Mental Health Clinical Nurse Specialist, or Mental Health Nurse. U.S. citizenship or permanent resident status and membership in the American Nurses Association are required. Selection is based on commitment to a career in substance abuse in psychiatric/mental health issues affecting minority populations.

Financial data The program provides an annual stipend of $22,476 and tuition assistance up to $5,000.

Duration 3 to 5 years.

Additional information Funds for this program are provided by the Substance Abuse and Mental Health Services Administration (SAMHSA).

Number awarded 1 or more each year.

Deadline March of each year.

[739]
AMERICAN NURSES ASSOCIATION MINORITY FELLOWSHIP PROGRAM YOUTH

American Nurses Association
Attn: SAMHSA Minority Fellowship Programs
8515 Georgia Avenue, Suite 400
Silver Spring, MD 20910-3492
(301) 628-5247   Toll Free: (800) 274-4ANA
Fax: (301) 628-5339 E-mail: janet.jackson@ana.org
Web: www.emfp.org

Summary To provide financial assistance to Native American and other minority nurses who are interested in working on a master's degree in psychiatric/mental health nursing for service to young people.

Eligibility This program is open to nurses who are members of the American Nurses Association and members of an ethnic or racial minority group, including but not limited to Blacks or African Americans, Hispanics or Latinos, American Indians and Alaska Natives, Asians and Asian Americans, and Native Hawaiians and other Pacific Islanders. Applicants must be enrolled full time in an accredited master's degree behavioral health (psychiatric/mental health/substance abuse) nursing program. They must intend to apply for certification to become a Psychiatric Mental Health Nurse Practitioners, a fellowship-approved certification in substance abuse, or another sub-specialty that is associated with behavioral health services for children, adolescents, and youth transitioning into adulthood (ages 16 through 25). U.S. citizenship or permanent resident status is required. Selection is based on commitment to a career that provides behavioral health services to young people.

Financial data The stipend is $11,500 per year. Funds are disbursed directly to the fellow.

Duration 1 year; may be renewed.

Additional information Funds for this program are provided by the Substance Abuse and Mental Health Services Administration (SAMHSA).

Number awarded 1 or more each year.

Deadline March of each year.

[740]
AMERICAN POLITICAL SCIENCE ASSOCIATION MINORITY FELLOWS PROGRAM

American Political Science Association
Attn: Diversity and Inclusion Programs
1527 New Hampshire Avenue, N.W.
Washington, DC 20036-1206
(202) 349-9362   Fax: (202) 483-2657
E-mail: kmealy@apsanet.org
Web: www.apsanet.org/mfp

Summary To provide financial assistance to Native American and other underrepresented minorities interested in working on a doctoral degree in political science.

Eligibility This program is open to African Americans, Asian Pacific Americans, Latino(a)s, and Native Americans who are in their senior year at a college or university or currently enrolled in a master's degree program. Applicants must be planning to enroll in a doctoral program in political science to prepare for a career in teaching and research. They must be U.S. citizens and able to demonstrate financial need. Along with their application, they must submit a 500-word personal statement that includes why they are interested in attending graduate school in political science, what specific fields within the discipline they plan to study, and how they intend to contribute to research within the discipline. Selection is based on interest in teaching and potential for research in political science.

Financial data The stipend is $2,000 per year.

Duration 2 years.

Additional information In addition to the fellows who receive stipends from this program, students who are selected as fellows without stipend are recommended for admission and financial support to every doctoral political science program in the country. This program was established in 1969.

Number awarded Up to 12 fellows receive stipends each year.

Deadline March or October of each year.

[741]
AMERICAN SOCIETY OF HEMATOLOGY MINORITY GRADUATE STUDENT ABSTRACT ACHIEVEMENT AWARD

American Society of Hematology
Attn: Awards Manager
2021 L Street, N.W., Suite 900
Washington, DC 20036
(202) 776-0544   Fax: (202) 776-0545
E-mail: awards@hematology.org
Web: www.hematology.org

Summary To recognize and reward Native American and other underrepresented minority graduate students who present outstanding abstracts at the annual meeting of the American Society of Hematology (ASH).

Eligibility This award is available to students who are enrolled in the first 3 years of work on a Ph.D. in the field of hematology and submit an abstract to the annual ASH meeting that is accepted for oral or poster presentation. Applicants must be a member of a racial or ethnic group that has been shown to be underrepresented in health-related sciences in the United States and Canada, including American Indians, Alaska Natives, Blacks or African Americans, Hispanics or Latinos, Native Hawaiians, other Pacific Islanders, African Canadians, Inuit, and First Nation Peoples. They must be working under the direction of an ASH member.

Financial data The award is $1,500.

Duration The award is presented annually.

Number awarded Varies each year; recently, 4 were presented.

Deadline The deadline for applying for these awards is the same as that for submitting abstracts for the annual meeting. Usually, that date is in early August.

[742]
AMERICAN SPEECH-LANGUAGE-HEARING FOUNDATION SCHOLARSHIP FOR MINORITY STUDENTS

American Speech-Language-Hearing Foundation
Attn: Programs Administrator
2200 Research Boulevard
Rockville, MD 20850-3289
(301) 296-8703   Toll Free: (800) 498-2071, ext. 8703
Fax: (301) 296-8567
E-mail: foundationprograms@asha.org
Web: www.ashfoundation.org

Summary To provide financial assistance to Native American and other minority graduate students in communication sciences and disorders programs.

Eligibility This program is open to full-time graduate students who are enrolled in communication sciences and disorders programs, with preference given to U.S. citizens who are members of a racial or ethnic minority group. Applicants must submit an essay, up to 5 pages in length, on a topic that relates to the future of leadership in the discipline. Selection is based on academic promise and outstanding academic achievement.

Financial data The stipend is $5,000. Funds must be used for educational support (e.g., tuition, books, school living expenses), not for personal or conference travel.

Duration 1 year.

Number awarded Up to 3 each year.

Deadline May of each year.

[743]
AMERICAN THEOLOGICAL LIBRARY ASSOCIATION DIVERSITY SCHOLARSHIP

American Theological Library Association
Attn: Diversity Committee
300 South Wacker Drive, Suite 2100
Chicago, IL 60606-6701
(312) 454-5100   Toll Free: (888) 665-ATLA
Fax: (312) 454-5505   E-mail: memberrep@atla.com
Web: www.atla.com

Summary To provide funding to library students from Native American and other underrepresented groups who are members of the American Theological Library Association (ATLA) interested in working on a master's degree in theological librarianship.

Eligibility This program is open to ATLA members from underrepresented groups (religious, racial, ethnic, or gender) who are enrolled at an ALA-accredited master's degree program in library and information studies. Applicants must submit personal statements on what diversity means to them, why their voice has not yet been heard, how they will increase diversity in their immediate context, and how they plan to increase diversity and participate fully in the ATLA.

Financial data The stipend is $2,400.

Duration 1 year.

Number awarded 1 each year.

Deadline April of each year.

[744]
AMS GRADUATE FELLOWSHIPS

American Meteorological Society
Attn: Development and Student Program Manager
45 Beacon Street
Boston, MA 02108-3693
(617) 227-2426, ext. 3907   Fax: (617) 742-8718
E-mail: dFernandez@ametsoc.org
Web: www2.ametsoc.org

Summary   To encourage Native American and other under-represented students entering their first year of graduate school to work on an advanced degree in the atmospheric and related oceanic and hydrologic sciences.

Eligibility   This program is open to students entering their first year of graduate study and planning to work on an advanced degree in the atmospheric or related oceanic or hydrologic sciences. Applicants must be U.S. citizens or permanent residents and have a GPA of 3.25 or higher. Along with their application, they must submit 200-word essays on 1) their most important achievements that qualify them for this scholarship; and 2) their career goals in the atmospheric or related sciences. Selection is based on academic record as an undergraduate. The sponsor specifically encourages applications from women, minorities, and students with disabilities who are traditionally underrepresented in the atmospheric and related sciences.

Financial data   The stipend is $25,000 per academic year.

Duration   9 months.

Additional information   This program was initiated in 1991. It is funded by high-technology firms and government agencies.

Number awarded   Varies each year; recently, 8 were awarded.

Deadline   January of each year.

[745]
AMY HUNTER-WILSON, M.D. MEMORIAL SCHOLARSHIP

Wisconsin Medical Society
Attn: Wisconsin Medical Society Foundation
330 East Lakeside Street
Madison, WI 53715
(608) 442-3789   Toll Free: (866) 442-3800, ext. 3789
Fax: (608) 442-3802 E-mail: elizabeth.ringle@wismed.org
Web: www.wisconsinmedicalsociety.org

Summary   To provide financial assistance to American Indians interested in working on a degree in medicine, nursing, or allied health care.

Eligibility   This program is open to members of federally-recognized American Indian tribes who are 1) full-time students enrolled in a health career program at an accredited institution; 2) adults returning to school in an allied health field; and 3) adults working in a non-professional health-related field returning for a professional license or degree. Applicants must be working on a degree or advanced training as a doctor of medicine, nurse, physician assistant, technician, or other health-related professional. Along with their application, they must submit a personal statement of 1 to 2 pages on their family background, achievements, current higher educational status, career goals, and financial need. Preference is given to residents of Wisconsin who are students at educational institutions in the state. U.S. citizenship

is required. Selection is based on financial need, academic achievement, personal qualities and strengths, and letters of recommendation.

Financial data   Stipends range from $2,000 to $4,000.

Duration   1 year.

Number awarded   Varies each year; recently, 1 at $4,000, 1 at $2,500, and 2 at $2,000 each were awarded.

Deadline   January of each year.

[746]
ANDREW GRONHOLDT SCHOLARSHIP AWARD

The Aleut Corporation
Attn: Aleut Foundation
703 West Tudor Road, Suite 102
Anchorage, AK 99503-6650
(907) 646-1929   Toll Free: (800) 232-4882
Fax: (907) 646-1949   E-mail: taf@thealeutfoundation.org
Web: www.thealeutfoundation.org

Summary   To provide financial assistance to Native Alaskans who are shareholders of The Aleut Corporation or their descendants and working on a degree in the arts at a school in any state.

Eligibility   This program is open to Native Alaskans who are original enrollees or descendants of original enrollees of The Aleut Corporation (TAC). Applicants must have completed at least 1 year of a bachelor's, 2- or 4-year vocational, or master's degree in the arts at a school in any state. They must be enrolled full time and have a GPA of 3.0 or higher. Along with their application, they must include a letter of intent, up to 500 words in length, that describes their educational goals and objectives and their expected graduation date.

Financial data   A stipend is awarded (amount not specified).

Duration   1 year.

Additional information   The Aleut Corporation is 1 of 13 Alaska Native Regional Corporations created under the Alaska Native Claims Settlement Act of 1971.

Number awarded   1 each year.

Deadline   June of each year.

[747]
ANDREW W. MELLON INTERNSHIPS AT THE NATIONAL MUSEUM OF THE AMERICAN INDIAN

National Museum of the American Indian
Attn: Conservation Office
Cultural Resources Center
4220 Silver Hill Road, MRC 538
Suitland, MD 20746-2863
(301) 238-1424   Fax: (301) 238-3201
E-mail: NMAIcrcconserv@si.edu
Web: www.nmai.si.edu

Summary   To provide graduate students and professionals involved in conservation of museum collections with an opportunity to participate in an internship at the Smithsonian Institution's National Museum of the American Indian (NMAI).

Eligibility   This program is open to 1) students who are currently enrolled in or have recently completed graduate degree programs in conservation; and 2) practicing conservation professionals. of recognized conservation training programs. Applicants must be interested in an internship at the NMAI

Cultural Resources Center in Suitland, Maryland to cultivate practical skills and foster an understanding of the contexts of material culture, the philosophies of conservation of the NMAI, and the ethics of the conservation profession. The program involves collaboration with Native people in developing appropriate methods of caring for and interpreting cultural materials. Candidates who demonstrate a career interest in the conservation of material culture of the indigenous peoples of North, Central, and South America are especially welcome. Proficiency in English is required.

Financial data Interns receive a stipend (amount not specified).

Duration 10 weeks, beginning in June.

Number awarded Varies each year.

Deadline January of each year.

[748]
ANN EUBANK HEALTH SCHOLARSHIP

Chickasaw Foundation
2020 Arlington, Suite 4
P.O. Box 1726
Ada, OK 74821-1726
(580) 421-9030   Fax: (580) 421-9031
E-mail: ChickasawFoundation@chickasaw.net
Web: www.chickasawfoundation.org/Scholarships.aspx

Summary To provide financial assistance to members of the Chickasaw Nation who are working or an undergraduate or graduate degree in a health care field.

Eligibility This program is open to Chickasaw students who are currently working full time on an undergraduate or graduate degree in a health care-related field. Applicants must have a GPA of 3.0 or higher. They must submit 2 letters of recommendation; a copy of their Chickasaw Nation citizenship card; official high school or college transcripts; ACT or SAT scores; a 2-page list of honors, achievements, awards, club memberships, societies, and civic involvement; and a 1-page essay on their long-term goals and plans for achieving those. Financial need is not considered in the selection process.

Financial data A stipend is awarded (amount not specified).

Duration 1 year.

Number awarded 1 each year.

Deadline June of each year.

[749]
ANTHC SCHOLARSHIPS

Alaska Native Tribal Health Consortium
Attn: Education, Development and Training Department
3900 Ambassador Drive, Suite 101
Anchorage, AK 99508
(907) 729-1301   Toll Free: (800) 684-8361
Fax: (907) 729-3638   E-mail: learning@anthc.org
Web: www.anthc.org/scholarship-opportunities

Summary To provide financial assistance for college or graduate school to Natives and American Indians who are residents of Alaska and interested in a career in health care.

Eligibility This program is open to Alaska Natives and American Indians who are undergraduate or graduate students interested in preparing for a career in the field of health care. Applicants must be residents of Alaska working full time

on an associate, bachelor's, master's, or Ph.D. degree. Along with their application, they must submit a personal statement answering several questions on their interest in Alaska Native health care. Selection is based on the statement, letters of recommendation, presentation of the application, and involvement in the Native community.

Financial data The stipend is $5,000 per year.

Duration 1 year; may be renewed if recipients maintain a GPA of 2.5 or higher and complete at least 6 credits each term.

Number awarded 10 each year.

Deadline June of each year.

[750]
ANTHONY A. WELMAS GRADUATE SCHOLARSHIP

American Indian College Fund
Attn: Scholarship Department
8333 Greenwood Boulevard
Denver, CO 80221
(303) 426-8900   Toll Free: (800) 776-FUND
Fax: (303) 426-1200
E-mail: scholarships@collegefund.org
Web: www.collegefund.org

Summary To provide financial assistance to Native American students who are working on a graduate degree in any field.

Eligibility This program is open to American Indians and Alaska Natives who have proof of enrollment or descendancy in a federally-recognized tribe. Applicants must be working on a graduate or professional degree in any field. They must have a GPA of 3.0 or higher. Applications are available only online and include required essays on specified topics. U.S. citizenship is required.

Financial data The stipend is $1,000.

Duration 1 year.

Number awarded 1 or more each year.

Deadline May of each year.

[751]
APA MINORITY MEDICAL STUDENT SUMMER MENTORING PROGRAM

American Psychiatric Association
Attn: Division of Diversity and Health Equity
1000 Wilson Boulevard, Suite 1825
Arlington, VA 22209-3901
(703) 907-8653   Toll Free: (888) 35-PSYCH
Fax: (703) 907-7852   E-mail: mking@psych.org
Web: www.psychiatry.org/minority-fellowship

Summary To provide funding to Native American and other minority medical students who are interested in working on a summer project with a psychiatrist mentor.

Eligibility This program is open to minority medical students who are interested in psychiatric issues. Minorities include American Indians, Alaska Natives, Native Hawaiians, Asian Americans, Hispanic/Latinos, and African Americans. Applicants must be interested in working with a psychiatrist mentor, primarily on clinical work with underserved minority populations and mental health care disparities. Work settings may be in a research, academic, or clinical environment. Most of them are inner-city or rural and deal with psychiatric subspecialties, particularly substance abuse and geriatrics. Selection is based on interest of the medical student and specialty of the mentor, practice setting, and geographic proximity of the mentor to the student. U.S. citizenship or permanent resident status is required.

Financial data Fellowships provide $1,500 for living and out-of-pocket expenses directly related to the conduct of the fellowship.

Duration Summer months.

Additional information This program is funded by the Substance Abuse and Mental Health Services Administration.

Number awarded Varies each year.

Deadline March of each year.

[752]
APAGS COMMITTEE FOR THE ADVANCEMENT OF RACIAL AND ETHNIC DIVERSITY (CARED) GRANT PROGRAM

American Psychological Association
Attn: American Psychological Association of Graduate
  Students
750 First Street, N.E.
Washington, DC 20002-4242
(202) 336-6014   Fax: (202) 336-5694
E-mail: apags@apa.org
Web: www.apa.org/about/awards/apags-cema.aspx

Summary To provide funding to graduate students who are members of the American Psychological Association of Graduate Students (APAGS) and who wish to develop a project that increases membership and participation of Native American and other ethnic minority students within the association.

Eligibility This program is open to members of APAGS who are enrolled at least half time in a master's or doctoral program at an accredited university. Applicants must be interested in developing a project to increase the membership and participation of ethnic minority graduate students within APAGS, advertise education and training opportunities for ethnic minorities, and enhance the recruitment and retention efforts for ethnic minority students in psychology. Examples include, but are not limited to, workshops, conferences, speaker series, mentorship programs, and the development of student organizations with a focus on multiculturalism or ethnic minority concerns.

Financial data The grant is $1,000.

Duration The grant is presented annually.

Additional information This grant was first awarded in 1997.

Number awarded 4 each year.

Deadline November of each year.

[753]
ARCTIC EDUCATION FOUNDATION SCHOLARSHIPS

Arctic Slope Regional Corporation
Attn: Arctic Education Foundation
P.O. Box 129
Barrow, AK 99723
(907) 852-8633   Toll Free: (800) 770-2772
Fax: (907) 852-2774   E-mail: arcticed@asrc.com
Web: www.arcticed.com

Summary To provide financial assistance to Inupiat Natives who are shareholders or descendants of shareholders of the Arctic Slope Regional Corporation (ASRC) and interested in attending college or graduate school in any state.

Eligibility This program is open to U.S. citizens who are 1) a northern Alaskan Inupiat Native currently residing in the Arctic Slope region of Alaska; 2) an original shareholder of the ASRC; or 3) a direct lineal descendant of an original ASRC shareholder. Applicants must be attending or planning to attend a college, university, or vocational/technical school in any state as a full- or part-time undergraduate or graduate student. Along with their application, they must submit documentation of financial need and a short paragraph on their personal plans upon completion of study.

Financial data For students in vocational training programs, the maximum stipend is $2,875 per semester ($5,750 per year). For full-time undergraduate students at 4-year colleges and universities, the maximum stipend is $6,750 per year. For graduate students, the maximum stipend is $10,750 per year.

Duration 1 year; may be renewed.

Additional information The Arctic Slope Regional Corporation is 1 of 13 Alaska Native Regional Corporations created under the Alaska Native Claims Settlement Act of 1971.

Number awarded Varies each year.

Deadline February of each year for spring quarter; April of each year for summer school; July of each year for fall semester or quarter; or November of each year for spring semester or winter quarter.

[754]
ARENT FOX DIVERSITY SCHOLARSHIPS

Arent Fox LLP
Attn: Attorney Recruitment and Development Manager
1717 K Street, N.W.
Washington, DC 20036
(202) 715-8503   Fax: (202) 857-6395
E-mail: lawrecruit@arentfox.com
Web: www.arentfox.com

Summary To provide financial assistance and work experience to Native American and other underrepresented law students.

Eligibility This program is open to first-year law students who are members of a diverse population that historically has been underrepresented in the legal profession, including people of color, women, and LGBT individuals. Applicants must be U.S. citizens or otherwise authorized to work in the United States. They must also be willing to work as a summer intern at the sponsoring law firm's offices in Los Angeles, New York City, or Washington, D.C. Along with their application, they must submit a resume, an undergraduate transcript and law school grades when available, a 5- to 10-page legal writing sample, 3 letters of recommendation, and a 1-page essay on how they have successfully navigated the challenges and barriers in your life and how they believe those experiences will help them excel as a lawyer. Selection is based on academic performance during college and law school, oral and writing communication skills, leadership qualities, and community involvement.

Financial data The scholarship stipend is $15,000. The summer salary is $3,000 per week.

Duration 1 year.

Additional information These scholarships were first offered in 2006. Recipients are also offered summer internships with Arent Fox in Los Angeles, New York City, or Washington, D.C.

Number awarded 3 each year.

Deadline January of each year.

[755]
ARKANSAS CONFERENCE ETHNIC AND LANGUAGE CONCERNS COMMITTEE SCHOLARSHIPS

United Methodist Church-Arkansas Conference
Attn: Committee on Ethnic and Language Concerns
800 Daisy Bates Drive
Little Rock, AR 72202
(501) 324-8045   Toll Free: (877) 646-1816
Fax: (501) 324-8018   E-mail: mallen@arumc.org
Web: www.arumc.org/docs-and-forms

Summary To provide financial assistance to Native American and other ethnic minority Methodist students from Arkansas who are interested in attending college or graduate school in any state.

Eligibility This program is open to ethnic minority undergraduate and graduate students who are active members of local congregations affiliated with the Arkansas Conference of the United Methodist Church (UMC). Applicants must be currently enrolled in an accredited institution of higher education in any state. Along with their application, they must submit an essay explaining how this scholarship will make them a leader in the UMC. Preference is given to students attending a UMC-affiliated college or university.

Financial data The stipend is $500 per semester ($1,000 per year) for undergraduates or $1,000 per semester ($2,000 per year) for graduate students.

Duration 1 year; may be renewed.

Number awarded 5 each year: 1 in each UMC Arkansas district.

Deadline February or September of each year.

[756]
ARL CAREER ENHANCEMENT PROGRAM

Association of Research Libraries
Attn: Director of Diversity Programs
21 Dupont Circle, N.W., Suite 800
Washington, DC 20036
(202) 296-2296   Fax: (202) 872-0884
E-mail: mpuente@arl.org
Web: www.arl.org

Summary To provide an opportunity for Native Americand and members of other minority racial and ethnic groups to gain work experience at a library that is a member of the Association of Research Libraries (ARL).

Eligibility This program is open to members of racial and ethnic minority groups that are underrepresented as professionals in academic and research libraries (American Indian or Alaska Native, Asian, Black or African American, Native Hawaiian or other Pacific Islander, or Hispanic or Latino). Applicants must have completed at least 12 credit hours of an M.L.I.S. degree program at an ALA-accredited institution. They must be interested in an internship at 1 of 7 ARL mem-

ber institutions. Along with their application, they must submit a 500-word essay on what attracts them to an internship opportunity in an ARL library, their professional interests as related to the internship, and their goals for the internship.

Financial data Fellows receive a stipend of $4,800 for the internship, housing reimbursement up to $2,500, relocation assistance up to $1,000, and financial support (approximately $1,400) to attend the annual ARL Leadership Institute.

Duration The internship lasts 6 to 12 weeks (or 240 hours).

Additional information This program is funded by the Institute of Museum and Library Services. Recently, the 7 participating ARL institutions were the University of Arizona, University of California at San Diego, University of Kentucky, University of Michigan, University of Washington, National Library of Medicine, and North Carolina State University.

Number awarded Varies each year; recently, 13 of these fellows were selected.

Deadline October of each year.

[757]
ARL INITIATIVE TO RECRUIT A DIVERSE WORKFORCE

Association of Research Libraries
Attn: Director of Diversity Programs
21 Dupont Circle, N.W., Suite 800
Washington, DC 20036
(202) 296-2296   Fax: (202) 872-0884
E-mail: mpuente@arl.org
Web: www.arl.org

Summary To provide financial assistance to Native American and members of other minority racial and ethnic groups who are interested in preparing for a career as an academic or research librarian.

Eligibility This program is open to members of racial and ethnic minority groups that are underrepresented as professionals in academic and research libraries (American Indian or Alaska Native, Asian, Black or African American, Native Hawaiian or other Pacific Islander, or Hispanic or Latino). Applicants must be interested in working on an M.L.I.S. degree at an ALA-accredited program. They must be citizens or permanent residents of the United States (including Puerto Rico) or Canada.

Financial data The stipend is $5,000 per year.

Duration 2 years.

Additional information This program began in 2000. Funding is currently provided by the Institute of Museum and Library Services and by the contributions of 52 libraries that are members of the Association of Research Libraries (ARL).

Number awarded Varies each year; recently, 15 were awarded.

Deadline April of each year.

[758]
ARL/SAA MOSAIC SCHOLARSHIPS

Society of American Archivists
Attn: Chair, Awards Committee
17 North State Street, Suite 1425
Chicago, IL 60602-4061
(312) 606-0722   Toll Free: (866) 722-7858
Fax: (312) 606-0728   E-mail: info@archivists.org
Web: www2.archivists.org

Summary To provide financial assistance to Native American and other minority students who are working on a graduate degree in archival science.

Eligibility This program is open to minority graduate students, defined as those of American Indian/Alaska Native, Asian, Black/African American, Hispanic/Latino, or Native Hawaiian/other Pacific Islander descent. Applicants must be enrolled or planning to enroll full or part time in a master's degree program or a multi-course program in archival science, archival management, digital archives, special collections, or a related program. They may have completed no more than half of the credit requirements for a degree. Along with their application, they must submit a 500-word essay outlining their interests and future goals in the archives profession. U.S. or Canadian citizenship or permanent resident status is required.

Financial data The stipend is $10,000.

Duration 1 year.

Additional information This program began in 2009. A second iteration of the program began in 2013 in partnership with the Association of Research Libraries (ARL) and financial support provided by the Institute of Museum and Library Sciences (IMLS).

Number awarded 1 or 2 each year.

Deadline June of each year.

[759]
ARNOLD & PORTER DIVERSITY SCHOLARSHIP

Arnold & Porter LLP
Attn: Professional Development Manager
555 Twelfth Street, N.W.
Washington, DC 20004-1206
(202) 942-5000   Fax: (202) 942-5999
Web: arnoldporter.webfactional.com

Summary To provide financial assistance to Native American and other law students who contribute to the diversity of their law school and the legal profession.

Eligibility This program is open to students enrolled in the first year at an ABA-accredited law school who contribute to the diverse background of the law school body, demonstrate strong academic achievement, and demonstrate an interest in promoting diversity in the legal profession. The sponsor defines diversity to include female, minority, disabled, and LGBT students. Applicants must submit a resume, official law transcript, and a personal statement that describes their personal background and the importance of diversity in their life and the legal profession. They may also submit information on their financial need, but that is not required.

Financial data The stipend is $10,000; funds are paid directly to the law school to help finance the second year.

Duration 1 year.

Number awarded 1 or more each year.

Deadline March of each year.

[760]
ARTHUR C. PARKER SCHOLARSHIPS

Society for American Archaeology
Attn: Native American Scholarship Fund
1111 14th Street, N.W., Suite 800
Washington, DC 20005-5622
(202) 789-8200   Fax: (202) 789-0284
E-mail: nasf@saa.org
Web: ecommerce.saa.org

Summary To provide financial assistance to Native American students and professionals interested in additional training in archaeological methods.

Eligibility This program is open to high school seniors, college undergraduates, graduate students, and personnel of tribal or other Native cultural preservation programs. Applicants must be Native Americans or Pacific Islanders from the United States, including U.S. Trust Territories, or indigenous people from Canada. They must be interested in attending a training program in archaeological methods offered by an accredited college or university, including field work, analytical techniques, and curation. Individuals may apply themselves, or they may be nominated by a high school teacher, current professor, or cultural preservation program supervisor. Along with the application, they must submit a 2-page personal statement describing why they are interested in their proposed program and in archaeology, and the contributions they hope to make to the future of archaeology.

Financial data The stipend is $4,000.

Duration 1 year.

Additional information Partial support of this program is provided by the National Science Foundation (NSF).

Number awarded 4 each year: 1 funded by the Society for American Archaeology and 3 by the NSF.

Deadline December of each year.

[761]
ASA MINORITY FELLOWSHIP PROGRAM GENERAL FELLOWSHIP

American Sociological Association
Attn: Minority Affairs Program
1430 K Street, N.W., Suite 600
Washington, DC 20005-2504
(202) 383-9005, ext. 322   Fax: (202) 638-0882
TDD: (202) 638-0981 E-mail: minority.affairs@asanet.org
Web: www.asanet.org

Summary To provide financial assistance to doctoral students in sociology who are Native American or members of other minority groups.

Eligibility This program is open to U.S. citizens, permanent residents, and noncitizen nationals who are Blacks/African Americans, Latinos (e.g., Mexican Americans, Puerto Ricans, Cubans), American Indians or Alaskan Natives, Asian Americans (e.g., southeast Asians, Japanese, Chinese, Koreans), or Pacific Islanders (e.g., Filipinos, Samoans, Hawaiians, Guamanians). Applicants must be entering or continuing students in sociology at the doctoral level. Along with their application, they must submit 3-page essays on 1) the reasons why they decided to undertake graduate study in sociology, their primary research interests, and why they hope to do with a Ph.D. in sociology; and 2) what led them to select the doctoral program they attend or hope to attend and how they see that doctoral program preparing them for a professional career in sociology. Selection is based on commitment to research, focus of research experience, academic achievement, writing ability, research potential, and financial need.

Financial data The stipend is $18,000 per year.

Duration 1 year; may be renewed up to 2 additional years.

Additional information This program, which began in 1974, is supported by individual members of the American Sociological Association (ASA) and by several affiliated organizations (Alpha Kappa Delta, Sociologists for Women in Society, the Association of Black Sociologists, the Midwest Sociological Society, and the Southwestern Sociological Association).

Number awarded Varies each year; since the program began, more than 500 of these fellowships have been awarded.

Deadline January of each year.

[762]
ASCO MEDICAL STUDENT ROTATION FOR UNDERREPRESENTED POPULATIONS

American Society of Clinical Oncology
Attn: Conquer Cancer Foundation of ASCO
2318 Mill Road, Suite 800
Alexandria, VA 22314
(571) 483-1700
E-mail: grants@conquercancerfoundation.org
Web: www.conquercancerfoundation.org

Summary To provide funding to medical students from Native American and other underrepresented groups interested in a clinical research oncology rotation.

Eligibility This program is open to U.S. citizens, nationals, and permanent residents who are currently enrolled at a U.S. medical school. Applicants must be a member of a group currently underrepresented in medicine, defined as American Indian/Alaska Native, Black/African American, Hispanic/Latino, or Native Hawaiian/Pacific Islander. They must be interested in a rotation either in a cancer patient care setting or a cancer clinical research setting; the rotation may take place either at their own school or another institution but must have a faculty member who belongs to the American Society of Clinical Oncology (ASCO) and is willing to serve as a mentor. Selection is based on interest in preparing for a career in oncology; demonstration of leadership, volunteerism and/ or commitment to underserved populations or heath disparities; letters of recommendation; and overall academic record.

Financial data Students receive a stipend of $5,000 plus $1,500 for future travel to the annual meeting of the American Society of Clinical Oncology (ASCO). Their mentor receives a grant of $2,000.

Duration 8 to 10 weeks.

Additional information This program, which began in 2009, is currently sponsored by Lilly and Genentech BioOncology.

Number awarded Varies each year; recently, 4 were awarded.

Deadline January of each year.

[763]
ASSE DIVERSITY COMMITTEE GRADUATE SCHOLARSHIP

American Society of Safety Engineers
Attn: ASSE Foundation
Scholarship Award Program
520 North Northwest Highway
Park Ridge, IL 60068-2538
(847) 699-2929   Fax: (847) 296-3769
E-mail: assefoundation@asse.org
Web: foundation.asse.org/scholarships-and-grants

Summary To provide financial assistance to graduate students who are Native Americans or members of other diverse groups and are working on a degree related to occupational safety.

Eligibility This program is open to students who are working on a graduate degree in occupational safety, health, environment, industrial hygiene, occupational health nursing, or a closely-related field (e.g., industrial or environmental engineering). Applicants must be full- or part-time students who have completed at least 9 semester hours and have a GPA of 3.5 or higher. A goal of this program is to support individuals regardless of race, ethnicity, gender, religion, personal beliefs, age, sexual orientation, physical challenges, geographic location, university, or specific area of study. U.S. citizenship is not required. Membership in the American Society of Safety Engineers (ASSE) is not required, but preference is given to members.

Financial data The stipend is $1,000 per year.

Duration 1 year; recipients may reapply.

Number awarded 1 each year.

Deadline November of each year.

[764]
A.T. ANDERSON MEMORIAL SCHOLARSHIP

American Indian Science and Engineering Society
Attn: Director of Membership and Communications
2305 Renard Place, S.E., Suite 200
Albuquerque, NM 87106
(505) 765-1052, ext. 110   Fax: (505) 765-5608
E-mail: lpaz@aises.org
Web: www.aises.org/scholarships/at-anderson

Summary To provide financial assistance to members of the American Indian Science and Engineering Society (AISES) who are majoring in designated fields as undergraduate or graduate students.

Eligibility This program is open to AISES members who are full-time undergraduate or graduate students at an accredited 4-year college or university. Applicants must be American Indian tribal members, Alaskan Natives, or Native Hawaiians and have a Certificate of Degree of Indian or Alaska Native Blood (CDIB) showing at least 25% Native blood. They must have a GPA of 3.0 or higher and be working on a degree in engineering, mathematics, medical sciences, natural resources, physical science, technology, or the sciences. Selection is based on academic performance, a personal statement, letters of recommendation, and activities (e.g., jobs, volunteer efforts, internships, extracurricular involvement, hobbies).

Financial data The annual stipend is $1,000 for undergraduates or $2,000 for graduate students.

Duration 1 year; nonrenewable.

Additional information This program began in 1983. Current sponsors include the AMB Foundation, Bayer, Boeing, Chrysler, Helen Roberti Foundation, Lockheed Martin, Northrup Grumman, Oracle, and the San Manuel Band of Mission Indians.

Number awarded Varies each year; recently, 80 were awarded.

Deadline April of each year.

[765]
ATKINS NORTH AMERICA LEADERSHIP SCHOLARSHIP

Conference of Minority Transportation Officials
Attn: National Scholarship Program
100 M Street, S.E., Suite 917
Washington, DC 20003
(202) 506-2917   E-mail: info@comto.org
Web: www.comto.org/page/scholarships

Summary To provide financial assistance to Native American and other minority undergraduate and graduate students interested in working on a degree in transportation or a related field.

Eligibility This program is open to minority 1) undergraduates who have completed at least 12 semester hours of study; and 2) graduate students. Applicants must be studying transportation, engineering, planning, or a related discipline. Along with their application they must submit a cover letter on their transportation-related career goals and life aspirations. Financial need is not considered in the selection process.

Financial data The stipend is $3,000. Funds are paid directly to the recipient's college or university.

Duration 1 year.

Additional information This program is sponsored by Atkins North America.

Number awarded 1 each year.

Deadline April of each year.

[766]
BAKER DONELSON DIVERSITY SCHOLARSHIPS

Baker, Donelson, Bearman, Caldwell & Berkowitz, P.C.
Attn: Director of Attorney Recruiting
3414 Peachtree Road N.E., Suite 1600
Atlanta, GA 30326
(404) 577-6000   Fax: (404) 221-6501
E-mail: lklein@bakerdonelson.com
Web: www.bakerdonelson.com

Summary To provide financial assistance to law students who are Native Americans or members of other groups underrepresented at large law firms.

Eligibility This program is open to students who have completed the first year at an ABA-accredited law school. Applicants must be members of a group traditionally underrepresented at large law firms, including (but not limited to) ethnic minority, female, and LGBT students. Along with their application, they must submit a 10-page legal writing sample and a 1-page personal statement on challenges they have faced in pursuit of their legal career that have helped them to understand the value of diversity and its inclusion in the legal profession. Finalists are interviewed.

Financial data The stipend is $10,000.

Duration 1 year.

Additional information Recipients are also offered summer internships at Baker Donelson offices in Atlanta (Georgia), Baton Rouge (Louisiana), Birmingham (Alabama), Chattanooga (Tennessee), Fort Lauderdale (Florida), Houston (Texas), Jackson (Mississippi), Johnson City (Tennessee), Knoxville (Tennessee), Macon (Georgia), Mandeville (Louisiana), Memphis (Tennessee), Montgomery (Alabama), Nashville (Tennessee), New Orleans (Louisiana), Orlando (Florida), and Washington (D.C).

Number awarded 3 each year.

Deadline June of each year.

[767]
BAKERHOSTETLER DIVERSITY FELLOWSHIP PROGRAM

BakerHostetler LLP
Attn: Attorney Recruitment and Development Manager
PNC Center
1900 East Ninth Street, Suite 3200
Cleveland, OH 44114-3482
(216) 621-0200   Fax: (216) 696-0740
E-mail: ddriscole@bakerlaw.com
Web: www.bakerlaw.com

Summary To provide financial assistance and summer work experience to Native American and other minority law school students who are interested in employment with BakerHostetler.

Eligibility This program is open to full-time second-year students at ABA-accredited law schools who are members of underrepresented groups (Black/African American, Hispanic, Asian American/Pacific Islander, American Indian/Alaskan Native, 2 or more races, or gay, lesbian, bisexual, transgender). Applicants must be interested in a summer associate position with BakerHostetler and possible full-time employment following graduation. They must be U.S. citizens or otherwise authorized to work in the United States. Along with their application, they must submit a 500-word personal statement presenting their views of or experience with diversity, including why they are interested in Baker Hostetler and how they will be able to contribute to the diversity objectives of the firm. Selection is based on academic performance in college and law school, personal achievements, community involvement, oral and written communication skills, demonstrated leadership achievements, and a sincere interest and commitment to join BakerHostetler.

Financial data The stipend is $25,000, of which $10,000 is paid within the first 30 days of starting a summer associate position with the firm and the remaining $15,000 is contingent upon receiving and accepting a full-time offer with the firm.

Duration Summer associate positions are for 8 weeks.

Additional information Summer associate positions may be performed at any of the firm's offices in Atlanta, Chicago, Cincinnati, Cleveland, Columbus, Costa Mesa, Denver, Houston, Los Angeles, New York, Orlando, Seattle, or Washington, D.C.

Number awarded 1 or more each year.

Deadline October of each year.

[768]
BALFOUR PHI DELTA PHI MINORITY SCHOLARSHIP AWARD

Phi Delta Phi International Legal Fraternity
Attn: Executive Director
P.O. Box 11570
Fort Lauderdale, FL 33339
(202) 223-6801   Toll Free: (800) 368-5606
Fax: (202) 223-6808   E-mail: info@phideltaphi.org
Web: www.phideltaphi.org/?page=BalfourMinorityGuide

Summary To provide financial assistance to Native American and other minorities who are members of Phi Delta Phi International Legal Fraternity.

Eligibility This program is open to law students who have been members of the legal fraternity for at least 1 year. Applicants must be minorities, defined to include African Americans, Asian/Pacific Islanders, American Indians/Alaskan Natives, Hispanic, or LGBT students. They must affirm that they intend to practice law in inner-cities of the United States, especially in New England. Along with their application, they must submit a 750-word essay on why they consider themselves qualified to serve as role models for minority youth. Priority is given to students at law schools in New England, especially Massachusetts.

Financial data The stipend is $3,000.

Duration 1 year.

Additional information This program began in 1997 with funding from the Lloyd G. Balfour Foundation.

Number awarded 1 each year.

Deadline October of each year.

[769]
BARNES & THORNBURG DIVERSITY SCHOLARSHIP

Barnes & Thornburg LLP
Attn: Jonathan P. Froemel, Careers Partner
One North Wacker Drive, Suite 440
Chicago, IL 60606-2833
(312) 214-8315   Fax: (312) 759-5946
E-mail: jonathan.froemel@btlaw.com
Web: www.btlaw.com

Summary To provide financial assistance and work experience at Barnes & Thornburg to Native American and other law students who will contribute to diversity in the profession.

Eligibility This program is open to first-year students at ABA-accredited law schools who demonstrate a commitment to contributing to the diversity and inclusion goals of the sponsoring firm and the legal profession. Applicants must be interested in summer associateships at offices of the sponsoring law firm. Selection is based on academic achievement that demonstrates promise for a successful legal career, demonstrated leadership ability, excellent writing and interpersonal skills, and an essay describing how their background and personal attributes or characteristics will contribute to the diversity goals of the firm.

Financial data The program provides a paid associateship (salary not specified) during the summer following their first year of law school, a stipend of $5,000 for the second year of law school, a salary of $5,000 for a second summer associateship, and a grant of $5,000 if they are offered and accept an offer to join the firm as an entry-level associate.

Duration 2 years, including summers.

Additional information Students may also apply to the firm's Careers Partners, and perform their summer associateship, at its offices in Fort Wayne, Grand Rapids, Indianapolis, Minneapolis, or South Bend.

Number awarded 1 each year.

Deadline February of each year.

[770]
BARNEY UHART MEMORIAL SCHOLARSHIP PROGRAM

Chugach Alaska Corporation
Attn: Chugach Heritage Foundation
3800 Centerpoint Drive, Suite 1200
Anchorage, AK 99503
(907) 261-0400   Toll Free: (800) 858-2768
Fax: (907) 261-8896 E-mail: scholarships@chugach.com
Web: www.chugachheritagefoundation.org

Summary To provide financial assistance to college seniors and graduate students who are original shareholders of the Chugach Alaska Corporation or their descendants and interested in an internship with the Corporation or a subsidiary.

Eligibility This program is open to original shareholders and the descendants of original enrollees of the Chugach Alaska Corporation who are willing to relocate temporarily to intern with a Corporation subsidiary or at corporate headquarters. Applicants must be enrolled or planning to enroll full time at an accredited college or university in any state as a senior or graduate student and have a GPA of 3.0 or higher. They must be working on a degree in specified fields; recently, those were accounting, business, communications, education, engineering, finance, or information technology. Selection is based on academic excellence, community involvement, leadership qualities, and management interest.

Financial data The stipend is $5,000; the internship is a paid position.

Duration 1 year.

Additional information The Chugach Alaska Corporation is 1 of 13 Alaska Native Regional Corporations created under the Alaska Native Claims Settlement Act of 1971.

Number awarded 2 each year.

Deadline January of each year.

[771]
BERDACH RESEARCH GRANTS

Gay Indian Studies Association
Attn: Foundation
13730 Loumont Street
Whittier, CA 90601

Summary To provide financial assistance to American Indian graduate students interested in conducting research on the phenomenon of berdaches in the southwestern United States.

Eligibility This program is open to graduate students who wish to conduct research (for a master's degree thesis or a doctoral dissertation) on the topic of berdaches (male Indians who lived as women) among the tribes of the southwestern United States. Applicants must be gay males who are enrolled members of a federally-recognized Indian tribal organization in the United States. They must be able to demonstrate a "congruence between their own personal experiences and the topic of their proposed research."

Financial data The grant is $10,000. Funds must be used for research purposes only; the research may be historical (in libraries and archives) or contemporary (involving field studies as well as library research).

Duration This is a 1-time grant.

Additional information Funding for this program is provided by the National Science Foundation. Requests for applications should be accompanied by a self-addressed stamped envelope, the student's e-mail address, and the source where they found the scholarship information.

Number awarded 2 or more each year.

Deadline December of each year.

[772]
BERING STRAITS FOUNDATION HIGHER EDUCATION SCHOLARSHIPS

Bering Straits Native Corporation
Attn: Bering Straits Foundation
110 Front Street, Suite 300
P.O. Box 1008
Nome, AK 99762-1008
(907) 443-4305   Toll Free: (800) 478-5079 (within AK)
Fax: (907) 443-8129
E-mail: foundation@beringstraits.com
Web: www.beringstraits.com/foundation/scholarships

Summary To provide financial assistance to Alaska Natives who are shareholders or descendants of shareholders of the Bering Straits Native Corporation and entering or enrolled in an undergraduate or graduate program in any state.

Eligibility This program is open to Native Alaskans who are shareholders or lineal descendants of shareholders of the Bering Straits Native Corporation. Applicants must be graduating or have graduated from high school with a GPA of 3.0 or higher (or have earned a GED). They must be accepted or currently enrolled (as an undergraduate or graduate student) at an accredited college or university in any state as a full-time student and be able to demonstrate financial need. Along with their application, they must submit a personal statement on their educational goals and objectives, their community and school activities, and honors and awards they have received.

Financial data The stipend is $1,000 per semester for students who maintain a GPA of 3.0 or higher or $400 per semester for students whose GPA is from 2.5 to 2.99. Funds are paid directly to the recipient's school.

Duration 1 semester; may be renewed if the recipient maintains a GPA of 2.5 or higher.

Additional information The Bering Straits Native Corporation is 1 of 13 Alaska Native Regional Corporations created under the Alaska Native Claims Settlement Act of 1971.

Number awarded Varies each year.

Deadline April of each year for high school seniors; June of each year for the fall semester for continuing undergraduates; December of each year for the spring semester.

[773]
BIA HIGHER EDUCATION GRANTS FOR HOPI TRIBAL MEMBERS

Hopi Tribe
Attn: Grants and Scholarships Program
P.O. Box 123
Kykotsmovi, AZ 86039
(928) 734-3542   Toll Free: (800) 762-9630
Fax: (928) 734-9575   E-mail: JTorivio@hopi.nsn.us
Web: www.hopi-nsn.gov

Summary To provide financial assistance to students of Hopi ancestry who are working on an undergraduate, graduate, or postgraduate degree.

Eligibility This program is open to students who are working or planning to work full time on an associate, baccalaureate, graduate, or postgraduate degree. Applicants must be enrolled members of the Hopi Tribe and able to demonstrate financial need. They must have a GPA of 2.0 or higher as an incoming freshman, 2.25 or higher as an entering sophomore, 2.5 as an entering junior or senior, or 3.0 as a graduate or professional student.

Financial data The maximum grant is $2,500 per semester ($5,000 per year).

Duration 1 semester; may be renewed for up to 10 terms of undergraduate study or up to 5 terms of graduate study, provided the recipient remains enrolled full time and meets the required GPA for their academic level.

Additional information This program is funded by the Bureau of Indian Affairs (BIA).

Number awarded Varies each year.

Deadline June of each year for fall; October of each year for winter; November of each year for spring.

[774]
BILL BERNBACH DIVERSITY SCHOLARSHIPS

American Association of Advertising Agencies
Attn: AAAA Foundation
1065 Avenue of the Americas, 16th Floor
New York, NY 10018
(212) 262-2500   E-mail: bbscholarship@ddb.com
Web: www.aaaa.org

Summary To provide financial assistance to Native American and other multicultural students interested in working on an undergraduate or graduate degree in advertising at designated schools.

Eligibility This program is open to African Americans, Asian Americans, Hispanic Americans, and Native Americans (including American Indians, Alaska Natives, Native Hawaiians, and other Pacific Islanders) who are interested in studying the advertising creative arts at designated institutions as a full-time student. Applicants must be working on or have already received an undergraduate degree and be able to demonstrate creative talent and promise. They must be U.S. citizens, nationals, or permanent residents. Along with their application, they must submit 10 samples of creative work in their respective field of expertise.

Financial data The stipend is $5,000.

Duration 1 year.

Additional information This program, which began in 1998, is currently sponsored by DDB Worldwide. The participating schools are the Art Center College of Design (Pasadena, California), Creative Circus (Atlanta, Georgia), Miami Ad School (Miami Beach, Florida), University of Oklahoma (Norman, Oklahoma), University of Texas at Austin, VCU Brandcenter (Richmond, Virginia), Savannah College of Art and Design (Savannah, Georgia), University of Oregon (Eugene), City College of New York, School of Visual Arts (New York, New York), Fashion Institute of Technology (New York, New York), and Howard University (Washington, D.C.).

Number awarded 3 each year.

Deadline May of each year.

[775]
BILL RABBIT LEGACY ART SCHOLARSHIP

Cherokee Nation Foundation
800 South Muskogee
Tahlequah, OK 74464
(918) 207-0950 Fax: (918) 207-0951
E-mail: contact@cherokeenationfoundation.org
Web: cherokeenation.academicworks.com

Summary To provide financial assistance to citizens of the Cherokee Nation who are interested in attending a university in any state and majoring in specified fields of art.

Eligibility This program is open to citizens of the Cherokee Nation who are high school seniors or students currently enrolled as full-time undergraduate or graduate students at a 4-year college or university in any state. Applicants must have a GPA of 3.0 or higher and be studying drawing, painting, sculpture, pottery, traditional beadwork, or textiles. They are not required to reside in the Cherokee Nation area. Along with their application, they must submit 3 samples of their work, a 650-word essay on the world they come from and how it has shaped their dreams and aspiration, and a 500-word essay on their desire to pursue higher education, their chosen field of study, how they plan to serve the Cherokee people after they complete their higher education, and whether or not they speak the Cherokee language. Selection is based on the clarity and presentation of the essay; academic information (including transcripts and ACT scores); school, cultural and community activities; future plans to serve Cherokee people; and financial need.

Financial data A stipend is awarded (amount not specified).

Duration 1 year; may be renewed up to 3 additional years, provided the recipient maintains a GPA of 3.0 or higher.

Number awarded 1 or more each year.

Deadline January of each year.

[776]
BISHOP THOMAS HOYT, JR. FELLOWSHIP

St. John's University
Attn: Collegeville Institute for Ecumenical and Cultural Research
2475 Ecumenical Drive
P.O. Box 2000
Collegeville, MN 56321-2000
(320) 363-3366 Fax: (320) 363-3313
E-mail: staff@CollegevilleInstitute.org
Web: www.collegevilleinstitute.org

Summary To provide funding to Native American and other students of color who wish to complete their doctoral dissertation while in residence at the Collegeville Institute for Ecu-

menical and Cultural Research of St. John's University in Collegeville, Minnesota.

Eligibility This program is open to people of color completing a doctoral dissertation in ecumenical and cultural research. Applicants must be interested in a residency at the Collegeville Institute for Ecumenical and Cultural Research of St. John's University. Along with their application, they must submit a 1,000-word description of the research project they plan to complete while in residence at the Institute.

Financial data The stipend covers the residency fee of $2,500, which includes housing and utilities.

Duration 1 year.

Additional information Residents at the Institute engage in research, publication, and education on the important intersections between faith and culture. They seek to discern and communicate the meaning of Christian identity and unity in a religiously and culturally diverse world.

Number awarded 1 each year.

Deadline January of each year.

[777]
BLOSSOM KALAMA EVANS MEMORIAL SCHOLARSHIPS

Hawai'i Community Foundation
Attn: Scholarship Department
827 Fort Street Mall
Honolulu, HI 96813
(808) 566-5570 Toll Free: (888) 731-3863
Fax: (808) 521-6286
E-mail: scholarships@hcf-hawaii.org
Web: hcf.scholarships.ngwebsolutions.com

Summary To provide financial assistance to residents of Hawaii of native ancestry who are interested in working on an undergraduate or graduate degree at a school in the state.

Eligibility This program is open to residents of Hawaii who are of Native Hawaiian ancestry and enrolled as full-time juniors, seniors, or graduate students at a 4-year college or university in the state. Applicants must be able to demonstrate academic achievement (GPA of 2.7 or higher), good moral character, and financial need. Along with their application, they must submit a short statement indicating their reasons for attending college, their planned course of study, their career goals, what community service means to them, and how they plan to use their knowledge to serve the needs of the Native Hawaiian community. Preference is given to applicants interested in studying Hawaiian language or Hawaiian studies.

Financial data The amounts of the awards depend on the availability of funds and the need of the recipient. Recently, the average value of the scholarships awarded by the foundation was $2,800.

Duration 1 year.

Number awarded Varies each year; recently, 9 were awarded.

Deadline February of each year.

[778]
BOIS FORTE HIGHER EDUCATION PROGRAM

Bois Forte Band of Chippewa
Attn: Department of Education and Training
5344 Lakeshore Drive
P.O. Box 16
Nett Lake, MN 55772
(218) 757-3124   Toll Free: (800) 221-8129
Fax: (218) 757-3126 E-mail: bmason@boisforte-NSN.gov
Web: www.boisforte.com/divisions/education.htm

Summary To provide financial assistance for undergraduate or graduate study to enrolled members of the Bois Forte Band of Chippewa Indians.

Eligibility Eligible to apply for this assistance are enrolled members of the Bois Forte Band of Chippewa Indians. Applicants must have been accepted at an institution of higher education and had their financial need determined by that institution based on the Free Application for Federal Student Aid (FAFSA). Minnesota residents must apply to the Indian Scholarship Assistance Program of the Minnesota Indian Scholarship Program. Applicants wishing to attend school outside of Minnesota must complete an out-of-state application form. Applicants must also apply for financial assistance from all other available sources, including but not limited to public and private grants and scholarships. They must not be in default of any tribal, federal, or state student education loan or in non-compliance with child support payments. Applicants are interviewed. Financial assistance is awarded on a first-come, first-served basis.

Financial data The maximum amount awarded is $5,000 per year for undergraduates or $6,250 per year for graduate students.

Duration 1 year; may be renewed for a total of 10 semesters of full-time enrollment or part-time equivalent provided recipients maintain a GPA of 2.0 or higher.

Additional information Students may receive financial assistance for summer school.

Number awarded Varies each year.

Deadline Applications may be submitted any time after January 1 but should be received no later than 8 weeks prior to the first day of school.

[779]
BRADLEY ARANT BOULT CUMMINGS ANNUAL DIVERSITY SCHOLARSHIP

Bradley Arant Boult Cummings LLP
Attn: Recruiting Manager
One Federal Place
1819 Fifth Avenue North
Birmingham, AL 35203-2119
(205) 521-8000   Fax: (205) 488-6445
E-mail: vkranzusch@babc.com
Web: www.babc.com/diversity_scholarship

Summary To provide financial assistance and summer work experience to law students who are Native Americans or members of other groups traditionally underrepresented in the legal profession.

Eligibility This program is open to students currently enrolled in the first or second year of at ABA-accredited law schools. Applicants must reflect the diversity of the legal marketplace and be from a group traditionally underrepresented in the legal profession based on their age, ancestry, gender, color, national origin, disability, place of birth, religion, sexual orientation, or veteran status. They must be interested in a summer clerkship at 1 of the sponsoring firm's offices. Along with their application, they must submit a 750-word essay on the importance of diversity in the legal profession and the ways in which their receipt of the scholarship would further the sponsor's desire to improve diversity in the legal profession. Selection is based on that essay, academic qualifications, involvement in community activities, significant work and personal achievements, and financial need.

Financial data The stipend is $10,000 for a second-year student or $5,000 for a first-year student. A salary (amount not specified) is paid for the summer clerkship.

Duration 1 summer and 1 academic year.

Additional information The firm's law offices are located in Birmingham, Charlotte, Huntsville, Jackson, Montgomery, Nashville, Tampa, and Washington, D.C.

Number awarded 2 each year: 1 to a first-year student and 1 to a second-year student.

Deadline February of each year.

[780]
BREAKTHROUGH TO NURSING SCHOLARSHIPS

National Student Nurses' Association
Attn: Foundation
45 Main Street, Suite 606
Brooklyn, NY 11201
(718) 210-0705   Fax: (718) 210-0710
E-mail: nsna@nsna.org
Web: www.nsna.org

Summary To provide financial assistance to Native American and other minority undergraduate and graduate students who wish to prepare for careers in nursing.

Eligibility This program is open to students currently enrolled in state-approved schools of nursing or pre-nursing associate degree, baccalaureate, diploma, generic master's, generic doctoral, R.N. to B.S.N., R.N. to M.S.N., or L.P.N./L.V.N. to R.N. programs. Graduating high school seniors are not eligible. Support for graduate education is provided only for a first degree in nursing. Applicants must be members of a racial or ethnic minority underrepresented among registered nurses (American Indian or Alaska Native, Hispanic or Latino, Native Hawaiian or other Pacific Islander, Black or African American, or Asian). They must be committed to providing quality health care services to underserved populations. Along with their application, they must submit a 200-word description of their professional and educational goals and how this scholarship will help them achieve those goals. Selection is based on academic achievement, financial need, and involvement in student nursing organizations and community health activities. U.S. citizenship or permanent resident status is required.

Financial data Stipends range from $1,000 to $2,000.

Duration 1 year.

Additional information Applications must be accompanied by a $10 processing fee.

Number awarded Varies each year; recently, 13 were awarded: 10 sponsored by the American Association of Critical-Care Nurses and 3 sponsored by the Mayo Clinic.

Deadline January of each year.

[781]
BROWN AND CALDWELL MINORITY SCHOLARSHIP

Brown and Caldwell
Attn: HR/Scholarship Program
1527 Cole Boulevard, Suite 300
Lakewood, CO 80401
(303) 239-5400   Fax: (303) 239-5454
E-mail: scholarships@brwncald.com
Web: www.brownandcaldwell.com/Scholarships.asp?id=1

Summary To provide financial assistance to Native American and other minority students working on an undergraduate or graduate degree in an environmental or engineering field.

Eligibility This program is open to members of minority groups (African Americans, Hispanics, Asians, Pacific Islanders, Native Americans, or Alaska Natives) who are full-time juniors, seniors, or graduate students at an accredited 4-year college or university. Applicants must have a GPA of 3.0 or higher and a declared major in civil, chemical, or environmental engineering or an environmental science (e.g., biology, ecology, geology, hydrogeology). They must be U.S. citizens or permanent residents. Along with their application, they must submit an essay (up to 250 words) on a topic that changes annually but relates to their personal development. Financial need is not considered in the selection process.

Financial data The stipend is $5,000.

Duration 1 year.

Number awarded 1 each year.

Deadline May of each year.

[782]
BUCKFIRE & BUCKFIRE LAW SCHOOL DIVERSITY SCHOLARSHIP

Buckfire & Buckfire, P.C.
Attn: Scholarships
25800 Northwestern Highway, Suite 890
Southfield, MI 48075
(248) 569-4646   Toll Free: (800) 606-1717
Fax: (248) 569-6737 E-mail: marketing@buckfirelaw.com
Web: www.buckfirelaw.com/library/general

Summary To provide financial assistance to law students who come from a Native American or other minority background or have a commitment to diversity.

Eligibility This program is open to U.S. citizens who are members of an ethnic, racial, or other minority or who demonstrate a defined commitment to issues of diversity within their academic career. Applicants must be attending an accredited law school and have a GPA of 3.0 or higher. Selection is based on academic achievement and an essay on how they will utilize their law degree to promote diversity.

Financial data The stipend is $2,000.

Duration 1 year.

Additional information This program began in 2013.

Number awarded 1 each year.

Deadline May of each year.

[783]
BUCKFIRE & BUCKFIRE MEDICAL SCHOOL DIVERSITY SCHOLARSHIP

Buckfire & Buckfire, P.C.
Attn: Scholarships
25800 Northwestern Highway, Suite 890
Southfield, MI 48075
(248) 569-4646   Toll Free: (800) 606-1717
Fax: (248) 569-6737 E-mail: marketing@buckfirelaw.com
Web: www.buckfirelaw.com/library/general

Summary To provide financial assistance to medical students who come from a Native American or other minority background or have a commitment to diversity.

Eligibility This program is open to U.S. citizens who are members of an ethnic, racial, or other minority or who demonstrate a defined commitment to issues of diversity within their academic career. Applicants must have completed at least 1 semester at an accredited medical school and have a GPA of 3.0 or higher. Selection is based on academic achievement and an essay on how they will utilize their medical degree to promote diversity.

Financial data The stipend is $2,000.

Duration 1 year.

Additional information This program began in 2014.

Number awarded 1 each year.

Deadline May of each year.

[784]
BUTLER RUBIN DIVERSITY SCHOLARSHIP

Butler Rubin Saltarelli & Boyd LLP
Attn: Diversity Partner
70 West Madison Street, Suite 1800
Chicago, IL 60602
(312) 696-4478   Fax: (312) 873-4328
E-mail: jaldort@butlerrubin.com
Web: www.butlerrubin.com/about/diversity

Summary To provide financial assistance and summer work experience to Native American and other diverse law students who are interested in the area of business litigation.

Eligibility This program is open to law students of backgrounds that will contribute to diversity in the legal profession. Applicants must be interested in the private practice of law in the area of business litigation and in a summer associateship in that field with Butler Rubin Saltarelli & Boyd in Chicago. Selection is based on academic performance and achievement, intention to remain in the Chicago area following graduation, and interpersonal and communication skills.

Financial data The stipend is $10,000 per year; funds are to be used for tuition and other expenses associated with law school. For the summer associateship, a stipend is paid.

Duration 1 year; may be renewed.

Additional information This program began in 2006.

Number awarded 1 each year.

Deadline Deadline not specified.

[785]
CALIFORNIA BAR FOUNDATION 1L DIVERSITY SCHOLARSHIPS

State Bar of California
Attn: California Bar Foundation
180 Howard Street
San Francisco, CA 94105-1639
(415) 856-0780   Fax: (415) 856-0788
E-mail: scholarships@calbarfoundation.org
Web: www.calbarfoundation.org

Summary To provide financial assistance to residents of any state who are Native Americans or members of other groups historically underrepresented in the legal profession and entering law school in California.

Eligibility This program to open to residents of any state who are entering their first year at a law school in California. Applicants must be able to contribute to greater diversity in the legal profession. Diversity includes a broad array of backgrounds and life experiences, including students from groups or with skills or attributes that are underrepresented in the legal profession. Students from socially and economically disadvantaged backgrounds are especially encouraged to apply. Along with their application, they must submit a 500-word essay describing their commitment to serving the community and, if applicable, any significant obstacles or hurdles they have overcome to attend law school. Financial need is considered in the selection process.

Financial data The stipend is $7,500.

Duration 1 year.

Additional information This program began in 2008. Each year, the foundation grants awards named after sponsors that donate funding for the scholarships.

Number awarded Varies each year; recently, 33 were awarded.

Deadline May of each year.

[786]
CALIFORNIA COMMUNITY SERVICE-LEARNING PROGRAM

National Medical Fellowships, Inc.
Attn: Scholarship Program
347 Fifth Avenue, Suite 510
New York, NY 10016
(212) 483-8880   Toll Free: (877) NMF-1DOC
Fax: (212) 483-8897 E-mail: scholarships@nmfonline.org
Web: www.nmfonline.org

Summary To provide funding to Native American and other underrepresented medical students in California who wish to participate in a community service program for underserved areas of the state.

Eligibility This program is open to members of underrepresented minority groups (African American, Hispanic/Latino, Native American, Vietnamese, or Cambodian) who are U.S. citizens or DACA certified. Applicants must be currently enrolled in an accredited medical school in California. They must be interested in a self-directed service-learning experience that provides 200 hours of community service in medically-underserved areas of the state. Selection is based on demonstrated leadership early in career and commitment to serving medically underserved communities.

Financial data The stipend is $5,000.

Additional information Funding for this program, which began in 2013 and is administered by National Medical Fellowships (NMF), is provided by the California Wellness Foundation.

Number awarded 10 each year.

Deadline March of each year.

[787]
CALIFORNIA PLANNING FOUNDATION DIVERSITY IN PLANNING SCHOLARSHIP

American Planning Association-California Chapter
Attn: California Planning Foundation
c/o Kelly Main
California Polytechnic State University at San Luis Obispo
City and Regional Planning Department
Office 21-116B
San Luis Obispo, CA 93407-0283
(805) 756-2285   Fax: (805) 756-1340
E-mail: cpfapplications@gmail.com
Web: www.californiaplanningfoundation.org

Summary To provide financial assistance to Native Americans and other undergraduate and graduate students in accredited planning programs at California universities who will increase diversity in the profession.

Eligibility This program is open to students entering their final year for an undergraduate or master's degree in an accredited planning program at a university in California. Applicants must be students who will increase diversity in the planning profession. Along with their application, they must submit 1) a 500-word personal statement explaining why planning is important to them, their potential contribution to the profession of planning in California, and how this scholarship would help them to complete their degree; 2) a 500-word description of their experience in planning (e.g., internships, volunteer experiences, employment); and 3) a 500-word essay on what they consider to be 1 of the greatest planning challenges in California today. Selection is based on academic performance, increasing diversity in the planning profession, commitment to serve the planning profession in California, and financial need.

Financial data The stipend is $3,000. The award includes a 1-year student membership in the American Planning Association (APA) and payment of registration for the APA California Conference.

Duration 1 year.

Additional information The accredited planning programs are at 3 campuses of the California State University system (California State Polytechnic University at Pomona, California Polytechnic State University at San Luis Obispo, and San Jose State University), 3 campuses of the University of California (Berkeley, Irvine, and Los Angeles), and the University of Southern California.

Number awarded 1 each year.

Deadline March of each year.

[788]
CALISTA EDUCATION AND CULTURE SCHOLARSHIP PROGRAM

Calista Corporation
Attn: Calista Education and Culture, Inc.
5015 Business Park Boulevard, Suite 3000
Anchorage, AK 99503
(907) 275-2800   Toll Free: (800) 277-5516
Fax: (907) 275-2936
E-mail: scholarships@calistacorp.com
Web: www.calistaeducation.org/scholarships.html

Summary To provide financial assistance to Alaska Natives who are shareholders or descendants of shareholders of the Calista Corporation and interested in working on an undergraduate or graduate degree at a school in any state.

Eligibility This program is open to Alaska Natives who are shareholders or lineal descendants of shareholders of the Calista Corporation. Applicants must be at least a high school graduate or have earned a GED and be in good academic standing with a GPA of 2.0 or higher. They must be working on an undergraduate or graduate degree at a college or university in any state. Along with their application, they must submit a 1-page essay on their educational and career goals. Financial need is considered in the selection process.

Financial data The amount awarded for undergraduates depends upon the recipient's GPA: awards for full-time students are $500 per semester for a GPA of 2.0 to 2.49, $750 per semester for a GPA of 2.5 to 2.99, and $1,000 per semester a GPA of 3.0 or higher. Awards for part-time students are half those amounts. Stipends are $750 per semester for full-time trade school students or $375 per semester for part-time trade school student. For graduate students, the stipend is $1,500 per semester for full-time students or $750 for part-time students. The funds are paid in 2 equal installments; the second semester check is not issued until grades from the previous semester's work are received.

Duration 1 year; recipients may reapply.

Additional information The Calista Corporation is 1 of 13 Alaska Native Regional Corporations created under the Alaska Native Claims Settlement Act of 1971. This program was established in 1994.

Number awarded Varies each year; recently, scholarships worth $309,125 were awarded.

Deadline June of each year for fall term; November of each year for spring trm.

[789]
CANFIT PROGRAM GRADUATE SCHOLARSHIPS

Communities-Adolescents-Nutrition-Fitness
Attn: Scholarship Program
P.O. Box 3989
Berkeley, CA 94703
(510) 644-1533, ext. 112   Toll Free: (800) 200-3131
Fax: (510) 843-9705   E-mail: info@canfit.org
Web: www.canfit.org/scholarships

Summary To provide financial assistance to Native American and other minority graduate students who are working on a degree in nutrition, physical education, or public health in California.

Eligibility This program is open to American Indians, Alaska Natives, African Americans, Asian Americans, Pacific Islanders, and Latinos/Hispanics from California who are enrolled in 1) an approved master's or doctoral program in nutrition, public health, or physical education in the state; or 2) a pre-professional practice program approved by the American Dietetic Association at an accredited university in the state. Applicants must have completed 12 to 15 units of graduate course work and have a cumulative GPA of 3.0 or higher. Along with their application, they must submit 1) documentation of financial need; 2) letters of recommendation from 2 individuals; 3) a 1- to 2-page letter describing their academic goals and involvement in community nutrition and/or physical education activities; and 4) an essay of 500 to 1,000 words on a topic related to healthy foods for youth from low-income communities of color.

Financial data A stipend is awarded (amount not specified).

Number awarded 1 or more each year.

Deadline March of each year.

[790]
CAP LATHROP BROADCAST AND TELECOMMUNICATIONS SCHOLARSHIP

Cook Inlet Region, Inc.
Attn: The CIRI Foundation
3600 San Jeronimo Drive, Suite 256
Anchorage, AK 99508-2870
(907) 793-3575   Toll Free: (800) 764-3382
Fax: (907) 793-3585   E-mail: tcf@thecirifoundation.org
Web: www.thecirifoundation.org/scholarships

Summary To provide financial assistance for undergraduate or graduate studies in media-related fields to Alaska Natives and their lineal descendants.

Eligibility This program is open to Alaska Native enrollees under the Alaska Native Claims Settlement Act (ANCSA) of 1971 and their lineal descendants. Applicants may be enrollees of any of the 13 ANCSA regional corporations, but preference is given to original enrollees/descendants of Cook Inlet Region, Inc. (CIRI) who have a GPA of 2.5 or higher. There are no Alaska residency requirements or age limitations. Applicants must be accepted or enrolled full time in a 2-year undergraduate, 4-year undergraduate, or graduate degree program. They must be majoring in a media-related field (e.g., telecommunications, broadcast, business, engineering, journalism) and planning to work in the telecommunications or broadcast industry in Alaska after graduation. Along with their application, they must submit a 500-word statement on their educational and career goals and how they are contributing, or planning to contribute, to a positive Alaska Native community. Selection is based on that statement, academic achievement, rigor of course work or degree program, student financial contribution, financial need, grade level, previous work performance, community service, and relationship of degree program to career goals.

Financial data The stipend is $4,000 per year. Funds must be used for tuition, university fees, books, required class supplies, and campus housing and meal plans for students who must live away from their permanent home to attend college. Checks are sent directly to the recipient's school.

Duration 1 year (2 semesters).

Additional information CIRI is 1 of 13 regional corporations established according to the terms of the Alaska Native Claims Settlement Act (ANCSA) of 1971. This program began in 1997. Recipients must plan to work in the broadcast or telecommunications industry in Alaska upon completion of their academic degree.

Number awarded   1 each year.

Deadline   May of each year.

[791]
CARL H. MARRS SCHOLARSHIP FUND

Cook Inlet Region, Inc.
Attn: The CIRI Foundation
3600 San Jeronimo Drive, Suite 256
Anchorage, AK 99508-2870
(907) 793-3575   Toll Free: (800) 764-3382
Fax: (907) 793-3585   E-mail: tcf@thecirifoundation.org
Web: www.thecirifoundation.org/about/donors

Summary   To provide financial assistance for undergraduate or graduate studies in business-related fields to Alaska Natives who are original enrollees to Cook Inlet Region, Inc. (CIRI) and their lineal descendants.

Eligibility   This program is open to Alaska Native enrollees to CIRI under the Alaska Native Claims Settlement Act (ANCSA) of 1971 and their lineal descendants. There are no Alaska residency requirements or age limitations. Applicants must be accepted or enrolled full time in a 4-year undergraduate or a graduate degree program in business administration, economics, finance, organizational management, accounting, or a similar field. They must have a GPA of 3.7 or higher. Along with their application, they must submit a 500-word statement on their educational and career goals and how they are contributing, or planning to contribute, to a positive Alaska Native community. Selection is based on that statement, academic achievement, rigor of course work or degree program, student financial contribution, financial need, grade level, previous work performance, community service, and relationship of degree program to career goals.

Financial data   The stipend is $20,000 per year.

Duration   1 year; may be renewed.

Additional information   CIRI is 1 of 13 regional corporations established according to the terms of the Alaska Native Claims Settlement Act (ANCSA) of 1971. This program began in 2001.

Number awarded   Varies each year; recently, 2 were awarded.

Deadline   May of each year.

[792]
CARMEN E. TURNER SCHOLARSHIPS

Conference of Minority Transportation Officials
Attn: National Scholarship Program
100 M Street, S.E., Suite 917
Washington, DC 20003
(202) 506-2917   E-mail: info@comto.org
Web: www.comto.org/page/scholarships

Summary   To provide financial assistance for college or graduate school to members of the Conference of Minority Transportation Officials (COMTO) and their families.

Eligibility   This program is open to undergraduate and graduate students who have been members or whose parents, guardians, or grandparents have been members of COMTO for at least 1 year. Applicants must be working on a degree in a field related to transportation and have a GPA of

2.5 or higher. Along with their application they must submit a cover letter on their transportation-related career goals and life aspirations. Financial need is not considered in the selection process.

Financial data   The stipend is $3,500. Funds are paid directly to the recipient's college or university.

Duration   1 year.

Number awarded   1 each year.

Deadline   April of each year.

[793]
CARRINGTON-HSIA-NIEVES SCHOLARSHIP FOR MIDWIVES OF COLOR

American College of Nurse-Midwives
Attn: ACNM Foundation, Inc.
8403 Colesville Road, Suite 1550
Silver Spring, MD 20910-6374
(240) 485-1850   Fax: (240) 485-1818
E-mail: foundation@acnmf.org
Web: www.midwife.org

Summary   To provide financial assistance to Native American and other midwives of color who are members of the American College of Nurse-Midwives (ACNM) and engaged in doctoral or postdoctoral study.

Eligibility   This program is open to ACNM members of color who are certified nurse midwives (CNM) or certified midwives (CM). Applicants must be enrolled in a program of doctoral or postdoctoral education. Along with their application, they must submit brief statements on their 5-year academic career plans, their intended use of the funds, and their intended future participation in the local, regional, and/or national activities of the ACNM and in activities that otherwise contribute substantially to midwifery research, education, or practice.

Financial data   The stipend is $5,000.

Duration   1 year.

Number awarded   1 each year.

Deadline   October of each year.

[794]
CATCHING THE DREAM SCHOLARSHIPS

Catching the Dream
Attn: Scholarship Affairs Office
8200 Mountain Road, N.E., Suite 203
Albuquerque, NM 87110-7835
(505) 262-2351   Fax: (505) 262-0534
E-mail: NScholarsh@aol.com
Web: www.catchingthedream.org

Summary   To provide financial assistance for college to American Indian undergraduate and graduate students interested in studying a field related to economic development for tribes.

Eligibility   This program is open to American Indians who can provide proof that they are at least one-quarter Indian blood and a member of a U.S. tribe that is federally-recognized, state-recognized, or terminated. Applicants must be enrolled or planning to enroll full time at an accredited U.S. college or university as entering freshmen, undergraduate students, graduate students, or Ph.D. candidates. Along with their application, they must submit 1) documentation that they have read the sponsor's web site on "How to Find and Win

Scholarships" and have applied for at least 50 other scholarships or financial aid programs; 2) official transcripts including standardized test scores (ACT, SAT, GRE, MCAT, LSAT, etc.); and 3) an essay of 3 to 5 pages explaining their career plans (especially how those plans include working with and benefiting Indians), what their Indian heritage means to them, and their leadership experience. Selection is based on merit and potential for improving the lives of Indian people.

Financial data Stipends range from $500 to $5,000 per year.

Duration 1 year.

Additional information The sponsor formerly offered 3 separate programs: the MESBEC (Mathematics, Engineering, Science, Business, Education, Computers) Program; the Native American Leadership in Education (NALE) Program; and the Tribal Business Management (TBM) Program.

Number awarded Varies; generally, 30 to 35 each year.

Deadline April of each year for fall semester or quarter; September of each year for spring semester or winter quarter; March of each year for summer school.

[795]
CATHY L. BROCK SCHOLARSHIP

Institute for Diversity in Health Management
Attn: Membership and Education Specialist
155 North Wacker Avenue
Chicago, IL 60606
(312) 422-2658   E-mail: cbiddle@aha.org
Web: www.diversityconnection.org

Summary To provide financial assistance to Native American and other graduate students in health care management, especially financial operations, who will contribute to ethnic diversity in the profession.

Eligibility This program is open to U.S. citizens who represent ethnically diverse cultural backgrounds. Applicants must be enrolled in the first or second year of a master's degree program in health administration or a comparable program and have a GPA of 3.0 or higher. Along with their application, they must submit 1) a personal statement of 1 to 2 pages on their interest in health care management and their career goals; 2) an essay on what they see as the most challenging issue facing America's hospitals and health systems; and 3) a 500-word essay on their interest and background in health care finance. Selection is based on academic achievement, commitment to a career in health care finance, and financial need.

Financial data The stipend is $1,000.

Duration 1 year.

Number awarded 1 each year.

Deadline January of each year.

[796]
CERT COLLEGE SCHOLARSHIPS

Council of Energy Resource Tribes
Attn: Program Assistant
3545 South Tamarac Drive, Suite 320
Denver, CO 80237
(303) 282-7576, ext. 12   Fax: (303) 282-7584
E-mail: clebeau@certredearth.com
Web: 74.63.154.129/tribaladvance-education-college.html

Summary To provide financial assistance to American Indians who are interested in studying fields related to mathematics, business, science, engineering, or other technical fields on the undergraduate or graduate school level.

Eligibility This program is open to Indian high school seniors, college students, and graduate students who have participated in a qualifying program conducted by the Council of Energy Resource Tribes (CERT). Applicants must be enrolled or planning to enroll full time at an accredited 2- or 4-year tribal, public, or private college or university and major in business, engineering, science, mathematics, computer technology, or a related field. Along with their application, they must submit official tribal affiliation documents, university or college enrollment verification, and their most recent academic transcripts. Financial need is not considered in the selection process.

Financial data The stipend is $1,000 per year.

Duration 1 year; may be renewed up to 4 additional years, provided the recipient maintains a GPA of 2.5 or higher.

Number awarded Varies each year.

Deadline September of each year for fall semester; February of each year for spring semester.

[797]
CHAHTA FOUNDATION DOCTORATE SCHOLARSHIP

Chahta Foundation
Attn: Scholarship Specialist
P.O. Box 1849
Durant, OK 74702
(580) 924-8280, ext. 2546
Toll Free: (800) 522-6170, ext. 2546
Fax: (580) 745-9023
E-mail: scholarship@chahtafoundation.com
Web: www.chahtafoundation.com

Summary To provide financial assistance to Choctaw tribal members who are working on a doctoral degree in any field at a college in any state.

Eligibility This program is open to members of the Choctaw nation who are working on a doctoral degree in any field at a college or university in any state. Applicants must submit a financial needs analysis, 2 letters of recommendation, an essay on how they will "pay this scholarship forward" in their school or community, and a resume that includes information on their honors, awards, activities, education, and work experience. They must have a GPA of 3.0 or higher.

Financial data The stipend is $10,000.

Duration 1 year; nonrenewable.

Number awarded 1 each year.

Deadline March of each year.

[798]
CHAHTA FOUNDATION GRADUATE SCHOLARSHIP

Chahta Foundation
Attn: Scholarship Specialist
P.O. Box 1849
Durant, OK 74702
(580) 924-8280, ext. 2546
Toll Free: (800) 522-6170, ext. 2546
Fax: (580) 745-9023
E-mail: scholarship@chahtafoundation.com
Web: www.chahtafoundation.com

Summary   To provide financial assistance to Choctaw tribal members who are working on a graduate degree in any field at a college in any state.

Eligibility   This program is open to members of the Choctaw nation who are working on a graduate degree in any field at a college or university in any state. Applicants must submit a financial needs analysis, 2 letters of recommendation, an essay on how they will "pay this scholarship forward" in their school or community, and a resume that includes information on their honors, awards, activities, education, and work experience. They must have a GPA of 3.0 or higher.

Financial data   The stipend is $6,000.

Duration   1 year; nonrenewable.

Number awarded   1 each year.

Deadline   March of each year.

[799]
CHAHTA FOUNDATION HERITAGE SCHOLARSHIP

Chahta Foundation
Attn: Scholarship Specialist
P.O. Box 1849
Durant, OK 74702
(580) 924-8280, ext. 2546
Toll Free: (800) 522-6170, ext. 2546
Fax: (580) 745-9023
E-mail: scholarship@chahtafoundation.com
Web: www.chahtafoundation.com

Summary   To provide aid-for-service grants to Choctaw tribal members who are working on a doctoral degree in medicine at a school in any state.

Eligibility   This program is open to members of the Choctaw nation who are currently enrolled in a medical doctoral degree program in any state. Applicants must be willing to sign a service agreement to provide 2 years of service with the Choctaw Nation Health Division or make a monetary payback of funds. They must have a GPA of 2.75 or higher. Along with their application, they must submit a resume, transcript, a financial need analysis, and 2 letters of recommendation.

Financial data   The basic stipend is $40,000, including $15,000 per semester and $10,000 for summer session. An additional $1,000 is provided as a living stipend each month, up to $5,000 per semester.

Duration   1 year.

Number awarded   A selected number are awarded each year.

Deadline   March of each year.

[800]
CHARLES A. EASTMAN DISSERTATION FELLOWSHIP FOR NATIVE AMERICAN SCHOLARS

Dartmouth College
Attn: Office of Graduate Studies
37 Dewey Field Road
6062 Wentworth Hall, Room 304
Hanover, NH 03755-1419
(603) 646-2106   Fax: (603) 646-8762
Web: graduate.dartmouth.edu

Summary   To provide funding to Native American and other doctoral students who are interested in working on their dissertation at Dartmouth College.

Eligibility   This program is open to doctoral candidates who have completed all requirements for the Ph.D. except the dissertation and are planning a career in higher education. Applicants must be Native Americans or other graduate students with a demonstrated commitment and ability to advance educational diversity. They must be interested in working on their dissertation at Dartmouth College. All academic fields that are taught in the Dartmouth undergraduate Arts and Sciences curriculum are eligible. Selection is based on academic achievement and promise; demonstrated commitment to increasing opportunities for underrepresented minorities and increasing cross-racial understanding; and potential for serving as an advocate and mentor for minority undergraduate and graduate students.

Financial data   The stipend is $36,000. In addition, fellows receive office space, library privileges, and a $2,500 research allowance.

Duration   1 year, beginning in September.

Additional information   The fellows are affiliated with a department or program at Dartmouth College. Fellows are expected to be in residence at Dartmouth College for the duration of the program and to complete their dissertation during that time. They are also expected to teach a course, either as the primary instructor or as part of a team.

Number awarded   1 each year.

Deadline   January of each year.

[801]
CHARLES B. RANGEL GRADUATE FELLOWSHIP PROGRAM

Howard University
Attn: Ralph J. Bunche International Affairs Center
2218 Sixth Street, N.W.
Washington, DC 20059
(202) 806-4367   Toll Free: (877) 633-0002
Fax: (202) 806-5424 E-mail: rangelprogram@howard.edu
Web: www.rangelprogram.org

Summary   To provide financial assistance for graduate study in a field related to the work of the Foreign Service, especially to Native American and members of other underrepresented minority groups.

Eligibility   This program is open to U.S. citizens who are either graduating college seniors or recipients of an undergraduate degree. Applicants must be planning to enter graduate school to work on a master's degree in international affairs or other area of interest to the Foreign Service of the U.S. Department of State (e.g., public administration, public policy, business administration, foreign languages, economics, political science, or communications). They must have a GPA of 3.2 or higher. The program encourages applications from members of minority groups historically underrepresented in the Foreign Service and those who can demonstrate financial need.

Financial data The program provides a stipend of $20,000 per year for tuition and fees, $15,000 per year for room, board, books, and other education-related expenses, and a stipend of $10,000 per year for housing, transportation, and related expenses for summer internships.

Duration 2 years.

Additional information This program is offered jointly by Howard University and the U.S. Department of State. Fellows are provided an internship working on international issues for members of Congress during the summer after they are selected and before they begin graduate study. They are provided a second internship at a U.S. embassy overseas during the summer before their second year of graduate study. Fellows who complete the program and Foreign Service entry requirements receive appointments as Foreign Service Officers. Each fellow who obtains a master's degree is committed to at least 5 years of service as a Foreign Service Officer. If recipients do not complete the program successfully or do not fulfill the 3-year service obligation, they may be subject to a reimbursement obligation.

Number awarded 20 each year.

Deadline January of each year.

[802]
CHEROKEE NATION BUSINESSES SCHOLARSHIP

Cherokee Nation Foundation
800 South Muskogee
Tahlequah, OK 74464
(918) 207-0950   Fax: (918) 207-0951
E-mail: contact@cherokeenationfoundation.org
Web: www.cherokeenationfoundation.org/scholarships

Summary To provide scholarship/loans and work experience to citizens of the Cherokee Nation who are interested in completing a bachelor's or master's degree in a business-related field at a university in any state and working for Cherokee Nation Businesses.

Eligibility This program is open to citizens of the Cherokee Nation who are currently enrolled full time at a college or university in any state and working on an upper level bachelor's, professional, or master's degree. Their field of study must be accounting, corporate law, finance, engineering (biomedical, chemical, electrical, or mechanical), marketing, or mass communications. Applicants must be willing to 1) complete a paid summer internship for Cherokee Nation Businesses; and 2) sign a contract to work for Cherokee Nation Businesses for 2 years after graduation. They are not required to reside in the Cherokee Nation area. Along with their application, they must submit an 800-word essay on their desire to pursue higher education, their chosen field of study, how they plan to serve the Cherokee people after they complete their higher education, and whether or not they speak the Cherokee language. Financial need is considered in the selection process.

Financial data A stipend is awarded (amount not specified).

Duration 1 year; may be renewed up to 3 additional years, provided the recipient maintains a GPA that is in good standing at their school, performs the required internship, and completes a course in Cherokee Nation history.

Number awarded 1 or more each year.

Deadline January of each year.

[803]
CHEVRON CORPORATION SCHOLARSHIPS OF THE AMERICAN INDIAN SCIENCE AND ENGINEERING SOCIETY

American Indian Science and Engineering Society
Attn: Director of Membership and Communications
2305 Renard Place, S.E., Suite 200
Albuquerque, NM 87106
(505) 765-1052, ext. 110   Fax: (505) 765-5608
E-mail: lpaz@aises.org
Web: www.aises.org

Summary To provide financial assistance to members of the American Indian Science and Engineering Society (AISES) who are working on an undergraduate or graduate degree in a field of interest to Chevron Corporation.

Eligibility This program is open to AISES members who are full-time undergraduate or graduate students at an accredited 4-year college or university. Applicants must be American Indian tribal members, Alaskan Natives, Native Hawaiians, First Nations members, or other indigenous peoples of North America and have a Certificate of Degree of Indian or Alaska Native Blood (CDIB) showing at least 25% Native blood. They must have a GPA of 3.3 or higher and be working on a degree in business or a field of science, technology, engineering, or mathematics (STEM) that is beneficial to Chevron. In the selection process, priority is given to 1) freshmen and sophomores who have a related internship or nontechnical work experience; 2) juniors who have at least 1 leadership role in AISES and at least 1 technical internship related to their field of study; 3) seniors who have least 1 leadership role in AISES, at least 1 technical internship related to their field of study, and have not committed to an offer of employment with a company other than Chevron; and graduate students who have a least 1 technical internship related to their field of study and a master's thesis or doctoral dissertation on a topic that is related to the energy industry. All applicants must be able to demonstrate knowledge and interest in Chevron and the energy industry and have at least 1 noteworthy achievement or recognition.

Financial data The stipend is $5,000.

Duration 1 year; nonrenewable.

Additional information This program is funded by Chevron Corporation.

Number awarded 1 or more each year.

Deadline April of each year.

[804]
CHEYENNE AND ARAPAHO HIGHER EDUCATION GRANTS

Cheyenne and Arapaho Tribes of Oklahoma
Attn: Higher Education Program
100 Red Moon Circle
P.O. Box 167
Concho, OK 73022
(405) 422-7653   Toll Free: (800) 247-4612
Fax: (405) 422-8211   E-mail: heducation@c-a-tribes.org
Web: www.c-a-tribes.org/higher-education

Summary To provide financial assistance to enrolled Cheyenne-Arapaho tribal members who are interested in working on an undergraduate or graduate degree at a college in any state.

Eligibility This program is open to Cheyenne-Arapaho Indians who reside in any state and are at least a high school graduate (or the equivalent), approved for admission by a college or university, and in financial need. Applicants may be enrolled or planning to enroll at a 2- or 4-year college or university (not a vocational or technical school) in any state. The vast majority of students assisted under this program are at the undergraduate level, although graduate and/or married students are eligible for consideration and assistance. Summer and part-time students may apply as well, as long as application is made well in advance of enrollment and is accompanied by an official need evaluation.

Financial data The stipend is $2,000 per year.

Duration 1 year; renewable.

Number awarded 40 to 80 each year.

Deadline May of each year for fall semester; October for spring semester; or March for summer session.

[805]
CHF/ALYESKA MATCH SCHOLARSHIPS

Chugach Alaska Corporation
Attn: Chugach Heritage Foundation
3800 Centerpoint Drive, Suite 1200
Anchorage, AK 99503
(907) 261-0400   Toll Free: (800) 858-2768
Fax: (907) 261-8896 E-mail: scholarships@chugach.com
Web: www.chugachheritagefoundation.org

Summary To provide financial assistance to undergraduate and graduate students who are original shareholders of the Chugach Alaska Corporation or their descendants and attending college in any state to prepare for a career in the oil industry.

Eligibility This program is open to original shareholders and the descendants of original enrollees of the Chugach Alaska Corporation. Applicants must be enrolled or planning to enroll at an accredited college or university in any state as an undergraduate or graduate student to work on a degree in engineering (chemical, civil, electrical, mechanical; environmental health and safety; construction and project management; computer science, information technology, management information systems; instrumentation, process technology, supervisory control and data acquisition (SCADA); accounting, business administration, economics, of finance; or applied technology and industry trades such as welding, diesel and heavy equipment, electrician, maritime, culinary. They must have a GPA of 2.5 or higher and an interest in working within the Trans-Alaska Pipeline Services (TAPS) and the oil industry. Along with their application, a personal statement of career goals.

Financial data The stipend is $7,500 per academic year.

Duration 1 year; may be renewed.

Additional information The Chugach Alaska Corporation is 1 of 13 Alaska Native Regional Corporations created under the Alaska Native Claims Settlement Act of 1971. This program is sponsored by the Alyeska Pipeline Service Company.

Number awarded Varies each year.

Deadline Students must submit applications within 4 weeks after the start of the term. Awards are presented on a first-come, first-served basis.

[806]
CHICKASAW FOUNDATION GENERAL PURPOSE EDUCATION SCHOLARSHIPS

Chickasaw Foundation
2020 Arlington, Suite 4
P.O. Box 1726
Ada, OK 74821-1726
(580) 421-9030   Fax: (580) 421-9031
E-mail: ChickasawFoundation@chickasaw.net
Web: www.chickasawfoundation.org/Scholarships.aspx

Summary To provide financial assistance to members of the Chickasaw Nation who are interested in working on an undergraduate or graduate degree.

Eligibility This program is open to Chickasaw students who are currently enrolled at an accredited institution of higher education as a full-time undergraduate or graduate student. Applicants may be majoring in any field, but they must have a GPA of 2.0 or higher. Along with their application, they must submit high school or college transcripts; 2 letters of recommendation; a copy of their Chickasaw Nation citizenship card; a 2-page list of honors, achievements, awards, club memberships, societies, and civic involvement; and a 1-page essay on their long-term goals and plans for achieving those. Financial need is not considered in the selection process.

Financial data A stipend is awarded (amount not specified).

Duration 1 year.

Number awarded Varies each year; recently, 5 were awarded.

Deadline June of each year.

[807]
CHICKASAW FOUNDATION HEALTH PROFESSIONS SCHOLARSHIP

Chickasaw Foundation
2020 Arlington, Suite 4
P.O. Box 1726
Ada, OK 74821-1726
(580) 421-9030   Fax: (580) 421-9031
E-mail: ChickasawFoundation@chickasaw.net
Web: www.chickasawfoundation.org/Scholarships.aspx

Summary To provide financial assistance to members of the Chickasaw Nation who are interested in working on an undergraduate, graduate, or vocational/technical degree in a health-related field.

Eligibility This program is open to undergraduate, graduate, and vocational/technical students who are members of the Chickasaw Nation. Academic students must be preparing for a career as a dentist, dental hygienist, nurse, physician assistant, nurse practitioner, medical doctor, laboratory technologist, pharmacist, imaging technologist, behavioral health counselor, or biomedical engineer. Vocational students must be engaged in training as an emergency medical technician, licensed practical nurse, or electrician or plumber for the health arena. Applicants must have a GPA of 3.0 or higher. Along with their application, they must submit high school or college transcripts; 2 letters of recommendation; a copy of their Certificate of Degree of Indian Blood (CDIB) if relevant; a copy of their Chickasaw Nation citizenship card; a 2-page list of honors, achievements, awards, club memberships, societies, and civic involvement; and a 1-page essay on their long-term goals and plans for achieving those. Financial need is not considered in the selection process.

Financial data A stipend is awarded (amount not specified).

Duration 1 year.

Number awarded 1 each year.

Deadline June of each year.

[808]
CHICKASAW FOUNDATION JUDICIAL SCHOLARSHIP

Chickasaw Foundation
2020 Arlington, Suite 4
P.O. Box 1726
Ada, OK 74821-1726
(580) 421-9030   Fax: (580) 421-9031
E-mail: ChickasawFoundation@chickasaw.net
Web: www.chickasawfoundation.org/Scholarships.aspx

Summary To provide financial assistance to members of the Chickasaw Nation who are interested in working on an undergraduate or graduate degree in a field related to law.

Eligibility This program is open to Chickasaw students who are currently enrolled at an accredited 4-year college or university as a full-time undergraduate or law student. Applicants must be working on a degree in law, pre-law, legal studies, paralegal, or any major associated with law or a bachelor's degree obtained with the intention of pursuing a law degree. They must have a GPA of 3.2 or higher. Along with their application, they must submit high school, college, and/or law school transcripts; 2 letters of recommendation; a copy of their Chickasaw Nation citizenship card; a 2-page list of honors, achievements, awards, club memberships, societies, and civic involvement; and a 1-page essay on their long-term goals and plans for achieving those. Financial need is not considered in the selection process.

Financial data A stipend is awarded (amount not specified).

Duration 1 year.

Number awarded 1 each year.

Deadline June of each year.

[809]
CHICKASAW FOUNDATION NONPROFIT MANAGEMENT SCHOLARSHIP

Chickasaw Foundation
2020 Arlington, Suite 4
P.O. Box 1726
Ada, OK 74821-1726
(580) 421-9030   Fax: (580) 421-9031
E-mail: ChickasawFoundation@chickasaw.net
Web: www.chickasawfoundation.org/Scholarships.aspx

Summary To provide financial assistance to members of the Chickasaw Nation working on an undergraduate or graduate degree in a field related to nonprofit management.

Eligibility This program is open to members of the Chickasaw Nation who are currently enrolled as full-time graduate students or undergraduates at a 4-year college or university. Applicants must be working on nonprofit management certification or another field of study related to the nonprofit sector. They must have a GPA of 3.0 or higher. Along with their application, they must submit high school or college transcripts; 2 letters of recommendation; a copy of their Chickasaw Nation citizenship card; a 2-page list of honors, achievements, awards, club memberships, societies, and civic involvement; and a 1-page essay on their long-term goals and plans for achieving those. Financial need is not considered in the selection process.

Financial data A stipend is awarded (amount not specified).

Duration 1 year.

Number awarded 1 each year.

Deadline June of each year.

[810]
CHIPS QUINN SCHOLARS PROGRAM

Newseum Institute
Attn: Chips Quinn Scholars Program
555 Pennsylvania Avenue, N.W.
Washington, DC 20001
(202) 292-6271   Fax: (202) 292-6275
E-mail: kcatone@freedomforum.org
Web: www.newseuminstitute.org

Summary To provide work experience to Native American and other minority college students and recent graduates who are majoring in journalism.

Eligibility This program is open to students of color who are college juniors, seniors, graduate students, or recent graduates with journalism majors or career goals in newspapers. Candidates must be nominated or endorsed by journalism faculty, campus media advisers, editors of newspapers, or leaders of minority journalism associations. Along with their application, they must submit a resume, transcripts, 2 letters of recommendation, and an essay of 200 to 400 words on why they want to be a Chips Quinn Scholar. Reporters and copy editors must also submit 6 samples of published articles they have written; photographers must submit 15 to 25 photographs on a DVD; multimedia journalists and graphic designers should submit 6 to 10 samples of their work on a DVD. Applicants must have a car and be available to work as a full-time intern during the spring or summer. U.S. citizenship or permanent resident status is required. Campus newspaper experience is strongly encouraged.

Financial data Students chosen for this program receive a travel stipend to attend a Multimedia training program in Nashville, Tennessee prior to reporting for their internship, a $500 housing allowance from the Freedom Forum, and a competitive salary during their internship.

Duration Internships are for 10 to 12 weeks, in spring or summer.

Additional information This program began in 1991 in memory of the late John D. Quinn Jr., managing editor of the *Poughkeepsie Journal*. Funding is provided by the Freedom Forum, formerly the Gannett Foundation. After graduating from college and obtaining employment with a newspaper, alumni of this program are eligible to apply for fellowship support to attend professional journalism development activities.

Number awarded Approximately 70 each year. Since the program began, more than 1,300 scholars have been selected.

Deadline September of each year.

[811]
CHRISTENSEN CONSERVATION LEADERS SCHOLARSHIP

Wildlife Conservation Society
Attn: Graduate Scholarship Program
2300 Southern Boulevard
Bronx, NY 10460
(718) 220-5100   E-mail: kmastro@wcs.org
Web: www.wcs.org

Summary To provide funding to graduate students from other countries and from North American indigenous groups who are interested in conducting conservation research anywhere in the world.

Eligibility This program is open to entering a master's or doctoral degree program who are 1) residents of Africa, Asia/Pacific, or Latin America; or 2) members of North American indigenous groups. Applicants must be interested in conducting research on terrestrial or marine conservation issues at the local, regional, or national level. They must be nominated by the program director of the Wildlife Conservation Society (WCS) for their country and be citizens of that country. Current graduate students are not eligible, and applicants do not need to have selected the graduate school they plan to attend when they apply. Along with their application, they must submit 1) a 500-word essay on the key conservation issues in their country; 2) a 500-word essay on why they are preparing for a career as a conservationist; 3) an 850-word essay on their conservation career to date; 4) an 850-word essay on the specific area of studies in which they plan to specialize; 5) a 250-word essay on why this is the right time for them to begin graduate studies; and 6) information on their financial circumstances. Selection is based on the applicant's abilities, their potential to become leaders of the conservation movement in their home country, and the relevance of their proposed study and future work to WCS conservation priorities.

Financial data Fellows receive a grant of $30,000 to $36,000 for tuition, room, board, and a stipend. Other benefits include graduate school application fees, preparation and sitting fees for examinations such as the GRE and TOEFL, visa processing fees, English language training as needed, 1 round-trip airfare, a textbook allowance, a laptop computer and printer, settling-in allowance, and health insurance as required.

Duration 1 year.

Number awarded Varies each year.

Deadline April of each year.

[812]
CHUGACH HERITAGE FOUNDATION GRADUATE SCHOLARSHIPS

Chugach Alaska Corporation
Attn: Chugach Heritage Foundation
3800 Centerpoint Drive, Suite 1200
Anchorage, AK 99503
(907) 261-0400   Toll Free: (800) 858-2768
Fax: (907) 261-8896 E-mail: scholarships@chugach.com
Web: www.chugachheritagefoundation.org

Summary To provide financial assistance to graduate students who are original shareholders of the Chugach Alaska Corporation or their descendants and attending college in any state.

Eligibility This program is open to original shareholders and the descendants of original enrollees of the Chugach Alaska Corporation. Applicants must be enrolled or planning to enroll at an accredited college or university in any state as a graduate student. They must have a GPA of 2.5 or higher as an entering graduate student or 3.0 or higher as a continuing graduate student. Selection is based on academic excellence, community involvement, and leadership qualities.

Financial data The stipend is $10,500 per year for full-time students or a prorated amount for part-time students.

Duration 1 year; may be renewed if the recipient maintains a GPA of 3.0 or higher.

Additional information The Chugach Alaska Corporation is 1 of 13 Alaska Native Regional Corporations created under the Alaska Native Claims Settlement Act of 1971.

Number awarded Varies each year.

Deadline June of each year.

[813]
CIRI FOUNDATION ACHIEVEMENT SCHOLARSHIPS

Cook Inlet Region, Inc.
Attn: The CIRI Foundation
3600 San Jeronimo Drive, Suite 256
Anchorage, AK 99508-2870
(907) 793-3575   Toll Free: (800) 764-3382
Fax: (907) 793-3585   E-mail: tcf@thecirifoundation.org
Web: www.thecirifoundation.org/scholarships

Summary To provide financial assistance for undergraduate or graduate studies to Alaska Natives who are original enrollees to Cook Inlet Region, Inc. (CIRI) and their lineal descendants.

Eligibility This program is open to Alaska Native enrollees to CIRI under the Alaska Native Claims Settlement Act (ANCSA) of 1971 and their lineal descendants. There are no Alaska residency requirements or age limitations. Applicants must be accepted or enrolled full time in a 4-year or graduate degree program. They must have a GPA of 3.0 or higher. Along with their application, they must submit a 500-word statement on their educational and career goals and how they are contributing, or planning to contribute, to a positive Alaska Native community. Selection is based on that statement, academic achievement, rigor of course work or degree program, student financial contribution, financial need, grade level, previous work performance, community service, and relationship of degree program to career goals.

Financial data   The stipend is $8,000 per year.

Duration   1 year (2 semesters).

Additional information   CIRI is 1 of 13 regional corporations established according to the terms of the Alaska Native Claims Settlement Act (ANCSA) of 1971.

Number awarded   Varies each year.

Deadline   May of each year.

[814]
CIRI FOUNDATION EXCELLENCE SCHOLARSHIPS

Cook Inlet Region, Inc.
Attn: The CIRI Foundation
3600 San Jeronimo Drive, Suite 256
Anchorage, AK 99508-2870
(907) 793-3575   Toll Free: (800) 764-3382
Fax: (907) 793-3585   E-mail: tcf@thecirifoundation.org
Web: www.thecirifoundation.org/scholarships

Summary   To provide financial assistance for undergraduate or graduate studies to Alaska Natives who are original enrollees to Cook Inlet Region, Inc. (CIRI) and their lineal descendants.

Eligibility   This program is open to Alaska Native enrollees to CIRI under the Alaska Native Claims Settlement Act (ANCSA) of 1971 and their lineal descendants. There are no Alaska residency requirements or age limitations. Applicants must be accepted or enrolled full time in a 4-year undergraduate or a graduate degree program. They must have a GPA of 3.5 or higher. Along with their application, they must submit a 500-word statement on their educational and career goals and how they are contributing, or planning to contribute, to a positive Alaska Native community. Selection is based on that statement, academic achievement, rigor of course work or degree program, student financial contribution, financial need, grade level, previous work performance, community service, and relationship of degree program to career goals.

Financial data   The stipend is $10,000 per year.

Duration   1 year (2 semesters).

Additional information   CIRI is 1 of 13 regional corporations established according to the terms of the Alaska Native Claims Settlement Act (ANCSA) of 1971.

Number awarded   Varies each year; recently, 7 were awarded.

Deadline   May of each year.

[815]
CIRI FOUNDATION GENERAL SEMESTER SCHOLARSHIPS

Cook Inlet Region, Inc.
Attn: The CIRI Foundation
3600 San Jeronimo Drive, Suite 256
Anchorage, AK 99508-2870
(907) 793-3575   Toll Free: (800) 764-3382
Fax: (907) 793-3585   E-mail: tcf@thecirifoundation.org
Web: www.thecirifoundation.org/scholarships

Summary   To provide financial assistance for undergraduate or graduate studies to Alaska Natives who are original

enrollees to Cook Inlet Region, Inc. (CIRI) and their lineal descendants.

Eligibility   This program is open to Alaska Native enrollees to CIRI under the Alaska Native Claims Settlement Act (ANCSA) of 1971 and their lineal descendants. There are no Alaska residency requirements or age limitations. Applicants must be accepted or enrolled full or part time in a 2-year, 4-year, or graduate degree program. They must have a GPA of 2.5 or higher. Along with their application, they must submit a 500-word statement on their educational and career goals and how they are contributing, or planning to contribute, to a positive Alaska Native community. Selection is based on that statement, academic achievement, rigor of course work or degree program, student financial contribution, financial need, grade level, previous work performance, community service, and relationship of degree program to career goals.

Financial data   The stipend is $2,500 per semester for full-time students or $2,250 per semester for part-time students.

Duration   1 semester; recipients may reapply.

Additional information   CIRI is 1 of 13 regional corporations established according to the terms of the Alaska Native Claims Settlement Act (ANCSA) of 1971.

Number awarded   Varies each year; recently, 213 were awarded.

Deadline   May or November of each year.

[816]
CIRI FOUNDATION INTERNSHIP PROGRAM

Cook Inlet Region, Inc.
Attn: The CIRI Foundation
3600 San Jeronimo Drive, Suite 256
Anchorage, AK 99508-2870
(907) 793-3575   Toll Free: (800) 764-3382
Fax: (907) 793-3585   E-mail: tcf@thecirifoundation.org
Web: www.thecirifoundation.org/internships

Summary   To provide on-the-job training to Alaska Natives who are original enrollees to the Cook Inlet Region, Inc. (CIRI) and their lineal descendants.

Eligibility   This program is open to Alaska Native enrollees to CIRI under the Alaska Native Claims Settlement Act (ANCSA) of 1971 and their lineal descendants. Applicants must 1) be enrolled in a 2- or 4-year academic or graduate degree program with a GPA of 2.5 or higher; 2) have recently completed an undergraduate or graduate degree program; or 3) be enrolled or have recently completed a technical skills training program at an accredited or otherwise approved postsecondary institution. Along with their application, they must submit a 500-word statement on their areas of interest, their educational and career goals, how their career goals relate to their educational goals, and the type of work experience they would like to gain as it relates to their career and educational goals.

Financial data   The intern's wage is based on a trainee position and is determined by the employer of the intern with the approval of the foundation (which pays one half of the intern's wages).

Duration   Internships are approved on a quarterly basis for 480 hours of part-time or full-time employment. Interns may reapply on a quarter-by-quarter basis, not to exceed 12 consecutive months.

Additional information The foundation and the intern applicant work together to identify an appropriate placement experience. The employer hires the intern. Placement may be with Cook Inlet Region, Inc. (CIRI), a firm related to the foundation, or a business or service organization located anywhere in the United States. The intern may be placed with more than 1 company during the internship period. Interns may receive academic credit. CIRI is 1 of 13 regional corporations established according to the terms of the Alaska Native Claims Settlement Act (ANCSA) of 1971.

Number awarded Varies each year.

Deadline March, June, September, or November of each year.

[817]
CIRI FOUNDATION SPECIAL EXCELLENCE SCHOLARSHIPS

Cook Inlet Region, Inc.
Attn: The CIRI Foundation
3600 San Jeronimo Drive, Suite 256
Anchorage, AK 99508-2870
(907) 793-3575   Toll Free: (800) 764-3382
Fax: (907) 793-3585   E-mail: tcf@thecirifoundation.org
Web: www.thecirifoundation.org/scholarships

Summary To provide financial assistance for undergraduate or graduate studies in selected fields to Alaska Natives who are original enrollees to Cook Inlet Region, Inc. (CIRI) and their lineal descendants.

Eligibility This program is open to Alaska Native enrollees to CIRI under the Alaska Native Claims Settlement Act (ANCSA) of 1971 and their lineal descendants. There are no Alaska residency requirements or age limitations. Applicants must be accepted or enrolled full time in a 4-year undergraduate or a graduate degree program. They must have a GPA of 3.7 or higher. Preference is given to students working on a degree in business, education, mathematics, sciences, health services, or engineering. Along with their application, they must submit a 500-word statement on their educational and career goals and how they are contributing, or planning to contribute, to a positive Alaska Native community. Selection is based on that statement, academic achievement, rigor of course work or degree program, student financial contribution, financial need, grade level, previous work performance, community service, and relationship of degree program to career goals.

Financial data The stipend is $20,000 per year.

Duration 1 year; may be renewed.

Additional information CIRI is 1 of 13 regional corporations established according to the terms of the Alaska Native Claims Settlement Act (ANCSA) of 1971.This program began in 1997.

Number awarded 1 or more each year.

Deadline May of each year.

[818]
CITIZEN POTAWATOMI NATION TRIBAL ROLLS SCHOLARSHIPS

Citizen Potawatomi Nation
Attn: Office of Tribal Rolls
1601 South Gordon Cooper Drive
Shawnee, OK 74801-9002
(405) 878-5779   Toll Free: (800) 880-9880
Fax: (405) 878-4653
Web: www.potawatomi.org/services/education

Summary To provide financial assistance for college or graduate school to members of the Citizen Potawatomi Nation.

Eligibility This program is open to enrolled members of the Citizen Potawatomi Nation who are attending or planning to attend an undergraduate or graduate degree program, vocational technical career courses, or other accredited educational program in any state. Applicants must have a GPA of 2.0 or higher and be able to demonstrate financial need.

Financial data Stipends are $1,500 per semester for full-time students or $750 per semester for part-time students.

Duration 1 semester; may be renewed, provided the recipient maintains a GPA of 2.0 or higher.

Number awarded Varies each year; recently, 125 were awarded, including 94 to undergraduates, 10 to vocational/technical students, and 21 to graduate students.

Deadline July of each year for fall session, November of each year for spring or winter session, or May for summer session.

[819]
CLA SCHOLARSHIP FOR MINORITY STUDENTS IN MEMORY OF EDNA YELLAND

California Library Association
1055 East Colorado Boulevard, Fifth Floor
Pasadena, CA 91106
(626) 204-4071   E-mail: info@cla-net.org
Web: www.cla-net.org/?page=110

Summary To provide financial assistance to Native American and students of other ethnic minority origin in California who are attending graduate school in any state to prepare for a career in library or information science.

Eligibility This program is open to California residents who are members of ethnic minority groups (American Indian/Alaska Native, African American/Black, Latino/Hispanic, Asian American, or Pacific Islander). Applicants must have completed at least 1 course in a master's program at an accredited graduate library school in any state. Evidence of financial need and U.S. citizenship or permanent resident status must be submitted. Finalists are interviewed.

Financial data The stipend is $2,500.

Duration 1 academic year.

Additional information This fellowship is named for the executive secretary of the California Library Association from 1947 to 1963 who worked to promote the goals of the California Library Association and the profession. Until 1985, it was named the Edna Yelland Memorial Scholarship.

Number awarded 3 each year.

Deadline July of each year.

[820]
COBELL SCHOLARSHIPS

Indigenous Education, Inc.
6501 Americas Parkway, N.E., Suite 825
P.O. Box 26837
Albuquerque, NM 87125
(505) 313-0032   Toll Free: (844) 551-0650
Web: www.cobellscholar.org

Summary To provide financial assistance to Native Americans interested in attending college.

Eligibility This program is open to American Indians and Alaska Natives who submit a tribal enrollment form. Applicants must be enrolled or planning to enroll in a vocational diploma, associate, bachelor's, master's, doctoral, or professional degree or certificate. They must be able to demonstrate financial need.

Financial data Recently, stipends averaged more than $5,000.

Duration 1 year; nonrenewable.

Additional information This program was established in 2009 with $3.4 billion as settlement of a lawsuit filed by Elouise Cobell against the federal government for misuse of Indian Trust funds.

Number awarded Varies each year; recently, 368 students received more than $1,900,000 in scholarships (more than $1,500,000 for undergraduates and nearly $400,000 for graduate students.

Deadline May of each year.

[821]
COMMERCIAL AND FEDERAL LITIGATION SECTION DIVERSITY FELLOWSHIP

The New York Bar Foundation
One Elk Street
Albany, NY 12207
(518) 487-5651   Fax: (518) 487-5699
E-mail: moclair@tnybf.org
Web: www.tnybf.org/fellandschol

Summary To provide an opportunity for residents of any state who are Native Americans or other students from diverse backgrounds and attending law school in New York to gain summer work experience in a litigation position in the public sector in the state.

Eligibility This program is open to Black/African American, Latino/a, Native American or Alaskan Native, or Asian/Pacific Islander students from any state who are enrolled in the first year at a law school in New York. Applicants must have demonstrated an interest in commercial and federal litigation. They must be interested in working in a litigation position during the summer in the public sector in New York. Selection is based on content and quality of application materials, demonstrated interest in litigation, work experience, academic record, leadership experience, extracurricular activities, community service, quality of written expression, maturity, integrity, and professionalism.

Financial data The stipend is $6,000.

Duration 10 weeks during the summer.

Additional information This program began in 2007 with support from the Commercial and Federal Litigation Section of the New York State Bar Association. It is administered by The New York Bar Foundation.

Number awarded 1 each year.

Deadline January of each year.

[822]
COMMISSION ON DIETETIC REGISTRATION DIVERSITY SCHOLARSHIPS

Academy of Nutrition and Dietetics
Attn: Foundation
120 South Riverside Plaza, Suite 2000
Chicago, IL 60606-6995
(312) 899-4821   Toll Free: (800) 877-1600, ext. 4821
Fax: (312) 899-4796   E-mail: blabrador@eatright.org
Web: www.eatrightfoundation.org/foundation/scholarships

Summary To provide financial assistance to Native Americans and members of other underrepresented minority groups who are enrolled in an undergraduate or graduate program in dietetics.

Eligibility This program is open to students enrolled at a CADE-accredited/approved college or university in the undergraduate coordinated dietetics program, the undergraduate didactic program in dietetics, a dietetic internship program, a dietetic technician program, or a dietetic graduate program. Applicants must be members of underrepresented minority groups (African American, Hispanic, Native American). They must be U.S. citizens or permanent residents and show promise of being a valuable, contributing member of the profession. Membership in the Academy of Nutrition and Dietetics is encouraged but not required.

Financial data The stipend is $5,000.

Duration 1 year.

Number awarded 20 each year.

Deadline March of each year.

[823]
COMMITTEE ON ETHNIC MINORITY RECRUITMENT SCHOLARSHIP

United Methodist Church-California-Pacific Annual
   Conference
Attn: Board of Ordained Ministry
1720 East Linfield Street
Glendora, CA 91740
(626) 824-2284   E-mail: admin@bom.calpacumc.org
Web: www.calpacumc.org/ordainedministry/scholarships

Summary To provide financial assistance to Nativ Americans and members of other ethnic minority groups in the California-Pacific Annual Conference of the United Methodist Church (UMC) who are attending a seminary in any state to qualify for ordination as an elder or deacon.

Eligibility This program is open to members of ethnic minority groups in the UMC California-Pacific Annual Conference who are enrolled at a seminary in any state approved by the UMC University Senate. Applicants must have been approved as certified candidates by their district committee and be seeking Probationary Deacon or Elder's Orders. They may apply for 1 or more types of assistance: tuition scholarships, grants for books and school supplies (including computers), or emergency living expense grants.

Financial data Tuition stipends are $1,000 per year; books and supplies grants range up to $1,000 per year; emergency living expense grants depend on need and the availability of funds.

Duration 1 year; may be renewed up to 2 additional years.

Additional information The California-Pacific Annual Conference includes churches in southern California, Hawaii, Guam, and Saipan.

Number awarded Varies each year.

Deadline August of each year for fall term; December of each year for spring term.

[824]
CONSORTIUM FOR GRADUATE STUDY IN MANAGEMENT FELLOWSHIPS

Consortium for Graduate Study in Management
229 Chesterfield Business Parkway
Chesterfield, MO 63005
(636) 681-5553   Fax: (636) 681-5499
E-mail: recruiting@cgsm.org
Web: www.cgsm.org

Summary To provide financial assistance and work experience to Native Americans and other underrepresented racial minorities interested in preparing for a management career in business.

Eligibility This program is open to African Americans, Hispanic Americans (Chicanos, Cubans, Dominicans, and Puerto Ricans), and Native Americans who have graduated from college and are interested in preparing for a career in business. Other U.S. citizens and permanent residents who can demonstrate a commitment to the sponsor's mission of enhancing diversity in business education are also eligible. An undergraduate degree in business or economics is not required. Applicants must be planning to work on an M.B.A. degree at 1 of the consortium's 18 schools.

Financial data The fellowship pays full tuition and required fees. Summer internships with the consortium's cooperative sponsors, providing paid practical experience, are also offered.

Duration Up to 4 semesters.

Additional information This program began in 1966. The participating schools are Carnegie Mellon University, Cornell University, Dartmouth College, Emory University, Georgetown University, Indiana University, University of Michigan, New York University, University of California at Berkeley, University of California at Los Angeles, University of North Carolina at Chapel Hill, University of Rochester, University of Southern California, University of Texas at Austin, University of Virginia, Washington University, University of Wisconsin at Madison, and Yale University. Fellowships are tenable at member schools only. Application fees are $150 for students applying to 1 or 2 schools, $200 for 3 schools, $240 for 4 schools, $275 for 5 schools, or $300 for 6 schools.

Number awarded Varies each year; recently, 420 were awarded.

Deadline January of each year.

[825]
CONSTANGY DIVERSITY SCHOLARS AWARD

Constangy, Brooks, Smith and Prophete LLP
Attn: Chair, Diversity Council
200 West Forsyth Street, Suite 1700
Jacksonville, FL 32202-4317
(904) 356-8900   Fax: (904) 356-8200
E-mail: mzabijaka@constangy.com
Web: www.constangy.com/f-4.html

Summary To provide financial assistance to Native American and other students enrolled in law schools in selected states.

Eligibility This program is open to second-year students enrolled in accredited law schools located in 1 of 3 regions: South (Alabama, Florida, Georgia, South Carolina, Tennessee), Midwest/West Coast (California, Illinois, Kansas, Missouri, Texas, Wisconsin), or East (Massachusetts, New Jersey, North Carolina, Virginia/Washington D.C.). Applicants must submit a personal statement on why diversity is important to them personally and in the legal profession. They must have a GPA of 3.0 or higher. Selection is based on academic achievement, commitment to diversity, and personal achievement in overcoming obstacles.

Financial data The stipend is $2,500.

Duration 1 year.

Number awarded 1 each year.

Deadline November of each year.

[826]
CONSUELO W. GOSNELL MEMORIAL SCHOLARSHIPS

National Association of Social Workers
Attn: NASW Foundation
750 First Street, N.E., Suite 800
Washington, DC 20002-4241
(202) 408-8600, ext. 298   Fax: (202) 336-8292
E-mail: naswfoundation@naswdc.org
Web: www.naswfoundation.org/gosnell.asp

Summary To provide financial assistance to Native American, Hispanic American, and other students interested in working on a master's degree in social work.

Eligibility This program is open to students who have applied to or been accepted into an accredited M.S.W. program. Applicants must have demonstrated a commitment to work with, or have a special affinity with, American Indian, Alaska Native, or Hispanic/Latino populations in the United States. They must be members of the National Association of Social Workers (NASW), have the potential for completing an M.S.W. program, and have a GPA of 3.0 or higher. Applicants who have demonstrated a commitment to working with public or voluntary nonprofit agencies or with local grassroots groups in the United States are also eligible. Financial need is considered in the selection process.

Financial data The stipends range up to $4,000 per year.

Duration Up to 1 year; may be renewed for 1 additional year.

Number awarded Up to 10 each year.

Deadline February of each year.

[827]
COOK INLET TRIBAL COUNCIL TRIBAL HIGHER EDUCATION PROGRAM

Cook Inlet Tribal Council, Inc.
c/o The CIRI Foundation
3600 San Jeronimo Drive, Suite 256
Anchorage, AK 99508-2870
(907) 793-3575   Toll Free: (800) 764-3382
Fax: (907) 793-3585   E-mail: tcf@thecirifoundation.org
Web: www.thecirifoundation.org/citc-scholarship

Summary To provide financial assistance to Alaska Native shareholders of the Cook Inlet Region, Inc. (CIRI) and their descendants who are working on an undergraduate or graduate degree.

Eligibility This program is open to Alaska Native shareholders of CIRI and their descendants, regardless of residence, who are enrolled or planning to enroll full time at an accredited college, university, training institution, or vocational/technical school. Applicants must be working on a certificate, associate, bachelor's, master's, or doctoral degree. Along with their application they must submit a letter of reference, a 200-word statement of purpose, their Certificate of Degree of Alaska Native Blood (CDIB), a letter of acceptance from the school, transcripts, their Student Aid Report, a budget forecast, and (for males) documentation of Selective Service registration. Awards are presented on a first-come, first-served basis as long as funds are available.

Financial data This program provides supplementary matching financial aid. Awards are intended to be applied to tuition, fees, course-required books and supplies, and on-campus housing and meal plans only. Total funding over a lifetime educational career is limited to $30,000 for undergraduate degrees and certificates, $20,000 for a master's degree, or $20,000 for a doctoral degree.

Duration 1 year; may be renewed up to 4 additional years if the recipient maintains a GPA of 2.0 or higher.

Additional information Students whose CDIB gives their village as Tyonek, Kenai, Ninilchik, Knik, or Salamatof must apply directly to their village organization.

Number awarded Varies each year, depending on the availability of funds.

Deadline May of each year for fall; November of each year for spring.

[828]
COQUILLE INDIAN TRIBE COMPUTER EQUIPMENT PROGRAM

Coquille Indian Tribe
Attn: Department of Culture, Education and Library Services
495 Miluk Drive
Coos Bay, OR 97420
(541) 756-0904   Toll Free: (800) 622-5869
Fax: (541) 888-2418
E-mail: rhondaferguson@coquilletribe.org
Web: www.coquilletribe.org/higheredprograms.htm

Summary To provide funding for the purchase of computer equipment to members of the Coquille Indian Tribe who are working full time on an undergraduate or graduate degree.

Eligibility This program is open to enrolled members of the Coquille Indian Tribe who have been enrolled for at least 2 semesters as a full- or part-time undergraduate or graduate student at an accredited college, university, or community college in any state. Applicants must be seeking funding for the purchase of computer equipment.

Financial data The grant is $1,200; funds must be used for purchase of computer equipment or programming, and not for training, shipping, and/or maintenance of equipment.

Duration This is a 1-time grant.

Number awarded Varies each year.

Deadline Deadline not specified.

[829]
COQUILLE INDIAN TRIBE HIGHER EDUCATION GRANTS

Coquille Indian Tribe
Attn: Department of Culture, Education and Library Services
495 Miluk Drive
Coos Bay, OR 97420
(541) 756-0904   Toll Free: (800) 622-5869
Fax: (541) 888-2418
E-mail: bridgettwheeler@coquilletribe.org
Web: www.coquilletribe.org/higheredprograms.htm

Summary To provide financial assistance to members of the Coquille Indian Tribe who are attending or planning to attend college or graduate school in any state.

Eligibility This program is open to enrolled members of the Coquille Indian Tribe who are entering or continuing undergraduate or graduate students at an accredited college, university, or community college in any state. Along with their application, they must submit a personal statement on their short- and long-term career goals and if they plan to work for the tribe after graduation. Financial need is also considered in the selection process.

Financial data Maximum stipends are $12,000 per year for graduate students, $9,000 per year for full-time undergraduates at 4-year colleges and universities or $7,500 per year for students at 2-year community colleges. Part-time students are eligible to receive funding for tuition and books only.

Duration 1 year; may be renewed up to 4 additional years.

Number awarded Varies each year.

Deadline June of each year for fall semester or quarter, October of each year for spring semester or winter quarter; January of each year for spring quarter; March of each year for summer term.

[830]
CORRIS BOYD SCHOLARS PROGRAM

Association of University Programs in Health Administration
Attn: Prizes, Fellowships and Scholarships
2000 14th Street North, Suite 780
Arlington, VA 22201
(703) 894-0940, ext. 122   Fax: (703) 894-0941
E-mail: lmeckley@aupha.org
Web: www.aupha.org

Summary To provide financial assistance to Native American and other minority students entering graduate schools affiliated with the Association of University Programs in Health Administration (AUPHA).

Eligibility This program is open to students of color (African Americans, American Indians, Alaska Natives, Asian Americans, Latino/Hispanic, Native Hawaiians, Pacific Islanders) who have been accepted to a master's degree program in health care management at an AUPHA member institution. Applicants must be U.S. citizens or permanent residents and have a GPA of 3.0 or higher. Along with their application, they must submit a personal statement explaining why they are choosing to prepare for a career in health administration. Selection is based on leadership qualities, academic achievement, community involvement, and commitment to health care and health care management as a career path; financial need may be considered if all other factors are equal.

Financial data The stipend is $40,000.

Duration 1 year.

Additional information This program began in 2006.

Number awarded 2 each year.

Deadline April of each year.

[831]
CREDIT SUISSE MBA FELLOWSHIP

Credit Suisse
Attn: Diversity and Inclusion Programs
Eleven Madison Avenue
New York, NY 10010-3629
(212) 325-2000   Fax: (212) 325-6665
E-mail: campus.diversity@credit-suisse.com
Web: www.credit-suisse.com

Summary To provide financial assistance and work experience at offices of Credit Suisse to Native American and other underrepresented minority graduate students working on a master's degree as preparation for a career in investment banking.

Eligibility This program is open to students entering their first year of a full-time M.B.A. program who are female, Black/African American, Hispanic/Latino, or Native American. Applicants must be able to demonstrate a strong interest in a career in investment banking. Selection is based on academic excellence, leadership ability, and interest in the financial services industry.

Financial data The stipend is $15,000 for the first year; for the second year, students may elect to have $30,000 paid directly to their university or to have $15,000 paid to them for tuition and for academic and living expenses.

Duration 1 year (the first year of graduate school), followed by a summer internship at 1 of the offices of Credit Suisse. Students who successfully complete the internship and accept an office of full-time employment with the firm are eligible for a second year of funding.

Additional information Offices of Credit Suisse are located in Chicago, Houston, Los Angeles, New York, and San Francisco.

Number awarded 1 or more each year.

Deadline November of each year.

[832]
CREEK NATION POST GRADUATE PROGRAM

Muscogee (Creek) Nation of Oklahoma
Attn: Higher Education Program
P.O. Box 580
Okmulgee, OK 74447
(918) 732-7690   Toll Free: (800) 482-1979, ext. 7690
Fax: (918) 732-7694   E-mail: highered@mcn-nsn.gov
Web: www.muscogeenation-nsn.gov

Summary To provide financial assistance to enrolled citizens of the Muscogee (Creek) Nation interested in working on a graduate degree at a college or university in any state.

Eligibility This program is open to enrolled citizens of the Muscogee (Creek) Nation (with no minimum blood quantum required) who are enrolled or planning to enroll in an accredited college or university in any state to work on a master's, doctoral, or professional degree. Applicants must have a GPA of 3.0 or higher. They must submit copies of their Certificate of Degree of Indian Blood (CDIB) and tribal enrollment card.

Financial data The stipend is $250 per credit hour per year, to a maximum of $4,500 per academic year.

Duration 1 year; may be renewed for up to 1 additional year (for master's degree students) or up to 2 additional years (for doctoral students).

Number awarded Varies each year.

Deadline October of each year for fall semester; February of each year for spring semester; June of each year for summer semester.

[833]
CRST EDUCATION HARDSHIP GRANT

Cheyenne River Sioux Tribe
Attn: Education Services Office
2001 Main Street
P.O. Box 590
Eagle Butte, SD 57625
(605) 964-8311   E-mail: dal7882@lakotanetwork.com
Web: www.sioux.org/educational-services-department.html

Summary To provide financial assistance to members of the Cheyenne River Sioux Tribe who are attending college or graduate school in any state but are not eligible for funding through other tribal programs.

Eligibility This program is open to enrolled Cheyenne River Sioux tribal members who are attending a college, university, or vocational/technical school in any state. Applicants must be ineligible for other tribal education programs because they 1) are graduate students (master's degree only); 2) have been suspended from the tribe's higher education or adult vocational training programs; or 3) have exceeded the number of semesters allowed by the higher education program. Funding is awarded in the following priority order: undergraduate students attending college off-reservation, moving expenses for students attending college off-reservation, undergraduate students at Oglala Lakota College, graduate students attending college off-reservation, and graduate students enrolled in online distance learning programs.

Financial data A stipend is awarded (amount not specified).

Duration 1 year; may be renewed.

Number awarded Varies each year.

Deadline September of each year for fall semester; February of each year for spring semester.

[834]
DALMAS A. TAYLOR MEMORIAL SUMMER MINORITY POLICY FELLOWSHIP

Society for the Psychological Study of Social Issues
208 I Street, N.E.
Washington, DC 20002-4340
(202) 675-6956   Toll Free: (877) 310-7778
Fax: (202) 675-6902   E-mail: awards@spssi.org
Web: www.spssi.org

Summary To enable Native Americans and other graduate students of color to be involved in the public policy activities of the American Psychological Association (APA) during the summer.

Eligibility This program is open to graduate students who are members of an ethnic minority group (including, but not limited to, African American, Alaskan Native, American Indian, Asian American, Hispanic, and Pacific Islander) and/or have demonstrated a commitment to a career in psychology or a related field with a focus on ethnic minority issues. Applicants must be interested in spending a summer in Washington, D.C. to work on public policy issues in conjunction with the Minority Fellowship Program of the APA. Their application must indicate why they are interested in the fellowship, their previous and current research experiences, their interest and involvement in ethnic minority psychological issues, and how the fellowship would contribute to their career goals.

Financial data The stipend is $3,000. The sponsor also provides travel expenses and up to $1,500 for living expenses.

Duration 8 to 12 weeks.

Additional information This program began in 2000. The sponsor is Division 9 of the APA.

Number awarded 1 each year.

Deadline February of each year.

[835]
DAVE CALDWELL SCHOLARSHIP

American Water Works Association
Attn: Scholarship Coordinator
6666 West Quincy Avenue
Denver, CO 80235-3098
(303) 794-7771   Toll Free: (800) 926-7337
Fax: (303) 347-0804   E-mail: scholarships@awwa.org
Web: www.awwa.org

Summary To provide financial assistance to outstanding Native American and other minority students interested in working on a graduate degree in the field of water supply and treatment.

Eligibility This program is open to minority and female students working on a graduate degree in the field of water supply and treatment at a college or university in Canada, Guam, Mexico, Puerto Rico, or the United States. Students who have been accepted into graduate school but have not yet begun graduate study are encouraged to apply. Applicants must submit a 2-page resume, official transcripts, 3 letters of recommendation, a proposed curriculum of study, a 1-page

statement of educational plans and career objectives demonstrating an interest in the drinking water field, and a 3-page proposed plan of research. Selection is based on academic record and potential to provide leadership in applied research and consulting in the drinking water field.

Financial data The stipend is $10,000.

Duration 1 year; nonrenewable.

Additional information Funding for this program comes from the engineering firm Brown and Caldwell.

Number awarded 1 each year.

Deadline January of each year.

[836]
DAVID AND CAROLYN NIMMO GRADUATE BUSINESS SCHOLARSHIP

Chickasaw Foundation
2020 Arlington, Suite 4
P.O. Box 1726
Ada, OK 74821-1726
(580) 421-9030   Fax: (580) 421-9031
E-mail: ChickasawFoundation@chickasaw.net
Web: www.chickasawfoundation.org/Scholarships.aspx

Summary To provide financial assistance to members of the Chickasaw Nation who are working on a master's degree in business.

Eligibility This program is open to Chickasaw students who are currently enrolled full time at an accredited college or university and working on an M.B.A. degree. Applicants must have a GPA of 3.0 or higher. Along with their application, they must submit high school or college transcripts; 2 letters of recommendation; a copy of their Chickasaw Nation citizenship card; a 2-page list of honors, achievements, awards, club memberships, societies, and civic involvement; and a 1-page essay on their long-term goals and plans for achieving those. Financial need is not considered in the selection process.

Financial data A stipend is awarded (amount not specified).

Duration 1 year.

Number awarded 1 each year.

Deadline June of each year.

[837]
DAVID EATON SCHOLARSHIP

Unitarian Universalist Association
Attn: Ministerial Credentialing Office
24 Farnsworth Street
Boston, MA 02210-1409
(617) 948-6403   Fax: (617) 742-2875
E-mail: mcoadministrator@uua.org
Web: www.uua.org

Summary To provide financial assistance to Native American and other minority women preparing for the Unitarian Universalist (UU) ministry.

Eligibility This program is open to women from historically marginalized groups who are currently enrolled or planning to enroll full or at least half time in a UU ministerial training program with aspirant or candidate status. Applicants must be citizens of the United States or Canada. Priority is given first to those who have demonstrated outstanding ministerial ability and secondarily to students with the greatest financial need (especially persons of color).

Financial data The stipend ranges from $1,000 to $15,000 per year.

Duration 1 year.

Number awarded 1 or 2 each year.

Deadline April of each year.

[838]
DAVID SANKEY MINORITY SCHOLARSHIP IN METEOROLOGY

National Weather Association
Attn: Executive Director
3100 Monitor Avenue, Suite 123
Norman, OK 73072
(405) 701-5167   Fax: (405) 701-5227
E-mail: exdir@nwas.org
Web: www.nwas.org

Summary To provide financial assistance to Native Americans and members of other underrepresented groups working on an undergraduate or graduate degree in meteorology.

Eligibility This program is open to members of underrepresented ethnic groups who are either entering their sophomore or higher year of undergraduate study or enrolled as graduate students. Applicants must be working on a degree in meteorology. Along with their application, they must submit a 1-page statement explaining why they are applying for this scholarship. Selection is based on that statement, academic achievement, and 2 letters of recommendation.

Financial data The stipend is $1,000.

Duration 1 year.

Additional information This program began in 2002.

Number awarded 1 each year.

Deadline April of each year.

[839]
DAVIS WRIGHT TREMAINE 1L DIVERSITY SCHOLARSHIP PROGRAM

Davis Wright Tremaine LLP
Attn: Diversity Scholarship Program
1201 Third Avenue, Suite 2200
Seattle, WA 98101-3045
(206) 757-8761   Toll Free: (877) 398-8416
Fax: (206) 757-7700   E-mail: BrookDormaier@dwt.com
Web: www.dwt.com/1ldiversityscholarship

Summary To provide financial assistance and summer work experience to Native Americans and other law students of diverse backgrounds.

Eligibility This program is open to first-year law students of color, women, LGBT students, and others of diverse backgrounds. Applicants must have a record of academic achievement as an undergraduate and in the first year of law school that demonstrates promise for a successful career in law, a commitment to civic involvement that promotes diversity and will continue after entering the legal profession, and a commitment to practicing in the Northwest after law school. Although demonstrated need may be taken into account, applicants need not disclose their financial circumstances.

Financial data The award consists of a $7,500 stipend for second-year tuition and expenses and a paid summer clerkship.

Duration 1 academic year and summer.

Number awarded 3 each year: 1 in the Seattle office, 1 in the Portland office, and 1 in the New York City office.

Deadline January of each year.

[840]
DEEP CARBON OBSERVATORY DIVERSITY GRANTS

American Geosciences Institute
Attn: Grant Coordinator
4220 King Street
Alexandria, VA 22302-1502
(703) 379-2480   Fax: (703) 379-7563
E-mail: hrhp@agiweb.org
Web: www.americangeosciences.org

Summary To provide funding to geoscientists who are Native Americans or members of other underrepresented ethnic groups and interested in participating in research and other activities of the Deep Carbon Observatory (DCO) project.

Eligibility This program is open to traditionally underrepresented geoscientists (e.g., African Americans, Native Americans, Native Alaskans, Hispanics, Latinos, Latinas, Native Hawaiians, Native Pacific Islanders, Filipinos, of mixed racial/ethnic backgrounds) who are U.S. citizens or permanent residents. Applicants must be interested in participating in the DCO, a global research program focused on understanding carbon in Earth, and must have research interests that are aligned with its mission. They may be doctoral students, postdoctoral researchers, or early-career faculty members or research staff.

Financial data Grants average $5,000.

Duration 1 year.

Additional information This program is funded by the Alfred P. Sloan Foundation.

Number awarded 4 or 5 each year.

Deadline April of each year.

[841]
DELAWARE ATHLETIC TRAINERS' ASSOCIATION ETHNIC DIVERSITY ADVISORY COMMITTEE SCHOLARSHIP

Delaware Athletic Trainers' Association
c/o Education Committee Chair
University of Delaware
159 Fred Rust Ice Arena
Newark, DE 19716
(302) 831-6402   E-mail: kaminski@udel.edu
Web: www.delata.org/scholarship-applications.html

Summary To provide financial assistance to Native Americans and other ethnic minority members of the National Athletic Trainers' Association (NATA) from Delaware who are working on an undergraduate or graduate degree in the field.

Eligibility This program is open to NATA members who are members of ethnic diversity groups and residents of Delaware or attending college in that state. Applicants must be enrolled full time in an undergraduate athletic training education program or a graduate athletic training program and have a GPA of 2.5 or higher. They must intend to prepare for the profession of athletic training. Along with their application, they must submit an 800-word statement on their athletic training background, experience, philosophy, and goals.

Selection is based equally on academic performance and athletic training clinical achievement.

Financial data   A stipend is awarded (amount not specified).

Duration   1 year.

Number awarded   1 or more each year.

Deadline   February of each year.

[842]
DINSMORE & SHOHL LLP DIVERSITY SCHOLARSHIP PROGRAM

Dinsmore & Shohl LLP
Attn: Director of Recruiting and Legal Personnel
255 East Fifth Street, Suite 1900
Cincinnati, OH 45202
(513) 977-8488   Fax: (513) 977-8141
E-mail: dinsmore.legalrecuiting@dinsmore.com
Web: www.dinsmorecareers.com

Summary   To provide financial assistance and summer work experience with the sponsoring firm to Native Americans and other law students who will contribute to diversity in the legal profession.

Eligibility   This program is open to first-year law students who have made a meaningful commitment to diversity in the legal profession. The sponsor defines diversity as "the confluence of cultures, histories, sexual orientations, religions, and dialects that together make up the whole of our society." Applicants must have a demonstrated record of academic or professional achievement and leadership qualities through past work experience, community involvement, or student activities. They must also be interested in a summer associateship with Dinsmore & Shohl LLP. Along with their application, they must submit a 500-word personal statement explaining their interest in the scholarship program and how diversity has impacted their life.

Financial data   The program provides an academic scholarship of $5,000 and a paid associateship at the firm.

Duration   The academic scholarship is for 1 year. The summer associateship is for 12 weeks.

Additional information   Associateships are available at firm offices in Charleston (West Virginia), Cincinnati (Ohio), or Morgantown (West Virginia).

Number awarded   Varies each year.

Deadline   December of each year.

[843]
DISSERTATION FELLOWSHIPS OF THE CONSORTIUM FOR FACULTY DIVERSITY

Consortium for Faculty Diversity at Liberal Arts Colleges
c/o Gettysburg College
Provost's Office
300 North Washington Street
Campus Box 410
Gettysburg, PA 17325
(717) 337-6796   E-mail: sgockows@gettysburg.edu
Web: www.gettysburg.edu

Summary   To provide an opportunity for Native American and other doctoral candidates who will promote diversity to work on their dissertation while in residence at selected liberal arts colleges.

Eligibility   This program is open to U.S. citizens and permanent residents who have completed all the requirements for the Ph.D. or M.F.A. except the dissertation. Applicants must be interested in a residency at a member institution of the Consortium for Faculty Diversity at Liberal Arts Colleges during which they will complete their dissertation. They must be able to contribute to diversity at the institution.

Financial data   Dissertation fellows receive a stipend based on the average salary paid to instructors at the participating college. Modest funds are made available to finance the fellow's proposed research, subject to the usual institutional procedures.

Duration   1 year.

Additional information   The following schools are participating in the program: Allegheny College, Amherst College, Bard College, Bowdoin College, Bryn Mawr College, Bucknell University, Carleton College, Centenary College of Louisiana, Centre College, College of the Holy Cross, Colorado College, Denison University, DePauw University, Dickinson College, Gettysburg College, Grinnell College, Gustavus Adolphus College, Hamilton College, Haverford College, Hobart and William Smith Colleges, Juniata College, Lafayette College, Lawrence University, Luther College, Macalester College, Mount Holyoke College, Muhlenberg College, Oberlin College, Pitzer College, Pomona College, Reed College, Scripps College, Skidmore College, Smith College, Southwestern University, St. Lawrence University, St. Olaf College, Swarthmore College, The College of Wooster, Trinity College, University of Richmond, Vassar College, and Wellesley College. Fellows are expected to teach at least 1 course in each academic term of residency, participate in departmental seminars, and interact with students.

Number awarded   Varies each year.

Deadline   October of each year.

[844]
DISSERTATION FELLOWSHIPS OF THE FORD FOUNDATION DIVERSITY FELLOWSHIP PROGRAM

The National Academies of Sciences, Engineering, and Medicine
Attn: Fellowships Office
500 Fifth Street, N.W.
Washington, DC 20001
(202) 334-2872   Fax: (202) 334-3419
E-mail: FordApplications@nas.edu
Web: sites.nationalacademies.org

Summary   To provide funding for dissertation research to Native American and other graduate students whose success will increase the racial and ethnic diversity of U.S. colleges and universities.

Eligibility   This program is open to citizens, permanent residents, and nationals of the United States who are Ph.D. or Sc.D. degree candidates committed to a career in teaching and research at the college or university level. Applicants must be completing a degree in 1 of the following fields: American studies, anthropology, archaeology, art and theater history, astronomy, chemistry, communications, computer science, cultural studies, earth sciences, economics, education, engineering, ethnic studies, ethnomusicology, geography, history, international relations, language, life sciences, linguistics, literature, mathematics, performance study, philosophy, physics, political science, psychology, religious studies, sociology, urban planning, and women's studies. Also eligible are interdisciplinary programs such as African American studies, Native American studies, area studies, peace studies, and social justice. Students in practice-oriented areas, terminal master's degrees, other doctoral degrees (e.g., Ed.D., D.F.A., Psy.D.), professional degrees (e.g., medicine, law, public health), or joint degrees (e.g., M.D./Ph.D., J.D./Ph.D., M.F.A./Ph.D.) are not eligible. The following are considered as positive factors in the selection process: evidence of superior academic achievement; promise of continuing achievement as scholars and teachers; membership in a group whose underrepresentation in the American professoriate has been severe and longstanding, including Black/African Americans, Puerto Ricans, Mexican Americans/Chicanos/Chicanas, Native American Indians, Alaska Natives (Eskimos, Aleuts, and other indigenous people of Alaska), and Native Pacific Islanders (Hawaiians, Micronesians, or Polynesians); capacity to respond in pedagogically productive ways to the learning needs of students from diverse backgrounds; sustained personal engagement with communities that are underrepresented in the academy and an ability to bring this asset to learning, teaching, and scholarship at the college and university level; and likelihood of using the diversity of human experience as an educational resource in teaching and scholarship.

Financial data The stipend is $25,000; stipend payments are made through fellowship institutions.

Duration 9 to 12 months.

Additional information The competition for this program is conducted by the National Research Council on behalf of the Ford Foundation. Fellows may not accept remuneration from another fellowship or similar external award while supported by this program; however, supplementation from institutional funds, educational benefits from the Department of Veterans Affairs, or educational incentive funds may be received concurrently with Ford Foundation support. Dissertation fellows are required to submit an interim progress report 6 months after the start of the fellowship and a final report at the end of the 12 month tenure.

Number awarded Approximately 36 each year.

Deadline November of each year.

[845]
DIVERSIFYING HIGHER EDUCATION FACULTY IN ILLINOIS

Illinois Board of Higher Education
Attn: DFI Program
431 East Adams Street, Second Floor
Springfield, IL 62701-1404
(217) 782-2551   Fax: (217) 782-8548
TDD: (888) 261-2881   E-mail: DFI@ibhe.org
Web: www.ibhe.state.il.us/DFI/default.htm

Summary To provide fellowship/loans to Native American and other minority students interested in enrolling in graduate school programs in Illinois to prepare for a career in higher education.

Eligibility This program is open to U.S. citizens and permanent residents who 1) are residents of Illinois and have received a baccalaureate degree from an educational institution in the state; or 2) have received a baccalaureate degree from an accredited educational institution in any state and

have lived in Illinois for at least the 3 previous years. Applicants must be members of a minority group traditionally underrepresented in graduate school enrollment in Illinois (African Americans, Hispanic Americans, Alaskan Natives, Asian Americans, American Indians, Native Alaskans, Native Hawaiians, or other Pacific Islanders) and have been admitted to a graduate program in the state to work on a doctoral or master's degree and prepare for a career in teaching or administration at an Illinois postsecondary institution or Illinois higher education governing board. They must have a GPA of 2.75 or higher in the last 60 hours of undergraduate work or 3.2 or higher in at least 9 hours of graduate study. Along with their application, they must submit statements on 1) their professional goals (including their intended employment setting, intended position in Illinois higher education, plans for achieving their intended goals, and current and/or past experiences that would be helpful in achieving their intended goals; and 2) their underrepresented status (including how their underrepresented status influenced their personal and academic development and why they should be awarded a fellowship designated specifically for underrepresented groups in higher education). Financial need is considered in the selection process.

Financial data Stipends are $10,000 for new fellows or $13,000 per year for renewal fellows. Some participating institutions also provide a tuition waiver or scholarship. This is a fellowship/loan program. Recipients must agree to accept a position, in teaching or administration, at an Illinois postsecondary educational institution, on an Illinois higher education governing or coordinating board, or at a state agency in an education-related position. Recipients failing to fulfill the conditions of the award are required to repay 20% of the total award.

Duration Up to 2 years for master's degree students; up to 4 years for doctoral students.

Additional information The Illinois General Assembly established this program in 2004 as a successor to 2 earlier programs (both established in 1985); the Illinois Consortium for Educational Opportunity Program (ICEOP) and the Illinois Minority Graduate Incentive Program (IMGIP).

Number awarded Varies each year; recently, 111 new and renewal fellows were receiving support through this program.

Deadline February of each year.

[846]
DIVERSITY IN PSYCHOLOGY AND LAW RESEARCH AWARD

American Psychological Association
Attn: Division 41 (American Psychology-Law Society)
c/o Kathy Gaskey, Administrative Officer
P.O. Box 11488
Southport, NC 28461-3936
(910) 933-4018   Fax: (910) 933-4018
E-mail: apls@ec.rr.com
Web: www.apadivisions.org

Summary To provide funding to Native American and other student members of the American Psychology-Law Society (AP-LS) who are interested in conducting a research project related to diversity.

Eligibility This program is open to undergraduate and graduate student members of AP-LS who are interested in conducting research on issues related to psychology, law, multiculturalism, and/or diversity (e.g., research pertaining to psycholegal issues on race, gender, culture, sexual orientation). Students from underrepresented groups are strongly encouraged to apply; underrepresented groups include, but are not limited to: racial and ethnic minorities; first-generation college students; lesbian, gay, bisexual, and transgender students; and students with physical disabilities. Applicants must submit a project description that includes a statement of the research problem, the project's likely impact on the field of psychology and law broadly, methodology, budget, and an overview of relevant literature. Selection is based on the impact of the project on diversity and multiculturalism and the expected completion within the allocated time.

Financial data The grant is $1,000.

Duration The project must be completed within 1 year.

Number awarded Up to 5 each year.

Deadline November of each year.

[847]
DIVERSITY SUMMER FELLOWSHIP IN HEALTH LAW

The New York Bar Foundation
One Elk Street
Albany, NY 12207
(518) 487-5651   Fax: (518) 487-5699
E-mail: moclair@tnybf.org
Web: www.tnybf.org/fellandschol

Summary To provide an opportunity for Native American and other diverse residents of any state attending law school in New York to gain work experience in health law with an attorney or facility in the state.

Eligibility This program is open to diverse students from any state who are enrolled at a law school in New York. They must be interested in working on health law with a health care attorney or facility in New York. Along with their application, they must submit a writing sample on any topic, preferably health law. Selection is based on content and quality of application materials, demonstrated interest in health law, work experience, academic record, leadership experience, extracurricular activities, community service, quality of written expression, maturity, integrity, and professionalism.

Financial data The stipend is $5,000.

Duration 8 weeks during the summer.

Additional information This program began in 2011 by the Health Law Section of the New York State Bar Association. It is administered by The New York Bar Foundation.

Number awarded 2 each year.

Deadline December of each year.

[848]
DOCTORAL DIVERSITY FELLOWSHIPS IN SCIENCE, TECHNOLOGY, ENGINEERING, AND MATHEMATICS

State University of New York
Attn: Office of Diversity, Equity and Inclusion
State University Plaza, T1000A
353 Broadway
Albany, NY 12246
(518) 320-1189   E-mail: carlos.medina@suny.edu
Web: system.suny.edu/odei/diversity-programs

Summary To provide financial assistance to Native American and other residents of any state who are working on a doctoral degree in a field of science, technology, engineering, or mathematics (STEM) at campuses of the State University of New York (SUNY) and contribute to the diversity of the student body.

Eligibility This program is open to U.S. citizens and permanent residents who are residents of any state and enrolled as doctoral students at any of the participating SUNY institutions. Applicants must be working on a degree in a field of STEM. They must be able to demonstrate how they will contribute to the diversity of the student body, primarily by having overcome a disadvantage or other impediment to success in higher education. Economic disadvantage, although not a requirement, may be the basis for eligibility. Membership in a racial or ethnic group that is underrepresented at the applicant's school or program may serve as a plus factor in making awards, but may not form the sole basis of selection.

Financial data The stipend is $20,000 per year. A grant of $2,000 to support research and professional development is also provided.

Duration 3 years; may be renewed for up to 2 additional years.

Number awarded 2 each year.

Deadline March of each year.

[849]
DONALD W. BANNER DIVERSITY SCHOLARSHIP

Banner & Witcoff, Ltd.
Attn: Christopher Hummel
1100 13th Street, N.W., Suite 1200
Washington, DC 20005-4051
(202) 824-3000   Fax: (202) 824-3001
E-mail: chummel@bannerwitcoff.com
Web: www.bannerwitcoff.com/about/diversity

Summary To provide financial assistance to Native American and other law students who come from groups historically underrepresented in intellectual property law.

Eligibility This program is open to students enrolled in the first or second year of a J.D. program at an ABA-accredited law school in the United States. Applicants must come from a group historically underrepresented in intellectual property law; that underrepresentation may be the result of race, sex, ethnicity, sexual orientation, disability, education, culture, religion, age, or socioeconomic background. Selection is based on academic merit, commitment to the pursuit of a career in intellectual property law, written communication skills, oral communication skills (determined through an interview), leadership qualities, and community involvement.

Financial data The stipend is $5,000 per year.

Duration 1 year (the second or third year of law school); students who accept and successfully complete the firm's summer associate program may receive an additional $5,000 for a subsequent semester of law school.

Number awarded 1 each year.

Deadline October of each year.

[850]
DORSEY & WHITNEY DIVERSITY FELLOWSHIPS

Dorsey & Whitney LLP
Attn: Senior Recruiting Coordinator
50 South Sixth Street, Suite 1500
Minneapolis, MN 55402-1498
(612) 340-2600   Toll Free: (800) 759-4929
Fax: (612) 340-2868
E-mail: schueffner.sarah@dorsey.com
Web: www.dorsey.com/careers/lawstudents

Summary To provide financial assistance for law school to Native Americans and other students from diverse backgrounds who are interested in working during the summer at offices of the sponsoring law firm.

Eligibility This program is open to first-year students at ABA-accredited law schools who have accepted a summer associate position at an office of the sponsor in Minneapolis or Seattle. Applicants must be able to demonstrate academic achievement and a commitment to promoting diversity in the legal community, including work as women, ethnic minorities, or LGBT individuals. Along with their application, they must submit a personal statement on the ways in which they have promoted and will continue to promote diversity in the legal community, what diversity means to them, and why they are interested in the sponsoring law firm.

Financial data Fellows receive a stipend of $7,500 for the second year of law school and, if they complete a summer associate position in the following summer, another stipend of $7,500 for the third year of law school. If they join the firm following graduation, they receive an additional $5,000.

Duration 1 year; may be renewed for 1 additional year.

Additional information This program began in 2006.

Number awarded 1 each year.

Deadline January of each year.

[851]
DOYON FOUNDATION BASIC SCHOLARSHIPS

Doyon, Limited
Attn: Doyon Foundation
615 Bidwell Avenue, Suite 101
Fairbanks, AK 99701
(907) 459-2048   Toll Free: (888) 478-4755, ext. 2048
Fax: (907) 459-2065   E-mail: foundation@doyon.com
Web: www.doyonfoundation.com/static/facts.aspx

Summary To provide financial assistance to undergraduate and graduate students at schools in any state who are shareholders or descendants of shareholders of Doyon, Limited.

Eligibility This program is open to undergraduate or graduate students who are shareholders or the descendants of shareholders of Doyon, Limited. Applicants must be accepted or enrolled at an accredited college, university, technical institute, or vocational school. Both part-time and full-time students are eligible, but full-time students must be accepted into a degree program.

Financial data Stipends are $1,200 per semester for full-time students or $800 per semester for part-time students.

Duration 1 year. Undergraduate students may reapply if they maintain a GPA of 2.0 or higher; graduate or master's degree students may reapply if they maintain a GPA of 3.0 or

higher; and specialist or doctoral students may reapply if they maintain a GPA of 3.25 or higher.

Additional information Doyon, Limited is 1 of 13 Alaska Native Regional Corporations created under the Alaska Native Claims Settlement Act of 1971.

Number awarded Varies each year; recently, scholarships were awarded to 175 full-time students and 57 part-time students.

Deadline March of each year for summer school, May of each year for fall semester, November of each year for spring semester.

[852]
DOYON FOUNDATION COMPETITIVE SCHOLARSHIPS

Doyon, Limited
Attn: Doyon Foundation
615 Bidwell Avenue, Suite 101
Fairbanks, AK 99701
(907) 459-2048   Toll Free: (888) 478-4755, ext. 2048
Fax: (907) 459-2065   E-mail: foundation@doyon.com
Web: www.doyonfoundation.com/static/facts.aspx

Summary To provide financial assistance to undergraduate and graduate students at schools in any state who are shareholders or descendants of shareholders of Doyon, Limited.

Eligibility This program is open to undergraduate or graduate students who are shareholders or the descendants of shareholders of Doyon, Limited. Applicants must be accepted or enrolled full or part time at an accredited college, university, or vocational/technical school in any state. Undergraduates must be enrolled in a 4-year bachelor's degree program; graduate students must be enrolled in any post-baccalaureate program; vocational/technical students must be enrolled in a 1- to 3-year certificate or associate degree program. Along with their application, they must submit a personal essay on their educational goals, professional goals, extracurricular and community service activities or volunteerism, and cultural awareness and contributions to a healthy Native community. Selection is based on the essay (40 points), GPA (40 points), letters of recommendation (30 points), and personal impression (10 points).

Financial data Stipends are $5,000 per year for undergraduates, $7,000 per year for master's students, and $9,000 per year for doctoral students.

Duration 1 year. Undergraduate students may reapply if they maintain a GPA of 2.0 or higher; graduate or master's degree students may reapply if they maintain a GPA of 3.0 or higher; and specialist or doctoral students may reapply if they maintain a GPA of 3.25 or higher.

Additional information Doyon, Limited is 1 of 13 Alaska Native Regional Corporations created under the Alaska Native Claims Settlement Act of 1971. This program includes the Morris Thompson Scholarship Fund and the Rosemarie Maher Memorial Fund. Recipients must attend school on a full-time basis. Scholarship recipients of $5,000 or more are encouraged to complete at least 1 summer internship during their 4 years of study. Scholarship recipients of less than $5,000 are encouraged to do 1 of the following: serve on a local or regional board or commission, volunteer at least 20 hours, or give presentations on their field of study. A written report detailing the internship or service and lessons learned is required upon completion of the internship.

Number awarded Varies each year; recently, 26 were awarded.

Deadline May of each year for academic year scholarships; November of each year for spring semester.

[853]
DR. BERYL BLUE SPRUCE MEMORIAL FELLOWSHIP

American Indian Graduate Center
Attn: Executive Director
3701 San Mateo Boulevard, N.E., Suite 200
Albuquerque, NM 87110-1249
(505) 881-4584   Toll Free: (800) 628-1920
Fax: (505) 884-0427   E-mail: fellowships@aigc.com
Web: www.aigcs.org/scholarships/graduate-fellowships

Summary To provide financial assistance to citizens of Indian Pueblos interested in working on a degree in medical or nursing obstetrics and gynecology.

Eligibility This program is open to enrolled members of Indian Pueblos who can document one-fourth degree federally-recognized Indian blood. Applicants must be enrolled full time at a university in the United States and working on a graduate degree in nursing with an emphasis on obstetrics and gynecology or a medical degree in those fields. Along with their application, they must submit a 500-word essay on how receiving this fellowship will enable them to continue to build, promote, and honor self-sustaining American Indian and Alaska Native communities. Financial need is also considered in the selection process.

Financial data Stipends range from $500 to $5,000 per academic year, depending on the availability of funds and the recipient's unmet financial need.

Duration 1 year; may be renewed.

Number awarded 1 each year.

Deadline May of each year.

[854]
DR. DAVID K. MCDONOUGH SCHOLARSHIP IN OPHTHALMOLOGY/ENT

National Medical Fellowships, Inc.
Attn: Scholarship Program
347 Fifth Avenue, Suite 510
New York, NY 10016
(212) 483-8880   Toll Free: (877) NMF-1DOC
Fax: (212) 483-8897 E-mail: scholarships@nmfonline.org
Web: www.nmfonline.org

Summary To provide financial assistance to Native American and other underrepresented minority students specializing in ophthalmology or ear, nose, and throat (ENT) specialties at medical schools in New York City.

Eligibility This program is open to African American, Afro-Latino, and Native American medical students enrolled at a school in New York City. Applicants must be preparing for a career in ophthalmology or ENT specialties. They must be U.S. citizens or DACA students. Selection is based on leadership, commitment to serving medically underserved communities, and financial need.

Financial data The stipend is $5,000.

Duration 1 year.

Number awarded 1 each year.

Deadline September of each year.

[855]
DR. DAVID MONASH/HARRY LLOYD AND ELIZABETH PAWLETTE MARSHALL MEDICAL STUDENT SERVICE SCHOLARSHIPS

National Medical Fellowships, Inc.
Attn: Scholarship Program
347 Fifth Avenue, Suite 510
New York, NY 10016
(212) 483-8880   Toll Free: (877) NMF-1DOC
Fax: (212) 483-8897 E-mail: scholarships@nmfonline.org
Web: www.nmfonline.org

Summary To provide funding for a community health project to Native American and other underrepresented medical students in Chicago who are committed to remaining in the area and working to reduce health disparities.

Eligibility This program is open to residents of any state who are currently enrolled in their second through fourth year at a medical school in Chicago. U.S. citizenship is required. Applicants must be interested in conducting a community health project in an underserved community. They must identify as an underrepresented minority student in health care (defined as African American, Hispanic/Latino, American Indian, Alaska Native, Native Hawaiian, Vietnamese, Cambodian, or Pacific Islander) and/or socioeconomically disadvantaged student. Along with their application, they must submit documentation of financial status; a short biography; a resume; 2 letters of recommendation; a personal statement of 500 to 1,000 words on their personal and professional motivation for a medical career, their commitment to primary care and service in a health and/or community setting, their motivation for working to reduce health disparities, and their commitment to improving health care; a personal statement of 500 to 1,000 words on the experiences that are preparing them to practice in an underserved community; and a 150- to 350-word description of their proposed community service project. Selection is based on demonstrated leadership early in career and commitment to serving medically underserved communities in Chicago.

Financial data The stipend is $5,000.

Duration 1 year.

Additional information This program began in 2010 with support from the Chicago Community Trust.

Number awarded 6 each year.

Deadline May of each year.

[856]
DR. GEORGE BLUE SPRUCE FELLOWSHIP

American Indian Graduate Center
Attn: Executive Director
3701 San Mateo Boulevard, N.E., Suite 200
Albuquerque, NM 87110-1249
(505) 881-4584   Toll Free: (800) 628-1920
Fax: (505) 884-0427   E-mail: fellowships@aigc.com
Web: www.aigcs.org/scholarships/graduate-fellowships

Summary To provide financial assistance to Native American students interested in working on a degree in dentistry.

Eligibility This program is open to enrolled members of federally-recognized American Indian tribes and Alaska

Native groups and students who can document one-fourth degree federally-recognized Indian blood. Applicants must be enrolled full time at a dental school in the United States. Along with their application, they must submit a 500-word essay on how receiving this fellowship will enable them to continue to build, promote, and honor self-sustaining American Indian and Alaska Native communities. Financial need is also considered in the selection process.

Financial data Stipends range from $500 to $5,000 per academic year, depending on the availability of funds and the recipient's unmet financial need.

Duration 1 year; may be renewed.

Number awarded 1 each year.

Deadline May of each year.

[857]
DR. JOSEPHINE P. WHITE EAGLE GRADUATE FELLOWSHIPS

Ho-Chunk Nation
Attn: Higher Education Division
P.O. Box 667
Black River Falls, WI 54615
(715) 284-4915   Toll Free: (800) 362-4476
Fax: (715) 284-1760
E-mail: higher.education@ho-chunk.com
Web: www.ho-chunknation.com/highered/scholarships.aspx

Summary To provide financial assistance to enrolled members of the Ho-Chunk Nation who are working on a master's or doctoral degree in any field.

Eligibility This program is open to enrolled members of the Ho-Chunk Nation who have been accepted at an accredited college or university in the United States. Applicants must be working on a master's or doctoral degree. Along with their application, they must submit an essay about their educational and career goals and documentation of financial need.

Financial data The stipend is $24,000 per year for full-time students or $18,000 per year for part-time students.

Duration 1 year; may be renewed for a total of 6 semesters for a master's degree, 8 semesters for a J.D. degree, 10 semesters for an academic or professional doctoral degree (3 academic years of study and 2 years to complete a dissertation), or 10 semesters for a professional medical degree (e.g., M.D., D.D.S., D.P.T., D.N.P.). Renewal is provided only if the recipient maintains a GPA of 3.0 or higher.

Number awarded Varies each year.

Deadline April of each year for the fall term; September of each year for the spring term.

[858]
DR. NANCY FOSTER SCHOLARSHIP PROGRAM

National Oceanic and Atmospheric Administration
Attn: Office of National Marine Sanctuaries
1305 East-West Highway
N/ORM 6 SSMC4, Room 11146
Silver Spring, MD 20910
(301) 713-7245   Fax: (301) 713-9465
E-mail: fosterscholars@noaa.gov
Web: fosterscholars.noaa.gov/aboutscholarship.html

Summary To provide financial assistance to graduate students, especially Native Americans and other minorities, who are interested in working on a degree in fields related to marine sciences.

Eligibility This program is open to U.S. citizens, particularly women and members of minority groups, currently working on or intending to work on a master's or doctoral degree in oceanography, marine biology, or maritime archaeology, including all science, engineering, and resource management of ocean and coastal areas. Applicants must submit a description of their academic, research, and career goals, and how their proposed course of study or research will help them to achieve those goals. They must be enrolled full time and have a GPA of 3.3 or higher. As part of their program, they must be interested in participating in a summer research collaboration at a facility of the National Oceanic and Atmospheric Administration (NOAA). Selection is based on academic record and a statement of career goals and objectives (20%); quality of project and applicability to program priorities (30%); recommendations and/or endorsements (15%); additional relevant experience related to diversity of education, extracurricular activities, honors and awards, written and oral communication skills, and interpersonal skills (20%); and financial need (15%).

Financial data The program provides a stipend of $30,000 per academic year, a tuition allowance of up to $12,000 per academic year, and up to $10,000 of support for a 4- to 6-week research collaboration at a NOAA facility is provided.

Duration Master's degree students may receive up to 2 years of stipend and tuition support and 1 research collaboration (for a total of $94,000). Doctoral students may receive up to 4 years of stipend and tuition support and 2 research collaborations (for a total of $188,000).

Additional information This program began in 2001.

Number awarded Varies each year; recently, 3 were awarded.

Deadline December of each year.

[859]
DR. ROE B. LEWIS MEMORIAL SCHOLARSHIPS

Southwest Indian Agricultural Association
1664 East Florence boulevard
Casa Grande, AZ 85122-4779
(520) 562-6722   Fax: (520) 562-2840
E-mail: swiaa@g.com
Web: www.swindianag.com/construction.html

Summary To provide financial assistance to American Indians working on an undergraduate or graduate degree in a field related to agriculture or natural resources.

Eligibility This program is open to American Indians enrolled in a federally-recognized band, nation, or tribe. Applicants must be working on an undergraduate or graduate degree in agriculture or natural resources at an accredited college, university, or vocational/technical school. Along with their application, they must submit an essay explaining how they plan to use their education to promote, educate, and/or improve agriculture on southwest reservations. First-year undergraduates must have a GPA of 2.5 or higher; all other students must have a GPA of 3.0 or higher. Financial need is not considered in the selection process.

Financial data The stipend is $1,000.

Duration 1 year.

Number awarded 3 each year: 2 to undergraduates and 1 to a graduate student.

Deadline November of each year.

[860]
DRI LAW STUDENT DIVERSITY SCHOLARSHIP

DRI-The Voice of the Defense Bar
Attn: Deputy Executive Director
55 West Monroe Street, Suite 2000
Chicago, IL 60603
(312) 795-1101   Fax: (312) 795-0747
E-mail: dri@dri.org
Web: www.dri.org/About

Summary To provide financial assistance to Native American and other minority law students.

Eligibility This program is open to full-time students entering their second or third year of law school who are African American, Hispanic, Asian, Native American, women, or other students who will come from backgrounds that would add to the cause of diversity, including sexual orientation. Applicants must submit an essay, up to 1,000 words, on a topic that changes annually but relates to the work of defense attorneys. Selection is based on that essay, demonstrated academic excellence, service to the profession, service to the community, and service to the cause of diversity. Students affiliated with the American Association for Justice as members, student members, or employees are not eligible. Finalists are invited to participate in personal interviews.

Financial data The stipend is $10,000.

Duration 1 year.

Additional information This program began in 2004.

Number awarded 2 each year.

Deadline May of each year.

[861]
EDNA FURBUR FELLOWSHIP

American Indian Graduate Center
Attn: Executive Director
3701 San Mateo Boulevard, N.E., Suite 200
Albuquerque, NM 87110-1249
(505) 881-4584   Toll Free: (800) 628-1920
Fax: (505) 884-0427   E-mail: fellowships@aigc.com
Web: www.aigcs.org/scholarships/graduate-fellowships

Summary To provide financial assistance to female Native American graduate students interested in working on a degree related to the arts.

Eligibility This program is open to women who are enrolled members of federally-recognized American Indian tribes and Alaska Native groups or who can document one-fourth degree federally-recognized Indian blood. Applicants must be enrolled full time in a graduate program in the creative fine arts, visual works, crafts, music, performing, dance, literary arts, creative writing, or poetry. Along with their application, they must submit a 500-word essay on how receiving this fellowship will enable them to continue to build, promote, and honor self-sustaining American Indian and Alaska Native communities. Financial need is also considered in the selection process.

Financial data Stipends range from $500 to $5,000 per academic year, depending on the availability of funds and the recipient's unmet financial need.

Duration 1 year; may be renewed.

Number awarded 1 each year.

Deadline May of each year.

[862]
EDSA MINORITY SCHOLARSHIP

Landscape Architecture Foundation
Attn: Leadership in Landscape Scholarship Program
1129 20th Street, N.W., Suite 202
Washington, DC 20036
(202) 331-7070   Fax: (202) 331-7079
E-mail: scholarships@lafoundation.org
Web: www.lafoundation.org

Summary To provide financial assistance to Native American and other minority college students who are interested in studying landscape architecture.

Eligibility This program is open to African American, Hispanic, Native American, and minority college students of other cultural and ethnic backgrounds. Applicants must be entering their final 2 years of undergraduate study in landscape architecture or working on a graduate degree in that field. Along with their application, they must submit a 500-word essay on a design or research effort they plan to pursue (explaining how it will contribute to the advancement of the profession and to their ethnic heritage), 3 work samples, and 2 letters of recommendation. Selection is based on professional experience, community involvement, extracurricular activities, and financial need.

Financial data The stipend is $5,000.

Additional information This scholarship was formerly designated the Edward D. Stone, Jr. and Associates Minority Scholarship.

Number awarded 1 each year.

Deadline February of each year.

[863]
EDUCATIONAL FOUNDATION OF THE COLORADO SOCIETY OF CERTIFIED PUBLIC ACCOUNTANTS MINORITY SCHOLARSHIPS

Colorado Society of Certified Public Accountants
Attn: Educational Foundation
7887 East Belleview Avenue, Suite 200
Englewood, CO 80111
(303) 773-2877   Toll Free: (800) 523-9082 (within CO)
Fax: (303) 773-6344
Web: www.cocpa.org

Summary To provide financial assistance to Native American and other minority upper-division and graduate students in Colorado who are majoring in accounting.

Eligibility This program is open to Colorado minority residents (Black or African American, Hispanic or Latino, Native American, Asian American) who are upper-division or graduate students at colleges and universities in the state and have completed at least 6 semester hours of accounting courses. Applicants must have a GPA of at least 3.0 overall and 3.25 in accounting classes. They must be U.S. citizens or noncitizens legally living and studying in Colorado with a valid visa that enables them to become employed. Financial need is not considered in the selection process.

Financial data The stipend is $2,500. Funds are paid directly to the recipient's school to be used for books, C.P.A. review materials, tuition, fees, and dormitory room and board.

Duration 1 year; recipients may reapply.

Number awarded 1 or more each year.

Deadline May of each year for fall semester or quarter; November of each year for winter quarter or spring semester.

[864]
EDWARD L. KRUGER MEMORIAL *ITTISH AAISHA* SCHOLARSHIP

Chickasaw Foundation
2020 Arlington, Suite 4
P.O. Box 1726
Ada, OK 74821-1726
(580) 421-9030   Fax: (580) 421-9031
E-mail: ChickasawFoundation@chickasaw.net
Web: www.chickasawfoundation.org/Scholarships.aspx

Summary To provide financial assistance to members of the Chickasaw Nation who are working on a graduate degree in pharmacy.

Eligibility This program is open to Chickasaw students who are currently enrolled full time in a graduate school of pharmacy. Applicants must have a GPA of 3.0 or higher. Along with their application, they must submit high school or college transcripts; 2 letters of recommendation; a copy of their Chickasaw Nation citizenship card; a 2-page list of honors, achievements, awards, club memberships, societies, and civic involvement; and a 1-page essay on their long-term goals and plans for achieving those. Financial need is not considered in the selection process.

Financial data A stipend is awarded (amount not specified).

Duration 1 year.

Number awarded 1 each year.

Deadline June of each year.

[865]
ELIZABETH AND SHERMAN ASCHE MEMORIAL SCHOLARSHIP

Association on American Indian Affairs, Inc.
Attn: Director of Scholarship Programs
966 Hungerford Drive, Suite 12-B
Rockville, MD 20850
(240) 314-7155   Fax: (240) 314-7159
E-mail: general.aaia@indian-affairs.org
Web: www.indian-affairs.org

Summary To provide financial assistance to Native Americans interested in working on an undergraduate or graduate degree in health or science.

Eligibility This program is open to American Indian and Alaskan Native full-time undergraduate and graduate students working on a degree in health or science. Applicants must submit proof of tribal enrollment and an essay of 2 to 3 pages on 1 of the following topics: 1) why the sponsor's International Repatriation Project is important and how they would inform others about it; 2) the Annie E. Casey Foundation's Juvenile Detention Alternatives Initiative and tribal and community-based alternatives to detention for juveniles; or 3) how tribal leaders can promote higher education in their family

and community. They must have a GPA of 2.5 or higher. Selection is based on merit and need.

Financial data The stipend is $1,500.

Duration 1 year. Recipients may reapply.

Number awarded Varies each year; recently, 6 were awarded.

Deadline May of each year.

[866]
ELLIOTT C. ROBERTS SCHOLARSHIP

Institute for Diversity in Health Management
Attn: Membership and Education Specialist
155 North Wacker Avenue
Chicago, IL 60606
(312) 422-2658   E-mail: cbiddle@aha.org
Web: www.diversityconnection.org

Summary To provide financial assistance to Native Americans and other graduate students in health care management who will contribute to ethnic diversity in the profession.

Eligibility This program is open to U.S. citizens who represent ethnically diverse cultural backgrounds. Applicants must be enrolled in the second year of a master's degree program in health administration or a comparable program and have a GPA of 3.0 or higher. Along with their application, they must submit 1) a personal statement of 1 to 2 pages on their interest in health care management and their career goals; 2) an essay on what they see as the most challenging issue facing America's hospitals and health systems; and 3) a 500-word essay on their interest and background in health care finance. Selection is based on academic achievement, commitment to community service, and financial need.

Financial data The stipend is $1,000.

Duration 1 year.

Number awarded 1 each year.

Deadline January of each year.

[867]
ELLIS INJURY LAW DIVERSITY SCHOLARSHIPS

Ellis Law Corporation
Attn: Scholarship
883 North Douglas Street
El Segundo, CA 90245
Toll Free: (888) 559-7672
E-mail: scholarships@alelaw.com
Web: www.ellisinjurylaw.com/scholarships

Summary To provide financial assistance to pre-law and law students who either are members of an ethnic minority group or have been involved in diversity issues.

Eligibility This program is open to students accepted or enrolled at 1) a 4-year college or university with the intention of working on a law degree; and 2) an ABA-accredited law school. Applicants must be either members of an ethnic/racial minority or individuals who have made a demonstrative commitment to diversity within their school and/or community. They must have a GPA of 3.0 or higher. Along with their application, they must submit an essay of 1,500 to 2,000 words answering 3 questions about recent Supreme Court decisions regarding affirmative action. Selection is based on that essay and transcripts.

Financial data The stipend is $1,000.

Duration 1 year.

Additional information This program began in 2014.

Number awarded 3 each year.

Deadline December of each year.

[868]
EMERGING ARCHIVAL SCHOLARS PROGRAM

Archival Education and Research Institute
Center for Information as Evidence
c/o UCLA Graduate School of Education and Information
  Studies
Office of External Relations
2043 Moore Hall
Los Angeles, CA 90095-1521
(310) 206-0375   Fax: (310) 794-5324
Web: aeri.gseis.ucla.edu/fellowships.htm

Summary To provide an opportunity for Native American and other minority undergraduate and graduate students to learn more about the field of archival studies and to be exposed to research in the field.

Eligibility This program is open to undergraduates who have completed their junior year and to students who have completed the first year of a master's degree program. Applicants must be African American, Hispanic/Latino, Asian/Pacific Islander, Native American, Puerto Rican, or any other person who will add diversity to the field of archival studies. They must have a GPA of 3.0 or higher, but they may be working on a degree in any field and are not required to have prior knowledge of or experience in archival studies. U.S. citizenship or permanent resident status is required. Applicants must be interested in attending the week-long Archival Education and Research Institute (AERI), held at a different university each summer, where they are assigned both a faculty research mentor and a Ph.D. student mentor who introduce them to doctoral research and careers in archival studies.

Financial data Grants provide payment of round-trip travel, accommodation, and most meals.

Duration These grants are offered annually.

Additional information This program, first offered in 2009, is supported by the Institute of Museum and Library Services. Scholars who indicate an interest in continuing on to a doctoral program in archival studies after completing the AERI may be invited to participate in a supervised research project that will last up to 1 year and to present results of their research in a poster session at the AERI of the following year.

Number awarded Up to 7 each year.

Deadline April of each year.

[869]
EPISCOPAL NATIVE AND INDIGENOUS MINISTRIES THEOLOGICAL EDUCATION SCHOLARSHIPS

Episcopal Church Center
Attn: Domestic and Foreign Missionary Society
Scholarship Committee
815 Second Avenue, Fifth Floor
New York, NY 10017-4503
(212) 716-6168   Toll Free: (800) 334-7626
Fax: (212) 867-0395
E-mail: ahercules@episcopalchurch.org
Web: www.episcopalchurch.org

Summary To provide financial assistance to Native and Indigenous Americans interested in seeking ordination and serving in a ministry involving Native Americans and Alaska Natives in the Episcopal Church.

Eligibility This program is open to Native and Indigenous American students pursuing theological education, including diocesan programs as well as seminary education. Applicants must be a member of a Native or Indigenous American constituency in the Episcopal Church and have begun the process of seeking ordination through a local Episcopal diocese. Scholarships are presented both for full- and part-time study.

Financial data The maximum stipend is $5,000 per year.

Duration 1 year; may be renewed up to 3 additional years.

Additional information This program receives support from several funds of the sponsoring agency: the Mary E. Hinman Fund (established in 1879), the Missionary Education Fund (established in 1880), the Walter Nichols Hart Fund (established in 1884), the Joy Lyons Fund (established in 1885), the Thomas Balch Fund (established in 1886), the George C. Morris Fund, the Christiana Mason Gibson Memorial Fund (established in 1892), the Mortimer Scholarship Fund (established in 1893), the Theological Education Scholarship Fund (established in 1983), the Martin Luther King, Jr. Legacy Fund (established in 1991), the Howard A. Welch Fund (established in 2000), and the Episcopal Diocese of Michigan Native American Scholarship Fund (established in 2007).

Number awarded Varies each year; recently, 7 of these scholarships, with a value of $21,154, were awarded.

Deadline April of each year.

[870]
ESTHER NGAN-LING CHOW AND MAREYJOYCE GREEN SCHOLARSHIP

Sociologists for Women in Society
Attn: Administrative Officer
University of Kansas
Department of Sociology
1415 Jayhawk Boulevard, Room 716
Lawrence, KS 66045
(785) 864-9405   E-mail: swsao@outlook.com
Web: www.socwomen.org

Summary To provide funding to Native American and other women of color who are conducting dissertation research in sociology.

Eligibility This program is open to women from a racial/ethnic group that faces discrimination in the United States. Applicants must be in the early stages of writing a doctoral dissertation in sociology on a topic relating to the concerns that women of color face domestically and/or internationally. They must be able to demonstrate financial need. Both domestic and international students are eligible to apply. Along with their application, they must submit a personal statement that details their short- and long-term career and research goals; a resume or curriculum vitae; 2 letters of recommendation; and a 5-page dissertation proposal that includes the purpose of the research, the work to be accomplished through support from this scholarship, and a time line for completion.

Financial data The stipend is $15,000. An additional grant of $500 is provided to enable the recipient to attend the winter meeting of Sociologists for Women in Society (SWS), and travel expenses to attend the summer meeting are reimbursed.

Duration 1 year.

Additional information This program began in 2007 and was originally named the Women of Color Dissertation Scholarship.

Number awarded 1 each year.

Deadline March of each year.

[871]
ETHEL AND EMERY FAST SCHOLARSHIP

Ethel and Emery Fast Scholarship Foundation, Inc.
12620 Rolling Road
Potomac, MD 20854
(301) 762-1102   Fax: (301) 279-0201
E-mail: qccarol@erols.com

Summary To provide financial assistance to qualified Native Americans enrolled as undergraduates or graduate students.

Eligibility Applicants must 1) be Native Americans enrolled in a federally-recognized tribe; 2) have successfully completed 1 year of their undergraduate or graduate school program; 3) be enrolled in school full time; and 4) be able to demonstrate financial need. Along with their application, they must submit documentation of Native American eligibility, an original transcript, a letter confirming enrollment, a federal income tax return, a statement of financial need, and a personal statement (up to 2 pages) describing their current situation, their future aspirations in terms of their academic pursuits, and how this scholarship will assist them in attaining their goals.

Financial data A stipend is awarded (amount not specified). Funds are paid directly to the recipient's college or university and can only be used to pay for tuition, room, board, and fees.

Duration 1 year.

Number awarded Varies each year.

Deadline August of each year for the fall semester; January of each year for the spring semester.

[872]
ETHEL CURRY SCHOLARSHIPS

Minnesota Department of Education
Attn: Manager, Minnesota Indian Education
1500 Highway 36 West
Roseville, MN 55113-4266
(651) 582-8832   Toll Free: (800) 657-3927
E-mail: ladonna.mustin@state.mn.us
Web: www.education.state.mn.us

Summary To provide financial assistance to Native Americans in Minnesota who are interested in working on an undergraduate or graduate degree.

Eligibility This program is open to Indians who are enrolled in a Minnesota-based tribe or community. Applicants must be attending or planning to attend an accredited postsecondary institution in Minnesota as an undergraduate or graduate student. Undergraduates must have a GPA of 2.0 or higher; graduate students must have a GPA of 3.0 or higher. Along with their application, they must submit a 400-word

essay on why they should be awarded this scholarship. Selection is based on merit.

Financial data A stipend is awarded (amount not specified).

Duration Up to 4 years.

Number awarded Varies each year; recently, 9 were awarded.

Deadline May of each year.

[873]
ETHNIC IN-SERVICE TRAINING FUND FOR CLINICAL PASTORAL EDUCATION (EIST-CPE)

United Methodist Church
Attn: General Board of Higher Education and Ministry
Office of Loans and Scholarships
1001 19th Avenue South
P.O. Box 340007
Nashville, TN 37203-0007
(615) 340-7342   Fax: (615) 340-7367
E-mail: umscholar@gbhem.org
Web: www.gbhem.org

Summary To provide financial assistance to United Methodist Church clergy and candidates for ministry who are Native American or members of other minority groups interested in preparing for a career as a clinical pastor.

Eligibility This program is open to U.S. citizens and permanent residents who are members of ethnic or racial minority groups and have been active, full members of a United Methodist Church for at least 1 year prior to applying. Applicants must be United Methodist clergy, certified candidates for ministry, or seminary students accepted into an accredited Clinical Pastor Education (CPE) or an accredited American Association of Pastoral Counselors (AAPC) program. They must be preparing for a career as a chaplain, pastoral counselor, or in pastoral care.

Financial data Grants range up to $2,000.

Duration 1 year.

Number awarded 1 each year.

Deadline February of each year.

[874]
EUGENE DANIEL SCHOLARSHIPS

Osage Nation Education Department
Attn: Career Training and Scholarship
105 Buffalo Avenue
Hominy, OK 74035
(918) 287-5301   Fax: (918) 885-2136
E-mail: scholarship@osagenation-nsn.gov
Web: www.osagenation-nsn.gov

Summary To provide financial assistance to members of the Osage Nation who are interested in working on an undergraduate or graduate degree in a medical-related field.

Eligibility This program is open to Osage tribal students who are enrolled full time in a certification, associate, baccalaureate, master's, or doctoral program at an accredited college or technical school. Applicants must be working on a degree in a medical-related field and have a GPA of 3.0 or higher. They must be able to demonstrate financial need.

Financial data The stipend is $500 per semester. Funds are paid directly to the student's school to be applied toward tuition, fees, and books.

Duration 2 semesters.

Number awarded 4 each year.

Deadline June of each year.

[875]
EXTERNSHIP IN ADDICTION PSYCHIATRY

American Psychiatric Association
Attn: Minority Medical Student Awards
1000 Wilson Boulevard, Suite 1825
Arlington, VA 22209-3901
(703) 907-7894   Toll Free: (888) 357-7849
Fax: (703) 907-1087   E-mail: Mfpstudents@psych.org
Web: www.psychiatry.org

Summary To provide an opportunity for Native American and other minority medical students to spend an elective residency learning about substance abuse disorders, prevention, and early intervention.

Eligibility This program is open to student members of the American Psychiatric Association (APA) who come from racial/ethnic minorities and are currently enrolled at accredited U.S. medical school. Applicants must be interested in working with a mentor at a designated site to gain exposure to how psychiatrists treat patients with substance abuse disorders and participate in an interactive didactic experiential learning program. Mentors and sites are selected where there is an approved substance abuse training program and a significant number of substance abuse disorder patients from minority and underserved populations. U.S. citizenship or permanent resident status is required.

Financial data The program provides a stipend of $1,500 for living expenses and funding for travel to and from the mentoring site.

Duration 1 month during the summer.

Number awarded 6 each year.

Deadline March of each year.

[876]
EXXONMOBIL GEOSCIENCES SCHOLARSHIP PROGRAM

American Indian Science and Engineering Society
Attn: Director of Membership and Communications
2305 Renard Place, S.E., Suite 200
Albuquerque, NM 87106
(505) 765-1052, ext. 110   Fax: (505) 765-5608
E-mail: lpaz@aises.org
Web: www.aises.org/scholoarships/aises-exxonmobil

Summary To provide funding to members of the American Indian Science and Engineering Society (AISES) who are interested in conducting field work or research related to geosciences.

Eligibility This program is open to AISES members who are full-time undergraduate or graduate students at an accredited 4-year college or university. Applicants must be American Indian tribal members, Alaskan Natives, or Native Hawaiians and have a Certificate of Degree of Indian or Alaska Native Blood (CDIB) showing at least 25% Native blood. They must be seeking funding for geosciences field camps (normally undergraduates) or field-based research (typically master's or doctoral students). Along with their application, they must submit documentation of acceptance into a geoscience field camp or an approved plan for field-based research. A GPA of at least 3.0 is required.

Financial data The stipend is $3,000.

Duration 1 year; nonrenewable.

Additional information This program is funded by Exxon-Mobil.

Number awarded Up to 7 each year.

Deadline April of each year.

[877]
EXXONMOBIL SCHOLARSHIP OF KONIAG INCORPORATED

Koniag Incorporated
Attn: Koniag Education Foundation
4241 B Street, Suite 303B
Anchorage, AK 99503
(907) 562-9093   Toll Free: (888) 562-9093
Fax: (907) 562-9023
E-mail: scholarships@koniageducation.org
Web: www.koniageducation.org

Summary To provide financial assistance to Alaska Natives who are Koniag Incorporated shareholders or descendants and working on an undergraduate or graduate degree in science or mathematics related to the oil and gas industry.

Eligibility This program is open to undergraduate and graduate students who are Alaska Native shareholders of Koniag Incorporated or descendants of those original enrollees. Applicants must have a GPA of 3.0 or higher and be working full time on a degree in a field of science or mathematics related to the oil and gas industry. Along with their application, they must submit a 300-word essay about their personal and family history, community involvement, volunteer activities, and educational and life goals. Financial need is not considered in the selection process.

Financial data The stipend is $5,000 per year. Funds are sent directly to the recipient's school and may be used for tuition, books, supplies, room, board, and transportation.

Duration 1 year; may be renewed.

Additional information Koniag Incorporated is 1 of 13 Alaska Native Regional Corporations created under the Alaska Native Claims Settlement Act of 1971. This program is supported by ExxonMobil.

Number awarded 1 to 3 each year.

Deadline May of each year.

[878]
FAEGRE BAKER DANIELS DIVERSITY AND INCLUSION FELLOWSHIPS

Faegre Baker Daniels
Attn: Diversity and Pro Bono Coordinator
300 North Meridian Street, Suite 2700
Indianapolis, IN 46204
(317) 237-8298   Fax: (317) 237-1000
E-mail: brita.horvath@faegrebd.com
Web: www.faegrebd.com/fellowship

Summary To provide financial assistance and summer work experience to Native Americans and other students from diverse backgrounds entering the second year of law school.

Eligibility This program is open to residents of any state who are entering their second year at an accredited law school. Applicants must reflect diversity, defined to mean that they come from varied ethnic, racial, cultural, and lifestyle backgrounds, as well as those with disabilities or unique viewpoints. They must also be interested in a place in the sponsor's associate program during the summer between their second and third year of law school. Along with their application, they must submit a 2-page personal statement describing how or why they will contribute meaningfully to diversity and inclusion at the sponsoring firm and/or in the legal profession.

Financial data The stipend is $10,000.

Duration 1 year.

Additional information This law firm was formerly Baker & Daniels LLP. Recipients of these fellowships may elect to conduct their associateship at offices in Boulder, Chicago, Denver, Des Moines, Fort Wayne, Indianapolis, Minneapolis, Silicon Valley (East Palo Alto), South Bend, and Washington, D.C.

Number awarded 3 each year.

Deadline September of each year.

[879]
FELLOWSHIPS FOR LATINO/A, ASIAN AND FIRST NATIONS DOCTORAL STUDENTS

Forum for Theological Exploration
Attn: Fellowship Program
160 Clairemont Avenue, Suite 300
Decatur, GA 30030
(678) 369-6755   Fax: (678) 369-6757
E-mail: dhutto@fteleaders.org
Web: www.fteleaders.org

Summary To provide funding to Latino/as, Asians, and members of First Nations who are working on a doctoral degree in religious, theological, or biblical studies.

Eligibility This program is open to students of Latino/a, Asian, or First Nations descent who are U.S. or Canadian citizens or permanent residents working full time on a Ph.D. or Th.D. degree. Applicants must be past the course work stage; they are not required to have been advanced to candidacy, but they must have had their dissertation topic approved and be in a position to devote full time to writing. Students who are working on a Doctor of Ministry (D.Min.) degree are not eligible.

Financial data The stipend is $25,000.

Duration 1 year.

Additional information Fellows also receive reimbursement of expenses to attend the sponsor's Christian Leadership Forum. This sponsor was formerly named the The Fund for Theological Education, Inc.

Number awarded Varies each year; recently, 12 were awarded.

Deadline January of each year.

[880]
FINNEGAN DIVERSITY SCHOLARSHIP

Finnegan, Henderson, Farabow, Garrett & Dunner, LLP
Attn: Attorney Recruitment Manager
901 New York Avenue, N.W.
Washington, DC 20001-4413
(202) 408-4034   Fax: (202) 408-4400
E-mail: diversityscholarship@finnegan.com
Web: www.finnegan.com/careers/summerprogram/overview

Summary To provide financial assistance and work experience to Native Americans and other law students from diverse groups who are interested in a career in intellectual property law.

Eligibility This program is open to law students who have demonstrated a commitment to a career in intellectual property law and are currently enrolled either as a first-year full-time student or second-year part-time student. Applicants must contribute to enhancing diversity; the sponsor defines diversity broadly, and has considered members of racial, ethnic, disabled, and sexual orientation groups that have been historically underrepresented in the legal profession. They must have earned an undergraduate degree in life sciences, chemistry, engineering, or computer science, or have substantial prior trademark experience. Selection is based on academic performance at the undergraduate, graduate (if applicable), and law school level; relevant work experience; community service; leadership skills; and special accomplishments.

Financial data The stipend is $15,000 per year.

Duration 1 year; may be renewed 1 additional year as long as the recipient completes a summer associateship with the sponsor and maintains of GPA of 3.0 or higher.

Additional information The sponsor, the world's largest intellectual property law firm, established this scholarship in 2003. Summer associateships are available at its offices in Washington, D.C., Atlanta, Boston, Palo Alto, or Reston.

Number awarded 1 each year.

Deadline January of each year.

[881]
FIRST GENERATION INDIAN DESCENT TUITION ASSISTANCE PROGRAM

Poarch Band of Creek Indians
Attn: Tuition Program Coordinator
5811 Jack Springs Road
Atmore, AL 36502
(251) 368-9136, ext. 2535   Fax: (251) 368-4502
E-mail: mjohnson@pci-nsn.gov
Web: www.poarchcreekindians.org

Summary To provide financial assistance to undergraduate and graduate students who are first-generation descendants of members of the Poarch Band of Creek Indians.

Eligibility This program is open to first-generation descendants of enrolled tribal members of the Poarch Band of Creek Indians. Applicants must be attending or planning to attend an approved postsecondary institution as an undergraduate or graduate student. They must have a GPA of 2.0 or higher and be able to document financial need.

Financial data Total maximum awards are $5,000 for students participating in a certificate program not culminating in a degree and not part of the federal student aid program,

$10,000 for students participating in a certificate program not culminating in a degree but part of the federal student aid program, $20,000 for an associate degree program, or $50,000 for a bachelor's, master's, or graduate degree program.

Duration 1 year; may be renewed until the recipient reaches a lifetime benefit cap of $50,000.

Additional information This program began in 2006 and was named the Fred L. McGhee First Generation Indian Descent Scholarship Program. The current name was adopted in 2013.

Number awarded Varies each year.

Deadline Applications may be submitted at any time.

[882]
FIRST TRANSIT SCHOLARSHIP

Conference of Minority Transportation Officials
Attn: National Scholarship Program
100 M Street, S.E., Suite 917
Washington, DC 20003
(202) 506-2917   E-mail: info@comto.org
Web: www.comto.org/page/scholarships

Summary To provide financial assistance to Native American and other minority upper-division and graduate students in engineering or other field related to transportation.

Eligibility This program is open to minority juniors, seniors, and graduate students in transporation, planning, engineering or other technical transportation-related disciplines. Applicants must submit a cover letter on their transportation-related career goals and life aspirations. Financial need is not considered in the selection process.

Financial data The stipend is $6,000. Funds are paid directly to the recipient's college or university.

Duration 1 year.

Additional information This program is sponsored by First Transit Inc.

Number awarded 1 each year.

Deadline April of each year.

[883]
FISH & RICHARDSON DIVERSITY FELLOWSHIP PROGRAM

Fish & Richardson P.C.
Recruiting Department
Attn: Fellowship Program
12390 El Camino Real
San Diego, CA 92130
(858) 678-5070   Fax: (858) 678-5099
E-mail: diversity@fr.com
Web: www.fr.com/about/diversity

Summary To provide financial assistance for law school to Native Americans and other students who will contribute to diversity in the legal profession.

Eligibility This program is open to students enrolled in the first year at a law school anywhere in the country. Applicants must be African American/Black, American Indian/Alaskan Native, Hispanic/Latino, Native Hawaiian/Pacific Islander, Asian, person with disabilities, military veteran, or openly GLBT. Along with their application, they must submit a 500-word essay describing their background, what led them to the legal field, their interest in the sponsoring law firm, and what they could contribute to its practice and the profession. They must also indicate their first 3 choices of an office of the firm where they are interested in a summer associate clerkship.

Financial data The stipend is $10,000, of which $5,000 is paid after completion of their first-year summer clerkship with the firm and an additional $5,000 is paid after the student receives and accepts an associate offer with the firm after completion of a second-year summer clerkship.

Duration 1 year; may be extended for a second year.

Additional information Recipients are also offered a paid associate clerkship during the summer following their first and second year of law school at an office of the firm in the location of their choice in Atlanta, Austin, Boston, Dallas, Delaware, Houston, New York, San Diego, Silicon Valley, Twin Cities, or Washington, D.C. This program began in 2005.

Number awarded 1 or more each year.

Deadline January of each year.

[884]
FLORENCE YOUNG MEMORIAL SCHOLARSHIP

Association on American Indian Affairs, Inc.
Attn: Director of Scholarship Programs
966 Hungerford Drive, Suite 12-B
Rockville, MD 20850
(240) 314-7155   Fax: (240) 314-7159
E-mail: general.aaia@indian-affairs.org
Web: www.indian-affairs.org/graduate-applications.html

Summary To provide financial assistance to Native Americans interested in working on a graduate degree in specified fields.

Eligibility This program is open to American Indian and Alaskan Native full-time students working on a graduate degree in art, public health, or law. Applicants must submit proof of tribal enrollment and an essay of 2 to 3 pages on 1 of the following topics: 1) why the sponsor's International Repatriation Project is important and how they would inform others about it; 2) the Annie E. Casey Foundation's Juvenile Detention Alternatives Initiative and tribal and community-based alternatives to detention for juveniles; or 3) how tribal leaders can promote higher education in their family and community. They must have a GPA of 2.5 or higher. Selection is based on merit and need.

Financial data The stipend is $1,500.

Duration 1 year; recipients may reapply.

Number awarded Varies each year; recently, 2 were awarded.

Deadline May of each year.

[885]
FLORIDA LIBRARY ASSOCIATION MINORITY SCHOLARSHIPS

Florida Library Association
541 East Tennessee Street, Suite 103
Tallahassee, FL 32308
(850) 270-9205   Fax: (850) 270-9405
E-mail: flaexecutivedirector@comcast.net
Web: www.flalib.org/scholarships.php

Summary To provide financial assistance to Native American and other minority students working on a graduate degree in library and information science in Florida.

Eligibility This program is open to residents of Florida who are working on a graduate degree in library and information science at schools in the state. Applicants must be members of a minority group: Black/African American, American Indian/Alaska Native, Asian/Pacific Islander, or Hispanic/Latino. They must have some experience in a Florida library, must be a member of the Florida Library Association, and must commit to working in a Florida library for at least 1 year after graduation. Along with their application, they must submit 1) a list of activities, honors, awards, and/or offices held during college and outside college; 2) an essay of 1 to 2 pages on why they are entering librarianship; and 3) an essay of 1 to 2 pages on their career goals with respect to Florida libraries. Financial need is considered in the selection process.

Financial data   The stipend is $2,000.

Duration   1 year.

Number awarded   1 each year.

Deadline   January of each year.

[886]
FOLEY & LARDNER DIVERSITY FELLOWSHIP

Foley & Lardner LLP
Attn: Director of Legal Recruiting
555 South Flower Street
Los Angeles, CA 90071-2411
(213) 972-4535   E-mail: rbradley@foley.com
Web: www.foley.com/careers/lawstudents/#!/student/1417/2

Summary   To provide financial assistance and work experience to first-year Native American and other law students who will contribute to diversity in the legal profession.

Eligibility   This program is open to students completing the first year of full-time study at an ABA-accredited law school. Applicants must have demonstrated a commitment to promoting diversity and inclusion in the legal profession and the broader community. They must be interested in a summer associateship at an office of the sponsoring firm. Selection is based on involvement in diversity-related student organizations, involvement in community activities, undergraduate and law school academic achievement, and interest in employment with the sponsoring firm.

Financial data   The total stipend is $20,000, of which $10,000 is paid following successful completion of the summer associate program and $10,000 within 30 days after joining the firm as an associate/law graduate.

Duration   1 summer and 1 academic year.

Additional information   This program began in 1998. The sponsoring firm has offices in Boston, Chicago, Detroit, Jacksonville, Los Angeles, Madison, Miami, Milwaukee, New York, Orlando, Sacramento, San Diego, San Francisco, Silicon Valley, Tallahassee, Tampa, and Washington, D.C.

Number awarded   2 each year.

Deadline   April of each year.

[887]
FORT PECK TRIBES GRADUATE ASSISTANCE PROGRAM

Fort Peck Assiniboine and Sioux Tribes
Attn: Education Department
501 Medicine Bear Road
P.O. Box 1027
Poplar, MT 59255-1027
(406) 768-5136   Toll Free: (800) 799-2926
Fax: (406) 768-3556
Web: www.fortpecktribes.org/education.html

Summary   To provide financial assistance to Assiniboine and Sioux members of the Fort Peck Tribes in Montana who are interested in attending graduate school in any state.

Eligibility   This program is open to enrolled members of the Fort Peck Assiniboine and Sioux Tribes. Applicants must have been accepted into a master's or doctoral degree program at a college or university in any state. Along with their application, they must submit transcripts from any colleges they may have attended, a copy of the acceptance letter from the graduate school they attend, a copy of their registration for fall term verifying full-time enrollment, a Certificate of Degree of Indian Blood (CDIB), and evidence of financial need. Graduate students who are enrolled in correspondence courses, in extension courses, or as part-time students are not eligible.

Financial data   The stipend depends on the availability of funds.

Duration   1 semester; may be renewed, although only 1 master's degree or 1 doctoral degree will be funded.

Additional information   These awards are presented only if funds are available at the end of the fiscal year after all eligible undergraduate students have been supported.

Number awarded   Varies each year.

Deadline   September of each year.

[888]
FOSTER PEPPER DIVERSITY FELLOWSHIP

Foster Pepper PLLC
Attn: Manager, Attorney Recruitment and Professional
   Development
1111 Third Avenue, Suite 3400
Seattle, WA 98101-3299
(206) 447-4400   Toll Free: (800) 995-5902
Fax: (206) 447-9700   E-mail: browb@foster.com
Web: www.foster.com/careers.aspx

Summary   To provide financial assistance and work experience to Native American and other law students of color who are interested in practicing law in Seattle, Washington following graduation.

Eligibility   This program is open to students of color or other diverse background who are enrolled in the first year at an ABA-accredited law school. Applicants must be able to demonstrate 1) a record of academic achievement that offers great promise for a successful career during the remainder of law school and in the legal profession; 2) meaningful contributions to the diversity of the law school student body and, upon entering the legal profession, the legal community; and 3) a commitment to practice law in Seattle following graduation from law school. Along with their application, they must submit a 500-word personal statement describing their interest in practicing law in Seattle, their interest in the sponsoring firm and its summer program, and how they would contribute to the diversity of the firm and the Seattle legal community.

Financial data The stipend is $7,500.

Duration 1 year.

Additional information This program began in 2008. The program also includes a paid summer associate position in the firm's Seattle office.

Number awarded 1 or more each year.

Deadline January of each year.

[889]
FRANCES C. ALLEN FELLOWSHIPS

Newberry Library
Attn: Committee on Awards
60 West Walton Street
Chicago, IL 60610-3305
(312) 255-3666   Fax: (312) 255-3513
E-mail: research@newberry.org
Web: www.newberry.org/short-term-fellowships

Summary To provide funding to Native American women graduate students who wish to use the resources of the D'Arcy McNickle Center for the History of the American Indian at the Newberry Library.

Eligibility This program is open to women of American Indian heritage who are interested in using the library for a project appropriate to its collections. Applicants must be enrolled in a graduate or pre-professional program, especially in the humanities or social sciences. Recommendations are required; at least 2 must come from academic advisers or instructors who can comment on the significance of the applicant's proposed project and explain how it will help in the achievement of professional goals.

Financial data The basic stipend is $2,500 per month; supplemental funding may be available on a case by case basis.

Duration From 1 month to 1 year.

Additional information These grants were first awarded in 1983. Fellows must spend a significant portion of their time at the library's D'Arcy McNickle Center.

Number awarded Varies each year; recently, 2 were awarded.

Deadline December of each year.

[890]
FRANCIS M. KEVILLE MEMORIAL SCHOLARSHIP

Construction Management Association of America
Attn: CMAA Foundation
7926 Jones Branch Drive, Suite 800
McLean, VA 22101-3303
(703) 677-3361   E-mail: foundation@cmaanet.org
Web: www.cmaafoundation.org

Summary To provide financial assistance to Native American and other minority undergraduate and graduate students working on a degree in construction management.

Eligibility This program is open to women and members of minority groups who are enrolled as full-time undergraduate or graduate students. Applicants must have completed at least 1 year of study and have at least 1 full year remaining for a bachelor's or master's degree in construction management

or a related field. Along with their application, they must submit essays on why they are interested in a career in construction management and why they should be awarded this scholarship. Selection is based on that essay (20%), academic performance (40%), recommendation of the faculty adviser (15%), and extracurricular activities (25%); a bonus of 5% is given to student members of the Construction Management Association of America (CMAA).

Financial data The stipend is $5,000. Funds are disbursed directly to the student's university.

Duration 1 year.

Number awarded 1 each year.

Deadline April of each year.

[891]
FRANK W. HILL MEMORIAL SCHOLARSHIP

Bristol Bay Native Corporation
Attn: BBNC Education Foundation
111 West 16th Avenue, Suite 400
Anchorage, AK 99501-6299
(907) 278-3602   Toll Free: (800) 426-3602
Fax: (907) 265-7886   E-mail: bbncef@bbnc.net
Web: www.bbnc.net

Summary To provide financial assistance to shareholders of Bristol Bay Native Corporation (BBNC) who are currently working on an undergraduate or graduate degree in education at a college in any state.

Eligibility This program is open to BBNC shareholders who are enrolled full time as a junior, senior, or graduate student at a college or university in any state and working on a degree in education. Applicants must have a GPA of 2.5 or higher and be able to demonstrate financial need. Along with their application, they must submit an essay on how they became interested in their proposed field of study, any special circumstances they want to be considered, and their desire to work in the region or for a BBNC subsidiary company. Selection is based on the essay (30%), cumulative GPA (40%), financial need (20%), a resume (5%), and letters of recommendation (5%).

Financial data The stipend is $1,000.

Duration 1 year.

Additional information The BBNC is 1 of 13 Alaska Native Regional Corporations created under the Alaska Native Claims Settlement Act of 1971. This program began in 2012.

Number awarded 1 or more each year.

Deadline April of each year.

[892]
FRANKLIN C. MCLEAN AWARD

National Medical Fellowships, Inc.
Attn: Scholarship Program
347 Fifth Avenue, Suite 510
New York, NY 10016
(212) 483-8880   Toll Free: (877) NMF-1DOC
Fax: (212) 483-8897 E-mail: scholarships@nmfonline.org
Web: www.nmfonline.org

Summary To provide financial assistance to Native American and other underrepresented minority medical students who demonstrate academic achievement.

Eligibility This program is open to African Americans, Hispanics/Latinos, Native Americans, Vietnamese, Cambodians, and Pacific Islanders who are entering their senior year of medical school. They must be U.S. citizens or DACA students. Selection is based on academic achievement, leadership, and community service.

Financial data The stipend is $5,000.

Duration 1 year.

Additional information This program began in 1968.

Number awarded 1 each year.

Deadline September of each year.

[893]
FREDRIKSON & BYRON FOUNDATION MINORITY SCHOLARSHIP

Fredrikson & Byron Foundation
Attn: Attorney Recruiting Administrator
200 South Sixth Street, Suite 4000
Minneapolis, MN 55402-1425
(612) 492-7000   Fax: (612) 492-7077
E-mail: cokerson@fredlaw.com
Web: www.fredlaw.com/firm/scholarship.htm

Summary To provide financial assistance and summer work experience to Native American and other minority law students from any state who are interested in practicing in the upper Midwest.

Eligibility This program is open to African American or Black, Asian or Pacific Islander, Hispanic, Native American, and Alaska Native students enrolled in their first year of law school. Applicants must be interested in practicing law in the upper Midwest, covering the Minneapolis-St. Paul, Bismarck, Fargo, or Des Moines areas. Along with their application, they must submit brief statements on their expectations and objectives in applying for this scholarship; the factors they will use to measure success in their legal career; what they see as potential issues, obstacles, and opportunities facing new lawyers in a large private practice firm; and their interest in a summer associate position in private practice, including their interest in practicing law in the upper Midwest. Financial need is not considered.

Financial data The fellowship stipend is $10,000. The internship portion of the program provides a $1,000 weekly stipend.

Duration 1 year.

Additional information Fellows are also eligible to participate in an internship at the firm's offices.

Number awarded 1 each year.

Deadline March of each year.

[894]
G. WILLIAM RICE MEMORIAL SCHOLARSHIP

Oklahoma Bar Association
Attn: Indian Law Section
P.O. Box 1548
Ada, OK 74821
E-mail: debra.gee@chickasaw.net

Summary To provide financial assistance to students who plan to practice Indian law in Oklahoma.

Eligibility This program is open to law students in their second or third year who intend to practice Indian law in Oklahoma. Applicants must submit a cover letter describing their

commitment to practice Indian law in Oklahoma, a resume describing their Indian law-related activities, a transcript, and an academic or professional letter of recommendation.

Financial data The stipend is $2,500.

Duration 1 year.

Number awarded 1 each year.

Deadline May of each year.

[895]
GABE STEPETIN SCHOLARSHIP AWARD

The Aleut Corporation
Attn: Aleut Foundation
703 West Tudor Road, Suite 102
Anchorage, AK 99503-6650
(907) 646-1929   Toll Free: (800) 232-4882
Fax: (907) 646-1949   E-mail: taf@thealeutfoundation.org
Web: www.thealeutfoundation.org

Summary To provide financial assistance to Native Alaskans who are shareholders of The Aleut Corporation or their descendants and working on a degree in business at a school in any state.

Eligibility This program is open to Native Alaskans who are original enrollees or descendants of original enrollees of The Aleut Corporation (TAC). Applicants must have completed at least 1 year of a bachelor's, 2- or 4-year vocational, or master's degree in business at a school in any state. They must be enrolled full time and have a GPA of 3.0 or higher. Along with their application, they must include a letter of intent, up to 500 words in length, that describes their educational goals and objectives and their expected graduation date.

Financial data A stipend is awarded (amount not specified).

Duration 1 year.

Additional information The Aleut Corporation is 1 of 13 Alaska Native Regional Corporations created under the Alaska Native Claims Settlement Act of 1971.

Number awarded 1 each year.

Deadline June of each year.

[896]
GAIUS CHARLES BOLIN DISSERTATION AND POST-MFA FELLOWSHIPS

Williams College
Attn: Dean of the Faculty
880 Main Street
Hopkins Hall, Third Floor
P.O. Box 141
Williamstown, MA 01267
(413) 597-4351   Fax: (413) 597-3553
E-mail: gburda@williams.edu
Web: faculty.williams.edu

Summary To provide financial assistance to Native Americans and members of other underrepresented groups who are interested in teaching courses at Williams College while working on their doctoral dissertation or building their post-M.F.A. professional portfolio.

Eligibility This program is open to members of underrepresented groups, including ethnic minorities, first-generation college students, women in predominantly male fields, and scholars with disabilities. Applicants must be 1) doctoral candidates in any field who have completed all work for a Ph.D. except for the dissertation; or 2) artists who completed an M.F.A. degree within the past 2 years and are building their professional portfolio. They must be willing to teach a course at Williams College. Along with their application, they must submit a full curriculum vitae, a graduate school transcript, 3 letters of recommendation, a copy of their dissertation prospectus or samples of their artistic work, and a description of their teaching interests within a department or program at Williams College. U.S. citizenship or permanent resident status is required.

Financial data   Fellows receive $38,000 for the academic year, plus housing assistance, office space, computer and library privileges, and a research allowance of up to $4,000.

Duration   2 years.

Additional information   Bolin fellows are assigned a faculty adviser in the appropriate department. This program was established in 1985. Fellows are expected to teach a 1-semester course each year. They must be in residence at Williams College for the duration of the fellowship.

Number awarded   2 each year.

Deadline   November of each year.

[897]
GEM M.S. ENGINEERING FELLOWSHIP PROGRAM

National Consortium for Graduate Degrees for Minorities
  in Engineering and Science (GEM)
Attn: Manager, Fellowships Administration
1430 Duke Street
Alexandria, VA 22314
(703) 562-3646   Fax: (202) 207-3518
E-mail: info@gemfellowship.org
Web: www.gemfellowship.org

Summary   To provide financial assistance and summer work experience to Native American and other underrepresented minority students interested in working on a master's degree in engineering or computer science.

Eligibility   This program is open to U.S. citizens and permanent residents who are members of ethnic groups underrepresented in engineering: American Indians/Native Americans, Blacks/African Americans, or Latinos/Hispanic Americans. Applicants must be a senior or graduate of an ABET-accredited engineering or computer science program and have an academic record that indicates the ability to pursue graduate studies in engineering (including a GPA of 2.8 or higher). They must agree to apply to at least 3 of the 106 GEM member universities that offer a master's degree and to intern during summers with a sponsoring GEM employer.

Financial data   Full fellows receive 1) a stipend of $4,000 per semester; 2) full tuition and fees at the GEM member university; and 3) a salary during the summer work assignment as a GEM summer intern. Associate fellows receive the stipend and payment of tuition and fees, but are not offered a summer salary. University fellows receive only payment of tuition from a participating university.

Duration   Up to 4 semesters; full fellows also receive summer work internships lasting 10 to 14 weeks for up to 2 summers.

Additional information   During the summer internship, each fellow is assigned an engineering project in a research setting. Each project is based on the fellow's interest and

background and is carried out under the supervision of an experienced engineer. At the conclusion of the internship, each fellow writes a project report. Recipients must work on a master's degree in the same engineering discipline as their baccalaureate degree.

Number awarded   Varies each year; recently, 48 full fellowships, 6 associate fellowships, and 11 university fellowships were awarded.

Deadline   November of each year.

[898]
GEM PH.D. ENGINEERING FELLOWSHIP PROGRAM

National Consortium for Graduate Degrees for Minorities
  in Engineering and Science (GEM)
Attn: Manager, Fellowships Administration
1430 Duke Street
Alexandria, VA 22314
(703) 562-3646   Fax: (202) 207-3518
E-mail: info@gemfellowship.org
Web: www.gemfellowship.org

Summary   To provide financial assistance and summer work experience to Native American and other underrepresented minority students interested in obtaining a Ph.D. degree in engineering.

Eligibility   This program is open to U.S. citizens and permanent residents who are members of ethnic groups underrepresented in engineering: American Indians/Native Americans, Blacks/African Americans, and Latinos/Hispanic Americans. Applicants must be college seniors, master's degree students, or graduates of an ABET-accredited program in engineering and have an academic record that indicates the ability to work on a doctoral degree in engineering (including a GPA of 3.0 or higher). They must agree to apply to at least 3 of the 102 GEM member universities that offer a doctoral degree in engineering and to intern during summer with a sponsoring GEM employer.

Financial data   For full fellows, the stipend is $16,000 for the first year; in subsequent years, fellows receive full payment of tuition and fees plus an additional stipend and assistantship from their university that is equivalent to funding received by other doctoral students in their department. They also receive a paid internship during the summer following their first year of study. Associate fellows receive the same first-year stipend and payment of tuition and fees for subsequent years, but the additional stipend paid by the university is optional.

Duration   3 to 5 years for the fellowship; 12 weeks during the summer immediately after sponsorship for the internship.

Additional information   This program is valid only at 1 of the 106 participating GEM member universities; contact GEM for a list. The fellowship award is designed to support the student in the first year of the doctoral program without working. Subsequent years may be subsidized by the respective universities and will usually include either a teaching or research assistantship. Recipients must participate in the GEM summer internship; failure to agree to accept the internship cancels the fellowship.

Number awarded   Varies each year; recently, 26 full fellowships and 15 associate fellowships were awarded.

Deadline   November of each year.

[899]
GEM PH.D. SCIENCE FELLOWSHIP PROGRAM

National Consortium for Graduate Degrees for Minorities
in Engineering and Science (GEM)
Attn: Manager, Fellowships Administration
1430 Duke Street
Alexandria, VA 22314
(703) 562-3646   Fax: (202) 207-3518
E-mail: info@gemfellowship.org
Web: www.gemfellowship.org

Summary   To provide financial assistance and summer work experience to Native American and other underrepresented minority students interested in working on a Ph.D. degree in the life sciences, mathematics, or physical sciences.

Eligibility   This program is open to U.S. citizens and permanent residents who are members of ethnic groups underrepresented in the natural sciences: American Indians/Native Americans, Blacks/African Americans, and Latinos/Hispanic Americans. Applicants must be college seniors, master's degree students, or recent graduates in the biological sciences, mathematics, or physical sciences (chemistry, computer science, environmental sciences, and physics) with an academic record that indicates the ability to pursue doctoral studies (including a GPA of 3.0 or higher). They must agree to apply to at least 3 of the 106 GEM member universities that offer a doctoral degree in science and to intern during summer with a sponsoring GEM employer.

Financial data   For full fellows, the stipend is $16,000 for the first year; in subsequent years, fellows receive full payment of tuition and fees plus an additional stipend and assistantship from their university that is equivalent to funding received by other doctoral students in their department. They also receive a paid internship during the summer following their first year of study. Associate fellows receive the same first-year stipend and payment of tuition and fees for subsequent years, but the additional stipend paid by the university is optional.

Duration   3 to 5 years for the fellowship; 12 weeks during the summer immediately after sponsorship for the internship.

Additional information   This program is valid only at 1 of 106 participating GEM member universities; contact GEM for a list. The fellowship award is designed to support the student in the first year of the doctoral program without working. Subsequent years are subsidized by the respective university and will usually include either a teaching or research assistantship. Recipients must participate in the GEM summer internship; failure to agree to accept the internship cancels the fellowship. Recipients must enroll in the same scientific discipline as their undergraduate major.

Number awarded   Varies each year; recently, 28 full fellowships and 14 associate fellowships were awarded.

Deadline   November of each year.

[900]
GENERATION GOOGLE SCHOLARSHIPS FOR CURRENT UNIVERSITY STUDENTS

Google Inc.
Attn: Scholarships
1600 Amphitheatre Parkway
Mountain View, CA 94043-8303
(650) 253-0000   Fax: (650) 253-0001
E-mail: generationgoogle@google.com
Web: www.google.com

Summary   To provide financial assistance to Native Americans and members of other underrepresented groups enrolled as undergraduate or graduate students in a computer-related field.

Eligibility   This program is open to students enrolled as full-time undergraduate or graduate students at a college or university in the United States or Canada. Applicants must be members of a group underrepresented in computer science: African Americans, Hispanics, American Indians, or Filipinos/Native Hawaiians/Pacific Islanders. They must be working on a degree in computer science, computer engineering, or a closely-related field. Selection is based on academic achievement, leadership, and passion for computer science and technology.

Financial data   The stipend is $10,000 per year for U.S. students or $C5,000 for Canadian students.

Duration   1 year; may be renewed.

Additional information   Recipients are also invited to attend Google's Computer Science Summer Institute at Mountain View, California, Seattle, Washington, or Cambridge, Massachusetts in the summer.

Number awarded   Varies each year.

Deadline   February of each year.

[901]
GE-NMF PRIMARY CARE LEADERSHIP PROGRAM

National Medical Fellowships, Inc.
Attn: Scholarship Program
347 Fifth Avenue, Suite 510
New York, NY 10016
(212) 483-8880   Toll Free: (877) NMF-1DOC
Fax: (212) 483-8897   E-mail: pclpinfo@nmfonline.org
Web: www.nmfonline.org

Summary   To provide funding to Native American and other underrepresented medical and nursing students who wish to participate in a summer mentored clinical experience in selected communities.

Eligibility   This program is open to members of underrepresented minority groups (African American, Hispanic/Latino, American Indian, Native Hawaiian, Alaska Native, Vietnamese, Cambodian, or Native Pacific Islander) and/or socioeconomically disadvantaged students. U.S. citizenship is required. Applicants must be currently enrolled in an accredited medical school or graduate-level nursing degree program. They must be interested in a mentored clinical service-learning experience that includes a site-specific independent project at a community health center in Atlanta, Boston/Lynn, Chicago, Houston, Los Angeles, Miami, Mound Bayou (Mississippi), New York, Phoenix, Rochester (New York), or Seattle. Along with their application, they must submit documentation of financial status; a short biography; a resume; 2 letters of recommendation; and a 500-word personal statement on their experiences working in or being part of a medically underserved population and how those experiences have impacted their educational path, professional aspirations, and decision to apply to this program.

Financial data The stipend is $5,000. Funds are expected to cover travel, living, and lodging expenses.

Duration Scholars are required to complete 200 clinical service-learning hours within a 6- to 8-week period during the summer following receipt of the award.

Additional information Funding for this program, which began in 2012 and is administered by National Medical Fellowships (NMF), is provided by the GE Foundation.

Number awarded Varies each year, recently, 59 were granted: 2 in Atlanta, 2 in Boston/Lynn, 8 in Chicago, 5 in Houston, 12 in Los Angeles, 8 in Miami, 2 in Bound Bayou, 2 in New York, 8 in Phoenix, 4 in Rochester, and 6 in Seattle.

Deadline March of each year.

[902]
GEOCORPS AMERICA DIVERSITY INTERNSHIPS

Geological Society of America
Attn: Program Officer, GeoCorps America
3300 Penrose Place
P.O. Box 9140
Boulder, CO 80301-9140
(303) 357-1025   Toll Free: (800) 472-1988, ext. 1025
Fax: (303) 357-1070   E-mail: mdawson@geosociety.org
Web: rock.geosociety.org

Summary To provide work experience at national parks to student members of the Geological Society of America (GSA) who are Native Americans or members of other underrepresented groups.

Eligibility This program is open to all GSA members, but applications are especially encouraged from groups historically underrepresented in the sciences (African Americans, American Indians, Alaska Natives, Hispanics, Native Hawaiians, other Pacific Islanders, and persons with disabilities). Applicants must be interested in a short-term work experience in facilities of the U.S. government. Geoscience knowledge and skills are a significant requirement for most positions, but students from diverse disciplines (e.g., chemistry, physics, engineering, mathematics, computer science, ecology, hydrology, meteorology, the social sciences, and the humanities) are also invited to apply. Activities involve research; interpretation and education; inventory and monitoring; or mapping, surveying, and GIS. Prior interns are not eligible. U.S. citizenship or possession of a proper visa is required.

Financial data Each internship provides a $2,750 stipend. Also provided are free housing or a housing allowance of $1,500 to $2,000.

Duration 3 months during the spring, summer, fall, or winter.

Additional information This program is offered by the GSA in partnership with the National Park Service, the U.S. Forest Service, and the Bureau of Land Management.

Number awarded Varies each year.

Deadline March of each year for spring or summer positions; June of each year for fall or winter positions.

[903]
GEOCORPS AMERICAN INDIAN INTERNSHIPS

Geological Society of America
Attn: Program Officer, GeoCorps America
3300 Penrose Place
P.O. Box 9140
Boulder, CO 80301-9140
(303) 357-1025   Toll Free: (800) 472-1988, ext. 1025
Fax: (303) 357-1070   E-mail: mdawson@geosociety.org
Web: rock.geosociety.org

Summary To provide work experience in national parks to American Indians and Native Alaskans who are student members of the Geological Society of America (GSA).

Eligibility This program is open to all GSA members, but applications are especially encouraged from American Indians, Alaska Natives, and persons with a strong connection to an American Indian tribe or community. Applicants must be interested in a short-term work experience in facilities of the U.S. government. Geoscience knowledge and skills are a significant requirement for most positions, but students from diverse disciplines (e.g., chemistry, physics, engineering, mathematics, computer science, ecology, hydrology, meteorology, the social sciences, and the humanities) are also invited to apply. Activities involve research; interpretation and education; inventory and monitoring; or mapping, surveying, and GIS. Prior interns are not eligible. U.S. citizenship or permanent resident status is required.

Financial data Each internship provides a $2,750 stipend. A travel allowance of $500 (or $1,000 for positions in Alaska) and free housing or a housing allowance of $1,500 to $2,000 are also provided.

Duration 3 months during the spring, summer, fall, or winter.

Additional information This program is offered by the GSA in partnership with the National Park Service.

Number awarded 1 or more each year.

Deadline March of each year for spring or summer positions; June of each year for fall or winter positions.

[904]
GEOLOGICAL SOCIETY OF AMERICA
GRADUATE STUDENT RESEARCH GRANTS

Geological Society of America
Attn: Program Officer-Grants, Awards and Recognition
3300 Penrose Place
P.O. Box 9140
Boulder, CO 80301-9140
(303) 357-1060   Toll Free: (888) 443-4472, ext. 1060
Fax: (303) 357-1070   E-mail: awards@geosociety.org
Web: www.geosociety.org/grants/gradgrants.htm

Summary To provide funding to Native American and other underrepresented graduate student members of the Geological Society of America (GSA) interested in conducting research at universities in the United States, Canada, Mexico, or Central America.

Eligibility This program is open to GSA members working on a master's or doctoral degree at a university in the United States, Canada, Mexico, or Central America. Applicants must be interested in conducting geological research. Minorities, women, and persons with disabilities are strongly encouraged to apply. Selection is based on the scientific merits of the proposal, the capability of the investigator, and the reasonableness of the budget.

Financial data Grants range up to $2,500 and recently averaged $1,851. Funds can be used for the cost of travel, room and board in the field, services of a technician or field assistant, funding of chemical and isotope analyses, or other expenses directly related to the fulfillment of the research contract. Support is not provided for the purchase of ordinary field equipment, for maintenance of the families of the grantees and their assistants, as reimbursement for work already accomplished, for institutional overhead, for adviser participation, or for tuition costs.

Duration 1 year.

Additional information In addition to general grants, GSA awards a number of specialized grants.

Number awarded Varies each year; recently, the society awarded nearly 400 grants worth more than $723,000 through this and all of its specialized programs.

Deadline January of each year.

[905]
GEORGE A. STRAIT MINORITY SCHOLARSHIP ENDOWMENT

American Association of Law Libraries
Attn: Chair, Scholarships Committee
105 West Adams Street, Suite 3300
Chicago, IL 60603
(312) 939-4764   Fax: (312) 431-1097
E-mail: scholarships@aall.org
Web: www.aallnet.org

Summary To provide financial assistance to Native American and other minority college seniors or college graduates who are interested in becoming law librarians.

Eligibility This program is open to college graduates with meaningful law library experience who are members of minority groups and intend to have a career in law librarianship. Applicants must be degree candidates at an ALA-accredited library school or an ABA-accredited law school. Along with their application, they must submit a personal statement that discusses their interest in law librarianship, reason for applying for this scholarship, career goals as a law librarian, and any other pertinent information.

Financial data The stipend is $3,500.

Duration 1 year.

Additional information This program, established in 1990, is currently supported by Thomson Reuters.

Number awarded Varies each year; recently, 6 were awarded.

Deadline March of each year.

[906]
GEORGE K. NOLAN TRIBAL JUDICIAL SCHOLARSHIP

Sault Tribe of Chippewa Indians
Attn: Higher Education Department
523 Ashmun Street
Sault Ste. Marie, MI 49783
(906) 635-6050, ext. 26312   Toll Free: (800) 793-0660
Fax: (906) 635-7785   E-mail: BMacArthur@saulttribe.net
Web: www.saulttribe.com

Summary To provide financial assistance to members of the Sault Tribe of Chippewa Indians who are working on an undergraduate or graduate degree in a field related to law.

Eligibility This program is open to members of the Sault Tribe who are attending a 2- or 4-year college or university as a full-time sophomore or higher. Applicants must be working on an undergraduate or graduate degree in law enforcement, legal studies, political science, public administration, or tribal law. Along with their application, they must submit an essay of 1,000 to 2,000 words on a topic that changes annually but relates to their Indian heritage.

Financial data The stipend is $1,000.

Duration 1 year.

Number awarded 1 each year.

Deadline May of each year.

[907]
GERALD PEET FELLOWSHIP

American Indian Graduate Center
Attn: Executive Director
3701 San Mateo Boulevard, N.E., Suite 200
Albuquerque, NM 87110-1249
(505) 881-4584   Toll Free: (800) 628-1920
Fax: (505) 884-0427   E-mail: fellowships@aigc.com
Web: www.aigcs.org/scholarships/graduate-fellowships

Summary To provide financial assistance to Native American students interested in working on a graduate degree in medicine or other health-related field.

Eligibility This program is open to enrolled members of federally-recognized American Indian tribes and Alaska Native groups and students who can document one-fourth degree federally-recognized Indian blood. Applicants must be enrolled full time at a graduate or medical school in the United States and working on a degree in medicine or other health-related field. Along with their application, they must submit a 500-word essay on how receiving this fellowship will enable them to continue to build, promote, and honor self-sustaining American Indian and Alaska Native communities. Financial need is also considered in the selection process.

Financial data Stipends range from $500 to $5,000 per academic year, depending on the availability of funds and the recipient's unmet financial need.

Duration 1 year; may be renewed.

Number awarded 1 each year.

Deadline May of each year.

[908]
GERBER SCHOLARSHIP IN PEDIATRICS

National Medical Fellowships, Inc.
Attn: Scholarship Program
347 Fifth Avenue, Suite 510
New York, NY 10016
(212) 483-8880   Toll Free: (877) NMF-1DOC
Fax: (212) 483-8897 E-mail: scholarships@nmfonline.org
Web: www.nmfonline.org

Summary To provide financial assistance to Native American and other underrepresented minority medical students who are interested in pediatrics.

Eligibility This program is open to African Americans, Hispanics/Latinos, Native Americans, Vietnamese, Cambodians, and Pacific Islanders who are enrolled in medical school.

Applicants must be interested in pediatrics with an emphasis on nutrition They must be U.S. citizens or DACA students. Selection is based on leadership, commitment to serving medically underserved communities, and financial need.

Financial data The stipend is $5,000.

Duration 1 year.

Additional information This program, which began in 1997, is supported by Gerber.

Number awarded 2 each year.

Deadline September of each year.

[909]
GO RED MULTICULTURAL SCHOLARSHIP FUND

American Heart Association
Attn: Go Red for Women
7272 Greenville Avenue
Dallas, TX 75231-4596
Toll Free: (800) AHA-USA1
E-mail: GoRedScholarship@heart.org
Web: www.goredforwomen.org

Summary To provide financial assistance to Native American women and others from from multicultural backgrounds who are preparing for a career in a field of health care.

Eligibility This program is open to women who are currently enrolled at an accredited college, university, health care institution, or program and have a GPA of 3.0 or higher. Applicants must be U.S. citizens or permanent residents of Hispanic, African American, Asian/Pacific Islander, Native American, or other minority origin. They must be working on an undergraduate or graduate degree as preparation for a career as a nurse, physician, or allied health care worker. Selection is based on community involvement, a personal essay, transcripts, and 2 letters of recommendation.

Financial data The stipend is $2,500.

Duration 1 year.

Additional information This program, which began in 2012, is supported by Macy's.

Number awarded 16 each year.

Deadline December of each year.

[910]
GOLDMAN SACHS MBA FELLOWSHIP

Goldman Sachs
Attn: Human Capital Management
200 West Street, 25th Floor
New York, NY 10282
E-mail: Iris.Birungi@gs.com
Web: www.goldmansachs.com

Summary To provide financial assistance and work experience to Native American and other underrepresented minority students interested in working on an M.B.A. degree.

Eligibility This program is open to graduate students of Black, Hispanic, or Native American descent who are interested in working on an M.B.A. degree. Applicants must be preparing for a career in the financial services industry. Along with their application, they must submit 2 essays of 500 words or less on the following topics: 1) why they are preparing for a career in the financial services industry; and 2) their current involvement with a community-based organization. Selection is based on analytical skills and the ability to identify significant problems, gather facts, and analyze situations in depth;

interpersonal skills, including, but not limited to, poise, confidence, and professionalism; academic record; evidence of hard work and commitment; ability to work well with others; and commitment to community involvement.

Financial data Fellows receive $25,000 toward payment of tuition and living expenses for the first year of business school; an internship at a domestic office of Goldman Sachs during the summer after the first year of business school; and (after successful completion of the summer internship and acceptance of an offer to return to the firm after graduation as a full-time regular employee) either payment of tuition costs for the second year of business school or an additional $25,000 toward tuition and living costs.

Duration Up to 2 years.

Additional information This program was initiated in 1997.

Number awarded 1 or more each year.

Deadline November of each year.

[911]
GOLDSTEIN AND SCHNEIDER SCHOLARSHIPS BY THE MACEY FUND

Society for Industrial and Organizational Psychology Inc.
Attn: SIOP Foundation
440 East Poe Road, Suite 101
Bowling Green, OH 43402
(419) 353-0032   Fax: (419) 352-2645
E-mail: siopfoundation@siop.org
Web: www.siop.org/SIOPAwards/thornton.aspx

Summary To provide funding to Native American and other minority student members of the Society for Industrial and Organizational Psychology (SIOP) who are conducting doctoral research.

Eligibility This program is open to student affiliate members of SIOP who are enrolled full time in a doctoral program in industrial and organizational (I/O) psychology or a closely-related field at an accredited college or university. Applicants must be members of an ethnic minority group (Native American/Alaskan Native, Asian/Pacific American, African/Caribbean American, or Latino/Hispanic American). They must have an approved dissertation plan that has potential to make significant theoretical and application contributions to the field of I/O psychology.

Financial data The stipend is $3,000. Students may elect to have the funds paid to them directly or to be deposited into a "professional development" account at their university.

Duration 1 academic year.

Additional information The SIOP is Division 14 of the American Psychological Association. This program consists of the Benjamin Schneider Scholarship (offered in odd-numbered years) and the Irwin L. Goldstein Scholarship (offered in even-numbered years).

Number awarded 1 each year.

Deadline October of each year.

[912]
GOODWIN DIVERSITY FELLOWSHIPS

Goodwin Procter LLP
Attn: National Hiring Partner
100 Northern Avenue
Boston, MA 02210
(617) 570-1000   Fax: (617) 523-1231
E-mail: fellowships@goodwinlaw.com
Web: www.goodwinlaw.com/careers/1l-diversity-fellowship

Summary To provide financial assistance and work experience to Native Americans and other students from diverse backgrounds who are interested in public interest law.

Eligibility This program is open to first-year law students who self-identify as a member of an historically underrepresented group in the legal profession (including racially and ethnically diverse and LGBT students). Applicants must actively express an interest in working in the sponsoring firm's summer program in public interest law. If they are applying for the Goodwin MassMutual Diversity Fellowship, they must express an interest in working with MassMutual's legal department in Springfield, Massachusetts for 2 weeks as part of the summer program and specializing in the investment or insurance business or in a legal focus to advance business objectives. Selection is based on academic performance, leadership abilities, involvement in diversity organizations, commitment to community service, interpersonal skills, other special achievements and honors, and interest in working with the firm during the summer.

Financial data The stipend is $7,500.

Duration 1 year; nonrenewable.

Additional information This program began in 2005. In 2007, it added the Goodwin MassMutual Diversity Fellowship, created in conjunction with its long-standing client, Massachusetts Mutual Life Insurance Company (MassMutual). Summer positions are available at the firm's offices in Boston, Los Angeles, New York, Silicon Valley (Menlo Park), San Francisco, and Washington, D.C.

Number awarded 6 each year, including 1 Goodwin MassMutual Diversity Fellowship.

Deadline October of each year.

[913]
GORDON STAFFORD SCHOLARSHIP IN ARCHITECTURE

Stafford King Wiese Architects
Attn: Scholarship Selection Committee
622 20th Street
Sacramento, CA 95811
(916) 930-5900   Fax: (916) 290-0100
E-mail: info@skwaia.com
Web: www.skwarchitects.com/about/scholarship

Summary To provide financial assistance to Native Americans and members of other minority groups from California interested in studying architecture at a college in any state.

Eligibility This program is open to California residents currently enrolled at accredited schools of architecture in any state as first-year new or first-year transfer students and working on a bachelor's or 5-year master's degree. Applicants must be able to demonstrate minority status (defined as Black, Hispanic, Native American, Pacific Asian, or Asian Indian). They must submit a 500-word statement expressing their desire to prepare for a career in architecture. Finalists are interviewed and must travel to Sacramento, California at their own expense for the interview.

Financial data The stipend is $3,000 per year. That includes $1,500 deposited in the recipient's school account and $1,500 paid to the recipient directly.

Duration 1 year; may be renewed up to 4 additional years.

Additional information This program began in 1995.

Number awarded Up to 5 each year.

Deadline June of each year.

[914]
GRACE WALL BARREDA MEMORIAL FELLOWSHIP

American Indian Graduate Center
Attn: Executive Director
3701 San Mateo Boulevard, N.E., Suite 200
Albuquerque, NM 87110-1249
(505) 881-4584   Toll Free: (800) 628-1920
Fax: (505) 884-0427   E-mail: fellowships@aigc.com
Web: www.aigcs.org/scholarships/graduate-fellowships

Summary To provide financial assistance to Native American students interested in working on a graduate degree in environmental studies or public health.

Eligibility This program is open to enrolled members of federally-recognized American Indian tribes and Alaska Native groups and students who can document one-fourth degree federally-recognized Indian blood. Applicants must be enrolled full time at a graduate school in the United States and working on a degree in environmental studies or public health. Along with their application, they must submit a 500-word essay on how receiving this fellowship will enable them to continue to build, promote, and honor self-sustaining American Indian and Alaska Native communities. Financial need is also considered in the selection process.

Financial data Stipends range from $500 to $5,000 per academic year, depending on the availability of funds and the recipient's unmet financial need.

Duration 1 year; may be renewed.

Number awarded 1 each year.

Deadline May of each year.

[915]
GRADUATE RESEARCH FELLOWSHIP PROGRAM OF THE NATIONAL SCIENCE FOUNDATION

National Science Foundation
Directorate for Education and Human Resources
Attn: Division of Graduate Education
4201 Wilson Boulevard, Room 875S
Arlington, VA 22230
(703) 331-3542   Toll Free: (866) NSF-GRFP
Fax: (703) 292-9048   E-mail: info@nsfgrfp.org
Web: www.nsf.gov/funding/pgm_summ.jsp?pims_id=6201

Summary To provide financial assistance to Native American and other graduate students interested in working on a master's or doctoral degree in fields supported by the National Science Foundation (NSF).

Eligibility This program is open to U.S. citizens, nationals, and permanent residents who wish to work on research-based master's or doctoral degrees in a field of science, technology, engineering, or mathematics (STEM) supported by NSF (including astronomy, chemistry, computer and information sciences and engineering, geosciences, engineering, life sciences, materials research, mathematical sciences, physics, psychology, social sciences, or STEM education and learning). Other work in medical, dental, law, public health, or practice-oriented professional degree programs, or in joint science-professional degree programs, such as M.D./Ph.D. and J.D./Ph.D. programs, is not eligible. Applications normally should be submitted during the senior year in college or in the first year of graduate study; eligibility is limited to those who have completed no more than 12 months of graduate study since completion of a baccalaureate degree. Applicants who have already earned an advanced degree in science, engineering, or medicine (including an M.D., D.D.S., or D.V.M.) are ineligible. Selection is based on 1) intellectual merit of the proposed activity: strength of the academic record, proposed plan of research, previous research experience, references, appropriateness of the choice of institution; and 2) broader impacts of the proposed activity: how well does the activity advance discovery and understanding, how well does it broaden the participation of underrepresented groups (e.g., women, minorities, persons with disabilities, veterans), to what extent will it enhance the infrastructure for research and education, will the results be disseminated broadly to enhance scientific and technological understanding, what may be the benefits of the proposed activity to society).

Financial data The stipend is $32,000 per year; an additional $12,000 cost-of-education allowance is provided to the recipient's institution.

Duration Up to 3 years, usable over a 5-year period.

Number awarded Approximately 2,000 each year.

Deadline October of each year.

[916]
GRAHAM & DUNN DIVERSITY FELLOWSHIP

Graham & Dunn, PC
Attn: Marisa Velling Lindell
Pier 70
2801 Alaskan Way, Suite 300
Seattle, WA 98121
(206) 340-9639   Fax: (206) 340-9599
E-mail: mlindell@grahamdunn.com
Web: www.grahamdunn.com/careers/careers-law-students

Summary To provide financial assistance and work experience at Graham & Dunn to Native American and other law students who will increase the diversity of the firm and the legal profession.

Eligibility This program is open to first-year law students of color and all first-year law students of diverse and underrepresented groups. Applicants must be interested in a summer clerkship at the firm's Seattle office. They must demonstrate a commitment to fostering diversity in the legal community; demonstrate a record of academic, employment, community, and/or other achievement indicating potential for success in law school and in the legal profession; and be committed to practicing law in Seattle for the long term.

Financial data The program provides a paid summer clerkship (salary not specified) and a stipend of $7,500 for the second year of law school.

Duration 1 summer and 1 academic year.

Number awarded 1 each year.

Deadline January of each year.

[917]
GRAND PORTAGE TRIBAL SCHOLARSHIP PROGRAM

Grand Portage Reservation Tribal Council
Attn: Education Director
P.O. Box 428
Grand Portage, MN 55605
(218) 475-2812   Fax: (218) 475-2284

Summary To provide financial assistance for undergraduate or graduate study to Grand Portage Reservation Chippewa Tribe members in Minnesota.

Eligibility This program is open to enrolled members of the Grand Portage Reservation of Chippewa who are residents of Minnesota. Applicants must be enrolled or planning to enroll at an accredited college, university, or vocational school in Minnesota at least three-quarter time as an undergraduate or half time as a graduate student They must be able to demonstrate financial need.

Financial data The amount of the award is based on the need of the recipient.

Duration 1 year; may be renewed for a total of 10 semesters or 15 quarters to complete a 4-year degree program if recipients maintain full-time enrollment and a GPA of 2.0 or higher. Adjustments are considered for part-time and/or graduate study.

Number awarded Varies each year.

Deadline At least 2 weeks before school starts.

[918]
GRAND TRAVERSE BAND HIGHER EDUCATION GRANTS

Grand Traverse Band of Ottawa and Chippewa Indians
Attn: Higher Education Specialist
845 Business Park Drive
Traverse City, MI 49686
(231) 534-7760   Toll Free: (866) 534-7760
Fax: (231) 534-7773
E-mail: melissa.alberts@gtbindians.com
Web: www.gtbindians.org/higher_education.asp

Summary To provide financial assistance to members of the Grand Traverse Band (GTB) of Ottawa and Chippewa Indians who are interested in attending college or graduate school in any state.

Eligibility This program is open to enrolled GTB members who are working on or planning to work on an associate, bachelor's, master's, or doctoral degree at a public college or university in Michigan. Applicants must be able to document financial need. Along with their application, they must submit a personal statement on how they plan to serve their Indian community after they have successfully completed their course of study.

Financial data Stipends for associate degree students are $200 per credit hour, to a maximum of $7,200 per year; stipends for bachelor's degree students are $250 per credit hour, to a maximum of $9,000 per year; stipends for graduate students are $600 per credit hour, to a maximum of $10,800 per year.

Duration 1 semester; may be renewed as long as the recipient maintains a GPA of 2.0 or higher. Support is provided for up to 12 credits above the number required for an undergraduate degree or up to 6 credits above the number required for a graduate degree.

Number awarded Varies each year.

Deadline Deadline not specified.

[919]
GREAT LAKES SECTION IFT DIVERSITY SCHOLARSHIP

Institute of Food Technologists-Great Lakes Section
c/o Andrea Kirk, Scholarship Chair
Post Foods, LLC
275 Cliff Street
Battle Creek, MI 49014
E-mail: greatlakesift@gmail.com
Web: www.greatlakesift.org/student-scholarships

Summary To provide financial assistance to Native American and other minority members of the Great Lakes Section of the Institute of Food Technologists (IFT) from any state who are working on an undergraduate or graduate degree related to food technology at a college in Michigan.

Eligibility This program is open to minority residents of any state who are members of the IFT Great Lakes Section (GLS) and working full time on an undergraduate or graduate degree in food science, nutrition, food engineering, food packaging, or related fields at a college or university in Michigan. Applicants must have a GPA of 3.0 or higher and plans for a career in the food industry. Along with their application, they must submit a 1-page personal statement that covers their academic program, future plans and career goals, extracurricular activities (including involvement in community, university, GLS, or national IFT activities), and work experience. Financial need is not considered in the selection process.

Financial data The stipend is $1,000.

Duration 1 year; nonrenewable.

Number awarded 1 each year.

Deadline February of each year.

[920]
GREENSPOON MARDER DIVERSITY SCHOLARSHIP PROGRAM FOR LAW STUDENTS

Community Foundation of Sarasota County
Attn: Grants and Scholarships Coordinator
2635 Fruitville Road
P.O. Box 49587
Sarasota, FL 34230-6587
(941) 556-7114   Fax: (941) 952-7115
E-mail: eyoung@cfsarasota.org
Web: www.cfsarasota.org

Summary To provide financial assistance to Native American and other minority students from any state attending designated law schools (most of which are in Florida).

Eligibility This program is open to racial and ethnic minority students from any state who are members of groups traditionally underrepresented in the legal profession. Applicants must be entering their second year of full-time study at the University of Florida Levin College of Law, Florida State University College of Law, Stetson University College of Law, Nova Southeastern University Shepard Broad Law Center, St. Thomas University School of Law, Howard University College of Law, Texas Southern University Thurgood Marshall School of Law, Florida Coastal School of Law, or Florida International University College of Law. They must have a GPA of 2.6 or higher. Along with their application, they must submit a 1,000-word personal statement that describes their personal strengths, their contributions through community service, any special or unusual circumstances that may have affected their academic performance, or their personal and family history of educational or socioeconomic disadvantage; it should include aspects of their minority racial or ethnic identity that are relevant to their application. Applicants may also include information about their financial circumstances if they wish to have those considered in the selection process. U.S. citizenship or permanent resident status is required.

Financial data The stipend is $2,500 per semester.

Duration 1 semester (the spring semester of the second year of law school); may be renewed 1 additional semester (the fall semester of the third year).

Additional information This program was established by the Florida law firm Ruden McClosky, which was acquired by the firm Greenspoon Marder in 2011. It is administered by the Community Foundation of Sarasota County, but the law firm selects the recipients.

Number awarded 1 or more each year.

Deadline July of each year.

[921]
HANA SCHOLARSHIPS

United Methodist Church
Attn: General Board of Higher Education and Ministry
Office of Loans and Scholarships
1001 19th Avenue South
P.O. Box 340007
Nashville, TN 37203-0007
(615) 340-7342   Fax: (615) 340-7367
E-mail: umscholar@gbhem.org
Web: www.gbhem.org

Summary To provide financial assistance to upper-division and graduate Methodist students who are of Hispanic, Asian, Native American, or Pacific Islander ancestry.

Eligibility This program is open to full-time juniors, seniors, and graduate students at accredited colleges and universities in the United States who have been active, full members of a United Methodist Church (UMC) for at least 3 years prior to applying. Applicants must have at least 1 parent who is Hispanic, Asian, or Native American. They must be able to demonstrate involvement in their Hispanic, Asian, or Native American (HANA) community in the UMC. Selection is based on that involvement, academic ability (GPA of at least 2.85), and financial need. U.S. citizenship or permanent resident status is required.

Financial data Stipends range from $1,000 to $3,000.

Duration 1 year; recipients may reapply.

Number awarded 50 each year.

Deadline February of each year.

[922]
HARRIS BEACH SECOND YEAR LAW SCHOOL SCHOLARSHIP

Harris Beach PLLC
Attn: Human Resources
99 Garnsey Road
Pittsford, NY 14534
(585) 419-8728   Fax: (585) 419-8801
E-mail: mdomanti@harrisbeach.com
Web: www.harrisbeach.com/careers/diversity

Summary To provide financial assistance to Native American and other students at law schools in any state who are interested in practicing in New York state and will contribute to diversity of the legal profession.

Eligibility This program is open to second-year students at law schools in any state who are can demonstrate a strong commitment to live and work in New York. Applicants must reflect the diversity of the sponsoring law firm, which focuses on race, gender, religion, and sexual orientation, but also includes regional, cultural, generational, and other differences. Along with their application, they must submit essays on 1) how they can contribute to a diverse work environment at the sponsoring law firm; and 2) what excites them and engages their heart and mind.

Financial data The stipend is $7,500. Funds are paid directly to the recipient's law school.

Duration 1 year.

Number awarded 1 or more each year.

Deadline September of each year.

[923]
HARTER SECREST & EMERY LLP DIVERSITY SCHOLARSHIP

Harter Secrest & Emery LLP
Attn: Legal Recruiter
1600 Bausch & Lomb Place
Rochester, NY 14604-2711
(585) 231-1414   Fax: (585) 232-2152
E-mail: cgordon@hselaw.com
Web: www.hselawcareers.com/law-student/diversity

Summary To provide financial assistance and summer work experience in Rochester, New York to Nativ American and other law students from any state who will contribute to the diversity of the legal profession.

Eligibility This program is open to students who are currently enrolled full time in their first year at an ABA-accredited law school. Students who are members of populations historically underrepresented in the legal profession are encouraged to apply. They must also be interested in a summer associateship at the sponsoring law firm's main office in Rochester, New York. The firm's commitment to diversity includes people of all races, ethnic backgrounds, ages, lifestyles, sexual orientation, religious beliefs, and physical capabilities. Selection is based on academic record, interest and capacity for a successful career during the remainder of law school and in the legal profession, and contribution to the diversity of the student body at law school. A disclosure of financial circumstances is not required, but a demonstrated need for financial assistance may be taken into consideration. The finalists are invited to an interview.

Financial data The stipend for the academic year is $7,500, paid directly to the student's law school. The salary for the summer associateship is the same as for all associates of the firm.

Duration The summer associateship is for 12 weeks following the first year of law school. The academic stipend is for the second year.

Additional information This program began in 2005 for students at Cornell University Law School. In 2008, it was expanded to students at all ABA-accredited law schools.

Number awarded 1 each year.

Deadline January of each year.

[924]
HAWAI'I'S DAUGHTERS GUILD OF CALIFORNIA SCHOLARSHIPS

Hawai'i's Daughters Guild of California
P.O. Box 3305
Gardena, CA 90247
E-mail: HDG.Scholarship@gmail.com
Web: www.hawaiidaughtersguild.webs.com

Summary To provide financial assistance for college or graduate school to women of Polynesian ancestry from California.

Eligibility This program is open to California residents who are women of Polynesian ancestry and graduating high school seniors, full-time undergraduates, or full-time graduate students. Applicants must have a GPA of 3.0 or higher and be able to demonstrate financial need. Along with their application, they must submit transcripts, 3 letters of recommendation, an autobiographical essay, and proof of ancestry. Selection is based on goals as described in the autobiographical essay, academic achievement, extracurricular activities, community service, and financial need.

Financial data A stipend is awarded (amount not specified).

Duration 1 year.

Number awarded Varies each year.

Deadline March of each year.

[925]
HAYNES/HETTING AWARD

Philanthrofund Foundation
Attn: Scholarship Committee
1409 Willow Street, Suite 109
Minneapolis, MN 55403-2241
(612) 870-1806   Toll Free: (800) 435-1402
Fax: (612) 871-6587   E-mail: info@PfundOnline.org
Web: www.pfundonline.org/scholarships.html

Summary To provide funds to African American and Native American Minnesota students who have supported gay, lesbian, bisexual, and transgender (GLBT) activities.

Eligibility This program is open to residents of Minnesota and students attending a Minnesota educational institution who are African American or Native American. Applicants must be self-identified as GLBT or from a GLBT family. They may be attending or planning to attend a trade school, technical college, college, or university (as an undergraduate or graduate student). Selection is based on the applicant's 1) affirmation of GLBT or allied identity; 2) evidence of experience and skills in service and leadership; and 3) evidence of service, leading, and working for change in GLBT communities, including serving as a role model, mentor, and/or adviser.

Financial data   The stipend is $5,000. Funds must be used for tuition, books, fees, or dissertation expenses.

Duration   1 year.

Number awarded   1 each year.

Deadline   January of each year.

[926]
HCMP DIVERSITY FELLOWSHIP

Hillis Clark Martin & Peterson P.S.
Attn: Recruiting Coordinator
1221 Second Avenue, Suite 500
Seattle, WA 98101-2925
(206) 623-1745   Fax: (206) 623-7789
E-mail: brenda.partridge@hcmp.com
Web: www.hcmp.com/careers/diversity-fellowship

Summary   To provide financial assistance and work experience to Native American and other law students whose background and life experiences will contribute to the diversity of the legal community.

Eligibility   This program is open to students enrolled in the first year at an ABA-accredited law school. The firm seeks "people of different races, ethnicities, ages, religions, sexual orientation, and cultures, but also people of diverse ideas, abilities, styles, backgrounds, experiences, and beliefs." Applicants must submit a resume, transcripts, a personal statement of 1 to 2 pages describing their background and addressing the selection criteria, a legal writing sample, and a list of 3 references. Selection is based on distinction in academic performance, accomplishments and activities, commitment to community service, and leadership ability.

Financial data   The stipend is $7,500.

Duration   1 year.

Additional information   The program includes a salaried summer associate position following the first year of law school.

Number awarded   1 or more each year.

Deadline   January of each year.

[927]
HEALTH POLICY RESEARCH SCHOLARS

Robert Wood Johnson Foundation
50 College Road East
Princeton, NJ 08540-6614
Toll Free: (877) 843-RWJF   E-mail: mail@rwjf.org
Web: www.rwjf.org

Summary   To provide funding to Native American and other doctoral students from diverse backgrounds interested in working on a degree related to health policy.

Eligibility   This program is open to full-time doctoral students in the first or second year of their program. Applicants must be from underrepresented populations or disadvantaged backgrounds (e.g., first-generation college students, individuals from lower socioeconomic backgrounds, members of racial and ethnic groups underrepresented in doctoral programs, people with disabilities). They must be working on a degree in a field related to health policy, such as urban planning, political science, economics, ethnography, education, social work, or sociology; the program is not intended for stu-

dents working on a clinical doctorate without a research focus. Prior experience or knowledge in health policy is neither required nor expected.

Financial data   The stipend is $30,000 per year. Scholars are also eligible for $10,000 research grants if their dissertation is related to health policy.

Duration   Up to 4 years. Participants may continue in the program without the annual stipend for a fifth year or until they complete their doctoral program, whichever occurs first.

Number awarded   Up to 50 each year.

Deadline   March of each year.

[928]
HEALTH PROFESSIONS SCHOLARSHIP PROGRAM

Indian Health Service
Attn: Scholarship Program
5600 Fishers Lane
Mail Stop OHR (11E53A)
Rockville, MD 20857
(301) 443-6197   Fax: (301) 443-6048
Web: www.ihs.gov/scholarship/scholarships

Summary   To provide loans-for-service to American Indian and Alaska Native students enrolled in health professions and allied health professions programs.

Eligibility   This program is open to American Indians and Alaska Natives who are members of federally-recognized tribes. Applicants must be at least high school graduates and enrolled in a full-time study program leading to a degree in a health-related professions school within the United States. Priority is given to upper-division and graduate students. Qualifying fields of study recently included chemical dependency counseling (master's degree), clinical psychology (Ph.D. or Psy.D.), coding specialist (A.A.S.), counseling psychology (Ph.D.), dentistry (D.D.S. or D.M.D.), diagnostic radiology technology (associate or B.S.), environmental engineering (B.S., junior or senior), environmental health/sanitarian (B.S., junior or senior), health records administration (R.H.I.T. or R.H.I.A.), medical technology (B.S., junior or senior), allopathic and osteopathic medicine (M.D. or D.O.), nursing (A.D.N., B.S.N., C.R.N.A., N.P., certified nurse midwife, certified registered nurse anesthetist, geriatric nursing, pediatric nursing, psychiatric and mental health nursing, women's health nursing), optometry (O.D.), pharmacy (Pharm.D.), physician assistant (P.A.C.), physical therapy (M.S. or D.P.T.), podiatry (D.P.M.), public health nutritionist (M.S.), respiratory therapy (B.S.), social work (master's degree with concentration in direct or clinical practice), or ultrasonography (B.S. or certificate). Along with their application, they must submit a brief narrative that includes why they are requesting the scholarship, their career goals, and how those goals will help to meet the health needs of American Indian and Alaska Native people. Selection is based on that narrative (30 points); academic performance (40 points); and faculty, employer, and tribal recommendations (30 points).

Financial data   Awards provide a payment directly to the school for tuition and required fees; a stipend for living expenses of at least $1,500 per month for 12 months; a lump sum to cover the costs of books, laboratory expenses, and other necessary educational expenses; a payment of $300 for travel expenses; and up to $400 for approved tutorial costs. Upon completion of their program of study, recipients are required to provide payback service of 1 year for each year of scholarship support at the Indian Health Service, at a tribal health program, at an urban Indian health program, or in private practice in a designated health professional shortage area serving a substantial number of Indians. Recipients who fail to complete their service obligation must repay all funds received (although no interest is charged).

Duration 1 year; may be renewed for up to 3 additional years.

Number awarded Varies each year.

Deadline February of each year for continuing students; March of each year for new applicants.

[929]
HERMAN G. GREEN, PHD MEMORIAL SCHOLARSHIP

South Carolina Professional Association for Access and Equity
Attn: Financial Secretary
P.O. Box 71297
North Charleston, SC 29415
(843) 670-4890   E-mail: anderson4569@bellsouth.net
Web: www.scpaae.org/#!scholarships/c11tv

Summary To provide financial assistance to Native American and other graduate students at colleges and universities in South Carolina who are recognized as underrepresented minorities on their campus.

Eligibility This program is open to residents of any state who have completed at least 9 semester hours of graduate study at a college or university in South Carolina. Applicants must be recognized as an underrepresented ethnic minority on their campus. They must have a GPA of 3.5 or higher. Along with their application, they must submit 1) a personal letter on their public service, academic and career goals, honors and awards, leadership skills and organization participation, community service, and a statement of why they would like to receive this scholarship; and 2) a paragraph defining access and equity and describing how they can assist in achieving access and equity within South Carolina. Financial need is not considered in the selection process.

Financial data The stipend is $1,200.

Duration 1 year.

Number awarded 1 or more each year.

Deadline February of each year.

[930]
HINCKLEY ALLEN SCHOLARSHIP PROGRAM

Hinckley Allen
Attn: Director of Legal Recruitment and Integration
28 State Street
Boston, MA 02109
(617) 345-9000   Fax: (617) 345-9020
E-mail: dyergeau@hinckleyallen.com
Web: www.hinckleyallen.com/diversity/diversity-inclusion

Summary To provide financial assistance and work experience at the sponsor's Boston office to Native American and other law students who are committed to diversity.

Eligibility This program is open to students currently enrolled in the first year at an ABA-accredited law school. Applicants must be able to demonstrate an excellent academic record, leadership, and a commitment to diversity.

They must be interested in a summer associateship at the sponsoring law firm in Boston. Along with their application, they must submit a resume, transcript, writing sample, and a personal statement on their life experiences and how they will contribute to the diversity of the firm and the legal profession.

Financial data The selected student receives a summer salary and a scholarship for law school of $10,000.

Duration 10 weeks for the associateship; 1 academic year for the scholarship.

Number awarded 1 or more each year.

Deadline January of each year.

[931]
HO-CHUNK NATION SUMMER PROGRAM AWARDS

Ho-Chunk Nation
Attn: Higher Education Division
P.O. Box 667
Black River Falls, WI 54615
(715) 284-4915   Toll Free: (800) 362-4476
Fax: (715) 284-1760
E-mail: higher.education@ho-chunk.com
Web: www.ho-chunknation.com/highered/scholarships.aspx

Summary To provide financial assistance to Ho-Chunk undergraduate or graduate students who wish to continue their postsecondary studies during the summer.

Eligibility Applicants must be enrolled members of the Ho-Chunk Nation; have been accepted at an accredited public vocational or technical school, college, or university in the United States in an undergraduate or graduate program; and be interested in attending summer school on a full-time basis.

Financial data This program pays up to $3,500 to undergraduate recipients and up to $9,000 to graduate school recipients. Funds must be used for tuition, fees, or books. Funds are paid directly to the recipient's school.

Duration 1 term for a 1-year degree or certificate, 3 terms for an associate degree, 6 terms for a bachelor's degree, 8 terms for a master's degree, or 10 terms for a doctoral or professional degree.

Additional information Undergraduate recipients must earn a GPA of 2.0 or higher in the summer classes; graduate school recipients must earn 3.0 or higher.

Number awarded Varies each year.

Deadline February of each year.

[932]
HOLLY A. CORNELL SCHOLARSHIP

American Water Works Association
Attn: Scholarship Coordinator
6666 West Quincy Avenue
Denver, CO 80235-3098
(303) 794-7771   Toll Free: (800) 926-7337
Fax: (303) 347-0804   E-mail: scholarships@awwa.org
Web: www.awwa.org

Summary To provide financial assistance to Native American and other minority students interested in working on an master's degree in the field of water supply and treatment.

Eligibility This program is open to minority and female students working on a master's degree in the field of water supply and treatment at a college or university in Canada, Guam, Mexico, Puerto Rico, or the United States. Students who have been accepted into graduate school but have not yet begun graduate study are encouraged to apply. Applicants must submit a 2-page resume, official transcripts, 3 letters of recommendation, a proposed curriculum of study, a 1-page statement of educational plans and career objectives demonstrating an interest in the drinking water field, and a 3-page proposed plan of research. Selection is based on academic record and potential to provide leadership in the field of water supply and treatment.

Financial data The stipend is $7,500.

Duration 1 year; nonrenewable.

Additional information Funding for this program, which began in 1990, comes from the consulting firm CH2M Hill.

Number awarded 1 each year.

Deadline January of each year.

[933]
HOMER "DEE" WELLS MEMORIAL SCHOLARSHIP

Chickasaw Foundation
2020 Arlington, Suite 4
P.O. Box 1726
Ada, OK 74821-1726
(580) 421-9030   Fax: (580) 421-9031
E-mail: ChickasawFoundation@chickasaw.net
Web: www.chickasawfoundation.org/Scholarships.aspx

Summary To provide financial assistance to members of the Chickasaw Nation who are working on an undergraduate or graduate degree in construction management or engineering.

Eligibility This program is open to members of the Chickasaw Nation who are currently enrolled full time in the second year of an associate degree program, as a junior or senior in an undergraduate program, or as a graduate student. Applicants must be working on a degree in construction management or engineering. They must have a GPA of 3.0 or higher. Along with their application, they must submit high school or college transcripts; 2 letters of recommendation; a copy of their Chickasaw Nation citizenship card; a 2-page list of honors, achievements, awards, club memberships, societies, and civic involvement; and a 1-page essay on their long-term goals and plans for achieving those. Financial need is not considered in the selection process.

Financial data A stipend is awarded (amount not specified).

Duration 1 year.

Number awarded 1 or more each year.

Deadline June of each year.

[934]
HOPI EDUCATION AWARDS PROGRAM

Hopi Tribe
Attn: Grants and Scholarships Program
P.O. Box 123
Kykotsmovi, AZ 86039
(928) 734-3542   Toll Free: (800) 762-9630
Fax: (928) 734-9575   E-mail: JTorivio@hopi.nsn.us
Web: www.hopi-nsn.gov

Summary To provide financial assistance to needy students of Hopi ancestry who are working on an undergraduate, graduate, or postgraduate degree.

Eligibility This program is open to students who are working full time on an associate, baccalaureate, graduate, or postgraduate degree. Applicants must be enrolled members of the Hopi Tribe and able to demonstrate financial need. Undergraduates must have a GPA of 2.5 or higher and graduate students must have a GPA of 3.0 or higher.

Financial data The maximum grant is $2,500 per semester ($5,000 per year).

Duration 1 semester; may be renewed for up to 10 terms of undergraduate study or up to 5 terms of graduate study, provided the recipient maintains full-time enrollment and a GPA of 2.5 or higher as an undergraduate or 3.0 or higher as a graduate student.

Additional information This grant is awarded as a secondary source of financial aid to eligible students who are also receiving aid from the Bureau of Indian Affairs (BIA) Higher Education program.

Number awarded Varies each year.

Deadline June of each year for fall; October of each year for winter; November of each year for spring.

[935]
HOPI TRIBAL PRIORITY AWARDS

Hopi Tribe
Attn: Grants and Scholarships Program
P.O. Box 123
Kykotsmovi, AZ 86039
(928) 734-3542   Toll Free: (800) 762-9630
Fax: (928) 734-9575   E-mail: JTorivio@hopi.nsn.us
Web: www.hopi-nsn.gov

Summary To provide scholarship/loans to Hopi students who are interested in working on a graduate degree in an area of interest to the Hopi Tribe.

Eligibility This program is open to enrolled members of the Hopi Tribe who are full-time graduate students working on a degree in a subject area that is of priority interest to the Hopi Tribe. Recently, those areas were law, economic development, business/finance, environmental/natural resources, education, or social sciences. Applicants must have a GPA of 3.5 or higher. Along with their application, they must submit personal statements on their reasons for applying for this scholarship, their career goals as related to the Hopi Tribe priorities, and how they intend to apply directly their educational goals to meet the needs of the Hopi People.

Financial data This program provides payment of all tuition and fees, books and supplies, transportation, room and board, and a stipend of $1,500 per month. Recipients must agree to provide 1 year of professional services to the Hopi Tribe or other service agencies that serve the Hopi People for each year funding is awarded.

Duration 1 year; may be renewed, provided the recipient maintains a GPA of 3.5 or higher.

Number awarded Up to 5 each year.

Deadline June of each year.

[936]
HOPI TUITION AND BOOK AWARD

Hopi Tribe
Attn: Grants and Scholarships Program
P.O. Box 123
Kykotsmovi, AZ 86039
(928) 734-3542   Toll Free: (800) 762-9630
Fax: (928) 734-9575   E-mail: JTorivio@hopi.nsn.us
Web: www.hopi-nsn.gov

Summary To provide financial assistance to students of Hopi ancestry who are interested in working on an undergraduate or graduate degree at a college in any state but cannot demonstrate financial need.

Eligibility This program is open to students who are interested in working full or part time on an associate, baccalaureate, graduate, or postgraduate degree. Applicants must be enrolled members of the Hopi Tribe who have no unmet financial need. Undergraduates must have a GPA of 2.5 or higher and graduate students must have a GPA of 3.0 or higher.

Financial data The maximum grant is $2,500 per semester ($5,000 per year).

Duration 1 semester; may be renewed for up to 10 terms of undergraduate study or up to 5 terms of graduate study, provided the recipient maintains full-time enrollment and a GPA of 2.5 or higher as an undergraduate or 3.0 or higher as a graduate student.

Number awarded Varies each year.

Deadline June of each year for fall; October of each year for winter; November of each year for spring.

[937]
HOWARD KECK/WESTMIN ENDOWMENT SCHOLARSHIP FUND

Cook Inlet Region, Inc.
Attn: The CIRI Foundation
3600 San Jeronimo Drive, Suite 256
Anchorage, AK 99508-2870
(907) 793-3575   Toll Free: (800) 764-3382
Fax: (907) 793-3585   E-mail: tcf@thecirifoundation.org
Web: www.thecirifoundation.org/about/donors

Summary To provide financial assistance for undergraduate or graduate studies in any field to Alaska Natives who are original enrollees to Cook Inlet Region, Inc. (CIRI) and their lineal descendants.

Eligibility This program is open to Alaska Native enrollees to CIRI under the Alaska Native Claims Settlement Act (ANCSA) of 1971 and their lineal descendants. There are no Alaska residency requirements or age limitations. Applicants must be accepted or enrolled full time in a 2-year undergraduate, 4-year undergraduate, or graduate degree program. They may be studying in any field but must have a GPA of 2.5 or higher. Along with their application, they must submit a 500-word statement on their educational and career goals and how they are contributing, or planning to contribute, to a positive Alaska Native community. Selection is based on that statement, academic achievement, rigor of course work or degree program, student financial contribution, financial need, grade level, previous work performance, community service, and relationship of degree program to career goals.

Financial data The stipend is $20,000 per year, $10,000 per year, $8,000 per year, or $2,500 per semester, depending on GPA.

Duration 1 semester or 1 year.

Additional information CIRI is 1 of 13 regional corporations established according to the terms of the Alaska Native Claims Settlement Act (ANCSA) of 1971. This fund was established in 1986 by Howard Keck/Westmin Ltd.

Number awarded Varies each year; recently, 5 were awarded.

Deadline May of each year for annual scholarships; May or November of each year for semester scholarships.

[938]
HOWARD MAYER BROWN FELLOWSHIP

American Musicological Society
6010 College Station
Brunswick, ME 04011-8451
(207) 798-4243   Toll Free: (877) 679-7648
Fax: (207) 798-4254   E-mail: ams@ams-net.org
Web: www.ams-net.org/fellowships/hmb.php

Summary To provide financial assistance to Native American and other minority students who are working on a doctoral degree in the field of musicology.

Eligibility This program is open to members of minority groups historically underrepresented in the field of musicology. In the United States, that includes African Americans, Native Americans, Hispanic Americans, and Asian Americans. In Canada, it refers to aboriginal people and visible minorities. Applicants must have completed at least 1 year of full-time academic work at an institution with a graduate program in musicology and be planning to complete a Ph.D. degree in the field. There are no restrictions on research area, age, or sex. U.S. or Canadian citizenship or permanent resident status is required.

Financial data The stipend is $20,000.

Duration 1 year; nonrenewable.

Additional information This fellowship was first awarded in 1995.

Number awarded 1 each year.

Deadline December of each year.

[939]
HP ENGINEERING INC SCHOLARSHIP

Cherokee Nation Foundation
800 South Muskogee
Tahlequah, OK 74464
(918) 207-0950   Fax: (918) 207-0951
E-mail: contact@cherokeenationfoundation.org
Web: cherokeenation.academicworks.com

Summary To provide financial assistance to citizens of several Cherokee nations who are enrolled at a college or university in any state and working on an undergraduate or graduate degree in electrical or mechanical engineering.

Eligibility This program is open to citizens of the Cherokee Nation, the United Keetoowah Band, or the Eastern Band of Cherokee Indians. Applicants must be juniors, seniors, or graduate students in an ABET-accredited undergraduate or graduate program in electrical or mechanical engineering. They must agree to spend a 2-day job shadow experience at HP Engineering offices in Tulsa, Oklahoma and Rogers,

Arkansas. Along with their application, they must submit a description of their most meaningful achievements and how those relate to their field of study and their future goals. Selection is based on the clarity and presentation of the essay; academic information (including transcripts and ACT scores); school, cultural and community activities; future plans to serve Cherokee people; and financial need.

Financial data   The stipend is $1,000.

Duration   1 year.

Additional information   This program is sponsored by HP Engineering Inc.

Number awarded   1 or more each year.

Deadline   February of each year.

[940]
HUGGINS-QUARLES AWARD

Organization of American Historians
Attn: Award and Committee Coordinator
112 North Bryan Street
Bloomington, IN 47408-4141
(812) 855-7311   Fax: (812) 855-0696
E-mail: khamm@oah.org
Web: www.oah.org

Summary   To provide funding to Native American and other minority graduate students who are completing dissertations in American history.

Eligibility   This program is open to graduate students of color (African American, Latino(a), Asian American, Native American) at the dissertation research stage of their Ph.D. programs. Their dissertation must deal with a topic related to American history. Along with their application, they must submit a cover letter that also indicates their progress on the dissertation, a curriculum vitae, a 5-page dissertation proposal (including an explanation of the project's significance and contribution to the field and a description of the most important primary sources) and a 1-page itemized budget explaining travel and research plans.

Financial data   The grant is $1,500 (if 1 is presented) or $750 (if 2 are presented). Funds are to be used to assist with costs of travel to collections to complete research on the dissertation.

Additional information   This program was established in honor of Benjamin Quarles and the late Nathan Huggins, both outstanding historians of the African American past.

Number awarded   1 or 2 each year.

Deadline   November of each year.

[941]
HUGH J. ANDERSEN MEMORIAL SCHOLARSHIPS

National Medical Fellowships, Inc.
Attn: Scholarship Program
347 Fifth Avenue, Suite 510
New York, NY 10016
(212) 483-8880   Toll Free: (877) NMF-1DOC
Fax: (212) 483-8897 E-mail: scholarships@nmfonline.org
Web: www.nmfonline.org

Summary   To provide financial assistance to Native American and other underrepresented minority medical students at schools in Minnesota.

Eligibility   This program is open to African Americans, Hispanics/Latinos, Native Americans, Vietnamese, Cambodians, and Pacific Islanders who are entering the second or third year of medical school. Applicants must be Minnesota residents enrolled at an accredited medical school in Minnesota. They must be U.S. citizens or DACA students. Selection is based on leadership, commitment to serving medically underserved communities, and financial need.

Financial data   The stipend is $5,000.

Duration   1 year.

Additional information   This program began in 1982.

Number awarded   2 each year.

Deadline   September of each year.

[942]
IDA M. POPE MEMORIAL SCHOLARSHIPS

Hawai'i Community Foundation
Attn: Scholarship Department
827 Fort Street Mall
Honolulu, HI 96813
(808) 566-5570   Toll Free: (888) 731-3863
Fax: (808) 521-6286
E-mail: scholarships@hcf-hawaii.org
Web: hcf.scholarships.ngwebsolutions.com

Summary   To provide financial assistance to Native Hawaiian women who are interested in working on an undergraduate or graduate degree in designated fields at a school in any state.

Eligibility   This program is open to female residents of Hawaii who are Native Hawaiian, defined as a descendant of the aboriginal inhabitants of the Hawaiian islands prior to 1778. Applicants must be enrolled full time at a 2- or 4-year college or university in any state and working on an undergraduate or graduate degree in health, science, mathematics, or education (including counseling and social work). They must be able to demonstrate academic achievement (GPA of 3.5 or higher), good moral character, and financial need. Along with their application, they must submit a short statement indicating their reasons for attending college, their planned course of study, their career goals, and what community service means to them.

Financial data   The amounts of the awards depend on the availability of funds and the need of the recipient. Recently, the average value of the scholarships awarded by the foundation was $2,800.

Duration   1 year; may be renewed.

Number awarded   Varies each year; recently, 61 were awarded.

Deadline   February of each year.

[943]
ILLINOIS NURSES FOUNDATION CENTENNIAL SCHOLARSHIP

Illinois Nurses Association
Attn: Illinois Nurses Foundation
P.O. Box 636
Manteno, IL 60950
(815) 468-8804   Fax: (773) 304-1419
E-mail: info@ana-illinois.org
Web: www.ana-illinois.org

Summary To provide financial assistance to nursing undergraduate and graduate students who are American Indians or members of other underrepresented groups.

Eligibility This program is open to students working on an associate, bachelor's, or master's degree at an accredited NLNAC or CCNE school of nursing. Applicants must be members of a group underrepresented in nursing (African Americans, Hispanics, American Indians, Asians, and males). Undergraduates must have earned a passing grade in all nursing courses taken to date and have a GPA of 2.85 or higher. Graduate students must have completed at least 12 semester hours of graduate work and have a GPA of 3.0 or higher. All applicants must be willing to 1) act as a spokesperson to other student groups on the value of the scholarship to continuing their nursing education; and 2) be profiled in any media or marketing materials developed by the Illinois Nurses Foundation. Along with their application, they must submit a narrative of 250 to 500 words on how they, as nurses, plan to affect policy at either the state or national level that impacts on nursing or health care generally, or how they believe they will impact the nursing profession in general.

Financial data A stipend is awarded (amount not specified).

Duration 1 year.

Number awarded 1 or more each year.

Deadline March of each year.

[944]
INDIANA CLEO FELLOWSHIPS

Indiana Supreme Court
Attn: Division of State Court Administration
30 South Meridian Street, Suite 500
Indianapolis, IN 46204
(317) 232-2542   Toll Free: (800) 452-9963
Fax: (317) 233-6586 E-mail: ashley.rozier@courts.in.gov
Web: www.in.gov/judiciary/cleo/2402.htm

Summary To provide financial assistance to Native American and other disadvantaged minority college seniors from any state interested in attending law school in Indiana.

Eligibility This program is open to residents of Indiana who attend college in the state or attend college out of state and are recommended by the admissions officer at a law school in the state. Applicants must be minority, low income, first-generation college, or limited English proficiency college seniors who have applied to an Indiana law school. Selected applicants are invited to participate in the Indiana Conference for Legal Education Opportunity (Indiana CLEO) Summer Institute, held at a law school in the state. Admission to that program is based on GPA, LSAT scores, 3 letters of recommendation, a resume, a personal statement, and financial need. Students who successfully complete the Institute and are admitted to an Indiana law school receive these fellowships.

Financial data All expenses for the Indiana CLEO Summer Institute are paid. The fellowship stipend is $9,000 per year.

Duration The Indiana CLEO Summer Institute lasts 6 weeks. Fellowships are for 1 year and may be renewed up to 2 additional years.

Additional information The first Summer Institute was held in 1997.

Number awarded 30 students are invited to participate in the summer institute; the number of those selected to receive a fellowship varies each year.

Deadline February of each year.

[945]
INTELLECTUAL PROPERTY LAW SECTION WOMEN AND MINORITY SCHOLARSHIP

State Bar of Texas
Attn: Intellectual Property Law Section
c/o Bhaveeni D. Parmar, Scholarship Selection
  Committee
Law Office of Bhaveeni Parmar PLLC
4447 North Central Expressway, Suite 110-295
Dallas, Texas 75205
E-mail: bhaveeni@parmarlawoffice.com
Web: www.texasbariplaw.org

Summary To provide financial assistance to Native American and other minority and female students at law schools in Texas who plan to practice intellectual property law.

Eligibility This program is open to women and members of minority groups (African Americans, Hispanics, Asian Americans, and Native Americans) from any state who are currently enrolled at an ABA-accredited law school in Texas. Applicants must be planning to practice intellectual property law in Texas. Along with their application, they must submit a 2-page essay explaining why they plan to prepare for a career in intellectual property law in Texas, any qualifications they believe are relevant for their consideration for this scholarship, and (optionally) any issues of financial need they wish to have considered.

Financial data The stipend is $5,000.

Duration 1 year.

Number awarded 2 each year: 1 to a women and 1 to a minority.

Deadline May of each year.

[946]
INTERMOUNTAIN SECTION AWWA DIVERSITY SCHOLARSHIP

American Water Works Association-Intermountain
  Section
Attn: Member Services Coordinator
3430 East Danish Road
Sandy, UT 84093
(801) 712-1619, ext. 2   Fax: (801) 487-6699
E-mail: nicoleb@ims-awwa.org
Web: ims-awwa.site-ym.com/group/StudentPO

Summary To provide financial assistance to Native American and other minority undergraduate and graduate students working on a degree in the field of water quality, supply, and treatment at a university in the Intermountain West.

Eligibility This program is open to 1) women; and 2) students who identify as Hispanic or Latino, Black or African American, Native Hawaiian or other Pacific Islander, Asian, or American Indian or Alaska Native. Applicants must be entering or enrolled in an undergraduate or graduate program at a college or university in the Intermountain West (defined to include all or portions of Arizona, Colorado, Idaho, Montana, Nevada, New Mexico, Utah, or Wyoming) that relates to water quality, supply, or treatment. Along with their application, they must submit a 2-page essay on their academic interests and career goals and how those relate to water quality, supply, or treatment. Selection is based on that essay, letters of recommendation, and potential to contribute to the field of water quality, supply, and treatment in the Intermountain West.

Financial data The stipend is $1,000. The winner also receives a 1-year student membership in the Intermountain Section of the American Water Works Association (AWWA).

Duration 1 year; nonrenewable.

Number awarded 1 each year.

Deadline November of each year.

[947]
IRA L. AND MARY L. HARRISON MEMORIAL SCHOLARSHIP

Baptist Convention of New Mexico
Attn: Missions Mobilization Team
5325 Wyoming Boulevard, N.E.
P.O. Box 94485
Albuquerque, NM 87199-4485
(505) 924-2315   Toll Free: (800) 898-8544
Fax: (505) 924-2320   E-mail: cpairett@bcnm.com
Web: www.bcnm.com/scholarships

Summary To provide financial assistance to Native American Southern Baptist students from New Mexico who are attending designated colleges or Baptist seminaries.

Eligibility This program is open to undergraduate and seminary students who are Native American members of churches affiliated with the Baptist Convention of New Mexico. Applicants must have a GPA of 2.0 or higher and be able to demonstrate financial need. Undergraduates must be attending Wayland Baptist University at its main campus in Plainview, Texas or at its New Mexico external campuses in Clovis or Albuquerque. Graduate students must be attending 1 of the 6 Southern Baptist seminaries: Southeastern Baptist Theological Seminary (Wake Forest, North Carolina); Southern Baptist Theological Seminary (Louisville, Kentucky); Southwestern Baptist Theological Seminary (Fort Worth, Texas); New Orleans Baptist Theological Seminary (New Orleans, Louisiana); Midwestern Baptist Theological Seminary (Kansas City, Missouri); or Golden Gate Baptist Theological Seminary (Mill Valley, California).

Financial data A stipend is awarded (amount not specified).

Duration 1 year; may be renewed.

Number awarded 1 or more each year.

Deadline March, June, August, or December of each year.

[948]
IRTS BROADCAST SALES ASSOCIATE PROGRAM

International Radio and Television Society Foundation
Attn: Director, Special Projects
1697 Broadway, 10th Floor
New York, NY 10019
(212) 867-6650   Toll Free: (888) 627-1266
Fax: (212) 867-6653   E-mail: submit@irts.org
Web: 406.144.myftpupload.com

Summary To provide summer work experience to Native American and other minority graduate students interested in working in broadcast sales in the New York City area.

Eligibility This program is open to graduating college seniors and students already enrolled in graduate school who are members of a minority (African American, Hispanic/Latino, Asian/Pacific Islander, American Indian/Alaskan Native) group. Applicants must be interested in working during the summer in a sales training program traditionally reserved for actual station group employees. They must be a communications major or have demonstrated a strong interest in the field through extracurricular activities or other practical experience, but they are not required to have experience in broadcast sales.

Financial data Travel, housing, and a living allowance are provided.

Duration 9 weeks during the summer.

Additional information The program consists of a 1-week orientation to the media and entertainment business, followed by an 8-week internship experience in the sales division of a network stations group.

Number awarded Varies each year.

Deadline February of each year.

[949]
ISAAC J. "IKE" CRUMBLY MINORITIES IN ENERGY GRANT

American Association of Petroleum Geologists
  Foundation
Attn: Grants-in-Aid Program
1444 South Boulder Avenue
P.O. Box 979
Tulsa, OK 74101-0979
(918) 560-2644   Toll Free: (855) 302-2743
Fax: (918) 560-2642   E-mail: foundation@aapg.org
Web: foundation.aapg.org

Summary To provide funding to Native American and other minority graduate students who are interested in conducting research related to earth science aspects of the petroleum industry.

Eligibility This program is open to women and ethnic minorities (Black, Hispanic, Asian, or Native American, including American Indian, Eskimo, Hawaiian, or Samoan) who are working on a master's or doctoral degree. Applicants must be interested in conducting research related to the search for and development of petroleum and energy-minerals resources and to related environmental geology issues. Selection is based on student's academic and employment history (10 points), scientific merit of proposal (30 points), suitability to program objectives (30 points), financial merit of proposal (20 points), and endorsement by faculty or department adviser (10 points).

Financial data Grants range from $500 to $3,000. Funds are to be applied to research-related expenses (e.g., a summer of field work). They may not be used to purchase capital equipment or to pay salaries, tuition, room, or board.

Duration 1 year. Doctoral candidates may receive a 1-year renewal.

Number awarded 1 each year.

Deadline February of each year.

[950]
ITHANA (EDUCATION) SCHOLARSHIP

Chickasaw Foundation
2020 Arlington, Suite 4
P.O. Box 1726
Ada, OK 74821-1726
(580) 421-9030   Fax: (580) 421-9031
E-mail: ChickasawFoundation@chickasaw.net
Web: www.chickasawfoundation.org/Scholarships.aspx

Summary To provide financial assistance to members of the Chickasaw Nation who can demonstrate financial need and are working on an undergraduate or graduate degree in any field.

Eligibility This program is open to members of the Chickasaw Nation who are currently working full-time on an undergraduate or graduate degree in any field. Applicants must be able to demonstrate that they are a leader or contributor to society with a strong Christian character. They must have a GPA of 2.5 or higher. Along with their application, they must submit high school or college transcripts; 2 letters of recommendation; a copy of their Chickasaw Nation citizenship card; documentation of financial need; a 2-page list of honors, achievements, awards, club memberships, societies, and civic involvement; and a 1-page essay on their long-term goals and plans for achieving those.

Financial data A stipend is awarded (amount not specified).

Duration 1 year.

Number awarded Varies each year; recently, 3 were awarded.

Deadline June of each year.

[951]
J. MICHAEL PRINCE GRADUATE SCHOLARSHIP

Chahta Foundation
Attn: Scholarship Specialist
P.O. Box 1849
Durant, OK 74702
(580) 924-8280, ext. 2546
Toll Free: (800) 522-6170, ext. 2546
Fax: (580) 745-9023
E-mail: scholarship@chahtafoundation.com
Web: www.chahtafoundation.com

Summary To provide financial assistance to Choctaw tribal members who are working on a master's degree in business at a school in any state.

Eligibility This program is open to members of the Choctaw nation who are entering an M.B.A. degree program in any state. Applicants must have an undergraduate GPA of 3.0 or higher. Along with their application, they must submit a resume, transcript, a financial need analysis, and a letter of recommendation.

Financial data The stipend is $1,000.

Duration 1 year.

Additional information This program began in 2014.

Number awarded A selected number are awarded each year.

Deadline March of each year.

[952]
JACK L. STEPHENS GRADUATE SCHOLARSHIP

Conference of Minority Transportation Officials-Fort
   Lauderdale Chapter
Attn: Scholarship Committee
Victor Garcia, South Florida Regional Transportation
   Authority
801 N.W. 33rd Street
Pompano Beach, FL 33064
(954) 788-7925   Toll Free: (800) GO-SFRTA
Fax: (854) 788-7961   TDD: (800) 273-7545
E-mail: victorgarcia@comtoftlauderdale.org
Web: www.comtoftlauderdale.org/scholarship-program

Summary To provide financial assistance to Native American and other minority students working on a transportation-related graduate degree at a college in Florida.

Eligibility This program is open to minority students currently enrolled at accredited colleges and universities in Florida. Applicants must be working on a master's or doctoral degree in a transportation-related field and have a GPA of 2.5 or higher. They must be U.S. citizens or permanent residents. Along with their application, they must submit an essay of 500 to 750 words on their transportation-related career goals and life aspirations. Financial need is not considered in the selection process.

Financial data The stipend is $2,500.

Duration 1 year; nonrenewable.

Additional information This program began in 2015.

Number awarded 1 each year.

Deadline April of each year.

[953]
JACOB WILLIAMS SCHOLARSHIP

United Methodist Foundation of Indiana
8401 Fishers Center Drive
Fishers, IN 46038-2318
(317) 788-7879   Toll Free: (877) 391-8811
Fax: (317) 788-0089
E-mail: foundation@UMFIndiana.org
Web: www.umfindiana.org/endowments

Summary To provide financial assistance to Native American and other ethnic minority ministerial students from Indiana who are attending a seminary in any state that is approved by the United Methodist Church (UMC).

Eligibility This program is open to members of ethnic minority groups who are candidates for ordination and certified by a District Committee of the Indiana Conference of the UMC. Applicants must be enrolled full time at an approved seminary in any state. They must be seeking ordination as a deacon or elder. Along with their application, they must submit documentation of financial need and a statement of their vocational goals.

Financial data Stipends are awarded at the rate of $100 per credit hour (per semester) and $200 per projected decade of service remaining (per semester).

Duration 1 year; may be renewed.

Number awarded 1 or more each year.

Deadline May of each year for fall semester; October of each year for spring semester.

[954]
JAMES AND CAROLEE CUNDIFF GRANTS

Chickasaw Foundation
2020 Arlington, Suite 4
P.O. Box 1726
Ada, OK 74821-1726
(580) 421-9030　　　　　　　　Fax: (580) 421-9031
E-mail: ChickasawFoundation@chickasaw.net
Web: www.chickasawfoundation.org/Scholarships.aspx

Summary　To provide financial assistance to members of the Chickasaw Nation who can demonstrate financial need and are working on an undergraduate or graduate degree in any field.

Eligibility　This program is open to members of the Chickasaw Nation who are currently enrolled as full-time undergraduate or graduate students at a 2- or 4-year college or university in any state. Applicants must be able to demonstrate that they are a leader or contributor to society with a strong Christian character. Along with their application, they must submit high school or college transcripts; 2 letters of recommendation; a copy of their Chickasaw Nation citizenship card; documentation of financial need; a 2-page list of honors, achievements, awards, club memberships, societies, and civic involvement; and a 1-page essay on their long-term goals and plans for achieving those.

Financial data　A stipend is awarded (amount not specified).

Duration　1 year.

Number awarded　10 each year.

Deadline　June of each year.

[955]
JAMES B. MORRIS SCHOLARSHIPS

James B. Morris Scholarship Fund
Attn: Scholarship Selection Committee
P.O. Box 12145
Des Moines, IA 50312
(515) 864-0922
Web: www.morrisscholarship.org

Summary　To provide financial assistance to Native American and other minority undergraduate, graduate, and law students from Iowa.

Eligibility　This program is open to minority students (African Americans, Asian/Pacific Islanders, Hispanics, or Native Americans) who are interested in working on an undergraduate or graduate degree. Applicants must be either Iowa residents attending a college or university anywhere in the United States or non-Iowa residents who are attending a college or university in Iowa. Along with their application, they must submit an essay of 250 to 500 words on why they are applying for this scholarship, activities or organizations in which they are involved, and their future plans. Selection is based on the essay, academic achievement (GPA of 2.5 or higher), community service, and financial need. U.S. citizenship is required.

Financial data　The stipend ranges from $1,000 to $2,500 per year.

Duration　1 year; may be renewed.

Additional information　This fund was established in 1978 in honor of the J.B. Morris family, who founded the Iowa branch of the National Association for the Advancement of Colored People and published the *Iowa Bystander* newspaper. The program includes the Ann Chapman Scholarships, the Vincent Chapman, Sr. Scholarships, the Catherine Williams Scholarships, and the Brittany Hall Memorial Scholarships. Support for additional scholarships is provided by EMC Insurance Group and Wells Fargo Bank.

Number awarded　Varies each year; recently, 22 were awarded.

Deadline　February of each year.

[956]
JAMES ECHOLS SCHOLARSHIP

California Association for Health, Physical Education,
　Recreation and Dance
Attn: Chair, Scholarship Committee
1501 El Camino Avenue, Suite 3
Sacramento, CA 95815-2748
(916) 922-3596　　　Toll Free: (800) 499-3596 (within CA)
Fax: (916) 922-0133　　　E-mail: reception@cahperd.org
Web: www.cahperd.org

Summary　To provide financial assistance to Native American and other minority student members of the California Association for Health, Physical Education, Recreation and Dance.

Eligibility　This program is open to California residents who have been members of the association for at least 60 days and are attending a 2- or 4-year college or university in the state. Applicants must be undergraduate or graduate students working on a degree in health education, physical education, recreation, or dance and have completed at least 60 semester hours of college work. Selection is based on scholastic proficiency (a GPA of 3.0 or higher); leadership ability in school, community, and professional activities; and personal qualities of enthusiasm, cooperativeness, responsibility, initiative, and ability to work with others. This scholarship is awarded to the highest-ranked minority (Asian, African American, Latino, or Native American) applicant.

Financial data　The stipend is $1,000.

Duration　1 year.

Number awarded　1 each year.

Deadline　November of each year.

[957]
JANIE HARDWICK BENSON MEMORIAL SCHOLARSHIP

Chickasaw Foundation
2020 Arlington, Suite 4
P.O. Box 1726
Ada, OK 74821-1726
(580) 421-9030　　　　　　　　Fax: (580) 421-9031
E-mail: ChickasawFoundation@chickasaw.net
Web: www.chickasawfoundation.org/Scholarships.aspx

Summary　To provide financial assistance to members of the Chickasaw Nation who are working or an undergraduate or graduate degree in nursing.

Eligibility　This program is open to Chickasaw students who are currently working full time on an undergraduate or graduate degree in nursing (A.D.N., B.S.N., or M.S.N.). Applicants must have a GPA of 2.75 or higher. Along with their application, they must submit high school or college transcripts; 2 letters of recommendation; a copy of their Chickasaw Nation citizenship card; a 2-page list of honors, achievements, awards, club memberships, societies, and civic involvement; and a 1-page essay on their long-term goals and plans for achieving those. Financial need is not considered in the selection process.

Financial data A stipend is awarded (amount not specified).

Duration 1 year.

Number awarded 1 each year.

Deadline June of each year.

[958]
JEANETTE ELMER FELLOWSHIP

American Indian Graduate Center
Attn: Executive Director
3701 San Mateo Boulevard, N.E., Suite 200
Albuquerque, NM 87110-1249
(505) 881-4584   Toll Free: (800) 628-1920
Fax: (505) 884-0427   E-mail: fellowships@aigc.com
Web: www.aigcs.org/scholarships/graduate-fellowships

Summary To provide financial assistance to Native American students who are interested in working on a graduate degree in library science.

Eligibility This program is open to enrolled members of federally-recognized American Indian tribes who are enrolled full time at a graduate school in the United States. Along with their application, they must submit a 500-word essay on how receiving this fellowship will enable them to continue to build, promote, and honor self-sustaining American Indian and Alaska Native communities. Financial need is also considered in the selection process.

Financial data Stipends range from $500 to $5,000 per academic year, depending on the availability of funds and the recipient's unmet financial need.

Duration 1 year; may be renewed.

Number awarded 1 each year.

Deadline May of each year.

[959]
JEANNE SPURLOCK RESEARCH FELLOWSHIP IN SUBSTANCE ABUSE AND ADDICTION FOR MINORITY MEDICAL STUDENTS

American Academy of Child and Adolescent Psychiatry
Attn: Department of Research, Training, and Education
3615 Wisconsin Avenue, N.W.
Washington, DC 20016-3007
(202) 587-9663   Fax: (202) 966-5894
E-mail: training@aacap.org
Web: www.aacap.org

Summary To provide funding to Native American and other minority medical students who are interested in working during the summer on the topics of drug abuse and addiction with a child and adolescent psychiatrist researcher-mentor.

Eligibility This program is open to African American, Asian American, Native American, Alaska Native, Mexican American, Hispanic, and Pacific Islander students in accredited U.S. medical schools. Applicants must present a plan for a program of research training in drug abuse and addiction that involves significant contact with a mentor who is an experienced child and adolescent psychiatrist researcher. The plan should include program planning discussions; instruction in

research planning and implementation; regular meetings with the mentor, laboratory director, and research group; and assigned readings. The mentor must be a member of the American Academy of Child and Adolescent Psychiatry (AACAP). Research assignments may include responsibility for part of the observation or evaluation, developing specific aspects of the research mechanisms, conducting interviews or tests, using rating scales, and psychological or cognitive testing of subjects. The training plan also should include discussion of ethical issues in research, such as protocol development, informed consent, collection and storage of raw data, safeguarding data, bias in analyzing data, plagiarism, protection of patients, and ethical treatment of animals. U.S. citizenship or permanent resident status is required.

Financial data The stipend is $4,000. Fellows also receive reimbursement of travel expenses to attend the annual meeting of the American Academy of Child and Adolescent Psychiatry.

Duration 12 weeks during the summer.

Additional information Upon completion of the training program, the student is required to submit a brief paper summarizing the research experience. The fellowship pays expenses for the fellow to attend the academy's annual meeting and present this paper. This program is co-sponsored by the National Institute on Drug Abuse.

Number awarded Up to 5 each year.

Deadline February of each year.

[960]
JESS GREEN LAW STUDENT SCHOLARSHIP

National Tribal Gaming Commissions/Regulators
Attn: Scholarship Committee
P.O. Box 454
Oneida, WI 54155
E-mail: dawnr@thehillgroup.org
Web: www.ntgcr.com/scholarships

Summary To provide financial assistance to Native Americans interested in working on law degree in a field related to the gaming industry.

Eligibility This program is open to enrolled members of federally-recognized American Indian tribes and Alaska Native groups. Applicants must be enrolled or planning to enroll full time at an accredited law school in the United States and have a GPA of 2.5 or higher. Along with their application, they must submit a 4-page essay on their personal background (including whether or not they speak their tribal language or are learning their tribal language and other cultural skills), their degree plan for higher education, why they have chosen that field of study, how they plan to serve their tribal people when they complete their higher education, and why they should be selected for this scholarship. Selection is based on that essay, academic grade point average, exhibition of leadership, community involvement, letter of recommendations, accomplishments and professional development.

Financial data The stipend is $2,500.

Duration 1 year.

Number awarded 1 each year.

Deadline June of each year.

[961]
JO MORSE SCHOLARSHIP

Alaska Library Association
Attn: Scholarship Committee
c/o Alaska State Library
395 Whittier Street
Juneau, AK 99801
(907) 465-2916   Toll Free: (888) 820-4525
Fax: (907) 465-2151
E-mail: julie.neiderhauser@alaska.gov
Web: www.akla.org/scholarships

Summary To provide financial assistance to Alaska residents, especially Native Alaskans, who are interested in working on a certificate in school librarianship and, upon graduation, working in a school library in Alaska.

Eligibility This program is open to Alaska residents who hold a State of Alaska teaching certificate. Applicants must be eligible for acceptance or currently enrolled in a graduate school library media specialist certificate program during the academic year, semester, or quarter for which the scholarship is awarded and be willing to make a commitment to work in an Alaska school library for at least 1 year after graduation as a paid employee or volunteer. Both on-campus and distance education programs qualify. Preference is given to applicants meeting the federal definition of Alaska Native ethnicity. Selection is based on financial need, demonstrated scholastic ability and writing skills, an essay on professional goals and objectives in pursuing a library media specialist certificate, and 3 letters of recommendation (at least 1 of which must be from a librarian).

Financial data The stipend is $4,000.

Duration 1 year.

Number awarded 1 each year.

Deadline January of each year.

[962]
JOAN HAMILTON MEMORIAL SCHOLARSHIP

American Civil Liberties Union of Alaska
1057 West Fireweed Lane, Suite 207
Anchorage, AK 99503
(907) 258-0044   Fax: (907) 258-0288
E-mail: scholarship@acluak.org
Web: www.acluak.org/pages/joan-hamilton-scholarship.html

Summary To provide financial assistance to Alaska residents who are interested in attending college or law school in any state to prepare for a career serving Alaska Natives and/or residents of rural Alaska.

Eligibility This program is open to residents of Alaska who are enrolled in a postsecondary educational or vocational program in any state. Applicants must be preparing for a career related to the law (e.g., lawyer, VSO, guardian ad litem, paralegal) in order to become advocates of Alaska Native rights and "defend the constitutional rights and civil liberties of the peoples of rural Alaska." Along with their application, they must submit an essay of 2 to 4 pages that includes what they consider important challenges facing Alaska Native communities and/or residents of rural Alaska, the actions they have taken and plan to take to support Native Alaska communities and/or residents of rural Alaska, how a law-related career would enable them to address the challenges facing Alaska Native communities and/or residents of rural

Alaska, and how they envision their education to allow them to further the work of this program's sponsor and namesake.

Financial data The stipend is $2,500 per year.

Duration 1 year; may be renewed.

Number awarded 1 each year.

Deadline March of each year.

[963]
JOHN A. MAYES EDAC SCHOLARSHIP

National Athletic Trainers' Association
Attn: Ethnic Diversity Advisory Committee
1620 Valwood Parkway, Suite 115
Carrollton, TX 75006
(214) 637-6282   Toll Free: (800) 879-6282
Fax: (214) 637-2206
Web: www.nata.org

Summary To provide financial aid to Native Americans and other ethnically diverse graduate students who are preparing for a career as an athletic trainer.

Eligibility This program is open to members of ethnically diverse groups who have been accepted into an entry-level master's athletic training degree program or into a doctoral-level athletic training and/or sports medicine degree program. Applicants must be sponsored by a certified athletic trainer who is a member of the National Athletic Trainers' Association (NATA). They must have a cumulative undergraduate GPA of 3.2 or higher. First priority is given to a student working on an entry-level athletic training master's degree; second priority is given to a student entering the second year of an athletic training master's degree program; third priority is given to a student working on a doctoral degree in athletic training or sports medicine. Special consideration is given to applicants who have been members of NATA for at least 2 years.

Financial data The stipend is $2,300.

Duration 1 year.

Additional information This program began in 2009.

Number awarded 1 each year.

Deadline February of each year.

[964]
JOHN CARTER BROWN LIBRARY INDIGENOUS STUDIES FELLOWSHIP

Brown University
John Carter Brown Library
Attn: Fellowships Coordinator
P.O. Box 1894
Providence, RI 02912
(401) 863-5010   Fax: (401) 863-3477
E-mail: Valerie_Andrews@Brown.edu
Web: www.brown.edu

Summary To support scholars and graduate students interested in conducting research on the history and/or anthropology of the native peoples of the Americas at the John Carter Brown Library.

Eligibility This fellowship is open to U.S-based and foreign graduate students, scholars, and independent researchers. Graduate students must have passed their preliminary or general examinations. Tribal historians with nontraditional academic backgrounds are also eligible. Applicants must be interested in conducting research on the history and/or anthropology of native peoples of the Americas. Selection is based on the applicant's scholarly qualifications, the merits and significance of the project, and the particular need that the holdings of the John Carter Brown Library will fill in the development of the project.

Financial data The stipend is $2,100 per month.

Duration From 2 to 4 months.

Additional information This program began in 2014. Fellows are expected to be in regular residence at the library and to participate in the intellectual life of Brown University for the duration of the program.

Number awarded 1 or more each year.

Deadline December of each year.

[965]
JOHN D. VOELKER FOUNDATION NATIVE AMERICAN SCHOLARSHIP

John D. Voelker Foundation
P.O. Box 15222
Lansing, MI 48901-5222
(517) 377-0716
Web: www.voelkerfdn.org/Scholarships.asp

Summary To provide financial assistance to students enrolled in Wisconsin or Michigan tribes who live in any state and are interested in working on a law degree.

Eligibility This program is open to students who are enrolled members of a federally-recognized Michigan or Wisconsin tribe (applicants may live in any state) and are interested in studying law to prepare for a career that will benefit Native American people. Applicants do not need to be currently enrolled in law school, but if they apply as undergraduates they must ultimately intend to attend law school. Selection is based on academic achievements and financial need (preference is given to applicants with the greatest need).

Financial data The amount awarded varies annually; recently, the scholarships were at least $4,000 each. In most cases, the recipient's law school matches this foundation's stipend as a result of an arrangement between it and the Michigan Inter-Tribal Council.

Duration 1 year.

Additional information Recipients must provide an annual report on their progress.

Number awarded 1 or more each year.

Deadline Deadline not specified.

[966]
JOHN HOPE FRANKLIN DISSERTATION FELLOWSHIP

American Philosophical Society
Attn: Director of Grants and Fellowships
104 South Fifth Street
Philadelphia, PA 19106-3387
(215) 440-3429   Fax: (215) 440-3436
E-mail: LMusumeci@amphilsoc.org
Web: amphilsoc.org/grants/johnhopefranklin

Summary To provide funding to Native American and other underrepresented minority graduate students conducting research for a doctoral dissertation.

Eligibility This program is open to African American, Hispanic American, and Native American graduate students working on a degree at a Ph.D. granting institution in the United States. Other talented students who have a demonstrated commitment to eradicating racial disparities and enlarging minority representation in academia are also eligible. Applicants must have completed all course work and examinations preliminary to the doctoral dissertation and be able to devote full-time effort, with no teaching obligations, to researching or writing their dissertation. The proposed research should relate to a topic in which the holdings of the Library of the American Philosophical Society (APS) are particularly strong: quantum mechanics, nuclear physics, computer development, the history of genetics and eugenics, the history of medicine, Early American political and cultural history, natural history in the 18th and 19th centuries, the development of cultural anthropology, or American Indian culture and linguistics.

Financial data The grant is $25,000; an additional grant of $5,000 is provided to support the cost of residency in Philadelphia.

Duration 12 months, to begin at the discretion of the grantee.

Additional information This program began in 2005. Recipients are expected to spend a significant amount of time in residence at the APS Library.

Number awarded 1 each year.

Deadline March of each year.

[967]
JOHN MCLENDON MEMORIAL MINORITY POSTGRADUATE SCHOLARSHIP AWARD

National Association of Collegiate Directors of Athletics
Attn: NACDA Foundation
24651 Detroit Road
Westlake, OH 44145
(440) 788-7474   Fax: (440) 892-4007
E-mail: knewman@nacda.com
Web: www.nacda.com/mclendon/scholarship.html

Summary To provide financial assistance to Native American and other minority college seniors who are interested in working on a graduate degree in athletics administration.

Eligibility This program is open to minority college students who are seniors, are attending school on a full-time basis, have a GPA of 3.2 or higher, intend to attend graduate school to earn a degree in athletics administration, and are involved in college or community activities. Also eligible are college graduates who have at least 2 years' experience in an athletics administration position. Candidates must be nominated by an official of a member institution of the National Association of Collegiate Directors of Athletics (NACDA) or (for college graduates) a supervisor.

Financial data The stipend is $10,000.

Duration 1 year.

Additional information Recipients must maintain full-time status during the senior year to retain their eligibility. They must attend NACDA-member institutions.

Number awarded 5 each year.

Deadline Nominations must be submitted by April of each year.

[968]
JOHN N. COLBERG SCHOLARSHIP FUND

Cook Inlet Region, Inc.
Attn: The CIRI Foundation
3600 San Jeronimo Drive, Suite 256
Anchorage, AK 99508-2870
(907) 793-3575   Toll Free: (800) 764-3382
Fax: (907) 793-3585   E-mail: tcf@thecirifoundation.org
Web: www.thecirifoundation.org/about/donors

Summary   To provide financial assistance for undergraduate or graduate studies leading to a career in the law to Alaska Natives who are original enrollees to Cook Inlet Region, Inc. (CIRI) and their lineal descendants.

Eligibility   This program is open to Alaska Native enrollees to CIRI under the Alaska Native Claims Settlement Act (ANCSA) of 1971 and their lineal descendants. There are no Alaska residency requirements or age limitations. Applicants must be accepted or enrolled full time in a 4-year undergraduate or a graduate degree program. Preference is given to students who are working on a degree leading to the study of law and have a GPA of 2.5 or higher. Along with their application, they must submit a 500-word statement on their educational and career goals and how they are contributing, or planning to contribute, to a positive Alaska Native community. Selection is based on that statement, academic achievement, rigor of course work or degree program, student financial contribution, financial need, grade level, previous work performance, community service, and relationship of degree program to career goals.

Financial data   The stipend is $2,500 per semester.

Duration   1 semester or 1 year.

Additional information   CIRI is 1 of 13 regional corporations established according to the terms of the Alaska Native Claims Settlement Act (ANCSA) of 1971. This program began in 2003.

Number awarded   1 or more each year.

Deadline   May of each year.

[969]
JOHN RAINER MEMORIAL FELLOWSHIP

American Indian Graduate Center
Attn: Executive Director
3701 San Mateo Boulevard, N.E., Suite 200
Albuquerque, NM 87110-1249
(505) 881-4584   Toll Free: (800) 628-1920
Fax: (505) 884-0427   E-mail: fellowships@aigc.com
Web: www.aigcs.org/scholarships/graduate-fellowships

Summary   To provide financial assistance to Native American students interested in working on a graduate degree in any field.

Eligibility   This program is open to enrolled members of federally-recognized American Indian tribes and Alaska Native groups and students who can document one-fourth degree federally-recognized Indian blood. Applicants must be enrolled full time at a graduate school in the United States. Along with their application, they must submit a 500-word essay on how receiving this fellowship will enable them to continue to build, promote, and honor self-sustaining American Indian and Alaska Native communities. Financial need is also considered in the selection process. Males and females are considered separately.

Financial data   The stipend is $1,000, of which $500 may be applied to the cost of education and $500 must be used to support participation in volunteer activities that afford an opportunity to develop leadership skills.

Duration   1 year; nonrenewable.

Number awarded   2 each year: 1 to a male and 1 to a female.

Deadline   May of each year.

[970]
JOHN SHURR JOURNALISM AWARD

Cherokee Nation Foundation
800 South Muskogee
Tahlequah, OK 74464
(918) 207-0950   Fax: (918) 207-0951
E-mail: contact@cherokeenationfoundation.org
Web: cherokeenation.academicworks.com

Summary   To provide financial assistance to citizens of the Cherokee Nation who are enrolled at a college or university in any state and working on an undergraduate or graduate degree in journalism.

Eligibility   This program is open to citizens of the Cherokee Nation who are currently enrolled in an undergraduate or graduate program in journalism or mass communications at a college or university in any state. Applicants must have a GPA of 3.0 or higher. They are not required to reside in the Cherokee Nation area. Along with their application, they must submit writing samples and an essay describing their journalism career goals. Selection is based on the clarity and presentation of the essay; academic information (including transcripts and ACT scores); school, cultural and community activities; future plans to serve Cherokee people; and financial need.

Financial data   The stipend is $1,000 per semester ($2,000 per year).

Duration   1 year. Renewal for the second semester requires the recipient to earn a GPA of 3.0 or higher in the first semester.

Additional information   Recipients are expected to apply for an 8-week paid internship with *The Cherokee Phoenix* newspaper in Tahlequah, Oklahoma during the summer following their scholarship year.

Number awarded   1 each year.

Deadline   January of each year.

[971]
JOHN STANFORD MEMORIAL WLMA SCHOLARSHIP

Washington Library Association-School Library Division
c/o Susan Kaphammer, Scholarship Chair
521 North 24th Avenue
Yakima, WA 98902
(509) 972-5999   E-mail: scholarships@wlma.org
Web: www.wla.org/school-scholarships

Summary   To provide financial assistance to Native Americans and other ethnic minorities in Washington who are interested in attending a school in any state to prepare for a library media career.

Eligibility   This program is open to residents of Washington who are working toward a library media endorsement or graduate degree in the field at a school in any state. Applicants must be members of an ethnic minority group. They must be working or planning to work in a school library. Along with their application, they must submit a 3-page letter that includes a description of themselves and their achievements to date, their interest and work in the library field, their personal and professional activities, their goals and plans for further education and professional development, how they expect the studies funded by this award to impact their professional practice and contributions to the Washington school library community, and their financial need.

Financial data The stipend is $1,000.

Duration 1 year.

Additional information The School Library Division of the Washington Library Association was formerly the Washington Library Media Association (WLMA).

Number awarded 1 each year.

Deadline May of each year.

[972]
JOHNSON & JOHNSON/AACN MINORITY NURSE FACULTY SCHOLARS PROGRAM

American Association of Colleges of Nursing
One Dupont Circle, N.W., Suite 530
Washington, DC 20036
(202) 463-6930   Fax: (202) 785-8320
E-mail: scholarship@aacn.nche.edu
Web: www.aacn.nche.edu/students/scholarships/minority

Summary To provide fellowship/loans to Native American and other minority students who are working on a graduate degree in nursing to prepare for a career as a faculty member.

Eligibility This program is open to members of racial and ethnic minority groups (Alaska Native, American Indian, Black or African American, Native Hawaiian or other Pacific Islander, Hispanic or Latino, or Asian American) who are enrolled full time at a school of nursing. Applicants must be working on 1) a doctoral nursing degree (e.g., Ph.D., D.N.P.); or 2) a clinically-focused master's degree in nursing (e.g., M.S.N., M.S.). They must commit to 1) serve in a teaching capacity at a nursing school for a minimum of 1 year for each year of support they receive; 2) provide 6-month progress reports to the American Association of Colleges of Nursing (AACN) throughout the entire funding process and during the payback period; 3) agree to work with an assigned mentor throughout the period of the scholarship grant; and 4) attend an annual leadership training conference to connect with their mentor, fellow scholars, and colleagues. Selection is based on ability to contribute to nursing education; leadership potential; development of goals reflecting education, research, and professional involvement; ability to work with a mentor/adviser throughout the award period; proposed research and/or practice projects that are significant and show commitment to improving nursing education and clinical nursing practice in the United States; proposed research and/or clinical education professional development plan that exhibits quality, feasibility, and innovativeness; and evidence of commitment to a career in nursing education and to recruiting, mentoring, and retaining other underrepresented minority nurses. Preference is given to students enrolled in doctoral nursing programs. Applicants must be U.S. citizens, permanent residents, refugees, or qualified immigrants.

Financial data The stipend is $18,000 per year. The award includes $1,500 that is held in escrow to cover the costs for the recipient to attend the leadership training confer-

ence. Recipients are required to sign a letter of commitment that they will provide 1 year of service in a teaching capacity at a nursing school in the United States for each year of support received; if they fail to complete that service requirement, they must repay all funds received.

Duration 1 year; may be renewed 1 additional year.

Additional information This program, established in 2007, is sponsored by the Johnson & Johnson Campaign for Nursing's Future.

Number awarded 5 each year.

Deadline April of each year.

[973]
JOSEPH K. LUMSDEN MEMORIAL SCHOLARSHIP

Sault Tribe of Chippewa Indians
Attn: Higher Education Department
523 Ashmun Street
Sault Ste. Marie, MI 49783
(906) 635-6050, ext. 26312   Toll Free: (800) 793-0660
Fax: (906) 635-7785   E-mail: BMacArthur@saulttribe.net
Web: www.saulttribe.com

Summary To provide financial assistance to members of the Sault Tribe of Chippewa Indians who are upper-division or graduate students at a university in any state.

Eligibility This program is open to members of the Sault Tribe who are college juniors or higher and are one-quarter Indian blood quantum or more. Applicants must be enrolled full time at a 4-year college or university in any state and have a cumulative GPA of 3.0 or higher. Along with their application, they must submit an essay of 1,000 to 2,000 words on a topic that changes annually but relates to their Indian heritage.

Financial data The stipend is $1,000 per year.

Duration 1 year; may be renewed.

Number awarded 1 each year.

Deadline May of each year.

[974]
JOSEPHINE FORMAN SCHOLARSHIP

Society of American Archivists
Attn: Chair, Awards Committee
17 North State Street, Suite 1425
Chicago, IL 60602-4061
(312) 606-0722   Toll Free: (866) 722-7858
Fax: (312) 606-0728   E-mail: info@archivists.org
Web: www2.archivists.org

Summary To provide financial assistance to Native American and other minority graduate students working on a degree in archival science.

Eligibility This program is open to members of minority groups (American Indian/Alaska Native, Asian, Black/African American, Hispanic/Latino, or Native Hawaiian/other Pacific Islander) currently enrolled in or accepted to a graduate program or a multi-course program in archival administration. The program must offer at least 3 courses in archival science and students may have completed no more than half of the credit requirements toward their graduate degree. Selection is based on potential for scholastic and personal achievement and commitment both to the archives profession and to advancing diversity concerns within it. U.S. citizenship or permanent resident status is required.

Financial data The stipend is $10,000.

Duration 1 year.

Additional information Funding for this program, established in 2011, is provided by the General Commission on Archives and History of the United Methodist Church.

Number awarded 1 each year.

Deadline February of each year.

[975]
JOSIAH MACY JR. FOUNDATION SCHOLARSHIPS

National Medical Fellowships, Inc.
Attn: Scholarship Program
347 Fifth Avenue, Suite 510
New York, NY 10016
(212) 483-8880   Toll Free: (877) NMF-1DOC
Fax: (212) 483-8897 E-mail: scholarships@nmfonline.org
Web: www.nmfonline.org

Summary To provide financial assistance to Native American and other underrepresented minority medical students who demonstrate financial need.

Eligibility This program is open to African Americans, Hispanics/Latinos, Native Americans, Vietnamese, Cambodians, and Pacific Islanders who are entering their second or third year of medical school. They must be U.S. citizens or DACA students. Selection is based on leadership, commitment to serving medically underserved communities, and financial need.

Financial data A stipend is awarded (amount not specified).

Duration 1 year.

Additional information This program is sponsored by the Josiah Macy Jr. Foundation.

Number awarded 4 each year.

Deadline September of each year.

[976]
JOURNEY TOWARD ORDAINED MINISTRY SCHOLARSHIP

United Methodist Church
Attn: General Board of Higher Education and Ministry
Office of Loans and Scholarships
1001 19th Avenue South
P.O. Box 340007
Nashville, TN 37203-0007
(615) 340-7344   Fax: (615) 340-7367
E-mail: umscholar@gbhem.org
Web: www.gbhem.org

Summary To provide financial assistance to Native American and other minority United Methodist students preparing for ministry at a Methodist-related institution.

Eligibility This program is open to members of racial or ethnic minority groups who are 30 years of age or younger and have been active, full members of a United Methodist Church for at least 2 years prior to applying. Applicants must be enrolled as full-time undergraduate or graduate students at a United Methodist-related institution in a program that leads to ordained ministry. Undergraduates must have a GPA

of 2.85 or higher and graduate students must have a GPA of 3.0 or higher.

Financial data The stipend is $5,000.

Duration 1 year.

Number awarded 1 or more each year.

Deadline February of each year.

[977]
JTBF SUMMER JUDICIAL INTERNSHIP PROGRAM

Just the Beginning Foundation
c/o Maria Shade Harris, Chief Operating Officer
233 South Wacker Drive, Suite 6600
Chicago, IL 60606
(312) 258-5930   E-mail: mharris@jtb.org
Web: www.jtb.org/about/our-programs

Summary To provide work experience to Native American and other economically disadvantaged law students who plan to seek judicial clerkships after graduation.

Eligibility This program is open to students currently enrolled in their second or third year of law school who are members of minority or economically disadvantaged groups. Applicants must intend to work as a clerk in the federal or state judiciary upon graduation or within 5 years of graduation.

Financial data Program externs receive a summer stipend in an amount determined by the sponsor.

Duration Students must perform at least 35 hours per week of work for at least 8 weeks during the summer.

Additional information This program began in 2005. Law students are matched with federal and state judges across the country who provide assignments to the participants that will enhance their legal research, writing, and analytical skills (e.g., drafting memoranda). Students are expected to complete at least 1 memorandum of law or other key legal document each semester of the externship. Course credit may be offered, but students may not receive academic credit and a stipend simultaneously.

Number awarded Varies each year.

Deadline January of each year.

[978]
JUDICIAL INTERN OPPORTUNITY PROGRAM

American Bar Association
Attn: Section of Litigation
321 North Clark Street
Chicago, IL 60654-7598
(312) 988-6348   Fax: (312) 988-6234
E-mail: Gail.Howard@americanbar.org
Web: www.americanbar.org

Summary To provide an opportunity for Native American and other economically disadvantaged law students to gain experience as judicial interns in selected courts during the summer.

Eligibility This program is open to first- and second-year students at ABA-accredited law schools who are 1) members of racial or ethnic groups that are traditionally underrepresented in the legal profession (African Americans, Asians, Hispanics/Latinos, Native Americans); 2) students with disabilities; 3) students who are economically disadvantaged; or 4) students who identify themselves as lesbian, gay, bisexual, or transgender. Applicants must be interested in a judicial internship at courts in selected areas and communities. They may indicate a preference for the area in which they wish to work, but they may not specify a court or a judge. Along with their application, they must submit a current resume, a 10-page legal writing sample, and a 2-page statement of interest that outlines their qualifications for the internship. Screening interviews are conducted by staff of the American Bar Association, either in person or by telephone. Final interviews are conducted by the judges with whom the interns will work. Some spots are reserved for students with an interest in intellectual property law.

Financial data The stipend is $2,000.

Duration 6 weeks during the summer.

Additional information Recently, internships were available in the following locations: Chicago along with surrounding cities and circuits throughout Illinois; Houston, Dallas, and the southern and eastern districts of Texas; Miami, Florida; Phoenix, Arizona; Los Angeles, California; New York City; Philadelphia, Pennsylvania; San Francisco, California; Seattle, Washington; and Washington, D.C. Some internships in Chicago, Los Angeles, Texas, and Washington, D.C. are reserved for students with an interest in intellectual property law.

Number awarded Varies each year; recently, 194 of these internships were awarded, including 31 at courts in Illinois, 17 in Dallas, 14 in Houston, 14 in Miami, 17 in Phoenix, 23 in Los Angeles, 30 in San Francisco, 10 in New York, 12 in Philadelphia, 8 in Seattle, and 18 in Washington, D.C.

Deadline January of each year.

[979]
JUDITH McMANUS PRICE SCHOLARSHIPS

American Planning Association
Attn: Leadership Affairs Associate
205 North Michigan Avenue, Suite 1200
Chicago, IL 60601
(312) 431-9100   Fax: (312) 786-6700
E-mail: mgroh@planning.org
Web: www.planning.org/scholarships/apa

Summary To provide financial assistance to Native American and other underrepresented students enrolled in undergraduate or graduate degree programs at recognized planning schools.

Eligibility This program is open to undergraduate and graduate students in urban and regional planning who are women or members of the following minority groups: African American, Hispanic American, or Native American. Applicants must be citizens of the United States and able to document financial need. They must intend to work as practicing planners in the public sector. Along with their application, they must submit a 2-page personal and background statement describing how their education will be applied to career goals and why they chose planning as a career path. Selection is based (in order of importance), on: 1) commitment to planning as reflected in their personal statement and on their resume; 2) academic achievement and/or improvement during the past 2 years; 3) letters of recommendation; 4) financial need; and 5) professional presentation.

Financial data Stipends range from $2,000 to $4,000 per year. The money may be applied to tuition and living expenses only. Payment is made to the recipient's university and divided by terms in the school year.

Duration 1 year; recipients may reapply.

Additional information This program began in 2002.

Number awarded Varies each year; recently, 3 were awarded.

Deadline April of each year.

[980]
JULIE CUNNINGHAM LEGACY SCHOLARSHIP

Conference of Minority Transportation Officials
Attn: National Scholarship Program
100 M Street, S.E., Suite 917
Washington, DC 20003
(202) 506-2917   E-mail: info@comto.org
Web: www.comto.org/page/scholarships

Summary To provide financial assistance to Native American and other minority graduate students who are working on a degree in transportation to prepare for a leadership role in that industry.

Eligibility This program is open to minorities who are working on a graduate degree with an interest in leadership in transportation. Applicants must have a GPA of 3.0 or higher. They must be able to demonstrate strong leadership skills, active commitment to community service and diversity, and a commitment to the Conference of Minority Transportation Officials (COMTO) on a local or national level. Along with their application they must submit a cover letter on their transportation-related career goals and life aspirations. Financial need is not considered in the selection process.

Financial data The stipend is $7,500. Funds are paid directly to the recipient's college or university.

Duration 1 year.

Number awarded 1 each year.

Deadline April of each year.

[981]
JUNE CURRAN PORCARO SCHOLARSHIP

Sault Tribe of Chippewa Indians
Attn: Higher Education Department
523 Ashmun Street
Sault Ste. Marie, MI 49783
(906) 635-6050, ext. 26312   Toll Free: (800) 793-0660
Fax: (906) 635-7785   E-mail: BMacArthur@saulttribe.net
Web: www.saulttribe.com

Summary To provide financial assistance to members of the Sault Tribe of Chippewa Indians who have been homeless, displaced, or in the foster care system and are interested in attending college or graduate school in any state to work on a degree in human services.

Eligibility This program is open to members of the Sault Tribe who have been homeless, displaced, or in the foster care system. Applicants must be working on an undergraduate or graduate degree in human services at a college or university in any state to prepare for a career of helping people who are homeless, displaced, or involved in the foster care system. They must be able to demonstrate financial need. Along with their application, they must submit an essay of 1,000 to 2,000 words on a topic that changes annually but relates to their Indian heritage.

Financial data The stipend is $1,000.

Duration 1 year.

Additional information Recipients must agree to provide at least 40 hours of volunteer service at an accredited homeless shelter during the school year for which they receive the award.

Number awarded 1 each year.

Deadline May of each year.

[982]
JUSTICE RUDOLPH HARGRAVE WRITING COMPETITION

Sovereignty Symposium, Inc.
c/o Julie Rorie
Oklahoma Judicial Center
2100 North Lincoln Boulevard
Oklahoma City, OK 73105
(405) 556-9371 E-mail: sovereignty.symposium@oscn.net
Web: www.thesovereigntysymposium.com

Summary To recognize and reward law students who write outstanding papers on Native American law.

Eligibility This competition is open to students at accredited law schools who submit papers for presentation at the Sovereignty Symposium. Papers may deal with any issue concerning Native American law.

Financial data First prize is $1,500, second $1,000, and third $750.

Duration The competition is held annually.

Number awarded 3 each year.

Deadline April of each year.

[983]
KAISER PERMANENTE COLORADO DIVERSITY SCHOLARSHIP PROGRAM

Kaiser Permanente
Attn: Diversity Development Department
10065 East Harvard Avenue, Suite 400
Denver, CO 80231
Toll Free: (877) 457-4772
E-mail: co-diversitydevelopment@kp.org

Summary To provide financial assistance to Colorado residents who are Native Americans of members of other underrepresented groups and interested in working on an undergraduate or graduate degree in a health care field at a public college in the state.

Eligibility This program is open to all residents of Colorado, including those who identify as 1 or more of the following: African American, Asian Pacific, Latino, lesbian, gay, bisexual, transgender, intersex, Native American, U.S. veteran, and/or a person with a disability. Applicants must be enrolled or planning to enroll full time at a publicly-funded college, university, or technical school in Colorado as 1) a graduating high school senior with a GPA of 2.7 or higher; 2) a GED recipient with a GED score of 520 or higher; 3) an undergraduate student; or 4) a graduate or doctoral student. They must be preparing for a career in health care (e.g., athletic training, audiology, cardiovascular perfusion technology, clinical medical assisting, cytotechnology, dental assisting, dental hygiene, diagnostic medicine, dietetics, emergency medical technology, medicine, nursing, occupational therapy, pharmacy, phlebotomy, physical therapy, physician assistant, radiology, respiratory therapy, social work, sports medicine, surgical technology). Selection is based on academic achievement, character qualities, community outreach and volunteering, and financial need.

Financial data Stipends range from $1,400 to $2,600 per year.

Duration 1 year; may be renewed.

Number awarded Varies each year; recently, 17 were awarded.

Deadline March of each year.

[984]
KATRIN H. LAMON FELLOWSHIP

School for Advanced Research
Attn: Director of Scholar Programs
660 Garcia Street
P.O. Box 2188
Santa Fe, NM 87504-2188
(505) 954-7201   E-mail: scholar@sarsf.org
Web: www.sarweb.org

Summary To provide funding to Native American pre- and postdoctoral scholars interested in conducting research in the social sciences or humanities while in residence at the School for Advanced Research (SAR) in Santa Fe, New Mexico.

Eligibility This program is open to Native American Ph.D. candidates and scholars with doctorates who are interested in conducting research at SAR in the humanities or the social sciences. Applicants must submit a 150-word abstract describing the purpose, goals, and objectives of their research project; a 4-page proposal; a bibliography; a curriculum vitae; a brief statement of tribal affiliation; and 3 letters of recommendation. Predoctoral applicants must also submit a brief letter of nomination from their department. Preference is given to applicants whose field work or basic research and analysis are complete and who need time to write up their research.

Financial data The fellowship provides an apartment and office on the school's campus, a stipend of up to $40,000 for scholars or $30,000 for Ph.D. candidates, library assistance, and other benefits.

Duration 9 months, beginning in September.

Additional information Funding for this program is provided by the Katrin H. Lamon Endowment for Native American Art and Education. Participants must spend their 9-month residency at the school in New Mexico.

Number awarded 1 each year.

Deadline October of each year.

[985]
KATRIN LAMON FUND

American Indian Graduate Center
Attn: Executive Director
3701 San Mateo Boulevard, N.E., Suite 200
Albuquerque, NM 87110-1249
(505) 881-4584   Toll Free: (800) 628-1920
Fax: (505) 884-0427   E-mail: fellowships@aigc.com
Web: www.aigcs.org/scholarships/graduate-fellowships

Summary To provide financial assistance to Native American students interested in working on a graduate degree in literature or journalism.

Eligibility This program is open to enrolled members of federally-recognized American Indian tribes and Alaska Native groups, as well as students who can document one-fourth degree federally-recognized Indian blood. Applicants must be enrolled full time at a graduate school in the United States and working on a degree in literature or journalism. Along with their application, they must submit a 500-word essay on how receiving this fellowship will enable them to continue to build, promote, and honor self-sustaining American Indian and Alaska Native communities. Financial need is also considered in the selection process.

Financial data Stipends range from $500 to $5,000 per academic year, depending on the availability of funds and the recipient's unmet financial need.

Duration 1 year; may be renewed.

Number awarded 1 each year.

Deadline May of each year.

[986]
KATTEN MUCHIN ROSENMAN MINORITY SCHOLARSHIPS

Katten Muchin Rosenman LLP
Attn: Attorney Recruiting Specialist
525 West Monroe Street
Chicago, IL 60661-3693
(312) 902-5200   Fax: (312) 902-1061
E-mail: stephanie.london@kattenlaw.com
Web: www.kattenlaw.com/minority-scholarship

Summary To provide financial assistance and summer work experience in Chicago or New York City to Native American and other minority law students from any state.

Eligibility This program is open to minority students from any state who have completed their first year of law school. Applicants must have applied for and been accepted as a summer associate at the sponsoring law firm's Chicago or New York office. Along with their application, they must submit 250-word statements on 1) their strongest qualifications for this award; 2) their reasons for preparing for law as a profession; and 3) their views on diversity and how their personal experience and philosophy will be an asset to the firm. Selection is based on academic achievement, leadership experience, and personal qualities that reflect the potential for outstanding contributions to the firm and the legal profession.

Financial data Participants receive the standard salary for the summer internship and a stipend of $15,000 for the academic year.

Duration 1 year.

Number awarded 2 each year; 1 for an internship in Chicago and 1 for an internship in New York City.

Deadline September of each year.

[987]
KAY LONGCOPE SCHOLARSHIP AWARD

National Lesbian & Gay Journalists Association
2120 L Street, N.W., Suite 850
Washington, DC 20037
(202) 588-9888   Fax: (202) 588-1818
E-mail: info@nlgfa.org
Web: www.nlgja.org/resources/longcope

Summary To provide financial assistance to lesbian, gay, bisexual, and transgender (LGBT) undergraduate and gradu-

ate students of color who are interested in preparing for a career in journalism.

Eligibility This program is open to LGBT students of color who are current or incoming undergraduate or graduate students at a college, university, or community college. Applicants must be planning a career in journalism and be committed to furthering the sponsoring organization's mission of fair and accurate coverage of the LGBT community. They must demonstrate an awareness of the issues facing the LGBT community and the importance of fair and accurate news coverage. For undergraduates, a declared major in journalism and/or communications is desirable but not required; non-journalism majors may demonstrate their commitment to a journalism career through work samples, internships, and work on a school news publication, online news service, or broadcast affiliate. Graduate students must be enrolled in a journalism program. Along with their application, they must submit a 1-page resume, 5 work samples, official transcripts, 3 letters of recommendation, and a 750-word news story on a designated subject involving the LGBT community. U.S. citizenship or permanent resident status is required. Selection is based on journalistic and scholastic ability.

Financial data The stipend is $3,000.

Duration 1 year.

Additional information This program began in 2008.

Number awarded 1 each year.

Deadline May of each year.

[988]
KEGLER, BROWN, HILL & RITTER MINORITY MERIT SCHOLARSHIP

Kegler, Brown, Hill & Ritter
Attn: Human Resources Manager
Capitol Square, Suite 1800
65 East State Street
Columbus, OH 43215
(614) 462-5467   Toll Free: (800) 860-7885
Fax: (614) 464-2634
E-mail: jnistelbeck@keglerbrown.com
Web: www.keglerbrown.com

Summary To provide financial assistance and summer work experience at Kegler, Brown, Hill & Ritter in Columbus, Ohio to Native American and other minority students at law schools in any state.

Eligibility This program is open to first-year students of minority descent at law schools in any state. Applicants must be interested in a summer clerkship with the firm following their first year of law school. Along with their application, they must submit brief essays on 1) a major accomplishment that has shaped their life, how it influenced their decision to prepare for a career in law, and how it prepared them for a future as a lawyer; 2) what diversity means to them; 3) why they have applied for the scholarship; and 4) any training and/or experience they believe to be relevant to the clerkship. Selection is based on academic performance, accomplishments, activities, and potential contributions to the legal community.

Financial data The program provides a $10,000 stipend for law school tuition and a paid summer clerkship position.

Duration 1 year.

Additional information This program began in 2004.

Number awarded   2 each year.
Deadline   January of each year.

[989]
KENNETH COMER CHEROKEE SCHOLARSHIP

Cherokee Nation Foundation
800 South Muskogee
Tahlequah, OK 74464
(918) 207-0950   Fax: (918) 207-0951
E-mail: contact@cherokeenationfoundation.org
Web: cherokeenation.academicworks.com

Summary   To provide financial assistance to citizens of the Cherokee Nation who are working on a graduate degree in psychology or counseling psychology at a school in Oklahoma.

Eligibility   This program is open to citizens of the Cherokee Nation who are currently enrolled at a college or university in Oklahoma. Applicants must be working on a graduate degree in psychology or counseling psychology that will enable them to become a licensed professional counselor or licensed drug and alcohol counselor. Along with their application, they must submit 1) a 650-word essay on their story, how they came to be the person they are today, their passions and future expectations, how they will benefit from this scholarship, and how the scholarship will benefit from them; and 2) a description of their most meaningful achievements and how those relate to their field of study and their future goals.

Financial data   The stipend is $5,000.

Duration   1 year.

Number awarded   1 or more each year.

Deadline   January of each year.

[990]
KENNETH COMER CHICKASAW SCHOLARSHIP

Chickasaw Foundation
2020 Arlington, Suite 4
P.O. Box 1726
Ada, OK 74821-1726
(580) 421-9030   Fax: (580) 421-9031
E-mail: ChickasawFoundation@chickasaw.net
Web: www.chickasawfoundation.org/Scholarships.aspx

Summary   To provide financial assistance to members of the Chickasaw Nation who are working on a graduate degree in counseling psychology.

Eligibility   This program is open to Chickasaw graduate students who are currently enrolled at an accredited college or university. Applicants must be planning to become a licensed professional counselor, a licensed drug and alcohol counselor, and certified problem gaming counselor. Along with their application, they must submit high school or college transcripts; 2 letters of recommendation; a copy of their Chickasaw Nation citizenship card; a 2-page list of honors, achievements, awards, club memberships, societies, and civic involvement; and a 1-page essay on their long-term goals and plans for achieving those. Financial need is not considered in the selection process.

Financial data   A stipend is awarded (amount not specified).

Duration   1 year.

Number awarded   1 each year.

Deadline   June of each year.

[991]
KENTUCKY LIBRARY ASSOCIATION SCHOLARSHIP FOR MINORITY STUDENTS

Kentucky Library Association
c/o Executive Director
5932 Timber Ridge Drive, Suite 101
Prospect, KY 40059
(502) 223-5322   Fax: (502) 223-4937
E-mail: info@kylibasn.org
Web: www.klaonline.org/scholarships965.cfm

Summary   To provide financial assistance to Native Americans and members of other minority groups who are residents of Kentucky or attending school there and are working on an undergraduate or graduate degree in library science.

Eligibility   This program is open to members of minority groups (defined as American Indian, Alaskan Native, Black, Hispanic, Pacific Islander, or other ethnic group) who are entering or continuing at a graduate library school accredited by the American Library Association (ALA) or an undergraduate library program accredited by the National Council for Teacher Education (NCATE). Applicants must be residents of Kentucky or a student in a library program in the state. Along with their application, they must submit a statement of their career objectives, why they have chosen librarianship as a career, and their reasons for applying for this scholarship. Selection is based on that statement, cumulative undergraduate and graduate GPA (if applicable), academic merit and potential, and letters of recommendation. U.S. citizenship or permanent resident status is required.

Financial data   The stipend is $1,000.

Duration   1 year; nonrenewable.

Number awarded   1 or more each year.

Deadline   June of each year.

[992]
KENTUCKY MINORITY EDUCATOR RECRUITMENT AND RETENTION SCHOLARSHIPS

Kentucky Department of Education
Attn: Office of Next-Generation Learners
500 Mero Street, 19th Floor
Frankfort, KY 40601
(502) 564-1479   Fax: (502) 564-4007
TDD: (502) 564-4970
E-mail: jennifer.baker@education.ky.gov
Web: www.education.ky.gov

Summary   To provide forgivable loans to Native Americans and other minority undergraduate and graduate students enrolled in Kentucky public institutions who want to become teachers.

Eligibility   This program is open to residents of Kentucky who are undergraduate or graduate students pursuing initial teacher certification at a public university or community college in the state. Applicants must have a GPA of 2.75 or higher and either maintain full-time enrollment or be a part-time student within 18 semester hours of receiving a teacher education degree. They must be U.S. citizens and meet the Kentucky definition of a minority student.

Financial data   Stipends are $5,000 per year at the 8 state universities in Kentucky or $2,000 per year at community and technical colleges. This is a scholarship/loan program. Recipients are required to teach 1 semester in Kentucky for each semester or summer term the scholarship is received. If they fail to fulfill that requirement, the scholarship converts to a loan payable at 6% annually.

Duration 1 year; may be renewed up to 3 additional years.

Additional information The Kentucky General Assembly established this program in 1992.

Number awarded Varies each year.

Deadline Each state college of teacher education sets its own deadline.

[993]
KING & SPALDING DIVERSITY FELLOWSHIP PROGRAM

King & Spalding, LLP
Attn: Associate Director of Human Resources and
  Diversity
1180 Peachtree Street
Atlanta, GA 30309
(404) 572-4643   Fax: (404) 572-5100
E-mail: cabney@kslaw.com
Web: www.kslaw.com

Summary To provide financial assistance and summer work experience at U.S. offices of King & Spalding to Native American and other law students who will contribute to the diversity of the legal community.

Eligibility This program is open to second-year law students who 1) come from a minority ethnic or racial group (American Indian/Alaskan Native, Asian American/Pacific Islander, Black/African American, Hispanic, or multi-racial); 2) are a member of the gay, lesbian, bisexual, or transgender (GLBT) community; or 3) have a disability. Applicants must receive an offer of a clerkship at a U.S. office of King & Spalding during their second-year summer. Along with their application, they must submit a 500-word personal statement that describes their talents, qualities, and experiences and how they would contribute to the diversity of the firm.

Financial data Fellows receive a stipend of $10,000 for their second year of law school and a paid summer associate clerkship at a U.S. office of the firm during the following summer.

Duration 1 year.

Additional information The firm's U.S. offices are located in Atlanta, Austin, Charlotte, Houston, Los Angeles, New York, San Francisco, Silicon Valley, and Washington.

Number awarded Up to 4 each year.

Deadline August of each year.

[994]
KIRBY MCDONALD EDUCATION ENDOWMENT FUND

Cook Inlet Region, Inc.
Attn: The CIRI Foundation
3600 San Jeronimo Drive, Suite 256
Anchorage, AK 99508-2870
(907) 793-3575   Toll Free: (800) 764-3382
Fax: (907) 793-3585   E-mail: tcf@thecirifoundation.org
Web: www.thecirifoundation.org/about/donors

Summary To provide financial assistance for undergraduate or graduate studies in designated fields to Alaska Natives who are original enrollees to Cook Inlet Region, Inc. (CIRI) and their lineal descendants.

Eligibility This program is open to Alaska Native enrollees to CIRI under the Alaska Native Claims Settlement Act (ANCSA) of 1971 and their lineal descendants. There are no Alaska residency requirements or age limitations. Applicants must be accepted or enrolled full time in a 4-year undergraduate or a graduate degree program. Preference is given to students in the culinary arts, business administration, or engineering. They must have a GPA of 2.5 or higher. Along with their application, they must submit a 500-word statement on their educational and career goals and how they are contributing, or planning to contribute, to a positive Alaska Native community. Selection is based on that statement, academic achievement, rigor of course work or degree program, student financial contribution, financial need, grade level, previous work performance, community service, and relationship of degree program to career goals.

Financial data The stipend is $10,000 per year, $8,000 per year, or $2,500 per semester, depending on GPA.

Duration 1 semester or 1 year.

Additional information CIRI is 1 of 13 regional corporations established according to the terms of the Alaska Native Claims Settlement Act (ANCSA) of 1971. This program began in 1991.

Number awarded 1 or more each year.

Deadline May of each year for annual scholarships; May or November of each year for semester scholarships.

[995]
KIRKLAND & ELLIS LLP DIVERSITY FELLOWSHIP PROGRAM

Kirkland & Ellis LLP
Attn: Attorney Recruiting Manager
333 South Hope Street
Los Angeles, CA 90071
(213) 680-8436   Fax: (213) 680-8500
E-mail: cherie.beffa@kirkland.com
Web: www.kirkland.com

Summary To provide financial assistance and summer work experience at an office of Kirkland & Ellis to Native American and other diverse law students from any state.

Eligibility This program is open to second-year students at ABA-accredited law schools who reflect the firm's efforts to reach out to racial, ethnic, women's, and LGBT student groups. Applicants must have been accepted as summer associates at a domestic office of the sponsoring law firm (Chicago, Los Angeles, New York, Palo Alto, San Francisco, Washington, D.C.) and be likely to practice at 1 of those offices after graduation. Along with their application, they must submit a 1-page personal statement that describes ways in which they have promoted and will continue to promote diversity in the legal community, along with their interest in the firm. Selection is based on merit.

Financial data Fellows receive a salary during their summer associateship and a $25,000 stipend at the conclusion of the summer. Stipend funds are to be used for payment of educational expenses during the third year of law school.

Duration 1 year.

Additional information This program, which replaced the Kirkland & Ellis Minority Fellowship Program, was established at 14 law schools in 2004. In 2006, it began accepting applications from students at all ABA-accredited law schools.

Number awarded   Varies each year; recently, 10 were awarded. Since the program began, it has awarded 140 fellowships worth more than $2.3 million.

Deadline   August of each year.

[996]
K&L GATES DIVERSITY FELLOWSHIP

Kirkpatrick & Lockhart Preston Gates Ellis LLP
Attn: Legal Recruitment and Development Assistant
925 Fourth Avenue, Suite 2900
Seattle, WA 98104
(206) 370-5760   E-mail: tia.chang@klgates.com
Web: www.klgates.com/aboutus/diversity

Summary   To provide financial assistance and summer work experience in Seattle to Native American and other law students from any state who come from diverse backgrounds.

Eligibility   This program is open to first-year students at ABA-accredited law schools in the United States. Applicants must identify with 1 of the firm's affinity groups at the firmwide and local office levels, including those for women lawyers; lesbian, gay, bisexual and transgender (LGBT) lawyers; lawyers of color; working parents; and lawyers with disabilities. Along with their application, they must submit a 500-word personal statement describing the contribution they would make to the legal profession in general and the sponsoring firm in particular.

Financial data   Fellows receive a paid associateship with the Seattle office of the sponsoring firm during the summer following their first year of law school and an academic scholarship of $10,000 for their second year of law school.

Duration   1 year.

Number awarded   1 each year.

Deadline   January of each year.

[997]
KONIAG EDUCATION FOUNDATION GENERAL SCHOLARSHIPS

Koniag Incorporated
Attn: Koniag Education Foundation
4241 B Street, Suite 303B
Anchorage, AK 99503
(907) 562-9093   Toll Free: (888) 562-9093
Fax: (907) 562-9023
E-mail: scholarships@koniageducation.org
Web: www.koniageducation.org/scholarships/general

Summary   To provide financial assistance to Alaska Natives who are Koniag Incorporated shareholders or descendants and plan to attend college or graduate school in any state.

Eligibility   This program is open to high school seniors, high school and GED graduates, college students, and graduate students who are Alaska Native shareholders of Koniag Incorporated or descendants of those original enrollees. Applicants must have a GPA of 2.5 or higher and be enrolled or planning to enroll full or part time at a college or university in any state. Along with their application, they must submit a 300-word essay about their personal and family history, community involvement, volunteer activities, and educational and

life goals. Financial need is not considered in the selection process.

Financial data   Stipends range up to $2,500 per year. Funds are sent directly to the recipient's school and may be used for tuition, books, supplies, room, board, and transportation.

Duration   1 year; may be renewed, provided recipients maintain a GPA of 2.0 or higher.

Additional information   Koniag Incorporated is 1 of 13 Alaska Native Regional Corporations created under the Alaska Native Claims Settlement Act of 1971.

Number awarded   Varies each year.

Deadline   March of each year.

[998]
KPMG MINORITY ACCOUNTING DOCTORAL SCHOLARSHIPS

KPMG Foundation
Attn: Scholarship Administrator
Three Chestnut Ridge Road
Montvale, NJ 07645-0435
(201) 307-7161   Fax: (201) 624-7763
E-mail: us-kpmgfoundation@kpmg.com
Web: www.kpmgfoundation.org

Summary   To provide funding to Native American and other underrepresented minority students working on a doctoral degree in accounting.

Eligibility   Applicants must be African Americans, Hispanic Americans, or Native Americans. They must be U.S. citizens or permanent residents and accepted or enrolled in a full-time accounting doctoral program. Along with their application, they must submit a brief letter explaining their reason for working on a Ph.D. in accounting.

Financial data   The stipend is $10,000 per year.

Duration   1 year; may be renewed up to 4 additional years.

Additional information   These funds are not intended to replace funds normally made available by the recipient's institution. The foundation recommends that the recipient's institution also award, to the recipient, a $5,000 annual stipend, a teaching or research assistantship, and a waiver of tuition and fees.

Number awarded   Approximately 12 each year.

Deadline   April of each year.

[999]
LAC DU FLAMBEAU GRADUATE ASSISTANCE PROGRAM

Lac du Flambeau Band of Lake Superior Chippewa
    Indians
Attn: Gikendaasowin (Education) Center
562 Peace Pipe Road
P.O. Box 67
Lac du Flambeau, WI 54538
(715) 588-7925   Fax: (715) 588-9063
E-mail: ldfedu@ldftribe.com
Web: www.ldftribe.com

Summary   To provide financial assistance to tribal members of the Lac du Flambeau Band of Lake Superior Chippewa Indians who are interested in working on a graduate degree.

Eligibility This program is open to enrolled Lac du Flambeau members who are working on or planning to work full or part time on a master's or doctoral degree. Applicants must be able to demonstrate financial need.

Financial data The maximum stipend is $3,500 per semester for full-time work or $1,750 per semester for part-time work.

Duration 1 semester; may be renewed up to 5 additional semesters of full-time master's degree study or 7 additional semesters of full-time doctoral study; renewal is granted only if the recipient maintains a GPA of 3.0 or higher.

Number awarded Varies each year.

Deadline The priority deadline is June of each year for fall semester, November of each year for spring semester, or March of each year for summer session.

[1000]
LAGRANT FOUNDATION GRADUATE SCHOLARSHIPS

Lagrant Foundation
Attn: Senior Talent Acquisition and Fundraising Manager
633 West Fifth Street, 48th Floor
Los Angeles, CA 90071
(323) 469-8680, ext. 223   Fax: (323) 469-8683
E-mail: erickainiguez@lagrant.com
Web: www.lagrantfoundation.org

Summary To provide financial assistance to Native American and other minority graduate students who are working on a degree in advertising, public relations, or marketing.

Eligibility This program is open to African Americans, Asian American/Pacific Islanders, Hispanics/Latinos, and Native Americans/American Indians who are full-time graduate students at an accredited institution. Applicants must have a GPA of 3.2 or higher and be working on a master's degree in advertising, marketing, or public relations. They must have at least 2 academic semesters remaining to complete their degree. Along with their application, they must submit 1) a 1- to 2-page essay outlining their career goals; why it is important to increase ethnic representation in the fields of advertising, marketing, and public relations; and the role of an advertising, marketing, or public relations practitioner; 2) a paragraph describing the graduate school and/or community activities in which they are involved; 3) a brief paragraph describing any honors and awards they have received; 4) a letter of reference; 5) a resume; and 6) an official transcript. U.S. citizenship or permanent resident status is required.

Financial data The stipend is $5,000.

Duration 1 year.

Number awarded Varies each year; recently, 19 were awarded.

Deadline February of each year.

[1001]
LARRY MATFAY SCHOLARSHIP

Koniag Incorporated
Attn: Koniag Education Foundation
4241 B Street, Suite 303B
Anchorage, AK 99503
(907) 562-9093   Toll Free: (888) 562-9093
Fax: (907) 562-9023
E-mail: scholarships@koniageducation.org
Web: www.koniageducation.org/scholarships/larry-matfay

Summary To provide financial assistance to Alaska Natives who are Koniag Incorporated shareholders or descendants and enrolled in undergraduate or graduate study in a field related to Alutiiq culture.

Eligibility This program is open to college juniors, seniors, and graduate students who are Alaska Native shareholders of Koniag Incorporated or descendants of those original enrollees. Applicants must have a GPA of 2.5 or higher and be working full time on a degree in Alaska Native or American Indian studies, anthropology, health care, history, linguistics, rural development, or another discipline that involves research and learning about Alutiiq culture. Along with their application, they must submit a 300-word essay about their personal and family history, community involvement, volunteer activities, and educational and life goals. Financial need is not considered in the selection process.

Financial data The stipend is $1,000 per year. Funds are sent directly to the recipient's school and may be used for tuition, books, supplies, room, board, and transportation.

Duration 1 year; may be renewed.

Additional information Koniag Incorporated is 1 of 13 Alaska Native Regional Corporations created under the Alaska Native Claims Settlement Act of 1971.

Number awarded 1 each year.

Deadline May of each year.

[1002]
LATHAM & WATKINS DIVERSITY SCHOLARS PROGRAM

Latham & Watkins LLP
Attn: Senior Manager of Global Attorney Recruiting
885 Third Avenue
New York, NY 10022-4834
(212) 906-1332   Fax: (212) 751-4864
E-mail: elizabeth.krichmar@lw.com
Web: www.lw.com/AboutUs/Diversity

Summary To provide financial assistance to Native American and other minority law students interested in working for a global law firm.

Eligibility Applicants must be second-year law students at an ABA-accredited law school and plan to practice law in a major city in the United States. Applicants must contribute to the firm's efforts to achieve a rich mixture of men and women of different races, ethnic backgrounds, sexual orientations, cultures, and primary languages. Along with their application, they must submit a 500-word personal statement that describes what led them to prepare for a legal career, their ability to contribute to the diversity objectives of global law firms; the life experiences that have shaped their values and that provide them with a unique perspective, including any obstacles or challenges they have overcome; their academic and/or leadership achievements; and their intent to practice in a global law firm environment.

Financial data The stipend is $10,000.

Duration 1 year; nonrenewable.

Additional information This program began in 2005. Recipients are not required to work for Latham & Watkins after graduation.

Number awarded 6 each year.

Deadline September of each year.

[1003]
LAUNCHING LEADERS MBA SCHOLARSHIP

JPMorgan Chase
Campus Recruiting
Attn: Launching Leaders
277 Park Avenue, Second Floor
New York, NY 10172
(212) 270-6000
E-mail: bronwen.x.baumgardner@jpmorgan.com
Web: careers.jpmorgan.com

Summary To provide financial assistance and work experience to Native American and other underrepresented minority students enrolled in the first year of an M.B.A. program.

Eligibility This program is open to Black, Hispanic, and Native American students enrolled in the first year of an M.B.A. program. Applicants must have a demonstrated commitment to working in financial services. Along with their application, they must submit essays on 1) a hypothetical proposal on how to use $50 million from a donor to their school to benefit all of its students; and 2) the special background and attributes they would contribute to the sponsor's diversity agenda and their motivation for applying to this scholarship program. They must be interested in a summer associate position in the sponsor's investment banking, sales and trading, or research divisions.

Financial data The stipend is $40,000 for the first year of study; a paid summer associate position is also provided.

Duration 1 year; may be renewed 1 additional year if the recipient successfully completes the 10-week summer associate program.

Number awarded Varies each year.

Deadline October of each year.

[1004]
LAWRENCE MATSON MEMORIAL ENDOWMENT FUND SCHOLARSHIPS

Cook Inlet Region, Inc.
Attn: The CIRI Foundation
3600 San Jeronimo Drive, Suite 256
Anchorage, AK 99508-2870
(907) 793-3575　　　　Toll Free: (800) 764-3382
Fax: (907) 793-3585　　　E-mail: tcf@thecirifoundation.org
Web: www.thecirifoundation.org/about/donors

Summary To provide financial assistance for undergraduate or graduate studies in selected liberal arts to Alaska Natives who are original enrollees to Cook Inlet Region, Inc. (CIRI) and their lineal descendants.

Eligibility This program is open to Alaska Native enrollees to CIRI under the Alaska Native Claims Settlement Act (ANCSA) of 1971 and their lineal descendants. There are no Alaska residency requirements or age limitations. Applicants

must be accepted or enrolled full time in a 4-year undergraduate or a graduate degree program in the following liberal arts fields: language, education, social sciences, arts, communications, or law. They must have a GPA of 2.5 or higher. Along with their application, they must submit a 500-word statement on their educational and career goals and how they are contributing, or planning to contribute, to a positive Alaska Native community. Selection is based on that statement, academic achievement, rigor of course work or degree program, student financial contribution, financial need, grade level, previous work performance, community service, and relationship of degree program to career goals.

Financial data The stipend is $10,000 per year, $8,000 per year, or $2,500 per semester, depending on GPA.

Duration 1 semester or 1 year.

Additional information CIRI is 1 of 13 regional corporations established according to the terms of the Alaska Native Claims Settlement Act (ANCSA) of 1971. This fund was established in 1989.

Number awarded Varies each year; recently, 3 were awarded: 1 at $10,000 per year, 1 at $8,000 per year, and 1 at $2,500 per semester.

Deadline May of each year for annual scholarships; May or November of each year for semester scholarships.

[1005]
LEADERSHIP FOR DIVERSITY SCHOLARSHIP

California School Library Association
Attn: CSL Foundation
6444 East Spring Street, Number 237
Long Beach, CA 90815-1553
Toll Free: (888) 655-8480　　　　Fax: (888) 655-8480
E-mail: info@csla.net
Web: www.csla.net/awards-2/scholarships

Summary To provide financial assistance to Native American and other students who reflect the diversity of California's population and are interested in earning a credential as a library media teacher in the state.

Eligibility This program is open to students who are members of a traditionally underrepresented group enrolled in a college or university library media teacher credential program in California. Applicants must intend to work as a library media teacher in a California school library media center for a minimum of 3 years. Along with their application, they must submit a 250-word statement on what they can contribute to the profession, their commitment to serving the needs of multicultural and multilingual students, and their financial need.

Financial data The stipend is $1,500.

Duration 1 year.

Number awarded 1 each year.

Deadline September of each year.

[1006]
LEECH LAKE POSTSECONDARY GRANT PROGRAM

Leech Lake Band of Ojibwe
Attn: Education Division
190 Sailstar Drive, N.W.
Cass Lake, MN 56633
(218) 335-8253   Toll Free: (866) 638-7738
Fax: (218) 335-8339
Web: www.llojibwe.com

Summary To provide financial assistance to Minnesota Chippewa Tribe members who are interested in postsecondary education at a school in any state.

Eligibility This program is open to enrolled members of the Leech Lake Band of Ojibwe who have been residents of Minnesota for at least 1 year. Applicants may be high school seniors or graduates, current undergraduates, short-term training students, or full- or part-time graduate students. They must be interested in attending a postsecondary institution in any state. Financial need is considered in the selection process.

Financial data Stipends range up to $3,000 per year, depending on need.

Duration 1 year; may be renewed.

Additional information Applicants for this program must also apply for the Minnesota Indian Scholarship Program, financial aid administered by their institution, and any other aid for which they may be eligible (e.g., work-study, Social Security, veteran's benefits).

Number awarded Varies each year.

Deadline For vocational school students, at least 8 weeks before school starts; for college or university students, June of each year.

[1007]
LEON BRADLEY SCHOLARSHIPS

American Association of School Personnel Administrators
Attn: Scholarship Program
11863 West 112th Street, Suite 100
Overland Park, KS 66210
(913) 327-1222   Fax: (913) 327-1223
E-mail: aaspa@aaspa.org
Web: www.aaspa.org/leon-bradley-scholarship

Summary To provide financial assistance to Native American and other minority undergraduates, paraprofessionals, and graduate students preparing for a career in teaching and school leadership at colleges in designated southeastern states.

Eligibility This program is open to members of minority groups (American Indian, Alaskan Native, Asian, Pacific Islander, Black, Hispanic, Middle Easterner) currently enrolled full time at a college or university in Alabama, Florida, Georgia, Kentucky, North Carolina, South Carolina, Tennessee, or Virginia. Applicants must be 1) undergraduates in their final year (including student teaching) of an initial teaching certification program; 2) paraprofessional career-changers in their final year (including student teaching) of an initial teaching certification program; or 3) graduate students who have served as a licensed teacher and are working on a school administrator credential. They must have an overall GPA of 3.0 or higher. Priority is given to applicants who 1) can demonstrate work experience that has been applied to college expenses; 2) have received other scholarship or financial aid support; or 3) are seeking initial certification and/or endorsement in a state-identified critical area.

Financial data Stipends are $2,500 for undergraduates in their final year, $1,500 for paraprofessionals in their final year, and $1,500 for graduate students.

Duration 1 year.

Number awarded 4 each year: 1 undergraduate, 1 paraprofessional, and 2 graduate students.

Deadline May of each year.

[1008]
LIBRARY AND INFORMATION TECHNOLOGY ASSOCIATION MINORITY SCHOLARSHIPS

American Library Association
Attn: Library and Information Technology Association
50 East Huron Street
Chicago, IL 60611-2795
(312) 280-4270   Toll Free: (800) 545-2433, ext. 4270
Fax: (312) 280-3257   TDD: (888) 814-7692
E-mail: lita@ala.org
Web: www.ala.org/lita/awards

Summary To provide financial assistance to Native American and other minority graduate students interested in preparing for a career in library automation.

Eligibility This program is open to U.S. or Canadian citizens who are interested in working on a master's degree in library/information science and preparing for a career in the field of library and automated systems. Applicants must be a member of 1 of the following ethnic groups: American Indian, Alaskan Native, Asian, Pacific Islander, African American, or Hispanic. They may not have completed more than 12 credit hours of course work for their degree. Selection is based on academic excellence, leadership potential, evidence of a commitment to a career in library automation and information technology, and prior activity and experience in those fields. Financial need is considered when all other factors are equal.

Financial data Stipends are $3,000 or $2,500. Funds are paid directly to the recipient.

Duration 1 year.

Additional information This program includes scholarships funded by Online Computer Library Center (OCLC) and by Library Systems & Services, Inc. (LSSI).

Number awarded 2 each year: 1 at $3,000 (funded by OCLC) and 1 at $2,500 (funded by LSSI).

Deadline February of each year.

[1009]
LILLE HOPE MCGARVEY SCHOLARSHIP AWARD

The Aleut Corporation
Attn: Aleut Foundation
703 West Tudor Road, Suite 102
Anchorage, AK 99503-6650
(907) 646-1929   Toll Free: (800) 232-4882
Fax: (907) 646-1949   E-mail: taf@thealeutfoundation.org
Web: www.thealeutfoundation.org

Summary To provide financial assistance to Native Alaskans who are shareholders of The Aleut Corporation or their descendants and working on a degree in the medical field at a school in any state.

Eligibility This program is open to Native Alaskans who are original enrollees or descendants of original enrollees of The Aleut Corporation (TAC). Applicants must have completed at least 1 year of a bachelor's, 2- or 4-year vocational, or master's degree in a medical field at a school in any state. They must be enrolled full time and have a GPA of 3.0 or higher. Along with their application, they must include a letter of intent, up to 500 words in length, that describes their educational goals and objectives and their expected graduation date.

Financial data A stipend is awarded (amount not specified).

Duration 1 year.

Additional information The Aleut Corporation is 1 of 13 Alaska Native Regional Corporations created under the Alaska Native Claims Settlement Act of 1971.

Number awarded 1 each year.

Deadline June of each year.

[1010]
LILLIAN FOWLER MEMORIAL SCHOLARSHIP

Chickasaw Foundation
2020 Arlington, Suite 4
P.O. Box 1726
Ada, OK 74821-1726
(580) 421-9030   Fax: (580) 421-9031
E-mail: ChickasawFoundation@chickasaw.net
Web: www.chickasawfoundation.org/Scholarships.aspx

Summary To provide financial assistance to members of the Chickasaw Nation who are working or an undergraduate or graduate degree in health care or social work.

Eligibility This program is open to Chickasaw students who are currently working full time on an undergraduate or graduate degree in social work or a health Applicants must have a GPA of 3.0 or higher. Along with their application, they must submit high school or college transcripts; 2 letters of recommendation; a copy of their Chickasaw Nation citizenship card; a 2-page list of honors, achievements, awards, club memberships, societies, and civic involvement; and a 1-page essay on their long-term goals and plans for achieving those. Financial need is not considered in the selection process.

Financial data A stipend is awarded (amount not specified).

Duration 1 year.

Number awarded 1 each year.

Deadline June of each year.

[1011]
LIONEL C. BARROW MINORITY DOCTORAL STUDENT SCHOLARSHIP

Association for Education in Journalism and Mass
  Communication
Attn: Communication Theory and Methodology Division
234 Outlet Pointe Boulevard, Suite A
Columbia, SC 29210-5667
(803) 798-0271   Fax: (803) 772-3509
E-mail: aejmc@aejmc.org
Web: www.aejmc.us

Summary To provide financial assistance to minorities who are interested in working on a doctorate in mass communication.

Eligibility This program is open to Native American and other minority students enrolled in a Ph.D. program in journalism and/or mass communication. Applicants must submit 2 letters of recommendation, a resume, and a brief letter outlining their research interests and career plans. Membership in the association is not required, but applicants must be U.S. citizens or permanent residents. Selection is based on the likelihood that the applicant's work will contribute to communication theory and/or methodology.

Financial data The stipend is $2,000.

Duration 1 year.

Additional information This program began in 1972.

Number awarded 1 each year.

Deadline May of each year.

[1012]
LITTLE RIVER BAND OF OTTAWA INDIANS HIGHER EDUCATION SCHOLARSHIP

Little River Band of Ottawa Indians
Attn: Education Department
2608 Government Center Drive
Manistee, MI 49660
(231) 398-6735   Toll Free: (888) 723-8288
Fax: (231) 398-6655   E-mail: yparsons@lrboi-nsn.gov
Web: www.lrboi-nsn.gov/membership-services/education

Summary To provide financial assistance to members of the Little River Band of Ottawa Indians who are interested in attending college or graduate school.

Eligibility This program is open to tribal citizens of the Little River Band of Ottawa Indians who are attending or planning to attend an accredited college or university. Applicants must be interested in working on an associate, bachelor's, master's, or Ph.D. degree. They must have applied for all other available financial aid and still show unmet need. In the selection process, priority is given first to residents of Michigan, second to students attending schools in Michigan, and third to students attending schools in other states.

Financial data The stipend is $3,500 per semester ($7,000 per year). Recipients are also eligible to apply for book stipends of $200 to $500 (depending on the number of credits in which they are enrolled). Funds are paid to the recipient's institution.

Duration 1 year; may be renewed, provided the recipient maintains a GPA of 2.0 or higher.

Number awarded Varies each year.

Deadline Deadline not specified.

[1013]
LITTLE RIVER BAND OF OTTAWA INDIANS VOCATIONAL EDUCATION ASSISTANCE PROGRAM

Little River Band of Ottawa Indians
Attn: Education Department
2608 Government Center Drive
Manistee, MI 49660
(231) 398-6735   Toll Free: (888) 723-8288
Fax: (231) 398-6655   E-mail: yparsons@lrboi-nsn.gov
Web: www.lrboi-nsn.gov/membership-services/education

Summary To provide financial assistance to members of the Little River Band of Ottawa Indians who are interested in attending vocational school.

Eligibility This program is open to tribal citizens of the Little River Band of Ottawa Indians who are at least 18 years of age. Applicants must be interested in attending an accredited vocational/technical program for training to obtain reasonable and satisfactory employment. They must have applied for all other available financial aid and still show unmet need. In the selection process, priority is given first to residents of Michigan, second to students attending schools in Michigan, and third to students attending schools in other states.

Financial data The stipend is $4,000 per term. Funds are paid to the recipient's institution.

Duration Recipients are entitled to a maximum of 24 months of support (or 36 months for nursing programs).

Number awarded Varies each year.

Deadline Deadline not specified.

[1014]
LOWENSTEIN SANDLER SCHOLARS PROGRAM

Lowenstein Sandler LLP
Attn: Chair, Diversity Committee
65 Livingston Avenue
Roseland, NJ 07068
(973) 597-6308   Fax: (973) 597-6309
E-mail: mhildebrand@lowenstein.com
Web: www.lowenstein.com/about/diversity

Summary To provide financial assistance and work experience with the sponsoring firm to Native American and other students at designated law schools who will contribute to diversity.

Eligibility This program is open to students currently enrolled full time in their first year at Columbia University School of Law, Cornell University Law School, Duke University School of Law, Georgetown Law Center, Harvard Law School, Howard University School of Law, New York University School of Law, Rutgers University School of Law at Newark, Seton Hall University School of Law, University of Pennsylvania Law School, or Yale Law School. Applicants must be interested in a summer associateship with Lowenstein Sandler at its offices in Roseland, New Jersey. They must contribute to the firm's efforts to recruit, retain, and promote lawyers from diverse social, economic, cultural, and personal backgrounds. Along with their application, they must submit a cover letter describing their career goals, the reasons they would like to be accepted to this program, and their expected contribution to the firm's diverse community; a current resume; transcripts; a writing sample from a first-semester legal writing course; a 500-word personal essay describing their most significant challenge and how they met it; and 2 references.

Financial data Selected students receive a salary of $2,700 per week for an associateship during the summer after the first year of law school and a scholarship of $10,000 towards second-year tuition.

Duration 11 weeks for the associateship and 1 academic year for the scholarship. The scholarship may be renewed for the third year of law school if the recipient accepts an associate position for the summer after the second year and maintains a GPA of 3.0 or higher.

Additional information This program began in 2009.

Number awarded Up to 4 each year.

Deadline January of each year.

[1015]
LTK ENGINEERING SCHOLARSHIP

Conference of Minority Transportation Officials
Attn: National Scholarship Program
100 M Street, S.E., Suite 917
Washington, DC 20003
(202) 506-2917   E-mail: info@comto.org
Web: www.comto.org/page/scholarships

Summary To provide financial assistance to Native American and other minority upper-division and graduate students in engineering or other field related to transportation.

Eligibility This program is open to full-time minority juniors, seniors, and graduate students in engineering or other technical transportation-related disciplines. Applicants must have a GPA of 3.0 or higher. Along with their application they must submit a cover letter on their transportation-related career goals and life aspirations. Financial need is not considered in the selection process.

Financial data The stipend is $6,000. Funds are paid directly to the recipient's college or university.

Duration 1 year.

Additional information This program is sponsored by LTK Engineering Services.

Number awarded 1 each year.

Deadline April of each year.

[1016]
LTK ENGINEERING TRANSPORTATION
PLANNING SCHOLARSHIP

Conference of Minority Transportation Officials
Attn: National Scholarship Program
100 M Street, S.E., Suite 917
Washington, DC 20003
(202) 506-2917   E-mail: info@comto.org
Web: www.comto.org/page/scholarships

Summary To provide financial assistance to Native American and other minority upper-division and graduate students in planning or other field related to transportation.

Eligibility This program is open to full-time minority juniors, seniors, and graduate students in planning of other technical transportation-related disciplines. Applicants must have a GPA of 3.0 or higher. Along with their application they must submit a cover letter on their transportation-related career goals and life aspirations. Financial need is not considered in the selection process.

Financial data The stipend is $5,000. Funds are paid directly to the recipient's college or university.

Duration 1 year.

Additional information This program is sponsored by LTK Engineering Services.

Number awarded 1 each year.

Deadline April of each year.

[1017]
LULA BYNUM BOURLAND MEMORIAL SCHOLARSHIP

Chickasaw Foundation
2020 Arlington, Suite 4
P.O. Box 1726
Ada, OK 74821-1726
(580) 421-9030   Fax: (580) 421-9031
E-mail: ChickasawFoundation@chickasaw.net
Web: www.chickasawfoundation.org/Scholarships.aspx

Summary   To provide financial assistance to members of the Chickasaw Nation who are working on an undergraduate or graduate degree in Native American studies, peace education studies, or alternatives to growth.

Eligibility   This program is open to members of the Chickasaw Nation who are currently enrolled as full-time juniors, seniors, or graduate students at a 4-year college or university. Applicants must be working on a degree in Native American studies, peace education studies, sustainable resource studies, or a related field of alternatives to perpetual growth as an economic model. Along with their application, they must submit high school or college transcripts; 2 letters of recommendation; a copy of their Chickasaw Nation citizenship card; a 2-page list of honors, achievements, awards, club memberships, societies, and civic involvement; and a 1-page essay on their long-term goals and plans for achieving those. Financial need is not considered in the selection process.

Financial data   A stipend is awarded (amount not specified).

Duration   1 year.

Number awarded   1 or more each year.

Deadline   June of each year.

[1018]
MAE LASSLEY/OSAGE SCHOLARSHIPS

Osage Scholarship Fund
c/o Roman Catholic Diocese of Tulsa
P.O. Box 690240
Tulsa, OK 74169-0240
(918) 294-1904   Fax: (918) 294-0920
E-mail: sarah.jameson@dioceseoftulsa.org
Web: www.osagenation-nsn.gov

Summary   To provide financial assistance to Osage Indians who are Roman Catholics attending college or graduate school.

Eligibility   This program is open to Roman Catholics who are attending or planning to attend a college or university as a full-time undergraduate or graduate student. Applicants must be Osage Indians on the rolls in Pawhuska, Oklahoma and have a copy of their Certificate of Degree of Indian Blood (CDIB) or Osage tribal membership card. Undergraduates must have a GPA of 2.5 or higher; graduate students must have a GPA of 3.0 or higher. Selection is based on academic ability and financial need.

Financial data   The stipend is $1,000 per year.

Duration   1 year; may be renewed if the recipient maintains full-time enrollment and a GPA of 2.5 or higher as an undergraduate or 3.0 or higher as a graduate student.

Number awarded   Normally, 10 each year: 2 for students attending St. Gregory's University in Shawnee, Oklahoma as freshmen and 8 for any college or university.

Deadline   April of each year.

[1019]
MAGNEL LARSEN DRABEK SCHOLARSHIP

Koniag Incorporated
Attn: Koniag Education Foundation
4241 B Street, Suite 303B
Anchorage, AK 99503
(907) 562-9093   Toll Free: (888) 562-9093
Fax: (907) 562-9023
E-mail: scholarships@koniageducation.org
Web: www.koniageducation.org

Summary   To provide financial assistance to Alaska Natives who are Koniag Incorporated shareholders or descendants and working on an undergraduate or graduate degree in education, arts, or cultural studies.

Eligibility   This program is open to undergraduate and graduate students who are Alaska Native shareholders of Koniag Incorporated or descendants of those original enrollees. Applicants must have a GPA of 2.5 or higher and be working full time on a degree in education, arts, or cultural studies. Along with their application, they must submit a 300-word essay about their personal and family history, community involvement, volunteer activities, and educational and life goals. Financial need is not considered in the selection process.

Financial data   The stipend is $2,000 per year. Funds are sent directly to the recipient's school and may be used for tuition, books, supplies, room, board, and transportation.

Duration   1 year; may be renewed.

Additional information   Koniag Incorporated is 1 of 13 Alaska Native Regional Corporations created under the Alaska Native Claims Settlement Act of 1971.

Number awarded   1 each year.

Deadline   May of each year.

[1020]
MARGARET L. BROWN SCHOLARSHIP FUND

Cook Inlet Region, Inc.
Attn: The CIRI Foundation
3600 San Jeronimo Drive, Suite 256
Anchorage, AK 99508-2870
(907) 793-3575   Toll Free: (800) 764-3382
Fax: (907) 793-3585   E-mail: tcf@thecirifoundation.org
Web: www.thecirifoundation.org/about/donors

Summary   To provide financial assistance for undergraduate or graduate studies in designated fields to Alaska Natives who are original enrollees to Cook Inlet Region, Inc. (CIRI) and their lineal descendants.

Eligibility   This program is open to Alaska Native enrollees to CIRI under the Alaska Native Claims Settlement Act (ANCSA) of 1971 and their lineal descendants. There are no Alaska residency requirements or age limitations. Applicants must be accepted or enrolled full time in a 4-year undergraduate or a graduate degree program in land use policy and planning, conversation economics, environmental science, education policy, or related fields. They must have a GPA of 3.7 or higher. Along with their application, they must submit a

500-word statement on their educational and career goals and how they are contributing, or planning to contribute, to a positive Alaska Native community. Selection is based on that statement, academic achievement, rigor of course work or degree program, student financial contribution, financial need, grade level, previous work performance, community service, and relationship of degree program to career goals.

Financial data The stipend is $20,000 per year.

Duration 1 year; may be renewed.

Additional information CIRI is 1 of 13 regional corporations established according to the terms of the Alaska Native Claims Settlement Act (ANCSA) of 1971. This program began in 2013.

Number awarded 1 or more each year.

Deadline May of each year.

[1021]
MARILYN A. JACKSON MEMORIAL AWARD

Omaha Presbyterian Seminary Foundation
7101 Mercy Road, Suite 216
Omaha, NE 68106-2616
(402) 397-5138   Toll Free: (888) 244-6714
Fax: (402) 397-4944   E-mail: opsf@opsf-omaha.org
Web: www.omahapresbyterianseminaryfoundation.org

Summary To provide financial assistance to students at Presbyterian theological seminaries who are willing to serve in designated states, especially Native Americans and members of other ethnic minority groups.

Eligibility This program is open to members of a Presbyterian Church, under the care of a presbytery as a candidate/inquirer, and accepted or enrolled to work on a master's degree in divinity at 1 of the following 10 Presbyterian theological institutions: Austin Presbyterian Theological Seminary (Austin, Texas); Columbia Theological Seminary (Decatur, Georgia); University of Dubuque Theological Seminary (Dubuque, Iowa); Johnson C. Smith Theological Seminary (Atlanta, Georgia); Louisville Presbyterian Theological Seminary (Louisville, Kentucky); McCormick Theological Seminary (Chicago, Illinois); Pittsburgh Theological Seminary (Pittsburgh, Pennsylvania); Princeton Theological Seminary (Princeton, New Jersey); San Francisco Theological Seminary (San Anselmo, California); or Union Theological Seminary and Presbyterian School of Christian Education (Richmond, Virginia). Applicants must be willing to serve in a small Presbyterian church for 5 years in Colorado, Iowa, Kansas, Minnesota, Missouri, Montana, Nebraska, North Dakota, Oklahoma, South Dakota, Utah, Wisconsin, or Wyoming. Along with their application, they must submit answers to 7 questions about themselves and their commitment to pastoral service. Preference is given to members of ethnic minority groups from the following synods: Lakes and Prairies (Iowa, Minnesota, Nebraska, North Dakota, South Dakota, Wisconsin), Mid-America (Delaware, Maryland, North Carolina, Virginia, Washington, D.C.), Rocky Mountains (Colorado, Montana, Utah, Wyoming), and Sun (Arkansas, Louisiana, Oklahoma, Texas). Financial need is considered in the selection process.

Financial data The stipend is $7,500.

Duration 1 year.

Number awarded 1 each year.

Deadline April of each year.

[1022]
MARJORIE BOWENS-WHEATLEY SCHOLARSHIPS

Unitarian Universalist Association
Attn: UU Women's Federation
258 Harvard Street
Brookline, MA 02446
(617) 838-6989   E-mail: uuwf@uua.org
Web: www.uuwf.org

Summary To provide financial assistance to Native American and other women of color who are working on an undergraduate or graduate degree to prepare for Unitarian Universalist ministry or service.

Eligibility This program is open to women of color who are either 1) aspirants or candidates for the Unitarian Universalist ministry; or 2) candidates in the Unitarian Universalist Association's professional religious education or music leadership credentialing programs. Applicants must submit a 1- to 2-page narrative that covers their call to UU ministry, religious education, or music leadership; their passions; how their racial/ethnic/cultural background influences their goals for their calling; and how the work of the program's namesake relates to their dreams and plans for their UU service.

Financial data The stipend is $1,500.

Duration 1 year.

Additional information This program began in 2009.

Number awarded Varies each year; recently, 2 were awarded.

Deadline March of each year.

[1023]
MARK T. BANNER SCHOLARSHIP FOR LAW STUDENTS

Richard Linn American Inn of Court
c/o Amy Ziegler, Scholarship Chair
Green Burns & Crain
300 South Wacker Drive, Suite 2500
Chicago, IL 60606
(312) 987-2926   Fax: (312) 360-9315
E-mail: marktbannerscholarship@linninn.org
Web: www.linninn.org/Pages/scholarship.shtml

Summary To provide financial assistance to law students who are Native Americans or members of other groups historically underrepresented in intellectual property law.

Eligibility This program is open to students at ABA-accredited law schools in the United States who are members of groups historically underrepresented (by race, sex, ethnicity, sexual orientation, or disability) in intellectual property law. Applicants must submit a 3-page statement on how ethics, civility, and professionalism have been their focus; how diversity has impacted them; and their commitment to a career in intellectual property law. Selection is based on academic merit; written and oral communication skills; leadership qualities; community involvement; commitment, qualities and actions toward ethics, civility and professionalism; and commitment to a career in IP law.

Financial data The stipend is $5,000.

Duration 1 year.

Number awarded 1 each year.

Deadline November of each year.

[1024]
MARTHA MILLER TRIBUTARY SCHOLARSHIP

Sault Tribe of Chippewa Indians
Attn: Higher Education Department
523 Ashmun Street
Sault Ste. Marie, MI 49783
(906) 635-6050, ext. 26312   Toll Free: (800) 793-0660
Fax: (906) 635-7785   E-mail: BMacArthur@saulttribe.net
Web: www.saulttribe.com

Summary To provide financial assistance to members of the Sault Tribe of Chippewa Indians who are attending college in any state and working on an undergraduate or graduate degree in human services or social work.

Eligibility This program is open to members of the Sault Tribe who are enrolled full time at a 2- or 4-year college or university in any state. Applicants must be working on an undergraduate or graduate degree in social work, social services, or other field of study related to human services. Along with their application, they must submit an essay of 1,000 to 2,000 words on a topic that changes annually but relates to their Indian heritage.

Financial data The stipend is $1,000.

Duration 1 year.

Number awarded 1 each year.

Deadline May of each year.

[1025]
MARTIN LUTHER KING, JR. MEMORIAL SCHOLARSHIP FUND

California Teachers Association
Attn: CTA Foundation for Teaching and Learning
1705 Murchison Drive
P.O. Box 921
Burlingame, CA 94011-0921
(650) 697-1400   E-mail: scholarships@cta.org
Web: www.cta.org

Summary To provide financial assistance for college or graduate school to Native Americans and other racial and ethnic minorities who are members of the California Teachers Association (CTA), children of members, or members of the Student CTA.

Eligibility This program is open to members of racial or ethnic minority groups (African Americans, American Indians/Alaska Natives, Asians/Pacific Islanders, and Hispanics) who are 1) active CTA members; 2) dependent children of active, retired, or deceased CTA members; or 3) members of Student CTA. Applicants must be interested in preparing for a teaching career in public education or already engaged in such a career.

Financial data Stipends vary each year; recently, they ranged up to $6,000.

Duration 1 year.

Number awarded Varies each year; recently, 24 were awarded: 1 to a CTA member, 10 to children of CTA members, and 13 to Student CTA members.

Deadline February of each year.

[1026]
MARTIN LUTHER KING JR. SCHOLARSHIP AWARDS

American Correctional Association
Attn: Scholarship Award Committee
206 North Washington Street, Suite 200
Alexandria, VA 22314
(703) 224-0000   Toll Free: (800) ACA-JOIN
Fax: (703) 224-0179   E-mail: execoffice@aca.org
Web: www.aca.org

Summary To provide financial assistance for undergraduate or graduate study to Native American and other minorities interested in a career in the criminal justice field.

Eligibility Members of the American Correctional Association (ACA) may nominate a minority person for these awards. Nominees do not need to be ACA members, but they must have been accepted to or be enrolled in an undergraduate or graduate program in criminal justice at a 4-year college or university. Along with the nomination package, they must submit a 250-word essay describing their reflections on the ideals and philosophies of Dr. Martin Luther King and how they have attempted to emulate those qualities in their lives. They must provide documentation of financial need, academic achievement, and commitment to the principles of Dr. King.

Financial data A stipend is awarded (amount not specified). Funds are paid directly to the recipient's college or university.

Duration 1 year.

Number awarded 1 each year.

Deadline May of each year.

[1027]
MARY BALL CARRERA SCHOLARSHIP

National Medical Fellowships, Inc.
Attn: Scholarship Program
347 Fifth Avenue, Suite 510
New York, NY 10016
(212) 483-8880   Toll Free: (877) NMF-1DOC
Fax: (212) 483-8897   E-mail: scholarships@nmfonline.org
Web: www.nmfonline.org

Summary To provide financial assistance to Native American women who are attending medical school.

Eligibility This program is open to Native American women who are enrolled in the first or second year of an accredited medical school in the United States. Applicants must be able to demonstrate academic achievement, leadership, and community service, but selection is based primarily on financial need.

Financial data The stipend is $2,500.

Duration 1 year; nonrenewable.

Number awarded 1 or more each year.

Deadline September of each year.

[1028]
MARY E. TINKER SCHOLARSHIPS

Osage Nation Education Department
Attn: Career Training and Scholarship
105 Buffalo Avenue
Hominy, OK 74035
(918) 287-5301   Fax: (918) 885-2136
E-mail: scholarship@osagenation-nsn.gov
Web: www.osagenation-nsn.gov

Summary To provide financial assistance to members of the Osage Nation who are interested in working on a graduate degree in any field.

Eligibility This program is open to Osage tribal students who are enrolled for at least 6 credit hours in a graduate degree program at an accredited college or university. Applicants must have a GPA of 2.0 or higher and be able to demonstrate financial need. In the selection process, preference is given to students with the highest GPA.

Financial data The stipend is $525 per semester. Funds are paid directly to the student's school to be applied toward tuition, fees, and books.

Duration 2 semesters.

Number awarded 10 each year.

Deadline June of each year.

[1029]
MARY MUNSON RUNGE SCHOLARSHIP

American Pharmacists Association
Attn: APhA Foundation
2215 Constitution Avenue, N.W.
Washington, DC 20037-2985
(202) 429-7503   Toll Free: (800) 237-APhA
Fax: (202) 638-3793   E-mail: bwall@aphanet.org
Web: www.aphafoundation.org

Summary To provide financial assistance to members of the Academy of Student Pharmacists of the American Pharmacists Association (APhA-ASP), especially Native Americans and members of other underrepresented minority groups.

Eligibility This program is open to full-time pharmacy students who have been actively involved in their school's APhA-ASP chapter. Applicants must have completed at least 1 year in the professional sequence of courses with a GPA of 2.75 or higher. Preference is given to members of underrepresented minority groups (American Indians or Alaska Natives, Blacks or African Americans, Hispanics or Latinos, Native Hawaiians or other Pacific Islanders). Along with their application, they must submit a 500-word essay on a topic that changes annually but relates to the future of the pharmacy profession, 2 letters of recommendation, a current resume or curriculum vitae, and a list of pharmacy and non-pharmacy related activities. Selection is based on the essay (20 points), academic performance (10 points), pharmacy-related activities (25 points), non-pharmacy/community activities (25 points), and letters of recommendation (20 points).

Financial data The stipend is $1,000.

Duration 1 year; recipients may reapply.

Number awarded 1 each year.

Deadline November of each year.

[1030]
MCGHEE-TULLIS TUITION ASSISTANCE PROGRAM

Poarch Band of Creek Indians
Attn: Tuition Program Coordinator
5811 Jack Springs Road
Atmore, AL 36502
(251) 368-9136, ext. 2535   Fax: (251) 368-4502
E-mail: mjohnson@pci-nsn.gov
Web: www.poarchcreekindians.org

Summary To provide funding to members of the Poarch Band of Creek Indians for payment of tuition or repayment of educational loans.

Eligibility This program is open to enrolled members of the Poarch Band of Creek Indians who are enrolled or planning to enroll in 1) a certificate program leading to an increased chance of employment and/or increase in salary; 2) a vocational/technical school; or 3) a college or university program leading to an undergraduate, graduate, or professional degree. Applicants must be seeking funding 1) to pay the cost of tuition, books, and mandatory fees; or 2) to repay their educational loans incurred prior to their current enrollment.

Financial data Total maximum awards are $10,000 for students participating in a certificate program not culminating in a degree and not part of the federal student aid program, $20,000 for students participating in a certificate program not culminating in a degree but part of the federal student aid program, $30,000 for an associate degree program, $50,000 for a bachelor's degree, $75,000 for a master's degree, or $100,000 for a doctoral degree; those limits are cumulative. Tribal members may also apply for a supplemental grant for purchase of specialized tools required for their program and a 1-time grant of $1,000 for the purchase of a laptop or desktop computer.

Duration Available funds are disbursed as requested, until exhaustion of the lifetime allotment.

Number awarded Varies each year.

Deadline Applications may be submitted at any time.

[1031]
MCGLINCHEY STAFFORD DIVERSITY FELLOWSHIP PROGRAM

McGlinchey Stafford PLLC
Attn: Legal Recruiting Coordinator
601 Poydras Street, 12th Floor
New Orleans, LA 70130
(504) 654-1239   E-mail: aschwener@mcglinchey.com
Web: www.mcglinchey.com/DiversityFellowshipProgram

Summary To provide financial assistance and work experience at the Baton Rouge office of McGlinchey Stafford to Native American and other law students who will contribute diversity to the profession.

Eligibility This program is open to first-year students at accredited law schools in the United States who will add diversity to the legal profession. Applicants must be interested in a clerkship at the firm's Baton Rouge office with the possibility of another clerkship following the second year of law school. Selection is based on academic credentials, leadership skills, and an essay on their interest in this fellowship and how they would contribute to the diversity of the firm and its community.

Financial data The program includes a stipend of $5,000 for the second year of law school and a paid clerkship (salary not specified).
Duration 1 summer and 1 academic year; may be renewed for another summer.
Number awarded 1 each year.
Deadline January of each year.

[1032]
MCGUIREWOODS DIVERSITY SCHOLARSHIP PROGRAM

McGuireWoods LLP
Attn: Attorney Recruiting Manager
77 West Wacker Drive, Suite 4100
Chicago, IL 60601-1818
(312) 849-8100   Fax: (312) 849-3690
E-mail: apretty@mcguirewoods.com
Web: www.mcguirewoods.com/Our-Firm/Diversity.aspx

Summary To provide financial assistance to Native American law students and others who come from various groups that are traditionally underrepresented in law schools and the legal profession.
Eligibility This program is open to first-year law students who are committed to contributing to and supporting diversity within the legal profession. The sponsor defines diversity to include considerations of age, sex, gender identity, race, ethnicity, national origin, disability, religion, sexual orientation, marital status, and veteran status, as well as educational and professional backgrounds. It also considers other factors, such as whether a student is the first family member to attend college, from an economically disadvantaged family, a member of a group currently underrepresented in law schools and law firms, from a family with little or no legal education or experience, an alumnus of a college or university whose graduates are historically underrepresented in law school, or demonstrating a strong commitment to promoting diversity in their graduate school, law school, and community. Selection is based on law school and undergraduate academic performance, personal achievements, involvement in community activities and diversity-related student organizations, and a personal statement explaining their commitment to diversity in the legal profession.
Financial data The stipend is $5,000.
Duration 1 year.
Number awarded Up to 8 each year.
Deadline May of each year.

[1033]
MCKINNEY FAMILY FUND SCHOLARSHIP

Cleveland Foundation
Attn: Scholarship Processing
1422 Euclid Avenue, Suite 1300
Cleveland, OH 44115-2001
(216) 861-3810   Fax: (216) 861-1729
E-mail: mbaker@clevefdn.org
Web: www.clevelandfoundation.org

Summary To provide financial assistance to residents of Ohio, especially Native Americans and members of other minority groups, who are interested in attending college or graduate school in any state.

Eligibility This program is open to U.S. citizens who have been residents of Ohio for at least 2 years. Applicants must be high school seniors or graduate students and interested in working full or part time on an associate, bachelor's, master's, or doctoral degree at an accredited college or university in any state. They must have a GPA of 2.5 or higher. Preference is given to applicants of minority descent. Selection is based on evidence of sincerity toward obtaining an academic credential. Financial need may be used as a tiebreaker.
Financial data The stipend is $2,000 per year. Funds are paid directly to the school and must be applied to tuition, fees, books, supplies, and equipment required for course work.
Duration 1 year; may be renewed up to 3 additional.
Number awarded 1 or more each year.
Deadline March of each year.

[1034]
MEDICAL STUDENT ELECTIVE IN HIV PSYCHIATRY

American Psychiatric Association
Attn: Office of HIV Psychiatry
1000 Wilson Boulevard, Suite 1825
Arlington, VA 22209-3901
(703) 907-8668   Toll Free: (888) 357-7849
Fax: (703) 907-1087   E-mail: aids@psych.org
Web: www.psychiatry.org

Summary To provide an opportunity for Native American and other minority medical students to spend an elective residency learning about HIV psychiatry.
Eligibility This program is open to medical students entering their fourth year at an accredited M.D. or D.O. degree-granting institution. Preference is given to minority candidates and those who have primary interests in services related to HIV/AIDS and substance abuse and its relationship to the mental health or the psychological well-being of ethnic minorities. Applicants should be interested in a psychiatry, internal medicine, pediatrics, or research career. They must be interested in participating in a program that includes intense training in HIV mental health (including neuropsychiatry), a clinical and/or research experience working with a mentor, and participation in the Committee on AIDS of the American Psychiatric Association (APA). U.S. citizenship is required.
Financial data A small stipend is provided (amount not specified).
Duration 1 month.
Additional information The heart of the program is in establishing a mentor relationship at 1 of several sites, becoming involved with a cohort of medical students interested in HIV medicine/psychiatry, participating in an interactive didactic/experimental learning program, and developing expertise in areas related to ethnic minority mental health research or psychiatric services. Students selected for the program who are not APA members automatically receive membership.
Number awarded Varies each year.
Deadline March of each year.

[1035]
MENTAL HEALTH AND SUBSTANCE ABUSE FELLOWSHIP PROGRAM

Council on Social Work Education
Attn: Minority Fellowship Program
1701 Duke Street, Suite 200
Alexandria, VA 22314-3457
(703) 683-2050   Fax: (703) 683-8099
E-mail: mfpy@cswe.org
Web: www.cswe.org

Summary To provide financial assistance to Native American and other racial minority members interested in preparing for a clinical career in the mental health fields.

Eligibility This program is open to U.S. citizens, noncitizen nationals, and permanent residents who have been underrepresented in the field of social work. These include but are not limited to the following groups: American Indians/Alaskan Natives, Asian/Pacific Islanders (e.g., Chinese, East Indians, South Asians, Filipinos, Hawaiians, Japanese, Koreans, and Samoans), Blacks, and Hispanics (e.g., Mexicans/Chicanos, Puerto Ricans, Cubans, Central or South Americans). Applicants must be interested in and committed to a career in mental health and/or substance abuse with specialization in the delivery of services of ethnic and racial minority groups. They must have a degree in social work and be accepted to or enrolled in a full-time master's or doctoral degree program. Selection is based on evidence of strong fit with and commitment to behavioral health services for underserved racial/ethnic populations; life experiences relevant to and/or volunteer or work experience with racial/ethnic populations; high quality scholarly writing showing ability to think and write at the doctoral level; academic evidence of ability to achieve timely degree completion; and fit of the sponsor's mission with the applicant's behavioral health services or research agenda.

Financial data The program provides a monthly stipend (amount not specified), specialized training, and support for professional development.

Duration 1 academic year; renewable for 2 additional years if funds are available and the recipient makes satisfactory progress toward the degree objectives.

Additional information The program has been funded since 1978 by the Center for Mental Health Services (CMHS), the Center for Substance Abuse Prevention (CSAP), and the Center for Substance Abuse Treatment (CSAT) within the Substance Abuse and Mental Health Services Administration. The master's degree program was added in 2014.

Number awarded Varies each year; recently, 40 master's degree students, 12 new doctoral fellows and 12 returning doctoral fellows were appointed.

Deadline February of each year.

[1036]
MENTAL HEALTH RESEARCH DISSERTATION GRANT TO INCREASE WORKFORCE DIVERSITY

National Institute of Mental Health
Attn: Division of Extramural Activities
6001 Executive Boulevard, Room 6138
Bethesda, MD 20892-9609
(301) 443-3534   Fax: (301) 443-4720
TDD: (301) 451-0088   E-mail: armstrda@mail.nih.gov
Web: www.grants.nih.gov

Summary To provide research funding to Native American and other doctoral candidates from underrepresented groups planning to prepare for a research career in any area relevant to mental health and/or mental disorders.

Eligibility This program is open to doctoral candidates conducting dissertation research in a field related to mental health and/or mental disorders at a university, college, or professional school with an accredited doctoral degree granting program. Applicants must be 1) members of an ethnic or racial group that has been determined by the National Science Foundation to be underrepresented in health-related sciences (i.e., African Americans, Hispanic Americans, Alaska Natives, American Indians, Native Hawaiians, and other Pacific Islanders); 2) individuals with disabilities; or 3) individuals from socially, culturally, economically, or educationally disadvantaged backgrounds that have inhibited their ability to prepare for a career in health-related research. They must be U.S. citizens, nationals, or permanent residents.

Financial data The stipend is $23,376. An additional grant up to $15,000 is provided for additional research expenses, fringe benefits (including health insurance), travel to scientific meetings, and research costs of the dissertation. Facilities and administrative costs are limited to 8% of modified total direct costs.

Duration Up to 2 years; nonrenewable.

Number awarded Varies each year.

Deadline Applications must be submitted by February, June, or October of each year.

[1037]
MESCALERO APACHE TRIBAL SCHOLARSHIP

Mescalero Apache Tribe
Attn: Tribal Education Department
148 Cottonwood Drive
P.O. Box 227
Mescalero, NM 88340
(575) 464-9243   Fax: (575) 464-4506
E-mail: mescaleroed@matisp.net
Web: mescaleroapachetribe.com/tribaledu

Summary To provide financial assistance for undergraduate or graduate education to members of the Mescalero Apache Tribe.

Eligibility This program is open to enrolled members of the Mescalero Apache Tribe who are high school seniors, high school graduates, or currently-enrolled undergraduate or graduate students. Applicants must have a GPA of 2.0 or higher and be able to demonstrate financial need. They must enroll full or part time at an accredited college, university, or community college in any state.

Financial data The amount awarded varies, up to $10,000 per year.

Duration 1 year; may be renewed for up to 3 additional years, provided the recipient maintains a GPA of 2.0 or higher as an undergraduate or 3.0 or higher as a graduate student.

Number awarded Varies each year.

Deadline May of each year for the academic year and fall term; October of each year for the spring term; March of each year for the summer session.

[1038]
MICHIGAN INDIAN TUITION WAIVER PROGRAM

Michigan Department of Civil Rights
Attn: Michigan Indian Tuition Waiver
110 West Michigan Avenue, Suite 800
Lansing, MI 48933
(517) 335-3165   Fax: (517) 241-0546
TDD: (517) 241-1965
E-mail: MDCR-INFO@michigan.gov
Web: www.michigan.gov

Summary To exempt members of Indian tribes from tuition at Michigan postsecondary institutions.

Eligibility This program is open to Michigan residents who have lived in the state for at least 12 months and can certify at least one-quarter North American Indian blood from a federally-recognized tribe. Applicants must be attending a public college, university, or community college in Michigan. The program includes full- and part-time study, academic-year and summer school, and undergraduate and graduate work.

Financial data All qualified applicants are entitled to waiver of tuition at Michigan public institutions.

Duration Indian students are entitled to the waiver as long as they attend college in Michigan.

Additional information This program began in 1976 as the result of an agreement between the state of Michigan and the federal government under which the state agreed to provide free tuition to North American Indians in exchange for the Mt. Pleasant Indian School, which the state acquired as a training facility for the developmentally disabled.

Number awarded Varies each year.

Deadline Deadline not specified.

[1039]
MICKEY LELAND ENERGY FELLOWSHIPS

Oak Ridge Institute for Science and Education
Attn: MLEF Fellowship Program
1299 Bethel Valley Road, Building SC-200
P.O. Box 117, MS 36
Oak Ridge, TN 37831-0117
(865) 574-6440   Fax: (865) 576-0734
E-mail: barbara.dunkin@orau.org
Web: orise.orau.gov/mlef/index.html

Summary To provide summer work experience at fossil energy sites of the Department of Energy (DOE) to Native American, other underrepresented minority, and female students or postdoctorates.

Eligibility This program is open to U.S. citizens currently enrolled full time at an accredited college or university. Applicants must be undergraduate, graduate, or postdoctoral students in fields of science, technology (IT), engineering, or mathematics (STEM) and have a GPA of 3.0 or higher. They must be interested in a summer work experience at a DOE fossil energy research facility. Along with their application, they must submit a 100-word statement on why they want to participate in this program. A goal of the program is to recruit women and underrepresented minorities into careers related to fossil energy, although all qualified students are encouraged to apply.

Financial data Weekly stipends are $600 for undergraduates, $750 for master's degree students, or $850 for doctoral and postdoctoral students. Travel costs for a round trip to and from the site and for a trip to a designated place for technical presentations are also paid.

Duration 10 weeks during the summer.

Additional information This program began as 3 separate activities: the Historically Black Colleges and Universities Internship Program established in 1995, the Hispanic Internship Program established in 1998, and the Tribal Colleges and Universities Internship Program, established in 2000. Those 3 programs were merged into the Fossil Energy Minority Education Initiative, renamed the Mickey Leland Energy Fellowship Program in 2000. Sites to which interns may be assigned include the National Energy Technology Laboratory (Morgantown, West Virginia, Albany, Oregon and Pittsburgh, Pennsylvania), Pacific Northwest National Laboratory (Richland, Washington), Sandia National Laboratory (Livermore, California), Lawrence Berkeley National Laboratory (Berkeley, California), Los Alamos National Laboratory (Los Alamos, New Mexico), Strategic Petroleum Reserve Project Management Office (New Orleans, Louisiana), or U.S. Department of Energy Headquarters (Washington, D.C.).

Number awarded Varies each year; recently, 30 students participated in this program.

Deadline December of each year.

[1040]
MIDWIVES OF COLOR-WATSON MIDWIFERY STUDENT SCHOLARSHIP

American College of Nurse-Midwives
Attn: ACNM Foundation, Inc.
8403 Colesville Road, Suite 1550
Silver Spring, MD 20910-6374
(240) 485-1850   Fax: (240) 485-1818
E-mail: foundation@acnmf.org
Web: www.midwife.org

Summary To provide financial assistance for midwifery education to Native American and other students of color who belong to the American College of Nurse-Midwives (ACNM).

Eligibility This program is open to ACNM members of color who are currently enrolled in an accredited basic midwife education program and have successfully completed 1 academic or clinical semester/quarter or clinical module. Applicants must submit they must submit a 150-word essay on their 5-year midwifery career plans; a 150-word essay on their intended future participation in the local, regional, and/or national activities of the ACNM; a 150-word essay on their need for financial assistance; and a 100-word statement on how they would use the funds if they receive the scholarship. Selection is based on academic excellence, leadership potential, and financial need.

Financial data The stipend is $3,000.

Duration 1 year.

Number awarded Varies each year; recently, 3 were awarded.

Deadline February of each year.

[1041]
MILBANK DIVERSITY SCHOLARS PROGRAM

Milbank, Tweed, Hadley & McCloy LLP
Attn: Diversity Committee Chair
28 Liberty Street
New York, NY 10005
(212) 530-5545   Fax: (212) 822-5545
E-mail: etaylor@milbank.com
Web: www.milbank.com

Summary To provide financial assistance and work experience to law students, especially Native Americans members of other groups underrepresented at large law firms.

Eligibility This program is open to students who have completed their first year of a full-time J.D. program at an ABA-accredited law school. Joint degree candidates must have successfully completed 2 years of a J.D. program. Applications are particularly encouraged from members of groups traditionally underrepresented at large law firms who will contribute to the firm's goal of recruiting people regardless of race, religion, color, age, gender, veteran status, national origin, gender identity and expression, sexual orientation, physical challenge, or marital or family status. Applicants must submit a 500-word essay on 1) the challenges they have faced in pursuit of a legal career that have helped them understand the value of diversity and inclusion in the legal profession; and 2) the personal contributions they would make to furthering the diversity objectives of the sponsoring law firm. Selection is based on academic achievement, demonstrated leadership ability, writing and interpersonal skills, and interest in the firm's practice.

Financial data The stipend is $25,000. A paid associate position during the summer after the second year of law school is also provided. If the student is offered and accepts a permanent position with the firm after graduation, an additional $25,000 scholarship stipend is also awarded.

Duration 1 year (the third year of law school).

Additional information Scholars may be offered a permanent position with the firm, but there is no guarantee of such an offer.

Number awarded At least 2 each year.

Deadline August of each year.

[1042]
MILLER JOHNSON WEST MICHIGAN DIVERSITY LAW SCHOOL SCHOLARSHIP

Grand Rapids Community Foundation
Attn: Education Program Officer
185 Oakes Street S.W.
Grand Rapids, MI 49503-4008
(616) 454-1751, ext. 103   Fax: (616) 454-6455
E-mail: rbishop@grfoundation.org
Web: www.grfoundation.org/scholarshipslist

Summary To provide financial assistance to Native Americans and other minorities from Michigan who are attending law school in any state.

Eligibility This program is open to U.S. citizens who are students of color (African American, Asian, Hispanic, Native American, Pacific Islander) and residents of Michigan. Applicants must be attending an accredited law school in any state. They must have a GPA of 3.0 or higher and be able to demonstrate financial need.

Financial data The stipend is $5,000. Funds are paid directly to the recipient's institution.

Duration 1 year.

Number awarded 1 each year.

Deadline March of each year.

[1043]
MILLER NASH DIVERSITY FELLOWSHIPS

Miller Nash Graham & Dunn LLP
Attn: Director of Recruiting
111 S.W. Fifth Avenue, Suite 3400
Portland, OR 97204-3699
(503) 224-5858   Fax: (503) 224-0155
E-mail: MNrecruiting@millernash.com
Web: www.millernash.com

Summary To provide financial assistance and work experience to Native American and other law students who contribute to diversity and are interested in living and working in the Pacific Northwest following graduation from law school.

Eligibility This program is open to first-year students at ABA-accredited law schools in any state. Applicants must be able to demonstrate academic excellence, interpersonal skills, leadership qualities, contributions to diversity (including gender, age, race, disability, nationality, and sexual orientation), and meaningful contributions to the community. They must intend to work, live, and practice law in the Pacific Northwest. Along with their application, they must submit a personal statement of 2 to 4 pages that includes a description of organizations or projects in which they currently participate or have participated that address diversity issues or support diversity in their legal, business, or local communities.

Financial data Fellows receive a paid summer clerk position and a stipend of $7,500 for law school.

Duration 1 year (including 12 weeks for the summer clerk position); nonrenewable.

Number awarded 2 each year: 1 for a summer clerk position in Portland and 1 in Seattle.

Deadline January of each year.

[1044]
MINNESOTA AMERICAN INDIAN BAR ASSOCIATION LAW STUDENT SCHOLARSHIPS

Minnesota American Indian Bar Association
Attn: MAIBA Scholarship Committee
P.O. Box 3712
Minneapolis, MN 55403
(612) 339-0517   Fax: (612) 349-6059
E-mail: angeldaher@msn.com
Web: www.maiba.org/scholarship

Summary To provide financial assistance to Native American students from any state who are enrolled at law schools in Minnesota.

Eligibility This program is open to students who are enrolled members of an Indian tribe or band or recognized by their community of residence or origin as being Indian. Applicants must be a second- or third-year law student at a Minnesota law school, demonstrate that they are currently in academic good standing, demonstrate that they have unmet financial need, submit a written personal statement, and submit at least 1 letter of recommendation.

Financial data The stipend ranges from $500 to $3,000.

Duration　1 year.

Number awarded　Varies each year; recently, 3 were awarded.

Deadline　October of each year.

[1045]
MINNESOTA INDIAN SCHOLARSHIP PROGRAM

Minnesota Office of Higher Education
Attn: Minnesota Indian Scholarship Program
1450 Energy Park Drive, Suite 350
St. Paul, MN 55108-5227
(651) 642-0567　　　　　　Toll Free: (800) 657-3866
Fax: (651) 642-0675　　　　TDD: (800) 627-3529
E-mail: info.ohe@state.mn.us
Web: www.ohe.state.mn.us/mPg.cfm?pageID=149

Summary　To provide financial assistance to Native Americans in Minnesota who are interested in working on an undergraduate or graduate degree in any field.

Eligibility　Applicants must be at least one-fourth degree Indian ancestry; members of a recognized Indian tribe; at least high school graduates (or approved equivalent); accepted by an accredited college, university, or vocational school in Minnesota; and residents of Minnesota for at least 1 year. Undergraduates must be attending college at least three-fourths time; graduate students must be enrolled at least half time.

Financial data　The stipend depends on need, to a maximum of $4,000 per year for undergraduates or $6,000 per year for graduate students. Awards are paid directly to the student's school or college.

Duration　1 year; may be renewed up to 4 additional years plus an additional 5 years of graduate study.

Number awarded　Approximately 700 each year.

Deadline　June of each year.

[1046]
MINORITIES IN GOVERNMENT FINANCE SCHOLARSHIP

Government Finance Officers Association
Attn: Scholarship Committee
203 North LaSalle Street, Suite 2700
Chicago, IL 60601-1210
(312) 977-9700　　　　　　Fax: (312) 977-4806
Web: www.gfoa.org

Summary　To provide financial assistance to Native American and other minority upper-division and graduate students who are preparing for a career in state and local government finance.

Eligibility　This program is open to upper-division and graduate students who are preparing for a career in public finance by working on a degree in public administration, accounting, finance, political science, economics, or business administration (with a specific focus on government or nonprofit management). Applicants must be members of a minority group, citizens or permanent residents of the United States or Canada, and able to provide a letter of recommendation from a representative of their school. Selection is based on career plans, academic record, plan of study, letters of recommendation, and GPA. Financial need is not considered.

Financial data　The stipend is $6,000.

Duration　1 year.

Additional information　This program defines minorities as Blacks or African Americans, American Indians or Alaskan Natives, Hispanics or Latinos, Native Hawaiians or other Pacific Islanders, or Asians.

Number awarded　1 each year.

Deadline　February of each year.

[1047]
MINORITY AND UNDERREPRESENTED ENVIRONMENTAL LITERACY PROGRAM

Missouri Department of Higher Education
Attn: Student Financial Assistance
205 Jefferson Street
P.O. Box 1469
Jefferson City, MO 65102-1469
(573) 751-2361　　　　　　Toll Free: (800) 473-6757
Fax: (573) 751-6635　　　　E-mail: info@dhe.mo.gov
Web: www.dhe.mo.gov/ppc/grants/muelp_0310_final.php

Summary　To provide financial assistance to Native American and other underrepresented students from Missouri who are or will be working on a bachelor's or master's degree in an environmental field.

Eligibility　This program is open to residents of Missouri who are high school seniors or current undergraduate or graduate students enrolled or planning to enroll full time at a college or university in the state. Priority is given to members of the following underrepresented minority ethnic groups: African Americans, Hispanic or Latino Americans, Native Americans and Alaska Natives, and Native Hawaiians and Pacific Islanders. Applicants must be working on or planning to work on a bachelor's or master's degree in 1) engineering (civil, chemical, environmental, mechanical, or agricultural); 2) environmental studies (geology, biology, wildlife management, natural resource planning, natural resources, or a closely-related course of study); 3) environmental chemistry; or 4) environmental law enforcement. They must be U.S. citizens or permanent residents or otherwise lawfully present in the United States. Graduating high school seniors must have a GPA of 3.0 or higher; students currently enrolled in college or graduate school must have a GPA of 2.5 or higher. Along with their application, they must submit a 1-page essay on why they are applying for this scholarship, 3 letters of recommendation, a resume of school and community activities, and transcripts that include SAT or ACT scores. Financial need is not considered in the selection process.

Financial data　Stipends vary each year; recently, they averaged approximately $3,045 per year.

Duration　1 year; may be renewed if the recipient maintains a GPA of 2.5 or higher and full-time enrollment.

Additional information　This program was established by the Missouri Department of Natural Resources but transferred to the Department of Higher Education in 2009.

Number awarded　Varies each year.

Deadline　May of each year.

[1048]
MINORITY FACULTY DEVELOPMENT SCHOLARSHIP AWARD IN PHYSICAL THERAPY

American Physical Therapy Association
Attn: Honors and Awards Program
1111 North Fairfax Street
Alexandria, VA 22314-1488
(703) 684-APTA   Toll Free: (800) 999-APTA, ext. 8082
Fax: (703) 684-7343   TDD: (703) 683-6748
E-mail: honorsandawards@apta.org
Web: www.apta.org

Summary To provide financial assistance to Native American and other minority faculty members in physical therapy who are interested in working on a post-professional doctoral degree.

Eligibility This program is open to U.S. citizens and permanent residents who are members of the following minority groups: African American or Black, Asian, Native Hawaiian or other Pacific Islander, American Indian or Alaska Native, or Hispanic/Latino. Applicants must be full-time faculty members, teaching in an accredited or developing professional physical therapist education program, who will have completed the equivalent of 2 full semesters of post-professional doctoral course work. They must possess a license to practice physical therapy in a U.S. jurisdiction and be enrolled as a student in an accredited post-professional doctoral program whose content has a demonstrated relationship to physical therapy. Along with their application, they must submit a personal essay on their professional goals, including their plans to contribute to the profession and minority services. Selection is based on contributions in the area of minority affairs and services and contributions to the profession of physical therapy. Preference is given to members of the American Physical Therapy Association (APTA).

Financial data A stipend is awarded (amount not specified).

Duration 1 year.

Additional information This program began in 1999.

Number awarded 1 or more each year.

Deadline November of each year.

[1049]
MINORITY FELLOWSHIPS IN ENVIRONMENTAL LAW

New York State Bar Association
Attn: Environmental Law Section
One Elk Street
Albany, NY 12207
(518) 463-3200   Fax: (518) 487-5517
E-mail: lbataille@nysba.org
Web: www.nysba.org

Summary To provide an opportunity for Native American and other minority law students from New York to gain summer work experience in environmental law.

Eligibility This program is open to law students who are African American, Latino, Native American, Alaskan Native, Asian, or Pacific Islander. Applicants must be residents of New York or attending law school in that state. They must be interested in a summer internship working on legal matters for a government environmental agency or public interest environmental organization in New York State. Selection is based on interest in environmental issues, academic record (undergraduate and/or law school), personal qualities, leadership abilities, and financial need.

Financial data The stipend is $6,000.

Duration At least 10 weeks during the summer.

Additional information This program began in 1992.

Number awarded 1 each year.

Deadline December of each year.

[1050]
MINORITY MEDICAL STUDENT AWARD PROGRAM OF THE AMERICAN SOCIETY OF HEMATOLOGY

American Society of Hematology
Attn: Awards Manager
2021 L Street, N.W., Suite 900
Washington, DC 20036
(202) 776-0544   Fax: (202) 776-0545
E-mail: awards@hematology.org
Web: www.hematology.org

Summary To provide an opportunity for Native American and other underrepresented minority medical students to conduct a research project in hematology.

Eligibility This program is open to medical students enrolled in D.O., M.D., or M.D./Ph.D. programs in the United States or Canada who are members of minority groups. For purposes of this program, minority is defined as a member of a racial or ethnic group that has been shown to be underrepresented in health-related sciences in the United States and Canada, including American Indians, Alaska Natives, Blacks or African Americans, Hispanics or Latinos, Native Hawaiians, other Pacific Islanders, African Canadians, Inuit, and First Nation Peoples. Applicants must be interested in conducting a research project in hematology at their home institution or at another institution that has agreed to host them. They must work with 2 mentors who are members of the American Society of Hematology (ASH): a research mentor who oversees the participant's work and progress and a career development mentor (who is from the same minority group as the student) who participates for the duration of the program. U.S. or Canadian citizenship or permanent resident status is required.

Financial data The grant includes $5,000 for research support, an additional $1,000 to support travel to the annual meeting of the ASH, and another $1,000 for making a short presentation about the research experience at a special reception at the ASH annual meeting. Research mentors receive an allowance of $2,000 for supplies and $1,000 for attendance at the ASH annual meeting. Career development mentors receives $1,000 as a travel allowance each time they accompany the student to an ASH annual meeting during their remaining years of medical school and residency.

Duration 8 to 12 weeks.

Additional information This program is supported by Amgen, Celgene Corporation, Cephalon Oncology, and Genentech BioOncology.

Number awarded Up to 10 each year.

Deadline March of each year.

[1051]
MINORITY MEDICAL STUDENT SUMMER EXTERNSHIP IN ADDICTION PSYCHIATRY

American Psychiatric Association
Attn: Division of Diversity and Health Equity
1000 Wilson Boulevard, Suite 1825
Arlington, VA 22209-3901
(703) 907-8653   Toll Free: (888) 35-PSYCH
Fax: (703) 907-7852   E-mail: mking@psych.org
Web: www.psychiatry.org/minority-fellowship

Summary To provide funding to Native American and other minority medical students who are interested in working on a research externship during the summer with a mentor who specializes in addiction psychiatry.

Eligibility This program is open to minority medical students who have a specific interest in services related to substance abuse treatment and prevention. Minorities include American Indians, Alaska Natives, Native Hawaiians, Asian Americans, Hispanics/Latinos, and African Americans. Applicants must be interested in working with a mentor who specializes in addiction psychiatry. Work settings provide an emphasis on working clinically with or studying underserved minority populations and issues of co-occurring disorders, substance abuse treatment, and mental health disparity. Most of them are in inner-city or rural settings.

Financial data Externships provide $1,500 for travel expenses to go to the work setting of the mentor and up to another $1,500 for out-of-pocket expenses directly related to the conduct of the externship.

Duration 1 month during the summer.

Additional information Funding for this program is provided by the Substance Abuse and Mental Health Services Administration (SAMHSA).

Number awarded 10 each year.

Deadline March of each year.

[1052]
MINORITY TEACHERS OF ILLINOIS SCHOLARSHIP PROGRAM

Illinois Student Assistance Commission
Attn: Scholarship and Grant Services
1755 Lake Cook Road
Deerfield, IL 60015-5209
(847) 948-8550   Toll Free: (800) 899-ISAC
Fax: (847) 831-8549   TDD: (800) 526-0844
E-mail: isac.studentservices@isac.illinois.gov
Web: www.isac.org

Summary To provide scholarship/loans to Native Americans and other minority students in Illinois who plan to become teachers at the preschool, elementary, or secondary level.

Eligibility Applicants must be Illinois residents, U.S. citizens or eligible noncitizens, members of a minority group (African American/Black, Hispanic American, Asian American, or Native American), and high school graduates or holders of a General Educational Development (GED) certificate. They must be enrolled at least half time as an undergraduate or graduate student, have a GPA of 2.5 or higher, not be in default on any student loan, and be enrolled or accepted for enrollment in a teacher education program.

Financial data Grants up to $5,000 per year are awarded. This is a scholarship/loan program. Recipients must agree to teach full time 1 year for each year of support received. The teaching agreement may be fulfilled at a public, private, or parochial preschool, elementary school, or secondary school in Illinois; at least 30% of the student body at those schools must be minority. It must be fulfilled within the 5-year period following the completion of the undergraduate program for which the scholarship was awarded. The time period may be extended if the recipient serves in the U.S. armed forces, enrolls full time in a graduate program related to teaching, becomes temporarily disabled, is unable to find employment as a teacher at a qualifying school, or takes additional courses on at least a half-time basis to obtain certification as a teacher in Illinois. Recipients who fail to honor this work obligation must repay the award with 5% interest.

Duration 1 year; may be renewed for a total of 8 semesters or 12 quarters.

Number awarded Varies each year.

Deadline Priority consideration is given to applications received by February of each year.

[1053]
MITCH SPERRY MEMORIAL LAW SCHOLARSHIP

Chickasaw Foundation
2020 Arlington, Suite 4
P.O. Box 1726
Ada, OK 74821-1726
(580) 421-9030   Fax: (580) 421-9031
E-mail: ChickasawFoundation@chickasaw.net
Web: www.chickasawfoundation.org/Scholarships.aspx

Summary To provide financial assistance to members of the Chickasaw Nation who are interested in working on an undergraduate or graduate degree in a field related to law.

Eligibility This program is open to Chickasaw students who are currently enrolled at an accredited 4-year college or university as a full-time undergraduate or law student. Applicants must be working on a degree in law, pre-law, legal studies, paralegal, or any major associated with law or a bachelor's degree obtained with the intention of pursuing a law degree. They must have a GPA of 3.0 or higher. Along with their application, they must submit high school, college, and/or law school transcripts; 2 letters of recommendation; a copy of their Chickasaw Nation citizenship card; a 2-page list of honors, achievements, awards, club memberships, societies, and civic involvement; and a 1-page essay on their long-term goals and plans for achieving those. Financial need is not considered in the selection process.

Financial data A stipend is awarded (amount not specified).

Duration 1 year.

Number awarded 1 each year.

Deadline June of each year.

[1054]
MLA/NLM SPECTRUM SCHOLARSHIPS

Medical Library Association
Attn: Grants Coordinator
65 East Wacker Place, Suite 1900
Chicago, IL 60601-7246
(312) 419-9094, ext. 15   Fax: (312) 419-8950
E-mail: awards@mail.mlahq.org
Web: www.mlanet.org/p/cm/ld/fid=449

Summary To provide financial assistance to Native American and members of other minority groups interested in preparing for a career as a medical librarian.

Eligibility This program is open to members of minority groups (African Americans, Hispanics, Asian, Native Americans, and Pacific Islanders) who are attending library schools accredited by the American Library Association (ALA). Applicants must be interested in preparing for a career as a health sciences information professional.

Financial data The stipend is $3,250.

Duration 1 year.

Additional information This program, established in 2001, is jointly sponsored by the Medical Library Association (MLA) and the National Library of Medicine (NLM) of the U.S. National Institutes of Health (NIH). It operates as a component of the Spectrum Initiative Scholarship program of the ALA.

Number awarded 2 each year.

Deadline February of each year.

[1055]
MLA SCHOLARSHIP FOR MINORITY STUDENTS

Medical Library Association
Attn: Grants Coordinator
65 East Wacker Place, Suite 1900
Chicago, IL 60601-7246
(312) 419-9094, ext. 15   Fax: (312) 419-8950
E-mail: awards@mail.mlahq.org
Web: www.mlanet.org/p/cm/ld/fid=304

Summary To assist Native American and other minority students interested in preparing for a career in medical librarianship.

Eligibility This program is open to racial minority students (Asians, Blacks or African Americans, Hispanics or Latinos, Aboriginals, North American Indians or Alaskan Natives, Native Hawaiians, or other Pacific Islanders) who are entering an ALA-accredited graduate program in librarianship or who have completed less than half of their academic requirements for a master's degree in library science. They must be interested in preparing for a career in medical librarianship. Selection is based on academic record, letters of reference, professional potential, and the applicant's statement of career objectives. U.S. or Canadian citizenship or permanent resident status is required.

Financial data The stipend is $5,000.

Duration 1 year.

Additional information This program began in 1973.

Number awarded 1 each year.

Deadline November of each year.

[1056]
MONTANA AMERICAN INDIAN STUDENT WAIVER

Office of the Commissioner of Higher Education
Attn: Montana University System
State Scholarship Coordinator
2500 Broadway
P.O. Box 203201
Helena, MT 59620-3201
(406) 444-6570   Toll Free: (800) 537-7508
Fax: (406) 444-1469   E-mail: snewlun@montana.edu
Web: www.mus.edu

Summary To provide financial assistance to Montana Indians interested in attending college or graduate school in the state.

Eligibility Eligible to apply are Native American students (one-quarter Indian blood or more) who have been residents of Montana for at least 1 year prior to application, have graduated from an accredited high school or federal Indian school, and can demonstrate financial need.

Financial data Students eligible for this benefit are entitled to attend any unit of the Montana University System without payment of undergraduate or graduate registration or incidental fees.

Duration Students are eligible for continued fee waiver as long as they maintain reasonable academic progress and full-time status (12 or more credits for undergraduates, 9 or more credits for graduate students).

Number awarded Varies; more than $1 million in waivers are approved each year.

Deadline Deadline not specified.

[1057]
MOONIENE OGEE MEMORIAL SCHOLARSHIP

Chickasaw Foundation
2020 Arlington, Suite 4
P.O. Box 1726
Ada, OK 74821-1726
(580) 421-9030   Fax: (580) 421-9031
E-mail: ChickasawFoundation@chickasaw.net
Web: www.chickasawfoundation.org/Scholarships.aspx

Summary To provide financial assistance to members of the Chickasaw Nation who are working on an undergraduate or graduate degree in education.

Eligibility This program is open to Chickasaw students who are currently working full time on an undergraduate, graduate, or doctoral degree in education. Applicants must have a GPA of 2.5 or higher. Along with their application, they must submit high school or college transcripts; 2 letters of recommendation; a copy of their Chickasaw Nation citizenship card; a 2-page list of honors, achievements, awards, club memberships, societies, and civic involvement; and a 1-page essay on their long-term goals and plans for achieving those. Financial need is not considered in the selection process.

Financial data A stipend is awarded (amount not specified).

Duration 1 year.

Number awarded 1 each year.

Deadline June of each year.

[1058]
MORGAN LEWIS DIVERSITY FELLOWSHIP PROGRAM

Morgan Lewis
Attn: Lindsay Callantine, Firmwide Director of Attorney
  Recruiting
1701 Market Street
Philadelphia, PA 19103-2921
(215) 963-5105   Fax: (215) 963-5001
E-mail: diversityfellowship@morganlewis.com
Web: www.morganlewis.com/careers/life-at-morgan-lewis

Summary To provide work experience at offices of Morgan Lewis to Native American and other law students who will contribute diversity to the profession.

Eligibility This program is open to students entering the second year of law school who will promote diversity at the firm and within the legal community. Applicants must have demonstrated academic excellence, have outstanding leadership skills, have an interest in employment with Morgan Lewis, and have a demonstrated interest in promoting diversity.

Financial data The program provides a paid summer associateship (salary not specified) and a stipend of $15,000, of which half is paid when the associate accepts an offer of employment and half is paid upon commencement of associate employment.

Duration 1 year and 1 summer.

Additional information This program began in 2008. The firm's U.S. offices where associates may elect to perform their service are located in Boston, Chicago, Dallas, Harrisburg, Houston, Irvine, Los Angeles, Miami, New York, Palo Alto, Philadelphia, Pittsburgh, Princeton, San Francisco, Washington, and Wilmington.

Number awarded Up to 4 each year.

Deadline September of each year.

[1059]
MORGAN STANLEY MBA FELLOWSHIP

Morgan Stanley
Attn: Diversity Recruiting
1585 Broadway
New York, NY 10036
(212) 762-0211   Toll Free: (888) 454-3965
Fax: (212) 507-4972
E-mail: mbafellowship@morganstanley.com
Web: www.morganstanley.com

Summary To provide financial assistance and work experience to Native Americans and members of other underrepresented groups who are working on an M.B.A. degree.

Eligibility This program is open to full-time M.B.A. students who are women, African Americans, Hispanics, Native Americans, or lesbian/gay/bisexual/transgender. Selection is based on assigned essays, academic achievement, recommendations, extracurricular activities, leadership qualities, and on-site interviews.

Financial data The program provides full payment of tuition and fees and a paid summer internship.

Duration 1 year; may be renewed for a second year, providing the student remains enrolled full time in good academic standing and completes the summer internship following the first year.

Additional information The paid summer internship is offered within Morgan Stanley institutional securities (equity research, fixed income, institutional equity, investment banking), investment management, or private wealth management. This program was established in 1999.

Number awarded 1 or more each year.

Deadline December of each year.

[1060]
MORRISON & FOERSTER 1L DIVERSITY FELLOWSHIP PROGRAM

Morrison & Foerster
Attn: Natalie Kernisant, Attorney Recruiting Diversity
  Manager
425 Market Street
San Francisco, CA 94105-2482
(415) 268-7000   Fax: (415) 268-7522
E-mail: diversityfellowship@mofo.com
Web: www.mofo.com

Summary To provide financial assistance and work experience at Morrison & Foerster to law students who are Native Americans or members of other underrepresented groups.

Eligibility This program is open to members of a diverse population that has historically been underrepresented in the legal profession (women, minorities, and LGBT persons) who are U.S. citizens or otherwise authorized to work in the United States. Applicants must be enrolled full time in their first year at an ABA-accredited law school. They must be interested in participating in a program that includes summer employment at the sponsoring law firm. Selection is based on academic performance, demonstrated leadership qualities, and community involvement.

Financial data The program provides paid internships during the summers following the first and second years of law school and a stipend of $15,000, paid in 2 equal installments: first following agreement to return for the second summer internship and second following acceptance of full-time associate employment following law school graduation.

Duration 2 years, including summers.

Additional information Recipients may perform their summer internship at the firm's offices in Denver, Los Angeles, New York, Palo Alto, Sacramento, San Diego, San Francisco, northern Virginia, or Washington, D.C.

Number awarded Up to 10 each year.

Deadline January of each year.

[1061]
MOSS ADAMS FOUNDATION SCHOLARSHIP

Educational Foundation for Women in Accounting
Attn: Foundation Administrator
136 South Keowee Street
Dayton, OH 45402
(937) 424-3391   Fax: (937) 222-5749
E-mail: info@efwa.org
Web: www.efwa.org/scholarships_graduate.php

Summary To provide financial support to women, including minority women, who are working on an accounting degree.

Eligibility This program is open to women who are enrolled in an accounting degree program at an accredited college or university. Applicants must meet 1 of the following criteria: 1) women pursuing a fifth-year requirement either through general studies or within a graduate program; 2) women returning to school as current or reentry juniors or seniors; or 3) minority women. Selection is based on aptitude for accounting and business, commitment to the goal of working on a degree in accounting (including evidence of continued commitment after receiving this award), clear evidence that the candidate has established goals and a plan for achieving those goals (both personal and professional), financial need, and a demonstration of how the scholarship will impact her life. U.S. citizenship is required.

Financial data The stipend is $1,000.

Duration 1 year.

Additional information This program was established by Rowling, Dold & Associates LLP, a woman-owned C.P.A. firm based in San Diego. It was renamed when that firm merged with Moss Adams LLP.

Number awarded 2 each year: 1 to an undergraduate and 1 to a graduate student.

Deadline April of each year.

[1062]
MSCPA MINORITY SCHOLARSHIPS

Missouri Society of Certified Public Accountants
Attn: MSCPA Educational Foundation
540 Maryville Centre Drive, Suite 200
P.O. Box 958868
St. Louis, MO 63195-8868
(314) 997-7966   Toll Free: (800) 264-7966 (within MO)
Fax: (314) 997-2592   E-mail: dhull@mocpa.org
Web: www.mocpa.org/students/scholarships

Summary To provide financial assistance to Native American and other minority residents of Missouri who are working on an undergraduate or graduate degree in accounting at a university in the state.

Eligibility This program is open to members of minority groups underrepresented in the accounting profession (Black/African American, Hispanic/Latino, Native American, Asian American) who are currently working full time on an undergraduate or graduate degree in accounting at a college or university in Missouri. Applicants must either be residents of Missouri or the children of members of the Missouri Society of Certified Public Accountants (MSCPA). They must be U.S. citizens, have completed at least 30 semester hours of college work, have a GPA of 3.3 or higher, and be student members of the MSCPA. Selection is based on the GPA, involvement in MSCPA, educator recommendations, and leadership potential. Financial need is not considered.

Financial data The stipend is $1,250 per year.

Duration 1 year; may be renewed.

Number awarded Varies each year; recently, 3 were awarded.

Deadline February of each year.

[1063]
MSIPP INTERNSHIPS

Department of Energy
Office of Environmental Management
Savannah River National Laboratory
Attn: MSIPP Program Manager
Building 773-41A, 232
Aiken, SC 29808
(803) 725-9032   E-mail: connie.yung@srnl.doe.gov
Web: srnl.doe.gov/msipp/internships.htm

Summary To provide an opportunity for undergraduate and graduate students at Minority Serving Institutions (MSIs) to work on a summer research project at designated National Laboratories of the U.S. Department of Energy (DOE).

Eligibility This program is open to full-time undergraduate and graduate students enrolled at an accredited MSI. Applicants must be interested in working during the summer on a research project at a participating DOE National Laboratory. They must be working on a degree in a field of science, technology, engineering, or mathematics (STEM); the specific field depends on the particular project on which they wish to work. Their GPA must be 3.0 or higher. U.S. citizenship is required.

Financial data The stipend depends on the cost of living at the location of the host laboratory.

Duration 10 weeks during the summer.

Additional information This program is administered at the Savannah River National Laboratory (SRNL) in Aiken, South Carolina, which serves as the National Laboratory for the DOE Office of Environmental Management. The other participating National Laboratories are Argonne National Laboratory (ANL) in Argonne, Illinois, Idaho National Laboratory (INL) in Idaho Falls, Idaho, Los Alamos National Laboratory (LANL) in Los Alamos, New Mexico, Oak Ridge National Laboratory (ORNL) in Oak Ridge, Tennessee, and Pacific Northwest National Laboratory (PNNL) in Richland, Washington. The program began in 2016.

Number awarded Varies each year. Recently, the program offered 11 research projects at SRNL, 12 at ANL, 1 at INL, 7 at LANL, 4 at ORNL, and 7 at PNNL.

Deadline March of each year.

[1064]
MULTICULTURAL AUDIENCE DEVELOPMENT INITIATIVE INTERNSHIPS

Metropolitan Museum of Art
Attn: Internship Programs
1000 Fifth Avenue
New York, NY 10028-0198
(212) 570-3710   Fax: (212) 570-3782
E-mail: mmainterns@metmuseum.org
Web: www.metmuseum.org

Summary To provide summer work experience at the Metropolitan Museum of Art to Native American and other college undergraduates, graduate students, and recent graduates from diverse backgrounds.

Eligibility This program is open to members of diverse groups who are undergraduate juniors and seniors, students currently working on a master's degree, or individuals who completed a bachelor's or master's degree within the past year. Ph.D. students may be eligible to apply during the first

12 months of their program, provided they have not yet achieved candidacy. Students from various academic backgrounds are encouraged to apply, but they must be interested in preparing for a career in the arts and museum fields. Freshmen and sophomores are not eligible.

Financial data   The stipend is $3,750.

Duration   10 weeks, beginning in June.

Additional information   Interns are assigned to departmental projects (curatorial, administration, or education) at the Metropolitan Museum of Art; other assignments may include giving gallery talks and working at the Visitor Information Center. The assignment is for 35 hours a week. The internships are funded by the Multicultural Audience Initiative at the museum.

Number awarded   1 or more each year.

Deadline   January of each year.

[1065]
MUNGER TOLLES & OLSON DIVERSITY SUMMER PROGRAM

Munger Tolles & Olson LLP
Attn: Kevinn C. Villard, Director of Legal Recruiting
355 South Grand Avenue, 35th Floor
Los Angeles, CA 90071-1560
(213) 683-9242   E-mail: Kevinn.Villard@mto.com
Web: www.mto.com/careers/1L-Diversity-Summer-Program

Summary   To provide summer work experience in public interest law at Munger Tolles & Olson to Native American and other law students who will contribute to diversity of the law profession.

Eligibility   This program is open to first-year law students who contribute to the diversity of the sponsoring firm and the legal community, including 1) members of racial or ethnic minority groups; 2) are gay, lesbian, bisexual, or transgender; 3) are physically challenged; or 4) are from disadvantaged socioeconomic backgrounds. Applicants must be interested in a summer associateship at the firm's offices in Los Angeles or San Francisco that includes performing work for a nonprofit organization in those areas. Selection is based on 1) academic, employment, community, and other achievements indicating the potential for success in law school and in the legal profession; 2) contribution to diversity of the firm and the legal community; and 3) a personal statement describing their interest in the program and how they would contribute to the diversity of the legal profession.

Financial data   Participates receive a stipend (amount not specified) from the firm for the entire length of the program, including their service to a nonprofit organization.

Duration   11 weeks during the summer, including 7 weeks in an office and 4 weeks at a nonprofit organization.

Number awarded   Up to 6 each year.

Deadline   February of each year.

[1066]
NASA EDUCATION AERONAUTICS SCHOLARSHIP AND ADVANCED STEM TRAINING AND RESEARCH FELLOWSHIP

National Aeronautics and Space Administration
Attn: National Scholarship Deputy Program Manager
Office of Education and Public Outreach
Ames Research Center
Moffett Field, CA 94035
(650) 604-6958   E-mail: elizabeth.a.cartier@nasa.gov
Web: nspires.nasaprs.com

Summary   To provide financial assistance to Nativ Americans and members of other underrepresented groups interested in working on a graduate degree in fields of science, technology, engineering, and mathematics (STEM) of interest to the U.S. National Aeronautics and Space Administration (NASA).

Eligibility   This program (identified as AS&ASTAR) is open to students who have a bachelor's degree and have historically been underrepresented in NASA-related fields (women, minorities, persons with disabilities, and veterans). Applicants must be working on a research-based master's or doctoral degree in a NASA-related field of STEM, including chemistry, computer and information science and engineering, geosciences (e.g., geophysics, hydrology, oceanography, paleontology, planetary science), engineering (e.g., aeronautical, aerospace, biomedical, chemical, civil, computer, electrical, electronic, environmental, industrial, materials, mechanical, nuclear, ocean, optical, systems), life sciences (e.g., biochemistry, cell biology, environmental biology, genetics, neurosciences, physiology), materials research, mathematical sciences, or physics and astronomy). They must arrange with a researcher at a NASA Center to serve as a technical adviser in collaboration with the student's faculty adviser. Research must be conducted at a NASA Center as a team project involving the student, the faculty adviser, and the NASA technical adviser. In the selection process, consideration is given to the proposed use of NASA facilities, content, and people. Applications must include a plan for a Center-Based Research Experience (CBRE) to be conducted during the summer at the NASA facility. Students must be U.S. citizens and have a GPA of 3.0 or higher.

Financial data   Grants provide a stipend of $25,000 for master's degree students or $30,000 for doctoral candidates, $10,000 for tuition offset and fees, $8,000 as a CBRE allowance, $1,000 as a health insurance allowance, $4,500 as a faculty adviser allowance, and $1,500 as a fellow professional development allowance.

Duration   1 year; may be renewed up to 2 additional years.

Additional information   The participating NASA facilities are Ames Research Center (Moffett Field, California), Armstrong Flight Research Center (Edwards, California), Glenn Research Center (Cleveland, Ohio), Goddard Space Flight Center (Greenbelt, Maryland), Jet Propulsion Laboratory (Pasadena, California), Johnson Space Center (Houston, Texas), Kennedy Space Center (Kennedy Space Center, Florida), Langley Research Center (Hampton, Virginia), Marshall Space Flight Center (Marshall Space Flight Center, Alabama), and Stennis Space Center (Stennis Space Center, Mississippi).

Number awarded   At least 13 each year.

Deadline   June of each year.

[1067]
NASP-ERT MINORITY SCHOLARSHIP PROGRAM

National Association of School Psychologists
Attn: Education and Research Trust
4340 East-West Highway, Suite 402
Bethesda, MD 20814
(301) 657-0270   Toll Free: (866) 331-NASP
Fax: (301) 657-0275   TDD: (301) 657-4155
E-mail: kbritton@naspweb.org
Web: www.nasponline.org

Summary To provide financial assistance to Native Americans and other minority graduate students who are members of the National Association of School Psychologists (NASP) and enrolled in a school psychology program.

Eligibility This program is open to minority students who are NASP members enrolled full or part time in a regionally-accredited school psychology program in the United States. Applicants must have a GPA of 3.0 or higher. Doctoral candidates are not eligible. Applications must be accompanied by 1) a resume that includes undergraduate and/or graduate schools attended, awards and honors, student and professional activities, work and volunteer experiences, research and publications, workshops or other presentations, and any special skills, training, or experience, such as bilingualism, teaching experience, or mental health experience; and 2) a statement, up to 1,000 words, of professional goals. Selection is based on adherence to instructions; completeness of the application; applicant's experience, interests and growth as reflected on their resume; applicant's professional goals statement; recommendations; financial standing; and degree of scholarship. U.S. citizenship is required.

Financial data The stipend is $5,000 per year.

Duration 1 year; may be renewed up to 2 additional years.

Additional information This program, which began in 1995, includes the Deborah Peek Crockett Minority Scholarship Award, the Wayne Gressett Memorial Minority Scholarship Award, and the Pearson Minority Scholarship Award.

Number awarded Varies each year; recently, 4 were awarded.

Deadline November of each year.

[1068]
NATIONAL MEDICAL FELLOWSHIPS EMERGENCY SCHOLARSHIP FUND

National Medical Fellowships, Inc.
Attn: Scholarship Program
347 Fifth Avenue, Suite 510
New York, NY 10016
(212) 483-8880   Toll Free: (877) NMF-1DOC
Fax: (212) 483-8897 E-mail: scholarships@nmfonline.org
Web: www.nmfonline.org

Summary To provide financial assistance to Native American and other minority medical students who are facing financial emergencies.

Eligibility This program is open to U.S. citizens who are enrolled in the third or fourth year of an accredited M.D. or D.O. degree-granting program in the United States and are facing extreme financial difficulties because of unforeseen training-related expenses. The emergency must be sudden, unexpected, and unbudgeted. Applicants must be African Americans, Latinos, Native Hawaiians, Alaska Natives, American Indians, Pacific Islanders, Vietnamese, or Cambodians

who permanently reside in the United States. They must be interested in primary care practice in underserved communities.

Financial data Assistance ranges up to $5,000.

Duration 1 year; nonrenewable.

Additional information This program began in 2008.

Number awarded Varies each year; recently, 3 were awarded.

Deadline Applications may be submitted at any time.

[1069]
NATIONAL MUSEUM OF THE AMERICAN INDIAN 10-WEEK INTERNSHIPS IN CONSERVATION

National Museum of the American Indian
Attn: Conservation Office
Cultural Resources Center
4220 Silver Hill Road, MRC 538
Suitland, MD 20746-2863
(301) 238-1424   Fax: (301) 238-3201
E-mail: NMAIcrcconserv@si.edu
Web: www.nmai.si.edu

Summary To provide undergraduate and graduate students with an opportunity to learn more about conservation during an internship at the Smithsonian Institution's National Museum of the American Indian (NMAI).

Eligibility This program is open to undergraduate and graduate students with a background in studio art, anthropology, art history, museum studies, chemistry, or biology. Native American students interested in conservation and museum care practices are especially welcome. Applicants must be interested in participating in a program at the NMAI Cultural Resources Center in Suitland, Maryland that involves collaboration with Native people in developing appropriate methods of handling, preserving, and interpreting cultural materials.

Financial data Interns receive a stipend (amount not specified).

Duration 10 weeks, in summer or winter.

Number awarded Varies each year.

Deadline February of each year for summer; September of each year for winter.

[1070]
NATIONAL MUSEUM OF THE AMERICAN INDIAN CONSERVATION 6-MONTH PRE-PROGRAM INTERNSHIP

National Museum of the American Indian
Attn: Conservation Office
Cultural Resources Center
4220 Silver Hill Road, MRC 538
Suitland, MD 20746-2863
(301) 238-1424   Fax: (301) 238-3201
E-mail: NMAIcrcconserv@si.edu
Web: www.nmai.si.edu

Summary To provide an opportunity for students planning to enter a graduate training program in art conservation to learn more about the field during an internship at the Smithsonian Institution's National Museum of the American Indian (NMAI).

Eligibility This program is open to students preparing to apply to a graduate level training program in art conservation. Applicants must be interested in participating in a program at the NMAI Cultural Resources Center in Suitland, Maryland that will provide them with an understanding of Native American ethnographic and archaeological materials and approaches to conservation. They must have a GPA of 3.0 or higher. Along with their application, they must submit a personal statement that includes why they want to become a conservator, what they hope to accomplish through this internship, how it would relate to their academic achievement and professional development, and what in particular about NMAI interests them and leads them to apply for the internship.

Financial data Interns receive a stipend (amount not specified).

Duration 6 months, beginning in September or October.

Additional information Interns perform supervised condition examinations, write reports and treatment proposals, perform photo documentation, and treat objects requested for exhibitions or loans.

Number awarded 1 each year.

Deadline February of each year.

[1071]
NATIONAL PHYSICAL SCIENCE CONSORTIUM GRADUATE FELLOWSHIPS

National Physical Science Consortium
c/o University of Southern California
3716 South Hope Street, Suite 348
Los Angeles, CA 90007-4344
(213) 821-2409   Toll Free: (800) 854-NPSC
Fax: (213) 821-6329   E-mail: npsc@npsc.org
Web: www.npsc.org

Summary To provide financial assistance and summer work experience to Nativ Americans and other underrepresented minorities interested in working on a Ph.D. in designated science and engineering fields.

Eligibility This program is open to U.S. citizens who are seniors graduating from college with a GPA of 3.0 or higher, enrolled in the first year of a doctoral program, completing a terminal master's degree, or returning from the workforce and holding no more than a master's degree. Students currently in the third or subsequent year of a Ph.D. program or who already have a doctoral degree in any field (Ph.D., M.D., J.D., Ed.D.) are ineligible. Applicants must be interested in working on a Ph.D. in fields that vary but emphasize astronomy, chemistry, computer science, engineering (chemical, computer, electrical, environmental, or mechanical), geology, materials science, mathematical sciences, or physics. The program welcomes applications from all qualified students and continues to emphasize the recruitment of underrepresented minority (African American, Hispanic, Native American Indian, Eskimo, Aleut, and Pacific Islander) and women physical science and engineering students. Fellowships are provided to students at more than 100 universities that are members of the consortium. Selection is based on academic standing (GPA), course work taken in preparation for graduate school, university and/or industry research experience, letters of recommendation, and GRE scores.

Financial data The fellowship pays tuition and fees plus an annual stipend of $20,000. It also provides on-site paid summer employment to enhance technical experience. The exact value of the fellowship depends on academic standing, summer employment, and graduate school attended; the total amount generally exceeds $200,000.

Duration Support is initially provided for 2 or 3 years, depending on the employer-sponsor. If the fellow makes satisfactory progress and continues to meet the conditions of the award, support may continue for a total of up to 6 years or completion of the Ph.D., whichever comes first.

Additional information This program began in 1989. Tuition and fees are provided by the participating universities. Stipends and summer internships are provided by sponsoring organizations. Students must submit separate applications for internships, which may have additional eligibility requirements. Internships are currently available at Lawrence Livermore National Laboratory in Livermore, California (astronomy, chemistry, computer science, geology, materials science, mathematics, and physics); National Institute of Standards and Technology in Gaithersburg, Maryland (various fields of STEM); National Security Agency in Fort Meade, Maryland (astronomy, chemistry, computer science, geology, materials science, mathematics, and physics); Sandia National Laboratory in Livermore, California (biology, chemistry, computer science, environmental science, geology, materials science, mathematics, and physics); and Sandia National Laboratory in Albuquerque, New Mexico (chemical engineering, chemistry, computer science, materials science, mathematics, mechanical engineering, and physics). Fellows must submit a separate application for dissertation support in the year prior to the beginning of their dissertation research program, but not until they can describe their intended research in general terms.

Number awarded Varies each year; recently, 11 were awarded.

Deadline November of each year.

[1072]
NATIONAL SPACE GRANT COLLEGE AND FELLOWSHIP PROGRAM

National Aeronautics and Space Administration
Attn: Office of Education
300 E Street, S.W.
Mail Suite 6M35
Washington, DC 20546-0001
(202) 358-1069   Fax: (202) 358-7097
E-mail: aleksandra.korobov@nasa.gov
Web: www.nasa.gov

Summary To provide financial assistance to Native American and other undergraduate and graduate students interested in preparing for a career in a space-related field.

Eligibility This program is open to undergraduate and graduate students at colleges and universities that participate in the National Space Grant program of the U.S. National Aeronautics and Space Administration (NASA) through their state consortium. Applicants must be interested in a program of study and/or research in a field of science, technology, engineering, or mathematics (STEM) related to space. A specific goal of the program is to recruit and train U.S. citizens, especially underrepresented minorities, women, and persons with disabilities, for careers in aerospace science and technology. Financial need is not considered in the selection process.

Financial data Each consortium establishes the terms of the fellowship program in its state.

Additional information NASA established the Space Grant program in 1989. It operates through 52 consortia in each state, the District of Columbia, and Puerto Rico. Each consortium includes selected colleges and universities in that state as well as other affiliates from industry, museums, science centers, and state and local agencies.

Number awarded Varies each year.

Deadline Each consortium sets its own deadlines.

[1073]
NATIONAL TRIBAL GAMING COMMISSIONS/ REGULATORS SCHOLARSHIPS

National Tribal Gaming Commissions/Regulators
Attn: Scholarship Committee
P.O. Box 454
Oneida, WI 54155
E-mail: dawnr@thehillgroup.org
Web: www.ntgcr.com/scholarships

Summary To provide financial assistance to Native Americans interested in working on an undergraduate or graduate degree in a field related to the gaming industry.

Eligibility This program is open to enrolled members of federally-recognized American Indian tribes and Alaska Native groups. Applicants must be high school seniors, rising undergraduates, or potential graduate students enrolled or planning to enroll full time at an accredited college or university in the United States and have a GPA of 2.5 or higher. They must be preparing for a career in the gaming, business, financial, or hospitality industries. Along with their application, they must submit a 4-page essay on their personal background (including whether or not they speak their tribal language or are learning their tribal language and other cultural skills), their degree plan for higher education, why they have chosen that field of study, how they plan to serve their tribal people when they complete their higher education, and why they should be selected for this scholarship. Selection is based on the essay, academic ability (judged on GPA, class rank, SAT and/or ACT scores, and curriculum rigor), leadership, honors and awards received, community involvement, 3 letters of recommendation, intellectual skills beyond the classroom, accomplishments, professional development, and financial need.

Financial data The stipend is $2,500.

Duration 1 year.

Number awarded 2 each year.

Deadline June of each year for fall semester; December of each year for spring semester.

[1074]
NATIONAL URBAN FELLOWS PROGRAM

National Urban Fellows, Inc.
Attn: Program Director
1120 Avenue of the Americas, Fourth Floor
New York, NY 10036
(212) 730-1700   Fax: (212) 730-1823
E-mail: info@nuf.org
Web: www.nuf.org/fellows-overview

Summary To provide mid-career public sector professionals, especially people of color and women, with an opportunity to strengthen leadership skills through a master's degree program coupled with a mentorship.

Eligibility This program is open to U.S. citizens who have a bachelor's degree, have at 5 to 7 years of professional work experience with 2 years in a management capacity, have demonstrated leadership capacity with potential for further growth, have a GPA of 3.0 or higher, and can demonstrate a commitment to public service. Applicants must submit a 1-page autobiographical statement, a 2-page personal statement, and a 2-page statement on their career goals. They may be of any racial or ethnic background, but the program's goal is to increase the number of competent administrators from underrepresented ethnic and cultural groups at all levels of public and private urban management organizations. Semifinalists are interviewed.

Financial data The stipend is $25,000. Fellows are required to pay a $500 registration fee and a $7,500 co-investment tuition payment upon acceptance and enrollment in the program.

Duration 14 months.

Additional information The program begins with a summer semester of study at Bernard M. Baruch College of the City University of New York. Following this, fellows spend 9 months in mentorship assignments with a senior administrator in a government agency, a major nonprofit, or a foundation. The final summer is spent in another semester of study at Baruch College. Fellows who successfully complete all requirements are granted a master's of public administration from that college. A $150 processing fee must accompany each application.

Number awarded Approximately 40 to 50 each year.

Deadline December of each year.

[1075]
NATIVE AGRICULTURE AND FOOD SYSTEMS COLLEGE SCHOLARSHIP PROGRAM

First Nations Development Institute
Attn: Senior Program Officer
2432 Main Street
Longmont, CO 80501
(303) 774-7836, ext. 208   Fax: (303) 774-7841
E-mail: mwhiting@firstnations.org
Web: www.firstnations.org/grantmaking/scholarship

Summary To provide financial assistance to Native Americans who are working on an undergraduate or graduate degree in an agriculture-related field.

Eligibility This program is open to enrolled members of a current or terminated federal or state tribe who are enrolled as full-time undergraduate or graduate students and can demonstrate a commitment to helping their Native community reclaim local food-system control. Applicants must be working on a degree in agriculture or a related field, including (but not limited to) agribusiness management, agriscience technologies, agronomy, animal husbandry, aquaponics, fisheries and wildlife, food production and safety, food-related policy and legislation, horticulture, irrigation science, plant-based nutrition, and sustainable agriculture or food systems. They must have a GPA of 3.0 or higher. Along with their application, they must submit an essay of 250 to 500 words on how they have been involved in their tribal community and how they will use their degree to help their tribe reclaim control of their traditional or local food system.

Financial data The stipend is $1,000.

Duration 1 year.

Additional information This program began in 2014.

Number awarded 6 each year.

Deadline November of each year.

[1076]
NATIVE AMERICAN HEALTH EDUCATION FUND SCHOLARSHIP

Triangle Community Foundation
Attn: Scholarships and Donor Services Officer
P.O. Box 12729
Durham, NC 27701
(919) 474-8370, ext. 4015   Fax: (919) 941-9208
E-mail: sarah@trianglecf.org
Web: www.trianglecf.org

Summary To provide financial assistance to Native Americans who are attending college or graduate school to prepare for a career in a health-related field.

Eligibility This program is open to Native American students currently enrolled at a college or graduate school. Applicants must be preparing for a career in medicine, nursing, dietetics and nutrition, medical technology, physical therapy, pharmacy, social work, medical research (biochemistry), or other health-related fields. They must be able to demonstrate a desire to return to their community or Reservation to improve health care.

Financial data The stipend ranges up to $1,000.

Duration 1 year.

Additional information This program, sponsored by the Native American Health Education Fund, awarded its first scholarship in 1990.

Number awarded Varies each year. Since the program began, it has awarded 106 scholarships.

Deadline June of each year.

[1077]
NATIVE AMERICAN JOURNALISTS ASSOCIATION SCHOLARSHIPS

Native American Journalists Association
c/o University of Oklahoma
Gaylord College
395 West Lindsey Street
Norman, OK 73019-4201
(405) 325-1649   Fax: (405) 325-6945
E-mail: info@naja.com
Web: www.naja.com/students/naja-scholarships

Summary To provide financial assistance to student members of the Native American Journalists Association (NAJA) who are interested in a career in journalism or journalism education.

Eligibility This program is open to NAJA members who are high school seniors, undergraduates, or graduate students working on or planning to work on a degree in journalism. Applicants must include proof of enrollment in a federal- or state-recognized tribe; work samples; transcripts; a cover letter on their financial need, area of interest (print, broadcast, photojournalism, new media, journalism education), and reasons for preparing for a career in journalism; and 2 letters of recommendation.

Financial data The stipend is $1,000.

Duration 1 year.

Additional information Support for this program is provided by the Joseph Grimm Foundation, the Haskell Indian Nations University, and CNN.

Number awarded Varies each year; recently, 3 were awarded.

Deadline March of each year.

[1078]
NATIVE AMERICAN NATURAL RESOURCE RESEARCH SCHOLARSHIP

Intertribal Timber Council
Attn: Education Committee
1112 N.E. 21st Avenue, Suite 4
Portland, OR 97232-2114
(503) 282-4296   Fax: (503) 282-1274
E-mail: itc1@teleport.com
Web: www.itcnet.org/about_us/scholarships.html

Summary To provide funding to Native American undergraduate or graduate students interested in conducting tribally-relevant research on a natural resource issue.

Eligibility This program is open to undergraduate or graduate students who are enrolled members of a federally-recognized Indian tribe or Alaska Native Corporation. Applicants must be planning to conduct natural resource research that is tribally-relevant. They must submit a 4-page research proposal that includes 1) an abstract that explains the merit of the research and how it is relevant to tribal natural resource interests; 2) a timeline and methodology; 3) a dissemination plan, including a tribal component; and 4) budget and budget justification.

Financial data The grant ranges up to $4,000.

Duration 1 year.

Additional information This program is offered in partnership with the U.S. Forest Service.

Number awarded 1 each year.

Deadline January of each year.

[1079]
NATIVE AMERICAN RIGHTS FUND SUMMER CLERKSHIPS

Native American Rights Fund
Attn: Clerkship Program
1506 Broadway
Boulder, CO 80302-6296
(303) 447-8760   Fax: (303) 443-7776
E-mail: cjohnson@narf.org
Web: www.narf.org/contact/clerk.htm

Summary To provide summer work experience at offices of the Native American Rights Fund (NARF) to law students with an interest in Indian law.

Eligibility This program is open to law students who are experienced in Indian law or have a background in Indian affairs. Applicants for summer clerkships must have completed their second year of law school and be able to work at NARF offices in Boulder (Colorado), Anchorage (Alaska), or Washington, D.C. They must be able to demonstrate completion of course work in Indian law and natural resources law, experience in drafting legal memoranda, excellent research abilities, excellent written and oral communication skills and familiarity with tribal communities and cultures.

Financial data The stipend is $20 per hour.

Duration Clerks work full time for 10 to 12 weeks.

Additional information Law clerk projects consist primarily of legal research and writing.

Number awarded Varies each year.

Deadline September of each year.

[1080]
NATIVE AMERICAN SUPPLEMENTAL GRANTS

Presbyterian Church (USA)
Attn: Office of Financial Aid for Service
100 Witherspoon Street
Louisville, KY 40202-1396
(502) 569-5224   Toll Free: (888) 728-7228, ext. 5224
Fax: (502) 569-8766   TDD: (800) 833-5955
E-mail: finaid@pcusa.org
Web: www.presbyterianmission.org

Summary To provide financial assistance to Native American students interested in preparing for church occupations within the Presbyterian Church (USA).

Eligibility This program is open to Native American and Alaska Native students who are enrolled full time at a PCUSA seminary or accredited theological institution approved by their presbytery's Committee on Preparation for Ministry (CPM). Applicants must be working on 1) an M.Div. degree and enrolled as an inquirer or candidate by a PCUSA presbytery; or 2) an M.A.C.E. degree and preparing for a church occupation. They must be PCUSA members, U.S. citizens or permanent residents, able to demonstrate financial need, and recommended by the financial aid officer at their theological institution. Along with their application, they must submit a 1,000-word essay on what they believe God is calling them to do in ministry.

Financial data Stipends range from $500 to $1,500 per year. Funds are intended as supplements to students who have been awarded a Presbyterian Study Grant but still demonstrate remaining financial need.

Duration 1 year; may be renewed up to 2 additional years.

Number awarded Varies each year; the sponsor awards approximately 130 grants for this and 3 related programs each year.

Deadline June of each year.

[1081]
NATIVE AMERICAN VISITING STUDENT AWARDS

Smithsonian Institution
Attn: Office of Fellowships and Internships
Minority Awards Program
470 L'Enfant Plaza, Suite 7102
P.O. Box 37012, MRC 902
Washington, DC 20013-7012
(202) 633-7070   Fax: (202) 633-7069
E-mail: siofi@si.edu
Web: www.smithsonianofi.com

Summary To provide funding to Native American graduate students interested in working on a project related to Native American topics at the Smithsonian Institution.

Eligibility Native Americans who are formally or informally related to a Native American community are eligible to apply. Applicants must be advanced graduate students who are proposing to undertake a project that is related to a Native Amer-

ican topic and requires the use of Native American resources at the Smithsonian Institution.

Financial data Students receive a grant of $175 per day for short-term awards or $600 per week for long-term awards. Also provided are allowances for travel and research.

Duration Up to 21 days for short-term awards; 3 to 10 weeks for long-term awards.

Additional information Recipients carry out independent research projects in association with the Smithsonian's research staff. Fellows are required to be in residence at the Smithsonian for the duration of the fellowship.

Number awarded Varies each year.

Deadline January of each year for summer or fall residency; September of each year for spring residency.

[1082]
NATIVE HAWAIIAN HEALTH SCHOLARSHIP PROGRAM

Papa Ola Lokahi, Inc.
Attn: Native Hawaiian Health Scholarship Program
894 Queen Street
Honolulu, HI 96813
(808) 597-6550   Fax: (808) 597-6552
E-mail: adminassist@nhhsp.org
Web: www.papaolalokahi.org

Summary To provide scholarship/loans to Native Hawaiians for training in the health professions in exchange for service, after graduation, in a federally-designated health professional shortage area (HPSA) or other facility for Native Hawaiians.

Eligibility Applicants must be Native Hawaiians training in allopathic or osteopathic medicine (M.D. or D.O.); dentistry (D.D.S. or D.M.D.); clinical psychology (Ph.D. or Psy.D.); nursing (A.D.N., B.S.N. or M.S.N.); nurse midwifery (M.S.N.); primary care nurse practitioner, including adult/geriatrics, community/public health, family health, pediatrics, and women's health (M.S.N.); social work, (M.S.W.); dental hygiene (D.H.); primary care physician assistant (master's level); optometry (O.D.): pharmacy (Pharm.D.); public health (M.P.H.); dietitian or nutritionist (master's level); or marriage and family therapy (M.F.T.). They may be studying in any state. Recipients must agree to serve in a designated health care facility in Hawaii upon completion of training. First priority is given to former scholars who have completed their previous service obligation and are seeking another year of support. Second priority is given to applicants who appear to have characteristics that increase the probability they will continue to serve underserved Native Hawaiians after the completion of their service obligations.

Financial data Full coverage of tuition and fees is paid directly to the health professional school. A stipend, recently set at $1,330 per month, is paid directly to the scholar. This is a scholarship/loan program. Participants are obligated to provide full-time clinical primary health care services to populations in 1) a Native Hawaiian Health Care System; or 2) an HPSA in Hawaii, medically underserved area (MUA), or another area or facility in Hawaii designated by the U.S. Department of Health and Human Services. Participants owe 1 year of service in the National Health Service Corps for each full or partial year of support received under this program. The minimum service obligation is 2 years.

Duration 1 year; may be renewed for up to 3 additional years.

Additional information This program, which began in 1991, is administered by the U.S. Health Resources and Services Administration, Bureau of Health Professions, through a contract with Papa Ola Lokahi, Inc.

Number awarded Normally, 10 each year.

Deadline February of each year.

[1083]
NAVAJO NATION DISSERTATION FUNDING

Navajo Nation
Attn: Office of Navajo Nation Scholarship and Financial
  Assistance
P.O. Box 1870
Window Rock, AZ 86515-1870
(928) 871-7444   Toll Free: (800) 243-2956
Fax: (928) 871-7410
E-mail: rosegraham@navajo-nsn.gov
Web: www.onnsfa.org/FundingTypes/GraduateFund.aspx

Summary To provide financial assistance to members of the Navajo Nation who are working on a doctoral dissertation.

Eligibility This program is open to enrolled members of the Navajo Nation who are conducting dissertation research for a doctoral degree. Applicants must have completed all course work and have been advanced to candidacy. They must submit an itemized dissertation budget.

Financial data Funding is limited to direct costs for field work and research necessary to complete the dissertation.

Duration 1 year; may be renewed if the recipient is making satisfactory progress on the dissertation.

Number awarded Varies each year.

Deadline April of each year.

[1084]
NAVAJO NATION GRADUATE TRUST FUND AND FELLOWSHIP

Navajo Nation
Attn: Office of Navajo Nation Scholarship and Financial
  Assistance
P.O. Box 1870
Window Rock, AZ 86515-1870
(928) 871-7444   Toll Free: (800) 243-2956
Fax: (928) 871-7410
E-mail: rosegraham@navajo-nsn.gov
Web: www.onnsfa.org/FundingTypes/GraduateFund.aspx

Summary To provide financial assistance to members of the Navajo Nation who wish to work on a graduate degree.

Eligibility This program is open to enrolled members of the Navajo Nation who are enrolled or planning to enroll as graduate students. Preference is given to students at institutions that provide matching funds to the Navajo Nation or its student participants. Candidates for a second graduate degree at the same level (master's, education terminal degree, or doctorate) are not eligible. Applicants must submit transcripts and documentation of financial need.

Financial data Stipends for full-time graduate students range from $5,000 to $10,000 per year, depending on the need of the recipient; for part-time graduate students, the stipend is $500 per 3 semester credit hours or equivalent amount of quarter credit hours.

Duration 1 year; may be renewed for a total of 5 semesters (6 semesters for law students) provided the recipient maintains a GPA of at least 3.0 (or 2.0 for medical, veterinary, and law students).

Number awarded Varies each year.

Deadline April of each year.

[1085]
NAVAL RESEARCH LABORATORY SUMMER RESEARCH PROGRAM FOR HBCU/MI UNDERGRADUATES AND GRADUATES

Naval Research Laboratory
Attn: Personnel Operations Branch
4555 Overlook Avenue, S.W.
Washington, DC 20375-5320
(202) 767-8313
Web: www.nrl.navy.mil/hbcu/description

Summary To provide research experience at the Naval Research Laboratory (NRL) to undergraduate and graduate students in fields of science, technology, engineering, and mathematics (STEM) at Tribal Colleges and Universities and other minority institutions.

Eligibility This program is open to undergraduate and graduate students who have completed at least 1 year of study at an Historically Black College or University (HBCU), Minority Institution (MI), or Tribal College or University (TCU). Applicants must be working on a degree in a field of STEM and have a cumulative GPA of 3.0 or higher. They must be interested in participating in a research program at NRL under the mentorship of a senior staff scientist. U.S. citizenship or permanent resident status is required.

Financial data The stipend is $810 per week for undergraduates or $1,050 per week for graduate students. Subsidized housing is provided at a motel in the area.

Duration 10 weeks during the summer.

Additional information This program is conducted in accordance with a planned schedule and a working agreement between NRL, the educational institution, and the student.

Number awarded Varies each year.

Deadline February of each year.

[1086]
NBC UNIVERSAL SCHOLARSHIP

American Indian College Fund
Attn: Scholarship Department
8333 Greenwood Boulevard
Denver, CO 80221
(303) 426-8900   Toll Free: (800) 776-FUND
Fax: (303) 426-1200
E-mail: scholarships@collegefund.org
Web: www.collegefund.org

Summary To provide financial assistance to Native American students interested in attending a Tribal College or University (TCU) or mainstream university to prepare for a career in media.

Eligibility This program is open to American Indians and Alaska Natives who are planning to enroll as an undergraduate or graduate student at an eligible TCU or mainstream university. Applicants must have declared a major in broadcasting, entertainment, film, journalism, media, or telecommunications and have a GPA of 3.0 or higher. They must be able to demonstrate an interest in a career in media (either in front of or behind the camera) and an internship in the Los Angeles or New York offices of NBC Universal. Applications are available only online and include required essays on specified topics. U.S. citizenship is required.

Financial data The stipend is $5,000 at mainstream universities or $5,250 at TCUs.

Duration 1 year.

Additional information This scholarship is sponsored by NBCUniversal, in partnership with the American Indian College Fund.

Number awarded 1 or more each year.

Deadline May of each year.

[1087]
NBCC MINORITY FELLOWSHIP PROGRAM

National Board for Certified Counselors
Attn: NBCC Foundation
3 Terrace Way
Greensboro, NC 27403
(336) 232-0376   Fax: (336) 232-0010
E-mail: foundation@nbcc.org
Web: nbccf-mfpdr.applicantstack.com/x/detail/a2b3qvixcgjm

Summary To provide financial assistance to doctoral candidates, especially Nativ Americans and those from other racially and ethnically diverse populations, and who are interested in working on a degree in mental health and/or substance abuse counseling.

Eligibility This program is open to U.S. citizens and permanent residents who are enrolled full time in an accredited doctoral degree mental health and/or substance abuse and addictions counseling program. Applicants must have a National Certified Counselor or equivalent credential. They must commit to provide mental health and substance abuse services to racially and ethnically diverse populations. African Americans, Alaska Natives, American Indians, Asian Americans, Hispanics/Latinos, Native Hawaiians, and Pacific Islanders are especially encouraged to apply. Applicants must be able to commit to providing substance abuse and addictions counseling services to underserved minority populations for at least 2 years after graduation.

Financial data The stipend is $20,000.

Duration 1 year.

Additional information This program began in 2012 with support from the Substance Abuse and Mental Health Services Administration.

Number awarded 23 each year.

Deadline June of each year.

[1088]
NBCC MINORITY FELLOWSHIP PROGRAM (MASTER'S ADDICTIONS)

National Board for Certified Counselors
Attn: NBCC Foundation
3 Terrace Way
Greensboro, NC 27403
(336) 232-0376   Fax: (336) 232-0010
E-mail: foundation@nbcc.org
Web: nbccf-mfp.applicantstack.com/x/detail/a2hlw8mozup7

Summary To provide financial assistance to students, especially Native Americans and members of other racially and ethnically diverse populations, who are interested in working on a master's degree in substance abuse and addictions counseling.

Eligibility This program is open to U.S. citizens and permanent residents who are enrolled full time in an accredited master's degree substance abuse and addictions counseling program. Applicants must demonstrate knowledge of and experience with racially and ethnically diverse populations. They must be able to commit to applying for the National Certified Counselor credential prior to graduation and to providing substance abuse and addictions counseling services to underserved minority transition-age youth populations (16-25 years of age) for at least 2 years after graduation. African Americans, Alaska Natives, American Indians, Asian Americans, Hispanics/Latinos, Native Hawaiians, and Pacific Islanders are especially encouraged to apply.

Financial data The stipend is $11,000.

Duration 1 year.

Additional information This program began in 2012 with support from the Substance Abuse and Mental Health Services Administration.

Number awarded 40 each year.

Deadline June of each year.

[1089]
NBCC MINORITY FELLOWSHIP PROGRAM (MASTER'S MENTAL HEALTH)

National Board for Certified Counselors
Attn: NBCC Foundation
3 Terrace Way
Greensboro, NC 27403
(336) 232-0376   Fax: (336) 232-0010
E-mail: foundation@nbcc.org
Web: nbccf-mfp.applicantstack.com/x/detail/a2hlw8m1394v

Summary To provide financial assistance to students who have knowledge of and experience with racially and ethnically diverse populations and are interested in working on a master's degree in mental health counseling.

Eligibility This program is open to U.S. citizens and permanent residents who are enrolled full time in an accredited master's degree mental health counseling program. Applicants must demonstrate knowledge of and experience with racially and ethnically diverse populations. They must be able to commit to applying for the National Certified Counselor credential prior to graduation and to providing mental health counseling services to underserved minority transition-age youth populations (16-25 years of age) for at least 2 years after graduation. African Americans, Alaska Natives, American Indians, Asian Americans, Hispanics/Latinos, Native Hawaiians, and Pacific Islanders are especially encouraged to apply.

Financial data The stipend is $5,000.

Duration 1 year.

Additional information This program is supported by the Substance Abuse and Mental Health Services Administration.

Number awarded 40 each year.

Deadline June of each year.

[1090]
NCAA ETHNIC MINORITY ENHANCEMENT POSTGRADUATE SCHOLARSHIP FOR CAREERS IN ATHLETICS

National Collegiate Athletic Association
Attn: Office for Diversity and Inclusion
700 West Washington Street
P.O. Box 6222
Indianapolis, IN 46206-6222
(317) 917-6683   Fax: (317) 917-6888
E-mail: lthomas@ncaa.org
Web: www.ncaa.org

Summary To provide funding to Native American and other ethnic minority graduate students who are interested in preparing for a career in intercollegiate athletics.

Eligibility This program is open to members of minority groups who have been accepted into a program at a National Collegiate Athletic Association (NCAA) member institution that will prepare them for a career in intercollegiate athletics (athletics administrator, coach, athletic trainer, or other career that provides a direct service to intercollegiate athletics). Applicants must be U.S. citizens, have performed with distinction as a student body member at their respective undergraduate institution, have a cumulative undergraduate GPA of 3.2 or higher, and be entering the first semester or term of full-time postgraduate study. Selection is based on the applicant's involvement in extracurricular activities, course work, commitment to preparing for a career in intercollegiate athletics, and promise for success in that career. Financial need is not considered.

Financial data The stipend is $7,500; funds are paid to the college or university of the recipient's choice.

Duration 1 year; nonrenewable.

Number awarded 13 each year.

Deadline February of each year.

[1091]
NEIGHBORHOOD DIABETES EDUCATION PROGRAM

National Medical Fellowships, Inc.
Attn: Scholarship Program
347 Fifth Avenue, Suite 510
New York, NY 10016
(212) 483-8880   Toll Free: (877) NMF-1DOC
Fax: (212) 483-8897 E-mail: scholarships@nmfonline.org
Web: www.nmfonline.org

Summary To provide funding to Native American and other underrepresented medical and nursing students who wish to participate in a neighborhood diabetes education project in New York City.

Eligibility This program is open to members of underrepresented minority groups (African American, Hispanic/Latino, Native American, Vietnamese, or Cambodian) who are U.S. citizens. Applicants must be currently enrolled in an accredited medical school or graduate-level nursing degree program in Connecticut, New Jersey, New York, or Pennsylvania. They must be interested in a mentored service-learning experience that provides 200 hours of proactive diabetes education at a variety of community sites and health care settings in New York City. Selection is based on demonstrated leadership early in career and commitment to serving medically underserved communities.

Financial data The stipend is $5,000.

Additional information Funding for this program, which began in 2015 and is administered by National Medical Fellowships (NMF), is provided by the Empire BlueCross BlueShield Foundation.

Number awarded 10 each year.

Deadline March of each year.

[1092]
NELLIE STONE JOHNSON SCHOLARSHIP

Nellie Stone Johnson Scholarship Program
P.O. Box 40309
St. Paul, MN 55104
(651) 738-1404   Toll Free: (866) 738-5238
E-mail: info@nelliestone.org
Web: www.nelliestone.org/scholarship-program

Summary To provide financial assistance to Native American and other racial minority union members and their families who are interested in working on an undergraduate or graduate degree in any field at a Minnesota state college or university.

Eligibility This program is open to students in undergraduate and graduate programs at a 2- or 4-year institution that is a component of Minnesota State Colleges and Universities (MnSCU). Applicants must be a minority (Asian, American Indian, Alaska Native, Black/African American, Chicano(a) or Latino(a), Native Hawaiian, or Pacific Islander) and a union member or the child, grandchild, or spouse of a minority union member. They must submit a 2-page essay about their background, educational goals, career goals, and commitment to the causes of human or civil rights. Undergraduates must have a GPA of 2.0 or higher; graduate students must have a GPA of 3.0 or higher. Preference is given to Minnesota residents. Selection is based on the essay, commitment to human or civil rights, extracurricular activities, volunteer activities, community involvement, academic standing, and union verification.

Financial data Stipends are $1,200 per year for full-time students or $500 per year for part-time students.

Duration 1 year; may be renewed up to 3 additional years for students working on a bachelor's degree, 1 additional year for students working on a master's degree, or 1 additional year for students in a community or technical college program.

Number awarded Varies each year; recently, 18 were awarded.

Deadline May of each year.

[1093]
NEW MEXICO MINORITY DOCTORAL LOAN-FOR-SERVICE PROGRAM

New Mexico Higher Education Department
Attn: Financial Aid Division
2048 Galisteo Street
Santa Fe, NM 87505-2100
(505) 476-8460   Toll Free: (800) 279-9777
Fax: (505) 476-8454   E-mail: fin.aid@state.nm.us
Web: www.hed.state.nm.us/students/minoritydoc.aspx

Summary To provide loans-for-service to Native Americans and other underrepresented minorities who reside in

New Mexico and are interested in working on a doctoral degree in selected fields.

Eligibility This program is open to ethnic minorities and women who are residents of New Mexico and have received a baccalaureate degree from a public 4-year college or university in the state in mathematics, engineering, the physical or life sciences, or any other academic discipline in which ethnic minorities and women are demonstrably underrepresented in New Mexico academic institutions. Applicants must have been admitted as a full-time doctoral student at an approved university in any state. They must be sponsored by a New Mexico institution of higher education which has agreed to employ them in a tenure-track faculty position after they obtain their degree. U.S. citizenship is required.

Financial data Loans average $15,000. This is a loan-for-service program; for every year of service as a college faculty member in New Mexico, a portion of the loan is forgiven. If the entire service agreement is fulfilled, 100% of the loan is eligible for forgiveness. Penalties may be assessed if the service agreement is not satisfied.

Duration 1 year; may be renewed up to 3 additional years.

Number awarded Up to 12 each year.

Deadline March of each year.

[1094]
NEW YORK COMMUNITY TRUST/NMF MEDICAL EDUCATION AND POLICY SCHOLARSHIP

National Medical Fellowships, Inc.
Attn: Scholarship Program
347 Fifth Avenue, Suite 510
New York, NY 10016
(212) 483-8880   Toll Free: (877) NMF-1DOC
Fax: (212) 483-8897 E-mail: scholarships@nmfonline.org
Web: www.nmfonline.org

Summary To provide funding for medical education or health policy research to Native American and other underrepresented minority students at designated medical schools in New York City.

Eligibility This program is open to African Americans, Hispanics/Latinos, Native Americans, Vietnamese, Cambodians, and Pacific Islanders who are enrolled at Montefiore Medical Center, Icahn School of Medicine at Mount Sinai, or Columbia University's College of Physicians and Surgeons. Applicants must be interested in conducting medical education or health policy research. They must be U.S. citizens or DACA students. Selection is based on leadership, commitment to serving medically underserved communities, and financial need.

Financial data The stipend is $6,000.

Duration 1 year.

Additional information This program is sponsored by the New York Community Trust.

Number awarded 1 each year.

Deadline September of each year.

[1095]
NEW YORK COMMUNITY TRUST/NMF MEDICAL RESEARCH SCHOLARSHIPS

National Medical Fellowships, Inc.
Attn: Scholarship Program
347 Fifth Avenue, Suite 510
New York, NY 10016
(212) 483-8880   Toll Free: (877) NMF-1DOC
Fax: (212) 483-8897 E-mail: scholarships@nmfonline.org
Web: www.nmfonline.org

Summary To provide funding for community health research to Native American and other underrepresented minority students at medical schools in New York City.

Eligibility This program is open to African Americans, Hispanics/Latinos, Native Americans, Vietnamese, Cambodians, and Pacific Islanders who are entering their second through fourth year at a medical school in New York City. Applicants must be interested in conducting community health research that addresses health inequities in the city. They must be U.S. citizens or DACA students. Selection is based on leadership, commitment to serving medically underserved communities, and financial need.

Financial data The stipend is $6,000.

Duration 1 year.

Additional information This program was established by the New York Community Trust in 2013.

Number awarded 2 each year.

Deadline September of each year.

[1096]
NEW YORK EXCEPTIONAL UNDERGRADUATE/ GRADUATE STUDENT SCHOLARSHIP

Conference of Minority Transportation Officials
Attn: National Scholarship Program
100 M Street, S.E., Suite 917
Washington, DC 20003
(202) 506-2917   E-mail: info@comto.org
Web: www.comto.org/page/scholarships

Summary To provide financial assistance to Native American or other minority students who are members or relatives of members of the Conference of Minority Transportation Officials (COMTO) in New York and working on an undergraduate or graduate degree in transportation.

Eligibility This program is open to minorities who have been members or relatives of members of COMTO in New York for at least 1 year. Applicants must be enrolled full time at an accredited college, university, or vocational/technical institute and working on an undergraduate or graduate degree in a transportation-related discipline. They must have a GPA of 3.5 or higher. Along with their application they must submit a cover letter on their transportation-related career goals and life aspirations. Financial need is not considered in the selection process.

Financial data The stipend is $5,000. Funds are paid directly to the recipient's college or university.

Duration 1 year.

Number awarded 1 each year.

Deadline April of each year.

[1097]
NEWBERRY CONSORTIUM IN AMERICAN INDIAN AND INDIGENOUS STUDIES GRADUATE STUDENT FELLOWSHIPS

Newberry Library
Attn: Committee on Awards
60 West Walton Street
Chicago, IL 60610-3305
(312) 255-3666　　　　　　　　Fax: (312) 255-3513
E-mail: research@newberry.org
Web: www.newberry.org/short-term-fellowships

Summary To provide funding to doctoral students at member institutions of the Newberry Consortium in American Indian and Indigenous Studies (NCAIS) who wish to conduct dissertation research in American Indian studies at various sites, especially the D'Arcy McNickle Center for the History of the American Indian at the Newberry Library.

Eligibility This program is open to advanced graduate students at NCAIS institutions who are interested in conducting dissertation research in American Indian studies at the Newberry Library. Applicants must submit their curriculum vitae, 2 letters of recommendation, and a 2- to 3-page summary of an approved dissertation proposal, including a discussion of the methodology to be employed and the specific Newberry or other library collections to be consulted. They may be interested in conducting research at the Newberry, at other libraries, at archives, or in the field.

Financial data Grants provide a stipend of $2,500 per month.

Duration From 1 to 2 months.

Additional information The Newberry Library inaugurated the NCAIS in 2009, following the end of its partnership with the 13 universities of Committee on Institutional Cooperation (CIC). It is limited to 18 universities in the United States and Canada; for a list of those universities, contact the Newberry. Fellows are expected to present their research at the consortium's annual graduate student conference or at a Newberry-sponsored seminar in American Indian and Indigenous studies.

Number awarded Varies each year; recently, 7 were awarded.

Deadline December of each year.

[1098]
NEXSEN PRUET DIVERSITY SCHOLARSHIPS

Nexsen Pruet
Attn: Diversity Scholarship
1230 Main Street, Suite 700
P.O. Drawer 2426
Columbia, SC 29202-2426
(803) 771-8900　　　　　　　　Fax: (803) 727-1469
E-mail: diversity@nexsenpruet.com
Web: www.nexsenpruet.com/scholarships

Summary To provide financial assistance to Native Americans and members of other minority groups attending designated law schools in North and South Carolina.

Eligibility This program is open to minority students currently enrolled in the first year at the University of North Carolina School of Law, University of South Carolina School of Law, Wake Forest University School of Law, North Carolina Central University School of Law, Charleston School of Law, Charlotte School of Law, Elon University School of Law, or Campbell University School of Law. Applicants must be interested in practicing law in North or South Carolina after graduation. Along with their application, they must submit information on their academic achievements; their contributions to promoting diversity in their community, school, or work environment; and their ability to overcome challenges in the pursuit of their goals. They must also submit essays of 250 words each on 1) their reasons for preparing for a legal career; 2) their interest in the private practice of law in North Carolina and/or South Carolina; 3) any obstacles, including but not limited to financial obstacles, that the scholarship will help them overcome; and 4) what they see as potential obstacles, issues, and opportunities facing new minority lawyers.

Financial data The stipend is $3,000 per year.

Duration 1 year; recipients may reapply.

Additional information Recipients are considered for summer employment in an office of the firm after completion of their first year of law school.

Number awarded 3 each year.

Deadline December of each year.

[1099]
NMAI INTERNSHIP PROGRAM

National Museum of the American Indian
Attn: Internship Program
Fourth Street and Independence Avenue, S.W.
MRC 590
P.O. Box 37012
Washington, DC 20013
(202) 633-6645　　　　　　　　Fax: (202) 633-6899
E-mail: NMAIinterns@si.edu
Web: www.nmai.si.edu/connect/internships/

Summary To provide work and/or research opportunities for Native American students in the area of museum practice and related programming at the Smithsonian Institution's National Museum of the American Indian (NMAI).

Eligibility These internships are intended primarily for American Indian, Native Hawaiian, and Alaska Native students currently enrolled in undergraduate or graduate academic programs with a cumulative GPA of 3.0 or higher. Applicants must be interested in guided work/research experiences using the resources of the NMAI or other Smithsonian Institution facilities. Along with their application, they must submit a personal statement on their interest in the museum field, what they hope to accomplish through an internship, how it would relate to their academic and professional development, and what in particular about the NMAI interests them and leads them to apply for an internship.

Financial data Stipends range from $100 to $400 per week.

Duration 3 sessions of 10 weeks each are held annually.

Additional information Intern projects vary by department. Most projects provide the intern with museum practice and program development experience. Some projects may be more research oriented. Interns who receive a stipend must work 40 hours per week. Positions are available at the Cultural Resources Center in Suitland, Maryland, the George Gustav Heye Center in New York, or the administrative offices in Washington, D.C.

Number awarded Varies each year. More than 100 students have participated in the program since it began in 1994.

Deadline February of each year for summer; July of each year for fall; November of each year for spring.

[1100]
NMF NATIONAL ALUMNI COUNCIL SCHOLARSHIP PROGRAM

National Medical Fellowships, Inc.
Attn: Scholarship Program
347 Fifth Avenue, Suite 510
New York, NY 10016
(212) 483-8880   Toll Free: (877) NMF-1DOC
Fax: (212) 483-8897 E-mail: scholarships@nmfonline.org
Web: www.nmfonline.org

Summary To provide financial assistance to Native American and other underrepresented minority medical students who are committed to the health of underserved communities.

Eligibility This program is open to African Americans, Hispanics/Latinos, Native Americans, Vietnamese, Cambodians, and Pacific Islanders who are entering their fourth year of medical school. Applicants must have demonstrated commitment to the health of underserved communities through community service and leadership potential at an early stage in their professional careers. They must be U.S. citizens or DACA students. Financial need is considered in the selection process.

Financial data The stipend is $5,000.

Duration 1 year.

Number awarded 8 each year.

Deadline September of each year.

[1101]
NNALSA WRITING COMPETITION

National Native American Law Students Association
Attn: President
1001 Marquette Avenue, N.W.
Albuquerque, NM 87102
(505) 289-0810   E-mail: nnalsa.president@gmail.com
Web: www.nationalnalsa.org/#!writing-competition/e5d6c

Summary To recognize and reward members of the National Native American Law Students Association (NNALSA) who submit outstanding articles on Indian law.

Eligibility This competition is open to NNALSA members who submit articles, from 25 to 50 pages in length in standard legal essay format, on a topic of importance to Indians, including federal Indian law and policy, tribal law and policy, international law and policy concerning indigenous peoples, or comparative law. Selection is based on originality, timeliness of topic, quality and creativity of analysis, knowledge and use of relevant law, grammar, punctuation, and citation style.

Financial data The first-place winner receives $1,000 and publication in a law journal of the sponsoring university. The second-place winner receives $500 and the third-place winner receives $250.

Duration The competition is held annually.

Additional information This competition was first held in 2002. Each year, the Native American law student association at a different university sponsors the competition.

Number awarded 3 each year.

Deadline February of each year.

[1102]
NOAA EDUCATIONAL PARTNERSHIP PROGRAM WITH MINORITY SERVING INSTITUTIONS GRADUATE RESEARCH AND TRAINING SCHOLARSHIP PROGRAM

National Oceanic and Atmospheric Administration
Attn: Office of Education
1315 East-West Highway
SSMC3, Room 10600
Silver Spring, MD 20910-6233
(301) 628-2900   E-mail: gsp@noaa.gov
Web: www.noaa.gov/office-education/epp-msi/grtsp

Summary To provide financial assistance and summer research experience to graduate students at Tribal Colleges and Universities and other Minority Serving Institutions who are majoring in scientific fields of interest to the National Oceanic and Atmospheric Administration (NOAA).

Eligibility This program is open to full-time graduate students working on master's or doctoral degrees at Minority Serving Institutions, including Alaska Native Serving Institutions (ANSIs), Hispanic Serving Institutions (HSIs), Historically Black Colleges and Universities (HBCUs), Native Hawaiian Serving Institutions (NHSIs), and Tribal Colleges and Universities (TCUs). Applicants must be working on a degree in biology, chemistry, computer science, economics, engineering, environmental law, geography, geology, mathematics, physical science, physics, or social science. They must have a GPA of 3.5 or higher. The program includes a training program during the summer at a NOAA research facility. Selection is based on academic records, a statement of career interests and goals, and compatibility of applicant's background with the interests of NOAA. U.S. citizenship is required.

Financial data Doctoral candidates receive a stipend of $45,000 to support tuition and fees and up to $10,000 to support research travel and to present findings at conferences; master's degree candidates receive $36,000 to support tuition and fees and up to $7,000 to support research travel and to present findings at conferences.

Duration 1 year; may be renewed 1 additional year for doctoral students, provided the recipient maintains a GPA of 3.5 or higher.

Number awarded Varies each year; recently, 9 were awarded.

Deadline January of each year.

[1103]
NOAH THOMAS LEASK FAMILY SCHOLARSHIPS

Sault Tribe of Chippewa Indians
Attn: Higher Education Department
523 Ashmun Street
Sault Ste. Marie, MI 49783
(906) 635-6050, ext. 26312   Toll Free: (800) 793-0660
Fax: (906) 635-7785 E-mail: BMacArthur@saulttribe.net
Web: www.saulttribe.com

Summary To provide financial assistance to members of the Sault Tribe of Chippewa Indians interested in attending college in any state to work on an undergraduate or graduate degree in any field.

Eligibility This program is open to members of the Sault Tribe who are enrolled full time at a 2- or 4-year college or university in any state. Applicants must be working on an undergraduate or graduate degree in any field. Along with their application, they must submit an essay of 1,000 to 2,000 words on a topic that changes annually but relates to their Indian heritage.

Financial data The stipend is $1,000.

Duration 1 year.

Number awarded 35 each year.

Deadline May of each year.

[1104]
NORTH TEXAS EXCEPTIONAL UNDERGRADUATE/GRADUATE STUDENT SCHOLARSHIP

Conference of Minority Transportation Officials
Attn: National Scholarship Program
100 M Street, S.E., Suite 917
Washington, DC 20003
(202) 506-2917   E-mail: info@comto.org
Web: www.comto.org/page/scholarships

Summary To provide financial assistance to Native American and other minority residents of Texas who are working on an undergraduate or graduate degree in transportation.

Eligibility This program is open to minorities who are residents of Texas enrolled at an accredited college, university, or vocational/technical institute and working on an undergraduate or graduate degree in a transportation-related discipline. Applicants must have a GPA of 2.5 or higher. Along with their application they must submit a cover letter on their transportation-related career goals and life aspirations. Financial need is not considered in the selection process. Membership in the Conference of Minority Transportation Officials (COMTO) is considered a plus but is not required.

Financial data The stipend is $4,500. Funds are paid directly to the recipient's college or university.

Duration 1 year.

Number awarded 1 each year.

Deadline April of each year.

[1105]
NORTHERN ARAPAHO TRIBAL SCHOLARSHIPS

Northern Arapaho Tribe
Attn: Sky People Higher Education
533 Ethete Road
P.O. Box 920
Fort Washakie WY 82514
(307) 332-5286   Toll Free: (800) 815-6795
Fax: (307) 332-9104 E-mail: assistant@skypeopleed.org
Web: www.skypeopleed.org/?page_id=117

Summary To provide financial assistance for college or graduate school to members of the Northern Arapaho Tribe.

Eligibility This program is open to anyone who can certify at least one-fourth degree Northern Arapaho Indian Blood, but preference is given to enrolled members of the Northern Arapaho tribe. Applicants must be enrolled or planning to enroll full time at an accredited college, university, or graduate school in any state. Funding priorities are 1) high school

seniors ready to graduate; 2) continuing students with a GPA of 2.25 or higher; 3) high school or GED graduates; and 4) late applicants.

Financial data The amount of the awards depends on the financial need of the recipients.

Duration 1 year; may be renewed for a total of 5 academic years, provided the recipient remains enrolled full time and maintains a GPA of 2.25 or higher.

Additional information This program is supported by Northern Arapaho tribal funds.

Number awarded Varies each year.

Deadline June of each year for the academic year; November of each year for the spring semester; April of each year for summer school.

[1106]
NORTHWEST INDIAN BAR ASSOCIATION LEGAL EDUCATION SCHOLARSHIP

Northwest Indian Bar Association
c/o Sarah Roubidoux Lawson
Schwabe, Williamson & Wyatt
1420 Fifth Avenue, Suite 3400
Seattle, WA 98101
(206) 407-1507   Fax: (206) 292-0460
E-mail: slawson@schwabe.com
Web: www.nwiba.org/#!blank/c1iwz

Summary To provide financial assistance to Native Americans from the Northwest who are interested in attending law school in the area.

Eligibility This program is open to 1) residents of Alaska, Idaho, Oregon, or Washington who are attending an accredited law school in any area; and 2) residents of any area attending law school in those states. Applicants must have a tribal or native affiliation as an American Indian, Canadian First Nation, Native Hawaiian, or Alaska Native. They must intend to work in the field of American Indian or Alaska Native law or policy in the area. Along with their application, they must submit a 1-page essay describing their commitment and career goals as they will benefit or provide service to American Indian, Canadian First Nation, or Alaska Native people.

Financial data Stipends recently ranged from $500 to $1,500.

Duration 1 year.

Additional information This program began in 2003. It is funded by several Native tribal organizations and the Indian Law Section of the Washington State Bar Association.

Number awarded Several each year.

Deadline November of each year.

[1107]
NSCA MINORITY SCHOLARSHIPS

National Strength and Conditioning Association
Attn: NSCA Foundation
1885 Bob Johnson Drive
Colorado Springs, CO 80906-4000
(719) 632-6722, ext. 152   Toll Free: (800) 815-6826
Fax: (719) 632-6367   E-mail: foundation@nsca.org
Web: www.nsca.com/foundation/nsca-scholarships

Summary To provide financial assistance to Native Americans and other minorities who are interested in working on an undergraduate or graduate degree in strength training and conditioning.

Eligibility This program is open to Blacks, Hispanics, Asian Americans, and Native Americans who are 17 years of age and older. Applicants must have been accepted into an accredited postsecondary institution to work on an undergraduate or graduate degree in the strength and conditioning field. Along with their application, they must submit a 500-word essay on their personal and professional goals and how receiving this scholarship will assist them in achieving those goals. Selection is based on that essay, academic achievement, strength and conditioning experience, honors and awards, community involvement, letters of recommendation, and involvement in the National Strength and Conditioning Association (NSCA).

Financial data The stipend is $1,500.

Duration 1 year.

Additional information The NSCA is a nonprofit organization of strength and conditioning professionals, including coaches, athletic trainers, physical therapists, educators, researchers, and physicians. This program was first offered in 2003.

Number awarded Varies each year; recently, 5 were awarded.

Deadline March of each year.

[1108]
NTUA ENHANCED SCHOLARSHIP WITH INTERNSHIP

Navajo Tribal Utility Authority
Attn: HR Division/Training Department
P.O. Box 170
Fort Defiance, AZ 86504
(928) 729-5721, ext. 2152
Web: www.ntua.com/ntuascholarship.html

Summary To provide financial assistance and work experience to members of the Navajo Nation who are interested in working on an undergraduate or master's degree as preparation for a career in the utility industry.

Eligibility This program is open to enrolled members of the Navajo Nation who are enrolled to planning to enroll as full-time undergraduate or graduate students. Applicants must be preparing for a career in the multi-service utility industry by working on a degree in business, management, administration, accounting, engineering (civil, electrical, or environmental), information technology, or environment. They must also be interested in an internship with the Navajo Tribal Utility Authority (NTUA). Undergraduates must have a GPA of 2.0 or higher and graduate students must have at least a 3.0 GPA. Along with their application, they must submit a business letter describing their interest in the scholarship and describing how their degree aligns with the multi-service utility industry.

Financial data The stipend is $2,500 per year. The internship is paid.

Duration 1 year; may be renewed, provided undergraduates maintain a GPA of 2.0 or higher and graduate students maintain a GPA of 3.0 or higher.

Number awarded 1 or more each year.

Deadline April of each year.

[1109]
NTUA SCHOLARSHIP

Navajo Tribal Utility Authority
Attn: HR Division/Training Department
P.O. Box 170
Fort Defiance, AZ 86504
(928) 729-5721, ext. 2152
Web: www.ntua.com/ntuascholarship.html

Summary To provide financial assistance to members of the Navajo Nation who are interested in working on an undergraduate or master's degree as preparation for a career in the utility industry.

Eligibility This program is open to enrolled members of the Navajo Nation who are enrolled to planning to enroll as full-time undergraduate or graduate students. Applicants must be preparing for a career in the multi-service utility industry by working on a degree in business, management, administration, accounting, engineering (civil, electrical, or environmental), information technology, or environment. Undergraduates must have a GPA of 2.0 or higher and graduate students must have at least a 3.0 GPA. Along with their application, they must submit a business letter describing their interest in the scholarship and describing how their degree aligns with the multi-service utility industry.

Financial data The stipend is $2,000 per year.

Duration 1 year; may be renewed, provided undergraduates maintain a GPA of 2.0 or higher and graduate students maintain a GPA of 3.0 or higher.

Number awarded 1 or more each year.

Deadline April of each year.

[1110]
NYAL BRINGS GRADUATE SCHOLARSHIP

Dakota Indian Foundation
209 North Main Street
P.O. Box 340
Chamberlain, SD 57325-0340
(605) 234-5472   Fax: (605) 234-5858
Web: www.dakotaindianfoundation.org

Summary To provide financial assistance to American Indians (especially those of Sioux heritage) who are working on a graduate degree in Native American studies.

Eligibility This program is open to American Indians (priority given to those of Lakota, Dakota, or Nakota heritage) who are entering or enrolled at a college or university in any state as a graduate student. Applicants must be working on a degree in Native American studies, specifically the Lakota language or other subjects directly relevant to the preservation of Lakota culture. Along with their application, they must submit a personal statement that includes their qualifications for a scholarship, educational interest, career plans, extracurricular activities, and need for financial assistance.

Financial data The stipend is $1,000 per semester ($2,000 per year).

Duration 1 semester; recipients may reapply.

Number awarded Varies each year.

Deadline July of each year for the fall semester; January of each year for the spring semester.

[1111]
OACTA LAW STUDENT DIVERSITY SCHOLARSHIPS

Ohio Association of Civil Trial Attorneys
17 South High Street, Suite 200
Columbus, OH 43215
(614) 228-4727   E-mail: oacta@assnoffices.com
Web: www.oacta.org/About/diversity_scholarship.aspx

Summary To provide financial assistance to Native Americans and other minorities who are enrolled at law schools in Ohio.

Eligibility This program is open to students entering their second or third year at a law school in Ohio. Applicants must be women or members of minority ethnic or racial groups (African American, Hispanic, Asian, Pan Asian, or Native American). Along with their application, they must submit a law school transcript and a cover letter that addresses their academic, personal, and professional accomplishments and why they should be selected as a recipient of this scholarship. Selection is based on academic achievement in law school, professional interest in civil defense practice, service to community, and service to the cause of diversity.

Financial data The stipend is $1,250.

Duration 1 year.

Number awarded Up to 3 each year.

Deadline April of each year.

[1112]
OFFICE OF HAWAIIAN AFFAIRS HIGHER EDUCATION SCHOLARSHIP PROGRAM

Hawai'i Community Foundation
Attn: Scholarship Department
827 Fort Street Mall
Honolulu, HI 96813
(808) 566-5570   Toll Free: (888) 731-3863
Fax: (808) 521-6286
E-mail: scholarships@hcf-hawaii.org
Web: hcf.scholarships.ngwebsolutions.com

Summary To provide financial assistance for college or graduate school to Native Hawaiian residents of any state.

Eligibility This program is open to residents of any state who can document Native Hawaiian ancestry through the Office of Hawaiian Affairs Hawaiian Registry Program. Applicants must be enrolled full or part time at an accredited 2- or 4-year college or university as an undergraduate or graduate student. They must be able to demonstrate academic achievement (GPA of 2.0 or higher for undergraduates or 3.0 or higher for graduate students), good moral character, and financial need. Along with their application, they must submit a short statement indicating their reasons for attending college, their planned course of study, their career goals, and what community service means to them.

Financial data The amounts of the awards depend on the availability of funds and the need of the recipient. Recently, the average value of the scholarships awarded by the foundation was $2,800.

Duration 1 year; may be renewed.

Number awarded Varies each year.

Deadline February of each year.

[1113]
OKLAHOMA CAREERTECH FOUNDATION TEACHER RECRUITMENT/RETENTION SCHOLARSHIP FOR TEACHERS

Oklahoma CareerTech Foundation
Attn: Administrator
1500 West Seventh Avenue
Stillwater, OK 74074-4364
(405) 743-5453   Fax: (405) 743-5541
E-mail: leden@careertech.ok.gov
Web: www.okcareertech.org

Summary To provide financial assistance to Native American and other residents of Oklahoma who reflect the diversity of the state and are interested in attending a college or university in the state to earn a credential or certification for a career in the Oklahoma CareerTech system.

Eligibility This program is open to residents of Oklahoma who are incumbent CareerTech teachers working toward a CareerTech credential or certification at an institution of higher education in the state. Applicants must reflect the ethnic diversity of the state. Along with their application, they must submit brief statements on their interest and commitment to the CareerTech teaching profession and their financial need.

Financial data The stipend ranges from $500 per semester to $1,500 per year.

Duration 1 semester; may be renewed, provided the recipient maintains a GPA of 2.5 or higher.

Number awarded 1 or more each year.

Deadline May of each year.

[1114]
OLIVE WHITMAN MEMORIAL SCHOLARSHIP

Daughters of the American Revolution-New York State Organization
c/o Nancy Goodnough
59 Susquehanna Avenue
Coopertown, NY 13326
(607) 547-8794   E-mail: ngoodnaugh@gmail.com
Web: www.nydar.org

Summary To provide financial assistance for college or graduate school to Native American women in New York.

Eligibility This program is open to women who are at least 50% Native American and residents of New York. Applicants must be graduating or have graduated from a high school in the state with a "B+" average. They must be attending or planning to attend an accredited college, university, or graduate school in the state.

Financial data The stipend is $1,000.

Duration 1 year.

Number awarded 1 each year.

Deadline April of each year.

[1115]
OLIVER GOLDSMITH, M.D. SCHOLARSHIP

Kaiser Permanente Southern California
Attn: Residency Administration and Recruitment
393 East Walnut Street, Fifth Floor
Pasadena, CA 91188
Toll Free: (877) 574-0002   Fax: (626) 405-6581
E-mail: socal.residency@kp.org
Web: residency-scal-kaiserpermanente.org

Summary To provide financial assistance to Native American and other medical students who will help bring diversity to the profession.

Eligibility This program is open to students entering their third or fourth year of allopathic or osteopathic medical school. Members of all ethnic and racial groups are encouraged to apply, but applicants must have demonstrated their commitment to diversity through community service, clinical volunteering, or research. They may be attending medical school in any state, but they must intend to practice in southern California and they must be available to participate in a mentoring program and a clerkship at a Kaiser Permanente facility in that region.

Financial data The stipend is $5,000.

Duration 1 year.

Additional information This program began in 2004.

Number awarded 12 each year.

Deadline January of each year.

[1116]
OPERATION JUMP START III SCHOLARSHIPS

American Association of Advertising Agencies
Attn: AAAA Foundation
1065 Avenue of the Americas, 16th Floor
New York, NY 10018
(212) 262-2500   E-mail: ameadows@aaaa.org
Web: www.aaaa.org

Summary To provide financial assistance to Native American and other multicultural art directors and copywriters interested in working on an undergraduate or graduate degree in advertising.

Eligibility This program is open to African Americans, Asian Americans, Hispanic Americans, and Native Americans who are U.S. citizens or permanent residents. Applicants must be incoming graduate students at 1 of 6 designated portfolio schools or full-time juniors at 1 of 2 designated colleges. They must be able to demonstrate extreme financial need, creative talent, and promise. Along with their application, they must submit 10 samples of creative work in their respective field of expertise.

Financial data The stipend is $5,000 per year.

Duration Most awards are for 2 years.

Additional information Operation Jump Start began in 1997 and was followed by Operation Jump Start II in 2002. The current program began in 2006. The 6 designated portfolio schools are the AdCenter at Virginia Commonwealth University, the Creative Circus in Atlanta, the Portfolio Center in Atlanta, the Miami Ad School, the University of Texas at Austin, and Pratt Institute. The 2 designated colleges are the Minneapolis College of Art and Design and the Art Center College of Design at Pasadena, California.

Number awarded 20 each year.

Deadline Deadline not specified.

[1117]
OREGON STATE BAR SCHOLARSHIPS

Oregon State Bar
Attn: Diversity and Inclusion Department
16037 S.W. Upper Boones Ferry Road
P.O. Box 231935
Tigard, OR 97281-1935
(503) 620-0222
Toll Free: (800) 452-8260, ext. 338 (within OR)
Fax: (503) 684-1366   TDD: (503) 684-7416
E-mail: cling@osbar.org
Web: www.osbar.org/diversity/programs.html#scholar

Summary To provide financial assistance to entering and continuing students from any state enrolled at law schools in Oregon, especially Native Americans and others who will help the Oregon State Bar achieve its diversity and inclusion objectives.

Eligibility This program is open to students entering or continuing at 1 of the law schools in Oregon (Willamette, University of Oregon, and Lewis and Clark). Preference is given to students who will contribute to the Oregon State Bar's diversity and inclusion program, defined to include age, culture, disability, ethnicity, gender and gender identity or expression, geographic location, national origin, race, religion, sex, sexual orientation, and socio-economic status. Along with their application, they must submit a 500-word personal statement on either 1) how their status as a person of diversity has influenced their decision to become a lawyer and how will it influence them throughout their legal professional career; or 2) a challenge they have faced, how they met the challenge, and how that experience will affect the decisions they will make as a legal professional. They must also submit a sample of their legal writing. Selection is based on the personal statement (35%), legal writing ability (25%), academic achievement (15%), work experience and honors (10%), and financial need (15%).

Financial data The stipend is $2,000 per year. Funds are credited to the recipient's law school tuition account.

Duration 1 year; recipients may reapply.

Number awarded 10 each year.

Deadline March of each year.

[1118]
OSAGE NATION HIGHER EDUCATION SCHOLARSHIPS

Osage Nation Education Department
Attn: Career Training and Scholarship
105 Buffalo Avenue
Hominy, OK 74035
(918) 287-5301   Fax: (918) 885-2136
E-mail: scholarship@osagenation-nsn.gov
Web: www.osagenation-nsn.gov

Summary To provide financial assistance for college or graduate school to members of the Osage Nation.

Eligibility This program is open to Osage tribal students who are enrolled or planning to enroll at a 2- or 4-year college or university. Applicants are eligible for funding through 1 or more of the following types of aid: tuition and fees, books, room and board, and supplies and equipment. They must be able to demonstrate financial need.

Financial data Stipends are $150 per credit hour for students at associate degree colleges, $290 per credit hour for students at baccalaureate colleges, $330 per credit hour at research universities, or $360 per credit hour for students enrolled in professional or graduate programs.

Duration Students may receive support for up to 36 credit hours per academic year plus 12 credit hours for summer school.

Number awarded Varies each year.

Deadline June of each year for all semesters.

[1119]
PA STUDENT SCHOLARSHIPS

American Academy of Physician Assistants
Attn: Physician Assistant Foundation
2318 Mill Road, Suite 1300
Alexandria, VA 22314-6868
(703) 836-2272   Fax: (703) 684-1924
E-mail: pafoundation@aapa.org
Web: www.pa-foundation.org

Summary To provide financial assistance to student members of the American Academy of Physician Assistants (AAPA) who are Native American or other underrepresented minorities or disadvantaged students.

Eligibility This program is open to AAPA student members attending a physician assistant program accredited by the Commission on Accreditation of Allied Health Education Programs. Applicants must qualify as 1) an underrepresented minority (American Indian, Alaska Native, Black or African American, Hispanic or Latino, Native Hawaiian or other Pacific Islander, or Asian other than Chinese, Filipino, Japanese, Korean, Asian Indian, or Thai); 2) economically disadvantaged (with income below a specified level); or 3) educationally disadvantaged (from a high school with low SAT scores, from a school district in which less than half of graduates go on to college, has a diagnosed physical or mental impairment, English is not their primary language, the first member of their family to attend college). They must have completed at least 1 semester of PA studies.

Financial data Stipends are $2,500, $2,000, or $1,000.

Duration 1 year; nonrenewable.

Additional information This program includes the AAPA Past Presidents Scholarship, the Bristol-Myers Squibb Endowed Scholarship, the National Commission on Certification of Physician Assistants Endowed Scholarships, the Procter & Gamble Endowed Scholarship, and the PA Foundation Scholarships.

Number awarded Varies each year; recently, 32 were awarded: 3 at $2,500, 27 at $2,000, and 2 at $1,000.

Deadline January of each year.

[1120]
PATRICIA G. ARCHBOLD PREDOCTORAL SCHOLAR AWARD

National Hartford Center of Gerontological Nursing
  Excellence
Attn: Hartford Institute for Geriatric Nursing
NYU Rory Myers College of Nursing
433 First Avenue, Fifth Floor
New York, NY 10010
(202) 779-1439   E-mail: nhcgne@nyu.edu
Web: www.nhcgne.org

Summary To provide funding to Native American and other nurses from underrepresented minority groups who are interested in working on a doctoral degree in gerontological nursing.

Eligibility This program is open to registered nurses who are members of underrepresented minority groups (American Indians, Alaska Natives, Asians, Blacks or African Americans, Hispanics or Latinos/Latinas, Native Hawaiians or other Pacific Islanders) and have been admitted to a doctoral program as a full-time student. The institution they plan to attend must be a member of the National Hartford Center of Gerontological Nursing Excellence (NHCGNE). Applicants must plan an academic research career in geriatric nursing. They must identify a mentor/adviser with whom they will work and whose program of research in geriatric nursing is a good match with their own research interest area. Selection is based on potential for substantial long-term contributions to the knowledge base in geriatric nursing; leadership potential; evidence of commitment to a career in academic geriatric nursing; and evidence of involvement in educational, research, and professional activities. U.S. citizenship or permanent resident status is required.

Financial data The stipend is $50,000 per year. An additional stipend of $5,000 is available to fellows whose research includes the study of pain in the elderly.

Duration 2 years.

Additional information This program began in 2001 with funding from the John A. Hartford Foundation. In 2004, the Mayday Fund added support to scholars who focus on the study of pain in the elderly. Until 2013 it was known as the Building Academic Geriatric Nursing Capacity Program.

Number awarded 1 or more each year.

Deadline January of each year.

[1121]
PATRICIA M. LOWRIE DIVERSITY LEADERSHIP SCHOLARSHIP

Association of American Veterinary Medical Colleges
Attn: Diversity Committee
1101 Vermont Avenue, N.W., Suite 301
Washington, DC 20005-3536
(202) 371-9195, ext. 147   Toll Free: (877) 862-2740
Fax: (202) 842-0773   E-mail: lgreenhill@aavmc.org
Web: www.aavmc.org

Summary To provide financial assistance to Native American and other veterinary students who have promoted diversity in the profession.

Eligibility This program is open to second-, third-, and fourth-year students at veterinary colleges in the United States. Applicants must have a demonstrated record of contributing to enhancing diversity and inclusion through course projects, co-curricular activities, outreach, domestic and community engagement, research, and/or an early reputation for influencing others to be inclusive. Along with their application, they must submit a 3-page personal statement that describes 1) why diversity and inclusion are important to them personally and professionally; 2) how they intend to continue contributing to diversity and inclusion efforts in the veterinary profession after graduation; and 3) what it might mean to be honored as a recipient of this scholarship. They must also indicate how they express their race and/or ethnicity (American Indian or Alaskan, Asian, Black or African American, Hispanic, Native Hawaiian or Pacific Islander, or White) and how they express their gender (male, female, transgender spectrum, or other). Selection is based primarily on documentation of a demonstrated commitment to promoting diversity in academic veterinary medicine; consideration is also given to academic achievement, the student's broader community service record, and financial need.

Financial data The stipend is $6,000.

Duration 1 year; nonrenewable.

Additional information This program began in 2013.

Number awarded 1 each odd-numbered year.

Deadline October of each even-numbered year.

[1122]
PAUAHI FOUNDATION SCHOLARSHIP PROGRAM

Pauahi Foundation
Attn: Scholarships
567 South King Street, Suite 160
Honolulu, HI 96813-3036
(808) 534-3966   Fax: (808) 534-3890
E-mail: scholarships@pauahi.org
Web: www.pauahi.org/scholarships

Summary To provide financial assistance to college and graduate students, especially Native Hawaiians, who are working on a degree in various fields.

Eligibility This program includes many scholarships with different specifications, but all of them give preference to Native Hawaiians (descendants of the aboriginal inhabitants of the Hawaiian Islands prior to 1778). Most are for both undergraduate and graduate students, although some specify 1 or the other. Most are based on merit only, but some include or require financial need. Eligible fields of study cover a wide range of topics, and many are open to all fields. Most require full-time study, but some also allow half-time enrollment. Most are for residents and students in any state, but some require residence and/or study in Hawaii. Many, but not all, specify a minimum GPA. For a list of all the scholarships with their individual requirements, contact the foundation.

Financial data Stipends range from $500 to $5,000 per year.

Duration Most scholarships are for 1 year; some are renewable.

Number awarded Varies each year; the program includes 100 distinct scholarships, most of which provide only 1 award although some offer as many as 6.

Deadline February of each year.

[1123]
PAUL D. WHITE SCHOLARSHIP

BakerHostetler LLP
Attn: Recruiting Coordinator
312 Walnut Street, Suite 3200
Cincinnati, OH 45202-4074
(513) 929-3400   Fax: (513) 929-0303
E-mail: knickolas@bakerlaw.com
Web: www.bakerlaw.com/diversity/firmdiversityscholarship

Summary To provide financial assistance and summer work experience to Native American and other minority law school students.

Eligibility This program is open to first- and second-year law students of Black/African American, Hispanic/Latino, Asian, Native Hawaiian/Pacific Islander or American Indian/Alaska Native descent. Applicants must submit a 2-page statement on what they hope to gain from being a scholarship recipient and thus having a summer clerkship at a law firm such as BakerHostetler. Selection is based on that statement, law school performance, demonstrated leadership abilities (as evidenced by community and collegiate involvement), collegiate academic record, extracurricular activities, and work experience.

Financial data The program provides a stipend of $7,500 for the scholarship and a paid summer clerkship with the sponsoring firm. To date, the firm has expended more than $2.0 million in scholarships and clerkships.

Duration 1 year, including the following summer.

Additional information This program began in 1997. Clerkships may be performed at the firm's offices in Cincinnati or Orlando.

Number awarded 1 or more each year.

Deadline January of each year.

[1124]
PAUL HASTINGS DIVERSITY SCHOLARSHIP

Paul Hastings LLP
Attn: Director of Talent Acquisition
75 East 55th Street, First Floor
New York, NY 10022
(212) 318-6000   Fax: (212) 319-4090
Web: www.paulhastings.com

Summary To provide financial assistance and work experience at Paul Hastings LLP to second-year Native American and other law students who will contribute to the firm's diversity goals.

Eligibility This program is open to students currently enrolled full time in the second year at an ABA-accredited law school. Applicants must demonstrate a commitment to promoting diversity and contributing to the Paul Hastings firm's diversity goals (for its women, lawyers of color, LGBT lawyers, and other affinity groups) as a result of background, experience, personal attributes or characteristics. They must receive an offer to join a Paul Hastings summer program in 1 of its U.S. offices and be likely to practice after graduation in 1 of those offices. Along with their application, they must submit a 500-word personal statement on 1) their commitment to a particular practice area and the city where the Paul Hastings office is located; and 2) how they would contribute to building a diverse work environment if they were to join Paul Hastings following graduation from law school. Selection is based on that statement, demonstrated commitment to promoting diversity and contributing to the firm's diversity goals, undergraduate and law school academic performance, personal achievement, demonstrated leadership ability, oral and written communication skills, community service, and commitment to succeed as a lawyer in a large, private practice environment.

Financial data   The stipend is $10,000, of which $5,000 is paid upon acceptance of an offer to participate in the summer program and $5,000 upon acceptance of an offer to join the firm as a full-time associate.

Duration   1 summer and 1 academic year.

Additional information   The firm's offices are located in Atlanta, Chicago, Houston, Los Angeles, New York, Orange County (California), Palo Alto, San Diego, San Francisco, and Washington.

Number awarded   2 each year.

Deadline   September of each year.

[1125]
PEGGY PETERMAN SCHOLARSHIP

Tampa Bay Times
Attn: Director of Corporate Giving
490 First Avenue South
St. Petersburg, FL 33701
(727) 893-8780   Toll Free: (800) 333-7505, ext. 8780
Fax: (727) 892-2257   E-mail: waclawek@tampabay.com
Web: www.tampabay.com

Summary   To provide financial assistance to Native American and other minority undergraduate and graduate students who are interested in preparing for a career in the newspaper industry and who accept an internship at the *Tampa Bay Times*.

Eligibility   This program is open to minority college sophomores, juniors, seniors, and graduate students from any state who are interested in preparing for a career in the newspaper industry. Applicants must be interested in an internship at the *Tampa Bay Times* and must apply for that at the same time as they apply for this scholarship. They should have experience working on a college publication and at least 1 professional internship.

Financial data   The stipend is $5,000.

Duration   Internships are for 12 weeks during the summer. Scholarships are for 1 year.

Number awarded   1 each year.

Deadline   October of each year.

[1126]
PERKINS COIE DIVERSITY STUDENT FELLOWSHIPS

Perkins Coie LLP
Attn: Chief Diversity Officer
131 South Dearborn Street, Suite 1700
Chicago, IL 60603-5559
(312) 324-8593   Fax: (312) 324-9400
E-mail: diversity@perkinscoie.com
Web: www.perkinscoie.com

Summary   To provide financial assistance to Native American and other law students who reflect the diversity of communities in the country.

Eligibility   This program is open to students enrolled in the first year of a J.D. program at an ABA-accredited law school.

Applicants must contribute meaningfully to the diversity of the law school student body and the legal profession. Diversity is defined broadly to include members of racial, ethnic, disabled, and sexual orientation minority groups, as well as those who may be the first person in their family to pursue higher education. Applicants must submit a 1-page personal statement that describes their unique personal history, a legal writing sample, a current resume, and undergraduate and law school transcripts. They are not required to disclose their financial circumstances, but a demonstrated need for financial assistance may be taken into consideration.

Financial data   The stipend is $7,500.

Duration   1 year.

Additional information   Fellows are also offered a summer associateship at their choice of the firm's offices in Chicago, Madison, Phoenix, Portland, San Francisco, Seattle, or Washington, D.C.

Number awarded   Varies each year; recently, 7 were awarded.

Deadline   January of each year.

[1127]
PETER DOCTOR MEMORIAL INDIAN SCHOLARSHIP GRANTS

Peter Doctor Memorial Indian Scholarship Foundation, Inc.
c/o Clara Hill, Treasurer
P.O. Box 731
Basom, NY 14013
(716) 542-2025   E-mail: ceh3936@hughes.net

Summary   To provide financial assistance to New York Iroquois Indians currently enrolled at a college in any state on the undergraduate or graduate school level.

Eligibility   This program is open to enrolled New York Iroquois Indian students who have completed at least 1 year at a technical school, college, or university in any state. Both undergraduate and graduate students are eligible. There are no age limits or GPA requirements. Interviews may be required. Applicants must have tribal certification. Selection is based on need.

Financial data   Stipends range up to $1,500.

Duration   2 years for medical students; 1 year for all other recipients.

Number awarded   Varies each year.

Deadline   May of each year.

[1128]
PETER KALIFORNSKY MEMORIAL ENDOWMENT SCHOLARSHIP FUND

Cook Inlet Region, Inc.
Attn: The CIRI Foundation
3600 San Jeronimo Drive, Suite 256
Anchorage, AK 99508-2870
(907) 793-3575   Toll Free: (800) 764-3382
Fax: (907) 793-3585   E-mail: tcf@thecirifoundation.org
Web: www.thecirifoundation.org/about/donors

Summary   To provide financial assistance for undergraduate or graduate studies, especially in Alaska Native studies, to Alaska Natives who are original enrollees to Cook Inlet Region, Inc. (CIRI) and their lineal descendants.

Eligibility This program is open to Alaska Native enrollees to CIRI under the Alaska Native Claims Settlement Act (ANCSA) of 1971 and their lineal descendants. There are no Alaska residency requirements or age limitations. Applicants must be accepted or enrolled full time in a 4-year undergraduate or a graduate degree program. Preference is given to students in Alaska Native studies. They must have a GPA of 2.5 or higher. Along with their application, they must submit a 500-word statement on their educational and career goals and how they are contributing, or planning to contribute, to a positive Alaska Native community. Selection is based on that statement, academic achievement, rigor of course work or degree program, student financial contribution, financial need, grade level, previous work performance, community service, and relationship of degree program to career goals.

Financial data The stipend is $10,000 per year, $8,000 per year, or $2,500 per semester, depending on GPA.

Duration 1 semester or 1 year.

Additional information CIRI is 1 of 13 regional corporations established according to the terms of the Alaska Native Claims Settlement Act (ANCSA) of 1971. This program began in 1993.

Number awarded 1 or more each year.

Deadline May of each year for annual scholarships; May or November of each year for semester scholarships.

[1129]
PFATS-NFL CHARITIES MINORITY SCHOLARSHIPS

Professional Football Athletic Trainers Society
c/o Britt Brown, ATC, Associate Athletic Trainer
Dallas Cowboys
One Cowboys Parkway
Irving, TX 75063
(972) 497-4992   E-mail: bbrown@dallascowboys.net
Web: www.pfats.com/about/scholarships

Summary To provide financial assistance to Native American and other ethnic minority undergraduate and graduate students working on a degree in athletic training.

Eligibility This program is open to ethnic minority students who are working on an undergraduate or graduate degree in athletic training. Applicants must have a GPA of 2.5 or higher. Along with their application, they must submit a cover letter, a curriculum vitae, and a letter of recommendation from their supervising athletic trainer. Female athletic training students are encouraged to apply.

Financial data A stipend is awarded (amount not specified).

Duration 1 year.

Additional information Recipients also have an opportunity to work at summer training camp of a National Football League (NFL) team. Support for this program, which began in 1993, is provided by NFL Charities.

Number awarded 1 or more each year.

Deadline March of each year.

[1130]
PHILLIPS EXETER ACADEMY DISSERTATION YEAR FELLOWSHIP

Phillips Exeter Academy
Attn: Dean of Multicultural Affairs
20 Main Street
Exeter, NH 03833-2460
(603) 772-4311   Fax: (603) 777-4393
E-mail: teaching_opportunities@exeter.edu
Web: www.exeter.edu

Summary To provide an opportunity for Native American and other doctoral candidates from diverse backgrounds to work on their dissertation during a residency at Phillips Exeter Academy in Exeter, New Hampshire.

Eligibility This program is open to Ph.D. candidates in any discipline who are in the completion stage of their dissertation. Applicants must be prepared to devote full time to their writing during a residency at the academy. Along with their application, they must submit a curriculum vitae, 2 letters of reference, a 2- to 3-page synopsis of the dissertation, and a 500-word statement of purpose testifying to the appropriateness of the fellowship. Candidates who are interested in potentially teaching in an independent school setting and who are underrepresented in higher education are particularly encouraged to apply.

Financial data This program provides a stipend ($14,310), research and travel funds up to $1,000, room and board, benefits, access to facilities and resources of the school, and professional development opportunities.

Duration 1 academic year.

Additional information Fellows do not have any regular or prescribed duties. During the tenure of the program, fellows may not have any other full- or part-time job.

Number awarded 1 each year.

Deadline March of each year.

[1131]
PHILLIPS FUND GRANTS FOR NATIVE AMERICAN RESEARCH

American Philosophical Society
Attn: Director of Grants and Fellowships
104 South Fifth Street
Philadelphia, PA 19106-3387
(215) 440-3429   Fax: (215) 440-3436
E-mail: LMusumeci@amphilsoc.org
Web: www.amphilsoc.org/grants/phillips

Summary To provide funding to graduate students and scholars interested in conducting research on North American Indian anthropological linguistics and ethnohistory.

Eligibility Eligible to apply are scholars, preferably young scholars, working in the fields of Native American linguistics and ethnohistory and the history of Native Americans in the continental United States and Canada. Applications are not accepted for projects in archaeology, ethnography, psycholinguistics, or for the preparation of pedagogical materials. Graduate students may apply for support for research on their master's or doctoral dissertations.

Financial data Grants range up to $3,500 and average about $2,500. These funds are intended for such extra costs as travel, tapes, films, and informants' fees, but not for general maintenance or the purchase of books or permanent equipment.

Duration 1 year.

Number awarded Varies each year; recently, 17 were awarded.

Deadline February of each year.

[1132]
PI STATE NATIVE AMERICAN GRANTS-IN-AID

Delta Kappa Gamma Society International-Pi State Organization
c/o Arlene Ida, Native American Committee Chair
3 Sherwood Park Drive
Burnt Hills, NY 12027
E-mail: aiddski@nucap.rr.com
Web: www.deltakappagamma.org/NY

Summary To provide funding to Native American women from New York who plan to work in education or another service field.

Eligibility This program is open to Native American women from New York who are attending a 2- or 4-year college in the state. Applicants must be planning to work in education or another service field, but preference is given to those majoring in education. Both undergraduate and graduate students are eligible.

Financial data The grant is $500 per semester ($1,000 per year). Funds may be used for any career-related purpose, including purchase of textbooks.

Duration 1 semester; may be renewed for a total of 5 years and a total of $5,000 over a recipient's lifetime.

Number awarded Up to 5 each year.

Deadline May of each year for fall; January of each year for winter or spring.

[1133]
PLAINS ANTHROPOLOGICAL SOCIETY NATIVE AMERICAN STUDENT AWARDS

Plains Anthropological Society
c/o Mark Muñiz
St. Cloud State University
262 Stewart Hall
720 Fourth Avenue South
St. Cloud, MN 56301-4498
(320) 308-4162   E-mail: mpmuniz@stcloudstate.edu
Web: www.plainsanthropologicalsociety.org/scholarship

Summary To provide financial assistance to Native Americans working on an undergraduate or graduate degree in anthropology or archaeology at a college in the Great Plains area of the United States or Canada.

Eligibility This program is open to Native American students currently enrolled full time at a 4-year college or university and working on an undergraduate or graduate degree in anthropology or archaeology. Undergraduates may be attending a college or university in the United States or Canada that provides course work or research covering the Great Plains area of the United States (all or part of the states of Colorado, Kansas, Montana, Nebraska, New Mexico, North Dakota, Oklahoma, South Dakota, Texas, or Wyoming) or Canada (all or part of the provinces of Alberta, Manitoba, or Saskatchewan). Graduate students must be conducting research that relates to an aspect of the Great Plains, but

they do not need to be attending a university located in that region. All applicants must submit documentation of tribal enrollment, a letter of recommendation from a faculty member focusing on their accomplishments or potential in the field of anthropology, and a letter of interest outlining their prior experience and future goals in studying anthropology.

Financial data The stipend is $1,000.

Duration 1 year.

Number awarded 1 or more each year.

Deadline September of each year.

[1134]
POARCH BAND OF CREEK INDIANS ACADEMIC ACHIEVEMENT BONUS

Poarch Band of Creek Indians
Attn: Tuition Program Coordinator
5811 Jack Springs Road
Atmore, AL 36502
(251) 368-9136, ext. 2535   Fax: (251) 368-4502
E-mail: mjohnson@pci-nsn.gov
Web: www.poarchcreekindians.org

Summary To recognize and reward members of the Poarch Band of Creek Indians who achieve academic excellence while working on an undergraduate or graduate degree.

Eligibility These awards are presented to enrolled members of the Poarch Band of Creek Indians who are completing an associate, bachelor's, or master's degree program at a college or university in any state and have been enrolled in the tribe's tuition assistance program. To qualify, they must maintain a GPA of 3.5 or higher upon graduation.

Financial data The award is $2,000 for associate degree students, $4,000 for bachelor's degree students, or $2,000 for master's degree students. Other professional degree students are evaluated on a case-by-case basis.

Duration Each student is eligible to receive 1 of these awards.

Number awarded Varies each year.

Deadline Deadline not specified.

[1135]
PORTER PHYSIOLOGY DEVELOPMENT AWARDS

American Physiological Society
Attn: Education Office
9650 Rockville Pike, Room 3111
Bethesda, MD 20814-3991
(301) 634-7132   Fax: (301) 634-7098
E-mail: education@the-aps.org
Web: www.the-aps.org

Summary To provide financial assistance to Native Americans and other minorities who are members of the American Physiological Society (APS) interested in working on a doctoral degree in physiology.

Eligibility This program is open to U.S. citizens and permanent residents who are members of racial or ethnic minority groups (Hispanic or Latino, American Indian or Alaska Native, Asian, Black or African American, or Native Hawaiian or other Pacific Islander). Applicants must be currently enrolled in or accepted to a doctoral program in physiology at a university as full-time students. They must be APS members and have actively participated in its work. Selection is based on the applicant's potential for success (academic record, statement of interest, previous awards and experiences, letters of recommendation); applicant's proposed training environment (including quality of preceptor); and applicant's research and training plan (clarity and quality).

Financial data The stipend is $28,300 per year. No provision is made for a dependency allowance or tuition and fees.

Duration 1 year; may be renewed for 1 additional year and, in exceptional cases, for a third year.

Additional information This program is supported by the William Townsend Porter Foundation (formerly the Harvard Apparatus Foundation). The first Porter Fellowship was awarded in 1920. In 1966 and 1967, the American Physiological Society established the Porter Physiology Development Committee to award fellowships to minority students engaged in graduate study in physiology. The highest ranked applicant for these fellowships is designated the Eleanor Ison Franklin Fellow.

Number awarded Varies each year; recently, 6 were awarded.

Deadline January of each year.

[1136]
POST-BACCALAUREATE INTERNSHIP PROGRAM IN BIOSTATISTICS AND COMPUTATIONAL BIOLOGY

Harvard T.H. Chan School of Public Health
Department of Biostatistics
Attn: Diversity Coordinator
677 Huntington Avenue, SPH2, Fourth Floor
Boston, MA 02115
(617) 432-3175   Fax: (617) 432-5619
E-mail: biostat_diversity@hsph.harvard.edu
Web: www.hsph.harvard.edu

Summary To enable Native American and other underrepresented minority science post-baccalaureates to participate in a summer research internship at Harvard T.H. Chan School of Public Health that focuses on biostatistics and epidemiology.

Eligibility This program is open to students who have received a bachelor's degree and are interested in or planning to attend a graduate degree program in biostatistics or epidemiology. Applicants must be U.S. citizens or permanent residents who are 1) members of ethnic groups underrepresented in graduate education (African Americans, Hispanic/ Latinos, Native Americans, Pacific Islanders, biracial/multiracial); 2) first-generation college students; 3) low-income students; or 4) individuals with a disability. They must have a strong GPA, including course work in calculus, and a strong interest in mathematics, statistics, computer science, and other quantitative subjects.

Financial data Interns receive a salary (amount not specified) and support for travel.

Duration 2 to 3 months, starting in June.

Additional information Interns conduct biostatistical or epidemiologic research alongside a Harvard faculty mentor and graduate student mentor, participate in collaborative research projects, attend regular seminars, and receive directed mentoring and support for graduate school applications and selection.

Number awarded 2 each year.

Deadline January of each year.

[1137]
PREDOCTORAL FELLOWSHIP IN MENTAL HEALTH AND SUBSTANCE ABUSE SERVICES

American Psychological Association
Attn: Minority Fellowship Program
750 First Street, N.E.
Washington, DC 20002-4242
(202) 336-6127   Fax: (202) 336-6012
TDD: (202) 336-6123   E-mail: mfp@apa.org
Web: www.apa.org

Summary To provide financial assistance to Native American and other doctoral students committed to providing mental health and substance abuse services to ethnic minority populations.

Eligibility Applicants must be U.S. citizens, nationals, or permanent residents, enrolled full time in an accredited doctoral program, and committed to a career in psychology related to ethnic minority mental health and substance abuse services. Members of ethnic minority groups (African Americans, Hispanics/Latinos, American Indians, Alaskan Natives, Asian Americans, Native Hawaiians, and other Pacific Islanders) are especially encouraged to apply. Preference is given to students specializing in clinical, school, and counseling psychology. Selection is based on commitment to ethnic minority behavioral health services or policy, knowledge of ethnic minority behavioral health services, the fit between career goals and training environment selected, potential as a future leader in ethnic minority psychology as demonstrated through accomplishments and goals, scholarship and grades, and letters of recommendation.

Financial data The stipend varies but is based on the amount established by the National Institutes of Health for predoctoral students; recently that was $23,376 per year.

Duration 1 academic or calendar year; may be renewed for up to 2 additional years.

Additional information Funding is provided by the U.S. Substance Abuse and Mental Health Services Administration.

Number awarded Varies each year.

Deadline January of each year.

[1138]
PREDOCTORAL FELLOWSHIPS OF THE FORD FOUNDATION DIVERSITY FELLOWSHIP PROGRAM

The National Academies of Sciences, Engineering, and Medicine
Attn: Fellowships Office
500 Fifth Street, N.W.
Washington, DC 20001
(202) 334-2872   Fax: (202) 334-3419
E-mail: FordApplications@nas.edu
Web: sites.nationalacademies.org

Summary To provide financial assistance for graduate school to Native American and other students whose success will increase the racial and ethnic diversity of U.S. colleges and universities.

Eligibility This program is open to citizens, permanent residents, and nationals of the United States who are enrolled or planning to enroll full time in a Ph.D. or Sc.D. degree program and are committed to a career in teaching and research at the college or university level. Applicants may be undergraduates in their senior year, individuals who have completed undergraduate study or some graduate study, or current Ph.D. or Sc.D. students who can demonstrate that they can fully utilize a 3-year fellowship award. They must be working on or planning to work on a degree in 1 of the following fields: American studies, anthropology, archaeology, art and theater history, astronomy, chemistry, communications, computer science, cultural studies, earth sciences, economics, education, engineering, ethnic studies, ethnomusicology, geography, history, international relations, language, life sciences, linguistics, literature, mathematics, performance study, philosophy, physics, political science, psychology, religious studies, sociology, urban planning, and women's studies. Also eligible are interdisciplinary programs such as African American studies, Native American studies, area studies, peace studies, and social justice. Students in practice-oriented areas, terminal master's degrees, other doctoral degrees (e.g., Ed.D., D.F.A., Psy.D.), professional degrees (e.g., medicine, law, public health), or joint degrees (e.g., M.D./Ph.D., J.D./Ph.D., M.F.A./Ph.D.) are not eligible. The following are considered as positive factors in the selection process: evidence of superior academic achievement; promise of continuing achievement as scholars and teachers; membership in a group whose underrepresentation in the American professoriate has been severe and longstanding, including Black/African Americans, Puerto Ricans, Mexican Americans/Chicanos/Chicanas, Native American Indians, Alaska Natives (Eskimos, Aleuts, and other indigenous people of Alaska), and Native Pacific Islanders (Hawaiians, Micronesians, or Polynesians); capacity to respond in pedagogically productive ways to the learning needs of students from diverse backgrounds; sustained personal engagement with communities that are underrepresented in the academy and an ability to bring this asset to learning, teaching, and scholarship at the college and university level; and likelihood of using the diversity of human experience as an educational resource in teaching and scholarship.

Financial data The program provides a stipend to the student of $24,000 per year and an award to the host institution of $2,000 per year in lieu of tuition and fees.

Duration 3 years of support is provided, to be used within a 5-year period.

Additional information The competition for this program is conducted by the National Research Council on behalf of the Ford Foundation. Applicants who merit receiving the fellowship but to whom awards cannot be made because of insufficient funds are given Honorable Mentions; this recognition does not carry with it a monetary award but honors applicants who have demonstrated substantial academic achievement. The National Research Council publishes a list of those Honorable Mentions who wish their names publicized. Fellows may not accept remuneration from another fellowship or similar external award while on this program; however, supplementation from institutional funds, educational benefits from the Department of Veterans Affairs, or educational incentive funds may be received concurrently with Ford Foundation support. Predoctoral fellows are required to submit an interim progress report 6 months after the start of the fellowship and a final report at the end of the 12 month tenure.

Number awarded Approximately 60 each year.

Deadline November of each year.

[1139]
PRESBYTERIAN WOMEN OF COLOR GRANTS
Presbyterian Church (USA)
Attn: Office of Financial Aid for Service
100 Witherspoon Street
Louisville, KY 40202-1396
(502) 569-5224   Toll Free: (888) 728-7228, ext. 5224
Fax: (502) 569-8766   TDD: (800) 833-5955
E-mail: finaid@pcusa.org
Web: www.presbyterianmission.org

Summary To provide financial assistance to graduate students who are women of color and Presbyterian Church (USA) members interested in preparing for church occupations.

Eligibility This program is open to women of color who are full-time graduate students at a PCUSA seminary or accredited theological institution approved by their Committee on Preparation for Ministry. Applicants must be working on 1) an M.Div. degree and enrolled as an inquirer or candidate by a PCUSA presbytery; or 2) an M.A.C.E. degree and preparing for a church occupation. They must be PCUSA members, U.S. citizens or permanent residents, able to demonstrate financial need, and recommended by the financial aid officer at their theological institution. Along with their application, they must submit a 1,000-word essay on what they believe God is calling them to do in ministry.

Financial data Stipends range from $1,000 to $3,000 per year. Funds are intended as supplements to students who have been awarded a Presbyterian Study Grant but still demonstrate remaining financial need.

Duration 1 year; may be renewed up to 2 additional years.

Number awarded Varies each year; the sponsor awards approximately 130 grants for this and 3 related programs each year.

Deadline June of each year.

[1140]
PRINCE KUHI'O HAWAIIAN CIVIC CLUB SCHOLARSHIP
Prince Kuhi'o Hawaiian Civic Club
Attn: Scholarship Chair
P.O. Box 4728
Honolulu, HI 96812
(808) 678-0231   E-mail: pkhcc64@gmail.com
Web: www.pkhcc.com/scholarship.html

Summary To provide financial assistance for undergraduate or graduate studies to persons of Native Hawaiian descent.

Eligibility This program is open to high school seniors and full-time undergraduate or graduate students who are of Native Hawaiian descent (descendants of the aboriginal inhabitants of the Hawaiian Islands prior to 1778). Graduating high school seniors and current undergraduate students must have a GPA of 2.5 or higher; graduate students must have at least a 3.3 GPA. Along with their application, they must submit an essay on a topic that changes annually; recently, students were asked to write on the Hawaiian issue that influenced their decision to pursue their course of study at a college or university. Priority is given to members of the Prince Kuhi'o Hawaiian Civic Club in good standing, including directly-related family members. Special consideration is given to applicants majoring in Hawaiian studies and culture,

Hawaiian language, education, or journalism. Selection is based on academic achievement and leadership potential.

Financial data Stipends range from $500 to $1,000 per year.

Duration 1 year; may be renewed.

Number awarded Varies each year.

Deadline March of each year.

[1141]
PROCTER & GAMBLE AND DINSMORE & SHOHL LLP DIVERSITY SCHOLARSHIP PROGRAM

Dinsmore & Shohl LLP
Attn: Director of Recruiting and Legal Personnel
255 East Fifth Street, Suite 1900
Cincinnati, OH 45202
(513) 977-8488   Fax: (513) 977-8141
E-mail: dinsmore.legalrecruiting@dinsmore.com
Web: www.dinsmorecareers.com

Summary To provide financial assistance and summer work experience with Procter & Gamble to Native American and other law students who will contribute to diversity in the legal profession.

Eligibility This program is open to first-year law students who have made a meaningful commitment to diversity in the legal profession. The sponsor defines diversity as "the confluence of cultures, histories, sexual orientations, religions, and dialects that together make up the whole of our society." Applicants must have a demonstrated record of academic or professional achievement and leadership qualities through past work experience, community involvement, or student activities. They must also be interested in a summer associateship with both Procter & Gamble and with Dinsmore & Shohl LLP. Along with their application, they must submit a 500-word personal statement explaining their interest in the scholarship program and how diversity has impacted their life.

Financial data The program provides an academic scholarship of $10,000 and a paid associateship.

Duration The academic scholarship is for 1 year. The summer associateship is for 12 weeks, of which 6 weeks are at Dinsmore & Shohl and 6 weeks are in the legal department of Procter & Gamble.

Additional information Associateships are available in Cincinnati, Ohio.

Number awarded 1 each year.

Deadline December of each year.

[1142]
PROSKAUER SILVER SCHOLAR PROGRAM

Proskauer Rose LLP
Eleven Times Square
New York, NY 10036
(212) 969-3000   Fax: (212) 969-2900
E-mail: silverscholar@proskauer.com
Web: www.proskauer.com/diversity/silverscholar

Summary To provide financial assistance and work experience to law students who are Native Americans or members of other historically underrepresented groups in the legal profession and are interested in a summer associateship and a permanent position with the sponsoring law firm.

Eligibility This program is open to students currently enrolled full time in the first or second year at an ABA-accred-

ited law school. Applicants must be members of racial and/or ethnic minority groups, be differently abled, or be from disadvantaged socioeconomic backgrounds. First-year students must accept an offer to participate in the summer associate program, successfully complete that program in the following summer, return for at least 2 weeks during the summer after their second year of law school, and receive and accept an offer to join the firm; second-year students must accept an offer to participate in the summer associate program, successfully complete that program in the following summer, and receive and accept an offer to join the firm. Along with their application, they must a legal writing sample and a 500-word personal statement that addresses why diversity is important to them, how they have been a leader and advanced diversity in their community, and how diversity can be improved in the legal profession.

Financial data The stipend is $30,000, paid in installments.

Duration 1 year of academic study and 1 or 2 summers as a summer associate.

Additional information Summer associateships are available at the firm's offices in Boston, Los Angeles, and New York.

Number awarded 1 each year.

Deadline January of each year for first-year students; August of each year for second-year students.

[1143]
PUBLIC HONORS FELLOWSHIPS OF THE OREGON STATE BAR

Oregon State Bar
Attn: Diversity and Inclusion Department
16037 S.W. Upper Boones Ferry Road
P.O. Box 231935
Tigard, OR 97281-1935
(503) 620-0222
Toll Free: (800) 452-8260, ext. 338 (within OR)
Fax: (503) 684-1366   TDD: (503) 684-7416
E-mail: cling@osbar.org
Web: www.osbar.org/diversity/programs.html#honors

Summary To provide law students in Oregon with summer work experience in public interest law, especially Native Americans and others who will help the Oregon State Bar achieve its diversity and inclusion objectives.

Eligibility This program is open to students at law schools in Oregon who are not in the first or final year of study. Each school may nominate up to 5 students. Nominees must have demonstrated a career goal in public interest or public sector law. Preference is given to students who will contribute to the Oregon State Bar's diversity and inclusion program, defined to include age, culture, disability, ethnicity, gender and gender identity or expression, geographic location, national origin, race, religion, sex, sexual orientation, and socio-economic status. They must be interested in working in a law office during the summer; the employment should be in Oregon, although exceptions will be made if the job offers the student special experience not available within the state. Along with their application, they must submit a 500-word personal statement on either 1) how their status as a person of diversity has influenced their decision to become a lawyer and how will it influence them throughout their legal professional career; or 2) a challenge they have faced, how they met the challenge, and how that experience will affect the decisions they will make as a legal professional. They must also submit a sample of their legal writing. Selection is based on the personal statement (35%), legal writing ability (25%), academic achievement (15%), work experience and honors (10%), and financial need (15%). The information on those students is forwarded to prospective employers in Oregon and they arrange to interview the selectees.

Financial data Fellows receive a stipend of $5,000.

Duration 3 months during the summer.

Additional information There is no guarantee that all students selected by the sponsoring organization will receive fellowships at Oregon law firms.

Number awarded 6 each year: 2 from each of the law schools.

Deadline Each law school sets its own deadline.

[1144]
PUBLIC POLICY AND INTERNATIONAL AFFAIRS FELLOWSHIPS

Public Policy and International Affairs Fellowship Program
c/o University of Minnesota
Humphrey School of Public Affairs
130 Humphrey School
301 19th Avenue South
Minneapolis, MN 55455
Toll Free: (877) 774-2001   E-mail: hadd0029@umn.edu
Web: www.ppiaprogram.org/ppia

Summary To provide financial assistance to Native Americans and other students from underrepresented groups who have completed a specified summer institute and are interested in preparing for graduate study in the fields of public policy and/or international affairs.

Eligibility This program is open to people of color historically underrepresented in public policy and international affairs. Applicants must be U.S. citizens or permanent residents interested in a summer institute in public policy and international affairs. They must first apply directly to the summer institute. Following participation in that institute, they apply for graduate study in fields of their choice at 41 designated universities. For a list of participating institutions, contact the sponsor.

Financial data The participating programs in public policy and/or international affairs have agreed to waive application fees and grant fellowships of at least $5,000 to students who have participated in the summer institutes.

Duration 1 summer and 1 academic year.

Additional information This program was established in 1981 when the Alfred P. Sloan Foundation provided a grant to the Association for Public Policy Analysis and Management (APPAM). From 1981 through 1988, participants were known as Sloan Fellows. From 1889 through 1995, the program was supported by the Ford Foundation and administered by the Woodrow Wilson National Fellowship Administration, so participants were known as Woodrow Wilson Fellows in Public Policy and International Affairs. Beginning in 1995, the program's name was shortened to the Public Policy and International Affairs Fellowship Program (PPIA) and the Association of Professional Schools of International Affairs (APSIA) also became an institutional sponsor. In 1999, the Ford Foundation ended its support for PPIA effective with the student cohort that participated in summer institutes in 1999. The APPAM and APSIA incorporated PPIA as an independent organization and have continued to sponsor it. Since summer of 2001, summer institutes have been held at 5 universities: the Summer Program in Public Policy and International Affairs at the Gerald R. Ford School of Public Policy at the University of Michigan, the Humphrey School Junior Institute at the Humphrey School of Public Affairs at the University of Minnesota (which serves as host of the program), the UCP-PIA Junior Summer Institute at the Richard and Rhoda Goldman School of Public Policy at the University of California at Berkeley, the PPIA Junior Summer Institute at the Woodrow Wilson School of Public and International Affairs at Princeton University, and the PPIA Junior Summer Institute at the Heinz School of Public Policy and Management at Carnegie Mellon University. For information on those institutes, contact the respective school. Additional support is currently provided by the Foundation for Child Development and the William T. Grant Foundation.

Number awarded Varies each year.

Deadline Each of the 5 participating universities that offer summer institutes and each of the 41 universities that accept students for graduate study sets its own deadline.

[1145]
PUEBLO OF ISLETA HIGHER EDUCATION PROGRAM

Pueblo of Isleta
Attn: Scholarship Coordinator
P.O. Box 1270
Isleta, NM 87022
(505) 869-9790, ext. 9794   Fax: (505) 869-7573
E-mail: poi08001@isletapueblo.com
Web: www.isletapueblo.com/isleta-higher-education.html

Summary To provide financial assistance to members of the Pueblo of Isleta who are interested in attending college or graduate school in any state.

Eligibility This program is open to undergraduate and graduate students who are tribally enrolled members of the Pueblo of Isleta and can document at least one-half Isleta blood. Applicants must have applied for federal aid by submitting a Free Application for Federal Student Aid (FAFSA).

Financial data For full-time students who can demonstrate financial need, the maximum stipend for a 4-year undergraduate degree or graduate degree is $3,000 per academic term. For part-time students who can demonstrate financial need, the maximum stipend is $1,000 per academic term. For students enrolled in a course of study that normally does not lead to a 4-year degree, the maximum stipend is $1,000 per academic term. For students who are designated as "no-need" by their institution and are ineligible to receive other assistance, the maximum stipend is $5,000 per academic term. Students enrolled in special legal summer programs in preparation for entrance to an accredited institution for the following semester can receive up to a maximum award of $2,500.

Duration 1 year; students may receive support for an undergraduate degree for up to 5 years, for a master's degree for 2 years beyond the bachelor's degree, or for a doctoral degree for 3 years beyond the master's degree.

Number awarded Varies each year.

Deadline June of each year for the full academic year or fall semester; October of each year for the spring semester or winter quarter; March of each year for summer term.

[1146]
PUEBLO OF JEMEZ GRADUATE SCHOLARSHIP PROGRAM

Pueblo of Jemez
Attn: Education Services Center
5117 Highway 4
P.O. Box 100
Jemez Pueblo, NM 87024
(575) 834-9102   Toll Free: (888) 834-3936
Fax: (575) 834-7900
E-mail: higher_ed@jemezpueblo.org
Web: www.jemezpueblo.org

Summary To provide financial assistance to Jemez Pueblo students who demonstrate academic merit and are interested in earning a graduate degree at a school in any state.

Eligibility This program is open to Jemez Pueblo students working on or planning to work on a graduate degree at an accredited institution of higher education in any state as a full-time student. Applicants must have a GPA of 3.0 or higher and be able to demonstrate academic merit. They must be at least one quarter Jemez and recognized by the Jemez Pueblo census office (a Certificate of Indian Blood must be provided). Along with their application, they must submit 2 letters of recommendation, a copy of their letter of acceptance from the institution they are attending or planning to attend, and an official transcript from the high school or college they last attended.

Financial data The stipend depends on the need of the recipient.

Duration 1 semester; may be renewed if the recipient remains enrolled full time with a GPA of 3.5 or higher.

Number awarded Varies each year.

Deadline June of each year for fall; January of each year for spring.

[1147]
PUEBLO OF LAGUNA HIGHER EDUCATION GRADUATE PROGRAM

Pueblo of Laguna
Attn: Partners for Success
11 Rodeo Drive, Building A
P.O. Box 207
Laguna, NM 87026
(505) 552-9322   Fax: (505) 552-0623
E-mail: p.solimon@lagunaed.net
Web: partnersforsuccess.us/pfs—direct-education.html

Summary To provide financial assistance to members of the Pueblo of Laguna who are interested in attending graduate school in any state.

Eligibility This program is open to regular enrolled members of the Pueblo of Laguna. Applicants must have a bachelor's degree and be working on a graduate degree at an accredited college or university in the United States. Along with their application, they must submit a 2- to 3-page essay on the meaning on their graduate education to the Pueblo of Laguna and/or to the larger Indian community, including their

philosophy of leadership, enriching the lives of others, belief systems, cultural experiences, traditions, extracurricular activities at their institution relative to Native issues, tribal and community involvement, previous experience with Laguna, and how they will give back to Laguna Pueblo. Preference is given to applicants who demonstrate an intention to build and enhance local tribal community efforts, followed by fields that address Native American interests and national perspectives.

Financial data The stipend is $5,000 for the first year, $6,000 for the second year, $7,000 for the third year, and $9,000 for the fourth year.

Duration Up to 4 years.

Number awarded Varies each year.

Deadline July of each year.

[1148]
PUEBLO OF POJOAQUE HIGHER EDUCATION SCHOLARSHIP PROGRAM

Pueblo of Pojoaque
Attn: Higher Education
101 C Lightning Loop
Santa Fe, NM 87506
(505) 455-3369   Fax: (505) 455-3360
E-mail: puebloofpojoaque@gmail.com
Web: www.puebloofpojoaque.blogspot.com

Summary To provide financial assistance to Pueblo of Pojoaque tribal members interested in working on an undergraduate or graduate degree at a school in any state.

Eligibility This program is open to Pueblo of Pojoaque tribal members who can provide a certificate of tribal verification. Applicants must be working on or planning to work on a certificate, associate, bachelor's, master's, or doctoral degree at a school of higher education in any state. They must be able to verify that they have applied for all other available financial aid and that they still have financial need. Both full- and part-time undergraduate students are eligible, but graduate students must be enrolled full time.

Financial data Both full- and part-time students receive a grant to cover tuition, fees, and books, to a maximum of $2,000 per year. In addition, full-time students receive a monthly stipend (amount not specified).

Duration Support to full-time students is available for 1 year for certificate programs, 3 years for associate degrees, 5 years for bachelor's degrees, or 4 years for graduate degrees. Support to part-time students is available for 2 years for certificate programs, 4 years for associate degrees, or 7 years for bachelor's degrees. Renewal for full-time students requires that they complete at least 20 hours of nonprofit community service per semester. Renewal for all students requires that they maintain a GPA of 2.0 or higher.

Number awarded Varies each year.

Deadline April of each year.

[1149]
RACE RELATIONS MULTIRACIAL STUDENT SCHOLARSHIP

Christian Reformed Church
Attn: Office of Race Relations
1700 28th Street, S.E.
Grand Rapids, MI 49508
(616) 224-5883   Toll Free: (877) 864-3977
Fax: (616) 224-0834   E-mail: elugo@crcna.org
Web: www.crcna.org/race/scholarships

Summary To provide financial assistance to Native American and other undergraduate and graduate minority students interested in attending colleges related to the Christian Reformed Church in North America (CRCNA).

Eligibility This program is open to students of color in the United States and Canada. Normally, applicants are expected to be members of CRCNA congregations who plan to pursue their educational goals at Calvin Theological Seminary or any of the colleges affiliated with the CRCNA. They must be interested in training for the ministry of racial reconciliation in church and/or in society. Along with their application, they must submit paragraphs about their personal history and family, Christian faith, and Christian leadership goals. Students who have no prior history with the CRCNA must attend a CRCNA-related college or seminary for a full academic year before they are eligible to apply for this program. Students entering their sophomore year must have earned a GPA of 2.0 or higher as freshmen; students entering their junior year must have earned a GPA of 2.3 or higher as sophomores; students entering their senior year must have earned a GPA of 2.6 or higher as juniors.

Financial data First-year students receive $500 per semester. Other levels of students may receive up to $2,000 per academic year.

Duration 1 year.

Additional information This program was first established in 1971 and revised in 1991. Recipients are expected to train to engage actively in the ministry of racial reconciliation in church and in society. They must be able to work in the United States or Canada upon graduating and must consider working for 1 of the agencies of the CRCNA.

Number awarded Varies each year; recently, 31 students received a total of $21,000 in support.

Deadline March of each year.

[1150]
RACIAL ETHNIC PASTORAL LEADERSHIP PROGRAM

Synod of Southern California and Hawaii
Attn: Racial Ethnic Pastoral Leadership Program
14225 Roscoe Boulevard
Panorama, CA 91402
(213) 483-3840, ext. 112   Fax: (818) 891-0212
E-mail: ntucker@synod.org
Web: www.synod.org/#repl

Summary To provide financial assistance to Native Americans and members of other racial minority groups in the Presbyterian Church (USA) Synod of Southern California and Hawaii who are preparing for a career as a pastor or other church vocation.

Eligibility Applicants must be under care of their church's Session and enrolled with a Presbytery within the Synod of Southern California and Hawaii. They must be members of racial ethnic groups interested in becoming a Presbyterian pastor or other church worker (e.g., commissioned ruling elder, certified Christian educator) and serving in a racial ethnic ministry within the PCUSA. Racial ethnic persons who already have an M.Div. degree, are from another denomination in correspondence with the PCUSA, and are seeking to meet PCUSA requirements for ordination or transfer may also be eligible if they plan to serve in a racial ethnic congregation or an approved specialized ministry. Applicants must submit documentation of financial need, recommendations from the appropriate presbytery committee or session, a current transcript, and essays on their goals and objectives. They must be enrolled full or part time in a PCUSA seminary or other seminary approved by the Committee on Preparation for Ministry of their Presbytery.

Financial data The stipend is $5,000 per year.

Duration 1 year; may be renewed.

Additional information This program began in 1984.

Number awarded Varies each year; recently, 5 students were receiving support from this program. Since the program began, it has awarded $372,375 to approximately 335 seminarians.

Deadline April of each year.

[1151]
RACIAL ETHNIC SUPPLEMENTAL GRANTS

Presbyterian Church (USA)
Attn: Office of Financial Aid for Service
100 Witherspoon Street
Louisville, KY 40202-1396
(502) 569-5224   Toll Free: (888) 728-7228, ext. 5224
Fax: (502) 569-8766   TDD: (800) 833-5955
E-mail: finaid@pcusa.org
Web: www.presbyterianmission.org

Summary To provide financial assistance to Native American and other minority graduate students who are Presbyterian Church (USA) members interested in preparing for church occupations.

Eligibility This program is open to racial/ethnic graduate students (Asian American, African American, Hispanic American, Native American, or Alaska Native) who are enrolled full time at a PCUSA seminary or accredited theological institution approved by their Committee on Preparation for Ministry. Applicants must be working on 1) an M.Div. degree and enrolled as an inquirer or candidate by a PCUSA presbytery; or 2) an M.A.C.E. degree and preparing for a church occupation. They must be PCUSA members, U.S. citizens or permanent residents, able to demonstrate financial need, and recommended by the financial aid officer at their theological institution. Along with their application, they must submit a 1,000-word essay on what they believe God is calling them to do in ministry.

Financial data Stipends range from $500 to $1,000 per year. Funds are intended as supplements to students who have been awarded a Presbyterian Study Grant but still demonstrate remaining financial need.

Duration 1 year; may be renewed up to 2 additional years.

Number awarded Varies each year; the sponsor awards approximately 130 grants for this and 3 related programs each year.

Deadline June of each year.

[1152]
RAMSEY COUNTY BAR FOUNDATION LAW STUDENT SCHOLARSHIP

Ramsey County Bar Foundation
Attn: Diversity Committee
E-1401 First National Bank Building
332 Minnesota Street
St. Paul, MN 55101
(651) 222-0846   Fax: (651) 223-8344
E-mail: Cheryl@ramseybar.org
Web: www.ramseybar.org/news/law-student-scholarship

Summary To provide financial assistance to Native Americans and members of other groups traditionally underrepresented in the legal profession who are attending law school in Minnesota.

Eligibility This program is open to residents of any state who are currently enrolled at a Minnesota law school. Applicants must be a member of a group traditionally underrepresented in the legal profession, including race, sex, ethnicity, sexual orientation, or disability. They must contribute meaningfully to diversity in their community, have a record of academic or professional achievement, and display leadership qualities through past work experience, community involvement, or student activities.

Financial data The stipend ranges up to $6,000.

Duration 1 year.

Number awarded 1 each year.

Deadline February of each year.

[1153]
RDW GROUP, INC. MINORITY SCHOLARSHIP FOR COMMUNICATIONS

Rhode Island Foundation
Attn: Donor Services Administrator
One Union Station
Providence, RI 02903
(401) 427-4011   Fax: (401) 331-8085
E-mail: rbogert@rifoundation.org
Web: www.rifoundation.org

Summary To provide financial assistance to Native American and other undergraduate and graduate students of color in Rhode Island who are interested in preparing for a career in communications at a school in any state.

Eligibility This program is open to undergraduate and graduate students at colleges and universities in any state who are Rhode Island residents of color. Applicants must intend to work on a degree in communications (including computer graphics, art, cinematography, or other fields that would prepare them for a career in advertising). They must be able to demonstrate financial need and a commitment to a career in communications. Along with their application, they must submit an essay (up to 300 words) on the impact they would like to have on the communications field.

Financial data The stipend is approximately $2,000 per year.

Duration 1 year; recipients may reapply.

Additional information This program is sponsored by the RDW Group, Inc.

Number awarded 1 each year.

Deadline April of each year.

[1154]
RED CLIFF BAND HIGHER EDUCATION GRANTS PROGRAM

Red Cliff Band of Lake Superior Chippewa
Attn: Education Department
88385 Pike Road, Highway 13
Bayfield, WI 54814
(715) 779-3706, ext. 229   Fax: (715) 779-3704
E-mail: Dee.Gokee@redcliff-nsn.gov
Web: www.redcliff-nsn.gov

Summary To provide financial assistance for college or graduate school to members of the Red Cliff Band of Lake Superior Chippewa.

Eligibility This program is open to enrolled tribal members of the Red Cliff Band who are working on or planning to work on an undergraduate or graduate degree. Applicants must be able to demonstrate financial need. In the selection process, first priority is given to enrolled members of the tribe who reside within the reservation, including the communities of Bayfield and LaPointe; second to enrolled members who reside in the neighboring communities of Cornucopia, Washburn, or Ashland; third to enrolled members of the tribe who reside in the state of Wisconsin and are attending school full time or, only if funding allows, part time; and fourth to enrolled members of the tribe who live in other states and are attending school full time or, only if funding allows, part time.

Financial data The maximum stipend for undergraduate students is $3,000 per academic year for full-time students or $1,500 per academic year for part-time students. The maximum stipend for graduate students is $2,500 per academic year.

Duration 1 year; may be renewed for a total of 10 semesters for undergraduates or 4 semesters for graduate students, provided the recipient maintains a GPA of 2.0 or higher as an undergraduate or 3.0 or higher as a graduate student.

Number awarded Varies each year.

Deadline June of each year.

[1155]
REED SMITH DIVERSE SCHOLARS PROGRAM

Reed Smith LLP
Attn: U.S. Director of Legal Recruiting
Three Logan Square, Suite 3100
1717 Arch Street
Philadelphia, PA 19103
(215) 851-8100   E-mail: dlevin@reedsmith.com
Web: www.reedsmith.com/diverse_scholars_program

Summary To provide financial assistance and summer work experience to Native American and other law students who are committed to diversity.

Eligibility This program is open to students who are completing their first year of law school and are authorized to work in the United States. Applicants must be able to demonstrate a record of academic excellence and a commitment to diversity and inclusion. The sponsor defines diversity to include race, ancestry, religion, color, sex, age, national origin, sexual orientation, gender identity and/or expression, disability, and veteran's status. Along with their application, they must submit a 750-word personal statement on why they believe it is important to strive for diversity and inclusion in the legal profession.

Financial data   The stipend is $20,000. Recipients are also offered a summer associate position at their choice of the firm's U.S. offices after completion of their second year of law school (in Chicago, Houston, Los Angeles, New York, Philadelphia, Pittsburgh, San Francisco, or Washington, D.C.).

Duration   1 year (the second year of law school).

Additional information   The firm established this program in 2008 as part of its commitment to promote diversity in the legal profession.

Number awarded   2 each year.

Deadline   July of each year.

[1156]
REED SMITH/KAISER PERMANENTE 1L DIVERSITY FELLOWSHIP PROGRAM

Reed Smith LLP
Attn: Manager of Legal Recruiting
101 Second Street, Suite 1800
San Francisco, CA 94195
(415) 543-8700   Fax: (415) 391-8269
E-mail: jsisco@reedsmith.com
Web: www.reedsmith.com/Diversity_Fellowship

Summary   To provide financial assistance and summer work experience in the San Francisco Bay area to Native American and other law students who are committed to diversity.

Eligibility   This program is open to students who are completing their first year of law school and are authorized to work in the United States. Applicants must be able to demonstrate a record of academic scholarship, dedication to community service and/or leadership, and an understanding of the importance of diversity and inclusion in the legal profession. The sponsor defines diversity to include race, ancestry, religion, color, sex, age, national origin, sexual orientation, gender identity and/or expression, disability, and veteran's status. They must be interested in a summer associate program at the sponsor's San Francisco office and the Oakland office of Kaiser Permanent Foundation Health Plan, Inc. Along with their application, they must submit a personal statement on the ways in which they consider themselves to be a "diverse" individual and how their life experiences as a diverse individual have impacted their academic and work experiences, have influenced their career choices, and will have in shaping or influencing their legal career.

Financial data   The program provides a summer associate salary and a stipend of $5,000 for the recipient's second year of law school.

Duration   10 weeks during the summer (7 weeks at the law firm's San Francisco office and 3 weeks at Kaiser's Oakland office) and 1 year of academic study.

Additional information   The firm established this program in 2008 as part of its commitment to promote diversity in the legal profession.

Number awarded   1 each year.

Deadline   March of each year.

[1157]
RETAIL REAL ESTATE DIVERSITY SCHOLARSHIP

International Council of Shopping Centers
Attn: ICSC Foundation
1221 Avenue of the Americas, 41st Floor
New York, NY 10020-1099
(646) 728-3628   Fax: (732) 694-1690
E-mail: foundation@icsc.org
Web: www.icsc.org

Summary   To provide financial assistance to Native American and other minority graduate students who are members of the International Council of Shopping Centers (ICSC) and preparing for a career as a retail real estate professional.

Eligibility   This program is open to U.S. citizens who are graduate student members of ICSC and working on a degree related to the retail real estate profession. Applicants must be a member of an underrepresented ethnic minority group (American Indian or Alaskan Native, Asian or Pacific Islander, African American, Hispanic, Caribbean). They must have a GPA of 3.0 or higher and be enrolled full time or enrolled part time while working.

Financial data   The stipend is $2,500.

Duration   1 year.

Number awarded   1 or more each year.

Deadline   January of each year.

[1158]
RICHARD D. HAILEY SCHOLARSHIP

American Association for Justice
Attn: AAJ Education
777 Sixth Street, N.W., Suite 200
Washington, DC 20001
(202) 684-9563   Toll Free: (800) 424-2725
Fax: (202) 965-0355   E-mail: education@justice.org
Web: www.justice.org

Summary   To provide financial assistance for law school to Native American and other minority student members of the American Association for Justice (AAJ).

Eligibility   This program is open to African American, Hispanic, Asian American, Native American, and biracial members of the association who are entering the first, second, or third year of law school. Applicants must submit a 500-word essay on how they meet the selection criteria: commitment to the association, involvement in student chapter and minority caucus activities, desire to represent victims, interest and proficiency of skills in trial advocacy, and financial need.

Financial data   The stipend is $1,000.

Duration   1 year.

Additional information   The American Association for Justice was formerly the Association of Trial Lawyers of America.

Number awarded   Up to 6 each year.

Deadline   May of each year.

[1159]
RICHARD S. WHITE FELLOWSHIP

Helsell Fetterman
Attn: White Fellowship
1001 Fourth Avenue, Suite 4200
Seattle, WA 98154-1154
(206) 292-1144   E-mail: rswfa@helsell.com
Web: www.helsell.com

Summary To provide financial assistance and summer work experience in the Seattle area to Native American and other law students who will further diversity within the legal profession.

Eligibility This program is open to students currently enrolled in the second year of an ABA-accredited law school (third year if working on an LL.M. degree). Applicants must demonstrate an interest in furthering diversity within the community and the profession; the firm's diversity initiatives focus on minorities, women, and GLBT students. They must possess an academic record, leadership abilities, and a commitment to personal and professional initiatives that indicate promise for a successful legal career, particularly in the practice areas represented at Halsell Fetterman and to building a practice in the Seattle area. Along with their application, they must submit a 1- to 2-page personal statement on a topic of their choice that illustrates their ability to enrich the diversity of the legal community.

Financial data The program provides a paid summer associateship at Halsell Fetterman and a stipend of $7,500 for the third year of law school, paid directly to the school.

Duration 12 weeks for the summer associateship; 1 academic year for the scholarship.

Additional information This program began in 2012.

Number awarded 1 each year.

Deadline August of each year.

[1160]
RICHARD (YOGI) CROWE MEMORIAL SCHOLARSHIP

Richard (Yogi) Crowe Memorial Scholarship Fund
P.O. Box 892
Cherokee, NC 28719
E-mail: jans_28719@yahoo.com
Web: www.yogicrowecherokeescholarship.org

Summary To provide financial assistance to members of the Eastern Band of Cherokee Indians who are working on a graduate degree.

Eligibility This program is open to enrolled members of the Eastern Band of Cherokee Indians who have been accepted by a graduate or doctoral school that requires the GMAT, GRE, LSAT, or MCAT for admission. Applicants must be willing to return to Cherokee, North Carolina and contribute to the betterment of the tribe for at least 2 years. Both part- and full-time students are eligible. Financial need is considered in the selection process.

Financial data The stipend depends on the availability of funds.

Duration 1 year.

Number awarded 1 or more each year.

Deadline March of each year for summer term; June of each year for fall semester; October of each year for spring semester.

[1161]
RIDDELL WILLIAMS DIVERSITY FELLOWSHIP

Riddell Williams P.S.
Attn: Recruiting and HR Manager
1001 Fourth Avenue, Suite 4500
Seattle, WA 98154-1192
(206) 624-3600   Fax: (206) 389-1708
E-mail: rmisich@riddellwilliams.com
Web: www.riddellwilliams.com/careers

Summary To provide financial assistance and work experience at Riddell Williams in Seattle to Native American and other law students who reflect diversity.

Eligibility This program is open to second-year students at ABA-accredited law schools who reflect diversity in the legal profession. Applicants must be interested in a summer associateship at the sponsoring law firm followed by support for the third year of law school. They should reflect the firm's definition of diversity, which it defines to include gender, race, national origin, religion, age, veteran status, political affiliation, marital status, disability, socioeconomic circumstances, geographic background, sexual orientation, and family circumstances. Particular emphasis is given to applicants who are members of groups that are historically underrepresented in the legal profession and at the firm. Selection is based on academic record, leadership ability, commitment to community service, personal and professional accomplishments that demonstrate promise for a successful legal career, ability to make continuing contributions to the diversity of the firm and the legal profession, interest in the firm's practice areas, and commitment to building their practice in the Seattle area.

Financial data The program provides a paid summer associateship (salary not specified) and a stipend of $7,500 for the third year of law school.

Duration 1 summer and 1 academic year.

Number awarded 1 each year.

Deadline September of each year.

[1162]
ROBERT D. WATKINS GRADUATE RESEARCH FELLOWSHIP

American Society for Microbiology
Attn: Education Board
1752 N Street, N.W.
Washington, DC 20036-2904
(202) 942-9283   Fax: (202) 942-9329
E-mail: fellowships@asmusa.org
Web: www.asm.org

Summary To provide funding for research in microbiology to Native American and other underrepresented minority doctoral students who are members of the American Society for Microbiology (ASM).

Eligibility This program is open to African Americans, Hispanics, Native Americans, Alaskan Natives, and Pacific Islanders enrolled as full-time graduate students who have completed their first year of doctoral study and who are members of the society. Applicants must propose a joint research plan in collaboration with a society member scientist. They must have completed all graduate course work requirements for the doctoral degree by the date of the activation of the fellowship. U.S. citizenship or permanent resident status is required. Selection is based on academic achievement, evidence of a successful research plan developed in collaboration with a research adviser/mentor, relevant career goals in the microbiological sciences, and involvement in activities that serve the needs of underrepresented groups.

Financial data Students receive $21,000 per year as a stipend; funds may not be used for tuition or fees.

Duration 3 years.

Number awarded Varies each year.

Deadline April of each year.

[1163]
ROBERT J. AND EVELYN CONLEY CREATIVE WRITING AWARD

Cherokee Nation Foundation
800 South Muskogee
Tahlequah, OK 74464
(918) 207-0950   Fax: (918) 207-0951
E-mail: contact@cherokeenationfoundation.org
Web: cherokeenation.academicworks.com

Summary To provide financial assistance to citizens of several Cherokee nations who are enrolled at a college or university in any state and working on an undergraduate or graduate degree in English or creative writing.

Eligibility This program is open to citizens of the Cherokee Nation, the United Keetoowah Band, or the Eastern Band of Cherokee Indians. Applicants must be currently enrolled in an undergraduate or graduate program in English or creative writing at a college or university in any state. They are not required to reside in the Cherokee Nation area. Along with their application, they must submit writing samples and an 800-word essay on their desire to pursue higher education, their chosen field of study, how they plan to serve the Cherokee people after they complete their higher education, and whether or not they speak the Cherokee language. Selection is based on the clarity and presentation of the essay; academic information (including transcripts and ACT scores); school, cultural and community activities; future plans to serve Cherokee people; and financial need.

Financial data The stipend is $1,000 per semester ($2,000 per year).

Duration 1 year. Renewal for the second semester requires the recipient to earn a GPA of 3.0 or higher in the first semester.

Number awarded 1 each year.

Deadline January of each year.

[1164]
ROBERT STRAUSS DIVERSITY SCHOLARSHIP

Akin Gump Strauss Hauer & Feld LLP
Attn: Legal Recruiting
Bank of America Tower
New York NY 10036-6745
(212) 872-1000   Fax: (212) 872-1002
E-mail: nylegalrecruiting@akingump.com
Web: www.akingump.com

Summary To provide financial assistance and work experience at Akin Gump to Native American and other law students who will contribute to diversity in the profession.

Eligibility This program is open to students from diversity backgrounds who are entering their second year at an ABA-accredited law school. Applicants must be interested in a summer associateship at the sponsoring firm's New York or Washington offices. They must have excellent undergraduate and law school academic records, evidence of leadership abilities, personal and professional accomplishments, and a demonstrated commitment to promoting diversity.

Financial data The program provides a paid associateship (salary not specified) at the firm's New York or Washington offices during the summer following their second year of law school and a stipend of $25,000 for the third year of law school. The first half of the stipend is paid upon the successful completion of the summer associateship and the second half is paid prior to the second semester of the students' third year, provided they have received and accepted an offer to join the firm as an associate following the completion of their legal education.

Duration 1 summer and 1 academic year.

Number awarded 2 each year.

Deadline August of each year.

[1165]
ROBERT TOIGO FOUNDATION FELLOWSHIPS

Robert Toigo Foundation
Attn: Fellowship Program Administrator
180 Grand Avenue, Suite 450
Oakland, CA 94612
(510) 763-5771   Fax: (510) 763-5778
E-mail: info@toigofoundation.org
Web: www.toigofoundation.org

Summary To provide financial assistance to Native American and other minority students working on a master's degree in business administration or a related field.

Eligibility This program is open to members of minority groups (African American, Hispanic/Latino, Native American/ Alaskan Native, South Asian American, or Asian American/ Pacific Islander) who are entering or enrolled in a program for an M.B.A., J.D./M.B.A., master's in real estate, or master's in finance. Applicants must be preparing for a career in finance, including (but not limited to) investment management, investment banking, corporate finance, real estate, private equity, venture capital, business development, pension fund investment, or financial services consulting. U.S. citizenship or permanent resident status is required.

Financial data The stipend is $2,500 per year.

Duration Up to 2 years.

Additional information The application fee is $50.

Number awarded Approximately 50 to 60 each year.

Deadline March of each year.

[1166]
ROBERTSON BIG CAT CONSERVATION FELLOWSHIP

Wildlife Conservation Society
Attn: Graduate Scholarship Program
2300 Southern Boulevard
Bronx, NY 10460
(718) 220-5100   E-mail: kmastro@wcs.org
Web: www.wcs.org

Summary To provide funding to graduate students from other countries and from North American indigenous groups who are interested in conducting conservation research relevant to big cats.

Eligibility This program is open to entering a master's or doctoral degree program who are 1) residents of big cat range countries in Africa, Asia, or Latin America; or 2) members of North American indigenous groups. Applicants must be interested in conducting research on big cat conservation issues at the local, regional, or national level. They must be nominated by the program director of the Wildlife Conservation Society (WCS) for their country and be citizens of that country. Current graduate students are not eligible, and applicants do not need to have selected the graduate school they plan to attend when they apply. Along with their application, they must submit 1) a 500-word essay on the key conservation issues in their country; 2) a 500-word essay on why they are preparing for a career as a conservationist; 3) an 850-word essay on their conservation career to date; 4) an 850-word essay on the specific area of studies in which they plan to specialize; 5) a 250-word essay on why this is the right time for them to begin graduate studies; and 6) information on their financial circumstances. Selection is based on the applicant's abilities, their potential to become leaders of the conservation movement in their home country, and the relevance of their proposed study and future work to WCS conservation priorities.

Financial data Fellows receive a grant of $30,000 to $36,000 for tuition, room, board, and a stipend. Other benefits include graduate school application fees, preparation and sitting fees for examinations such as the GRE and TOEFL, visa processing fees, English language training as needed, 1 round-trip airfare, a textbook allowance, a laptop computer and printer, settling-in allowance, and health insurance as required.

Duration 1 year.

Number awarded Varies each year.

Deadline April of each year.

[1167]
RODNEY T. MATHEWS, JR. MEMORIAL SCHOLARSHIP FOR CALIFORNIA INDIANS

Morongo Band of Mission Indians
Attn: Scholarship Coordinator
12700 Pumarra Road
Banning, CA 92220
(951) 572-6185   E-mail: trisha.smith@morongo.org
Web: www.morongonation.org/content/education-services

Summary To provide financial assistance for college or graduate school in any state to California Indians.

Eligibility This program is open to enrolled members of federally-recognized California Indian tribes who have been actively involved in the Native American community. Applicants must submit documentation of financial need, an academic letter of recommendation, and a letter of recommendation from the American Indian community. They must be enrolled full time at an accredited college or university in any state. Undergraduates must have a GPA of 2.75 or higher; graduate students must have a GPA of 3.5 or higher. Along with their application, they must submit 1) a 2-page personal statement on their academic, career, and personal goals; any extenuating circumstances they wish to have considered; how they view their Native American heritage and its importance to them; how they plan to "give back" to Native Americans after graduation; and their on-going active involvement in the Native American community both on and off campus;

and 2) a 2-page essay, either on what they feel are the most critical issues facing tribal communities today and how they see themselves working in relationship to those issues, or on where they see Native people in the 21st century in terms of survival, governance, and cultural preservation, and what role they see themselves playing in that future.

Financial data The maximum stipend is $10,000 per year. Funds are paid directly to the recipient's school for tuition, housing, textbooks, and required fees.

Duration 1 year; may be renewed 1 additional year.

Additional information Recipients are required to complete 60 hours of service with a designated California Indian community agency: California Indian Museum and Cultural Center, Indian Health Care Services, National Indian Justice Center, California Indian Legal Services, California Indian Professor Association, California Indian Culture and Awareness Conference, or California Democratic Party Native American Caucus.

Number awarded 4 each year.

Deadline March of each year.

[1168]
RONALD M. DAVIS SCHOLARSHIP

American Medical Association
Attn: AMA Foundation
330 North Wabash Avenue, Suite 39300
Chicago, IL 60611-5885
(312) 464-4193   Fax: (312) 464-4142
E-mail: amafoundation@ama-assn.org
Web: www.ama-assn.org

Summary To provide financial assistance to medical school students who are Native Americans or members of other underrepresented minority groups and planning to become a primary care physician.

Eligibility This program is open to first- and second-year medical students who are members of the following minority groups: African American/Black, American Indian, Native Hawaiian, Alaska Native, or Hispanic/Latino. Candidates must have an interest in becoming a primary care physician. Only nominations are accepted. Each medical school is invited to submit 2 nominees. U.S. citizenship or permanent resident status is required.

Financial data The stipend is $10,000.

Duration 1 year.

Additional information This program is offered by the AMA Foundation of the American Medical Association as a component of its Minority Scholars Awards. Support is provided by the National Business Group on Health.

Number awarded 1 each year.

Deadline March of each year.

[1169]
ROSA L. PARKS COLLEGE SCHOLARSHIP

Conference of Minority Transportation Officials
Attn: National Scholarship Program
100 M Street, S.E., Suite 917
Washington, DC 20003
(202) 506-2917   E-mail: info@comto.org
Web: www.comto.org/page/scholarships

Summary To provide financial assistance to Native American and other students who have a tie to the Conference of

Minority Transportation Officials (COMTO) and are interested in working on an undergraduate or master's degree in transportation.

Eligibility   This program is open to 1) undergraduates who have completed at least 60 semester credit hours in a transportation discipline; and 2) students working on a master's degree in transportation who have completed at least 15 credits. Applicants must be or have a parent, guardian, or grandparent who has been a COMTO member for at least 1 year. They must have a GPA of 3.0 or higher. Along with their application they must submit a cover letter on their transportation-related career goals and life aspirations. Financial need is not considered in the selection process.

Financial data   The stipend is $4,500. Funds are paid directly to the recipient's college or university.

Duration   1 year.

Number awarded   1 each year.

Deadline   April of each year.

[1170]
ROY M. HUHNDORF SCHOLARSHIP ENDOWMENT

Cook Inlet Region, Inc.
Attn: The CIRI Foundation
3600 San Jeronimo Drive, Suite 256
Anchorage, AK 99508-2870
(907) 793-3575   Toll Free: (800) 764-3382
Fax: (907) 793-3585   E-mail: tcf@thecirifoundation.org
Web: www.thecirifoundation.org/about/donors

Summary   To provide financial assistance for undergraduate or graduate studies in health science to Alaska Natives who are original enrollees to Cook Inlet Region, Inc. (CIRI) and their lineal descendants.

Eligibility   This program is open to Alaska Native enrollees to CIRI under the Alaska Native Claims Settlement Act (ANCSA) of 1971 and their lineal descendants. There are no Alaska residency requirements or age limitations. Applicants must be accepted or enrolled full time in a 4-year undergraduate or a graduate degree program. They must be working on a degree in health science and have a GPA of 2.5 or higher. Along with their application, they must submit a 500-word statement on their educational and career goals and how they are contributing, or planning to contribute, to a positive Alaska Native community. Selection is based on that statement, academic achievement, rigor of course work or degree program, student financial contribution, financial need, grade level, previous work performance, community service, and relationship of degree program to career goals.

Financial data   The stipend is $10,000 per year, $8,000 per year, or $2,500 per semester, depending on GPA.

Duration   1 semester or 1 year.

Additional information   CIRI is 1 of 13 regional corporations established according to the terms of the Alaska Native Claims Settlement Act (ANCSA) of 1971. This program began in 1995.

Number awarded   1 or more each year.

Deadline   May of each year for annual scholarships; May or November of each year for semester scholarships.

[1171]
RUKIN HYLAND DORIA & TINDALL EQUITY AND INCLUSION SCHOLARSHIP

Rukin Hyland Doria & Tindall LLP
Attn: Scholarship
100 Pine Street, Suite 2150
San Francisco, CA 94111
(415) 421-1800   Toll Free: (855) 557-5880
Web: www.rhdtlaw.com/equityscholarship

Summary   To provide financial assistance to Native American and other law students from underrepresented groups who are interested in a career in employment law.

Eligibility   This program is open to second-year law students who are members of underrepresented groups in the bar, including law students who are economically disadvantaged. Applicants must be able to demonstrate solid academic credentials, personal achievement outside the school environment, significant participation in community service, and an interest in employment law. They must have a cumulative GPA of 3.3 or higher. Along with their application, they must submit an essay of 750 to 1,000 words on how they hope that their work will promote fairness and justice in their community or in society as a whole.

Financial data   The stipend is $3,000.

Duration   1 year.

Additional information   This program began in 2014.

Number awarded   1 each year.

Deadline   August of each year.

[1172]
RUTH D. PETERSON FELLOWSHIPS FOR RACIAL AND ETHNIC DIVERSITY

American Society of Criminology
Attn: Awards Committee
1314 Kinnear Road, Suite 212
Columbus, OH 43212-1156
(614) 292-9207   Fax: (614) 292-6767
E-mail: asc@asc41.com
Web: www.asc41.com

Summary   To provide financial assistance to Native American and other ethnic minority doctoral students in criminology and criminal justice.

Eligibility   This program is open to students of color, especially members of ethnic groups underrepresented in the field of criminology and criminal justice, including (but not limited to) Asians, Blacks, Indigenous peoples, and Latina/os. Applicants must have been accepted into a doctoral program in the field. Along with their application, they must submit an up-to-date curriculum vitae; a personal statement on their race or ethnicity; copies of undergraduate and graduate transcripts; a statement of need and prospects for other financial assistance; a letter describing career plans, salient experiences, and nature of interest in criminology and criminal justice; and 3 letters of reference.

Financial data   The stipend is $6,000.

Duration   1 year.

Additional information   This program began in 1988 as the American Society of Criminology Graduate Fellowships for Ethnic Minorities. Its current name was adopted in 2016.

Number awarded   3 each year.

Deadline   February of each year.

[1173]
RUTH L. KIRSCHSTEIN NATIONAL RESEARCH SERVICE AWARDS FOR INDIVIDUAL PREDOCTORAL FELLOWSHIPS TO PROMOTE DIVERSITY IN HEALTH-RELATED RESEARCH

National Institutes of Health
Office of Extramural Research
Attn: Grants Information
6705 Rockledge Drive, Suite 4090
Bethesda, MD 20892-7983
(301) 435-0714   Fax: (301) 480-0525
TDD: (301) 451-5936   E-mail: grantsinfo@nih.gov
Web: www.grants.nih.gov

Summary To provide financial assistance to Native American and students from other underrepresented groups interested in working on a doctoral degree and preparing for a career in biomedical and behavioral research.

Eligibility This program is open to students enrolled or accepted for enrollment in a Ph.D. or equivalent research degree program; a formally combined M.D./Ph.D. program; or other combined professional doctoral/research Ph.D. program in the biomedical, behavioral, or clinical sciences. Students in health professional degree programs (e.g., M.D., D.O., D.D.S., D.V.M.) are not eligible. Applicants must be 1) members of an ethnic or racial group underrepresented in biomedical or behavioral research; 2) individuals with disabilities; or 3) individuals from socially, culturally, economically, or educationally disadvantaged backgrounds that have inhibited their ability to prepare for a career in health-related research. They must be U.S. citizens, nationals, or permanent residents.

Financial data The fellowship provides an annual stipend of $23,376, a tuition and fee allowance (60% of costs up to $16,000 or 60% of costs up to $21,000 for dual degrees), and an institutional allowance of $4,200 ($3,100 at for-profit and federal institutions) for travel to scientific meetings, health insurance, and laboratory and other training expenses.

Duration Up to 5 years for Ph.D. students or up to 6 years for M.D./Ph.D. or other combined research degree programs.

Additional information These fellowships are offered by most components of the National Institutes of Health (NIH). Contact the NIH for a list of names and telephone numbers of responsible officers at each component.

Number awarded Varies each year.

Deadline April, August, or December of each year.

[1174]
RUTH MUSKRAT BRONSON FELLOWSHIP

American Indian Graduate Center
Attn: Executive Director
3701 San Mateo Boulevard, N.E., Suite 200
Albuquerque, NM 87110-1249
(505) 881-4584   Toll Free: (800) 628-1920
Fax: (505) 884-0427   E-mail: fellowships@aigc.com
Web: www.aigcs.org/scholarships/graduate-fellowships

Summary To provide financial assistance to Native American students interested in working on a graduate degree in nursing or other health-related field.

Eligibility This program is open to enrolled members of federally-recognized American Indian tribes and Alaska Native groups who can document one-fourth degree federally-recognized Indian blood. Applicants must be enrolled full time at a graduate school in the United States. First priority is given to nursing students; second priority is given to students in other health-related fields. Along with their application, they must submit a 500-word essay on how receiving this fellowship will enable them to continue to build, promote, and honor self-sustaining American Indian and Alaska Native communities. Financial need is also considered in the selection process.

Financial data Stipends range from $500 to $5,000 per academic year, depending on the availability of funds and the recipient's unmet financial need.

Duration 1 year; may be renewed.

Number awarded 1 or 2 each year.

Deadline May of each year.

[1175]
RUTH WEBB MINORITY SCHOLARSHIP

California Academy of Physician Assistants
2318 South Fairview Street
Santa Ana, CA 92704-4938
(714) 427-0321   Fax: (714) 427-0324
E-mail: capa@capanet.org
Web: www.capanet.org

Summary To provide financial assistance to Native American and other minority student members of the California Academy of Physician Assistants (CAPA) enrolled in physician assistant programs in California.

Eligibility This program is open to student members of CAPA enrolled in primary care physician assistant programs in California. Applicants must be members of a minority group (African American, Hispanic, Asian/Pacific Islander, or Native American/Alaskan Native). They must have maintained good academic standing and conducted activities to promote the physician assistant profession. Along with their application, they must submit an essay describing the activities they have performed to promote the physician assistant profession, the importance of representing minorities in their community, and why they should be awarded this scholarship. Financial need is considered in the selection process.

Financial data The stipend is $2,000.

Duration 1 year.

Number awarded 1 each year.

Deadline December of each year.

[1176]
SAGINAW CHIPPEWA INDIAN TRIBAL SCHOLARSHIP PROGRAM

Saginaw Chippewa Indian Tribe of Michigan
Attn: Higher Education Coordinator
7070 East Broadway Road
Mt. Pleasant, MI 48858
(989) 775-4505   Fax: (989) 775-4529
E-mail: skutt@sagchip.org
Web: www.sagchipschool.net/higher-ed/Scholarships

Summary To provide financial assistance for college, graduate school, or vocational training to members of the Saginaw Chippewa Indian Tribe of Michigan.

Eligibility This program is open to enrolled members of the Saginaw Chippewa Indian Tribe of Michigan who are attending or planning to attend an accredited 2- or 4-year college, university, or vocational/trade institution in any state. Applicants must be interested in working on an undergraduate or graduate degree or vocational certificate as a full- or part-time student. They must apply for all available financial aid using the FAFSA standard form; residents of Michigan who plan to attend college in that state must also apply for the Michigan Indian Tuition Waiver. U.S. citizenship is required.

Financial data The stipend for vocational training is $125 per week, to a maximum of $2,000. The stipend for undergraduate and graduate study is $1,000 per semester ($2,000 per year) for part-time students enrolled in 6 to 8 undergraduate credit hours or 3 to 5 graduate credit hours, $1,500 per semester ($3,000 per year) for part-time students enrolled in 9 to 11 undergraduate credit hours or 6 to 8 graduate credit hours, or $2,000 per semester ($4,000 per year) for full-time students.

Duration 1 year; may be renewed, provided the recipient maintains a GPA of 2.0 or higher. Students are limited to receiving 1 each of vocational certificates, associate degree, bachelor's degree, master's degree, or doctoral degree.

Number awarded Varies each year.

Deadline October of each year for fall semester or quarter; February of each year for winter quarter or spring quarter or semester; or June of each year for summer term.

[1177]
SALAMATOF NATIVE ASSOCIATION, INC. SCHOLARSHIP AND GRANT PROGRAM

Cook Inlet Region, Inc.
Attn: The CIRI Foundation
3600 San Jeronimo Drive, Suite 256
Anchorage, AK 99508-2870
(907) 793-3575　　　　Toll Free: (800) 764-3382
Fax: (907) 793-3585　　E-mail: tcf@thecirifoundation.org
Web: www.thecirifoundation.org

Summary To provide financial assistance for undergraduate or graduate studies to Alaska Natives who are original enrollees of the Salamatof Native Association, Inc. (SNAI) and their spouses and lineal descendants.

Eligibility This program is open to Alaska Native enrollees to SNAI under the Alaska Native Claims Settlement Act (ANCSA) of 1971 and their spouses and lineal descendants. There are no Alaska residency requirements or age limitations. Applicants must be accepted or enrolled full or part time in a 2-year, 4-year undergraduate, technical skills training, or graduate degree program. They must have a GPA of 2.5 or higher. Along with their application, they must submit a 500-word statement on their educational and career goals and how they are contributing, or planning to contribute, to a positive Alaska Native community. Selection is based on that statement, academic achievement, rigor of course work or degree program, student financial contribution, financial need, grade level, previous work performance, community service, and relationship of degree program to career goals.

Financial data Stipends range from $2,250 to $2,500 per term.

Duration 1 year; recipients must reapply each year.

Additional information Cook Inlet Region, Inc. (CIRI) is 1 of 13 regional corporations established according to the terms of the Alaska Native Claims Settlement Act (ANCSA) of 1971. This program began in 1992 by the Salamatof Native Association, Inc. which provides funds matched by the CIRI Foundation.

Number awarded Varies each year; recently, 3 were awarded.

Deadline May or December of each year for academic programs; June of each year for vocational programs.

[1178]
SAN CARLOS APACHE TRIBE HIGHER EDUCATION GRANTS

San Carlos Apache Tribe
Attn: Department of Education
1 San Carlos Avenue
San Carlos, AZ 85550
(928) 475-2336　　　　　　Fax: (928) 475-2507
Web: www.scateducationdepartment.com

Summary To provide financial assistance for college or graduate school in any state to members of the San Carlos Apache Tribe.

Eligibility This program is open to members of the San Carlos Apache Tribe who are attending or planning to attend an accredited 2- or 4-year college or university in any state. Applicants must be interested in working on an associate, baccalaureate, or graduate degree as a full- or part-time student. They must be able to demonstrate financial need and have 1) a GPA of 2.0 or higher or a GED score of 45 or higher; and 2) an ACT score of 22 or higher or an SAT combined critical reading and mathematics score of 930 or higher. In the selection process, awards are presented in the following priority order: first, full-time undergraduate students who reside on the San Carlos Reservation in southeastern Arizona; second, graduate students who reside on the reservation; third, part-time students who reside on the reservation; fourth, students who reside off the reservation; and fifth, students who do not demonstrate financial need (assisted only if funds are available).

Financial data The stipend depends on the financial need of the recipient, to a maximum of $4,000 per semester at a 2-year college or $5,000 per semester at a 4-year college or university.

Duration 1 year; may be renewed up to a total of 64 credit hours at a 2-year college, up to 125 credit hours at a 4-year college or university. Renewal requires the recipient to maintain a GPA of 2.0 or higher as an undergraduate or 3.0 or higher as a graduate student.

Number awarded Varies each year.

Deadline June of each year for fall semester; November of each year for spring semester.

[1179]
SASP ADVANCED STUDENT DIVERSITY SCHOLARSHIPS

American Psychological Association
Attn: Division 16 (School Psychology)
750 First Street, N.E.
Washington, DC 20002-4242
(202) 336-6165　　　　　　Fax: (202) 218-3599
TDD: (202) 336-6123　　E-mail: cchambers@apa.org
Web: www.apadivisions.org/division-16/awards/sasp.aspx

Summary To provide financial assistance to continuing graduate student members of the Student Affiliates in School

Psychology (SASP) of Division 16 (School Psychology) of the American Psychological Association (APA) who are Native Americans or from other underrepresented cultural backgrounds.

Eligibility This program is open to SASP members who come from underrepresented cultural backgrounds. Applicants must be working on a graduate degree to prepare for a career as a school psychologist. They must be entering their third, fourth, or fifth year of graduate study.

Financial data The stipend is $1,000.

Duration 1 year; nonrenewable.

Number awarded 1 each year.

Deadline April of each year.

[1180]
SAULT TRIBE SPECIAL NEEDS SCHOLARSHIPS

Sault Tribe of Chippewa Indians
Attn: Higher Education Department
523 Ashmun Street
Sault Ste. Marie, MI 49783
(906) 635-6050, ext. 26312   Toll Free: (800) 793-0660
Fax: (906) 635-7785   E-mail: BMacArthur@saulttribe.net
Web: www.saulttribe.com

Summary To provide financial assistance for education at any level to members of the Sault Tribe of Chippewa Indians who have a disability.

Eligibility This program is open to members of the Sault Tribe who have a documented physical or emotional disability. Applicants must be enrolled in an educational program at any level. Along with their application, they must submit a letter from themselves or a parent describing the proposed use of the funds and an itemized list of the expected costs.

Financial data The stipend is $1,000.

Duration 1 year.

Number awarded 4 each year: 2 for students under 18 years of age and 2 for students 18 years of age or older.

Deadline May of each year.

[1181]
SCHOLARSHIP FOR A THEOLOGICAL LIBRARIANSHIP COURSE

American Theological Library Association
Attn: Diversity Committee
300 South Wacker Drive, Suite 2100
Chicago, IL 60606-6701
(312) 454-5100   Toll Free: (888) 665-ATLA
Fax: (312) 454-5505   E-mail: memberrep@atla.com
Web: www.atla.com

Summary To provide funding to Native American library students from other underrepresented groups who are members of the American Theological Library Association (ATLA) interested in taking a course in theological librarianship.

Eligibility This program is open to ATLA members from underrepresented groups (religious, racial, ethnic, or gender) who wish to attend a theological librarianship course at an ALA-accredited master's program in library and information studies. Applicants must submit personal statements on what diversity means to them, why their voice has not yet been heard, how their voice will add diversity to the theological librarianship course, how they will increase diversity in their

immediate context, and how they plan to increase diversity and participate fully in the ATLA.

Financial data The stipend is $1,200.

Duration Up to 1 year.

Number awarded 1 each year.

Deadline April of each year.

[1182]
SCHOLARSHIPS FOR MINORITY ACCOUNTING STUDENTS

American Institute of Certified Public Accountants
Attn: Academic and Career Development Division
220 Leigh Farm Road
Durham, NC 27707-8110
(919) 402-4931   Fax: (919) 419-4705
E-mail: scholarships@aicpa.org
Web: www.aicpa.org

Summary To provide financial assistance to Native Americans and other minorities interested in studying accounting at the undergraduate or graduate school level.

Eligibility This program is open to minority undergraduate and graduate students, enrolled full time, who have a GPA of 3.3 or higher (both cumulatively and in their major) and intend to pursue a C.P.A. credential. The program defines minority students as those whose heritage is Black or African American, Hispanic or Latino, Native American, or Asian American. Undergraduates must have completed at least 30 semester hours, including at least 6 semester hours of a major in accounting. Graduate students must be working on a master's degree in accounting, finance, taxation, or a related program. Applicants must be U.S. citizens or permanent residents and student affiliate members of the American Institute of Certified Public Accountants (AICPA). Along with their application, they must submit 500-word essays on 1) why they want to become a C.P.A. and how attaining that licensure will contribute to their goals; and 2) how they would spread the message about accounting and the C.P.A. profession in their community and school. In the selection process, some consideration is given to financial need.

Financial data Stipends range up to $5,000 per year. Funds are disbursed directly to the recipient's school.

Duration 1 year; may be renewed up to 3 additional years or until completion of a bachelor's or master's degree, whichever is earlier.

Additional information This program began in 1969. Additional support is provided by the Accounting Education Foundation of the Texas Society of Certified Public Accountants, the New Jersey Society of Certified Public Accountants, Robert Half International, and the Virgin Islands Society of Certified Public Accountants.

Number awarded Varies each year; recently, 97 students received funding through this program.

Deadline March of each year.

[1183]
SCHWABE, WILLIAMSON & WYATT SUMMER ASSOCIATE DIVERSITY SCHOLARSHIP

Schwabe, Williamson & Wyatt, Attorneys at Law
Attn: Diversity Committee Chair
1211 S.W. Fifth Avenue, Suite 1900
Portland, OR 97204
(503) 796-2903   Fax: (503) 796-2900
E-mail: agamblin@schwabe.com
Web: www.schwabe.com/recruitdiversity.aspx

Summary To provide financial assistance and summer work experience in Portland, Oregon or Seattle, Washington to Native American and other law students who will bring to the legal profession differences related to race, gender, ethnicity, religion, disability, and sexual orientation.

Eligibility This program is open to first-year students working on a J.D. degree at an ABA-accredited law school. Applicants must 1) contribute to the diversity of the law school student body and the legal community; 2) possess a record of academic achievement, capacity, and leadership as an undergraduate and in law school that indicates promise for a successful career in the legal profession; and 3) demonstrate a commitment to practice law in the Pacific Northwest upon completion of law school. They must be interested in a paid summer associateship at the sponsoring law firm's office in Portland, Oregon or Seattle, Washington. Along with their application, they must submit a resume, undergraduate and law school transcripts, a legal writing sample, and a 1- to 2-page personal statement explaining their interest in the scholarship and how they will contribute to diversity in the legal community.

Financial data The program provides a paid summer associateship during the summer following completion of the first year of law school and an academic scholarship of $7,500 to help pay tuition and other expenses during the recipient's second year of law school.

Duration 1 year.

Number awarded 1 each year.

Deadline January of each year.

[1184]
SEALASKA HERITAGE INSTITUTE 7(I) SCHOLARSHIPS

Sealaska Corporation
Attn: Sealaska Heritage Institute
105 South Seward Street, Suite 201
Juneau, AK 99801
(907) 463-4844   E-mail: scholarships@sealaska.com
Web: scholarship.sealaskaheritage.org/Account/LogOn

Summary To provide financial assistance for undergraduate or graduate study in any state to Native Alaskans who have a connection to Sealaska Corporation and are majoring in designated fields.

Eligibility This program is open to 1) Alaska Natives who are shareholders of Sealaska Corporation; and 2) Native lineal descendants of Alaska Natives enrolled to Sealaska Corporation, whether or not the applicant owns Sealaska Corporation stock. Applicants must be enrolled or accepted for enrollment as full-time undergraduate or graduate students at a college or university in any state. Along with their application, they must submit 2 essays: 1) their personal history and

educational goals; and 2) their expected contributions to the Alaska Native or Native American community. Financial need is also considered in the selection process. The following areas of study qualify for these awards: natural resources (environmental sciences, engineering, conservation biology, environmental law, fisheries, forestry, geology, marine science/biology, mining technology, wildlife management); business administration (accounting, computer information systems, economics, finance, human resources management, industrial management, information systems management, international business, international commerce and trade, and marketing); and other special fields (cadastral surveys, chemistry, equipment/machinery operators, industrial safety specialists, health specialists, plastics engineers, trade specialists, physics, mathematics, and marine trades and occupations).

Financial data The amount of the award depends on the availability of funds, the number of qualified applicants, class standing, and cumulative GPA.

Duration 1 year; may be renewed up to 6 years for a bachelor's degree, up to 3 years for a master's degree, up to 2 years for a doctorate, or up to 3 years for vocational study. The maximum total support is limited to 9 years. Renewal depends on recipients' maintaining full-time enrollment and a GPA of 2.0 or higher.

Additional information Funding for this program is provided from Alaska Native Claims Settlement Act (ANSCA) Section 7(i) revenue sharing provisions. Sealaska Corporation is 1 of 13 Alaska Native Regional Corporations created under the Alaska Native Claims Settlement Act of 1971.

Number awarded Varies each year.

Deadline February of each year.

[1185]
SEALASKA HERITAGE SCHOLARSHIPS

Sealaska Corporation
Attn: Sealaska Heritage Institute
105 South Seward Street, Suite 201
Juneau, AK 99801
(907) 463-4844   E-mail: scholarships@sealaska.com
Web: scholarship.sealaskaheritage.org/Account/LogOn

Summary To provide financial assistance for undergraduate or graduate study in any state to Native Alaskans who have a connection to Sealaska Corporation.

Eligibility This program is open to 1) Alaska Natives who are shareholders of Sealaska Corporation; and 2) Native lineal descendants of Alaska Natives enrolled to Sealaska Corporation, whether or not they own Sealaska Corporation stock. Applicants must be enrolled or accepted for enrollment as full-time undergraduate or graduate students at a college or university in any state. Undergraduates must have a GPA of 2.0 or higher; graduate students must have a GPA of 3.0 or higher. Along with their application, they must submit 2 essays: 1) their personal history and educational goals; and 2) their expected contributions to the Alaska Native or Native American community. Financial need is also considered in the selection process.

Financial data The amount of the award depends on the availability of funds, the number of qualified applicants, class standing, and cumulative GPA.

Duration 1 year; may be renewed up to 6 years for a bachelor's degree, up to 3 years for a master's degree, up to 2 years for a doctorate, or up to 3 years for vocational study. The maximum total support is limited to 9 years. Renewal depends on recipients' maintaining full-time enrollment and a GPA of 2.0 or higher as an undergraduate or 3.0 or higher as a graduate student.

Additional information Sealaska Corporation is 1 of 13 Alaska Native Regional Corporations created under the Alaska Native Claims Settlement Act of 1971.

Number awarded Varies each year.

Deadline February of each year.

[1186]
SELECTED PROFESSIONS FELLOWSHIPS FOR WOMEN OF COLOR

American Association of University Women
Attn: AAUW Educational Foundation
1111 16th Street, N.W.
Washington, DC 20036-4873
(202) 785-7700   Toll Free: (800) 326-AAUW
Fax: (202) 872-1425   TDD: (202) 785-7777
E-mail: aauw@applyists.com
Web: www.aauw.org

Summary To aid women of color who are in their final year of graduate training in the fields of business administration, law, or medicine.

Eligibility This program is open to women who are working full time on a degree in fields in which women of color have been historically underrepresented: business administration (M.B.A.), law (J.D.), or medicine (M.D., D.O.). They must be African Americans, Mexican Americans, Puerto Ricans and other Hispanics, Native Americans, Alaska Natives, Asian Americans, or Pacific Islanders. U.S. citizenship or permanent resident status is required. Applicants in business administration must be entering their second year of study; applicants in law must be entering their third year of study; applicants in medicine may be entering their third or fourth year of study. Special consideration is given to applicants who 1) demonstrate their intent to enter professional practice in disciplines in which women are underrepresented, to serve underserved populations and communities, or to pursue public interest areas; and 2) are nontraditional students. Selection is based on professional promise and personal attributes (50%), academic excellence and related academic success indicators (40%), and financial need (10%).

Financial data Stipends range from $5,000 to $18,000.

Duration 1 year, beginning in July.

Additional information The filing fee is $35.

Number awarded Varies each year; recently, a total of 25 Selected Professions Fellowships were awarded.

Deadline January of each year.

[1187]
SEMICONDUCTOR RESEARCH CORPORATION MASTER'S SCHOLARSHIP PROGRAM

Semiconductor Research Corporation
Attn: Global Research Collaboration
1101 Slater Road, Suite 120
P.O. Box 12053
Research Triangle Park, NC 27709-2053
(919) 941-9400   Fax: (919) 941-9450
E-mail: students@src.org
Web: www.src.org/student-center/fellowship/#tab2

Summary To provide financial assistance to Native Americans and other minorities interested in working on a master's degree in a field of microelectronics relevant to the interests of the Semiconductor Research Corporation (SRC).

Eligibility This program is open to women and members of underrepresented minority groups (African Americans, Hispanics, and Native Americans). Applicants must be U.S. citizens or have permanent resident, refugee, or political asylum status in the United States. They must be admitted to an SRC participating university to work on a master's degree in a field relevant to microelectronics under the guidance of an SRC-sponsored faculty member and under an SRC-funded contract. Selection is based on academic achievement.

Financial data The fellowship provides full tuition and fee support, a competitive stipend (recently, $2,536 per month), an annual grant of $2,000 to the university department with which the student recipient is associated, and travel expenses to the Graduate Fellowship Program Annual Conference.

Duration Up to 2 years.

Additional information This program began in 1997 for underrepresented minorities and expanded to include women in 1999.

Number awarded Approximately 12 each year.

Deadline January of each year.

[1188]
SENECA NATION HIGHER EDUCATION PROGRAM

Seneca Nation of Indians
Attn: Higher Education Department, Cattaraugus Territory
12861 Route 438
Irving, NY 14081
(716) 532-3341   Fax: (716) 532-3269
E-mail: snihighered@sni.org
Web: sni.org

Summary To provide financial assistance for college or graduate school to members of the Seneca Nation of Indians in New York.

Eligibility This program is open to members of the Seneca Nation of Indians who are enrolled or planning to enroll in an associate, bachelor's, master's, or doctoral program. They must have applied for all other forms of financial aid for which they qualify, e.g., full-time undergraduates who are New York residents must apply for New York State Indian Aid (NYSIA) and the New York State Tuition Assistance Program (TAP); part-time undergraduates who are New York residents must apply for Aid for Part-Time Study (APTS); non-residents of New York must apply for funding from their state of residence; graduate students must apply for an American Indian Graduate Center (AIGC) fellowship. Applicants with permanent residence on the reservation qualify for level 1 awards; those with permanent residence within New York qualify for level 2 awards; those with permanent residence outside New York qualify for level 3 awards. Financial need is considered in the selection process.

Financial data Maximum awards per academic year for tuition and fees are $15,000 for level 1 students, $12,000 for level 2 students, or $10,000 for level 3 students. Other benefits for all recipients include $1,400 per year for books and supplies for full-time students or $140 per 3-credit hours for part-time students; payment of room and board in dormitories or college-approved housing for full-time students; a transportation allowance for commuters of $1,000 per year for full-time students or $100 per 3-credit hours for part-time students; a supplies allowance of $600 per year for full-time students or $60 per 3-credit hours for part-time students; a computer allowance of $1,200; a required equipment/tools allowance of $1,200; and a child care expense allowance of $750 per semester for full-time students or $375 per semester for part-time students.

Duration 1 year; may be renewed.

Number awarded Varies each year.

Deadline July of each year for fall semester or quarter; October of each year for winter quarter; December of each year for spring semester or quarter; May of each year for summer semester or quarter.

[1189]
SEO CAREER LAW PROGRAM

Sponsors for Educational Opportunity
Attn: Career Program
55 Exchange Place
New York, NY 10005
(212) 979-2040   Toll Free: (800) 462-2332
Fax: (646) 706-7113
E-mail: careerprogram@seo-usa.org
Web: www.seo-usa.org/Career/Corporate_Law

Summary To provide summer work experience to Native Americans and other students of color interested in studying law.

Eligibility This program is open to students of color who are college seniors or recent graduates planning to attend law school in the United States. Applicants must be interested in a summer internship at a participating law firm that specializes in corporate law, including initial public offerings of stock, mergers and acquisitions, joint ventures, corporate reorganizations, cross-border financing, including securities, tax, bankruptcy, antitrust, real estate and white-collar crime. They must have a cumulative GPA of 3.0 or higher. Personal interviews are required.

Financial data Interns receive a competitive stipend of up to $1,300 per week.

Duration 10 weeks during the summer.

Additional information This program began in 1980. Internships are available in New York City, Washington, D.C., Houston, Los Angeles, San Francisco, Menlo Park, Palo Alto, or Atlanta.

Number awarded Varies each year.

Deadline February of each year.

[1190]
SEQUOYAH GRADUATE FELLOWSHIPS

Association on American Indian Affairs, Inc.
Attn: Director of Scholarship Programs
966 Hungerford Drive, Suite 12-B
Rockville, MD 20850
(240) 314-7155   Fax: (240) 314-7159
E-mail: general.aaia@indian-affairs.org
Web: www.indian-affairs.org/graduate-applications.html

Summary To provide financial assistance to Native Americans interested in working on a graduate degree in any field.

Eligibility This program is open to American Indians and Alaskan Natives working full time on a graduate degree. Applicants must submit proof of tribal enrollment and an essay of 2 to 3 pages on 1 of the following topics: 1) why the sponsor's International Repatriation Project is important and how they would inform others about it; 2) the Annie E. Casey Foundation's Juvenile Detention Alternatives Initiative and tribal and community-based alternatives to detention for juveniles; or 3) how tribal leaders can promote higher education in their family and community. They must have a GPA of 2.5 or higher. Selection is based on merit and need.

Financial data The stipend is $1,500.

Duration 1 year; recipients may reapply.

Number awarded Varies each year; recently, 7 were awarded.

Deadline May of each year.

[1191]
SHERRY R. ARNSTEIN MINORITY STUDENT SCHOLARSHIP

American Association of Colleges of Osteopathic
  Medicine
Attn: Scholarships
5550 Friendship Boulevard, Suite 310
Chevy Chase, MD 20815-7231
(301) 968-4142   Fax: (301) 968-4101
E-mail: jshepperd@aacom.org
Web: www.aacom.org

Summary To provide financial assistance to Native Americans and other underrepresented minority students entering or enrolled in osteopathic medical school.

Eligibility This program is open to African American, mainland Puerto Rican, Hispanic, Native American, Native Hawaiian, and Alaska Native students who are entering or currently enrolled in good standing in their first, second, or third year of osteopathic medical school. Applicants must submit a 4-page essay on what osteopathic medical schools can do to recruit and retain more underrepresented minority students, what they personally plan to do as a student and as a future D.O. to help increase minority student enrollment at a college of osteopathic medicine, and how and why they were drawn to osteopathic medicine.

Financial data The stipend is $2,500.

Duration 1 year; nonrenewable.

Number awarded 2 each year: 1 entering and 1 continuing student.

Deadline March of each year.

[1192]
SIDLEY DIVERSITY AND INCLUSION SCHOLARSHIP

Sidley Austin LLP
Attn: Scholarships
One South Dearborn Street
Chicago, IL 60603
(312) 853-7000 Fax: (312) 853-7036
E-mail: scholarship@sidley.com
Web: www.sidleycareers.com

Summary To provide financial assistance and work experience to Native American and other law students who come from a diverse background.

Eligibility The program is open to students entering their second year of law school; preference is given to students at schools where the sponsor conducts on-campus interviews or participates in a resume collection. Applicants must have a demonstrated ability to contribute meaningfully to the diversity of the law school and/or legal profession, including minority, LGBT, and disabled lawyers. Along with their application, they must submit a 500-word essay that includes their thoughts on and efforts to improve diversity, how they might contribute to the sponsor's commitment to improving diversity, and their interest in practicing law at a global firm (specifically the sponsor). Selection is based on academic achievement and leadership qualities.

Financial data The stipend is $20,000.

Duration 1 year.

Additional information This program began in 2011. Recipients are expected to participate in the sponsor's summer associate program following their second year of law school. They must apply separately for the associate position. The firm has offices in Boston, Chicago, Dallas, Houston, Los Angeles, New York, Palo Alto, San Francisco, and Washington, D.C.

Number awarded Up to 15 each year.

Deadline September of each year.

[1193]
SIDNEY B. WILLIAMS, JR. INTELLECTUAL PROPERTY LAW SCHOOL SCHOLARSHIPS

Thurgood Marshall College Fund
Attn: Senior Manager of Scholarship Programs
1770 St. James Place, Suite 414
Houston, TX 77056
(713) 955-1073 Fax: (202) 448-1017
E-mail: deshuandra.walker@tmcf.org
Web: tmcf.org

Summary To provide financial assistance to Native American and other underrepresented minority law school students who are interested in preparing for a career in intellectual property law.

Eligibility This program is open to members of underrepresented minority groups currently enrolled in or accepted to an ABA-accredited law school. Applicants must be U.S. citizens with a demonstrated intent to engage in the full-time practice of intellectual property law. Along with their application, they must submit a 250-word essay on how this scholarship will make a difference to them in meeting their goal of engaging in the full-time practice of intellectual property law and why they intend to do so. Selection is based on 1) demonstrated commitment to developing a career in intellectual property law; 2) academic performance at the undergraduate, graduate, and law school levels (as applicable); 3) general factors, such as leadership skills, community activities, or special accomplishments; and 4) financial need.

Financial data The stipend is $10,000 per year. Funds may be used for tuition, fees, books, supplies, room, board, and a patent bar review course.

Duration 1 year; may be renewed up to 2 additional years if the recipient maintains a GPA of 2.0 or higher.

Additional information This program, which began in 2002, is administered by the Thurgood Marshall College Fund with support from the American Intellectual Property Law Education Foundation.

Number awarded Varies each year; recently, 12 were awarded.

Deadline March of each year.

[1194]
SMITHSONIAN MINORITY AWARDS PROGRAM

Smithsonian Institution
Attn: Office of Fellowships and Internships
470 L'Enfant Plaza, Suite 7102
P.O. Box 37012, MRC 902
Washington, DC 20013-7012
(202) 633-7070 Fax: (202) 633-7069
E-mail: siofi@si.edu
Web: www.smithsonianofi.com

Summary To provide funding to Native American and other minority undergraduate and graduate students interested in conducting research at the Smithsonian Institution.

Eligibility This program is open to members of U.S. minority groups underrepresented in the Smithsonian's scholarly programs. Applicants must be undergraduates or beginning graduate students interested in conducting research in the Institution's disciplines and in the museum field. They must be U.S. citizens or permanent residents and have a GPA of 3.0 or higher.

Financial data Students receive a grant of $600 per week.

Duration Up to 10 weeks.

Additional information Recipients must carry out independent research projects in association with the Smithsonian's research staff. Eligible fields of study currently include animal behavior, ecology, and environmental science (including an emphasis on the tropics); anthropology (including archaeology); astrophysics and astronomy; earth sciences and paleobiology; evolutionary and systematic biology; history of science and technology; history of art (especially American, contemporary, African, Asian, and 20th-century art); American crafts and decorative arts; social and cultural history of the United States; and folklife. Students are required to be in residence at the Smithsonian for the duration of the fellowship.

Number awarded Varies each year; recently, 25 were granted: 2 for fall, 19 for summer, and 4 for spring.

Deadline January of each year for summer and fall residency; September of each year for spring residency.

[1195]
SMITHSONIAN MINORITY STUDENT INTERNSHIP

Smithsonian Institution
Attn: Office of Fellowships and Internships
470 L'Enfant, Suite 7102
P.O. Box 37012, MRC 902
Washington, DC 20013-7012
(202) 633-7070   Fax: (202) 633-7069
E-mail: siofi@si.edu
Web: www.smithsonianofi.com/minority-internship-program

Summary To provide Native American and other minority undergraduate or graduate students with the opportunity to work on research or museum procedure projects in specific areas of history, art, or science at the Smithsonian Institution.

Eligibility Internships are offered to minority students who are actively engaged in undergraduate or graduate study or have graduated within the past 4 months. Applicants must be U.S. citizens or permanent residents who have an overall GPA of 3.0 or higher. Applicants must be interested in conducting research in any of the following fields of interest to the Smithsonian: animal behavior, ecology, and environmental science (including an emphasis on the tropics); anthropology (including archaeology); astrophysics and astronomy; earth sciences and paleobiology; evolutionary and systematic biology; history of science and technology; history of art (especially American, contemporary, African, Asian, and 20th-century art); American crafts and decorative arts; social and cultural history of the United States; and folklife.

Financial data The program provides a stipend of $600 per week; travel allowances may also be offered.

Duration 10 weeks during the summer or academic year.

Number awarded Varies each year.

Deadline January of each year for summer or fall; September of each year for spring.

[1196]
SMITHSONIAN NATIVE AMERICAN INTERNSHIPS

Smithsonian Institution
Attn: Office of Fellowships and Internships
Minority Awards Program
470 L'Enfant Plaza, Suite 7102
P.O. Box 37012, MRC 902
Washington, DC 20013-7012
(202) 633-7070   Fax: (202) 633-7069
E-mail: siofi@si.edu
Web: www.smithsonianofi.com

Summary To support Native American students interested in conducting projects related to Native American topics that require the use of Native American resources at the Smithsonian Institution.

Eligibility Applicants must be Native American students who are actively engaged in graduate or undergraduate study and are interested in working with Native American resources at the Smithsonian Institution. Along with their application, they must submit a 2- to 4-page essay in which they describe their past and present academic history and other experiences which they feel have prepared them for an internship, what they hope to accomplish through an internship and how it would relate to their academic and career goals, and what

about the Smithsonian in particular interests them and leads them to apply for the internship.

Financial data Interns receive a stipend of $600 per week, a travel allowance, and a small research allowance.

Duration Up to 10 weeks.

Additional information Interns pursue directed research projects supervised by Smithsonian staff members. Recipients must be in residence at the Smithsonian Institution for the duration of the program.

Number awarded Varies each year.

Deadline January of each year for summer residency or fall residency; September of each year for spring residency.

[1197]
SOCIETY FOR AMERICAN ARCHAEOLOGY NATIVE AMERICAN GRADUATE ARCHAEOLOGY SCHOLARSHIP

Society for American Archaeology
Attn: Native American Scholarship Fund
1111 14th Street, N.W., Suite 800
Washington, DC 20005-5622
(202) 789-8200   Fax: (202) 789-0284
E-mail: nasf@saa.org
Web: ecommerce.saa.org

Summary To provide financial assistance to Native Americans interested in working on a graduate degree in archaeology.

Eligibility This program is open to Native Americans who are enrolled or planning to enroll at an accredited college or university in a graduate program in archaeology. Applicants must submit a 2-page personal statement describing why they are interested in their proposed program and in archaeology, and the contributions they hope to make to the future of archaeology.

Financial data The stipend is $10,000.

Duration 1 year.

Additional information This program began in 2009.

Number awarded 1 each year.

Deadline December of each year.

[1198]
SOCIETY FOR THE STUDY OF SOCIAL PROBLEMS RACIAL/ETHNIC MINORITY GRADUATE SCHOLARSHIP

Society for the Study of Social Problems
Attn: Executive Officer
University of Tennessee
901 McClung Tower
Knoxville, TN 37996-0490
(865) 689-1531   Fax: (865) 689-1534
E-mail: sssp@utk.edu
Web: www.sssp1.org

Summary To provide funding to Native American and other ethnic and racial minority members of the Society for the Study of Social Problems (SSSP) who are interested in conducting research for their doctoral dissertation.

Eligibility This program is open to SSSP members who are Black or African American, Hispanic or Latino, Asian or Asian American, Native Hawaiian or other Pacific Islander, or American Indian or Alaska Native. Applicants must have completed all requirements for a Ph.D. (course work, examinations, and approval of a dissertation prospectus) except the dissertation. They must have a GPA of 3.25 or higher and be able to demonstrate financial need. Their field of study may be any of the social and/or behavioral sciences that will enable them to expand their perspectives in the investigation into social problems. U.S. citizenship or permanent resident status is required.

Financial data The stipend is $15,000. Additional grants provide $500 for the recipient to 1) attend the SSSP annual meeting prior to the year of the work to receive the award; and 2) attend the meeting after the year of the award to present a report on the work completed.

Duration 1 year.

Number awarded 1 each year.

Deadline January of each year.

[1199]
SOCIETY OF AMERICAN INDIAN GOVERNMENT EMPLOYEES ACADEMIC SCHOLARSHIPS

Society of American Indian Government Employees
c/o Southern California Scholarship Committee
1340 South Ventura Road
Oxnard, CA 93033
E-mail: Vvmed4d@yahoo.com
Web: www.saige.org/scholar/acscholarship.html

Summary To provide financial assistance to members of the Society of American Indian Government Employees (SAIGE) who are interested in working on an undergraduate or graduate degree.

Eligibility This program is open to American Indians and Alaska Natives who have term, seasonal, career conditional, or career appointments as federal employees. Applicants must be interested in working on a bachelor's, master's, or Ph.D. degree at an accredited postsecondary school. They must have a GPA of 2.5 or higher and be members of SAIGE. Along with their application, they must submit a 1-page essay describing their educational and workforce advancement goals and how this scholarship will help them achieve their goals, a letter of recommendation, and a narrative of extracurricular and community service activities.

Financial data Stipends range from $300 to $500 per semester, or $500 to $1,000 per academic year. Funding is provided as reimbursement for tuition costs upon receipt of a passing grade.

Duration 1 semester; may be renewed upon reapplication.

Additional information This program began in 2005.

Number awarded 1 or more each semester.

Deadline May of each year for fall semester; October of each year for spring semester.

[1200]
SOVEREIGN NATIONS SCHOLARSHIP FUND GRADUATE AWARDS

American Indian College Fund
Attn: Scholarship Department
8333 Greenwood Boulevard
Denver, CO 80221
(303) 426-8900   Toll Free: (800) 776-FUND
Fax: (303) 426-1200
E-mail: scholarships@collegefund.org
Web: www.collegefund.org

Summary To provide financial assistance to Native American students who are working on a graduate degree in any field.

Eligibility This program is open to American Indians and Alaska Natives who can document proof of enrollment or descendancy. Applicants must be planning to enroll full time in a graduate or professional degree program (e.g., M.A., M.S., J.D., Ph.D., M.D.) at a mainstream institution. They must have a GPA of 3.0 or higher and be able to demonstrate exceptional academic achievement. Applications are available only online and include required essays on specified topics. U.S. citizenship is required.

Financial data The stipend is $2,000 per year.

Duration 1 year; may be renewed.

Number awarded Varies each year.

Deadline May of each year.

[1201]
SPECTRUM SCHOLARSHIP PROGRAM

American Library Association
Attn: Office for Diversity
50 East Huron Street
Chicago, IL 60611-2795
(312) 280-5048   Toll Free: (800) 545-2433, ext. 5048
Fax: (312) 280-3256   TDD: (888) 814-7692
E-mail: spectrum@ala.org
Web: www.ala.org/offices/diversity/spectrum

Summary To provide financial assistance to Native American and other minority students interested in working on a degree in librarianship.

Eligibility This program is open to ethnic minority students (African American or Black, Asian, Native Hawaiian or other Pacific Islander, Latino or Hispanic, and American Indian or Alaska Native). Applicants must be U.S. or Canadian citizens or permanent residents who have completed no more than a third of the requirements for a master's or school library media degree. They must be enrolled full or part time at an ALA-accredited school of library and information studies or an ALA-recognized NCATE school library media program. Selection is based on academic leadership, outstanding service, commitment to a career in librarianship, statements indicating the nature of the applicant's library and other work experience, letters of reference, and personal presentation.

Financial data The stipend is $5,000.

Duration 1 year; nonrenewable.

Additional information This program began in 1998. It is administered by a joint committee of the American Library Association (ALA).

Number awarded Varies each year; recently, 69 were awarded.

Deadline February of each year.

[1202]
SREB DOCTORAL AWARDS

Southern Regional Education Board
Attn: Coordinator, Institute and Scholar Services
592 Tenth Street N.W.
Atlanta, GA 30318-5776
(404) 879-5516   Fax: (404) 872-1477
E-mail: tammy.wright@sreb.org
Web: www.sreb.org/types-awards

Summary To provide financial assistance to Native Americans and other minority students who wish to work on a doctoral degree, especially in fields of science, technology, engineering, or mathematics (STEM), at designated universities in the southern states.

Eligibility This program is open to U.S. citizens and permanent residents who are members of racial/ethnic minority groups (Native Americans, Hispanic Americans, Asian Americans, and African Americans) and have or will receive a bachelor's or master's degree. Applicants must be entering or enrolled in the first year of a Ph.D. program at a designated college or university in the following 11 states: Alabama, Arkansas, Georgia, Kentucky, Louisiana, Maryland, Mississippi, South Carolina, Tennessee, Virginia, West Virginia. Enrollment at a graduate school in 5 of those states (Georgia, Mississippi, South Carolina, Tennessee, and Virginia) is available only to residents of those states. Residents of any state in the country may attend a university in the other 5 states. Applicants must indicate an interest in becoming a full-time college or university professor. The program does not support students working on other doctoral degrees (e.g., M.D., D.B.A., D.D.S., J.D., D.V.M., Ed.D., Pharm.D., D.N.P., D.P.T.). Preference is given to applicants in STEM disciplines with particularly low minority representation, although all academic fields are eligible.

Financial data Scholars receive a waiver of tuition and fees (in or out of state) for up to 5 years, an annual stipend of $20,000 for 3 years, an annual allowance of $500 for research and professional development activities, and reimbursement of travel expenses to attend the Compact for Faculty Diversity's annual Institute on Teaching and Mentoring.

Duration Up to 5 years.

Additional information This program began in 1993 as part of the Compact for Faculty Diversity, supported by the Pew Charitable Trusts and the Ford Foundation.

Number awarded Varies each year; recently, the program was supporting more than 300 scholars.

Deadline March of each year.

[1203]
ST. CROIX CHIPPEWA INDIANS HIGHER EDUCATION GRANTS PROGRAM

St. Croix Chippewa Indians of Wisconsin
Attn: Education Coordinator
24663 Angeline Avenue
Webster, WI 54893
(715) 349-2195, ext. 5300   Toll Free: (800) 236-2195
Fax: (715) 349-7905
Web: www.stcciw.com

Summary To provide financial assistance for college or graduate school to tribal members of the St. Croix Chippewa Indians of Wisconsin.

Eligibility This program is open to enrolled tribal members of the St. Croix Chippewa Indians who are working on or planning to work on an undergraduate or graduate degree at a 4-year college or university. Applicants must be able to demonstrate financial need. Along with their application, they must submit a 350-word personal essay that includes their strengths and weaknesses, how they feel their life experiences have prepared them for their life goals, and who has inspired them in their life.

Financial data Full-time (12 credits or more) undergraduates may receive up to $3,000 per semester, half-time (6 to 11 credits) up to $1,500 per semester, and part-time (less than 6 credits) up to $750 per semester. Funds may be used for tuition, fees, books, and room in a dormitory. Full-time (6 credits or more) graduate students may receive up to $2,500 for tuition and up to $500 for books per semester) and half-time (3 to 5 credits) up to $1,250 for tuition and $500 for books per semester. Summer students (6 credits or more) may receive up to $1,500 for tuition, fees, books, and room in a dormitory.

Duration 1 year; may be renewed for a total of 10 semesters, provided the recipient maintains a GPA of 2.0 or higher as an undergraduate or 3.0 or higher as a graduate student.

Number awarded Varies each year.

Deadline June of each year for fall term; October of each year for winter or spring term; March of each year for summer term.

[1204]
STOEL RIVES FIRST-YEAR DIVERSITY FELLOWSHIPS

Stoel Rives LLP
Attn: Senior Lawyer Recruiting Manager
760 S.W. Ninth Avenue, Suite 3000
Portland, OR 97205
(503) 224-3380   Fax: (503) 220-2480
E-mail: dorianna.phillips@stoel.com
Web: www.stoel.com/diversity.aspx?Show=2805

Summary To provide financial assistance for law school and work experience to Native American and other law students who bring diversity to the profession and are interested in a summer associate position with designated offices of Stoel Rives.

Eligibility This program is open to first-year law students who contribute to the diversity of the student body at their law school and who will contribute to the diversity of the legal community. The first defines diversity to include differing life experiences, cultures, and backgrounds, as well as gender, race, national origin, religion, sexual orientation, gender identity, disability, marital status, and age. Applicants must be willing to accept a summer associate position at Stoel Rives offices in Portland, Salt Lake City, or Seattle. Selection is based on academic excellence, leadership ability, personal and professional accomplishments, commitment to community service, commitment to living in Portland, Salt Lake City, or Seattle, and meaningful contribution to the diversity of the legal community.

Financial data The program provides a stipend of $7,500 to help defray expenses of law school and a salaried summer associate position.

Duration 1 year.

Additional information This program began in 2004.

Number awarded At least 2 each year.

Deadline January of each year.

[1205]
SUMMER RESEARCH OPPORTUNITY PROGRAM IN PATHOLOGY

American Society for Investigative Pathology
Attn: Executive Officer
9650 Rockville Pike, Suite E133
Bethesda, MD 20814-3993
(301) 634-7130   Fax: (301) 634-7990
E-mail: asip@asip.org
Web: www.asip.org/awards/sropp.cfm

Summary To provide an opportunity for Native Americans and members of other underrepresented minority groups to participate in a summer research program in pathology.

Eligibility This program is open to students who are members of underrepresented minority groups. Applicants must be interested in visiting prominent research laboratories and institutions during the summer to learn and participate in new research in the mechanisms of disease.

Financial data The program provides housing at the host laboratory and a grant of $2,800 to cover travel costs to and from the site, living expenses, and a stipend.

Duration 10 weeks during the summer.

Additional information This program operates in partnership with the Intersociety Council for Pathology Information.

Number awarded Varies each year; recently, 2 laboratories were selected and 1 student was assigned to each.

Deadline March of each year.

[1206]
SUMMER TRANSPORTATION INTERNSHIP PROGRAM FOR DIVERSE GROUPS

Department of Transportation
Attn: Summer Transportation Internship Program for
  Diverse Groups
Eighth Floor E81-105
1200 New Jersey Avenue, S.E.
Washington, DC 20590
(202) 366-2907   E-mail: Crystal.Taylor@dot.gov
Web: www.fhwa.dot.gov/education/stipdg.cfm

Summary To enable Native Americans and undergraduate, graduate, and law students from other diverse groups to gain work experience during the summer at facilities of the U.S. Department of Transportation (DOT).

Eligibility This program is open to all qualified applicants, but it is designed to provide women, persons with disabilities, and members of diverse social and ethnic groups with summer opportunities in transportation. Applicants must be U.S. citizens currently enrolled in a degree-granting program of study at an accredited institution of higher learning at the undergraduate (community or junior college, university, college, or Tribal College or University) or graduate level. Undergraduates must be entering their junior or senior year; students attending a Tribal or community college must have completed their first year of school; law students must be entering their second or third year of school. Students who will graduate during the spring or summer are not eligible unless they have been accepted for enrollment in graduate school. The program accepts applications from students in all majors who are interested in working on transportation-related topics and issues. Preference is given to students with a GPA of 3.0 or higher. Undergraduates must submit a 1-page essay on their transportation interests and how participation in this program will enhance their educational and career plans and goals. Graduate students must submit a writing sample representing their educational and career plans and goals. Law students must submit a legal writing sample.

Financial data The stipend is $4,000 for undergraduates or $5,000 for graduate and law students. The program also provides housing and reimbursement of travel expenses from interns' homes to their assignment location.

Duration 10 weeks during the summer.

Additional information Assignments are at the DOT headquarters in Washington, D.C., a selected modal administration, or selected field offices around the country.

Number awarded 80 to 100 each year.

Deadline January of each year.

[1207]
SUSAN KELLY POWER AND HELEN HORNBECK TANNER FELLOWSHIP

Newberry Library
Attn: Committee on Awards
60 West Walton Street
Chicago, IL 60610-3305
(312) 255-3666   Fax: (312) 255-3513
E-mail: research@newberry.org
Web: www.newberry.org/short-term-fellowships

Summary To provide funding to American Indian doctoral candidates and postdoctorates who wish to use the resources of the D'Arcy McNickle Center for the History of the American Indian at the Newberry Library.

Eligibility This program is open to Ph.D. candidates and postdoctoral scholars of American Indian heritage. Applicants must be interested in conducting research in any field of the humanities while in residence at the McNickle Center.

Financial data The stipend is $2,500 per month.

Duration 1 week to 2 months.

Additional information This program began in 2002.

Number awarded 1 each year.

Deadline December of each year.

[1208]
SUSIE QIMMIQSAK BEVINS ENDOWMENT SCHOLARSHIP FUND

Cook Inlet Region, Inc.
Attn: The CIRI Foundation
3600 San Jeronimo Drive, Suite 256
Anchorage, AK 99508-2870
(907) 793-3575   Toll Free: (800) 764-3382
Fax: (907) 793-3585   E-mail: tcf@thecirifoundation.org
Web: www.thecirifoundation.org/about/donors

Summary To provide financial assistance for undergraduate or graduate studies in the literary, performing, and visual arts to Alaska Natives who are original enrollees to Cook Inlet Region, Inc. (CIRI) and their lineal descendants.

Eligibility This program is open to Alaska Native enrollees to CIRI under the Alaska Native Claims Settlement Act (ANCSA) of 1971 and their lineal descendants. There are no Alaska residency requirements or age limitations. Applicants must be accepted or enrolled full time in a 2-year, 4-year, or graduate degree program in the literary, visual, or performing arts. They should have a GPA of 2.5 or higher. Along with their application, they must submit a 500-word statement on their educational and career goals and how they are contributing, or planning to contribute, to a positive Alaska Native community. Selection is based on that statement, academic achievement, rigor of course work or degree program, student financial contribution, financial need, grade level, previous work performance, community service, and relationship of degree program to career goals.

Financial data   The stipend is $2,000 per semester.

Duration   1 semester; recipients may reapply.

Additional information   CIRI is 1 of 13 regional corporations established according to the terms of the Alaska Native Claims Settlement Act (ANCSA) of 1971. This program began in 1990.

Number awarded   1 or more each year.

Deadline   May or November of each year.

[1209]
SYNOD OF LAKES AND PRAIRIES RACIAL ETHNIC SCHOLARSHIPS

Synod of Lakes and Prairies
Attn: Committee on Racial Ethnic Ministry
2115 Cliff Drive
Eagen, MN 55122-3327
(651) 357-1140   Toll Free: (800) 328-1880, ext. 202
Fax: (651) 357-1141   E-mail: mkes@lakesandprairies.org
Web: www.lakesandprairies.org

Summary   To provide financial assistance to Native American and other minority residents of the Presbyterian Church (USA) Synod of Lakes and Prairies who are working on an undergraduate or graduate degree at a college or seminary in any state as preparation for service to the church.

Eligibility   This program is open to members of Presbyterian churches who reside within the Synod of Lakes and Prairies (Iowa, Minnesota, Nebraska, North Dakota, South Dakota, and Wisconsin). Applicants must be members of ethnic minority groups studying at least half time for service in the Presbyterian Church (USA) as a teaching elder, ordained minister, commissioned ruling elder, lay professional, or volunteer. They must be in good academic standing, making progress toward an undergraduate or graduate degree, and able to demonstrate financial need. Along with their application, they must submit essays of 200 to 500 words on 1) what the church needs to do to be faithful to its mission in the world today; and 2) the people, practices, or events that influence their commitment to Christ in ways that renew their fair and strengthen their service.

Financial data   Stipends range from $850 to $3,500.

Duration   1 year.

Number awarded   Varies each year; recently, 9 were awarded.

Deadline   September of each year.

[1210]
TEXAS MEDICAL ASSOCIATION MINORITY SCHOLARSHIP PROGRAM

Texas Medical Association
Attn: Director, Educational Loans, Scholarships and
  Awards
401 West 15th Street, Suite 100
Austin, TX 78701-1680
(512) 370-1600   Toll Free: (800) 880-1300, ext. 1600
Fax: (512) 370-1693
E-mail: gail.schatte@tmaloanfunds.com
Web: www.tmaloanfunds.com/Content/Template.aspx?id=9

Summary   To provide financial assistance to Native Americans and members of other underrepresented minority groups from any state who are entering medical school in Texas.

Eligibility   This program is open to members of minority groups that are underrepresented in the medical profession (African American, Mexican American, Native American). Applicants must have been accepted at a medical school in Texas; students currently enrolled are not eligible. Along with their application, they must submit a 750-word essay on how they, as a physician, would improve the health of all Texans.

Financial data   The stipend is $2,500 per year.

Duration   4 years.

Additional information   This program began in 1999.

Number awarded   12 each year: 1 at each of the medical schools in Texas.

Deadline   February of each year.

[1211]
TEXAS YOUNG LAWYERS ASSOCIATION DIVERSITY SCHOLARSHIP PROGRAM

Texas Young Lawyers Association
Attn: Diversity Committee
1414 Colorado, Fourth Floor
P.O. Box 12487
Austin, TX 78711-2487
(512) 427-1529   Toll Free: (800) 204-2222, ext. 1529
Fax: (512) 427-4117   E-mail: btrevino@texasbar.com
Web: www.tyla.org

Summary   To provide financial assistance to residents of any state who are Native Americans or members of other diverse groups attending law school in Texas.

Eligibility   This program is open to members of recognized diverse groups, including diversity based on gender, national origin, race, ethnicity, sexual orientation, gender identity, disability, socioeconomic status, and geography. Applicants must be attending an ABA-accredited law school in Texas. Along with their application, they must submit a brief essay on 1) why they believe diversity is important to the practice of law; and 2) what the Texas Young Lawyers Association and the State Bar of Texas can do to promote and support diversity in the legal profession. Selection is based on those essays, academic performance, demonstrated commitment to diversity, letters of recommendation, and financial need.

Financial data   The stipend is $1,000.

Duration   1 year.

Number awarded   At least 9 each year: at least 1 at each accredited law school in Texas.

Deadline   October of each year.

[1212]
THE LEADERSHIP INSTITUTE SCHOLARSHIPS

The Leadership Institute for Women of Color Attorneys, Inc.
Attn: Scholarship Chair
1266 West Paces Ferry Road, N.W., Suite 263
Atlanta, GA 30327
(404) 443-5715   E-mail: hhorton@mcquirewoods.com
Web: www.leadingwomenofcolor.org

Summary To provide financial assistance to women of color who are attending law school.

Eligibility This program is open to Native American and other women of color who have completed at least 1 year at an accredited law school and have a GPA of 3.0 or higher. Applicants must be U.S. citizens who can demonstrate a commitment to the legal profession. Along with their application, they must submit brief statements on their work experience, extracurricular activities, why they think it is important for women of color to serve in the legal profession, what they believe is necessary for success in the legal profession, and what they plan to do with their law degree.

Financial data The stipend is $3,000.

Duration 1 year.

Number awarded 5 each year.

Deadline December of each year.

[1213]
THERESA A. MIKE SCHOLARSHIP

Theresa A. Mike Foundation
Attn: Scholarship Committee
46-200 Harrison Place
Coachella, CA 92236
(760) 863-5108
Web: www.theresamike.org/index-3.html

Summary To provide financial assistance to American Indians from any state and residents of the Coachella Valley of California who are interested in attending college or graduate school in any state.

Eligibility This program is open to 1) employees and dependents of employees of any entity of the Twenty-Nine Palms Band of Mission Indians; 2) enrolled members of a federally-recognized Native American Indian Tribe; or 3) current residents or graduates of high schools in the Coachella Valley or Morongo Basin of California. Applicants must be enrolled or planning to enroll full time at a college or graduate school in any state. They must have a GPA of 3.0 or higher. Along with their application, they must submit an essay of at least 1,000 words that covers their career goals and how they became interested in their chosen career, why education is important to them, and how other aspects of their life relate to their educational and career goals. Financial need may also be considered in the selection process.

Financial data A stipend is awarded (amount not specified).

Duration 1 year.

Additional information This program began in 1997.

Number awarded Varies each year.

Deadline June of each year.

[1214]
THOMAS G. NEUSOM SCHOLARSHIPS

Conference of Minority Transportation Officials
Attn: National Scholarship Program
100 M Street, S.E., Suite 917
Washington, DC 20003
(202) 506-2917   E-mail: info@comto.org
Web: www.comto.org/page/scholarships

Summary To provide financial assistance for college or graduate school to Native American and other minority members of the Conference of Minority Transportation Officials (COMTO) and their families.

Eligibility This program is open to undergraduate and graduate students who have been members of COMTO or whose parents, guardians, or grandparents have been members for at least 1 year. Applicants must be working (either full or part time) on a degree in a field related to transportation and have a GPA of 2.5 or higher. Along with their application they must submit a cover letter on their transportation-related career goals and life aspirations. Financial need is not considered in the selection process.

Financial data The stipend is $5,500. Funds are paid directly to the recipient's college or university.

Duration 1 year.

Number awarded 1 each year.

Deadline April of each year.

[1215]
THOMAS R. PICKERING FOREIGN AFFAIRS FELLOWSHIPS

The Washington Center for Internships
Attn: Foreign Affairs Fellowship Program
1333 16th Street, N.W.
Washington, DC 20036-2205
(202) 238-7900   Fax: (202) 238-7700
E-mail: info@twc.org
Web: www.twc.edu

Summary To provide forgivable loans to undergraduate and graduate students, especially Native Americans and members of other underrepresented groups, interested in preparing for a career with the Department of State's Foreign Service.

Eligibility This program is open to U.S. citizens who are entering their senior year of undergraduate study or their first year of graduate study. Applicants must be planning to work on a 2-year full-time master's degree program relevant to the work of the U.S. Foreign Service, including public policy, international affairs, public administration, business, economics, political science, sociology, or foreign languages. They must be preparing for a career in the Foreign Service. Applications are especially encouraged from women, members of minority groups historically underrepresented in the Foreign Service, and students with financial need.

Financial data The program pays for tuition, room, board, books, mandatory fees, and 1 round-trip ticket from the fellow's residence to academic institution, to a maximum of $37,500 per academic year.

Duration 2 years: the senior year of undergraduate study and the first year of graduate study for college seniors; the first 2 years of graduate school for entering graduate students.

Additional information This program is funded by the State Department and administered by The Washington Center for Internships. Fellows must commit to a minimum of 5 years of service in an appointment as a Foreign Service Officer following graduation and successful completion of the Foreign Service examination. If they fail to fulfill that commitment, they must refund all money received.

Number awarded Approximately 40 each year: 20 college seniors and 20 entering graduate students.

Deadline January of each year.

[1216]
TOMIAR RUDY ORTEGA, SR. SCHOLARSHIP

Pukúu, Cultural Community Services
1019 Second Street, Suite 2
San Fernando, CA 91340
(818) 336-6105   Fax: (818) 837-0796
Web: www.pukuu.org/services/scholarship

Summary To provide financial assistance to Native Americans who live in California and are attending college or graduate school in any state.

Eligibility This program is open to American Indians and Alaskan Natives who live in California and can document tribal or village enrollment or descendancy. Applicants must be enrolled at an accredited college or university in any state. They must be able to document completion of community service within the previous 12 months. Undergraduates must have a GPA of 2.75 or higher and graduate students must have a GPA of 3.5 or higher. Along with their application, they must submit a 2-page essay on their academic, career, and personal goals, including how they view their Native American heritage and its importance to them, how they plan to "give back" to Native Americans after graduation, and their on-going active involvement in the Native American community both on and off campus.

Financial data The stipend is $1,000.

Duration 1 year.

Number awarded 2 each year.

Deadline August of each year.

[1217]
TONKON TORP FIRST-YEAR DIVERSITY FELLOWSHIP PROGRAM

Tonkon Torp LLP
Attn: Director of Attorney Professional Development and
   Recruiting
888 S.W. Fifth Avenue, Suite 1600
Portland, OR 97204
(503) 221-1440   Fax: (503) 972-3798
E-mail: heather.decker@tonkon.com
Web: www.tonkon.com

Summary To provide financial assistance and summer work experience in Portland, Oregon to first-year law students who are persons of color or have other diverse backgrounds.

Eligibility This program is open to students who have diverse backgrounds and are currently enrolled in their first year at an ABA-accredited law school. Applicants must be able to demonstrate 1) a record of academic achievement that indicates a strong likelihood of a successful career during the remainder of law school and in the legal profession; 2) a

commitment to practice law in Portland, Oregon following graduation from law school; and 3) an ability to contribute meaningfully to the diversity of the law school student body and, after entering the legal profession, the legal community. They are not required to disclose their financial circumstances, but a demonstrated need for financial assistance may be taken into consideration.

Financial data The recipient is offered a paid summer associateship at Tonkon Torp in Portland, Oregon for the summer following the first year of law school and, depending on the outcome of that experience, may be invited for a second summer following the second year of law school. Following the successful completion of that second associateship, the recipient is awarded an academic scholarship of $7,500 for the third year of law school.

Duration The program covers 2 summers and 1 academic year.

Additional information For 2 weeks during the summer, the fellow works in the legal department of Portland General Electric Company, Oregon's largest electric utility and a client of the sponsoring firm.

Number awarded 1 each year.

Deadline January of each year.

[1218]
TRAILBLAZER SCHOLARSHIP

Conference of Minority Transportation Officials
Attn: National Scholarship Program
100 M Street, S.E., Suite 917
Washington, DC 20003
(202) 506-2917   E-mail: info@comto.org
Web: www.comto.org/page/scholarships

Summary To provide financial assistance for college or graduate school to Native American and other minority members of the Conference of Minority Transportation Officials (COMTO) and their families.

Eligibility This program is open to undergraduate and graduate students who have been members of COMTO or whose parents, guardians, or grandparents have been members for at least 1 year. Applicants must be working (either full or part time) on a degree in a field related to transportation and have a GPA of 2.5 or higher. Along with their application they must submit a cover letter on their transportation-related career goals and life aspirations. Financial need is not considered in the selection process.

Financial data The stipend is $2,500. Funds are paid directly to the recipient's college or university.

Duration 1 year.

Number awarded 1 each year.

Deadline April of each year.

[1219]
TRANS-PAC ALASKA SCHOLARSHIP

Koniag Incorporated
Attn: Koniag Education Foundation
4241 B Street, Suite 303B
Anchorage, AK 99503
(907) 562-9093   Toll Free: (888) 562-9093
Fax: (907) 562-9023
E-mail: scholarships@koniageducation.org
Web: www.koniageducation.org/scholarships

Summary To provide financial assistance to Alaska Natives who are Koniag Incorporated shareholders or descendants and enrolled in undergraduate or graduate study in a field related to natural resources.

Eligibility This program is open to college juniors, seniors, and graduate students who are Alaska Native shareholders of Koniag Incorporated or descendants of those original enrollees. Applicants must have a GPA of 3.0 or higher and be working full time on a degree related to natural resources (e.g., forestry). Along with their application, they must submit a 300-word essay about their personal and family history, community involvement, volunteer activities, and educational and life goals. Financial need is not considered in the selection process.

Financial data The stipend is $5,000 per year. Funds are sent directly to the recipient's school and may be used for tuition, books, supplies, room, board, and transportation.

Duration 1 year; may be renewed.

Additional information Koniag Incorporated is 1 of 13 Alaska Native Regional Corporations created under the Alaska Native Claims Settlement Act of 1971. This program is supported by Transpac Group, a log and lumber export company.

Number awarded 2 each year.

Deadline May of each year.

[1220]
TURTLE MOUNTAIN BAND OF CHIPPEWA INDIANS SCHOLARSHIP PROGRAM

Turtle Mountain Band of Chippewa Indians
Attn: Tribal Scholarship Office
P.O. Box 900
Belcourt, ND 58316
(701) 477-8102   Fax: (701) 477-8053
Web: www.tmbci.org/programs/?program_id=35

Summary To provide financial assistance for full-time undergraduate or graduate study in any state to enrolled members of the Turtle Mountain Band of Chippewa.

Eligibility Applicants must be enrolled members of the Turtle Mountain Band of Chippewa, be full-time students enrolled in an academic program at an accredited postsecondary institution in any state on either the undergraduate or graduate school level, and have a GPA of 2.0 or higher. Undergraduate applicants must be enrolled for at least 12 quarter or 12 semester credit hours (or 6 semester/quarter hours for a summer session); graduate school applicants must be enrolled for at least 1 course. Along with their application, they must submit a Certificate of Degree of Indian Blood (CDIB), a letter of acceptance/admission from their college, the award notice sent by the college's financial aid office, a high school transcript or GED certificate, and any college transcripts. Priority is given to applicants in the following order: seniors who need to attend summer school in order to graduate, juniors who need summer school in order to become seniors, students who need summer school to acquire their 2-year degree, sophomores, freshmen, and graduate students.

Financial data A stipend is awarded (amount not specified).

Duration The maximum number of terms the scholarship program will fund a student for an undergraduate degree is 10 semesters or 15 quarters; the maximum number of terms for a student at a 2-year college is 3 years, 6 semesters, or 9 quarters.

Additional information Once recipients earn 65 or more credit hours at a 2-year college, they must transfer to a 4-year institution.

Number awarded Varies each year.

Deadline August of each year.

[1221]
UDALL FOUNDATION NATIVE AMERICAN CONGRESSIONAL INTERNSHIPS

Morris K. Udall and Stewart L. Udall Foundation
Attn: Program Manager, Internship Program
130 South Scott Avenue
Tucson, AZ 85701-1922
(520) 901-8561   Fax: (520) 670-5530
E-mail: info@udall.gov
Web: www.udall.gov

Summary To provide an opportunity for Native American upper-division and graduate students to work in a Congressional office during the summer.

Eligibility This program is open to American Indians and Alaska Natives who are enrolled members of recognized tribes and have an interest in tribal government and policy. Applicants must have a GPA of 3.0 or higher as a junior, senior, graduate student, law student, or recent graduate of a tribal or 4-year college. They must be able to participate in an internship in Washington, D.C., where they will gain practical experience in the legislative process, Congressional matters, and governmental proceedings that specifically relate to Native American issues. Fields of study of previous interns have included American Indian studies, political science, law and pre-law, psychology, social work, history, business and public administration, anthropology, community and urban planning, architecture, communications, health sciences, public health, biology, engineering, sociology, environmental studies and natural resources, economics, and justice studies. Applicants must demonstrate strong research and writing skills; organizational abilities and time management skills; maturity, responsibility, and flexibility; interest in learning how the federal government "really works;" commitment to their tribal community; knowledge of Congressman Morris K. Udall's legacy with regard to Native Americans; and awareness of issues and challenges currently facing Indian Country.

Financial data Interns receive round-trip airfare to Washington, D.C.; dormitory lodging at a local university; a $42 daily allowance sufficient for meals, transportation, and incidentals; and an educational stipend of $1,200 to be paid at the conclusion of the internship.

Duration 10 weeks during the summer.

Additional information These internships were first offered in 1996.

Number awarded 12 each year.

Deadline January of each year.

[1222]
UNDERREPRESENTED MINORITY DENTAL STUDENT SCHOLARSHIP

American Dental Association
Attn: ADA Foundation
211 East Chicago Avenue
Chicago, IL 60611
(312) 440-2547   Fax: (312) 440-3526
E-mail: adaf@ada.org
Web: www.adafoundation.org/en/how-to-apply/education

Summary To provide financial assistance to Native American and other underrepresented minorities who wish to enter the field of dentistry.

Eligibility This program is open to U.S. citizens from a minority group that is currently underrepresented in the dental profession: Native American, African American, or Hispanic. Applicants must have a GPA of 3.25 or higher and be entering their second year of full-time study at a dental school in the United States accredited by the Commission on Dental Accreditation. Selection is based upon academic achievement, a written summary of personal and professional goals, letters of reference, and demonstrated financial need.

Financial data The maximum stipend is $2,500. Funds are sent directly to the student's financial aid office to be used to cover tuition, fees, books, supplies, and living expenses.

Duration 1 year.

Additional information This program, established in 1991, is supported by the Harry J. Bosworth Company, Colgate-Palmolive, Sunstar Americas, and Procter & Gamble Company. Students receiving a full scholarship from any other source are ineligible to receive this scholarship.

Number awarded Approximately 25 each year.

Deadline November of each year.

[1223]
UNITED HEALTH FOUNDATION/NMF DIVERSE MEDICAL SCHOLARS PROGRAM

National Medical Fellowships, Inc.
Attn: Scholarship Program
347 Fifth Avenue, Suite 510
New York, NY 10016
(212) 483-8880   Toll Free: (877) NMF-1DOC
Fax: (212) 483-8897 E-mail: scholarships@nmfonline.org
Web: www.nmfonline.org

Summary To provide financial assistance to underrepresented minority students at medical schools in designated areas who are interested in conducting a community health project.

Eligibility This program is open to African Americans, Hispanics/Latinos, Native Americans, Vietnamese, Cambodians, and Pacific Islanders who are currently enrolled at an accredited medical school in the greater New York City metropolitan area (including Connecticut, New Jersey, New York, and Pennsylvania), Florida (Orlando, Tampa, and greater Miami), Arizona (Phoenix), New Mexico (Albuquerque), Tennessee (Nashville), Texas (San Antonio), Wisconsin (Milwaukee), or Georgia (Atlanta). Applicants must have demonstrated leadership and a commitment to serving medically underserved communities. They must be interested in conducting a self-directed health project of 200 hours at a site of choice in an underserved community in the same area as their medical school. U.S. citizenship or DACA status is required.

Financial data The grant is $7,000.

Duration 1 year; recipients may apply for a second year of funding.

Additional information This program, sponsored by United Health Foundation, began in 2007.

Number awarded 30 each year.

Deadline October of each year.

[1224]
UNITED HEALTHCARE/LAWYERS COLLABORATIVE FOR DIVERSITY CLERKSHIP

Lawyers Collaborative for Diversity
Attn: Program Coordinator
P.O. Box 230637
Hartford, CT 06123-0637
(860) 275-0668
E-mail: kdavis@lawyerscollaborativefordiversity.org
Web: www.lcdiversity.com/scholarships.htm

Summary To provide summer work experience at United Healthcare Services in Hartford, Connecticut to Native American and other underrepresented students at law schools in Connecticut and western Massachusetts.

Eligibility This program is open to women and students of color in their first year at law schools in Connecticut or western Massachusetts. Applicants must be interested in a summer internship at United Healthcare Services in Harford, Connecticut. Along with their application, they must submit 500-word essays on 1) why they should be selected for this opportunity; and 2) their thoughts about diversity in Connecticut's legal community.

Financial data The stipend is $5,000.

Duration 8 weeks during the summer.

Additional information This program is sponsored by United HealthCare Services, Inc.

Number awarded 1 each year.

Deadline February of each year.

[1225]
UNITED METHODIST NATIVE AMERICAN SEMINARY AWARDS

United Methodist Church
Attn: General Board of Higher Education and Ministry
Office of Loans and Scholarships
1001 19th Avenue South
P.O. Box 340007
Nashville, TN 37203-0007
(615) 340-7344   Fax: (615) 340-7367
E-mail: umscholar@gbhem.org
Web: www.gbhem.org

Summary To provide financial assistance to Native American seminary students preparing for ministry within the United Methodist Church.

Eligibility This program is open to Native Americans accepted and/or enrolled as a full-time student at a school of theology approved by the University Senate of the United Methodist Church. At least 1 parent must be American Indian, Native American, or Alaska Native. Applicants must have been active, full members of a United Methodist Church for at least 3 years prior to applying. They must be able to demonstrate financial need, a GPA of 2.5 or higher, and involvement in their Native American community.

Financial data Stipends range from $3,000 to $10,000. Half of the funds are provided in the form of a grant and half in the form of a loan that is forgiven if the recipient serves at least 2 years in a Native American congregation or ministry/fellowship that is recognized by the United Methodist Church.

Duration 1 year.

Number awarded Varies each year; recently, 12 were awarded.

Deadline February of each year.

[1226]
UNITED METHODIST WOMEN OF COLOR SCHOLARS PROGRAM

United Methodist Church
Attn: General Board of Higher Education and Ministry
Office of Loans and Scholarships
1001 19th Avenue South
P.O. Box 340007
Nashville, TN 37203-0007
(615) 340-7342   Fax: (615) 340-7367
E-mail: umscholar@gbhem.org
Web: www.gbhem.org

Summary To provide financial assistance to Methodist women of color who are working on a doctoral degree to prepare for a career as an educator at a United Methodist seminary.

Eligibility This program is open to women of color (have at least 1 parent who is African American, African, Hispanic, Asian, Native American, Alaska Native, or Pacific Islander) who have an M.Div. degree. Applicants must have been active, full members of a United Methodist Church for at least 3 years prior to applying. They must be enrolled full time in a degree program at the Ph.D. or Th.D. level to prepare for a career teaching at a United Methodist seminary.

Financial data The maximum stipend is $10,000 per year.

Duration 1 year; may be renewed up to 3 additional years.

Number awarded Varies each year; recently, 10 were awarded.

Deadline January of each year.

[1227]
UNITED SOUTH AND EASTERN TRIBES SCHOLARSHIP FUND

United South and Eastern Tribes, Inc.
Attn: Scholarship Fund
711 Stewarts Ferry Pike, Suite 100
Nashville, TN 37214
(615) 467-1542   Fax: (615) 872-7417
E-mail: mstephens@usetinc.org
Web: www.usetinc.org/resources/scholarships

Summary To provide supplemental financial assistance for college to Native Americans who are in the United South and Eastern Tribes (USET) service area.

Eligibility This program is open to Indian students who live in the service area of the USET, which covers portions of the following states: Alabama, Connecticut, Florida, Louisiana, Maine, Massachusetts, Mississippi, New York, North Carolina, Rhode Island, South Carolina, and Texas. Special consideration is given to applicants who are enrolled members of

1 of the following 26 federally-recognized United South and Eastern Tribes: Alabama Coushatta Tribe of Texas; Aroostook Band of Micmac Indians (Maine); Catawba Indian Nation (South Carolina); Cayuga Nation (New York); Chitimacha Tribe of Louisiana; Coushatta Tribe of Louisiana; Eastern Band of Cherokee Indians (North Carolina); Houlton Band of Maliseet Indians (Maine); Jena Band of Choctaw Indians (Louisiana); Mashantucket Pequot Tribe (Connecticut); Mashpee Wampanoag Tribe (Massachusetts); Miccosukee Tribe of Florida; Mississippi Band of Choctaw Indians; Mohegan Tribe of Connecticut; Narragansett Tribe (Rhode Island); Oneida Nation (New York); Passamaquoddy Tribe Indian Township (Maine); Passamaquoddy Pleasant Point (Maine); Penobscot Nation (Maine); Poarch Band of Creek Indians (Alabama); Seminole Tribe of Florida; Seneca Nation (New York); Shinnecock Indian Nation (New York); St. Regis Band of Mohawk Indians (New York); Tunica Biloxi Tribe of Louisiana; Wampanoag Tribe of Gay Head (Massachusetts);. Applicants must be currently enrolled or accepted at a postsecondary educational institution, have satisfactory scholastic standing, and be able to demonstrate need for financial assistance. Undergraduates must submit a 250-word essay on their future goals, obstacles overcome, and challenges; graduate students must submit a 500-word essay on their future goals, reasons for attending graduate school, obstacles overcome, and challenges.

Financial data The stipend for undergraduates is at least $750 and for graduate students at least $1,000.

Duration 1 year.

Number awarded Varies each year.

Deadline April of each year.

[1228]
UTC/LCD DIVERSITY SCHOLARS PROGRAM

Lawyers Collaborative for Diversity
Attn: Program Coordinator
P.O. Box 230637
Hartford, CT 06123-0637
(860) 275-0668
E-mail: kdavis@lawyerscollaborativefordiversity.org
Web: www.lcdiversity.com/scholarships.htm

Summary To provide financial assistance and summer work experience to Native American and other underrepresented students at law schools in Connecticut and western Massachusetts.

Eligibility This program is open to women and people of color from any state who are currently enrolled in the first year at a law school in Connecticut or western Massachusetts. Applicants must be available to work as an intern during the summer following their first year. Along with their application, they must submit 500-word essays on 1) why diversity is important to them and how the Connecticut legal community can improve diversity in the legal profession; and 2) why they should be selected for this program.

Financial data The program provides a stipend of $2,000 per year for the second and third years of law school, a paid internship during the summer after the first year at a member firm of the Lawyers Collaborative for Diversity (LCD), and an unpaid internship with a legal department of United Technologies Corporation during that same summer.

Duration The scholarship is for 2 years; the paid internship is for 5 weeks during the summer; the unpaid internship is for 3 weeks during the summer.

Additional information This program is sponsored by United Technologies Corporation (UTC).

Number awarded 2 each year.

Deadline January of each year.

[1229]
VEDDER PRICE DIVERSITY SCHOLARSHIP

Vedder Price P.C.
Attn: Manager of Legal Recruiting
222 North LaSalle Street, Suite 2600
Chicago, IL 60601-1003
(312) 609-7500   Fax: (312) 609-5005
E-mail: abrummel@vedderprice.com
Web: www.vedderprice.com/diversity-scholarship

Summary To provide financial assistance and summer work experience to Native American and other students at designated law schools in Illinois who will contribute to diversity in the legal profession.

Eligibility This program is open to students currently enrolled in the first year at designated law schools in Illinois. Applicants must be a student of color, GLBT, a person with a disability, or anyone whose background or experience would otherwise contribute to the diversity of the sponsoring law firm and the legal profession. Along with their application, they must submit a 2-page personal statement describing 1) their talents, qualities, and experiences; and 2) how they would contribute to the diversity of the firm and the legal profession, based on their personal and academic background and experiences. They must also be available to accept a guaranteed associateship with the firm during the summer following their first year of law school.

Financial data The scholarship stipend is $5,000 per year.

Duration 1 year; may be renewed as long as the recipient remains enrolled in good standing in law school.

Additional information This program began in 2005. The participating law schools include Chicago-Kent College of Law, DePaul University College of Law, John Marshall Law School, Loyola University Chicago School of Law, University of Chicago Law School, Northwestern University School of Law, and the University of Illinois College of Law.

Number awarded 1 each year.

Deadline December of each year.

[1230]
VICTOR MATSON, SR. TRIBUTARY SCHOLARSHIP

Sault Tribe of Chippewa Indians
Attn: Higher Education Department
523 Ashmun Street
Sault Ste. Marie, MI 49783
(906) 635-6050, ext. 26312   Toll Free: (800) 793-0660
Fax: (906) 635-7785   E-mail: BMacArthur@saulttribe.net
Web: www.saulttribe.com

Summary To provide financial assistance to members of the Sault Tribe of Chippewa Indians interested in attending college in any state to work on an undergraduate or graduate degree in a field related to fisheries or natural resources.

Eligibility This program is open to members of the Sault Tribe who are enrolled full time at a 2- or 4-year college or university in any state. Applicants must be working on an undergraduate or graduate degree in the field of fisheries or natural resources management or a related area. Along with their application, they must submit an essay of 1,000 to 2,000 words on a topic that changes annually but relates to their Indian heritage.

Financial data The stipend is $1,000.

Duration 1 year.

Number awarded 1 each year.

Deadline May of each year.

[1231]
VINE DELORIA JR. MEMORIAL SCHOLARSHIP

American Indian College Fund
Attn: Scholarship Department
8333 Greenwood Boulevard
Denver, CO 80221
(303) 426-8900   Toll Free: (800) 776-FUND
Fax: (303) 426-1200
E-mail: scholarships@collegefund.org
Web: www.collegefund.org

Summary To provide financial assistance to Native American students who are working on a graduate degree.

Eligibility This program is open to American Indians and Alaska Natives who can document proof of enrollment or descendancy. Applicants must be enrolled in a graduate or professional degree program (e.g., M.A., M.S., J.D., Ph.D., M.D.) in any field. They must have a GPA of 3.0 or higher and be able to demonstrate financial need. Applications are available only online and include required essays on specified topics. U.S. citizenship is required.

Financial data The stipend is $1,000.

Duration 1 year.

Number awarded Varies each year.

Deadline May of each year.

[1232]
VINSON & ELKINS DIVERSITY FELLOWSHIPS

Vinson & Elkins L.L.P.
Attn: Senior Diversity and Inclusion Coordinator
1001 Fannin Street, Suite 2500
Houston, TX 77002-6760
(713) 758-3272   Fax: (713) 758-2346
E-mail: abutts@velaw.com
Web: www.velaw.com

Summary To provide financial assistance to Native American and other minority law students who are interested in working in a law firm setting.

Eligibility This program is open to students who are entering the second year at an ABA-accredited law school and are members of a racial or ethnic group that has been historically underrepresented in the legal profession (Asian, American Indian/Alaskan Native, Black/African American, Hispanic/Latino, multiracial, or Native Hawaiian or other Pacific Islander). Applicants must be able to demonstrate a strong undergraduate and law school record, excellent writing skills, and an interest in working in a large law firm setting. Along with their application, they must submit a 500-word narrative discussing their interest in the sponsoring firm and describing how their unique experiences will contribute to the firm's commitment to diversity in the legal profession.

Financial data The stipend is $7,000 per year.

Duration 2 years (the second and third year of law school).

Additional information This program began in 2007. Fellows are also considered for summer associate positions at the sponsor's offices in Austin, Dallas, Houston, New York, San Francisco, or Washington, D.C. following their first year of law school.

Number awarded 4 each year.

Deadline January of each year.

[1233]
VIRGINIA MATTHEWS MEMORIAL SCHOLARSHIP

American Indian Library Association
c/o Holly Tomren, Scholarship Review Board Chair
Drexel University
Hagerty Library, Room 122
3300 Market Street
Philadelphia, PA 19104
(215) 895-2761   E-mail: htomren@gmail.com
Web: www.ailanet.org/awards/scholarships

Summary To provide financial assistance to American Indians interested in working on a master's degree in library and/or information science.

Eligibility This program is open to enrolled members of a federally-recognized American Indian tribe who live and work in the American Indian community. Applicants must have been admitted to a master's degree program in library and/or information science accredited by the American Library Association. They must be able to demonstrate sustained involvement in the American Indian community and sustained commitment to American Indian concerns and initiatives. Preference is given to applicants who are employed in a tribal library or who are currently employed in a library serving American Indian populations. Financial need is considered in the selection process.

Financial data The stipend is $2,000.

Duration 1 year; may be renewed 1 additional year.

Additional information This program began in 2002 and was given its current name in 2012.

Number awarded 1 each year.

Deadline April of each year.

[1234]
VISITING RESEARCH INTERNSHIP PROGRAM

Harvard Medical School
Office for Diversity Inclusion and Community Partnership
Attn: Program for Faculty Development and Diversity
  Inclusion
164 Longwood Avenue, Second Floor
Boston, MA 02115-5810
(617) 432-1892   Fax: (617) 432-3834
E-mail: pfdd_dcp@hms.harvard.edu
Web: mfdp.med.harvard.edu

Summary To provide an opportunity for medical students, especially Native American and other underrepresented minorities, to conduct a mentored research project at Harvard Medical School during the summer.

Eligibility This program is open to first- and second-year medical students, particularly underrepresented minority and/or disadvantaged individuals, in good standing at accredited U.S. medical schools. Applicants must be interested in conducting a summer research project at Harvard Medical School under the mentorship of a faculty advisor. They must be interested in a research and health-related career, especially in clinical or translational research or research that transforms scientific discoveries arising from laboratory, clinical, or population studies into clinical or population-based applications to improve health. U.S. citizenship, nationality, or permanent resident status is required.

Financial data Participants receive a stipend (amount not specified), housing, and reimbursement of transportation costs to Boston up to $400.

Duration 8 weeks during the summer.

Additional information This program, established in 2008, is funded by the National Center for Research Resources of the National Institutes of Health NIH). It is a joint enterprise of Harvard University, its 10 schools, its 17 Academic Healthcare Centers, Boston College School of Nursing, MIT, the Cambridge Health Alliance, and other community partners. Interns attend weekly seminars with Harvard faculty focusing on such topics as research methodology, health disparities, ethics, and career paths. They also have the opportunity to participate in offerings of other Harvard Medical School programs, such a career development seminars and networking dinners.

Number awarded Varies each year; recently, 6 medical students were admitted to this program.

Deadline December of each year.

[1235]
WAH-TIAH-KAH SCHOLARSHIP

Osage Minerals Council
813 Grandview
P.O. Box 779
Pawhuska, OK 74056
(918) 287-5346
Web: www.osagenation-nsn.gov

Summary To provide financial assistance to Osage students who are interested in attending college or graduate school to prepare for a career in the petroleum industry.

Eligibility This program is open to full-time undergraduate and graduate students who can prove Osage Indian blood in any degree. Applicants must be working on or planning to work on a degree in a field related to petroleum. Along with their application, they must submit a copy of their Osage Certificate of Degree of Indian Blood (CDIB), transcripts, 2 letters of recommendation, ACT or SAT scores, and a personal statement of their educational and career goals.

Financial data A stipend is awarded (amount not specified).

Duration 1 semester; may be renewed for up to 7 additional semesters, provided the recipient reapplies each semester and maintains a GPA of 2.0 or higher.

Number awarded Varies each year.

Deadline June of each year for fall term; December of each year for spring term.

[1236]
WAK-WEI SCHOLARSHIPS

Yakama Nation
Department of Human Services
Attn: Higher Education Program
107 Teo Road
P.O. Box 151
Toppenish, WA 98948
(509) 865-5121, ext. 4542   Toll Free: (800) 543-2802
Fax: (509) 865-6994   E-mail: murry@yakama.com
Web: www.yakama.us/programs.php

Summary To provide financial assistance to Yakama tribal members interested in working on an undergraduate or graduate degree at a school in any state.

Eligibility This program is open to enrolled members of the Yakama nation who are enrolled or planning to enroll full time at a 2- or 4-year college or university in any state. High school seniors must have a GPA of 3.0 or higher; students returning to college after an absence must have a GPA of 2.0 or higher. Financial need is the major factor in the selection process.

Financial data The stipend is $500 per year for freshmen and sophomores or $1,000 per year for juniors, seniors, and graduate students.

Duration 1 year; recipients may reapply.

Number awarded 7 each year: 4 for freshmen and sophomores and 3 for juniors and seniors.

Deadline June of each year.

[1237]
WALTER CHARLEY MEMORIAL SCHOLARSHIPS

Ahtna, Incorporated
Attn: Ahtna Heritage Foundation
P.O. Box 213
Glennallen, AK 99588
(907) 822-5778   Fax: (907) 822-5338
E-mail: ahtnaheritage@yahoo.com
Web: www.ahtnaheritagefoundation.com/scholarships.html

Summary To provide financial assistance to shareholders of Ahtna, Incorporated in Alaska and their descendants who plan to attend college or graduate school in any state.

Eligibility This program is open to Ahtna shareholders (original, gifted, inherited, or Class L) who are high school graduates or GED recipients. Applicants must be 1) attending or planning to attend a college, university, or vocational school in any state as an undergraduate or graduate student; or 2) accepted in a program specializing in a recognized area or field of study. They must have a GPA of 2.0 or higher and be able to demonstrate financial need.

Financial data For undergraduates, the stipend is $2,000 per semester ($4,000 per year) for full-time students or $1,000 per semester ($2,000 per year) for part-time students. For graduate students, the stipend is $3,000 per semester ($6,000 per year) for full-time students or $1,500 per semester ($3,000 per year) for part-time students.

Duration 1 year; may be renewed, provided the recipient maintains a GPA of 2.0 or higher.

Additional information Ahtna, Incorporated is 1 of 13 regional corporations established according to the terms of the Alaska Native Claims Settlement Act (ANCSA) of 1971.

Number awarded Varies each year.

Deadline July of each year for fall semester; December of each year for spring semester.

[1238]
WARNER NORCROSS & JUDD LAW SCHOOL SCHOLARSHIP

Grand Rapids Community Foundation
Attn: Education Program Officer
185 Oakes Street S.W.
Grand Rapids, MI 49503-4008
(616) 454-1751, ext. 103   Fax: (616) 454-6455
E-mail: rbishop@grfoundation.org
Web: www.grfoundation.org/scholarshipslist

Summary To provide financial assistance to Native Americans and other minorities from Michigan who are attending law school.

Eligibility This program is open to students of color who are attending or planning to attend an accredited law school. Applicants must be residents of Michigan or attending law school in the state. They must be U.S. citizens or permanent residents and have a GPA of 2.5 or higher. Financial need is considered in the selection process.

Financial data The stipend is $5,000. Funds are paid directly to the recipient's institution.

Duration 1 year.

Additional information Funding for this program is provided by the law firm Warner Norcross & Judd LLP.

Number awarded 1 each year.

Deadline March of each year.

[1239]
WASHINGTON AMERICAN INDIAN ENDOWED SCHOLARSHIP PROGRAM

Washington Student Achievement Council
Attn: American Indian Endowed Scholarship Program
917 Lakeridge Way
P.O. Box 43430
Olympia, WA 98504-3430
(360) 753-7843   Toll Free: (888) 535-0747
Fax: (360) 753-7808   TDD: (360) 753-7809
E-mail: aies@wsac.wa.gov
Web: www.wsac.wa.gov

Summary To provide financial assistance to American Indian undergraduate and graduate students in Washington.

Eligibility This program is open to Washington residents who have close social and cultural ties to an American Indian tribe and/or community in the state. Applicants must demonstrate financial need and be enrolled, or planning to enroll, as a full-time undergraduate or graduate student at a Washington state public or independent college, university, or career school. Along with their application, they must submit essays on 1) their close social and cultural ties to an American Indian community in Washington; and 2) how they plan to serve a Washington American Indian community upon completing their education and how their contribution is intended to affect the community. Selection is based on academic merit, financial need, and commitment to serve the American Indian community in Washington.

Financial data Stipends range from about $500 to $2,000 per year.

Duration 1 year, may be renewed up to 4 additional years.

Additional information This program was created by the Washington legislature in 1990 with a state appropriation to an endowment fund and matching contributions from tribes, individuals, and organizations.

Number awarded Varies each year; recently, 16 students received $17,300 in support from this program.

Deadline January of each year.

[1240]
WASHOE TRIBE INCENTIVE SCHOLARSHIPS

Washoe Tribe
Attn: Education Department
1246 Waterloo Lane
Gardnerville, NV 89410
(775) 782-6320, ext. 2808   Toll Free: (800) 76-WASHOE
Fax: (775) 782-6790   E-mail: education@washoetribe.us
Web: www.washoetribe.us

Summary To provide financial assistance to members of the Washoe Tribe working on an undergraduate or graduate degree at a school in any state.

Eligibility This program is open to members of the Washoe Tribe who are currently working full time on an associate, baccalaureate, graduate, or postgraduate degree at a school in any state. Applicants must have a GPA of 3.0 or higher. Along with their application they must submit proof of Washoe enrollment, a copy of their college grade report, and a copy of their current class schedule. Selection is based on a first-come, first-served basis; financial need is not considered.

Financial data The stipend varies each year; recently, stipends were $2,000 per semester.

Duration 1 year; recipients may reapply.

Number awarded 20 each year.

Deadline January or June of each year.

[1241]
WAYNE ANTHONY BUTTS SCHOLARSHIP

National Medical Fellowships, Inc.
Attn: Scholarship Program
347 Fifth Avenue, Suite 510
New York, NY 10016
(212) 483-8880   Toll Free: (877) NMF-1DOC
Fax: (212) 483-8897 E-mail: scholarships@nmfonline.org
Web: www.nmfonline.org

Summary To provide financial assistance to Native American and other underrepresented minority students at medical schools in the New York City metropolitan area.

Eligibility This program is open to African Americans, Hispanics/Latinos, Native Americans, Vietnamese, Cambodians, and Pacific Islanders who are entering their first or second year of medical school. Applicants must be enrolled at a school in the New York City metropolitan area. They must be U.S. citizens or DACA students. Selection is based on leadership, commitment to serving medically underserved communities, and financial need.

Financial data The stipend is $3,000.

Duration 1 year.

Additional information This program began in 2013.

Number awarded 1 each year.

Deadline September of each year.

[1242]
WELLS FARGO AMERICAN INDIAN SCHOLARSHIP PROGRAM

American Indian Graduate Center
Attn: Executive Director
3701 San Mateo Boulevard, N.E., Suite 200
Albuquerque, NM 87110-1249
(505) 881-4584   Toll Free: (800) 628-1920
Fax: (505) 884-0427   E-mail: fellowships@aigc.com
Web: www.aigcs.org/scholarships/graduate-fellowships

Summary To provide financial assistance to Native American graduate students interested in preparing for a career in banking, gaming operations, resort management, or administration.

Eligibility This program is open to enrolled members of federally-recognized American Indian tribes and Alaska Native groups who can provide a Certificate of Degree of Indian Blood (CDIB). Applicants must be working full time on a graduate or professional degree to prepare for a career in banking, resort management, gaming operations, or management and administration, including accounting, finance, human resources, and information systems. They must have a GPA of 3.0 or higher. Along with their application, they must submit an essay on their personal, educational, and professional goals. Financial need is also considered in the selection process.

Financial data A stipend is awarded (amount not specified).

Duration 1 year.

Additional information This program is supported by Wells Fargo Bank.

Number awarded 1 or more each year.

Deadline April of each year.

[1243]
WHITE EARTH SCHOLARSHIP PROGRAM

White Earth Indian Reservation Tribal Council
Attn: Scholarship Program
P.O. Box 418
White Earth, MN 56591
(218) 983-3285, ext. 5304   Toll Free: (800) 950-3248
Fax: (218) 983-3705
E-mail: leslie.nessman@whiteearth-nsn.gov
Web: www.whiteearth.com

Summary To provide financial assistance to Minnesota Chippewa Tribe members who are interested in attending college, vocational school, or graduate school in specified fields.

Eligibility This program is open to enrolled members of the White Earth Band of the Minnesota Chippewa Tribe who can demonstrate financial need. Applicants must be attending or planning to attend a college, university, or vocational school in any state. Graduate students must be working on a degree in business, education, human services, law, or medicine.

Financial data A stipend is awarded (amount not specified).

Duration 1 year; may be renewed, provided undergraduates maintain a GPA of 2.0 or higher and graduate students maintain a GPA of 3.0 or higher.

Additional information Applicants for this program must also apply for financial aid administered by their institution and any other aid for which they may be eligible (e.g., work-study, Social Security, veteran's benefits).

Number awarded Varies each year.

Deadline May of each year.

[1244]
WHITE MOUNTAIN APACHE TRIBAL SCHOLARSHIPS

White Mountain Apache Tribe
Attn: Office of Higher Education
205 West Fatco Road
P.O. Box 250
Whiteriver, AZ 85941
(928) 338-5800   Toll Free: (877) 7-APACHE
Fax: (928) 338-1869   E-mail: lgoklish@wmat.us
Web: www.wmat.nsn.us/high_ed.html

Summary To provide financial assistance to members of the White Mountain Apache Tribe who are interested in attending college or graduate school in any state.

Eligibility This program is open to members of the White Mountain Apache Tribe who are enrolled or planning to enroll full time at a college, university, or vocational/technical school in any state. Applicants must be interested in working on an undergraduate or graduate degree in any field. Along with their application, they must submit a 150-word essay on their educational goals and plans for utilizing their scholarship.

Financial data A stipend is awarded (amount not specified).

Duration 1 year; may be renewed, provided the recipient remains enrolled full time and maintains a GPA of 1.7 or higher as a freshman, 2.0 as a sophomore through senior, or 3.0 as a graduate student.

Additional information This program is funded by the U.S. Bureau of Indian Affairs (BIA).

Number awarded Varies each year.

Deadline March of each year for fall; September of each year for spring.

[1245]
WIEA SCHOLARSHIPS

Wisconsin Indian Education Association
Attn: Scholarship Coordinator
P.O. Box 910
Keshena, WI 54135
(715) 799-5110   Fax: (715) 799-5102
E-mail: vnuske@mitw.org
Web: www.wiea.org/index.php/About/Scholarships

Summary To provide financial assistance for undergraduate or graduate study to members of Wisconsin Indian tribes.

Eligibility This program is open to residents of Wisconsin who can provide proof of tribal enrollment. Applicants must fall into 1 of the following categories: 1) entering freshman at a 4-year college or university; 2) new or continuing student at a tribal college or vocational/technical school; 3) undergraduate student at a 4-year college or university; or 4) graduate or Ph.D. student. All applicants must be full-time students. Along with their application, they must submit a 1-page personal essay on how they will apply their education. Selection is based on that essay (25 points), letters of recommendation (10 points), and GPA (15 points if 3.5 or higher, 10 points if

3.00 to 3.49, 5 points if 2.50 to 2.99). Financial need is not considered.

Financial data The stipend is $1,000.

Duration 1 year; nonrenewable.

Additional information This program began in 1997. Eligible tribes include Menominee, Oneida, Stockbridge-Munsee, Forest County Potowatomi, Ho-Chunk, Bad River Chippewa, Lac Courte Oreilles Ojibwe, St. Croix Chippewa, Red Cliff Chippewa, Sakoagon (Mole Lake) Chippewa, Brotherton, and Lac du Flambeau Chippewa.

Number awarded 4 each year: 1 in each of the 4 categories.

Deadline April of each year.

[1246]
WIGA COLLEGE SCHOLARSHIPS

Washington Indian Gaming Association
1110 Capitol Way South, Suite 404
Olympia, WA 98501-2251
(360) 352-3248   Fax: (360) 352-4819
E-mail: abriel@reachone.com
Web: www.washingtonindiangaming.org

Summary To provide financial assistance to members of Indian tribes in Washington who are interested in attending college or graduate school in any state.

Eligibility This program is open to Washington residents who are enrolled members of tribes affiliated with the Washington Indian Gaming Association (WIGA) and to urban Indian students in the state. Applicants must be attending or accepted at a community college, undergraduate institution, or graduate school in any state. Native American students from outside Washington who attend college in the state are also eligible. Along with their application, they must submit a 250-word personal essay on why they are considering their intended major, how it will help them reach future career objectives, and how their education will benefit their home community (whether urban or rural). Financial need is also considered in the selection process.

Financial data Stipends are $2,200 per year for graduate or professional students, $2,000 per year for undergraduates at 4-year institutions, or $1,000 per year for students at community colleges or technical schools.

Duration 1 year; may be renewed, provided the recipient maintains a GPA of 2.5 or higher.

Number awarded Varies each year; recently, 41 were awarded: 7 to students at community colleges and technical schools, 25 to undergraduates at 4-year institutions, and 9 to graduate students.

Deadline March of each year.

[1247]
WILEY W. MANUEL LAW FOUNDATION SCHOLARSHIPS

Wiley W. Manuel Law Foundation
c/o Law Offices of George Holland
1970 Broadway, Suite 1030
Oakland, CA 94612
(510) 465-4100
Web: www.wileymanuel.org/forms.html

Summary To provide financial assistance to Native American and other minority students from any state enrolled at law schools in northern California.

Eligibility This program is open to minority students entering their third year at law schools in northern California. Applicants should exemplify the qualities of the late Justice Wiley Manuel, the first African American to serve on the California Supreme Court. Along with their application, they must submit a 250-word essay on why they should be awarded this scholarship. Financial need is also considered in the selection process.

Financial data The stipend is approximately $1,500.

Duration 1 year.

Number awarded Varies each year; recently, 12 were awarded.

Deadline August of each year.

[1248]
WILLIAM AND CHARLOTTE CADBURY AWARD

National Medical Fellowships, Inc.
Attn: Scholarship Program
347 Fifth Avenue, Suite 510
New York, NY 10016
(212) 483-8880   Toll Free: (877) NMF-1DOC
Fax: (212) 483-8897 E-mail: scholarships@nmfonline.org
Web: www.nmfonline.org

Summary To provide financial assistance to Native American and other underrepresented minority medical students who demonstrate academic achievement.

Eligibility This program is open to African Americans, Hispanics/Latinos, Native Americans, Vietnamese, Cambodians, and Pacific Islanders who are entering their senior year of medical school. They must be U.S. citizens or DACA students. Selection is based on academic achievement, leadership, and community service.

Financial data The stipend is $5,000.

Duration 1 year.

Additional information This program began in 1977.

Number awarded 1 each year.

Deadline September of each year.

[1249]
WILLIAM D. PHILLIPS SCHOLARSHIP FUND

Cook Inlet Region, Inc.
Attn: The CIRI Foundation
3600 San Jeronimo Drive, Suite 256
Anchorage, AK 99508-2870
(907) 793-3575   Toll Free: (800) 764-3382
Fax: (907) 793-3585   E-mail: tcf@thecirifoundation.org
Web: www.thecirifoundation.org/about/donors

Summary To provide financial assistance for undergraduate or graduate studies in public policy fields to Alaska Natives who are original enrollees to Cook Inlet Region, Inc. (CIRI) and their lineal descendants.

Eligibility This program is open to Alaska Native enrollees to CIRI under the Alaska Native Claims Settlement Act (ANCSA) of 1971 and their lineal descendants. There are no Alaska residency requirements or age limitations. Applicants must be accepted or enrolled full time in a 4-year undergraduate or a graduate degree program in government, public policy, public administration, budget and public finance, social

policy, education policy, or related fields. They must have a GPA of 3.7 or higher. Along with their application, they must submit a 500-word statement on their educational and career goals and how they are contributing, or planning to contribute, to a positive Alaska Native community. Selection is based on that statement, academic achievement, rigor of course work or degree program, student financial contribution, financial need, grade level, previous work performance, community service, and relationship of degree program to career goals.

Financial data The stipend is $20,000 per year.

Duration 1 year; may be renewed.

Additional information CIRI is 1 of 13 regional corporations established according to the terms of the Alaska Native Claims Settlement Act (ANCSA) of 1971.

Number awarded 1 or more each year.

Deadline May of each year.

[1250]
WILLIAM G. ANDERSON, D.O. MINORITY SCHOLARSHIP

American Osteopathic Foundation
Attn: Director, Internal and External Affairs
142 East Ontario Street
Chicago, IL 60611-2864
(312) 202-8235   Toll Free: (866) 455-9383
Fax: (312) 202-8216   E-mail: ehart@aof-foundation.org
Web: www.aof.org

Summary To provide financial assistance to Native American and other minority students enrolled in colleges of osteopathic medicine.

Eligibility This program is open to minority (African American, Native American, Asian American, Pacific Islander, or Hispanic) students entering their second, third, or fourth year at an accredited college of osteopathic medicine. Applicants must demonstrate 1) interest in osteopathic medicine, its philosophy, and its principles; 2) academic achievement; 3) leadership efforts in addressing the educational, societal, and health needs of minorities; 4) leadership efforts in addressing inequities in medical education and health care; 5) accomplishments, awards and honors, special projects, and extracurricular activities that demonstrate the applicant's ability to be a leader.

Financial data The stipend is $7,500.

Duration 1 year.

Additional information This program began in 1998.

Number awarded 1 each year.

Deadline April of each year.

[1251]
WILLIAM K. SCHUBERT M.D. MINORITY NURSING SCHOLARSHIP

Cincinnati Children's Hospital Medical Center
Attn: Office of Diversity and Inclusion, MLC 9008
3333 Burnet Avenue
Cincinnati, OH 45229-3026
(513) 803-6416   Toll Free: (800) 344-2462
Fax: (513) 636-5643   TDD: (513) 636-4900
E-mail: diversity@cchmc.org
Web: www.cincinnatichildrens.org

Summary To provide financial assistance to Native Americans and members of other underrepresented groups interested in working on a bachelor's or master's degree in nursing to prepare for licensure in Ohio.

Eligibility This program is open to members of groups underrepresented in the nursing profession (males, American Indians or Alaska Natives, Blacks or African Americans, Hawaiian Natives or other Pacific Islanders, Hispanics or Latinos, or Asians). Applicants must be enrolled or accepted in a professional bachelor's or master's registered nurse program at an accredited school of nursing to prepare for initial licensure in Ohio. They must have a GPA of 2.75 or higher. Along with their application, they must submit a 750-word essay that covers 1) their long-range personal, educational, and professional goals; 2) why they chose nursing as a profession; 3) how their experience as a member of an underrepresented group has influenced a major professional and/or personal decision in their life; 4) any unique qualifications, experiences, or special talents that demonstrate their creativity; and 5) how their work experience has contributed to their personal development.

Financial data The stipend is $2,750 per year.

Duration 1 year. May be renewed up to 3 additional years for students working on a bachelor's degree or 1 additional year for students working on a master's degree; renewal requires that students maintain a GPA of 2.75 or higher.

Number awarded 1 or more each year.

Deadline April of each year.

[1252]
WILLIAM REECE SMITH, JR. DIVERSITY SCHOLARSHIPS

Carlton Fields Jorden Blut
Attn: Naila Townes Ahmed, Director of Legal Talent
  Management
Corporate Center Three at International Plaza
4221 West Boy Scout Boulevard, Suite 1000
Tampa, FL 33607-5780
(813) 229-4172   Toll Free: (888) 223-9191
Fax: (813) 229-4133   E-mail: nahmed@cfjblaw.com
Web: www.cfjblaw.com/diversity-scholarships

Summary To provide financial assistance and work experience at Carlton Fields Jorden Blut to Native American and other law students who come from a diverse background.

Eligibility This program is open to students completing their first year at an ABA-accredited law school who come from a diverse background, including ethnicity, race, gender, sexual orientation, culture, or disabilities. Applicants must be interested in a summer associateship at the sponsoring firm's law offices in Miami, Orlando, Tampa, or West Palm Beach. They must be able to demonstrate a record of achievement that holds great promise for a successful legal career, a high level of work intensity, a desire to practice law in a highly focused but collegial setting, demonstrated leadership ability, excellent writing and interpersonal skills, and academic achievement.

Financial data The program provides a stipend of $5,000 for law school and a paid summer associateship (salary not specified).

Duration 1 year.

Additional information This program began in 2011.

Number awarded 2 each year.

Deadline February of each year.

[1253]
WILLIAM RUCKER GREENWOOD SCHOLARSHIP

Association for Women Geoscientists-Potomac Chapter
Attn: Scholarships
P.O. Box 6644
Arlington, VA 22206-0644
E-mail: awgpotomacschol@hotmail.com
Web: www.awg.org/members/po_scholarships.htm

Summary To provide financial assistance to Native American and other minority women from any state working on an undergraduate or graduate degree in the geosciences at a college in the Potomac Bay region.

Eligibility This program is open to minority women who are residents of any state and currently enrolled as full-time undergraduate or graduate geoscience majors at an accredited, degree-granting college or university in Delaware, the District of Columbia, Maryland, Virginia, or West Virginia. Selection is based on the applicant's 1) participation in geoscience or earth science educational activities; and 2) potential for leadership as a future geoscience professional.

Financial data The stipend is $1,000. The recipient also is granted a 1-year membership in the Association for Women Geoscientists (AWG).

Duration 1 year.

Number awarded 1 each year.

Deadline April of each year.

[1254]
WILSON-HOOPER SCHOLARSHIP

Chahta Foundation
Attn: Scholarship Specialist
P.O. Box 1849
Durant, OK 74702
(580) 924-8280, ext. 2546
Toll Free: (800) 522-6170, ext. 2546
Fax: (580) 745-9023
E-mail: scholarship@chahtafoundation.com
Web: www.chahtafoundation.com

Summary To provide financial assistance to members of the Choctaw Nation who are preparing for a career in veterinary technology or veterinary medicine.

Eligibility This program is open to Choctaw students who are attending an institution of higher education and working on an association degree in veterinary technology or a doctoral degree in veterinary medicine. They must have a GPA of 3.0 or higher. Along with their application, they must submit essays on 1) why they want to become a veterinarian; and 2) their preference in working with small animals, large animals, or exotics. In the selection process, emphasis is placed on desire and ability rather than financial need.

Financial data The stipend ranges from $500 to $4,000 per year.

Duration 1 year; recipients may reapply.

Additional information This program began in 2014.

Number awarded 1 or more each year.

Deadline May of each year.

[1255]
WINNEBAGO TRIBE HIGHER EDUCATION ASSISTANCE

Winnebago Tribe of Nebraska
Attn: Higher Education Director
100 Bluff Street
P.O. Box 687
Winnebago, NE 68071
(402) 878-2631   Fax: (402) 878-2637
E-mail: patrice.bass@winnebagotribe.com
Web: www.winnebagotribe.com

Summary To provide financial assistance to members of the Winnebago Tribe of Nebraska who are interested in attending vocational school, college, or graduate school in any state.

Eligibility This program is open to enrolled members of the Winnebago Tribe of Nebraska who are attending or planning to attend an institution of higher education in any state. Applicants must be working full or part time on a vocational certificate or an associate, bachelor's, master's, or doctoral degree and have a GPA of 2.5 or higher. They must submit a copy of their Certificate of Degree of Indian Blood (CDIB), transcripts, and documentation of financial need. In the selection process, first priority is given to students who live on the reservation, second to students who live off the reservation, third to students who live in Nebraska, and fourth to students who live in other states.

Financial data For undergraduates, funding is intended only to supplement other assistance available to the student. For full-time graduate students, the stipend is $15,000 per year. For part-time graduate students, the stipend depends on the need of the recipient.

Duration 1 semester; may be renewed, provided the recipient maintains a GPA of 2.5 or higher as an undergraduate or 3.0 or higher as a graduate student.

Number awarded Varies each year.

Deadline April of each year for fall, academic year, or summer school; October of each year for spring or winter.

[1256]
WINSTON & STRAWN DIVERSITY SCHOLARSHIP PROGRAM

Winston & Strawn LLP
Attn: Amanda Sommerfeld, Diversity Committee Chair
333 South Grand Avenue
Los Angeles, CA 90071-1543
(213) 615-1724   Fax: (213) 615-1750
E-mail: asommerfeld@winston.com
Web: www.winston.com

Summary To provide financial assistance to Native American and other diverse law students who are interested in practicing in a city in which Winston & Strawn LLP has an office.

Eligibility This program is open to second-year law students who represent the varied experiences of different races, ethnic groups, genders, sexual orientation, ages, religions, national origins and disabilities. Applicants must submit a resume, law school transcript, and 500-word personal statement. Selection is based on 1) interest in practicing law after graduation in a large law firm in a city in which Winston & Strawn has an office (currently, Charlotte, Chicago, Houston, Los Angeles, Menlo Park, New York, Newark, San Fran-

cisco, and Washington, D.C.); 2) law school and undergraduate record, including academic achievements and involvement in extracurricular activities; 3) demonstrated leadership skills; 4) and interpersonal skills.

Financial data The stipend is $10,000.

Duration 1 year (the third year of law school).

Additional information This program began in 2004.

Number awarded 3 each year.

Deadline September of each year.

[1257]
WISCONSIN INDIAN STUDENT ASSISTANCE GRANTS

Wisconsin Higher Educational Aids Board
131 West Wilson Street, Suite 902
P.O. Box 7885
Madison, WI 53707-7885
(608) 266-0888   Fax: (608) 267-2808
E-mail: cindy.cooley@wi.gov
Web: www.heab.state.wi.us/programs.html

Summary To provide financial assistance to Native Americans in Wisconsin who are interested in attending college or graduate school in the state.

Eligibility Wisconsin residents who have at least 25% Native American blood (of a certified tribe or band) are eligible to apply if they are able to demonstrate financial need and are interested in attending college on the undergraduate or graduate school level. Applicants must attend a Wisconsin institution (public, independent, or proprietary). They may be enrolled either full or part time.

Financial data The stipend ranges from $250 to $1,100 per year. Additional funds are available on a matching basis from the U.S. Bureau of Indian Affairs.

Duration Up to 5 years.

Number awarded Varies each year.

Deadline Generally, applications can be submitted at any time.

[1258]
WOMAN WHO MOVES THE NATION SCHOLARSHIP

Conference of Minority Transportation Officials
Attn: National Scholarship Program
100 M Street, S.E., Suite 917
Washington, DC 20003
(202) 506-2917   E-mail: info@comto.org
Web: www.comto.org/page/scholarships

Summary To provide financial assistance to Native American and other minority women who are working on an undergraduate or graduate degree in specified fields to prepare for a management career in a transportation-related organization.

Eligibility This program is open to minority women who are working on an undergraduate or graduate degree with intent to lead in some capacity as a supervisor, manager, director, or other position in transit or a transportation-related organization. Applicants may be studying business, entrepreneurship, political science, or other specialized area. They must have a GPA of 3.0 or higher. Along with their application they must submit a cover letter on their transportation-related career goals and life aspirations. Financial need is not considered in the selection process.

Financial data The stipend is $5,000. Funds are paid directly to the recipient's college or university.

Duration 1 year.

Number awarded 1 each year.

Deadline April of each year.

[1259]
WSP/PARSONS BRINCKERHOFF WOMEN IN LEADERSHIP SCHOLARSHIP

Conference of Minority Transportation Officials
Attn: National Scholarship Program
100 M Street, S.E., Suite 917
Washington, DC 20003
(202) 506-2917   E-mail: info@comto.org
Web: www.comto.org/page/scholarships

Summary To provide financial assistance to Native American and other minority women who are working on a master's degree in civil engineering or other transportation-related field.

Eligibility This program is open to minority women who are working full time on a master's degree in civil engineering with intent to prepare for a leadership role in transportation. They must have a GPA of 3.0 or higher. Along with their application they must submit a cover letter on their transportation-related career goals and life aspirations. Financial need is not considered in the selection process.

Financial data The stipend is $3,000. Funds are paid directly to the recipient's college or university.

Duration 1 year.

Additional information This program is sponsored by WSP USA, formerly Parsons Brinckerhoff, Inc.

Number awarded 1 each year.

Deadline April of each year.

[1260]
XEROX TECHNICAL MINORITY SCHOLARSHIP PROGRAM

Xerox Corporation
Attn: Technical Minority Scholarship Program
150 State Street, Fourth Floor
Rochester, NY 14614
Toll Free: (877) 747-3625   E-mail: xtmsp@rballiance.com
Web: www.xerox.com/jobs/minority-scholarships/enus.html

Summary To provide financial assistance to Native Americans and other minorities interested in undergraduate or graduate education in the sciences and/or engineering.

Eligibility This program is open to minorities (people of African American, Asian, Pacific Islander, Native American, Native Alaskan, or Hispanic descent) working full time on a bachelor's, master's, or doctoral degree in chemistry, computing and software systems, engineering (chemical, computer, electrical, imaging, manufacturing, mechanical, optical, or software), information management, laser optics, materials science, physics, or printing management science. Applicants must be U.S. citizens or permanent residents with a GPA of 3.0 or higher and attending a 4-year college or university.

Financial data Stipends range from $1,000 to $10,000.

Duration 1 year.

Number awarded Varies each year; recently, 128 were awarded.

Deadline September of each year.

[1261]
YAKAMA NATION CREDIT ENTERPRISE SCHOLARSHIP

Yakama Nation
Department of Human Services
Attn: Higher Education Program
107 Teo Road
P.O. Box 151
Toppenish, WA 98948
(509) 865-5121, ext. 4540   Toll Free: (800) 543-2802
Fax: (509) 865-6994   E-mail: murry@yakama.com
Web: www.yakama.us/programs.php

Summary To provide financial assistance to undergraduate and graduate students who are Yakama tribal members majoring in a business-related field at a school in any state.

Eligibility This program is open to enrolled members of the Yakama nation who are enrolled or planning to enroll full time at a college or university in any state. Applicants must be working on an undergraduate or graduate degree in accounting, banking, business, real estate, or a closely-related field.

Financial data A stipend is awarded (amount not specified).

Duration 1 year.

Number awarded 1 or more each year.

Deadline June of each year.

[1262]
YAKAMA NATION HIGHER EDUCATION SCHOLARSHIP

Yakama Nation
Department of Human Services
Attn: Higher Education Program
107 Teo Road
P.O. Box 151
Toppenish, WA 98948
(509) 865-5121, ext. 4540   Toll Free: (800) 543-2802
Fax: (509) 865-6994   E-mail: murry@yakama.com
Web: www.yakama.us/programs.php

Summary To provide financial assistance to Yakama tribal members interested in working on an undergraduate or graduate degree at a school in any state.

Eligibility This program is open to enrolled members of the Yakama nation who are enrolled or planning to enroll at a postsecondary institution in any state. Applicants must be interested in working on an undergraduate or graduate degree on a part-time or full-time basis. Along with their application, they must submit a personal letter describing their educational and employment goals. Financial need is considered in the selection process.

Financial data The stipend is $1,500 per year for full-time undergraduates or $3,000 per year for full-time graduate students. Part-time students are eligible for funding for tuition and books only.

Duration 1 year; may be renewed.

Number awarded Varies each year.

Deadline June of each year for fall semester or quarter or for academic year; October of each year for spring semester or winter quarter; January of each year for spring quarter; April of each year for high school seniors and summer school.

[1263]
YAVAPAI-APACHE NATION HIGHER EDUCATION GRANTS

Yavapai-Apache Nation
Attn: Higher Education Department
2400 West Datsi Street
Camp Verde, AZ 86322
(928) 649-7111   Fax: (928) 567-6485
Web: www.yavapai-apache.org/administration

Summary To provide financial assistance to members of the Yavapai-Apache Nation who are interested in attending college or graduate school in any state.

Eligibility This program is open to members of the Yavapai-Apache Nation who are enrolled or planning to enroll at an accredited institution of higher education in any state. Applicants must be interested in working full or part time on a vocational certificate or an associate, bachelor's, master's, or doctoral degree. Along with their application, they must submit 1) a brief essay on their educational goals and how they will utilize their education; and 2) documentation of financial need.

Financial data The stipend is $20,000 per year for undergraduate and vocational students or $30,000 per year for graduate students.

Duration 1 semester; may be renewed up to 5 additional full-time semesters for students working on an associate degree, 9 additional full-time semesters for students working on a bachelor's degree, 9 additional full-time semesters for students working on a graduate degree, or until completion of a program for vocational students. Renewal requires the recipient to maintain a GPA of 2.0 or higher.

Number awarded Varies each year.

Deadline June of each year for fall and academic year; September of each year for spring only; March of each year for summer; August of each year for vocational/technical school.

[1264]
YUM! BRANDS AND DINSMORE & SHOHL LLP DIVERSITY SCHOLARSHIP PROGRAM

Dinsmore & Shohl LLP
Attn: Director of Recruiting and Legal Personnel
255 East Fifth Street, Suite 1900
Cincinnati, OH 45202
(513) 977-8488   Fax: (513) 977-8141
E-mail: dinsmore.legalrecruiting@dinsmore.com
Web: www.dinsmorecareers.com

Summary To provide financial assistance and summer work experience with Yum! Brands to Native Americans and other law students who will contribute to diversity in the legal profession.

Eligibility This program is open to first-year law students who have made a meaningful commitment to diversity in the legal profession. The sponsor defines diversity as "the confluence of cultures, histories, sexual orientations, religions, and

dialects that together make up the whole of our society." Applicants must have a demonstrated record of academic or professional achievement and leadership qualities through past work experience, community involvement, or student activities. They must also be interested in a summer associateship with both Yum! Brands and with Dinsmore & Shohl LLP. Along with their application, they must submit a 500-word personal statement explaining their interest in the scholarship program and how diversity has impacted their life.

Financial data The program provides an academic scholarship of $5,000 and a paid associateship.

Duration The academic scholarship is for 1 year. The summer associateship is for 12 weeks, of which 6 weeks are at Dinsmore & Shohl and 6 weeks are in the legal department of Yum! Brands.

Additional information Associateships are in Louisville, Kentucky.

Number awarded 1 each year.

Deadline December of each year.

[1265]
ZELLE HOFMANN DIVERSITY IN LAW SCHOLARSHIP

Zelle Hofmann Voelbel & Mason LLP
Attn: Diversity Coordinator
500 Washington Avenue South, Suite 4000
Minneapolis, MN 55415
(612) 339-2000   Toll Free: (800) 899-5291
Fax: (612) 336-9100   E-mail: pstpeter@zelle.com
Web: www.zelle.com/careers-diversity-outreach.html

Summary To provide financial assistance to law students who are Native Americans or members of other groups historically underrepresented in the private practice of law.

Eligibility This program is open to first-year law students who either 1) are a member of a population or group whose background and perspectives are historically underrepresented in the private practice of law; or 2) demonstrate a long-standing commitment to diversity that will be furthered by award of the scholarship. The firm's diversity initiatives have focused on women, ethnic minorities, and LGBT students. Selection is based on academic performance, writing skills, demonstrated leadership skills, an interest in litigation (including antitrust and insurance litigation), financial need, and a desire to practice in a city where the sponsor maintains an office.

Financial data The stipend is $15,000 per year.

Duration 2 years: the second and third year of law school.

Additional information Students may be offered, but are under no obligation to accept, a paid summer clerkship at the firm's offices in Boston, Dallas, Minneapolis, or San Francisco. Other cities where the firm has offices are Miami, New York, Philadelphia, and Washington.

Number awarded 1 each year.

Deadline March of each year.

[1266]
ZUNI HIGHER EDUCATION SCHOLARSHIPS

Pueblo of Zuni
Attn: Education and Career Development Center
01 Twin Buttes Drive
P.O. Box 339
Zuni, NM 87327
(505) 782-5998   Fax: (505) 782-6080
E-mail: zecdc@ashiwi.org
Web: www.ashiwi.org/zecdc/Tribal.Scholarship.html

Summary To provide financial assistance for college or graduate school in any state to members of the Pueblo of Zuni.

Eligibility This program is open to enrolled members of the Pueblo of Zuni who are high school seniors or graduates. Applicants must have earned a GPA of 2.0 or higher and be interested in working on an associate, bachelor's, or graduate degree as a full-time student at a college or university in any state. They must have also applied for a federal Pell Grant. Along with their application, they must submit a personal statement on why they are seeking this scholarship.

Financial data The amount awarded depends on the need of the recipient, up to $5,000 per year.

Duration 1 year; may be renewed if the recipient maintains a GPA of 2.0 or higher.

Number awarded Varies each year.

Deadline June of each year for the fall semester; October of each year for the spring semester; April of each year for the summer session.

Professionals/ Postdoctorates

Listed alphabetically by program title and described in detail here are 94 grants, awards, residencies, and other sources of "free money" available to American Indian, Native Alaskan (including Eskimos and Aleuts), and Native Hawaiian professionals and postdoctorates. This funding can be used to support research, creative activities, training programs, and/or residencies in the United States.

[1267]
AMERICAN INDIAN STUDIES VISITING SCHOLAR AND VISITING RESEARCHER PROGRAM

University of California at Los Angeles
Institute of American Cultures
Attn: American Indian Studies Center
3220 Campbell Hall
P.O. Box 951548
Los Angeles, CA 90095-1548
(310) 825-7315   Fax: (310) 206-7060
E-mail: rwhiteeyes@aisc.ucla.edu
Web: www.iac.ucla.edu/fellowships_visitingscholar.html

Summary To provide funding to scholars interested in conducting research in Native American studies at UCLA's American Indian Studies Center.

Eligibility Applicants must have completed a doctoral degree in Native American or related studies. They must be interested in teaching or conducting research at UCLA's American Indian Studies Center. Visiting Scholar appointments are available to people who currently hold permanent academic appointments; Visiting Researcher appointments are available to postdoctorates who recently received their degree. UCLA faculty, students, and staff are not eligible. U.S. citizenship or permanent resident status is required.

Financial data Fellows receive a stipend of $35,000, health benefits, and up to $4,000 in research support. Visiting Scholars are paid through their home institution; Visiting Researchers receive their funds directly from UCLA.

Duration 9 months, beginning in October.

Additional information Fellows must teach or do research in the programs of the center. The award is offered in conjunction with UCLA's Institute of American Cultures (IAC).

Number awarded 1 each year.

Deadline January of each year.

[1268]
AMERICAN NURSES ASSOCIATION MINORITY FELLOWSHIP PROGRAM

American Nurses Association
Attn: SAMHSA Minority Fellowship Programs
8515 Georgia Avenue, Suite 400
Silver Spring, MD 20910-3492
(301) 628-5247   Toll Free: (800) 274-4ANA
Fax: (301) 628-5339   E-mail: janet.jackson@ana.org
Web: www.emfp.org

Summary To provide financial assistance to Native American and other minority nurses who are doctoral candidates interested in psychiatric, mental health, and substance abuse issues that impact the lives of ethnic minority people.

Eligibility This program is open to nurses who have a master's degree and are members of an ethnic or racial minority group, including but not limited to Blacks or African Americans, Hispanics or Latinos, American Indians and Alaska Natives, Asians and Asian Americans, and Native Hawaiians and other Pacific Islanders. Applicants must be enrolled full time in an accredited doctoral nursing program. They must be certified as a Mental Health Nurse Practitioner, Mental Health Clinical Nurse Specialist, or Mental Health Nurse. U.S. citizenship or permanent resident status and membership in the American Nurses Association are required. Selection is based on commitment to a career in substance abuse in psychiatric/mental health issues affecting minority populations.

Financial data The program provides an annual stipend of $22,476 and tuition assistance up to $5,000.

Duration 3 to 5 years.

Additional information Funds for this program are provided by the Substance Abuse and Mental Health Services Administration (SAMHSA).

Number awarded 1 or more each year.

Deadline March of each year.

[1269]
ANAC STUDENT DIVERSITY MENTORSHIP SCHOLARSHIP

Association of Nurses in AIDS Care
Attn: Awards Committee
3538 Ridgewood Road
Akron, OH 44333-3122
(330) 670-0101   Toll Free: (800) 260-6780
Fax: (330) 670-0109   E-mail: anac@anacnet.org
Web: www.nursesinaidscare.org

Summary To provide financial assistance to student nurses from Native American and other minority groups who are interested in HIV/AIDS nursing and in attending the national conference of the Association of Nurses in AIDS Care (ANAC).

Eligibility This program is open to student nurses from a diverse racial or ethnic background, defined to include African Americans, Hispanics/Latinos, Asians/Pacific Islanders, and American Indians/Alaskan Natives. Candidates must have a genuine interest in HIV/AIDS nursing, be interested in attending the ANAC national conference, and desire to develop a mentorship relationship with a member of the ANAC Diversity Specialty Committee. They may be 1) pre-licensure students enrolled in an initial R.N. or L.P.N./L.V.N. program (i.e. L.P.N./L.V.N., A.D.N., diploma, B.S./B.S.N.); or 2) current licensed R.N. students with an associate or diploma degree who are enrolled in a bachelor's degree program. Nominees may be recommended by themselves, nursing faculty members, or ANAC members, but their nomination must be supported by an ANAC member. Along with their nomination form, they must submit a 2,000-character essay describing their interest or experience in HIV/AIDS care and why they want to attend the ANAC conference.

Financial data Recipients are awarded a $1,000 scholarship (paid directly to the school), up to $599 in reimbursement of travel expenses to attend the ANAC annual conference, free conference registration, an award plaque, a free ticket to the awards ceremony at the conference, and a 2-year ANAC membership.

Duration 1 year.

Additional information The mentor will be assigned at the conference and will maintain contact during the period of study.

Number awarded 1 each year.

Deadline August of each year.

[1270]
ANDREW W. MELLON FELLOWSHIPS AT THE NATIONAL MUSEUM OF THE AMERICAN INDIAN

National Museum of the American Indian
Attn: Conservation Office
Cultural Resources Center
4220 Silver Hill Road, MRC 538
Suitland, MD 20746-2863
(301) 238-1424   Fax: (301) 238-3201
E-mail: NMAIcrcconserv@si.edu
Web: www.nmai.si.edu

Summary To provide recent college graduates involved in conservation of museum collections with an opportunity to participate in a training program at the Smithsonian Institution's National Museum of the American Indian (NMAI).

Eligibility This program is open to recent graduates of recognized conservation training programs. Applicants must be preparing for a career in the conservation of material culture of the indigenous peoples of North, Central, and South America. They must be interested in participating in a training program at the NMAI Cultural Resources Center in Suitland, Maryland that involves collaboration with Native people in developing appropriate methods of caring for and interpreting cultural materials. The program is intended to cultivate practical skills as well as foster a solid understanding of the contexts of material culture, the philosophies of conservation at NMAI, and the ethics of the conservation profession. Current projects involved the preparation of artifacts for loans and for exhibits at NMAI sites. Fellowships are awarded without regard to the age, sex, race, or nationality of the applicant; proficiency in English is required.

Financial data Fellows receive a stipend (amount not specified) and funds for travel and research.

Duration 1 year; may be renewed 1 additional year.

Number awarded 1 each year.

Deadline March of each year.

[1271]
ANDREW W. MELLON INTERNSHIPS AT THE NATIONAL MUSEUM OF THE AMERICAN INDIAN

National Museum of the American Indian
Attn: Conservation Office
Cultural Resources Center
4220 Silver Hill Road, MRC 538
Suitland, MD 20746-2863
(301) 238-1424   Fax: (301) 238-3201
E-mail: NMAIcrcconserv@si.edu
Web: www.nmai.si.edu

Summary To provide graduate students and professionals involved in conservation of museum collections with an opportunity to participate in an internship at the Smithsonian Institution's National Museum of the American Indian (NMAI).

Eligibility This program is open to 1) students who are currently enrolled in or have recently completed graduate degree programs in conservation; and 2) practicing conservation professionals. of recognized conservation training programs. Applicants must be interested in an internship at the NMAI Cultural Resources Center in Suitland, Maryland to cultivate practical skills and foster an understanding of the contexts of material culture, the philosophies of conservation of the NMAI, and the ethics of the conservation profession. The program involves collaboration with Native people in developing appropriate methods of caring for and interpreting cultural materials. Candidates who demonstrate a career interest in the conservation of material culture of the indigenous peoples of North, Central, and South America are especially welcome. Proficiency in English is required.

Financial data Interns receive a stipend (amount not specified).

Duration 10 weeks, beginning in June.

Number awarded Varies each year.

Deadline January of each year.

[1272]
ANISFIELD-WOLF BOOK AWARDS

Cleveland Foundation
1422 Euclid Avenue, Suite 1300
Cleveland, OH 44115-2001
(216) 861-3810   Fax: (216) 861-1729
E-mail: Hello@anisfield-wolf.org
Web: www.anisfield-wolf.org

Summary To recognize and reward recent books that have contributed to an understanding of racism or appreciation of the rich diversity of human cultures.

Eligibility Works published in English during the preceding year that "contribute to our understanding of racism or our appreciation of the rich diversity of human cultures" are eligible to be considered. Entries may be either scholarly or imaginative (fiction, poetry, memoir). Plays and screenplays are not eligible, nor are works in progress. Manuscripts and self-published works are not eligible, and no grants are made for completing or publishing manuscripts.

Financial data The prize is $10,000. If more than 1 author is chosen in a given year, the prize is divided equally among the winning books.

Duration The award is presented annually.

Additional information This program began in 1936.

Number awarded 2 each year: 1 for fiction or poetry and 1 for nonfiction, biography, or scholarly research.

Deadline December of each year.

[1273]
ANNE RAY FELLOWSHIP

School for Advanced Research
Attn: Director of Scholar Programs
660 Garcia Street
P.O. Box 2188
Santa Fe, NM 87504-2188
(505) 954-7201   E-mail: scholar@sarsf.org
Web: www.sarweb.org

Summary To provide funding to Native American scholars interested in conducting research in the social sciences, arts, or humanities while in residence at the School for Advanced Research (SAR) in Santa Fe, New Mexico.

Eligibility This program is open to Native American scholars who are interested in conducting research at SAR in the humanities, arts, or the social sciences. Applicants must be interested in providing mentorship to recent Native graduates or graduate students. Along with their application, they must submit a 150-word abstract describing the purpose, goals, and objectives of their research project; a 4-page proposal; a bibliography; a curriculum vitae; a brief statement of tribal affiliation; a 3-page statement identifying their experience and interest in serving as a mentor; and 3 letters of recommendation. Preference is given to applicants whose field work or basic research and analysis are complete and who need time to write up their research.

Financial data The fellowship provides an apartment and office on the school's campus, a stipend of up to $40,000, library assistance, and other benefits.

Duration 9 months, beginning in September.

Additional information Funding for this program, which began in 2009, is provided by the Anne Ray Charitable Trust. In addition to working on their own research, the fellow serves as a mentor to 2 Native interns working at the Indian Arts Research Center on the SAR campus. Participants must spend their 9-month residency at the school in New Mexico.

Number awarded 1 each year.

Deadline October of each year.

[1274]
ARTHUR C. PARKER SCHOLARSHIPS

Society for American Archaeology
Attn: Native American Scholarship Fund
1111 14th Street, N.W., Suite 800
Washington, DC 20005-5622
(202) 789-8200   Fax: (202) 789-0284
E-mail: nasf@saa.org
Web: ecommerce.saa.org

Summary To provide financial assistance to Native American students and professionals interested in additional training in archaeological methods.

Eligibility This program is open to high school seniors, college undergraduates, graduate students, and personnel of tribal or other Native cultural preservation programs. Applicants must be Native Americans or Pacific Islanders from the United States, including U.S. Trust Territories, or indigenous people from Canada. They must be interested in attending a training program in archaeological methods offered by an accredited college or university, including field work, analytical techniques, and curation. Individuals may apply themselves, or they may be nominated by a high school teacher, current professor, or cultural preservation program supervisor. Along with the application, they must submit a 2-page personal statement describing why they are interested in their proposed program and in archaeology, and the contributions they hope to make to the future of archaeology.

Financial data The stipend is $4,000.

Duration 1 year.

Additional information Partial support of this program is provided by the National Science Foundation (NSF).

Number awarded 4 each year: 1 funded by the Society for American Archaeology and 3 by the NSF.

Deadline December of each year.

[1275]
ARTIST'S COMMUNITY WORKSHOP PROGRAM OF THE NATIONAL MUSEUM OF THE AMERICAN INDIAN

National Museum of the American Indian
Attn: Artist Leadership Program
Cultural Resources Center
4220 Silver Hill Road
Suitland, MD 20746-2863
(301) 238-1544   Fax: (301) 238-3200
E-mail: ALP@si.edu
Web: www.nmai.si.edu/connect/artist-leadership-program

Summary To provide Native American professional artists with an opportunity to organize and conduct a workshop within their local community.

Eligibility This program is open to Native artists from the western Hemisphere and Hawaii who are recognized by their community and can demonstrate significant artistic accomplishments in any media (e.g., visual arts, media arts, sculpture, textile and fiber arts, performance arts, literature). Students enrolled in a degree program are ineligible. Applicants must be interested in planning and managing a free workshop for artists in their local community. The workshop may cover such themes as skills that the artist has mastered, new techniques learned during a collections research visit to Washington, D.C., or new or revised cultural art techniques. Along with their application, they must submit a 500-word research proposal, a 500-word project proposal, a digital portfolio of 10 images or 5 minutes, 2 letters of support, a resume, and a 75-word statement describing their purpose, goal, and intended results.

Financial data The grant is $7,000 to cover project costs, supplies, and materials.

Duration Participants first spend 10 days in Washington, D.C. consulting with staff of the National Museum of the American Indian (NMAI), after which they return to their community and complete a project within 1 year.

Additional information This is a 2-part program. In the first part, participants visit Washington, D.C. for 10 days to conduct research in collections of the NMAI and other local museums, participate in interviews with Collections and Education staff, conduct lunch-time presentations for NMAI staff and the museum public, and visit area galleries. Following the completion of that visit, participants return to their community to share the knowledge learned from the experience and research visit and conduct their project. They select the workshop location, create an agenda and syllabus, obtain materials, and facilitate advertising and registration. The workshop they offer should provide 1 to 3 days of instruction to at least 10 community members interested in learning artistic skills.

Number awarded 4 each year.

Deadline June of each year.

[1276]
ASH-AMFDP AWARDS

American Society of Hematology
Attn: Awards Manager
2021 L Street, N.W., Suite 900
Washington, DC 20036
(202) 776-0544   Fax: (202) 776-0545
E-mail: awards@hematology.org
Web: www.hematology.org

Summary To provide an opportunity for Native American and other historically disadvantaged postdoctoral physicians to conduct a research project in hematology.

Eligibility This program is open to postdoctoral physicians who are members of historically disadvantaged groups, defined as individuals who face challenges because of their race, ethnicity, socioeconomic status, or other similar factors. Applicants must be committed to a career in academic medicine in hematology and to serving as a role model for students and faculty of similar backgrounds. They must identify a mentor at their institution to work with them and give them research and career guidance. Selection is based on excellence in educational career; willingness to devote 4 consecutive years to research; and commitment to an academic career, improving the health status of the underserved, and decreasing health disparities. U.S. citizenship or permanent resident status is required.

Financial data The grant includes a stipend of up to $75,000 per year, a grant of $30,000 per year for support of research activities, complimentary membership in the American Society of Hematology (ASH), and travel support to attend the ASH annual meeting.

Duration 4 years.

Additional information This program, first offered in 2006, is a partnership between the ASH and the Robert Wood Johnson Foundation, whose Minority Medical Faculty Development Program (MMFDP) was renamed the Harold Amos Medical Faculty Development Program (AMFDP) in honor of the first African American to chair a department at the Harvard Medical School. Scholars must spend at least 70% of their time in research activities.

Number awarded At least 1 each year.

Deadline March of each year.

[1277]
AWARDS FOR FACULTY AT TRIBAL COLLEGES AND UNIVERSITIES

National Endowment for the Humanities
Attn: Division of Research Programs
400 Seventh Street, S.W.
Washington, DC 20506
(202) 606-8200   Toll Free: (800) NEH-1121
Fax: (202) 606-8204   TDD: (866) 372-2930
E-mail: FacultyAwards@neh.gov
Web: www.neh.gov

Summary To provide funding for research to faculty at Tribal Colleges and Universities (TCUs).

Eligibility This program is open to faculty members at TCUs who are interested in conducting research of value to humanities scholars, students, or general audiences. Eligible projects include conducting research in primary and secondary sources; producing articles, monographs, books, digital materials, archaeological site reports, translations, editions, or other scholarly resources; or conducting basic research leading to the improvement of an existing undergraduate course or the achievement or institutional or community research goals. Applicants must be U.S. citizens or foreign nationals who have lived in the United States for at least 3 years. They are not required to have advanced degrees, but individuals enrolled in a degree-granting program are ineligible.

Financial data The grant is $4,200 per month, to a maximum of $50,400 for 12 months.

Duration 2 to 12 months.

Number awarded Approximately 3 each year.

Deadline April of each year.

[1278]
BIA HIGHER EDUCATION GRANTS FOR HOPI TRIBAL MEMBERS

Hopi Tribe
Attn: Grants and Scholarships Program
P.O. Box 123
Kykotsmovi, AZ 86039
(928) 734-3542   Toll Free: (800) 762-9630
Fax: (928) 734-9575   E-mail: JTorivio@hopi.nsn.us
Web: www.hopi-nsn.gov

Summary To provide financial assistance to students of Hopi ancestry who are working on an undergraduate, graduate, or postgraduate degree.

Eligibility This program is open to students who are working or planning to work full time on an associate, baccalaureate, graduate, or postgraduate degree. Applicants must be enrolled members of the Hopi Tribe and able to demonstrate financial need. They must have a GPA of 2.0 or higher as an incoming freshman, 2.25 or higher as an entering sophomore, 2.5 as an entering junior or senior, or 3.0 as a graduate or professional student.

Financial data The maximum grant is $2,500 per semester ($5,000 per year).

Duration 1 semester; may be renewed for up to 10 terms of undergraduate study or up to 5 terms of graduate study, provided the recipient remains enrolled full time and meets the required GPA for their academic level.

Additional information This program is funded by the Bureau of Indian Affairs (BIA).

Number awarded Varies each year.

Deadline June of each year for fall; October of each year for winter; November of each year for spring.

[1279]
CARRINGTON-HSIA-NIEVES SCHOLARSHIP FOR MIDWIVES OF COLOR

American College of Nurse-Midwives
Attn: ACNM Foundation, Inc.
8403 Colesville Road, Suite 1550
Silver Spring, MD 20910-6374
(240) 485-1850   Fax: (240) 485-1818
E-mail: foundation@acnmf.org
Web: www.midwife.org

Summary To provide financial assistance to Native American and other midwives of color who are members of the American College of Nurse-Midwives (ACNM) and engaged in doctoral or postdoctoral study.

Eligibility This program is open to ACNM members of color who are certified nurse midwives (CNM) or certified midwives (CM). Applicants must be enrolled in a program of doctoral or postdoctoral education. Along with their application, they must submit brief statements on their 5-year academic career plans, their intended use of the funds, and their intended future participation in the local, regional, and/or national activities of the ACNM and in activities that otherwise contribute substantially to midwifery research, education, or practice.

Financial data The stipend is $5,000.

Duration 1 year.

Number awarded 1 each year.

Deadline October of each year.

[1280]
CHEST DIVERSITY COMMITTEE MINORITY INVESTIGATOR RESEARCH GRANT

American College of Chest Physicians
Attn: The CHEST Foundation
2595 Patriot Boulevard
Glenview, IL 60026
(224) 521-9527　　　　Toll Free: (800) 343-2227
Fax: (224) 521-9801　　　E-mail: grants@chestnet.org
Web: www.chestnet.org

Summary To provide funding to Native American and other minority physicians who are interested in conducting clinical or translational research on topics of interest to the American College of Chest Physicians (ACCP).

Eligibility This program is open to members of the ACCP who are members of an underrepresented group (African American, Latin American, Hispanic American, Asian/Pacific Island American, Native American, women). Applicants must be interested in conducting a clinical or translational research project that contributes to the understanding of the pathophysiology or treatment of conditions or diseases related to pulmonary, cardiovascular, critical care, or sleep medicine. They may be at later career stages, but special consideration is given to those within 5 years of completing an advanced training program.

Financial data The grant is $25,000.

Duration 1 year, beginning in July.

Additional information This program is supported in part by AstraZeneca.

Number awarded 1 each year.

Deadline April of each year.

[1281]
CHICKASAW FOUNDATION CAREER TECHNOLOGY SCHOLARSHIP

Chickasaw Foundation
2020 Arlington, Suite 4
P.O. Box 1726
Ada, OK 74821-1726
(580) 421-9030　　　　Fax: (580) 421-9031
E-mail: ChickasawFoundation@chickasaw.net
Web: www.chickasawfoundation.org/Scholarships.aspx

Summary To provide financial assistance for vocational school to employees of the Chickasaw Nation.

Eligibility This program is open to employees of the Chickasaw Nation who are currently enrolled at a career technology, vocational/technical, or trade school. Applicants must be at least 18 years of age and have a GPA of 2.0 or higher. Along with their application, they must submit high school or college transcripts; 2 letters of recommendation; a copy of their Chickasaw Nation citizenship card; a copy of their Chickasaw Nation employee identification badge; a 2-page list of honors, achievements, awards, club memberships, societies, and civic involvement; and a 1-page essay on their long-term

goals and plans for achieving those. Financial need is not considered in the selection process.

Financial data A stipend is awarded (amount not specified).

Duration 1 year.

Number awarded 1 each year.

Deadline June or February of each year.

[1282]
CHIPS QUINN SCHOLARS PROGRAM

Newseum Institute
Attn: Chips Quinn Scholars Program
555 Pennsylvania Avenue, N.W.
Washington, DC 20001
(202) 292-6271　　　　Fax: (202) 292-6275
E-mail: kcatone@freedomforum.org
Web: www.newseuminstitute.org

Summary To provide work experience to Native American and other minority college students and recent graduates who are majoring in journalism.

Eligibility This program is open to students of color who are college juniors, seniors, graduate students, or recent graduates with journalism majors or career goals in newspapers. Candidates must be nominated or endorsed by journalism faculty, campus media advisers, editors of newspapers, or leaders of minority journalism associations. Along with their application, they must submit a resume, transcripts, 2 letters of recommendation, and an essay of 200 to 400 words on why they want to be a Chips Quinn Scholar. Reporters and copy editors must also submit 6 samples of published articles they have written; photographers must submit 15 to 25 photographs on a DVD; multimedia journalists and graphic designers should submit 6 to 10 samples of their work on a DVD. Applicants must have a car and be available to work as a fulltime intern during the spring or summer. U.S. citizenship or permanent resident status is required. Campus newspaper experience is strongly encouraged.

Financial data Students chosen for this program receive a travel stipend to attend a Multimedia training program in Nashville, Tennessee prior to reporting for their internship, a $500 housing allowance from the Freedom Forum, and a competitive salary during their internship.

Duration Internships are for 10 to 12 weeks, in spring or summer.

Additional information This program began in 1991 in memory of the late John D. Quinn Jr., managing editor of the *Poughkeepsie Journal.* Funding is provided by the Freedom Forum, formerly the Gannett Foundation. After graduating from college and obtaining employment with a newspaper, alumni of this program are eligible to apply for fellowship support to attend professional journalism development activities.

Number awarded Approximately 70 each year. Since the program began, more than 1,300 scholars have been selected.

Deadline September of each year.

[1283]
CIRI FOUNDATION INTERNSHIP PROGRAM

Cook Inlet Region, Inc.
Attn: The CIRI Foundation
3600 San Jeronimo Drive, Suite 256
Anchorage, AK 99508-2870
(907) 793-3575   Toll Free: (800) 764-3382
Fax: (907) 793-3585   E-mail: tcf@thecirifoundation.org
Web: www.thecirifoundation.org/internships

Summary To provide on-the-job training to Alaska Natives who are original enrollees to the Cook Inlet Region, Inc. (CIRI) and their lineal descendants.

Eligibility This program is open to Alaska Native enrollees to CIRI under the Alaska Native Claims Settlement Act (ANCSA) of 1971 and their lineal descendants. Applicants must 1) be enrolled in a 2- or 4-year academic or graduate degree program with a GPA of 2.5 or higher; 2) have recently completed an undergraduate or graduate degree program; or 3) be enrolled or have recently completed a technical skills training program at an accredited or otherwise approved postsecondary institution. Along with their application, they must submit a 500-word statement on their areas of interest, their educational and career goals, how their career goals relate to their educational goals, and the type of work experience they would like to gain as it relates to their career and educational goals.

Financial data The intern's wage is based on a trainee position and is determined by the employer of the intern with the approval of the foundation (which pays one half of the intern's wages).

Duration Internships are approved on a quarterly basis for 480 hours of part-time or full-time employment. Interns may reapply on a quarter-by-quarter basis, not to exceed 12 consecutive months.

Additional information The foundation and the intern applicant work together to identify an appropriate placement experience. The employer hires the intern. Placement may be with Cook Inlet Region, Inc. (CIRI), a firm related to the foundation, or a business or service organization located anywhere in the United States. The intern may be placed with more than 1 company during the internship period. Interns may receive academic credit. CIRI is 1 of 13 regional corporations established according to the terms of the Alaska Native Claims Settlement Act (ANCSA) of 1971.

Number awarded Varies each year.

Deadline March, June, September, or November of each year.

[1284]
CIVIL SOCIETY INSTITUTE FELLOWSHIPS

Vermont Studio Center
80 Pearl Street
P.O. Box 613
Johnson, VT 05656
(802) 635-2727   Fax: (802) 635-2730
E-mail: info@vermontstudiocenter.org
Web: www.vermontstudiocenter.org/fellowships

Summary To provide funding to Native American and other minority artists from the East Coast who are interested in a residency at the Vermont Studio Center in Johnson, Vermont.

Eligibility Eligible to apply for this support are painters, sculptors, printmakers, new and mixed-media artists, photographers who are members of a minority group and residents of the East Coast. Preference is given to applicants from New Haven (Connecticut), Jersey City (New Jersey), or Baltimore (Maryland). Applicants must be interested in a residency at the center in Johnson, Vermont. Visual artists must submit up to 20 slides or visual images of their work, poets must submit up to 10 pages, and other writers must submit 10 to 15 pages. Selection is based on artistic merit and financial need.

Financial data The residency fee of $3,950 covers studio space, room, board, lectures, and studio visits. The fellowship pays all residency fees plus a $500 travel stipend.

Duration 4 weeks.

Additional information This program is sponsored by the Institute for Civil Society.

Number awarded 3 each year (1 for each term).

Deadline February, June, or September of each year.

[1285]
DEEP CARBON OBSERVATORY DIVERSITY GRANTS

American Geosciences Institute
Attn: Grant Coordinator
4220 King Street
Alexandria, VA 22302-1502
(703) 379-2480   Fax: (703) 379-7563
E-mail: hrhp@agiweb.org
Web: www.americangeosciences.org

Summary To provide funding to geoscientists who are Native Americans or members of other underrepresented ethnic groups and interested in participating in research and other activities of the Deep Carbon Observatory (DCO) project.

Eligibility This program is open to traditionally underrepresented geoscientists (e.g., African Americans, Native Americans, Native Alaskans, Hispanics, Latinos, Latinas, Native Hawaiians, Native Pacific Islanders, Filipinos, of mixed racial/ethnic backgrounds) who are U.S. citizens or permanent residents. Applicants must be interested in participating in the DCO, a global research program focused on understanding carbon in Earth, and must have research interests that are aligned with its mission. They may be doctoral students, postdoctoral researchers, or early-career faculty members or research staff.

Financial data Grants average $5,000.

Duration 1 year.

Additional information This program is funded by the Alfred P. Sloan Foundation.

Number awarded 4 or 5 each year.

Deadline April of each year.

[1286]
DISSERTATION AWARD IN LATIN AMERICAN POLITICS

Harvard University
David Rockefeller Center for Latin American Studies
Attn: Thesis Prize Committee
CGIS South Building
1730 Cambridge Street
Cambridge, MA 02138
(617) 495-3366   Fax: (617) 496-2802
E-mail: ned_strong@fas.harvard.edu
Web: www.drclas.harvard.edu

Summary To recognize and reward authors of outstanding doctoral dissertations in Latin American politics.

Eligibility This award is available to doctoral students at universities in the United States or abroad who passed their thesis defense for the Ph.D. during the preceding 2 calendar years. The dissertation must present outstanding original research on a Latin American and Caribbean political topic undertaken in any of the social sciences or history. Authors must be nominated by their thesis adviser. Nominations of qualified women, members of underrepresented minority groups, and scholars from outside the United States are especially encouraged.

Financial data The award is $4,000.

Duration The award is presented annually.

Number awarded 1 each year.

Deadline May of each year.

[1287]
DOROTHY BRACY/JANICE JOSEPH MINORITY AND WOMEN NEW SCHOLAR AWARD

Academy of Criminal Justice Sciences
7339A Hanover Parkway
P.O. Box 960
Greenbelt, MD 20768-0960
(301) 446-6300   Toll Free: (800) 757-ACJS
Fax: (301) 446-2819   E-mail: info@acjs.org
Web: www.acjs.org/Awards

Summary To recognize and reward Native American and other minority junior scholars who have made outstanding contributions to the field of criminal justice.

Eligibility This award is available to members of the Academy of Criminal Justice Sciences (ACJS) who are members of a group that has experienced historical discrimination, including minorities and women. Applicants must have obtained a Ph.D. in a field of criminal justice within the past 7 years and be able to demonstrate a strong record as a new scholar in the areas of research, teaching, and service.

Financial data The award is $1,000.

Duration The award is presented annually.

Number awarded 1 each year.

Deadline October of each year.

[1288]
DR. DAVID MONASH/HARRY LLOYD AND ELIZABETH PAWLETTE MARSHALL RESIDENCY SCHOLARSHIPS

National Medical Fellowships, Inc.
Attn: Scholarship Program
347 Fifth Avenue, Suite 510
New York, NY 10016
(212) 483-8880   Toll Free: (877) NMF-1DOC
Fax: (212) 483-8897 E-mail: scholarships@nmfonline.org
Web: www.nmfonline.org

Summary To provide funding for repayment of student loans and other expenses to Native American and other underrepresented medical residents in Chicago who are committed to remaining in the area and working to reduce health disparities.

Eligibility This program is open to residents of any state who graduated from a medical school in Chicago and are currently engaged in a clinical residency program in the area in primary care, community/family medicine, or a related field. U.S. citizenship is required. Applicants must be seeking funding for repayment of student loans and other residency-related expenses. They must identify as an underrepresented minority student in health care (defined as African American, Hispanic/Latino, American Indian, Alaska Native, Native Hawaiian, Vietnamese, Cambodian, or Pacific Islander) and/or socioeconomically disadvantaged student. Along with their application, they must submit documentation of financial status; a short biography; a resume; 2 letters of recommendation; a personal statement of 500 to 1,000 words on their personal and professional motivation for a medical career, their commitment to primary care and service in a health and/or community setting, their motivation for working to reduce health disparities, and their commitment to improving health care; a personal statement of 500 to 1,000 words on the experiences that are preparing them to practice in an underserved community; and a copy of a residency contract from a Chicago clinical residency program. Selection is based on demonstrated leadership early in career and commitment to serving medically underserved communities in Chicago.

Financial data The grant is $25,000, of which 80% must be used to decrease medical school debt.

Duration 1 year.

Additional information This program began in 2010 with support from the Chicago Community Trust.

Number awarded 4 each year.

Deadline May of each year.

[1289]
DUPONT MINORITIES IN ENGINEERING AWARD

American Society for Engineering Education
Attn: Awards Administration
1818 N Street, N.W., Suite 600
Washington, DC 20036-2479
(202) 331-3550   Fax: (202) 265-8504
E-mail: board@asee.org
Web: www.asee.org

Summary To recognize and reward outstanding achievements by engineering educators to increase diversity by ethnicity and gender in science, engineering, and technology.

Eligibility Eligible for nomination are engineering or engineering technology educators who, as part of their educational activity, either assume or are charged with the responsibility of motivating underrepresented students to enter and continue in engineering or engineering technology curricula at the college or university level, graduate or undergraduate. Nominees must demonstrate leadership in the conception, organization, and operation of pre-college and college activities designed to increase participation by underrepresented students in engineering and engineering technology.

Financial data The award consists of $1,500, a certificate, and a grant of $500 for travel expenses to the ASEE annual conference.

Duration The award is granted annually.

Additional information Funding for this award is provided by DuPont. It was originally established in 1956 as the Vincent Bendix Minorities in Engineering Award.

Number awarded 1 each year.

Deadline January of each year.

[1290]
EARLY CAREER PATIENT-ORIENTED DIABETES RESEARCH AWARD

Juvenile Diabetes Research Foundation International
Attn: Senior Director, Research Administration
26 Broadway, 14th Floor
New York, NY 10004
(212) 479-7519   Toll Free: (800) 533-CURE
Fax: (212) 785-9595   E-mail: emilligan@jdrf.org
Web: grantcenter.jdrf.org

Summary To provide funding to physician scientists (particularly women, minorities, and persons with disabilities) who are interested in pursuing a program of clinical diabetes-related research training.

Eligibility This program is open to investigators in diabetes-related research who have an M.D. or M.D./Ph.D. degree and a faculty appointment at the late training or assistant professor level. Applicants must be sponsored by an investigator who is affiliated full time with an accredited institution, who pursues patient-oriented clinical research, and who agrees to supervise the applicant's training. There are no citizenship requirements. Applications are encouraged from women, members of minority groups underrepresented in the sciences, and people with disabilities. Areas of relevant research can include: mechanisms of human disease, therapeutic interventions, clinical trials, and the development of new technologies. The proposed research may be conducted at foreign or domestic, for-profit or nonprofit, or public or private institutions, including universities, colleges, hospitals, laboratories, units of state or local government, or eligible agencies of the federal government.

Financial data The total award may be up to $150,000 each year, up to $75,000 of which may be requested for research (including a technician, supplies, equipment, and travel). The salary request must be consistent with the established salary structure of the applicant's institution. Equipment purchases in years other than the first must be strongly justified. Indirect costs may not exceed 10%.

Duration The award is for 5 years and is generally nonrenewable.

Number awarded Varies each year.

Deadline July of each year.

[1291]
EARTHWORKS PRIZE FOR INDIGENOUS POETRY

Kenyon Review
c/o Kenyon College
102 West Wiggin Street
Gambier, OH 43022-9623
(740) 427-5208   Fax: (740) 427-5417
E-mail: earthworks@kenyon.edu
Web: www.kenyonreview.org/contests/earthworks-prize

Summary To recognize and reward Indigenous poets from any country who submit outstanding manuscripts.

Eligibility This competition is open to poets from any country who can verify tribal affiliation and/or Indigenous ancestry (e.g., Native American, First Nations, Alaska Native, Métis, Inuit, Native Hawaiian, Chamorro, Maori, Torres Straits Islander). Applicants may have published no more than 1 book of poetry. They must submit a poetry manuscript from 50 to 70 pages in length. Individual poems from the manuscript may have been published previously in magazines or anthologies, but the complete collection must be unpublished.

Financial data The prize is $1,000.

Duration The prize is presented annually.

Additional information This prize is offered by *The Kenyon Review* in partnership with Salt Publishing, UK.

Number awarded 1 each year.

Deadline August of each year.

[1292]
EDWARD A. BOUCHET AWARD

American Physical Society
Attn: Honors Program
One Physics Ellipse
College Park, MD 20740-3844
(301) 209-3268   Fax: (301) 209-0865
E-mail: honors@aps.org
Web: www.aps.org/programs/honors/awards/bouchet.cfm

Summary To recognize and reward outstanding research in physics by Native Americans and members of other underrepresented minority groups.

Eligibility Nominees for this award must be African Americans, Hispanic Americans, or Native Americans who have made significant contributions to physics research and are effective communicators.

Financial data The award consists of a grant of $3,500 to the recipient, a travel allowance for the recipient to visit 3 academic institutions to deliver lectures, and an allowance for travel expenses to the meeting of the American Physical Society (APS) at which the prize is presented.

Duration The award is presented annually.

Additional information This award was established in 1994 by a grant from the Research Corporation and is currently funded by institutional and individual donations. As part of the award, the recipient visits 3 academic institutions where the impact of the visit on minority students will be significant. The purpose of those visits is to deliver technical lectures on the recipient's field of specialization, to visit classrooms where appropriate, to assist the institution with precollege outreach efforts where appropriate, and to talk informally with faculty and students about research and teaching careers in physics.

Number awarded 1 each year.

Deadline June of each year.

[1293]
E.E. JUST ENDOWED RESEARCH FELLOWSHIP FUND

Marine Biological Laboratory
Attn: Division of Research
7 MBL Street
Woods Hole, MA 02543-1015
(508) 289-7173 Fax: (508) 457-1924
E-mail: research@mbl.edu
Web: www.mbl.edu/research/whitman-awards

Summary To provide funding to Native American and other minority scientists who wish to conduct summer research at the Marine Biological Laboratory (MBL) in Woods Hole, Massachusetts.

Eligibility This program is open to minority faculty members who are interested in conducting summer research at the MBL. Applicants must submit a statement of the potential impact of this award on their career development. The program encourages applications focused on 1) evolutionary, genetic, and genomic approaches in developmental biology with an emphasis on novel marine organisms; and 2) integrated imaging and computational approaches to illuminate cellular function and biology emerging from the study of marine and other organisms.

Financial data Grants range from $5,000 to $25,000, typically to cover laboratory rental and/or housing costs. Awardees are responsible for other costs, such as supplies, shared resource usage, affiliated staff who accompany them, or travel.

Duration 4 to 10 weeks during the summer.

Number awarded 1 each year.

Deadline December of each year.

[1294]
ERIC AND BARBARA DOBKIN NATIVE ARTIST FELLOWSHIP FOR WOMEN

School for Advanced Research
Attn: Indian Arts Research Center
660 Garcia Street
P.O. Box 2188
Santa Fe, NM 87504-2188
(505) 954-7205 Fax: (505) 954-7207
E-mail: iarc@sarsf.org
Web: www.sarweb.org/index.php?artists

Summary To provide an opportunity for Native American women artists to improve their skills through a spring residency at the Indian Arts Research Center in Santa Fe, New Mexico.

Eligibility This program is open to Native American women who excel in the arts, including sculpture, performance, basketry, painting, printmaking, digital art, mixed media, photography, pottery, writing, and filmmaking. Applicants should be attempting to explore new avenues of creativity, grapple with new ideas to advance their work, and

strengthen existing talents. Along with their application, they must submit a current resume, examples of their current work, and a 2-page statement that explains why they are applying for this fellowship, how it will help them realize their professional and/or personal goals as an artist, and the scope of the project they plan to complete during the residency.

Financial data The fellowship provides a stipend of $3,000 per month, housing, studio space, supplies allowance, and travel reimbursement to and from the center.

Duration 3 months, beginning in March.

Additional information Fellows work with the staff and research curators at the Indian Arts Research Center, an academic division of the School of American Research that is devoted solely to Native American art scholarship. The center has a significant collection of Pueblo pottery, Navajo and Pueblo Indian textiles, and early 20th-century Indian paintings, as well as holdings of jewelry and silverwork, basketry, clothing, and other ethnological materials. This fellowship was established in 2001.

Number awarded 1 each year.

Deadline January of each year.

[1295]
ETHNIC IN-SERVICE TRAINING FUND FOR CLINICAL PASTORAL EDUCATION (EIST-CPE)

United Methodist Church
Attn: General Board of Higher Education and Ministry
Office of Loans and Scholarships
1001 19th Avenue South
P.O. Box 340007
Nashville, TN 37203-0007
(615) 340-7342 Fax: (615) 340-7367
E-mail: umscholar@gbhem.org
Web: www.gbhem.org

Summary To provide financial assistance to United Methodist Church clergy and candidates for ministry who are Native American or members of other minority groups interested in preparing for a career as a clinical pastor.

Eligibility This program is open to U.S. citizens and permanent residents who are members of ethnic or racial minority groups and have been active, full members of a United Methodist Church for at least 1 year prior to applying. Applicants must be United Methodist clergy, certified candidates for ministry, or seminary students accepted into an accredited Clinical Pastor Education (CPE) or an accredited American Association of Pastoral Counselors (AAPC) program. They must be preparing for a career as a chaplain, pastoral counselor, or in pastoral care.

Financial data Grants range up to $2,000.

Duration 1 year.

Number awarded 1 each year.

Deadline February of each year.

[1296]
FIRST BOOK GRANT PROGRAM FOR MINORITY SCHOLARS

Louisville Institute
Attn: Executive Director
1044 Alta Vista Road
Louisville, KY 40205-1798
(502) 992-5432   Fax: (502) 894-2286
E-mail: info@louisville-institute.org
Web: www.louisville-institute.org

Summary To provide funding to Native Americans and other scholars of color interested in completing a major research and book project that focuses on an aspect of Christianity in North America.

Eligibility This program is open to members of racial/ethnic minority groups (African Americans, Hispanics, Native Americans, Asian Americans, Arab Americans, and Pacific Islanders) who have an earned doctoral degree (normally the Ph.D. or Th.D.). Applicants must be a non-tenured faculty member in a full-time, tenure-track position at an accredited institution of higher education (college, university, or seminary) in North America. They must be able to negotiate a full academic year free from teaching and committee responsibilities in order to engage in a scholarly research project leading to the publication of their first (or second) book focusing on an aspect of Christianity in North America. Selection is based on the intellectual quality of the research and writing project, its potential to contribute to scholarship in religion, and the potential contribution of the research to the vitality of North American Christianity.

Financial data The grant is $40,000. Awards are intended to make possible a full academic year of sabbatical research and writing by providing up to half of the grantee's salary and benefits for that year. Funds are paid directly to the grantee's institution, but no indirect costs are allowed.

Duration 1 academic year; nonrenewable.

Additional information The Louisville Institute is located at Louisville Presbyterian Theological Seminary and is supported by the Lilly Endowment. These grants were first awarded in 2003. Grantees may not accept other awards that provide a stipend during the tenure of this award, and they must be released from all teaching and committee responsibilities during the award year.

Number awarded Varies each year; recently, 3 were awarded.

Deadline January of each year.

[1297]
FOLK AND TRADITIONAL ARTS APPRENTICESHIP AWARDS

Hawai'i State Foundation on Culture and the Arts
Attn: Folk and Traditional Arts Program
250 South Hotel Street, Second Floor
Honolulu, HI 96813
(808) 586-0771   Fax: (808) 586-0308
TDD: (808) 586-0740
E-mail: denise.miyahana@hawaii.gov
Web: sfca.hawaii.gov/grants-programs/folk-traditional-arts

Summary To enable master folk artists in Hawaii to share their knowledge and skills with experienced individuals.

Eligibility This program is open to practitioners of any traditional art form in any culture in Hawaii. A master artist and an apprentice must apply together as a team for an apprenticeship. It is the responsibility of the applicants to meet and agree to undertake a master-apprentice training relationship with each other prior to submitting the application. Both the master and the apprentice must be residents of Hawaii. Master artists must explain how they learned the traditional art form they wish to teach; how long they have been actively involved in the art form; their community activities, performances, lectures, teaching, and awards; why preserving the art form and their cultural heritage is important to them; why they wish to participate in the apprenticeship; and why they would like to teach the apprentice. Prospective apprentices must explain how they first became interested in the tradition they wish to study; how long they have been actively involved in the tradition; their current skill level; why they wish to participate in the apprenticeship award; why they wish to work with this particular master artist; and how they plan to preserve this tradition and share it with others after their apprenticeship award is completed.

Financial data Grants range from $2,800 to $5,000. Funds are intended to be used to cover fees for the master folk artist and essential material or travel expenses associated with the apprenticeship.

Duration The apprenticeship should involve a minimum of 80 to a maximum of 130 total hours of contact over a period of 6 to 7 months.

Additional information The foundation may wish to document a portion of the apprenticeship with still photographs and/or audio or videotapes. Funding for this program is provided by the State Foundation on Culture and the Arts and the National Endowment for the Arts. Funding is not available for apprenticeships conducted abroad. Similarly, the funds may not be used to cover out-of-state travel expenses. Upon completion of the program, the master folk artist and the apprentice are asked to give a brief community presentation covering what was learned during the course of study.

Number awarded Approximately 17 each year.

Deadline March of each year.

[1298]
GAIUS CHARLES BOLIN DISSERTATION AND POST-MFA FELLOWSHIPS

Williams College
Attn: Dean of the Faculty
880 Main Street
Hopkins Hall, Third Floor
P.O. Box 141
Williamstown, MA 01267
(413) 597-4351   Fax: (413) 597-3553
E-mail: gburda@williams.edu
Web: faculty.williams.edu

Summary To provide financial assistance to Native Americans and members of other underrepresented groups who are interested in teaching courses at Williams College while working on their doctoral dissertation or building their post-M.F.A. professional portfolio.

Eligibility This program is open to members of underrepresented groups, including ethnic minorities, first-generation college students, women in predominantly male fields, and scholars with disabilities. Applicants must be 1) doctoral candidates in any field who have completed all work for a Ph.D. except for the dissertation; or 2) artists who completed an M.F.A. degree within the past 2 years and are building their professional portfolio. They must be willing to teach a course at Williams College. Along with their application, they must submit a full curriculum vitae, a graduate school transcript, 3 letters of recommendation, a copy of their dissertation prospectus or samples of their artistic work, and a description of their teaching interests within a department or program at Williams College. U.S. citizenship or permanent resident status is required.

Financial data Fellows receive $38,000 for the academic year, plus housing assistance, office space, computer and library privileges, and a research allowance of up to $4,000.

Duration 2 years.

Additional information Bolin fellows are assigned a faculty adviser in the appropriate department. This program was established in 1985. Fellows are expected to teach a 1-semester course each year. They must be in residence at Williams College for the duration of the fellowship.

Number awarded 2 each year.

Deadline November of each year.

[1299]
GEORGE A. STRAIT MINORITY SCHOLARSHIP ENDOWMENT

American Association of Law Libraries
Attn: Chair, Scholarships Committee
105 West Adams Street, Suite 3300
Chicago, IL 60603
(312) 939-4764   Fax: (312) 431-1097
E-mail: scholarships@aall.org
Web: www.aallnet.org

Summary To provide financial assistance to Native American and other minority college seniors or college graduates who are interested in becoming law librarians.

Eligibility This program is open to college graduates with meaningful law library experience who are members of minority groups and intend to have a career in law librarianship. Applicants must be degree candidates at an ALA-accredited library school or an ABA-accredited law school. Along with their application, they must submit a personal statement that discusses their interest in law librarianship, reason for applying for this scholarship, career goals as a law librarian, and any other pertinent information.

Financial data The stipend is $3,500.

Duration 1 year.

Additional information This program, established in 1990, is currently supported by Thomson Reuters.

Number awarded Varies each year; recently, 6 were awarded.

Deadline March of each year.

[1300]
GERALD OSHITA MEMORIAL FELLOWSHIP

Djerassi Resident Artists Program
Attn: Admissions
2325 Bear Gulch Road
Woodside, CA 94062-4405
(650) 747-1250   Fax: (650) 747-0105
E-mail: drap@djerassi.org
Web: www.djerassi.org/oshita.html

Summary To provide an opportunity for Native Americans and other composers of color to participate in the Djerassi Resident Artists Program.

Eligibility This program is open to composers of Asian, African, Latino, or Native American ethnic background. Applicants must be interested in utilizing a residency to compose, study, rehearse, and otherwise advance their own creative projects.

Financial data The fellow is offered housing, meals, studio space, and a stipend of $2,500.

Duration 1 month, from late March through mid-November.

Additional information This fellowship was established in 1994. The program is located in northern California, 45 miles south of San Francisco, on 600 acres of rangeland, redwood forests, and hiking trails. There is a $45 non-refundable application fee.

Number awarded 1 each year.

Deadline February of each year.

[1301]
HARPO FOUNDATION NATIVE AMERICAN FELLOWSHIPS

Vermont Studio Center
80 Pearl Street
P.O. Box 613
Johnson, VT 05656
(802) 635-2727   Fax: (802) 635-2730
E-mail: info@vermontstudiocenter.org
Web: www.vermontstudiocenter.org/fellowships

Summary To provide funding to Native American artists who are interested in a residency at the Vermont Studio Center in Johnson, Vermont.

Eligibility Eligible to apply for this support are American Indian, Native Hawaiian, and Alaskan Native visual artists. Applicants must be interested in a residency at the center in Johnson, Vermont. They must submit up to 20 slides or visual images of their work and a 300-word statement about their work and their plans for the residency. Selection is based on artistic merit and financial need.

Financial data The residency fee of $3,950 covers studio space, room, board, lectures, and studio visits. The fellowship pays all residency fees plus a $500 travel stipend.

Duration 4 weeks.

Additional information This program is sponsored by the Harpo Foundation.

Number awarded 2 each year.

Deadline February, June, or September of each year.

[1302]
HO-CHUNK NATION GRADUATION ACHIEVEMENT AWARDS

Ho-Chunk Nation
Attn: Higher Education Division
P.O. Box 667
Black River Falls, WI 54615
(715) 284-4915   Toll Free: (800) 362-4476
Fax: (715) 284-1760
E-mail: higher.education@ho-chunk.com
Web: www.ho-chunknation.com

Summary To recognize and reward Ho-Chunk students who received financial assistance from the tribe and completed an undergraduate or graduate degree.

Eligibility Applicants must be enrolled in the Ho-Chunk Nation and have received financial assistance from the tribe to work on a postsecondary degree. Funds are paid to these students when they complete any of the following degrees: 1-year certificate or diploma, associate degree (2 years), bachelor's degree (4 years), master's or professional degree, J.D. degree, or doctoral degree.

Financial data Awards are $300 for a 1-year certificate or degree, $750 for an associate degree, $1,500 for a bachelor's degree, $3,000 for a master's degree, $4,000 for a J.D. degree, or $5,000 for a doctoral degree.

Duration Students are eligible for only 1 award per degree.

Number awarded Varies each year.

Deadline Applications must be submitted within 1 year of completion of the degree.

[1303]
HOPI EDUCATION AWARDS PROGRAM

Hopi Tribe
Attn: Grants and Scholarships Program
P.O. Box 123
Kykotsmovi, AZ 86039
(928) 734-3542   Toll Free: (800) 762-9630
Fax: (928) 734-9575   E-mail: JTorivio@hopi.nsn.us
Web: www.hopi-nsn.gov

Summary To provide financial assistance to needy students of Hopi ancestry who are working on an undergraduate, graduate, or postgraduate degree.

Eligibility This program is open to students who are working full time on an associate, baccalaureate, graduate, or postgraduate degree. Applicants must be enrolled members of the Hopi Tribe and able to demonstrate financial need. Undergraduates must have a GPA of 2.5 or higher and graduate students must have a GPA of 3.0 or higher.

Financial data The maximum grant is $2,500 per semester ($5,000 per year).

Duration 1 semester; may be renewed for up to 10 terms of undergraduate study or up to 5 terms of graduate study, provided the recipient maintains full-time enrollment and a GPA of 2.5 or higher as an undergraduate or 3.0 or higher as a graduate student.

Additional information This grant is awarded as a secondary source of financial aid to eligible students who are also receiving aid from the Bureau of Indian Affairs (BIA) Higher Education program.

Number awarded Varies each year.

Deadline June of each year for fall; October of each year for winter; November of each year for spring.

[1304]
IDAHO FOLK AND TRADITIONAL ARTS APPRENTICESHIP AWARDS

Idaho Commission on the Arts
Attn: Traditional Arts
2410 North Old Penitentiary Road
P.O. Box 83720
Boise, ID 83720-0008
(208) 334-2119   Toll Free: (800) 278-3863
Fax: (208) 334-2488   E-mail: info@arts.idaho.gov
Web: www.arts.idaho.gov/grants/trap.aspx

Summary To provide funding to masters of traditional art forms in Idaho and apprentices who wish to learn from them.

Eligibility This program is open to traditional arts masters and apprentices who have been residents of Idaho for at least 1 year. Applicants must be interested in establishing a partnership in which the apprentice will learn by observation and practice within the family, tribe, occupational, or other group. Master artists should have learned skills informally and have received peer recognition for achieving the highest level of artistry according to community standards. Apprentices should have some background in the proposed art form, wish to learn from a recognized master, and be committed to continue practicing after the apprenticeship has ended. Art forms must represent shared cultural traditions of both applicants. Priority is given to art forms with few practitioners. In-family apprenticeships are encouraged. Selection is based on quality (master is recognized by peers and by community standards, the apprentice will benefit from working with the master at this time, the apprentice is committed to advancing his or her skills in the art form and carrying on the tradition); community (master and apprentice share the same cultural background, the art form is significant to their community, the art form is endangered within the particular traditional culture or there are few artists practicing it); and feasibility (the goals for the apprenticeship are clear, the budget is appropriate, the work plan provides appropriate time for interaction to achieve meaningful results).

Financial data The maximum grant is $3,000.

Duration From 4 to 10 months, depending on the particular art form and on the proposed work plan.

Number awarded Varies each year; recently, 7 of these fellowships were awarded.

Deadline January of each year.

[1305]
INDIGENOUS FELLOWSHIP PROGRAM OF THE DENVER MUSEUM

Denver Museum of Nature & Science
Attn: Department of Anthropology
Native American Science Initiative
2001 Colorado Boulevard
Denver, CO 80205
(303) 370-6367   E-mail: nascience@dmns.org
Web: www.dmns.org

Summary To provide an opportunity for Native American artists, elders, curators, scholars, and others to conduct research using the resources of the Department of Anthropology at the Denver Museum of Nature & Science.

Eligibility This program is open to artists, elders, curators, scholars, and other individuals from indigenous communities. Applicants must be interested in conducting original research using the anthropological resources of the museum. They must submit a description of the project they would like to pursue as a visiting fellow.

Financial data Fellows receive payment of all travel, meal, and hotel expenses plus an honorarium of $1,000.

Duration 1 week.

Number awarded 1 or more each year.

Deadline Applications may be submitted at any time.

[1306]
J. ROBERT GLADDEN ORTHOPAEDIC SOCIETY BASIC RESEARCH GRANTS

J. Robert Gladden Orthopaedic Society
Attn: Scientific Committee
9400 West Higgins Road, Suite 500
Rosemont, IL 60018
(847) 698-1633   Fax: (847) 823-4921
E-mail: jrgos@aaos.org
Web: www.gladdensociety.org

Summary To provide funding to Native Americans and other minority group members of the J. Robert Gladden Orthopaedic Society (JRGOS) who are interested in conducting a basic research project.

Eligibility This program is open to members of underrepresented minority groups who are JRGOS members and interested in conducting a basic research project. Applicants must be affiliated with a research institution that provides laboratory space and basic facilities. They must be able to demonstrate the compatibility of their project's clinical relevance with the mission and goals of the society. Preference is given to applicants planning to work with a senior JRGOS member.

Financial data The grant is $25,000.

Duration 1 year.

Additional information This program is sponsored by DePuy/Johnson & Johnson.

Number awarded 1 or more each year.

Deadline September of each year.

[1307]
JOHN CARTER BROWN LIBRARY INDIGENOUS STUDIES FELLOWSHIP

Brown University
John Carter Brown Library
Attn: Fellowships Coordinator
P.O. Box 1894
Providence, RI 02912
(401) 863-5010   Fax: (401) 863-3477
E-mail: Valerie_Andrews@Brown.edu
Web: www.brown.edu

Summary To support scholars and graduate students interested in conducting research on the history and/or anthropology of the native peoples of the Americas at the John Carter Brown Library.

Eligibility This fellowship is open to U.S-based and foreign graduate students, scholars, and independent researchers. Graduate students must have passed their preliminary or

general examinations. Tribal historians with nontraditional academic backgrounds are also eligible. Applicants must be interested in conducting research on the history and/or anthropology of native peoples of the Americas. Selection is based on the applicant's scholarly qualifications, the merits and significance of the project, and the particular need that the holdings of the John Carter Brown Library will fill in the development of the project.

Financial data The stipend is $2,100 per month.

Duration From 2 to 4 months.

Additional information This program began in 2014. Fellows are expected to be in regular residence at the library and to participate in the intellectual life of Brown University for the duration of the program.

Number awarded 1 or more each year.

Deadline December of each year.

[1308]
JOHN MCLENDON MEMORIAL MINORITY POSTGRADUATE SCHOLARSHIP AWARD

National Association of Collegiate Directors of Athletics
Attn: NACDA Foundation
24651 Detroit Road
Westlake, OH 44145
(440) 788-7474   Fax: (440) 892-4007
E-mail: knewman@nacda.com
Web: www.nacda.com/mclendon/scholarship.html

Summary To provide financial assistance to Native American and other minority college seniors who are interested in working on a graduate degree in athletics administration.

Eligibility This program is open to minority college students who are seniors, are attending school on a full-time basis, have a GPA of 3.2 or higher, intend to attend graduate school to earn a degree in athletics administration, and are involved in college or community activities. Also eligible are college graduates who have at least 2 years' experience in an athletics administration position. Candidates must be nominated by an official of a member institution of the National Association of Collegiate Directors of Athletics (NACDA) or (for college graduates) a supervisor.

Financial data The stipend is $10,000.

Duration 1 year.

Additional information Recipients must maintain full-time status during the senior year to retain their eligibility. They must attend NACDA-member institutions.

Number awarded 5 each year.

Deadline Nominations must be submitted by April of each year.

[1309]
KATRIN H. LAMON FELLOWSHIP

School for Advanced Research
Attn: Director of Scholar Programs
660 Garcia Street
P.O. Box 2188
Santa Fe, NM 87504-2188
(505) 954-7201   E-mail: scholar@sarsf.org
Web: www.sarweb.org

Summary To provide funding to Native American pre- and postdoctoral scholars interested in conducting research in the social sciences or humanities while in residence at the

School for Advanced Research (SAR) in Santa Fe, New Mexico.

Eligibility This program is open to Native American Ph.D. candidates and scholars with doctorates who are interested in conducting research at SAR in the humanities or the social sciences. Applicants must submit a 150-word abstract describing the purpose, goals, and objectives of their research project; a 4-page proposal; a bibliography; a curriculum vitae; a brief statement of tribal affiliation; and 3 letters of recommendation. Predoctoral applicants must also submit a brief letter of nomination from their department. Preference is given to applicants whose field work or basic research and analysis are complete and who need time to write up their research.

Financial data The fellowship provides an apartment and office on the school's campus, a stipend of up to $40,000 for scholars or $30,000 for Ph.D. candidates, library assistance, and other benefits.

Duration 9 months, beginning in September.

Additional information Funding for this program is provided by the Katrin H. Lamon Endowment for Native American Art and Education. Participants must spend their 9-month residency at the school in New Mexico.

Number awarded 1 each year.

Deadline October of each year.

[1310]
KING-CHAVEZ-PARKS VISITING PROFESSORS PROGRAM

University of Michigan
Attn: Office of the Provost and Executive Vice President
  for Academic Affairs
503 Thompson Street
3084 Fleming Administration Building
Ann Arbor, MI 48109-1340
(734) 764-3982   Fax: (734) 764-4546
E-mail: provost@umich.edu
Web: www.provost.umich.edu

Summary To provide an opportunity for Native American and other minority scholars to visit and teach at the University of Michigan.

Eligibility Outstanding minority (African American, Asian/Pacific American, Latino/a-Hispanic American, and Native American) scholars, performers, or practitioners are eligible to be nominated by University of Michigan faculty members to visit and lecture there. Nominations that include collaborations with other educational institutions in Michigan are of high priority.

Financial data Visiting Professors receive round-trip transportation and an appropriate honorarium.

Duration Visits range from 1 to 5 days.

Additional information This program was established in 1986. Visiting Professors are expected to lecture or teach at the university, offer at least 1 event open to the general public, and meet with minority campus/community groups, including local K-12 schools.

Number awarded Varies each year.

Deadline Nominations may be submitted at any time, but they must be received at least 30 days before a funding decision is required.

[1311]
LAGUNA ACOMA CONNECTIONS PROGRAM

Pueblo of Laguna
Attn: Partners for Success
11 Rodeo Drive, Building A
P.O. Box 207
Laguna, NM 87026
(505) 552-9322   Fax: (505) 552-0623
E-mail: p.solimon@lagunaed.net
Web: partnersforsuccess.us/pfs—apply.html

Summary To provide vocational rehabilitation to American Indian adults with disabilities who reside on the Laguna and Acoma reservations in New Mexico.

Eligibility This program is open to residents of the Laguna and Acoma reservations who either apply directly or are referred by an agency, family member, or community member. Applicants must have a physical or mental impairment that is a barrier to employment and require services in order to prepare for, enter, or obtain employment. Along with their applicatiopn, they must submit a 3-paragraph statement that covers 1) the type of degree or certificate they plan to earn; 2) the type of work they will seek upon completion; 3) their personal commitment or desire to complete a program; 4) any personal achievements; and 5) previous education.

Financial data This program provides services based on individual need and interest, availability of jobs, and selection of career goals.

Duration Services are provided until the participant obtains employment.

Number awarded Varies each year; recently, this program served 57 Indians with disabilities.

Deadline Applications may be submitted at any time.

[1312]
LEE & LOW BOOKS NEW VISIONS AWARD

Lee & Low Books
95 Madison Avenue, Suite 1205
New York, NY 10016
(212) 779-4400   Fax: (212) 683-1894
E-mail: general@leeandlow.com
Web: www.leeandlow.com

Summary To recognize and reward outstanding unpublished fantasy or mystery books for young readers by Native American and other writers of color.

Eligibility The contest is open to writers of color who are residents of the United States. Applicants must submit a manuscript of a fantasy, science fiction, or mystery book directed to readers at the middle grade or young adult level. They may not previously have published a middle grade or young adult novel published.

Financial data The award is a $1,000 cash grant plus the standard publication contract, including the standard advance and royalties. The Honor Award winner receives a cash grant of $500.

Duration The competition is held annually.

Additional information This program began in 2012. Manuscripts may not be sent to any other publishers while under consideration for this award.

Number awarded 2 each year.

Deadline October of each year.

[1313]
LEE & LOW BOOKS NEW VOICES AWARD

Lee & Low Books
95 Madison Avenue, Suite 1205
New York, NY 10016
(212) 779-4400   Fax: (212) 683-1894
E-mail: general@leeandlow.com
Web: www.leeandlow.com

Summary To recognize and reward outstanding unpublished children's picture books by Native American and other writers of color.

Eligibility The contest is open to writers of color who are residents of the United States and who have not previously published a children's picture book. Writers who have published in other venues, (e.g., children's magazines, young adult fiction and nonfiction) are eligible. Manuscripts previously submitted to the sponsor are not eligible. Submissions should be no more than 1,500 words and must address the needs of children of color by providing stories with which they can identify and relate and that promote a greater understanding of each other. Submissions may be fiction or nonfiction for children between the ages of 5 and 12. Folklore and animal stories are not considered. Up to 2 submissions may be submitted per entrant.

Financial data The award is a $1,000 cash grant plus the standard publication contract, including the standard advance and royalties. The Honor Award winner receives a cash grant of $500.

Duration The competition is held annually.

Additional information This program began in 2000. Manuscripts may not be sent to any other publishers while under consideration for this award.

Number awarded 2 each year.

Deadline September of each year.

[1314]
LEON BRADLEY SCHOLARSHIPS

American Association of School Personnel Administrators
Attn: Scholarship Program
11863 West 112th Street, Suite 100
Overland Park, KS 66210
(913) 327-1222   Fax: (913) 327-1223
E-mail: aaspa@aaspa.org
Web: www.aaspa.org/leon-bradley-scholarship

Summary To provide financial assistance to Native American and other minority undergraduates, paraprofessionals, and graduate students preparing for a career in teaching and school leadership at colleges in designated southeastern states.

Eligibility This program is open to members of minority groups (American Indian, Alaskan Native, Asian, Pacific Islander, Black, Hispanic, Middle Easterner) currently enrolled full time at a college or university in Alabama, Florida, Georgia, Kentucky, North Carolina, South Carolina, Tennessee, or Virginia. Applicants must be 1) undergraduates in their final year (including student teaching) of an initial teaching certification program; 2) paraprofessional career-changers in their final year (including student teaching) of an initial teaching certification program; or 3) graduate students who have served as a licensed teacher and are working on a school administrator credential. They must have an overall GPA of 3.0 or higher. Priority is given to applicants who 1) can demonstrate work experience that has been applied to college expenses; 2) have received other scholarship or financial aid support; or 3) are seeking initial certification and/or endorsement in a state-identified critical area.

Financial data Stipends are $2,500 for undergraduates in their final year, $1,500 for paraprofessionals in their final year, and $1,500 for graduate students.

Duration 1 year.

Number awarded 4 each year: 1 undergraduate, 1 paraprofessional, and 2 graduate students.

Deadline May of each year.

[1315]
LOFT SPOKEN WORD IMMERSION GRANTS

The Loft Literary Center
Attn: Immersion Grant Program Director
1011 Washington Avenue South, Suite 200
Minneapolis, MN 55415
(612) 215-2585   Fax: (612) 215-2576
E-mail: bphi@loft.org
Web: www.loft.org/programs__awards/grants__awards

Summary To provide funding to spoken word Native Americans and other poets of color who are interested in developing and implementing community learning and enrichment projects of their own design.

Eligibility This program is open to spoken word poets of color currently residing in the United States; the program defines poets of color to include Native Americans, Pacific Islanders, Africans, African Americans, Asians, South Asians, Asian Americans, Latino/as, Chicano/as, Arabs, Middle Easterners, and mixed race. Applicants must proposed to develop and implement a project that enriches their art as well as the community's. Proposal objectives and activities may include, but are not limited to, personal artistic growth; developing and teaching workshops or open mics in a non-traditional space; research and immersion into community-specific art forms; multidisciplinary and cross-community spoken word projects; ELL, bilingual, and multilingual immersion; or improving speaking, performance, and presentation skills. Tuition for non-degree granting programs (e.g., writers' conferences, community-based education) may be approved, but tuition for classes leading to a degree is not eligible. Selection is based on quality of a work sample; merit of the project design (originality, feasibility, clarity of the stated objectives, community immersion and enrichment, artistic growth of the artist); and the applicant's potential ability to complete the project.

Financial data The grant is $7,500.

Duration Projects must conclude within a year and a half.

Additional information Funding for this program comes from the Surdna Foundation.

Number awarded 4 each year, of whom 1 must be a resident of Minnesota.

Deadline October of each year.

[1316]
LYMAN T. JOHNSON POSTDOCTORAL FELLOWSHIP

University of Kentucky
Attn: Vice President for Research
311 Main Building, 0032
Lexington, KY 40506-0032
(859) 257-5090   Fax: (859) 323-2800
E-mail: vprgrants@uky.edu
Web: www.research.uky.edu

Summary To provide an opportunity for recent postdoctorates, especially Native Americans and other minorities, to conduct research at the University of Kentucky (U.K.).

Eligibility This program is open to U.S. citizens and permanent residents who have completed a doctoral degree within the past 2 years. Applicants must be interested in conducting an individualized research program under the mentorship of a U.K. professor. They should indicate, in their letter of application, how their participation in this program would contribute to the compelling interest of diversity at U.K. Race, ethnicity, and national origin are among the factors that contribute to diversity. Selection is based on evidence of scholarship with competitive potential for a tenure-track faculty appointment at a research university, compatibility of specific research interests with those in doctorate-granting units at U.K., quality of the research proposal, support from mentor and references, and effect of the appointment on the educational benefit of diversity within the research or professional area.

Financial data The fellowship provides a stipend of $35,000 plus $5,000 for support of research activities.

Duration Up to 2 years.

Additional information In addition to conducting an individualized research program under the mentorship of a U.K. professor, fellows actively participate in research, teaching, and service to the university, their profession, and the community. This program began in 1992.

Number awarded 2 each year.

Deadline October of each year.

[1317]
LYNN C. GIBSON MEMORIAL SCHOLARSHIP

Chickasaw Foundation
2020 Arlington, Suite 4
P.O. Box 1726
Ada, OK 74821-1726
(580) 421-9030   Fax: (580) 421-9031
E-mail: ChickasawFoundation@chickasaw.net
Web: www.chickasawfoundation.org/Scholarships.aspx

Summary To provide financial assistance for vocational study of secretarial science to members of the Chickasaw Nation.

Eligibility This program is open to members of the Chickasaw Nation who are currently enrolled in a career technology program that leads to certification as a secretarial or administrative assistant. Applicants must have a grade average of "B" or higher. Along with their application, they must submit high school or college transcripts; 2 letters of recommendation; a copy of their Chickasaw Nation citizenship card; a 2-page list of honors, achievements, awards, club memberships, societies, and civic involvement; and a 1-page essay on their long-

term goals and plans for achieving those. Financial need is not considered in the selection process.

Financial data A stipend is awarded (amount not specified).

Duration 1 year.

Number awarded 1 each year.

Deadline June or February of each year.

[1318]
MAINE ARTS COMMISSION TRADITIONAL ARTS APPRENTICESHIP PROGRAM

Maine Arts Commission
Attn: Senior Director for Grants and Arts Accessibility
193 State Street
25 State House Station
Augusta, ME 04333-0025
(207) 287-2750   Fax: (207) 287-2725
TDD: (877) 887-3878   E-mail: kathy.shaw@maine.gov
Web: mainearts.maine.gov

Summary To provide an opportunity for Native American and other traditional artists in Maine to share their skills with and train qualified apprentices.

Eligibility This program is open to master artists who practice a significant and/or endangered traditional art form in Maine. Traditional arts are defined as artistic practices that reflect a community's shared cultural heritage and are learned in an informal way, usually by example rather than through academic or institutional means. Apprentices should be from the same ethnic, religious, occupational, or familial group as the master artist. Both master and apprentice must have resided in Maine for at least 1 year. Masters must be 18 years of age or older, but apprentices may be of any age. Selection is based on artistic strength of master (20%), creative practice of apprentice (20%), community impact (30%), capacity (20%), and application quality (10%).

Financial data The maximum grant is $4,000. Funds are available for the master artist's teaching fee, apprentices' supplies and travel costs, and documentation of the apprenticeship.

Duration 8 to 12 months.

Additional information Master artists and apprentices work together on a one-to-one basis. The work may be in art, crafts, dance, occupational skills, or music.

Number awarded Varies each year; recently, 6 of these grants were awarded.

Deadline May of each year.

[1319]
MANY VOICES FELLOWSHIPS

Playwrights' Center
Attn: Artistic Programs Administrator
2301 East Franklin Avenue
Minneapolis, MN 55406-1024
(612) 332-7481, ext. 115   Fax: (612) 332-6037
E-mail: julia@pwcenter.org
Web: www.pwcenter.org/programs/many-voices-fellowships

Summary To provide funding to Native American and other playwrights of color from Minnesota and other states so they can spend a year in residence at the Playwrights' Center in Minneapolis.

Eligibility This program is open to playwrights of color who are citizens or permanent residents of the United States; residents of Minnesota and of other states are eligible. Applicants must be interested in playwriting and creating theater in a supportive artist community at the Playwrights' Center.

Financial data Fellows receive a $10,000 stipend, $2,500 for living expenses, and $1,500 in play development funds.

Duration 9 months, beginning in October.

Additional information This program, which began in 1994, is funded by the Jerome Foundation. Fellows must be in residence at the Playwrights' Center for the duration of the program.

Number awarded 2 each year: 1 to a resident of Minnesota and 1 to a resident of any state.

Deadline November of each year.

[1320]
MARTIN LUTHER KING, JR. MEMORIAL SCHOLARSHIP FUND

California Teachers Association
Attn: CTA Foundation for Teaching and Learning
1705 Murchison Drive
P.O. Box 921
Burlingame, CA 94011-0921
(650) 697-1400   E-mail: scholarships@cta.org
Web: www.cta.org

Summary To provide financial assistance for college or graduate school to Native Americans and other racial and ethnic minorities who are members of the California Teachers Association (CTA), children of members, or members of the Student CTA.

Eligibility This program is open to members of racial or ethnic minority groups (African Americans, American Indians/Alaska Natives, Asians/Pacific Islanders, and Hispanics) who are 1) active CTA members; 2) dependent children of active, retired, or deceased CTA members; or 3) members of Student CTA. Applicants must be interested in preparing for a teaching career in public education or already engaged in such a career.

Financial data Stipends vary each year; recently, they ranged up to $6,000.

Duration 1 year.

Number awarded Varies each year; recently, 24 were awarded: 1 to a CTA member, 10 to children of CTA members, and 13 to Student CTA members.

Deadline February of each year.

[1321]
MASTER ARTIST AND APPRENTICE GRANTS IN TRADITIONAL NATIVE ARTS

Alaska State Council on the Arts
Attn: Community and Native Arts Program Director
161 Klevin Street, Suite 102
Anchorage, AK 99508-1506
(907) 269-6610   Toll Free: (888) 278-7424
Fax: (907) 269-6601   TDD: (800) 770-8973
E-mail: aksca.info@alaska.gov
Web: www.eed.state.ak.us/aksca/grants3.html

Summary To provide funding to masters and apprentices interested in supporting and encouraging the maintenance and development of the traditional arts of Alaska's native people.

Eligibility This program is open to apprentices and masters in a traditional Alaska Native art form, including but not limited to visual arts, crafts, music, dance, storytelling, and singing. The apprentice applicants must be residents of Alaska, have demonstrated experience in the art form in which they are interested, be 18 years of age or older, and have identified and located a master artist willing to accept apprentices. The master applicants must be able to provide evidence of excellence in the art form, agree to take on the applicant as an apprentice, be recognized for their proficiency and skill in an art form by members of their own cultural community, and be 18 years of age or older. Priority is given to apprentices who wish to study an art form within their own cultural tradition. Selection is based on quality of the work of the apprentice (35 points), quality of the work of the master artist (20 points), lesson plan (35 points), and total budget and materials list (10 points).

Financial data The maximum grant is $2,000. The funds are to be used to pay the fees of the master artist and to cover essential expenses of the apprenticeship (primarily materials and, in rare cases, travel).

Duration These are usually 1-time grants.

Number awarded Varies each year.

Deadline February, May, August, or November of each year.

[1322]
MICKEY LELAND ENERGY FELLOWSHIPS

Oak Ridge Institute for Science and Education
Attn: MLEF Fellowship Program
1299 Bethel Valley Road, Building SC-200
P.O. Box 117, MS 36
Oak Ridge, TN 37831-0117
(865) 574-6440   Fax: (865) 576-0734
E-mail: barbara.dunkin@orau.org
Web: orise.orau.gov/mlef/index.html

Summary To provide summer work experience at fossil energy sites of the Department of Energy (DOE) to Native American, other underrepresented minority, and female students or postdoctorates.

Eligibility This program is open to U.S. citizens currently enrolled full time at an accredited college or university. Applicants must be undergraduate, graduate, or postdoctoral students in fields of science, technology (IT), engineering, or mathematics (STEM) and have a GPA of 3.0 or higher. They must be interested in a summer work experience at a DOE fossil energy research facility. Along with their application, they must submit a 100-word statement on why they want to participate in this program. A goal of the program is to recruit women and underrepresented minorities into careers related to fossil energy, although all qualified students are encouraged to apply.

Financial data Weekly stipends are $600 for undergraduates, $750 for master's degree students, or $850 for doctoral and postdoctoral students. Travel costs for a round trip to and from the site and for a trip to a designated place for technical presentations are also paid.

Duration 10 weeks during the summer.

Additional information This program began as 3 separate activities: the Historically Black Colleges and Universities

Internship Program established in 1995, the Hispanic Internship Program established in 1998, and the Tribal Colleges and Universities Internship Program, established in 2000. Those 3 programs were merged into the Fossil Energy Minority Education Initiative, renamed the Mickey Leland Energy Fellowship Program in 2000. Sites to which interns may be assigned include the National Energy Technology Laboratory (Morgantown, West Virginia, Albany, Oregon and Pittsburgh, Pennsylvania), Pacific Northwest National Laboratory (Richland, Washington), Sandia National Laboratory (Livermore, California), Lawrence Berkeley National Laboratory (Berkeley, California), Los Alamos National Laboratory (Los Alamos, New Mexico), Strategic Petroleum Reserve Project Management Office (New Orleans, Louisiana), or U.S. Department of Energy Headquarters (Washington, D.C.).

Number awarded Varies each year; recently, 30 students participated in this program.

Deadline December of each year.

[1323]
MINORITY FACULTY DEVELOPMENT SCHOLARSHIP AWARD IN PHYSICAL THERAPY

American Physical Therapy Association
Attn: Honors and Awards Program
1111 North Fairfax Street
Alexandria, VA 22314-1488
(703) 684-APTA   Toll Free: (800) 999-APTA, ext. 8082
Fax: (703) 684-7343   TDD: (703) 683-6748
E-mail: honorsandawards@apta.org
Web: www.apta.org

Summary To provide financial assistance to Native American and other minority faculty members in physical therapy who are interested in working on a post-professional doctoral degree.

Eligibility This program is open to U.S. citizens and permanent residents who are members of the following minority groups: African American or Black, Asian, Native Hawaiian or other Pacific Islander, American Indian or Alaska Native, or Hispanic/Latino. Applicants must be full-time faculty members, teaching in an accredited or developing professional physical therapist education program, who will have completed the equivalent of 2 full semesters of post-professional doctoral course work. They must possess a license to practice physical therapy in a U.S. jurisdiction and be enrolled as a student in an accredited post-professional doctoral program whose content has a demonstrated relationship to physical therapy. Along with their application, they must submit a personal essay on their professional goals, including their plans to contribute to the profession and minority services. Selection is based on contributions in the area of minority affairs and services and contributions to the profession of physical therapy. Preference is given to members of the American Physical Therapy Association (APTA).

Financial data A stipend is awarded (amount not specified).

Duration 1 year.

Additional information This program began in 1999.

Number awarded 1 or more each year.

Deadline November of each year.

[1324]
MINORITY POSTDOCTORAL FELLOWSHIP AWARDS IN DIABETES

American Diabetes Association
Attn: Research Programs
1701 North Beauregard Street
Alexandria, VA 22311
(703) 549-1500, ext. 2362   Toll Free: (800) DIABETES
Fax: (703) 549-1715
E-mail: grantquestions@diabetes.org
Web: professional.diabetes.org

Summary To provide financial assistance to Native American and other minority postdoctoral fellows for additional research training in diabetes.

Eligibility This program is open to members of underrepresented minority groups (African American, Hispanic or Latino, American Indian or Alaskan Native, Native Hawaiian or Pacific Islander) who have an M.D., Ph.D., D.O., D.P.M., or Pharm.D. degree and less than 10 years of postdoctoral experience. Applicants must be authorized to work in the United States or its territories. They must be interested in a program of research (basic, clinical, or translational) training related to diabetes under the supervision of a mentor. Selection is based on the potential of the project and investigator to significantly impact the field of diabetes research and/or advance the prevention, cure or treatment of diabetes; applicant's scientific potential and potential for establishing a successful and independent career in diabetes-related research; quality and originality of the research proposal and experimental approach, and its relevance to diabetes; tangible evidence of the applicant's performance in research in the form of peer-reviewed scientific publications or equivalent; and evidence of a strong commitment from the mentor toward providing quality training and support in preparation for an independent career in diabetes research.

Financial data The investigator's stipend ranges from $42,000 to $55,272 per year, depending on the number of years of postdoctoral experience. Other support includes a $5,000 training allowance (travel to diabetes-related scientific meetings, computer, books, publication costs, equipment, training courses/workshops, reagents, laboratory supplies) and a $5,000 fringe benefits allowance. Indirect costs are not covered.

Duration Up to 3 years.

Number awarded Varies each year.

Deadline April of each year.

[1325]
MLA PRIZE FOR STUDIES IN NATIVE AMERICAN LITERATURES, CULTURES, AND LANGUAGES

Modern Language Association of America
Attn: Office of Programs
85 Broad Street, Suite 500
New York, NY 10004-2434
(646) 576-5141   Fax: (646) 458-0030
E-mail: awards@mla.org
Web: www.mla.org

Summary To recognize and reward members of the Modern Language Association (MLA) who have written outstanding books on Native American literature.

Eligibility This award is presented to authors of outstanding scholarly work in the field of Native American literatures, cultures, or languages. The work must broaden and examine understanding of the cultural expressions of first peoples or nations in the United States, Canada, or Mexico. Works in Indigenous languages, literatures, or cultures focusing on other geographic areas may also be considered if they bring fresh perspectives to the field. Authors must be members of MLA.

Financial data The prize is $1,000 and a certificate.

Duration The prize is awarded biennially.

Additional information This prize was first awarded in 2014.

Number awarded 1 each even-numbered year.

Deadline April of each even-numbered year.

[1326]
MULTICULTURAL AUDIENCE DEVELOPMENT INITIATIVE INTERNSHIPS

Metropolitan Museum of Art
Attn: Internship Programs
1000 Fifth Avenue
New York, NY 10028-0198
(212) 570-3710   Fax: (212) 570-3782
E-mail: mmainterns@metmuseum.org
Web: www.metmuseum.org

Summary To provide summer work experience at the Metropolitan Museum of Art to Native American and other college undergraduates, graduate students, and recent graduates from diverse backgrounds.

Eligibility This program is open to members of diverse groups who are undergraduate juniors and seniors, students currently working on a master's degree, or individuals who completed a bachelor's or master's degree within the past year. Ph.D. students may be eligible to apply during the first 12 months of their program, provided they have not yet achieved candidacy. Students from various academic backgrounds are encouraged to apply, but they must be interested in preparing for a career in the arts and museum fields. Freshmen and sophomores are not eligible.

Financial data The stipend is $3,750.

Duration 10 weeks, beginning in June.

Additional information Interns are assigned to departmental projects (curatorial, administration, or education) at the Metropolitan Museum of Art; other assignments may include giving gallery talks and working at the Visitor Information Center. The assignment is for 35 hours a week. The internships are funded by the Multicultural Audience Initiative at the museum.

Number awarded 1 or more each year.

Deadline January of each year.

[1327]
NATIONAL URBAN FELLOWS PROGRAM

National Urban Fellows, Inc.
Attn: Program Director
1120 Avenue of the Americas, Fourth Floor
New York, NY 10036
(212) 730-1700   Fax: (212) 730-1823
E-mail: info@nuf.org
Web: www.nuf.org/fellows-overview

Summary To provide mid-career public sector professionals, especially people of color and women, with an opportunity to strengthen leadership skills through a master's degree program coupled with a mentorship.

Eligibility This program is open to U.S. citizens who have a bachelor's degree, have at 5 to 7 years of professional work experience with 2 years in a management capacity, have demonstrated leadership capacity with potential for further growth, have a GPA of 3.0 or higher, and can demonstrate a commitment to public service. Applicants must submit a 1-page autobiographical statement, a 2-page personal statement, and a 2-page statement on their career goals. They may be of any racial or ethnic background, but the program's goal is to increase the number of competent administrators from underrepresented ethnic and cultural groups at all levels of public and private urban management organizations. Semifinalists are interviewed.

Financial data The stipend is $25,000. Fellows are required to pay a $500 registration fee and a $7,500 co-investment tuition payment upon acceptance and enrollment in the program.

Duration 14 months.

Additional information The program begins with a summer semester of study at Bernard M. Baruch College of the City University of New York. Following this, fellows spend 9 months in mentorship assignments with a senior administrator in a government agency, a major nonprofit, or a foundation. The final summer is spent in another semester of study at Baruch College. Fellows who successfully complete all requirements are granted a master's of public administration from that college. A $150 processing fee must accompany each application.

Number awarded Approximately 40 to 50 each year.

Deadline December of each year.

[1328]
NATIVO LODGE RISING ARTISTS FELLOWSHIPS

Southwestern Association for Indian Arts, Inc.
215 Washington Avenue
P.O. Box 969
Santa Fe, NM 87504-0969
(505) 983-5220   Fax: (505) 983-7647
E-mail: info@swaia.org
Web: www.swaia.org

Summary To provide a residency to Native American artists from New Mexico who are interested in advancing their education and careers.

Eligibility This program is open to Native American artists from New Mexico who are working in all mediums. Preference is given to emerging Native artists, but all levels are eligible. Applicants must be interested in a residency at the Nativo Lodge in Albuquerque where they can explore the creative process and push the boundaries of their respective art forms and creative expression. They have the opportunity to redesign a room at the Lodge into a studio of their own specifications where they can work. Along with their application, they must submit a concept drawing of the proposed room design, 4 images of their current work, an artist statement, and a biography.

Financial data Fellows receive a stipend of $3,000, free lodging at the Nativo, an advance of $1,000 for materials, a grant of $1,000 during the work process, and a grant of $1,000 after the work has been completed.

Duration The grants are awarded annually.

Additional information This program began in 2012.

Number awarded 2 each year.

Deadline October of each year.

[1329]
NBCC MINORITY FELLOWSHIP PROGRAM

National Board for Certified Counselors
Attn: NBCC Foundation
3 Terrace Way
Greensboro, NC 27403
(336) 232-0376   Fax: (336) 232-0010
E-mail: foundation@nbcc.org
Web: nbccf-mfpdr.applicantstack.com/x/detail/a2b3qvixcgjm

Summary To provide financial assistance to doctoral candidates, especially Nativ Americans and those from other racially and ethnically diverse populations, and who are interested in working on a degree in mental health and/or substance abuse counseling.

Eligibility This program is open to U.S. citizens and permanent residents who are enrolled full time in an accredited doctoral degree mental health and/or substance abuse and addictions counseling program. Applicants must have a National Certified Counselor or equivalent credential. They must commit to provide mental health and substance abuse services to racially and ethnically diverse populations. African Americans, Alaska Natives, American Indians, Asian Americans, Hispanics/Latinos, Native Hawaiians, and Pacific Islanders are especially encouraged to apply. Applicants must be able to commit to providing substance abuse and addictions counseling services to underserved minority populations for at least 2 years after graduation.

Financial data The stipend is $20,000.

Duration 1 year.

Additional information This program began in 2012 with support from the Substance Abuse and Mental Health Services Administration.

Number awarded 23 each year.

Deadline June of each year.

[1330]
NEWBERRY CONSORTIUM IN AMERICAN INDIAN AND INDIGENOUS STUDIES FACULTY FELLOWSHIPS

Newberry Library
Attn: Committee on Awards
60 West Walton Street
Chicago, IL 60610-3305
(312) 255-3666   Fax: (312) 255-3513
E-mail: research@newberry.org
Web: www.newberry.org/long-term-fellowships

Summary To provide funding to faculty at member institutions of the Newberry Consortium in American Indian and Indigenous Studies (NCAIS) who wish to conduct research in American Indian studies at the D'Arcy McNickle Center for the History of the American Indian at the Newberry Library.

Eligibility This program is open to faculty at NCAIS institutions who are interested in conducting research in American Indian studies at the Newberry Library. Applicants must submit their curriculum vitae; a 300-word project abstract, a 1,500-word project description that discusses the topic, significance, conceptual framework, and specific Newberry col-

lections to be used; and 3 letters of recommendation. They may apply for either a long-term or a short-term fellowship.

Financial data The stipend is $4,200 per month for long-term fellowships or $5,000 for short-term fellowships.

Duration 4 to 6 months for long-term fellowships; 1 month for short-term fellowships.

Additional information The Newberry Library inaugurated the NCAIS in 2009, following the end of its partnership with the 13 universities of Committee on Institutional Cooperation (CIC). It is limited to 18 universities in the United States and Canada; for a list of those universities, contact the Newberry. Fellows are expected to present research, participate in both the McNickle Center Seminar in American Indian and Indigenous Studies and the Newberry Library Fellows' Seminar, and be available for consultation with the NCAIS Graduate Student Fellows.

Number awarded 1 or more each year.

Deadline November of each year for long-term fellowships; December of each year for short-term fellowships.

[1331]
NORTH AMERICAN INDIAN PROSE AWARD

University of Nebraska Press
1111 Lincoln Mall
Lincoln, NE 68588-0630
(402) 472-3581   Toll Free: (800) 755-1105
Fax: (402) 472-6214   E-mail: pressmail@unl.edu
Web: www.nebraskapress.unl.edu

Summary To recognize and reward outstanding book-length nonfiction manuscripts written by authors of American Indian descent.

Eligibility This competition is open to authors of North American Indian descent. They are invited to submit book-length nonfiction manuscripts, including biographies, autobiographies, histories, literary criticisms, essays, nonfiction works for children, and political commentaries. The competition excludes fiction, poetry, drama, collections of interviews, and work previously published in book form. Selection is based on literary merit, originality, and familiarity with North American Indian life.

Financial data The winner receives a cash advance of $1,000 and publication of the award-winning manuscript by the University of Nebraska Press.

Duration The award is presented annually.

Number awarded 1 each year.

Deadline June of each year.

[1332]
OKLAHOMA CAREERTECH FOUNDATION TEACHER RECRUITMENT/RETENTION SCHOLARSHIP FOR TEACHERS

Oklahoma CareerTech Foundation
Attn: Administrator
1500 West Seventh Avenue
Stillwater, OK 74074-4364
(405) 743-5453   Fax: (405) 743-5541
E-mail: leden@careertech.ok.gov
Web: www.okcareertech.org

Summary To provide financial assistance to Native American and other residents of Oklahoma who reflect the diversity of the state and are interested in attending a college or university in the state to earn a credential or certification for a career in the Oklahoma CareerTech system.

Eligibility This program is open to residents of Oklahoma who are incumbent CareerTech teachers working toward a CareerTech credential or certification at an institution of higher education in the state. Applicants must reflect the ethnic diversity of the state. Along with their application, they must submit brief statements on their interest and commitment to the CareerTech teaching profession and their financial need.

Financial data The stipend ranges from $500 per semester to $1,500 per year.

Duration 1 semester; may be renewed, provided the recipient maintains a GPA of 2.5 or higher.

Number awarded 1 or more each year.

Deadline May of each year.

[1333]
OSAGE NATION GRADUATE DEGREE AWARDS

Osage Nation Education Department
Attn: Career Training and Scholarship
105 Buffalo Avenue
Hominy, OK 74035
(918) 287-5301   Fax: (918) 885-2136
E-mail: scholarship@osagenation-nsn.gov
Web: www.osagenation-nsn.gov

Summary To recognize and reward members of the Osage Nation who complete a graduate degree.

Eligibility This award is provided to Osage tribal students who complete a master's or doctoral degree.

Financial data The award is $2,000 for a master's degree or $3,000 for a doctoral degree.

Duration Tribal members may receive 1 master's award and 1 doctoral award in a lifetime.

Number awarded Varies each year.

Deadline June of each year.

[1334]
PACIFIC ISLANDERS IN COMMUNICATIONS MEDIA FUND GRANTS

Pacific Islanders in Communications
Attn: Program Director
615 Pi'ikoi Street, Suite 1504
Honolulu, HI 96814
(808) 591-0059   Fax: (808) 591-1114
E-mail: mediafund@piccom.org
Web: www.piccom.org/pages/media-fund

Summary To provide funding to producers of public television programs that relate to the Pacific Islander experience.

Eligibility This program is open to independent producers and public television stations interested in developing programs that originate from the Pacific Islander experience and are intended for national public broadcast audiences. Applicants must have artistic, budgetary, and editorial control and must own the copyright of the proposed project. They must be at least 18 years of age, be citizens or legal residents of the United States or its territories, and have previous film or television experience. Student productions are not eligible. All projects must be delivered in standard public television lengths and meet accepted technical, ethical, and journalistic standards for national public television broadcast. Programs may be of any genre, but they must be intended for broadcast on national public television. For purposes of this program, Pacific Islanders are defined as descendants of the first peoples of American Samoa, Guam, Hawai'i, and the Northern Mariana Islands. Selection is based on the power of the finished product to shed light on the Pacific Islander experience; ability of the program to provoke thoughtful dialogue about the subject; knowledge and understanding of the subject as well as a thoughtful and sensitive approach; potential of the finished project to be shown on national public television; production and fundraising plans; ability of the producer and the production team to complete the project within budget and on schedule; and extent to which Pacific Islanders hold key creative production positions.

Financial data Maximum awards are $15,000 for research and development grants or $50,000 for production and completion grants.

Number awarded Varies each year; recently, 3 research and development grants, 5 production grants, and 1 completion grant were awarded.

Deadline February, July, or October of each year.

[1335]
PATRICIA M. LOWRIE DIVERSITY LEADERSHIP SCHOLARSHIP

Association of American Veterinary Medical Colleges
Attn: Diversity Committee
1101 Vermont Avenue, N.W., Suite 301
Washington, DC 20005-3536
(202) 371-9195, ext. 147   Toll Free: (877) 862-2740
Fax: (202) 842-0773   E-mail: lgreenhill@aavmc.org
Web: www.aavmc.org

Summary To provide financial assistance to Native American and other veterinary students who have promoted diversity in the profession.

Eligibility This program is open to second-, third-, and fourth-year students at veterinary colleges in the United States. Applicants must have a demonstrated record of contributing to enhancing diversity and inclusion through course projects, co-curricular activities, outreach, domestic and community engagement, research, and/or an early reputation for influencing others to be inclusive. Along with their application, they must submit a 3-page personal statement that describes 1) why diversity and inclusion are important to them personally and professionally; 2) how they intend to continue contributing to diversity and inclusion efforts in the veterinary profession after graduation; and 3) what it might mean to be honored as a recipient of this scholarship. They must also indicate how they express their race and/or ethnicity (American Indian or Alaskan, Asian, Black or African American, Hispanic, Native Hawaiian or Pacific Islander, or White) and how they express their gender (male, female, transgender spectrum, or other). Selection is based primarily on documentation of a demonstrated commitment to promoting diversity in academic veterinary medicine; consideration is also given to academic achievement, the student's broader community service record, and financial need.

Financial data The stipend is $6,000.

Duration 1 year; nonrenewable.

Additional information This program began in 2013.

Number awarded 1 each odd-numbered year.

Deadline October of each even-numbered year.

[1336]
PAULA DE MERIEUX RHEUMATOLOGY FELLOWSHIP AWARD

American College of Rheumatology
Attn: Rheumatology Research Foundation
2200 Lake Boulevard N.E.
Atlanta, GA 30319
(404) 633-3777   Fax: (404) 633-1870
E-mail: foundation@rheumatology.org
Web: rheumresearch.org/Awards/Education_Training

Summary   To provide funding to Native American and other underrepresented minorities interested in a program of training for a career providing clinical care to people affected by rheumatic diseases.

Eligibility   This program is open to trainees at ACGME-accredited institutions. Applications must be submitted by the training program director at the institution who is responsible for selection and appointment of trainees. The program must train and prepare fellows to provide clinical care to those affected by rheumatic diseases. Trainees must be women or members of underrepresented minority groups, defined as Black Americans, Hispanics, and Native Americans (Native Hawaiians, Alaska Natives, and American Indians). They must be U.S. citizens, nationals, or permanent residents. Selection is based on the institution's pass rate of rheumatology fellows, publication history of staff and previous fellows, current positions of previous fellows, and status of clinical faculty.

Financial data   The grant is $50,000, to be used as salary for the trainee. Other trainee costs (e.g., fees, health insurance, travel, attendance at scientific meetings) are to be incurred by the recipient's institutional program. Supplemental or additional support to offset the cost of living may be provided by the grantee institution.

Duration   Up to 1 year.

Additional information   This fellowship was first awarded in 2005.

Number awarded   1 each year.

Deadline   July of each year.

[1337]
PEN OPEN BOOK AWARD

PEN American Center
Attn: Literary Awards Associate
588 Broadway, Suite 303
New York, NY 10012
(212) 334-1660, ext. 4813   Fax: (212) 334-2181
E-mail: awards@pen.org
Web: www.pen.org/content/pen-open-book-award-5000

Summary   To recognize and reward outstanding authors of color from any country.

Eligibility   This award is presented to an author of color (African, Arab, Asian, Caribbean, Latino, and Native American) whose book-length writings were published in the United States during the current calendar year. Works of fiction, literary nonfiction, biography/memoir, poetry, and other works of literary character are strongly preferred. U.S. citizenship or residency is not required. Nominations must be submitted by publishers or literary agents. Self-published books are not eligible.

Financial data   The prize is $5,000.

Duration   The prizes are awarded annually.

Additional information   This prize was formerly known as the Beyond Margins Award. The entry fee is $75.

Number awarded   1 or 2 each year.

Deadline   August of each year.

[1338]
PHILLIPS FUND GRANTS FOR NATIVE AMERICAN RESEARCH

American Philosophical Society
Attn: Director of Grants and Fellowships
104 South Fifth Street
Philadelphia, PA 19106-3387
(215) 440-3429   Fax: (215) 440-3436
E-mail: LMusumeci@amphilsoc.org
Web: www.amphilsoc.org/grants/phillips

Summary   To provide funding to graduate students and scholars interested in conducting research on North American Indian anthropological linguistics and ethnohistory.

Eligibility   Eligible to apply are scholars, preferably young scholars, working in the fields of Native American linguistics and ethnohistory and the history of Native Americans in the continental United States and Canada. Applications are not accepted for projects in archaeology, ethnography, psycholinguistics, or for the preparation of pedagogical materials. Graduate students may apply for support for research on their master's or doctoral dissertations.

Financial data   Grants range up to $3,500 and average about $2,500. These funds are intended for such extra costs as travel, tapes, films, and informants' fees, but not for general maintenance or the purchase of books or permanent equipment.

Duration   1 year.

Number awarded   Varies each year; recently, 17 were awarded.

Deadline   February of each year.

[1339]
POSTDOCTORAL FELLOWSHIPS OF THE CONSORTIUM FOR FACULTY DIVERSITY

Consortium for Faculty Diversity at Liberal Arts Colleges
c/o Gettysburg College
Provost's Office
300 North Washington Street
Campus Box 410
Gettysburg, PA 17325
(717) 337-6796   E-mail: sgockows@gettysburg.edu
Web: www.gettysburg.edu

Summary   To make available the facilities of liberal arts colleges to scholars who recently received their doctoral/advanced degree and will enhance diversity at their college.

Eligibility   This program is open to scholars in the liberal arts and engineering who are U.S. citizens or permanent residents and received the Ph.D. or M.F.A. degree within the past 5 years. Applicants must be interested in a residency at a participating institution that is part of the Consortium for Faculty Diversity at Liberal Arts Colleges. They must be able to enhance diversity at the institution.

Financial data   Fellows receive a stipend equivalent to the average salary paid by the host college to beginning assistant professors. Modest funds are made available to finance the fellow's proposed research, subject to the usual institutional procedures.

Duration 1 year.

Additional information The following schools are participating in the program: Allegheny College, Amherst College, Bard College, Bowdoin College, Bryn Mawr College, Bucknell University, Carleton College, Centenary College of Louisiana, Centre College, College of the Holy Cross, Colorado College, Denison University, DePauw University, Dickinson College, Gettysburg College, Grinnell College, Gustavus Adolphus College, Hamilton College, Haverford College, Hobart and William Smith Colleges, Juniata College, Lafayette College, Lawrence University, Luther College, Macalester College, Mount Holyoke College, Muhlenberg College, Oberlin College, Pitzer College, Pomona College, Reed College, Scripps College, Skidmore College, Smith College, Southwestern University, St. Lawrence University, St. Olaf College, Swarthmore College, The College of Wooster, Trinity College, University of Richmond, Vassar College, and Wellesley College. Fellows are expected to teach at least 60% of a regular full-time faculty member's load, participate in departmental seminars, and interact with students.

Number awarded Varies each year; recently, 23 of the 43 member institutions made a total of 51 appointments through this program.

Deadline October of each year.

[1340]
POSTDOCTORAL FELLOWSHIPS OF THE FORD FOUNDATION DIVERSITY FELLOWSHIP PROGRAM

The National Academies of Sciences, Engineering, and
  Medicine
Attn: Fellowships Office
500 Fifth Street, N.W.
Washington, DC 20001
(202) 334-2872   Fax: (202) 334-3419
E-mail: FordApplications@nas.edu
Web: sites.nationalacademies.org

Summary To provide funding for postdoctoral research to be conducted in the United States or any other country to Native American and other scholars whose success will increase the racial and ethnic diversity of U.S. colleges and universities.

Eligibility This program is open to U.S. citizens, permanent residents, and nationals who earned a Ph.D. or Sc.D. degree within the past 7 years and are committed to a career in teaching and research at the college or university level. The following are considered as positive factors in the selection process: evidence of superior academic achievement; promise of continuing achievement as scholars and teachers; membership in a group whose underrepresentation in the American professoriate has been severe and longstanding, including Black/African Americans, Puerto Ricans, Mexican Americans/Chicanos/Chicanas, Native American Indians, Alaska Natives (Eskimos, Aleuts, and other indigenous people of Alaska), and Native Pacific Islanders (Hawaiians, Micronesians, or Polynesians); capacity to respond in pedagogically productive ways to the learning needs of students from diverse backgrounds; sustained personal engagement with communities that are underrepresented in the academy and an ability to bring this asset to learning, teaching, and

scholarship at the college and university level; and likelihood of using the diversity of human experience as an educational resource in teaching and scholarship. Eligible areas of study include American studies, anthropology, archaeology, art and theater history, astronomy, chemistry, communications, computer science, cultural studies, earth sciences, economics, education, engineering, ethnic studies, ethnomusicology, geography, history, international relations, language, life sciences, linguistics, literature, mathematics, performance study, philosophy, physics, political science, psychology, religious studies, sociology, urban planning, and women's studies. Also eligible are interdisciplinary programs such as African American studies, Native American studies, area studies, peace studies, and social justice. Awards are not available for practice-oriented programs or professional programs such as medicine, law, or public health. Research may be conducted at an appropriate institution of higher education in the United States (normally) or abroad, including universities, museums, libraries, government or national laboratories, privately sponsored nonprofit institutes, government chartered nonprofit research organizations, or centers for advanced study. Applicants should designate a faculty member or other scholar to serve as host at the proposed fellowship institution. They are encouraged to choose a host institution other than that where they are affiliated at the time of application.

Financial data The stipend is $45,000. Funds may be supplemented by sabbatical leave pay or other sources of support that do not carry with them teaching or other responsibilities. The employing institution receives an allowance of $1,500, paid after fellowship tenure is completed; the employing institution is expected to match the grant and to use the allowance and the match to assist with the fellow's continuing research expenditures.

Duration 9 to 12 months.

Additional information Fellows may not accept another major fellowship while they are being supported by this program.

Number awarded Approximately 24 each year.

Deadline November of each year.

[1341]
REGINALD F. LEWIS FELLOWSHIP FOR LAW TEACHING

Harvard Law School
Attn: Lewis Committee
Griswold Two South
1525 Massachusetts Avenue
Cambridge, MA 02138
(617) 495-3109
E-mail: LewisFellowship@law.harvard.edu
Web: hls.harvard.edu

Summary To provide funding to law school graduates, especially Native Americans and others of color, who are preparing for a career in law teaching and are interested in a program of research and training at Harvard Law School.

Eligibility This program is open to recent graduates of law school who have demonstrated an interest in law scholarship and teaching. Applicants must be interested in spending time in residence at Harvard Law School where they will audit courses, attend workshops, and follow a schedule of research under the sponsorship of the committee. The program encourages the training of prospective law teachers who will enhance the diversity of the profession and especially encourages applications from candidates of color.

Financial data The stipend is $50,000 per year.

Duration 2 years.

Number awarded 1 each year.

Deadline January of each year.

[1342]
RESEARCH AND TRAINING PROGRAM ON POVERTY AND PUBLIC POLICY POSTDOCTORAL FELLOWSHIPS

University of Michigan
Gerald R. Ford School of Public Policy
Attn: National Poverty Center
Joan and Sanford Weill Hall
735 South State Street, Room 5100
Ann Arbor, MI 48109-3091
(734) 764-3490   Fax: (734) 763-9181
E-mail: npcinfo@umich.edu
Web: npc.umich.edu/opportunities/visiting

Summary To provide funding to Native American and other minority postdoctorates interested in conducting research and pursuing intensive training on poverty-related public policy issues at the University of Michigan.

Eligibility This program is open to U.S. citizens and permanent residents who are members of a minority group that is underrepresented in the social sciences. Applicants must have received the Ph.D. degree within the past 5 years and be engaged in research on poverty and public policy. Along with their application, they must submit a research proposal that represents either a significant extension upon previous work or a new poverty research project; a 1- to 2-page statement that specifies the ways in which residence at the University of Michigan will foster their career development and research goals and provides information about how their racial/ethnic/regional/economic background qualifies them as a members of a group that is underrepresented in the social sciences; a curriculum vitae; and a sample of their scholarly writing. Preference is given to proposals that would benefit from resources available at the University of Michigan and from interactions with affiliated faculty.

Financial data The stipend is $50,000 per calendar year.

Duration 1 or 2 years.

Additional information This program is funded by the Ford Foundation. Fellows spend the year participating in a seminar on poverty and public policy and conducting their own research. Topics currently pursued include the effects of the recession and the American Recovery and Reinvestment Act of 2009 on workers, families, and children; evolution of the social safety net; longitudinal analyses of youth development; family formation and healthy marriages; immigration and poverty; investing in low-income families: the accumulation of financial assets and human capital; and qualitative and mixed-methods research on poverty. Fellows must be in residence at the University of Michigan for the duration of the program.

Number awarded 1 or more each year.

Deadline January of each year.

[1343]
ROLLIN AND MARY ELLA KING NATIVE ARTIST FELLOWSHIP

School for Advanced Research
Attn: Indian Arts Research Center
660 Garcia Street
P.O. Box 2188
Santa Fe, NM 87504-2188
(505) 954-7205   Fax: (505) 954-7207
E-mail: iarc@sarsf.org
Web: www.sarweb.org/index.php?artists

Summary To provide an opportunity for Native American visual artists from the Southwest to improve their skills through a fall residency at the Indian Arts Research Center in Santa Fe, New Mexico.

Eligibility This program is open to Native Americans who excel in the visual arts and are residents of Arizona, Colorado, New Mexico, or Utah. Applicants should be attempting to explore new avenues of creativity, grapple with new ideas to advance their work, and strengthen existing talents. Along with their application, they must submit a current resume, examples of their current work, and a 2-page statement that explains why they are applying for this fellowship, how it will help them realize their professional and/or personal goals as an artist, and describing the project they plan to complete during the residency.

Financial data The fellowship provides a stipend of $3,000 per month, housing, studio space, supplies allowance, and travel reimbursement to and from the center.

Duration 3 months, beginning in September.

Additional information Fellows work with the staff and research curators at the Indian Arts Research Center, an academic division of the School of American Research that is devoted solely to Native American art scholarship. The center has a significant collection of Pueblo pottery, Navajo and Pueblo Indian textiles, and early 20th-century Indian paintings, as well as holdings of jewelry and silverwork, basketry, clothing, and other ethnological materials. This fellowship was established in 2001.

Number awarded 1 each year.

Deadline January of each year.

[1344]
RON AND SUSAN DUBIN NATIVE ARTIST FELLOWSHIP

School for Advanced Research
Attn: Indian Arts Research Center
660 Garcia Street
P.O. Box 2188
Santa Fe, NM 87504-2188
(505) 954-7205   Fax: (505) 954-7207
E-mail: iarc@sarsf.org
Web: www.sarweb.org/index.php?artists

Summary To provide an opportunity for Native American artists to improve their skills through a summer residency at the Indian Arts Research Center in Santa Fe, New Mexico.

Eligibility This program is open to Native American artists; priority is given to individuals who excel in the visual arts that relate to the center's collecting emphasis, but artists who work in the verbal and performing arts are also considered. Along with their application, they must submit a current resume, examples of their current work, and a 2-page statement that explains why they are applying for this fellowship, how it will help them realize their professional and/or personal goals as an artist, and describing the project they plan to complete during the residency.

Financial data The fellowship provides a stipend of $3,000 per month, housing, studio space, supplies allowance, and travel reimbursement to and from the center.

Duration 2 months, beginning in June.

Additional information Fellows work with the staff and research curators at the Indian Arts Research Center, an academic division of the School of American Research that is devoted solely to Native American art scholarship. The center has a significant collection of Pueblo pottery, Navajo and Pueblo Indian textiles, and early 20th-century Indian paintings, as well as holdings of jewelry and silverwork, basketry, clothing, and other ethnological materials. This fellowship was first awarded in 1994.

Number awarded 1 each year.

Deadline January of each year.

[1345]
SAR INDIGENOUS WRITER-IN-RESIDENCE FELLOWSHIP

School for Advanced Research
Attn: Director of Scholar Programs
660 Garcia Street
P.O. Box 2188
Santa Fe, NM 87504-2188
(505) 954-7237   Fax: (505) 954-7207
E-mail: scholar@sarsf.org
Web: www.sarweb.org

Summary To provide an opportunity for Native American writers to improve their skills through a winter residency at the Indian Arts Research Center in Santa Fe, New Mexico.

Eligibility This program is open to writers indigenous to the United States or Canada. Applicants must be interested in a program of residence at the Center to work on their creative projects. Along with their application, they must submit a current resume; a 10-page sample of their current work; a 4-page proposal that describes the project they intend to work on during their fellowship, the ideas or techniques they will explore, a timeline for the project's completion, why obtaining this fellowship is important to them as a writer at this stage of their career, and how the fellowship will help them reach their goals and/or develop as a writer; and a statement of 500 to 1,000 words explaining, justifying, and contextualizing their body of work.

Financial data The fellowship provides a stipend of $6,000, housing, studio space, supplies allowance, and travel reimbursement to and from the center.

Duration 7 weeks, in January and February.

Additional information Fellows work with the staff and research curators at the Indian Arts Research Center, an academic division of the School of American Research (SAR) that is devoted solely to Native American scholarship. This fellowship was first awarded in 2011.

Number awarded Varies each year; recently, 5 fellows were appointed.

Deadline January of each year.

[1346]
SARAH STANLEY GORDON EDWARDS AND ARCHIBALD CASON EDWARDS ENDOWMENT FOR FELLOWSHIPS

Virginia Center for the Creative Arts
Attn: Admissions Committee
154 San Angelo Drive
Amherst, VA 24521
(434) 946-7236   Fax: (434) 946-7239
E-mail: vcca@vcca.com
Web: www.vcca.com

Summary To provide support to female painters, especially Native Americans, who are interested in a residency at the Virginia Center for the Creative Arts in Sweet Briar, Virginia.

Eligibility This program is open to female painters older than 25 years of age who are interested in a residency at the center so they can concentrate solely on their creative work. Preference is given to Native American painters. Applicants must submit samples of their work completed within the past 4 years.

Financial data The fellowship provides payment of all residency costs, including a private bedroom, separate studio, and 3 prepared meals a day.

Duration 2 weeks.

Additional information This program began in 2016. The application fee is $40.

Number awarded 1 each year.

Deadline January of each year for June to September residencies; May of each year for October to January residencies; September of each year for February to May residencies.

[1347]
SMITHSONIAN MINORITY STUDENT INTERNSHIP

Smithsonian Institution
Attn: Office of Fellowships and Internships
470 L'Enfant, Suite 7102
P.O. Box 37012, MRC 902
Washington, DC 20013-7012
(202) 633-7070   Fax: (202) 633-7069
E-mail: siofi@si.edu
Web: www.smithsonianofi.com/minority-internship-program

Summary To provide Native American and other minority undergraduate or graduate students with the opportunity to work on research or museum procedure projects in specific areas of history, art, or science at the Smithsonian Institution.

Eligibility Internships are offered to minority students who are actively engaged in undergraduate or graduate study or have graduated within the past 4 months. Applicants must be U.S. citizens or permanent residents who have an overall GPA of 3.0 or higher. Applicants must be interested in conducting research in any of the following fields of interest to the Smithsonian: animal behavior, ecology, and environmental science (including an emphasis on the tropics); anthropology (including archaeology); astrophysics and astronomy; earth sciences and paleobiology; evolutionary and systematic biology; history of science and technology; history of art (especially American, contemporary, African, Asian, and 20th-century art); American crafts and decorative arts; social and cultural history of the United States; and folklife.

Financial data The program provides a stipend of $600 per week; travel allowances may also be offered.
Duration 10 weeks during the summer or academic year.
Number awarded Varies each year.
Deadline January of each year for summer or fall; September of each year for spring.

[1348]
SMITHSONIAN NATIVE AMERICAN COMMUNITY SCHOLAR AWARDS

Smithsonian Institution
Attn: Office of Fellowships and Internships
470 L'Enfant, Suite 7102
P.O. Box 37012, MRC 902
Washington, DC 20013-7012
(202) 633-7070   Fax: (202) 633-7069
E-mail: siofi@si.edu
Web: www.smithsonianofi.com

Summary To provide opportunities for Native Americans to work on projects related to Native American topics at the Smithsonian Institution.

Eligibility Native Americans who are formally or informally related to a Native American community are eligible to apply. Applicants must be proposing to undertake a project that is related to a Native American topic and requires the use of Native American resources at the Smithsonian Institution.

Financial data Scholars receive a stipend of $175 per day and allowances for travel and research.
Duration Up to 21 days.
Additional information Projects are carried out in association with the Smithsonian's research staff. Fellows are required to be in residence at the Smithsonian for the duration of the fellowship.
Number awarded Varies each year.
Deadline January of each year for summer or fall residency; September of each year for spring residency.

[1349]
SUSAN KELLY POWER AND HELEN HORNBECK TANNER FELLOWSHIP

Newberry Library
Attn: Committee on Awards
60 West Walton Street
Chicago, IL 60610-3305
(312) 255-3666   Fax: (312) 255-3513
E-mail: research@newberry.org
Web: www.newberry.org/short-term-fellowships

Summary To provide funding to American Indian doctoral candidates and postdoctorates who wish to use the resources of the D'Arcy McNickle Center for the History of the American Indian at the Newberry Library.

Eligibility This program is open to Ph.D. candidates and postdoctoral scholars of American Indian heritage. Applicants must be interested in conducting research in any field of the humanities while in residence at the McNickle Center.
Financial data The stipend is $2,500 per month.
Duration 1 week to 2 months.
Additional information This program began in 2002.
Number awarded 1 each year.
Deadline December of each year.

[1350]
SWAIA DISCOVERY FELLOWSHIPS

Southwestern Association for Indian Arts, Inc.
215 Washington Avenue
P.O. Box 969
Santa Fe, NM 87504-0969
(505) 983-5220   Fax: (505) 983-7647
E-mail: info@swaia.org
Web: swaia.org

Summary To provide funding to American Indian artists, filmmakers, and writers interested in advancing their education and careers.

Eligibility This program is open to American Indian artists whose work conforms to the standards and classification definitions of the Southwestern Association for Indian Arts (SWAIA): jewelry; pottery; paintings, drawings, graphics, and photography; Pueblo wooden carving; sculpture; textiles; basketry; beadwork and quillwork; film and video; writing (poetry and fiction); and diverse arts. Both emerging and established artists are eligible. Their work may be traditional or contemporary. Applicants must be interested in pursuing an opportunity to travel, develop marketing plans, purchase supplies, expand their studies, develop their portfolio, or explore new directions. Funding is not provided to full-time students or for use as a scholarship. Along with their application, they must submit a formal artist statement of 1 to 2 pages explaining and contextualizing their art work by discussing their motivations to create, materials that they use, or cultural impact they wish to develop with their fellowship. They must also submit samples of their work (4 digital images for visual artists, a 5-minute CD or DVD for filmmakers, or 10 pages of writing for authors), an explanation of how they plan to use the grant, and a formal resume.

Financial data Fellows receive a grant of $3,500 and a complimentary booth at the Santa Fe Indian Market; in lieu of a booth, writers participate in SWAIA's Native literary and performance event during Indian Market Week.
Duration The grants are awarded annually.
Additional information SWAIA established a fellowship program in 1980. Beginning in 2010, it began offering 2 types of fellowships: these Discovery Fellowships (similar to the prior fellowships) and Residency Fellowships (for artists interested in a residency at the Santa Fe Art Institute). The application fee is $25.
Number awarded 3 each year.
Deadline May of each year.

[1351]
SWAIA INDIAN MARKET AWARDS

Southwestern Association for Indian Arts, Inc.
215 Washington Avenue
P.O. Box 969
Santa Fe, NM 87504-0969
(505) 983-5220   Fax: (505) 983-7647
E-mail: info@swaia.org
Web: www.swaia.org/Exhibitors/index.html

Summary To recognize and reward outstanding Indian artists who participate in the Santa Fe Indian Market.

Eligibility This program is open to artists who have a Certificate of Degree of Indian Blood (CDIB) as an enrolled member of a federally-recognized tribe or Alaska Native corporation and a New Mexico Taxation and Revenue CRS Identification Number. Artists must be 18 years of age and older. The 10 divisions are 1) jewelry; 2) pottery; 3) paintings, drawings, graphics, and photography; 4) Pueblo wooden carvings; 5) sculpture; 6) textiles; 7) diverse art forms; 8) beadwork and quillwork; 9); youth; and 10) basketry. Along with their application, artists must submit slides of each medium that they wish to show at the annual Santa Fe Indian Market. The work must comply with standards of the Southwestern Association for Indian Arts (SWAIA) and be representative of the art work they plan to sell at the Market. An eleventh division is available for artists who are 17 years of age or younger, with 3 subdivisions: ages 9 and under, ages 10 through 13, and ages 14 through 17.

Financial data A total of more than $100,000 in prize money is awarded each year. Awards vary each year, but they have included $1,000 for Best of Show and $500 for first place in each category.

Duration The Market is held on 2 days in August of each year.

Additional information Special awards range up to $2,500; they include the Institute of American Indian Arts Distinguished Alumni Award, the Innovation Award, the Tony Da Award for Pottery, the Joe Caté Award for Beadmaking, the Jean Seth Award for Painting, the Traditional Pueblo Pottery Award ($1,000), the *Native Peoples* Magazine Creativity Award, the Anita Da Award for Youth Pottery, the *Santa Fe New Mexican* Indian Market Award for Youth Artists, the Best of Classification IX for Youth, and the Best of Division A for Ages 9 and Under. Artists are responsible for payment of a $35 online application fee or $50 hard-copy application fee, a $10 city of Santa Fe business license fee, a $10 city of Santa Fe booth permit fee, and a booth fee of $400 to $750.

Number awarded Varies each year.

Deadline Applications must be submitted by January of each year.

[1352]
TRIBAL COLLEGES RESEARCH GRANTS PROGRAM

Department of Agriculture
National Institute of Food and Agriculture
Attn: National Program Leader-Tribal Programs
1400 Independence Avenue, S.W.
Stop 2201
Washington, DC 20250-2201
(202) 690-0402　　　　E-mail: tgrosser@nifa.usda.gov
Web: nifa.usda.gov

Summary To provide funding to scholars at Tribal Colleges who are interested in conducting agricultural research.

Eligibility This program is open to investigators at the Tribal Colleges designated as the 1994 Land-Grant Institutions. Applicants must be interested in conducting research that relates to the action plan of the sponsoring agency: local and global food supply and security, responding to climate and energy needs, sustainable use of natural resources, human nutrition and childhood obesity, food safety, education and science literacy, and rural prosperity/rural-urban interdependence. Collaboration is required between the applicant 1994 Land Grant Institution and at least 1 of the following: 1) an 1890 or 1862 Land Grant college or university; 2) a non-Land Grant college of agriculture; 3) an approved forestry

school; or 4) the Agricultural Research Service of the Department of Agriculture. Applicants may be seeking funding for 1) New Discovery projects, for institutions that already possess the necessary research maturity to conduct scientific research that least to an enhanced body of knowledge and a level of problem solving for relevant issues; 2) Capacity Building projects, for developing existing research capacity with a focus on enhancing research infrastructure, instrumentation, and faculty expertise; or 3) Student Research experience, for projects that consist of individual or group student research investigations.

Financial data Maximum grants for New Discovery projects are $200,000 with minimal student involvement or $220,000 with significant student involvement, $85,000 for Capacity Building projects, or $65,000 for Student Research experience; all amounts are per project, not per year.

Duration 36 months for New Discovery projects; 24 months for Capacity Building projects or Student Research experience.

Number awarded Varies each year; recently, $1,700,000 was available for grants through this program.

Deadline February of each year.

[1353]
UC BERKELEY'S CHANCELLOR'S POSTDOCTORAL FELLOWSHIP PROGRAM FOR ACADEMIC DIVERSITY

University of California at Berkeley
Attn: Division of Equity and Inclusion
402 Sproul Hall
Berkeley, CA 94720-5920
(510) 643-8235　　　　E-mail: ppfpinfo@berkeley.edu
Web: diversity.berkeley.edu

Summary To provide an opportunity for Native American and other recent postdoctorates who will increase diversity at the University of California at Berkeley (UCB) to conduct research on the campus.

Eligibility This program is open to U.S. citizens and permanent residents who received a doctorate within 3 years of the start of the fellowship. The program solicits applications from scholars whose research, teaching, and service will contribute to diversity and equal opportunity at the university. The contributions to diversity may include public service towards increasing equitable access in fields where women and minorities are underrepresented or research focusing on underserved populations or understanding inequalities related to race, gender, disability, or LGBT issues. Applicants should have the potential to bring to their academic and research careers the perspective that comes from their non-traditional educational background or understanding of the experiences of members of groups historically underrepresented in higher education.

Financial data The stipend is $44,500 per year (11 months, plus 1 month vacation). The award also includes health insurance, vision and dental benefits, and up to $5,000 for research-related and program travel expenses.

Duration 1 year; may be renewed 1 additional year.

Additional information This program operates in addition to the University of California President's Postdoctoral Fellowship Program for Academic Diversity. Interested candidates may apply to either program.

Number awarded Varies each year; recently, 3 were awarded.

Deadline October of each year.

[1354]
UC DAVIS CHANCELLOR'S POSTDOCTORAL FELLOWSHIP PROGRAM

University of California at Davis
Attn: Office of Graduate Studies
250 Mrak Hall
One Shields Avenue
Davis, CA 95616
(530) 752-0650   Fax: (530) 752-6222
E-mail: gradservices@ucdavis.edu
Web: gradstudies.ucdavis.edu

Summary To provide an opportunity for Native American and other recent postdoctorates who will increase diversity at the University of California at Davis (UCD) to conduct research at the university.

Eligibility This program is open to scholars who have a Ph.D. in any field from an accredited university. Applicants must be interested in conducting research at UC Davis under the mentorship of an established scholar in their field. The program particularly solicits applications from scholars whose research, teaching, and service will contribute to the diversity and equal opportunity at the university. Those contributions may include public service addressing the needs of our increasingly diverse society, efforts to improve equitable access to higher education, or research focusing on under-served populations or understanding inequities related to race, gender, disability, or LGBT status. They must be able to demonstrate that they are legally authorized to work in the United States without restrictions or limitations; individuals granted deferred action status under the Deferred Action for Childhood Arrivals (DACA) program are encouraged to apply. Selection is based on academic accomplishments, strength of research proposal, and potential for faculty careers that will contribute to diversity through their teaching, research, and service.

Financial data The stipend is at least $44,500 per year (11 months, plus 1 month vacation). The award also includes health insurance, vision and dental benefits, and up to $5,000 for research-related and program travel expenses.

Duration 1 year; may be renewed 1 additional year.

Additional information This program, which began in 2012, operates in addition to the University of California President's Postdoctoral Fellowship Program for Academic Diversity. Interested candidates may apply to either program.

Number awarded Varies each year; recently, 7 were appointed.

Deadline October of each year.

[1355]
UC SAN DIEGO CHANCELLOR'S POSTDOCTORAL FELLOWSHIP PROGRAM FOR ACADEMIC DIVERSITY

University of California at San Diego
Attn: Office of the Vice Chancellor for Equity, Diversity and Inclusion
302 University Center, Room 102
La Jolla, CA 92093-0029
(858) 246-1923   E-mail: mcg005@ucsd.edu
Web: facultyexcellence.ucsd.edu/funding/cpfp1/index.html

Summary To provide an opportunity for Native American and other recent postdoctorates who will increase diversity at the University of California at San Diego (UCSD) to conduct research at the university.

Eligibility This program is open to U.S. citizens and permanent residents who received a doctorate within 3 years of the start of the fellowship and are interested in conducting research at UCSD. The program particularly solicits applications from scholars whose research, teaching, and service will contribute to the diversity and equal opportunity at the university. Those contributions may include public service towards increasing equitable access in fields where women and minorities are under-represented. In some fields, the contributions may include research focusing on underserved populations or understanding inequalities related to race, gender, disability, or LGBT. The program is seeking applicants with the potential to bring to their academic and research careers the critical perspective that comes from their nontraditional educational background or understanding of the experiences of members of groups historically under-represented in higher education in the United States.

Financial data The stipend is $44,500 per year (11 months, plus 1 month vacation). The award also includes health insurance, vision and dental benefits, and up to $5,000 for research-related and program travel expenses.

Duration 1 year; may be renewed 1 additional year.

Additional information This program operates in addition to the University of California President's Postdoctoral Fellowship Program for Academic Diversity. Interested candidates may apply to either program.

Number awarded 2 each year.

Deadline October of each year.

[1356]
UCLA CHANCELLOR'S POSTDOCTORAL FELLOWSHIP PROGRAM

University of California at Los Angeles
Attn: Office for Diversity and Faculty Development
3109 Murphy Hall
P.O. Box 951407
Los Angeles, CA 90095-1407
(310) 206-7411   Fax: (310) 206-8427
E-mail: facdiversity@conet.ucla.edu
Web: faculty.diversity.ucla.edu

Summary To provide an opportunity for Native American and other recent postdoctorates who will increase diversity at the University of California at Los Angeles (UCLA) to conduct research at the university.

Eligibility This program is open to U.S. citizens and permanent residents who received a doctorate within 3 years of the start of the fellowship. Applicants must be interested in conducting research at UCLA. The program particularly solicits applications from scholars whose research, teaching, and service will contribute to the diversity and equal opportunity at the university. Those contributions may include public service addressing the needs of our increasingly diverse society, efforts to improve equitable access to higher education, or research focusing on underserved populations or understanding inequities related to race, gender, disability, or LGBT status.

Financial data The stipend is at least $44,500 per year (11 months, plus 1 month vacation). The award also includes health insurance, vision and dental benefits, and up to $5,000 for research-related and program travel expenses.

Duration 1 year; may be renewed 1 additional year.

Additional information This program operates in addition to the University of California President's Postdoctoral Fellowship Program for Academic Diversity. Interested candidates may apply to either program.

Number awarded 2 each year.

Deadline October of each year.

[1357]
UDALL FOUNDATION NATIVE AMERICAN CONGRESSIONAL INTERNSHIPS

Morris K. Udall and Stewart L. Udall Foundation
Attn: Program Manager, Internship Program
130 South Scott Avenue
Tucson, AZ 85701-1922
(520) 901-8561   Fax: (520) 670-5530
E-mail: info@udall.gov
Web: www.udall.gov

Summary To provide an opportunity for Native American upper-division and graduate students to work in a Congressional office during the summer.

Eligibility This program is open to American Indians and Alaska Natives who are enrolled members of recognized tribes and have an interest in tribal government and policy. Applicants must have a GPA of 3.0 or higher as a junior, senior, graduate student, law student, or recent graduate of a tribal or 4-year college. They must be able to participate in an internship in Washington, D.C., where they will gain practical experience in the legislative process, Congressional matters, and governmental proceedings that specifically relate to Native American issues. Fields of study of previous interns have included American Indian studies, political science, law and pre-law, psychology, social work, history, business and public administration, anthropology, community and urban planning, architecture, communications, health sciences, public health, biology, engineering, sociology, environmental studies and natural resources, economics, and justice studies. Applicants must demonstrate strong research and writing skills; organizational abilities and time management skills; maturity, responsibility, and flexibility; interest in learning how the federal government "really works;" commitment to their tribal community; knowledge of Congressman Morris K. Udall's legacy with regard to Native Americans; and awareness of issues and challenges currently facing Indian Country.

Financial data Interns receive round-trip airfare to Washington, D.C.; dormitory lodging at a local university; a $42 daily allowance sufficient for meals, transportation, and inci-

dentals; and an educational stipend of $1,200 to be paid at the conclusion of the internship.

Duration 10 weeks during the summer.

Additional information These internships were first offered in 1996.

Number awarded 12 each year.

Deadline January of each year.

[1358]
UNIVERSITY OF NORTH CAROLINA POSTDOCTORAL PROGRAM FOR FACULTY DIVERSITY

University of North Carolina at Chapel Hill
Attn: Office of Postdoctoral Affairs
301 Bynum Hall, CB 4100
Chapel Hill, NC 27599-4100
(919) 843-4793   Fax: (919) 962-6769
E-mail: jennifer_pruitt@unc.edu
Web: www.research.unc.edu/carolina-postdocs/applicants

Summary To support Native American and other minority scholars who are interested in teaching and conducting research at the University of North Carolina (UNC).

Eligibility This program is open to scholars, especially members of underrepresented groups (African Americans, Native Americans, and Hispanic Americans) who have completed their doctoral degree within the past 5 years. Applicants must be interested in teaching and conducting research at UNC. Preference is given to U.S. citizens and permanent residents. Selection is based on the evidence of scholarship potential and ability to compete for tenure-track appointments at UNC and other research universities.

Financial data Fellows receive $47,476 per year, plus an allowance of $2,000 for research and travel. Health benefits are also available.

Duration Up to 2 years.

Additional information Fellows must be in residence at the Chapel Hill campus for the duration of the program. They teach 1 course per year and spend the rest of the time in research. This program began in 1983.

Number awarded 4 or 5 each year.

Deadline November of each year.

[1359]
VISION MAKER MEDIA PUBLIC MEDIA CONTENT FUND

Vision Maker Media
Attn: Public Media Content Fund
1800 North 33rd Street
Lincoln, NE 68503
(402) 472-0497   Fax: (402) 472-8675
E-mail: visionmaker@unl.edu
Web: www.visionmakermedia.org/filmmakers

Summary To provide funding for the creation of Native American theme programs intended for broadcast to public television audiences.

Eligibility This program invites producers to submit competitive proposals for the research and development, scripting, or completion of culture-specific programs that originate from the Native North American experience and are intended for national public television audiences. All program categories are eligible, except industrial or promotional films and videos, student productions, projects that are commercial in nature, projects for which 4-year exclusive public television broadcast rights are not available, projects or production entities that are foreign-owned or controlled, projects intended solely for theatrical release, and projects funded in part by a government entity or group featured in the content of the program. Applicants must be U.S. citizens or legal residents at least 21 years of age. They must have previous television or filmmaking experience. Selection is based on quantity and quality of Native American participation in creative, technical, and advisory roles; power of the finished program to illuminate the Native American experience through public television; originality of concept and style; strength of the production team to complete the project within budget, schedule, and the highest quality standards; sound production and fundraising plans; reasonable budget estimates and considerations; potential interest to a national audience; and strength of sample work.

Financial data Grants range from $5,000 to $20,000 for research and development, up to half of the project's total budget for production or post-production, or from $5,000 to $35,000 for new media projects.

Duration Up to 1 year.

Additional information This program is underwritten by the Corporation for Public Broadcasting.

Number awarded Varies each year.

Deadline February of each year.

[1360]
YOUTH PUBLIC ART PROJECT PROGRAM OF THE NATIONAL MUSEUM OF THE AMERICAN INDIAN

National Museum of the American Indian
Attn: Artist Leadership Program
Cultural Resources Center
4220 Silver Hill Road
Suitland, MD 20746-2863
(301) 238-1544   Fax: (301) 238-3200
E-mail: ALP@si.edu
Web: www.nmai.si.edu/connect/artist-leadership-program

Summary To provide Native American professional artists with an opportunity to organize and conduct a collaborative art project focused on youth within their local community.

Eligibility This program is open to Native artists from the western Hemisphere and Hawaii who are recognized by their community and can demonstrate significant artistic accomplishments in any media (e.g., visual arts, media arts, sculpture, textile and fiber arts, performance arts, literature). Students enrolled in a degree program are ineligible. Applicants must be interested in creating a public art project within their home community in collaboration with a local youth organization. The project must result in a finished product such as a sculpture, mural, theatrical work, musical performance, or video. Along with their application, they must submit a 500-word research proposal, 500-word project proposal, digital portfolio of 10 images or 5 minutes, 2 letters of support, a resume, and a 75-word statement describing their purpose, goal, and intended results.

Financial data The grant is $7,000 to cover project costs, supplies, and materials.

Duration Participants first spend 10 days in Washington, D.C. consulting with staff of the National Museum of the American Indian (NMAI), after which they return to their community and complete a project within 1 year.

Additional information This is a 2-part program. In the first part, participants visit Washington, D.C. for 10 days to conduct research in collections of the NMAI and other local museums, participate in interviews with Collections and Education staff, conduct lunch-time presentations for NMAI staff and the museum public, and visit area galleries. Following the completion of that visit, participants return to their community to share the knowledge learned from the experience and research visit and conduct their project. They must provide at least 10 art/production lessons to at least 5 community youth during the project schedule.

Number awarded 4 each year.

Deadline June of each year.

Indexes

Program Title Index

If you know the name of a particular funding program open to Native Americans and want to find out where it is covered in the directory, use the Program Title Index. Here, program titles are arranged alphabetically, word by word. To assist you in your search, every program is listed by all its known names or abbreviations. In addition, we've used an alphabetical code (within parentheses) to help you determine if the program is aimed at you: U = Undergraduates; G = Graduate Students; P = Professionals/Postdoctorates. Here's how the code works: if a program is followed by (U) 241, the program is described in the Undergraduates chapter, in entry 241. If the same program title is followed by another entry number—for example, (P) 1301—the program is also described in the Professionals/Postdoctorates chapter, in entry 1301. Remember: the numbers cited here refer to program entry numbers, not to page numbers in the book.

U–Undergraduates　　　　**G–Graduate Students**　　　　**P–Professionals/Postdoctorates**

Comer Chickasaw Scholarship. *See* Kenneth Comer Chickasaw Scholarship, entry (G) 990

Commercial and Federal Litigation Section Diversity Fellowship, (G) 821

Commission on Dietetic Registration Diversity Scholarships, (U) 173, (G) 822

Committee for the Advancement of Racial and Ethnic Diversity (CARED) Grant Program. *See* APAGS Committee for the Advancement of Racial and Ethnic Diversity (CARED) Grant Program, entry (G) 752

Committee on Ethnic Minority Recruitment Scholarship, (G) 823

Communications Internship Award for Students of Color, (U) 174

Communications Scholarship for Ethnic Minority Students. *See* Leonard M. Perryman Communications Scholarship for Ethnic Minority Students, entry (U) 374

ComputerCraft Corporation Scholarship, (U) 175

COMTO Colorado Scholarships, (U) 176

Conley Creative Writing Award. *See* Robert J. and Evelyn Conley Creative Writing Award, entries (U) 563, (G) 1163

Connecticut Education Foundation Scholarships for Minority High School Students, (U) 177

Connecticut Minority Teacher Incentive Grants, (U) 178

Connecticut Native American Intertribal Urban Council Scholarship, (U) 179

Connecticut Society of Certified Public Accountants Diversity Scholarships, (U) 180

Connie Greene Scholarship. *See* LCDR Janet Cochran and CDR Connie Greene Scholarship, entry (U) 369

Consortium for Graduate Study in Management Fellowships, (G) 824

Constangy Diversity Scholars Award, (G) 825

Consuelo W. Gosnell Memorial Scholarships, (G) 826

Continental Society Daughters of Indian Wars Scholarship, (U) 181

Cook Inlet Tribal Council Tribal Higher Education Program, (U) 182, (G) 827

Coquille Indian Tribe Adult Vocational Training Grants, (U) 183

Coquille Indian Tribe Computer Equipment Program, (U) 184, (G) 828

Coquille Indian Tribe Higher Education Grants, (U) 185, (G) 829

Cornell Scholarship. *See* Holly A. Cornell Scholarship, entry (G) 932

Corp Scholarship. *See* Don Corp Scholarship, entry (U) 202

Corris Boyd Scholars Program, (G) 830

Council of Energy Resource Tribes College Scholarships. *See* CERT College Scholarships, entries (U) 125, (G) 796

Cox Art Scholarship for a Native American Woman. *See* Helen Trueheart Cox Art Scholarship for a Native American Woman, entry (U) 287

Credit Suisse MBA Fellowship, (G) 831

Creek Nation of Oklahoma Scholarship Grants, (U) 186

Creek Nation Post Graduate Program, (G) 832

Creek Nation Tribal Funds Grant Program, (U) 187

Creek Nation Tribal Incentive Grant Program, (U) 188

Crockett Minority Scholarship Award. *See* NASP-ERT Minority Scholarship Program, entry (G) 1067

Crowe Memorial Scholarship. *See* Richard (Yogi) Crowe Memorial Scholarship, entry (G) 1160

CRST Education Hardship Grant, (U) 189, (G) 833

Crumbly Minorities in Energy Grant. *See* Isaac J. "Ike" Crumbly Minorities in Energy Grant, entry (G) 949

Cub McKerchie Tributary Scholarship. *See* Mary and Harold "Cub" McKerchie Tributary Scholarship, entry (U) 399

Cuba Wadlington, Jr. and Michael P. Johnson Scholarship, (U) 190

Cundiff Grants. *See* James and Carolee Cundiff Grants, entries (U) 325, (G) 954

Cunningham Legacy Scholarship. *See* Julie Cunningham Legacy Scholarship, entry (G) 980

Cyprus Tohono Corporation Four Year Scholarship, (U) 191

D

Da Award for Pottery. *See* SWAIA Indian Market Awards, entry (P) 1351

Da Award for Youth Pottery. *See* SWAIA Indian Market Awards, entry (P) 1351

Dakota Indian Foundation Scholarship, (U) 192

Dalmas A. Taylor Memorial Summer Minority Policy Fellowship, (G) 834

Damon P. Moore Scholarship, (U) 193

Daniel Scholarships. *See* Eugene Daniel Scholarships, entries (U) 230, (G) 874

Daniel T. Jenks Scholarship. *See* Mary K. Moreland and Daniel T. Jenks Scholarship, entry (U) 402

Dargan Minority Scholarship. *See* Thomas Dargan Minority Scholarship, entry (U) 622

Dave Caldwell Scholarship, (G) 835

David and Carolyn Nimmo Graduate Business Scholarship, (G) 836

David Eaton Scholarship, (G) 837

David K. McDonough Scholarship in Ophthalmology/ENT. *See* Dr. David K. McDonough Scholarship in Ophthalmology/ENT, entry (G) 854

David Monash/Harry Lloyd and Elizabeth Pawlette Marshall Medical Student Service Scholarships. *See* Dr. David Monash/Harry Lloyd and Elizabeth Pawlette Marshall Medical Student Service Scholarships, entry (G) 855

David Monash/Harry Lloyd and Elizabeth Pawlette Marshall Residency Scholarships. *See* Dr. David Monash/Harry Lloyd and Elizabeth Pawlette Marshall Residency Scholarships, entry (P) 1288

David Sankey Minority Scholarship in Meteorology, (U) 194, (G) 838

Davis Educational Fund. *See* Unto These Hills Educational Fund Scholarship, entry (U) 642

Davis Ethnic/Minority Scholarship Program. *See* Mary Hill Davis Ethnic/Minority Scholarship Program, entry (U) 401

Davis Scholarship. *See* Ronald M. Davis Scholarship, entry (G) 1168

Davis Wright Tremaine 1L Diversity Scholarship Program, (G) 839

de Merieux Rheumatology Fellowship Award. *See* Paula de Merieux Rheumatology Fellowship Award, entry (P) 1336

Deanna Snyder, Sr. Chairman's Scholarship. *See* Barry and Deanna Snyder, Sr. Chairman's Scholarship, entry (U) 89

Deborah Peek Crockett Minority Scholarship Award. *See* NASP-ERT Minority Scholarship Program, entry (G) 1067

Dee Wells Memorial Scholarship. *See* Homer "Dee" Wells Memorial Scholarship, entries (U) 295, (G) 933

Deep Carbon Observatory Diversity Grants, (G) 840, (P) 1285

Deere Scholarship for Female and Minority Students. *See* John Deere Scholarship for Female and Minority Students, entry (U) 338

Delaware Athletic Trainers' Association Ethnic Diversity Advisory Committee Scholarship, (U) 195, (G) 841

Deloria Jr. Memorial Scholarship. *See* Vine Deloria Jr. Memorial Scholarship, entry (G) 1231

U–Undergraduates   G–Graduate Students   P–Professionals/Postdoctorates

U–Undergraduates   **G–Graduate Students**   **P–Professionals/Postdoctorates**

U–Undergraduates   **G–Graduate Students**   **P–Professionals/Postdoctorates**

U–Undergraduates   G–Graduate Students   P–Professionals/Postdoctorates

Mental Health and Substance Abuse Fellowship Program, (G) 1035

Mental Health Research Dissertation Grant to Increase Workforce Diversity, (G) 1036

MESBEC Program. *See* Catching the Dream Scholarships, entries (U) 124, (G) 794

Mescalero Apache Tribal Scholarship, (U) 410, (G) 1037

Michael Baker Scholarship for Diversity in Engineering, (U) 411

Michael Memorial HPC Fellowships. *See* ACM/IEEE-CS George Michael Memorial HPC Fellowships, entry (G) 697

Michael P. Johnson Scholarship. *See* Cuba Wadlington, Jr. and Michael P. Johnson Scholarship, entry (U) 190

Michigan Chapter COMTO Scholarships, (U) 412

Michigan Indian Elders Association Scholarship, (U) 413

Michigan Indian Tuition Waiver Program, (U) 414, (G) 1038

Mickey Leland Energy Fellowships, (U) 415, (G) 1039, (P) 1322

Mickey Williams Minority Scholarships. *See* PDEF Mickey Williams Minority Scholarships, entry (U) 525

Midwives of Color-Watson Midwifery Student Scholarship, (U) 416, (G) 1040

Mike Dunn Memorial Scholarship. *See* James Michael "Mike" Dunn Memorial Scholarship, entry (U) 328

Mike Scholarship. *See* Theresa A. Mike Scholarship, entries (U) 621, (G) 1213

Milbank Diversity Scholars Program, (G) 1041

Miller Johnson West Michigan Diversity Law School Scholarship, (G) 1042

Miller Nash Diversity Fellowships, (G) 1043

Miller Native American Vocational Scholarship. *See* Verl and Dorothy Miller Native American Vocational Scholarship, entry (U) 648

Miller Tributary Scholarship. *See* Martha Miller Tributary Scholarship, entries (U) 396, (G) 1024

Minnesota American Indian Bar Association Law Student Scholarships, (G) 1044

Minnesota Association of Counselors of Color Student of Color Scholarship. *See* MnACC Student of Color Scholarship, entry (U) 432

Minnesota Indian Scholarship Program, (U) 417, (G) 1045

Minnesota Social Service Association Diversity Scholarship, (U) 418

Minorities in Government Finance Scholarship, (U) 419, (G) 1046

Minority Affairs Committee's Award for Outstanding Scholastic Achievement, (U) 420

Minority and Underrepresented Environmental Literacy Program, (U) 421, (G) 1047

Minority Faculty Development Scholarship Award in Physical Therapy, (G) 1048, (P) 1323

Minority Fellowships in Environmental Law, (G) 1049

Minority Medical Student Award Program of the American Society of Hematology, (G) 1050

Minority Medical Student Summer Externship in Addiction Psychiatry, (G) 1051

Minority Nurse Faculty Scholars Program. *See* Johnson & Johnson/AACN Minority Nurse Faculty Scholars Program, entry (G) 972

Minority Postdoctoral Fellowship Awards in Diabetes, (P) 1324

Minority Scholarship Award for Academic Excellence in Physical Therapy, (U) 422

Minority Scholarship Awards for College Students in Chemical Engineering, (U) 423

Minority Scholarship Awards for Incoming College Freshmen in Chemical Engineering, (U) 424

Minority Scholarship in Classics and Classical Archaeology, (U) 425

Minority Serving Institutions Partnership Program Internships. *See* MSIPP Internships, entries (U) 443, (G) 1063

Minority Teacher Education Scholarships, (U) 426

Minority Teachers of Illinois Scholarship Program, (U) 427, (G) 1052

Minority University Research and Education Project (MUREP) Scholarships. *See* NASA Scholarship and Research Opportunities (SRO) Minority University Research and Education Project (MUREP) Scholarships, entry (U) 449

Miss Cherokee Scholarships, (U) 428

Missouri Minority Teaching Scholarship Program, (U) 429

Missouri Society of Certified Public Accountants Minority Scholarships. *See* MSCPA Minority Scholarships, entries (U) 442, (G) 1062

Mitch Musgrove Memorial Scholarship, (U) 430

Mitch Sperry Memorial Law Scholarship, (U) 431, (G) 1053

Mitchell Memorial Scholarship. *See* Anna Belle Mitchell Memorial Scholarship, entry (U) 55

MLA/NLM Spectrum Scholarships, (G) 1054

MLA Prize for Studies in Native American Literatures, Cultures, and Languages, (P) 1325

MLA Scholarship for Minority Students, (G) 1055

MnACC Student of Color Scholarship, (U) 432

Modern Language Association of America Prize for Studies in Native American Literatures, Cultures, and Languages. *See* MLA Prize for Studies in Native American Literatures, Cultures, and Languages, entry (P) 1325

Mohawk Higher Education Program, (U) 433

Monash/Harry Lloyd and Elizabeth Pawlette Marshall Medical Student Service Scholarships. *See* Dr. David Monash/Harry Lloyd and Elizabeth Pawlette Marshall Medical Student Service Scholarships, entry (G) 855

Monash/Harry Lloyd and Elizabeth Pawlette Marshall Residency Scholarships. *See* Dr. David Monash/Harry Lloyd and Elizabeth Pawlette Marshall Residency Scholarships, entry (P) 1288

Montana American Indian Student Waiver, (U) 434, (G) 1056

Montgomery Summer Research Diversity Fellowships, (U) 435

Mooniene Ogee Memorial Scholarship, (U) 436, (G) 1057

Moore Scholarship. *See* Damon P. Moore Scholarship, entry (U) 193

Moreland and Daniel T. Jenks Scholarship. *See* Mary K. Moreland and Daniel T. Jenks Scholarship, entry (U) 402

Morgan Lewis Diversity Fellowship Program, (G) 1058

Morgan Stanley MBA Fellowship, (G) 1059

Morgan Stanley Tribal Scholars Program, (U) 437

Morgan Transportation Achievement Scholarship. *See* Garrett A. Morgan Transportation Achievement Scholarship, entry (U) 254

Morris K. Udall Scholarships, (U) 438

Morris Scholarship. *See* Addie B. Morris Scholarship, entries (U) 9, (G) 701

Morris Thompson Scholarship Fund. *See* Doyon Foundation Competitive Scholarships, entries (U) 207, (G) 852

Morrison & Foerster 1L Diversity Fellowship Program, (G) 1060

Morse Scholarship. *See* Jo Morse Scholarship, entry (G) 961

Mosaic Scholarships. *See* ARL/SAA Mosaic Scholarships, entry (G) 758

Mosley Scholarships. *See* Dwight Mosley Scholarships, entry (U) 211

Moss Adams Diversity Scholarships, (U) 439

U–Undergraduates　　　　**G–Graduate Students**　　　　**P–Professionals/Postdoctorates**

U–Undergraduates   **G–Graduate Students**   **P–Professionals/Postdoctorates**

U–Undergraduates   **G–Graduate Students**   **P–Professionals/Postdoctorates**

U–Undergraduates   **G–Graduate Students**   **P–Professionals/Postdoctorates**

Sponsoring Organization Index

The Sponsoring Organization Index makes it easy to identify agencies that offer financial aid to Native Americans. In this index, the sponsoring organizations are listed alphabetically, word by word. In addition, we've used an alphabetical code (within parentheses) to help you identify the intended recipients of the funding offered by the organizations: U = Undergraduates; G = Graduate Students; P = Professionals/Postdoctorates. For example, if the name of a sponsoring organization is followed by (U) 241, a program sponsored by that organization is described in the Undergraduate chapter, in entry 241. If that sponsoring organization's name is followed by another entry number—for example, (P) 1301—the same or a different program sponsored by that organization is described in the Professionals/Postdoctorates chapter, in entry 1301. Remember: the numbers cited here refer to program entry numbers, not to page numbers in the book.

A

Academic Library Association of Ohio, (G) 694
Academy of Applied Science, (U) 559
Academy of Criminal Justice Sciences, (P) 1287
Academy of Nutrition and Dietetics, (U) 173, (G) 822
Accenture LLP, (U) 2
Accountancy Board of Ohio, (U) 4
Accounting and Financial Women's Alliance, (U) 371
Acoustical Society of America, (G) 699
Act Six, (U) 5
Actuarial Foundation, (U) 6
Acxiom Corporation, (U) 7, (G) 700
Adler Pollock & Sheehan P.C., (G) 702
Ahtna, Incorporated, (U) 14-16, 654, (G) 708, 1237
Ainahau o Kaleponi Hawaiian Civic Club, (U) 19
Airport Minority Advisory Council, (U) 31, 85
Akin Gump Strauss Hauer & Feld LLP, (G) 1164
Alabama Indian Affairs Commission, (U) 22, (G) 715
Alabama Society of Certified Public Accountants, (U) 72
Alaska Library Association, (G) 716, 961
Alaska Native Tribal Health Consortium, (U) 60, (G) 749
Alaska State Council on the Arts, (P) 1321
Albuquerque Community Foundation, (U) 497
The Aleut Corporation, (U) 23-25, 53, 253, 376, (G) 718-719, 746, 895, 1009
Alfred P. Sloan Foundation, (G) 840, (P) 1285
Allan R. Bloomfield, (G) 720
Allina Health System, (U) 224
Alpha Kappa Delta, (G) 761
Alyeska Pipeline Service Company, (U) 28-30, 135, (G) 805
AMB Foundation, (U) 78, (G) 764
American Academy of Child and Adolescent Psychiatry, (G) 959
American Academy of Physician Assistants, (U) 520, (G) 1119
American Anthropological Association, (G) 725

American Association for Justice, (G) 1158
American Association for Respiratory Care, (U) 334
American Association of Advertising Agencies, (U) 50, 96, 196, 513, (G) 774, 1116
American Association of Airport Executives Foundation, (U) 1
American Association of Blacks in Energy. Atlanta Chapter, (U) 561
American Association of Blacks in Energy. Philadelphia Chapter, (U) 533
American Association of Colleges of Nursing, (G) 972
American Association of Colleges of Osteopathic Medicine, (G) 1191
American Association of Critical-Care Nurses, (U) 106, (G) 780
American Association of Law Libraries, (G) 905, (P) 1299
American Association of Petroleum Geologists Foundation, (G) 949
American Association of Physicists in Medicine, (U) 33
American Association of Railroad Superintendents, (U) 9, (G) 701
American Association of School Personnel Administrators, (U) 373, (G) 1007, (P) 1314
American Association of University Women, (G) 1186
American Bar Association. Fund for Justice and Education, (G) 726
American Bar Association. Section of Litigation, (G) 978
American Bar Foundation, (U) 435
American Bus Association, (U) 34
American Chemical Society, (U) 35
American Civil Liberties Union of Alaska, (U) 335, (G) 962
American College of Chest Physicians, (P) 1280
American College of Healthcare Executives, (G) 717
American College of Nurse-Midwives, (U) 416, (G) 793, 1040, (P) 1279
American College of Rheumatology, (P) 1336
American Correctional Association, (U) 398, (G) 1026
American Dental Association, (G) 1222

U–Undergraduates   **G–Graduate Students**   **P–Professionals/Postdoctorates**

U–Undergraduates   **G–Graduate Students**   **P–Professionals/Postdoctorates**

U–Undergraduates   **G–Graduate Students**   **P–Professionals/Postdoctorates**

U–Undergraduates   **G–Graduate Students**   **P–Professionals/Postdoctorates**

U–Undergraduates　　　　**G–Graduate Students**　　　　**P–Professionals/Postdoctorates**

Residency Index

Some programs listed in this book are set aside for Native Americans who are residents of a particular state or region. Others are open to applicants wherever they may live. The Residency Index will help you pinpoint programs available in your area as well as programs that have no residency restrictions at all (these are listed under the term "United States"). To use this index, look up the geographic areas that apply to you (always check the listings under "United States"), jot down the entry numbers listed for the educational level that applies to you (Undergraduates, Graduate Students, or Professionals/Postdoctorates), and use those numbers to find the program descriptions in the directory. To help you in your search, we've provided some "see" and "see also" references in the index entries. Remember: the numbers cited here refer to program entry numbers, not to page numbers in the book.

A

Alabama: **Undergraduates,** 22, 641; **Graduate Students,** 715, 1227. *See also* United States

Alaska: **Undergraduates,** 28, 60, 65, 154, 257, 335, 346, 536, 583; **Graduate Students,** 716, 749, 753, 961-962, 1106; **Professionals/Postdoctorates,** 1321. *See also* Northwestern states; United States

American Samoa: **Professionals/Postdoctorates,** 1334. *See also* United States territories

Arizona: **Undergraduates,** 62, 71, 111, 191, 251, 297-298, 468, 471, 478, 535, 607; **Professionals/Postdoctorates,** 1343. *See also* United States

Arizona, southeastern: **Undergraduates,** 575; **Graduate Students,** 1178. *See also* Arizona

Arkansas: **Undergraduates,** 69; **Graduate Students,** 755, 1021. *See also* United States

Ashland, Wisconsin: **Undergraduates,** 556; **Graduate Students,** 1154. *See also* Wisconsin

B

Baltimore, Maryland: **Professionals/Postdoctorates,** 1284. *See also* Maryland

Bayfield, Wisconsin: **Undergraduates,** 556; **Graduate Students,** 1154. *See also* Wisconsin

Burnett County, Wisconsin: **Undergraduates,** 224. *See also* Wisconsin

C

California: **Undergraduates,** 36, 58-59, 71, 111, 113, 116-118, 270, 280, 297, 327, 370, 378, 397, 478, 564, 572, 604, 625, 629-630; **Graduate Students,** 730, 787, 789, 819, 913, 924, 956, 1005, 1025, 1167, 1175, 1216; **Professionals/Postdoctorates,** 1320. *See also* United States

California, southern: **Graduate Students,** 823, 1150. *See also* California

Campbellsville, Kentucky. *See* Kentucky

D

Colorado: **Undergraduates,** 62, 111, 126, 171-172, 176, 216, 286, 349, 462, 629-630; **Graduate Students,** 863, 983, 1021; **Professionals/Postdoctorates,** 1343. *See also* United States

Connecticut: **Undergraduates,** 27, 177, 179-180, 314, 629-630, 641; **Graduate Students,** 1227. *See also* Northeastern states; United States

Cornucopia, Wisconsin: **Undergraduates,** 556; **Graduate Students,** 1154. *See also* Wisconsin

D

Delaware: **Undergraduates,** 195, 533; **Graduate Students,** 841, 1021. *See also* Northeastern states; Southeastern states; United States

District of Columbia. *See* Washington, D.C.

F

Florida: **Undergraduates,** 164, 237, 297, 426, 487, 629-630, 641; **Graduate Students,** 885, 1227. *See also* Southeastern states; United States

G

Georgia: **Undergraduates,** 237, 561. *See also* Southeastern states; United States

Guam: **Undergraduates,** 170; **Graduate Students,** 823, 835, 932; **Professionals/Postdoctorates,** 1334. *See also* United States territories

H

Hawaii: **Undergraduates,** 56, 102, 165, 214, 225, 279, 307, 336, 350, 463, 542; **Graduate Students,** 777, 823, 942, 1082, 1140, 1150; **Professionals/Postdoctorates,** 1275, 1297, 1334. *See also* United States

I

Idaho: **Undergraduates,** 536; **Graduate Students,** 1106; **Professionals/Postdoctorates,** 1304. *See also* Northwestern states; United States

Tenability Index

Some programs listed in this book can be used only in specific cities, counties, states, or regions. Others may be used anywhere in the United States (or even abroad). The Tenability Index will help you locate funding that is restricted to a specific area as well as funding that has no tenability restrictions (these are listed under the term "United States"). To use this index, look up the geographic areas where you'd like to go (always check the listings under "United States"), jot down the entry numbers listed for the recipient group that represents you (Undergraduates, Graduate Students, Professionals/Postdoctorates), and use those numbers to find the program descriptions in the directory. To help you in your search, we've provided some "see" and "see also" references in the index entries. Remember: the numbers cited here refer to program entry numbers, not to page numbers in the book.

Subject Index

There are hundreds of specific subject fields covered in this directory. Use the Subject Index to identify this focus, as well as the recipient level supported (Undergraduates, Graduate Students, or Professionals/Postdoctorates) by the available funding programs. To help you pinpoint your search, we've included many "see" and "see also" references. Since a large number of programs are not restricted by subject, be sure to check the references listed under the "General programs" heading in the subject index (in addition to the specific terms that directly relate to your interest areas); hundreds of funding opportunities are listed there that can be used to support activities in any subject area—although the programs may be restricted in other ways. Remember: the numbers cited in this index refer to program entry numbers, not to page numbers in the book.

A

Academic librarianship. *See* Libraries and librarianship, academic

Accounting: **Undergraduates,** 4, 28-31, 62, 72, 85-88, 120, 130, 135, 164, 180, 190-191, 216, 239, 251, 275, 312, 371, 375, 419, 430, 439-442, 465, 489, 494, 498, 501-502, 552, 579, 583-584, 588, 615, 629-630, 650, 664, 689; **Graduate Students,** 709, 770, 791, 802, 805, 863, 998, 1046, 1061-1062, 1108-1109, 1182, 1184, 1242, 1261. *See also* Finance; General programs

Acoustical engineering. *See* Engineering, acoustical

Acoustics: **Graduate Students,** 699. *See also* General programs; Physics

Acquired Immunodeficiency Syndrome. *See* AIDS

Acting. *See* Performing arts

Actuarial sciences: **Undergraduates,** 6, 446, 615. *See also* General programs; Statistics

Addiction. *See* Alcohol use and abuse; Drug use and abuse

Administration. *See* Business administration; Education, administration; Management; Personnel administration; Public administration

Adolescents: **Graduate Students,** 959. *See also* Child development; General programs

Advertising: **Undergraduates,** 50, 96, 174, 196, 314, 363, 508, 513, 555; **Graduate Students,** 723, 774, 1000, 1116, 1153. *See also* Communications; General programs; Marketing; Public relations

Aeronautical engineering. *See* Engineering, aeronautical

Aeronautics: **Undergraduates,** 337; **Graduate Students,** 1066. *See also* Aviation; Engineering, aeronautical; General programs; Physical sciences

Aerospace engineering. *See* Engineering, aerospace

Aerospace sciences. *See* Space sciences

Affirmative action: **Undergraduates,** 310. *See also* Equal opportunity; General programs

African American studies: **Graduate Students,** 844, 1138; **Professionals/Postdoctorates,** 1340. *See also* General programs; Minority studies

Aged and aging: **Undergraduates,** 144; **Graduate Students,** 706. *See also* General programs; Social sciences

Agribusiness: **Undergraduates,** 315, 457, 494, 645; **Graduate Students,** 1075. *See also* Agriculture and agricultural sciences; Business administration; General programs

Agricultural economics. *See* Economics, agricultural

Agricultural education. *See* Education, agricultural

Agricultural engineering. *See* Engineering, agricultural

Agriculture and agricultural sciences: **Undergraduates,** 210, 315, 341, 457, 645; **Graduate Students,** 859, 1075; **Professionals/Postdoctorates,** 1352. *See also* Biological sciences; General programs

Agrimarketing and sales. *See* Agribusiness

Agronomy: **Undergraduates,** 341, 457, 645; **Graduate Students,** 1075. *See also* Agriculture and agricultural sciences; General programs

AIDS: **Undergraduates,** 51, 277; **Graduate Students,** 1034; **Professionals/Postdoctorates,** 1269. *See also* Disabilities; General programs; Immunology; Medical sciences

Air conditioning industry. *See* Cooling industry

Alcohol use and abuse: **Undergraduates,** 156, 284; **Graduate Students,** 875, 928, 990, 1035, 1088. *See also* Drug use and abuse; General programs; Health and health care

Alzheimer's Disease: **Graduate Students,** 706. *See also* Aged and aging; Disabilities; General programs; Medical sciences

American history. *See* History, American

American Indian affairs. *See* Native American affairs

American Indian language. *See* Language, Native American

American Indian studies. *See* Native American studies

American literature. *See* Literature, American

American studies: **Graduate Students,** 844, 1138; **Professionals/Postdoctorates,** 1340. *See also* General programs; Humanities

Anesthetic nurses and nursing. *See* Nurses and nursing, anesthesiology

Tourism: **Undergraduates,** 20, 34, 291, 450, 664; **Graduate Students,** 713, 1242. *See also* General programs

Toxicology: **Undergraduates,** 35. *See also* General programs; Medical sciences

Trade unions. *See* Labor unions and members

Trademarks law. *See* Intellectual property law

Transportation: **Undergraduates,** 9, 34, 80-82, 121, 127, 234, 254, 292, 311, 323-324, 385-386, 412, 447-448, 477, 491-492, 565, 614, 623, 626, 628, 683, 687; **Graduate Students,** 701, 765, 792, 882, 952, 980, 1015-1016, 1096, 1104, 1169, 1206, 1214, 1218, 1258-1259. *See also* Aviation; Engineering, transportation; General programs; Space sciences

Transportation engineering. *See* Engineering, transportation

Transportation law: **Undergraduates,** 614; **Graduate Students,** 1206. *See also* General programs; Law, general

Travel and tourism. *See* Tourism

Tribal law. *See* Indian law

Tropical studies: **Undergraduates,** 593-594; **Graduate Students,** 1194-1195; **Professionals/Postdoctorates,** 1347. *See also* General programs

Tuberculosis. *See* Lung disease

TV. *See* Television

Typing. *See* Secretarial sciences

U

Unions and unionization. *See* Labor unions and members

Universities. *See* Education, higher; Libraries and librarianship, academic

Unrestricted programs. *See* General programs

Urban affairs: **Graduate Students,** 1074; **Professionals/Postdoctorates,** 1327. *See also* General programs; Urban and regional planning

Urban and regional planning: **Undergraduates,** 80-82, 113, 176, 234, 311, 323-324, 344, 386, 393, 438, 447-448, 636; **Graduate Students,** 765, 787, 844, 882, 927, 979, 1016, 1020, 1138, 1221; **Professionals/Postdoctorates,** 1340, 1357. *See also* General programs; Urban affairs

Urban studies: **Professionals/Postdoctorates,** 1352. *See also* General programs; Urban affairs

Utilities: **Undergraduates,** 62, 501-502; **Graduate Students,** 1108-1109. *See also* Energy; General programs

V

Veterinary sciences: **Undergraduates,** 22, 315, 676; **Graduate Students,** 715, 1121, 1254; **Professionals/Postdoctorates,** 1335. *See also* Animal science; General programs; Sciences

Veterinary technology: **Undergraduates,** 676; **Graduate Students,** 1254. *See also* Animal science; General programs

Video. *See* Filmmaking; Television

Visual arts: **Undergraduates,** 445, 616; **Graduate Students,** 861, 1208; **Professionals/Postdoctorates,** 1275, 1284, 1301, 1304, 1343-1344, 1350, 1360. *See also* General programs; Humanities; names of specific visual arts

Vocational education. *See* Education, vocational

Voice: **Undergraduates,** 79. *See also* General programs; Music; Performing arts

W

Water resources: **Undergraduates,** 62, 313; **Graduate Students,** 835, 932, 946. *See also* Environmental sciences; General programs; Natural resources

Weather. *See* Climatology

Weaving: **Professionals/Postdoctorates,** 1350-1351. *See also* Arts and crafts; General programs

Web design. *See* Internet design and development

Web journalism. *See* Journalism, online

Welding: **Undergraduates,** 28, 62, 135; **Graduate Students,** 805. *See also* Building trades; General programs

Welding engineering. *See* Engineering, welding

Welfare. *See* Social services

Wildlife management: **Undergraduates,** 421, 457, 584; **Graduate Students,** 811, 1047, 1075, 1166, 1184. *See also* Environmental sciences; General programs

Women's studies and programs: **Graduate Students,** 844, 1138; **Professionals/Postdoctorates,** 1340. *See also* General programs

Work. *See* Employment

Worker's compensation. *See* Employment law

World literature. *See* Literature

Y

Youth. *See* Adolescents; Child development

Calendar Index

Since most funding programs have specific deadline dates, some may have already closed by the time you begin to look for money. You can use the Calendar Index to identify which programs are still open. To do that, go to the recipient category (Undergraduates, Graduate Students, or Professionals/ Postdoctorates) that interests you, think about when you'll be able to complete your application forms, go to the appropriate months, jot down the entry numbers listed there, and use those numbers to find the program descriptions in the directory. Keep in mind that the numbers cited here refer to program entry numbers, not to page numbers in the book.

Made in the USA
Middletown, DE
16 June 2018